OXFORD

The world's most trusted dictionaries

LEARNER'S GERMAN Dictionary

Editors

Valerie Grundy • Nicholas Rollin • Eva Vennebusch
Helen Warren • Sally Wehmeier

Consultant

René Koglbauer

OXFORD

UNIVERSITY PRESS

OXFORD
UNIVERSITY PRESS

Great Clarendon Street, Oxford OX2 6DP

Oxford University Press is a department of the University of Oxford.
It furthers the University's objective of excellence in research,
scholarship, and education by publishing worldwide in

Oxford   New York

Auckland   Cape Town   Dar es Salaam   Hong Kong   Karachi
Kuala Lumpur   Madrid   Melbourne   Mexico City   Nairobi
New Delhi   Shanghai   Taipei   Toronto

With offices in

Argentina   Austria   Brazil   Chile   Czech Republic   France   Greece
Guatemala   Hungary   Italy   Japan   Poland   Portugal   Singapore
South Korea   Switzerland   Thailand   Turkey   Ukraine   Vietnam

Oxford is a registered trade mark of Oxford University Press
in the UK and in certain other countries

© Oxford University Press 2017

Database right Oxford University Press (maker)

Illustrations © El primo Ramón (Borja Ramón López Cotelo)

Photocredits: Car mechanic and goalkeeper©wavebreakmedia/Shutterstock • Eating out
©Monkey Business Images/Shutterstock • Cinema©Nestor Rizhniak/Shutterstock.com
• Wind turbines©Ferenc Cegledi/Shutterstock • Glastonbury Festival©antb/Shutterstock

First published 2009
Second edition 2012
This edition 2017

British Library Cataloguing in Publication Data
Data available

ISBN: 978-0-19-840797-3

10 9 8 7 6 5 4 3 2

Printed in China by Golden Cup

Contents

Contents

Introduction

This bilingual dictionary has been specifically written for students of German – from those just starting out all the way up to those preparing for exams. It presents essential information in a format designed to be clear and easy to consult.

In the UK, this dictionary provides support to all students preparing for GCSE, and is the ideal dictionary to use when preparing for role play activities and written exams.

There are two main alphabetical sections: **GERMAN – ENGLISH** and **ENGLISH – GERMAN**. These sections are divided by a thematic centre section in full colour.

TIP *To help you find words quickly, the first word on each page is printed top left and the last word on the page is printed top right.*

GERMAN – ENGLISH

Look up German words – listed alphabetically – to find their meaning in English. When a word has more than one meaning, make sure you choose the one that is most relevant.

TIP *Make sure you check not only the main translation but also the translations in the example sentences.*

ENGLISH – GERMAN

Look up English words – listed alphabetically – to find out how to say them in German. Next to the English word you will see what type of word it is, e.g. *NOUN*, *VERB*, etc. When you look up a noun, the German translation has the correct article in front of it (der for masculine nouns, die for feminine nouns, das for neuter nouns). To help you choose the right word and use it correctly, don't forget to read through the example sentences provided.

TIP *When looking up a verb, check the verb tables in the centre section, where there is more information about the forms of many verbs, in particular irregular and modal verbs.*

TIP *To find out more about the German translation that you are given, look it up on the GERMAN – ENGLISH side of the dictionary afterwards.*

Using your German colour section

In the colour section you will find key vocabulary to help you prepare for your exams. There are useful phrases for role play and sample questions and answers for the photo card activities. These will help you to build your own answers using them as a guide.

It also includes verb tables for regular verbs and the most common irregular verbs as well as for modal verbs, e.g. müssen, sollen, wollen.

Get to know your dictionary

User-friendly layout

- **Two-colour layout**

  In this dictionary all the German words are in blue and all the English is in black. This makes it easy to identify the words you need.

- **Easy to navigate**

  The alphabet runs down the side of each page indicating what letter you are looking at, and whether you are on the **GERMAN – ENGLISH** or **ENGLISH – GERMAN** side of the dictionary:

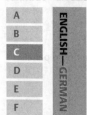

- **The key symbol**

  The key symbol is explained along the bottom of every right-hand page.

  ℓ indicates key words

- **The diamond symbol**

  The diamond symbol is explained at the bottom of every left-hand page.

  ◇ indicates irregular verb

Clear entries

- **Word classes written out in full**

  NOUN, VERB, ADJECTIVE, ADVERB, CONJUNCTION, PREPOSITION or *DETERMINER* are all written out clearly after the headword:

  to boast *VERB*
  prahlen
  He was boasting about his new bike.
  Er prahlte mit seinem neuen Rad.

- **Gender of nouns doubly clear**

  The gender of each German noun is shown by the article that is used before it, e.g. der Musiker, die Musikerin, das Fest. Der shows you masculine words, die shows you feminine words and das neuter words.

  Sometimes, die does not show a feminine word but is used to show that the noun is plural. In these cases, you will find *PLURAL NOUN* next to the German noun, e.g.

  die **Atomwaffen** *PLURAL NOUN*
  nuclear weapons

- **All variations shown**
The plural forms of nouns are given too.

> der **Motor**, *PLURAL* die **Motoren**
> engine, motor

- **Pointers to other word classes**
Where a word can do more than one job (be a noun *and* a
verb, for example), a helpful symbol ▸ reminds you to check
the whole of the dictionary entry.

> ℘ **fish** *NOUN*
> der Fisch, (*PL* die Fische)

> to **fish** *NOUN*
> fischen, (*with a rod*) angeln

Extra help with verbs
- **Very common verbs**
Common verbs are given special treatment in tinted panels:

> ℘ **gehen** *VERB*◇, *IMPERFECT* **ging** *PERFECT* **ist**
> **gegangen**
> 1 **to go**
>   Ich gehe schlafen. I'm going to bed.
> 2 **to walk**
>   Seid ihr zu Fuß nach Hause gegangen?
>   Did you walk home?

- **Verb tables in centre section**
The centre section contains full conjugations for regular
verbs and the most common irregular verbs.

- **Irregular forms of verbs**
If you look up past participles and non-infinitive forms of
a verb, you are directed to the relevant headword:

trank ▸ *SEE* **trinken**

Extra help with difficult points of German
- **Extra help with grammar and spelling**
'Word tips' give extra help with tricky grammatical points
and reminders on how German spelling is different from
English. Often there is an example sentence given within
the word tip:

WORD TIP The past participle is gemusst when
müssen is the main verb: Er hat nach Hause
gemusst. The past participle is müssen when it
is an auxiliary verb: Sie hat es tun müssen.

- **Typical problematic areas**

  Extra help is given with traditionally problematic areas, such as talking about jobs and professions:

  WORD TIP Professions, hobbies, and sports don't take an article in German: Er ist Lehrer.

- **False friends**

  False friends are shown on the **GERMAN – ENGLISH** side of the dictionary:

  WORD TIP The German word Billion does not mean **billion** in English; the German translation for the English **billion** is Milliarde.

Language in context – example sentences

- **Thousands of example sentences**

  Thousands of 'real language' examples are given on both sides of the dictionary – to help you understand German in context and express what you really want to say.

  ℗ **nehmen** *VERB*◇, *PRESENT* **nimmt**, *IMPERFECT* **nahm**, *PERFECT* **hat genommen**
  1 to take
  2 to have
    Ich nehme eine Suppe. I'll have soup.
  3 Was nehmen Sie dafür? How much do you want for it?
  4 jemanden zu sich nehmen to have somebody live with you
  5 sich etwas nehmen to take something
    Sie nahm sich ein Bonbon. She took a sweet.
    Nimm dir ein Stück Kuchen. Help yourself to a piece of cake.

  ℗ **phone** *NOUN*
    das Telefon, (*PL* die **Telefone**),
    (*mobile*) das **Handy**, (*PL* die **Handys**)
    She's on the phone. Sie telefoniert.
    I was on the phone to Sophie. Ich habe mit Sophie telefoniert.

- **World German**

  All German-speaking countries are represented on both sides of the dictionary:

  das **Obers**
    (*in Southern Germany and Austria*) cream

Additional features

- ### Core vocabulary highlighted

  The dictionary includes all the key curriculum words you
  need and a key symbol highlights the key words you must
  know to prepare for your exams.

  ♪ **billig** *ADJECTIVE*
      cheap

- ### Using your German colour section

  The full-colour centre section will help you communicate in
  both written and spoken German.

- ### Mini-infos

  Boxed notes provide interesting cultural information
  throughout the alphabetical entries:

  ### 🔵 RECHTSCHREIBREFORM

  German spelling reform. In 1996 the German-
  speaking countries signed an agreement on
  new German spelling rules. These new rules are
  compulsory only in schools as there is no law
  relating to orthography. Since then Germany
  and Austria have made a number of changes
  to the rules. However, Germany, but not
  Austria, reversed some of the 1996 changes.
  As a result, German spelling follows the Duden
  dictionary, while Austrian school teachers have
  to consult the Österreichisches Wörterbuch
  instead. Switzerland has been in a different
  position from the beginning as there have
  always been some differences in Swiss German.
  For example, the letter 'ß' was never used.

  ### 🔵 SCHOOL

  At the age of 10, pupils move from primary
  school (Grundschule or Volksschule) to
  one of three types of school in Germany:
  Hauptschule, Realschule, or Gymnasium. In
  some areas, there are comprehensive schools
  (Gesamtschulen). In Austria, pupils move to
  a Hauptschule or Gymnasium. The Austrian
  government wants to introduce a new type
  of school, the 'neue Mittelschule', with some
  of the features of a comprehensive school.
  In Switzerland, some cantons have only
  one type of secondary school, while others
  divide their pupils up into three types, too.
  The Hauptschule focuses on more practical
  subjects, the Gymnasium on more academic
  subjects. The Realschule is between the two.

- **Language functions covered**

Exam syllabus language functions, such as requests and demands, are covered within example sentences:

ℰ **bitte** *ADVERB*

 1 **please** (*when asking for something*)
 'Möchten Sie Kuchen?' – 'Ja, bitte.' 'Would you like some cake?' – 'Yes, please.'

 2 **you're welcome, that's all right** (*in reply to thanks*)
 'Vielen Dank für Ihre Hilfe.' – 'Bitte schön/ sehr.' 'Thank you very much for your help.' – 'That's all right.'

 3 Wie bitte? (*when you haven't understood something*) Sorry?, Pardon?

 4 **Come in!** (*after a knock on the door*)

ℰ **gern(e)** *ADVERB*

 1 **gladly**

 2 jemanden gern haben to like somebody etwas gern tun to like doing something
 Ich tanze gern. I like dancing.
 Ich hätte gerne einen Kaffee. I'd like a coffee.
 Welchen Belag hättest du gerne? Which topping would you like?

 3 Ja, gern! Yes, I'd love to!

 4 Gern geschehen! You're welcome!

 5 Das glaube ich gern. I can well believe that.

Aa

der **Aal**, *PLURAL* die **Aale**
eel

℘ **ab** *PREPOSITION (+ DAT)*
from
ab Montag from Monday
ab dem 1. Juni from 1 June
Kinder ab sechs Jahren zahlen fünf Euro.
Children from the age of six pay five euros.

ab *ADVERB*
1 **off**
Der Knopf ist ab. The button has come off.
Ab ins Bett! *(informal)* Off (you go) to bed!
2 **ab und zu occasionally**
Ab und zu fahre ich mit dem Rad zur
Schule. Occasionally I cycle to school.

abbiegen *VERB*◇, *IMPERFECT* **bog ab**, *PERFECT* **ist
abgebogen**
1 **to turn off**
nach rechts abbiegen to turn off to the
right
2 **to turn**
Biegen Sie an der Ampel (nach) links ab!
Turn left at the lights.

die **Abbildung**, *PLURAL* die **Abbildungen**
illustration

abbrechen *VERB*◇, *PRESENT* **bricht
ab**, *IMPERFECT* **brach ab**, *PERFECT* **hat
abgebrochen**
1 **to break off** *(a branch, negotiations)*
Ruth brach ein paar Zweige ab. Ruth broke
off a few twigs.
2 **to pull down** *(a building)*
3 **to cut short**
Leider mussten wir unsere Ferien
vorzeitig abbrechen. Unfortunately we
had to cut short our holidays.
Er hat sein Studium aus finanziellen
Gründen abgebrochen. He left university
for financial reasons.
4 *PERFECT* **ist abgebrochen**
Der Ast ist abgebrochen. The branch has
broken off.

℘ der **Abend**, *PLURAL* die **Abende**
evening
heute Abend this evening, tonight
gestern Abend yesterday evening, last
night
Am Abend sehen wir fern. In the evening
we watch TV.
Wann esst ihr zu Abend? When do you
have dinner?

das **Abendbrot**
evening meal

℘ das **Abendessen**, *PLURAL* die **Abendessen**
supper, dinner *(in the evening)*
Was gibt es zum Abendessen? What are
we having for supper?

der **Abendkurs**, *PLURAL* die **Abendkurse**
evening class

℘ **abends** *ADVERB*
in the evening

℘ das **Abenteuer**, *PLURAL* die **Abenteuer**
adventure

der **Abenteuerfilm**, *PLURAL* die
Abenteuerfilme
adventure film

abenteuerlich *ADJECTIVE*
1 **risky**
2 **bizarre**

℘ der **Abenteuerspielplatz**, *PLURAL* die
Abenteuerspielplätze
adventure playground

℘ **aber** *CONJUNCTION*
but
Das Top ist schön, aber zu teuer. The top is
nice, but it's too expensive.

aber *ADVERB*
really
Das war aber nett von dir. That was really
nice of you.
Du bist aber groß! Aren't you tall!
'Bist du fertig?' – 'Aber ja!' 'Are you
ready?' – 'But of course!'
Jetzt ist aber Schluss! That's it now!

abergläubisch *ADJECTIVE*
superstitious

℘ **abfahren** *VERB*◇, *PRESENT* **fährt ab**, *IMPERFECT*
fuhr ab, *PERFECT* **ist abgefahren**
to leave
Peter fährt morgen ganz früh ab. Peter is
leaving very early tomorrow morning.
Wann fährt der Zug nach Berlin ab? When
does the Berlin train leave?

℘ die **Abfahrt**, *PLURAL* die **Abfahrten**
1 **departure**
2 **run** *(on a ski slope)*
3 **exit** *(on a motorway)*

der **Abfall**, *PLURAL* die **Abfälle**
rubbish

der **Abfalleimer**, *PLURAL* die **Abfalleimer**
rubbish bin

abfliegen *VERB*◇, *IMPERFECT* **flog ab**, *PERFECT* **ist abgeflogen**

1 **to take off**
Die Maschine ist mit zehn Minuten Verspätung abgeflogen. The plane took off ten minutes late.

2 **to leave** *(by plane)*
Ich fliege um 11 Uhr ab. My plane leaves at 11 o'clock.

der **Abflug**, *PLURAL* die **Abflüge**
departure

das **Abflussrohr**, *PLURAL* die **Abflussrohre**
outlet, **drain**

abfragen *VERB*, *PERFECT* **hat abgefragt**

1 **to test**
Sie fragt ihn Vokabeln ab. She's testing him on his vocabulary.

2 **to call up** *(on a computer)*
Die Informationen kann man am Computer abfragen. You can call up the information on the computer.

♀ die **Abgase** *PLURAL NOUN*
exhaust fumes

abgeben *VERB*◇, *PRESENT* **gibt ab**, *IMPERFECT* **gab ab**, *PERFECT* **hat abgegeben**

1 **to hand in** *(homework, an application, lost property)*

2 **to pass** *(in football)*
Er hat den Ball an Max abgegeben. He passed the ball to Max.

3 **sich mit etwas abgeben** to spend time on something
Mit solchen Leuten würde ich mich nicht abgeben. I wouldn't associate with people like that.

4 **jemandem etwas abgeben** to give somebody something
Gibst du mir ein Stück von deiner Schokolade ab? Would you give me a piece of your chocolate?
Gib deinem Bruder etwas (davon) ab! Share it with your brother!

5 Er wird einen guten Lehrer abgeben. He'll make a good teacher.

abgelegen *ADJECTIVE*
remote

abgemacht *ADJECTIVE*
agreed

der/die **Abgeordnete**, *PLURAL* die **Abgeordneten**
member of parliament

> **DER ABGEORDNETE**
>
> In Germany, members of parliament (MPs) are called Abgeordnete zum Bundestag. In Austria and Switzerland they are called Abgeordnete zum Nationalrat. The word Abgeordnete is also used for the members of the federal state parliaments in Austria and Germany.

abgesehen *ADVERB*
abgesehen davon apart from that

abgießen *VERB*◇, *IMPERFECT* **goss ab**, *PERFECT* **hat abgegossen**

1 **to pour away**

2 **to drain** *(vegetables)*

der **Abhang**, *PLURAL* die **Abhänge**
slope

abhängen[1] *VERB*◇, *IMPERFECT* **hing ab**, *PERFECT* **hat abgehangen**
von jemandem abhängen to depend on somebody
Das hängt von dir ab. That depends on you.
von etwas abhängen to depend on something
Es hängt vom Wetter ab, ob wir am Wochenende nach Wales fahren. Whether or not we go to Wales at the weekend depends on the weather.

abhängen[2] *VERB*, *PERFECT* **hat abgehängt**

1 **to unhitch** *(a trailer)*

2 **to uncouple** *(a train carriage)*

3 *(informal)* **to shake off**
Die Einbrecher hängten die Polizei schnell ab. The burglars soon shook off the police.

♀ **abhängig** *ADJECTIVE*
abhängig sein von to be dependent on

abheben *VERB*◇, *IMPERFECT* **hob ab**, *PERFECT* **hat abgehoben**

1 **to lift off**

2 **to withdraw** *(money)*

3 **to answer the phone**
Ich habe schon zweimal angerufen, aber niemand hat abgehoben. I've rung twice before, but nobody answered.

abheften *VERB*, *PERFECT* **hat abgeheftet**
to file

♀ **abholen** *VERB*, *PERFECT* **hat abgeholt**

1 **to collect**
Er holte das Paket bei der Post ab. He collected the parcel from the post office.

2 to pick up
Ich hole dich am Bahnhof ab. I'll pick you up at the station.

die **Abholzung**
1 deforestation
2 cutting down

das **Abi**, *PLURAL* die **Abis**
(*informal*) A levels

ℓ das **Abitur**
A levels
Er hat gerade sein Abitur gemacht. He's just done his A levels.

> **ABITUR**
>
> The end-of-school exam taken by students in Germany at the age of 18 or 19. This exam qualifies students to go to university.

der **Abiturient**, *PLURAL* die **Abiturienten**
A-level student (*male*)

die **Abiturientin**, *PLURAL* die **Abiturientinnen**
A-level student (*female*)

das **Abkommen**, *PLURAL* die **Abkommen**
agreement

abkürzen *VERB*, *PERFECT* **hat abgekürzt**
1 to abbreviate
Sein Name wird oft zu Chris abgekürzt. His name is often abbreviated to Chris.
2 Wir haben den Weg abgekürzt. We took a short cut.

ℓ die **Abkürzung**, *PLURAL* die **Abkürzungen**
1 abbreviation
Die Abkürzung für Europäische Union ist EU. The abbreviation for European Union is EU.
2 short cut
Wir haben eine gute Abkürzung gefunden. We found a good short cut.

abladen *VERB*◇, *PRESENT* **lädt ab**, *IMPERFECT* **lud ab**, *PERFECT* **hat abgeladen**
to unload

das **Ablaufdatum**, *PLURAL* die **Ablaufdaten**
expiry date

ablaufen *VERB*◇, *PRESENT* **läuft ab**, *IMPERFECT* **lief ab**, *PERFECT* **ist abgelaufen**
1 to expire (*passport, contract*)
2 to drain away
Lass bitte das Badewasser ablaufen. Please let the bathwater out.

ablegen *VERB*, *PERFECT* **hat abgelegt**
1 to take off (*a coat*)
2 Sie trägt die abgelegte Kleidung ihrer

Schwester. She wears her sister's cast-offs.
3 to put down (*an object*)
Ich habe den Schlüssel neben dem Fernseher abgelegt. I put down the key next to the TV.
4 to cast off (*of a ship*)

ablehnen *VERB*, *PERFECT* **hat abgelehnt**
1 to turn down (*a position, money, an invitation*)
2 to reject (*an applicant, a suggestion*)

ℓ **ablenken** *VERB*, *PERFECT* **hat abgelenkt**
1 to distract
Du lenkst mich von meiner Arbeit ab. You're distracting me from my work.
Er wollte seinen Freund von seinen Sorgen ablenken. He wanted to take his friend's mind off his worries.
2 to divert (*attention, suspicion*)
Sie versuchte, vom Thema abzulenken. She tried to change the subject.

abliefern *VERB*, *PERFECT* **hat abgeliefert**
1 to deliver
2 to hand in (*an essay, a form, lost property*)
3 to drop off
Wer wird die Kinder bei der Party abliefern? Who's going to drop the children off at the party?

ℓ **abmachen** *VERB*, *PERFECT* **hat abgemacht**
1 to take off
Kannst du den Deckel abmachen? Can you take off the lid?
2 to agree
Wir müssen noch einen Termin für unser nächstes Treffen abmachen. We still have to agree on a date for our next meeting.
Abgemacht! Agreed!
3 to sort out
Das müsst ihr untereinander abmachen. You'll have to sort that out amongst yourselves.

die **Abmachung**, *PLURAL* die **Abmachungen**
agreement

ℓ **abnehmen** *VERB*◇, *PRESENT* **nimmt ab**, *IMPERFECT* **nahm ab**, *PERFECT* **hat abgenommen**
1 to take off (*remove*)
Er nahm dem Jungen das Messer ab. He took the knife off the boy.
Sie nehmen einem schnell zwanzig Euro ab. They'll soon take twenty euros off you.
2 to take down (*washing*)
3 Kann ich dir etwas abnehmen? (*carry*) Can I take something (for you)? (*help*) Can I do anything for you?
4 to buy

A
B
C
D
E
F
G
H
I
J
K
L
M
N
O
P
Q
R
S
T
U
V
W
X
Y
Z

5 to decrease *(in number)*

6 to lose weight
Er hat schon vier Kilo abgenommen. He's already lost four kilos.

7 to answer *(the phone)*
Niemand hat abgenommen. Nobody answered.

8 Das nehme ich dir nicht ab. *(informal)*
I don't buy that.

das **Abonnement**, *PLURAL* die **Abonnements**
subscription

abonnieren *VERB, PERFECT* **hat abonniert**
to subscribe to

abraten *VERB◇, PRESENT* **rät ab**, *IMPERFECT* **riet ab**, *PERFECT* **hat abgeraten**
jemandem von etwas abraten to advise somebody against something
Der Arzt hat mir davon abgeraten. The doctor advised me against it.

abräumen *VERB, PERFECT* **hat abgeräumt**
to clear away
Kannst du den Tisch abräumen? Can you clear the table?

abreagieren *VERB, PERFECT* **hat abreagiert**
1 Er hat seine Wut an seinem kleinen Bruder abreagiert. He took his anger out on his little brother.

2 sich abreagieren to let off steam
Nach der Schule müssen sich die Kinder erst abreagieren. After school, the children first have to let off steam.

♀ die **Abreise**
departure

abreisen *VERB, PERFECT* **ist abgereist**
to leave

abreißen *VERB◇, IMPERFECT* **riss ab**, *PERFECT* **hat abgerissen**
1 to tear down *(a poster, notice)*
2 to demolish *(a building)*
3 *PERFECT* **ist abgerissen** to come off *(a button, for example)*

Abs. *ABBREVIATION*
(=Absender) sender

♀ die **Absage**, *PLURAL* die **Absagen**
1 refusal
2 cancellation *(of an event)*

absagen *VERB, PERFECT* **hat abgesagt**
1 to cancel
2 to turn down
Sie hat unsere Einladung abgesagt. She turned down our invitation.

der **Absatz**, *PLURAL* die **Absätze**
1 heel *(of a shoe)*
2 paragraph

absaven *VERB, PERFECT* **hat abgesavt**
1 to save on computer
2 *(informal)* to ensure

abschaffen *VERB, PERFECT* **hat abgeschafft**
1 to abolish *(a regulation, capital punishment)*
2 to get rid of
Wir haben unser Auto abgeschafft. We got rid of our car.

abschalten *VERB, PERFECT* **hat abgeschaltet**
to switch off

abscheulich *ADJECTIVE*
horrible

abschicken *VERB, PERFECT* **hat abgeschickt**
to send off

♀ der **Abschied**, *PLURAL* die **Abschiede**
1 parting
2 farewell
3 Sie mussten Abschied nehmen. They had to say goodbye.

der **Abschleppdienst**
breakdown service, vehicle recovery service

> ● **DER ABSCHLEPPDIENST**
>
> In Austria and Germany, car owners are often members of a car club, similar to the AA in Britain. In Austria there are two clubs, ARBÖ (Auto-, Motor- und Radfahrerbund Österreich) and ÖAMTC (Österreichische Automobil-, Motorrad- und Touring-Club). The German club is called ADAC (Allgemeine Deutsche Automobil Club).

abschleppen *VERB, PERFECT* **hat abgeschleppt**
1 to tow away *(a car)*
2 Warum muss ich mich mit den Koffern abschleppen? *(informal)* Why do I have to struggle along with the suitcases?
3 Wie schafft er es, dass er so viele Mädchen abschleppt? *(informal)* How does he manage to pick up so many girls?

der **Abschleppwagen**, *PLURAL* die **Abschleppwagen**
breakdown truck

abschließen *VERB◇, IMPERFECT* **schloss ab**, *PERFECT* **hat abgeschlossen**
to lock

♀ der **Abschluss**, *PLURAL* die **Abschlüsse**
1 end, conclusion

◇ irregular verb; *SEP* separable verb; for more help with verbs see centre section

Zum Abschluss gab es ein Feuerwerk.
There were fireworks at the end.

2 final examination
Sie macht nächstes Jahr ihren Abschluss.
She's doing her final examination next
year.

die **Abschlussprüfung**, PLURAL die
Abschlussprüfungen
final examination

das **Abschlusszeugnis**, PLURAL die
Abschlusszeugnisse
school-leaving certificate

abschneiden VERB◇, IMPERFECT **schnitt ab**,
PERFECT **hat abgeschnitten**
1 to cut off
Ich schneide dir eine Scheibe Brot ab. I'll
cut you a slice of bread.
2 to do
Bei der Arbeit hat sie gut/schlecht
abgeschnitten. She did well/badly in the
test.

abschrecken VERB, PERFECT **hat**
abgeschreckt
to deter

abschreiben VERB◇, IMPERFECT **schrieb ab**,
PERFECT **hat abgeschrieben**
to copy

das **Abseilen**
abseiling

abseits ADVERB
1 away
Er stand etwas abseits. He stood a little
way away.
2 offside (in soccer)

der **Absender**, PLURAL die **Absender**
sender

absetzen VERB, PERFECT **hat abgesetzt**
1 to take off (your hat, glasses)
2 to put down (a bag, suitcase)
3 to drop off
Ich setze euch am Kino ab. I'll drop you off
at the cinema.
4 Sie hat die Pille abgesetzt. She's stopped
taking the pill.

die **Absicht**, PLURAL die **Absichten**
intention

absichtlich ADVERB
intentionally

absolut ADJECTIVE
absolute
absolut ADVERB
absolutely

Das ist absolut unmöglich. That's
absolutely impossible.

abspülen VERB, PERFECT **hat abgespült**
1 to rinse, to rinse off
2 to do the washing up

der **Abstand**, PLURAL die **Abstände**
1 distance
Sie folgten in zwanzig Meter Abstand.
They followed at a distance of twenty
metres.
Bei Regen muss man Abstand halten.
When it's raining, you have to keep your
distance.
2 interval

abstauben VERB, PERFECT **hat abgestaubt**
to dust

abstellen VERB, PERFECT **hat abgestellt**
1 to turn off (the radio, a tap)
2 to put down (a suitcase, the shopping)
3 to park (the car)

der **Abstellraum**, PLURAL die **Abstellräume**
storeroom

die **Abstimmung**, PLURAL die
Abstimmungen
vote

abstreiten VERB◇, IMPERFECT **stritt ab**,
PERFECT **hat abgestritten**
to deny

abstürzen VERB, PERFECT **ist abgestürzt**
1 to fall
2 to crash (of a plane)

der **Abszess**, PLURAL die **Abszesse**
abscess

abtauen VERB, PERFECT **hat abgetaut**
to defrost (the fridge)

das **Abteil**, PLURAL die **Abteile**
compartment

abteilen VERB, PERFECT **hat abgeteilt**
1 to divide up
2 to divide off

ℱ die **Abteilung**, PLURAL die **Abteilungen**
department

ℱ die **Abtreibung**, PLURAL die **Abtreibungen**
abortion

ℱ **abtrocknen** VERB, PERFECT **hat abgetrocknet**
1 to dry up
2 Er trocknete sich ab. He dried himself.

abwägen VERB◇, IMPERFECT **wog ab**,
PERFECT **hat abgewogen**
to weigh up

ℱ **indicates key words**

abwählen VERB, PERFECT **hat abgewählt**
1 to vote off
2 to drop (school subject)

abwärts ADVERB
down

der **Abwasch**
washing-up

ℐ **abwaschen** VERB◇, PRESENT **wäscht ab**, IMPERFECT **wusch ab**, PERFECT **hat abgewaschen**
1 to wash up (the dishes)
2 to wash off (dirt, marks)

das **Abwasser**, PLURAL die **Abwässer**
sewage

die **Abwechslung**, PLURAL die **Abwechslungen**
change
Heute gibt es zur Abwechslung Fisch.
Today we're having fish for a change.

abwerten VERB, PERFECT **hat abgewertet**
to devalue

abwertend ADJECTIVE
pejorative

ℐ **abwesend** ADJECTIVE
absent

die **Abwesenheit**
absence

abwischen VERB, PERFECT **hat abgewischt**
to wipe

abzählen VERB, PERFECT **hat abgezählt**
to count

das **Abzeichen**, PLURAL die **Abzeichen**
badge

abziehen VERB◇, IMPERFECT **zog ab**, PERFECT **hat abgezogen**
1 to take off (a sheet, backing)
Ich zog die Betten ab. I stripped the beds.
2 to take out (a key)
3 to deduct, to take away
4 to withdraw (troops)
5 PERFECT **ist abgezogen** to escape (of steam, smoke)
6 PERFECT **ist abgezogen** (informal) to push off
Sie sind gleich nach dem Essen abgezogen. They pushed off straight after the meal.

abzielen VERB, PERFECT **hat abgezielt**
auf jemanden abzielen to be aimed at somebody
Der Film zielt auf Teenager ab. The film is aimed at teenagers.
Diese Bemerkung zielte auf dich ab! That remark was aimed at you.

die **Abzweigung**, PLURAL die **Abzweigungen**
turning

ℐ **ach** EXCLAMATION
oh!
Ach so! Oh, I see!

die **Achsel**, PLURAL die **Achseln**
shoulder

die **Achselhöhle**, PLURAL die **Achselhöhlen**
armpit

ℐ **acht** NUMBER
eight
um acht (Uhr) at eight (o'clock)
um halb acht at half past seven

die **Acht**[1], PLURAL die **Achten**
eight
Die Kinder schrieben eine Acht. The children wrote an eight.

ℐ die **Acht**[2]
1 sich in Acht nehmen to be careful
Nimm dich in Acht! Be careful!
2 etwas außer Acht lassen to ignore something
Kleinere Fehler wurden außer Acht gelassen. Minor errors were ignored.
3 ▸ SEE achtgeben

das **Achtel**, PLURAL die **Achtel**
eighth
Sie bestellte ein Achtel Weißwein. She ordered an eighth of a litre of white wine.

achten VERB, PERFECT **hat geachtet**
1 to respect (a person, an opinion)
2 auf etwas achten to pay attention to something
3 auf jemanden achten to look after somebody
4 Achte nicht darauf! Don't take any notice of it!

achter, achte, achtes ADJECTIVE
eighth
jede achte Kiste every eighth crate
mein achter Geburtstag my eighth birthday
Sie ging als Achte durchs Ziel. She finished eighth.

ℐ die **Achterbahn**, PLURAL die **Achterbahnen**
roller coaster

◇ **irregular verb; SEP separable verb; for more help with verbs see centre section**

achtgeben VERB◊, PRESENT **gibt acht**, IMPERFECT **gab acht**, PERFECT **hat achtgegeben**
1 to pay attention
Er sollte in der Schule besser achtgeben.
He should pay more attention at school.
Gib acht! Watch out!
2 auf jemanden/etwas achtgeben to look after somebody/something
Sie muss auf ihre Schwester achtgeben.
She has to look after her sister.

achthundert NUMBER
eight hundred

achtmal ADVERB
eight times

ℰ die **Achtung**
1 respect
Ich habe große Achtung vor diesen Leuten. I have great respect for these people.
2 Achtung! Look out!
Achtung, fertig, los! On your marks, get set, go!
'Achtung Stufe' 'Mind the step'

ℰ **achtzehn** NUMBER
eighteen

ℰ **achtzig** NUMBER
eighty

der **Acker**, PLURAL die **Äcker**
field

der **ADAC** ABBREVIATION
(=Allgemeiner Deutscher Automobil-Club)
German motoring organization

addieren VERB, PERFECT **hat addiert**
to add

die **Ader**, PLURAL die **Adern**
vein

ℰ das **Adjektiv**, PLURAL die **Adjektive**
adjective

der **Adler**, PLURAL die **Adler**
eagle

adoptieren VERB, PERFECT **hat adoptiert**
to adopt

die **Adoption**, PLURAL die **Adoptionen**
adoption

die **Adoptiveltern** PLURAL NOUN
adoptive parents

das **Adoptivkind**, PLURAL die **Adoptivkinder**
adopted child

ℰ die **Adresse**, PLURAL die **Adressen**
address

adressieren VERB, PERFECT **hat adressiert**
to address
An wen soll ich den Brief adressieren?
Who shall I address the letter to?

der **Advent**
Advent

der **Adventskalender**, PLURAL die **Adventskalender**
Advent calendar

der **Adventskranz**, PLURAL die **Adventskränze**
Advent wreath

ℰ das **Adverb**, PLURAL die **Adverbien**
adverb

das **Aerobic**
aerobics

ℰ der **Affe**, PLURAL die **Affen**
1 monkey
2 ape

die **Affenklammer** (informal) PLURAL die **Affenklammern**
(informal) at-sign

ℰ **Afrika** NEUTER NOUN
Africa
Sie kommt aus Afrika. She's from Africa.
Er fliegt nach Afrika. He's flying to Africa.

der **Afrikaner**, PLURAL die **Afrikaner**
African (male)

die **Afrikanerin**, PLURAL die **Afrikanerinnen**
African (female)

afrikanisch ADJECTIVE
African

> **WORD TIP** Adjectives never have capitals in German, even for regions, countries, or nationalities.

ℰ die **AG**, PLURAL die **AGs** ABBREVIATION
1 (=Aktiengesellschaft) plc (=Public limited company)
2 (=Arbeitsgruppe) study group, school club

der **Agentenroman**, PLURAL die **Agentenromane**
spy novel

die **Agentur**, PLURAL die **Agenturen**
agency

aggressiv ADJECTIVE
aggressive

ℰ indicates key words

ähneln *VERB*, *PERFECT* **hat geähnelt**
1 to resemble
Er ähnelt seinem Vater sehr. He's very like his father.
2 sich ähneln to be alike
Sie ähneln sich sehr. They are very much alike.

ahnen *VERB*, *PERFECT* **hat geahnt**
1 to know
Das konnte ich wirklich nicht ahnen. I had no way of knowing that.
Wer soll denn ahnen, dass ...? Who would have thought that ...?
2 to suspect
So etwas habe ich doch schon geahnt. I did suspect something like that.

ℰ **ähnlich** *ADJECTIVE*
1 similar
Gib mir ein ähnliches Beispiel. Give me a similar example.
2 Er ist seinem Onkel ähnlich. He is like his uncle.
Sie sieht ihrer Mutter ähnlich. She looks like her mother.
Es schmeckt ähnlich wie Huhn. It tastes like chicken.
3 Das sieht dir ähnlich! *(informal)* That's just like you!

ℰ **die Ähnlichkeit**, *PLURAL* die **Ähnlichkeiten**
similarity

ℰ **die Ahnung**
1 idea
Hast du eine Ahnung, wie er heißt? Have you got any idea what he's called?
2 Keine Ahnung! No idea!
Er hat von Mode absolut keine Ahnung. He doesn't know a thing about fashion.
3 premonition

ahnungslos *ADJECTIVE*
unsuspecting

der Ahorn, *PLURAL* die **Ahorne**
maple

das Aids
Aids

der Akademiker, *PLURAL* die **Akademiker**
university graduate *(male)*

die Akademikerin, *PLURAL* die **Akademikerinnen**
university graduate *(female)*

akademisch *ADJECTIVE*
academic

der Akkusativ, *PLURAL* die **Akkusative**
accusative *(in grammar)*

die Akne
acne

die Akte, *PLURAL* die **Akten**
file

die Aktenmappe, *PLURAL* die **Aktenmappen**
portfolio case

ℰ **die Aktentasche**, *PLURAL* die **Aktentaschen**
briefcase

die Aktion, *PLURAL* die **Aktionen**
1 action
Wir müssen sofort in Aktion treten. We have to take action straight away.
2 campaign
Sie starteten eine Aktion für den Frieden. They started a peace campaign.

ℰ **aktiv** *ADJECTIVE*
active

das Aktiv
active *(in grammar)*

die Aktivität, *PLURAL* die **Aktivitäten**
activity

die Aktualisierung, *PLURAL* die **Aktualisierungen**
1 update
2 updating

ℰ **aktuell** *ADJECTIVE*
1 topical
In dem Artikel geht es um ein aktuelles Thema. The article is about a topical issue.
2 Das ist nicht mehr aktuell. It's no longer relevant.
3 current
Ich sehe mir im Fernsehen gern aktuelle Sendungen an. I like watching current-affairs programmes on TV.

WORD TIP The German word aktuell does not mean actual in English; the German word for actual and actually is eigentlich.

ℰ **der Akzent**, *PLURAL* die **Akzente**
1 accent
Sie spricht mit starkem Akzent. She speaks with a strong accent.
2 accent *(on a letter)*
3 stress
Wir legen den Akzent auf die Praxis. We stress the practical work.

albern *ADJECTIVE*
silly

◇ irregular verb; *SEP* separable verb; for more help with verbs see centre section

albern ADVERB
in a silly way

der **Albtraum**, PLURAL die **Albträume**
nightmare

das **Album**, PLURAL die **Alben**
album

die **Algebra**
algebra

ℰ der **Alkohol**
alcohol

ℰ **alkoholfrei** ADJECTIVE
non-alcoholic

der **Alkoholiker**, PLURAL die **Alkoholiker**
alcoholic (male)

die **Alkoholikerin**, PLURAL die
Alkoholikerinnen
alcoholic (female)

alkoholisch ADJECTIVE
alcoholic

das **All**
space
Sie haben einen Satelliten ins All
geschickt. They sent a satellite into space.

alle ▸ SEE **aller**

die **Allee**, PLURAL die **Alleen**
avenue

ℰ **allein** ADJECTIVE
1 alone
Sie waren allein im Zimmer. They were
alone in the room.
Die Eltern ließen die Kinder allein. The
parents left the children alone.
2 on your own
Sie hat das ganz allein gezeichnet. She
drew it all on her own.
3 von allein by yourself, by itself
(automatically)
Die Tür ging von allein auf. The door
opened by itself.
4 Allein der Gedanke daran ist ekelhaft. The
mere thought (of it) is disgusting.

alleinerziehend ADJECTIVE
single
Sie ist eine alleinerziehende Mutter. She's
a single mother.
der/die Alleinerziehende single parent

alleinstehend ADJECTIVE
single
Er ist alleinstehend. He's single.

ℰ **aller, alle, alles** ADJECTIVE, PRONOUN
1 all
Alle meine Freunde kommen auch. All
my friends are coming too.
Er hat alles Geld ausgegeben. He has
spent all the money.
Sie gingen alle miteinander in die Stadt.
They went all together into town.
Fliegen können in alle Richtungen
sehen. Flies can see in all directions at
once.
2 Alle Jungen in der Schule machen mit.
All the boys in the school are taking part.
Alles Gute! All the best!
Es gab Getränke aller Art. There were all
kinds of drinks.
3 alle (plural) all
Alle waren da. They were all there.
Wir alle wollen helfen. All of us want to
help.
Wir haben alle gesehen. We saw all of
them.
4 Sie weinte ohne allen Grund. She was
crying for no reason.
5 alle beide both of them
6 every
alle Tage every day
Sie sah alle fünf Minuten auf die Uhr. She
looked at her watch every five minutes.
7 alles everything, everybody (people)
Hier finden Sie alles unter einem Dach.
Here, you will find everything under one
roof.
Alles aufstehen! Stand up everybody.
8 alle sein (informal) to be all gone
Die Milch ist alle. The milk is all gone.

WORD TIP The German expression alle Tage
does not mean all day in English; the German
expression for all day is den ganzen Tag.

allerbester, allerbeste, allerbestes
ADJECTIVE
1 very best
2 Du warst am allerbesten. You were best
of all.

ℰ **allerdings** ADVERB
1 though
Das Essen ist gut, allerdings ziemlich
teuer. The food's good, though rather
expensive.
2 certainly (yes)
'Tut das weh?' – 'Allerdings!' 'Does it
hurt?' – 'It certainly does!'

die **Allergie**, PLURAL die **Allergien**
allergy

ℰ **allergisch** ADJECTIVE
allergic

Er ist allergisch gegen Nüsse. He's allergic to nuts.

Allerheiligen NEUTER NOUN
All Saints' Day

> **ALLERHEILIGEN**
>
> Allerheiligen is celebrated on 1 November: All Saint's Day. A public holiday in Austria and most Roman Catholic parts of Germany. People visit cemeteries and put wreaths and flowers on the graves.

allerlei ADJECTIVE
all sorts of
Sie ließen sich allerlei Ausreden einfallen. They came up with all sorts of excuses.

allerletzter, allerletzte, allerletztes
ADJECTIVE
very last

alles ▸ SEE **aller**

ℰ **allgemein** ADJECTIVE
1 **general**
2 **im Allgemeinen** in general
allgemein ADVERB
1 **generally**
2 **Es ist allgemein bekannt, dass ...** It is common knowledge that ...

allmählich ADJECTIVE
gradual
allmählich ADVERB
gradually
Wir sollten allmählich gehen. It's time we got going.

ℰ der **Alltag**
1 **daily routine, everyday life**
2 **weekday**

alltäglich ADJECTIVE
everyday (event, sight)

alltags ADVERB
on weekdays

ℰ die **Alpen** PLURAL NOUN
die Alpen the Alps

> **ALPEN**
>
> The Alps cover much of Austria and Switzerland, and stretch along the southern border of Germany. They are a popular holiday area in both summer and winter. The highest peaks in the three countries are: Großglockner 3798m (Austria), Monte Rosa 4634m (Switzerland), Zugspitze 2964m (Germany).

ℰ das **Alphabet**, PLURAL die **Alphabete**
alphabet

alphabetisch ADJECTIVE
alphabetical

ℰ **als** CONJUNCTION
1 **when**
Als meine Freundin hier war, ... When my friend was here, ...
Erst als der Lehrer hereinkam, hörten sie auf. They stopped only when the teacher came in.
2 **than** (in comparisons)
Er ist jünger als sie. He's younger than her.
3 **lieber ... als ... rather ... than ...**
Ich würde lieber ins Kino gehen, als vor dem Fernseher zu sitzen. I'd rather go to the cinema than sit in front of the TV.
4 **as**
Als Frau kann ich das verstehen. As a woman, I can sympathize.
Gerade als ich gehen wollte, klingelte das Telefon. Just as I was about to leave the phone rang.
5 **als ob** as if
Als ob ich das nicht wüsste! As if I didn't know that!

ℰ **also** ADVERB, CONJUNCTION
1 **so, therefore**
Ich konnte ihn telefonisch nicht erreichen, also habe ich ihm eine Mail geschickt. I couldn't get through to him on the phone, so I sent him an email.
2 **then**
Also kommst du mit? You're coming too, then?
Also gut! All right then!
3 **well**
Also, wie gesagt, ... Well, as I said before, ...
4 **Na also!** There you are!

> **WORD TIP** The German word also does not mean also in English; the German word for also is auch.

ℰ **alt** ADJECTIVE
1 **old**
Wie alt bist du? How old are you?
Er ist alt geworden. He has grown old.
2 Ich finde, wir sollten alles beim Alten lassen. I think we should leave everything as it was.

der **Altar**, PLURAL die **Altäre**
altar

das **Altenheim**, PLURAL die **Altenheime**
old people's home

◇ irregular verb; SEP separable verb; for more help with verbs see centre section

der **Altenpfleger**, PLURAL die **Altenpfleger**
geriatric nurse (male)

WORD TIP Professions, hobbies, and sports don't take an article in German: Er ist Altenpfleger.

die **Altenpflegerin**, PLURAL die **Altenpflegerinnen**
geriatric nurse (female)

WORD TIP Professions, hobbies, and sports don't take an article in German: Sie ist Altenpflegerin.

ℙ das **Alter**, PLURAL die **Alter**
1 age
In deinem Alter solltest du das wissen. At your age, you should know that.
Er ist im Alter von zwanzig gestorben. He died at the age of twenty.
2 old age
Viele Menschen sind im Alter allein. Many people are alone in old age.

älter ADJECTIVE
1 older
Mein Rad ist älter als deins. My bike is older than yours.
2 elder
Mein älterer Bruder ist sechzehn. My elder brother is sixteen.
3 elderly
Sie ist eine ältere Dame. She is an elderly lady.

altern VERB, PERFECT **ist gealtert**
to age

die **Alternative**, PLURAL die **Alternativen**
alternative

ℙ der **Altersgenosse**, PLURAL die **Altersgenossen**
person of your own age (male)

ℙ die **Altersgenossin**, PLURAL die **Altersgenossinnen**
person of your own age (female)

die **Altersgrenze**, PLURAL die **Altersgrenzen**
age limit

das **Altersheim**, PLURAL die **Altersheime**
old people's home

ältester, älteste, ältestes ADJECTIVE
1 oldest
2 eldest
Er ist der älteste Sohn. He is the eldest son.

das **Altglas**
glass for recycling

ℙ der **Altglascontainer**, PLURAL die **Altglascontainer**
bottle bank

ℙ **altmodisch** ADJECTIVE
old-fashioned

ℙ das **Altpapier**
waste paper

ℙ der **Altpapiercontainer**, PLURAL die **Altpapiercontainer**
paper recycling skip

die **Altstadt**, PLURAL die **Altstädte**
old town

die **Alufolie**
kitchen foil

das **Aluminium**
aluminium

ℙ **am** ▸ SEE **an dem**
1 am Freitag on Friday
2 am Abend in the evening
3 am nächsten Tag the next day
4 am vorigen Samstag last Saturday
5 am besten the best
6 am teuersten (the) most expensive
7 am längsten the longest
8 am liebsten most of all, the most

die **Ameise**, PLURAL die **Ameisen**
ant

ℙ **Amerika** NEUTER NOUN
America

der **Amerikaner**, PLURAL die **Amerikaner**
American (male)

die **Amerikanerin**, PLURAL die **Amerikanerinnen**
American (female)

amerikanisch ADJECTIVE
American

WORD TIP Adjectives never have capitals in German, even for regions, countries, or nationalities.

ℙ die **Ampel**, PLURAL die **Ampeln**
traffic lights

ℙ die **Amsel**, PLURAL die **Amseln**
blackbird

das **Amt**, PLURAL die **Ämter**
office

amtlich ADJECTIVE
official

amüsant ADJECTIVE
amusing

amüsieren *VERB*, *PERFECT* **hat amüsiert**
1 to amuse
2 sich amüsieren to enjoy yourself
  Amüsier dich gut! Enjoy yourself!
3 Er hat sich über die Witze amüsiert. He
  found the jokes funny.
  Sie haben sich über seine Frisur amüsiert.
  They made fun of his haircut.

ℓ **an** *PREPOSITION* (+ DAT or + ACC)
1 (the dative is used when talking about
  position; the accusative shows movement
  or a change of place) **at**
  Sie stehen an der Spitze. (DAT) They are
  at the top.
  Wir setzten uns an den Tisch. (ACC) We
  sat down at the table.
  Er arbeitet an der Schule. (DAT) He works
  at the school.
2 **on** (attached to, when talking about time)
  Das Bild hängt an der Wand. (DAT) The
  picture is on the wall.
  Sie klebte das Poster an die Wand. (ACC)
  She stuck the poster on the wall.
  An dem Tag regnete es. It rained on that
  day.
  Ich habe am fünften März Geburtstag.
  My birthday is on the fifth of March.
3 **to**
  Er schickte einen Brief an seinen Freund.
  (ACC) He sent a letter to his friend.
4 **of**
  Sie starb an Krebs. She died of cancer.
5 Ich denke an dich. I'm thinking of you.
6 Erinnerst du dich an ihn? Do you
  remember him?
7 Halte dich an die Regeln! Stick to the
  rules!
8 an (und für) sich actually
  An sich ist das kein Problem. Actually,
  it's no problem.
9 Es liegt an dir, jetzt etwas zu
  unternehmen. It's up to you to do
  something now.

WORD TIP an + dem gives am; an + das gives
ans

---

an *ADVERB*
1 **on**
  Das Licht ist an. The light's on.
2 Es kostet an die dreißig Euro. It's about
  thirty euros.
3 Von heute an wird alles anders. From
  today, everything will change.

analysieren *VERB*, *PERFECT* **hat analysiert**
to analyse

die Ananas, *PLURAL* **die Ananas**
pineapple

das Anästhetikum, *PLURAL* **die Anästhetika**
anaesthetic

anbauen *VERB*, *PERFECT* **hat angebaut**
to grow
Sie bauen Gemüse an. They grow
vegetables.

ℓ **anbieten** *VERB*◇, *IMPERFECT* **bot an**, *PERFECT* **hat
angeboten**
to offer
Anna bot (mir) an, mich nach Hause zu
bringen. Anna offered to take me home.

der Anblick, *PLURAL* **die Anblicke**
sight

anbrennen *VERB*◇, *IMPERFECT* **brannte an**,
PERFECT **ist angebrannt**
to burn
Das Essen ist angebrannt. The food's
burnt.

ℓ **das Andenken**, *PLURAL* **die Andenken**
1 souvenir
2 Ich schenke es dir zum Andenken an
  unsere Ferien. I'm giving it to you to
  remind us of our holiday.

ℓ **anderer, andere, anderes** *ADJECTIVE*
1 **other**
  Ich nehme das andere T-Shirt. I'll have the
  other T-shirt.
2 **different**
  Reden wir über ein anderes Thema. Let's
  talk about a different subject.
3 ein anderer/eine andere/ein anderes
  another
  Ich zeige es dir ein anderes Mal. I'll show it
  to you another time.

anderer andere anderes *PRONOUN*
1 der/die/das andere the other one
  Er meint nicht dieses Buch, sondern das
  andere. He doesn't mean that book, but
  the other one.
  die anderen the others
  Die anderen kommen später. The others
  are coming later.
2 andere other ones (things, toys, etc.)
3 ein anderer/eine andere/ein anderes a
  different one (thing) someone else (person)
4 kein anderer no one else
5 unter anderem among other things
6 etwas anderes something else
7 alles andere everything else

andererseits *ADVERB*
on the other hand

andermal ADVERB
ein andermal another time

ℓ **ändern** VERB, PERFECT **hat geändert**
1 to change
2 to alter (a garment)
3 sich ändern to change
   Sie hat sich sehr geändert. She's changed a lot.

ℓ **anders** ADVERB
1 differently
   Ich mache das anders. I do it differently.
2 different
   Er sieht heute anders aus. He looks different now.
3 anders als different from
   Du bist ganz anders als ich. You're quite different from me.
4 niemand anders nobody else
   jemand anders somebody else
   Kann nicht jemand anders dir helfen? Couldn't somebody else help you?
5 irgendwo anders somewhere else

anderthalb NUMBER
one and a half

die **Anerkennung**
1 appreciation
2 recognition (of a king, state)

der **Anfall**, PLURAL die **Anfälle**
fit

ℓ der **Anfang**, PLURAL die **Anfänge**
1 beginning, start
   Am Anfang war es schwer. In the beginning, it was difficult.
   Sie war von Anfang an dagegen. She was against it from the start.
2 zu Anfang at first

ℓ **anfangen** VERB◇, PRESENT **fängt an**, IMPERFECT **fing an**, PERFECT **hat angefangen**
1 to begin, to start
   Die Schule fängt um acht an. School starts at eight.
   Er fing mit seinen Hausaufgaben an. He started (on) his homework.
2 Sie fängt nächste Woche bei einer anderen Firma an. She starts working for a different firm next week.
3 Was soll ich damit anfangen? What am I supposed to do with that?
4 Damit kann ich nichts anfangen. That's no good to me (it's no use)., It doesn't mean anything to me (I don't understand it).

der **Anfänger**, PLURAL die **Anfänger**
beginner (male)

die **Anfängerin**, PLURAL die **Anfängerinnen**
beginner (female)

ℓ **anfassen** VERB, PERFECT **hat angefasst**
1 to touch
   Ihr dürft hier nichts anfassen! You are not allowed to touch anything here!
2 to tackle (a problem, a task)
3 to treat (a person)
   Fass ihn nicht so hart an! Don't treat him so harshly!
4 Kannst du mit anfassen? Can you lend a hand?
5 sich anfassen to feel
   Es fasst sich weich an. It feels soft.

anfragen VERB, PERFECT **hat angefragt**
to enquire, to ask

anfreunden VERB, PERFECT **hat sich angefreundet**
1 sich (mit jemandem) anfreunden to make friends (with somebody)
   Sie freundet sich mit allen möglichen Leuten an. She makes friends with all sorts of people.
2 sich anfreunden to become friends
   Wir haben uns angefreundet. We've become friends.

die **Anführungszeichen** PLURAL NOUN
inverted commas

die **Angabe**, PLURAL die **Angaben**
1 piece of information
2 serve (in tennis)
3 showing off
   Das ist nur Angabe! He is/She is/They are only showing off!

ℓ **angeben** VERB◇, PRESENT **gibt an**, IMPERFECT **gab an**, PERFECT **hat angegeben**
1 to give (your name, a reason)
2 to show off
   Warum gibt er immer so an? Why is he always showing off?
3 to indicate (on a map)
4 to serve (in tennis)

der **Angeber**, PLURAL die **Angeber**
show-off (male)

die **Angeberin**, PLURAL die **Angeberinnen**
show-off (female)

angeberisch ADJECTIVE
boastful, showy

ℓ das **Angebot**, PLURAL die **Angebote**
offer

ρ **angehen** VERB◇, IMPERFECT **ging an**, PERFECT **ist angegangen**
1 **to come on** *(a radio, heating, a light)*
2 **to concern**
Das geht auch dich etwas an. It concerns you too.
Das geht dich nichts an. It's none of your business.
3 PERFECT **hat angegangen to tackle** *(problems, difficulty, work)*

der/die **Angehörige**, PLURAL die **Angehörigen**
relative

die **Angel**, PLURAL die **Angeln**
fishing rod

die **Angelegenheit**, PLURAL die **Angelegenheiten**
1 **matter**
2 **business**
Das ist meine Angelegenheit. That's my business.

ρ **angeln** VERB, PERFECT **hat geangelt**
1 **to fish**
Möchtest du angeln gehen? Would you like to go fishing?
2 **to catch** *(a fish)*

die **Angelrute**, PLURAL die **Angelruten**
fishing rod

angemessen ADJECTIVE
appropriate

angenehm ADJECTIVE
pleasant

angenehm EXCLAMATION
Pleased to meet you! *(when introduced to somebody)*

ρ der/die **Angestellte**, PLURAL die **Angestellten**
employee

angewiesen ADJECTIVE
dependent
Sie sind auf Spenden angewiesen. They are dependent on donations.
Wir sind auf ihn angewiesen. We are dependent on him.

angewöhnen VERB, PERFECT **hat angewöhnt**
1 jemandem etwas angewöhnen **to get somebody used to something**
Sie hat den Kindern angewöhnt, im Haushalt zu helfen. She's got the children used to helping with the housework.
2 sich etwas angewöhnen **to get into the habit of doing something**
Ich habe es mir angewöhnt, früh

aufzustehen. I've got into the habit of getting up early.

die **Angewohnheit**, PLURAL die **Angewohnheiten**
habit

angreifen VERB◇, IMPERFECT **griff an**, PERFECT **hat angegriffen**
1 **to attack**
2 **to affect** *(your health, voice)*
3 *(used in Southern Germany and Austria)* **to touch**

der **Angriff**, PLURAL die **Angriffe**
attack

ρ die **Angst**, PLURAL die **Ängste**
fear
Sie hatten Angst. They were afraid.
Hast du Angst vor ihm? Are you afraid of him?
Das machte mir Angst. It frightened me.
Ich habe Angst vor der Prüfung. I'm worried about the exam.
Sie hat Angst um ihre Tochter. She's worried about her daughter.

ängstlich ADJECTIVE
1 **nervous**
2 **frightened**
3 **anxious**

angucken VERB, PERFECT **hat angeguckt**
1 **to look at**
Er guckte mich nicht an. He didn't look at me.
2 sich etwas angucken **to look at something**
Guck dir das mal an! Look at that!
3 sich etwas angucken **to watch something** *(on TV)*
Den Film haben wir uns im Kino angeguckt. We saw the film at the cinema.

anhaben VERB◇ *(informal)*, PRESENT **hat an**, IMPERFECT **hatte an**, PERFECT **hat angehabt**
to have on
Sie hat heute das neue Kleid an. She's got her new dress on today.

anhalten VERB◇, PRESENT **hält an**, IMPERFECT **hielt an**, PERFECT **hat angehalten**
1 **to stop**
2 Ich hielt den Atem an. I held my breath.
3 **to last**
Das schöne Wetter wird nicht lange anhalten. The good weather won't last long.

der **Anhalter**, PLURAL die **Anhalter**
1 **hitchhiker** *(male)*
2 per Anhalter fahren **to hitchhike**

◇ **irregular verb;** SEP **separable verb; for more help with verbs see centre section**

Sie fuhren per Anhalter nach Berlin. They hitchhiked to Berlin.

die **Anhalterin**, PLURAL die **Anhalterinnen**
hitchhiker *(female)*

der **Anhang**, PLURAL die **Anhänge**
1 appendix *(in a book)*
2 attachment *(in an email)*

anhängen VERB, PERFECT **hat angehängt**
to attach
Ich habe das Protokoll angehängt. I've attached the minutes.

der **Anhänger**, PLURAL die **Anhänger**
1 supporter *(male)*
2 trailer
3 label *(on a suitcase)*
4 pendant
5 loop *(for hanging up)*

die **Anhängerin**, PLURAL die **Anhängerinnen**
supporter *(female)*

ℙ **anhören** VERB, PERFECT **hat angehört**
1 to listen to *(music)*
Sie hörte sich eine Lied an. She listened to a song.
Ich kann ihn mir nicht länger anhören. I can't listen to him any longer.
2 sich anhören to sound
Das hört sich gut an. That sounds good.
3 jemandem etwas anhören to hear something in somebody's voice
Man hörte ihr die Verzweiflung an. You could hear the despair in her voice.

anklagen VERB, PERFECT **hat angeklagt**
to accuse

die **Ankleidekabine**, PLURAL die **Ankleidekabinen**
changing cubicle

anklicken VERB, PERFECT **hat angeklickt**
etwas anklicken to click on something
Du musst das Icon anklicken. You have to click on the icon.

ℙ **ankommen** VERB◇, IMPERFECT **kam an**, PERFECT **ist angekommen**
1 to arrive
Wir sind gut angekommen. We have arrived safely.
2 (bei jemandem) gut ankommen *(informal)* to go down well *(with somebody)*
Der neue Song kam bei den Fans gut an. *(informal)* The new song went down well with the fans.
3 ankommen auf to depend on
Es kommt ganz darauf an. It all depends.
4 es drauf ankommen lassen *(informal)* to

take a chance
5 Auf ein paar Minuten kommt es nicht an. A few minutes don't matter.

ankreuzen VERB, PERFECT **hat angekreuzt**
to mark with a cross

ankündigen VERB, PERFECT **hat angekündigt**
to announce

die **Ankündigung**, PLURAL die **Ankündigungen**
announcement

ℙ die **Ankunft**, PLURAL die **Ankünfte**
arrival

die **Ankunftstafel**, PLURAL die **Ankunftstafeln**
arrivals board

die **Ankunftszeit**, PLURAL die **Ankunftszeiten**
time of arrival

die **Anlage**, PLURAL die **Anlagen**
1 gardens
2 investment
Das Haus ist eine gute Anlage. The house is a good investment.
3 plant *(industrial, for recycling, for example)*
4 enclosure *(with a letter, etc.)*
als Anlage enclosed
Als Anlage sende ich Ihnen ... Please find enclosed ...
5 system *(music, loudspeakers, etc.)*
6 installation *(military)*

der **Anlass**, PLURAL die **Anlässe**
1 cause
Was war der Anlass ihres Streits? What was the cause of their row?
Das gibt Anlass zur Sorge. It gives cause for concern.
2 occasion
Die Eröffnung war ein festlicher Anlass. The opening was a festive occasion.
Aus Anlass ihres Geburtstags lud sie die ganze Familie ein. She invited the whole family on her birthday.

die **Anleitung**, PLURAL die **Anleitungen**
instructions

anmachen VERB, PERFECT **hat angemacht**
1 to turn on *(the light, radio, TV)*
2 to light *(a fire)*
3 to dress *(salad)*
4 *(informal)* to chat up *(a person)*

das **Anmeldeformular**, PLURAL die **Anmeldeformulare**
registration form

ℙ anmelden VERB, PERFECT **hat angemeldet**
1 to register *(a car, change of address)*
2 jemanden anmelden to enrol somebody
3 jemanden anmelden to make an appointment for somebody
   Sind Sie angemeldet? Do you have an appointment?
4 sich anmelden to say that you're coming
5 sich anmelden to register your new address *(in Germany and Austria, a change of address has to be registered at the 'Einwohnermeldeamt')*
   sich polizeilich anmelden to register with the police
6 sich anmelden to make an appointment
   Sie hat sich beim Arzt angemeldet. She has made an appointment with the doctor.
7 sich anmelden to check in *(at a hotel)*
8 sich anmelden to enrol
   Er hat sich zu einem Abendkurs angemeldet. He has enrolled for an evening class.

ℙ die Anmeldung, PLURAL die **Anmeldungen**
1 registration *(in Germany and Austria a change of address has to be registered at the 'Einwohnermeldeamt')*
2 appointment *(with the doctor)*
3 reception *(at a hotel)*

annehmbar ADJECTIVE
acceptable

annehmen VERB◇, PRESENT **nimmt an**, IMPERFECT **nahm an**, PERFECT **hat angenommen**
1 to accept *(an invitation, help, a verdict)*
2 to take *(a call, name)*
3 to adopt *(a child, habit)*
4 to assume
   Angenommen, dass … Assuming that …

die Annonce, PLURAL die **Annoncen**
(small) ad

anonym ADJECTIVE
anonymous
anonym ADVERB
anonymously

der Anorak, PLURAL die **Anoraks**
1 anorak
2 cagoule

anordnen VERB, PERFECT **hat angeordnet**
1 to arrange
2 to order

ℙ anpassen VERB, PERFECT **hat sich angepasst**
sich anpassen to adapt

anpassungsfähig ADJECTIVE
adaptable

anprobieren VERB, PERFECT **hat anprobiert**
to try on

ℙ der Anruf, PLURAL die **Anrufe**
(phone) call

der Anrufbeantworter, PLURAL die **Anrufbeantworter**
answering machine

ℙ anrufen VERB◇, IMPERFECT **rief an**, PERFECT **hat angerufen**
to ring, to phone, to call
Ich rufe schnell mal meine Mutter an. I'll just quickly ring my mother.

ans
▶ SEE **an das**
Gehst du ans Telefon? Would you answer the phone?

die Ansage, PLURAL die **Ansagen**
announcement

der Ansager, PLURAL die **Ansager**
announcer *(male)*

die Ansagerin, PLURAL die **Ansagerinnen**
announcer *(female)*

anschalten VERB, PERFECT **hat angeschaltet**
to switch on

anschauen VERB, PERFECT **hat angeschaut**
1 to look at
2 sich etwas anschauen to look at something, to watch something *(on TV)*
   Sie schauten sich den neuen Film an. They saw the new film.

anscheinend ADVERB
apparently

der Anschlag, PLURAL die **Anschläge**
1 notice
2 attack
   War es ein Anschlag auf den Präsidenten? Was it an attack on the president?

das Anschlagbrett, PLURAL die **Anschlagbretter**
noticeboard

anschlagen VERB◇, PRESENT **schlägt an**, IMPERFECT **schlug an**, PERFECT **hat angeschlagen**
1 to put up *(a notice, an announcement)*
2 to chip

anschließen VERB◇, IMPERFECT **schloss an**, PERFECT **hat angeschlossen**
1 to connect

◇ **irregular verb;** SEP **separable verb; for more help with verbs see centre section**

2 sich an etwas anschließen to follow something
An den Vortrag schließt sich eine Diskussion an. The talk will be followed by a discussion.

3 sich jemandem anschließen to join somebody
Sie schlossen sich der Gruppe an. They joined the group.

anschließend ADVERB
1 afterwards
2 anschließend an after
Anschließend an das Turnier findet die Preisverleihung statt. After the tournament, the prizes will be presented.

der **Anschluss**, PLURAL die **Anschlüsse**
1 connection
2 Hast du schon Anschluss gefunden? Have you made any friends yet?
3 im Anschluss an after
Im Anschluss an den Vortrag findet eine Diskussion statt. After the talk there will be a discussion.

anschnallen VERB, PERFECT **hat sich angeschnallt**
sich anschnallen to fasten your seat belt

die **Anschrift**, PLURAL die **Anschriften**
address

die **Anschuldigung**, PLURAL die **Anschuldigungen**
accusation

ℰ **ansehen** VERB◇, PRESENT **sieht an**, IMPERFECT **sah an**, PERFECT **hat angesehen**
1 to look at
Sie sah mich nicht an. She didn't look at me.
2 sich etwas ansehen to look at something
Sehen Sie sich das Bild an. Look at the picture.
Sie sahen sich die Altstadt an. They looked round the old town.
3 sich etwas ansehen to watch something (on TV)
Heute abend sehen wir uns das Endspiel an. Tonight we're going to watch the final.
Hast du dir den Film schon angesehen? Have you seen the film yet?
4 to regard
Ich sehe ihn als meinen Freund an. I regard him as a friend.

das **Ansehen**
1 respect
2 reputation

die **Ansicht**, PLURAL die **Ansichten**
view, opinion
Meiner Ansicht nach hat es sich nicht gelohnt. In my view it was a waste of time.

die **Ansichtskarte**, PLURAL die **Ansichtskarten**
picture postcard

ℰ der **Anspitzer**, PLURAL die **Anspitzer**
pencil sharpener

ansprechen VERB◇, PRESENT **spricht an**, IMPERFECT **sprach an**, PERFECT **hat angesprochen**
1 to speak to
2 to appeal to
Ihre Musik spricht mich an. Their music appeals to me.
3 to mention
Er sprach den Skandal an, in den sie verwickelt war. He mentioned the scandal she was involved in.
4 auf etwas ansprechen to respond to something (a treatment, for example)

ℰ der **Anspruch**, PLURAL die **Ansprüche**
1 demand
Wir stellen keine Ansprüche. We make no demands.
2 claim (for compensation)
3 Sie haben Anspruch auf Sozialhilfe. They are entitled to social security.
4 etwas in Anspruch nehmen to take advantage of something (an offer, for example)
5 Das nimmt viel Zeit in Anspruch. It takes up a lot of time.

anständig ADJECTIVE
1 decent
2 respectable

anstarren VERB, PERFECT **hat angestarrt**
to stare at

anstatt PREPOSITION (+ GEN)
instead of

anstatt CONJUNCTION
Anstatt zu arbeiten, sitzen sie zu Hause herum. Instead of working they sit around at home.

ansteckend ADJECTIVE
infectious

ansteigen VERB◇, IMPERFECT **stieg an**, PERFECT **ist angestiegen**
to increase, to rise

anstelle PREPOSITION (+ GEN)
instead of

ℰ indicates key words

_ℓ_ **anstellen** _VERB_, _PERFECT_ **hat angestellt**
1 **to employ**
2 **to turn on** (the TV, radio)
3 (informal) **to do**
   Was stellt ihr heute Abend noch an? What are you doing tonight?
   Wie kann ich es nur anstellen, dass ...? What can I do to ...?
4 **sich anstellen to queue**
   Wir mussten uns stundenlang anstellen. We had to queue for hours.
5 **sich anstellen to make a fuss**
   Stell dich nicht so an! Don't make such a fuss!

_ℓ_ der **Anstieg**, _PLURAL_ die **Anstiege**
1 **increase**
2 **way up, ascent**

anstreichen _VERB◇_, _IMPERFECT_ **strich an**, _PERFECT_ **hat angestrichen**
to paint

der **Anstreicher**, _PLURAL_ die **Anstreicher**
decorator (male)

> **WORD TIP** Professions, hobbies, and sports don't take an article in German: Er ist Anstreicher.

die **Anstreicherin**, _PLURAL_ die **Anstreicherinnen**
decorator (female)

> **WORD TIP** Professions, hobbies, and sports don't take an article in German: Sie ist Anstreicherin.

_ℓ_ **anstrengen** _VERB_, _PERFECT_ **hat angestrengt**
1 **to tire**
   Ihr Besuch hat mich sehr angestrengt. Their visit tired me out.
2 **sich anstrengen to make an effort**

_ℓ_ **anstrengend** _ADJECTIVE_
tiring, taxing, hard work
Die Proben für das Musical sind anstrengend. The rehearsals for the musical are hard work.

die **Anstrengung**, _PLURAL_ die **Anstrengungen**
effort

die **Antarktis**
die Antarktis the Antarctic
in der Antarktis in the Antarctic

der **Anteil**, _PLURAL_ die **Anteile**
1 **share**
   Was ist mein Anteil an dem Gewinn? What is my share of the profits?
2 **Anteil nehmen to sympathize**

Er nahm Anteil an ihren Sorgen. He sympathized with their worries.
3 Oma nahm Anteil am Leben ihrer Enkel. Gran took an interest in her grandchildren's lives.

die **Antenne**, _PLURAL_ die **Antennen**
aerial

das **Antibiotikum**, _PLURAL_ die **Antibiotika**
antibiotic

antik _ADJECTIVE_
1 **antique**
2 **ancient**

die **Antiquitäten** _PLURAL NOUN_
antiques

das **Antiseptikum**, _PLURAL_ die **Antiseptika**
antiseptic

das **Antivirenprogramm**, _PLURAL_ die **Antivirenprogramme**
anti-virus software

der **Antrag**, _PLURAL_ die **Anträge**
application
Sie müssen erst einen Antrag stellen. You have to make an application first.

das **Antragsformular**, _PLURAL_ die **Antragsformulare**
application form

_ℓ_ die **Antwort**, _PLURAL_ die **Antworten**
answer, reply
Sie gab mir keine Antwort. She didn't give me an answer.

_ℓ_ **antworten** _VERB_, _PERFECT_ **hat geantwortet**
to answer, to reply
auf etwas antworten to answer something
Auf meine Frage hat er nicht geantwortet. He didn't answer my question.
jemandem antworten to reply to somebody
Hat sie dir geantwortet? Did she reply to you?

der **Anwalt**, _PLURAL_ die **Anwälte**
lawyer (male)

> **WORD TIP** Professions, hobbies, and sports don't take an article in German: Er ist Anwalt.

die **Anwältin**, _PLURAL_ die **Anwältinnen**
lawyer (female)

> **WORD TIP** Professions, hobbies, and sports don't take an article in German: Sie ist Anwältin.

die **Anweisung**, _PLURAL_ die **Anweisungen**
instruction

◇ irregular verb; _SEP_ separable verb; for more help with verbs see centre section

anwenden VERB, PERFECT **hat angewendet**
1 **to use** (a method, process, medicine)
2 **to apply** (a rule, law)

die Anwendung, PLURAL die **Anwendungen**
1 **use**
2 **application** (in computing)

anwesend ADJECTIVE
present

die Anwesenheit
presence
Er gab es in meiner Anwesenheit zu. He admitted it in my presence.

die Anzahl
number

anzahlen VERB, PERFECT **hat angezahlt**
to pay a deposit
Ich habe hundert Euro angezahlt. I paid a deposit of a hundred euros.
Sie hat das Auto angezahlt. She paid a deposit on the car.

die Anzahlung, PLURAL die **Anzahlungen**
deposit

das Anzeichen, PLURAL die **Anzeichen**
sign

ℙ **die Anzeige**, PLURAL die **Anzeigen**
1 **advertisement**
2 **report** (to the police)
Sie hat Anzeige gegen ihn erstattet. She reported him to the police.

anzeigen VERB, PERFECT **hat angezeigt**
1 **to report**
jemanden anzeigen to report somebody to the police
2 **to show** (the time, a date)

ℙ **anziehen** VERB◇, IMPERFECT **zog an**, PERFECT **hat angezogen**
1 **to attract**
2 **to put on** (clothes, the brakes)
3 **to dress** (a child or doll)
Sie ist immer gut angezogen. She's always well dressed.
4 **to tighten** (a knot, a screw)
5 **sich anziehen** to get dressed
Zieh dich schnell an! Get dressed quickly!
6 Was soll ich anziehen? What shall I wear?

ℙ **der Anzug**, PLURAL die **Anzüge**
suit

anzünden VERB, PERFECT **hat angezündet**
to light

der Aperitif, PLURAL die **Aperitifs**
apéritif

ℙ **der Apfel**, PLURAL die **Äpfel**
apple

🔵 **APFELSTRUDEL**

A traditional Austrian dessert made of thin pastry rolled round a filling of apples and raisins. It is sometimes served with whipped cream.

der Apfelmost
cider

ℙ **der Apfelsaft**, PLURAL die **Apfelsäfte**
apple juice

die Apfelsine, PLURAL die **Apfelsinen**
orange

ℙ **die Apotheke**, PLURAL die **Apotheken**
chemist's, pharmacy

der Apotheker, PLURAL die **Apotheker**
chemist, pharmacist (male)

WORD TIP Professions, hobbies, and sports don't take an article in German: Er ist Apotheker.

die Apothekerin, PLURAL die **Apothekerinnen**
chemist, pharmacist (female)

WORD TIP Professions, hobbies, and sports don't take an article in German: Sie ist Apothekerin.

der Apparat, PLURAL die **Apparate**
1 **set** (TV, radio)
2 **camera**
3 **phone**
Am Apparat! Speaking!
4 **gadget**

das Appartement, PLURAL die **Appartements**
flat

der Appetit
appetite
Guten Appetit! Enjoy your meal!

appetitlich ADJECTIVE
1 **appetizing**
2 **attractive**

die Aprikose, PLURAL die **Aprikosen**
apricot

ℙ **der April**
April
im April in April
Sie hat am ersten April Geburtstag. Her birthday is on the first of April.
April, April! April fool!
Er hat mich in den April geschickt. He played an April fool trick on me.

der **Aprilscherz**, PLURAL die **Aprilscherze**
April Fool's joke

das **Aquarium**, PLURAL die **Aquarien**
1 aquarium
2 tank (for fish)

der **Äquator**
equator

der **Araber**, PLURAL die **Araber**
Arab (male)

die **Araberin**, PLURAL die **Araberinnen**
Arab (female)

arabisch ADJECTIVE
1 Arab
die arabischen Länder the Arab countries
2 Arabian
3 Arabic (number, language)
arabische Zahlen Arabic numerals
die arabische Sprache Arabic

> **WORD TIP** Adjectives never have capitals in German, even for regions, countries, or nationalities.

ℓ die **Arbeit**, PLURAL die **Arbeiten**
1 work
Ich habe viel Arbeit. I have a lot of work.
Sie kam von der Arbeit. She came from work.
2 job
Er sucht Arbeit. He's looking for a job.
3 test (at school)
Morgen schreiben wir eine Arbeit. We have a test tomorrow.
4 Du hast dir aber viel Arbeit gemacht! You've really gone to a lot of trouble!

ℓ **arbeiten** VERB, PERFECT **hat gearbeitet**
to work

der **Arbeiter**, PLURAL die **Arbeiter**
worker (male)

die **Arbeiterin**, PLURAL die **Arbeiterinnen**
worker (female)

der **Arbeitgeber**, PLURAL die **Arbeitgeber**
employer (male)

die **Arbeitgeberin**, PLURAL die **Arbeitgeberinnen**
employer (female)

der **Arbeitnehmer**, PLURAL die **Arbeitnehmer**
employee (male)

die **Arbeitnehmerin**, PLURAL die **Arbeitnehmerinnen**
employee (female)

das **Arbeitsamt**, PLURAL die **Arbeitsämter**
jobcentre

das **Arbeitsblatt**, PLURAL die **Arbeitsblätter**
worksheet, spreadsheet

die **Arbeitsgemeinschaft**, PLURAL die **Arbeitsgemeinschaften**
1 team
2 study group

die **Arbeitsgruppe**, PLURAL die **Arbeitsgruppen**
1 study group
2 school club

ℓ **arbeitslos** ADJECTIVE
unemployed

der/die **Arbeitslose**, PLURAL die **Arbeitslosen**
unemployed person
die Arbeitslosen the unemployed

die **Arbeitslosigkeit**
unemployment

der **Arbeitsplatz**, PLURAL die **Arbeitsplätze**
1 job
2 desk

das **Arbeitspraktikum**, PLURAL die **Arbeitspraktika**
work experience

ℓ die **Arbeitsstunde**, PLURAL die **Arbeitsstunden**
working hour

die **Arbeitszeit**, PLURAL die **Arbeitszeiten**
working hours

ℓ das **Arbeitszimmer**, PLURAL die **Arbeitszimmer**
study

der **Architekt**, PLURAL die **Architekten**
architect (male)

> **WORD TIP** Professions, hobbies, and sports don't take an article in German: Er ist Architekt.

die **Architektin**, PLURAL die **Architektinnen**
architect (female)

> **WORD TIP** Professions, hobbies, and sports don't take an article in German: Sie ist Architektin.

die **Architektur**
architecture

◇ irregular verb; SEP separable verb; for more help with verbs see centre section

ARD

die **ARD** *ABBREVIATION* (=Arbeitsgemeinschaft der öffentlich-rechtlichen Rundfunkanstalten der Bundesrepublik Deutschland) (a German public TV channel)

ℱ der **Ärger**
1 annoyance
2 trouble
Wir hatten schon wieder Ärger mit dem Auto! We had trouble with the car again!

ärgerlich *ADJECTIVE*
1 annoying
2 annoyed
Er war darüber sehr ärgerlich. He was very annoyed about it.

ℱ **ärgern** *VERB*, *PERFECT* **hat geärgert**
1 to annoy
2 sich ärgern to be annoyed, to get annoyed
Ich habe mich darüber geärgert. I was annoyed about it.
Sie hat sich über Tom geärgert. She got annoyed with Tom.

das **Argument**, *PLURAL* die **Argumente**
argument, point (in a discussion)
Das ist ein gutes Argument. That's a good point.

WORD TIP Careful: The German word for argument in the sense of 'fight' is Streit.

die **Arktis**
die Arktis the Arctic
in der Arktis in the Arctic

ℱ **arm** *ADJECTIVE*
poor
die Armen the poor (people)

ℱ der **Arm**, *PLURAL* die **Arme**
1 arm
2 (informal) jemanden auf den Arm nehmen to pull somebody's leg
Willst du mich auf den Arm nehmen? Are you pulling my leg?

das **Armband**, *PLURAL* die **Armbänder**
bracelet

die **Armbanduhr**, *PLURAL* die **Armbanduhren**
wristwatch

die **Armee**, *PLURAL* die **Armeen**
army

der **Ärmel**, *PLURAL* die **Ärmel**
sleeve

der **Ärmelkanal**
(English) Channel

ℱ die **Armut**
poverty

arrangieren *VERB*, *PERFECT* **hat arrangiert**
1 to arrange
2 sich arrangieren to come to an arrangement, to reach a compromise
Sie haben sich jetzt arrangiert. They have come to an arrangement now.

ℱ die **Art**, *PLURAL* die **Arten**
1 way
Auf diese Art schaffen wir es nie. We'll never manage it in this way.
Er machte es auf seine Art. He did it in his own way.
2 kind, sort
Diese Art (von) Buch mag ich nicht. I don't like this kind of book.
Sie verkaufen Bücher aller Art. They sell books of all kinds.
3 species
Der Gorilla ist eine vom Aussterben bedrohte Art. The gorilla is an endangered species.
4 nature
Es ist nicht seine Art, das zu tun. It's not (in) his nature to do that.

die **Arterie**, *PLURAL* die **Arterien**
artery

artig *ADJECTIVE*
well-behaved

der **Artikel**, *PLURAL* die **Artikel**
article
der bestimmte/unbestimmte Artikel the definite/indefinite article (in grammar)

die **Artischocke**, *PLURAL* die **Artischocken**
artichoke

die **Arznei**, *PLURAL* die **Arzneien**
medicine

das **Arzneimittel**, *PLURAL* die **Arzneimittel**
drug

ℱ der **Arzt**, *PLURAL* die **Ärzte**
doctor (male)

WORD TIP Professions, hobbies, and sports don't take an article in German: Er ist Arzt.

ℱ die **Ärztin**, *PLURAL* die **Ärztinnen**
doctor (female)

WORD TIP Professions, hobbies, and sports don't take an article in German: Sie ist Ärztin.

ärztlich *ADJECTIVE*
medical

ärztlich

ℱ indicates key words

ärztlich ADVERB
Du solltest dich ärztlich behandeln lassen.
You should have medical treatment.

die **Asche**, PLURAL die **Aschen**
ash

der **Aschenbecher**, PLURAL die
Aschenbecher
ashtray

der **Aschermittwoch**
Ash Wednesday

der **Asiat**, PLURAL die **Asiaten**
Asian (male)

die **Asiatin**, PLURAL die **Asiatinnen**
Asian (female)

asiatisch ADJECTIVE
Asian

> **WORD TIP** Adjectives never have capitals in German, even for regions, countries, or nationalities.

♀ **Asien** NEUTER NOUN
Asia
Sie fliegen nach Asien. They fly to Asia.

das **Ass**, PLURAL die **Asse**
ace

aß ▸ SEE **essen**

der **Assistent**, PLURAL die **Assistenten**
assistant (male)

die **Assistentin**, PLURAL die **Assistentinnen**
assistant (female)

♀ der **Ast**, PLURAL die **Äste**
branch

♀ das **Asthma**
asthma

die **Astrologie**
astrology

der **Astronaut**, PLURAL die **Astronauten**
astronaut (male)

> **WORD TIP** Professions, hobbies, and sports don't take an article in German: Er ist Astronaut.

die **Astronautin**, PLURAL die
Astronautinnen
astronaut (female)

> **WORD TIP** Professions, hobbies, and sports don't take an article in German: Sie ist Astronautin.

die **Astronomie**
astronomy

das **Asyl**
1 asylum
Sie baten um politisches Asyl. They applied for political asylum.
2 hostel (for the homeless)

der **Asylbewerber**, PLURAL die
Asylbewerber
asylum seeker (male)

die **Asylbewerberin**, PLURAL die
Asylbewerberinnen
asylum seeker (female)

das **Atelier**, PLURAL die **Ateliers**
(artist's) studio

der **Atem**
breath
Er war außer Atem. He was out of breath.

die **Atembeschwerden** PLURAL NOUN
breathing difficulties

atemlos ADJECTIVE
breathless

die **Atemlosigkeit**
breathlessness

Athen NEUTER NOUN
Athens

der **Athlet**, PLURAL die **Athleten**
athlete (male)

die **Athletik**
athletics

die **Athletin**, PLURAL die **Athletinnen**
athlete (female)

der **Atlantik**
der Atlantik the Atlantic (Ocean)
Die Insel liegt im Atlantik. The island is in the Atlantic.

der **Atlas**, PLURAL die **Atlanten**
atlas

♀ **atmen** VERB, PERFECT **hat geatmet**
to breathe

die **Atmosphäre**, PLURAL die **Atmosphären**
atmosphere

das **Atom**, PLURAL die **Atome**
atom

atomar ADJECTIVE
atomic

die **Atombombe**, PLURAL die **Atombomben**
atomic bomb

die **Atomwaffen** PLURAL NOUN
nuclear weapons

◇ irregular verb; SEP separable verb; for more help with verbs see centre section

atomwaffenfrei *ADJECTIVE*
 nuclear-free

attraktiv *ADJECTIVE*
 attractive

ätzend *ADJECTIVE*
1 corrosive
2 **scathing**, **caustic** *(wit, remark)*
3 *(informal)* **vile**

au *EXCLAMATION*
1 ouch!
2 oh! *(when surprised or enthusiastic)*
 Au ja! Oh yes!

ℰ **auch** *ADVERB*
1 **also**, **too**
 Sophie war auch dabei. Sophie was also there./Sophie was there too.
 Ich auch! Me too!
 nicht nur ... sondern auch ... not only ... but also ...
2 'Ich gehe jetzt.' – 'Ich auch.' 'I'm going now.' – 'So am I.'
 'Er schläft.' – 'Sie auch.' 'He's asleep.' – 'So is she.'
3 'Ich bin nicht müde.' – 'Ich auch nicht.' 'I'm not tired.' – 'Neither am I.'
 Das weiß ich auch nicht. I don't know either.
4 Auch wenn das stimmt, ... Even if that's true ...
5 Wann ich auch anrufe, er ist nie da. Whenever I phone, he's not at home.
 Was er auch versuchte, es half nichts. Whatever he tried, nothing helped.
 Wo du auch bist, ich denke an dich. Wherever you are, I'm thinking of you.
 Wer es auch getan hat, ist ein Feigling. Whoever did it is a coward.
6 Wie dem auch sei, ich gehe hin! Anyway, I'm going there!
7 Lügst du auch nicht? You're not lying, are you?

ℰ **auf** *PREPOSITION* (+ DAT or + ACC)
1 *(the dative is used when talking about position; the accusative shows movement or a change of place)* **on**
 Das Buch liegt auf dem Tisch. *(DAT)* The book's on the table.
 Er hat das Buch auf den Tisch gelegt. *(ACC)* He put the book on the table.
2 Ich war auf der Party. *(DAT)* I was at the party.
 Ich gehe auf eine Party. *(ACC)* I'm going to a party.
 Ich war auf der Post. *(DAT)* I was at the

---

post office.
 Er ist auf die Post gegangen. *(ACC)* He went to the post office.
3 Sie spielen auf der Straße. *(DAT)* They play in the street.
4 Sag es auf Deutsch! Say it in German!
 Auf diese Art geht es schneller. It's quicker this way.
5 **for** *(indicating time or distance)*
 Er ist auf ein paar Tage verreist. He's gone away for a few days.
6 Auf seinen Rat hin ging ich zum Arzt. On his advice, I went to the doctor's.
7 Auf Wiedersehen! Goodbye!
8 Auf Wiederhören! Goodbye! *(on the telephone)*

> **WORD TIP** auf + das gives aufs

auf *ADVERB*
1 **open**
 Die Tür ist auf. The door is open.
 Mund auf! Open your mouth!
2 **up** *(out of bed)*
 auf sein to be up
 Er ist schon auf. He's already up.
3 auf einmal suddenly
 Auf einmal ging das Licht aus. Suddenly the lights went out.
4 auf einmal at once *(at the same time)*
 Die Kunden kamen alle auf einmal. The customers all came at once.
5 auf und ab up and down
 Sie ging im Flur auf und ab. She walked up and down in the corridor.

aufbekommen *VERB*◇, *IMPERFECT* **bekam auf**, *PERFECT* **hat aufbekommen**
1 to get open
 Er bekam das Fenster nicht auf. He couldn't get the window open.
2 Hausaufgaben aufbekommen to be given homework
 Freitags bekommen wir keine Hausaufgaben auf. We don't get any homework on Fridays.

aufbewahren *VERB*, *PERFECT* **hat aufbewahrt**
 to keep

aufblasen *VERB*◇, *PRESENT* **bläst auf**, *IMPERFECT* **blies auf**, *PERFECT* **hat aufgeblasen**
 to blow up

aufbleiben *VERB*◇, *IMPERFECT* **blieb auf**, *PERFECT* **ist aufgeblieben**
1 to stay open
 Wie lange bleiben die Geschäfte auf? How long do the shops stay open?

ℰ indicates key words

2 to stay up (not go to bed)
Die älteren Kinder durften noch aufbleiben. The older children were allowed to stay up.

aufbringen VERB◇, IMPERFECT **brachte auf**, PERFECT **hat aufgebracht**
1 **to raise** (money)
2 **to find** (patience, strength)
3 **to open**
Ich bringe die Tür nicht auf. I can't open the door.
4 Dafür kann ich kein Verständnis aufbringen. I can't understand it.

aufeinander ADVERB
1 **one on top of the other**
die Bretter aufeinander legen to put the planks one on top of the other
2 **aufeinander liegen** to lie on top of each other
3 **aufeinander folgen** to follow one another
4 **aufeinander warten** to wait for each other
5 **aufeinander schießen** to shoot at each other
6 **aufeinander fahren** to collide with each other

ℙ der **Aufenthalt**, PLURAL die **Aufenthalte**
1 **stay**
Guten Aufenthalt! Enjoy your stay!
2 **stop** (pause in a journey)
Der Zug hat zehn Minuten Aufenthalt in Köln. The train stops in Cologne for ten minutes.

ℙ der **Aufenthaltsraum**, PLURAL die **Aufenthaltsräume**
1 **lounge**
2 **common room**

die **Auffahrt**, PLURAL die **Auffahrten**
1 **drive**
2 **slip road**

auffallend ADJECTIVE
striking

auffangen VERB◇, PRESENT **fängt auf**, IMPERFECT **fing auf**, PERFECT **hat aufgefangen**
to catch

aufführen VERB, PERFECT **hat aufgeführt**
1 **to perform** (a play)
2 **to list** (words, items)
3 **sich aufführen** to behave

die **Aufführung**, PLURAL die **Aufführungen**
performance

ℙ **auffüllen** VERB, PERFECT **hat aufgefüllt**
1 **to fill up**
2 **to stock up**

ℙ die **Aufgabe**, PLURAL die **Aufgaben**
1 **task, job**
Es ist meine Aufgabe, morgens die Katze zu füttern. It is my job to feed the cat in the morning.
2 **exercise** (at school)
3 **question** (in a test or an exam)
Die zweite Aufgabe habe ich nicht verstanden. I didn't understand the second question.
4 **Aufgaben homework**
Hast du deine Aufgaben gemacht? Have you done your homework?

ℙ **aufgeben** VERB◇, PRESENT **gibt auf**, IMPERFECT **gab auf**, PERFECT **hat aufgegeben**
1 **to give up**
Ich gebe auf! I give up!
2 **to post** (a letter, a parcel)
3 **to check in** (luggage)
4 **to place** (an advertisement, order)
5 **to set** (homework)
Heute hat sie uns keine Hausaufgaben aufgegeben. She didn't set us any homework today.

aufgebracht ADJECTIVE
angry

aufgehen VERB◇, IMPERFECT **ging auf**, PERFECT **ist aufgegangen**
1 **to open** (of a door or flower, for example)
Die Knospen gehen auf. The buds are opening.
2 **to come undone** (of a knot or zip, for example)
Der Knopf ist aufgegangen. The button has come undone.
3 **to rise** (of the sun, moon)
4 **to realize**
Mir ist aufgegangen, dass ... I've realized that ...
5 **to work out** (in maths)
Die Gleichung ging auf. The equation worked out.
Zehn durch drei geht nicht auf. Three into ten won't go.

aufgeregt ADJECTIVE
excited

aufgeschlossen ADJECTIVE
open-minded

aufgrund PREPOSITION (+ GEN)
1 **because of**
2 **on the strength of**

aufhaben VERB◇, PRESENT **hat auf**, IMPERFECT **hatte auf**, PERFECT **hat aufgehabt**
1 **to have on** (a hat)

◇ irregular verb; SEP separable verb; for more help with verbs see centre section

2 Er hat die Augen auf. His eyes are open.

3 etwas aufhaben to have homework to do
Hast du heute in Mathe etwas auf? Do you have any maths homework today?
Heute haben wir viel auf. We have a lot of homework today.

4 to be open
Der Laden hat abends auf. The shop is open in the evening.

aufhalten VERB◇, PRESENT **hält auf**, IMPERFECT **hielt auf**, PERFECT **hat aufgehalten**

1 to hold open (a door)

2 to hold up, to keep (somebody from doing something)
Ich will dich nicht aufhalten. I don't want to hold you up.

3 Der Bettler hielt die Hand auf. The beggar held out his hand.

4 Ich kann kaum die Augen aufhalten. I can hardly keep my eyes open.

5 to check (inflation, an advance, unemployment)

6 sich aufhalten to stay

7 sich mit etwas aufhalten to spend your time on something
Halte dich nicht mit den Einzelheiten auf! Don't spend your time on the details!

aufhängen VERB, PERFECT **hat aufgehängt**

1 to hang up (washing)

2 sich aufhängen to hang yourself

aufheben VERB◇, IMPERFECT **hob auf**, PERFECT **hat aufgehoben**

1 to pick up (from the ground)

2 to keep

3 to abolish (a law)

4 gut aufgehoben sein to be well looked after
Im Kindergarten sind sie gut aufgehoben. They are well looked after at kindergarten.

aufheitern VERB, PERFECT **hat aufgeheitert**

1 to cheer up

2 sich aufheitern to brighten up (of the weather)

die **Aufheiterung**, PLURAL die **Aufheiterungen**

1 entertainment

2 sunny interval

ℐ **aufhören** VERB, PERFECT **hat aufgehört**
to stop
Mit 65 hörte sie auf zu arbeiten. She stopped working at 65.

aufklären VERB, PERFECT **hat aufgeklärt**

1 to solve (a crime)

2 to explain (an event, incident)

3 ein Kind aufklären to tell a child the facts of life
Werden die Kinder in der Schule aufgeklärt? Do the children learn the facts of life in school?

4 sich aufklären to be solved (a misunderstanding or mystery)
Das Rätsel hat sich aufgeklärt. The mystery has been solved.

5 sich aufklären to clear up
Das Wetter klärt sich auf. The weather is clearing up.

der **Aufkleber**, PLURAL die **Aufkleber**
sticker

der **Auflauf**, PLURAL die **Aufläufe**
bake
Heute gibt es Kartoffel-Spinat-Auflauf. We are having potato and spinach bake today.

auflegen VERB, PERFECT **hat aufgelegt**

1 to put on

2 to hang up (when phoning)

3 to lay
Wir müssen noch ein Gedeck auflegen. We have to lay another place. (at table)

4 to publish
neu auflegen to reprint
Das Buch wird neu aufgelegt. The book is being reprinted.

auflösen VERB, PERFECT **hat aufgelöst**

1 to dissolve

2 to close (an account)

3 sich auflösen to dissolve

4 sich auflösen to break up (of a crowd, demonstration)

5 Der Nebel hat sich aufgelöst. The fog has lifted.

6 Sie war in Tränen aufgelöst. She was in floods of tears.

ℐ **aufmachen** VERB, PERFECT **hat aufgemacht**

1 to open
Wer hat ihm aufgemacht? Who opened the door to him?

2 to undo (a zip, knot)

3 sich aufmachen to set out
Sie machten sich um 8 Uhr auf. They set out at 8 o'clock.

aufmerksam ADJECTIVE

1 attentive

2 auf etwas aufmerksam werden to notice something
Ich bin darauf aufmerksam geworden, dass Bücher aus der Klasse verschwinden. I have noticed that books are disappearing from the classroom.

3 jemanden auf etwas aufmerksam

A
B
C
D
E
F
G
H
I
J
K
L
M
N
O
P
Q
R
S
T
U
V
W
X
Y
Z

ℐ indicates key words

machen to draw somebody's attention to
something
Er machte mich auf einen Fehler
aufmerksam. He drew my attention to a
mistake.

aufmuntern VERB, PERFECT **hat**
aufgemuntert
to cheer up

die **Aufnahme**, PLURAL die **Aufnahmen**
1 photograph
2 recording
3 admission (to hospital, to a club)
4 welcome

die **Aufnahmeprüfung**, PLURAL die
Aufnahmeprüfungen
entrance exam

die **Aufnahmetaste**, PLURAL die
Aufnahmetasten
record button

ℰ **aufnehmen** VERB◇, PRESENT **nimmt**
auf, IMPERFECT **nahm auf**, PERFECT **hat**
aufgenommen
1 to receive (guests)
2 to take up (an idea, activity, a theme)
3 to admit (to hospital, to a club)
4 to photograph
5 to film
6 to record (a song, a programme, a film)
7 es mit jemandem aufnehmen können to
be a match for somebody
Mit Federer kann er es nicht aufnehmen.
He's no match for Federer.
8 to take (food, news)
Sie nahm die Nachricht gelassen auf. She
took the news calmly.

ℰ **aufpassen** VERB, PERFECT **hat aufgepasst**
1 to pay attention
2 to watch out
3 auf jemanden aufpassen to look after
somebody
Er passte auf seinen kleinen Bruder auf.
He looked after his little brother.
4 auf etwas aufpassen to keep an eye on
something
Pass auf meine Tasche auf. Keep an eye on
my bag.

ℰ **aufräumen** VERB, PERFECT **hat aufgeräumt**
to tidy up

aufrecht ADJECTIVE
upright

aufregen VERB, PERFECT **hat aufgeregt**
1 to excite
2 to annoy

3 sich aufregen to get worked up

aufregend ADJECTIVE
exciting

aufs ▸ SEE **auf das**

ℰ der **Aufsatz**, PLURAL die **Aufsätze**
essay

aufschieben VERB◇, IMPERFECT **schob auf**,
PERFECT **hat aufgeschoben**
1 to slide open (a window, door)
2 to put off (an arrangement)

ℰ **aufschlagen** VERB◇, PRESENT **schlägt**
auf, IMPERFECT **schlug auf**, PERFECT **hat**
aufgeschlagen
to open

aufschließen VERB◇, IMPERFECT **schloss auf**,
PERFECT **hat aufgeschlossen**
to unlock

der **Aufschnitt**
sliced cold meat and cheese

ℰ **aufschreiben** VERB◇, IMPERFECT **schrieb auf**,
PERFECT **hat aufgeschrieben**
to write down

aufsehen VERB◇, PRESENT **sieht auf**, IMPERFECT
sah auf, PERFECT **hat aufgesehen**
to look up

das **Aufsehen**
sensation, stir
Der Film erregte Aufsehen. The film
caused a stir.

der **Aufseher**, PLURAL die **Aufseher**
1 supervisor (male)
2 warder (in a prison) (male)
3 attendant (in a museum) (male)

WORD TIP Professions, hobbies, and sports
don't take an article in German: Er ist Aufseher.

die **Aufseherin**, PLURAL die **Aufseherinnen**
1 supervisor (female)
2 warder (in a prison) (female)
3 attendant (in a museum) (female)

WORD TIP Professions, hobbies, and sports
don't take an article in German: Sie ist
Aufseherin.

aufsetzen VERB, PERFECT **hat aufgesetzt**
1 to put on (glasses, a hat)
2 to draft (a contract)
3 sich aufsetzen to sit up

die **Aufsicht**
1 supervision
2 supervisor

◇ irregular verb; SEP separable verb; for more help with verbs see centre section

der **Aufstand**, PLURAL die **Aufstände**
rebellion

ϸ **aufstehen** VERB✧, IMPERFECT **stand auf**, PERFECT
ist aufgestanden
1 **to get up**
Ich stehe um sieben Uhr auf. I get up at
seven o'clock.
2 PERFECT **hat aufgestanden to be open**
Die Haustür steht auf! The front door is
open!

ϸ **aufstellen** VERB, PERFECT **hat aufgestellt**
1 **to put up**
2 **to set up** *(skittles, chess pieces)*
3 **to pick** *(a player, team)*
Hat der Trainer die Mannschaft schon
aufgestellt? Has the coach picked the team
yet?
4 **to draw up** *(a list)*
5 **sich aufstellen to line up**

die **Aufstiegsmöglichkeiten** PLURAL NOUN
prospects of promotion

auftauen VERB, PERFECT **ist aufgetaut**
1 **to thaw**
2 **to defrost**
Die Erdbeeren sind aufgetaut. The
strawberries have defrosted.
3 PERFECT **hat aufgetaut**
etwas auftauen to defrost something
Ich habe die Erdbeeren aufgetaut. I've
defrosted the strawberries.

aufteilen VERB, PERFECT **hat aufgeteilt**
to divide up

ϸ der **Auftrag**, PLURAL die **Aufträge**
1 **job**
2 **order** *(in business)*
etwas in Auftrag geben to order
something
3 **instructions**
Er hat den Auftrag ausgeführt. He carried
out the instructions.
4 **im Auftrag von on behalf of**

auftreten VERB✧, PRESENT **tritt auf**, IMPERFECT
trat auf, PERFECT **ist aufgetreten**
1 **to appear** *(on stage)*
2 **to arise** *(of a problem, difficulty)*
3 **to behave**
4 **to tread**

aufwachen VERB, PERFECT **ist aufgewacht**
to wake up

aufwachsen VERB✧, PRESENT **wächst
auf**, IMPERFECT **wuchs auf**, PERFECT **ist
aufgewachsen**
to grow up

ϸ **aufwecken** VERB, PERFECT **hat aufgeweckt**
jemanden aufwecken to wake somebody
up

aufziehen VERB✧, IMPERFECT **zog auf**, PERFECT
hat aufgezogen
1 **to wind up** *(a clock or toy)*
2 **to draw** *(curtains)*
3 jemanden aufziehen *(informal)* to tease
somebody
4 **to bring up** *(a child)*

ϸ der **Aufzug**, PLURAL die **Aufzüge**
lift
Ich fahre mit dem Aufzug runter. I'm
going down in the lift.

ϸ das **Auge**, PLURAL die **Augen**
1 **eye**
2 unter vier Augen in private

ϸ der **Augenarzt**, PLURAL die **Augenärzte**
ophthalmologist *(male)*

> **WORD TIP** Professions, hobbies, and sports don't
> take an article in German: Er ist Augenarzt.

ϸ die **Augenärztin**, PLURAL die
Augenärztinnen
ophthalmologist *(female)*

> **WORD TIP** Professions, hobbies, and sports don't
> take an article in German: Sie ist Augenärztin.

der **Augenblick**, PLURAL die **Augenblicke**
moment
im Augenblick at the moment

die **Augenbraue**, PLURAL die **Augenbrauen**
eyebrow

ϸ der **August**
August
im August in August

die **Aula**, PLURAL die **Aulen**
hall, assembly hall

der **Au-pair-Junge**, PLURAL die **Au-pair-
Jungen**
au pair *(boy)*

das **Au-pair-Mädchen**, PLURAL die **Au-pair-
Mädchen**
au pair *(girl)*

ϸ **aus** PREPOSITION (+ DAT)
1 **out of**
Er hat es aus dem Fenster geworfen. He
threw it out of the window.
2 **from**
Sie kommt aus Spanien. She's from
Spain.

Das wissen wir aus Erfahrung. We know that from experience.
3 **made of**
Es ist aus Holz. It is made of wood.
4 Sie haben es nur aus Spaß getan. They did it just for fun.
5 Hüte sind aus der Mode gekommen. Hats have gone out of fashion.
6 Ich habe es aus Versehen weggeworfen. I threw it away by mistake.
7 **aus diesem Grund** for that reason
Aus welchem Grund? Why?
8 Aus ihr ist eine gute Rechtsanwältin geworden. She made a good lawyer.
Aus ihm ist nichts geworden. He never made anything of his life.

aus ADVERB
1 **off** (of a TV, radio)
Das Licht ist aus. The light is off.
Licht aus! Lights out!
2 **finished**
Wenn das Spiel aus ist, … When the game has finished …
3 **von mir aus** as far as I'm concerned
Von mir aus kannst du ins Kino gehen. As far as I'm concerned, you can go to the cinema.
4 **von sich aus** of your own accord
Er hat von sich aus sein Zimmer aufgeräumt. He tidied up his bedroom of his own accord.

ausbauen VERB, PERFECT **hat ausgebaut**
1 **to extend** (a building)
2 **to convert** (a loft)

ausbeuten VERB, PERFECT **hat ausgebeutet**
to exploit

ausbilden VERB, PERFECT **hat ausgebildet**
to train

ℰ die **Ausbildung**
1 **training**
2 **education**

der **Ausbildungsplatz**, PLURAL die **Ausbildungsplätze**
training place

ausbreiten VERB, PERFECT **hat ausgebreitet**
1 **to unfold**
2 **to spread** (out)
3 **to stretch out** (your arms)

ausbuhen VERB, PERFECT **hat ausgebuht**
to boo
Die Menge buhte den Schiedsrichter aus. The crowd booed the referee.

die **Ausdauer**
stamina

das **Ausdauertraining**
stamina training

ausdehnen VERB, PERFECT **hat ausgedehnt**
1 **to extend, to prolong**
2 **to expand**

der **Ausdruck**[1], PLURAL die **Ausdrücke**
expression
etwas zum Ausdruck bringen to express something
Er kann seine Gefühle nicht zum Ausdruck bringen. He can't express his feelings.

der **Ausdruck**[2], PLURAL die **Ausdrucke**
printout

ausdrucken VERB, PERFECT **hat ausgedruckt**
to print out

ausdrücken VERB, PERFECT **hat ausgedrückt**
1 **to squeeze** (oranges, lemons)
2 **to express**
3 **sich ausdrücken** to express yourself

auseinander ADVERB
1 **apart**
2 **auseinander schreiben** to write as separate words

auseinandergehen VERB◇, IMPERFECT **ging auseinander**, PERFECT **ist auseinandergegangen**
to part

auseinanderhalten VERB◇, PRESENT **hält auseinander**, IMPERFECT **hielt auseinander**, PERFECT **hat auseinandergehalten**
to tell apart

auseinandernehmen VERB◇, PRESENT **nimmt auseinander**, IMPERFECT **nahm auseinander**, PERFECT **hat auseinandergenommen**
to take apart

auseinandersetzen VERB, PERFECT **hat sich auseinandergesetzt**
1 **sich mit einem Problem auseinandersetzen** to get to grips with a problem
2 **sich mit jemandem auseinandersetzen** to have it out with somebody

die **Ausfahrt**, PLURAL die **Ausfahrten**
1 **exit**
2 'Ausfahrt freihalten' 'Keep clear'

der **Ausfall**, PLURAL die **Ausfälle**
1 **failure** (of an engine, brakes)

breakdown *(of a machine, heating)*
2 **loss** *(of hair, teeth)*
3 **cancellation** *(of an event)*

ausfallen *VERB◇, PRESENT* **fällt aus**, *IMPERFECT* **fiel aus**, *PERFECT* **ist ausgefallen**
1 **to be cancelled**
Sie ließen das Konzert ausfallen. They cancelled the concert.
2 **to fall out** *(hair)*
3 **to fail** *(an engine, brakes, a signal)*
4 **to break down** *(a machine, a car, heating)*
5 **to turn out**
Die Verluste sind nicht so hoch ausgefallen wie erwartet. The losses turned out to be lower than expected.
Das Zeugnis ist gut ausgefallen. The report was good.

der **Ausflug**, *PLURAL* die **Ausflüge**
outing, trip
Morgen machen wir einen Ausflug. Tomorrow we're going on an outing.

die **Ausfuhr**
export

ausführen *VERB, PERFECT* **hat ausgeführt**
1 **to carry out** *(a plan)*
2 **to export** *(goods)*
3 **to take out**
Er hat seine Freundin zum Essen ausgeführt. He took his girlfriend out for a meal.
4 Kannst du den Hund ausführen? Can you take the dog for a walk?

ausführlich *ADJECTIVE*
detailed
ausführlich *ADVERB*
in detail

ℙ **ausfüllen** *VERB, PERFECT* **hat ausgefüllt**
1 **to fill in**
Hilfst du mir, das Formular auszufüllen? Would you help me fill in the form?
2 Ihr Beruf als Lehrerin füllt sie ganz aus. Teaching gives her great satisfaction.

die **Ausgabe**, *PLURAL* die **Ausgaben**
1 **edition**
2 **issue**
3 Ausgaben **expenditure**

ℙ der **Ausgang**, *PLURAL* die **Ausgänge**
1 **exit**
'Kein Ausgang' 'No exit'
2 **end, ending**
3 **result** *(of a game, discussion)*

ℙ **ausgeben** *VERB◇, PRESENT* **gibt aus**, *IMPERFECT* **gab aus**, *PERFECT* **hat ausgegeben**
1 **to spend**
2 **to hand out**
3 Der Automat gibt die Fahrkarten aus. The machine issues the tickets.
4 **to serve** *(food)*
5 sich ausgeben als **to pretend to be**
Er gab sich als ihr Bruder aus. He pretended to be her brother.
6 einen ausgeben *(informal)* **to treat everybody** *(to a round of drinks, for example)*
Ich geb euch einen aus! *(informal)* I'll treat you!

ausgebildet *ADJECTIVE*
trained, qualified

ausgebucht *ADJECTIVE*
fully booked

ausgeglichen *ADJECTIVE*
1 **well-balanced**
2 **stable**

ℙ **ausgehen** *VERB◇, PRESENT* **geht aus**, *IMPERFECT* **ging aus**, *PERFECT* **ist ausgegangen**
1 **to go out**
Er geht oft mit seinen Freunden aus. He often goes out with his friends.
2 **to run out** *(of supplies)*
3 **to end**
Wie geht die Geschichte aus? How does the story end?
4 von etwas ausgehen **to assume something**
Ich gehe davon aus, dass ihr die Fälle schon gelernt habt. I'm assuming that you have learnt the cases already.

ausgenommen *ADVERB*
apart from

ausgerechnet *ADVERB*
1 Ausgerechnet heute regnet es. Today of all days it's raining.
2 Warum ausgerechnet sie? Why her of all people?

ausgeschlossen *ADJECTIVE*
out of the question

ℙ **ausgestorben** *ADJECTIVE*
extinct
eine ausgestorbene Art an extinct species

ausgewogen *ADJECTIVE*
balanced

ℙ **ausgezeichnet** *ADJECTIVE*
excellent

ausgleichen VERB, IMPERFECT **glich aus**, PERFECT **hat ausgeglichen**
to equalize
Sie glichen in der letzten Minute aus. They equalized in the last minute.

aushalten VERB◇, PRESENT **hält aus**, IMPERFECT **hielt aus**, PERFECT **hat ausgehalten**
1 to stand
2 Es ist nicht zum Aushalten! It's unbearable!

die **Aushilfe**, PLURAL die **Aushilfen**
temporary assistant, temp

aushöhlen VERB, PERFECT **hat ausgehöhlt**
to hollow out

auskennen VERB◇, IMPERFECT **kannte sich aus**, PERFECT **hat sich ausgekannt**
1 sich auskennen to know your way around
Kennst du dich in Köln aus? Do you know your way around Cologne?
2 Sie kennt sich gut mit Computern aus. She knows a lot about computers.

auskommen VERB◇, IMPERFECT **kam aus**, PERFECT **ist ausgekommen**
1 to manage
Wir mussten mit fünfzig Euro auskommen. We had to manage on fifty euros.
2 to get on
Er kommt gut mit seiner Schwester aus. He gets on well with his sister.

ℙ die **Auskunft**, PLURAL die **Auskünfte**
1 information
2 information desk
3 enquiries (when phoning)

auslachen VERB, PERFECT **hat ausgelacht**
to laugh at

ausladen VERB◇, PRESENT **lädt aus**, IMPERFECT **lud aus**, PERFECT **hat ausgeladen**
1 to unload
2 jemanden ausladen (informal) to put somebody off
Sie haben mich wieder ausgeladen! They asked me not to come!

ℙ das **Ausland**
1 abroad
Sein Vater lebt im Ausland. His father lives abroad.
In den Ferien reisen sie immer ins Ausland. In the holidays they always travel abroad.
2 foreign countries
Was denkt das Ausland? What do other countries think?

ℙ der **Ausländer**, PLURAL die **Ausländer**
foreigner (male)
Jeder vierte Berliner ist Ausländer. Every fourth inhabitant of Berlin is a foreigner.

ℙ die **Ausländerin**, PLURAL die **Ausländerinnen**
foreigner (female)

ℙ **ausländisch** ADJECTIVE
foreign

das **Auslandsgespräch**, PLURAL die **Auslandsgespräche**
international call

ℙ **auslassen** VERB◇, PRESENT **lässt aus**, IMPERFECT **ließ aus**, PERFECT **hat ausgelassen**
to leave out

ausleeren VERB, PERFECT **hat ausgeleert**
to empty out

ℙ **ausleihen** VERB◇, IMPERFECT **lieh aus**, PERFECT **hat ausgeliehen**
1 (sich) etwas ausleihen to borrow something
Ich habe (mir) sein Handy ausgeliehen. I borrowed his mobile phone.
2 to lend
Leihst du mir dein Fahrrad aus? Can you lend me your bike?

ℙ **ausmachen** VERB, PERFECT **hat ausgemacht**
1 to turn off (the heating, light)
2 to put out (a cigarette)
3 to arrange
Wir haben ausgemacht, dass wir uns heute Abend treffen. We've arranged to meet up this evening.
4 Das macht mir nichts aus. I don't mind.
Macht es Ihnen etwas aus, wenn ...? Would you mind if ...?
5 Das macht viel aus! It makes a great difference!

die **Ausnahme**, PLURAL die **Ausnahmen**
exception

ausnutzen VERB, PERFECT **hat ausgenutzt**
1 to use
2 to take advantage of
3 to exploit

ℙ **auspacken** VERB, PERFECT **hat ausgepackt**
to unpack

ℙ der **Auspuff**, PLURAL die **Auspuffe**
exhaust

ℙ die **Auspuffgase** PLURAL NOUN
exhaust fumes

◇ irregular verb; SEP separable verb; for more help with verbs see centre section

ausrechnen *VERB*, *PERFECT* **hat ausgerechnet**
to work out

℘ die **Ausrede**, *PLURAL* die **Ausreden**
excuse

℘ **ausreichend** *ADJECTIVE*
1 **sufficient**
2 **adequate** *(also as a school mark)*

die **Ausreise**, *PLURAL* die **Ausreisen**
departure *(from a country)*

ausrichten *VERB*, *PERFECT* **hat ausgerichtet**
1 jemandem etwas ausrichten to tell
somebody something
Kann ich etwas ausrichten? Can I take a
message?
2 to organize *(an event)*
Welches Land richtet 2016 die
Olympischen Spiele aus? Which country
will host the Olympic Games in 2016?

ausrufen *VERB*◇, *IMPERFECT* **rief aus**, *PERFECT*
hat ausgerufen
1 to call out
2 to call, to declare
Sie riefen allgemeine Wahlen aus. They
called a general election.
Der Notstand wurde ausgerufen. A state
of emergency was declared.

das **Ausrufezeichen**, *PLURAL* die
Ausrufezeichen
exclamation mark

ausruhen *VERB*, *PERFECT* **hat sich ausgeruht**
sich ausruhen to have a rest

ausrüsten *VERB*, *PERFECT* **hat ausgerüstet**
to equip

die **Ausrüstung**
equipment

℘ **ausschalten** *VERB*, *PERFECT* **hat
ausgeschaltet**
1 to switch off *(a light, radio, machine)*
2 to eliminate *(an opponent)*

ausschneiden *VERB*◇, *IMPERFECT* **schnitt aus**,
PERFECT **hat ausgeschnitten**
to cut out

der **Ausschuss**, *PLURAL* die **Ausschüsse**
committee

℘ **aussehen** *VERB*◇, *PRESENT* **sieht aus**, *IMPERFECT*
sah aus, *PERFECT* **hat ausgesehen**
to look
Er sieht aus wie seine Mutter. He looks like
his mother.

℘ das **Aussehen**
looks, appearance

℘ **außen** *ADVERB*
1 **(on the) outside**
von außen from the outside
Von außen sah man nichts. You couldn't
see anything from the outside.
2 nach außen outwards
Das Fenster geht nach außen auf. The
window opens outwards.

der **Außenminister**, *PLURAL* die
Außenminister
Foreign Secretary, Foreign Minister

℘ **außer** *PREPOSITION* (+ DAT)
1 **apart from, except (for)**
Alle außer ihm halfen mit. Everyone
except (for) him helped.
außer sonntags except Sundays
2 out of
Sie waren bald außer Sicht. Soon they
were out of sight.
Der Getränkeautomat ist außer Betrieb.
The drinks machine is out of order.
3 Er ist außer Haus. He is out.
4 Sie war außer sich, als sie es erfuhr. She
was beside herself when she found out.

außer *CONJUNCTION*
außer (wenn) ... unless ...

℘ **außerdem** *ADVERB*
1 **as well**
2 **besides**

äußerer, äußere, äußeres *ADJECTIVE*
1 **external** *(injury, circumstances)*
2 **outer** *(layer, circle)*
3 **outward** *(appearance, effect)*

außergewöhnlich *ADJECTIVE*
unusual

außerhalb *PREPOSITION* (+ GEN)
outside

außerhalb *ADVERB*
außerhalb wohnen to live out of town

der/die **Außerirdische**, *PLURAL* die
Außerirdischen
alien *(from outer space)*

äußerlich *ADJECTIVE*
1 **external**
2 **outward** *(appearance)*

außerordentlich *ADJECTIVE*
extraordinary

äußerst *ADVERB*
extremely

die **Äußerung**, *PLURAL* die **Äußerungen**
remark

℘ indicates key words

P die **Aussicht**, PLURAL die **Aussichten**
  1 prospect
    Er hat eine Lehrstelle in Aussicht. He has
    the prospect of an apprenticeship.
    Sie haben keine Aussichten auf Erfolg.
    They have no chance of success.
  2 view
    Wir möchten ein Zimmer mit Aussicht
    aufs Meer. We would like a room with a
    view of the sea.

die **Aussprache**, PLURAL die **Aussprachen**
  1 pronunciation
  2 talk

P **aussprechen** VERB◇, PRESENT **spricht
  aus**, IMPERFECT **sprach aus**, PERFECT **hat
  ausgesprochen**
  1 to pronounce
  2 to express
  3 Lassen Sie ihn aussprechen! Let him finish!
    (speaking)
  4 sich aussprechen to talk
    Sie hat sich mit ihrer Freundin
    ausgesprochen. She had a talk with her
    friend.
  5 sich gegen etwas aussprechen to come
    out against something
    sich für etwas aussprechen to come out in
    favour of something
  6 Der Lehrer hat sich lobend über ihn
    ausgesprochen. The teacher has spoken
    highly of him.

P **aussteigen** VERB◇, IMPERFECT **stieg aus**,
  PERFECT **ist ausgestiegen**
  1 to get off
  2 to get out

ausstellen VERB, PERFECT **hat ausgestellt**
  1 to display (in a shop)
  2 to exhibit
  3 to make out (a certificate, bill)
  4 to issue (a passport)
  5 to switch off

P die **Ausstellung**, PLURAL die **Ausstellungen**
  exhibition

aussterben VERB◇, PRESENT **stirbt
  aus**, IMPERFECT **starb aus**, PERFECT **ist
  ausgestorben**
  to die out

ausstreichen VERB◇, IMPERFECT **strich aus**,
  PERFECT **hat ausgestrichen**
  to cross out

P **aussuchen** VERB, PERFECT **hat ausgesucht**
  1 to choose
  2 sich etwas aussuchen to choose
    something

Such dir einfach ein Lied aus. Just choose
a song.

P der **Austausch**
  exchange

austauschen VERB, PERFECT **hat
  ausgetauscht**
  1 to exchange
  2 to replace
  3 to substitute (a player)

P die **Austauschschule**, PLURAL die
  Austauschschulen
  exchange school

P der **Austauschschüler**, PLURAL die
  Austauschschüler
  exchange student (male)

P die **Austauschschülerin**, PLURAL die
  Austauschschülerinnen
  exchange student (female)

P **austragen** VERB◇, PRESENT **trägt aus**, IMPERFECT
  trug aus, PERFECT **hat ausgetragen**
  1 to deliver (post, newspapers)
    Er trägt Zeitungen aus. He does a
    newspaper round.
  2 to hold (a race)

P **Australien** NEUTER NOUN
  Australia
  aus Australien from Australia

der **Australier**, PLURAL die **Australier**
  Australian (male)

die **Australierin**, PLURAL die
  Australierinnen
  Australian (female)

australisch ADJECTIVE
  Australian

> **WORD TIP** Adjectives never have capitals
> in German, even for regions, countries, or
> nationalities.

austreten VERB◇, PRESENT **tritt aus**, IMPERFECT
  trat aus, PERFECT **hat ausgetreten**
  1 to stamp out (a cigarette or fire)
  2 to wear out (shoes)
  3 PERFECT **ist ausgetreten**
    Sie ist aus dem Tennisverein ausgetreten.
    She's left the tennis club.
    Ich trete aus! I'm leaving!
  4 (informal) PERFECT **ist ausgetreten** to go
    to the loo
    Ich muss mal austreten. I have to go to
    the loo.

austrinken VERB◇, IMPERFECT **trank aus**,
  PERFECT **hat ausgetrunken**
  to drink up

◇ irregular verb; SEP separable verb; for more help with verbs see centre section

𝓟 der **Ausverkauf**, PLURAL die **Ausverkäufe**
sale

𝓟 **ausverkauft** ADJECTIVE
1 sold out
2 ein ausverkauftes Haus a full house (at the cinema or theatre)

𝓟 die **Auswahl**, PLURAL die **Auswahlen**
choice, selection
Das Geschäft hat wenig Auswahl. The shop has a limited selection.

𝓟 **auswählen** VERB, PERFECT **hat ausgewählt**
to choose

der **Auswanderer**, PLURAL die **Auswanderer**
emigrant (male)

die **Auswanderin**, PLURAL die **Auswanderinnen**
emigrant (female)

auswandern VERB, PERFECT **ist ausgewandert**
to emigrate
Sie wollen nach Amerika auswandern. They want to emigrate to America.

die **Auswanderung**
emigration

auswärts ADVERB
1 away (in sport)
auswärts spielen to play away
2 auswärts essen to eat out
3 Sie arbeitet auswärts. She doesn't work locally.

das **Auswärtsspiel**, PLURAL die **Auswärtsspiele**
away game

der **Ausweg**, PLURAL die **Auswege**
way out

der **Ausweis**, PLURAL die **Ausweise**
1 identity card
2 card (for students or members)
3 passport

𝓟 **auswendig** ADVERB
by heart

auswirken VERB, PERFECT **hat sich ausgewirkt**
sich auf etwas auswirken to have an effect on something

auszeichnen VERB, PERFECT **hat ausgezeichnet**
sich auszeichnen to stand out

𝓟 **ausziehen** VERB◇, IMPERFECT **zog aus**, PERFECT **hat ausgezogen**
1 to take off (clothes)
2 to undress
3 sich ausziehen to get undressed
4 PERFECT **ist ausgezogen** to move out (move house)
Wir ziehen nächste Woche aus. We're moving out next week.

der/die **Auszubildende**, PLURAL die **Auszubildenden**
trainee

𝓟 das **Auto**, PLURAL die **Autos**
1 car
Sie waschen jede Woche das Auto. They wash the car every week.
2 Auto fahren to drive
Kannst du Auto fahren? Do you drive?

die **Autobahn**, PLURAL die **Autobahnen**
motorway

das **Autobahnkreuz**, PLURAL die **Autobahnkreuze**
motorway interchange

𝓟 die **Autobahnraststätte**, PLURAL die **Autobahnraststätten**
motorway service area

der **Autobus**, PLURAL die **Autobusse**
bus

der **Autofahrer**, PLURAL die **Autofahrer**
motorist

autofrei ADJECTIVE
car-free

das **Autogramm**, PLURAL die **Autogramme**
autograph

der **Automat**, PLURAL die **Automaten**
machine

automatisch ADJECTIVE
automatic

𝓟 der **Autor**, PLURAL die **Autoren**
author (male)

𝓟 die **Autorin**, PLURAL die **Autorinnen**
author (female)

autoritär ADJECTIVE
authoritarian

die **Autorität**
authority

der **Autoskooter**, PLURAL die **Autoskooter**
bumper car, dodgem car

A
B
C
D
E
F
G
H
I
J
K
L
M
N
O
P
Q
R
S
T
U
V
W
X
Y
Z

der **Autostopp**
per Autostopp fahren to hitchhike
Sie fuhren per Autostopp nach Hause.
They hitchhiked home.

das **Autotelefon**, PLURAL die **Autotelefone**
car phone

℗ der **Autounfall**, PLURAL die **Autounfälle**
car accident

der **Autoverleih**, PLURAL die **Autoverleihe**
car hire (firm)

die **Autowäsche**
car wash

die **Autowerkstatt**, PLURAL die
Autowerkstätten
garage

die **Axt**, PLURAL die **Äxte**
axe

der/die **Azubi**, PLURAL die **Azubis** ABBREVIATION
(=Auszubildende)
(informal) trainee
Sie ist Azubi. She's a trainee.

Bb

℗ das **Baby**, PLURAL die **Babys**
baby

babysitten VERB, PERFECT **hat babygesittet/
gebabysittet**
to babysit
Sie geht heute Abend bei Müllers
babysitten. She's babysitting at the
Müller's tonight.
Sie verdienen sich mit Babysitten etwas
Geld dazu. They earn some extra money
doing babysitting.

WORD TIP This word is mainly used in the
infinitive form babysitten. ▶ SEE **Babysitting**

℗ der **Babysitter**, PLURAL die **Babysitter**
babysitter (male)

℗ die **Babysitterin**, PLURAL, **Babysitterinnen**
babysitter (female)

das **Babysitting**
babysitting
Sie macht am Wochenende oft
Babysitting. She often babysits at the
weekend.

der **Bach**, PLURAL die **Bäche**
stream

die **Backe**, PLURAL die **Backen**
cheek

℗ **backen** VERB, PRESENT **bäckt**, IMPERFECT
backte, PERFECT **hat gebacken**
to bake

der **Bäcker**, PLURAL die **Bäcker**
1 baker (male)
2 baker's
Beim Bäcker kann man auch Milch kaufen.
You can also buy milk at the baker's.

WORD TIP Professions, hobbies, and sports
don't take an article in German: Er ist Bäcker.

die **Bäckerei**, PLURAL die **Bäckereien**
baker's

🄞 **BÄCKEREI**

Bakeries usually sell many different kinds of
bread. They also sell rolls, called Brötchen in
many parts of Germany and Semmel in Austria,
which are baked very early in the morning so
that people can buy them for breakfast.

die **Bäckerin**, PLURAL die **Bäckerinnen**
baker (female)

WORD TIP Professions, hobbies, and sports
don't take an article in German: Sie ist Bäckerin.

der **Backofen**, PLURAL die **Backöfen**
oven

die **Backpflaume**, PLURAL die **Backpflaumen**
prune

℗ das **Bad**, PLURAL die **Bäder**
1 bath
2 bathroom

der **Badeanzug**, PLURAL die **Badeanzüge**
swimsuit

die **Badehose**, PLURAL die **Badehosen**
swimming trunks

der **Bademeister**, PLURAL die **Bademeister**
swimming-pool attendant (male)

WORD TIP Professions, hobbies, and sports
don't take an article in German: Er ist
Bademeister.

die **Bademeisterin**, PLURAL,
Bademeisterinnen
swimming-pool attendant (female)

WORD TIP Professions, hobbies, and sports
don't take an article in German: Sie ist
Bademeisterin.

die **Bademütze**, PLURAL die **Bademützen**
bathing cap

◇ irregular verb; SEP separable verb; for more help with verbs see centre section

baden *VERB, PERFECT* **hat gebadet**
1 **to have a bath**
Heute Abend möchte ich baden. I'd like to have a bath tonight.
2 **to swim** *(in the sea)*
Es war zu kalt, um im Meer zu baden. It was too cold to swim in the sea.
3 **to bath** *(wash somebody)*
Er hat das Baby gebadet. He bathed the baby.

der **Badeort**, *PLURAL* die **Badeorte**
1 **seaside resort**
2 **spa town**

das **Badetuch**, *PLURAL* die **Badetücher**
bath towel

die **Badewanne**, *PLURAL* die **Badewannen**
bath *(tub)*

das **Badezimmer**, *PLURAL* die **Badezimmer**
bathroom

das **Badminton**
badminton

die **Bahn**, *PLURAL* die **Bahnen**
1 **railway**
Mein Vater war bei der Bahn. My father worked for the railway.
2 **train**
mit der Bahn by train
Warum fahrt ihr nicht mit der Bahn? Why don't you go by train?
3 **tram**
Wann kommt die nächste Bahn? When is the next tram due?
4 **track** *(in sport)*
5 **lane** *(on a track, in a pool)*
6 **path** *(of a satellite, rocket)*
7 **auf die schiefe Bahn geraten** to go off the rails

die **Bahnfahrt**, *PLURAL* die **Bahnfahrten**
train journey

ℰ der **Bahnhof**, *PLURAL* die **Bahnhöfe**
(railway) station

die **Bahnhofshalle**, *PLURAL* die **Bahnhofshallen**
station concourse

der **Bahnsteig**, *PLURAL* die **Bahnsteige**
platform

der **Bahnübergang**, *PLURAL* die **Bahnübergänge**
level crossing

ℰ **bald** *ADVERB*
1 **soon**
Bis bald! See you soon!

2 **Wird's bald!** *(informal)* Get a move on!
3 **almost**
Ich hätte bald vergessen, ihn anzurufen. I almost forgot to ring him.

WORD TIP The German word bald does not mean bald in English; the German expression for He's bald is Er hat eine Glatze.

baldig *ADJECTIVE*
speedy

der **Balkan**
der Balkan the Balkans

der **Balken**, *PLURAL* die **Balken**
beam

ℰ der **Balkon**, *PLURAL* die **Balkons**
balcony

der **Ball**, *PLURAL* die **Bälle**
1 **ball**
Die Kinder spielten Ball. The children were playing ball.
2 **ball** *(event)*
Warst du schon einmal auf einem Ball? Have you ever been to a ball?

das **Ballett**, *PLURAL* die **Ballette**
ballet

der **Balletttänzer**, *PLURAL* die **Balletttänzer**
ballet dancer *(male)*

WORD TIP Professions, hobbies, and sports don't take an article in German: Er ist Balletttänzer.

die **Balletttänzerin**, *PLURAL* die **Balletttänzerinnen**
ballet dancer *(female)*

WORD TIP Professions, hobbies, and sports don't take an article in German: Sie ist Balletttänzerin.

der **Ballon**, *PLURAL* die **Ballons**
balloon

ℰ die **Banane**, *PLURAL* die **Bananen**
banana

band ▸ SEE **binden**

ℰ das **Band**[1], *PLURAL* die **Bänder**
1 **ribbon**
2 **tape** *(for recording)*
Er hat es auf Band aufgenommen. He taped it.
3 **production line**
Sie arbeiten am Band. They work on a production line.
4 **am laufenden Band** *(informal)* nonstop

ℰ der **Band**[2], *PLURAL* die **Bände**
volume *(book)*

A
B
C
D
E
F
G
H
I
J
K
L
M
N
O
P
Q
R
S
T
U
V
W
X
Y
Z

die **Band³**, PLURAL die **Bands**
band, group

die **Bande**, PLURAL die **Banden**
gang

die **Bank¹**, PLURAL die **Bänke**
bench

♀ die **Bank²**, PLURAL die **Banken**
bank
Ich muss erst zur Bank gehen. I have to go
to the bank first.

♀ die **Bankkauffrau**, PLURAL die
Bankkauffrauen
bank clerk (female)

> **WORD TIP** Professions, hobbies, and sports
> don't take an article in German: Sie ist
> Bankkauffrau.

♀ der **Bankkaufmann**, PLURAL die
Bankkaufleute
bank clerk (male)

> **WORD TIP** Professions, hobbies, and sports
> don't take an article in German: Er ist
> Bankkaufmann.

das **Bankkonto**, PLURAL die **Bankkonten**
bank account

die **Banknote**, PLURAL die **Banknoten**
banknote

der **Bankomat™**, PLURAL die **Bankomaten**
(in Austria) cash dispenser

bankrott ADJECTIVE
bankrupt
Die Firma ist bankrott. The firm is
bankrupt.

der **Bankrott**, PLURAL die **Bankrotte**
bankruptcy
Die Firma hat Bankrott gemacht. The firm
has gone bankrupt.

bar ADJECTIVE, ADVERB
(in) cash

die **Bar**, PLURAL die **Bars**
bar

der **Bär**, PLURAL die **Bären**
bear

barfuß ADJECTIVE
barefoot

das **Bargeld**
cash

der **Barren**, PLURAL die **Barren**
1 bar
2 parallel bars

der **Bart**, PLURAL die **Bärte**
beard
Der Witz hat einen Bart. That joke is
ancient.

bärtig ADJECTIVE
bearded

Basel NEUTER NOUN
Basle

die **Basis**, PLURAL die **Basen**
basis

♀ der **Basketball**
basketball

der **Bass**, PLURAL die **Bässe**
bass

basta! EXCLAMATION
and that's that!

basteln VERB, PERFECT **hat gebastelt**
1 to make
Die Kinder haben Geschenke gebastelt.
The children made presents.
2 to make things
Sie bastelt gern. She likes making things.

der **Bastler**, PLURAL die **Bastler**
DIY enthusiast

bat ▸ SEE **bitten**

die **Batterie**, PLURAL die **Batterien**
battery

der **Bau**, PLURAL die **Bauten**
1 construction
Die Turnhalle ist noch im Bau. The gym is
still under construction.
2 building
Das Museum war ein riesiger Bau. The
museum was a huge building.
3 building site
Mein Bruder arbeitet auf dem Bau. My
brother works on a building site.

die **Bauarbeiten** PLURAL NOUN
building work

♀ der **Bauarbeiter**, PLURAL die **Bauarbeiter**
builder, construction worker (male)

> **WORD TIP** Professions, hobbies, and sports
> don't take an article in German: Er ist
> Bauarbeiter.

♀ die **Bauarbeiterin**, PLURAL die
Bauarbeiterinnen
builder, construction worker (female)

> **WORD TIP** Professions, hobbies, and sports
> don't take an article in German: Sie ist
> Bauarbeiterin.

◇ irregular verb; SEP separable verb; for more help with verbs see centre section

ℯ der **Bauch**, PLURAL die **Bäuche**
stomach, belly

der **Bauchnabel**, PLURAL die **Bauchnabel**
navel, belly button

die **Bauchschmerzen** PLURAL NOUN
stomach ache

bauen VERB, PERFECT **hat gebaut**
1 to build
2 Er hat einen Unfall gebaut. *(informal)* He
had an accident.

der **Bauer**, PLURAL die **Bauern**
1 farmer *(male)*
2 pawn *(in chess)*

> **WORD TIP** Professions, hobbies, and sports
> don't take an article in German: Er ist Bauer.

die **Bäuerin**, PLURAL die **Bäuerinnen**
1 farmer *(female)*
2 farmer's wife

> **WORD TIP** Professions, hobbies, and sports
> don't take an article in German: Sie ist Bäuerin.

das **Bauernhaus**, PLURAL die **Bauernhäuser**
farmhouse

der **Bauernhof**, PLURAL die **Bauernhöfe**
farm

der **Bauingenieur**, PLURAL die
Bauingenieure
civil engineer *(male)*

> **WORD TIP** Professions, hobbies, and sports
> don't take an article in German: Er ist
> Bauingenieur.

die **Bauingenieurin**, PLURAL die
Bauingenieurinnen
civil engineer *(female)*

> **WORD TIP** Professions, hobbies, and sports
> don't take an article in German: Sie ist
> Bauingenieurin.

das **Baujahr**, PLURAL die **Baujahre**
year of manufacture *(of a car)*

ℯ der **Baum**, PLURAL die **Bäume**
tree

die **Baumwolle**
cotton

die **Bausparkasse**, PLURAL die
Bausparkassen
building society

ℯ die **Baustelle**, PLURAL die **Baustellen**
building site, construction site

der **Bauunternehmer**, PLURAL die
Bauunternehmer
building contractor *(male)*

> **WORD TIP** Professions, hobbies, and sports don't
> take an article in German: Er ist Bauunternehmer.

die **Bauunternehmerin**, PLURAL die
Bauunternehmerinnen
building contractor *(female)*

> **WORD TIP** Professions, hobbies, and sports
> don't take an article in German: Sie ist
> Bauunternehmerin.

bay(e)risch ADJECTIVE
Bavarian

> **WORD TIP** Adjectives never have capitals in
> German, even for regions, countries, or nationalities.

der **Bayer**, PLURAL die **Bayern**
Bavarian *(male)*

die **Bayerin**, PLURAL die **Bayerinnen**
Bavarian *(female)*

Bayern NEUTER NOUN
Bavaria
Ich komme aus Bayern. I'm from Bavaria.

ℯ **beabsichtigen** VERB, PERFECT **hat
beabsichtigt**
to intend

beachten VERB, PERFECT **hat beachtet**
1 to take notice of
Beachte ihn einfach nicht! Just don't take
any notice of him.
2 to observe *(a rule, ban)*
Auch Radfahrer müssen die
Verkehrsregeln beachten. Cyclists have to
observe the traffic regulations, too.
3 to follow *(advice)*

der **Beamte**, PLURAL die **Beamten**
1 civil servant *(male) (in Germany all public
employees, such as teachers and policemen,
are 'Beamte')*
2 official *(male)*

> **WORD TIP** Professions, hobbies, and sports
> don't take an article in German: Er ist Beamter.

die **Beamtin**, PLURAL die **Beamtinnen**
1 civil servant *(female)*
2 official *(female)*

> **WORD TIP** Professions, hobbies, and sports
> don't take an article in German: Sie ist Beamtin.

beanspruchen VERB, PERFECT **hat
beansprucht**
1 to claim *(benefit, damages)*
2 to take up *(time, space)*

Meine Hausaufgaben beanspruchen viel Zeit. My homework takes up a lot of my time.
3 **to demand** *(energy, attention)*
Die Arbeit beansprucht sie sehr. Her work is very demanding.
4 **to take advantage of** *(hospitality, services)*

die **Beanstandung**, PLURAL die **Beanstandungen**
complaint

beantragen VERB, PERFECT **hat beantragt**
to apply for

ℱ **beantworten** VERB, PERFECT **hat beantwortet**
to answer

bearbeiten VERB, PERFECT **hat bearbeitet**
1 **to deal with**
Sie haben den Antrag noch nicht bearbeitet. They haven't dealt with the application yet.
2 **to adapt** *(a play, book)*
Wer hat das Buch für das Fernsehen bearbeitet? Who adapted the book for television?
3 **to treat** *(wood, for example)*
Er hat die Oberfläche mit Wachs bearbeitet. He's treated the surface with wax.
4 jemanden bearbeiten *(informal)* **to work on somebody** *(persuade)*
Sie hat ihren Vater bearbeitet, dass er ihr einen Laptop kauft. She worked on her dad so that he bought her a laptop.

beaufsichtigen VERB, PERFECT **hat beaufsichtigt**
to supervise

ℱ der **Becher**, PLURAL die **Becher**
1 **beaker, mug**
2 **pot, carton** *(of yoghurt, cream)*

das **Becherglas**, PLURAL die **Bechergläser**
tumbler

das **Becken**, PLURAL die **Becken**
1 **basin** *(in the kitchen, bathroom)*
2 **pool** *(for swimming)*
3 **pelvis**

bedanken VERB, PERFECT **hat sich bedankt**
sich bedanken to say thank you
Vergiss nicht, dich zu bedanken! Don't forget to say thank you.
Ich habe mich bei ihm bedankt. I thanked him.

der **Bedarf**
1 **need**

2 bei Bedarf if required
3 **demand**
je nach Bedarf according to demand

bedauerlicherweise ADVERB
unfortunately

bedauern VERB, PERFECT **hat bedauert**
1 **to regret**
Ich bedaure kein Wort. I don't regret a single word.
2 Ich bedaure sehr, dass du nicht kommen kannst. I'm very sorry that you can't come. Bedaure! Sorry!
3 jemanden bedauern to feel sorry for somebody

bedecken VERB, PERFECT **hat bedeckt**
to cover

bedeckt ADJECTIVE
1 **covered**
2 **overcast** *(weather)*
Gestern war es den ganzen Tag bedeckt. It was overcast all day yesterday.

ℱ **bedenken** VERB◇, IMPERFECT **bedachte**, PERFECT **hat bedacht**
to consider

Bedenken PLURAL NOUN
1 **doubts**
Ich habe noch Bedenken. I still have some doubts.
2 ohne Bedenken without hesitation

bedenklich ADJECTIVE
1 **worrying**
Die Situation ist sehr bedenklich. The situation is very worrying.
2 **dubious**
Er hat bedenkliche Mittel angewendet, um sein Ziel zu erreichen. He's used dubious methods to achieve his aims.
3 **serious**

ℱ **bedeuten** VERB, PERFECT **hat bedeutet**
to mean
Was bedeutet das? What does it mean?

bedeutend ADJECTIVE
1 **important**
2 **considerable**

die **Bedeutung**, PLURAL die **Bedeutungen**
1 **meaning**
2 **importance**

ℱ **bedienen** VERB, PERFECT **hat bedient**
1 **to serve**
Hier wird man sehr schnell bedient. You get served very quickly here.
2 **to operate** *(a machine)*

◇ irregular verb; SEP separable verb; for more help with verbs see centre section

3 sich bedienen to help yourself
Bitte, bedienen Sie sich! Please help
yourselves.

der/die Bedienstete, *PLURAL* **die
Bediensteten**
servant

die Bedienung, *PLURAL* **die Bedienungen**
1 service
Bedienung inbegriffen. Service included.
2 waiter, waitress
3 shop assistant
4 operation *(of a machine)*

die Bedingung, *PLURAL* **die Bedingungen**
condition
Ich gehe hin, aber nur unter der
Bedingung, dass du mitkommst. I'll go,
but only on condition that you come with
me.

bedrohen *VERB, PERFECT* **hat bedroht**
to threaten

ℓ **bedroht** *ADJECTIVE*
1 threatened
2 endangered *(species)*

die Bedrohung, *PLURAL* **die Bedrohungen**
threat

das Bedürfnis, *PLURAL* **die Bedürfnisse**
need

bedürftig *ADJECTIVE*
needy

das Beefsteak, *PLURAL* **die Beefsteaks**
1 steak
2 deutsches Beefsteak hamburger

ℓ **beeilen** *VERB, PERFECT* **hat sich beeilt**
sich beeilen to hurry (up)
Beeilt euch! Hurry up!

beeindrucken *VERB, PERFECT* **hat
beeindruckt**
to impress

beeinflussen *VERB, PERFECT* **hat beeinflusst**
to influence

beenden *VERB, PERFECT* **hat beendet**
to end

die Beerdigung, *PLURAL* **die Beerdigungen**
funeral

die Beere, *PLURAL* **die Beeren**
berry

das Beet, *PLURAL* **die Beete**
1 flower bed
2 patch *(of vegetables)*

befahl ▸ SEE **befehlen**

der Befehl, *PLURAL* **die Befehle**
1 order
2 command
Wer hat den Befehl über die Armee? Who
is in command of the army?

befehlen *VERB◇, PRESENT* **befiehlt,** *IMPERFECT*
befahl, *PERFECT* **hat befohlen**
1 jemandem befehlen, etwas zu tun to
order somebody to do something
2 to give orders
Sie befiehlt gerne. She likes to give orders.

befestigen *VERB, PERFECT* **hat befestigt**
1 to fix
Wie hast du es an der Wand befestigt?
How did you fix it to the wall?
2 to fasten

befinden *VERB◇, IMPERFECT* **befand sich,**
PERFECT **hat sich befunden**
sich befinden to be
Sie befindet sich zur Zeit in Deutschland.
She's in Germany at the moment.

befolgen *VERB, PERFECT* **hat befolgt**
to follow

befördern *VERB, PERFECT* **hat befördert**
1 to carry *(people by bus or train)*
2 to transport *(goods by train or lorry)*
3 to promote
Er ist zum Kommissar befördert worden.
He's been promoted to inspector.

die Beförderung, *PLURAL* **die
Beförderungen**
1 transport
2 promotion

befragen *VERB, PERFECT* **hat befragt**
to question

befreien *VERB, PERFECT* **hat befreit**
1 to free
2 sich befreien to free yourself
3 to exempt
Er ist vom Wehrdienst befreit. He's
exempt from military service.

die Befreiung
liberation

befreunden *VERB, PERFECT* **hat sich
befreundet**
sich befreunden to make friends

befreundet *ADJECTIVE*
befreundet sein to be friends
Sie ist mit meiner Schwester befreundet.
She's friends with my sister.
Wir sind schon lange gut befreundet.

We've been close friends for a long time.

befriedigen VERB, PERFECT **hat befriedigt**
to satisfy

befriedigend ADJECTIVE
satisfactory *(also as a school mark)*

die **Befugnis**, PLURAL die **Befugnisse**
authority

begabt ADJECTIVE
gifted, talented

die **Begabung**
gift, talent

begann ▸SEE **beginnen**

begegnen VERB, PERFECT **ist begegnet**
1 jemandem begegnen to meet somebody
Heute morgen ist mir Anna begegnet. I
met Anna this morning.
2 sich begegnen to meet (each other)
Wir sind uns in der Stadt begegnet. We
met in town.
3 etwas begegnen to meet something
Solchen Vorurteilen bin ich noch nie
begegnet. I've never met such prejudice.

die **Begegnung**, PLURAL die **Begegnungen**
meeting

begehen VERB◇, IMPERFECT **beging**, PERFECT **hat
begangen**
to commit *(a crime, suicide)*

begeistern VERB, PERFECT **hat begeistert**
1 jemanden (für etwas) begeistern to
fill somebody with enthusiasm (for
something)
Der Lehrer hat seine Schüler für das Fach
begeistert. The teacher filled his students
with enthusiasm for the subject.
2 sich für etwas begeistern to be keen on
something
Er begeistert sich für Hip-Hop. He's keen
on Hip-Hop.

begeistert ADJECTIVE
enthusiastic

die **Begeisterung**
enthusiasm

der **Beginn**
beginning
Zu Beginn des Jahres war er krank. He was
ill at the beginning of the year.

ℓ **beginnen** VERB◇, IMPERFECT **begann**, PERFECT
hat begonnen
to begin, to start

begleiten VERB, PERFECT **hat begleitet**
to accompany
Er hat sie auf dem Klavier begleitet. He
accompanied her on the piano.

beglückwünschen VERB, PERFECT **hat
beglückwünscht**
to congratulate

begonnen ▸SEE **beginnen**

begraben VERB◇, PRESENT **begräbt**, IMPERFECT
begrub, PERFECT **hat begraben**
to bury

begreifen VERB◇, IMPERFECT **begriff**, PERFECT
hat begriffen
to understand

begrenzen VERB, PERFECT **hat begrenzt**
to limit

der **Begriff**, PLURAL die **Begriffe**
1 term
Das ist ein Begriff aus der Malerei. It is a
painting term.
2 concept
Sie haben einen anderen Begriff von
Freiheit. They have a different concept of
freedom.
Davon kann ich mir keinen Begriff
machen. I can't imagine that.
3 im Begriff sein, etwas zu tun to be about
to do something
Er war im Begriff zu gehen. He was about
to leave.
4 für meine Begriffe to my mind
Das ist für meine Begriffe eine Schande.
To my mind, it's a disgrace.
5 schwer von Begriff sein *(informal)* to be
slow on the uptake

begründen VERB, PERFECT **hat begründet**
etwas begründen to give a reason for
something, to justify something

die **Begründung**, PLURAL die **Begründungen**
reason, justification

begrüßen VERB, PERFECT **hat begrüßt**
1 to greet
2 to welcome

die **Begrüßung**
welcome

begünstigen VERB, PERFECT **hat begünstigt**
to favour

behaart ADJECTIVE
hairy

behaglich ADJECTIVE
cosy

behalten *VERB*◇, *PRESENT* **behält**, *IMPERFECT* **behielt**, *PERFECT* **hat behalten**
1 **to keep**
Du kannst die CD behalten. You can keep the CD.
2 **to remember**
Ich habe das Wort nicht behalten. I can't remember the word.

der **Behälter**, *PLURAL* die **Behälter**
container

behandeln *VERB*, *PERFECT* **hat behandelt**
1 **to treat**
Sie ist sehr schlecht behandelt worden. She's been treated very badly.
Darf er schon Patienten behandeln? Is he allowed to treat patients yet?
Welcher Arzt hat Sie behandelt? Which doctor treated you?
2 **to deal with** *a subject, question*
Das Buch behandelt das Drogenproblem. The book deals with the problem of drugs.

die **Behandlung**, *PLURAL* die **Behandlungen**
treatment

behaupten *VERB*, *PERFECT* **hat behauptet**
1 **to claim**
2 sich behaupten **to assert yourself**

die **Behauptung**, *PLURAL* die **Behauptungen**
claim

beherrschen *VERB*, *PERFECT* **hat beherrscht**
1 **to rule over** *(a country, people)*
2 **to control**
3 sich beherrschen **to control yourself**
4 **to know** *(a trick, rules)*

behilflich *ADJECTIVE*
jemandem bei etwas behilflich sein to help somebody with something
Kann ich Ihnen behilflich sein? Can I help you?

behindert *ADJECTIVE*
disabled
Ist er behindert? Does he have a disability?

◇ der/die **Behinderte**, *PLURAL* die **Behinderten**
disabled person
die Behinderten the disabled

◇ das **Behindertenheim**, *PLURAL* die **Behindertenheime**
home for people with disabilities

die **Behinderung**
1 obstruction
2 disability

die **Behörde**, *PLURAL* die **Behörden**
authority, authorities

behüten *VERB*, *PERFECT* **hat behütet**
to protect

◇ **bei** *PREPOSITION* (+ *DAT*)
1 **near** *close to*
Wir gehen in die Diskothek beim Bahnhof. We're going to the disco near the station.
2 **at** *(indicating a place or time)*
Wir treffen uns bei mir. We're meeting at my place.
Er ist beim Arzt. He's at the doctor's.
Sie übernachtet bei ihrer Freundin. She's staying the night at her friend's house.
Wir fuhren bei Tagesanbruch ab. We left at dawn.
3 **with** *(indicating where someone lives)*
Er wohnt bei seinen Eltern. He lives with his parents.
4 **for** *(indicating where someone works)*
Sie arbeitet bei einem Verlag. She works for a publisher.
5 Bei uns in der Schule wird eine Sekretärin gesucht. In our school they are looking for a secretary.
6 Er ist bei guter Gesundheit. He's in good health.
7 bei Regen if it rains
bei Nebel in fog
bei Tag by day
8 etwas bei sich haben to have something on you
Hast du deinen Pass bei dir? Do you have your passport on you?
9 bei Morris *(on a letter)* c/o Morris
10 sich bei jemandem entschuldigen to apologize to somebody
11 Bei der hohen Miete bleibt kein Geld für ein Auto übrig. With the high rent, there's no money left for a car.
12 Beim Fahren muss man sich konzentrieren. You have to concentrate while driving.
Ich war beim Lesen, als das Telefon klingelte. I was reading when the phone rang.
Sie waren beim Frühstück. They were having breakfast.

WORD TIP bei + dem gives beim

beibringen *VERB*◇, *PRESENT* **bringt bei**, *IMPERFECT* **brachte bei**, *PERFECT* **hat beigebracht**
jemandem etwas beibringen to teach somebody something
Meine Brieffreundin hat mir viele neue Wörter beigebracht. My penfriend has

taught me many new words.

die Beichte, PLURAL die **Beichten**
confession

beichten VERB, PERFECT **hat gebeichtet**
to confess

ℰ **beide** ADJECTIVE, PRONOUN
1 both
Ihr beide habt gewonnen./Ihr habt beide
gewonnen. Both of you have won.
Er hat seine beiden Eltern verloren. He has
lost both his parents.
2 two
Die beiden Schwestern sehen sich ähnlich.
The two sisters look alike.
Die ersten beiden bekommen einen Preis.
The first two get a prize.
Such dir eins von beiden aus. Choose one
of the two.
3 keiner von beiden neither (of them)
War es Max oder Tom? – Keiner von
beiden. Was it Max or Tom? – Neither (of
them).
4 beides both
Er spielt beides, Klavier und Gitarre. He
plays both the piano and the guitar.
5 dreißig beide thirty all (in tennis)

beieinander ADVERB
together

der Beifahrer, PLURAL die **Beifahrer**
passenger (male)

die Beifahrerin, PLURAL die **Beifahrerinnen**
passenger (female)

der Beifall
applause

das Beil, PLURAL die **Beile**
axe

die Beilage, PLURAL die **Beilagen**
1 supplement (to a paper)
2 side dish (with a meal)
Als Beilage gab es Reis und Erbsen. It was
served with rice and peas.

beiläufig ADJECTIVE
casual

beilegen VERB, PERFECT **hat beigelegt**
1 to enclose
Sie legte dem Brief ein Foto bei. She
enclosed a photo with the letter.
2 to settle (an argument)

das Beileid
condolences
jemandem sein Beileid aussprechen to
offer your condolences to somebody

Ich möchte Ihnen mein Beileid
aussprechen. I would like to offer my
condolences.
Mein aufrichtiges Beileid! My deepest
sympathy!

beiliegen VERB◇, PRESENT **liegt bei**, IMPERFECT
lag bei, PERFECT **hat beigelegen**
to be enclosed
Ein Scheck liegt bei. Please find enclosed
a cheque.

beiliegend ADJECTIVE
enclosed

beim ▸ SEE **bei dem**

ℰ **das Bein**, PLURAL die **Beine**
leg

beinahe ADVERB
almost

der Beinbruch, PLURAL die **Beinbrüche**
broken leg
Das ist doch kein Beinbruch! (informal) It's
not the end of the world.

beisammen ADVERB
together

beiseite ADVERB
aside
Er schob das Kind beiseite. He pushed the
child aside.

beiseitelegen VERB, PERFECT **hat
beiseitegelegt**
etwas beiseitelegen to put something by
Sie haben immer etwas Geld
beiseitegelegt. They have always put some
money by.

beiseiteschaffen VERB, PERFECT **hat
beiseitegeschafft**
etwas beiseiteschaffen to hide something
away
Wir müssen das Geld beiseiteschaffen. We
have to hide the money away.

ℰ **das Beispiel**, PLURAL die **Beispiele**
example
zum Beispiel for example
Sie ging mit gutem Beispiel voran. She set
a good example.

beispielsweise ADVERB
for example

beißen VERB◇, IMPERFECT **biss**, PERFECT **hat
gebissen**
1 to bite
2 to sting (of smoke, for example)
3 sich beißen to clash

Die Farben beißen sich. The colours clash.

der **Beitrag**, PLURAL die **Beiträge**
1 contribution
Er hat einen wichtigen Beitrag zum Projekt geleistet. He has made an important contribution to the project.
2 premium (insurance fee)
3 article (in a newspaper)
4 report (on television, the radio)

beitragen VERB✧, PRESENT **trägt bei**, IMPERFECT **trug bei**, PERFECT **hat beigetragen**
zu etwas beitragen to contribute to something

beitreten VERB✧, PRESENT **tritt bei**, IMPERFECT **trat bei**, PERFECT **ist beigetreten**
to join
Ich trete dem Fußballverein bei. I'm joining the football club.

bekam ▸SEE **bekommen**

bekämpfen VERB, PERFECT **hat bekämpft**
1 to fight
2 sich bekämpfen to fight

ℛ **bekannt** ADJECTIVE
1 well known
2 familiar
Das kommt mir bekannt vor. That seems familiar.
3 mit jemandem bekannt sein to know somebody
Sie ist mit meiner Mutter bekannt. She knows my mother.
4 für etwas bekannt sein to be (well) known for something
Österreich ist für gutes Essen bekannt. Austria is well known for its good food.
5 jemanden bekannt machen to introduce somebody
Er machte uns mit seiner Schwester bekannt. He introduced us to his sister.
6 Das ist mir bekannt. I know that.
7 etwas bekannt geben/machen to announce something
Sie gaben ihre Verlobung bekannt. They announced their engagement.
8 bekannt werden to become known, to come out
Erst jetzt wurde bekannt, dass ... It has only just come out that ...

ℛ der/die **Bekannte**, PLURAL die **Bekannten**
1 acquaintance
2 friend

bekanntlich ADVERB
as everybody knows
Rauchen ist bekanntlich schädlich. As

everybody knows, smoking is bad for you.

beklagen VERB, PERFECT **hat sich beklagt**
sich beklagen to complain

die **Bekleidung**
clothes, clothing

ℛ **bekommen** VERB✧, IMPERFECT **bekam**, PERFECT **hat bekommen**
1 to get
Was hast du zum Geburtstag bekommen? What did you get for your birthday?
Ich bekam Angst. I got frightened.
2 to catch (a bus, train)
Hast du deinen Zug noch bekommen? Did you manage to catch your train?
3 ein Kind bekommen to have a baby
4 Was bekommen Sie? (in a shop) Can I help you?, What would you like?
5 Was bekommen Sie dafür? How much is it?
6 PERFECT **ist bekommen**
jemandem bekommen to agree with somebody
Fettes Essen bekommt mir nicht. Fatty food doesn't agree with me.
7 PERFECT **ist bekommen**
jemandem gut bekommen to do somebody good
Die Ferien sind mir gut bekommen. The holiday did me good.

WORD TIP The German word bekommen does not mean to become in English; the German word for become is werden.

der **Belag**, PLURAL die **Beläge**
1 covering
2 coating
3 topping (on bread)

belasten VERB, PERFECT **hat belastet**
1 to burden
2 to put weight on (foot)
3 to pollute (the environment, atmosphere)
4 to debit (an account)
5 to incriminate

belästigen VERB, PERFECT **hat belästigt**
1 to bother
2 to harass

die **Belastung**
1 strain
2 load
3 burden
4 pollution

belaufen VERB✧, PRESENT **beläuft**, IMPERFECT **belief**, PERFECT **belaufen**
sich auf etwas belaufen to amount

to something
Die Rechnung beläuft sich auf 500 Euro.
The bill amounts to 500 euros.

belegen VERB, PERFECT **hat belegt**
1 to enrol for
Er belegte einen Spanischkurs. He
enrolled for a Spanish class.
2 den ersten Platz belegen to come first
3 Sie belegte eine Scheibe Brot mit Käse.
She put some cheese on a slice of bread.
4 to prove
Wissenschaftler haben belegt, dass sich
die Erde erwärmt. Scientists have proved
that the earth is warming up.

belegt ADJECTIVE
1 occupied
Der Platz ist belegt. This seat is taken.
2 ein belegtes Brot an open sandwich
3 Die Nummer ist belegt. *(when phoning)*
The number's engaged.

beleidigen VERB, PERFECT **hat beleidigt**
to insult

die **Beleidigung**, PLURAL die **Beleidigungen**
insult

die **Beleuchtung**
lighting

Belgien NEUTER NOUN
Belgium

der **Belgier**, PLURAL die **Belgier**
Belgian *(male)*

die **Belgierin**, PLURAL die **Belgierinnen**
Belgian *(female)*

belgisch ADJECTIVE
Belgian

> **WORD TIP** Adjectives never have capitals
> in German, even for regions, countries, or
> nationalities.

die **Belichtung**
exposure

beliebig ADJECTIVE
any
Denk dir eine beliebige Zahl aus. Think of
any number you like.

beliebig ADVERB
beliebig lange as long as you like
Kann man beliebig lange im Schwimmbad
bleiben? Can you stay in the pool as long
as you like?
beliebig viele as many as you like
Sie können beliebig viele Karten nehmen.
You can take as many cards as you like.

ρ **beliebt** ADJECTIVE
popular

die **Beliebtheit**
popularity

bellen VERB, PERFECT **hat gebellt**
to bark

belohnen VERB, PERFECT **hat belohnt**
to reward

die **Belohnung**, PLURAL die **Belohnungen**
reward

belügen VERB◇, IMPERFECT **belog**, PERFECT **hat**
belogen
to lie to
Er hat mich belogen. He lied to me.

bemerkbar ADJECTIVE
sich bemerkbar machen to attract
attention, to become noticeable

bemerken VERB, PERFECT **hat bemerkt**
1 to notice
Er hat es nicht bemerkt. He didn't notice
it.
2 to remark
3 nebenbei bemerkt by the way

ρ die **Bemerkung**, PLURAL die **Bemerkungen**
remark

bemitleiden VERB, PERFECT **hat bemitleidet**
to pity

ρ **bemühen** VERB, PERFECT **hat sich bemüht**
1 sich bemühen to try, to make an effort
Sie haben sich sehr bemüht. They made a
big effort.
2 sich um etwas bemühen to try to get
something
Er bemüht sich um eine Stelle. He's trying
to get a job.
3 sich um jemanden bemühen to try to help
somebody
Sie bemühte sich um die alte Dame. She
tried to help the old lady.
4 Bitte, bemühen Sie sich nicht! Please don't
trouble yourself!

die **Bemühung**, PLURAL die **Bemühungen**
effort

benachrichtigen VERB, PERFECT **hat**
benachrichtigt
1 to inform
2 to notify

benachteiligen VERB, PERFECT **hat**
benachteiligt
to put at a disadvantage

◇ irregular verb; SEP separable verb; for more help with verbs see centre section

benachteiligt *ADJECTIVE*
disadvantaged

benehmen *VERB⋄*, *PRESENT* **benimmt sich**,
IMPERFECT **benahm sich**, *PERFECT* **hat sich
benommen**
　sich benehmen to behave
　Benimm dich! Behave yourself!

das **Benehmen**
　behaviour

beneiden *VERB*, *PERFECT* **hat beneidet**
　to envy
　jemanden um etwas beneiden to envy
　somebody something

benoten *VERB*, *PERFECT* **hat benotet**
　to mark

ℓ **benutzen** *VERB*, *PERFECT* **hat benutzt**
　to use

der **Benutzer**, *PLURAL* die **Benutzer**
　user *(male)*

benutzerfreundlich *ADJECTIVE*
　user-friendly

die **Benutzerin**, *PLURAL* die **Benutzerinnen**
　user *(female)*

die **Benutzung**
　use

das **Benzin**
　petrol

beobachten *VERB*, *PERFECT* **hat beobachtet**
　to observe, to watch
　Ich habe dich die ganze Zeit beobachtet! I
　was watching you all the time!

bequem *ADJECTIVE*
1　**comfortable**
　Die Schuhe sind sehr bequem. The shoes
　are very comfortable.
2　Machen Sie es sich bequem. Make yourself
　at home.
3　**lazy**
　Sei nicht so bequem! Don't be so lazy!
4　**easy**
　Sie haben eine bequeme Lösung
　gefunden. They found an easy way out.

beraten *VERB⋄*, *PRESENT* **berät**, *IMPERFECT*
beriet, *PERFECT* **hat beraten**
1　**to advise**
　Kannst du mich beraten, welches
　Wörterbuch ich kaufen soll? Can you
　advise me which dictionary I should buy?
　Wir wurden gut/schlecht beraten. We
　were given good/bad advice.
2　sich beraten lassen to get advice

Sie sollten sich von einem Anwalt beraten
lassen. You should get legal advice.
3　gut/schlecht beraten sein to be well/ill
　advised
4　**to discuss** *(a plan, matter)*
5　sich über etwas beraten to discuss
　something

der **Berater**, *PLURAL* die **Berater**
　adviser *(male)*

die **Beraterin**, *PLURAL* die **Beraterinnen**
　adviser *(female)*

ℓ die **Beratung**, *PLURAL* die **Beratungen**
1　**advice**
2　**discussion**
3　**consultation** *(with a doctor, lawyer)*

berauben *VERB*, *PERFECT* **hat beraubt**
　to rob

berechnen *VERB*, *PERFECT* **hat berechnet**
1　**to charge**
　Dafür haben sie mir zehn Euro berechnet.
　They charged me ten euros for it.
2　jemandem zu viel berechnen to
　overcharge somebody
3　**to calculate**

berechtigen *VERB*, *PERFECT* **hat berechtigt**
　jemanden berechtigen, etwas zu tun to
　give someone the right to do something

berechtigt *ADJECTIVE*
　justified

ℓ der **Bereich**, *PLURAL* die **Bereiche**
1　**area, sector**
2　**field** *(in a profession)*
　Ich möchte gerne im Bereich Tourismus
　arbeiten. I would like to work in the field
　of tourism.

ℓ **bereit** *ADJECTIVE*
1　**ready**
2　bereit sein, etwas zu tun to be prepared to
　do something
　Sie waren nicht bereit, so viel Geld
　auszugeben. They were not prepared to
　spend so much money.

bereiten *VERB*, *PERFECT* **hat bereitet**
1　**to make** *(coffee, tea)*
2　**to cause** *(trouble, difficulty)*
　Leider hat es uns Schwierigkeiten
　bereitet. Unfortunately it caused us some
　problems.
3　**to give** *(a surprise, pleasure)*

bereits *ADVERB*
　already

ℓ **indicates key words**

bereuen *VERB*, *PERFECT* **hat bereut**
to regret

♪ der **Berg**, *PLURAL* die **Berge**
1 mountain
2 hill

> ### BERG
> The highest mountains in the German-speaking countries are: Großglockner 3798m (Austria), the Zugspitze 2964m (Germany), Monte Rosa 4634m (Switzerland). The most famous Swiss mountain, the Matterhorn, at 4478m is only the second highest mountain in the country.

bergab *ADVERB*
downhill

der **Bergarbeiter**, *PLURAL* die **Bergarbeiter**
miner

> **WORD TIP** Professions, hobbies, and sports don't take an article in German: Er ist Bergarbeiter.

bergauf *ADVERB*
uphill

die **Bergbahn**, *PLURAL* die **Bergbahnen**
mountain railway

bergen *VERB*◇, *PRESENT* **birgt**, *IMPERFECT* **barg**, *PERFECT* **hat geborgen**
to rescue

der **Bergsee**, *PLURAL* die **Bergseen**
mountain lake

das **Bergsteigen**
mountaineering

der **Bergsteiger**, *PLURAL* die **Bergsteiger**
mountaineer, climber *(male)*

die **Bergsteigerin**, *PLURAL* die **Bergsteigerinnen**
mountaineer, climber *(female)*

die **Bergwacht**
mountain rescue

das **Bergwerk**, *PLURAL* die **Bergwerke**
mine

♪ der **Bericht**, *PLURAL* die **Berichte**
report

berichten *VERB*, *PERFECT* **hat berichtet**
1 to report
Die Zeitungen haben nichts davon berichtet. The newspapers didn't report anything about it.
2 jemandem über etwas berichten to tell somebody about something
Er hat mir über seine Ferien in Amerika berichtet. He told me about his holiday in

America.

der **Berliner**, *PLURAL* die **Berliner**
doughnut

> **WORD TIP** Berliner can refer to a resident of Berlin as well as the food.

> ### BERLINER MAUER
> The Berlin Wall was built in 1961 as a physical barrier between West Berlin and East Berlin, the capital of the former German Democratic Republic (often referred to as 'East Germany'). The Berlin Wall was taken down in 1989 and Germany was reunited. Some parts of the Berlin Wall still remain and have been painted as a reminder of Germany's divided history.

Bern *NEUTER NOUN*
Berne

> ### BERN
> Bern is the 'federal' city of Switzerland. In order to respect federal sensibilities, Swiss law does not designate an official capital city.

berücksichtigen *VERB*, *PERFECT* **hat berücksichtigt**
to take into account

♪ der **Beruf**, *PLURAL* die **Berufe**
1 occupation
2 profession
Ich bin Lehrerin von Beruf. I'm a teacher by profession.
3 trade
4 Was sind Sie von Beruf? What do you do for a living?

beruflich *ADJECTIVE*
1 professional
2 vocational *(training)*
beruflich *ADVERB*
1 Sie ist beruflich erfolgreich. She is successful in her career.
2 Er ist beruflich viel unterwegs. He is away a lot on business.

die **Berufsausbildung**
(vocational) training
Er macht eine Berufsausbildung als Installateur. He is training to be a plumber.

der **Berufsberater**, *PLURAL* die **Berufsberater**
careers adviser *(male)*

> **WORD TIP** Professions, hobbies, and sports don't take an article in German: Er ist Berufsberater.

die **Berufsberaterin**, *PLURAL* die
Berufsberaterinnen
careers adviser *(female)*

WORD TIP Professions, hobbies, and sports
don't take an article in German: Sie ist
Berufsberaterin.

die **Berufsberatung**
careers advice

das **Berufspraktikum**, *PLURAL* die
Berufspraktika
work experience

ℰ die **Berufsschule**, *PLURAL* die **Berufsschulen**
technical college, vocational school

berufstätig *ADJECTIVE*
working

der **Berufsverkehr**
rush-hour traffic

beruhigen *VERB*, *PERFECT* **hat beruhigt**
1 to calm (down)
2 to reassure
3 sich beruhigen to calm down

das **Beruhigungsmittel**, *PLURAL* die
Beruhigungsmittel
sedative, tranquillizer

ℰ **berühmt** *ADJECTIVE*
famous

berühren *VERB*, *PERFECT* **hat berührt**
1 to touch
2 to touch on *(a topic, an issue)*
3 to affect
Ihre Geschichte berührte ihn seltsam. He
was strangely affected by her story.
4 sich berühren to touch

besaß ▸ SEE besitzen

beschädigen *VERB*, *PERFECT* **hat beschädigt**
to damage

die **Beschädigung**, *PLURAL* die
Beschädigungen
damage

beschaffen *VERB*, *PERFECT* **hat beschafft**
to get
Kannst du mir nicht einen Job beschaffen?
Can't you get me a job?

beschäftigen *VERB*, *PERFECT* **hat beschäftigt**
1 to occupy *(keep busy)*
2 to employ *(people)*
3 sich beschäftigen to occupy yourself
4 sich mit jemandem beschäftigen to spend
time with somebody
Das Au-pair-Mädchen beschäftigt sich mit

den Kindern. The au pair spends time with
the children.
5 sich mit etwas beschäftigen to deal with
something
Er beschäftigte sich mit einem neuen Fall.
He was dealing with a new case.
Sein Aufsatz beschäftigt sich mit der
Umweltverschmutzung. His essay deals
with environmental pollution.

beschäftigt *ADJECTIVE*
1 busy
2 employed

die **Beschäftigung**, *PLURAL* die
Beschäftigungen
1 occupation
2 activity

beschämt *ADJECTIVE*
ashamed

der **Bescheid**, *PLURAL* die **Bescheide**
1 jemandem Bescheid sagen to let
somebody know
Bitte sag mir Bescheid, wenn du fertig
bist. Please let me know when you have
finished.
2 über etwas Bescheid wissen to know
about something
Darüber weiß er schon Bescheid. He
already knows about it.

bescheiden *ADJECTIVE*
modest

die **Bescheinigung**, *PLURAL* die
Bescheinigungen
1 certificate
Sie brauchen eine ärztliche
Bescheinigung. You need a doctor's
certificate.
2 (written) confirmation

die **Bescherung**, *PLURAL* die **Bescherungen**
1 giving out of Christmas presents
Bei uns ist die Bescherung immer am
Heiligabend. We always give out the
Christmas presents on Christmas Eve.
2 Das ist ja eine schöne Bescherung!
(informal) What a mess!

beschimpfen *VERB*, *PERFECT* **hat beschimpft**
to swear at

beschlagnahmen *VERB*, *PERFECT* **hat
beschlagnahmt**
to confiscate

beschleunigen *VERB*, *PERFECT* **hat
beschleunigt**
1 to speed up
2 to accelerate
Der Lastwagen hinter uns hat plötzlich

beschleunigt. The lorry behind us suddenly accelerated.

ℰ **beschließen** *VERB⬦*, *IMPERFECT* **beschloss**, *PERFECT* **hat beschlossen**
to decide

der **Beschluss**, *PLURAL* die **Beschlüsse**
decision

beschränken *VERB*, *PERFECT* **hat beschränkt**
to limit

beschränkt *ADJECTIVE*
1 limited
2 narrow-minded
3 dim, stupid
Sie ist ein bisschen beschränkt. She's a bit dim.

die **Beschränkung**, *PLURAL* die **Beschränkungen**
limit

ℰ **beschreiben** *VERB⬦*, *IMPERFECT* **beschrieb**, *PERFECT* **hat beschrieben**
to describe

ℰ die **Beschreibung**, *PLURAL* die **Beschreibungen**
description

beschuldigen *VERB*, *PERFECT* **hat beschuldigt**
to accuse

die **Beschuldigung**, *PLURAL* die **Beschuldigungen**
accusation

beschützen *VERB*, *PERFECT* **hat beschützt**
to protect

die **Beschwerde**, *PLURAL* die **Beschwerden**
1 complaint
2 Beschwerden trouble
Sie hat Beschwerden beim Schlucken. She has trouble swallowing.

ℰ **beschweren** *VERB*, *PERFECT* **hat sich beschwert**
sich beschweren to complain
Ich habe mich bei den Nachbarn über ihn beschwert. I've complained to the neighbours about him.

beschwipst *ADJECTIVE*
tipsy

beseitigen *VERB*, *PERFECT* **hat beseitigt**
to remove

der **Besen**, *PLURAL* die **Besen**
broom

besetzen *VERB*, *PERFECT* **hat besetzt**
1 to occupy

2 to fill (a post, role)

besetzt *ADJECTIVE*
1 occupied
2 besetzt sein to be engaged (a phone, toilet)
3 taken (a table, seat)
Der Platz ist besetzt. This seat is taken.
4 full (of a train, bus)
Der Zug ist voll besetzt. The train is full up.

das **Besetztzeichen**, *PLURAL* die **Besetztzeichen**
engaged tone

die **Besetzung**, *PLURAL* die **Besetzungen**
1 cast
2 team
3 occupation (of a country)

ℰ **besichtigen** *VERB*, *PERFECT* **hat besichtigt**
1 to look round, to visit (a town, museum)
2 to see (sights, a house)

ℰ die **Besichtigung**, *PLURAL* die **Besichtigungen**
visit

besinnungslos *ADJECTIVE*
unconscious

der **Besitz**
1 property
2 possession
Er wurde festgenommen, weil er im Besitz von Drogen war. He was arrested for possession of drugs.

besitzen *VERB⬦*, *IMPERFECT* **besaß**, *PERFECT* **hat besessen**
1 to own
Sie besitzen ein Haus in Italien. They own a house in Italy.
2 to have (talent, a quality)

der **Besitzer**, *PLURAL* die **Besitzer**
owner (male)

die **Besitzerin**, *PLURAL* die **Besitzerinnen**
owner (female)

ℰ **besonderer, besondere, besonderes** *ADJECTIVE*
1 special
Das ist nur unter besonderen Umständen erlaubt. It's allowed only in special circumstances.
2 particular
Sie öffnete das Geschenk ohne besondere Begeisterung. She opened the present without any particular enthusiasm.
3 Der Verdächtige hat keine besonderen Kennzeichen. The suspect has no distinguishing features.

⬦ **irregular verb;** *SEP* **separable verb; for more help with verbs see centre section**

die **Besonderheit**, PLURAL die
  Besonderheiten
1 special feature
2 peculiarity

ℰ**besonders** ADVERB
  particularly, especially

besorgen VERB, PERFECT **hat besorgt**
  to get
  Ich kann dir Karten besorgen. I can get
  you tickets.

besorgt ADJECTIVE
  worried

ℰ**besprechen** VERB◇, PRESENT **bespricht**,
  IMPERFECT **besprach**, PERFECT **hat
  besprochen**
1 to discuss
  Ich muss es erst mit meinen Eltern
  besprechen. I'll have to discuss it with my
  parents first.
2 to review (a book, film)

die **Besprechung**, PLURAL die
  Besprechungen
1 meeting (at work)
2 discussion
3 review (of a film, play)

ℰ**besser** ADJECTIVE, ADVERB
  better
  Sie weiß immer alles besser. She always
  knows better.
  Geht es Ihnen besser? Are you feeling
  better?

die **Besserung**
1 improvement
2 Gute Besserung! Get well soon!

beständig ADJECTIVE
1 constant
2 settled (weather)

der **Bestandteil**, PLURAL die **Bestandteile**
  component

bestätigen VERB, PERFECT **hat bestätigt**
1 to confirm
2 to acknowledge (receipt)
3 sich bestätigen to be confirmed, to prove
  to be true
  Mein Verdacht hat sich bestätigt. My
  suspicion was confirmed.

beste ▸ SEE **bester**

bestechen VERB◇, PRESENT **besticht**, IMPERFECT
  bestach, PERFECT **hat bestochen**
1 to bribe
2 to win over

die **Bestechung**, PLURAL die **Bestechungen**
  bribery

das **Besteck**, PLURAL die **Bestecke**
  cutlery

bestehen VERB◇, IMPERFECT **bestand**, PERFECT
  hat bestanden
1 to exist
2 to be
  Es besteht die Gefahr, dass ... There is a
  danger that ...
  Noch besteht die Hoffnung, dass ... There
  is still hope that ...
3 to pass
  Hast du die Prüfung bestanden? Did you
  pass the exam?
4 auf etwas bestehen to insist on something
  Ich bestehe darauf! I insist!
5 aus etwas bestehen to consist of
  something
  Das Getränk besteht aus Zucker, Wasser
  und Farbstoff. The drink consists of sugar,
  water and colouring.
6 aus etwas bestehen to be made of
  something
  Der Stuhl besteht aus Metall. The chair is
  made of metal.

ℰ**bestellen** VERB, PERFECT **hat bestellt**
1 to order (goods)
2 to reserve (tickets)
3 to tell
  jemandem etwas bestellen to tell
  somebody something
  Kannst du ihr bestellen, dass ich morgen
  komme? Can you tell her that I'm coming
  tomorrow?
4 Bestell ihm schöne Grüße! Give him my
  regards.
5 Kann ich etwas bestellen? Can I take a
  message?
6 to send for
  jemanden zu sich bestellen to send for
  somebody

ℰ die **Bestellung**, PLURAL die **Bestellungen**
1 order
2 reservation (for tickets)

bestens ADVERB
  very well
  Das hat ja bestens geklappt. That worked
  out very well.

ℰ**bester, beste, bestes** ADJECTIVE
1 best
  Das ist sein bestes Buch. That's his best
  book.
2 Ich halte es für das Beste, wenn ... I think
  it would be best if ...

sein Bestes tun to do your best
Du hast dein Bestes getan. You did your best.

3 einen Witz zum Besten geben to tell a joke

4 jemanden zum Besten halten to pull somebody's leg
Wollen Sie mich zum Besten halten? Are you trying to pull my leg?

am besten ADVERB
   best
   Du bleibst am besten zu Hause. You'd best stay at home.
   Es ist am besten, wenn wir gleich anfangen. It's best if we get started straight away.
   Der erste Song hat mir am besten gefallen. I liked the first song best of all.

ℙ **bestimmen** VERB, PERFECT **hat bestimmt**
1 to fix (a time, price)
2 to decide (on)
   Das möchte ich allein bestimmen. I'd like to decide (on) that on my own.
   Er bestimmt immer, was wir machen. He always decides what we're going to do.
3 to be in charge
   Wer bestimmt bei der Gruppenarbeit? Who's in charge when you work in a group?
4 to rule
   Ihr Leben wird von der Arbeit bestimmt. Her life is ruled by work.
5 to determine
   Wie bestimmen die Wissenschaftler das Alter der Knochen? How do the scientists determine the age of the bones?
6 für jemanden bestimmt sein to be meant for somebody
7 für etwas bestimmt sein to be intended for something (a donation for a good cause, for example)

ℙ **bestimmt** ADJECTIVE
1 certain
   Die Straße ist zu bestimmten Zeiten geschlossen. The road is closed at certain times.
2 particular
   Suchen Sie etwas Bestimmtes? Are you looking for anything in particular?
3 definite (also in grammar)
bestimmt ADVERB
1 certainly, definitely
   Ich komme ganz bestimmt. I'm definitely coming.
2 Er hat es bestimmt vergessen. He's bound to have forgotten.
3 Du weißt es doch bestimmt noch. Surely you must remember it.

die **Bestimmung**, PLURAL die **Bestimmungen**
   regulation

bestrafen VERB, PERFECT **hat bestraft**
   to punish

bestreiten VERB◇, IMPERFECT **bestritt**, PERFECT **hat bestritten**
1 to deny
   Er bestritt, jemals am Tatort gewesen zu sein. He denied that he had ever been to the scene of the crime.
2 to dispute
   Das möchte ich nicht bestreiten. I'm not disputing it.
3 to pay for

bestürzt ADJECTIVE
   upset

ℙ der **Besuch**, PLURAL die **Besuche**
1 visit
2 a visitor, visitors
   Wir haben Besuch: Anne ist da. We have a visitor: Anne's here.
3 Am Wochenende waren sie bei Freunden zu Besuch. At the weekend, they were staying with friends.
   zu Besuch kommen to be visiting
   Morgen kommt Julia zu uns zu Besuch. Julia's coming to see us tomorrow.
4 attendance (at school)
   Der regelmäßige Besuch der Schule ist wichtig. Regular attendance at school is important.

ℙ **besuchen** VERB, PERFECT **hat besucht**
1 to visit (a friend, relative)
2 to go to (an exhibition, the theatre)
   die Schule besuchen to go to school
3 to attend (a lecture)

der **Besucher**, PLURAL die **Besucher**
   visitor (male)

die **Besucherin**, PLURAL die **Besucherinnen**
   visitor (female)

betätigen VERB, PERFECT **hat betätigt**
1 to operate (a machine, lever)
2 die Bremse betätigen to apply the brakes
3 Viele Studenten betätigen sich politisch. Many students are involved in politics.
4 In den Ferien habe ich Zeit, mich künstlerisch zu betätigen. In the holidays, I have time to do art.
5 Früher betätigte er sich als Reporter. He used to work as a reporter.

◇ irregular verb; SEP separable verb; for more help with verbs see centre section

das **Betäubungsmittel**, PLURAL die
  Betäubungsmittel
  anaesthetic

die **Bete**
  Rote Bete beetroot

beteiligen VERB, PERFECT **hat beteiligt**
1 sich an etwas beteiligen to take part in
  something
  Hast du dich an dem Wettbewerb
  beteiligt? Did you take part in the
  competition?
2 jemanden an etwas beteiligen to give
  somebody a share in something
  Er ist mit zehn Prozent an dem Geschäft
  beteiligt. He has a ten percent share in the
  business.

beten VERB, PERFECT **hat gebetet**
  to pray

der **Beton**
  concrete

betonen VERB, PERFECT **hat betont**
  to stress

die **Betonung**, PLURAL die **Betonungen**
  stress

der **Betrag**, PLURAL die **Beträge**
  amount

betragen VERB◇, PRESENT **beträgt**, IMPERFECT
  betrug, PERFECT **hat betragen**
1 to amount to, to come to
  Die Gesamtsumme beträgt 75 Franken.
  The total comes to 75 Swiss francs.
2 sich betragen to behave
  Haben sich die Kinder gut betragen? Did
  the children behave well?

das **Betragen**
  behaviour

der **Betreff**, PLURAL die **Betreffe**
  subject matter
  Betreff: Ihr Schreiben vom ... re your letter
  of ...

betreffen VERB◇, PRESENT **betrifft**, IMPERFECT
  betraf, PERFECT **hat betroffen**
  to concern
  Was mich betrifft, ... As far as I'm
  concerned, ...

betreten VERB◇, PRESENT **betritt**, IMPERFECT
  betrat, PERFECT **hat betreten**
1 to enter
2 'Betreten verboten' 'Keep out', 'Keep off'
  (the grass, for example)

der **Betrieb**, PLURAL die **Betriebe**
1 business, firm
  Sie arbeitet bei einem kleinen Betrieb. She
  works for a small firm.
2 activity
  Es war viel Betrieb. It was very busy.
3 operation
  Ist der neue Terminal schon in Betrieb? Is
  the new terminal in operation yet?
4 'Außer Betrieb' 'out of order'

die **Betriebsferien** PLURAL NOUN
  firm's holiday
  'Betriebsferien' 'Closed for the holidays'

der **Betriebsleiter**, PLURAL die **Betriebsleiter**
  manager (male)

  WORD TIP Professions, hobbies, and sports don't
  take an article in German: Er ist Betriebsleiter.

die **Betriebsleiterin**, PLURAL die
  Betriebsleiterinnen
  manager (female)

  WORD TIP Professions, hobbies, and sports don't
  take an article in German: Sie ist Betriebsleiterin.

℘ das **Betriebspraktikum**, PLURAL die
  Betriebspraktika
  work experience

das **Betriebssystem**, PLURAL die
  Betriebssysteme
  operating system

betrinken VERB◇, IMPERFECT **betrank sich**,
  PERFECT **hat sich betrunken**
  sich betrinken to get drunk

betroffen ADJECTIVE
  shocked, upset

betrog ▸ SEE betrügen

der **Betrug**
1 deception
2 fraud
  Was für ein Betrug! What a swindle!

betrügen VERB◇, IMPERFECT **betrog**, PERFECT
  hat betrogen
1 to cheat
  Sie haben ihn um tausend Euro betrogen.
  They cheated him out of a thousand euros.
2 to be unfaithful to, to cheat on
  Sie hat ihren Mann betrogen. She's been
  unfaithful to her husband.

betrunken ADJECTIVE
  drunk

℘ das **Bett**, PLURAL die **Betten**
  bed

Sie ging um 22 Uhr ins Bett. She went to bed at 10 o'clock.
Kannst du bitte die Betten machen? Can you make the beds, please?

der **Bettbezug**, PLURAL die **Bettbezüge**
duvet cover

die **Bettdecke**, PLURAL die **Bettdecken**
duvet

betteln VERB, PERFECT **hat gebettelt**
to beg

das **Bettlaken**, PLURAL die **Bettlaken**
sheet

der **Bettler**, PLURAL die **Bettler**
beggar (male)

die **Bettlerin**, PLURAL die **Bettlerinnen**
beggar (female)

das **Betttuch**, PLURAL die **Betttücher**
sheet

die **Bettwäsche**
bed linen

das **Bettzeug**
bedding

beugen VERB, PERFECT **hat gebeugt**
1 to bend
Er beugte sich nach vorn. He bent forwards.
Sie beugte sich über ihr Heft. She bent over her exercise book.
2 to lean
Ich beugte mich aus dem Fenster. I leant out of the window.
3 to decline, to conjugate (in grammar)
4 sich etwas beugen to submit to something, to bow to something
Wir haben uns schließlich der Mehrheit gebeugt. In the end, we bowed to the majority.

die **Beule**, PLURAL die **Beulen**
1 bump
2 lump
3 dent

beurteilen VERB, PERFECT **hat beurteilt**
to judge

der **Beutel**, PLURAL die **Beutel**
bag

die **Bevölkerung**, PLURAL die **Bevölkerungen**
population

ℓ **bevor** CONJUNCTION
1 before

Mach deine Hausaufgaben, bevor du in die Stadt gehst. Do your homework before you go into town.
2 bevor ... nicht until ...
Bevor er nicht unterschrieben hat, ist der Vertrag nicht gültig. Until he has signed, the contract is not valid.

bevorzugen VERB, PERFECT **hat bevorzugt**
to prefer

bewachen VERB, PERFECT **hat bewacht**
to guard

bewaffnen VERB, PERFECT **hat bewaffnet**
to arm

bewaffnet ADJECTIVE
armed

bewahren VERB, PERFECT **hat bewahrt**
jemanden vor etwas bewahren to protect someone from something

bewährt ADJECTIVE
1 reliable
2 tried and tested (method, design)
Ich nehme immer mein bewährtes Rezept. I always use my tried and tested recipe.

bewegen[1] VERB, PERFECT **hat bewegt**
1 to move
2 sich bewegen to move
Er konnte sich nicht bewegen. He could not move.
3 sich bewegen to take exercise
Du musst dich mehr bewegen. You have to take more exercise.

bewegen[2] VERB◇, IMPERFECT **bewog**, PERFECT **hat bewogen**
jemanden dazu bewegen, etwas zu tun to persuade somebody to do something

beweglich ADJECTIVE
1 movable
2 agile

bewegt ADJECTIVE
1 eventful
2 moved (emotionally)

die **Bewegung**, PLURAL die **Bewegungen**
1 movement
Jede Bewegung tut weh. Every movement hurts.
2 exercise
Bekommen die Kinder genug Bewegung? Are the children getting enough exercise?
3 eine Maschine in Bewegung setzen to start (up) a machine
4 sich in Bewegung setzen to start to move

◇ irregular verb; SEP separable verb; for more help with verbs see centre section

der **Beweis**, PLURAL die **Beweise**
1 proof
   Hast du einen Beweis dafür, dass er es
   war? Do you have any proof that it was
   him?
2 evidence
   Die Polizei fand belastende Beweise. The
   police found incriminating evidence.
3 token, sign

beweisen VERB◇, IMPERFECT **bewies**, PERFECT
   hat bewiesen
1 to prove
2 to show

bewerben VERB◇, PRESENT **bewirbt sich**,
   IMPERFECT **bewarb sich**, PERFECT **hat sich**
   beworben
   sich bewerben to apply
   Sie hat sich um eine Stelle beworben. She
   has applied for a job.

der **Bewerber**, PLURAL die **Bewerber**
   applicant *(male)*

die **Bewerberin**, PLURAL die **Bewerberinnen**
   applicant *(female)*

die **Bewerbung**, PLURAL die **Bewerbungen**
   application

der **Bewerbungsbrief**, PLURAL die
   Bewerbungsbriefe
   letter of application

das **Bewerbungsformular**, PLURAL die
   Bewerbungsformulare
   application form

das **Bewerbungsgespräch**, PLURAL die
   Bewerbungsgespräche
   job interview

bewohnen VERB, PERFECT **hat bewohnt**
   to live in

der **Bewohner**, PLURAL die **Bewohner**
1 resident *(male)*
2 inhabitant *(male)*

die **Bewohnerin**, PLURAL die
   Bewohnerinnen
1 resident *(female)*
2 inhabitant *(female)*

bewölkt ADJECTIVE
   cloudy

die **Bewölkung**
   clouds

bewundern VERB, PERFECT **hat bewundert**
   to admire

die **Bewunderung**
   admiration

bewusst ADJECTIVE
1 conscious
2 deliberate
3 sich etwas bewusst sein to be aware of
   something
   Ich war mir der Folgen bewusst. I was
   aware of the consequences.

bewusstlos ADJECTIVE
   unconscious

das **Bewusstsein**
1 consciousness
2 Er war bei vollem Bewusstsein. He was
   fully conscious.
3 Mir kam zu(m) Bewusstsein, dass ... I
   realized that ...

bezahlbar ADJECTIVE
   affordable

𝒫 **bezahlen** VERB, PERFECT **hat bezahlt**
1 to pay
   Ich habe 10 Euro für das Ticket bezahlt. I
   paid 10 euros for the ticket.
2 to pay for *(goods, food)*
   Er hat das Essen bezahlt. He paid for the
   meal.

die **Bezahlung**
   payment

bezeichnend ADJECTIVE
   typical

beziehen VERB◇, IMPERFECT **bezog**, PERFECT **hat**
   bezogen
1 to cover
2 Ich habe das Bett frisch bezogen. I put
   clean sheets on the bed.
3 to move into
   Wann kannst du die neue Wohnung
   beziehen? When will you be able to move
   into the new flat?
4 to get *(goods, a pension)*
5 to take *(a newspaper)*
6 sich auf etwas/jemanden beziehen to refer
   to something/somebody
7 Es bezieht sich. It's clouding over.

die **Beziehung**, PLURAL die **Beziehungen**
1 connection
2 relationship
3 Beziehungen contacts
   Anna hat gute Beziehungen. Anna has
   good contacts.
4 diplomatische Beziehungen diplomatic
   relations
5 in dieser Beziehung in this respect

6 eine Beziehung zu etwas haben to be able to relate to something (to art, pop music, for example)
Er hat keine Beziehung zur modernen Kunst. He can't relate to modern art.

beziehungsweise CONJUNCTION
1 or rather
2 respectively

der **Bezirk**, PLURAL die **Bezirke**
district

der **Bezug**, PLURAL die **Bezüge**
1 cover (of a cushion, duvet, etc.)
2 connection
keinen Bezug zu etwas haben to be unable to relate to something
Sie hat keinen Bezug zu Mathe. She can't relate to maths.
3 auf etwas Bezug nehmen to refer to something
4 in Bezug auf regarding
5 mit Bezug auf Ihr Angebot with reference to your offer

bezweifeln VERB, PERFECT **hat bezweifelt**
to doubt

der **BH**, PLURAL die **BHs**
bra

Bhf. ABBREVIATION ▶ SEE **Bahnhof**

die **Bibel**, PLURAL die **Bibeln**
bible

♪ die **Bibliothek**, PLURAL die **Bibliotheken**
library

der **Bibliothekar**, PLURAL die **Bibliothekare**
librarian (male)

WORD TIP Professions, hobbies, and sports don't take an article in German: Er ist Bibliothekar.

die **Bibliothekarin**, PLURAL die **Bibliothekarinnen**
librarian (female)

WORD TIP Professions, hobbies, and sports don't take an article in German: Sie ist Bibliothekarin.

biegen VERB◇, IMPERFECT **bog**, PERFECT **hat gebogen**
1 to bend
2 sich biegen to bend
3 PERFECT **ist gebogen to turn**
Als wir um die Ecke bogen, sahen wir den Bus. When we turned the corner we saw the bus.

die **Biene**, PLURAL die **Bienen**
bee

♪ das **Bier**, PLURAL die **Biere**
beer

der **Bierdeckel**, PLURAL die **Bierdeckel**
beer mat

der **Bierkeller**, PLURAL die **Bierkeller**
beer cellar

bieten VERB◇, IMPERFECT **bot**, PERFECT **hat geboten**
1 to offer
Er bot mir 50 Euro für das Fahrrad. He offered me 50 euros for the bike.
Die Schweiz hat viel zu bieten. Switzerland has plenty to offer.
2 to bid (at an auction)
3 Es bietet sich die Möglichkeit, einen Abstecher nach Italien zu machen. There is a possibility of making a detour to Italy.
4 to present (a sight)
5 sich etwas bieten lassen to put up with something
Das lasse ich mir nicht bieten! I won't put up with it!

der **Bikini**, PLURAL die **Bikinis**
bikini

♪ das **Bild**, PLURAL die **Bilder**
1 picture
2 photo
3 scene

bilden VERB, PERFECT **hat gebildet**
1 to form
2 sich bilden to form
3 sich bilden to educate yourself

der **Bildschirm**, PLURAL die **Bildschirme**
screen

bildschön ADJECTIVE
(very) beautiful

die **Bildung**
1 formation
2 education

♪ **billig** ADJECTIVE
cheap

die **Billion**, PLURAL die **Billionen**
trillion (a million million)
Es kostet drei Billionen Euro. It costs three trillion euros.

WORD TIP The German word Billion does not mean billion in English; the German translation for the English billion is Milliarde.

◇ irregular verb; SEP separable verb; for more help with verbs see centre section

𝒫 **bin** ▸ SEE **sein**

die **Binde**, PLURAL die **Binden**
1 bandage
2 sanitary towel

binden VERB◇, IMPERFECT **band**, PERFECT **hat gebunden**
1 to tie
2 to bind (a book)
3 to make up (a bouquet)
4 to thicken (a sauce)
5 sich binden to commit yourself

der **Bindestrich**, PLURAL die **Bindestriche**
hyphen

der **Bindfaden**, PLURAL die **Bindfäden**
(piece of) string

die **Bindung**, PLURAL die **Bindungen**
1 tie (responsibility)
2 relationship
3 binding (on a ski)

bio- PREFIX
organic, bio-

die **Biografie**, PLURAL die **Biografien**
biography

die **Biokost**
health food

der **Biokraftstoff**, PLURAL die **Biokraftstoffe**
biofuel

die **Biolebensmittel** PLURAL NOUN
organic food

𝒫 die **Biologie**
biology

biologisch ADJECTIVE
biological

der **Biomüll**
organic waste

die **Birke**, PLURAL die **Birken**
birch tree

die **Birne**, PLURAL die **Birnen**
1 pear
2 (light) bulb

𝒫 **bis** PREPOSITION (+ ACC)
1 as far as
Dieser Zug fährt nur bis Passau. This train only goes as far as Passau.
2 up to
Kinder bis zehn zahlen die Hälfte. Children up to ten pay half.
Die Fahrt dauert bis zu drei Stunden.

The journey takes up to three hours.
bis jetzt up to now
3 until, till (with time)
Die Party geht bis Mitternacht. The party goes on until midnight.
4 by
Ich muss bis zehn zu Hause sein. I have to be home by ten.
Bis dahin bist du wieder gesund. You will be better by then.
5 bis auf except for
Alle sind durchgefallen, bis auf die zwei Mädchen. Everyone failed except for the two girls.
6 Bis bald! See you soon!
Bis morgen! See you tomorrow!
7 to
von München bis Salzburg from Munich to Salzburg
von Montag bis Freitag from Monday to Friday
zwei bis drei Euro two to three euros

bis CONJUNCTION
until, till
Sie bleibt, bis es dunkel wird. She's staying until it gets dark.

der **Bischof**, PLURAL die **Bischöfe**
bishop

bisher ADVERB
so far

bisherig ADJECTIVE
previous

biss ▸ SEE **beißen**

der **Biss**, PLURAL die **Bisse**
bite

𝒫 **bisschen** PRONOUN
1 bit
ein bisschen a bit
ein bisschen Brot a bit of bread
2 kein bisschen not a bit

bissig ADJECTIVE
1 vicious
'Vorsicht bissiger Hund!' 'Beware of the dog!'
2 cutting (remark, tone)

𝒫 **bist** ▸ SEE **sein**

𝒫 **bitte** ADVERB
1 please (when asking for something)
'Möchten Sie Kuchen?' – 'Ja, bitte.' 'Would you like some cake?' – 'Yes, please.'

2 you're welcome, that's all right (in reply to thanks)
'Vielen Dank für Ihre Hilfe.' – 'Bitte schön/sehr.' 'Thank you very much for your help.' – 'That's all right.'
3 Wie bitte? (when you haven't understood something) Sorry?, Pardon?
4 Come in! (after a knock on the door)

die **Bitte**, PLURAL die **Bitten**
request

bitten VERB⬦, IMPERFECT **bat**, PERFECT **hat gebeten**
to ask
jemanden um etwas bitten to ask somebody for something

bitter ADJECTIVE
bitter

blamieren VERB, PERFECT **hat blamiert**
1 to disgrace
Er hat die ganze Klasse blamiert. He disgraced the whole class.
2 jemanden blamieren to embarrass somebody
3 sich blamieren to make a fool of yourself

die **Blase**, PLURAL die **Blasen**
1 bubble
2 blister
3 bladder

blasen VERB⬦, PRESENT **bläst**, IMPERFECT **blies**, PERFECT **hat geblasen**
to blow

das **Blasinstrument**, PLURAL die **Blasinstrumente**
wind instrument

die **Blaskapelle**, PLURAL die **Blaskapellen**
brass band

blass ADJECTIVE
pale

das **Blatt**, PLURAL die **Blätter**
1 leaf
2 sheet
Ich brauche ein Blatt Papier. I need a sheet of paper.
3 page
4 newspaper

♀ **blau** ADJECTIVE
1 blue
Sie trug ein blau gestreiftes Kleid. She wore a dress with blue stripes.
2 Er hat ein blaues Auge. He had a black eye.

3 ein blauer Fleck a bruise
4 blau sein (informal) to be drunk
5 eine Fahrt ins Blaue a mystery tour
6 blau machen (informal) to take the day off

das **Blech**, PLURAL die **Bleche**
1 sheet metal
2 tin
3 baking tray
4 brass (in music)

das **Blei**
lead (the metal)

♀ **bleiben** VERB⬦, IMPERFECT **blieb**, PERFECT **ist geblieben**
1 to stay, to remain
Ich bleibe zu Hause. I'm staying at home.
2 Bleiben Sie am Apparat. Hold the line.
3 bei etwas bleiben to stick to something
Ich bleibe bei meiner Meinung. I'm sticking to my opinion.
4 Versuchen Sie, ruhig zu bleiben. Try to keep calm.
5 Wo bleibt er so lange? Where has he got to?
6 etwas bleiben lassen to not do something
Wenn du nicht mitkommen willst, dann lass es eben bleiben. If you don't want to come, then don't.

bleich ADJECTIVE
pale

das **Bleichmittel**, PLURAL die **Bleichmittel**
bleach

bleifrei ADJECTIVE
unleaded

♀ der **Bleistift**, PLURAL die **Bleistifte**
pencil

der **Bleistiftspitzer**, PLURAL die **Bleistiftspitzer**
pencil sharpener

blenden VERB, PERFECT **hat geblendet**
1 to dazzle
2 to blind

blendend ADJECTIVE
1 marvellous
2 Es geht mir blendend. I feel great.
Wir haben uns blendend amüsiert. We had a great time.

♀ der **Blick**, PLURAL die **Blicke**
1 look
2 glance

56

3 view
Wir hatten ein Zimmer mit Blick aufs Meer. We had a room with a sea view.

4 auf den ersten Blick at first sight
Es war Liebe auf den ersten Blick. It was love at first sight.

5 eye
Ein Fotograf braucht einen guten Blick für interessante Motive. A photographer has to have a good eye for interesting subjects.

blicken VERB, PERFECT **hat geblickt**
1 to look
2 sich blicken lassen to show your face
Lass dich nie wieder bei uns blicken! Don't show your face here again!

blieb ►SEE **bleiben**

blies ►SEE **blasen**

blind ADJECTIVE
blind

der **Blinddarm**, PLURAL die **Blinddärme**
appendix

die **Blinddarmentzündung**, PLURAL die **Blinddarmentzündungen**
appendicitis

der/die **Blinde**, PLURAL die **Blinden**
blind person, blind man/woman

blinken VERB, PERFECT **hat geblinkt**
1 to flash
2 to indicate (of a car)

der **Blinker**, PLURAL die **Blinker**
indicator

blinzeln VERB, PERFECT **hat geblinzelt**
to blink

der **Blitz**, PLURAL die **Blitze**
1 (flash of) lightning
2 flash (for example on a camera)

blitzen VERB, PERFECT **hat geblitzt**
1 to flash
2 to sparkle
3 Es blitzt. There is some lightning.

das **Blitzlicht**, PLURAL die **Blitzlichter**
flash (for example on a camera)

die **Blockflöte**, PLURAL die **Blockflöten**
recorder
Er spielt Blockflöte. He plays the recorder.

ℰ **blöd** ADJECTIVE
stupid, daft, silly

der **Blödsinn**
nonsense

das or der **Blog**, PLURAL die **Blogs**
blog

ℰ **blond** ADJECTIVE
blond, blonde, fair-haired

bloß ADVERB
1 only
Es kostet bloß fünf Euro. It's only five euros.
2 Warum hat er das bloß gemacht? Why on earth did he do it?
3 Was mache ich bloß? Whatever shall I do?
4 Fass das bloß nicht an! Don't touch it!

bloß ADJECTIVE
1 bare (feet)
Man kann es mit bloßem Auge nicht sehen. You can't see it with the naked eye.
2 mere (words, suspicion)
Der bloße Gedanke daran macht mir Angst. The mere thought of it scares me.

blühen VERB, PERFECT **hat geblüht**
to be in bloom

ℰ die **Blume**, PLURAL die **Blumen**
flower

das **Blumenbeet**, PLURAL die **Blumenbeete**
flower bed

der **Blumenhändler**, PLURAL die **Blumenhändler**
florist (male)

WORD TIP Professions, hobbies, and sports don't take an article in German: Er ist Blumenhändler.

die **Blumenhändlerin**, PLURAL die **Blumenhändlerinnen**
florist (female)

WORD TIP Professions, hobbies, and sports don't take an article in German: Sie ist Blumenhändlerin.

der **Blumenkohl**
cauliflower

ℰ die **Bluse**, PLURAL die **Blusen**
blouse

ℰ das **Blut**
blood

der **Blutdruck**
blood pressure

die **Blüte**, PLURAL die **Blüten**
blossom

bluten VERB, PERFECT **hat geblutet**
to bleed

das **Blutgefäß**, *PLURAL* die **Blutgefäße**
blood vessel

blutig *ADJECTIVE*
bloody

die **Blutprobe**, *PLURAL* die **Blutproben**
blood test

die **Blutwurst**, *PLURAL* die **Blutwürste**
black pudding

der **Bock**, *PLURAL* die **Böcke**
1 buck
2 billy goat
3 ram
4 Bock auf etwas haben *(informal)* to fancy something
Hast du Bock auf Kino? *(informal)* Do you fancy going to the cinema?
Ich hab keinen Bock. *(informal)* I don't feel like it.
5 einen Bock schießen *(informal)* to make a blunder
Da hat er mal wieder einen Bock geschossen! *(informal)* He really made a blunder there!

die **Bockwurst**, *PLURAL* die **Bockwürste**
frankfurter

der **Boden**, *PLURAL* die **Böden**
1 ground
2 floor
3 soil
4 bottom *(of a container)*
5 loft, attic

ℓ der **Bodensee**
Lake Constance

WORD TIP The article is always used: Wir fahren an den Bodensee.

bog ▸SEE **biegen**

der **Bogen**, *PLURAL* die **Bögen**
1 curve
2 arch
3 bow *(for shooting, for string instruments)*
4 turn *(in skiing)*

das **Bogenschießen**
archery

ℓ die **Bohne**, *PLURAL* die **Bohnen**
bean

bohren *VERB*, *PERFECT* **hat gebohrt**
to drill

der **Bohrer**, *PLURAL* die **Bohrer**
drill

die **Bohrinsel**, *PLURAL* die **Bohrinseln**
oil rig

die **Bohrmaschine**, *PLURAL* die **Bohrmaschinen**
electric drill

die **Bombe**, *PLURAL* die **Bomben**
bomb

ℓ der or das **Bonbon**, *PLURAL* die **Bonbons**
sweet

WORD TIP In Austria, it is always das Bonbon.

das **Boot**, *PLURAL* die **Boote**
boat

das **Bord**[1], *PLURAL* die **Borde**
shelf

der **Bord**[2]
an Bord on board
Wir gingen an Bord des Dampfers. We went on board the steamer.
über Bord overboard

die **Bordkarte**, *PLURAL* die **Bordkarten**
boarding card

borgen, *PERFECT* **hat geborgt**
1 to borrow
2 sich etwas borgen to borrow something
Ich habe es mir von ihr geborgt. I borrowed it from her.
3 jemandem etwas borgen to lend somebody something
Evi hat mir ihr Buch geborgt. Evi lent me her book.

die **Börse**, *PLURAL* die **Börsen**
stock market

der **Börsenmakler**, *PLURAL* die **Börsenmakler**
stockbroker *(male)*

WORD TIP Professions, hobbies, and sports don't take an article in German: Er ist Börsenmakler.

die **Börsenmaklerin**, *PLURAL* die **Börsenmaklerinnen**
stockbroker *(female)*

WORD TIP Professions, hobbies, and sports don't take an article in German: Sie ist Börsenmaklerin.

die **Borste**, *PLURAL* die **Borsten**
bristle

böse *ADJECTIVE*
1 bad
2 evil
3 naughty *(child)*
4 angry

◇ irregular verb; *SEP* separable verb; for more help with verbs see centre section

Der Lehrer wurde böse. The teacher got angry.
Ich bin ihm böse. I'm angry with him.
5 auf jemanden böse sein to be cross with somebody
Bist du immer noch böse auf mich? Are you still cross with me?

boshaft ADJECTIVE
malicious

bot ▸ SEE **bieten**

der **Bote**, PLURAL die **Boten**
messenger (male)

die **Botin**, PLURAL die **Botinnen**
messenger (female)

die **Botschaft**, PLURAL die **Botschaften**
1 message
2 embassy
Wo ist die britische Botschaft? Where is the British Embassy?

der **Botschafter**, PLURAL die **Botschafter**
ambassador (male)

die **Botschafterin**, PLURAL die **Botschafterinnen**
ambassador (female)

die **Bowle**, PLURAL die **Bowlen**
punch (for drinking)

boxen VERB, PERFECT **hat geboxt**
1 to box
2 to punch

der **Boxer**, PLURAL die **Boxer**
boxer (male)

WORD TIP Professions, hobbies, and sports don't take an article in German: Er ist Boxer.

die **Boxerin**, PLURAL die **Boxerinnen**
boxer (female)

WORD TIP Professions, hobbies, and sports don't take an article in German: Sie ist Boxerin.

brach ▸ SEE **brechen**

brachte ▸ SEE **bringen**

die **Branche**, PLURAL die **Branchen**
1 (line of) business
2 industry

das **Branchenverzeichnis**, PLURAL die **Branchenverzeichnisse**
classified directory

der **Brand**, PLURAL die **Brände**
fire

die **Brandung**
surf

brannte ▸ SEE **brennen**

der **Brasilianer**, PLURAL die **Brasilianer**
Brazilian (male)

die **Brasilianerin**, PLURAL die **Brasilianerinnen**
Brazilian (female)

brasilianisch ADJECTIVE
Brazilian

WORD TIP Adjectives never have capitals in German, even for regions, countries, or nationalities.

Brasilien NEUTER NOUN
Brazil

braten VERB◊, PRESENT **brät**, IMPERFECT **briet**, PERFECT **hat gebraten**
1 to fry
2 to roast

der **Braten**, PLURAL die **Braten**
1 roast
2 joint (of meat)

die **Bratensoße**, PLURAL die **Bratensoßen**
gravy

das **Brathähnchen**, PLURAL die **Brathähnchen**
roast chicken

ℙ die **Bratkartoffeln** PLURAL NOUN
fried potatoes

die **Bratpfanne**, PLURAL die **Bratpfannen**
frying pan

die **Bratwurst**, PLURAL die **Bratwürste**
sausage

der **Brauch**, PLURAL die **Bräuche**
custom, tradition

brauchbar ADJECTIVE
1 usable
2 useful

ℙ **brauchen** VERB, PERFECT **hat gebraucht**
1 to need
Ich brauche eine neue Batterie für meine Kamera. I need a new battery for my camera.
Du brauchst nur auf den Knopf zu drücken. All you need to do is press the button.
Du brauchst nicht zu gehen. You needn't go.
2 to have to
Sie braucht es nur zu sagen. She only

has to say.
3 to take *(time)*
Wie lange brauchst du mit dem Auto?
How long does it take you by car?
4 Ich könnte es gut brauchen. I could do
with it.
Diese Erkältung kann ich jetzt wirklich
nicht brauchen. I could do without this
cold now.

brauen *VERB, PERFECT* **hat gebraut**
to brew

die Brauerei, *PLURAL* **die Brauereien**
brewery

☞ **braun** *ADJECTIVE*
1 brown
2 tanned
Sie waren braun (gebrannt). They were
tanned.
Im Urlaub ist sie braun geworden. She got
a tan on holiday.

die Bräune
tan

die Brause, *PLURAL* **die Brausen**
1 shower
2 fizzy drink

die Braut, *PLURAL* **die Bräute**
bride

der Bräutigam, *PLURAL* **die Bräutigame**
bridegroom

die Brautjungfer, *PLURAL* **die Brautjungfern**
bridesmaid

das Brautpaar, *PLURAL* **die Brautpaare**
bride and groom

brav *ADJECTIVE*
good

> **WORD TIP** The German word brav does not
> mean brave in English; the German word for
> brave is tapfer.

die BRD *ABBREVIATION*
(=Bundesrepublik Deutschland) **FRG** Federal
Republic of Germany

> **WORD TIP** The article is always used: Sie fuhren
> in die BRD.

☞ **brechen** *VERB◇, PRESENT* **bricht**, *IMPERFECT*
brach, *PERFECT* **hat gebrochen**
1 to break *(an agreement, a plate)*
2 sich etwas brechen to break something
Sie hat sich den Arm gebrochen. She
broke her arm.
3 to vomit, to be sick
Bei der Busfahrt musste er brechen. He

was sick on the bus.
4 *PERFECT* **ist gebrochen to break**
Der Ast ist gebrochen. The branch broke.

breit *ADJECTIVE*
1 wide
2 broad
3 die breite Masse the general public
das Breitband broadband

die Breite, *PLURAL* **die Breiten**
width

☞ **die Bremse**, *PLURAL* **die Bremsen**
1 brake
2 horsefly

bremsen *VERB, PERFECT* **hat gebremst**
1 to brake
Ich musste scharf bremsen. I had to brake
hard.
2 etwas bremsen to slow something down
(development, production)
3 jemanden bremsen *(informal)* to stop
somebody
Er ist nicht mehr zu bremsen. There's no
stopping him.

das Bremslicht, *PLURAL* **die Bremslichter**
brake light

das Bremspedal, *PLURAL* **die Bremspedale**
brake pedal

brennen *VERB◇, IMPERFECT* **brannte**, *PERFECT*
hat gebrannt
1 to burn
2 to be on *(of a light)*
Er hat wieder das Licht brennen lassen.
He's left the light on again.
3 to sting *(of a wound or sore)*
4 to be on fire
Das Haus brennt. The house is on fire.
Es brennt! Fire!
5 darauf brennen, etwas zu tun to be dying
to do something
Sie brannte darauf, das Geschenk
auszupacken. She was dying to open the
present.

die Brennnessel, *PLURAL* **die Brennnesseln**
stinging nettle

der Brennpunkt, *PLURAL* **die Brennpunkte**
focus

der Brennstoff, *PLURAL* **die Brennstoffe**
fuel

das Brett, *PLURAL* **die Bretter**
1 board
2 plank
3 shelf

◇ irregular verb; *SEP* separable verb; for more help with verbs see centre section

das **Brettspiel**, PLURAL die **Brettspiele**
board game

die **Brezel**, PLURAL die **Brezeln**
pretzel

● BREZELN

These are salted rolls in the shape of a figure of
eight, a speciality in South Germany. In Austria
they are called Pretzeln.

bricht ▸ SEE **brechen**

ℰ der **Brief**, PLURAL die **Briefe**
letter

ℰ der **Brieffreund**, PLURAL die **Brieffreunde**
penfriend, pen pal (male)

ℰ die **Brieffreundin**, PLURAL die
Brieffreundinnen
penfriend, pen pal (female)

die **Brieffreundschaft**, PLURAL die
Brieffreundschaften
correspondence with a penfriend
Wir haben eine Brieffreundschaft. We are
penfriends.

ℰ der **Briefkasten**, PLURAL die **Briefkästen**
1 letterbox
2 postbox

ℰ die **Briefmarke**, PLURAL die **Briefmarken**
stamp

ℰ die **Brieftasche**, PLURAL die **Brieftaschen**
wallet

der **Briefträger**, PLURAL die **Briefträger**
postman

WORD TIP Professions, hobbies, and sports
don't take an article in German: Er ist
Briefträger.

die **Briefträgerin**, PLURAL die
Briefträgerinnen
postwoman

WORD TIP Professions, hobbies, and sports
don't take an article in German: Sie ist
Briefträgerin.

der **Briefumschlag**, PLURAL die
Briefumschläge
envelope

der **Briefwechsel**
correspondence

brief ▸ SEE **braten**

der **Brillant**, PLURAL die **Brillanten**
diamond

ℰ die **Brille**, PLURAL die **Brillen**
glasses, spectacles

WORD TIP In German, die Brille is singular: Sie
trägt eine Brille.

ℰ **bringen** VERB✧, IMPERFECT **brachte**, PERFECT **hat
gebracht**
1 to bring
2 to take
Peter bringt dich nach Hause. Peter will
take you home.
3 Er brachte die Kinder ins Bett. He put the
children to bed.
4 to show (a film, programme)
5 to publish (an article)
6 to earn (interest)
7 to make (a profit)
8 jemanden dazu bringen, etwas zu tun to
get somebody to do something
Es bringt mich zum Lachen. It makes me
laugh.
9 etwas mit sich bringen to involve
something
Ein Umzug bringt viel Arbeit mit sich. A
move involves a lot of work.
10 etwas hinter sich bringen to get
something over and done with
Ich will die Prüfung endlich hinter mich
bringen. I want to get the exam over and
done with.
11 es weit bringen to go far
Sie wird es noch weit bringen. She will
go far.
12 es zu nichts bringen to get nowhere
Er hat es zu nichts gebracht. He got
nowhere.
13 jemanden auf eine Idee bringen to give
somebody an idea
Damit hast du mich auf eine gute Idee
gebracht. You gave me a good idea there.
14 Das bringt's nicht! (informal) That's no use!

die **Brise**, PLURAL die **Brisen**
breeze

der **Brite**, PLURAL die **Briten**
Briton (male)
die Briten the British

die **Britin**, PLURAL die **Britinnen**
Briton (female)

britisch ADJECTIVE
British

WORD TIP Adjectives never have capitals
in German, even for regions, countries, or
nationalities.

der **Brokkoli**
broccoli

ℰ **indicates key words**

die **Brombeere**, PLURAL die **Brombeeren**
blackberry

die **Brosche**, PLURAL die **Broschen**
brooch

♀ die **Broschüre**, PLURAL die **Broschüren**
brochure

♀ das **Brot**, PLURAL die **Brote**
1 bread
Sie essen viel Brot. They eat a lot of bread.
2 loaf of bread
Er kaufte zwei Brote. He bought two
loaves of bread.
3 slice of bread
Sie aß ein Brot mit Käse. She had a slice of
bread with cheese.

♀ das **Brötchen**, PLURAL die **Brötchen**
bread roll

der **Bruch**, PLURAL die **Brüche**
1 break
2 fracture
3 hernia
4 fraction

der **Bruchteil**, PLURAL die **Bruchteile**
fraction

♀ die **Brücke**, PLURAL die **Brücken**
bridge

♀ der **Bruder**, PLURAL die **Brüder**
brother

die **Brühe**, PLURAL die **Brühen**
1 clear soup
2 stock (for cooking)

der **Brühwürfel**, PLURAL die **Brühwürfel**
stock cube

brüllen VERB, PERFECT **hat gebrüllt**
to roar

brummen VERB, PERFECT **hat gebrummt**
1 to buzz
2 to growl (of a bear)
3 to hum (of an engine)

der **Brunnen**, PLURAL die **Brunnen**
1 well
2 fountain

Brüssel NEUTER NOUN
Brussels

die **Brust**, PLURAL die **Brüste**
1 chest
2 breast

das **Brustschwimmen**
breaststroke

brutal ADJECTIVE
brutal

die **Brutalität**
brutality

brutto ADVERB
gross

das **BSE** ABBREVIATION
(=bovine spongiforme Enzephalopathie) BSE

der **Bub**, PLURAL die **Buben**
(used in Southern Germany, Austria, and
Switzerland) boy

♀ das **Buch**, PLURAL die **Bücher**
book

die **Buche**, PLURAL die **Buchen**
beech

buchen VERB, PERFECT **hat gebucht**
to book

die **Bücherei**, PLURAL die **Büchereien**
library

das **Bücherregal**, PLURAL die **Bücherregale**
bookcase

der **Buchhalter**, PLURAL die **Buchhalter**
accountant, bookkeeper (male)

WORD TIP Professions, hobbies, and sports
don't take an article in German: Er ist
Buchhalter.

die **Buchhalterin**, PLURAL die
Buchhalterinnen
accountant, bookkeeper (female)

WORD TIP Professions, hobbies, and sports
don't take an article in German: Sie ist
Buchhalterin.

die **Buchhandlung**, PLURAL die
Buchhandlungen
bookshop

der **Buchladen**, PLURAL die **Buchläden**
bookshop

die **Büchse**, PLURAL die **Büchsen**
tin, can

der **Büchsenöffner**, PLURAL die
Büchsenöffner
tin opener

♀ der **Buchstabe**, PLURAL die **Buchstaben**
letter of the alphabet
ein großer Buchstabe a capital letter
ein kleiner Buchstabe a small letter

♢ irregular verb; SEP separable verb; for more help with verbs see centre section

_ℓ_ **buchstabieren** _VERB_, _PERFECT_ **hat**
  buchstabiert
  to spell

die **Bucht**, _PLURAL_ die **Buchten**
  bay

die **Buchung**, _PLURAL_ die **Buchungen**
  booking, reservation

bücken, _PERFECT_ **hat sich gebückt**
  sich bücken to bend down

der **Buddhismus**
  Buddhism

die **Bude**, _PLURAL_ die **Buden**
1 hut
2 stall
3 (informal) room
  Das ist meine Bude. That's my room.

das **Büfett**, _PLURAL_ die **Büfetts**
  buffet

der **Bügel**, _PLURAL_ die **Bügel**
  hanger

das **Bügeleisen**, _PLURAL_ die **Bügeleisen**
  iron

bügeln _VERB_, _PERFECT_ **hat gebügelt**
  to iron

die **Bühne**, _PLURAL_ die **Bühnen**
  stage

_ℓ_ **Bulgarien** _NEUTER NOUN_
  Bulgaria

der **Bulgarier**, _PLURAL_ die **Bulgarier**
  Bulgarian (male)

die **Bulgarierin**, _PLURAL_ die **Bulgarierinnen**
  Bulgarian (female)

bulgarisch _ADJECTIVE_
  Bulgarian

  WORD TIP Adjectives never have capitals
  in German, even for regions, countries, or
  nationalities.

der **Bulle**, _PLURAL_ die **Bullen**
1 bull
2 (informal) cop

der **Bummel**, _PLURAL_ die **Bummel**
  stroll (around town)

bummeln _VERB_, _PERFECT_ **ist gebummelt**
1 to stroll
  Wir sind durch die Stadt gebummelt. We
  strolled around town.

2 _PERFECT_ **hat gebummelt** to dawdle
  Nun bummel doch nicht so! Don't dawdle!

_ℓ_ der **Bund**[1], _PLURAL_ die **Bünde**
1 association
2 the (German) Federal Government
  Bund und Länder haben sich über die
  Reform geeinigt. The federal government
  and the state governments have come to
  an agreement on the reform.
3 der Bund (informal) the (German) armed
  forces
  Er muss zum Bund. (informal) He has to do
  his national service.
4 waistband

_ℓ_ das **Bund**[2], _PLURAL_ die **Bunde**
  bunch
  ein Bund Schnittlauch a bunch of chives

die **Bundesbahn**
  Federal Railway

der **Bundesbürger**, _PLURAL_ die
  Bundesbürger
  German citizen (male)

die **Bundesbürgerin**, _PLURAL_ die
  Bundesbürgerinnen
  German citizen (female)

das **Bundesheer**
  Austrian armed forces

_ℓ_ der **Bundeskanzler**, _PLURAL_ die
  Bundeskanzler
  Federal Chancellor (male)

🔵 **BUNDESKANZLER**

  The German Bundeskanzler is the equivalent
  of the British Prime Minister. The German
  equivalent of the Chancellor of the Exchequer
  is called the Finanzminister.

die **Bundeskanzlerin**, _PLURAL_ die
  Bundeskanzlerinnen
  Federal Chancellor (female)

das **Bundesland**, _PLURAL_ die **Bundesländer**
  (federal) state
  There are sixteen Bundesländer in Germany

A
B
C
D
E
F
G
H
I
J
K
L
M
N
O
P
Q
R
S
T
U
V
W
X
Y
Z

_ℓ_ indicates key words

and nine in Austria.

> **BUNDESLAND**
>
> Most of Germany's Bundesländer were
> formed after 1945: Baden-Württemberg,
> Bayern (Bavaria), Berlin, Brandenburg,
> Bremen, Hamburg, Hessen (Hesse),
> Mecklenburg-Vorpommern (Mecklenburg-
> Western Pomerania), Niedersachsen
> (Lower Saxony), Nordrhein-Westfalen
> (North Rhine-Westphalia), Rheinland-Pfalz
> (Rhineland-Palatinate), Saarland, Sachsen
> (Saxony), Sachsen-Anhalt (Saxony-Anhalt),
> Schleswig-Holstein, Thüringen (Thuringia).
> Austria has nine federal states, called
> Bundesländer: Burgenland, Kärnten
> (Carinthia), Niederösterreich (Lower Austria),
> Oberösterreich (Upper Austria), Salzburg,
> Steiermark (Styria), Tirol (Tyrol), Vorarlberg,
> Wien (Vienna).

die **Bundesliga**
(German) national football league

der **Bundespräsident**, *PLURAL* die
Bundespräsidenten
Federal President *(male)*

die **Bundespräsidentin**, *PLURAL* die
Bundespräsidentinnen
Federal President *(female)*

der **Bundesrat**
1 Upper House *(of the German and Austrian Parliament)*
2 Federal Council *(Swiss government)*

die **Bundesregierung**, *PLURAL* die
Bundesregierungen
Federal government

♭ die **Bundesrepublik**
Federal Republic

die **Bundesstraße**, *PLURAL* die
Bundesstraßen
A road, major road

der **Bundestag**
Lower House *(of the German Parliament)*

♭ die **Bundeswehr**
German armed forces

♭ der **Bungalow**, *PLURAL* die **Bungalows**
bungalow

bunt *ADJECTIVE*
colourful

♭ der **Buntstift**, *PLURAL* die **Buntstifte**
coloured pencil

die **Burg**, *PLURAL* die **Burgen**
castle

der **Bürger**, *PLURAL* die **Bürger**
citizen *(male)*

die **Bürgerin**, *PLURAL* die **Bürgerinnen**
citizen *(female)*

der **Bürgermeister**, *PLURAL* die
Bürgermeister
mayor *(male)*

> **WORD TIP** Professions, hobbies, and sports
> don't take an article in German: Er ist
> Bürgermeister.

die **Bürgermeisterin**, *PLURAL* die
Bürgermeisterinnen
mayor *(female)*

> **WORD TIP** Professions, hobbies, and sports
> don't take an article in German: Sie ist
> Bürgermeisterin.

der **Bürgersteig**, *PLURAL* die **Bürgersteige**
pavement

♭ das **Büro**, *PLURAL* die **Büros**
office

die **Büroklammer**, *PLURAL* die
Büroklammern
paper clip

die **Bürste**, *PLURAL* die **Bürsten**
brush

♭ **bürsten** *VERB*, *PERFECT* **hat gebürstet**
to brush
Sie bürstete sich die Haare. She brushed
her hair.

♭ der **Bus**, *PLURAL* die **Busse**
bus
Ich fahre mit dem Bus. I'm going by bus.

♭ der **Busbahnhof**, *PLURAL* die **Busbahnhöfe**
bus station

der **Busch**, *PLURAL* die **Büsche**
bush

der **Busen**, *PLURAL* die **Busen**
breasts, bosom

der **Busfahrer**, *PLURAL* die **Busfahrer**
bus driver *(male)*

> **WORD TIP** Professions, hobbies, and sports
> don't take an article in German: Er ist Busfahrer.

die **Busfahrerin**, *PLURAL* die **Busfahrerinnen**
bus driver *(female)*

> **WORD TIP** Professions, hobbies, and sports
> don't take an article in German: Sie ist
> Busfahrerin.

♭ die **Busfahrkarte**, *PLURAL* die
Busfahrkarten
bus ticket

ℰ die **Bushaltestelle**, PLURAL die **Bushaltestellen**
bus stop

die **Buslinie**, PLURAL die **Buslinien**
bus route

der **Bussard**, PLURAL die **Bussarde**
buzzard

das **Bußgeld**, PLURAL die **Bußgelder**
fine

der **Büstenhalter**, PLURAL die **Büstenhalter**
bra

die **Busverbindung**, PLURAL die **Busverbindungen**
1 bus connection
2 bus service

ℰ die **Butter**
butter

das **Butterbrot**, PLURAL die **Butterbrote**
sandwich, piece of bread and butter

bzw. ABBREVIATION ▸ SEE **beziehungsweise**

Cc

ca. ABBREVIATION
(=circa) approximately

ℰ das **Café**, PLURAL die **Cafés**
cafe

die **Cafeteria**, PLURAL die **Cafeterias**
cafeteria, snack bar

campen VERB, PERFECT **hat gecampt**
to camp

der **Camper**, PLURAL die **Camper**
camper (male)

die **Camperin**, PLURAL die **Camperinnen**
camper (female)

das **Camping**
camping

der **Campingbus**, PLURAL die **Campingbusse**
camper (vehicle)

der **Campingkocher**, PLURAL die **Campingkocher**
camping stove

ℰ der **Campingplatz**, PLURAL die **Campingplätze**
campsite

der **Cartoon**, PLURAL die **Cartoons**
1 cartoon
2 comic strip

ℰ die **CD**, PLURAL die **CDs**
CD

ℰ die **CD-Rom**, PLURAL die **CD-Roms**
CD-ROM

der **CD-Spieler**, PLURAL die **CD-Spieler**
CD player

das **Cello**, PLURAL die **Cellos**
cello
Sie spielt Cello. She plays the cello.

ℰ der **Cent**
cent (in euro and dollar systems)
25 Cent 25 cents

der **Champagner**, PLURAL die **Champagner**
champagne

ℰ der **Champignon**, PLURAL die **Champignons**
mushroom

die **Chance**, PLURAL die **Chancen**
chance, opportunity

das **Chaos**
chaos

chaotisch ADJECTIVE
chaotic

der **Charakter**, PLURAL die **Charaktere**
character

die **Charaktereigenschaft**, PLURAL die **Charaktereigenschaften**
characteristic

charmant ADJECTIVE
charming

der **Charme**
charm

der **Charterflug**, PLURAL die **Charterflüge**
charter flight

der **Chatroom**, PLURAL die **Chatrooms**
chat room

chatten VERB, PERFECT **hat gechattet**
to chat (on the Internet)

der **Chauvinist**, PLURAL die **Chauvinisten**
chauvinist

der **Chef**, PLURAL die **Chefs**
1 head (of a firm) (male)
2 boss (male)

> **WORD TIP** The German word Chef does not mean chef or cook in English; the German word for chef is Koch.

die **Chefin**, PLURAL die **Chefinnen**
1 head (of a firm) (female)
2 boss (female)

ℓ die **Chemie**
chemistry

die **Chemikalie**, PLURAL die **Chemikalien**
chemical

der **Chemiker**, PLURAL die **Chemiker**
chemist (male)

> **WORD TIP** Professions, hobbies, and sports don't take an article in German: Er ist Chemiker.

die **Chemikerin**, PLURAL die **Chemikerinnen**
chemist (female)

> **WORD TIP** Professions, hobbies, and sports don't take an article in German: Sie ist Chemikerin.

chemisch ADJECTIVE
1 chemical
2 Die chemische Reinigung der Jacke kostet 8 Euro. Dry-cleaning the jacket costs 8 euros.

der **Chicorée**
chicory

China NEUTER NOUN
China

der **Chinese**, PLURAL die **Chinesen**
Chinese (male)
die Chinesen the Chinese

die **Chinesin**, PLURAL die **Chinesinnen**
Chinese (female)

ℓ **chinesisch** ADJECTIVE
Chinese

> **WORD TIP** Adjectives never have capitals in German, even for regions, countries, or nationalities.

die **Chipkarte**, PLURAL die **Chipkarten**
smart card

ℓ die **Chips** PLURAL NOUN
crisps
Ich möchte eine Packung Chips. I'd like a packet of crisps.

> **WORD TIP** The German word Chips does not mean chips or French fries in English; the German word for chips is Pommes frites.

der **Chirurg**, PLURAL die **Chirurgen**
surgeon (male)

> **WORD TIP** Professions, hobbies, and sports don't take an article in German: Er ist Chirurg.

die **Chirurgin**, PLURAL die **Chirurginnen**
surgeon (female)

> **WORD TIP** Professions, hobbies, and sports don't take an article in German: Sie ist Chirurgin.

das **Chlor**
chlorine

ℓ der **Chor**, PLURAL die **Chöre**
choir

der **Christ**, PLURAL die **Christen**
Christian (male)

das **Christentum**
Christianity

die **Christin**, PLURAL die **Christinnen**
Christian (female)

christlich ADJECTIVE
Christian

> **WORD TIP** Adjectives never have capitals in German, even for religions.

Christus MASCULINE NOUN
Christ

circa ADVERB
approximately

die **Clique**, PLURAL die **Cliquen**
gang, crowd
Heute abend treffe ich mich mit meiner Clique. I'm meeting up with the gang tonight.

der **Clown**, PLURAL die **Clowns**
clown

cm ABBREVIATION
(=Zentimeter) centimetre

ℓ das or die **Cola**™, PLURAL die **Colas**
Coke™, cola

der **Comic**, PLURAL die **Comics**
cartoon

das **Comicheft**, PLURAL die **Comichefte**
comic

der **Computer**, PLURAL die **Computer**
computer
Ich spiele am Computer. I'm playing on the computer.

die **Computeranlage**, PLURAL die **Computeranlagen**
computer system

das **Computerprogramm**, PLURAL die **Computerprogramme**
computer program

◇ irregular verb; SEP separable verb; for more help with verbs see centre section

℘ das **Computerspiel**, PLURAL die
   Computerspiele
   computer game

der **Container**, PLURAL die **Container**
1 container
2 skip

cool ADJECTIVE
   (informal) cool

der **Cord**
   cord, corduroy

die **Cordhose**, PLURAL die **Cordhosen**
   cords

> **WORD TIP** In German, die Cordhose is singular:
> Er trug eine Cordhose.

die **Couch**, PLURAL die **Couchs**
   sofa

der **Couchtisch**, PLURAL die **Couchtische**
   coffee table

℘ der **Cousin**, PLURAL die **Cousins**
   cousin (male)

℘ die **Cousine**, PLURAL die **Cousinen**
   cousin (female)

die **Creme**, PLURAL die **Cremes**
1 cream
2 cream dessert

das **Curry**
1 curry
2 curry powder

℘ die **Currywurst**, PLURAL die **Currywürste**
   sausage with curry sauce

der **Cursor**, PLURAL die **Cursors**
   cursor

Dd

℘ **da** ADVERB
1 there
   da draußen out there
   da drüben over there
   Er ist da. He's there.
   Man muss pünktlich da sein. You have to
   be there on time.
2 Ist noch Brot da? Is there any bread left?
3 here
   Sind alle da? Is everyone here?
   Da sind deine Handschuhe. Here are your
   gloves.
4 Ist Sabine da? Is Sabine about?
   Ich bin wieder da. I'm back.

5 then
   Von da an war er glücklich. From then on,
   he was happy.
6 (therefore) so
   Der Bus war weg, da bin ich gelaufen. The
   bus had gone, so I walked.
7 Da kann man nichts machen. There's
   nothing you can do about it.
8 Das Hotel ist da, wo die Straße nach
   Stuttgart abzweigt. The hotel is at the
   turning for Stuttgart.

da CONJUNCTION
   as, since
   Da es regnet, fahren wir mit dem Auto. As
   it's raining we'll take the car.

dabei ADVERB
1 (included or next to) with it/him/her/them
   Sie hatten die Kinder dabei. They had the
   children with them.
2 dicht dabei close by
3 (referring to something already mentioned)
   about it
   Das Beste dabei ist, dass es nichts kostet.
   The best thing about it is that it's free.
4 at the same time
   Er malte ein Bild und sang dabei. He
   painted a picture and sang at the same
   time.
5 jemandem dabei helfen, etwas zu tun to
   help somebody do something
6 Was hast du dir denn dabei gedacht?
   What were you thinking of?
7 dabei sein to be there
   Er ist dabei gewesen. He was there.
8 dabei sein, etwas zu tun to be just doing
   something
   Ich war gerade dabei, meine
   Hausaufgaben zu machen. I was just doing
   my homework.
9 Was ist denn dabei? So what?
10 dabei bleiben to stick to it (an opinion, for
   example)
   Es bleibt dabei, wir treffen uns um acht.
   It's agreed then, we'll meet at eight.
11 (even though) and yet
   Dabei wollte er zuerst gar nicht
   mitmachen. And yet he didn't want to take
   part at first.

dabeibleiben VERB⬦, IMPERFECT **blieb dabei**,
   PERFECT **ist dabeigeblieben**
1 to stay on (at an organization)
2 to stick with it
   Er hat den Kurs angefangen, ist aber nicht
   dabeigeblieben. He started the course, but
   didn't stick with it.

♀ das **Dach**, PLURAL die **Dächer**
roof

der **Dachboden**, PLURAL die **Dachböden**
loft, attic

♀ das **Dachgeschoss**, PLURAL die
Dachgeschosse
attic

die **Dachrinne**, PLURAL die **Dachrinnen**
gutter (on roof edge)

dachte ▸ SEE **denken**

der **Dackel**, PLURAL die **Dackel**
dachshund

dadurch ADVERB
1 **through there**
Ihr müsst dadurch gehen. You have to go
through there.
2 **as a result**
Dadurch waren alle verärgert. As a result,
everybody was annoyed.
3 **in this way, that way**
Ich nehme die U-Bahn, dadurch bin ich
eine halbe Stunde eher da. I'll take the
tube. That way I'll be there half an hour
earlier.

dadurch CONJUNCTION
dadurch, dass because
Dadurch, dass es regnete, kamen nicht
viele. Not many people came because it
was raining.

dafür ADVERB
1 **for it/them**
Dafür kriegt man nicht viel. You won't get
much for it/them.
2 **instead**
Wenn er schon nicht auf die Party gehen
will, kann er dich dafür zum Essen
einladen. If he doesn't want to go to the
party, he can take you for a meal instead.
3 **but then** (on the other hand)
4 dafür, dass **considering (that)**
Dafür, dass sie erst zwölf ist, spielt sie
sehr gut. Considering that she's only
twelve, she plays really well.
5 Ich kann nichts dafür. It's not my fault.

dagegen ADVERB
1 **against it/them**
Ich bin dagegen. I'm against it.
2 **into it**
Das Auto ist dagegen gefahren. The car
drove into it.
3 **by comparison**
4 etwas dagegen haben **to mind**
Hast du was dagegen? Do you mind?
Ich habe nichts dagegen, dass er auch

kommt. I don't mind if he comes too.
5 **however, on the other hand**
Er ist sehr schüchtern; seine Schwester
dagegen gar nicht. He is very shy. His
sister, on the other hand, is not.

daheim ADVERB
at home

daher ADVERB
1 **from there**
Sie sind daher gekommen. They came
from there.
2 **that's why**
'Tim kommt zur Party.' – 'Ach, daher will
Susi auch hin!' 'Tim's coming to the party.'
– 'Oh, that's why Susi wants to go, too!'

dahin ADVERB
1 **there**
2 bis dahin (in the past) **until then** (in the
future) **by then**
Bis dahin geht es dir sicher wieder besser.
I'm sure you'll feel better by then.
3 jemanden dahin bringen, dass er etwas
tut **to get somebody to do something**
Wie kann ich meine Mutter dahin
bringen, dass sie es mir kauft? How can I
get my mother to buy it for me?

dahinten ADVERB
over there

dahinter ADVERB
1 **behind it/them**
2 dahinter kommen **to get to the bottom
of it**
Ich bin endlich dahinter gekommen. I
finally got to the bottom of it.

dalassen VERB◇, PRESENT **lässt da**, IMPERFECT
ließ da, PERFECT **hat dagelassen**
to leave there
Du kannst dein Sportzeug dalassen. You
can leave your sports kit there.

damals ADVERB
at that time, then
Wir wohnten damals in Berlin. We were
living in Berlin at that time.
Damals war alles anders. Everything was
different then.

♀ die **Dame**, PLURAL die **Damen**
1 **lady**
Sehr geehrte Damen und Herren! Ladies
and gentlemen!
2 **queen** (in chess or cards)
3 **draughts**

die **Damenbinde**, PLURAL die **Damenbinden**
sanitary towel

⬦ irregular verb; SEP separable verb; for more help with verbs see centre section

ℱ **damit** *ADVERB*
1 **with it/them**
Ich will damit spielen. I want to play with it.
Hör auf damit! Stop it!
2 **by it, by that**
Was meinst du damit? What do you mean by that?
3 Damit hat es noch Zeit. There's no hurry (about that).
4 **therefore, because of that**
Sie hat den zweiten Satz verloren und damit das Spiel. She lost the second set and therefore the match.

damit *CONJUNCTION*
so that
Ich habe es aufgeschrieben, damit du es nicht vergisst. I wrote it down so that you won't forget.

der **Damm**, *PLURAL* die **Dämme**
1 **dam**
2 **embankment**

dämmern *VERB, PERFECT* **hat gedämmert**
Es dämmert. It is getting light./It is getting dark.

die **Dämmerung**
1 **dawn**
2 **dusk**

der **Dampf**, *PLURAL* die **Dämpfe**
1 **steam**
2 giftige Dämpfe toxic fumes

dampfen *VERB, PERFECT* **hat gedampft**
to steam

dämpfen *VERB, PERFECT* **hat gedämpft**
1 **to steam** *(in cooking)*
2 **to muffle** *(a sound)*
3 **to dampen** *(somebody's enthusiasm)*

der **Dampfer**, *PLURAL* die **Dampfer**
steamer

ℱ **danach** *ADVERB*
1 **after it/them**
2 **afterwards**
Kurz danach haben sie sich getrennt. They split up shortly afterwards.
3 **accordingly**
Er ist schon achtzehn, aber er benimmt sich nicht danach. He's eighteen already, but he doesn't behave accordingly.
4 Wir suchen danach. We are looking for it.
5 Es sieht danach aus. It looks like it.
Mir ist nicht danach. I don't feel like it.

der **Däne**, *PLURAL* die **Dänen**
Dane *(male)*

daneben *ADVERB*
1 **next to it/them**
2 **by comparison**

Dänemark *NEUTER NOUN*
Denmark

die **Dänin**, *PLURAL* die **Däninnen**
Dane *(female)*

dänisch *ADJECTIVE*
Danish

> **WORD TIP** Adjectives never have capitals in German, even for regions, countries, or nationalities.

dank *PREPOSITION* (*+ GEN or + DAT*)
thanks to

der **Dank**
thanks
Mit Dank zurück. Thanks for the loan.
Vielen Dank! Thank you very much!

dankbar *ADJECTIVE*
1 **grateful**
Er war uns sehr dankbar. He was very grateful to us.
2 **rewarding** *(a job, task)*

ℱ **danke** *EXCLAMATION*
thank you, thanks
Danke schön! Thank you very much.
Nein, danke! No thank you./No thanks.

danken *VERB, PERFECT* **hat gedankt**
1 **to thank**
2 Nichts zu danken! Don't mention it!

ℱ **dann** *ADVERB*
then

daran *ADVERB*
1 **on it/them**
2 Daran hat er nicht gedacht. He didn't think of it.
3 Sie war nahe daran aufzugeben. She was on the point of giving up.
4 Daran ist nichts zu machen. There is nothing you can do about it.
5 Es liegt daran, dass ... It is because ...
6 Er ist daran gestorben. He died of it.

darauf *ADVERB*
1 **on it/them**
2 Möchten Sie darauf warten? Would you like to wait for it?
3 **to it**
Hat er darauf geantwortet? Did he to reply to it?
4 **after that**
Kurz darauf kam die Polizei. Shortly after that, the police arrived.
5 Am Tag darauf fuhren wir in Urlaub. The

A
B
C
D
E
F
G
H
I
J
K
L
M
N
O
P
Q
R
S
T
U
V
W
X
Y
Z

A
B
C
D
E
F
G
H
I
J
K
L
M
N
O
P
Q
R
S
T
U
V
W
X
Y
Z

day after, we went on holiday.
6 Es kommt darauf an, ob ... It depends whether ...

daraufhin ADVERB
as a result

daraus ADVERB
1 out of it/them, from it/them
2 Was ist daraus geworden? What has become of it?
3 Mach dir nichts daraus! Don't worry about it!

darf, darfst ▸ SEE **dürfen**

darin ADVERB
1 in it/them
2 in that respect
Darin gleichen sie sich. In that respect, they are similar.
Der Unterschied liegt darin, dass ... The difference is that ...

der **Darm**, PLURAL die **Därme**
intestine(s), bowel(s)

darstellen VERB, PERFECT **hat dargestellt**
1 to represent
2 to show
Dieses Gemälde stellt Szenen aus dem Bürgerkrieg dar. This painting shows scenes from the civil war.
3 to describe
Er stellt es so dar, als sei es meine Schuld. The way he describes it, it's all my fault.
4 to play (in the theatre)

der **Darsteller**, PLURAL die **Darsteller**
actor

die **Darstellerin**, PLURAL die **Darstellerinnen**
actress

darüber ADVERB
1 over it/them
2 about it/them
Ich möchte nicht darüber sprechen. I don't want to talk about it.
3 more
Die Karten kosten dreißig Euro oder darüber. The tickets cost thirty euros or more.

darum ADVERB
1 round it/them
2 Sie haben darum gebeten. They asked for it.
3 Ich sorge mich darum. I'm worried about it.
4 Es geht darum, zu gewinnen. The main thing is to win.

5 Darum geht es nicht. That's not the point.
6 that's why
Darum komme ich nicht. That's why I'm not coming.
7 because of that
Er tat es nur darum, weil er Geld brauchte. He only did it because he needed money.

darunter ADVERB
1 under it/them
2 Sie wohnen im Stock darunter. They live on the floor below.
3 among them
Mehrere Schüler, darunter zwei Zehnjährige, wurden beim Rauchen erwischt. A number of pupils, among them two ten-year-olds, were caught smoking.
4 less
Die Flüge kosten dreißig Euro oder darunter. The flights are thirty euros or less.
5 Was verstehen Sie darunter? What do you understand by that?

ℓ **das** ARTICLE
1 (neuter) the
das Haus the house
2 that
Das Mädchen war es. It was that girl.

das PRONOUN
1 which
Das Kleid, das ich im Schaufenster gesehen habe, ist schon weg. The dress which I saw in the window has gone.
2 'Welches Kleid meinst du?' – 'Das mit der Spitze.' 'Which dress do you mean?' – 'The one with the lace.'
3 who
Kennst du das Mädchen, das gegenüber wohnt? Do you know the girl who lives opposite?
4 that
Das wusste ich nicht. I didn't know that.
Das geht. That's all right.

dasein ▸ SEE **da**

das **Dasein**
existence

ℓ **dass** CONJUNCTION
1 that
Ich freue mich, dass ... I'm pleased that ...
2 Ich verstehe nicht, dass Karin ihn mag. I don't understand why Karin likes him.

dasselbe PRONOUN
the same, the same one

die **Datei**, PLURAL die **Dateien**
file

◇ irregular verb; SEP separable verb; for more help with verbs see centre section

die **Daten** *PLURAL NOUN*
data

die **Datenbank**, *PLURAL* die **Datenbanken**
database

die **Datenverarbeitung**
data processing

datieren *VERB*, *PERFECT* **hat datiert**
to date

der **Dativ**, *PLURAL* die **Dative**
dative *(in grammar)*

ℓ das **Datum**, *PLURAL* die **Daten**
date

ℓ die **Dauer**
1 duration
2 length
3 Sie werden für die Dauer von fünf Jahren
gewählt. They are elected for (a period of)
five years.
4 von Dauer sein to last
Es war nicht von Dauer. It did not last.
5 auf die Dauer in the long run
Auf die Dauer wird das zu teuer. It gets
too expensive in the long run.
auf Dauer permanently
Werden sie auf Dauer in Deutschland
bleiben? Are they going to live in Germany
permanently?

die **Dauerkarte**, *PLURAL* die **Dauerkarten**
season ticket

ℓ **dauern** *VERB*, *PERFECT* **hat gedauert**
1 to last
2 lange dauern to take a long time
Das hat aber lange gedauert! That took a
long time!
Es hat vier Wochen gedauert, bis der Brief
hier ankam. It took four weeks for the
letter to arrive.

dauernd *ADJECTIVE*
constant
dauernd *ADVERB*
constantly

die **Dauerwelle**, *PLURAL* die **Dauerwellen**
perm

der **Daumen**, *PLURAL* die **Daumen**
thumb

die **Daunendecke**, *PLURAL* die
Daunendecken
duvet

davon *ADVERB*
1 from it/them
2 about it

Ich weiß nichts davon. I don't know
anything about it.
3 of it/them
Er bekam die Hälfte davon. He got half
of it.
4 Das kommt davon! *(informal)* It serves you
right!
5 Was habe ich davon? What's the point?
6 Abgesehen davon war das Konzert super.
Apart from that, the concert was great.

davor *ADVERB*
1 in front of it/them
2 beforehand
3 Er hat Angst davor. He is afraid of it.
4 Sie war kurz davor zu kündigen. She was
on the point of handing in her notice.

dazu *ADVERB*
1 to it/them
2 as well
Es ist praktisch und dazu auch noch billig.
It's handy and cheap as well.
3 with it
Was isst du dazu? What are you having
with it?
4 Ich habe keine Lust dazu. I don't feel like it.
5 Ich bin nicht dazu gekommen. I didn't get
round to it.
6 Er ist nicht dazu bereit. He's not prepared
to do it.
7 jemanden dazu bringen, etwas zu tun to
get somebody to do something
Sie hat ihn dazu gebracht mitzuhelfen.
She got him to help.

ℓ **dazugeben** *VERB◇*, *PRESENT* **gibt dazu**,
IMPERFECT **gab dazu**, *PERFECT* **hat
dazugegeben**
to add

dazugehören *VERB*, *PERFECT* **hat dazugehört**
1 to belong to it/them
2 to go with it/them *(of accessories)*
Zum Geburtstag bekam sie ein Pferd und
alles, was dazugehört. For her birthday
she got a horse and everything you need
for riding.

dazukommen *VERB◇*, *IMPERFECT* **kam dazu**,
PERFECT **ist dazugekommen**
1 to arrive
2 to be added
3 Kommt noch etwas dazu? Would you like
anything else?

dazwischen *ADVERB*
1 in between
2 between them
Was ist der Unterschied dazwischen?
What is the difference between them?

dazwischenkommen VERB◇, PRESENT
kommt dazwischen, IMPERFECT
kam dazwischen, PERFECT **ist**
dazwischengekommen
to crop up
Wir können nicht hingehen, uns ist etwas
dazwischengekommen. We can't go,
something has cropped up.

die **DB** ABBREVIATION
(=Deutsche Bahn) German railways

die **DDR** ABBREVIATION
(=Deutsche Demokratische Republik) GDR,
East Germany
Leipzig liegt in der ehemaligen DDR.
Leipzig is in the former GDR.

WORD TIP The article is always used: Sie fuhren
in die DDR.

die **Debatte**, PLURAL die **Debatten**
debate

die **Decke**, PLURAL die **Decken**
1 blanket, cover
2 (table)cloth
Ich habe eine saubere Decke aufgelegt.
I've put on a clean tablecloth.
3 ceiling

der **Deckel**, PLURAL die **Deckel**
1 lid
2 top

♪**decken** VERB, PERFECT **hat gedeckt**
1 to cover
2 to lay (a table)
Kannst du den Tisch decken? Can you lay
the table?
3 jemanden decken to cover up for
somebody
4 einen Spieler decken to mark a player (in
sport)

definieren VERB, PERFECT **hat definiert**
to define

die **Definition**, PLURAL die **Definitionen**
definition

dehnbar ADJECTIVE
elastic

dehnen VERB, PERFECT **hat gedehnt**
to stretch

♪**dein** ADJECTIVE
your

♪**deiner, deine, dein(e)s** PRONOUN
yours
Meine Uhr ist kaputt, kann ich deine
haben? My watch is broken. Can I

take yours?

deinetwegen ADVERB
1 because of you
2 for your sake

deins ► SEE **deiner**

die **Deklination**, PLURAL die **Deklinationen**
declension (in grammar)

deklinieren VERB, PERFECT **hat dekliniert**
to decline (in grammar)

die **Dekoration**, PLURAL die **Dekorationen**
decoration

der **Delfin**, PLURAL die **Delfine**
dolphin

die **Delle**, PLURAL die **Dellen**
dent

♪**dem** ARTICLE
1 (dative) (to) the
2 Es liegt auf dem Tisch. It's on the table.
dem PRONOUN
1 to him
Gib es dem. Give it to him.
2 to it, to that one
3 to whom
Der Mann, dem ich das Geld gegeben
habe, hieß Max. The man I gave the money
to was called Max.
4 which, that
Das Messer, mit dem ich Zwiebeln
schneide, liegt in der Schublade. The knife
that I cut onions with is in the drawer.

demnächst ADVERB
shortly

die **Demokratie**, PLURAL die **Demokratien**
democracy

demokratisch ADJECTIVE
democratic

der **Demonstrant**, PLURAL die
Demonstranten
demonstrator (male)

die **Demonstrantin**, PLURAL die
Demonstrantinnen
demonstrator (female)

die **Demonstration**, PLURAL die
Demonstrationen
demonstration

demonstrieren VERB, PERFECT **hat**
demonstriert
to demonstrate

◇ irregular verb; SEP separable verb; for more help with verbs see centre section

ℙ **den** ARTICLE
1 *(masculine accusative)* **the**
  Hast du den Film schon gesehen? Have you seen the film yet?
2 *(plural dative)* **(to) the**
  Sie gab den Kindern Bonbons. She gave the children some sweets.
3 Ich habe mir den Arm gebrochen. I've broken my arm.

den PRONOUN
1 **him**
  Kennst du den? Do you know him?
2 **it, that one**
  Den kannst du gerne haben. You're welcome to it.
  Ich nehme den. I'll take that one.
3 **who(m)**
  Der Mann, den wir gesehen haben, kam mir bekannt vor. The man we saw seemed familiar to me.
4 **which, that**
  Der Mantel, den ich mir gekauft habe, ist schön warm. The coat I bought is nice and warm.

denen PRONOUN
1 *(dative plural)* **(to) them**
2 **that, (to) whom**
  Die Menschen, denen sie geholfen hat, sind ihr sehr dankbar. The people she helped are very grateful to her.

Den Haag NEUTER NOUN
  The Hague

denkbar ADJECTIVE
  conceivable

ℙ **denken** VERB◇, IMPERFECT **dachte**, PERFECT **hat gedacht**
1 **to think**
  Ich denke oft an dich. I often think of you.
2 Das kann ich mir denken. I can imagine.

das **Denkmal**, PLURAL die **Denkmäler**
  monument

ℙ **denn** CONJUNCTION
1 **because, for**
2 **than**
  mehr denn je more than ever

denn ADVERB
1 Wo denn? Where?
2 Was ist denn los? So what's the matter?
3 Warum denn nicht? Why ever not?
4 es sei denn, ... unless ...
  Ich komme, es sei denn, es regnet. I'm coming unless it rains.

dennoch CONJUNCTION
  nevertheless

deprimierend ADJECTIVE
  depressing

deprimiert ADJECTIVE
  depressed

ℙ **der** ARTICLE
1 *(masculine)* **the**
  der Mann the man
2 *(feminine and plural genitive)* **of the**
  Das ist die Katze der Frau. That's the woman's cat.
  Er nahm den Ball der Kinder. He took the children's ball.
3 *(feminine dative)* **(to) the**
  Ich gab es der Frau. I gave it to the woman.

der PRONOUN
1 **who**
  Der Mann, der hier wohnt, ist Millionär. The man who lives here is a millionaire.
2 **which**
  Der Regenschirm, der so schön groß war, ist verschwunden. The umbrella, which was such a nice big one, has disappeared.
3 der da that one
4 **him, he**

deren PRONOUN
1 **their**
  Wo sind die Kinder und deren Hund? Where are the children and their dog?
2 **whose**
3 **of which**

derselbe PRONOUN
  the same, the same one

ℙ **des** ARTICLE
  (masculine and neuter genitive singular) **of the**
  Das Klingeln des Telefons weckte ihn. The ringing of the phone woke him up.
  Das ist der Ball des Jungen. That's the boy's ball.

deshalb ADVERB
1 **therefore**
2 **that's why**

das **Desinfektionsmittel**, PLURAL die **Desinfektionsmittel**
  disinfectant

desinfizieren VERB, PERFECT **hat desinfiziert**
  to disinfect

dessen PRONOUN
1 **his**
2 **its**
3 **whose**
  Der Junge, dessen Mutter das Foto gemacht hat, ist mein Freund. The boy

ℙ indicates key words

whose mother took the photo is my friend.
4 of which

desto *ADVERB*
the
je mehr, desto besser the more the better

deswegen *CONJUNCTION*
1 therefore
2 that's why

der **Detektiv**, *PLURAL* die **Detektive**
detective

♀ **deutlich** *ADJECTIVE*
clear
deutlich *ADVERB*
clearly
Ich konnte ihn deutlich sehen. I could
clearly see him.

♀ **deutsch** *ADJECTIVE*
German

WORD TIP Adjectives never have capitals
in German, even for regions, countries, or
nationalities.

♀ das **Deutsch**
German
Wir lernen Deutsch. We are learning
German.
Sag es auf Deutsch! Say it in German!
Er spricht fließend Deutsch. He speaks
fluent German.

der/die **Deutsche**, *PLURAL* die **Deutschen**
German
Er ist Deutscher. He's German.
Sie ist Deutsche. She's German.

die **Deutsche Bahn**
German railways

♀ **Deutschland** *NEUTER NOUN*
Germany
Wir fahren nach Deutschland. We're going
to Germany.

🔵 **DEUTSCHLAND**

Capital: Berlin. Population: over 82 million.
Size: 357,021 square km. Official language:
German. Official currency: euro.

die **Devisen** *PLURAL NOUN*
foreign currency

♀ der **Dezember**
December
am ersten Dezember on the first of
December
im Dezember in December

die **Dezimalzahl**, *PLURAL* die **Dezimalzahlen**
decimal (number)

d. h. *ABBREVIATION*
(=*das heißt*) **i.e.**

Di. *ABBREVIATION*
(=*Dienstag*) **Tuesday**

das **Dia**, *PLURAL* die **Dias**
slide *(photographic)*

die **Diagnose**, *PLURAL* die **Diagnosen**
diagnosis

diagonal *ADJECTIVE*
diagonal

das **Diagramm**, *PLURAL* die **Diagramme**
diagram

der **Dialekt**, *PLURAL* die **Dialekte**
dialect

♀ der **Dialog**, *PLURAL* die **Dialoge**
dialogue

der **Diamant**, *PLURAL* die **Diamanten**
diamond

♀ die **Diät**, *PLURAL* die **Diäten**
diet
Der Arzt hat ihn auf Diät gesetzt. The
doctor has put him on a diet.

♀ **dich** *PRONOUN*
1 you
2 yourself

dicht *ADJECTIVE*
1 dense
2 thick *(fog)*
3 watertight
4 airtight
5 Er ist nicht ganz dicht. *(informal)* He's off
his head.
dicht *ADVERB*
1 densely
2 tightly
3 close
Geh nicht so dicht an den Käfig! Don't go
so close to the cage!
Der Ort liegt dicht bei Hamburg. The town
is close to Hamburg.

der **Dichter**, *PLURAL* die **Dichter**
poet *(male)*

die **Dichterin**, *PLURAL* die **Dichterinnen**
poet *(female)*

die **Dichtung**, *PLURAL* die **Dichtungen**
1 poetry
2 seal, washer

♀ **dick** *ADJECTIVE*
1 thick

2 swollen *(ankle, tonsils)*
3 fat *(person)*

der **Dickkopf**, PLURAL die **Dickköpfe**
1 stubborn person
2 Das Kind hat aber einen Dickkopf! The child is really stubborn!

dickköpfig ADJECTIVE
stubborn

dickköpfig ADVERB
stubbornly

ℰ **die** ARTICLE
(feminine and plural) the
die Frau the woman
die Bücher the books

die PRONOUN
1 *(feminine and plural)* who
Die Frau, die hier wohnt, ist sehr nett. The woman who lives here is very nice.
Die Kinder, die ich gefragt habe, wussten es nicht. The children I asked did not know.
2 which
Wo ist die Tasche, die ich gekauft habe? Where is the bag I bought?
3 she, her
4 them
Ich meine die. I mean them.
5 die da *(feminine)* that one, *(plural)* those

ℰ der **Dieb**, PLURAL die **Diebe**
thief *(male)*

ℰ die **Diebin**, PLURAL die **Diebinnen**
thief *(female)*

ℰ der **Diebstahl**, PLURAL die **Diebstähle**
1 theft
2 burglary

die **Diele**, PLURAL die **Dielen**
1 hall
2 floorboard

dienen VERB, PERFECT **hat gedient**
to serve

ℰ der **Dienst**, PLURAL die **Dienste**
1 service
2 duty
Wer hat heute Dienst? Who is on duty today?
Er hat auch am Wochenende Dienst. He also works weekends.

ℰ der **Dienstag**, PLURAL die **Dienstage**
Tuesday
am Dienstag on Tuesday

dienstags ADVERB
on Tuesdays

dienstfrei ADJECTIVE
1 ein dienstfreier Tag a day off
2 Er hat samstags dienstfrei. He is off duty on Saturdays.

dienstlich ADVERB
on business

die **Dienstreise**, PLURAL die **Dienstreisen**
business trip

ℰ **diese** ▸ SEE **dieser**

der **Diesel**
diesel

dieselbe PRONOUN
the same, the same one

ℰ **dieser**, **diese**, **dieses** ADJECTIVE
1 this
2 *(plural)* these
Diese Äpfel schmecken gut. These apples taste good.

dieser, **diese**, **dieses** PRONOUN
1 this one
Mir gefällt dieses am besten. I like this one best.
2 *(plural)* these ones

diesmal ADVERB
this time

digital ADJECTIVE
digital

die **Digitaluhr**, PLURAL die **Digitaluhren**
1 digital watch
2 digital clock

das **Diktat**, PLURAL die **Diktate**
dictation

diktieren VERB, PERFECT **hat diktiert**
to dictate

das **Ding**, PLURAL die **Dinge**
thing
vor allen Dingen above all
Das war ein Ding! *(informal)* That was quite something!

der/die/das **Dings**
(informal) thingummy

der **Dinosaurier**, PLURAL die **Dinosaurier**
dinosaur

das **Diplom**, PLURAL die **Diplome**
diploma

diplomatisch ADJECTIVE
diplomatic

ℰ **dir** PRONOUN
1 you, to you
Sie hat es dir gegeben. She gave it to you.

Ich verspreche dir, dass ... I promise you that ...

2 Sind sie Freunde von dir? Are they friends of yours?

3 yourself

direkt *ADJECTIVE*
direct

direkt *ADVERB*
directly

der Direktor, *PLURAL* **die Direktoren**
1 director *(male)*
2 head teacher, principal *(male)*
3 manager *(of a bank, firm) (male)*

> **WORD TIP** Professions, hobbies, and sports don't take an article in German: Er ist Direktor.

die Direktorin, *PLURAL* **die Direktorinnen**
1 director *(female)*
2 head teacher, principal *(female)*
3 manager *(of a bank, firm) (female)*

> **WORD TIP** Professions, hobbies, and sports don't take an article in German: Sie ist Direktorin.

die Direktübertragung, *PLURAL* **die Direktübertragungen**
live transmission, live broadcast

der Dirigent, *PLURAL* **die Dirigenten**
conductor *(male)*

> **WORD TIP** Professions, hobbies, and sports don't take an article in German: Er ist Dirigent.

die Dirigentin, *PLURAL* **die Dirigentinnen**
conductor *(female)*

> **WORD TIP** Professions, hobbies, and sports don't take an article in German: Sie ist Dirigentin.

dirigieren *VERB*, *PERFECT* **hat dirigiert**
to conduct

die Diskette, *PLURAL* **die Disketten**
disk

das Diskettenlaufwerk, *PLURAL* **die Diskettenlaufwerke**
disk drive

⟡ die Disko, *PLURAL* **die Diskos**
disco

die Diskothek, *PLURAL* **die Diskotheken**
disco, discotheque

die Diskriminierung
discrimination
Die Diskriminierung von Frauen ist

verboten. Discrimination against women is illegal.

die Diskussion, *PLURAL* **die Diskussionen**
discussion
zur Diskussion stehen to be under discussion

⟡ diskutieren *VERB*, *PERFECT* **hat diskutiert**
to discuss

die Disziplin, *PLURAL* **die Disziplinen**
discipline

diszipliniert *ADJECTIVE*
disciplined

die DJH *ABBREVIATION*
(=Deutsche Jugendherberge) German youth hostel (association)

die DM *ABBREVIATION*
(=Deutsche Mark) DM, Deutschmark
► SEE **Mark**

die D-Mark, *PLURAL* **die D-Mark**
Deutschmark, German mark
► SEE **Mark**

Do. *ABBREVIATION*
(=Donnerstag) Thursday

doch *ADVERB*
1 yes *(when you are contradicting somebody)*
'Hast du keinen Hunger?' – 'Doch!' 'Aren't you hungry?' – 'Yes, I am!'
2 after all
Sie hat ihn doch eingeladen. She invited him after all.
Sie ist doch nicht gekommen. She hasn't come after all.
3 Er hat doch meinen Brief bekommen? He did get my letter, didn't he?
Sie kommt doch? She's coming, isn't she?
4 anyway
Du hörst ja doch nicht auf mich. You won't listen to me anyway.
5 Pass doch auf! Do be careful!

doch *CONJUNCTION*
but

der Doktor, *PLURAL* **die Doktoren**
1 doctor
Er ist Doktor der Physik. He's a doctor of physics.
2 doctorate, PhD
Sie hat ihren Doktor gemacht. She did a doctorate.

die Doku, *PLURAL* **die Dokus**
(informal) documentary

das Dokument, *PLURAL* **die Dokumente**
document

ℰ der **Dokumentarfilm**, *PLURAL* die **Dokumentarfilme**
documentary

die **Dokumentarsendung**, *PLURAL* die **Dokumentarsendungen**
documentary (programme)

die **Dokumentation**, *PLURAL* die **Dokumentationen**
documentary

dolmetschen *VERB*, *PERFECT* **hat gedolmetscht**
to interpret

der **Dolmetscher**, *PLURAL* die **Dolmetscher**
interpreter *(male)*

WORD TIP Professions, hobbies, and sports don't take an article in German: Er ist Dolmetscher.

die **Dolmetscherin**, *PLURAL* die **Dolmetscherinnen**
interpreter *(female)*

WORD TIP Professions, hobbies, and sports don't take an article in German: Sie ist Dolmetscherin.

ℰ der **Dom**, *PLURAL* die **Dome**
cathedral

WORD TIP The German word Dom does not mean dome in English; the German word for dome is Kuppel.

die **Donau**
Danube

der **Döner**, *PLURAL* die **Döner**
doner kebab

der **Donner**
thunder

donnern *VERB*, *PERFECT* **hat gedonnert**
to thunder
Es donnert. It's thundering.

ℰ der **Donnerstag**, *PLURAL* die **Donnerstage**
Thursday
am Donnerstag on Thursday

donnerstags *ADVERB*
on Thursdays

ℰ **doof** *ADJECTIVE*
(informal) stupid, silly

das **Doppel**, *PLURAL* die **Doppel**
1 duplicate
2 doubles *(in sport)*

das **Doppelbett**, *PLURAL* die **Doppelbetten**
double bed

das **Doppelfenster**, *PLURAL* die **Doppelfenster**
double-glazed window
Wir haben Doppelfenster. We've got double glazing.

ℰ das **Doppelhaus**, *PLURAL* die **Doppelhäuser**
semi-detached house

der **Doppelklick**, *PLURAL* die **Doppelklicks**
double-click *(with mouse)*

der **Doppelpunkt**, *PLURAL* die **Doppelpunkte**
colon

die **Doppelstunde**, *PLURAL* die **Doppelstunden**
double period

doppelt *ADJECTIVE*
1 double
eine doppelte Portion a double portion
in doppelter Ausführung in duplicate
2 twice (the)
Wir brauchen die doppelte Menge. We need twice the amount.

doppelt *ADVERB*
1 doubly
2 twice
Es kostet doppelt so viel. It costs twice as much.
Ihr müsst euch jetzt doppelt anstrengen. You have to try twice as hard now.

ℰ das **Doppelzimmer**, *PLURAL* die **Doppelzimmer**
double room

ℰ das **Dorf**, *PLURAL* die **Dörfer**
village

der **Dorn**, *PLURAL* die **Dornen**
thorn

ℰ **dort** *ADVERB*
there
Sie sind dort drüben. They are over there.

dorther *ADVERB*
from there

dorthin *ADVERB*
there
Geht ihr jetzt dorthin? Are you going there now?

ℰ die **Dose**, *PLURAL* die **Dosen**
tin, can
Ich brauche eine Dose Tomaten. I need a tin of tomatoes.

dösen *VERB*, *PERFECT* **hat gedöst**
to doze

A
B
C
D
E
F
G
H
I
J
K
L
M
N
O
P
Q
R
S
T
U
V
W
X
Y
Z

77

der **Dosenöffner**, PLURAL die **Dosenöffner**
tin opener

die **Dosierung**, PLURAL die **Dosierungen**
dose

die **Dosis**, PLURAL die **Dosen**
dose

der **Dotter**, PLURAL die **Dotter**
yolk

downloaden VERB, PERFECT **hat
downgeloadet**
to download

der **Dozent**, PLURAL die **Dozenten**
lecturer (male)

> **WORD TIP** Professions, hobbies, and sports
> don't take an article in German: Er ist Dozent.

die **Dozentin**, PLURAL die **Dozentinnen**
lecturer (female)

> **WORD TIP** Professions, hobbies, and sports
> don't take an article in German: Sie ist
> Dozentin.

der **Drache**, PLURAL die **Drachen**
dragon

der **Drachen**, PLURAL die **Drachen**
kite
Heute will ich meinen Drachen steigen
lassen. I want to fly my kite today.

das **Drachenfliegen**
hang-gliding
In den Ferien gingen wir Drachenfliegen.
We went hang-gliding on holiday.

der **Draht**, PLURAL die **Drähte**
1 wire
2 Er ist auf Draht. (informal) He's on the ball.

das **Drama**, PLURAL die **Dramen**
drama

die **Dramatik**
drama

⚯ **dran** ADVERB
1 ▸ SEE daran
2 Ich bin dran. It's my turn.
Wer ist dran? Whose turn is it?
3 Du bist gut dran. You are well off.
4 Sie sind arm dran. They are in a bad way.
5 Ihr seid spät dran! You're late!

drängen VERB, PERFECT **hat gedrängt**
1 to push
2 to press, to urge (somebody)
3 sich drängen to crowd
Die Leute drängten sich vor der Kasse.
People crowded around the box office.

drankommen VERB⋄, IMPERFECT **kam dran**,
PERFECT **ist drangekommen**
to have your turn
Wer kommt dran? Whose turn is it?

drauf ADVERB
1 ▸ SEE darauf
2 drauf und dran sein, etwas zu tun to be on
the point of doing something
3 gut drauf sein (informal) to be in a good
mood

draußen ADVERB
outside

der **Dreck**
dirt

dreckig ADJECTIVE
dirty, filthy

das **Drehbuch**, PLURAL die **Drehbücher**
1 screenplay
2 script

drehen VERB, PERFECT **hat gedreht**
1 to turn
an etwas drehen to turn something
2 to shoot (a film)
3 sich drehen to turn
4 sich um etwas drehen to be about
something
Bei dem Streit dreht es sich um ihr
Taschengeld. The argument is about her
pocket money.

⚯ **drei** NUMBER
three

die **Drei**, PLURAL die **Dreien**
1 three
2 satisfactory (school mark)

das **Dreieck**, PLURAL die **Dreiecke**
triangle

dreieckig ADJECTIVE
triangular

dreifach ADJECTIVE
triple

dreihundert NUMBER
three hundred

das **Dreikönigsfest**, PLURAL die
Dreikönigsfeste
Epiphany

dreimal ADVERB
three times

das **Dreirad**, PLURAL die **Dreiräder**
tricycle

⋄ irregular verb; SEP separable verb; for more help with verbs see centre section

ℙ **dreißig** NUMBER
thirty

drei viertel NUMBER
three quarters

die **Dreiviertelstunde**, PLURAL die
Dreiviertelstunden
three quarters of an hour

ℙ **dreizehn** NUMBER
thirteen
um dreizehn Uhr at one p.m.

drin ADVERB
1 ▸ SEE **darin**, **drinnen**
2 drin sein (informal) to be possible
Jetzt ist noch alles drin. Anything is still
possible.
3 nicht drin sein (informal) to be out of the
question
Ein neuer Computer ist im Moment
nicht drin. A new computer is out of the
question at the moment.

ℙ **dringend** ADJECTIVE
urgent

drinnen ADVERB
1 inside
2 indoors

dritt ADVERB
Sie sind zu dritt. There are three of them.

dritte ▸ SEE **dritter**

das **Drittel**, PLURAL die **Drittel**
third

drittens ADVERB
thirdly

ℙ **dritter, dritte, drittes** ADJECTIVE
third
Ich sage es dir jetzt zum dritten Mal. I'm
telling you for the third time now.
Sie wurde Dritte. She came third.
die Dritte Welt the Third World
Jeder Dritte leidet unter einer Allergie.
One in three people suffers from an allergy.
Die Informationen dürfen nicht an einen
Dritten weitergegeben werden. The
information must not be passed on to a
third party.
das dritte Alter the third age

ℙ die **Droge**, PLURAL die **Drogen**
drug

drogenabhängig ADJECTIVE
addicted to drugs

der/die **Drogenabhängige**, PLURAL die
Drogenabhängigen
drug addict

die **Drogenabhängigkeit**
drug addiction

die **Drogenberatungsstelle**, PLURAL die
Drogenberatungsstellen
drug advisory centre

drogensüchtig ADJECTIVE
addicted to drugs

der/die **Drogensüchtige**, PLURAL die
Drogensüchtigen
drug addict

ℙ die **Drogerie**, PLURAL die **Drogerien**
chemist's

der **Drogist**, PLURAL die **Drogisten**
chemist (male)

> **WORD TIP** Professions, hobbies, and sports
> don't take an article in German: Er ist Drogist.

die **Drogistin**, PLURAL die **Drogistinnen**
chemist (female)

> **WORD TIP** Professions, hobbies, and sports
> don't take an article in German: Sie ist
> Drogistin.

drohen VERB, PERFECT **hat gedroht**
to threaten
jemandem drohen to threaten somebody

die **Drohung**, PLURAL die **Drohungen**
threat

die **Drossel**, PLURAL die **Drosseln**
thrush (bird)

drüben ADVERB
over there

der **Druck**
1 pressure
jemanden unter Druck setzen to put
pressure on somebody
2 printing
3 PLURAL die **Drucke** print

drucken VERB, PERFECT **hat gedruckt**
to print

drücken VERB, PERFECT **hat gedrückt**
1 to push
'Bitte drücken' 'Push'
2 to press
Sie drückte (auf) den Knopf. She pressed
the button.
3 jemanden drücken to hug somebody
4 to hurt, to pinch

A B C D E F G H I J K L M N O P Q R S T U V W X Y Z

79

Die Schuhe drücken. The shoes hurt.
5 **to bring down** *(the cost, prices)*
6 **sich vor etwas drücken** *(informal)* to get
out of something
Du hast dich mal wieder vor dem
Aufräumen gedrückt. You've got out of
tidying up again.

der **Drucker**, PLURAL die **Drucker**
printer

der **Druckknopf**, PLURAL die **Druckknöpfe**
press stud

die **Drucksache**, PLURAL die **Drucksachen**
printed matter

die **Druckschrift**, PLURAL die **Druckschriften**
block letters, block capitals
Bitte das Formular in Druckschrift
ausfüllen. Please complete the form in
block capitals.

die **Drüse**, PLURAL die **Drüsen**
gland

der **Dschungel**, PLURAL die **Dschungel**
jungle

ℰ **du** PRONOUN
1 **you**
2 **Darf ich du sagen?** Can I say 'du' to you?
Sie sind per du. They are on familiar terms.

WORD TIP The pronoun du is used when talking
to family members, close friends, or people of
your own age; otherwise Sie is used.

der **Dudelsack**, PLURAL die **Dudelsäcke**
bagpipes

der **Duft**, PLURAL die **Düfte**
fragrance, scent

duften VERB, PERFECT **hat geduftet**
to smell
Die Seife duftet nach Lavendel. The soap
smells of lavender.

dumm ADJECTIVE
1 **stupid**
2 **Das wird mir jetzt zu dumm.** *(informal)*
I've had enough of it.
3 **So etwas Dummes!** How annoying!
4 **Ich bin mal wieder der Dumme.** I've drawn
the short straw again.

dummerweise ADVERB
stupidly

die **Dummheit**, PLURAL die **Dummheiten**
1 **stupidity**
2 **stupid thing**
Mach keine Dummheiten! Don't do
anything stupid!

der **Dummkopf**, PLURAL die **Dummköpfe**
fool

der **Düne**, PLURAL die **Dünen**
dune

das **Düngemittel**
fertilizer

ℰ **dunkel** ADJECTIVE
1 **dark**
Er trug einen dunklen Anzug. He wore a
dark suit.
Wir fuhren im Dunkeln nach Hause. We
drove home in the dark.
2 **ein Dunkles** a dark beer
3 **vague** *(idea)*
4 **shady** *(business)*
5 **deep** *(voice)*

die **Dunkelheit**
darkness, dark
Sie kamen bei Einbruch der Dunkelheit an.
They arrived at dusk.

ℰ **dünn** ADJECTIVE
1 **thin**
2 **weak** *(coffee, tea)*

der **Dunst**, PLURAL die **Dünste**
haze

das **Duo**, PLURAL die **Duos**
duet

ℰ **durch** PREPOSITION (+ ACC)
1 **through**
Er ist durch das Fernsehen bekannt
geworden. He's become famous through
television.
2 **by**
Das Paket wurde durch Boten zugestellt.
The parcel was delivered by courier.
3 **Acht durch zwei ist vier.** Eight divided by
two is four.
4 **due to**
Durch das schlechte Wetter wurde der
Flug annulliert. Due to the bad weather the
flight was cancelled.

WORD TIP durch + das gives durchs

durch ADVERB
1 **through**
die ganze Nacht durch all through the
night
2 **den Winter durch** throughout the winter
3 **durch und durch** completely
4 **Es war acht Uhr durch.** *(informal)* It was
gone eight o'clock.

◇ irregular verb; *SEP* separable verb; for more help with verbs see centre section

durcharbeiten *VERB*, *PERFECT* **hat durchgearbeitet**
1 to work through
Sie haben die Nacht durchgearbeitet.
They worked through the night.
2 Ich habe mich durch das Buch durchgearbeitet. I worked my way through the book.

durchaus *ADVERB*
absolutely

durchblicken *VERB*, *PERFECT* **hat durchgeblickt**
1 *(informal)* to understand
Da blicke ich nicht durch. I don't understand it.
2 durchblicken lassen, dass ... to hint that ...
Sie ließ durchblicken, dass sie zu einem Kompromiss bereit war. She hinted that she was willing to compromise.

durchbrechen *VERB*◇, *PRESENT* **bricht durch**, *IMPERFECT* **brach durch**, *PERFECT* **hat durchgebrochen**
1 to break in two
Er brach den Ast durch. He broke the branch in two.
2 *PERFECT* **ist durchgebrochen** to snap
Das Brett ist durchgebrochen. The board has snapped.

durchdrehen *VERB*, *PERFECT* **ist durchgedreht**
(informal) to crack up

ℰ **durcheinander** *ADVERB*
1 in a mess
Mein Zimmer ist durcheinander. My room is (in) a mess.
2 confused
Ich bin ganz durcheinander. I'm completely confused.
3 Sie haben alle durcheinander geredet.
They all talked at once.

das **Durcheinander**
1 muddle
2 mess
In der Wohnung herrschte ein fürchterliches Durcheinander. The flat was a terrible mess.
3 confusion
Im allgemeinen Durcheinander entkam der Dieb. The thief escaped in the general confusion.

durcheinanderbringen *VERB*◇, *IMPERFECT* **brachte durcheinander**, *PERFECT* **hat durcheinandergebracht**
1 to muddle up

Sie haben die Akten durcheinandergebracht. You have muddled up the files.
Karl hat ihre Namen durcheinandergebracht. Karl got their names mixed up.
2 to confuse
Bring mich nicht durcheinander! Don't confuse me!.

durchfahren *VERB*◇, *PRESENT* **fährt durch**, *IMPERFECT* **fuhr durch**, *PERFECT* **ist durchgefahren**
1 to drive through
2 to go through
3 Der Zug fährt (in Stuttgart) durch. The train doesn't stop (in Stuttgart).

der **Durchfall**
diarrhoea

durchfallen *VERB*◇, *PRESENT* **fällt durch**, *IMPERFECT* **fiel durch**, *PERFECT* **ist durchgefallen**
1 to fall through
2 to fail
Er ist bei der Prüfung durchgefallen. He failed the exam.

durchführen *VERB*, *PERFECT* **hat durchgeführt**
to carry out

der **Durchgang**, *PLURAL* die **Durchgänge**
1 passage
2 'Durchgang verboten' 'No entry'
3 round *(in sport)*

der **Durchgangsverkehr**
through traffic

durchgehen *VERB*◇, *IMPERFECT* **ging durch**, *PERFECT* **ist durchgegangen**
1 to go through
2 jemandem etwas durchgehen lassen to let somebody get away with something

durchkommen *VERB*◇, *IMPERFECT* **kam durch**, *PERFECT* **ist durchgekommen**
1 to come through
2 to get through *(on the phone, in an exam)*
3 to pull through *(after an illness)*

durchlassen *VERB*◇, *PRESENT* **lässt durch**, *IMPERFECT* **ließ durch**, *PERFECT* **hat durchgelassen**
1 to let through
2 to let in

durchmachen *VERB*, *PERFECT* **hat durchgemacht**
1 to go through

2 to work through *(your lunch break, for example)*

3 Wir haben die Nacht durchgemacht. We made a night of it.

der **Durchmesser**, PLURAL die **Durchmesser** diameter

durchnehmen VERB◇, PRESENT **nimmt durch**, IMPERFECT **nahm durch**, PERFECT **hat durchgenommen**
to do *(a topic at school)*

durchs ▸ SEE **durch das**

die **Durchsage**, PLURAL die **Durchsagen** announcement

♪ der **Durchschnitt**, PLURAL die **Durchschnitte** average
im Durchschnitt on average

♪ **durchschnittlich** ADJECTIVE average
durchschnittlich ADVERB on average

die **Durchschnittstemperatur**, PLURAL die **Durchschnittstemperaturen** average temperature

durchsetzen VERB, PERFECT **hat durchgesetzt**

1 etwas durchsetzen to push something through

2 sich durchsetzen to assert yourself
Sie muss lernen sich durchzusetzen. She has to learn to assert herself.

3 sich durchsetzen to catch on *(of a fashion, an idea)*
Die Idee hat sich nicht durchgesetzt. The idea did not catch on.

durchsichtig ADJECTIVE transparent

durchstreichen VERB◇, IMPERFECT **strich durch**, PERFECT **hat durchgestrichen**
to cross out

durchsuchen VERB, PERFECT **hat durchsucht** to search

der **Durchzug** draught

♪ **dürfen** VERB◇, PRESENT **darf**, IMPERFECT **durfte**, PERFECT **hat gedurft, hat dürfen**

1 to be allowed
Sie darf das nicht. She's not allowed to do that.
Er hat nicht gedurft. He wasn't allowed to.
Klaus hat sie im Krankenhaus besuchen

dürfen. Klaus was allowed to visit her in hospital.

2 Darf ich? May I?

3 Das dürfen Sie nicht vergessen. You mustn't forget that.
Du darfst es nicht alles so ernst nehmen. You mustn't take it all so seriously.

4 Du darfst froh sein, dass sonst nichts passiert ist. You should be glad that nothing else happened.
Das darf einfach nicht passieren. That just shouldn't happen.
Das dürfte nicht schwierig sein. That shouldn't be difficult.

5 Das darf doch nicht wahr sein! I don't believe it!

6 Was darf es sein? *(said by shop assistant)* Can I help you?

7 Das dürfte der Grund sein. *(expressing probability)* That's probably the reason.

WORD TIP The past participle is gedurft when dürfen is the main verb, and dürfen when it is an auxiliary verb.

durfte, durften, durftest, durftet ▸ SEE **dürfen**

dürftig ADJECTIVE poor, meagre

die **Dürre**, PLURAL die **Dürren** drought

♪ der **Durst** thirst
Sie hatten Durst. They were thirsty.

durstig ADJECTIVE thirsty

♪ die **Dusche**, PLURAL die **Duschen** shower

♪ **duschen** VERB, PERFECT **hat geduscht** to have a shower
Ich habe (mich) noch nicht geduscht. I haven't had a shower yet.

das **Duschgel**, PLURAL die **Duschgels** shower gel

das **Düsenflugzeug**, PLURAL die **Düsenflugzeuge** jet (plane)

düster ADJECTIVE

1 dark

2 gloomy *(future, thoughts)*

das **Dutzend**, PLURAL die **Dutzende** dozen

duzen VERB, PERFECT **hat geduzt** to call somebody 'du'

◇ *irregular verb;* SEP *separable verb; for more help with verbs see centre section*

Wollen wir uns duzen? Shall we say 'du' to each other?

> **WORD TIP** The word du is used when talking to family members, close friends, or people of your own age; otherwise, Sie is used.

dynamisch *ADJECTIVE*
dynamic

der D-Zug, PLURAL die **D-Züge**
fast train, express

Ee

die Ebbe, PLURAL die **Ebben**
low tide
Das Foto zeigt den Strand bei Ebbe. The photo shows the beach at low tide.
Es ist Ebbe. The tide is out.

eben *ADJECTIVE*
1 flat
2 level
eben *ADVERB*
1 just
Gabi war eben hier. Gabi was just here.
Ich habe ihn eben noch gesehen. I've just seen him.
Das ist eben so. That's just the way it is.
2 exactly, precisely
Eben! Exactly!

die Ebene, PLURAL die **Ebenen**
1 plain
2 level
3 plane *(in geometry)*

ebenso *ADVERB*
just as
Ulla hat den Film ebenso oft gesehen wie du. Ulla's seen the film just as often as you.
Ich habe ebenso viel Arbeit wie du. I've got just as much work as you.

das Echo, PLURAL die **Echos**
echo

echt *ADJECTIVE*
real, genuine
Die Kette ist aus echtem Gold. The necklace is real gold.
echt *ADVERB*
(informal) really
Das Lied ist echt gut. The song is really good.

der Eckball, PLURAL die **Eckbälle**
corner (kick)

ℰ **die Ecke**, PLURAL die **Ecken**
corner
Die Schule ist gleich um die Ecke. The school is just round the corner.

eckig *ADJECTIVE*
square

der Edelstein, PLURAL die **Edelsteine**
precious stone

die EDV *ABBREVIATION*
(=elektronische Datenverarbeitung)
electronic data processing, EDP

der Efeu
ivy

ℰ **der Effekt**, PLURAL die **Effekte**
effect

effektiv *ADJECTIVE*
effective
effektiv *ADVERB*
really, actually

die EG *ABBREVIATION*
(=Europäische Gemeinschaft) EC

egal *ADJECTIVE*
1 all the same
Das ist uns egal. It's all the same to us.
2 Das Porto kostet fünf Euro, egal wie groß das Paket ist. Postage is five euros, no matter what size the parcel is.
Er muss mitmachen, egal ob er es will oder nicht. He has to take part, whether he wants to or not.

egoistisch *ADJECTIVE*
selfish

ehe *CONJUNCTION*
1 before
Ehe ich es vergesse, … Before I forget, …
2 ehe … nicht until …
Ehe ich nicht weiß, was er will, mache ich nichts. I won't do anything until I know what he wants.

die Ehe, PLURAL die **Ehen**
marriage

die Ehefrau, PLURAL die **Ehefrauen**
wife

ehemalig *ADJECTIVE*
former

der Ehemann, PLURAL die **Ehemänner**
husband

das Ehepaar, PLURAL die **Ehepaare**
married couple

eher ADVERB
1 **earlier, sooner**
Je eher, desto besser. The sooner the better.
2 **rather**
Eher gehe ich zu Fuß, als Geld für ein Taxi auszugeben. I'd rather walk than pay for a taxi.
3 **more**
Das ist schon eher möglich. That's more likely.

der **Ehering**, PLURAL die **Eheringe**
wedding ring

die **Ehre**, PLURAL die **Ehren**
honour

ehrenamtlich ADJECTIVE
honorary

der **Ehrgeiz**
ambition

ehrgeizig ADJECTIVE
ambitious

♀ **ehrlich** ADJECTIVE
honest

♀ die **Ehrlichkeit**
honesty

♀ das **Ei**, PLURAL die **Eier**
egg

die **Eiche**, PLURAL die **Eichen**
oak

das **Eichhörnchen**, PLURAL die **Eichhörnchen**
squirrel

der **Eid**, PLURAL die **Eide**
oath

die **Eidechse**, PLURAL die **Eidechsen**
lizard

das **Eidotter**, PLURAL die **Eidotter**
egg yolk

der **Eierbecher**, PLURAL die **Eierbecher**
egg cup

die **Eierschale**, PLURAL die **Eierschalen**
eggshell

der **Eifer**
eagerness

die **Eifersucht**
jealousy

eifersüchtig ADJECTIVE
jealous

Sie ist eifersüchtig auf mich. She is jealous of me.

eifrig ADJECTIVE
eager

das **Eigelb**, PLURAL die **Eigelb(e)**
egg yolk

eigen ADJECTIVE
own
Er ist erst siebzehn und hat schon ein eigenes Auto. He's only seventeen and he's already got his own car.

die **Eigenart**, PLURAL die **Eigenarten**
peculiarity

eigenartig ADJECTIVE
peculiar

die **Eigenschaft**, PLURAL die **Eigenschaften**
1 **quality**
2 **characteristic**

eigensinnig ADJECTIVE
obstinate

eigentlich ADJECTIVE
actual

eigentlich ADVERB
really, actually
Eigentlich habe ich keine Lust, heute ins Kino zu gehen. I don't really feel like going to the cinema today.
Eigentlich bin ich erleichtert. Actually, I'm relieved.

das **Eigentum**
property

der **Eigentümer**, PLURAL die **Eigentümer**
owner *(male)*

die **Eigentümerin**, PLURAL die **Eigentümerinnen**
owner *(female)*

eignen VERB, PERFECT **hat sich geeignet**
sich eignen to be suitable

die **Eile**
hurry

eilen VERB
1 PERFECT **ist geeilt** to hurry
2 PERFECT **hat geeilt** to be urgent
Das eilt nicht. It's not urgent.

eilig ADJECTIVE
1 **urgent**
2 **hurried**
3 Ich habe es eilig. I'm in a hurry.

◇ **irregular verb;** SEP **separable verb; for more help with verbs see centre section**

der **Eilzug**, *PLURAL* die **Eilzüge**
fast stopping train

℘ der **Eimer**, *PLURAL* die **Eimer**
bucket

ein *ADJECTIVE*
1 **one**
Sie haben nur ein Kind. They've got just one child.
eines Abends one evening
2 Wir sind einer Meinung. We are of the same opinion.
3 ein für alle Mal once and for all

℘ **ein, eine, ein** *ARTICLE*
a, an
ein Haus a house
eine Allergie an allergy
Wir machen heute einen Ausflug. We're going on an outing today.
Ich brauche ein bisschen mehr. I need a bit more.
Was für ein Kleid hast du gekauft? What sort of dress did you buy?

einander *PRONOUN*
each other, one another

einatmen *VERB, PERFECT* **hat eingeatmet**
to breathe in

die **Einbahnstraße**, *PLURAL* die **Einbahnstraßen**
one-way street

der **Einband**, *PLURAL* die **Einbände**
cover *(of a book)*

einbauen *VERB, PERFECT* **hat eingebaut**
1 **to fit**
2 **to install**

die **Einbauküche**, *PLURAL* die **Einbauküchen**
fitted kitchen

einbiegen *VERB◇, IMPERFECT* **bog ein**, *PERFECT* **ist eingebogen**
to turn
Der Radfahrer bog langsam in die Seitenstraße ein. The cyclist turned slowly down the side street.

einbilden *VERB, PERFECT* **hat sich eingebildet**
1 **sich einbilden to imagine**
Das bildest du dir nur ein. You're only imagining it.
2 Till bildet sich viel ein. Till is very conceited.

die **Einbildung**
imagination
Dieser Freund existiert nur in seiner Einbildung. This friend exists only in his

imagination.
Das ist alles nur Einbildung. It's all in the mind.

einbrechen *VERB◇, PRESENT* **bricht ein**, *IMPERFECT* **brach ein**, *PERFECT* **ist eingebrochen**
to break in
In unserem Haus sind Diebe eingebrochen. Thieves broke into our house.
Bei unseren Nachbarn ist eingebrochen worden. Our neighbours have been burgled.

der **Einbrecher**, *PLURAL* die **Einbrecher**
burglar

einbringen *VERB◇, IMPERFECT* **brachte ein**, *PERFECT* **hat eingebracht**
to bring in
Dieser Job bringt nicht viel Geld ein. This job doesn't bring in much money.

der **Einbruch**, *PLURAL* die **Einbrüche**
1 **burglary**
2 Wir müssen vor Einbruch der Dunkelheit zu Hause sein. We have to be home before it gets dark.
Sie kamen bei Einbruch der Nacht an. They arrived at nightfall.

einchecken *VERB, PERFECT* **hat eingecheckt**
to check in
Wann müssen wir am Flughafen einchecken? When do we have to check in at the airport?

eindeutig *ADJECTIVE*
1 **clear**
2 **definite** *(proof)*

der **Eindruck**, *PLURAL* die **Eindrücke**
impression
Er hat einen guten Eindruck auf mich gemacht. He made a good impression on me.

eindrucksvoll *ADJECTIVE*
impressive

eine ▸ SEE **ein, einer**

eineiig *ADJECTIVE*
identical *twins*

eineinhalb *NUMBER*
one and a half

℘ **einer, eine, ein(e)s** *PRONOUN*
1 **somebody, someone**
Kann mir mal einer helfen? Can someone help me?
2 **anybody, anyone**

Das glaubt kaum einer. Hardly anyone
believes that.
3 you
Das macht einen müde. It makes you tired.
4 one
Es muss einer von uns gewesen sein. It
must have been one of us.
Wie soll das einer wissen? How are you
supposed to know?

einerseits ADVERB
on the one hand
Einerseits sagt sie, dass sie kein Geld hat,
andererseits kauft sie sich dauernd neue
Sachen. On the one hand she claims to
have no money, on the other hand she's
constantly buying new things.

eines ▸ SEE **einer**

ℰ **einfach** ADJECTIVE
1 simple
2 easy
3 single (ticket, knot)
einfach ADVERB
simply

die **Einfachheit**
simplicity

die **Einfahrt**, PLURAL die **Einfahrten**
1 entrance
2 arrival (of a train)
3 slip road (on a motorway)

der **Einfall**, PLURAL die **Einfälle**
idea

einfallen VERB◇, PRESENT **fällt ein**, IMPERFECT
fiel ein, PERFECT **ist eingefallen**
1 jemandem einfallen to occur to somebody
Es fiel ihm nicht ein, sich zu
entschuldigen. It didn't occur to him to
apologize.
2 Ihr Name fällt mir nicht ein. I can't think
of her name.
3 Was fällt dir eigentlich ein? What do you
think you're doing?
4 sich etwas einfallen lassen to come up
with a good idea, to think of something
Lass dir etwas einfallen! Think of
something!

ℰ das **Einfamilienhaus**, PLURAL die
Einfamilienhäuser
detached house

der **Einfluss**, PLURAL die **Einflüsse**
influence

einfrieren VERB◇, IMPERFECT **fror ein**, PERFECT
ist eingefroren
1 to freeze (of a pipe, lake, computer)

Der Bildschirm ist wieder eingefroren.
The screen has frozen again.
2 PERFECT **hat eingefroren to freeze** (food in
the freezer)
Sie hat das Fleisch eingefroren. She has
frozen the meat.

die **Einfuhr**, PLURAL die **Einfuhren**
import

einführen VERB, PERFECT **hat eingeführt**
1 to import
2 to introduce

die **Einführung**, PLURAL die **Einführungen**
introduction

die **Eingabe**
input (of data)

ℰ der **Eingang**, PLURAL die **Eingänge**
entrance

ℰ die **Eingangshalle**, PLURAL die
Eingangshallen
hallway

eingeben VERB◇, PRESENT **gibt ein**, IMPERFECT
gab ein, PERFECT **hat eingegeben**
1 to input, to key in (data)
2 to give (medicine)

eingebildet ADJECTIVE
1 conceited
2 imaginary (illness)

der/die **Eingeborene**, PLURAL die
Eingeborenen
native

eingehen VERB◇, IMPERFECT **ging ein**, PERFECT
ist eingegangen
1 to shrink (of clothes)
2 to die (of plants)
3 to arrive (of goods)
4 auf etwas eingehen to go into something
Sie ging näher darauf ein. She went into it
in more detail.
5 auf etwas nicht eingehen to ignore
something
Am besten gehst du gar nicht auf seine
Fragen ein. The best thing is to ignore his
questions.
6 auf etwas eingehen to agree to something
Oliver ist auf unseren Plan eingegangen.
Oliver agreed to our plan.
7 to take (a risk)
Wir dürfen kein Risiko eingehen. We
mustn't take any risks.

eingeschrieben ADJECTIVE
registered
ein eingeschriebener Brief a registered
letter

◇ **irregular verb;** SEP **separable verb; for more help with verbs see centre section**

eingestellt *ADJECTIVE*
1 **prepared**
Wir sind auf schlechtes Wetter
eingestellt. We are prepared for bad
weather.
2 **minded**
Seine Oma ist sehr fortschrittlich
eingestellt. His granny is very
progressively minded.

eingewöhnen *VERB*, *PERFECT* **hat sich
eingewöhnt**
sich eingewöhnen to settle in

eingießen *VERB◇*, *IMPERFECT* **goss ein**, *PERFECT*
hat eingegossen
to pour

die **Eingliederung**
1 **integration**
2 **incorporation**

eingreifen *VERB◇*, *IMPERFECT* **griff ein**, *PERFECT*
hat eingegriffen
to intervene

der **Eingriff**, *PLURAL* die **Eingriffe**
1 **intervention**
2 **operation** *(surgical)*

einheimisch *ADJECTIVE*
1 **native**
2 **local**

der/die **Einheimische**, *PLURAL* die
Einheimischen
local

die **Einheit**, *PLURAL* die **Einheiten**
1 **unity**
2 **unit** *(of drink, soldiers)*

der **Einheitspreis**, *PLURAL* die **Einheitspreise**
1 **standard price**
2 **flat fare**

einholen *VERB*, *PERFECT* **hat eingeholt**
1 **to catch up with**
Geh schon vor, wir holen dich ein. Go
ahead, we'll catch you up.
2 **to make up** *(time, a delay)*
Das Flugzeug holte die Verspätung wieder
ein. The plane made up the delay.
3 **to buy**
einholen gehen to go shopping

einhundert *NUMBER*
one hundred

einig *ADJECTIVE*
1 **sich einig sein to agree**
2 **sich einig werden to reach agreement**

einige ▸ SEE **einiger**

einigen *VERB*, *PERFECT* **hat sich geeinigt**
sich einigen to come to an agreement
sich auf etwas einigen to agree on
something

♀ **einiger, einige, einiges** *ADJECTIVE*, *PRONOUN*
1 **some**
Sie sind vor einiger Zeit weggezogen.
They moved away some time ago.
2 **several**
Wir haben uns einige Male getroffen. We
met up several times.
3 **a few**
Nur einige waren noch da. There were
only a few left.
4 **einiges quite a lot**
Wir haben einiges gesehen. We saw quite
a lot (of things).
5 **einiges some things**
Einiges hat uns nicht gefallen. There were
some things we didn't like.

einigermaßen *ADVERB*
1 **fairly**
2 **fairly well**
3 'Wie geht es dir?' – 'Einigermaßen.' 'How
are you?' – 'So-so.'

einiges ▸ SEE **einiger**

die **Einigung**
agreement

der **Einkauf**, *PLURAL* die **Einkäufe**
1 **shopping**
Ich muss noch ein paar Einkäufe machen. I
have to do some shopping.
2 **purchase**
Sie zeigte uns ihre Einkäufe. She showed
us her purchases.

♀ **einkaufen** *VERB*, *PERFECT* **hat eingekauft**
1 **to buy**
Ich habe vergessen Milch einzukaufen. I
forgot to buy milk.
2 **to shop**
Wir kaufen meist im Supermarkt ein. We
usually shop at the supermarket.
einkaufen gehen to go shopping

♀ der **Einkaufsbummel**, *PLURAL* die
Einkaufsbummel
shopping trip

♀ die **Einkaufsliste**, *PLURAL* die **Einkaufslisten**
shopping list

die **Einkaufspassage**, *PLURAL* die
Einkaufspassagen
shopping arcade

♀ **indicates key words**

die **Einkaufstasche**, *PLURAL* die
Einkaufstaschen
shopping bag

der **Einkaufswagen**, *PLURAL* die
Einkaufswagen
shopping trolley

♀ das **Einkaufszentrum**, *PLURAL* die
Einkaufszentren
shopping centre

das **Einkommen**, *PLURAL* die **Einkommen**
income

♀ **einladen** *VERB*◇, *PRESENT* **lädt ein**, *IMPERFECT*
lud ein, *PERFECT* **hat eingeladen**
1 to invite
Sie haben uns zum Abendessen
eingeladen. They have invited us for
dinner.
Er hat mich ins Kino eingeladen. He took
me to the cinema.
2 to treat
Ich lade euch ein. I'll treat you.
3 to load *(goods)*

♀ die **Einladung**, *PLURAL* die **Einladungen**
invitation

einleben *VERB*, *PERFECT* **hat sich eingelebt**
sich einleben to settle in

die **Einleitung**, *PLURAL* die **Einleitungen**
introduction

♀ **einlösen** *VERB*, *PERFECT* **hat eingelöst**
to cash *(a cheque)*

♀ **einmal** *ADVERB*
1 once
Ich war erst einmal in Spanien. I've only
been to Spain once.
Wir gehen einmal pro Woche
schwimmen. We go swimming once a
week.
Es war einmal ... Once upon a time ...
2 one day *(in the future)*
Ich möchte einmal nach Brasilien fahren.
I'd like to go to Brazil one day.
3 auf einmal suddenly
Auf einmal gingen die Lichter aus.
Suddenly the lights went out.
4 auf einmal at the same time
Sie kamen alle auf einmal. They all came at
the same time.
5 nicht einmal not even
Er hat sich nicht einmal verabschiedet. He
didn't even say goodbye.
6 noch einmal again
Können Sie das bitte noch einmal
erklären? Could you explain that again,

please?
7 Es geht nun einmal nicht. It's just not
possible.

einmalig *ADJECTIVE*
1 unique
2 fantastic
3 single, one-off *(payment)*

einmischen *VERB*, *PERFECT* **hat sich
eingemischt**
sich einmischen to interfere

die **Einmündung**, *PLURAL* die
Einmündungen
1 junction *(of roads)*
2 confluence *(of rivers)*

einnehmen *VERB*◇, *PRESENT* **nimmt
ein**, *IMPERFECT* **nahm ein**, *PERFECT* **hat
eingenommen**
to take

einordnen *VERB*, *PERFECT* **hat eingeordnet**
1 to put in order
2 sich einordnen to fit in *(with other people)*
3 sich einordnen to get in lane *(when driving)*

♀ **einpacken** *VERB*, *PERFECT* **hat eingepackt**
1 to pack
2 to wrap *(a present)*

einplanen *VERB*, *PERFECT* **hat eingeplant**
to plan for

einreichen *VERB*, *PERFECT* **hat eingereicht**
to hand in

die **Einreise**, *PLURAL* die **Einreisen**
entry

einreisen *VERB*, *PERFECT* **ist eingereist**
in ein Land einreisen to enter a country
Er reiste nach Italien ein. He entered Italy.

♀ **einrichten** *VERB*, *PERFECT* **hat eingerichtet**
1 to furnish *(a room, a house)*
2 to set up *(an organization, an account)*
3 to arrange
Kannst du es so einrichten, dass du
vormittags kommst? Can you arrange to
come in the morning?
4 sich einrichten to furnish your home
5 sich auf etwas einrichten to be prepared
for something
Sie waren nicht auf den Schnee
eingerichtet. They were not prepared for
the snow.

die **Einrichtung**, *PLURAL* die **Einrichtungen**
1 furnishing
2 furnishings
3 setting up
4 institution

◇ **irregular verb;** *SEP* **separable verb; for more help with verbs see centre section**

staatliche Einrichtungen state institutions

ℰ **eins** NUMBER
one
Es steht eins zu eins. The score is one all.
Es ist eins. It's one o'clock.

eins PRONOUN ▸ SEE **einer**

eins ADJECTIVE
Mir ist alles eins. It's all the same to me.

die **Eins**, PLURAL die **Einsen**
1 **one**
2 **very good** (school mark)

einsam ADJECTIVE
lonely

die **Einsamkeit**
loneliness

einsammeln VERB, PERFECT **hat**
eingesammelt
to collect

der **Einsatz**
1 **use**
2 **stake** (when betting)

ℰ **einschalten** VERB, PERFECT **hat eingeschaltet**
1 **to switch on** (a radio, TV)
2 **sich einschalten to intervene**

ℰ **einschlafen** VERB◇, PRESENT **schläft**
ein, IMPERFECT **schlief ein**, PERFECT **ist**
eingeschlafen
to go to sleep

einschließen VERB◇, IMPERFECT **schloss ein**,
PERFECT **hat eingeschlossen**
1 **to lock in**
2 **sich einschließen to lock yourself in**
3 **to include**

einschließlich PREPOSITION (+ GEN)
including
Wir sind zehn Personen einschließlich der
Kinder. There are ten of us including the
children.

einschließlich ADVERB
inclusive

einschränken VERB, PERFECT **hat**
eingeschränkt
1 **to restrict**
2 **to cut back**
3 **sich einschränken to economize**

einschreiben VERB◇, IMPERFECT **schrieb sich**
ein, PERFECT **hat sich eingeschrieben**
1 **sich einschreiben to enrol** (at university)
2 **sich einschreiben to put your name down**
(on a list)
sich einschreiben to register (for a course)

das **Einschreiben**, PLURAL die **Einschreiben**
registered letter, registered parcel
Ich habe es per Einschreiben geschickt. I
sent it registered.

einsehen VERB◇, PRESENT **sieht ein**, IMPERFECT
sah ein, PERFECT **hat eingesehen**
1 **to realize**
2 **to see**
Das sehe ich nicht ein. I don't see why.

einseitig ADJECTIVE
one-sided

einsenden VERB◇, IMPERFECT **sendete ein/**
sandte ein, PERFECT **hat eingesendet/hat**
eingesandt
to send in

einsetzen VERB, PERFECT **hat eingesetzt**
1 **to put in** (a missing part)
2 **to use**
Während der Weltmeisterschaft wurden
Sonderzüge eingesetzt. Special trains
were put on during the World Cup.
3 **to deploy** (troops, weapons)
4 **to start** (of rain, snow)
5 **sich für jemanden einsetzen to support**
somebody
6 **sich für etwas einsetzen to fight for**
something

die **Einsicht**, PLURAL die **Einsichten**
1 **insight**
2 **sense**
3 Er ist zu der Einsicht gekommen, dass ...
He's come to realize that ...

einsperren VERB, PERFECT **hat eingesperrt**
to lock up

einsprachig ADJECTIVE
monolingual

der **Einspruch**, PLURAL die **Einsprüche**
objection

einst ADVERB
1 **once**
2 **one day** (in the future)

einstecken VERB, PERFECT **hat eingesteckt**
1 **to put in**
2 **to post** (a letter)
3 **etwas einstecken to put something in your**
pocket or bag, to take something
Hast du etwas Geld eingesteckt? Have you
taken some money?
4 (informal) **to take** (insults, criticism)
Er musste ziemlich viel Kritik einstecken.
He had to take a lot of criticism.

A B C D E F G H I J K L M N O P Q R S T U V W X Y Z

ℰ indicates key words

einsteigen VERB◇, IMPERFECT **stieg ein**, PERFECT **ist eingestiegen**
1 to get in
2 to get on *(a bus or train)*
Wir stiegen in den Bus ein. We got on the bus.

einstellen VERB, PERFECT **hat eingestellt**
1 to employ *(in a job)*
2 to adjust *(a machine)*
3 to focus *(a camera)*
4 to tune into *(a radio station)*
5 to stop
6 sich auf etwas einstellen to be prepared for something
Die Fahrgäste müssen sich auf neue Streiks einstellen. Passengers have to be prepared for more strikes.
7 sich auf etwas einstellen to adjust to something
Sie haben sich schnell auf die neue Situation eingestellt. They adjusted quickly to the new situation.

die **Einstellung**, PLURAL die **Einstellungen**
1 employment
2 adjustment
3 stopping
4 take *(of a film)*
5 attitude
Was ist seine politische Einstellung? What are his political views?

der **Einstieg**, PLURAL die **Einstiege**
1 entrance
2 start

einstürzen VERB, PERFECT **ist eingestürzt**
to collapse

einstweilen ADVERB
1 for the time being
2 meanwhile

eintausend NUMBER
one thousand

einteilen VERB, PERFECT **hat eingeteilt**
1 to divide up
2 to organize
Ich muss mir meine Zeit gut einteilen. I have to organize my time well.

der **Eintopf**, PLURAL die **Eintöpfe**
stew

der **Eintrag**, PLURAL die **Einträge**
entry

eintragen VERB◇, PRESENT **trägt ein**, IMPERFECT **trug ein**, PERFECT **hat eingetragen**
1 to enter, to write
2 sich eintragen to put your name down

einträglich ADJECTIVE
profitable

eintreffen VERB◇, PRESENT **trifft ein**, IMPERFECT **traf ein**, PERFECT **ist eingetroffen**
1 to arrive
2 to come true

eintreten VERB◇, PRESENT **tritt ein**, IMPERFECT **trat ein**, PERFECT **ist eingetreten**
1 to enter
2 in etwas eintreten to join something
Ich bin in den Tennisverein eingetreten. I joined the tennis club.
3 für jemanden eintreten to stand up for somebody

der **Eintritt**
1 entrance
2 admission
'Eintritt frei' 'Admission free'

das **Eintrittsgeld**, PLURAL die **Eintrittsgelder**
admission charge

die **Eintrittskarte**, PLURAL die **Eintrittskarten**
(admission) ticket

der **Eintrittspreis**, PLURAL die **Eintrittspreise**
admission charge

einverstanden ADJECTIVE
1 einverstanden sein to agree
Einverstanden! Okay!
2 mit jemandem einverstanden sein to approve of somebody

der **Einwand**, PLURAL die **Einwände**
objection

der **Einwanderer**, PLURAL die **Einwanderer**
immigrant *(male)*

die **Einwanderin**, PLURAL die **Einwanderinnen**
immigrant *(female)*

einwandern VERB, PERFECT **ist eingewandert**
to immigrate
Seine Großeltern sind nach Europa eingewandert. His grandparents came to Europe as immigrants.

die **Einwanderung**
immigration

einwärts ADVERB
inwards

die **Einwegflasche**, *PLURAL* die **Einwegflaschen**
non-returnable bottle

einweichen *VERB*, *PERFECT* **hat eingeweicht**
to soak *(washing)*

einwerfen *VERB*✧, *PRESENT* **wirft ein**, *IMPERFECT* **warf ein**, *PERFECT* **hat eingeworfen**
1 to post
2 to put in *(a coin, money)*
3 to throw in
4 to smash

ℐ der **Einwohner**, *PLURAL* die **Einwohner**
inhabitant *(male)*

ℐ die **Einwohnerin**, *PLURAL* die **Einwohnerinnen**
inhabitant *(female)*

das **Einwohnermeldeamt**, *PLURAL* die **Einwohnermeldeämter**
registration office *(where residents have to register a change of address)*

der **Einwurf**, *PLURAL* die **Einwürfe**
throw-in *(in sport)*

die **Einzahl**
singular *(in grammar)*

einzahlen *VERB*, *PERFECT* **hat eingezahlt**
to pay in

das **Einzel**, *PLURAL* die **Einzel**
singles *(in sport)*

die **Einzelfahrkarte**, *PLURAL* die **Einzelfahrkarten**
single ticket

das **Einzelhaus**, *PLURAL* die **Einzelhäuser**
detached house

die **Einzelheit**, *PLURAL* die **Einzelheiten**
detail

die **Einzelkarte**, *PLURAL* die **Einzelkarten**
single ticket

ℐ das **Einzelkind**, *PLURAL* die **Einzelkinder**
only child

einzeln *ADJECTIVE*
1 single
2 individual
3 odd *(sock, for example)*
einzeln *ADVERB*
1 individually
2 separately, one at a time
Bitte einzeln eintreten. Please enter one at a time.

der/die/das **Einzelne**, *PLURAL* die **Einzelnen**
1 der/die Einzelne the individual
2 Einzelne some
3 ein Einzelner/eine Einzelne/ein Einzelnes a single one
jeder/jede/jedes Einzelne every single one
4 im Einzelnen in detail
Er wollte nicht ins Einzelne gehen. He didn't want to go into detail.

ℐ das **Einzelzimmer**, *PLURAL* die **Einzelzimmer**
single room

einziehen *VERB*✧, *IMPERFECT* **zog ein**, *PERFECT* **hat eingezogen**
1 to collect *(payment)*
2 to draw in *(its feelers, claws)*
3 Sie musste den Kopf einziehen. She had to to duck.
4 *PERFECT* ist eingezogen to move in
Wann zieht ihr in die neue Wohnung ein? When are you moving into your new flat?
5 *PERFECT* ist eingezogen to soak in

einzig *ADJECTIVE*
only
Tom ist sein einziger Freund. Tom is his only friend.
Ich habe sie nur ein einziges Mal getroffen. I've only met her once.

der/die/das **Einzige**, *PLURAL* die **Einzigen**
1 der/die/das Einzige the only one
2 ein Einziger/eine Einzige/ein Einziges a single one
kein Einziger/keine Einzige/kein Einziges not a single one
3 Das ist das Einzige, was mich stört. That's the only thing that bothers me.

ℐ das **Eis**
1 ice
2 ice cream

ℐ die **Eisbahn**, *PLURAL* die **Eisbahnen**
ice rink

der **Eisbär**, *PLURAL* die **Eisbären**
polar bear

der **Eisbecher**, *PLURAL* die **Eisbecher**
ice cream sundae

das **Eiscafé**, *PLURAL* die **Eiscafés**
ice cream parlour, ice cream cafe

die **Eisdiele**, *PLURAL* die **Eisdielen**
ice cream parlour, ice cream shop

das **Eisen**
iron

die **Eisenbahn**, *PLURAL* die **Eisenbahnen**
railway

ℐ indicates key words

eisern | **Elfmeter**

eisern ADJECTIVE
iron

die Eishalle, PLURAL **die Eishallen**
ice rink, ice stadium

das Eishockey
ice hockey

eisig ADJECTIVE
icy

der Eiskaffee, PLURAL **die Eiskaffee(s)**
iced coffee

eiskalt ADJECTIVE
1 ice-cold (drink)
2 freezing cold

das Eislaufen
ice skating

der Eisläufer, PLURAL **die Eisläufer**
skater (on ice) (male)

die Eisläuferin, PLURAL **die Eisläuferinnen**
skater (on ice) (female)

die Eissorte, PLURAL **die Eissorten**
ice cream flavour

die Eissporthalle, PLURAL **die Eissporthallen**
ice rink

der Eiswürfel, PLURAL **die Eiswürfel**
ice cube

der Eiszapfen, PLURAL **die Eiszapfen**
icicle

die Eiszeit, PLURAL **die Eiszeiten**
ice age

eitel ADJECTIVE
vain

die Eitelkeit
vanity

der Eiter
pus

das Eiweiß
1 egg white
2 protein

der Ekel
disgust

♀ **ekelhaft** ADJECTIVE
disgusting

ekeln VERB, PERFECT **hat sich geekelt**
sich vor etwas ekeln to find something
disgusting

eklig ADJECTIVE
disgusting

das Ekzem, PLURAL **die Ekzeme**
eczema

♀ **der Elefant**, PLURAL **die Elefanten**
elephant

elegant ADJECTIVE
elegant, stylish

♀ **der Elektriker**, PLURAL **die Elektriker**
electrician

> **WORD TIP** Professions, hobbies, and sports
> don't take an article in German: Er ist Elektriker.

♀ **die Elektrikerin**, PLURAL **die Elektrikerinnen**
electrician

> **WORD TIP** Professions, hobbies, and sports
> don't take an article in German: Sie ist
> Elektrikerin.

elektrisch ADJECTIVE
electrical

die Elektrizität
electricity

das Elektrogerät, PLURAL **die Elektrogeräte**
electrical appliance

das Elektrogeschäft, PLURAL **die Elektrogeschäfte**
electrical shop

der Elektroherd, PLURAL **die Elektroherde**
electric cooker

die Elektronik
electronics

elektronisch ADJECTIVE
electronic

der Elektrorasierer, PLURAL **die Elektrorasierer**
electric razor

das Element, PLURAL **die Elemente**
element

elend ADJECTIVE
1 miserable
2 terrible

das Elend
misery

♀ **elf** NUMBER
eleven

die Elfe, PLURAL **die Elfen**
fairy

der Elfmeter, PLURAL **die Elfmeter**
penalty (in soccer)

◇ irregular verb; SEP separable verb; for more help with verbs see centre section

der **Ellbogen**, *PLURAL* die **Ellbogen**
elbow

ℰ die **Eltern** *PLURAL NOUN*
parents

der **Elternsprechabend**, *PLURAL* die
Elternsprechabende
parents' evening

das **Email**, *PLURAL* die **Emails**
enamel

ℰ die **E-Mail**, *PLURAL* die **E-Mails**
email

empfahl ▸ SEE **empfehlen**

der **Empfang**, *PLURAL* die **Empfänge**
1 reception
2 receipt *(of goods or a letter)*

empfangen *VERB◇*, *PRESENT* **empfängt**,
IMPERFECT **empfing**, *PERFECT* **hat**
empfangen
to receive

die **Empfängnisverhütung**
contraception

der **Empfangschef**, *PLURAL* die
Empfangschefs
head receptionist

ℰ die **Empfangsdame**, *PLURAL* die
Empfangsdamen
receptionist

> **WORD TIP** Professions, hobbies, and sports
> don't take an article in German: Sie ist
> Empfangsdame.

ℰ **empfehlen** *VERB◇*, *PRESENT* **empfiehlt**,
IMPERFECT **empfahl**, *PERFECT* **hat empfohlen**
to recommend

die **Empfehlung**, *PLURAL* die **Empfehlungen**
recommendation

ℰ **empfindlich** *ADJECTIVE*
1 sensitive
2 delicate
3 touchy

empfing ▸ SEE **empfangen**

empfohlen ▸ SEE **empfehlen**

empört *ADJECTIVE*
indignant

ℰ das **Ende**, *PLURAL* die **Enden**
1 end
Sie kommen Ende April. They're coming at
the end of April.
Biegen Sie am Ende der Straße links ab.

Turn left at the end of the road.
2 am Ende in the end
Am Ende ist alles gutgegangen. In the end
it all went well.
3 ending *(of a film, novel)*
4 zu Ende sein to be finished, to be over
Das Schuljahr ist schon zu Ende. The
school year is over already.
5 Ende gut, alles gut. All's well that ends
well.

ℰ **enden** *VERB*, *PERFECT* **hat geendet**
to end

endgültig *ADJECTIVE*
1 final *(result, decision)*
2 definite *(proof)*

die **Endivie**, *PLURAL* die **Endivien**
endive

endlich *ADVERB*
finally, at last
Na endlich! At last!

endlos *ADJECTIVE*
endless

das **Endspiel**, *PLURAL* die **Endspiele**
final

die **Endstation**, *PLURAL* die **Endstationen**
terminus

die **Endung**, *PLURAL* die **Endungen**
ending

ℰ die **Energie**
energy

energisch *ADJECTIVE*
energetic

ℰ **eng** *ADJECTIVE*
1 narrow
2 tight
3 close
Susi und Anne sind eng befreundet. Susi
and Anne are close friends.

engagiert *ADJECTIVE*
1 committed, dedicated
2 active

der **Engel**, *PLURAL* die **Engel**
angel

ℰ **England** *NEUTER NOUN*
England
Sie kommen aus England. They are from
England.

ℰ der **Engländer**, *PLURAL* die **Engländer**
Englishman

♀ die **Engländerin**, PLURAL die
Engländerinnen
Englishwoman

♀ **englisch** ADJECTIVE
English

> **WORD TIP** Adjectives never have capitals
> in German, even for regions, countries, or
> nationalities.

das **Englisch**
English
Sag es auf Englisch! Say it in English.

der **Enkel**, PLURAL die **Enkel**
grandson

die **Enkelin**, PLURAL die **Enkelinnen**
granddaughter

das **Enkelkind**, PLURAL die **Enkelkinder**
grandchild

enorm ADJECTIVE
1 huge, enormous
2 amazing (achievement)

entdecken VERB, PERFECT **hat entdeckt**
to discover

die **Entdeckung**, PLURAL die **Entdeckungen**
discovery

die **Ente**, PLURAL die **Enten**
duck

entfernen VERB, PERFECT **hat entfernt**
to remove

entfernt ADJECTIVE
1 distant
2 Die Stadt liegt zehn Kilometer entfernt.
The town is ten kilometres away.
entfernt ADVERB
distantly
Wir sind entfernt verwandt. We are
distantly related.

die **Entfernung**, PLURAL die **Entfernungen**
distance

entführen VERB, PERFECT **hat entführt**
1 to kidnap
2 to hijack

der **Entführer**, PLURAL die **Entführer**
1 hijacker (male)
2 kidnapper (male)

die **Entführerin**, PLURAL die **Entführerinnen**
1 hijacker (female)
2 kidnapper (female)

die **Entführung**, PLURAL die **Entführungen**
1 hijacking

2 kidnapping

entgegen PREPOSITION (+ DAT)
contrary to

entgegengesetzt ADJECTIVE
1 opposite
2 opposing (views)

entgegenkommen VERB◇, IMPERFECT
kam entgegen, PERFECT **ist
entgegengekommen**
1 to come towards
Uns kam ein Lastwagen entgegen. A lorry
was coming towards us.
2 Er hatte mich schon gesehen und kam mir
entgegen. He had already seen me and
came to meet me.
3 jemandem auf halbem Wege
entgegenkommen to meet somebody
halfway

entgegenkommend ADJECTIVE
1 obliging
2 der entgegenkommende Verkehr the
oncoming traffic

das **Entgelt**
payment

das **Enthaarungsmittel**, PLURAL die
Enthaarungsmittel
hair remover, depilatory

♀ **enthalten** VERB◇, PRESENT **enthält**, IMPERFECT
enthielt, PERFECT **hat enthalten**
1 to contain
2 sich enthalten to abstain
Sie enthielt sich (der Stimme). She
abstained.
3 in etwas enthalten sein to be included in
something
Die Mehrwertsteuer ist im Preis
enthalten. VAT is included in the price.

entkommen VERB◇, IMPERFECT **entkam**,
PERFECT **ist entkommen**
to escape

♀ **entlang** PREPOSITION (+ ACC or + DAT)
along
Wir radelten die Straße entlang. We
cycled along the road.
Der Weg führt am Fluss entlang. The path
runs along the river.

entlanggehen VERB◇, IMPERFECT **ging
entlang**, PERFECT **ist entlanggegangen**
to walk along

◇ irregular verb; SEP separable verb; for more help with verbs see centre section

entlanglaufen VERB◇, PRESENT **läuft entlang**, IMPERFECT **lief entlang**, PERFECT **ist entlanggelaufen**
to run along

entlassen VERB◇, PRESENT **entlässt**, IMPERFECT **entließ**, PERFECT **hat entlassen**
1 to dismiss *(from a job)*
2 to discharge *(from hospital)*
3 to release *(from prison)*

die **Entlassung**, PLURAL die **Entlassungen**
1 dismissal *(from a job)*
2 discharge *(from hospital)*
3 release *(from prison)*

entmutigen VERB, PERFECT **hat entmutigt**
to discourage

entrahmt ADJECTIVE
skimmed *(milk)*

entschädigen VERB, PERFECT **hat entschädigt**
to compensate

die **Entschädigung**
compensation

ℓ **entscheiden** VERB◇, IMPERFECT **entschied**, PERFECT **hat entschieden**
1 to decide (on)
2 sich entscheiden to decide
Ich habe mich noch nicht entschieden.
I haven't decided yet.

entscheidend ADJECTIVE
decisive, crucial

die **Entscheidung**, PLURAL die **Entscheidungen**
decision

die **Entschiedenheit**
decisiveness

entschließen VERB◇, IMPERFECT **entschloss sich**, PERFECT **hat sich entschlossen**
1 sich entschließen to decide
2 sich anders entschließen to change your mind
Karl hat sich anders entschlossen. Karl has changed his mind.

entschlossen ADJECTIVE
determined

der **Entschluss**, PLURAL die **Entschlüsse**
decision

ℓ **entschuldigen** VERB◇, PERFECT **hat entschuldigt**
1 to excuse
Entschuldigen Sie bitte, ... *(with a question or request)* Excuse me, ...
2 sich entschuldigen to apologize

Ich habe mich bei Mike entschuldigt.
I apologized to Mike.

ℓ die **Entschuldigung**, PLURAL die **Entschuldigungen**
1 apology
jemanden um Entschuldigung bitten to apologize to somebody
2 Entschuldigung! Sorry!
3 Entschuldigung, ... *(with a question or request)* Excuse me, ...
Entschuldigung, können Sie mir sagen, wie ich zum Bahnhof komme? Excuse me, could you tell me the way to the station?
4 excuse
5 note *(for the teacher, from parents)*

der **Entschuldigungsbrief**, PLURAL die **Entschuldigungsbriefe**
letter of apology

das **Entsetzen**
horror

entsetzlich ADJECTIVE
1 horrible
2 terrible

entsetzt ADJECTIVE
horrified

entsorgen VERB, PERFECT **hat entsorgt**
to dispose of *(waste)*

die **Entsorgung**
waste disposal

entspannen VERB, PERFECT **hat sich entspannt**
1 sich entspannen to relax
2 sich entspannen to become less tense *(of a situation)*

ℓ **entspannend** ADJECTIVE
relaxing

entsprechen VERB◇, PRESENT **entspricht**, IMPERFECT **entsprach**, PERFECT **hat entsprochen**
1 einer Sache entsprechen to be equivalent to something
2 einer Sache entsprechen to correspond to something *(the truth, a description)*
3 einer Sache entsprechen to meet something *(requirements)*
Es entspricht nicht den Anforderungen. It does not meet the requirements.

entsprechend ADJECTIVE
1 corresponding
2 appropriate

entsprechend PREPOSITION (+ DAT)
in accordance with

ℓ indicates key words

entstehen VERB◇, IMPERFECT **entstand**, PERFECT **ist entstanden**
1 to develop
2 to be caused
Bei dem Unfall entstand kein Schaden.
The accident didn't cause any damage.

enttäuschen VERB, PERFECT **hat enttäuscht**
to disappoint

enttäuschend ADJECTIVE
disappointing

♀ **enttäuscht** ADJECTIVE
disappointed

die **Enttäuschung**, PLURAL die **Enttäuschungen**
disappointment

♀ **entweder** CONJUNCTION
either
Die Party ist entweder heute oder morgen. The party is either today or tomorrow

entwerfen VERB◇, PRESENT **entwirft**, IMPERFECT **entwarf**, PERFECT **hat entworfen**
1 to design
2 to draw up

entwerten VERB, PERFECT **hat entwertet**
1 to devalue
2 to stamp (a ticket in a machine found on stations, trams, buses, and platforms; you have to stamp your ticket before each journey)

der **Entwerter**, PLURAL die **Entwerter**
ticket stamping machine (these machines are found on stations, trams, buses, and platforms; you have to stamp your ticket before each journey)

entwickeln VERB, PERFECT **hat entwickelt**
1 to develop
2 to display (ability, a characteristic)
3 sich entwickeln to develop

die **Entwicklung**, PLURAL die **Entwicklungen**
1 development
2 developing (of a film)

die **Entwicklungshilfe**
development aid

das **Entwicklungsland**, PLURAL die **Entwicklungsländer**
developing country

entwürdigend ADJECTIVE
degrading

der **Entwurf**, PLURAL die **Entwürfe**
1 design
2 draft

die **Entziehungskur**, PLURAL die **Entziehungskuren**
course of withdrawal treatment

entzückend ADJECTIVE
delightful

entzünden VERB, PERFECT **hat entzündet**
1 to light (a fire, match)
2 sich entzünden to become inflamed (of a wound)
3 sich entzünden to ignite (of gas, for example)

die **Entzündung**, PLURAL die **Entzündungen**
inflammation

der **Enzian**, PLURAL die **Enziane**
gentian

die **Epidemie**, PLURAL die **Epidemien**
epidemic

♀ **er** PRONOUN
1 he
2 (when referring to a thing or animal) it
'Wo ist mein Mantel?' – 'Er liegt auf dem Stuhl.' 'Where's my coat?' – 'It's on the chair.'
3 him (stressed)
Er war es. It was him.

erben VERB, PERFECT **hat geerbt**
to inherit

erblich ADJECTIVE
hereditary

erbrechen VERB◇, PRESENT **erbricht**, IMPERFECT **erbrach**, PERFECT **hat erbrochen**
1 to bring up (food)
2 sich erbrechen to be sick

die **Erbschaft**, PLURAL die **Erbschaften**
inheritance

die **Erbse**, PLURAL die **Erbsen**
pea

das **Erdbeben**, PLURAL die **Erdbeben**
earthquake

♀ die **Erdbeere**, PLURAL die **Erdbeeren**
strawberry

♀ die **Erde**
1 earth, soil
2 ground
Der Schal lag auf der Erde. The scarf was lying on the ground.
3 Earth

◇ irregular verb; SEP separable verb; for more help with verbs see centre section

4 earth *(for electricity)*

das **Erdgas**
natural gas

ℓ das **Erdgeschoss**, PLURAL die **Erdgeschosse**
ground floor
Unsere Wohnung ist im Erdgeschoss. Our
flat is on the ground floor.

ℓ die **Erdkunde**
geography

die **Erdnuss**, PLURAL die **Erdnüsse**
peanut

das **Erdöl**
oil

ereignen VERB, PERFECT **hat sich ereignet**
sich ereignen to happen

das **Ereignis**, PLURAL die **Ereignisse**
event

erfahren VERB◇, PRESENT **erfährt**, IMPERFECT
erfuhr, PERFECT **hat erfahren**
1 to hear, to learn
2 to experience
erfahren ADJECTIVE
experienced

ℓ die **Erfahrung**, PLURAL die **Erfahrungen**
experience

erfinden VERB◇, IMPERFECT **erfand**, PERFECT **hat**
erfunden
to invent

die **Erfindung**, PLURAL die **Erfindungen**
invention

der **Erfolg**, PLURAL die **Erfolge**
1 success
Erfolg haben to be successful
2 Erfolg versprechend promising
3 Viel Erfolg! Good luck!

erfolglos ADJECTIVE
unsuccessful

ℓ **erfolgreich** ADJECTIVE
successful

erfolgversprechend ▸ SEE **Erfolg**

erforderlich ADJECTIVE
necessary

erforschen VERB, PERFECT **hat erforscht**
1 to explore
2 to investigate

erfreulicherweise ADVERB
happily

erfreut ADJECTIVE
pleased

erfrieren VERB◇, IMPERFECT **erfror**, PERFECT **hat**
erfroren
1 to freeze to death
2 to be killed by frost *(plant)*

die **Erfrischung**, PLURAL die **Erfrischungen**
refreshment

das **Erfrischungsgetränk**, PLURAL die
Erfrischungsgetränke
soft drink

der **Erfrischungsstand**, PLURAL die
Erfrischungsstände
refreshment stall

erfüllen VERB, PERFECT **hat erfüllt**
to fulfil
sich erfüllen to come true

das **Ergebnis**, PLURAL die **Ergebnisse**
result

ergreifen VERB◇, IMPERFECT **ergriff**, PERFECT **hat**
ergriffen
1 to seize, to grab
2 to take *(measures, an opportunity)*
3 to take up *(a job, career)*
4 to move, to affect
Die Nachricht von ihrem Tod hat uns tief
ergriffen. We were deeply affected by the
news of her death.
5 die Flucht ergreifen to flee

ergreifend ADJECTIVE
moving

erhalten VERB◇, PRESENT **erhält**, IMPERFECT
erhielt, PERFECT **hat erhalten**
1 to receive
2 to preserve

erhältlich ADJECTIVE
obtainable

die **Erhaltung**
1 preservation
2 conservation
3 maintenance

erheben VERB◇, IMPERFECT **erhob**, PERFECT **hat**
erhoben
1 to raise
2 to charge *(a fee)*
3 Protest erheben to protest
4 sich erheben to rise up *(in a rebellion)*

erheblich ADJECTIVE
considerable

erheitern VERB, PERFECT **hat erheitert**
to amuse

A B C D E F G H I J K L M N O P Q R S T U V W X Y Z

ℓ indicates key words

erhitzen *VERB*, *PERFECT* **hat erhitzt**
to heat

erhöhen *VERB*, *PERFECT* **hat erhöht**
1 to increase
2 sich erhöhen to rise

die **Erhöhung**, *PLURAL* die **Erhöhungen**
increase

erholen *VERB*, *PERFECT* **hat sich erholt**
1 sich erholen to have a rest, to relax
Ich habe mich in den Ferien gut erholt. I had a good rest on holiday.
2 sich erholen to recover
Er hat sich von seiner Krankheit erholt. He has recovered from his illness.

erholsam *ADJECTIVE*
restful, relaxing

die **Erholung**
1 rest, relaxation
Sie ist zur Erholung in die Berge gefahren. She went to the mountains for a rest.
2 recovery

♪ **erinnern** *VERB*, *PERFECT* **hat erinnert**
1 to remind
Bitte erinnern Sie mich morgen noch einmal daran. Please remind me again tomorrow.
2 sich (an jemanden/etwas) erinnern to remember (somebody/something)
Ich erinnere mich noch gut an ihn. I remember him well.

die **Erinnerung**, *PLURAL* die **Erinnerungen**
1 memory
2 souvenir

erkälten *VERB*, *PERFECT* **hat sich erkältet**
1 sich erkälten to catch a cold
2 erkältet sein to have a cold
Ben ist erkältet. Ben has a cold.

♪ die **Erkältung**, *PLURAL* die **Erkältungen**
cold

erkennbar *ADJECTIVE*
recognizable

erkennen *VERB◇*, *IMPERFECT* **erkannte**, *PERFECT* **hat erkannt**
1 to recognize
2 to realize

erklären *VERB*, *PERFECT* **hat erklärt**
1 to explain
Kannst du mir das erklären? Can you explain it to me?
2 to declare
3 sich zu etwas bereit erklären to agree to something

die **Erklärung**, *PLURAL* die **Erklärungen**
1 explanation
2 declaration
3 eine öffentliche Erklärung a public statement

erkundigen *VERB*, *PERFECT* **hat sich erkundigt**
1 sich nach etwas erkundigen to enquire about something
Ich werde mich nach den Zügen erkundigen. I'm going to enquire about the trains.
2 sich nach jemandem erkundigen to ask after somebody
Susi hat sich nach dir erkundigt. Susi was asking after you.

die **Erkundigung**, *PLURAL* die **Erkundigungen**
enquiry

♪ **erlauben** *VERB*, *PERFECT* **hat erlaubt**
1 to allow
jemandem erlauben etwas zu tun to allow somebody to do something
2 sich etwas erlauben to treat yourself to something
3 Er denkt, dass er sich alles erlauben kann. He thinks he can do whatever he likes.
4 Erlauben Sie mal! *(informal)* Do you mind!

♪ die **Erlaubnis**
permission

erlaubt *ADJECTIVE*
allowed
Rauchen ist hier nicht erlaubt. Smoking is not allowed here.

erleben *VERB*, *PERFECT* **hat erlebt**
1 to experience
2 to have (a disappointment, a surprise, an experience)
3 to live to see
Er hat die Geburt seines Enkels nicht mehr erlebt. He didn't live to see the birth of his grandson.

das **Erlebnis**, *PLURAL* die **Erlebnisse**
experience

erledigen *VERB*, *PERFECT* **hat erledigt**
to deal with, to do

erledigt *ADJECTIVE*
1 settled
2 *(informal)* worn out

erleichtert *ADJECTIVE*
relieved

♦ irregular verb; *SEP* separable verb; for more help with verbs see centre section

die **Erleichterung**
relief

erleiden VERB◇, IMPERFECT **erlitt**, PERFECT **hat erlitten**
to suffer

der **Erlös**, PLURAL die **Erlöse**
proceeds

erloschen ADJECTIVE
1 out, extinguished
2 extinct (a volcano)

ermäßigen VERB, PERFECT **hat ermäßigt**
to reduce

ermäßigt ADJECTIVE
reduced

ℓ die **Ermäßigung**, PLURAL die **Ermäßigungen**
reduction, discount

ermorden VERB, PERFECT **hat ermordet**
to murder

ermüdend ADJECTIVE
tiring

ermutigen VERB, PERFECT **hat ermutigt**
to encourage

ernähren VERB, PERFECT **hat ernährt**
1 to feed
2 sich von etwas ernähren to live on something
Sie ernähren sich von Nudeln. They live on pasta.
3 to support (a family)

die **Ernährung**
1 diet
Eine gesunde Ernährung ist sehr wichtig. A healthy diet is very important.
2 nutrition

erneuern VERB, PERFECT **hat erneuert**
to renew

erneut ADJECTIVE
renewed
erneut ADVERB
once again

ℓ **ernst** ADJECTIVE
serious

der **Ernst**
1 seriousness
im Ernst seriously
2 Ist das dein Ernst? Are you serious?

ℓ **ernsthaft** ADJECTIVE
serious

ernstlich ADJECTIVE
serious

die **Ernte**, PLURAL die **Ernten**
harvest
Die Bauern bringen die Ernte ein. The farmers are gathering in the harvest.

ernten VERB, PERFECT **hat geerntet**
to harvest

erobern VERB, PERFECT **hat erobert**
to conquer

die **Eroberung**, PLURAL die **Eroberungen**
conquest

eröffnen, PERFECT **hat eröffnet**
to open

die **Eröffnung**, PLURAL die **Eröffnungen**
opening

die **Erpressung**, PLURAL die **Erpressungen**
blackmail

erraten VERB◇, PRESENT **errät**, IMPERFECT **erriet**, PERFECT **hat erraten**
to guess

erregen VERB, PERFECT **hat erregt**
1 to arouse
2 to cause
Sie erregte viel Aufsehen. She caused a sensation.

der **Erreger**, PLURAL die **Erreger**
germ

die **Erregung**
excitement

erreichen VERB, PERFECT **hat erreicht**
1 to reach
2 to catch (a train, a bus)
Hast du den letzten Zug noch erreicht? Did you manage to catch the last train?
3 to achieve (a goal, aim)
4 Irene ist telefonisch zu erreichen. Irene can be contacted by phone.

erröten VERB, PERFECT **ist errötet**
to blush

ℓ der **Ersatz**
replacement, substitute

das **Ersatzmittel**, PLURAL die **Ersatzmittel**
substitute (material, ingredient)

der **Ersatzreifen**, PLURAL die **Ersatzreifen**
spare tyre

der **Ersatzspieler**, PLURAL die **Ersatzspieler**
substitute (male)

A
B
C
D
E
F
G
H
I
J
K
L
M
N
O
P
Q
R
S
T
U
V
W
X
Y
Z

99

ℓ indicates key words

die **Ersatzspielerin**, PLURAL die
Ersatzspielerinnen
substitute *(female)*

das **Ersatzteil**, PLURAL die **Ersatzteile**
spare part

erschaffen VERB◇, IMPERFECT **erschuf**, PERFECT
erschaffen
to create

erscheinen VERB◇, IMPERFECT **erschien**, PERFECT
ist erschienen
to appear

erschöpft ADJECTIVE
exhausted

erschrecken¹ VERB, PERFECT **hat erschreckt**
jemanden erschrecken to scare somebody

erschrecken² VERB◇, PRESENT **erschrickt**,
IMPERFECT **erschrak**, PERFECT **ist**
erschrocken
(sich) erschrecken to get a fright

erschreckend ADJECTIVE
alarming

erschrocken ADJECTIVE
1 frightened
2 startled

ersetzen VERB, PERFECT **hat ersetzt**
1 to replace
2 Die Versicherung hat ihm den Schaden
ersetzt. The insurance paid him
compensation for the damage.

die **Ersparnisse** PLURAL NOUN
savings

ℰ **erst** ADVERB
1 first
Erst einmal essen wir etwas. First of all,
we'll have something to eat.
2 only
Ich habe die Neuigkeit eben erst erfahren.
I've only just heard the news.
3 not until
Das Endspiel ist erst nächste Woche. The
final is not until next week.
Oma war erst zufrieden, als die ganze
Familie da war. Granny was not happy until
all the family were there.

erstatten VERB, PERFECT **hat erstattet**
to reimburse

die **Erstattung**, PLURAL die **Erstattungen**
reimbursement

erstaunen VERB, PERFECT **hat erstaunt**
to astonish

erstaunlich ADJECTIVE
astonishing

erstaunt ADJECTIVE
amazed
Ich war erstaunt über seine Einstellung. I
was amazed at his attitude.

erste ▸ SEE **erster**

der/die/das **Erste**, PLURAL die **Ersten**
1 der/die Erste the first (one)
das Erste the first (thing)
2 Dirk kam als Erster. Dirk arrived first.
Marianne ging als Erste. Marianne left
first.
3 als Erster/Erste etwas tun to be the first to
do something
4 als Erstes first of all
5 fürs Erste for the time being

der **Erste-Hilfe-Kasten**, PLURAL die **Erste-**
Hilfe-Kästen
first-aid kit

erstens ADVERB
firstly

ℰ **erster, erste, erstes** ADJECTIVE
first
Mein erstes Rad war rot. My first bike was
red.
der erste Stock the first floor
der erste April the first of April
erste Hilfe first aid

erstklassig ADJECTIVE
first-class

erstmals ADVERB
for the first time

erteilen VERB, PERFECT **hat erteilt**
to give *(advice, information)*

ertragen VERB◇, PRESENT **erträgt**, IMPERFECT
ertrug, PERFECT **hat ertragen**
to bear

ertrinken VERB◇, IMPERFECT **ertrank**, PERFECT
ist ertrunken
to drown
Sie ertrank im See. She drowned in the
lake.

erwachsen ADJECTIVE
grown up

ℰ der/die **Erwachsene**, PLURAL die
Erwachsenen
adult, grown-up

ℰ **erwähnen** VERB, PERFECT **hat erwähnt**
to mention

◇ irregular verb; SEP separable verb; for more help with verbs see centre section

erwarten VERB, PERFECT **hat erwartet**
to expect

die **Erwartung**, PLURAL die **Erwartungen**
expectation

erweitern VERB, PERFECT **hat erweitert**
1 to widen
2 to expand

erwürgen VERB, PERFECT **hat erwürgt**
to strangle

ℰ **erzählen** VERB, PERFECT **hat erzählt**
to tell

die **Erzählung**, PLURAL die **Erzählungen**
story

erzeugen VERB, PERFECT **hat erzeugt**
1 to produce
2 to generate (electricity)

das **Erzeugnis**, PLURAL die **Erzeugnisse**
product

erziehen VERB◇, IMPERFECT **erzog**, PERFECT **hat erzogen**
1 to bring up
2 to educate

ℰ der **Erzieher**, PLURAL die **Erzieher**
1 educator (male)
2 teacher (male)

> **WORD TIP** Professions, hobbies, and sports don't take an article in German: Er ist Erzieher.

ℰ die **Erzieherin**, PLURAL die **Erzieherinnen**
1 educator (female)
2 teacher (female)

> **WORD TIP** Professions, hobbies, and sports don't take an article in German: Sie ist Erzieherin.

ℰ die **Erziehung**
1 upbringing
2 education

ℰ **es** PRONOUN
1 it
Es regnet. It is raining.
Es gefällt mir. I like it.
2 Es gibt ... There is .../There are ...
3 (when referring to a person) he/she
'Wo ist das Baby?' – 'Es schläft.' 'Where's the baby?' – 'He's/She's asleep.'

der **Esel**, PLURAL die **Esel**
donkey

essbar ADJECTIVE
edible

die **Essecke**, PLURAL die **Essecken**
dining area

ℰ **essen** VERB◇, PRESENT **isst**, IMPERFECT **aß**, PERFECT **hat gegessen**
to eat
Iss keine Bonbons. Don't eat sweets.

ℰ das **Essen**
1 meal
2 food

der **Essig**
vinegar

die **Essiggurke**, PLURAL die **Essiggurken**
gherkin

die **Esskastanie**, PLURAL die **Esskastanien**
sweet chestnut

ℰ das **Esszimmer**, PLURAL die **Esszimmer**
dining room

ℰ **Estland** NEUTER NOUN
Estonia

die **Etage**, PLURAL die **Etagen**
floor
Sie wohnen in der zweiten Etage. They live on the second floor.

das **Etagenbett**, PLURAL die **Etagenbetten**
bunk bed

ethnisch ADJECTIVE
ethnic

das **Etikett**, PLURAL die **Etikette(n)**
label

das **Etui**, PLURAL die **Etuis**
case

etwa ADVERB
1 about
Er ist etwa so groß wie du. He's about as tall as you.
2 for example
Sie hat Angst vor kleinen Tieren, wie etwa Mäusen. She's frightened of small animals, mice for example.
3 in etwa more or less
4 Hat Klaus etwa Angst gehabt? Klaus wasn't scared, was he?

ℰ **etwas** PRONOUN, ADVERB
1 something
2 anything
Sonst noch etwas? Anything else?
3 some
Er will auch etwas von dem Geld. He wants some of the money, too.
Noch etwas Kaffee? (Some) more coffee?
4 a little
Gib etwas Zucker in die Soße. Put a little sugar in the sauce.

ℰ indicates key words

Ihr müsst etwas lauter singen. You need to sing a little louder.

die **EU** *ABBREVIATION*
(=*Europäische Union*) EU

♂ **euch** *PRONOUN*
1 *(accusative)* you
Ich habe euch eingeladen. I've invited you.
2 *(dative)* to you
Eva hat es euch geschenkt. Eva gave it to you.
3 *(reflexive)* yourselves

♂ **euer** *ADJECTIVE*
your

die **Eule**, *PLURAL* die **Eulen**
owl

♂ **eurer, eure, eures** *PRONOUN*
yours

♂ der **Euro**
euro
Ein Euro hat hundert Cent. There are a hundred cents in a euro.
Es kostet drei Euro. It costs three euros.

WORD TIP In German, Euro is always used in the singular.

der **Eurocent**
cent

Euroland *NEUTER NOUN*
Eurozone

♂ **Europa** *NEUTER NOUN*
Europe

der **Europäer**, *PLURAL* die **Europäer**
European *(male)*

die **Europäerin**, *PLURAL* die **Europäerinnen**
European *(female)*

♂ **europäisch** *ADJECTIVE*
European

WORD TIP Adjectives never have capitals in German, even for regions, countries, or nationalities.

das **Eurostück**, *PLURAL* die **Eurostücke**
one-euro coin

der **Eurotunnel**
Channel Tunnel

evangelisch *ADJECTIVE*
Protestant

WORD TIP Adjectives never have capitals in German, even for religions.

eventuell *ADJECTIVE*
possible

eventuell *ADVERB*
1 possibly
2 perhaps

WORD TIP The German word eventuell does not mean eventually in English; the German word for eventually is schließlich.

ewig *ADJECTIVE*
eternal

ewig *ADVERB*
forever

die **Ewigkeit**
eternity

das **Examen**, *PLURAL* die **Examen**
examination, exam

das **Exemplar**, *PLURAL* die **Exemplare**
1 copy
2 specimen

existieren *VERB*, *PERFECT* **hat existiert**
to exist

die **Expedition**, *PLURAL* die **Expeditionen**
expedition

explodieren *VERB*, *PERFECT* **ist explodiert**
to explode

die **Explosion**, *PLURAL* die **Explosionen**
explosion

der **Export**, *PLURAL* die **Exporte**
export

exportieren *VERB*, *PERFECT* **hat exportiert**
to export
Russland exportiert viel Öl und Holz.
Russia exports a lot of oil and timber.

extra *ADVERB*
1 separately
2 extra
3 specially
4 *(informal)* on purpose

extrem *ADJECTIVE*
extreme

Ff

♂ **fabelhaft** *ADJECTIVE*
fabulous, fantastic

♂ die **Fabrik**, *PLURAL* die **Fabriken**
factory

WORD TIP The German word Fabrik does not mean fabric in English; the German word for fabric is Stoff.

♢ **irregular verb**; *SEP* **separable verb**; for more help with verbs see centre section

der **Fabrikarbeiter,** *PLURAL* die
Fabrikarbeiter
factory worker *(male)*

WORD TIP Professions, hobbies, and sports don't take an article in German: Er ist Fabrikarbeiter.

die **Fabrikarbeiterin,** *PLURAL* die
Fabrikarbeiterinnen
factory worker *(female)*

WORD TIP Professions, hobbies, and sports don't take an article in German: Sie ist Fabrikarbeiterin.

℘ das **Fach,** *PLURAL* die **Fächer**
1 compartment
2 pigeonhole *(for letters)*
3 subject *(at school)*

der **Facharzt,** *PLURAL* die **Fachärzte**
specialist *(male)*
Warst du schon beim Facharzt? Have you seen a specialist yet?
Er ist Facharzt für plastische Chirurgie. He's a plastic surgeon.

WORD TIP Professions, hobbies, and sports don't take an article in German: Er ist Facharzt.

die **Fachärztin,** *PLURAL* die **Fachärztinnen**
specialist *(female)*

WORD TIP Professions, hobbies, and sports don't take an article in German: Sie ist Fachärztin.

der **Fachausdruck,** *PLURAL* die
Fachausdrücke
technical term

℘ die **Fachfrau,** *PLURAL* die **Fachfrauen**
expert *(female)*

die **Fachhochschule,** *PLURAL* die
Fachhochschulen
college

℘ der **Fachmann,** *PLURAL* die **Fachleute**
expert *(male)*

die **Fachschule,** *PLURAL* die **Fachschulen**
technical college

fade *ADJECTIVE*
tasteless

der **Faden,** *PLURAL* die **Fäden**
thread

fähig *ADJECTIVE*
1 capable
2 able *(student)*

die **Fähigkeit,** *PLURAL* die **Fähigkeiten**
ability

die **Fahne,** *PLURAL* die **Fahnen**
flag

der **Fahrausweis,** *PLURAL* die **Fahrausweise**
ticket

die **Fahrbahn,** *PLURAL* die **Fahrbahnen**
1 carriageway
2 road

℘ die **Fähre,** *PLURAL* die **Fähren**
ferry

℘ **fahren** *VERB✧, PRESENT* **fährt,** *IMPERFECT* **fuhr,**
PERFECT **ist gefahren**
1 to go
Wir fahren mit dem Zug nach Wien. We're going to Vienna by train.
Ich bin mit dem Auto gefahren. I went by car.
2 to drive
Hanna ist sehr schnell gefahren. Hanna drove very fast.
3 to ride *(of a cyclist)*
4 to run *(of a train, bus)*
Der Zug fährt nicht an Sonn- und Feiertagen. The train doesn't run on Sundays and public holidays.
5 to leave
Wann fahrt ihr? When are you leaving?
6 Was ist in sie gefahren? *(informal)* What's got into her?
7 *PERFECT* **hat gefahren** to drive
Er hat Doris nach Hause gefahren. He drove Doris home.
Ich habe das Auto in die Garage gefahren. I drove the car into the garage.

℘ der **Fahrer,** *PLURAL* die **Fahrer**
driver *(male)*

die **Fahrerflucht**
Fahrerflucht begehen to commit a hit-and-run offence

℘ die **Fahrerin,** *PLURAL* die **Fahrerinnen**
driver *(female)*

der **Fahrgast,** *PLURAL* die **Fahrgäste**
passenger

das **Fahrgeld**
fare

℘ die **Fahrkarte,** *PLURAL* die **Fahrkarten**
ticket

die **Fahrkartenausgabe**
ticket office

der **Fahrkartenautomat,** *PLURAL* die
Fahrkartenautomaten
ticket machine

GERMAN—ENGLISH

der **Fahrkartenschalter**, *PLURAL* die
Fahrkartenschalter
ticket office

fahrlässig *ADJECTIVE*
negligent

der **Fahrlehrer**, *PLURAL* die **Fahrlehrer**
driving instructor *(male)*

> **WORD TIP** Professions, hobbies, and sports
> don't take an article in German: Er ist Fahrlehrer.

die **Fahrlehrerin**, *PLURAL* die
Fahrlehrerinnen
driving instructor *(female)*

> **WORD TIP** Professions, hobbies, and sports
> don't take an article in German: Sie ist
> Fahrlehrerin.

♭ der **Fahrplan**, *PLURAL* die **Fahrpläne**
timetable

der **Fahrpreis**, *PLURAL* die **Fahrpreise**
fare

die **Fahrprüfung**, *PLURAL* die
Fahrprüfungen
driving test
Wann machst du die Fahrprüfung? When
are you going to take your driving test?

♭ das **Fahrrad**, *PLURAL* die **Fahrräder**
bicycle

der **Fahrradfahrer**, *PLURAL* die
Fahrradfahrer
cyclist *(male)*

die **Fahrradfahrerin**, *PLURAL* die
Fahrradfahrerinnen
cyclist *(female)*

der **Fahrradweg**, *PLURAL* die **Fahrradwege**
cycle lane

der **Fahrschein**, *PLURAL* die **Fahrscheine**
ticket

die **Fahrschule**, *PLURAL* die **Fahrschulen**
driving school

der **Fahrstuhl**, *PLURAL* die **Fahrstühle**
lift

♭ die **Fahrt**, *PLURAL* die **Fahrten**
1 journey
Gute Fahrt! Have a good journey!
2 trip
3 drive
4 Er raste in voller Fahrt gegen einen Baum.
He hit a tree at full speed.

die **Fahrtdauer**
journey time

das **Fahrzeug**, *PLURAL* die **Fahrzeuge**
vehicle

fair *ADJECTIVE*
fair

der **Faktor**, *PLURAL* die **Faktoren**
factor

der **Falke**, *PLURAL* die **Falken**
falcon

der **Fall**, *PLURAL* die **Fälle**
1 case *(also in grammar)*
In diesem Fall hattest du Recht. In this
case, you were right.
2 für alle Fälle just in case
Ich habe für alle Fälle einen Schirm dabei.
I've brought an umbrella, just in case.
3 auf jeden Fall definitely
Ich komme auf jeden Fall. I'm definitely
coming.
4 auf keinen Fall on no account
Das darfst du auf keinen Fall Julia
erzählen. On no account should you tell
Julia.
5 fall

die **Falle**, *PLURAL* die **Fallen**
trap

fallen *VERB*♢, *PRESENT* **fällt**, *IMPERFECT* **fiel**,
PERFECT **ist gefallen**
1 to fall
2 etwas fallen lassen to drop something
Sie ließ die Vase fallen. She dropped the
vase.
Wir haben den Plan fallen lassen. We've
dropped the idea.
3 eine Bemerkung fallen lassen to make a
comment

fällen *VERB*, *PERFECT* **hat gefällt**
to fell, to cut down

fällig *ADJECTIVE*
due

falls *CONJUNCTION*
1 if
2 in case

der **Fallschirm**, *PLURAL* die **Fallschirme**
parachute

das **Fallschirmspringen**
parachuting

♭ **falsch** *ADJECTIVE*
1 wrong
Du hast ihn falsch verstanden. You got
him wrong.
2 false *(name, teeth, etc.)*
3 forged *(passport, etc.)*

♢ irregular verb; *SEP* separable verb; for more help with verbs see centre section

fälschen *VERB*, *PERFECT* **hat gefälscht**
 to forge

die **Fälschung**, *PLURAL* die **Fälschungen**
1 fake
2 forgery

die **Falte**, *PLURAL* die **Falten**
1 fold
2 crease
3 pleat
4 wrinkle

falten *VERB*, *PERFECT* **hat gefaltet**
 to fold

faltig *ADJECTIVE*
1 wrinkled
2 creased

familiär *ADJECTIVE*
 familiar

ℱ die **Familie**, *PLURAL* die **Familien**
 family

der/die **Familienangehörige**, *PLURAL* die
 Familienangehörigen
 relative

der **Familienname**, *PLURAL* die
 Familiennamen
 surname

der **Familienstand**, *PLURAL* die
 Familienstände
 marital status

das **Familienzimmer**, *PLURAL* die
 Familienzimmer
 family room

der **Fan**, *PLURAL* die **Fans**
 fan

fand ► SEE **finden**

ℱ **fangen** *VERB*◇, *PRESENT* **fängt**, *IMPERFECT* **fing**,
 PERFECT **hat gefangen**
 to catch

die **Fantasie**
1 imagination
2 Fantasien *(plural)* fantasies

fantasielos *ADJECTIVE*
 unimaginative

fantasievoll *ADJECTIVE*
 imaginative

ℱ **fantastisch** *ADJECTIVE*
 fantastic

ℱ die **Farbe**, *PLURAL* die **Farben**
1 colour

2 paint
3 dye
4 suit *(in playing cards)*

farbecht *ADJECTIVE*
 colour fast

färben *VERB*, *PERFECT* **hat gefärbt**
 to dye
 Sie färbt sich die Haare. She dyes her hair.

farbenblind *ADJECTIVE*
 colour-blind

farbig *ADJECTIVE*
 coloured

farblos *ADJECTIVE*
 colourless

der **Farbstift**, *PLURAL* die **Farbstifte**
 coloured pencil

der **Farbstoff**, *PLURAL* die **Farbstoffe**
1 dye
2 colour

der **Farbton**, *PLURAL* die **Farbtöne**
 shade

ℱ der **Fasching**
 carnival

> 🅘 **FASCHING**
>
> This is the period before Lent. Numerous
> fancy dress parties, parades, and balls (e.g.
> the Viennese Opera Ball) are held at the
> weekend, on the Monday (Rosenmontag)
> and Shrove Tuesday (Fastnachtsdienstag or
> Faschingsdienstag) before Ash Wednesday.
> A type of doughnut – a Berliner, also called
> Krapfen in South Germany and Austria – is
> sold.

der **Faschingsdienstag**, *PLURAL* die
 Faschingsdienstage
 Shrove Tuesday

die **Faser**, *PLURAL* die **Fasern**
 fibre

das **Fass**, *PLURAL* die **Fässer**
 barrel
 Bier vom Fass draught beer

fassen *VERB*, *PERFECT* **hat gefasst**
1 to grasp
2 to catch
 Es gelang der Polizei, den Dieb zu fassen.
 The police managed to catch the thief.
3 to hold *(of a container)*
4 to understand
 Es ist schwer zu fassen, wie jemand so
 etwas tun kann. It's hard to understand
 how anybody can do such a thing.
5 Das ist doch nicht zu fassen! It's

unbelievable!
6 sich fassen to compose yourself
7 einen Entschluss fassen to make a decision
8 Fassen Sie sich bitte kurz. Please be brief.

die **Fassung**, PLURAL die **Fassungen**
1 version
2 composure
3 jemanden aus der Fassung bringen to throw somebody, to upset somebody

fassungslos ADJECTIVE
speechless

fast ADVERB
1 almost
2 fast nie hardly ever

> **WORD TIP** The German word fast does not mean fast in English; the German word for fast is schnell.

fasten VERB, PERFECT **hat gefastet**
to fast

die **Fastenzeit**
Lent

♀ das **Fast Food**
fast food

die **Fastnacht**
carnival

♀ **faul** ADJECTIVE
1 lazy
2 rotten
3 Das ist doch nur eine faule Ausrede. It's just a lame excuse.
4 An der Sache ist etwas faul. (informal) There's something fishy about it.

faulen VERB, PERFECT **ist gefault**
to rot

♀ **faulenzen** VERB, PERFECT **hat gefaulenzt**
to laze about

die **Faust**, PLURAL die **Fäuste**
1 fist
2 auf eigene Faust off your own bat

faxen VERB, PERFECT **hat gefaxt**
to fax
Ich faxe Ihnen die Liste. I'll fax you the list.

das **Faxgerät**, PLURAL die **Faxgeräte**
fax machine

die **Faxnummer**, PLURAL die **Faxnummern**
fax number

das **FCKW**, PLURAL die **FCKWs** ABBREVIATION
(=Fluorchlorkohlenwasserstoff) **CFC**

♀ der **Februar**
February
im Februar in February

fechten VERB◇, PRESENT **ficht**, IMPERFECT **focht**, PERFECT **hat gefochten**
to fence

die **Feder**, PLURAL die **Federn**
1 feather
2 spring
3 nib (of a pen)

♀ der **Federball**, PLURAL die **Federbälle**
1 badminton
2 shuttlecock

das **Federbett**, PLURAL die **Federbetten**
duvet

der **Federhalter**, PLURAL die **Federhalter**
fountain pen

♀ das **Federmäppchen**, PLURAL die **Federmäppchen**
pencil case

die **Fee**, PLURAL die **Feen**
fairy

fegen VERB, PERFECT **hat gefegt**
to sweep

fehl ADJECTIVE
fehl am Platz out of place

♀ **fehlen** VERB, PERFECT **hat gefehlt**
1 to be missing
2 to be lacking
3 to be absent (from school)
4 Mir fehlt die Zeit. I haven't got the time. Es fehlt ihnen einfach das Geld für ein neues Auto. They simply haven't got the money for a new car.
5 Was fehlt dir? What's the matter?
6 Rudi fehlt mir. I miss Rudi.

♀ der **Fehler**, PLURAL die **Fehler**
1 mistake
2 fault

die **Feier**, PLURAL die **Feiern**
1 party
2 celebration

der **Feierabend**, PLURAL die **Feierabende**
1 finishing time
nach Feierabend after work
2 Feierabend machen to finish work
Wann machst du Feierabend? What time do you finish work?

die **Feierlichkeiten** PLURAL NOUN
festivities

feiern VERB, PERFECT **hat gefeiert**
to celebrate

*der **Feiertag**, PLURAL die **Feiertage**
1 holiday
Ist der 1. Mai ein gesetzlicher Feiertag? Is the first of May a public holiday?
2 der erste Feiertag Christmas Day
der zweite Feiertag Boxing Day

feig ▸ SEE **feige**

feige ADJECTIVE
cowardly
Du bist feige. You're a coward.

die **Feige**, PLURAL die **Feigen**
fig

der **Feigenbaum**, PLURAL die **Feigenbäume**
fig tree

der **Feigling**, PLURAL die **Feiglinge**
coward

die **Feile**, PLURAL die **Feilen**
file

fein ADJECTIVE
1 fine
2 delicate
3 refined
4 Für die Party haben sie sich fein gemacht. They dressed up for the party.

der **Feind**, PLURAL die **Feinde**
enemy (male)

die **Feindin**, PLURAL die **Feindinnen**
enemy (female)

feindlich ADJECTIVE
hostile

das **Feld**, PLURAL die **Felder**
1 field
2 pitch
3 box (on a form)
4 square (on a board game)

das **Fell**, PLURAL die **Felle**
fur, skin

der **Fels**
rock

der **Felsen**, PLURAL die **Felsen**
1 rock
2 cliff

feminin ADJECTIVE
feminine

der **Feminist**, PLURAL die **Feministen**
feminist (male)

die **Feministin**, PLURAL die **Feministinnen**
feminist (female)
Sie ist Feministin. She's a feminist.

*das **Fenster**, PLURAL die **Fenster**
window

der **Fensterladen**, PLURAL die **Fensterläden**
shutter

*die **Ferien** PLURAL NOUN
holidays
Ferien haben to be on holiday
Schöne Ferien! Have a nice holiday!

das **Ferienhaus**, PLURAL die **Ferienhäuser**
holiday home

*der **Ferienjob**, PLURAL die **Ferienjobs**
holiday job

die **Ferienwohnung**, PLURAL die **Ferienwohnungen**
holiday flat

fern ADJECTIVE
distant

fern ADVERB
far away

die **Fernbedienung**, PLURAL die **Fernbedienungen**
remote control

das **Ferngespräch**, PLURAL die **Ferngespräche**
long-distance call

ferngesteuert ADJECTIVE
remote-controlled

das **Fernglas**, PLURAL die **Ferngläser**
binoculars

fernhalten VERB◇, PRESENT **hält fern**, IMPERFECT **hielt fern**, PERFECT **hat ferngehalten**
sich fernhalten to keep away
jemanden von etwas fernhalten to keep somebody away from something

Fernost NEUTER NOUN
the Far East

das **Fernrohr**, PLURAL die **Fernrohre**
telescope

der **Fernsehapparat**, PLURAL die **Fernsehapparate**
television set

*fernsehen VERB◇, PRESENT **sieht fern**, IMPERFECT **sah fern**, PERFECT **hat ferngesehen**
to watch television

*indicates key words

℗ das **Fernsehen**
television
Was kommt im Fernsehen? What's on
television?

℗ der **Fernseher**, PLURAL die **Fernseher**
television (set)

das **Fernsehprogramm**, PLURAL die
Fernsehprogramme
1 TV listings
2 TV channel

der **Fernsehraum**, PLURAL die
Fernsehräume
television room

die **Fernsehsendung**, PLURAL die
Fernsehsendungen
television programme

die **Fernsehserie**, PLURAL die **Fernsehserien**
television series

das **Fernsehspiel**, PLURAL die **Fernsehspiele**
television play

℗ der **Fernsehturm**, PLURAL die **Fernsehtürme**
television tower

der **Fernsprecher**, PLURAL die **Fernsprecher**
telephone

die **Fernsteuerung**, PLURAL die
Fernsteuerungen
remote control

der **Fernunterricht**
correspondence course(s)

die **Ferse**, PLURAL die **Fersen**
heel

℗ **fertig** ADJECTIVE
1 finished
fertig sein to be finished
Bis heute Abend bin ich fertig. I'll be
finished by this evening.
Erst muss er mit den Hausaufgaben fertig
werden, dann darf er raus. He has to finish
his homework before he's allowed out.
2 shattered
Ich bin völlig fertig. I'm completely
shattered.
3 mit jemandem fertig sein (informal) to be
through with somebody
4 mit etwas fertig werden to cope with
something (problems, for example)
5 ready
Das Essen ist fertig! Food's ready!
6 etwas fertig machen prepare to get
something ready (complete) to finish
something
sich fertig machen to get ready

7 ▸ SEE **fertigbringen**, **fertigmachen**

fertig ADVERB
fertig essen to finish eating

fertigbringen VERB◇, IMPERFECT **brachte**
fertig, PERFECT **hat fertiggebracht**
es fertigbringen, etwas zu tun to bring
yourself to do something
Ich bringe es einfach nicht fertig. I just
can't bring myself to do it.

das **Fertiggericht**, PLURAL die
Fertiggerichte
ready meal

fertigmachen VERB, PERFECT **hat**
fertiggemacht
jemanden fertigmachen to wear
somebody out, to wear somebody down
Der ständige Stress macht mich fertig.
The constant stress is wearing me down.

fest ADJECTIVE
1 firm
2 fixed (salary, address)
3 close (friend)
4 solid
feste Nahrung solids
5 fest werden to harden

fest ADVERB
1 fest schlafen to be fast asleep
2 fest befreundet sein to be close friends
3 fest angestellt sein to have a permanent
job

℗ das **Fest**, PLURAL die **Feste**
1 party
2 celebration
3 festival

festbinden VERB◇, IMPERFECT **band fest**,
PERFECT **hat festgebunden**
to tie (up)

festhalten VERB◇, PRESENT **hält fest**, IMPERFECT
hielt fest, PERFECT **hat festgehalten**
1 to hold on to
2 sich festhalten to hold on
Halt dich an mir fest. Hold on to me.

die **Festigkeit**
strength

festlegen VERB, PERFECT **hat festgelegt**
1 to fix
2 sich auf etwas festlegen to commit
yourself to something

die **Festlegung**, PLURAL die **Festlegungen**
establishment

℗ **festlich** ADJECTIVE
festive

festmachen VERB, PERFECT **hat festgemacht**
1 **to fix**
Ich mache gleich einen Termin fest. I'll fix a date straight away.
2 **to fasten**

die **Festnahme**, PLURAL die **Festnahmen**
arrest

festnehmen VERB◇, PRESENT **nimmt fest**, IMPERFECT **nahm fest**, PERFECT **hat festgenommen**
to arrest

die **Festplatte**, PLURAL die **Festplatten**
hard disk

feststehen VERB◇, IMPERFECT **stand fest**, PERFECT **hat festgestanden**
to be certain
Eins steht fest, Daniel lade ich nicht mehr ein. One thing's certain - I'm not going to invite Daniel again.

feststellen VERB, PERFECT **hat festgestellt**
1 **to establish**
2 **to notice**

der **Festtag**, PLURAL die **Festtage**
1 **holiday**
2 **special day**

ℓ die **Fete**, PLURAL die **Feten**
party

ℓ **fett** ADJECTIVE
1 **fat** (person)
2 **greasy, fatty** (food)
3 **bold** (type)

ℓ das **Fett**, PLURAL die **Fette**
1 **fat**
2 **grease**

fettarm ADJECTIVE
low-fat

ℓ **fettig** ADJECTIVE
greasy

fettleibig ADJECTIVE
obese

der **Fetzen**, PLURAL die **Fetzen**
1 **scrap**
2 **rag**

feucht ADJECTIVE
1 **damp**
2 **humid**

die **Feuchtigkeit**
1 **moisture**
2 **humidity**

ℓ das **Feuer**
1 **fire**
2 **a light**
Hast du Feuer? Have you got a light?

der **Feuerlöscher**, PLURAL die **Feuerlöscher**
fire extinguisher

der **Feuermelder**, PLURAL die **Feuermelder**
fire alarm

die **Feuertreppe**, PLURAL die **Feuertreppen**
fire escape

die **Feuerwehr**, PLURAL die **Feuerwehren**
fire brigade

das **Feuerwehrauto**, PLURAL die **Feuerwehrautos**
fire engine

die **Feuerwehrfrau**, PLURAL die **Feuerwehrfrauen**
firefighter (female)

WORD TIP Professions, hobbies, and sports don't take an article in German: Sie ist Feuerwehrfrau.

der **Feuerwehrmann**, PLURAL die **Feuerwehrleute**
firefighter (male), **fireman**

WORD TIP Professions, hobbies, and sports don't take an article in German: Er ist Feuerwehrmann.

der **Feuerwehrwagen**, PLURAL die **Feuerwehrwagen**
fire engine

ℓ das **Feuerwerk**
fireworks

das **Feuerzeug**, PLURAL die **Feuerzeuge**
lighter

ficht ▸ SEE **fechten**

ℓ das **Fieber**
(high) temperature, fever
Sie hatte (hohes) Fieber. She had a (high) temperature.

fiel ▸ SEE **fallen**

fies ADJECTIVE
(informal) **nasty**

die **Figur**, PLURAL die **Figuren**
1 **figure**
2 **character** (in a book)

die **Filiale**, PLURAL die **Filialen**
branch

ℓ der **Film**, PLURAL die **Filme**
film

ℓ **indicates key words**

filmen *VERB*, *PERFECT* **hat gefilmt**
to film

die **Filmkomödie**, *PLURAL* die
Filmkomödien
comedy film

der **Filter**, *PLURAL* die **Filter**
filter

℘ der **Filzstift**, *PLURAL* die **Filzstifte**
felt-tip pen

das **Finale**, *PLURAL* die **Finale**
final

finanziell *ADJECTIVE*
financial

finanzieren *VERB*, *PERFECT* **hat finanziert**
to finance

℘ **finden** *VERB*◇, *IMPERFECT* **fand**, *PERFECT* **hat gefunden**
1 to find
2 to think
Wie fandest du den Test? What did you think of the test?
Findest du? Do you think so?
3 Ich finde nichts dabei. I don't mind.

fing ►SEE**fangen**

℘ der **Finger**, *PLURAL* die **Finger**
finger

der **Fingerabdruck**, *PLURAL* die
Fingerabdrücke
fingerprint

der **Fingernagel**, *PLURAL* die **Fingernägel**
fingernail

der **Finne**, *PLURAL* die **Finnen**
Finn *(male)*

die **Finnin**, *PLURAL* die **Finninnen**
Finn *(female)*

finnisch *ADJECTIVE*
Finnish

> **WORD TIP** Adjectives never have capitals in German, even for regions, countries, or nationalities.

Finnland *NEUTER NOUN*
Finland

finster *ADJECTIVE*
1 dark
im Finstern in the dark
2 sinister, shady

die **Finsternis**
darkness

℘ die **Firma**, *PLURAL* die **Firmen**
firm, company

der **Firmenwagen**, *PLURAL* die
Firmenwagen
company car

℘ der **Fisch**, *PLURAL* die **Fische**
1 fish
2 Fische Pisces
Helmut ist Fisch. Helmut is Pisces.

der **Fischer**, *PLURAL* die **Fischer**
fisherman

> **WORD TIP** Professions, hobbies, and sports don't take an article in German: Er ist Fischer.

die **Fischerin**, *PLURAL* die **Fischerinnen**
fisherwoman

> **WORD TIP** Professions, hobbies, and sports don't take an article in German: Sie ist Fischerin.

der **Fischhändler**, *PLURAL* die **Fischhändler**
fishmonger *(male)*

> **WORD TIP** Professions, hobbies, and sports don't take an article in German: Er ist Fischhändler.

die **Fischhändlerin**, *PLURAL* die
Fischhändlerinnen
fishmonger *(female)*

> **WORD TIP** Professions, hobbies, and sports don't take an article in German: Sie ist Fischhändlerin.

℘ **fit** *ADJECTIVE*
fit
Er hält sich durch Jogging fit. He keeps fit by jogging.

die **Fitness**
fitness

das **Fitnesstraining**
keep fit

das **Fitnesszentrum**, *PLURAL* die
Fitnesszentren
gym, fitness centre

fix *ADJECTIVE*
1 quick
2 Alles ist fix und fertig. It's all ready.
3 Ich bin fix und fertig. *(informal)* I'm shattered.

flach *ADJECTIVE*
1 flat
2 low
3 shallow
Die Erdbeeren kommen in die flache Schüssel. The strawberries go in the shallow bowl.

◇ **irregular verb;** *SEP* **separable verb; for more help with verbs see centre section**

die **Fläche**, PLURAL die **Flächen**
1 surface
2 area

flackern VERB, PERFECT **hat geflackert**
to flicker

die **Flagge**, PLURAL die **Flaggen**
flag

die **Flamme**, PLURAL die **Flammen**
flame

ℓ die **Flasche**, PLURAL die **Flaschen**
bottle

der **Flaschenöffner**, PLURAL die
Flaschenöffner
bottle opener

flauschig ADJECTIVE
1 fluffy
2 fleecy

der **Fleck**, PLURAL die **Flecken**
1 stain
2 spot
3 ein blauer Fleck a bruise

fleckig ADJECTIVE
1 stained
2 blotchy (skin)

die **Fledermaus**, PLURAL die **Fledermäuse**
bat

ℓ das **Fleisch**
1 meat
2 flesh

das **Fleischbällchen**, PLURAL die
Fleischbällchen
meatball

der **Fleischer**, PLURAL die **Fleischer**
butcher (male)

WORD TIP Professions, hobbies, and sports
don't take an article in German: Er ist Fleischer.

die **Fleischerei**, PLURAL die **Fleischereien**
butcher's

die **Fleischerin**, PLURAL die **Fleischerinnen**
butcher (female)

WORD TIP Professions, hobbies, and sports don't
take an article in German: Sie ist Fleischerin.

der **Fleiß**
hard (work)

ℓ **fleißig** ADJECTIVE
hard-working
fleißig ADVERB
hard (work)

flexibel ADJECTIVE
flexible
flexibel ADVERB
flexibly

flicken VERB, PERFECT **hat geflickt**
to mend

der **Flicken**, PLURAL die **Flicken**
patch (for mending)

die **Fliege**, PLURAL die **Fliegen**
1 fly
2 bow tie

ℓ **fliegen** VERB◇, IMPERFECT **flog**, PERFECT **ist
geflogen**
1 to fly
2 (informal) to fall
Ich bin vom Fahrrad geflogen. I fell off my
bike.
3 (informal) to be thrown out
Manfred ist von der Schule geflogen.
Manfred was thrown out of the school.
4 PERFECT **hat geflogen** to fly (a plane)

fliehen VERB◇, IMPERFECT **floh**, PERFECT **ist
geflohen**
to flee

die **Fliese**, PLURAL die **Fliesen**
tile

das **Fließband**, PLURAL die **Fließbänder**
1 conveyor belt
2 assembly line

fließen VERB◇, IMPERFECT **floss**, PERFECT **ist
geflossen**
to flow

fließend ADJECTIVE
1 fluent
Für diese Stelle ist fließendes Deutsch
erforderlich. Fluent German is an essential
requirement for this job.
2 running (water)
3 moving (traffic)
fließend ADVERB
fluently
Sie spricht fließend Englisch. She speaks
fluent English.

die **Flimmerkiste**, PLURAL die
Flimmerkisten
(informal) gogglebox

die **Flitterwochen** PLURAL NOUN
honeymoon
Sie fahren in den Flitterwochen nach
Venedig. They're going to Venice for their
honeymoon.

flitzen *VERB (informal)*, *PERFECT* **ist geflitzt**
1 to dash
2 to whizz

die **Flocke**, *PLURAL* die **Flocken**
flake

flog ▸ SEE **fliegen**

floh ▸ SEE **fliehen**

der **Floh**, *PLURAL* die **Flöhe**
flea

der **Flohmarkt**, *PLURAL* die **Flohmärkte**
flea market

Florenz *NEUTER NOUN*
Florence

der **Florist**, *PLURAL* die **Floristen**
florist *(male)*

> **WORD TIP** Professions, hobbies, and sports don't take an article in German: Er ist Florist.

die **Floristin**, *PLURAL* die **Floristinnen**
florist *(female)*

> **WORD TIP** Professions, hobbies, and sports don't take an article in German: Sie ist Floristin.

floss ▸ SEE **fließen**

die **Flosse**, *PLURAL* die **Flossen**
1 fin
2 flipper

♀ die **Flöte**, *PLURAL* die **Flöten**
1 flute
   Tom spielt Flöte. Tom plays the flute.
2 recorder
   Lisa spielt Flöte. Lisa plays the recorder.

flott *ADJECTIVE*
1 quick
2 stylish
flott *ADVERB*
1 quickly
2 stylishly

fluchen *VERB*, *PERFECT* **hat geflucht**
to curse

der **Flüchtling**, *PLURAL* die **Flüchtlinge**
refugee

♀ der **Flug**, *PLURAL* die **Flüge**
flight

der **Flugbegleiter**, *PLURAL* die **Flugbegleiter**
flight attendant *(male)*

> **WORD TIP** Professions, hobbies, and sports don't take an article in German: Er ist Flugbegleiter.

die **Flugbegleiterin**, *PLURAL* die **Flugbegleiterinnen**
flight attendant *(female)*

> **WORD TIP** Professions, hobbies, and sports don't take an article in German: Sie ist Flugbegleiterin.

das **Flugblatt**, *PLURAL* die **Flugblätter**
pamphlet

der **Flugdienstleiter**, *PLURAL* die **Flugdienstleiter**
air-traffic controller *(male)*

> **WORD TIP** Professions, hobbies, and sports don't take an article in German: Er ist Flugdienstleiter.

die **Flugdienstleiterin**, *PLURAL* die **Flugdienstleiterinnen**
air-traffic controller *(female)*

> **WORD TIP** Professions, hobbies, and sports don't take an article in German: Sie ist Flugdienstleiterin.

der **Flügel**, *PLURAL* die **Flügel**
1 wing
2 grand piano

der **Fluggast**, *PLURAL* die **Fluggäste**
(air) passenger

die **Fluggesellschaft**, *PLURAL* die **Fluggesellschaften**
airline

♀ der **Flughafen**, *PLURAL* die **Flughäfen**
airport

> **FLUGHAFEN**
> Germany's biggest airport is in Frankfurt.

der **Fluglotse**, *PLURAL* die **Fluglotsen**
air-traffic controller *(male)*

> **WORD TIP** Professions, hobbies, and sports don't take an article in German: Er ist Fluglotse.

die **Fluglotsin**, *PLURAL* die **Fluglotsinnen**
air-traffic controller *(female)*

> **WORD TIP** Professions, hobbies, and sports don't take an article in German: Sie ist Fluglotsin.

der **Flugplatz**, *PLURAL* die **Flugplätze**
1 airport
2 airfield

der **Flugschein**, *PLURAL* die **Flugscheine**
1 air ticket
2 pilot's licence

♀ das **Flugzeug**, *PLURAL* die **Flugzeuge**
plane, aircraft
Fahrt ihr mit dem Zug oder fliegt ihr mit

◇ irregular verb; *SEP* separable verb; for more help with verbs see centre section

dem Flugzeug? Are you going by train or by plane?

das **Fluor**
fluoride

der **Flur**, PLURAL die **Flure**
1 hall
2 corridor

> **WORD TIP** The German word Flur does not mean floor in English; the German word for floor is Boden.

ℓ der **Fluss**, PLURAL die **Flüsse**
river

flüssig ADJECTIVE
liquid

die **Flüssigkeit**, PLURAL die **Flüssigkeiten**
liquid

das **Flussufer**, PLURAL die **Flussufer**
river bank

flüstern VERB, PERFECT **hat geflüstert**
to whisper

die **Flut**, PLURAL die **Fluten**
1 high tide
Das Foto zeigt den Strand bei Flut. The photo shows the beach at high tide.
Es ist Flut. The tide is in.
2 flood (of letters, complaints)

das **Flutlicht**
floodlight

focht ▸ SEE **fechten**

der **Föhn**, PLURAL die **Föhne**
1 hairdryer
2 föhn wind, warm wind

🔵 **FÖHN**

The Föhn brings warm air from the Mediterranean to areas north of the Alps. Austria, Southern Germany, and parts of Switzerland are affected by it. Some people believe that it causes headaches and other health problems.

föhnen VERB, PERFECT **hat geföhnt**
to blow-dry

die **Folge**, PLURAL die **Folgen**
1 series
2 episode
3 consequence, result
Er starb an den Folgen eines Unfalls. He died as the result of an accident.
4 etwas zur Folge haben to result in something

ℓ **folgen** VERB, PERFECT **ist gefolgt**
1 to follow
Bitte folgen Sie mir. Follow me, please.
Ich kann dir nicht folgen. I can't follow what you're saying.
2 daraus folgt, dass ... it follows that ...
3 PERFECT **hat gefolgt** to obey

folgend ADJECTIVE
1 following
2 Er hat Folgendes gesagt: ... He said the following: ...

die **Folgerung**, PLURAL die **Folgerungen**
conclusion

folgsam ADJECTIVE
obedient

die **Folie**, PLURAL die **Folien**
foil

die **Folienkartoffel**, PLURAL die **Folienkartoffeln**
jacket potato (baked in foil)

die **Folterkammer**, PLURAL die **Folterkammern**
torture chamber

foltern VERB, PERFECT **hat gefoltert**
to torture

der **Fön**™, PLURAL die **Föne**
hairdryer

fordern VERB, PERFECT **hat gefordert**
to demand

fördern VERB, PERFECT **hat gefördert**
1 to promote
2 to sponsor

die **Forderung**, PLURAL die **Forderungen**
1 demand
2 claim

ℓ die **Forelle**, PLURAL die **Forellen**
trout

die **Form**, PLURAL die **Formen**
1 shape
2 form
Er ist in Form. He's on form.
3 tin (for baking)

das **Format**, PLURAL die **Formate**
format

formatieren VERB, PERFECT **hat formatiert**
to format

formen VERB, PERFECT **hat geformt**
1 to form
2 sich formen to take shape

förmlich ADJECTIVE
formal

ℓ indicates key words

förmlich ADVERB
1 formally
2 positively, practically
Wir mussten ihn förmlich zwingen. We practically had to force him.

♀ das **Formular**, PLURAL die **Formulare**
form

forschen VERB, PERFECT **hat geforscht**
1 to search
2 to research

der **Forscher**, PLURAL die **Forscher**
1 researcher, research scientist (male)
2 explorer (male)

WORD TIP Professions, hobbies, and sports don't take an article in German: Er ist Forscher.

die **Forscherin**, PLURAL die **Forscherinnen**
1 researcher, research scientist (female)
2 explorer (female)

WORD TIP Professions, hobbies, and sports don't take an article in German: Sie ist Forscherin.

die **Forschung**, PLURAL die **Forschungen**
research

der **Forst**, PLURAL die **Forste(n)**
forest

der **Förster**, PLURAL die **Förster**
forester (male)

WORD TIP Professions, hobbies, and sports don't take an article in German: Er ist Förster.

die **Försterin**, PLURAL die **Försterinnen**
forester (female)

WORD TIP Professions, hobbies, and sports don't take an article in German: Sie ist Försterin.

fort ADVERB
1 away
2 fort sein to have gone
Sind sie schon fort? Have they gone?
3 in einem fort on and on
Sie redet in einem fort. She talks on and on.
4 und so fort and so on

fortbewegen VERB, PERFECT **hat fortbewegt**
1 to move
2 sich fortbewegen to move

fortfahren VERB◇, PRESENT **fährt fort**, IMPERFECT **fuhr fort**, PERFECT **ist fortgefahren**
1 to leave
Wann fahrt ihr fort? When are you leaving?
2 to continue
Bitte fahren Sie fort. Please continue.

fortführen VERB, PERFECT **hat fortgeführt**
to continue

fortgeschritten ADJECTIVE
advanced

die **Fortpflanzung**, PLURAL die **Fortpflanzungen**
reproduction

der **Fortschritt**, PLURAL die **Fortschritte**
progress
Fortschritte machen to make progress

fortsetzen VERB, PERFECT **hat fortgesetzt**
to continue

die **Fortsetzung**, PLURAL die **Fortsetzungen**
1 continuation
2 instalment

♀ das **Foto**, PLURAL die **Fotos**
photo

der **Fotoapparat**, PLURAL die **Fotoapparate**
camera

der **Fotograf**, PLURAL die **Fotografen**
photographer (male)

WORD TIP Professions, hobbies, and sports don't take an article in German: Er ist Fotograf.

die **Fotografie**, PLURAL die **Fotografien**
1 photography
2 photograph

♀ **fotografieren** VERB, PERFECT **hat fotografiert**
1 to photograph, to take a photograph of
2 to take photographs

die **Fotografin**, PLURAL die **Fotografinnen**
photographer (female)

WORD TIP Professions, hobbies, and sports don't take an article in German: Sie ist Fotografin.

die **Fotokopie**, PLURAL die **Fotokopien**
photocopy

♀ **fotokopieren** VERB, PERFECT **hat fotokopiert**
to photocopy

Fr. ABBREVIATION
1 (=Frau) Mrs, Ms
2 (=Freitag) Friday

die **Fracht**, PLURAL die **Frachten**
freight, cargo

♀ die **Frage**, PLURAL die **Fragen**
question
(jemandem) eine Frage stellen to ask (somebody) a question
etwas in Frage stellen to question something

◇ irregular verb; SEP separable verb; for more help with verbs see centre section

Das kommt nicht in Frage. That's out of the question.

ℓ der **Fragebogen**, PLURAL die **Fragebogen**
questionnaire

ℓ **fragen** VERB, PERFECT **hat gefragt**
1 to ask
2 sich fragen to wonder

das **Fragezeichen**, PLURAL die **Fragezeichen**
question mark

fraglich ADJECTIVE
doubtful

der **Franken**[1], PLURAL die **Franken**
(Swiss) franc

Franken[2] NEUTER NOUN
Franconia

die **Frankfurter**, PLURAL die **Frankfurter**
frankfurter *(type of sausage)*

> **WORD TIP** The German word Frankfurter can refer to residents of Frankfurt as well as the food.

ℓ **Frankreich** NEUTER NOUN
France

der **Franzose**, PLURAL die **Franzosen**
Frenchman

die **Französin**, PLURAL die **Französinnen**
Frenchwoman

französisch ADJECTIVE
French

> **WORD TIP** Adjectives never have capitals in German, even for regions, countries, or nationalities.

ℓ das **Französisch**
French

fraß ▸ SEE **fressen**

ℓ die **Frau**, PLURAL die **Frauen**
1 woman
2 wife
3 Mrs, Ms

> **WORD TIP** Frau is usually used to address both married and unmarried women.

ℓ das **Fräulein**, PLURAL die **Fräulein**
1 young lady
2 Miss
Fräulein Schmidt Miss Schmidt

> **WORD TIP** Fräulein is no longer used to address unmarried women. Instead, Frau is used.

ℓ **frech** ADJECTIVE
cheeky, naughty

die **Frechheit**, PLURAL die **Frechheiten**
1 cheek
2 cheeky remark

ℓ **frei** ADJECTIVE
1 free
2 freelance
Er ist freier Journalist. He's a freelance journalist.
3 Ist dieser Platz frei? Is this seat taken?
4 Sie hat heute einen freien Tag. She has a day off today.
5 'Zimmer frei' 'Vacancies'
6 ▸ SEE **freinehmen**

ℓ das **Freibad**, PLURAL die **Freibäder**
open-air swimming pool

ℓ das **Freie**
im Freien in the open air

freigebig ADJECTIVE
generous

ℓ die **Freiheit**, PLURAL die **Freiheiten**
1 freedom
2 liberty
sich Freiheiten erlauben to take liberties

freilassen VERB◇, PRESENT **lässt frei**, IMPERFECT
ließ frei, PERFECT **hat freigelassen**
to release, to free

freinehmen VERB◇, PRESENT **nimmt
frei**, IMPERFECT **nahm frei**, PERFECT **hat
freigenommen**
1 to take off
Er nahm einen Tag frei. He took a day off.
2 sich freinehmen to take time off

der **Freistoß**, PLURAL die **Freistöße**
free kick

die **Freistunde**, PLURAL die **Freistunden**
free period

ℓ der **Freitag**, PLURAL die **Freitage**
Friday

freitags ADVERB
on Fridays

freiwillig ADJECTIVE
voluntary

der/die **Freiwillige**, PLURAL die **Freiwilligen**
volunteer

das **Freizeichen**, PLURAL die **Freizeichen**
dialling tone

ℓ die **Freizeit**
1 spare time
2 leisure

ℓ indicates key words

ℒ die **Freizeitbeschäftigung**, *PLURAL* die **Freizeitbeschäftigungen**
leisure activity

die **Freizeitkleidung**
leisure wear, casual clothes

der **Freizeitpark**, *PLURAL* die **Freizeitparks**
leisure park, theme park

das **Freizeitzentrum**, *PLURAL* die **Freizeitzentren**
leisure centre

fremd *ADJECTIVE*
1 foreign
2 strange
fremde Leute strangers
Ich bin hier fremd. I'm a stranger here.

der/die **Fremde**, *PLURAL* die **Fremden**
1 foreigner
2 stranger

der **Fremdenverkehr**
tourism

das **Fremdenverkehrsbüro**, *PLURAL* die **Fremdenverkehrsbüros**
tourist office

das **Fremdenzimmer**, *PLURAL* die **Fremdenzimmer**
room (to let)

ℒ die **Fremdsprache**, *PLURAL* die **Fremdsprachen**
foreign language

das **Fremdwort**, *PLURAL* die **Fremdwörter**
foreign word

fressen *VERB◇*, *PRESENT* **frisst**, *IMPERFECT* **fraß**, *PERFECT* **hat gefressen**
to eat

WORD TIP This word is normally used of animals.

die **Freude**, *PLURAL* die **Freuden**
1 joy
2 pleasure
mit Freuden with pleasure
3 an etwas Freude haben to be delighted with something
4 jemandem eine Freude machen to make somebody happy

ℒ **freuen** *VERB*, *PERFECT* **hat sich gefreut**
1 sich freuen to be pleased
Ich habe mich über das Geschenk sehr gefreut. I was very pleased with the present.
2 sich auf etwas freuen to look forward to something

Sie freute sich auf die Party. She was looking forward to the party.

ℒ der **Freund**, *PLURAL* die **Freunde**
1 friend *(male)*
2 boyfriend

ℒ die **Freundin**, *PLURAL* die **Freundinnen**
1 friend *(female)*
2 girlfriend

ℒ **freundlich** *ADJECTIVE*
1 friendly
2 kind

freundlicherweise *ADVERB*
kindly

die **Freundlichkeit**
friendliness

die **Freundschaft**, *PLURAL* die **Freundschaften**
friendship
mit jemandem Freundschaft schließen to make friends with somebody

ℒ der **Frieden**
peace

der **Friedhof**, *PLURAL* die **Friedhöfe**
cemetery

friedlich *ADJECTIVE*
peaceful

ℒ **frieren** *VERB◇*, *IMPERFECT* **fror**, *PERFECT* **hat gefroren**
1 to be cold
Frierst du? Are you cold?
Wir haben schrecklich gefroren. We were terribly cold.
2 Es friert. It's freezing., It's frosty.
3 *PERFECT* **ist gefroren** to freeze
Der Boden ist gefroren. The ground has frozen.

die **Frikadelle**, *PLURAL* die **Frikadellen**
rissole

ℒ **frisch** *ADJECTIVE*
fresh
sich frisch machen to freshen up
frisch *ADVERB*
freshly
'Frisch gestrichen' 'Wet paint'

ℒ der **Friseur**, *PLURAL* die **Friseure**
hairdresser *(male)*

WORD TIP Professions, hobbies, and sports don't take an article in German: Er ist Friseur.

◇ irregular verb; *SEP* separable verb; for more help with verbs see centre section

𝓟 die **Friseuse**, *PLURAL* die **Friseusen**
hairdresser *(female)*

> **WORD TIP** Professions, hobbies, and sports
> don't take an article in German: Sie ist Friseuse.

frisieren *VERB, PERFECT* **hat frisiert**
1 jemanden frisieren to do somebody's hair
2 sich frisieren to do your hair

frisst ▸ SEE **fressen**

𝓟 die **Frisur**, *PLURAL* die **Frisuren**
hairstyle, hairdo

Frl. *ABBREVIATION*
(=Fräulein) Miss

𝓟 **froh** *ADJECTIVE*
1 happy
Frohe Weihnachten! Happy Christmas!
2 über etwas froh sein to be glad about
something

fröhlich *ADJECTIVE*
cheerful

die **Fröhlichkeit**
cheerfulness

fromm *ADJECTIVE*
devout

fror ▸ SEE **frieren**

der **Frosch**, *PLURAL* die **Frösche**
frog

der **Frost**, *PLURAL* die **Fröste**
frost

frostig *ADJECTIVE*
frosty

das **Frottee**
towelling

das **Frottiertuch**, *PLURAL* die **Frottiertücher**
towel

die **Frucht**, *PLURAL* die **Früchte**
fruit

fruchtbar *ADJECTIVE*
fertile

das **Fruchteis**
fruit-flavoured ice cream

der **Früchtetee**, *PLURAL* die **Früchtetee(s)**
fruit tea

der **Fruchtsaft**, *PLURAL* die **Fruchtsäfte**
fruit juice

𝓟 **früh** *ADJECTIVE, ADVERB*
1 early
von früh auf from an early age

Die Kinder haben von früh auf im Geschäft
der Eltern mitgeholfen. The children
helped out in their parents' shop from an
early age.
2 heute früh this morning

die **Frühe**
in aller Frühe at the crack of dawn

früher *ADJECTIVE*
1 earlier
2 former
früher *ADVERB*
1 earlier
2 formerly
3 Früher war sie ganz anders. She used to be
quite different.
Das war früher ein Blumengeschäft. It
used to be a florist's.

frühestens *ADVERB*
at the earliest

das **Frühjahr**, *PLURAL* die **Frühjahre**
spring
im Frühjahr in spring

𝓟 der **Frühling**, *PLURAL* die **Frühlinge**
spring
im Frühling in spring

𝓟 das **Frühstück**, *PLURAL* die **Frühstücke**
breakfast

𝓟 **frühstücken** *VERB, PERFECT* **hat gefrühstückt**
to have breakfast

frühzeitig *ADJECTIVE*
early

der **Fuchs**, *PLURAL* die **Füchse**
fox

𝓟 **fühlen** *VERB, PERFECT* **hat gefühlt**
to feel
sich krank fühlen to feel ill

fuhr ▸ SEE **fahren**

führen *VERB, PERFECT* **hat geführt**
1 to lead
Sie führt mit fünf Punkten. She is five
points in the lead.
Unsere Mannschaft führt. Our team's
winning.
2 to run *(a shop or business)*
3 to show round
4 to keep *(a diary, list)*
5 ein Telefongespräch führen to make a
phone call

der **Führer**, *PLURAL* die **Führer**
1 leader
2 guide

117

𝓟 indicates key words

ᵖ der **Führerschein**, *PLURAL* die
Führerscheine
driving licence
den Führerschein machen to take your
driving test

die **Führung**, *PLURAL* die **Führungen**
1 leadership
2 guided tour
3 management *(of a shop)*
4 lead *(in sport)*
Nach der ersten Halbzeit lagen wir in
Führung. After the first half we were in
the lead.

die **Führungsposition**, *PLURAL* die
Führungspositionen
1 top position
2 pole position

füllen *VERB*, *PERFECT* **hat gefüllt**
1 to fill
2 to stuff *(a turkey, peppers)*
3 sich füllen to fill (up)

der **Füller**, *PLURAL* die **Füller**
fountain pen

der **Füllfederhalter**, *PLURAL* die
Füllfederhalter
fountain pen

die **Füllung**, *PLURAL* die **Füllungen**
filling

das **Fundament**, *PLURAL* die **Fundamente**
foundations

ᵖ das **Fundbüro**, *PLURAL* die **Fundbüros**
lost-property office

ᵖ **fünf** *NUMBER*
five
Es ist drei Uhr fünf. It's five past three.

die **Fünf**, *PLURAL* die **Fünfen**
1 five
2 poor *(school mark)*

WORD TIP Fünf is the worst mark in Austria, but
in Germany the worst mark is Sechs.

fünfhundert *NUMBER*
five hundred

das **Fünftel**, *PLURAL* die **Fünftel**
fifth

fünfter, fünfte, fünftes *ADJECTIVE*
fifth

ᵖ **fünfzehn** *NUMBER*
fifteen

ᵖ **fünfzig** *NUMBER*
fifty

der **Funke**, *PLURAL* die **Funken**
spark

funkeln *VERB*, *PERFECT* **hat gefunkelt**
1 to sparkle
2 to twinkle *(of a star)*

ᵖ **funktionieren** *VERB*, *PERFECT* **hat**
funktioniert
to work

ᵖ **für** *PREPOSITION (+ ACC)*
1 for
2 Was für ein ...? What sort of ... ?
3 für sich by yourself
Jetzt habe ich das Haus ganz für mich.
Now I've got the house to myself.
4 das Für und Wider the pros and cons

WORD TIP für + das gives fürs

---

die **Furcht**
fear

ᵖ **furchtbar** *ADJECTIVE*
terrible

fürchten *VERB*, *PERFECT* **hat gefürchtet**
1 to fear
2 sich fürchten to be afraid
Ich fürchte mich vor ihm. I'm afraid of him.
Ich fürchte, das geht nicht. I'm afraid
that's not possible.

fürchterlich *ADJECTIVE*
dreadful

füreinander *ADVERB*
for each other

fürs ► *SEE* für das

die **Fürsorge**
1 care
2 welfare
3 *(informal)* social security

ᵖ der **Fuß**, *PLURAL* die **Füße**
1 foot
zu Fuß on foot
Wir können zu Fuß in die Stadt gehen. We
can walk into town.
2 base

der **Fußabdruck**, *PLURAL* die **Fußabdrücke**
footprint

ᵖ der **Fußball**, *PLURAL* die **Fußbälle**
football

◇ **irregular verb;** *SEP* **separable verb; for more help with verbs see centre section**

der **Fußballplatz**, *PLURAL* die **Fußballplätze**
football pitch

das **Fußballspiel**, *PLURAL* die **Fußballspiele**
football match

der **Fußballspieler**, *PLURAL* die
Fußballspieler
footballer *(male)*

> **WORD TIP** Professions, hobbies, and sports
> don't take an article in German: Er ist
> Fußballspieler.

die **Fußballspielerin**, *PLURAL* die
Fußballspielerinnen
footballer *(female)*

> **WORD TIP** Professions, hobbies, and sports
> don't take an article in German: Sie ist
> Fußballspielerin.

der **Fußboden**, *PLURAL* die **Fußböden**
floor

der **Fußgänger**, *PLURAL* die **Fußgänger**
pedestrian

ℓ die **Fußgängerzone**, *PLURAL* die
Fußgängerzonen
pedestrian precinct

der **Fußweg**, *PLURAL* die **Fußwege**
footpath

das **Futter**
1 feed, food
Ich habe dem Hund schon Futter gegeben.
I've already given the dog his food.
2 lining *(of clothes)*

füttern *VERB, PERFECT* **hat gefüttert**
1 to feed
Kannst du den Hund und die Katze
füttern? Can you feed the dog and the cat?
2 to line
Ist die Jacke gefüttert? Is the coat lined?

ℓ das **Futur**, *PLURAL* die **Future**
future (tense) *(in grammar)*

Gg

g *ABBREVIATION*
(=*Gramm*) gram

gab ▸ SEE **geben**

die **Gabel**, *PLURAL* die **Gabeln**
fork

gähnen *VERB, PERFECT* **hat gegähnt**
to yawn

die **Galerie**, *PLURAL* die **Galerien**
gallery

galoppieren *VERB, PERFECT* **ist galoppiert**
to gallop

die **Gameshow**, *PLURAL* die **Gameshows**
game show

der **Gammler**, *PLURAL* die **Gammler**
drop-out *(male)*

die **Gammlerin**, *PLURAL* die **Gammlerinnen**
drop-out *(female)*

der **Gang**, *PLURAL* die **Gänge**
1 walk
2 corridor
3 aisle
ein Platz am Gang an aisle seat
4 course *(of a meal)*
5 gear *(of a car, bicycle)*
6 etwas in Gang setzen to get something
going
7 im Gang(e) sein to be in progress

gängig *ADJECTIVE*
1 common
2 popular *(goods)*

ℓ die **Gans**, *PLURAL* die **Gänse**
goose

das **Gänseblümchen**, *PLURAL* die
Gänseblümchen
daisy

die **Gänsehaut**
goose pimples

ℓ **ganz** *ADJECTIVE*
1 whole
ganz Deutschland the whole of Germany
2 im Großen und Ganzen on the whole
3 eine ganze Menge quite a lot
4 all
mein ganzes Geld all my money
die ganzen Leute all the people
5 etwas wieder ganz machen to mend
something

ganz *ADVERB*
1 quite
Es war ganz gut. It was quite good.
Das hat er ganz ordentlich gemacht. He
did that quite well.
2 really
Es war ganz toll. It was really good.
3 ganz und gar completely
4 ganz und gar nicht not at all

ganztägig *ADJECTIVE, ADVERB*
1 full-time
2 all-day

Die Cafeteria ist ganztägig geöffnet. The cafeteria is open all day.

ganztags ADVERB
1 full time
2 all day

⚆ die **Ganztagsschule**, PLURAL die **Ganztagsschulen**
1 all-day school
2 all-day schooling

die **Ganztagsstelle**, PLURAL die **Ganztagsstellen**
full-time job

⚆ **gar** ADJECTIVE
done, cooked

gar ADVERB
1 gar nicht not at all
gar nichts nothing
2 oder gar or even

⚆ die **Garage**, PLURAL die **Garagen**
garage

> **WORD TIP** This word refers only to a garage for parking. The German word for a garage for car repairs is Autowerkstatt.

die **Garantie**, PLURAL die **Garantien**
guarantee

garantieren VERB, PERFECT **hat garantiert**
to guarantee

die **Garderobe**, PLURAL die **Garderoben**
cloakroom
Wir können die Mäntel an der Garderobe abgeben. We can leave the coats in the cloakroom.

die **Gardine**, PLURAL die **Gardinen**
curtain

das **Garn**, PLURAL die **Garne**
thread

die **Garnele**, PLURAL die **Garnelen**
1 shrimp
2 prawn

⚆ der **Garten**, PLURAL die **Gärten**
garden

⚆ der **Gärtner**, PLURAL die **Gärtner**
gardener (male)

> **WORD TIP** Professions, hobbies, and sports don't take an article in German: Er ist Gärtner.

⚆ die **Gärtnerin**, PLURAL die **Gärtnerinnen**
gardener (female)

> **WORD TIP** Professions, hobbies, and sports don't take an article in German: Sie ist Gärtnerin.

das **Gas**, PLURAL die **Gase**
1 gas
2 Gas geben to accelerate

der **Gasherd**, PLURAL die **Gasherde**
gas cooker

das **Gaspedal**, PLURAL die **Gaspedale**
accelerator

⚆ die **Gasse**, PLURAL die **Gassen**
lane (narrow street)

⚆ der **Gast**, PLURAL die **Gäste**
1 guest
Wir haben heute Abend Gäste. We've got guests tonight.
2 bei jemandem zu Gast sein to be staying with somebody
3 visitor

der **Gastarbeiter**, PLURAL die **Gastarbeiter**
foreign worker, guest worker (male)

die **Gastarbeiterin**, PLURAL die **Gastarbeiterinnen**
foreign worker, guest worker (female)

das **Gästehaus**, PLURAL die **Gästehäuser**
guest house

das **Gästezimmer**, PLURAL die **Gästezimmer**
1 (hotel) room
2 spare room, guest room

⚆ die **Gastfamilie**, PLURAL die **Gastfamilien**
host family

gastfreundlich ADJECTIVE
hospitable

die **Gastfreundschaft**
hospitality

der **Gastgeber**, PLURAL die **Gastgeber**
host

die **Gastgeberin**, PLURAL die **Gastgeberinnen**
hostess

das **Gasthaus**, PLURAL die **Gasthäuser**
inn, pub

der **Gasthof**, PLURAL die **Gasthöfe**
inn

⚆ die **Gaststätte**, PLURAL die **Gaststätten**
restaurant

der **Gauner**, PLURAL die **Gauner**
crook (male)

die **Gaunerin**, PLURAL die **Gaunerinnen**
crook (female)

geb. ABBREVIATION ▸ SEE **geboren**

◇ irregular verb; SEP separable verb; for more help with verbs see centre section

das **Gebäck**
1 pastries
2 biscuits
3 rolls

> **WORD TIP** Careful: Don't confuse this with Gepäck.

gebären VERB◇, IMPERFECT **gebar**, PERFECT **hat geboren**
1 to give birth to
2 geboren werden to be born

ℱ das **Gebäude**, PLURAL die **Gebäude**
building

ℱ **geben** VERB◇, PRESENT **gibt**, IMPERFECT **gab**, PERFECT **hat gegeben**
1 to give
2 to deal (cards)
3 to teach (at school)
Herr Schmidt gibt Mathe und Deutsch.
Mr Schmidt teaches maths and German.
4 Geben Sie mir bitte Frau Scheck. Please put me through to Mrs Scheck.
5 es gibt ... there is .../there are ...
Es gibt viele gute Restaurants in München. There are lots of good restaurants in Munich.
Was gibt es im Kino? What's on at the cinema?
Was gibt es zum Mittagessen? What are we having for lunch?
6 Was gibt's Neues? What's the news?/ What's new?
7 sich geschlagen geben to admit defeat
8 Das gibt sich wieder. It'll get better.
9 Das gibt's doch nicht! I don't believe it!

---

das **Gebet**, PLURAL die **Gebete**
prayer

gebeten ▸SEE **bitten**

das **Gebiet**, PLURAL die **Gebiete**
1 area, region
2 field

gebildet ADJECTIVE
educated

das **Gebirge**, PLURAL die **Gebirge**
1 mountains
Sie gingen im Gebirge wandern. They went walking in the mountains.
2 mountain range

das **Gebiss**, PLURAL die **Gebisse**
1 teeth
2 false teeth, dentures

gebissen ▸SEE **beißen**

geblieben ▸SEE **bleiben**

geboren VERB ▸SEE **gebären**
geboren ADJECTIVE
1 born
2 née
Frau Hahn, geborene Müller Mrs Hahn, née Müller

geborgen ADJECTIVE
safe

geboten ▸SEE **bieten**

gebracht ▸SEE **bringen**

gebraten ADJECTIVE
fried

der **Gebrauch**, PLURAL die **Gebräuche**
1 use
Vor Gebrauch schütteln. Shake before use.
2 custom

gebrauchen VERB, PERFECT **hat gebraucht**
to use

die **Gebrauchsanweisung**, PLURAL die **Gebrauchsanweisungen**
instructions (for use)

gebraucht ADJECTIVE
used, second-hand

der **Gebrauchtwagen**, PLURAL die **Gebrauchtwagen**
second-hand car

gebrochen ▸SEE **brechen**

die **Gebühr**, PLURAL die **Gebühren**
fee, charge

gebührenfrei ADJECTIVE
free (of charge)

gebührenpflichtig ADJECTIVE
1 subject to a charge
2 eine gebührenpflichtige Straße a toll road

gebunden ▸SEE **binden**

ℱ die **Geburt**, PLURAL die **Geburten**
birth

die **Geburtenregelung**
birth control

das **Geburtsdatum**, PLURAL die **Geburtsdaten**
date of birth

der **Geburtsort**, PLURAL die **Geburtsorte**
place of birth

ℱ indicates key words

_ß_ der **Geburtstag**, PLURAL die **Geburtstage**
  birthday
  Ich habe heute Geburtstag. It's my
  birthday today.

die **Geburtsurkunde**, PLURAL die
  Geburtsurkunden
  birth certificate

gedacht ▸ SEE **denken**

das **Gedächtnis**, PLURAL die **Gedächtnisse**
  memory

gedämpft ADJECTIVE
  steamed

der **Gedanke**, PLURAL die **Gedanken**
1 thought
  Er war in Gedanken versunken. He was
  lost in thought.
2 sich Gedanken machen to worry
  Mach dir keine Gedanken! Don't worry!
3 jemanden auf andere Gedanken bringen
  to take somebody's mind off things

gedankenlos ADJECTIVE
  thoughtless

gedankenlos ADVERB
  without thinking

das **Gedeck**, PLURAL die **Gedecke**
1 place setting
2 set meal

_ß_ das **Gedicht**, PLURAL die **Gedichte**
  poem

das **Gedränge**
  crush

die **Geduld**
  patience

_ß_ **geduldig** ADJECTIVE
  patient

gedünstet ADJECTIVE
  steamed

gedurft ▸ SEE **dürfen**

geehrt ADJECTIVE
1 honoured
2 Sehr geehrte Frau Ross! Dear Mrs Ross, (at
  the beginning of a letter)

_ß_ **geeignet** ADJECTIVE
1 suitable
2 right

die **Gefahr**, PLURAL die **Gefahren**
1 danger
  Er ist jetzt außer Gefahr. He is out of
  danger now.

2 risk
  Betreten auf eigene Gefahr. Enter at your
  own risk.
  Gefahr laufen, etwas zu tun to run the risk
  of doing something

gefährdet ADJECTIVE
  at risk, endangered
  eine gefährdete Art an endangered species

_ß_ **gefährlich** ADJECTIVE
  dangerous

gefallen¹ ▸ SEE **fallen**

_ß_ **gefallen**² VERB◇, PRESENT **gefällt**, IMPERFECT
  gefiel, PERFECT **hat gefallen**
1 Es gefällt mir. I like it.
  Es hat mir sehr gut gefallen. I liked it a lot.
2 sich etwas gefallen lassen to put up with
  something
  Das lasse ich mir nicht mehr gefallen. I
  won't put up with it any longer.

der **Gefallen**¹, PLURAL die **Gefallen**
  favour
  Kannst du mir bitte einen Gefallen tun?
  Could you please do me a favour?

das **Gefallen**²
  pleasure
  Ich verstehe nicht, wie man an
  Horrorfilmen Gefallen finden kann. I don't
  understand how people get pleasure from
  horror films.
  Er tut es nur dir zu Gefallen. He only does
  it to please you.

der/die **Gefangene**, PLURAL die **Gefangenen**
  prisoner

das **Gefängnis**, PLURAL die **Gefängnisse**
  prison

gefärbt ADJECTIVE
  dyed

das **Gefäß**, PLURAL die **Gefäße**
  container

gefasst ADJECTIVE
1 calm, composed
2 auf etwas gefasst sein to be prepared for
  something

gefiel ▸ SEE **gefallen**

geflogen ▸ SEE **fliegen**

geflossen ▸ SEE **fließen**

das **Geflügel**
  poultry

◇ irregular verb; SEP separable verb; for more help with verbs see centre section

gefochten ▸SEE **fechten**

gefräßig ADJECTIVE
(informal) **greedy**

ℓ **gefrieren** VERB◇, IMPERFECT **gefror**, PERFECT **ist gefroren**
to freeze
Das Wasser ist gefroren. The water has frozen.

das **Gefrierfach**, PLURAL die **Gefrierfächer**
freezer (compartment)

die **Gefriertruhe**, PLURAL die **Gefriertruhen**
freezer

gefroren ADJECTIVE
frozen

das **Gefühl**, PLURAL die **Gefühle**
1 **feeling**
2 **sense, instinct**
etwas im Gefühl haben to have a feel for something

gefüllt ADJECTIVE
stuffed (peppers, for example)

gefunden ▸SEE **finden**

gegangen ▸SEE **gehen**

gegeben ▸SEE **geben**

gegebenenfalls ADVERB
if need be

ℓ **gegen** PREPOSITION (+ ACC)
1 **against**
Sie tat es gegen den Willen ihrer Eltern. She did it against her parents' will.
2 Er ist gegen die Mauer gefahren. He drove into the wall.
3 Gibt es ein Mittel gegen Grippe? Is there a cure for flu?
4 **towards** (a time)
gegen Abend towards evening
5 gegen vier Uhr around four o'clock
6 **compared with**
7 **versus** (in sport)

ℓ die **Gegend**, PLURAL die **Gegenden**
1 **area, region**
2 **neighbourhood**

gegeneinander ADVERB
against each other, against one another

das **Gegenmittel**, PLURAL die **Gegenmittel**
1 **remedy**
2 **antidote**

der **Gegensatz**, PLURAL die **Gegensätze**
1 **contrast**
2 **opposite**
3 Im Gegensatz zu mir ist er sehr musikalisch. Unlike me, he is very musical.

gegenseitig ADJECTIVE
mutual

gegenseitig ADVERB
sich gegenseitig helfen to help each other

der **Gegenstand**, PLURAL die **Gegenstände**
1 **object**
2 **subject** (in grammar or of a discussion)

ℓ das **Gegenteil**, PLURAL die **Gegenteile**
1 **opposite**
2 im Gegenteil on the contrary

ℓ **gegenüber** PREPOSITION (+ DAT)
1 **opposite**
Susi saß mir gegenüber. Susi sat opposite me.
2 **towards**
Sie waren uns gegenüber sehr freundlich. They were very friendly towards us.
3 **compared with**
Die Preise sind gegenüber dem Vorjahr gestiegen. Prices have risen compared with last year.
gegenüber ADVERB
opposite
Meine Freundin wohnt gegenüber. My friend lives opposite.

die **Gegenwart**
1 **present** (time)
2 **presence**

gegessen ▸SEE **essen**

der **Gegner**, PLURAL die **Gegner**
opponent (male)

die **Gegnerin**, PLURAL die **Gegnerinnen**
opponent (female)

gegrillt ADJECTIVE
grilled

Gehacktes NEUTER NOUN
mince

das **Gehalt**, PLURAL die **Gehälter**
salary

gehässig ADJECTIVE
spiteful

geheim ADJECTIVE
secret

ℓ das **Geheimnis**, PLURAL die **Geheimnisse**
secret

ℓ indicates key words

geheimnisvoll *ADJECTIVE*
mysterious

ℰ **gehen** *VERB◇*, *IMPERFECT* **ging** *PERFECT* **ist gegangen**
1 to go
Ich gehe schlafen. I'm going to bed.
2 to walk
Seid ihr zu Fuß nach Hause gegangen? Did you walk home?
3 über die Straße gehen to cross the road
4 Es geht mir gut. I'm fine.
Wie geht es Ihnen? How are you?
Es geht. It's not too bad.
5 Das geht nicht. That's impossible.
6 um etwas gehen to be about something
Worum geht es hier? What's it all about?
7 Die Uhr geht falsch. The clock's wrong.

das **Gehirn**, *PLURAL* die **Gehirne**
brain

die **Gehirnerschütterung**, *PLURAL* die **Gehirnerschütterungen**
concussion

gehoben ▸ SEE **heben**

geholfen ▸ SEE **helfen**

das **Gehör**
hearing

gehorchen *VERB*, *PERFECT* **hat gehorcht**
to obey
Der Hund gehorcht mir nicht. The dog does not obey me.

ℰ **gehören** *VERB*, *PERFECT* **hat gehört**
1 to belong
Es gehört mir. It belongs to me.
2 to take
Dazu gehört Mut. That takes courage.
3 sich gehören to be the done thing
Das gehört sich nicht. It isn't done.

gehorsam *ADJECTIVE*
obedient

der **Gehorsam**
obedience

der **Gehsteig**, *PLURAL* die **Gehsteige**
pavement

der **Gehweg**, *PLURAL* die **Gehwege**
pavement

der **Geier**, *PLURAL* die **Geier**
vulture

ℰ die **Geige**, *PLURAL* die **Geigen**
violin

Anna spielt Geige. Anna plays the violin.

geil *ADJECTIVE*
(informal) cool, wicked

die **Geisel**, *PLURAL* die **Geiseln**
hostage

der **Geist**, *PLURAL* die **Geister**
1 mind
2 ghost
3 wit

geistesabwesend *ADJECTIVE*
absent-minded

geisteskrank *ADJECTIVE*
mentally ill

die **Geisteskrankheit**, *PLURAL* die **Geisteskrankheiten**
mental illness

die **Geisteswissenschaften** *PLURAL NOUN*
arts, humanities

geistig *ADJECTIVE*
mental, intellectual

geistreich *ADJECTIVE*
witty, clever

geizig *ADJECTIVE*
mean

gekannt ▸ SEE **kennen**

gekocht *ADJECTIVE*
1 cooked
2 boiled

gekonnt ▸ SEE **können**

das **Gel**, *PLURAL* die **Gele**
gel

das **Gelächter**
laughter

gelähmt *ADJECTIVE*
paralysed

ℰ das **Gelände**, *PLURAL* die **Gelände**
1 grounds
Auf dem Gelände der Schule darf nicht geraucht werden. Smoking is not allowed in the school grounds.
2 area

das **Geländer**, *PLURAL* die **Geländer**
1 banister(s)
2 railing(s)

gelangweilt *ADJECTIVE*
bored

◇ irregular verb; *SEP* separable verb; for more help with verbs see centre section

gelassen *VERB* ▸ SEE **lassen**

gelassen *ADJECTIVE*
  calm

geläufig *ADJECTIVE*
1 common
2 Dieser Ausdruck ist mir nicht geläufig. I'm not familiar with this expression.

_ℓ_ **gelaunt** *ADJECTIVE*
  gut gelaunt sein to be in a good mood
  schlecht gelaunt sein to be in a bad mood

_ℓ_ **gelb** *ADJECTIVE*
  yellow

_ℓ_ das **Geld**, *PLURAL* die **Gelder**
  money

der **Geldautomat**, *PLURAL* die
  Geldautomaten
  cash machine

der **Geldbeutel**, *PLURAL* die **Geldbeutel**
  wallet, purse

_ℓ_ die **Geldbörse**, *PLURAL* die **Geldbörsen**
  wallet, purse

der **Geldschein**, *PLURAL* die **Geldscheine**
  banknote

die **Geldstrafe**, *PLURAL* die **Geldstrafen**
  fine

das **Geldstück**, *PLURAL* die **Geldstücke**
  coin

der **Geldwechsel**
1 bureau de change
2 currency exchange

gelegen ▸ SEE **liegen**

die **Gelegenheit**, *PLURAL* die **Gelegenheiten**
1 opportunity
2 occasion

gelegentlich *ADVERB*
  occasionally

das **Gelenk**, *PLURAL* die **Gelenke**
  joint

der/die **Geliebte**, *PLURAL* die **Geliebten**
  lover

geliehen ▸ SEE **leihen**

_ℓ_ **gelingen** *VERB*◇, *IMPERFECT* **gelang**, *PERFECT* **ist gelungen**
  to succeed
  Es ist mir gelungen, sie zu überreden.
  I succeeded in persuading her.

gelten *VERB*◇, *PRESENT* **gilt**, *IMPERFECT* **galt**, *PERFECT* **hat gegolten**
1 to be valid
  Das Ticket gilt zwei Stunden. The ticket is valid for two hours.
2 to apply *(of a rule)*
  Das gilt auch für dich. That applies to you, too.
3 jemandem gelten to be directed at somebody
  Ich glaube, diese Bemerkung galt mir. I think that remark was directed at me.
4 Sein Wort gilt viel. His word is worth a lot.
5 Das gilt nicht! That doesn't count!
6 als etwas gelten to be regarded as something
  Rom gilt als eine der schönsten Städte der Welt. Rome is regarded as one of the most beautiful cities in the world.

gelungen *VERB* ▸ SEE **gelingen**

gelungen *ADJECTIVE*
  successful

das **Gemälde**, *PLURAL* die **Gemälde**
  painting

_ℓ_ **gemein** *ADJECTIVE*
  mean, nasty

die **Gemeinde**, *PLURAL* die **Gemeinden**
1 community
2 congregation

gemeinsam *ADJECTIVE*
1 common
2 joint
gemeinsam *ADVERB*
  together
  Sie essen gemeinsam. They eat together.

die **Gemeinschaft**, *PLURAL* die
  Gemeinschaften
  community

_ℓ_ **gemischt** *ADJECTIVE*
  mixed

gemocht ▸ SEE **mögen**

_ℓ_ das **Gemüse**, *PLURAL* die **Gemüse**
  vegetables

der **Gemüsehändler**, *PLURAL* die
  Gemüsehändler
  greengrocer *(male)*

> **WORD TIP** Professions, hobbies, and sports don't take an article in German: Er ist Gemüsehändler.

A
B
C
D
E
F
G
H
I
J
K
L
M
N
O
P
Q
R
S
T
U
V
W
X
Y
Z

_ℓ_ indicates key words

die **Gemüsehändlerin**, PLURAL die
Gemüsehändlerinnen
greengrocer (female)

WORD TIP Professions, hobbies, and sports
don't take an article in German: Sie ist
Gemüsehändlerin.

_ꝑ_ der **Gemüseladen**, PLURAL die **Gemüseläden**
greengrocer's shop

gemusst ▸ SEE müssen

gemustert ADJECTIVE
patterned

gemütlich ADJECTIVE
1 cosy
2 Mach es dir gemütlich. Make yourself
comfortable.

das **Gen**, PLURAL die **Gene**
gene

genannt ▸ SEE nennen

_ꝑ_ **genau** ADJECTIVE
1 exact
2 accurate (scales, description)
3 meticulous
4 Ich weiß nichts Genaues. I don't know any
details.
genau ADVERB
1 exactly
2 carefully
Ich sah es mir genau an. I looked at it
carefully.
3 genau genommen strictly speaking

die **Genauigkeit**
accuracy

genauso ADVERB
1 just the same
2 just as
genauso gut just as good
genauso viel just as much, just as many
genauso lange just as long

die **Genehmigung**, PLURAL die
Genehmigungen
1 permission
2 permit
3 licence

die **Generation**, PLURAL die **Generationen**
generation

der **Generator**, PLURAL die **Generatoren**
generator

generell ADJECTIVE
general

die **Genetik**
genetics

genetisch ADJECTIVE
genetic

genetisch ADVERB
genetically

Genf NEUTER NOUN
Geneva

der **Genfer See**
Lake Geneva

WORD TIP This is always used with the article:
Der Genfer See ist der größte See in den Alpen.

genial ADJECTIVE
brilliant

das **Genick**, PLURAL die **Genicke**
(back of the) neck

das **Genie**, PLURAL die **Genies**
genius

genießbar ADJECTIVE
edible

genießen VERB◇, IMPERFECT **genoss**, PERFECT
hat genossen
to enjoy

genmanipuliert ADJECTIVE
genetically modified

genommen ▸ SEE nehmen

die **Gentechnik**
genetic engineering

_ꝑ_ **genug** ADVERB
enough

genügen VERB, PERFECT **hat genügt**
to be enough

genügend ADJECTIVE
1 enough
2 sufficient

der **Genuss**, PLURAL die **Genüsse**
1 enjoyment
2 consumption

_ꝑ_ **geöffnet** ADJECTIVE
open

die **Geografie/Geographie**
geography

die **Geometrie**
geometry

_ꝑ_ das **Gepäck**
luggage

WORD TIP Careful: Don't confuse this with
Gebäck.

◇ irregular verb; SEP separable verb; for more help with verbs see centre section

ℓ die **Gepäckaufbewahrung**, *PLURAL* die **Gepäckaufbewahrungen**
left-luggage office

die **Gepäckausgabe**
baggage reclaim

der **Gepäckträger**, *PLURAL* die **Gepäckträger**
1 porter
2 roof rack
3 carrier *(on a bike)*

gepflegt *ADJECTIVE*
1 well-kept
2 well-groomed
3 sophisticated

geplant *ADJECTIVE*
planned

gepunktet *ADJECTIVE*
1 spotted
2 dotted *(line)*

gerade *ADJECTIVE*
1 straight
Setz dich gerade hin. Sit up straight.
etwas gerade biegen to straighten something
2 upright
eine gerade Haltung an upright posture
3 even
eine gerade Zahl an even number

gerade *ADVERB*
1 just
Wir sind gerade erst gekommen. We've only just arrived.
Sie hat es gerade noch geschafft. She only just managed it.
2 nicht gerade not exactly
Es war nicht gerade billig. It wasn't exactly cheap.

ℓ **geradeaus** *ADVERB*
straight ahead

gerannt ▸ SEE **rennen**

das **Gerät**, *PLURAL* die **Geräte**
1 appliance
2 set *(TV or radio)*
3 tool
4 gadget
5 die Geräte apparatus *(in gymnastics)*

geraten *VERB*◇, *PRESENT* **gerät**, *IMPERFECT* **geriet**, *PERFECT* **ist geraten**
1 to get *(somewhere, into a state, etc.)*
Sie sind in Schwierigkeiten geraten. They got into difficulties.
Er geriet in Wut. He got angry.
2 an den Richtigen geraten to come to the right person

3 gut/schlecht geraten to turn out well/badly
4 nach jemandem geraten to take after somebody

das **Gerätetauchen**
scuba diving

geräuchert *ADJECTIVE*
smoked

geräumig *ADJECTIVE*
spacious

das **Geräusch**, *PLURAL* die **Geräusche**
noise, sound

gerecht *ADJECTIVE*
1 just
2 fair

die **Gerechtigkeit**
justice

das **Gerede**
gossip

das **Gericht**, *PLURAL* die **Gerichte**
1 court
2 dish *(of food)*

gerieben ▸ SEE **reiben**

gering *ADJECTIVE*
1 small *(amount)*
2 low *(value)*
3 short *(time, distance)*

das **Gerippe**, *PLURAL* die **Gerippe**
skeleton

gerissen *ADJECTIVE*
crafty

geritten ▸ SEE **reiten**

ℓ **gern(e)** *ADVERB*
1 gladly
2 jemanden gern haben to like somebody
etwas gern tun to like doing something
Ich tanze gern. I like dancing.
Ich hätte gerne einen Kaffee. I'd like a coffee.
Welchen Belag hättest du gerne? Which topping would you like?
3 Ja, gern! Yes, I'd love to!
4 Gern geschehen! You're welcome!
5 Das glaube ich gern. I can well believe that.

die **Gerste**
barley

der **Geruch**, *PLURAL* die **Gerüche**
smell

das **Gerücht**, *PLURAL* die **Gerüchte**
rumour

das **Gerümpel**
junk

gesalzen *VERB* ▸ SEE **salzen**
gesalzen *ADJECTIVE*
1 salted
2 gesalzene Preise *(informal)* steep prices

gesamt *ADJECTIVE*
1 whole
2 die gesamten Kosten the total cost
3 die gesamten Werke the complete works

℘ die **Gesamtschule**, *PLURAL* die
Gesamtschulen
comprehensive school

gesandt ▸ SEE **senden**

℘ das **Geschäft**, *PLURAL* die **Geschäfte**
1 shop
2 business
3 deal

die **Geschäftsfrau**, *PLURAL* die
Geschäftsfrauen
businesswoman

der **Geschäftsführer**, *PLURAL* die
Geschäftsführer
manager *(male)*

WORD TIP Professions, hobbies, and sports
don't take an article in German: Er ist
Geschäftsführer.

die **Geschäftsführerin**, *PLURAL* die
Geschäftsführerinnen
manager *(female)*

WORD TIP Professions, hobbies, and sports
don't take an article in German: Sie ist
Geschäftsführerin.

der **Geschäftsmann**, *PLURAL* die
Geschäftsleute
businessman

die **Geschäftszeiten** *PLURAL NOUN*
business hours, office hours

geschehen *VERB*◇, *PRESENT* **geschieht**,
IMPERFECT **geschah**, *PERFECT* **ist geschehen**
to happen

gescheit *ADJECTIVE*
clever

℘ das **Geschenk**, *PLURAL* die **Geschenke**
present, gift

℘ die **Geschichte**, *PLURAL* die **Geschichten**
1 story

2 history
3 business
Erinnere mich nicht an diese dumme
Geschichte. Don't remind me of that silly
business.

das **Geschick**
1 skill
2 fate

geschickt *ADJECTIVE*
1 skilful
2 clever

℘ **geschieden** *VERB* ▸ SEE **scheiden**
geschieden *ADJECTIVE*
divorced
Meine Eltern sind geschieden. My parents
are divorced.

geschienen ▸ SEE **scheinen**

das **Geschirr**
1 crockery
2 dishes

der **Geschirrspüler**, *PLURAL* die
Geschirrspüler
dishwasher

die **Geschirrspülmaschine**, *PLURAL* die
Geschirrspülmaschinen
dishwasher

das **Geschirrtuch**, *PLURAL* die
Geschirrtücher
tea towel

das **Geschlecht**, *PLURAL* die **Geschlechter**
1 sex
2 gender

℘ **geschlossen** *VERB* ▸ SEE **schließen**
geschlossen *ADJECTIVE*
closed

der **Geschmack**, *PLURAL* die **Geschmäcke**
taste

geschmacklos *ADJECTIVE*
1 tasteless
2 geschmacklos sein to be in bad taste

geschnitten ▸ SEE **schneiden**

geschossen ▸ SEE **schießen**

geschrieben ▸ SEE **schreiben**

geschrien ▸ SEE **schreien**

das **Geschwätz**
talk

geschwätzig *ADJECTIVE*
talkative

die **Geschwindigkeit**, *PLURAL* die
Geschwindigkeiten
speed

die **Geschwindigkeitsbegrenzung**, *PLURAL*
die **Geschwindigkeitsbegrenzungen**
speed limit

ℰ die **Geschwister** *PLURAL NOUN*
brothers and sisters, siblings

geschwommen ▸ SEE **schwimmen**

das **Geschwür**, *PLURAL* die **Geschwüre**
ulcer

ℰ **gesellig** *ADJECTIVE*
sociable

die **Gesellschaft**, *PLURAL* die **Gesellschaften**
1 society
2 company
Ich leiste dir Gesellschaft. I'll keep you
company.

gesessen ▸ SEE **sitzen**

ℰ das **Gesetz**, *PLURAL* die **Gesetze**
law

gesetzlich *ADJECTIVE*
legal
ein gesetzlicher Feiertag a public holiday
gesetzlich *ADVERB*
legally, by law

ℰ das **Gesicht**, *PLURAL* die **Gesichter**
face

der **Gesichtsausdruck**, *PLURAL* die
Gesichtsausdrücke
(facial) expression

gesollt ▸ SEE **sollen**

gespannt *ADJECTIVE*
1 eager
2 auf etwas gespannt sein to look forward
eagerly to something
auf jemanden gespannt sein to look
forward to seeing somebody
Ich bin schon ganz gespannt. I can't wait.
Ich bin gespannt, ob ... I wonder whether
...
3 tense
In Südafrika ist die Lage immer noch
gespannt. The situation in South Africa is
still tense.

das **Gespenst**, *PLURAL* die **Gespenster**
ghost

ℰ das **Gespräch**, *PLURAL* die **Gespräche**
1 conversation
im Gespräch sein to be under discussion

2 call *(on the phone)*

gesprächig *ADJECTIVE*
talkative

gesprochen ▸ SEE **sprechen**

gesprungen ▸ SEE **springen**

die **Gestalt**, *PLURAL* die **Gestalten**
1 figure
2 form

gestanden ▸ SEE **stehen**, **gestehen**

das **Geständnis**, *PLURAL* die **Geständnisse**
confession

gestatten *VERB*, *PERFECT* **hat gestattet**
1 to permit
2 nicht gestattet sein to be prohibited
3 Gestatten Sie? May I?

die **Geste**, *PLURAL* die **Gesten**
gesture

gestehen *VERB◇*, *IMPERFECT* **gestand**, *PERFECT*
hat gestanden
to confess

das **Gestell**, *PLURAL* die **Gestelle**
1 rack
2 stand
3 frame

ℰ **gestern** *ADVERB*
1 yesterday
2 gestern Nacht last night

gestohlen ▸ SEE **stehlen**

gestorben ▸ SEE **sterben**

gestreift *ADJECTIVE*
striped

ℰ **gesund** *ADJECTIVE*
1 healthy
2 wieder gesund werden to get well again
3 Schwimmen ist gesund. Swimming is
good for you.

ℰ die **Gesundheit**
1 health
2 Gesundheit! Bless you! *(said after someone
sneezes)*

gesungen ▸ SEE **singen**

getan ▸ SEE **tun**

ℰ das **Getränk**, *PLURAL* die **Getränke**
drink

die **Getränkekarte**, *PLURAL* die
Getränkekarten
drinks menu, wine list

A
B
C
D
E
F
G
H
I
J
K
L
M
N
O
P
Q
R
S
T
U
V
W
X
Y
Z

ℰ indicates key words

A
B
C
D
E
F
G
H
I
J
K
L
M
N
O
P
Q
R
S
T
U
V
W
X
Y
Z

der **Getränkemarkt**, PLURAL die **Getränkemärkte**
supermarket selling alcohol and soft drinks

getrauen VERB, PERFECT **hat sich getraut**
sich getrauen to dare

das **Getreide**
grain

getrennt ADJECTIVE
separate

getrennt ADVERB
1 getrennt leben to be separated
Meine Eltern leben getrennt. My parents are separated.
2 etwas getrennt schreiben to write something as two words
Schreibt man das zusammen oder getrennt? Is it written as one word or two?

das **Getriebe**, PLURAL die **Getriebe**
gearbox

getrieben ▸ SEE **treiben**

getroffen ▸ SEE **treffen**

getrunken ▸ SEE **trinken**

das **Getue**
fuss

geübt ADJECTIVE
1 experienced, skilful
2 mit geübtem Auge with a practised eye

das **Gewächshaus**, PLURAL die **Gewächshäuser**
greenhouse

℘ die **Gewalt**
1 power
2 force
mit Gewalt by force
3 violence

gewaltig ADJECTIVE
enormous

℘ **gewalttätig** ADJECTIVE
violent

gewann ▸ SEE **gewinnen**

das **Gewebe**, PLURAL die **Gewebe**
1 fabric
2 tissue

das **Gewehr**, PLURAL die **Gewehre**
rifle, gun

die **Gewerkschaft**, PLURAL die **Gewerkschaften**
trade union

gewesen ▸ SEE **sein**

das **Gewicht**, PLURAL die **Gewichte**
weight

der **Gewinn**, PLURAL die **Gewinne**
1 profit
2 winnings
3 prize

℘ **gewinnen** VERB◇, IMPERFECT **gewann**, PERFECT **hat gewonnen**
1 to win
Sie haben 3 zu 2 gewonnen. They won by 3 goals to 2.
2 to gain (time or influence)
an Bedeutung gewinnen to gain in importance

der **Gewinner**, PLURAL die **Gewinner**
winner (male)

die **Gewinnerin**, PLURAL die **Gewinnerinnen**
winner (female)

gewiss ADJECTIVE
certain
Ein gewisser Herr Schmidt möchte Sie sprechen. A Mr Schmidt would like to speak to you.

gewiss ADVERB
certainly, of course
'Darf ich?' – 'Aber gewiss doch.' 'May I?' – 'Of course.'

das **Gewissen**, PLURAL die **Gewissen**
conscience

gewissenhaft ADJECTIVE
conscientious

gewissermaßen ADVERB
1 more or less
2 as it were

℘ das **Gewitter**, PLURAL die **Gewitter**
thunderstorm

gewittrig ADJECTIVE
thundery

gewöhnen VERB, PERFECT **hat gewöhnt**
1 sich an etwas gewöhnen to get used to something
Sie mussten sich an den neuen Lehrer gewöhnen. They had to get used to the new teacher.
2 an etwas gewöhnt sein to be used to something
Ich bin an das frühe Aufstehen gewöhnt. I am used to getting up early.
3 jemanden an etwas gewöhnen to get somebody used to something
Sie gewöhnte die Kinder ans

◇ irregular verb; SEP separable verb; for more help with verbs see centre section

Zähneputzen. She got the children used to brushing their teeth.

℘ die **Gewohnheit**, PLURAL die **Gewohnheiten**
habit

gewöhnlich ADJECTIVE
1 usual
2 ordinary
gewöhnlich ADVERB
usually
wie gewöhnlich as usual

gewohnt ADJECTIVE
1 usual
2 etwas gewohnt sein to be used to something
Renate ist es nicht gewohnt, früh aufzustehen. Renate isn't used to getting up early.

gewollt ▸ SEE **wollen**

gewonnen ▸ SEE **gewinnen**

geworden ▸ SEE **werden**

geworfen ▸ SEE **werfen**

das **Gewürz**, PLURAL die **Gewürze**
spice

gewusst ▸ SEE **wissen**

die **Gezeiten** PLURAL NOUN
tides

gezogen ▸ SEE **ziehen**

gezwungen ▸ SEE **zwingen**

gibt ▸ SEE **geben**

gierig ADJECTIVE
greedy

gießen VERB◇, IMPERFECT **goss**, PERFECT **hat gegossen**
1 to pour
Er goss Kaffee in die Tasse. He poured coffee into the cup.
Es gießt. It's pouring.
2 to water
Vergiss nicht, die Blumen zu gießen. Don't forget to water the flowers.

die **Gießkanne**, PLURAL die **Gießkannen**
watering can

das **Gift**, PLURAL die **Gifte**
poison

WORD TIP The German word Gift does not mean gift in English; the German word for gift is Geschenk.

giftig ADJECTIVE
1 poisonous
2 toxic

der **Giftmüll**
toxic waste

das **Gigabyte**, PLURAL die **Gigabytes**
gigabyte
eine Festplatte mit 20 Gigabyte Speicherkapazität a 20 gigabyte hard disk

ging ▸ SEE **gehen**

der **Gipfel**, PLURAL die **Gipfel**
1 peak, summit
2 Das ist der Gipfel der Geschmacklosigkeit! That is the height of bad taste!

der **Gips**
plaster

die **Giraffe**, PLURAL die **Giraffen**
giraffe

das **Girokonto**, PLURAL die **Girokonten**
current account

℘ die **Gitarre**, PLURAL die **Gitarren**
guitar
Chris spielt Gitarre. Chris plays the guitar.

der **Gitarrist**, PLURAL die **Gitarristen**
guitarist, guitar player (male)

WORD TIP Professions, hobbies, and sports don't take an article in German: Er ist Gitarrist.

die **Gitarristin**, PLURAL die **Gitarristinnen**
guitarist, guitar player (female)

WORD TIP Professions, hobbies, and sports don't take an article in German: Sie ist Gitarristin.

das **Gitter**, PLURAL die **Gitter**
1 grid
2 bars

glänzen VERB, PERFECT **hat geglänzt**
to shine

glänzend ADJECTIVE
1 shining
2 brilliant
Die Show war ein glänzender Erfolg. The show was a brilliant success.

℘ das **Glas**, PLURAL die **Gläser**
1 glass (the material)
2 glass (for a drink)
Er trank ein Glas Wasser. He drank a glass of water.
3 jar

die **Glasscheibe**, PLURAL die **Glasscheiben**
pane (of glass)

131

die **Glasur**
1 icing
2 glaze

𝒫 **glatt** ADJECTIVE
1 smooth
2 slippery
3 eine glatte Absage a flat refusal

glatt ADVERB
1 smoothly
2 flatly
  etwas glatt ablehnen to flatly reject
  something
3 Das ist glatt gelogen. That's a downright
  lie.
4 Ich habe ihren Geburtstag glatt
  vergessen. I totally forgot about her
  birthday.

das **Glatteis**
(black) ice

die **Glatze**, PLURAL die **Glatzen**
  eine Glatze haben to be bald
  eine Glatze bekommen to go bald

der **Glaube**
1 faith
2 belief

𝒫 **glauben** VERB, PERFECT **hat geglaubt**
1 to believe
  Ich glaube ihr. I believe her.
  Glaubst du an Gott? Do you believe in
  God?
2 to think
  Glaubst du, dass sie die Wahrheit sagt? Do
  you think she is telling the truth?
  Das glaube ich nicht. I don't think so.
3 Das ist doch kaum/nicht zu glauben!
  That's incredible!

𝒫 **gleich** ADJECTIVE
1 same
2 identical
3 Das ist mir gleich. It's all the same to me.
  Ich bin nicht zu sprechen, ganz gleich,
  wer anruft. I'm not available, no matter
  who calls.

gleich ADVERB
1 the same
2 equally
3 immediately
  gleich danach immediately afterwards
  Er sitzt gleich neben Martin. He's sitting
  right next to Martin.
  Ich komme gleich. I'm coming (right
  away).
  Ich bin gleich wieder da. I'll be back in a
  minute.

gleichartig ADJECTIVE
  similar

gleichberechtigt ADJECTIVE
  equal

die **Gleichberechtigung**
  equality

gleichbleibend
  constant

gleichen VERB◇, IMPERFECT **glich**, PERFECT **hat
geglichen**
1 to be like
  Sie gleicht ihrer Mutter. She is like her
  mother.
2 sich gleichen to be alike
  Die Zwillinge gleichen sich. The twins are
  alike.

gleichfalls ADVERB
1 also
2 Danke gleichfalls! The same to you!

gleichgeschlechtlich ADJECTIVE
  same-sex

das **Gleichgewicht**
  balance

gleichgültig ADJECTIVE
1 indifferent
2 not important
  Das ist doch gleichgültig. It's not
  important.

die **Gleichheit**
  equality

die **Gleichung**, PLURAL die **Gleichungen**
  equation

gleichwertig ADJECTIVE
1 equivalent
2 of the same value
3 of the same standard

gleichzeitig ADVERB
  at the same time

𝒫 das **Gleis**, PLURAL die **Gleise**
1 track, line
  Die Gleise werden repariert. The tracks
  are being repaired.
2 platform
  Der Zug kommt auf Gleis vier an. The train
  is coming in on platform four.

das **Gleitschirmfliegen**
  paragliding

der **Gletscher**, PLURAL die **Gletscher**
  glacier

◇ irregular verb; SEP separable verb; for more help with verbs see centre section

glich ▸ SEE **gleichen**

das **Glied**, PLURAL die **Glieder**
1 limb
2 link

die **Gliederung**, PLURAL die **Gliederungen**
structure

glitschig ADJECTIVE
slippery

glitzern VERB, PERFECT **hat geglitzert**
to glitter

global ADJECTIVE
global, general
die globale Erwärmung global warming

die **Glocke**, PLURAL die **Glocken**
bell

ℙ das **Glück**
1 luck
Viel Glück! good luck!
Glück haben to be lucky
zum Glück luckily
2 happiness

ℙ **glücklich** ADJECTIVE
1 lucky
Es war ein glücklicher Zufall, dass ich ihn heute in der Stadt getroffen habe. It was a lucky coincidence that I met him in town today.
2 happy

glücklicherweise ADVERB
luckily, fortunately

der **Glückwunsch**, PLURAL die **Glückwünsche**
congratulations
Herzlichen Glückwunsch zum Geburtstag! Happy birthday!

die **Glückwunschkarte**, PLURAL die **Glückwunschkarten**
greetings card

die **Glühbirne**, PLURAL die **Glühbirnen**
light bulb

glühen VERB, PERFECT **hat geglüht**
to glow

der **Gokart**, PLURAL die **Gokarts**
go-kart
Gokart fahren to go karting

das **Gold**
gold

golden ADJECTIVE
1 gold

2 golden

der **Goldfisch**, PLURAL die **Goldfische**
goldfish

der **Golf**[1], PLURAL die **Golfe**
gulf

das **Golf**[2]
golf

der **Golfplatz**, PLURAL die **Golfplätze**
golf course

der **Golfschläger**, PLURAL die **Golfschläger**
golf club

der **Golfspieler**, PLURAL die **Golfspieler**
golfer (male)

die **Golfspielerin**, PLURAL die **Golfspielerinnen**
golfer (female)

der **Gorilla**, PLURAL die **Gorillas**
gorilla

goss ▸ SEE **gießen**

die **Gosse**, PLURAL die **Gossen**
gutter (in street)

der **Gott**, PLURAL die **Götter**
god

der **Gottesdienst**, PLURAL die **Gottesdienste**
(church) service

die **Göttin**, PLURAL die **Göttinnen**
goddess

das **Grab**, PLURAL die **Gräber**
grave

graben VERB◇, PRESENT **gräbt**, IMPERFECT **grub**, PERFECT **hat gegraben**
to dig

der **Grad**, PLURAL die **Grade**
degree

das **Graffiti**
graffiti

die **Grafik**, PLURAL die **Grafiken**
1 graphics
2 graphic art

der **Grafiker**, PLURAL die **Grafiker**
graphic designer (male)

WORD TIP Professions, hobbies, and sports don't take an article in German: Er ist Grafiker.

die **Grafikerin**, PLURAL die **Grafikerinnen**
graphic designer (female)

WORD TIP Professions, hobbies, and sports don't take an article in German: Sie ist Grafikerin.

ℙ indicates key words

Gramm   **grinsen**

♂ das **Gramm**, PLURAL die **Gramme**
gram

die **Grammatik**, PLURAL die **Grammatiken**
grammar

grammatikalisch ADJECTIVE
grammatical
ein grammatikalischer Fehler a
grammatical error

grantig ADJECTIVE
grumpy

die **Grapefruit**, PLURAL die **Grapefruits**
grapefruit

♂ das **Gras**, PLURAL die **Gräser**
grass

grässlich ADJECTIVE
horrible

die **Gräte**, PLURAL die **Gräten**
(fish) bone

gratis ADVERB
free of charge

gratulieren VERB, PERFECT **hat gratuliert**
to congratulate
Wir gratulieren! Congratulations!
Ich habe Gabi zum Geburtstag gratuliert.
I wished Gabi happy birthday.

♂ **grau** ADJECTIVE
grey

das **Graubrot**, PLURAL die **Graubrote**
brown bread (made from a mixture of rye
and wheat flour)
Sie kaufte zwei Graubrote. She bought
two loaves of brown bread.

der **Gräuel**, PLURAL die **Gräuel**
horror

grauen VERB, PERFECT **hat gegraut**
Mir graut es davor. I dread it.

grauenvoll ADJECTIVE
1 grim
2 horrific

grauhaarig ADJECTIVE
grey-haired

grausam ADJECTIVE
cruel

die **Grausamkeit**
cruelty

graziös ADJECTIVE
graceful

greifen VERB♦, IMPERFECT **griff**, PERFECT **hat
gegriffen**
1 to take hold of
2 to catch
3 nach etwas greifen to reach for something
4 um sich greifen to spread (of fire)

grell ADJECTIVE
1 glaring
2 garish
3 shrill

die **Grenze**, PLURAL die **Grenzen**
1 border
2 boundary
3 limit

grenzen VERB, PERFECT **hat gegrenzt**
an etwas grenzen to border on something

der **Grieche**, PLURAL die **Griechen**
Greek (male)

♂ **Griechenland** NEUTER NOUN
Greece

die **Griechin**, PLURAL die **Griechinnen**
Greek (female)

griechisch ADJECTIVE
Greek

> **WORD TIP** Adjectives never have capitals
> in German, even for regions, countries, or
> nationalities.

griff ▸ SEE **greifen**

der **Griff**, PLURAL die **Griffe**
1 grasp
2 handle

griffbereit ADJECTIVE
(ready) to hand
Sie hat das Wörterbuch immer griffbereit.
She always keeps the dictionary to hand.

der **Grill**, PLURAL die **Grills**
1 grill
2 barbecue

die **Grille**, PLURAL die **Grillen**
cricket (the insect)

grillen VERB, PERFECT **hat gegrillt**
1 to grill
2 to have a barbecue

das **Grillfest**, PLURAL die **Grillfeste**
barbecue (party)

die **Grillstube**, PLURAL die **Grillstuben**
grill (restaurant)

grinsen VERB, PERFECT **hat gegrinst**
to grin

♦ irregular verb; SEP separable verb; for more help with verbs see centre section

ℐ die **Grippe**, PLURAL die **Grippen**
　flu

grob ADJECTIVE
1　coarse
2　rough
3　rude
4　ein grober Fehler a bad mistake

der **Groschen**, PLURAL die **Groschen**
1　groschen (one hundredth of a Schilling in
　the former Austrian currency)
　▸ SEE **Schilling**
2　(informal)
　Der Groschen ist gefallen. The penny's
　dropped.

ℐ **groß** ADJECTIVE
1　big
2　great
　Gisela hatte große Angst. Gisela was very
　frightened.
3　tall
4　ein großer Buchstabe a capital letter
5　groß werden to grow up
6　die großen Ferien the summer holidays
7　im Großen und Ganzen on the whole
8　Groß und Klein young and old

groß ADVERB
　Was soll man da schon groß machen?
　What are you supposed to do?

großartig ADJECTIVE
　great

ℐ **Großbritannien** NEUTER NOUN
　Great Britain

der **Großbuchstabe**, PLURAL die
　Großbuchstaben
　capital (letter)

ℐ die **Größe**, PLURAL die **Größen**
1　size
2　height
3　greatness

ℐ die **Großeltern** PLURAL NOUN
　grandparents

großenteils ADVERB
　largely

der **Großmarkt**, PLURAL die **Großmärkte**
　hypermarket

ℐ die **Großmutter**, PLURAL die **Großmütter**
　grandmother

großschreiben VERB◇, IMPERFECT **schrieb
　groß**, PERFECT **hat großgeschrieben**
　to write with a capital letter
　Er schreibt dieses Wort groß. He writes
　the word with a capital letter.

ℐ die **Großstadt**, PLURAL die **Großstädte**
　city

größtenteils ADVERB
　for the most part

ℐ der **Großvater**, PLURAL die **Großväter**
　grandfather

großzügig ADJECTIVE
　generous

grub ▸ SEE **graben**

ℐ **grün** ADJECTIVE
1　green
　grüne Bohnen green beans
2　im Grünen in the country
3　die Grünen the Greens (political party)

die **Grünanlage**, PLURAL die **Grünanlagen**
　park

ℐ der **Grund**, PLURAL die **Gründe**
1　ground
2　bottom
3　reason
　aus diesem Grund for this reason
4　im Grunde genommen basically

gründen VERB, PERFECT **hat gegründet**
1　to set up, to found
2　sich auf etwas gründen to be based on
　something

die **Grundlage**, PLURAL die **Grundlagen**
　basis

gründlich ADJECTIVE
　thorough

gründlich ADVERB
1　thoroughly
2　completely
　Mein erster Versuch ging gründlich schief.
　My first attempt failed completely.

der **Grundsatz**, PLURAL die **Grundsätze**
　principle

grundsätzlich ADJECTIVE
1　fundamental
2　basic

grundsätzlich ADVERB
1　basically
2　on principle

die **Grundschule**, PLURAL die **Grundschulen**
　primary school

das **Grundstück**, PLURAL die **Grundstücke**
　plot (of land)

ℐ die **Gruppe**, PLURAL die **Gruppen**
　group

135

der **Gruselfilm**, PLURAL die **Gruselfilme**
horror film

gruselig ADJECTIVE
creepy, weird, scary

ℰ der **Gruß**, PLURAL die **Grüße**
greeting
Bestelle Lars einen schönen Gruß von mir.
Give my regards to Lars.
Mit herzlichen Grüßen ... With best
wishes ...

ℰ **grüßen** VERB, PERFECT **hat gegrüßt**
1 to greet
2 to say hello
3 Grüß Gott! (used in Southern Germany,
Austria, and Switzerland) Hello!
4 Grüße Thomas von mir. Give Thomas my
regards.
Lisa lässt grüßen. Lisa sends her regards.

gucken VERB, PERFECT **hat geguckt**
to look

das **Gulasch**, PLURAL die **Gulasche**
goulash

die **Gulaschsuppe**, PLURAL die
Gulaschsuppen
goulash soup

gültig ADJECTIVE
valid

die **Gültigkeit**
validity

der **Gummi**, PLURAL die **Gummis**
rubber

das **Gummiband**, PLURAL die **Gummibänder**
rubber band

das **Gummibärchen**, PLURAL die
Gummibärchen
jelly baby (in the shape of a bear)

der **Gummistiefel**, PLURAL die **Gummistiefel**
wellington (boot)

günstig ADJECTIVE
1 favourable
2 convenient

die **Gurgel**, PLURAL die **Gurgeln**
throat

gurgeln VERB, PERFECT **hat gegurgelt**
to gargle

die **Gurke**, PLURAL die **Gurken**
1 cucumber
2 gherkin
saure Gurken (pickled) gherkins

der **Gürtel**, PLURAL die **Gürtel**
belt

die **Gürteltasche**, PLURAL die **Gürteltaschen**
bum bag

ℰ **gut** ADJECTIVE
1 good (also as a school mark)
Das ist eine gute Idee. That's a good
idea.
Guten Abend! Good evening!
Guten Tag! Hello!
Guten Appetit! Enjoy your meal!
2 all right
Schon gut. That's all right.
Also gut, ich mache es. All right, I'll do it.
3 im Guten amicably
4 Alles Gute! All the best!

gut ADVERB
1 well
Er spricht sehr gut Deutsch. He speaks
German very well.
Gut gemacht! Well done!
2 good
Es schmeckt/riecht gut. It tastes/smells
good.
Der Flug dauert gut zwei Stunden. The
flight takes a good two hours.
3 fine, well
Uns geht's gut. We're fine.
'Wie geht es dir?' – 'Danke, gut.' 'How
are you?' – 'Fine, thanks.'
Ihm geht es nicht gut. He's not well.

---

das **Gut**, PLURAL die **Güter**
1 property
2 estate
3 Güter goods, freight

die **Güte**
1 goodness
Du meine Güte! My goodness!
2 quality

der **Güterzug**, PLURAL die **Güterzüge**
goods train

gutmütig ADJECTIVE
good-natured

ℰ der **Gutschein**, PLURAL die **Gutscheine**
1 (gift) voucher
2 coupon

ℰ das **Gymnasium**, PLURAL die **Gymnasien**
grammar school

WORD TIP The German word Gymnasium does
not mean gym in English; the German word for
gym is Turnhalle (in schools) or Fitnesszentrum
(for the public).

◇ irregular verb; SEP separable verb; for more help with verbs see centre section

die **Gymnastik**
1 gymnastics
2 keep-fit (exercises)

Hh

ℓ das **Haar**, PLURAL die **Haare**
1 hair
   Ich muss mir die Haare waschen. I have to
   wash my hair.
2 um ein Haar (informal) very nearly

die **Haarbürste**, PLURAL die **Haarbürsten**
hairbrush

haarig ADJECTIVE
hairy

der **Haarschnitt**, PLURAL die **Haarschnitte**
haircut

das **Haarwaschmittel**, PLURAL die
Haarwaschmittel
shampoo

ℓ **haben** VERB◇, PRESENT **hat**, IMPERFECT
hatte, PERFECT **hat gehabt**
1 to have (got)
   Ich habe ein neues Auto. I have/I've got
   a new car.
   etwas gegen jemanden haben to have
   something against somebody
2 (used with another verb, like 'have' in
   English, to form past tenses)
   Ich habe Werners Adresse verloren. I've
   lost Werner's address.
   Ich habe deine Mutter gestern
   angerufen. I rang your mother yesterday.
3 (used with certain nouns to form
   expressions)
   Angst haben to be frightened
   Hunger haben to be hungry
   Husten haben to have a cough
4 Heute haben wir Mittwoch. It's
   Wednesday today.
5 Die Kinder haben Ferien. The children
   are on holiday.
6 Was hat sie? What's the matter with her?
7 Ich hätte gern ... I'd like ...
   Ich hätte ihr geholfen. I would have
   helped her.
8 etwas nicht haben können (informal) to
   hate something
   Mein Vater kann diese Art von Musik
   nicht haben. My father hates that kind
   of music.

Das kann ich nicht haben. I can't stand it.
9 sich haben (informal) to make a fuss
   Hab dich nicht so! Don't make such a
   fuss!

der **Habicht**, PLURAL die **Habichte**
hawk

hacken VERB, PERFECT **hat gehackt**
1 to chop (up)
2 to peck (of a bird)

das **Hackfleisch**
minced meat

das **Hacksteak**, PLURAL die **Hacksteaks**
beefburger (without bread)

ℓ der **Hafen**, PLURAL die **Häfen**
harbour

🟠 **HAFEN**

Germany's busiest seaport is Hamburg.

die **Hafenstadt**, PLURAL die **Hafenstädte**
port

die **Haferflocken** PLURAL NOUN
porridge oats

haftbar ADJECTIVE
für etwas haftbar sein to be liable for
something

haften VERB, PERFECT **hat gehaftet**
1 to stick
2 für etwas haften to be responsible for
   something
3 für jemanden haften to be legally
   responsible for somebody
   Eltern haften für ihre Kinder. Parents are
   legally responsible for their children.

der **Hagel**
hail

hageln VERB, PERFECT **hat gehagelt**
to hail
Es hagelt. It's hailing.

der **Hagelschauer**, PLURAL die **Hagelschauer**
hailstorm

der **Hahn**, PLURAL die **Hähne**
1 cock, cockerel
2 tap

ℓ das **Hähnchen**, PLURAL die **Hähnchen**
chicken

der **Hai**, PLURAL die **Haie**
shark

ℓ indicates key words

der **Haken**, *PLURAL* die **Haken**
1 hook
2 tick
3 catch
Da muss ein Haken dran sein. There must
be a catch.

♭ **halb** *ADJECTIVE*
half
Ich habe es zum halben Preis bekommen.
I got it half price.
Es ist halb eins. It is half past twelve.

halb *ADVERB*
half
halb durch halfway through, *(steak)*
medium rare

♭ der **Halbbruder**, *PLURAL* die **Halbbrüder**
half-brother

halbfett *ADJECTIVE*
medium-fat

das **Halbfinale**, *PLURAL* die **Halbfinale**
semi-final

halbieren *VERB, PERFECT* **hat halbiert**
to halve

der **Halbkreis**, *PLURAL* die **Halbkreise**
semicircle

♭ die **Halbpension**
half board

♭ die **Halbschwester**, *PLURAL* die
Halbschwestern
half-sister

halbtags *ADVERB*
part-time

die **Halbtagsschule**, *PLURAL* die
Halbtagsschulen
1 half-day school
2 half-day schooling

die **Halbtagsstelle**, *PLURAL* die
Halbtagsstellen
part-time job

halbwegs *ADVERB*
more or less

die **Halbzeit**, *PLURAL* die **Halbzeiten**
1 half
in der ersten Halbzeit in the first half
2 half-time
während der Halbzeit during half-time

half ▶ SEE **helfen**

die **Hälfte**, *PLURAL* die **Hälften**
half
zur Hälfte half

Er hat die Aufgabe nur zur Hälfte
gemacht. He only did half the exercise.

die **Halle**, *PLURAL* die **Hallen**
1 hall
2 foyer

♭ das **Hallenbad**, *PLURAL* die **Hallenbäder**
indoor swimming pool

♭ **hallo** *EXCLAMATION*
hello!

♭ der **Hals**, *PLURAL* die **Hälse**
1 neck
2 throat
Mir tut der Hals weh. I've got a sore
throat.
3 Sie schrie aus vollem Hals. She shouted at
the top of her voice.
4 Hals über Kopf in a rush

das **Halsband**, *PLURAL* die **Halsbänder**
collar

die **Halskette**, *PLURAL* die **Halsketten**
necklace

♭ die **Halsschmerzen** *PLURAL NOUN*
sore throat
Paul hat Halsschmerzen. Paul's got a sore
throat.

♭ die **Halstablette**, *PLURAL* die **Halstabletten**
cough sweet

das **Halstuch**, *PLURAL* die **Halstücher**
scarf

halt *EXCLAMATION*
stop!

der **Halt**
hold
Ihre Füße fanden keinen Halt. Her feet
found no hold.
Jetzt hat es einen besseren Halt. It holds
better now.

haltbar *ADJECTIVE*
1 hard-wearing, durable
2 Mindestens haltbar bis ... Best before ...

♭ **halten** *VERB◇, PRESENT* **hält**, *IMPERFECT*
hielt, *PERFECT* **hat gehalten**
1 to hold
2 to keep
Er hat sein Versprechen gehalten. He has
kept his promise.
Kannst du das Essen warm halten? Can
you keep the food warm?
3 to stop

◇ **irregular verb;** *SEP* **separable verb; for more help with verbs see centre section**

Der Bus hält direkt vor seiner Haustür.
The bus stops right outside his door.
4 **to save** *(in sport)*
5 **to take** *(a paper, magazine)*
6 **to think**
　Die Lehrerin hält viel von Julia. The
　teacher thinks a lot of Julia.
　Ich halte ihn für ehrlich. I think he is
　honest.
7 Ich habe ihn für deinen Bruder gehalten.
　I took him for your brother.
8 **zu jemandem halten** to stand by
　somebody
9 **eine Rede halten** to make a speech
10 **sich halten** to keep *(of milk, fruit, etc.)*
11 **sich links/rechts halten** to keep to the
　left/right
12 **sich gut halten** to do well
13 **sich an etwas halten** to keep to
　something

die **Haltestelle**, PLURAL die **Haltestellen**
　stop

haltmachen
　to stop

die **Haltung**, PLURAL die **Haltungen**
1 posture
2 attitude
3 composure

♪ der **Hamburger**, PLURAL die **Hamburger**
　hamburger

> **WORD TIP** The German word Hamburger can
> refer to a resident of Hamburg as well as the food.

das **Hammelfleisch**
　mutton

der **Hammer**, PLURAL die **Hämmer**
　hammer

hämmern VERB, PERFECT **hat gehämmert**
　to hammer

♪ der **Hamster**, PLURAL die **Hamster**
　hamster

♪ die **Hand**, PLURAL die **Hände**
　hand
　Er hat mir die Hand gegeben. He shook
　hands with me.
　zu Händen von for the attention of

die **Handarbeit**, PLURAL die **Handarbeiten**
1 handicraft
2 hand-made article

der **Handball**
　handball

die **Handbremse**, PLURAL die **Handbremsen**
　handbrake
　Zieh die Handbremse! Put on the
　handbrake!

das **Handbuch**, PLURAL die **Handbücher**
　manual, handbook

der **Handel**
1 trade
2 deal
3 Das Spiel ist im August in den Handel
　gekommen. The game came on the market
　in August.

handeln VERB, PERFECT **hat gehandelt**
1 to trade, to deal
2 to haggle
　Er hat versucht mit dem Verkäufer zu
　handeln. He tried to haggle with the
　salesman.
3 to act
　Wir müssen schnell handeln. We have to
　act quickly.
4 **von etwas handeln** to be about something
　Wovon handelt das Buch? What is the
　book about?
5 **es handelt sich um ...** it's about ...
　Worum handelt es sich? What's it about?

die **Handelsschule**, PLURAL die
　Handelsschulen
　commercial college

die **Handfläche**, PLURAL die **Handflächen**
　palm

das **Handgelenk**, PLURAL die **Handgelenke**
　wrist

das **Handgepäck**
　hand luggage

handhaben VERB, PERFECT **hat gehandhabt**
　to handle

der **Händler**, PLURAL die **Händler**
　dealer *(male)*

die **Händlerin**, PLURAL die **Händlerinnen**
　dealer *(female)*

handlich ADJECTIVE
　handy

die **Handlung**, PLURAL die **Handlungen**
1 act
2 action
3 plot

die **Handschellen** PLURAL NOUN
　handcuffs

die **Handschrift**, PLURAL die **Handschriften**
　handwriting

A
B
C
D
E
F
G
H
I
J
K
L
M
N
O
P
Q
R
S
T
U
V
W
X
Y
Z

♪ **indicates key words**

der **Handschuh**, PLURAL die **Handschuhe**
glove

die **Handtasche**, PLURAL die **Handtaschen**
handbag

die **Handtrommel**, PLURAL die **Handtrommeln**
tambourine

ℰ das **Handtuch**, PLURAL die **Handtücher**
towel

der **Handwerker**, PLURAL die **Handwerker**
1 craftsman
2 workman

> **WORD TIP** Professions, hobbies, and sports don't take an article in German: Er ist Handwerker.

die **Handwerkerin**, PLURAL die **Handwerkerinnen**
1 craftswoman
2 worker (female)

> **WORD TIP** Professions, hobbies, and sports don't take an article in German: Sie ist Handwerkerin.

das **Handwerkszeug**
tools

ℰ das **Handy**, PLURAL die **Handys**
mobile (phone)

> **WORD TIP** The German word Handy does not mean handy in English; the German word for handy is praktisch, handlich.

der **Hang**, PLURAL die **Hänge**
slope

die **Hängematte**, PLURAL die **Hängematten**
hammock

hängen¹ VERB, PERFECT **hat gehängt**
1 to hang
Florian hat das Bild an die Wand gehängt. Florian hung the picture on the wall.
Sie hängte ihren Mantel in den Schrank. She hung her coat up in the wardrobe.
2 Sie haben den Wohnwagen an das Auto gehängt. They attached the caravan to the car.
3 sich an jemanden hängen to latch on to somebody

hängen² VERB◇, IMPERFECT **hing**, PERFECT **hat gehangen**
1 to hang
Mein Bild hat immer hier gehangen. My picture always used to hang here.
2 an jemandem hängen to be attached to somebody

Sie hängt sehr an ihrer Mutter. She's very attached to her mother.
3 an etwas hängen bleiben to catch on something, to stick to something
Ich bin mit dem Ärmel am Zaun hängen geblieben. I got my sleeve caught on the fence.

hängenbleiben ▸ SEE **hängen**²

Hannover NEUTER NOUN
Hanover

das **Hansaplast**™
(sticking) plaster

der **Happen**, PLURAL die **Happen**
mouthful
Ich habe heute keinen Happen gegessen. I haven't had a bite to eat all day.

die **Harfe**, PLURAL die **Harfen**
harp

die **Harke**, PLURAL die **Harken**
rake

harmlos ADJECTIVE
harmless

ℰ **hart** ADJECTIVE
1 hard
2 harsh
3 hart gekocht hard-boiled

ℰ das **Häschen**, PLURAL die **Häschen**
small rabbit

das **Haschisch**
hashish

der **Hase**, PLURAL die **Hasen**
hare

die **Haselnuss**, PLURAL die **Haselnüsse**
hazelnut

der **Hass**
hatred

ℰ **hassen** VERB, PERFECT **hat gehasst**
to hate

ℰ **hässlich** ADJECTIVE
1 ugly
Sie hat ein hässliches Gesicht. She's got an ugly face.
2 nasty
Das war sehr hässlich von dir. That was very nasty of you.

hast ▸ SEE **haben**

hastig ADJECTIVE
hasty

◇ irregular verb; SEP separable verb; for more help with verbs see centre section

hat, hatte, hatten, hattest, hattet
▸SEE **haben**

die Haube, PLURAL die **Hauben**
1 **bonnet** (for head or of a car)
2 **cap** (of a nurse)
3 (used in Austria and Southern Germany)
woolly hat

hauen VERB◇, PRESENT **haut**, IMPERFECT **haute**,
PERFECT **hat gehauen**
1 **to hit**
Er hat mich gehauen! He hit me!
2 **to thump, to bang**
3 jemanden übers Ohr hauen (informal) to
cheat somebody

der Haufen, PLURAL die **Haufen**
1 **heap**
2 **crowd** (of people)
3 ein Haufen (informal) heaps of, loads of
Ihre Eltern haben einen Haufen Geld. Her
parents have got loads of money.

haufenweise ADVERB
loads of
Gabi hat haufenweise CDs. Gabi has loads
of CDs.

häufig ADJECTIVE
frequent
häufig ADVERB
frequently

die Häufigkeit
frequency

der Hauptbahnhof, PLURAL die
Hauptbahnhöfe
main station

♀ der **Hauptdarsteller**, PLURAL die
Hauptdarsteller
leading actor

♀ die **Hauptdarstellerin**, PLURAL die
Hauptdarstellerinnen
leading actress

♀ das **Hauptgericht**, PLURAL die
Hauptgerichte
main course

die Hauptrolle, PLURAL die **Hauptrollen**
leading role

die Hauptsache, PLURAL die **Hauptsachen**
main thing

hauptsächlich ADJECTIVE
main
hauptsächlich ADVERB
mainly

♀ die **Hauptschule**, PLURAL die **Hauptschulen**
secondary (modern) school

die Hauptspeise, PLURAL die **Hauptspeisen**
main course

♀ die **Hauptstadt**, PLURAL die **Hauptstädte**
capital

♀ die **Hauptstraße**, PLURAL die **Hauptstraßen**
main road, main street

die Hauptverkehrszeit, PLURAL die
Hauptverkehrszeiten
rush hour

das Hauptwort, PLURAL die **Hauptwörter**
noun (in grammar)

♀ das **Haus**, PLURAL die **Häuser**
1 **house**
2 nach Hause home
Wir gingen nach Hause. We went home.
3 zu Hause at home
Sie ist nicht zu Hause. She's not at home.

die Hausarbeit, PLURAL die **Hausarbeiten**
1 **housework**
Die Kinder müssen bei der Hausarbeit
helfen. The children have to help with the
housework.
2 **homework**

♀ die **Hausaufgaben** PLURAL NOUN
homework
Hast du deine Hausaufgaben gemacht?
Have you done your homework?

♀ die **Hausfrau**, PLURAL die **Hausfrauen**
housewife

WORD TIP Professions, hobbies, and sports
don't take an article in German: Sie ist Hausfrau.

hausgemacht ADJECTIVE
home-made

♀ der **Haushalt**, PLURAL die **Haushalte**
1 **household**
2 **housework**
Er macht den Haushalt. He does the
housework.
Die Kinder helfen im Haushalt. The
children help in the house.
3 **budget**

das Haushaltswarengeschäft, PLURAL die
Haushaltswarengeschäfte
hardware shop

♀ der **Hausmann**, PLURAL die **Hausmänner**
house husband

WORD TIP Professions, hobbies, and sports
don't take an article in German: Er ist
Hausmann.

♀ **indicates key words**

der **Hausmeister**, PLURAL die **Hausmeister**
caretaker *(male)*

WORD TIP Professions, hobbies, and sports don't take an article in German: Er ist Hausmeister.

die **Hausmeisterin**, PLURAL die **Hausmeisterinnen**
caretaker *(female)*

WORD TIP Professions, hobbies, and sports don't take an article in German: Sie ist Hausmeisterin.

ℙ die **Hausnummer**, PLURAL die **Hausnummern**
house number

die **Hausordnung**, PLURAL die **Hausordnungen**
house rules

der **Hausschlüssel**, PLURAL die **Hausschlüssel**
front-door key

der **Hausschuh**, PLURAL die **Hausschuhe**
slipper

ℙ das **Haustier**, PLURAL die **Haustiere**
pet

die **Haustür**, PLURAL die **Haustüren**
front door

die **Hauswirtschaftslehre**
home economics

die **Haut**, PLURAL die **Häute**
1 skin
2 aus der Haut fahren *(informal)* to go up the wall

Hbf. ABBREVIATION
(=Hauptbahnhof) main station

die **Hebamme**, PLURAL die **Hebammen**
midwife

WORD TIP Professions, hobbies, and sports don't take an article in German: Sie ist Hebamme.

der **Hebel**, PLURAL die **Hebel**
lever

heben VERB◇, IMPERFECT **hob**, PERFECT **hat gehoben**
1 to lift
2 sich heben to rise

die **Hecke**, PLURAL die **Hecken**
hedge

das **Heer**, PLURAL die **Heere**
army

die **Hefe**
yeast

ℙ das **Heft**, PLURAL die **Hefte**
1 exercise book, notebook
2 issue *(of a magazine)*

heften VERB, PERFECT **hat geheftet**
1 to pin
2 to tack *(by sewing)*
3 to clip
4 to staple

heftig ADJECTIVE
1 violent
2 heavy *(snow, rain)*

die **Heftklammer**, PLURAL die **Heftklammern**
staple

das **Heftpflaster**, PLURAL die **Heftpflaster**
sticking plaster

die **Heftzwecke**, PLURAL die **Heftzwecken**
drawing pin

die **Heide**
heath

das **Heidekraut**
heather

die **Heidelbeere**, PLURAL die **Heidelbeeren**
bilberry, blueberry

heilen VERB, PERFECT **hat geheilt**
1 to cure
2 to heal

heilig ADJECTIVE
1 holy
2 jemandem heilig sein to be sacred to somebody
3 der heilige Franz von Assisi Saint Francis of Assisi

ℙ der **Heiligabend**, PLURAL die **Heiligabende**
Christmas Eve

der/die **Heilige**, PLURAL die **Heiligen**
saint

> 🔵 **HEILIGE DREI KÖNIGE**
>
> Heilige Drei Könige is celebrated on the 6 January and is the last day of the Christmas holidays. In Austria and parts of Germany, teenagers dress up as kings and go from house to house to collect money for projects that support poor children in the Third World.

der **Heilige Abend**, PLURAL die **Heiligen Abende**
Christmas Eve

das **Heilmittel**, PLURAL die **Heilmittel**
remedy

◇ **irregular verb;** SEP **separable verb; for more help with verbs see centre section**

heim ADVERB
home

das **Heim**, PLURAL die **Heime**
1 home
2 hostel

ℱ die **Heimat**, PLURAL die **Heimaten**
1 home
2 native land

heimatlos ADJECTIVE
homeless

die **Heimatstadt**, PLURAL die **Heimatstädte**
home town

die **Heimfahrt**, PLURAL die **Heimfahrten**
1 journey home
2 way home

heimgehen VERB◇, IMPERFECT **ging heim**,
PERFECT **ist heimgegangen**
to go home

heimlich ADJECTIVE
secret
heimlich ADVERB
secretly

das **Heimspiel**, PLURAL die **Heimspiele**
home game

der **Heimweg**, PLURAL die **Heimwege**
way home

ℱ das **Heimweh**
homesickness
Sie hatte Heimweh. She was homesick.

das **Heimwerken**
DIY

die **Heirat**, PLURAL die **Heiraten**
marriage

ℱ **heiraten** VERB, PERFECT **hat geheiratet**
to marry

heiser ADJECTIVE
hoarse

ℱ **heiß** ADJECTIVE
hot

ℱ **heißen** VERB◇, IMPERFECT **hieß**, PERFECT **hat**
geheißen
1 to be called
Wie heißt du? What's your name?
2 to mean
3 das heißt that is
4 es heißt they say
Es heißt, dass sie in den Fall verwickelt
war. They say that she was involved in the
case.

5 Wie heißt 'dog' auf Deutsch? What's the
German for 'dog'?

heiter ADJECTIVE
1 bright
2 cheerful

heizen VERB, PERFECT **hat geheizt**
1 to heat (a room)
2 to put the heating on
3 to have the heating on

der **Heizkörper**, PLURAL die **Heizkörper**
radiator

die **Heizung**, PLURAL die **Heizungen**
heating

ℱ **hektisch** ADJECTIVE
hectic

der **Held**, PLURAL die **Helden**
hero

die **Heldin**, PLURAL die **Heldinnen**
heroine

ℱ **helfen** VERB◇, PRESENT **hilft**, IMPERFECT **half**,
PERFECT **hat geholfen**
1 to help
Lisa hilft mir. Lisa is helping me.
2 Es hilft nichts, ... It's no good, ...
3 sich zu helfen wissen to know what to do
Ich weiß mir nicht zu helfen. I don't know
what to do.

der **Helfer**, PLURAL die **Helfer**
1 helper (male)
2 assistant (male)

die **Helferin**, PLURAL die **Helferinnen**
1 helper (female)
2 assistant (female)

ℱ **hell** ADJECTIVE
1 light (colour)
2 bright
3 eine helle Stimme a clear voice
4 helles Bier lager
ein Helles a lager
5 Das ist heller Wahnsinn. (informal) It's
sheer madness.

hellwach ADJECTIVE
wide awake

der **Helm**, PLURAL die **Helme**
helmet

ℱ das **Hemd**, PLURAL die **Hemden**
1 shirt
2 vest

der **Henkel**, PLURAL die **Henkel**
handle

ℱ indicates key words

die **Henne**, *PLURAL* die **Hennen**
hen

her *ADVERB*
1 **ago**
Das ist schon lange her. It was a long time ago.
Das ist drei Tage her. It was three days ago.
2 **here**
Komm her! Come here!
3 Sie liefen vor uns her. They walked in front of us.
4 **von etwas her** as far as something is concerned
Von der Farbe her gefällt es mir. I like it as far as the colour is concerned.
5 Wo bist du her? Where do you come from?
6 Wo hat Klaus das her? Where did Klaus get it from?
7 Her damit! *(informal)* Give it to me!

herab *ADVERB*
down

herablassend *ADJECTIVE*
condescending

herabsetzen *VERB*, *PERFECT* **hat herabgesetzt**
1 to reduce
2 to belittle

heran *ADVERB*
1 **an etwas heran** close to something, right up to something
bis an die Wand heran up to the wall
2 Immer heran! Come closer!

herankommen *VERB*◇, *IMPERFECT* **kam heran**, *PERFECT* **ist herangekommen**
1 to come near
2 **an jemanden herankommen** to come up to somebody
3 **an etwas herankommen** to reach something
Ich komme nicht heran. I can't get at it.

herauf *ADVERB*
up

heraufkommen *VERB*◇, *IMPERFECT* **kam herauf**, *PERFECT* **ist heraufgekommen**
to come up

heraufladen *VERB*◇, *PRESENT* **lädt herauf**, *IMPERFECT* **lud herauf**, *PERFECT* **hat heraufgeladen**
to upload

heraus *ADVERB*
out

herausbekommen *VERB*◇, *IMPERFECT* **bekam heraus**, *PERFECT* **hat herausbekommen**
1 to get out
2 to find out
3 to solve
4 Hast du noch Wechselgeld herausbekommen? Did you get any change?

herausbringen *VERB*◇, *IMPERFECT* **brachte heraus**, *PERFECT* **hat herausgebracht**
1 to publish *(a book)*
2 to release *(an album)*
3 to launch *(a product)*

herausfinden *VERB*◇, *IMPERFECT* **fand heraus**, *PERFECT* **hat herausgefunden**
1 to find out
2 to find your way out

herausgeben *VERB*◇, *PRESENT* **gibt heraus**, *IMPERFECT* **gab heraus**, *PERFECT* **hat herausgegeben**
1 to hand over
2 to bring out

herauskommen *VERB*◇, *IMPERFECT* **kam heraus**, *PERFECT* **ist herausgekommen**
to come out

herausnehmen *VERB*◇, *PRESENT* **nimmt heraus**, *IMPERFECT* **nahm heraus**, *PERFECT* **hat herausgenommen**
1 to take out
Sie nahm ihren Lippenstift aus der Tasche heraus. She took her lipstick out of her bag.
2 Er hat sich die Mandeln herausnehmen lassen. He's had his tonsils out.
3 es sich herausnehmen, etwas zu tun to have the nerve to do something
Du nimmst dir zu viel heraus. You're going too far.

herausstellen *VERB*, *PERFECT* **hat herausgestellt**
1 to put out
2 **sich herausstellen** to turn out
Es stellte sich heraus, dass ... It turned out that ...

herausziehen *VERB*◇, *IMPERFECT* **zog heraus**, *PERFECT* **hat herausgezogen**
to pull out

herb *ADJECTIVE*
1 sharp
2 dry *(wine)*
3 bitter *(disappointment)*

herbei *ADVERB*
over (here)

◇ **irregular verb**; *SEP* **separable verb**; for more help with verbs see centre section

Kommt herbei! Come over here!

die **Herberge**, PLURAL die **Herbergen**
hostel

die **Herbergseltern**, PLURAL NOUN
(hostel) wardens

der **Herbergsgast**, PLURAL die
Herbergsgäste
hostel guest

die **Herbergsmutter**, PLURAL die
Herbergsmütter
(hostel) warden *(female)*

der **Herbergsvater**, PLURAL die
Herbergsväter
(hostel) warden *(male)*

herbringen VERB◇, IMPERFECT **brachte her**,
PERFECT **hat hergebracht**
to bring (here)

ℒ der **Herbst**, PLURAL die **Herbste**
autumn
im Herbst in autumn

die **Herbstferien**, PLURAL NOUN
autumn half-term holidays

der **Herd**, PLURAL die **Herde**
cooker

die **Herde**, PLURAL die **Herden**
1 herd
2 flock

herein ADVERB
in
Herein! Come in!

hereinfallen VERB◇, PRESENT **fällt herein**,
IMPERFECT **fiel herein**, PERFECT **ist**
hereingefallen
to be taken in
Wir sind auf einen Betrüger
hereingefallen. We were taken in by a
swindler.

hereinkommen VERB◇, IMPERFECT **kam**
herein, PERFECT **ist hereingekommen**
to come in

hereinlassen VERB◇, PRESENT **lässt herein**,
IMPERFECT **ließ herein**, PERFECT **hat**
hereingelassen
to let in
Lass ihn nicht herein! Don't let him in here!

die **Herfahrt**, PLURAL die **Herfahrten**
1 journey here
2 way here

hergeben VERB◇, PRESENT **gibt her**, IMPERFECT
gab her, PERFECT **hat hergegeben**
1 to hand over
Gib die Tasche her! Hand over the bag!
2 to give away
3 sich für etwas hergeben to get involved in
something
Dafür gebe ich mich nicht her. I won't have
anything to do with it.

der **Hering**, PLURAL die **Heringe**
herring

herkommen VERB◇, IMPERFECT **kam her**,
PERFECT **ist hergekommen**
to come (here)
Wo kommt das her? Where does it come
from?

die **Herkunft**, PLURAL die **Herkünfte**
1 origin
2 background

das **Heroin**
heroin

ℒ der **Herr**, PLURAL die **Herren**
1 gentleman
2 Mr
Herr Huber Mr Huber
3 Sehr geehrte Herren! Dear Sirs, ... *(at the
beginning of a letter)*
4 Meine Herren! Gentlemen!
5 Herr Ober! Waiter!
6 master
7 der Herr the Lord

herrichten VERB, PERFECT **hat hergerichtet**
to get ready, to prepare
Sie richtet die Betten für die Gäste her.
She's getting the beds ready for the guests.

herrlich ADJECTIVE
marvellous

herrschen VERB, PERFECT **hat geherrscht**
1 to rule
2 to be
Es herrschte große Aufregung. There was
great excitement.

herstellen VERB, PERFECT **hat hergestellt**
to manufacture, to produce, to make
Das Gerät wird in Deutschland
hergestellt. The appliance is made in
Germany.

der **Hersteller**, PLURAL die **Hersteller**
manufacturer

die **Herstellung**, PLURAL die **Herstellungen**
manufacture, production

ℒ indicates key words

herüber ADVERB
over (here)

ℓ **herum** ADVERB
round, around
um ... herum round ...
Du hast die Batterie falsch herum
eingelegt. You put in the battery the
wrong way round.
Sie liefen im Kreis herum. They ran round
in a circle.

herumalbern VERB, PERFECT **hat
herumgealbert**
to fool around

herumdrehen VERB, PERFECT **hat
herumgedreht**
1 to turn (over or round)
2 sich herumdrehen to turn round

herumfahren VERB◇, PRESENT **fährt
herum**, IMPERFECT **fuhr herum**, PERFECT **ist
herumgefahren**
to drive around

herumführen VERB, PERFECT **hat
herumgeführt**
to show around

herumgehen VERB◇, IMPERFECT **ging herum**,
PERFECT **ist herumgegangen**
1 to go round
2 to walk around
Sie gingen im Park herum. They walked
around the park.
3 to pass (of time)

herunter ADVERB
down
Sie kam die Treppe herunter. She came
down the stairs.

herunterfallen VERB◇, PRESENT **fällt
herunter**, IMPERFECT **fiel herunter**, PERFECT
ist heruntergefallen
1 to fall down
2 to fall off

herunterkommen VERB◇, IMPERFECT
kam herunter, PERFECT **ist
heruntergekommen**
1 to come down
2 (informal) to go to rack and ruin

herunterladen VERB◇, PRESENT **lädt
herunter**, IMPERFECT **lud herunter**, PERFECT
hat heruntergeladen
to download

herunterlassen VERB◇, PRESENT **lässt
herunter**, IMPERFECT **ließ herunter**, PERFECT
hat heruntergelassen
to let down, to lower

hervor ADVERB
out

hervorragend ADJECTIVE
outstanding

hervorragend ADVERB
very well

hervorrufen VERB◇, IMPERFECT **rief hervor**,
PERFECT **hat hervorgerufen**
to cause

das **Herz**, PLURAL die **Herzen**
1 heart
2 hearts (in cards)

der **Herzanfall**, PLURAL die **Herzanfälle**
heart attack

der **Herzinfarkt**, PLURAL die **Herzinfarkte**
heart attack

herzlich ADJECTIVE
1 warm
2 sincere
3 Herzlichen Dank! Many thanks!
4 Mit herzlichen Grüßen ... Best wishes ...
5 Herzlichen Glückwunsch! Congratulations!
6 Herzlich willkommen in Passau. Welcome
to Passau.

herzlos ADJECTIVE
heartless

der **Herzschlag**, PLURAL die **Herzschläge**
1 heartbeat
2 pulse
3 heart attack
Er hat einen Herzschlag bekommen.
He had a heart attack.

heterosexuell ADJECTIVE
heterosexual

der/die **Heterosexuelle**, PLURAL die
Heterosexuellen
heterosexual

das **Heu**
hay

heulen VERB, PERFECT **hat geheult**
1 to howl
2 (informal) to cry

ℓ der **Heuschnupfen**
hay fever
Ich bekomme im Sommer immer
Heuschnupfen. I always suffer from hay
fever in the summer.

◇ irregular verb; SEP separable verb; for more help with verbs see centre section

_ℱ_ **heute** ADVERB
   today
   heute Abend this evening
   heute Morgen this morning
   heute Nachmittag this afternoon

heutig ADJECTIVE
1 today's
2 in der heutigen Zeit nowadays

_ℱ_ **heutzutage**
   nowadays
   Heutzutage sind Allergien häufig.
   Allergies are common nowadays.

die **Hexe**, PLURAL die **Hexen**
   witch

der **Hexenschuss**, PLURAL die **Hexenschüsse**
   lumbago

hielt ▸ SEE **halten**

_ℱ_ **hier** ADVERB
   here

hierher ADVERB
   here
   Komm sofort hierher! Come here
   immediately!

hierhin ADVERB
   here

hiesig ADJECTIVE
   local

hieß ▸ SEE **heißen**

_ℱ_ die **Hilfe**, PLURAL die **Hilfen**
1 help
2 aid

hilflos ADJECTIVE
   helpless

_ℱ_ **hilfsbereit** ADJECTIVE
   helpful

hilft ▸ SEE **helfen**

die **Himbeere**, PLURAL die **Himbeeren**
   raspberry

_ℱ_ der **Himmel**, PLURAL die **Himmel**
1 sky
2 heaven

himmlisch ADJECTIVE
   heavenly

_ℱ_ **hin** ADVERB
1 there
   hin und zurück there and back
2 hin und wieder now and again
3 hin und her back and forth, to and fro

4 auf meinen Rat hin on my advice
   auf Ihren Brief hin in reply to your letter
5 Wo ist Max hin? Where's Max gone?
6 Es ist nicht mehr lange hin. It's not long
   to go.
7 Ich bin hin. (informal) I'm done in.

hinauf ADVERB
   up

hinaufgehen VERB◇, IMPERFECT **ging hinauf**,
   PERFECT **ist hinaufgegangen**
   to go up

hinaus ADVERB
1 out
2 Die Zukunft der Firma ist auf Jahre hinaus
   gesichert. The company's future is secure
   for years to come.

hinausbringen VERB◇, IMPERFECT **brachte
   hinaus**, PERFECT **hat hinausgebracht**
1 to see out (a person)
2 to take out
   Kannst du bitte den Abfall hinausbringen?
   Could you take the rubbish out, please?

hinausgehen VERB◇, IMPERFECT **ging hinaus**,
   PERFECT **ist hinausgegangen**
1 to go out
2 über etwas hinausgehen to exceed
   something
3 Das Zimmer geht nach Norden hinaus.
   The room faces north.

hindern VERB, PERFECT **hat gehindert**
   to stop
   jemanden daran hindern, etwas zu tun to
   stop somebody from doing something

das **Hindernis**, PLURAL die **Hindernisse**
   obstacle

hinduistisch ADJECTIVE
   Hindu

   WORD TIP Adjectives never have capitals in
   German, even for religions.

hindurch ADVERB
1 through it/them
2 Der Zoo ist das ganze Jahr hindurch
   geöffnet. The zoo is open throughout the
   year.

hinein ADVERB
1 in
2 in etwas hinein into something

hineingehen VERB◇, IMPERFECT **ging hinein**,
   PERFECT **ist hineingegangen**
1 to go in
2 in etwas hineingehen to go into
   something

_ℱ_ indicates key words

hinfahren VERB◇, PRESENT **fährt hin**, IMPERFECT **fuhr hin**, PERFECT **ist hingefahren**
1 to go/drive there
2 PERFECT **hat hingefahren**
   jemanden hinfahren to take/drive somebody there

die **Hinfahrt**, PLURAL die **Hinfahrten**
1 journey there, way there
2 outward journey

hinfallen VERB◇, PRESENT **fällt hin**, IMPERFECT **fiel hin**, PERFECT **ist hingefallen**
   to fall over

hing ▸ SEE **hängen**

hingehen VERB◇, IMPERFECT **ging hin**, PERFECT **ist hingegangen**
1 to go there
   Wo geht ihr hin? Where are you going?
2 to go by (of time)

hinken VERB, PERFECT **hat/ist gehinkt**
   to limp

hinkommen VERB◇, IMPERFECT **kam hin**, PERFECT **ist hingekommen**
1 to get there
2 to go
   Wo kommt das Buch hin? Where does the book go?
3 mit etwas hinkommen (informal) to manage with something

hinlegen VERB, PERFECT **hat hingelegt**
1 to put down
   Leg die Zeitung unten hin. Put the paper down there.
2 sich hinlegen to lie down

ℓ **hinsetzen** VERB, PERFECT **hat sich hingesetzt**
   sich hinsetzen to sit down
   Petra setzte sich neben ihm hin. Petra sat down next to him.

hinten ADVERB
   at the back
   von hinten from behind

ℓ **hinter** PREPOSITION (+ DAT or + ACC)
1 (the dative is used when talking about position; the accusative shows movement or a change of place) behind
   Er sitzt hinter dir. (DAT) He's sitting behind you.
   Sie setzten sich hinter uns. (ACC) They sat down behind us.
2 after
   Die anderen Kinder rannten hinter ihm

3 her. (DAT) The other children ran after him.
4 hinter jemandem/etwas her sein (DAT) to be after somebody/something
   Die Polizei ist hinter ihnen her. The police are after them.
   Hinter dieser CD bin ich schon seit Wochen her. I've been after that CD for weeks.
5 etwas hinter sich bringen (ACC) to get something over with
   Erst muss ich die Prüfung hinter mich bringen. First I have to get the exam over with.

   WORD TIP hinter + das gives hinters

hintere ▸ SEE **hinterer**

hintereinander ADVERB
1 one behind the other
2 one after the other
   Er fiel dreimal hintereinander aufs Eis. He fell on the ice three times in a row.

hinterer, **hintere**, **hinteres** ADJECTIVE
1 back
2 Sein Büro ist am hinteren Ende des Gangs. His office is at the far end of the corridor.

der **Hintergrund**, PLURAL die **Hintergründe**
   background

hinterher ADVERB
   afterwards

der **Hintern**, PLURAL die **Hintern**
   bottom

das **Hinterrad**, PLURAL die **Hinterräder**
   back wheel

hinters ▸ SEE **hinter das**

hinüber ADVERB
1 over (there), across (there)
2 Mein Laptop ist hinüber. (informal) My laptop has had it.

hinübergehen VERB◇, IMPERFECT **ging hinüber**, PERFECT **ist hinübergegangen**
   to go over, to go across

hinunter ADVERB
   down

der **Hinweg**, PLURAL die **Hinwege**
   way there
   auf dem Hinweg on the way there

der **Hinweis**, PLURAL die **Hinweise**
1 hint
   Das war ein deutlicher Hinweis, dass er

◇ irregular verb; SEP separable verb; for more help with verbs see centre section

lieber allein fährt. It was an obvious hint that he prefers to go on his own.

2 reference
3 instruction
Hinweise zur Bedienung operating instructions

hinweisen VERB◇, IMPERFECT **wies hin**, PERFECT **hat hingewiesen**
to point
jemanden auf etwas hinweisen to point something out to somebody

das **Hirn**, PLURAL die **Hirne**
brain

die **Hirnhautentzündung**
meningitis

der **Hirsch**, PLURAL die **Hirsche**
1 deer
2 stag
3 venison

der **Hirt**, PLURAL die **Hirten**
shepherd (male)

die **Hirtin**, PLURAL die **Hirtinnen**
shepherdess

der **Historiker**, PLURAL die **Historiker**
historian (male)

WORD TIP Professions, hobbies, and sports don't take an article in German: Er ist Historiker.

die **Historikerin**, PLURAL die
Historikerinnen
historian (female)

WORD TIP Professions, hobbies, and sports don't take an article in German: Sie ist Historikerin.

historisch ADJECTIVE
1 historical
2 historic

die **Hitparade**, PLURAL die **Hitparaden**
charts

die **Hitze**
heat

hitzefrei ADJECTIVE
hitzefrei haben to be sent home early from school because of hot weather

🔵 **HITZEFREI**

Hitzefrei: 'heat free'. If the thermometer reaches 27 degrees centigrade many schools send their pupils home early.

die **Hitzewelle**, PLURAL die **Hitzewellen**
heatwave

der **Hitzschlag**, PLURAL die **Hitzschläge**
heatstroke

hob ▸ SEE **heben**

ℓ das **Hobby**, PLURAL die **Hobbys**
hobby

ℓ **hoch** ADJECTIVE
1 high
Der Zaun ist zu hoch. The fence is too high. Der Garten ist von einem hohen Zaun umgeben. The garden is surrounded by a high fence.
2 deep (snow)
3 great (age, weight)

WORD TIP With endings, hoch becomes hoher/hohe/hohes.

hoch ADVERB
1 highly
2 Er ging die Treppe hoch. He walked up the stairs.

das **Hoch**, PLURAL die **Hochs**
1 cheer
Ein dreifaches Hoch auf das Geburtstagskind! Three cheers for the birthday girl/boy!
2 high (pressure)

hochachtungsvoll ADVERB
Hochachtungsvoll, ... Yours faithfully, ...

hochbegabt ADJECTIVE
(very) gifted, (very) talented

hochhackig ADJECTIVE
high-heeled
hochhackige Schuhe high-heeled shoes

das **Hochhaus**, PLURAL die **Hochhäuser**
high-rise building

hochheben VERB◇, IMPERFECT **hob hoch**, PERFECT **hat hochgehoben**
to lift up
Sie hob das Kind hoch. She lifted up the child.

hochnäsig ADJECTIVE
stuck-up

die **Hochschule**, PLURAL die **Hochschulen**
university, college

der **Hochsprung**
high jump

höchst ADVERB
extremely

höchstens ADVERB
1 at the most
2 only, except perhaps

ℓ indicates key words

höchster, höchste, höchstes ADJECTIVE
1 highest
Der Großglockner ist der höchste Berg
Österreichs. The Grossglockner is Austria's
highest mountain.
2 Es ist höchste Zeit. It is high time.

die **Höchstgeschwindigkeit**, PLURAL die
Höchstgeschwindigkeiten
maximum speed

die **Höchsttemperatur**, PLURAL die
Höchsttemperaturen
maximum temperature

der **Höchstwert**, PLURAL die **Höchstwerte**
1 maximum value
2 maximum temperature

die **Hochzeit**, PLURAL die **Hochzeiten**
wedding

die **Hochzeitsfeier**, PLURAL die
Hochzeitsfeiern
wedding

der **Hochzeitstag**, PLURAL die
Hochzeitstage
1 wedding day
2 wedding anniversary

der **Hocker**, PLURAL die **Hocker**
stool

das **Hockey**
hockey

der **Hockeyschläger**, PLURAL die
Hockeyschläger
hockey stick

der **Hof**, PLURAL die **Höfe**
1 yard, courtyard
2 farm
3 court

ℓ **hoffen** VERB, PERFECT **hat gehofft**
to hope
auf etwas hoffen to hope for something

hoffentlich ADVERB
hopefully
Hoffentlich nicht! I hope not!

die **Hoffnung**, PLURAL die **Hoffnungen**
hope

hoffnungslos ADJECTIVE
hopeless

hoffnungsvoll ADJECTIVE
hopeful

ℓ **höflich** ADJECTIVE
polite

die **Höflichkeit**, PLURAL die **Höflichkeiten**
politeness, courtesy

die **Höhe**, PLURAL die **Höhen**
1 height
2 Das ist die Höhe! (informal) That's the
limit!

hoher, hohe, hohes ▸ SEE **hoch**

höher ADJECTIVE
1 higher
2 deeper

hohl ADJECTIVE
hollow

die **Höhle**, PLURAL die **Höhlen**
1 cave
2 den

ℓ **holen** VERB, PERFECT **hat geholt**
1 to get, to fetch
2 jemanden holen lassen to send for
somebody
3 sich etwas holen to get something

Holland NEUTER NOUN
Holland

der **Holländer**, PLURAL die **Holländer**
Dutchman

die **Holländerin**, PLURAL die **Holländerinnen**
Dutchwoman

holländisch ADJECTIVE
Dutch

> **WORD TIP** Adjectives never have capitals
> in German, even for regions, countries, or
> nationalities.

die **Hölle**, PLURAL die **Höllen**
hell

ℓ das **Holz**, PLURAL die **Hölzer**
wood

die **Holzkohle**
charcoal

die **Homöopathie**
homeopathy

homöopathisch ADJECTIVE
homeopathic

homosexuell ADJECTIVE
homosexual

der/die **Homosexuelle**, PLURAL die
Homosexuellen
homosexual

ℓ der **Honig**, PLURAL die **Honige**
honey

◇ **irregular verb**; SEP **separable verb**; for more help with verbs see centre section

horchen VERB, PERFECT **hat gehorcht**
1 to listen
2 to eavesdrop

𝒫 **hören** VERB, PERFECT **hat gehört**
1 to hear
2 to listen (to)
Ich höre gerne Musik. I like listening to music.

der **Hörer**, PLURAL die **Hörer**
1 listener (male)
2 receiver (of a phone)

die **Hörerin**, PLURAL die **Hörerinnen**
listener (female)

das **Hörgerät**, PLURAL die **Hörgeräte**
hearing aid

der **Horizont**, PLURAL die **Horizonte**
horizon

horizontal ADJECTIVE
horizontal

das **Horn**, PLURAL die **Hörner**
horn
David spielt Horn. David plays the horn.

𝒫 das **Horoskop**, PLURAL die **Horoskope**
horoscope

der **Horror**
horror

der **Horrorfilm**, PLURAL die **Horrorfilme**
horror film

𝒫 die **Hose**, PLURAL die **Hosen**
trousers

> **WORD TIP** In German, die Hose is singular:
> Deine Hose ist viel zu kurz. Also, this word does
> not mean hose in English; the German word for
> hose is Schlauch.

der **Hosenanzug**, PLURAL die **Hosenanzüge**
trouser suit

die **Hosenträger** PLURAL NOUN
braces

das or der **Hotdog**, PLURAL die **Hotdogs**
hot dog

𝒫 das **Hotel**, PLURAL die **Hotels**
hotel

das **Hotelverzeichnis**, PLURAL die
Hotelverzeichnisse
list of hotels

Hr. ABBREVIATION
(= Herr) Mr

𝒫 **hübsch** ADJECTIVE
1 pretty
2 nice

der **Hubschrauber**, PLURAL die
Hubschrauber
helicopter

der **Huf**, PLURAL die **Hufe**
hoof

das **Hufeisen**, PLURAL die **Hufeisen**
horseshoe

die **Hüfte**, PLURAL die **Hüften**
hip

der **Hügel**, PLURAL die **Hügel**
hill

das **Huhn**, PLURAL die **Hühner**
1 chicken
2 hen

die **Hummel**, PLURAL die **Hummeln**
bumblebee

der **Hummer**, PLURAL die **Hummer**
lobster

der **Humor**
1 humour
der schwarze Humor black humour
der Sinn für Humor sense of humour
2 sense of humour
Er hat keinen Humor. He has no sense of
humour.

humorlos ADJECTIVE
humourless

humorlos ADVERB
without humour

humorvoll ADJECTIVE
humorous

𝒫 der **Hund**, PLURAL die **Hunde**
dog
Kannst du den Hund ausführen? Can you
walk the dog?

die **Hundehütte**, PLURAL die **Hundehütten**
kennel

hundemüde ADJECTIVE
(informal) dog-tired

die **Hundepension**, PLURAL die
Hundepensionen
kennels (for boarding)

𝒫 **hundert** NUMBER
a hundred, one hundred

𝒫 der **Hunger**
hunger

𝒫 indicates key words

Ich habe Hunger. I'm hungry.

die **Hungersnot**
famine

hungrig ADJECTIVE
hungry

die **Hupe**, PLURAL die **Hupen**
horn

hurra EXCLAMATION
hooray!

husten VERB, PERFECT **hat gehustet**
to cough

ℙ der **Husten**
cough

der **Hustensaft**, PLURAL die **Hustensäfte**
cough mixture

ℙ der **Hut**, PLURAL die **Hüte**
hat

hüten VERB, PERFECT **hat gehütet**
1 to look after (a child, children)
2 sich hüten to be on your guard
3 sich hüten, etwas zu tun to take care not
to do something

die **Hütte**, PLURAL die **Hütten**
hut

die **Hygiene**
1 hygiene
2 health care

hygienisch ADJECTIVE
hygienic

hypnotisieren VERB, PERFECT **hat
hypnotisiert**
to hypnotize

die **Hypothek**, PLURAL die **Hypotheken**
mortgage

hysterisch ADJECTIVE
hysterical

Ii

der **IC**, PLURAL die **ICs** ABBREVIATION
(=Intercityzug) **intercity train**

der **ICE**, PLURAL die **ICEs** ABBREVIATION
(=Intercityexpresszug) **intercity express
train**

ℙ **ich** PRONOUN
I
Ich bin es. It's me.

das **Icon**, PLURAL die **Icons**
icon
Du musst das Icon anklicken. You have to
click on the icon.

ideal ADJECTIVE
ideal

ℙ die **Idee**, PLURAL die **Ideen**
idea

identifizieren VERB, PERFECT **hat identifiziert**
to identify

identisch ADJECTIVE
identical

der **Idiot**, PLURAL die **Idioten**
idiot

idiotisch ADJECTIVE
idiotic

idyllisch ADJECTIVE
idyllic

der **Igel**, PLURAL die **Igel**
hedgehog

ℙ **ihm** PRONOUN
1 him, to him
2 (when referring to a thing or animal) it, to it

ℙ **ihn** PRONOUN
1 him
2 (when referring to a thing or animal) it

ℙ **ihnen** PRONOUN
them, to them

ℙ **Ihnen** PRONOUN
you, to you (in formal use)
Wie geht es Ihnen? How are you?

ℙ **ihr** PRONOUN
1 you (plural)
2 her, to her
3 (when referring to a thing or animal) it, to it
ihr ADJECTIVE
1 her
2 (when referring to a thing or animal) its
3 their
Sie haben ihr Auto verkauft. They sold
their car.

ℙ **Ihr** ADJECTIVE
your (in formal use)
Ihr Sohn hat mir geschrieben. Your son
wrote to me.

ihrer, ihre, ihr(e)s PRONOUN
1 hers
Mein Rad ist rot, ihrs ist blau. My bike is
red, hers is blue.
2 theirs

◇ **irregular verb;** SEP **separable verb; for more help with verbs see centre section**

Das ist nicht ihre Katze, ihre ist schwarz.
That's not their cat. Theirs is black.

Ihrer, Ihre, Ihr(e)s *PRONOUN*
yours *(in formal use)*
Mein Job ist nicht so interessant wie Ihrer.
My job's not as interesting as yours.

ihretwegen *ADVERB*
1 **for her sake**
2 **for their sake**
3 **because of her**
4 **because of them**

Ihretwegen *ADVERB*
1 **for your sake** *(in formal use)*
2 **because of you** *(in formal use)*

die **Illusion**, *PLURAL* die **Illusionen**
illusion

die **Illustration**, *PLURAL* die **Illustrationen**
illustration

die **Illustrierte**, *PLURAL* die **Illustrierten**
magazine

ℰ **im** ▸ SEE **in dem**
1 **in**
im Wohnzimmer in the living room
im August in August
2 **at**
Was läuft im Kino? What's on at the
cinema?

das **Image**, *PLURAL* die **Images**
1 **image**
2 **reputation**

ℰ der **Imbiss**, *PLURAL* die **Imbisse**
1 **snack**
2 **snack bar**

die **Imbissbude**, *PLURAL* die **Imbissbuden**
hot-dog stand

die **Imbissstube**, *PLURAL* die **Imbissstuben**
snack bar, fast-food restaurant

der **Imitator**, *PLURAL* die **Imitatoren**
mimic, impressionist

imitieren *VERB*, *PERFECT* **hat imitiert**
to imitate

ℰ **immer** *ADVERB*
1 **always**
2 **immer wieder** again and again
3 **immer mehr** more and more
immer dunkler darker and darker
4 **immer noch** still
5 **immer, wenn er anruft** every time he rings
6 **wo/wer/wann immer** wherever/whoever/
whenever
7 **für immer** for ever

immerhin *ADVERB*
at least

immerzu *ADVERB*
all the time

das **Imperfekt**
imperfect *(in grammar)*
'Ich schlug' steht im Imperfekt. 'Ich
schlug' is in the imperfect.

der **Impfausweis**, *PLURAL* die **Impfausweise**
vaccination certificate

impfen *VERB*, *PERFECT* **hat geimpft**
to vaccinate

die **Impfung**, *PLURAL* die **Impfungen**
vaccination

imponieren *VERB*, *PERFECT* **hat imponiert**
to impress
Sein Mut hat mir imponiert. His courage
impressed me.

der **Import**, *PLURAL* die **Importe**
import

der **Importeur**, *PLURAL* die **Importeure**
importer

importieren *VERB*, *PERFECT* **hat importiert**
to import

imprägniert *ADJECTIVE*
waterproofed

imstande *ADVERB*
imstande sein, etwas zu tun to be able to
do something
Er ist nicht imstande, seine Hausaufgaben
allein zu machen. He's not able to do his
homework on his own.

ℰ **in** *PREPOSITION* (+ *DAT* or + *ACC*)
1 *(the dative is used when talking about
position; the accusative shows movement
or a change of place)* **in**
Es ist in der Küche. *(DAT)* It's in the
kitchen.
2 **into, in**
Ich habe es in meine Tasche gesteckt.
(ACC) I've put it in my bag.
3 **at**
Susi ist in der Schule. *(DAT)* Susi is at
school.
4 **to**
Wir gehen in die Schule. *(ACC)* We're
going to school.
5 **in diesem Jahr** this year
6 **in sein** to be in

153

> Rap ist in. Rap is in.
>
> **WORD TIP** in + dem gives im; in + das gives ins

inbegr. ABBREVIATION
(=inbegriffen) **included**

inbegriffen ADJECTIVE
included
Das Essen ist inbegriffen. Food is included.

indem CONJUNCTION
1 **while**
2 **by**

der **Inder**, PLURAL die **Inder**
Indian (male)

die **Inderin**, PLURAL die **Inderinnen**
Indian (female)

der **Indianer**, PLURAL die **Indianer**
(American) Indian, Native American
(male)

die **Indianerin**, PLURAL die **Indianerinnen**
(American) Indian, Native American
(female)

indianisch ADJECTIVE
(American) Indian, Native American

WORD TIP Adjectives never have capitals in German, even for regions, countries, or nationalities.

Indien NEUTER NOUN
India

indisch ADJECTIVE
Indian

WORD TIP Adjectives never have capitals in German, even for regions, countries, or nationalities.

indiskutabel ADJECTIVE
out of the question

individuell ADJECTIVE
individual

das **Individuum**, PLURAL die **Individuen**
individual

♂ die **Industrie**, PLURAL die **Industrien**
industry

das **Industriegebiet**, PLURAL die
Industriegebiete
industrial area

industriell ADJECTIVE
industrial

♂ die **Industriestadt**, PLURAL die
Industriestädte
industrial town, industrial city

die **Infektion**, PLURAL die **Infektionen**
infection

der **Infinitiv**, PLURAL die **Infinitive**
infinitive

infizieren VERB, PERFECT **hat infiziert**
1 **to infect**
2 **sich bei jemandem infizieren** to be infected by somebody

die **Inflation**, PLURAL die **Inflationen**
inflation

infolge PREPOSITION (+ GEN)
as a result of

infolgedessen ADVERB
consequently

♂ die **Informatik**
information technology

der **Informatiker**, PLURAL die **Informatiker**
IT specialist (male)

WORD TIP Professions, hobbies, and sports don't take an article in German: Er ist Informatiker.

die **Informatikerin**, PLURAL die
Informatikerinnen
IT specialist (female)

WORD TIP Professions, hobbies, and sports don't take an article in German: Sie ist Informatikerin.

♂ die **Information**, PLURAL die **Informationen**
(piece of) information

das **Informationsbüro**, PLURAL die
Informationsbüros
(tourist) information office

informieren VERB, PERFECT **hat informiert**
1 **to inform**
2 **gut/schlecht informiert sein** to be well/ill informed
Da bist du falsch informiert. You've been wrongly informed.
3 **sich über etwas informieren** to find out about something
Ich habe mich darüber genau informiert. I found out all about it.

der **Ingenieur**, PLURAL die **Ingenieure**
engineer (male)

WORD TIP Professions, hobbies, and sports don't take an article in German: Er ist Ingenieur.

die **Ingenieurin**, PLURAL die **Ingenieurinnen**
engineer (female)

WORD TIP Professions, hobbies, and sports don't take an article in German: Sie ist Ingenieurin.

◇ **irregular verb;** SEP **separable verb; for more help with verbs see centre section**

der **Ingwer**
  ginger

der **Inhaber**, PLURAL die **Inhaber**
1 **owner** (of a shop male)
2 **holder** (of an office) (male)

die **Inhaberin**, PLURAL die **Inhaberinnen**
1 **owner** (of a shop male)
2 **holder** (of a position) (female)

der **Inhalt**, PLURAL die **Inhalte**
1 **contents**
  Den Inhalt der Dose mit etwas Wasser
  verdünnen. Dilute the contents of the tin
  with a little water.
2 **content** (of a story, film)
  Er hat den Inhalt der Geschichte kurz für
  uns zusammengefasst. He gave us a quick
  summary of the content of the story.
3 **volume**
4 **area** (of a rectangle, circle, etc.)

das **Inhaltsverzeichnis**, PLURAL die
  Inhaltsverzeichnisse
  table of contents

die **Initiative**, PLURAL die **Initiativen**
  initiative
  die Initiative ergreifen to take the
  initiative

inkl. ABBREVIATION
  (=inklusive) **including**

inklusive PREPOSITION (+ GEN)
  including
inklusive ADVERB
  inclusive

das **Inland**
1 im Inland und im Ausland at home and
  abroad
2 im Inland und an der Küste inland and on
  the coast

inlineskaten VERB, PERFECT **hat**
  inlinegeskatet
  to go in-line skating, to go rollerblading

der **Inlineskater**, PLURAL die **Inlineskater**
  in-line skater, rollerblader

die **Inlineskates** PLURAL NOUN
  in-line skates, Rollerblades™

innen ADVERB
  inside
  nach innen inwards

ℙ die **Innenstadt**, PLURAL die **Innenstädte**
  town centre, city centre

das **Innere**
1 **interior**

2 **inside**

innerer, innere, inneres ADJECTIVE
1 **inner**
2 **inside**
3 **internal** (injuries)

innerhalb PREPOSITION (+ GEN)
1 **within**
2 **during**
innerhalb ADVERB
  innerhalb von within

innerlich ADJECTIVE
1 **internal**
2 **inner**
innerlich ADVERB
1 **internally**
2 **inwardly**

ℙ **ins**
  ▸SEE **in das**
  into, to
  ins Theater gehen to go to the theatre

insbesondere ADVERB
  especially

das **Insekt**, PLURAL die **Insekten**
  insect

ℙ die **Insel**, PLURAL die **Inseln**
  island

das **Inserat**, PLURAL die **Inserate**
  advertisement

inserieren VERB, PERFECT **hat inseriert**
  to advertise

insgesamt ADVERB
  in all

der **Instinkt**, PLURAL die **Instinkte**
  instinct

instinktiv ADJECTIVE
  instinctive

ℙ das **Instrument**, PLURAL die **Instrumente**
  instrument
  Spielen Sie ein Instrument? Do you play an
  instrument?

ℙ **intelligent** ADJECTIVE
  bright, intelligent

die **Intelligenz**
  intelligence

intensiv ADJECTIVE
  intensive

die **Intensivpflege**
  intensive care

ℙ indicates key words

die **Intensivstation**, *PLURAL* die
Intensivstationen
intensive care unit

der **Intercityexpresszug**, *PLURAL* die
Intercityexpresszüge
intercity express train

der **Intercityzug**, *PLURAL* die **Intercityzüge**
intercity train

℗ **interessant** *ADJECTIVE*
interesting

℗ das **Interesse**, *PLURAL* die **Interessen**
interest
Interesse an jemandem/etwas haben to
be interested in somebody/something

℗ **interessieren** *VERB*, *PERFECT* **hat interessiert**
1 to interest
Das interessiert mich nicht. I'm not
interested.
2 sich für jemanden/etwas interessieren to
be interested in somebody/something

das **Internat**, *PLURAL* die **Internate**
boarding school

international *ADJECTIVE*
international

die **Internatschule**, *PLURAL* die
Internatschulen
boarding school

℗ das **Internet**
Internet
Abends surft er im Internet. In the
evenings he surfs the Internet.

das **Internetcafé**, *PLURAL* die **Internetcafés**
Internet cafe
Wo gibt es hier ein Internetcafé? Where is
there an Internet cafe?

das **Internet-Mobbing**
cyberbullying

℗ die **Internetseite**, *PLURAL* die **Internetseiten**
web page

das **Internetshopping**
online shopping

℗ das **Interview**, *PLURAL* die **Interviews**
interview

inzwischen *ADVERB*
in the meantime, meanwhile

der **Irak**
der Irak Iraq

WORD TIP This is always used with an article:
Sie fahren in den Irak. Er wohnt im Irak.

der **Iran**
der Iran Iran

WORD TIP This is always used with an article:
Sie fahren in den Iran. Er wohnt im Iran.

der **Ire**, *PLURAL* die **Iren**
Irishman
Er ist Ire. He's Irish.
die Iren the Irish

irgend *ADVERB*
1 at all
wenn irgend möglich if at all possible
wenn du irgend kannst if you could
possibly manage it
2 irgend so eine Ausrede some such excuse

irgendein *ADJECTIVE*
1 some
2 any
3 irgendein anderer someone else, anyone
else

irgendeiner, irgendeine, irgendein(e)s
PRONOUN
1 any one
'Welche möchten Sie?' – 'Irgendeine.'
'Which one would you like?' – 'Any one.'
2 somebody, someone
3 anybody, anyone
Hat irgendeiner angerufen? Has anybody
phoned?

irgendetwas *PRONOUN*
1 something
2 anything

irgendjemand *PRONOUN*
1 somebody
2 anybody, anyone

irgendwann *ADVERB*
1 some time, at some time
2 any time, at any time

irgendwas *(informal)* ▶ SEE **irgendetwas**

irgendwie *ADVERB*
somehow

irgendwo *ADVERB*
1 somewhere
2 anywhere

die **Irin**, *PLURAL* die **Irinnen**
Irishwoman
Sie ist Irin. She's Irish.

◇ **irregular verb;** *SEP* **separable verb; for more help with verbs see centre section**

ℓ **irisch** ADJECTIVE
  Irish

> **WORD TIP** Adjectives never have capitals in German, even for regions, countries, or nationalities.

das **Irisch**
  Irish (language)

ℓ **Irland** NEUTER NOUN
  Ireland

die **Ironie**
  irony

ironisch ADJECTIVE
  ironic

irre ADJECTIVE
1 mad
2 (informal) incredible, fantastic
irre ADVERB
  irre gut (informal) incredibly good

irren VERB, PERFECT **ist geirrt**
1 to wander (about) (when lost)
2 PERFECT **hat sich geirrt**
  sich irren to be mistaken, to be wrong

irrsinnig ADJECTIVE
1 mad
2 (informal) incredible

der **Irrtum**, PLURAL die **Irrtümer**
  mistake

der **Islam**
  Islam

Island NEUTER NOUN
  Iceland

Israel NEUTER NOUN
  Israel

isst ▸ SEE **essen**

ist ▸ SEE **sein**

ℓ **Italien** NEUTER NOUN
  Italy

der **Italiener**, PLURAL die **Italiener**
  Italian (male)

die **Italienerin**, PLURAL die **Italienerinnen**
  Italian (female)

ℓ **italienisch** ADJECTIVE
  Italian

> **WORD TIP** Adjectives never have capitals in German, even for regions, countries, or nationalities.

Jj

ℓ **ja** ADVERB
1 yes
2 Ich glaube ja. I think so.
3 Du kommst doch, ja? You'll come, won't you?
  Es passt doch, ja? It fits, doesn't it?
4 Sag's ihm ja nicht! Don't (you dare) tell him, whatever you do!
  Seid ja vorsichtig! Do be careful!
5 Es ist ja noch früh. It's still early.
  Ich kann ihn ja mal fragen, ob er mitkommen will. I could always ask him if he wants to come.

die **Jacht**, PLURAL die **Jachten**
  yacht

ℓ die **Jacke**, PLURAL die **Jacken**
1 jacket
2 cardigan

das **Jackett**, PLURAL die **Jacketts**
  jacket

die **Jagd**, PLURAL die **Jagden**
1 hunt
2 hunting

jagen VERB, PERFECT **hat gejagt**
1 to hunt
2 to chase
  Drei Polizisten jagten den Einbrecher, aber er hängte sie schnell ab. Three policemen chased the burglar, but he soon shook them off.
  Meine Mutter hat mich aus dem Bett gejagt. (informal) My mother made me get up.
3 jemanden aus dem Haus jagen to throw somebody out of the house
4 Damit kannst du mich jagen. (informal) I can't stand that.

der **Jäger**, PLURAL die **Jäger**
1 hunter (male)
2 fighter (aircraft)

> **WORD TIP** Professions, hobbies, and sports don't take an article in German: Er ist Jäger.

die **Jägerin**, PLURAL die **Jägerinnen**
  hunter (female)

> **WORD TIP** Professions, hobbies, and sports don't take an article in German: Sie ist Jägerin.

jäh ADJECTIVE
  sudden

ℓ indicates key words

♂ das **Jahr**, PLURAL die **Jahre**
1 **year**
nächstes Jahr next year
Der Kurs ist für Kinder bis zu zwölf Jahren.
The course is for children up to the age of
twelve.
2 in den achtziger Jahren **in the eighties**
3 ein freiwilliges soziales Jahr (FSJ) **a
voluntary year** (during which community
work is done for subsistence payment)

jahrelang ADVERB
for years

der **Jahrestag**, PLURAL die **Jahrestage**
anniversary

♂ die **Jahreszeit**, PLURAL die **Jahreszeiten**
season

der **Jahrgang**, PLURAL die **Jahrgänge**
1 **year**
2 **vintage**

das **Jahrhundert**, PLURAL die **Jahrhunderte**
century

-jährig ADJECTIVE
eine dreißigjährige Frau **a woman aged
thirty**
eine zweijährige Verspätung **a two-year
delay**

jährlich ADJECTIVE, ADVERB
yearly
zweimal jährlich twice a year

der **Jahrmarkt**, PLURAL die **Jahrmärkte**
fair

das **Jahrtausend**, PLURAL die **Jahrtausende**
millennium

das **Jahrzehnt**, PLURAL die **Jahrzehnte**
decade

jähzornig ADJECTIVE
hot-tempered

jammern VERB, PERFECT **hat gejammert**
to moan

♂ der **Januar**
January
im Januar in January

Japan NEUTER NOUN
Japan

der **Japaner**, PLURAL die **Japaner**
Japanese (male)

die **Japanerin**, PLURAL die **Japanerinnen**
Japanese (female)

japanisch ADJECTIVE
Japanese

> **WORD TIP** Adjectives never have capitals
> in German, even for regions, countries, or
> nationalities.

jawohl ADVERB
1 **yes**
2 **certainly**

je ADVERB
1 **ever**
Es geht ihr besser denn je. **She feels better
than ever.**
2 **each**
Sie kosten je zwanzig Euro. **They are
twenty euros each.**
3 seit eh und je **always**
4 je nach **depending on**

je PREPOSITION (+ ACC)
per

je CONJUNCTION
1 je mehr, desto besser **the more the better**
2 je nachdem **it depends**

♂ die **Jeans**, PLURAL die **Jeans**
jeans
Er trug eine Jeans. **He was wearing jeans.**
Ich brauche eine neue Jeans. **I need a new
pair of jeans.**

> **WORD TIP** In German, die Jeans is singular:
> Meine Jeans ist zu klein.

jede ▸ SEE **jeder**

jedenfalls ADVERB
in any case

♂ **jeder, jede, jedes** ADJECTIVE
1 **every**
jedes Mal every time
jeden Tag every day
2 **each**
3 **any**
ohne jeden Grund without any reason

jeder jede jedes PRONOUN
1 **everybody, everyone**
2 **each one**
3 **anybody, anyone**
Das kann jeder. **Anybody can do that.**

jedermann PRONOUN
everybody, everyone

jederzeit ADVERB
at any time

jedes ▸ SEE **jeder**

jedoch ADVERB
however

◇ irregular verb; SEP separable verb; for more help with verbs see centre section

jemals *ADVERB*
ever

ℙ **jemand** *PRONOUN*
1 **somebody, someone**
Jemand hat das für dich abgegeben.
Somebody left this for you.
2 **anybody, anyone**
Hat jemand angerufen? Did anybody call?

jener, jene, jenes *ADJECTIVE*
1 *(used in formal language and in literature)*
that
2 **those** *(plural)*
jener jene jenes *PRONOUN*
1 **that one**
2 **those** *(plural)*

jenseits *PREPOSITION* (+ GEN)
(on) the other side of

der **Jetlag**
jet lag

ℙ **jetzt** *ADVERB*
now

ℙ der **Job**, PLURAL die **Jobs**
job

jobben *VERB* (informal), PERFECT **hat gejobbt**
to work

joggen *VERB*, PERFECT **ist gejoggt**
to jog

das **Jogging**
jogging

der **Jogginganzug**, PLURAL die
Jogginganzüge
tracksuit

der or das **Joghurt**, PLURAL die **Joghurt(s)**
yoghurt

das **Joghurteis**, PLURAL die **Joghurteis**
yoghurt ice cream

die **Johannisbeere**, PLURAL die
Johannisbeeren
1 die Rote Johannisbeere redcurrant
2 die Schwarze Johannisbeere blackcurrant

der **Journalist**, PLURAL die **Journalisten**
journalist *(male)*

> **WORD TIP** Professions, hobbies, and sports
> don't take an article in German: Er ist Journalist.

die **Journalistin**, PLURAL die **Journalistinnen**
journalist *(female)*

> **WORD TIP** Professions, hobbies, and sports
> don't take an article in German: Sie ist
> Journalistin.

der **Joystick**, PLURAL die **Joysticks**
joystick *(for computer games)*

jubeln *VERB*, PERFECT **hat gejubelt**
to cheer

das **Jubiläum**, PLURAL die **Jubiläen**
1 **anniversary**
2 **jubilee**

jucken *VERB*, PERFECT **hat gejuckt**
to be itchy

der **Jude**, PLURAL die **Juden**
Jew *(male)*

das **Judentum**
Judaism

die **Jüdin**, PLURAL die **Jüdinnen**
Jew *(female)*

jüdisch *ADJECTIVE*
Jewish

> **WORD TIP** Adjectives never have capitals in
> German, even for religions.

das **Judo**
judo

ℙ die **Jugend**
youth

ℙ die **Jugendherberge**, PLURAL die
Jugendherbergen
youth hostel

ℙ der **Jugendklub**, PLURAL die **Jugendklubs**
youth club

ℙ der/die **Jugendliche**, PLURAL die
Jugendlichen
1 **young person**
2 **die Jugendlichen** young people

ℙ das **Jugendmagazin**, PLURAL die
Jugendmagazine
teenage magazine

ℙ das **Jugendzentrum**, PLURAL die
Jugendzentren
youth centre

Jugoslawien *NEUTER NOUN*
Yugoslavia
Seine Eltern kommen aus dem
ehemaligen Jugoslawien. His parents are
from the former Yugoslavia.

jugoslawisch *ADJECTIVE*
Yugoslavian

> **WORD TIP** Adjectives never have capitals
> in German, even for regions, countries, or
> nationalities.

ℙ indicates key words

_ρ_ der **Juli**
July
im Juli in July

_ρ_ **jung** ADJECTIVE
1 young
2 Jung und Alt young and old

_ρ_ der **Junge**[1], PLURAL die **Jungen**
boy

das **Junge**[2], PLURAL die **Jungen**
young (animal)

jünger ADJECTIVE
younger

die **Jungfrau**, PLURAL die **Jungfrauen**
1 virgin
2 Virgo
Robert ist Jungfrau. Robert is Virgo.

der **Junggeselle**, PLURAL die **Junggesellen**
bachelor

jüngster, jüngste, jüngstes ADJECTIVE
1 youngest
2 latest (news, developments)
3 in jüngster Zeit recently

_ρ_ der **Juni**
June
im Juni in June

Jura
law (as a subject)

die **Jury**, PLURAL die **Jurys**
1 jury
2 judges (in competitions)

das or der **Juwel**, PLURAL die **Juwelen**
jewel
Juwelen jewellery

der **Juwelier**, PLURAL die **Juweliere**
jeweller (male)

> **WORD TIP** Professions, hobbies, and sports
> don't take an article in German: Er ist Juwelier.

die **Juwelierin**, PLURAL die **Juwelierinnen**
jeweller (female)

> **WORD TIP** Professions, hobbies, and sports
> don't take an article in German: Sie ist
> Juwelierin.

der **Jux**
(informal) laugh
Das hat er nur aus Jux gemacht. He did it
just for a laugh.

Kk

das **Kabel**, PLURAL die **Kabel**
1 cable
2 wire

der **Kabelanschluss**, PLURAL die
Kabelanschlüsse
1 cable connection
2 cable television

das **Kabelfernsehen**
cable television

der **Kabeljau**, PLURAL die **Kabeljaus**
cod

die **Kabine**, PLURAL die **Kabinen**
1 cabin
2 cubicle (for changing)
3 car (of a cable car)

die **Kachel**, PLURAL die **Kacheln**
tile

der **Käfer**, PLURAL die **Käfer**
beetle

_ρ_ der **Kaffee**, PLURAL die **Kaffee(s)**
coffee
Zwei Kaffee mit Milch, bitte. Two white
coffees, please.

> ● **KAFFEEHAUS**
>
> This is not only a place to drink your coffee,
> tea, or hot chocolate and enjoy a piece of cake,
> it is also a place to relax, to read newspapers,
> to meet friends – there is a real Kaffeehaus
> culture in cities such as Vienna. One of the
> most famous coffee houses in Vienna is the
> Landtmann opposite the town hall (Rathaus).

die **Kaffeekanne**, PLURAL die **Kaffeekannen**
coffee pot

die **Kaffeepause**, PLURAL die **Kaffeepausen**
coffee break

der **Käfig**, PLURAL die **Käfige**
cage

kahl ADJECTIVE
1 bald (head)
2 bare (tree, walls)

der **Kahn**, PLURAL die **Kähne**
1 barge
2 rowing boat

✧ **irregular verb**; SEP **separable verb**; for more help with verbs see centre section

der **Kaiser**, *PLURAL* die **Kaiser**
emperor

die **Kaiserin**, *PLURAL* die **Kaiserinnen**
empress

♟ der **Kakao**, *PLURAL* die **Kakao(s)**
1 cocoa
2 hot chocolate
Zwei Kakao, bitte. Two cups of hot
chocolate, please.

der **Kakerlak**, *PLURAL* die **Kakerlaken**
cockroach

der **Kaktus**, *PLURAL* die **Kakteen**
cactus

das **Kalb**, *PLURAL* die **Kälber**
1 calf
2 veal

das **Kalbfleisch**
veal

♟ der **Kalender**, *PLURAL* die **Kalender**
1 calendar
2 diary

der **Kalk**
1 lime
2 limescale
3 calcium

die **Kalorie**, *PLURAL* die **Kalorien**
calorie

kalorienarm *ADJECTIVE*
low-calorie, low in calories

kalorienreich *ADJECTIVE*
high-calorie, high in calories

♟ **kalt** *ADJECTIVE*
cold
Ist dir kalt? Are you cold?
Stell die Heizung an, den Kindern ist
kalt.
Put on the heating. The children are cold.
Abends essen wir kalt. We have a cold
meal in the evening.

die **Kälte**
1 cold
2 coldness
3 Es war fünf Grad Kälte. It was five degrees
below zero.

kam ▸ SEE **kommen**

das **Kamel**, *PLURAL* die **Kamele**
camel

die **Kamera**, *PLURAL* die **Kameras**
camera

der **Kamerad**, *PLURAL* die **Kameraden**
friend *(male)*

die **Kameradin**, *PLURAL* die **Kameradinnen**
friend *(female)*

die **Kamerafrau**, *PLURAL* die **Kamerafrauen**
camerawoman

> **WORD TIP** Professions, hobbies, and sports
> don't take an article in German: Sie ist
> Kamerafrau.

der **Kameramann**, *PLURAL* die
Kameramänner
cameraman

> **WORD TIP** Professions, hobbies, and sports
> don't take an article in German: Er ist
> Kameramann.

der **Kamin**, *PLURAL* die **Kamine**
fireplace
Wir saßen am Kamin. We sat by the fire.

der **Kamm**, *PLURAL* die **Kämme**
1 comb
2 ridge *(of a mountain)*

kämmen *VERB*, *PERFECT* **hat gekämmt**
1 to comb
2 sich kämmen to comb your hair

die **Kammer**, *PLURAL* die **Kammern**
1 store room
2 chamber

♟ die **Kampagne**, *PLURAL* die **Kampagnen**
campaign

der **Kampf**, *PLURAL* die **Kämpfe**
1 fight
2 contest
3 struggle

kämpfen *VERB*, *PERFECT* **hat gekämpft**
to fight

die **Kampfsportart**, *PLURAL* die
Kampfsportarten
martial art

Kanada *NEUTER NOUN*
Canada

der **Kanadier**, *PLURAL* die **Kanadier**
Canadian *(male)*

die **Kanadierin**, *PLURAL* die **Kanadierinnen**
Canadian *(female)*

A
B
C
D
E
F
G
H
I
J
K
L
M
N
O
P
Q
R
S
T
U
V
W
X
Y
Z

kanadisch *ADJECTIVE*
Canadian

> **WORD TIP** Adjectives never have capitals in German, even for regions, countries, or nationalities.

der Kanal, *PLURAL* **die Kanäle**
1 **canal**
2 **channel** (radio, TV)
3 **der Kanal** the (English) Channel
4 **sewer, drain**

die Kanalinseln *PLURAL NOUN*
die Kanalinseln the Channel Islands

die Kanalisation
sewers, drains

der Kanaltunnel, *PLURAL* **die Kanaltunnel**
Channel Tunnel

der Kanarienvogel, *PLURAL* **die Kanarienvögel**
canary

der Kandidat, *PLURAL* **die Kandidaten**
candidate (male)

die Kandidatin, *PLURAL* **die Kandidatinnen**
candidate (female)

das Känguru, *PLURAL* **die Kängurus**
kangaroo

℗ **das Kaninchen,** *PLURAL* **die Kaninchen**
rabbit

kann ▸ SEE **können**

das Kännchen, *PLURAL* **die Kännchen**
1 **pot**
Ein Kännchen Kaffee, bitte. A pot of coffee, please.
2 **jug** (of milk)

die Kanne, *PLURAL* **die Kannen**
1 **pot** (for coffee, tea)
2 **jug** (for water)
3 **can** (for oil)
4 **watering can**

kannst ▸ SEE **können**

kannte ▸ SEE **kennen**

die Kante, *PLURAL* **die Kanten**
edge

℗ **die Kantine,** *PLURAL* **die Kantinen**
canteen
Wir essen immer in der Kantine zu Mittag. We always have lunch in the canteen.

der Kanton, *PLURAL* **die Kantone**
canton, state (in Switzerland)

> **KANTONE**
> Switzerland has 26 cantons: Aargau, Appenzell Ausserrhoden, Appenzell Innerrhoden, Basel-Landschaft, Basel-Stadt, Bern, Freiburg, Genf (Geneva), Glarus, Graubünden, Jura, Luzern (Lucerne), Neuenburg, Niwalden, Obwalden, Schaffhausen, Schwyz, Solothurn, St. Gallen, Tessin (Ticino), Thurghau, Uri, Wardt, Wallis, Zug, Zürich (Zurich).

das Kanu, *PLURAL* **die Kanus**
canoe
Kanu fahren to go canoeing

die Kapelle, *PLURAL* **die Kapellen**
1 **chapel**
2 **(brass) band**

kapieren *VERB* (informal), *PERFECT* **hat kapiert**
to understand
Er hat es mir schon dreimal erklärt, aber ich kapier es einfach nicht. He's already explained it to me three times, but I just don't get it.

das Kapital
capital

der Kapitalismus
capitalism

der Kapitän, *PLURAL* **die Kapitäne**
captain

das Kapitel, *PLURAL* **die Kapitel**
chapter

℗ **die Kappe,** *PLURAL* **die Kappen**
cap

℗ **kaputt** *ADJECTIVE*
1 **broken**
2 An meinem Computer ist etwas kaputt. There's something wrong with my computer.
3 Ich bin kaputt. (informal) I'm shattered.

kaputtgehen *VERB*◇ (informal), *IMPERFECT* **ging kaputt,** *PERFECT* **ist kaputtgegangen**
1 **to break**
2 **to pack up**
Der Fernseher ist mitten im Fußballspiel kaputtgegangen. The television packed up in the middle of the football match.
3 **to wear out** (of clothing)
4 **to break up** (of a marriage or friendship)

kaputtmachen *VERB* (informal), *PERFECT* **hat kaputtgemacht**
1 **to break**

Er macht alle seine Spielsachen kaputt. He breaks all his toys.

2 to ruin *(clothes, furniture)*

3 to finish off, to wear out *(a person)*
Die viele Arbeit macht mich ganz kaputt. All this work is wearing me out.

4 sich kaputtmachen to wear yourself out

die **Kapuze**, PLURAL die **Kapuzen**
hood

der **Kapuzenpullover**, PLURAL die **Kapuzenpullover**
hoodie

der **Karamell**, PLURAL die **Karamells**
caramel

der **Karfreitag**
Good Friday

die **Karibik**
die Karibik the Caribbean

karibisch ADJECTIVE
Caribbean

> **WORD TIP** Adjectives never have capitals in German, even for regions, countries, or nationalities.

kariert ADJECTIVE

1 check
Sie trug einen karierten Rock. She wore a check skirt.

2 squared *(paper)*

ℐ der **Karneval**, PLURAL die **Karnevale**
carnival

⬤ KARNEVAL

This is the period before Lent, when many balls (e.g. the Viennese Opera Ball) and fancy dress parties are held. During the last weekend of the carnival period, many villages and towns celebrate carnival with parades.

das **Karo**, PLURAL die **Karos**

1 square

2 diamonds *(in cards)*

ℐ die **Karotte**, PLURAL die **Karotten**
carrot

der **Karpfen**, PLURAL die **Karpfen**
carp

die **Karriere**, PLURAL die **Karrieren**
career
Karriere machen to get to the top

ℐ die **Karte**, PLURAL die **Karten**

1 card, postcard
Ich schicke euch eine Karte aus Italien. I'll send you a card from Italy.

2 card *(for playing)*
Wir haben den ganzen Abend Karten gespielt. We played cards all evening.
gute/schlechte Karten haben to have a good/bad hand

3 ticket
Gibt es noch Karten für das Popfestival? Can you still get tickets for the pop festival?

4 menu
Können wir bitte die Karte sehen? Can we see the menu, please?

5 map
Ich kann Oberammergau nicht auf der Karte finden. I can't find Oberammergau on the map.

6 alles auf eine Karte setzen to put all your eggs in one basket

ℐ das **Kartenspiel**, PLURAL die **Kartenspiele**

1 card game

2 pack of cards

ℐ die **Kartoffel**, PLURAL die **Kartoffeln**
potato

der **Kartoffelbrei**
mashed potatoes

die **Kartoffelchips** PLURAL NOUN
potato crisps

> **WORD TIP** The German word Kartoffelchips does not mean **chips** or French fries in English; the German word for **chips** is Pommes frites.

der **Kartoffelsalat**, PLURAL die **Kartoffelsalate**
potato salad

der **Karton**, PLURAL die **Kartons**

1 cardboard

2 cardboard box

das **Karussell**, PLURAL die **Karussells**
merry-go-round
Karussell fahren to go on the merry-go-round

ℐ der **Käse**
cheese

der **Käsekuchen**, PLURAL die **Käsekuchen**
cheesecake

die **Kaserne**, PLURAL die **Kasernen**
barracks

die **Kasse**, PLURAL die **Kassen**

1 till

2 checkout
Bitte zahlen Sie an der Kasse. Please pay at the checkout.

3 cash desk *(in a bank)*

ℐ indicates key words

A B C D E F G H I J **K** L M N O P Q R S T U V W X Y Z

4 box office
Sie können die Karten an der Kasse abholen. You can collect the tickets from the box office.
5 ticket office *(at a sports stadium)*
Sie müssen sich an der Kasse anstellen. You have to queue at the ticket office.
6 health insurance
7 knapp bei Kasse sein *(informal)* to be short of money
gut bei Kasse sein *(informal)* to be in the money

♀ der **Kassenzettel**, PLURAL die **Kassenzettel**
receipt

die **Kassette**, PLURAL die **Kassetten**
1 cassette, tape
2 box *(for money, jewellery)*

der **Kassettenrekorder**, PLURAL die **Kassettenrekorder**
cassette recorder

kassieren VERB, PERFECT **hat kassiert**
1 to collect the money
2 to collect the fares
3 Wie viel hat er kassiert? How much did he charge you?
4 Darf ich bei Ihnen kassieren? Would you like to pay now? *(your bill in a restaurant)*
5 *(informal)* **to take away** *(a driving licence, for example)*

der **Kassierer**, PLURAL die **Kassierer**
cashier *(male)*

die **Kassiererin**, PLURAL die **Kassiererinnen**
cashier *(female)*

die **Kastanie**, PLURAL die **Kastanien**
chestnut

kastanienbraun ADJECTIVE
chestnut (brown)

der **Kasten**, PLURAL die **Kästen**
1 box
2 crate
Sie kauften einen Kasten Bier. They bought a crate of beer.
3 bin
4 letter box
5 Sie hat was auf dem Kasten. *(informal)* She's really clever.

der **Katalog**, PLURAL die **Kataloge**
catalogue

der **Katalysator**, PLURAL die **Katalysatoren**
catalytic converter

katastrophal ADJECTIVE
1 catastrophic

2 terrible
katastrophal ADVERB
terribly
Sie hat katastrophal schlecht abgeschnitten. She did terribly badly.

die **Katastrophe**, PLURAL die **Katastrophen**
catastrophe

die **Kategorie**, PLURAL die **Kategorien**
category

der **Kater**, PLURAL die **Kater**
1 tomcat, tom
2 *(informal)* **hangover**
Am nächsten Morgen hatte er einen Kater. He had a hangover the next morning.

die **Kathedrale**, PLURAL die **Kathedralen**
cathedral

der **Katholik**, PLURAL die **Katholiken**
Catholic *(male)*

die **Katholikin**, PLURAL die **Katholikinnen**
Catholic *(female)*

katholisch ADJECTIVE
Catholic

> **WORD TIP** Adjectives never have capitals in German, even for religions.

das **Kätzchen**, PLURAL die **Kätzchen**
kitten

♀ die **Katze**, PLURAL die **Katzen**
cat

kauen VERB, PERFECT **hat gekaut**
to chew

kauern VERB, PERFECT **hat gekauert**
to crouch

der **Kauf**, PLURAL die **Käufe**
1 purchase
2 Das war ein guter Kauf. That was a bargain.
3 etwas in Kauf nehmen to put up with something

♀ **kaufen** VERB, PERFECT **hat gekauft**
to buy

der **Käufer**, PLURAL die **Käufer**
buyer *(male)*

die **Käuferin**, PLURAL die **Käuferinnen**
buyer *(female)*

die **Kauffrau**, PLURAL die **Kauffrauen**
businesswoman

> **WORD TIP** Professions, hobbies, and sports don't take an article in German: Sie ist Kauffrau.

ℰ das **Kaufhaus**, PLURAL die **Kaufhäuser**
department store

der **Kaufmann**, PLURAL die **Kaufleute**
businessman

WORD TIP Professions, hobbies, and sports
don't take an article in German: Er ist
Kaufmann.

ℰ der **Kaugummi**, PLURAL die **Kaugummis**
chewing gum

die **Kaulquappe**, PLURAL die **Kaulquappen**
tadpole

kaum ADVERB
hardly, scarcely

die **Kaution**, PLURAL die **Kautionen**
1 deposit
2 bail

der **Kegel**, PLURAL die **Kegel**
1 cone
2 skittle

die **Kegelbahn**
skittle alley

kegeln VERB, PERFECT **hat gekegelt**
to play skittles

die **Kehle**, PLURAL die **Kehlen**
throat

der **Keim**, PLURAL die **Keime**
1 shoot
2 germ

ℰ **kein** ADJECTIVE
1 no
auf keinen Fall on no account
2 not any
Ich habe keine Zeit. I haven't got any time.
Er hat kein Geld. He hasn't got any money.
3 Es dauert keine zehn Minuten. It takes less
than ten minutes.

ℰ **keiner**, **keine**, **kein(e)s** PRONOUN
1 nobody, no one
2 none, not one
3 Von diesen Kleidern gefällt mir keins. I
don't like any of these dresses.
4 keiner von beiden neither (of them)

keinesfalls ADVERB
on no account

keineswegs ADVERB
by no means

keinmal ADVERB
not once

· **keins** ▸ SEE keiner

ℰ der **Keks**, PLURAL die **Kekse**
biscuit

ℰ der **Keller**, PLURAL die **Keller**
cellar

das **Kellergeschoss**, PLURAL die
Kellergeschosse
basement

ℰ der **Kellner**, PLURAL die **Kellner**
waiter

WORD TIP Professions, hobbies, and sports
don't take an article in German: Er ist Kellner.

ℰ die **Kellnerin**, PLURAL die **Kellnerinnen**
waitress

WORD TIP Professions, hobbies, and sports
don't take an article in German: Sie ist Kellnerin.

ℰ **kennen** VERB◇, IMPERFECT **kannte**, PERFECT **hat
gekannt**
to know

ℰ **kennenlernen** VERB, PERFECT **hat
kennengelernt**
1 to get to know
sich kennenlernen to get to know each
other
2 to meet (for the first time)
Ich habe Ulrike in London kennengelernt.
I met Ulrike in London.
Wo habt ihr euch kennengelernt? Where
did you meet?

die **Kenntnis**, PLURAL die **Kenntnisse**
1 knowledge
2 etwas zur Kenntnis nehmen to take note
of something

das **Kennzeichen**, PLURAL die **Kennzeichen**
1 mark
2 characteristic
3 registration (number) (of a vehicle)

der **Kerl**, PLURAL die **Kerle**
1 bloke
2 Eva ist ein netter Kerl. Eva's a nice girl.

der **Kern**, PLURAL die **Kerne**
1 pip
2 stone (of an apricot, peach)
3 kernel (of a nut)

die **Kernenergie**
nuclear power

das **Kernkraftwerk**, PLURAL die
Kernkraftwerke
nuclear power station

ℰ indicates key words

die **Kernwaffen** PLURAL NOUN
nuclear weapons

die **Kerze**, PLURAL die **Kerzen**
candle

der **Kerzenhalter**, PLURAL die **Kerzenhalter**
candlestick

der **Kessel**, PLURAL die **Kessel**
1 kettle
2 boiler

die **Kette**, PLURAL die **Ketten**
chain

die **Keule**, PLURAL die **Keulen**
1 club
2 leg (of lamb)
3 drumstick (of chicken)

kg ABBREVIATION
(=Kilogramm) kilogram

kichern VERB, PERFECT **hat gekichert**
to giggle

der **Kiefer**¹, PLURAL die **Kiefer**
jaw

die **Kiefer**², PLURAL die **Kiefern**
1 pine tree
2 pine (wood)

der **Kiefernzapfen**, PLURAL die
Kiefernzapfen
pine cone

der **Kieselstein**, PLURAL die **Kieselsteine**
pebble

ℙ das **Kilo**, PLURAL die **Kilo(s)**
kilo

ℙ das **Kilogramm**, PLURAL die **Kilogramme**
kilogram

ℙ der **Kilometer**, PLURAL die **Kilometer**
kilometre

ℙ das **Kind**, PLURAL die **Kinder**
child

der **Kindergarten**, PLURAL die **Kindergärten**
nursery school

das **Kindergeld**
child benefit

die **Kinderkrippe**, PLURAL die
Kinderkrippen
nursery, crèche

kinderleicht ADJECTIVE
very easy
Das ist kinderleicht. It's child's play.

das **Kindermädchen**, PLURAL die
Kindermädchen
nanny

WORD TIP Professions, hobbies, and sports don't
take an article in German: Sie ist Kindermädchen.

die **Kindertagesstätte**, PLURAL die
Kindertagesstätten
day nursery

der **Kinderwagen**, PLURAL die **Kinderwagen**
pram

die **Kindheit**
childhood

kindisch ADJECTIVE
childish

das **Kinn**, PLURAL die **Kinne**
chin

ℙ das **Kino**, PLURAL die **Kinos**
cinema

der **Kiosk**, PLURAL die **Kioske**
kiosk (for newspapers or snacks)

kippen VERB, PERFECT **hat gekippt**
1 to tip
2 PERFECT ist gekippt to fall (over)

ℙ die **Kirche**, PLURAL die **Kirchen**
church

kirchlich ADJECTIVE
1 church
2 religious

ℙ die **Kirsche**, PLURAL die **Kirschen**
cherry

das **Kissen**, PLURAL die **Kissen**
1 cushion
2 pillow

die **Kiste**, PLURAL die **Kisten**
1 crate
2 box

kitzeln VERB, PERFECT **hat gekitzelt**
to tickle

kitzlig ADJECTIVE
ticklish

die **Kiwi**, PLURAL die **Kiwis**
kiwi fruit

klagen VERB, PERFECT **hat geklagt**
to complain

die **Klammer**, PLURAL die **Klammern**
1 peg (for washing)
2 grip (for hair)
3 bracket

⬦ irregular verb; SEP separable verb; for more help with verbs see centre section

der **Klammeraffe** *(informal)* PLURAL die **Klammeraffen**
at *(@ in email addresses)*

die **Klamotten** PLURAL NOUN
gear *(clothes)*

klang ▸ SEE **klingen**

der **Klang**, PLURAL die **Klänge**
sound

die **Klappe**, PLURAL die **Klappen**
1 flap
2 clapperboard
3 *(informal)* trap *(mouth)*
Halt die Klappe! Shut up!

klappen VERB, PERFECT **hat geklappt**
1 nach vorne klappen to tilt forward
2 nach hinten klappen to tip back
3 nach oben klappen to lift up
4 nach unten klappen to put down
5 to work out
Hoffentlich klappt es. I hope it'll work out.

der **Klappstuhl**, PLURAL die **Klappstühle**
folding chair

klar ADJECTIVE
1 clear *(water, answer)*
klar werden to become clear
2 Jetzt ist mir alles klar. Now I understand.
3 sich klar werden to make up your mind
4 sich über etwas im Klaren sein to realize something

klar ADVERB
clearly
Na klar! *(informal)* Of course!

klären VERB, PERFECT **hat geklärt**
1 to clarify
2 to sort out
3 to purify *(sewage)*
4 sich klären to clear *(of the weather or the sky)*
5 sich klären to resolve itself, to be settled

die **Klarinette**, PLURAL die **Klarinetten**
clarinet
Annika spielt Klarinette. Annika plays the clarinet.

ℰ **klasse** ADJECTIVE
(informal) great, excellent

ℰ die **Klasse**, PLURAL die **Klassen**
1 class
Sie reist immer erster Klasse. She always travels first class.
2 year
Ich gehe in die sechste Klasse. I'm in year six.

die **Klassenarbeit**, PLURAL die **Klassenarbeiten**
(written) test

das **Klassenbuch**, PLURAL die **Klassenbücher**
class register *(kept by the teacher. It can also contain notes about students' behaviour, etc.)*

die **Klassenfahrt**, PLURAL die **Klassenfahrten**
school trip

der **Klassenkamerad**, PLURAL die **Klassenkameraden**
classmate *(male)*

die **Klassenkameradin**, PLURAL die **Klassenkameradinnen**
classmate *(female)*

der **Klassensprecher**, PLURAL die **Klassensprecher**
class representative *(male)*

die **Klassensprecherin**, PLURAL die **Klassensprecherinnen**
class representative *(female)*

ℰ das **Klassenzimmer**, PLURAL die **Klassenzimmer**
classroom

klassisch ADJECTIVE
classical

der **Klatsch**
gossip

klatschen VERB, PERFECT **hat geklatscht**
1 to clap
jemandem Beifall klatschen to applaud somebody
2 to slap
3 to gossip

klauen VERB *(informal)*, PERFECT **hat geklaut**
to pinch *(steal)*

ℰ das **Klavier**, PLURAL die **Klaviere**
piano
Dennis spielt Klavier. Dennis plays the piano.

kleben VERB, PERFECT **hat geklebt**
1 to stick
2 to glue
3 jemandem eine kleben *(informal)* to belt somebody

klebrig ADJECTIVE
sticky

der **Klebstoff**, PLURAL die **Klebstoffe**
glue

ℰ indicates key words

der **Klebstreifen**, PLURAL die **Klebstreifen**
sticky tape

der **Klecks**, PLURAL die **Kleckse**
stain

♀ das **Kleid**, PLURAL die **Kleider**
1 dress
Uschi hat sich zwei neue Kleider gekauft.
Uschi bought two new dresses.
2 Kleider clothes

der **Kleiderbügel**, PLURAL die **Kleiderbügel**
coat hanger

♀ der **Kleiderschrank**, PLURAL die
Kleiderschränke
wardrobe

♀ die **Kleidung**
clothes, clothing

♀ **klein** ADJECTIVE
1 small, little
Kannst du das Gemüse klein schneiden?
Could you chop up the vegetables?
2 short
Peter ist kleiner als Klaus. Peter is shorter
than Klaus.

der **Kleingarten**, PLURAL die **Kleingärten**
allotment (used mainly as garden)

das **Kleingeld**
change

der **Klempner**, PLURAL die **Klempner**
plumber (male)

> **WORD TIP** Professions, hobbies, and sports
> don't take an article in German: Er ist Klempner.

die **Klempnerin**, PLURAL die **Klempnerinnen**
plumber (female)

> **WORD TIP** Professions, hobbies, and sports
> don't take an article in German: Sie ist
> Klempnerin.

klettern VERB, PERFECT **ist geklettert**
to climb
Sie kletterten auf den Baum. They climbed
the tree.

der **Klick**, PLURAL die **Klicks**
click (with mouse)

das **Klicken**
click (noise)

der **Klient**, PLURAL die **Klienten**
client (male)

die **Klientin**, PLURAL die **Klientinnen**
client (female)

das **Klima**, PLURAL die **Klimas**
climate

die **Klimaanlage**, PLURAL die **Klimaanlagen**
air conditioning

der **Klimawandel**
climate change

die **Klinge**, PLURAL die **Klingen**
blade

die **Klingel**, PLURAL die **Klingeln**
bell

klingeln VERB, PERFECT **hat geklingelt**
to ring
Es hat geklingelt. There was a ring at the
door.

der **Klingelton**, PLURAL die **Klingeltöne**
ringtone

klingen VERB◇, IMPERFECT **klang**, PERFECT **hat
geklungen**
to sound

die **Klinik**, PLURAL die **Kliniken**
clinic

die **Klinke**, PLURAL die **Klinken**
handle

die **Klippe**, PLURAL die **Klippen**
rock, cliff

das **Klo**, PLURAL die **Klos**
(informal) loo

klopfen VERB, PERFECT **hat geklopft**
1 to knock
2 to beat

das **Klosett**, PLURAL die **Klosetts**
lavatory

der **Kloß**, PLURAL die **Klöße**
dumpling

das **Kloster**, PLURAL die **Kloster**
1 monastery
2 convent

der **Klotz**, PLURAL die **Klötze**
block

der **Klub**, PLURAL die **Klubs**
club

klug ADJECTIVE
1 clever, intelligent
2 Ich werde daraus nicht klug. I don't
understand it.

die **Klugheit**
intelligence

◇ irregular verb; SEP separable verb; for more help with verbs see centre section

der **Klumpen**, PLURAL die **Klumpen**
lump

km ABBREVIATION
(=Kilometer) kilometre

knabbern VERB, PERFECT **hat geknabbert**
to nibble

der **Knabe**, PLURAL die **Knaben**
boy

das **Knäckebrot**, PLURAL die **Knäckebrote**
crispbread

knacken VERB, PERFECT **hat geknackt**
to crack

der **Knall**, PLURAL die **Knalle**
bang

knallen VERB, PERFECT **hat geknallt**
1 to go bang
2 to pop (of a cork)
3 to slam (of a door)
4 to crack (of a whip)

knapp ADJECTIVE
1 scarce
2 tight (skirt, top)
3 knapp bei Kasse sein to be short of money
4 mit knapper Mehrheit by a narrow majority
5 just
Die Zugfahrt dauert eine knappe Stunde. The train trip is just under an hour.
Sie haben knapp verloren. They only just lost.
6 Das war knapp. (informal) That was a close shave.

knarren VERB, PERFECT **hat geknarrt**
to creak

der **Knauf**, PLURAL die **Knäufe**
knob

knautschen VERB, PERFECT **hat geknautscht**
1 to crumple
2 to crease

kneifen VERB ◇, IMPERFECT **kniff**, PERFECT **hat gekniffen**
1 to pinch
2 (informal) to chicken out
Sie hat mal wieder gekniffen und nichts gesagt. She chickened out yet again and didn't say anything.

die **Kneipe**, PLURAL die **Kneipen**
(informal) pub

kneten VERB, PERFECT **hat geknetet**
to knead

knicken VERB, PERFECT **hat geknickt**
1 to bend
2 to fold

ℰ das **Knie**, PLURAL die **Knie**
knee

knien VERB, PERFECT **hat gekniet**
1 to kneel
2 sich knien to kneel down

kniff ▸ SEE **kneifen**

knipsen VERB, PERFECT **hat geknipst**
(informal) to take a photo, to snap

der **Knoblauch**
garlic

die **Knoblauchzehe**, PLURAL die **Knoblauchzehen**
clove of garlic

der **Knöchel**, PLURAL die **Knöchel**
1 ankle
Mario hat sich beim Jogging den Knöchel verstaucht. Mario sprained his ankle when jogging.
2 knuckle

der **Knochen**, PLURAL die **Knochen**
bone

der **Knopf**, PLURAL die **Knöpfe**
button

der **Knoten**, PLURAL die **Knoten**
1 knot
2 bun (as a hairstyle)
3 lump

der **Knüller**, PLURAL die **Knüller**
scoop (in journalism)

knurren VERB, PERFECT **hat geknurrt**
1 to growl
2 to rumble
3 to grumble

knusprig ADJECTIVE
crisp, crusty (bread)

der **Koalabär**, PLURAL die **Koalabären**
koala bear

der **Koch**, PLURAL die **Köche**
1 cook (male)
2 chef (male)

WORD TIP Professions, hobbies, and sports don't take an article in German: Er ist Koch.

das **Kochbuch**, PLURAL die **Kochbücher**
cookery book

ℰ indicates key words

A B C D E F G H I J K L M N O P Q R S T U V W X Y Z

ℓ **kochen** VERB, PERFECT **hat gekocht**
1 to cook
2 to make *(tea, coffee)*
3 to boil
Das Wasser kocht. The water's boiling.

das **Kochfeld**, PLURAL die **Kochfelder**
ceramic hob

die **Köchin**, PLURAL die **Köchinnen**
1 cook *(female)*
2 chef *(female)*

WORD TIP Professions, hobbies, and sports don't take an article in German: Sie ist Köchin.

der **Kochtopf**, PLURAL die **Kochtöpfe**
saucepan

ℓ der **Koffer**, PLURAL die **Koffer**
suitcase

der **Kofferkuli**, PLURAL die **Kofferkulis**
baggage trolley

der **Kofferraum**, PLURAL die **Kofferräume**
boot

der **Kohl**
1 cabbage
2 *(informal)* rubbish
Rede keinen Kohl. Don't talk rubbish.

die **Kohle**, PLURAL die **Kohlen**
coal

die **Kohlrübe**, PLURAL die **Kohlrüben**
swede

das **Kokain**
cocaine

die **Kokosnuss**, PLURAL die **Kokosnüsse**
coconut

der **Kollege**, PLURAL die **Kollegen**
colleague *(male)*

die **Kollegin**, PLURAL die **Kolleginnen**
colleague *(female)*

Köln NEUTER NOUN
Cologne

das **Kölnischwasser**
eau de cologne

die **Kombination**, PLURAL die **Kombinationen**
combination

der **Komfort**
comfort

der **Komiker**, PLURAL die **Komiker**
comedian *(male)*

WORD TIP Professions, hobbies, and sports don't take an article in German: Er ist Komiker.

die **Komikerin**, PLURAL die **Komikerinnen**
comedian *(female)*

WORD TIP Professions, hobbies, and sports don't take an article in German: Sie ist Komikerin.

komisch ADJECTIVE
funny

das **Komma**, PLURAL die **Kommas**
1 comma
2 decimal point
zwei Komma fünf two point five

ℓ **kommen** VERB◇, IMPERFECT **kam** PERFECT **ist gekommen**
1 to come
2 to get
Wie komme ich zur U-Bahn? How do I get to the tube station?
Kommt gut nach Hause! Have a safe journey home!
3 etwas kommen lassen to send for something
4 Wie kommst du darauf? What gave you that idea?
5 hinter etwas kommen to find out about something
6 zur Schule kommen to start school
7 to go
Die Gabeln kommen in die Schublade. The forks go in the drawer.
ins Krankenhaus kommen to go into hospital
8 Wer kommt zuerst? Who's first?
Du kommst an die Reihe. It's your turn.
9 Wie kommt das? Why is that?
10 zu etwas kommen to acquire something
11 wieder zu sich kommen to come round *(after fainting or anaesthetic)*
12 dazu kommen, etwas zu tun to get round to doing something
Ich komme einfach nicht zum Einkaufen. I just can't get round to doing the shopping.
13 Das kommt davon! See what happens!

der **Kommissar**, PLURAL die **Kommissare**
(detective) inspector *(male)*

WORD TIP Professions, hobbies, and sports don't take an article in German: Er ist Kommissar.

◇ irregular verb; SEP separable verb; for more help with verbs see centre section

die **Kommissarin**, PLURAL die
Kommissarinnen
(detective) inspector *(female)*

WORD TIP Professions, hobbies, and sports don't take an article in German: Sie ist Kommissarin.

die **Kommode**, PLURAL die **Kommoden**
chest of drawers

der **Kommunismus**
communism

der **Kommunist**, PLURAL die **Kommunisten**
communist *(male)*

die **Kommunistin**, PLURAL die
Kommunistinnen
communist *(female)*

kommunizieren VERB, PERFECT **hat**
kommuniziert
to communicate

die **Komödie**, PLURAL die **Komödien**
comedy

der **Kompass**, PLURAL die **Kompasse**
compass

komplett ADJECTIVE
complete

das **Kompliment**, PLURAL die **Komplimente**
compliment

ℓ **kompliziert** ADJECTIVE
complicated

der **Komponist**, PLURAL die **Komponisten**
composer *(male)*

WORD TIP Professions, hobbies, and sports don't take an article in German: Er ist Komponist.

die **Komponistin**, PLURAL die
Komponistinnen
composer *(female)*

WORD TIP Professions, hobbies, and sports don't take an article in German: Sie ist Komponistin.

kompostieren VERB, PERFECT **hat**
kompostiert
to compost

das **Kompott**, PLURAL die **Kompotte**
stewed fruit

der **Kompromiss**, PLURAL die **Kompromisse**
compromise
einen Kompromiss schließen to
compromise

das **Konditional**
conditional *(in grammar)*

der **Konditor**, PLURAL die **Konditoren**
pastry cook *(male)*

WORD TIP Professions, hobbies, and sports don't take an article in German: Er ist Konditor.

die **Konditorei**, PLURAL die **Konditoreien**
patisserie, cake shop

die **Konditorin**, PLURAL die **Konditorinnen**
pastry cook *(female)*

WORD TIP Professions, hobbies, and sports don't take an article in German: Sie ist Konditorin.

das **Kondom**, PLURAL die **Kondome**
condom

die **Konfektion**
ready-made clothes

die **Konferenz**, PLURAL die **Konferenzen**
conference

der **Konflikt**, PLURAL die **Konflikte**
conflict

der **König**, PLURAL die **Könige**
king

die **Königin**, PLURAL die **Königinnen**
queen

königlich ADJECTIVE
royal

das **Königreich**, PLURAL die **Königreiche**
kingdom

die **Konjunktion**, PLURAL die
Konjunktionen
conjunction *(in grammar)*

der **Konkurrent**, PLURAL die **Konkurrenten**
competitor *(male)*

die **Konkurrentin**, PLURAL die
Konkurrentinnen
competitor *(female)*

die **Konkurrenz**
competition

ℓ **können** VERB◇, PRESENT **kann**, IMPERFECT
konnte, PERFECT **hat gekonnt, hat**
können

1 can
Kann ich Ihnen helfen? Can I help you?
Kannst du Auto fahren? Can you drive?
Kannst du Deutsch? Can you speak German?
Ich konnte nicht früher kommen. I couldn't come any earlier.
Das kann ich nicht. I can't do that.

2 to be able to
Er wird es vor Dienstag nicht machen können. He won't be able to do it before Tuesday.
3 may
Das kann gut sein. That may well be so.
Es kann sein, dass ... It may be that ...
4 Ich kann nichts dafür. It's not my fault.

WORD TIP The past participle is gekonnt when können is the main verb, and können when it is an auxiliary verb.

das Können
ability

der Könner, PLURAL die **Könner**
expert

könnt, konnte, konnten, konntest, konntet ▸ SEE **können**

der Konrektor, PLURAL die **Konrektoren**
deputy head, deputy headmaster

WORD TIP Professions, hobbies, and sports don't take an article in German: Er ist Konrektor.

die Konrektorin, PLURAL die **Konrektorinnen**
deputy head, deputy headmistress

WORD TIP Professions, hobbies, and sports don't take an article in German: Sie ist Konrektorin.

die Konserven PLURAL NOUN
tinned food

der Konsonant, PLURAL die **Konsonanten**
consonant

die Konstruktion, PLURAL die **Konstruktionen**
construction

der Konsul, PLURAL die **Konsuln**
consul

WORD TIP Professions, hobbies, and sports don't take an article in German: Er ist Konsul.

das Konsulat, PLURAL die **Konsulate**
consulate

konsultieren VERB, PERFECT **hat konsultiert**
to consult

der Kontakt, PLURAL die **Kontakte**
contact

kontaktfreudig ADJECTIVE
sociable

die Kontaktlinse, PLURAL die **Kontaktlinsen**
contact lens

ℙ **der Kontinent**, PLURAL die **Kontinente**
continent

das Konto, PLURAL die **Konten**
account

die Kontrolle, PLURAL die **Kontrollen**
1 check
2 control

der Kontrolleur, PLURAL die **Kontrolleure**
inspector (male)

WORD TIP Professions, hobbies, and sports don't take an article in German: Er ist Kontrolleur.

die Kontrolleurin, PLURAL die **Kontrolleurinnen**
inspector (female)

WORD TIP Professions, hobbies, and sports don't take an article in German: Sie ist Kontrolleurin.

kontrollieren VERB, PERFECT **hat kontrolliert**
1 to check
2 to control

konzentrieren VERB, PERFECT **hat konzentriert**
1 to concentrate
2 sich konzentrieren to concentrate

ℙ **das Konzert**, PLURAL die **Konzerte**
1 concert
2 concerto

ℙ **der Kopf**, PLURAL die **Köpfe**
1 head
2 sich den Kopf zerbrechen to rack your brains
3 seinen Kopf durchsetzen to get your own way
4 sich den Kopf waschen to wash your hair
5 auf dem Kopf upside down
6 ein Kopf Salat a lettuce

köpfen VERB, PERFECT **hat geköpft**
1 to head (in football)
2 to behead

der Kopfhörer, PLURAL die **Kopfhörer**
headphones

das Kopfkissen, PLURAL die **Kopfkissen**
pillow

der Kopfsalat, PLURAL die **Kopfsalate**
lettuce

ℙ **die Kopfschmerzen** PLURAL NOUN
headache
Ich habe Kopfschmerzen. I've got a headache.

die **Kopie**, PLURAL die **Kopien**
copy

𝒫 **kopieren** VERB, PERFECT **hat kopiert**
1 to copy
2 to photocopy

das **Kopiergerät**, PLURAL die **Kopiergeräte**
photocopier

der **Korb**, PLURAL die **Körbe**
1 basket
2 jemandem einen Korb geben to turn somebody down

der **Korbball**
netball

der **Kork**
cork

der **Korken**, PLURAL die **Korken**
cork

der **Korkenzieher**, PLURAL die **Korkenzieher**
corkscrew

das **Korn**, PLURAL die **Körner**
1 corn (in general)
2 grain (a seed)

der **Körper**, PLURAL die **Körper**
body

körperbehindert ADJECTIVE
disabled

der **Körpergeruch**, PLURAL die **Körpergerüche**
body odour, BO

körperlich ADJECTIVE
physical

die **Korrektur**, PLURAL die **Korrekturen**
correction

𝒫 **korrigieren** VERB, PERFECT **hat korrigiert**
to correct

Korsika NEUTER NOUN
Corsica

koscher ADJECTIVE
kosher

der **Kosename**, PLURAL die **Kosenamen**
pet name

die **Kosmetik**, PLURAL die **Kosmetika**
1 cosmetics
2 beauty care

die **Kost**
food

kostbar ADJECTIVE
precious

𝒫 **kosten** VERB, PERFECT **hat gekostet**
1 to cost
Wie viel kostet es? How much is it?
2 to taste

die **Kosten** PLURAL NOUN
1 cost
2 expenses

kostenlos ADJECTIVE
free (of charge)

köstlich ADJECTIVE
1 delicious
2 funny

das **Kostüm**, PLURAL die **Kostüme**
1 suit
2 costume

das **Kotelett**, PLURAL die **Koteletts**
chop

die **Krabbe**, PLURAL die **Krabben**
1 crab
2 shrimp

krabbeln VERB, PERFECT **ist gekrabbelt**
to crawl

der **Krach**
1 row (argument)
2 noise
3 crash

krachen VERB, PERFECT **hat gekracht**
1 to crash (thunder)
2 PERFECT **ist gekracht** to crack, to crash
Er ist gegen die Mauer gekracht. He crashed into the wall.

krächzen VERB, PERFECT **hat gekrächzt**
to croak

die **Kraft**, PLURAL die **Kräfte**
1 strength
Er hat nicht viel Kraft. He's not very strong.
2 force
in Kraft treten to come into force
3 power
geistige Kräfte mental powers
4 worker, employee
Sie ist eine zuverlässige Kraft. She is a reliable worker.

kräftig ADJECTIVE
1 strong
2 nourishing

kräftig ADVERB
1 strongly

2 hard
Du musst die Flasche kräftig schütteln.
You have to shake the bottle hard.

ℰ das **Kraftwerk**, PLURAL die **Kraftwerke**
power station

der **Kragen**, PLURAL die **Kragen**
collar

die **Krähe**, PLURAL die **Krähen**
crow

die **Kralle**, PLURAL die **Krallen**
claw

der **Kram**
stuff
Mach deinen Kram allein! (informal) Do it yourself!

kramen VERB, PERFECT **hat gekramt**
to rummage about

der **Krampf**, PLURAL die **Krämpfe**
cramp

der **Kran**, PLURAL die **Kräne**
crane (machine)

der **Kranich**, PLURAL die **Kraniche**
crane (bird)

ℰ **krank** ADJECTIVE
ill, sick
krank werden to fall ill

der/die **Kranke**, PLURAL die **Kranken**
patient

kränken VERB, PERFECT **hat gekränkt**
to hurt

ℰ das **Krankenhaus**, PLURAL die **Krankenhäuser**
hospital
Sie haben ihn gestern ins Krankenhaus eingeliefert. He was taken to hospital yesterday.

die **Krankenkasse**
health insurance
Bei welcher Krankenkasse sind Sie versichert? What health insurance have you got?

ℰ der **Krankenpfleger**, PLURAL die **Krankenpfleger**
nurse (male)

WORD TIP Professions, hobbies, and sports don't take an article in German: Er ist Krankenpfleger.

die **Krankenpflegerin**, PLURAL die **Krankenpflegerinnen**
nurse (female)

WORD TIP Professions, hobbies, and sports don't take an article in German: Sie ist Krankenpflegerin.

ℰ die **Krankenschwester**, PLURAL die **Krankenschwestern**
nurse (female)

WORD TIP Professions, hobbies, and sports don't take an article in German: Sie ist Krankenschwester.

die **Krankenversicherung**, PLURAL die **Krankenversicherungen**
medical insurance

der **Krankenwagen**, PLURAL die **Krankenwagen**
ambulance

die **Krankheit**, PLURAL die **Krankheiten**
illness, disease

der **Krapfen**, PLURAL die **Krapfen**
doughnut

krass ADJECTIVE
1 extreme
2 stark (contrast)
3 (informal) (very good) cool, wicked
4 (informal) (very bad) gross

kratzen VERB, PERFECT **hat gekratzt**
to scratch

der **Kratzer**, PLURAL die **Kratzer**
scratch

kraus ADJECTIVE
frizzy

ℰ das **Kraut**, PLURAL die **Kräuter**
1 herb
2 sauerkraut
3 (used in Southern Germany and Austria) cabbage

der **Kräutertee**, PLURAL die **Kräutertees**
herbal tea

der **Krawall**, PLURAL die **Krawalle**
1 riot
2 row

ℰ die **Krawatte**, PLURAL die **Krawatten**
tie

kreativ ADJECTIVE
creative

der **Krebs**, PLURAL die **Krebse**
1 crab
2 cancer
Er ist an Krebs gestorben. He died of cancer.

3 Cancer
Julia ist Krebs. Julia is Cancer.

der **Kredit**, PLURAL die **Kredite**
1 loan *(by a bank)*
Sie haben einen Kredit aufgenommen.
They took out a loan.
2 credit
Wir haben das Auto auf Kredit gekauft.
We bought the car on credit.

die **Kreditkarte**, PLURAL die **Kreditkarten**
credit card

die **Kreide**, PLURAL die **Kreiden**
chalk

kreieren VERB, PERFECT **hat kreiert**
to create

der **Kreis**, PLURAL die **Kreise**
1 circle
2 district

der **Kreislauf**
1 cycle
2 circulation

der **Kreisverkehr**, PLURAL die
Kreisverkehren
roundabout *(on road)*

das **Kreuz**, PLURAL die **Kreuze**
1 cross
2 (small of the) back
3 intersection *(of a motorway)*
4 clubs *(in cards)*

kreuzen VERB, PERFECT **hat gekreuzt**
1 to cross
2 sich kreuzen to cross

die **Kreuzfahrt**, PLURAL die **Kreuzfahrten**
1 cruise
eine Kreuzfahrt machen to go on a cruise
2 crusade

ℰ die **Kreuzung**, PLURAL die **Kreuzungen**
1 crossroads
2 cross *(of plants, animals)*

das **Kreuzworträtsel**, PLURAL die
Kreuzworträtsel
crossword (puzzle)

kriechen VERB◇, IMPERFECT **kroch**, PERFECT **ist**
gekrochen
to crawl

ℰ der **Krieg**, PLURAL die **Kriege**
war

kriegen VERB *(informal)*, PERFECT **hat gekriegt**
1 to get
2 ein Kind kriegen to have a baby

der **Krimi**, PLURAL die **Krimis**
thriller

der **Kriminalroman**, PLURAL die
Kriminalromane
crime novel

kriminell ADJECTIVE
criminal

der/die **Kriminelle**, PLURAL die **Kriminellen**
criminal

die **Krippe**, PLURAL die **Krippen**
1 manger
2 crib
3 crèche

die **Krise**, PLURAL die **Krisen**
crisis

der **Kristall**[1], PLURAL die **Kristalle**
crystal

das **Kristall**[2]
(glass) crystal, cut glass

kritisch ADJECTIVE
critical

kritisieren VERB, PERFECT **hat kritisiert**
1 to criticize
2 to review

kroch ▸ SEE **kriechen**

das **Krokodil**, PLURAL die **Krokodile**
crocodile

die **Krone**, PLURAL die **Kronen**
crown

die **Kröte**, PLURAL die **Kröten**
toad

die **Krücke**, PLURAL die **Krücken**
crutch

der **Krug**, PLURAL die **Krüge**
1 jug
2 mug

der **Krümel**, PLURAL die **Krümel**
crumb

krümelig ADJECTIVE
crumbly

krumm ADJECTIVE
1 bent
2 crooked

die **Kruste**, PLURAL die **Krusten**
crust

ℰ indicates key words

♀ die **Küche**, PLURAL die **Küchen**
1 kitchen
2 cooking, food
Anna liebt die italienische Küche. Anna
loves Italian food.
3 warme Küche hot food

♂ der **Kuchen**, PLURAL die **Kuchen**
cake

der **Kuckuck**, PLURAL die **Kuckucke**
cuckoo

die **Kuckucksuhr**, PLURAL die
Kuckucksuhren
cuckoo clock

die **Kugel**, PLURAL die **Kugeln**
1 ball
2 bullet
3 sphere
4 scoop
Wie viele Kugeln Eis möchtest du? How
many scoops of ice cream would you like?

der **Kugelschreiber**, PLURAL die
Kugelschreiber
ballpoint pen

♀ die **Kuh**, PLURAL die **Kühe**
cow

kühl ADJECTIVE
cool

kühlen VERB, PERFECT **hat gekühlt**
1 to cool, to chill
2 to refrigerate

der **Kühler**, PLURAL die **Kühler**
radiator

die **Kühlerhaube**, PLURAL die **Kühlerhauben**
bonnet (of a car)

♂ der **Kühlschrank**, PLURAL die **Kühlschränke**
fridge

die **Kühltruhe**, PLURAL die **Kühltruhen**
freezer

das **Küken**, PLURAL die **Küken**
chick

♂ der **Kuli**, PLURAL die **Kulis**
(informal) **Biro**™

♀ die **Kultur**, PLURAL die **Kulturen**
1 culture
2 civilization

der **Kulturbeutel**, PLURAL die **Kulturbeutel**
toilet bag

kulturell ADJECTIVE
cultural

der **Kummer**
1 sorrow
2 worry
3 trouble

kümmern VERB, PERFECT **hat gekümmert**
1 to concern
2 sich um jemanden/etwas kümmern to
look after somebody/something
Wer kümmert sich um den Garten? Who
looks after the garden?
3 sich darum kümmern, dass ... to see it
that ...
4 Kümmere dich um deine eigenen
Angelegenheiten! Mind your own
business!

♂ der **Kunde**, PLURAL die **Kunden**
1 customer (male)
2 client (male)

der **Kundendienst**
1 customer services (department)
2 after-sales service

kündigen VERB, PERFECT **hat gekündigt**
1 to cancel
2 to give notice
Die Firma hat ihm gekündigt. The
company gave him his notice.
3 (seine Stellung) kündigen to hand in your
notice
Er hat gekündigt. He has handed in his
notice.

die **Kundin**, PLURAL die **Kundinnen**
1 customer (female)
2 client (female)

die **Kundschaft**
customers

♀ die **Kunst**, PLURAL die **Künste**
1 art
2 skill

die **Kunstausstellung**, PLURAL die
Kunstausstellungen
art exhibition

der **Künstler**, PLURAL die **Künstler**
artist (male)

WORD TIP Professions, hobbies, and sports
don't take an article in German: Er ist Künstler.

die **Künstlerin**, PLURAL die **Künstlerinnen**
artist (female)

WORD TIP Professions, hobbies, and sports don't
take an article in German: Sie ist Künstlerin.

künstlerisch ADJECTIVE
artistic

◇ irregular verb; SEP separable verb; for more help with verbs see centre section

künstlich *ADJECTIVE*
artificial

der **Kunststoff**, *PLURAL* die **Kunststoffe**
plastic

das **Kunststück**, *PLURAL* die **Kunststücke**
1 trick
2 feat

das **Kunstwerk**, *PLURAL* die **Kunstwerke**
work of art

das **Kupfer**
copper

die **Kuppel**, *PLURAL* die **Kuppeln**
dome

die **Kupplung**, *PLURAL* die **Kupplungen**
1 clutch *(of a car)*
2 coupling

der **Kürbis**, *PLURAL* die **Kürbisse**
pumpkin

der **Kurier**, *PLURAL* die **Kuriere**
courier *(delivery person)*

der **Kurierdienst**, *PLURAL* die **Kurierdienste**
courier service

der **Kurort**, *PLURAL* die **Kurorte**
health resort, spa town

der **Kurs**, *PLURAL* die **Kurse**
1 course
2 exchange rate
3 price *(of shares)*

die **Kurve**, *PLURAL* die **Kurven**
1 curve
2 bend

ℓ **kurz** *ADJECTIVE*
1 short
  vor kurzem a short time ago
  kurze Hose(n) shorts
2 zu kurz kommen to get less than your fair
  share, to come off badly
kurz *ADVERB*
1 shortly
2 briefly
3 kurz gesagt in a word

die **Kurzarbeit**
short-time working

kurzärmelig *ADJECTIVE*
short-sleeved

kürzen *VERB*, *PERFECT* **hat gekürzt**
1 to shorten
2 to cut

kurzfristig *ADJECTIVE*
short-term
kurzfristig *ADVERB*
at short notice

kürzlich *ADVERB*
recently

kurzsichtig *ADJECTIVE*
short-sighted

die **Kurzwaren** *PLURAL NOUN*
haberdashery

das **Kuscheltier**, *PLURAL* die **Kuscheltiere**
cuddly toy

ℓ die **Kusine**, *PLURAL* die **Kusinen**
cousin *(female)*

der **Kuss**, *PLURAL* die **Küsse**
kiss

küssen *VERB*, *PERFECT* **hat geküsst**
1 to kiss
2 sich küssen to kiss

ℓ die **Küste**, *PLURAL* die **Küsten**
coast

das **Kuvert**, *PLURAL* die **Kuverts**
envelope

Ll

l *ABBREVIATION*
(= *Liter*) litre

ℓ das **Labor**, *PLURAL* die **Labors**
laboratory

die **Lache**, *PLURAL* die **Lachen**
pool

lächeln *VERB*, *PERFECT* **hat gelächelt**
to smile

ℓ **lachen** *VERB*, *PERFECT* **hat gelacht**
to laugh

lächerlich *ADJECTIVE*
ridiculous

der **Lachs**, *PLURAL* die **Lachse**
salmon

der **Lack**, *PLURAL* die **Lacke**
1 varnish
2 paint

lackieren *VERB*, *PERFECT* **hat lackiert**
1 to varnish
2 to spray *(with paint)*

A
B
C
D
E
F
G
H
I
J
K
L
M
N
O
P
Q
R
S
T
U
V
W
X
Y
Z

laden *VERB*◇, *PRESENT* **lädt**, *IMPERFECT* **lud**, *PERFECT* **hat geladen**
1 **to load**
Wir haben die Möbel in den Möbelwagen geladen. We loaded the furniture into the removal van.
2 **to charge** *(a battery)*
3 **to summon** *(a witness)*
Mein Bruder wurde als Zeuge geladen. My brother was summoned as a witness.

♀ der **Laden**, *PLURAL* die **Läden**
1 **shop**
Wann macht der Laden zu? When does the shop close?
2 **shutter**
Wenn es heiß ist, lassen wir die Läden den ganzen Tag zu. When it's hot we keep the shutters closed all day.

der **Ladendieb**, *PLURAL* die **Ladendiebe**
shoplifter *(male)*

die **Ladendiebin**, *PLURAL* die **Ladendiebinnen**
shoplifter *(female)*

die **Ladung**, *PLURAL* die **Ladungen**
1 **load**
2 **cargo**
3 **charge** *(of electricity or dynamite)*
4 **summons**

lag ▸ SEE **liegen**

♀ die **Lage**, *PLURAL* die **Lagen**
1 **situation**
Er ist in einer schwierigen Lage. He's in a difficult situation.
2 **location**
Sie suchen eine Wohnung in einer ruhigen Lage. They are looking for a flat in a quiet location.
3 **nicht in der Lage sein, etwas zu tun** to be not in a position to do something
4 **layer**

das **Lager**, *PLURAL* die **Lager**
1 **camp**
2 **warehouse**
3 **stock**
Wir haben das Buch auf Lager. We have the book in stock.
4 **stockroom**

lagern *VERB*, *PERFECT* **hat gelagert**
1 **to store**
2 **to camp**

lahm *ADJECTIVE*
lame

lähmen *VERB*, *PERFECT* **hat gelähmt**
to paralyse

die **Lähmung**
paralysis

der **Laib**, *PLURAL* die **Laibe**
loaf

das **Laken**, *PLURAL* die **Laken**
sheet

die **Lakritze**
liquorice

das **Lamm**, *PLURAL* die **Lämmer**
lamb

das **Lammfleisch**
lamb *(meat)*

♀ die **Lampe**, *PLURAL* die **Lampen**
lamp

der **Lampenschirm**, *PLURAL* die **Lampenschirme**
lampshade

das **Lancieren**
launch *(of product)*

♀ das **Land**, *PLURAL* die **Länder**
1 **country, countryside**
Wir wohnen auf dem Land. We live in the country.
2 **land**
3 **(federal) state** *(There are 16 Länder in Germany and 9 in Austria.)*

der **Landarbeiter**, *PLURAL* die **Landarbeiter**
agricultural worker *(male)*

die **Landarbeiterin**, *PLURAL* die **Landarbeiterinnen**
agricultural worker *(female)*

die **Landebahn**, *PLURAL* die **Landebahnen**
runway

landen *VERB*, *PERFECT* **ist gelandet**
1 **to land**
2 *(informal)* **to end up**
Die betrunkenen Teenager sind im Krankenhaus gelandet. The drunk teenagers ended up in hospital.

♀ die **Landkarte**, *PLURAL* die **Landkarten**
map

der **Landkreis**, *PLURAL* die **Landkreise**
district

ländlich *ADJECTIVE*
rural

◇ **irregular verb;** SEP **separable verb; for more help with verbs see centre section**

die **Landschaft**, PLURAL die **Landschaften**
1 countryside
2 landscape

das **Landschaftsschutzgebiet**, PLURAL die **Landschaftsschutzgebiete**
conservation area

die **Landstraße**, PLURAL die **Landstraßen**
country road

der **Landtag**
(federal) state parliament

die **Landwirtschaft**
agriculture, farming

landwirtschaftlich ADJECTIVE
agricultural

_ℓ_ **lang** ADJECTIVE
1 long
seit langem for a long time
2 tall

lang ADVERB
eine Woche lang for a week

langärmelig ADJECTIVE
long-sleeved

lange ADVERB
1 a long time
Ich hatte ihn lange nicht gesehen. I hadn't seen him for a long time.
Das ist schon lange her. That was a long time ago.
2 long
Wir wollen so lange wie möglich bleiben. We want to stay for as long as possible.
3 Er ist lange nicht so reich wie Bill Gates. He's nowhere near as rich as Bill Gates.

die **Länge**, PLURAL die **Längen**
1 length
2 longitude

langen VERB, PERFECT **hat gelangt**
1 to be enough
Das Geld langt nicht. (informal) It's not enough money.
Mir langt's! (informal) I've had enough!
2 to reach
Sie langte nach ihrer Handtasche. She reached for her handbag.
3 jemandem eine langen (informal) to slap somebody's face

der **Langlauf**
cross-country skiing

_ℓ_ **langsam** ADJECTIVE, ADVERB
1 slow(ly)
Sprechen Sie bitte langsam. Please speak slowly.

2 Die Musik geht mir langsam auf die Nerven. The music is starting to get on my nerves.

längst ADVERB
1 a long time ago
Das habe ich schon längst gemacht. I did it a long time ago.
2 for a long time
Er weiß es schon längst. He's known for a long time.
3 längst nicht nowhere near, not nearly
Es war längst nicht so schlimm, wie ich erwartet hatte. It was not nearly as bad as I had expected.

längster, **längste**, **längstes** ADJECTIVE
longest
Marion hat den längsten Aufsatz geschrieben. Marion wrote the longest essay.

langweilen VERB, PERFECT **hat gelangweilt**
1 to bore
2 sich langweilen to be bored
Langweilst du dich? Are you bored?

_ℓ_ **langweilig** ADJECTIVE
boring

der **Lappen**, PLURAL die **Lappen**
cloth, rag

der **Laptop**, PLURAL die **Laptops**
laptop

_ℓ_ der **Lärm**
noise
Die Nachbarn beschweren sich über den Lärm. The neighbours are complaining about the noise.

las ► SEE **lesen**

der **Laser**, PLURAL die **Laser**
laser

der **Laserdrucker**, PLURAL die **Laserdrucker**
laser printer

_ℓ_ **lassen** VERB◊, PRESENT **lässt**, IMPERFECT **ließ**, PERFECT **hat gelassen**, **hat lassen**
1 to let
Lass mich bitte schlafen. Please let me sleep.
Lass uns jetzt gehen. Let's go now.
2 jemandem etwas lassen to let somebody have something
3 to leave
Sie ließen die Kinder zu Hause. They left the children at home.
Lass mich! Leave me alone!

_ℓ_ indicates key words

4 jemanden warten lassen to keep somebody waiting
5 etwas reparieren lassen to have something repaired
6 Lass das! Stop it!
7 Die Tür lässt sich leicht öffnen. The door opens easily.
Das lässt sich alles machen. That can all be arranged.

WORD TIP The past participle is gelassen when lassen is the main verb: Meine Mutter hat mich nicht gelassen. The past participle is lassen when it is an auxiliary verb: Sie hat ihn gehen lassen.

lässig ADJECTIVE
casual

die **Last**, PLURAL die **Lasten**
1 load
2 jemandem zur Last fallen to be a burden on somebody

lästig ADJECTIVE
annoying

der **Lastkraftwagen**, PLURAL die **Lastkraftwagen**
lorry, truck

das **Latein**
Latin

die **Laterne**, PLURAL die **Laternen**
1 lantern
2 street light

das **Laub**
leaves

der **Lauch**
leek(s)

der **Lauf**, PLURAL die **Läufe**
1 run
2 course
im Laufe der Zeit in the course of time
im Laufe der Jahre over the years
3 race
4 barrel (of a gun)

die **Laufbahn**, PLURAL die **Laufbahnen**
career

ℰ **laufen** VERB◇, PRESENT **läuft**, IMPERFECT **lief**, PERFECT **ist gelaufen**
1 to run
Sie kann viel schneller laufen als ihr Bruder. She can run much faster than her brother.
2 to walk

Du kannst nach Hause laufen oder mit dem Bus fahren. You can walk home or go on the bus.
3 to be valid (of a passport, contract)
Der Pass läuft bis April 2011. The passport is valid until April 2011.
4 Ski laufen to ski
5 to be on (of a film, programme, or machine)
Was läuft im Kino? What's on at the cinema?

laufend ADJECTIVE
1 running
2 current (issue, month)
3 auf dem Laufenden sein to be up to date
Anita hält mich auf dem Laufenden. Anita keeps me up to date.

laufend ADVERB
continually, constantly

der **Läufer**, PLURAL die **Läufer**
1 runner (male)
2 rug
3 bishop (in chess)

die **Läuferin**, PLURAL die **Läuferinnen**
runner (female)

die **Laufmasche**, PLURAL die **Laufmaschen**
ladder (in your tights)

das **Laufwerk**, PLURAL die **Laufwerke**
drive (on a computer)

die **Laune**, PLURAL die **Launen**
mood
gute/schlechte Laune haben to be in a good/bad mood

ℰ **launisch** ADJECTIVE
moody

die **Laus**, PLURAL die **Läuse**
louse

ℰ **laut** ADJECTIVE
1 loud
2 noisy
Seid nicht so laut! Don't make so much noise!

laut ADVERB
1 loudly
2 noisily
3 aloud
Sie las das Gedicht laut vor. She read the poem aloud.
4 Er stellte das Radio lauter. He turned up the radio.

laut PREPOSITION (+ GEN or + DAT)
according to

der **Laut**, PLURAL die **Laute**
sound

◇ irregular verb; SEP separable verb; for more help with verbs see centre section

lauten *VERB, PERFECT* **hat gelautet**
1 to be
  Wie lautet Ihre Adresse? What is your
  address?
2 to go
  Wie lautet das Lied? How does the song
  go?

läuten *VERB, PERFECT* **hat geläutet**
  to ring

lauter *ADJECTIVE*
1 nothing but
2 louder

lautlos *ADJECTIVE*
  silent
lautlos *ADVERB*
  silently

der **Lautsprecher**, *PLURAL* die **Lautsprecher**
  (loud)speaker

die **Lautstärke**
  volume

lauwarm *ADJECTIVE*
  lukewarm

die **Lawine**, *PLURAL* die **Lawinen**
  avalanche

leben *VERB, PERFECT* **hat gelebt**
1 to live
2 to be alive
3 Leb wohl! Farewell!

ℰ das **Leben**, *PLURAL* die **Leben**
  life
  am Leben sein to be alive
  ums Leben kommen to die, to be killed

lebend *ADJECTIVE*
  living

lebendig *ADJECTIVE*
1 living
2 lebendig sein to be alive
3 lively

die **Lebensgefahr**
  mortal danger
  Sein Vater ist in Lebensgefahr. His father
  is critically ill.

lebensgefährlich *ADJECTIVE, ADVERB*
1 extremely dangerous
2 life-threatening *(injury)*
  Sie wurde lebensgefährlich verletzt. She
  was seriously injured.

die **Lebenshaltungskosten** *PLURAL NOUN*
  cost of living

lebenslänglich *ADJECTIVE*
  life
lebenslänglich *ADVERB*
  for life

der **Lebenslauf**, *PLURAL* die **Lebensläufe**
  CV

ℰ die **Lebensmittel** *PLURAL NOUN*
  food, groceries

das **Lebensmittelgeschäft**, *PLURAL* die
  Lebensmittelgeschäfte
  grocer's (shop)

ℰ die **Lebensmittelvergiftung**, *PLURAL* die
  Lebensmittelvergiftungen
  food poisoning

der **Lebensraum**, *PLURAL* die **Lebensräume**
1 habitat
2 living space

der **Lebensunterhalt**
  living
  Womit verdient sie ihren
  Lebensunterhalt? How does she earn a
  living?

die **Leber**, *PLURAL* die **Lebern**
  liver

der **Leberfleck**, *PLURAL* die **Leberflecke**
  mole

die **Leberwurst**
  liver sausage

das **Lebewesen**, *PLURAL* die **Lebewesen**
  living being, living thing

ℰ **lebhaft** *ADJECTIVE*
1 lively
2 vivid *(memory, colour)*

der **Lebkuchen**, *PLURAL* die **Lebkuchen**
  gingerbread

🛈 LEBKUCHEN

Lebkuchen are traditionally made at
Christmas. They may be covered in icing or
chocolate and are sometimes in the shape of a
star or heart.

leblos *ADJECTIVE*
  lifeless

das **Leck**, *PLURAL* die **Lecks**
  leak

lecken *VERB, PERFECT* **hat geleckt**
1 to lick
  Die Katze leckte ihre Jungen. The cat
  licked the kittens.
  Sie leckte an einem Eis. She was licking

an ice cream.

2 to leak

♪ **lecker** ADJECTIVE
delicious
Das Essen war sehr lecker. The food was really delicious.

♪ das **Leder**
leather

ledig ADJECTIVE
single

lediglich ADVERB
only, merely

♪ **leer** ADJECTIVE
1 empty
leer machen to empty
leer stehen to stand empty
2 blank
Ich brauche ein leeres Blatt Papier. I need a blank sheet of paper.

leeren VERB, PERFECT **hat geleert**
1 to empty
2 sich leeren to empty

der **Leerlauf**
neutral (gear)

die **Leerung**, PLURAL die **Leerungen**
collection (of post)

legal ADJECTIVE
legal

legen VERB, PERFECT **hat gelegt**
1 to put
2 to lay
3 sich legen to lie down
4 sich legen to die down (of a storm, noise)
Ihre Begeisterung hat sich gelegt. Their enthusiasm has worn off.

leger ADJECTIVE, ADVERB
casual(ly)
Sie waren leger gekleidet. They were casually dressed.

der **Lehm**
clay

die **Lehne**, PLURAL die **Lehnen**
1 back (of a chair)
2 arm (of a sofa or chair)

lehnen VERB, PERFECT **hat gelehnt**
1 to lean
2 sich an etwas lehnen to lean against something

der **Lehnstuhl**, PLURAL die **Lehnstühle**
easy chair

das **Lehrbuch**, PLURAL die **Lehrbücher**
textbook

♪ die **Lehre**, PLURAL die **Lehren**
1 apprenticeship
2 traineeship

lehren VERB, PERFECT **hat gelehrt**
to teach

♪ der **Lehrer**, PLURAL die **Lehrer**
1 teacher (male)
2 instructor (male)

> **WORD TIP** Professions, hobbies, and sports don't take an article in German: Er ist Lehrer.

♪ die **Lehrerin**, PLURAL die **Lehrerinnen**
1 teacher (female)
2 instructor (female)

> **WORD TIP** Professions, hobbies, and sports don't take an article in German: Sie ist Lehrerin.

das **Lehrerzimmer**, PLURAL die **Lehrerzimmer**
staff room

der **Lehrgang**, PLURAL die **Lehrgänge**
course

das **Lehrjahr**, PLURAL die **Lehrjahre**
year as an apprentice
Er ist im ersten Lehrjahr. He is in the first year of his apprenticeship.

♪ der **Lehrling**, PLURAL die **Lehrlinge**
1 apprentice
2 trainee

der **Lehrplan**, PLURAL die **Lehrpläne**
syllabus

lehrreich ADJECTIVE
informative

♪ die **Lehrstelle**, PLURAL die **Lehrstellen**
1 apprenticeship
2 traineeship

der **Leibwächter**, PLURAL die **Leibwächter**
bodyguard (male)

> **WORD TIP** Professions, hobbies, and sports don't take an article in German: Er ist Leibwächter.

die **Leibwächterin**, PLURAL die **Leibwächterinnen**
bodyguard (female)

> **WORD TIP** Professions, hobbies, and sports don't take an article in German: Sie ist Leibwächterin.

die **Leiche**, PLURAL die **Leichen**
(dead) body, corpse

℘ **leicht** *ADJECTIVE*
1 **light**
2 **easy**
   Der Test war ganz leicht. The test was really easy.
   Markus macht es sich immer leicht. Markus always takes the easy way out.
3 **slight**
   Er hat einen leichten Akzent. He speaks with a slight accent.

℘ die **Leichtathletik**
   athletics

leichtfallen *VERB*◇, *PRESENT* **fällt leicht**, *IMPERFECT* **fiel leicht**, *PERFECT* **ist leichtgefallen**
   jemandem leichtfallen to be easy for somebody
   Es ist ihm nicht leichtgefallen. It wasn't easy for him.

der **Leichtsinn**
1 **carelessness**
2 **recklessness**

leichtsinnig *ADVERB*
1 **carelessly**
2 **recklessly**

leichtsinnig *ADJECTIVE*
1 **careless**
2 **reckless**

leid *ADJECTIVE*
1 jemanden/etwas leid sein to be fed up with somebody/something
2 ▸SEE **leidtun**

das **Leid**
1 **suffering**
2 **harm**
3 ▸SEE **leidtun**

℘ **leiden** *VERB*◇, *IMPERFECT* **litt**, *PERFECT* **hat gelitten**
1 **to suffer**
2 jemanden gut leiden können to like somebody
   Ich kann Lisa nicht leiden. I can't stand Lisa.

leidenschaftlich *ADJECTIVE*
   passionate

℘ **leider** *ADVERB*
1 **unfortunately**
2 Leider ja. I'm afraid so.
   Leider nicht. I'm afraid not.

℘ **leidtun** *VERB*◇, *IMPERFECT* **tat leid**, *PERFECT* **hat leidgetan**
1 Es tut mir leid. I'm sorry.
2 Andreas tut mir leid. I feel sorry for Andreas.

leihen *VERB*◇, *IMPERFECT* **lieh**, *PERFECT* **hat geliehen**
1 **to lend**
   Kannst du mir fünf Euro leihen? Can you lend me five euros?
2 sich etwas leihen to borrow something
   Ich habe mir das Buch von Alex geliehen. I borrowed the book from Alex.

die **Leihgabe**, *PLURAL* die **Leihgaben**
   loan *(by or to a museum)*

der **Leihwagen**, *PLURAL* die **Leihwagen**
   hire car

der **Leim**, *PLURAL* die **Leime**
   glue

die **Leine**, *PLURAL* die **Leinen**
1 **rope**
2 **line** *(for washing)*
3 **lead** *(for a dog)*

das **Leinen**
   linen

die **Leinwand**, *PLURAL* die **Leinwände**
   screen *(in a cinema)*

℘ **leise** *ADJECTIVE*
   quiet

leise *ADVERB*
1 **quietly**
2 Sie stellte die Musik leiser. She turned the music down.

leisten *VERB*, *PERFECT* **hat geleistet**
1 **to achieve**
2 jemandem Hilfe leisten to help somebody
3 jemandem Gesellschaft leisten to keep somebody company
4 sich etwas leisten to treat yourself to something
   Er leistete sich einen neuen Mantel. He treated himself to a new coat.
5 sich etwas leisten können to be able to afford something
   Ich kann mir kein neues Auto leisten. I can't afford a new car.

die **Leistung**, *PLURAL* die **Leistungen**
1 **achievement**
2 **performance**
3 **service**
4 **payment**

der **Leistungsdruck**
   pressure to achieve

℘ der **Leistungskurs**, *PLURAL* die **Leistungskurse**
   main subject

℘ indicates key words

leistungsstark ADJECTIVE
powerful (battery)

leiten VERB, PERFECT **hat geleitet**
1 to lead
2 to direct
3 to manage, run (a business)
4 to conduct (a choir, orchestra)

die **Leiter**¹, PLURAL die **Leitern**
ladder

der **Leiter**², PLURAL die **Leiter**
1 leader (male)
2 head (male)
3 manager (male)
4 director (male)
5 conductor (of electricity)

die **Leiterin**, PLURAL die **Leiterinnen**
1 leader (female)
2 head (female)
3 manager (female)
4 director (female)

♀ die **Leitung**, PLURAL die **Leitungen**
1 management
2 (phone) line
3 (electric) wire, cable
4 pipe
5 direction
Das Schulorchester spielte unter der Leitung von Herrn Schmidt. The school orchestra was conducted by Mr Schmidt.

das **Leitungswasser**
tap water

die **Lektion**, PLURAL die **Lektionen**
lesson

die **Lektüre**, PLURAL die **Lektüren**
reading matter

lenken VERB, PERFECT **hat gelenkt**
1 to steer
2 to guide
3 den Verdacht auf jemanden lenken to throw suspicion on somebody

das **Lenkrad**, PLURAL die **Lenkräder**
steering wheel

die **Lenkstange**, PLURAL die **Lenkstangen**
handlebars

♀ **lernen** VERB, PERFECT **hat gelernt**
1 to learn
schwimmen lernen to learn to swim
2 to study, to revise
Sie müssen für die Prüfung lernen. They have to revise for the exam.

die **Lesbe**, PLURAL die **Lesben**
lesbian

lesbisch ADJECTIVE
lesbian

♀ **lesen** VERB◇, PRESENT **liest**, IMPERFECT **las**, PERFECT **hat gelesen**
to read

♀ der **Leser**, PLURAL die **Leser**
reader (male)

die **Leseratte**, PLURAL die **Leseratten**
bookworm

♀ die **Leserin**, PLURAL die **Leserinnen**
reader (female)

♀ **Lettland** NEUTER NOUN
Latvia

letzte ▸ SEE **letzter**

der/die/das **Letzte**, PLURAL die **Letzten**
1 der/die Letzte the last (one)
das Letzte the last (thing)
2 Boris kam als Letzter. Boris arrived last.

letztens ADVERB
1 recently
2 lastly

♀ **letzter, letzte, letztes** ADJECTIVE
1 last
das letzte Mal the last time
zum letzten Mal for the last time
2 latest (news, information)
3 in letzter Zeit recently

letztmöglich ADJECTIVE
last possible

leuchten VERB, PERFECT **hat geleuchtet**
to shine

der **Leuchter**, PLURAL die **Leuchter**
candlestick

die **Leuchtreklame**
neon sign

der **Leuchtturm**, PLURAL die **Leuchttürme**
lighthouse

leugnen VERB, PERFECT **hat geleugnet**
to deny

die **Leukämie**
leukaemia

♀ die **Leute** PLURAL NOUN
people

das **Lexikon**, PLURAL die **Lexika**
1 encyclopedia
2 dictionary

◇ irregular verb; SEP separable verb; for more help with verbs see centre section

das **Licht**, PLURAL die **Lichter**
  light

das **Lichtbild**, PLURAL die **Lichtbilder**
  photograph

der **Lichtschalter**, PLURAL die **Lichtschalter**
  light switch

das **Lid**, PLURAL die **Lider**
  (eye)lid

der **Lidschatten**, PLURAL die **Lidschatten**
  eye shadow

ℒ **lieb** ADJECTIVE
  dear
    Liebe Gabi! Dear Gabi, ... (at the beginning
    of a letter)
  3 **nice, sweet**
    Das ist lieb von euch. That's nice of you.
  4 **jemanden lieb haben** to be fond of
    somebody
  5 Es wäre mir lieber, wenn ... I'd prefer it
    if ...
  6 Diese Puppe ist ihr liebstes Spielzeug. This
    doll is her favourite toy.

ℒ die **Liebe**
  love

ℒ **lieben** VERB, PERFECT **hat geliebt**
  to love

liebenswürdig ADJECTIVE
  kind

ℒ **lieber** ADVERB
  1 **lieber mögen/haben** to like better
    Ich mag Nina lieber als Susi. I like Nina
    better than Susi.
  2 **rather**
    Er würde lieber ausgehen als zu Hause
    bleiben. He'd rather go out than stay at
    home.
  3 Lass das lieber! You'd better not do that!
  4 Ich trinke lieber Kaffee. I prefer coffee.

der **Liebesbrief**, PLURAL die **Liebesbriefe**
  love letter

der **Liebesfilm**, PLURAL die **Liebesfilme**
  romantic film

der **Liebeskummer**
  Liebeskummer haben to be lovesick

ℒ **liebevoll** ADJECTIVE
  loving, tender

der **Liebling**, PLURAL die **Lieblinge**
  1 **darling**
  2 **favourite**

ℒ **Lieblings-** PREFIX
  favourite
    Was ist dein Lieblingsfach? What is your
    favourite subject?

liebster, liebste, liebstes ADJECTIVE
  1 **dearest**
  2 **favourite**

liebsten ADVERB
  am liebsten best (of all)
    Ich mag Max am liebsten. I like Max best.

Liechtenstein NEUTER NOUN
  Liechtenstein

🔵 **LIECHTENSTEIN**

Capital: Vaduz. Population: approximately
35,000. Size: 160.4 square km. Main language
spoken: German. Official currency: Swiss franc.

ℒ das **Lied**, PLURAL die **Lieder**
  song

lief ▸ SEE **laufen**

liefern VERB, PERFECT **hat geliefert**
  1 to deliver
  2 to supply

die **Lieferung**, PLURAL die **Lieferungen**
  delivery

der **Lieferwagen**, PLURAL die **Lieferwagen**
  (delivery) van

ℒ **liegen** VERB◇, IMPERFECT **lag** PERFECT **hat
  gelegen**
  1 **to lie, to be**
    Er lag auf dem Boden. He was lying on
    the floor.
    Der Brief liegt auf dem Tisch. The letter
    is on the table.
    Es liegt viel Schnee. There's lots of snow.
  2 **to be, to be situated**
    Bern liegt in der Schweiz. Berne is in
    Switzerland.
  3 **liegen bleiben** to stay in bed
    Er ist (im Bett) liegen geblieben. He
    stayed in bed.
  4 **liegen bleiben** to be left behind
    Der Schal ist im Bus liegen geblieben.
    The scarf was left behind on the bus.
  5 **liegen bleiben** to be left unfinished
    Die Arbeit ist liegen geblieben. The work
    was left unfinished.
  6 **liegen bleiben** to settle (of snow)
    Der Schnee bleibt liegen. The snow is
    settling.
  7 **liegen lassen** to leave
    Ich habe meine Tasche bei Max liegen

ℒ **indicates key words**

lassen. I left my bag at Max's house.
8 Es liegt mir nicht. It doesn't suit me.
9 an etwas liegen to be due to something
10 Es liegt bei ihm. It's up to him.

der **Liegeplatz**, PLURAL die **Liegeplätze**
mooring, berth

der **Liegestuhl**, PLURAL die **Liegestühle**
deckchair

der **Liegewagen**, PLURAL die **Liegewagen**
couchette (coach)

ließ ▸ SEE **lassen**

liest ▸ SEE **lesen**

der **Lift**, PLURAL die **Lifte**
lift

die **Liga**, PLURAL die **Ligen**
league

ℓ **lila** ADJECTIVE
1 purple
2 mauve

die **Limo**, PLURAL die **Limo(s)** ▸ SEE **Limonade**

ℓ die **Limonade**, PLURAL die **Limonaden**
1 lemonade
2 fizzy drink

die **Limone**, PLURAL die **Limonen**
lime

ℓ das **Lineal**, PLURAL die **Lineale**
ruler

ℓ die **Linie**, PLURAL die **Linien**
1 line
2 route
Die Linie 6 fährt zum Bahnhof. The
number 6 goes to the station.

der **Linienflug**, PLURAL die **Linienflüge**
scheduled flight

die **Linke**
1 left
zu meiner Linken on my left
2 left hand
3 left side
4 die Linke the left (in politics)

linker, linke, linkes ADJECTIVE
1 left
2 left-wing

ℓ **links** ADVERB
1 on the left
In England fährt man links. In England
they drive on the left.

2 left
links abbiegen to turn left
von links from the left
nach links (to the) left
3 auf links (clothing) inside out
4 links sein to be left-wing
5 links stricken to purl (in knitting)
Du musst immer zwei links, zwei rechts
stricken. You have to purl two, knit two.

der **Linkshänder**, PLURAL die **Linkshänder**
left-hander (male)
Er ist Linkshänder. He's left-handed.

die **Linkshänderin**, PLURAL die
Linkshänderinnen
left-hander (female)
Sie ist Linkshänderin. She's left-handed.

die **Linse**, PLURAL die **Linsen**
1 lens
2 lentil

ℓ die **Lippe**, PLURAL die **Lippen**
lip

der **Lippenstift**, PLURAL die **Lippenstifte**
lipstick

Lissabon NEUTER NOUN
Lisbon

ℓ die **Liste**, PLURAL die **Listen**
list

listig ADJECTIVE
cunning

ℓ **Litauen** NEUTER NOUN
Lithuania

ℓ der **Liter**, PLURAL die **Liter**
litre

die **Literatur**
literature

litt ▸ SEE **leiden**

live ADVERB
live
Das Spiel wurde live übertragen. The
match was broadcast live.

WORD TIP In German, the word live is only used
in this sense. The German word for live, alive
is lebend.

die **Livesendung**, PLURAL die
Livesendungen
live broadcast

die **Lizenz**, PLURAL die **Lizenzen**
licence

◇ irregular verb; SEP separable verb; for more help with verbs see centre section

ℓ der **Lkw**, *PLURAL* die **Lkws** *ABBREVIATION*
(=*Lastkraftwagen*) **lorry, truck**

das **Lob**
praise

loben *VERB*, *PERFECT* **hat gelobt**
to praise

ℓ das **Loch**, *PLURAL* die **Löcher**
hole

die **Locke**, *PLURAL* die **Locken**
curl

locken *VERB*, *PERFECT* **hat gelockt**
1 **to tempt**
2 **sich locken to be curly**

locker *ADJECTIVE*
1 **loose**
2 **slack** *(rope)*
3 **relaxed** *(atmosphere, person)*

lockerlassen *VERB◇*, *PRESENT* **lässt locker**,
IMPERFECT **ließ locker**, *PERFECT* **hat**
lockergelassen
nicht lockerlassen *(informal)* **not to let up,**
not to give up

ℓ **lockig** *ADJECTIVE*
curly

ℓ der **Löffel**, *PLURAL* die **Löffel**
1 **spoon**
2 **spoonful**
ein Löffel Mehl a spoonful of flour

log ▸ SEE **lügen**

die **Logik**
logic

logisch *ADJECTIVE*
1 **logical**
2 *(informal)* **obvious**
Das ist doch logisch. That's obvious.
Ja, logisch! Yes, of course!

ℓ der **Lohn**, *PLURAL* die **Löhne**
1 **pay, wages**
2 **reward**

ℓ **lohnen** *VERB*, *PERFECT* **hat sich gelohnt**
sich lohnen to be worth it

das **Lokal**, *PLURAL* die **Lokale**
1 **bar**
2 **restaurant**

die **Lokomotive**, *PLURAL* die **Lokomotiven**
locomotive, engine

das **Lorbeerblatt**, *PLURAL* die
Lorbeerblätter
bay leaf

ℓ **los** *ADJECTIVE*
1 **Der Hund ist los. The dog is off the lead.**
2 **Die Schraube ist los. The screw is loose.**
3 **Es ist viel los. There's a lot going on.**
4 **etwas los sein to be rid of something**
5 **Was ist los? What's the matter?**

los *ADVERB*
1 **Los! Go on!**
2 **Achtung, fertig, los! Ready, steady, go!**

das **Los**, *PLURAL* die **Lose**
1 **(lottery) ticket**
2 **das große Los ziehen to hit the jackpot**
3 **lot** *fate*

losbinden *VERB◇*, *IMPERFECT* **band los**, *PERFECT*
hat losgebunden
to untie

löschen *VERB*, *PERFECT* **hat gelöscht**
1 **to put out**
2 **to delete**
3 **to erase**
4 **seinen Durst löschen to quench your thirst**

lose *ADJECTIVE*
loose

lösen *VERB*, *PERFECT* **hat gelöst**
1 **to solve**
2 **to undo**
3 **to buy** *(a ticket)*
4 **to release**
5 **to remove**
6 **sich lösen to come undone**
7 **sich lösen to be solved** *(of a puzzle or*
mystery)
sich (von selbst) lösen to be resolved *(of a*
problem)
8 **sich lösen to dissolve**
Die Tablette löst sich in Wasser. The tablet
dissolves in water.

ℓ **losfahren** *VERB◇*, *PRESENT* **fährt los**, *IMPERFECT*
fuhr los, *PERFECT* **ist losgefahren**
1 **to set off**
2 **to drive off**

losgehen *VERB◇*, *IMPERFECT* **ging los**, *PERFECT*
ist losgegangen
1 **to set off**
2 **to start**
3 **to come off** *(of a button)*
4 **to go off** *(of a bomb)*
5 **auf jemanden losgehen to go for**
somebody

loslassen *VERB◇*, *PRESENT* **lässt los**, *IMPERFECT*
ließ los, *PERFECT* **hat losgelassen**
1 **etwas loslassen to let go of something**
2 **to let go**

ℓ **indicates key words**

die **Losung**, PLURAL die **Losungen**
1 slogan
2 password
die Losung nennen to give the password

die **Lösung**, PLURAL die **Lösungen**
solution

loswerden VERB◇, PRESENT **wird los**, IMPERFECT
wurde los, PERFECT **ist losgeworden**
to get rid of

die **Lotterie**, PLURAL die **Lotterien**
lottery

das **Lotto**, PLURAL die **Lottos**
(national) lottery

ℓ der **Löwe**, PLURAL die **Löwen**
1 lion
2 Leo
Ben ist Löwe. Ben is a Leo.

die **Loyalität**
loyalty

ℓ die **Lücke**, PLURAL die **Lücken**
gap

ℓ die **Luft**, PLURAL die **Lüfte**
1 air
2 breath
die Luft anhalten to hold your breath
3 in die Luft gehen (informal) to blow your
top
4 jemanden wie Luft behandeln to ignore
somebody

der **Luftballon**, PLURAL die **Luftballons**
balloon

der **Luftdruck**
air pressure

das **Luftkissenboot**, PLURAL die
Luftkissenboote
hovercraft

die **Luftmatratze**, PLURAL die **Luftmatratzen**
air bed

die **Luftpost**
airmail
Ich habe den Brief per Luftpost geschickt.
I sent the letter by airmail.

die **Luftverschmutzung**
air pollution

die **Luftwaffe**
air force

die **Lüge**, PLURAL die **Lügen**
lie

lügen VERB◇, IMPERFECT **log**, PERFECT **hat**
gelogen
to lie

der **Lügner**, PLURAL die **Lügner**
liar (male)

die **Lügnerin**, PLURAL die **Lügnerinnen**
liar (female)

die **Lunge**, PLURAL die **Lungen**
lungs

die **Lungenentzündung**
pneumonia

die **Lupe**, PLURAL die **Lupen**
magnifying glass

ℓ die **Lust**
1 pleasure
2 Lust haben, etwas zu tun to feel like doing
something
Er hatte keine Lust, seine Hausaufgaben
zu machen. He didn't feel like doing his
homework.
Ich habe keine Lust. I don't feel like it.
Hast du Lust, mit uns ins Kino zu gehen?
Would you like to come to the cinema
with us?
3 Lust auf etwas haben to feel like
something, to fancy something
Hast du Lust auf ein Eis? Do you fancy an
ice cream?

ℓ **lustig** ADJECTIVE
1 funny
2 entertaining, fun
3 Dennis hat sich über mich lustig gemacht.
Dennis was making fun of me.

lutschen VERB, PERFECT **hat gelutscht**
to suck

der **Lutscher**, PLURAL die **Lutscher**
lollipop

ℓ **Luxemburg** NEUTER NOUN
Luxembourg

LUXEMBURG

Capital: Luxembourg. Population:
approximately 500,000. Size: 2586 square
km. Main languages spoken: German, French,
Lëtzebuergesch (everyday spoken language).
Official currency: euro.

der **Luxus**
luxury

Luzern NEUTER NOUN
Lucerne

◇ irregular verb; SEP separable verb; for more help with verbs see centre section

Mm

m *ABBREVIATION*
(=*Meter*) metre

ℰ **machen** *VERB, PERFECT* **hat gemacht**
1 to make
2 to do
 Was machst du da? What are you doing?
3 Was macht die Arbeit? How's work?
 Was macht Karin? How's Karin?
4 sich an die Arbeit machen to get down
 to work
5 schnell machen to hurry
6 Das macht nichts. It doesn't matter.
7 Mach schon! Hurry up!
8 Mach's gut! Take care! *(goodbye)*
9 to come to
 Das macht fünf Euro. That comes to five
 euros.
10 sich nichts aus etwas machen to be not
 very keen on something
 Laura macht sich nichts aus Schokolade.
 Laura isn't keen on chocolate.

---

die **Macht**, *PLURAL* die **Mächte**
 power
 an die Macht kommen to come to power

ℰ das **Mädchen**, *PLURAL* die **Mädchen**
 girl

der **Mädchenname**, *PLURAL* die
 Mädchennamen
1 maiden name
2 girl's name

die **Made**, *PLURAL* die **Maden**
 maggot

mag ▸SEE **mögen**

ℰ das **Magazin**, *PLURAL* die **Magazine**
 magazine

der **Magen**, *PLURAL* die **Mägen**
 stomach

ℰ die **Magenschmerzen** *PLURAL NOUN*
 stomach ache
 Ich habe Magenschmerzen. I've got
 stomach ache.

die **Magenverstimmung**, *PLURAL* die
 Magenverstimmungen
 stomach upset
 Er hatte eine Magenverstimmung. He had
 an upset stomach.

mager *ADJECTIVE*
1 thin
2 lean
3 low-fat

magersüchtig *ADJECTIVE*
 anorexic

die **Magie**
 magic

der **Magnet**, *PLURAL* die **Magnete(n)**
 magnet

magnetisch *ADJECTIVE*
 magnetic

magst ▸SEE **mögen**

das **Mahagoni**
 mahogany

mähen *VERB, PERFECT* **hat gemäht**
 to mow
 Samstags muss ich den Rasen mähen. On
 Saturdays I have to mow the lawn.

mahlen *VERB◇, PERFECT* **hat gemahlen**
 to grind

ℰ die **Mahlzeit**, *PLURAL* die **Mahlzeiten**
 meal
 Mahlzeit! Enjoy your meal!

ℰ der **Mai**
 May
 im Mai in May
 der Erste Mai May Day

der **Maifeiertag**
 May Day

das **Maiglöckchen**, *PLURAL* die
 Maiglöckchen
 lily of the valley

Mailand *NEUTER NOUN*
 Milan

mailen *VERB, PERFECT* **hat gemailt**
 to email

der **Mais**
1 maize
2 sweetcorn

die **Majonäse**
 mayonnaise

der **Majoran**
 marjoram

das **Make-up**
 make-up

die **Makkaroni** *PLURAL NOUN*
 macaroni

ℰ indicates key words

der **Makler**, PLURAL die **Makler**
estate agent (male)

> **WORD TIP** Professions, hobbies, and sports don't take an article in German: Er ist Makler.

die **Maklerin**, PLURAL die **Maklerinnen**
estate agent (female)

> **WORD TIP** Professions, hobbies, and sports don't take an article in German: Sie ist Maklerin.

𝒫 **mal** ADVERB
1 times
Zwei mal drei ist sechs. Two times three is six.
2 by
Mein Zimmer ist drei mal vier Meter groß. My room is three metres by four.
3 some time, one day
Ich möchte mal nach Brasilien fahren. I'd like to go to Brazil one day.
4 schon mal ever
Warst du schon mal in Paris? Have you ever been to Paris?
5 Ich war schon mal da. I've been there before.
6 nicht mal not even
7 Komm mal her! Come here!

das **Mal**, PLURAL die **Male**
1 time
nächstes Mal next time
zum ersten Mal for the first time
2 mark
3 mole

𝒫 **malen** VERB, PERFECT **hat gemalt**
to paint

der **Maler**, PLURAL die **Maler**
painter (male)

> **WORD TIP** Professions, hobbies, and sports don't take an article in German: Er ist Maler.

die **Malerei**
painting

die **Malerin**, PLURAL die **Malerinnen**
painter (female)

> **WORD TIP** Professions, hobbies, and sports don't take an article in German: Sie ist Malerin.

malerisch ADJECTIVE
picturesque

Mallorca NEUTER NOUN
Majorca

Malta NEUTER NOUN
Malta

die **Mama**, PLURAL die **Mamas**
mum

die **Mami**, PLURAL die **Mamis**
mum

𝒫 **man** PRONOUN
1 you, one
Wie macht man das? How do you do that?
Man kann ja nie wissen. One can never tell.
2 they, people
Man sagt, dass ... They say that ...
3 Man hat mir gesagt, dass ... I was told that ...

der **Manager**, PLURAL die **Manager**
manager (male)

> **WORD TIP** Professions, hobbies, and sports don't take an article in German: Er ist Manager.

die **Managerin**, PLURAL die **Managerinnen**
manager (female)

> **WORD TIP** Professions, hobbies, and sports don't take an article in German: Sie ist Managerin.

mancher, manche, manches ADJECTIVE
1 many a
so manches Mal many a time
2 manche (plural) some, many
An manchen Tagen will ich einfach nicht aufstehen. Some days I just don't want to get up.

mancher, manche, manches PRONOUN
1 (so) mancher/manche some people
Mancher lernt es nie. Some people never learn.
2 manche (plural) some people
3 manches some things

𝒫 **manchmal** ADVERB
sometimes

die **Mandarine**, PLURAL die **Mandarinen**
mandarin

die **Mandel**, PLURAL die **Mandeln**
1 almond
2 tonsil

die **Mandelentzündung**
tonsillitis

der **Mangel**, PLURAL die **Mängel**
1 lack
2 shortage
3 defect, fault

𝒫 **mangelhaft** ADJECTIVE
1 faulty
2 poor (also as a school mark)

◇ **irregular verb;** SEP **separable verb; for more help with verbs see centre section**

die **Manie**, PLURAL die **Manien**
mania

die **Manieren** PLURAL NOUN
manners
Er hat keine Manieren. He's got no manners.

ℙ der **Mann**, PLURAL die **Männer**
1 man
2 husband

das **Männchen**, PLURAL die **Männchen**
male (animal)

das **Mannequin**, PLURAL die **Mannequins**
model

männlich ADJECTIVE
1 male
2 manly
3 masculine (in grammar)

ℙ die **Mannschaft**, PLURAL die **Mannschaften**
1 team
2 crew

die **Manschette**, PLURAL die **Manschetten**
cuff

ℙ der **Mantel**, PLURAL die **Mäntel**
coat

ℙ die **Mappe**, PLURAL die **Mappen**
1 folder
2 briefcase
3 bag

> **WORD TIP** German word Mappe does not mean map in English; the German word for map is Karte or Stadtplan.

das **Märchen**, PLURAL die **Märchen**
fairy tale

die **Margarine**
margarine

der **Marienkäfer**, PLURAL die **Marienkäfer**
ladybird

die **Marine**, PLURAL die **Marinen**
navy

die **Mark**, PLURAL die **Mark**
mark (the currency of Germany until replaced by the euro)

die **Marke**, PLURAL die **Marken**
1 make, brand
Meine Mutter fährt seit Jahren die gleiche Marke. My mother has been driving the same make of car for years.
Adidas ist eine führende Marke. Adidas is a leading brand.
2 tag

3 stamp
4 coupon

das **Marketing**
marketing

markieren VERB, PERFECT **hat markiert**
1 to mark
2 to fake

ℙ der **Markt**, PLURAL die **Märkte**
1 market
2 Sie will ein neues Parfüm auf den Markt bringen. She wants to launch a new perfume.

ℙ der **Marktplatz**, PLURAL die **Marktplätze**
market place, market square

ℙ die **Marmelade**, PLURAL die **Marmeladen**
jam

der **Marmor**
marble

Marokko NEUTER NOUN
Morocco

der **Marsch**, PLURAL die **Märsche**
march

ℙ der **März**
March
im März in March

die **Masche**, PLURAL die **Maschen**
1 stitch
2 Maschen mesh
3 (informal) trick
die Masche raushaben to know how to do it
4 Das ist die neueste Masche. That's the latest thing.

die **Maschine**, PLURAL die **Maschinen**
1 machine
2 plane
3 typewriter
Maschine schreiben to type

die **Masern** PLURAL NOUN
measles

die **Maske**, PLURAL die **Masken**
mask

maskieren VERB, PERFECT **hat sich maskiert**
1 sich maskieren to dress up
2 sich maskieren to disguise yourself

maß ▶ SEE messen

das **Maß**[1], PLURAL die **Maße**
1 unit of measurement
2 measurement
3 extent, degree

in hohem Maße to a high degree
4 Maß halten to show moderation

die **Maß²**, PLURAL die **Maß**
litre (of beer)

die **Masse**, PLURAL die **Massen**
1 mass
Ich habe eine Masse Arbeit. I have masses of work to do.
2 crowd
3 mixture

massenhaft ADJECTIVE
masses of, loads of

die **Massenvernichtungswaffen** PLURAL NOUN
weapons of mass destruction

massieren VERB, PERFECT **hat massiert**
to massage

mäßig ADJECTIVE
moderate

die **Maßnahme**, PLURAL die **Maßnahmen**
measure

der **Maßstab**, PLURAL die **Maßstäbe**
1 standard
2 scale

der **Mast**, PLURAL die **Masten**
1 mast
2 pole
3 pylon

das **Material**, PLURAL die **Materialien**
1 material
2 materials

ℓ die **Mathe**
(informal) maths
Morgen haben wir Mathe. We've got maths tomorrow.

die **Mathematik**
mathematics

die **Matratze**, PLURAL die **Matratzen**
mattress

der **Matrose**, PLURAL die **Matrosen**
sailor

WORD TIP Professions, hobbies, and sports don't take an article in German: Er ist Matrose.

der **Matsch**
1 mud
2 slush

matschig ADJECTIVE
1 muddy
2 slushy

matt ADJECTIVE
1 weak
2 matt
3 dull
4 Matt! Checkmate!

die **Matte**, PLURAL die **Matten**
mat

die **Matura**
A levels
Sie hat gerade ihre Matura gemacht. She's just done her A levels.

ⓘ MATURA

The end-of-school exam taken by students in Austria and Switzerland at the age of 18. This exam qualifies students to go to university.

ℓ die **Mauer**, PLURAL die **Mauern**
wall

das **Maul**, PLURAL die **Mäuler**
mouth
Halt's Maul! (informal) Shut up!

der **Maulkorb**, PLURAL die **Maulkörbe**
muzzle

der **Maulwurf**, PLURAL die **Maulwürfe**
mole (animal)

der **Maurer**, PLURAL die **Maurer**
bricklayer (male)

WORD TIP Professions, hobbies, and sports don't take an article in German: Er ist Maurer.

die **Maurerin**, PLURAL die **Maurerinnen**
bricklayer (female)

WORD TIP Professions, hobbies, and sports don't take an article in German: Sie ist Maurerin.

ℓ die **Maus**, PLURAL die **Mäuse**
mouse

der **Mausklick**, PLURAL die **Mausklicks**
click of the mouse

die **Maut**, PLURAL die **Mauten**
toll (for road, bridge)

ⓘ MAUT/VIGNETTE

In order to be able to drive on Austrian or Swiss motorways, you need to buy a sticker called a Vignette, which you must display on the car windscreen.

das **Maximum**, PLURAL die **Maxima**
maximum

die **Mayonnaise**
mayonnaise

◇ irregular verb; SEP separable verb; for more help with verbs see centre section

ℰ der **Mechaniker**, PLURAL die **Mechaniker**
mechanic *(male)*

> **WORD TIP** Professions, hobbies, and sports don't take an article in German: Er ist Mechaniker.

ℰ die **Mechanikerin**, PLURAL die **Mechanikerinnen**
mechanic *(female)*

> **WORD TIP** Professions, hobbies, and sports don't take an article in German: Sie ist Mechanikerin.

mechanisch ADJECTIVE
mechanical

meckern VERB, PERFECT **hat gemeckert**
1 to bleat
2 to grumble

die **Medaille**, PLURAL die **Medaillen**
medal

ℰ die **Medien** PLURAL NOUN
media

die **Medienwissenschaft**
media studies

ℰ das **Medikament**, PLURAL die **Medikamente**
drug
Nehmen Sie Medikamente? Are you on any medication?

ℰ die **Medizin**, PLURAL die **Medizinen**
medicine

ℰ das **Meer**, PLURAL die **Meere**
sea, ocean

die **Meeresfrüchte** PLURAL NOUN
seafood

ℰ das **Meerschweinchen**, PLURAL die **Meerschweinchen**
guinea pig

das **Megabyte**, PLURAL die **Megabytes**
megabyte

das **Mehl**
flour

ℰ **mehr** ADVERB, PRONOUN
more
mehr als more than
nichts mehr no more
nie mehr never again

mehrere PRONOUN
several

mehreres PRONOUN
several things

mehrfach ADJECTIVE
1 multiple, many
2 repeated
mehrfach ADVERB
several times

die **Mehrfahrtenkarte**, PLURAL die **Mehrfahrtenkarten**
multi-ride ticket

das **Mehrfamilienhaus**, PLURAL die **Mehrfamilienhäuser**
house divided into flats

die **Mehrheit**, PLURAL die **Mehrheiten**
majority

mehrmalig ADJECTIVE
repeated

mehrmals ADVERB
several times

die **Mehrwertsteuer**
value added tax *(VAT)*

die **Mehrzahl**
1 majority
2 plural *(in grammar)*

meiden VERB⬦, IMPERFECT **mied**, PERFECT **hat gemieden**
to avoid

die **Meile**, PLURAL die **Meilen**
mile

ℰ **mein** ADJECTIVE
my

meine ▸ SEE mein, meiner

ℰ **meinen** VERB, PERFECT **hat gemeint**
1 to think
Was meinst du dazu? What do you think?
2 to mean
Er meint es gut. He means well.
3 to say

meiner, meine, mein(e)s PRONOUN
mine

meinetwegen ADVERB
1 for my sake
2 because of me
3 as far as I'm concerned
'Kann ich das Auto haben?' –
'Meinetwegen.' 'Can I take the car?'
– 'Sure.'

meins ▸ SEE meiner

ℰ die **Meinung**, PLURAL die **Meinungen**
opinion
meiner Meinung nach in my opinion

ℰ indicates key words

die **Meinungsumfrage**, PLURAL die
Meinungsumfragen
opinion poll

meist ADVERB
1 mostly
2 usually

meiste ADJECTIVE, PRONOUN
der/die/das meiste most
die meisten most
am meisten most, the most

ℰ **meistens** ADVERB
1 mostly
2 usually

der **Meister**, PLURAL die **Meister**
1 master
2 champion (male)

die **Meisterin**, PLURAL die **Meisterinnen**
champion (female)

die **Meisterschaft**, PLURAL die
Meisterschaften
championship

das **Meisterstück**, PLURAL die
Meisterstücke
1 masterpiece
2 master stroke

das **Meisterwerk**, PLURAL die **Meisterwerke**
masterpiece

ℰ **melden** VERB, PERFECT **hat gemeldet**
1 to report
2 to register
3 sich melden to report, to answer
Luise hat sich gemeldet. (in class) Luise put
up her hand.
4 sich bei jemandem melden to get in touch
with somebody

die **Melodie**, PLURAL die **Melodien**
melody, tune

die **Melone**, PLURAL die **Melonen**
1 melon
2 bowler (hat)

die **Menge**, PLURAL die **Mengen**
1 quantity
in großen Mengen in large quantities
Das ist eine Menge Geld. That's a lot of
money.
2 crowd
3 set (in mathematics)

ℰ der **Mensch**, PLURAL die **Menschen**
1 human being
2 person
kein Mensch nobody

jeder Mensch everybody
3 die Menschen people
Wie viele Menschen waren da? How many
people were there?
4 (as an exclamation)
Mensch! (informal) Wow!, Hey!
Mensch, hab ich mich geärgert! (informal)
I was damn annoyed.

menschenleer ADJECTIVE
deserted

das **Menschenrecht**, PLURAL die
Menschenrechte
human right

der **Menschenverstand**
gesunder Menschenverstand common
sense

die **Menschheit**
mankind

menschlich ADJECTIVE
1 human
2 humane

die **Mentalität**, PLURAL die **Mentalitäten**
mentality

das **Menü**, PLURAL die **Menüs**
1 meal
2 set menu, daily special
3 menu (in computer software)

WORD TIP The word Menü does not always
mean menu in English; the German word for the
menu in a restaurant is Speisekarte.

ℰ **merken** VERB, PERFECT **hat gemerkt**
1 to notice
Ich habe es nicht gemerkt. I didn't notice
it.
2 sich etwas merken to remember
something
Ich habe mir seinen Namen nicht
gemerkt. I don't remember his name.

das **Merkmal**, PLURAL die **Merkmale**
feature

merkwürdig ADJECTIVE
strange, odd

die **Messe**, PLURAL die **Messen**
1 mass (church service)
2 trade fair

messen VERB◇, PRESENT **misst**, IMPERFECT **maß**,
PERFECT **hat gemessen**
1 to measure
(bei jemandem) Fieber messen to take
somebody's temperature
2 sich mit jemandem messen können to be

◇ irregular verb; SEP separable verb; for more help with verbs see centre section

as good as somebody

℗ das **Messer**, PLURAL die **Messer**
knife

das **Messing**
brass

das **Metall**, PLURAL die **Metalle**
metal

℗ der **Meter**, PLURAL die **Meter**
metre

das **Metermaß**, PLURAL die **Metermaße**
tape measure

die **Methode**, PLURAL die **Methoden**
method

metrisch ADJECTIVE
metric

der **Metzger**, PLURAL die **Metzger**
butcher (male)

> **WORD TIP** Professions, hobbies, and sports don't take an article in German: Er ist Metzger.

℗ die **Metzgerei**, PLURAL die **Metzgereien**
butcher's (shop)

die **Metzgerin**, PLURAL die **Metzgerinnen**
butcher (female)

> **WORD TIP** Professions, hobbies, and sports don't take an article in German: Sie ist Metzgerin.

Mexiko NEUTER NOUN
Mexico

Mi. ABBREVIATION
(=Mittwoch) Wednesday

miauen VERB, PERFECT **hat miaut**
to miaow

℗ **mich** PRONOUN
1 me
2 myself

mied ▶ SEE **meiden**

mies ADJECTIVE
(informal) terrible, lousy

℗ die **Miete**, PLURAL die **Mieten**
1 rent
  Wie hoch ist die Miete für eure Wohnung?
  How much is the rent for your flat?
  Sie wohnen zur Miete. They live in rented
  accommodation.
2 hire charge

mieten VERB, PERFECT **hat gemietet**
1 to rent
2 to hire

der **Mieter**, PLURAL die **Mieter**
tenant (male)

die **Mieterin**, PLURAL die **Mieterinnen**
tenant (female)

das **Mietshaus**, PLURAL die **Mietshäuser**
block of flats

der **Mietvertrag**, PLURAL die **Mietverträge**
tenancy agreement, lease

der **Mietwagen**, PLURAL die **Mietwagen**
hire car

die **Migräne**, PLURAL die **Migränen**
migraine

der **Mikrochip**, PLURAL die **Mikrochips**
microchip

das **Mikrofon**, PLURAL die **Mikrofone**
microphone

das **Mikroskop**, PLURAL die **Mikroskope**
microscope

die **Mikrowelle**, PLURAL die **Mikrowellen**
1 microwave
2 (informal) microwave oven

der **Mikrowellenherd**, PLURAL die
Mikrowellenherde
microwave oven

℗ die **Milch**
milk

der **Milchshake**, PLURAL die **Milchshakes**
milk shake

mild ADJECTIVE
mild

das **Militär**
army

militärisch ADJECTIVE
military

die **Milliarde**, PLURAL die **Milliarden**
thousand million, billion
Es kostet zwei Milliarden Euro. It costs
two billion euros.

der **Millimeter**, PLURAL die **Millimeter**
millimetre

℗ die **Million**, PLURAL die **Millionen**
million

℗ der **Millionär**, PLURAL die **Millionäre**
millionaire (male)
Er ist angeblich Millionär. They say he's a
millionaire.

℗ indicates key words

♀ die **Millionärin**, PLURAL die **Millionärinnen**
millionaire (female)

die **Minderheit**, PLURAL die **Minderheiten**
minority

minderjährig ADJECTIVE
under age

der/die **Minderjährige**, PLURAL die
Minderjährigen
minor

mindestens ADVERB
at least

mindester, mindeste, mindestes ADJECTIVE,
PRONOUN
1 least, slightest
2 der/die/das Mindeste the least
zum Mindesten at least
nicht im Mindesten not in the least

das **Mindesthaltbarkeitsdatum**, PLURAL die
Mindesthaltbarkeitsdaten
best-before date

der **Mindestlohn**, PLURAL die **Mindestlöhne**
minimum wage

die **Mine**, PLURAL die **Minen**
1 mine
2 lead (pencil)
3 refill (ballpoint)

♀ das **Mineralwasser**, PLURAL die
Mineralwässer
mineral water

der **Minirock**, PLURAL die **Miniröcke**
miniskirt

der **Minister**, PLURAL die **Minister**
(government) minister (male)

> **WORD TIP** The German word Minister does not
> mean minister in the religious sense in English;
> the German word for minister in that sense is
> Pfarrer.

die **Ministerin**, PLURAL die **Ministerinnen**
(government) minister (female)

das **Ministerium**, PLURAL die **Ministerien**
ministry, department

minus ADVERB
minus

♀ die **Minute**, PLURAL die **Minuten**
minute

♀ **mir** PRONOUN
1 me, to me
2 myself, to myself

mischen VERB, PERFECT **hat gemischt**
1 to mix
2 to shuffle (cards)
3 sich mischen to mix

die **Mischung**, PLURAL die **Mischungen**
1 mixture
2 blend

miserabel ADJECTIVE (informal)
1 hopeless
2 dreadful

missbilligen VERB, PERFECT **hat missbilligt**
to disapprove of

der **Missbrauch**
1 abuse
2 misuse (of data, a system)

missbrauchen VERB, PERFECT **hat
missbraucht**
to abuse

der **Misserfolg**, PLURAL die **Misserfolge**
failure

das **Missgeschick**, PLURAL die
Missgeschicke
1 misfortune
2 mishap

misshandeln VERB, PRESENT **hat misshandelt**
to ill-treat, to mistreat

misslingen VERB◇, IMPERFECT **misslang**,
PERFECT **ist misslungen**
1 to be unsuccessful
Der erste Versuch ist misslungen. The first
attempt was unsuccessful.
2 Es misslang ihr. She failed.

misst ▸ SEE **messen**

misstrauen VERB, PERFECT **hat misstraut**
jemandem misstrauen to mistrust
somebody, to distrust somebody

das **Misstrauen**
mistrust, distrust

misstrauisch ADJECTIVE
suspicious

das **Missverständnis**, PLURAL die
Missverständnisse
misunderstanding

missverstehen VERB◇, IMPERFECT
missverstand, PERFECT **hat
missverstanden**
to misunderstand

der **Mist**
1 manure

2 *(informal)* **rubbish**

> **WORD TIP** The German word Mist does not mean mist in English; the German word for mist is Nebel.

die **Mistel**, *PLURAL* die **Misteln**
mistletoe

 ℓ **mit** *PREPOSITION (+ DAT)*
1 with
   mit großem Vergnügen with great
   pleasure
2 by
   mit der Post by post
   Wir sind mit der Bahn gefahren. We
   went by train.
3 at
   Die Kinder kommen mit sechs Jahren in
   die Schule. Children start school at the
   age of six.
   Sie fuhr mit Vollgas. She drove at full
   speed.
4 mit jemandem sprechen to speak to
   somebody
5 mit Bleistift in pencil
6 mit lauter Stimme in a loud voice
mit *ADVERB*
   as well, too
   Warst du mit dabei? Were you there
   too?

---

der **Mitarbeiter**, *PLURAL* die **Mitarbeiter**
1 colleague *(male)*
2 employee *(male)*

die **Mitarbeiterin**, *PLURAL* die
Mitarbeiterinnen
1 colleague *(female)*
2 employee *(female)*

mitbringen *VERB⬦*, *IMPERFECT* **brachte mit**,
PERFECT **hat mitgebracht**
1 to bring, to bring along
   Hast du den Hund mitgebracht? Have you
   brought the dog?
2 to take
   Ich bringe den Kindern Schokolade mit.
   I'm taking the children some chocolate.

miteinander *ADVERB*
   with each other, with one another

der **Mitesser**, *PLURAL* die **Mitesser**
blackhead

mitfahren *VERB⬦*, *PRESENT* **fährt mit**, *IMPERFECT*
fuhr mit, *PERFECT* **ist mitgefahren**
1 mit jemandem mitfahren to go with
   somebody
   Die Kinder fahren mit uns mit. The

children are coming with us.
2 bei jemandem mitfahren to get a lift with
   somebody
   Du kannst bei Peter mitfahren. You can
   get a lift with Peter.
   jemanden mitfahren lassen to give
   somebody a lift

mitgeben *VERB⬦*, *PRESENT* **gibt mit**, *IMPERFECT*
gab mit, *PERFECT* **hat mitgegeben**
to give

 ℓ das **Mitglied**, *PLURAL* die **Mitglieder**
member

mithalten *VERB⬦*, *PRESENT* **hält mit**, *IMPERFECT*
hielt mit, *PERFECT* **hat mitgehalten**
to keep up

 ℓ **mitkommen** *VERB⬦*, *IMPERFECT* **kam mit**,
PERFECT **ist mitgekommen**
1 to come too
2 to keep up

das **Mitleid**
1 pity
   Er tat es aus Mitleid. He did it out of pity.
2 sympathy
   Mit solchen Leuten habe ich kein Mitleid.
   I've got no sympathy for people like that.

 ℓ **mitmachen** *VERB*, *PERFECT* **hat mitgemacht**
1 to join in
   Hast du Lust, bei dem Spiel mitzumachen?
   Do you want to join in the game?
2 to take part
   Es ist ihr Ziel, bei der nächsten Olympiade
   mitzumachen. It's her goal to take part in
   the next Olympics.
3 to go through
   Sie hat viel mitgemacht. She's gone
   through a lot.

mitnehmen *VERB⬦*, *PRESENT* **nimmt
mit**, *IMPERFECT* **nahm mit**, *PERFECT* **hat
mitgenommen**
1 to take, to take along
   Anna hat die Kinder auf den Spielplatz
   mitgenommen. Anna has taken the
   children to the playground.
2 to give a lift to
3 to affect (badly)
4 zum Mitnehmen to take away

der **Mitschüler**, *PLURAL* die **Mitschüler**
schoolfriend *(male)*

die **Mitschülerin**, *PLURAL* die
Mitschülerinnen
schoolfriend *(female)*

 ℓ indicates key words

GERMAN—ENGLISH

A
B
C
D
E
F
G
H
I
J
K
L
M
N
O
P
Q
R
S
T
U
V
W
X
Y
Z

mitsingen

mitsingen VERB, IMPERFECT **sang mit**, PERFECT **hat mitgesungen**
to sing along

mitspielen VERB, PERFECT **hat mitgespielt**
1 to play
  Wer spielt beim Fußballspiel mit? Who's playing in the football match?
2 to join in
  Willst du mitspielen? Do you want to join in?
3 in einem Film mitspielen to be in a film

ℰ der **Mittag**, PLURAL die **Mittage**
1 midday
2 lunch
  zu Mittag essen to have lunch
3 lunch break

ℰ das **Mittagessen**, PLURAL die **Mittagessen**
lunch
  Wir waren beim Mittagessen. We were having lunch.
  Was gibt es zum Mittagessen? What's for lunch?

ℰ **mittags** ADVERB
1 at lunchtime
2 midday
  um zwölf Uhr mittags at noon

die **Mittagspause**, PLURAL die **Mittagspausen**
lunch break

die **Mittagszeit**
lunchtime

ℰ die **Mitte**, PLURAL die **Mitten**
1 middle
2 centre

mitteilen VERB, PERFECT **hat mitgeteilt**
to tell, to inform

die **Mitteilung**, PLURAL die **Mitteilungen**
1 announcement, statement
2 communication

ℰ das **Mittel**, PLURAL die **Mittel**
1 means
  Sie griffen zu drastischen Mitteln. They used drastic means.
2 remedy
  ein Mittel gegen Husten a cough remedy
3 öffentliche Mittel public funds

das **Mittelalter**
Middle Ages

mittelalterlich ADJECTIVE
medieval

Mitteleuropa NEUTER NOUN
Central Europe

mittelgroß ADJECTIVE
medium-sized

mittelmäßig ADJECTIVE
mediocre

das **Mittelmeer**
Mediterranean

der **Mittelpunkt**, PLURAL die **Mittelpunkte**
centre
  Sie steht gerne im Mittelpunkt. She likes to be the centre of attention.

der **Mittelstand**
middle class

der **Mittelstürmer**, PLURAL die **Mittelstürmer**
centre forward

mitten ADVERB
mitten in/auf in the middle of
mitten in der Nacht in the middle of the night

ℰ die **Mitternacht**
midnight

mittlerer, mittlere, mittleres ADJECTIVE
1 middle
2 medium
3 average
4 ▸SEE **Reife**

mittlerweile ADVERB
1 meanwhile
2 (by) now

ℰ der **Mittwoch**, PLURAL die **Mittwoche**
Wednesday

mittwochs ADVERB
on Wednesdays

der **Mixer**, PLURAL die **Mixer**
liquidizer, blender

Mo. ABBREVIATION
(=Montag) Monday

mobben VERB, PERFECT **hat gemobbt**
to bully

ℰ die **Möbel** PLURAL NOUN
furniture

der **Möbelwagen**, PLURAL die **Möbelwagen**
removal van

das **Mobiltelefon**, PLURAL die **Mobiltelefone**
mobile phone

◇ **irregular verb;** SEP **separable verb; for more help with verbs see centre section**

möbliert *ADJECTIVE*
furnished

mochte, möchte ▸ SEE **mögen**

♂ die **Mode**, *PLURAL* die **Moden**
fashion

das **Modell**, *PLURAL* die **Modelle**
model

der **Moderator**, *PLURAL* die **Moderatoren**
presenter *(male)*

WORD TIP Professions, hobbies, and sports don't take an article in German: Er ist Moderator.

die **Moderatorin**, *PLURAL* die
Moderatorinnen
presenter *(female)*

WORD TIP Professions, hobbies, and sports don't take an article in German: Sie ist Moderatorin.

♂ **modern** *ADJECTIVE*
modern

modernisieren *VERB*, *PERFECT* **hat**
modernisiert
to modernize

der **Modeschöpfer**, *PLURAL* die
Modeschöpfer
fashion designer *(male)*

WORD TIP Professions, hobbies, and sports don't take an article in German: Er ist Modeschöpfer.

die **Modeschöpferin**, *PLURAL* die
Modeschöpferinnen
fashion designer *(female)*

WORD TIP Professions, hobbies, and sports don't take an article in German: Sie ist Modeschöpferin.

modisch *ADJECTIVE*
fashionable

das **Mofa**, *PLURAL* die **Mofas**
moped

mogeln *VERB*, *PERFECT* **hat gemogelt**
to cheat

♂ **mögen** *VERB*◇, *PRESENT* **mag**, *IMPERFECT*
mochte, *PERFECT* **hat gemocht**, **hat**
mögen
1 to like
Ich mag ihn nicht. I don't like him.
Ich möchte ... I'd like ...
Ich möchte gern wissen, ... I'd like to
know ...
Möchtest du nach Hause? Would you like
to go home?

2 lieber mögen to prefer
Ich möchte lieber Tee. I would prefer tea.
3 etwas nicht tun mögen not to want to
do something
Ich mag nicht fragen. I don't want to ask.
Ich mag nicht mehr. I've had enough.
4 Das mag sein. Maybe.
5 Was mag das sein? Whatever can it be?

WORD TIP The past participle is gemocht when mögen is the main verb: Sie hat mich nie gemocht. The past participle is mögen when it is an auxiliary verb: Er hat nicht fragen mögen.

♂ **möglich** *ADJECTIVE*
1 possible
2 alles Mögliche all sorts of things

möglicherweise *ADVERB*
possibly

die **Möglichkeit**, *PLURAL* die **Möglichkeiten**
possibility

möglichst *ADVERB*
1 if possible
Kommt möglichst schon um 8 Uhr. Come
at eight o'clock if possible.
2 as ... as possible
Kommt möglichst früh! Come as early as
possible.

die **Möhre**, *PLURAL* die **Möhren**
carrot

die **Mohrrübe**, *PLURAL* die **Mohrrüben**
carrot

der **Mokka**, *PLURAL* die **Mokkas**
small black coffee

das **Molekül**, *PLURAL* die **Moleküle**
molecule

der **Moment**, *PLURAL* die **Momente**
moment
im Moment at the moment
Moment (mal)! Just a moment!

momentan *ADJECTIVE*
1 temporary
2 current

momentan *ADVERB*
1 temporarily
2 at the moment

♂ der **Monat**, *PLURAL* die **Monate**
month

monatelang *ADVERB*
for months

♂ indicates key words

monatlich ADJECTIVE, ADVERB
monthly

der **Mönch**, PLURAL die **Mönche**
monk

> **WORD TIP** Professions, hobbies, and sports don't take an article in German: Er ist Mönch.

der **Mond**, PLURAL die **Monde**
moon

der **Mondschein**
moonlight
im Mondschein by moonlight

♭ der **Montag**, PLURAL die **Montage**
Monday

montags ADVERB
on Mondays

das **Moped**, PLURAL die **Mopeds**
moped

die **Moral**
1 morals, morality
2 morale
3 moral (of a story)

moralisch ADJECTIVE
moral

der **Mord**, PLURAL die **Morde**
murder

der **Mörder**, PLURAL die **Mörder**
murderer (male)

> **WORD TIP** The German word Mörder does not mean murder in English; the German word for murder is Mord.

die **Mörderin**, PLURAL die **Mörderinnen**
murderer (female)

♭ **morgen** ADVERB
tomorrow
morgen früh tomorrow morning
morgen Nachmittag tomorrow afternoon
morgen Abend tomorrow evening

♭ der **Morgen**, PLURAL die **Morgen**
morning
am Morgen in the morning
heute Morgen this morning
Guten Morgen! Good morning!

der **Morgenmantel**, PLURAL die **Morgenmäntel**
dressing gown

♭ **morgens** ADVERB
in the morning

die **Moschee**, PLURAL die **Moscheen**
mosque

die **Mosel**
(River) Moselle

Moskau NEUTER NOUN
Moscow

das **Motiv**, PLURAL die **Motive**
1 motive
2 subject (of a picture, photo)
3 motif (in literature, music)

die **Motivation**
motivation

der **Motor**, PLURAL die **Motoren**
engine, motor

♭ das **Motorrad**, PLURAL die **Motorräder**
motorcycle, motorbike

die **Mousse**, PLURAL die **Mousses**
mousse

die **Möwe**, PLURAL die **Möwen**
seagull

die **Mücke**, PLURAL die **Mücken**
1 midge
2 mosquito

♭ **müde** ADJECTIVE
tired

die **Müdigkeit**
tiredness

die **Mühe**, PLURAL die **Mühen**
1 effort
Sie hat sich viel Mühe gegeben. She made a big effort.
2 trouble
Machen Sie sich keine Mühe. Don't go to any trouble.
3 mit Mühe und Not only just

die **Mühle**, PLURAL die **Mühlen**
1 mill
2 grinder

mühsam ADJECTIVE
laborious

♭ der **Müll**
rubbish

die **Müllabfuhr**
refuse collection

der **Mülleimer**, PLURAL die **Mülleimer**
rubbish bin

die **Mülltonne**, PLURAL die **Mülltonnen**
dustbin

◇ irregular verb; SEP separable verb; for more help with verbs see centre section

die **Mülltrennung**
separating rubbish

die **Müllvermeidung**
waste reduction

multikulti ADJECTIVE
(informal) multicultural

multikulturell ADJECTIVE
multicultural

der **Mumps**
mumps

ℙ **München** NEUTER NOUN
Munich

ℙ der **Mund**, PLURAL die **Münder**
mouth
Halt den Mund! (informal) Shut up!

der **Mundgeruch**
bad breath

die **Mundharmonika**, PLURAL die
Mundharmonikas
mouth organ
Daniel spielt Mundharmonika. Daniel
plays the mouth organ.

mündlich ADJECTIVE
1 oral
Wann ist die mündliche Prüfung? When is
the oral exam?
2 verbal
mündliche Kommunikation verbal
communication

das **Münster**, PLURAL die **Münster**
cathedral

ℙ die **Münze**, PLURAL die **Münzen**
coin

der **Münzfernsprecher**, PLURAL die
Münzfernsprecher
payphone

murmeln VERB, PERFECT **hat gemurmelt**
to mumble

mürrisch ADJECTIVE
surly

die **Muschel**, PLURAL die **Muscheln**
1 mussel
2 (sea)shell
3 mouthpiece
4 earpiece

das **Museum**, PLURAL die **Museen**
museum

das **Musical**, PLURAL die **Musicals**
musical

ℙ die **Musik**
music

ℙ **musikalisch** ADJECTIVE
musical

der **Musiker**, PLURAL die **Musiker**
musician (male)

WORD TIP Professions, hobbies, and sports
don't take an article in German: Er ist Musiker.

die **Musikerin**, PLURAL die **Musikerinnen**
musician (female)

WORD TIP Professions, hobbies, and sports don't
take an article in German: Sie ist Musikerin.

musizieren VERB, PERFECT **hat musiziert**
to make music

der **Muskat**
nutmeg

der **Muskel**, PLURAL die **Muskeln**
muscle

ℙ das **Müsli**
muesli

der **Muslim**, PLURAL die **Muslime** die
Muslims
Muslim (male)

die **Muslimin**, PLURAL die **Musliminnen**
Muslim (female)

muslimisch ADJECTIVE
Muslim

WORD TIP Adjectives never have capitals in
German, even for religions.

muss ▸SEE **müssen**

ℙ **müssen** VERB◇, PRESENT **muss**, IMPERFECT
musste, PERFECT **hat gemusst**, **hat**
müssen
1 etwas tun müssen to have to do
something
Sie muss es tun. She's got to do it.
Muss ich? Do I have to?
Muss das sein? Is it necessary?
2 Sie müssten es mal versuchen. You
should try it.
3 Sie müssen gleich hier sein. They'll be
here at any moment.
4 Ich muss mal. (informal) I need (to go to)
the loo.

WORD TIP The past participle is gemusst when
müssen is the main verb: Er hat nach Hause
gemusst. The past participle is müssen when it
is an auxiliary verb: Sie hat es tun müssen.

ℙ indicates key words

das **Muster**, PLURAL die **Muster**
1 pattern
2 sample

der **Mut**
courage
jemandem Mut machen to encourage
somebody

mutig ADJECTIVE
courageous

♀ die **Mutter**[1], PLURAL die **Mütter**
mother

die **Mutter**[2], PLURAL die **Muttern**
nut *(for a screw)*

das **Muttermal**, PLURAL die **Muttermale**
mole *(on the skin)*

♀ die **Muttersprache**, PLURAL die
Muttersprachen
mother tongue, first language

> **MUTTERSPRACHE**
>
> More people in the European Union have
> German as their mother tongue than English,
> French or Spanish.

der **Muttertag**, PLURAL die **Muttertage**
Mother's Day

die **Mutti**, PLURAL die **Muttis**
mum

♀ die **Mütze**, PLURAL die **Mützen**
1 cap
2 (woolly) hat

MwSt. ABBREVIATION
(=Mehrwertsteuer) VAT

der **Mythos**, PLURAL die **Mythen**
myth

Nn

na EXCLAMATION
well
Na ja, ... Well, ...
Na und? So what?
Na gut. All right then.

der **Nabel**, PLURAL die **Nabel**
navel

♀ **nach** PREPOSITION (+ DAT)
1 to
Wir fahren nach Italien. We're going
to Italy.
nach oben up
nach hinten back
Der Radfahrer bog nach rechts ab. The
cyclist turned right.
Sie griff nach ihrer Tasche. She reached
for her bag.
2 nach Hause home
Sie gingen nach Hause. They went home.
3 after
Nach Ihnen! After you!
Es ist zehn nach eins. It's ten past one.
4 according to
Nach Angaben der Polizei verlief die
Demonstration friedlich. According to
the police, the demonstration went off
peacefully.
meiner Meinung nach in my opinion

nach ADVERB
nach und nach bit by bit, gradually
nach wie vor still

nachahmen VERB, PERFECT **hat nachgeahmt**
to imitate

♀ der **Nachbar**, PLURAL die **Nachbarn**
neighbour *(male)*

♀ die **Nachbarin**, PLURAL die **Nachbarinnen**
neighbour *(female)*

die **Nachbarschaft**
neighbourhood

nachdem CONJUNCTION
1 after
2 je nachdem it depends
Abends gehe ich manchmal schwimmen,
je nachdem, wie schnell ich mit meinen
Hausaufgaben fertig werde. In the
evenings I sometimes go for a swim,
depending on how quickly I can finish my
homework.

nachdenken VERB ◇, IMPERFECT **dachte nach**,
PERFECT **hat nachgedacht**
to think
über etwas nachdenken to think about
something
Ich habe lange über ihr Angebot
nachgedacht und mich schließlich
dagegen entschieden. I thought about her
offer for a long time and finally decided
against it.

nachdenklich ADJECTIVE
thoughtful

nacheinander ADVERB
one after the other

◇ irregular verb; SEP separable verb; for more help with verbs see centre section

Die Bewerber kamen nacheinander herein. The applicants came in one after the other.

die **Nachfrage**, PLURAL die **Nachfragen**
demand
Es besteht keine Nachfrage. There's no demand for it.

nachgehen VERB◇, IMPERFECT **ging nach**, PERFECT **ist nachgegangen**
1 to be slow
Meine Uhr geht nach. My watch is slow.
2 jemandem nachgehen to follow somebody
Sie ging den anderen nach. She followed the others.
3 einer Sache nachgehen to look into something
Der Schuldirektor versprach, dem Vorfall nachzugehen. The head promised to look into the incident.

nachher ADVERB
1 afterwards
Erst gehen wir ins Kino und nachher wollen wir zu Lisa. We're going to the cinema first and then afterwards we'll go on to Lisa's.
2 later
Bis nachher! See you later!

ℰ die **Nachhilfe**
extra tuition

nachholen VERB, PERFECT **hat nachgeholt**
1 to catch up on
Ich hatte Grippe und muss jetzt viel Mathe nachholen. I've had flu and now I've got a lot of maths to catch up on.
2 to make up for (something missed)
3 eine Prüfung nachholen to do an exam at a later date

nachkommen VERB◇, IMPERFECT **kam nach**, PERFECT **ist nachgekommen**
1 to come later, to follow
2 Ich komme nicht nach. I can't keep up.
3 einem Versprechen nachkommen to keep a promise
seinen Verpflichtungen nachkommen to meet your commitments

nachlassen VERB◇, PRESENT **lässt nach**, IMPERFECT **ließ nach**, PERFECT **hat nachgelassen**
1 to ease
Der Wind ließ nach. The wind eased.
Meine Zahnschmerzen lassen nach. My toothache is getting better.
2 to let up
Der Regen ließ nicht nach. The rain

didn't let up.
3 to deteriorate
Opas Gedächtnis lässt nach. Grandad's memory is deteriorating.
4 etwas vom Preis nachlassen to take something off the price
Ich lasse Ihnen zwanzig Euro nach. I'll give you twenty euros off.

nachlässig ADJECTIVE
careless

nachlaufen VERB◇, PRESENT **läuft nach**, IMPERFECT **lief nach**, PERFECT **ist nachgelaufen**
jemandem nachlaufen to run after somebody
Philipp läuft allen Mädchen nach. (informal) Philipp chases all the girls.

nachmachen VERB, PERFECT **hat nachgemacht**
to copy

ℰ der **Nachmittag**, PLURAL die **Nachmittage**
afternoon

ℰ **nachmittags** ADVERB
in the afternoon

die **Nachnahme**
per Nachnahme cash on delivery

ℰ der **Nachname**, PLURAL die **Nachnamen**
surname

nachprüfen VERB, PERFECT **hat nachgeprüft**
to check
Er prüft nach, ob es stimmt. He's going to check if it is correct.

ℰ die **Nachricht**, PLURAL die **Nachrichten**
1 news
Ich warte noch immer auf eine Nachricht von ihm. I'm still waiting for news of him.
2 die Nachrichten the news (on radio, television)
Das kam in den Nachrichten. It was on the news.
3 message
Möchten Sie eine Nachricht hinterlassen? Can I take a message?

der **Nachrichtensprecher**, PLURAL die **Nachrichtensprecher**
newsreader (male)

WORD TIP Professions, hobbies, and sports don't take an article in German: Er ist Nachrichtensprecher.

die **Nachrichtensprecherin**, PLURAL die **Nachrichtensprecherinnen**
newsreader (female)

WORD TIP Professions, hobbies, and sports don't take an article in German: Sie ist Nachrichtensprecherin.

nachschauen VERB, PERFECT **hat nachgeschaut**
to look up
Schau doch mal im Wörterbuch nach! Look it up in the dictionary!

nachschlagen VERB◇, PRESENT **schlägt nach**, IMPERFECT **schlug nach**, PERFECT **hat nachgeschlagen**
to look up

nachsehen VERB◇, PRESENT **sieht nach**, IMPERFECT **sah nach**, PERFECT **hat nachgesehen**
1 to check
Sieh nach, wer da ist. Go and see who's there.
2 to look up
Ich habe im Internet nachgesehen. I looked it up on the Internet.
3 jemandem etwas nachsehen to forgive somebody something

nachsitzen VERB◇, IMPERFECT **saß nach**, PERFECT **hat nachgesessen**
to be in detention
Jan muss nachsitzen. Jan's got detention.

die **Nachspeise**, PLURAL die **Nachspeisen**
dessert, pudding

nächste ▸ SEE **nächster**

nächstens ADVERB
shortly

ℰ **nächster, nächste, nächstes** ADJECTIVE
1 next
Es ist in der nächsten Straße links. It's in the next road to the left.
2 nearest
Wo ist die nächste Apotheke? Where is the nearest pharmacy?
3 in nächster Nähe close by
nächstes PRONOUN
der/die/das Nächste (the) next
als Nächstes next

ℰ die **Nacht**, PLURAL die **Nächte**
night
Gute Nacht! Good night!

ℰ der **Nachteil**, PLURAL die **Nachteile**
disadvantage

der **Nachtfalter**, PLURAL die **Nachtfalter**
moth

das **Nachthemd**, PLURAL die **Nachthemden**
nightdress, nightshirt

die **Nachtigall**, PLURAL die **Nachtigallen**
nightingale

ℰ der **Nachtisch**, PLURAL die **Nachtische**
dessert, pudding

der **Nachtklub**, PLURAL die **Nachtklubs**
nightclub

das **Nachtleben**
nightlife

das **Nachtlokal**, PLURAL die **Nachtlokale**
all-night bar

nachträglich ADJECTIVE
1 subsequent
2 belated

nachträglich ADVERB
1 later
2 belatedly

nachts ADVERB
at night
Ich kann nachts nicht schlafen. I can't sleep at night.
Er rief um zwei Uhr nachts an. He called at two o'clock in the morning.

der **Nachttisch**, PLURAL die **Nachttische**
bedside table

der **Nacken**, PLURAL die **Nacken**
neck

nackt ADJECTIVE
1 naked
2 bare

die **Nacktschnecke**, PLURAL die **Nacktschnecken**
slug

die **Nadel**, PLURAL die **Nadeln**
1 needle
2 pin

der **Nagel**, PLURAL die **Nägel**
nail

die **Nagelbürste**, PLURAL die **Nagelbürsten**
nail brush

die **Nagelfeile**, PLURAL die **Nagelfeilen**
nail file

der **Nagellack**, PLURAL die **Nagellacke**
nail varnish

◇ irregular verb; SEP separable verb; for more help with verbs see centre section

nagelneu ADJECTIVE
 brand new

die **Nagelschere**, PLURAL die **Nagelscheren**
 nail scissors

nah PREPOSITION (+ DAT)
 near, close to

nahe, **nah** ADJECTIVE, ADVERB
 1 near, nearby
  in naher Zukunft in the near future
  der Nahe Osten the Middle East
  nahe daran sein, etwas zu tun to nearly do
  something
 2 close
  Er ist ein naher Verwandter von mir. He's
  a close relative of mine.
  Sitz nicht zu nah am Bildschirm. Don't sit
  too close to the screen.

♪ die **Nähe**
 1 proximity
 2 Die Schule ist in der Nähe der Kirche. The
  school is near the church.
  Er wohnt ganz in der Nähe. He lives
  nearby.
 3 aus der Nähe close up

nahelegen VERB, PERFECT **hat nahegelegt**
 jemandem nahelegen, etwas zu tun to
 urge somebody to do something

naheliegend ADJECTIVE
 obvious

♪ **nähen** VERB, PERFECT **hat genäht**
 1 to sew
 2 to stitch (a wound)

näher ADJECTIVE
 1 closer
 2 nähere Einzelheiten further details
 3 shorter (way, road)

näher ADVERB
 1 closer
  näher kommen to come closer
 2 more closely
 3 Näheres further details

nähern VERB, PERFECT **hat sich genähert**
 sich nähern to approach
 Wir näherten uns dem Dorf. We were
 approaching the village.

das **Nähgarn**
 cotton, sewing thread

nahm ▸ SEE **nehmen**

die **Nahrung**
 food

die **Naht**, PLURAL die **Nähte**
 seam

der **Nahverkehrszug**, PLURAL die
 Nahverkehrszüge
 local train

♪ der **Name**, PLURAL die **Namen**
 1 name
 2 im Namen von on behalf of
  Ich rufe im Namen von Herrn und Frau
  Schmidt an. I'm calling on behalf of Mr and
  Mrs Schmidt.

nämlich ADVERB
 1 because
  Ich komme nicht mit ins Kino, ich habe
  den Film nämlich schon gesehen. I'm not
  coming to the cinema because I've seen
  the film already.
 2 namely
  Es waren nur zwei Jungen aus unserer
  Klasse da, nämlich Tim und Marco. There
  were only two boys from our class there,
  namely Tim and Marco.
 3 Das war nämlich ganz anders. It was quite
  different, actually.

nannte ▸ SEE **nennen**

nanu EXCLAMATION
 well, well!

die **Narbe**, PLURAL die **Narben**
 scar

der **Narr**, PLURAL die **Narren**
 fool (male)

die **Närrin**, PLURAL die **Närrinnen**
 fool (female)

♪ die **Nase**, PLURAL die **Nasen**
 1 nose
 2 die Nase voll haben (informal) to have had
  enough

das **Nasenbluten**
 nosebleed
  Sie hatte Nasenbluten. She had a
  nosebleed.

das **Nashorn**, PLURAL die **Nashörner**
 rhinoceros

♪ **nass** ADJECTIVE
 wet

die **Nation**, PLURAL die **Nationen**
 nation

die **Nationalhymne**, PLURAL die
 Nationalhymnen
 national anthem

♪ indicates key words

die **Nationalität**, *PLURAL* die **Nationalitäten**
nationality

der **Nationalrat**,
Lower House *(of the Austrian or Swiss
parliament)*

⚲ die **Natur**
1 nature
von Natur aus by nature
2 die freie Natur the open countryside

der **Naturlehrpfad**, *PLURAL* die
Naturlehrpfade
nature trail

⚲ **natürlich** *ADJECTIVE*
natural
natürlich *ADVERB*
of course, naturally

die **Natürlichkeit**
naturalness

die **Naturschätze** *PLURAL NOUN*
natural resources

der **Naturschützer**, *PLURAL* die
Naturschützer
conservationist *(male)*

die **Naturschützerin**, *PLURAL* die
Naturschützerinnen
conservationist *(female)*

das **Naturschutzgebiet**, *PLURAL* die
Naturschutzgebiete
nature reserve

⚲ die **Naturwissenschaft**, *PLURAL* die
Naturwissenschaften
science

die **Naturwissenschaften**
science *(school subject)*
Das Fach Naturwissenschaften hat mich
schon immer interessiert. I've always been
interested in the sciences.

Neapel *NEUTER NOUN*
Naples

der **Nebel**, *PLURAL* die **Nebel**
1 fog
2 mist

nebelig *ADJECTIVE* ▶ SEE **neblig**

⚲ **neben** *PREPOSITION* (+ *DAT* or + *ACC*)
1 *(the dative is used when talking about
position; the accusative shows movement
or a change of place)* next to
Er hat neben mir gesessen. *(DAT)* He sat

next to me.
Er hat sich neben mich gesetzt. *(ACC)* He
sat down next to me.
2 apart from

nebenan *ADVERB*
next door

nebenbei *ADVERB*
1 as well, at the same time
Er liest die Zeitung und hört nebenbei
Musik. He reads the newspaper and listens
to music at the same time.
2 on the side
Nebenbei arbeitet sie noch in einem
Blumengeschäft. She works in a florist's
on the side.
Das mache ich so nebenbei. *(informal)* It's
just a sideline.
3 in passing
nebenbei bemerkt by the way

nebeneinander *ADVERB*
next to each other

nebenhergehen *VERB*◇, *IMPERFECT*
ging nebenher, *PERFECT* **ist
nebenhergegangen**
to walk alongside

der **Nebenjob**, *PLURAL* die **Nebenjobs**
(informal) sideline

⚲ **neblig** *ADJECTIVE*
1 foggy
2 misty

necken *VERB*, *PERFECT* **hat geneckt**
to tease

nee *ADVERB*
(informal) no

der **Neffe**, *PLURAL* die **Neffen**
nephew

negativ *ADJECTIVE*
negative

das **Negativ**, *PLURAL* die **Negative**
negative

⚲ **nehmen** *VERB*◇, *PRESENT* **nimmt**, *IMPERFECT*
nahm, *PERFECT* **hat genommen**
1 to take
2 to have
Ich nehme eine Suppe. I'll have soup.
3 Was nehmen Sie dafür? How much do
you want for it?
4 jemanden zu sich nehmen to have

◇ irregular verb; *SEP* separable verb; for more help with verbs see centre section

somebody live with you
5 sich etwas nehmen to take something
Sie nahm sich ein Bonbon. She took a sweet.
Nimm dir ein Stück Kuchen. Help yourself to a piece of cake.

der **Neid**
  envy, jealousy

ℱ **neidisch** ADJECTIVE
  envious, jealous

ℱ **nein** ADVERB
  no

die **Nelke**, PLURAL die **Nelken**
  carnation

nennen VERB◇, IMPERFECT **nannte**, PERFECT **hat genannt**
1 to call
2 to name
3 sich nennen to call yourself, to be called
4 Ihr Name wurde nicht genannt. Her name wasn't mentioned.

der **Nerv**, PLURAL die **Nerven**
  nerve
  Gabi geht mir auf die Nerven. Gabi gets on my nerves.

ℱ **nervig** ADJECTIVE
1 nerve-racking
2 irritating

ℱ **nervös** ADJECTIVE
  nervous, tense

die **Nervosität**
  nervousness, tension

die **Nessel**, PLURAL die **Nesseln**
  nettle

das **Nest**, PLURAL die **Nester**
1 nest
2 little place (a village)

ℱ **nett** ADJECTIVE
  nice

netto ADVERB
  net

das **Netz**, PLURAL die **Netze**
1 net
2 network
3 string bag
4 web (spider's)
5 Internet
  Sie surft stundenlang im Netz. She surfs the Internet for hours.

der **Netzball**
  netball

die **Netzkamera**, PLURAL die **Netzkameras**
  webcam

die **Netzkarte**, PLURAL die **Netzkarten**
  travel card (for a whole transport network)

das **Netzwerk**, PLURAL die **Netzwerke**
  network

ℱ **neu** ADJECTIVE
1 new
  Das Rad ist noch wie neu. The bike is as good as new.
2 neue Sprachen modern languages
3 seit neuestem recently
4 die neueste Mode the latest fashion
  das Neueste the latest news
  Er hat immer das Neueste an Audioausrüstung. He always has the latest audio equipment.
5 Das ist mir neu. That's news to me.

neu ADVERB
1 newly
2 only just
  Es ist neu eingetroffen. It has only just come in.
3 etwas neu schreiben to rewrite something

neuartig ADJECTIVE
  new
  ein neuartiger Flaschenöffner a new kind of bottle opener

neuerdings ADVERB
  recently

die **Neugier**
  curiosity

neugierig ADJECTIVE
  curious, inquisitive

die **Neuigkeit**, PLURAL die **Neuigkeiten**
  piece of news
  Gibt es irgendwelche Neuigkeiten? Is there any news?

das **Neujahr**
  New Year, New Year's Day

der **Neujahrstag**
  New Year's Day

neulich ADVERB
  the other day

ℱ **neun** NUMBER
  nine

die **Neun**, PLURAL die **Neunen**
  nine

A
B
C
D
E
F
G
H
I
J
K
L
M
N
O
P
Q
R
S
T
U
V
W
X
Y
Z

ℱ indicates key words

das **Neuntel**, PLURAL die **Neuntel**
 ninth

ℱ **neunter, neunte, neuntes** ADJECTIVE
 ninth

ℱ **neunzehn** NUMBER
 nineteen

ℱ **neunzig** NUMBER
 ninety

Neuseeland NEUTER NOUN
 New Zealand

ℱ **nicht** ADVERB
 1 not
  Sie ist nicht da. She's not there.
  Ich kann nicht. I can't.
  Iris hat nicht angerufen. Iris didn't ring.
  bitte nicht please don't
  Nicht! Don't!
  Nicht berühren! Don't touch!
 2 'Ich mag das nicht.' – 'Ich auch nicht.' 'I
  don't like it.' – 'Neither do I.'
 3 ..., nicht (wahr)? ..., isn't he/she/it/etc.?
  Du kennst ihn doch, nicht? You know him,
  don't you?
 4 gar nicht not at all
 5 nicht mehr no more

die **Nichte**, PLURAL die **Nichten**
 niece

der **Nichtraucher**, PLURAL die **Nichtraucher**
 non-smoker (male)
 Er ist Nichtraucher. He doesn't smoke.

die **Nichtraucherin**, PLURAL die
 Nichtraucherinnen
 non-smoker (female)
 Sie ist Nichtraucherin. She doesn't smoke.

ℱ **nichts** PRONOUN
 1 nothing
 2 not ... anything
  Ich habe nichts gewusst. I didn't know
  anything.
 3 nichts mehr nothing more
  Dazu habe ich nichts mehr zu sagen. I
  have nothing more to say.
 4 Das macht nichts. It doesn't matter.
 5 nichts ahnend unsuspecting

das **Nichtschwimmerbecken**, PLURAL die
 Nichtschwimmerbecken
 learners' pool (for non-swimmers and
 learners)

nicken VERB, PERFECT **hat genickt**
 to nod

das **Nickerchen**, PLURAL die **Nickerchen**
 nap
 ein Nickerchen machen to have a nap

ℱ **nie** ADVERB
 never

nieder ADJECTIVE
 low

nieder ADVERB
 down

die **Niederlage**, PLURAL die **Niederlagen**
 defeat

ℱ die **Niederlande** PLURAL NOUN
 die Niederlande the Netherlands

der **Niederländer**, PLURAL die **Niederländer**
 Dutchman
 die Niederländer the Dutch

die **Niederländerin**, PLURAL die
 Niederländerinnen
 Dutchwoman

niederländisch ADJECTIVE
 Dutch

> **WORD TIP** Adjectives never have capitals
> in German, even for regions, countries, or
> nationalities.

der **Niederschlag**
 rainfall, precipitation

niedlich ADJECTIVE
 sweet

niedrig ADJECTIVE
 1 low
 2 base

niemals ADVERB
 never

ℱ **niemand** PRONOUN
 nobody
 Wir haben niemand/niemanden
 gesehen. We didn't see anybody.

die **Niere**, PLURAL die **Nieren**
 kidney

nieseln VERB, PERFECT **hat genieselt**
 to drizzle
 Es nieselt. It's drizzling.

niesen VERB, PERFECT **hat geniest**
 to sneeze

der **Nikolaus**, PLURAL die **Nikoläuse**
Sankt Nikolaus, der Nikolaus Saint Nicholas

> **NIKOLAUS**
>
> Nikolaus is the equivalent of Santa Claus but he brings small presents and treats like nuts, oranges, chocolate and biscuits to children on 6 December, the feast of Saint Nicholas.

der **Nil**
der Nil the River Nile

das **Nilpferd**, PLURAL die **Nilpferde**
hippopotamus

nimmt ▶ SEE **nehmen**

nirgends, **nirgendwo** ADVERB
nowhere

das **Niveau**, PLURAL die **Niveaus**
1 level
2 standard

ℱ **noch** ADVERB
1 still
Es regnet immer noch. It's still raining.
Sie ist noch immer nicht da. She's still not arrived.
2 even
Seine neue Lied ist noch besser. His latest song is even better.
3 noch nicht not yet
Ich habe ihn noch nicht angerufen. I haven't called him yet.
4 noch nie never
Sie war noch nie in Rom. She's never been to Rome.
5 gerade noch only just
Wir haben den Bus gerade noch bekommen. We only just caught the bus.
6 else
Wer war noch da? Who else was there?
Was noch? What else?
Sonst noch etwas? Anything else?
7 noch (ein)mal again
8 Ich möchte noch ein Bier. I'd like another beer.
Noch etwas Kaffee? (Would you like some) more coffee?
9 Ich habe ihn noch gestern gesehen. I saw him only yesterday.
10 Sie haben noch und noch Geld. They have loads of money.
noch CONJUNCTION
nor
weder ... noch neither ... nor

nochmals ADVERB
again

das **Nomen**, PLURAL die **Nomen** or die **Nomina**
noun (in grammar)

der **Nominativ**, PLURAL die **Nominative**
nominative (in grammar)

die **Nonne**, PLURAL die **Nonnen**
nun

Nordamerika NEUTER NOUN
North America

der **Nordamerikaner**, PLURAL die **Nordamerikaner**
North American (male)

die **Nordamerikanerin**, PLURAL die **Nordamerikanerinnen**
North American (female)

nordamerikanisch ADJECTIVE
North American

> **WORD TIP** Adjectives never have capitals in German, even for regions, countries, or nationalities.

ℱ der **Norden**
north

Nordirland NEUTER NOUN
Northern Ireland

nördlich ADJECTIVE
1 northern
2 northerly (direction)
nördlich ADVERB, PREPOSITION (+ GEN)
nördlich der Stadt north of the town
nördlich von Wien to the north of Vienna

der **Nordosten**
north-east

der **Nordpol**
North Pole

die **Nordsee**
North Sea

der **Nordwesten**
north-west

nörgeln VERB, PERFECT **hat genörgelt**
to grumble

die **Norm**, PLURAL die **Normen**
1 norm
2 standard

normal ADJECTIVE
normal

das **Normalbenzin**
regular petrol

ℱ indicates key words

normalerweise ADVERB
normally

Norwegen NEUTER NOUN
Norway

der **Norweger**, PLURAL die **Norweger**
Norwegian (male)

die **Norwegerin**, PLURAL die
Norwegerinnen
Norwegian (female)

norwegisch ADJECTIVE
Norwegian

> **WORD TIP** Adjectives never have capitals
> in German, even for regions, countries, or
> nationalities.

die **Not**, PLURAL die **Nöte**
1 need
Sie spendeten Geld für Not leidende Kinder.
They donated money for children in need.
2 hardship, suffering
3 zur Not if necessary, at a pinch
4 mit knapper Not only just

die **Notaufnahme**, PLURAL die
Notaufnahmen
accident and emergency (hospital
department)

*der **Notausgang**, PLURAL die **Notausgänge**
emergency exit

die **Notbremse**, PLURAL die **Notbremsen**
emergency brake

*der **Notdienst**, PLURAL die **Notdienste**
1 emergency service
2 Notdienst haben to be on call

*die **Note**, PLURAL die **Noten**
1 note
Sie hat die falsche Note gespielt. She
played the wrong note.
Kannst du Noten lesen? Can you read music?
2 mark
Er hat immer gute Noten. He always gets
good marks.

> **NOTE**
> In Germany, the best mark is 1, the worst is 6.
> In Austria, the best mark is 1, the worst is 5. In
> Switzerland, the best mark is 6, the worst is
> 1. In Switzerland Halbnoten such as 3.5 or 5.5
> may also be given. These marks mean that the
> pupil's performance in a particular subject is
> between two marks.

der **Notendruck**
pressure to achieve high marks

der **Notfall**, PLURAL die **Notfälle**
emergency

notfalls ADVERB
if necessary, if need be

notieren VERB, PERFECT **hat notiert**
1 to note down
2 sich etwas notieren to make a note of
something
Ich habe es mir notiert. I've made a note
of it.

nötig ADJECTIVE
necessary

nötig ADVERB
urgently

*die **Notiz**, PLURAL die **Notizen**
1 note
Er machte sich Notizen. He took notes.
2 item (in a newspaper)
3 keine Notiz von etwas nehmen to take no
notice of something

der **Notizblock**, PLURAL die **Notizblöcke**
notepad

das **Notizbuch**, PLURAL die **Notizbücher**
notebook

die **Notlage**, PLURAL die **Notlagen**
crisis

der **Notruf**, PLURAL die **Notrufe**
1 emergency call
2 emergency number

notwendig ADJECTIVE
necessary

*der **November**
November
im November in November

NRW ABBREVIATION
(=Nordrhein-Westfalen) **North Rhine-
Westphalia**

nüchtern ADJECTIVE
1 sober
wieder nüchtern werden to sober up
2 auf nüchternen Magen on an empty
stomach
3 down to earth

*die **Nudel**, PLURAL die **Nudeln**
1 Nudeln noodles
2 Nudeln pasta
Heute gibt es Nudeln. We're having pasta
today.

*der **Nudelsalat**, PLURAL die **Nudelsalate**
pasta salad

*null NUMBER
1 zero, nought

◇ irregular verb; SEP separable verb; for more help with verbs see centre section

Es war zehn Grad unter null. It was ten degrees below zero.
2 **nil**
Es steht zwei zu null. It's two nil.
3 **love** (in tennis)
4 Sie hatte null Fehler. She had no mistakes. Ich habe null Ahnung. (informal) I haven't a clue.
5 in null Komma nichts (informal) in less than no time

die **Null**, PLURAL die **Nullen**
1 **zero, nought**
2 **failure**

♟ die **Nummer**, PLURAL die **Nummern**
1 **number**
2 **issue** (of a magazine)
3 **size** (of clothing)
4 **act**
5 auf Nummer sicher gehen to play safe

nummerieren VERB, PERFECT **hat nummeriert**
to number

das **Nummernschild**, PLURAL die **Nummernschilder**
number plate

♟ **nun** ADVERB
now
nun EXCLAMATION
well
Nun ja, ... Well, ...

♟ **nur** ADVERB
1 **only**
2 Was sollen wir nur tun? What on earth are we going to do?
3 Sie soll es nur versuchen! Just let her try!
4 Nur zu! Go ahead!

Nürnberg NEUTER NOUN
Nuremberg

♟ die **Nuss**, PLURAL die **Nüsse**
nut

♟ **nutzen, nützen** VERB, PERFECT **hat genutzt/ genützt**
1 **to use**
2 etwas nutzen to make the most of something
Du solltest diese Gelegenheit nutzen. You should make the most of this opportunity.
3 **to be useful**
4 nichts nutzen to be no use
Das nutzt mir nichts. That won't help me.
5 Das nutzt ja doch nichts. It's pointless.

der **Nutzen**
benefit

von Nutzen sein to be useful

♟ **nützlich** ADJECTIVE
useful

nutzlos ADJECTIVE
useless

Oo

♟ **ob** CONJUNCTION
1 **whether, if**
Wissen Sie, ob heute noch ein Zug nach Freising fährt? Do you know if there is another train to Freising today?
2 Ob Alex noch anruft? I wonder if Alex will ring.
3 Und ob! You bet!

obdachlos ADJECTIVE
homeless

der/die **Obdachlose**, PLURAL die **Obdachlosen**
homeless person
die Obdachlosen the homeless

♟ **oben** ADVERB
1 **on top**
oben auf on top of
Die Vase steht oben auf dem Schrank. The vase is on top of the cupboard.
2 **at the top**
von oben bis unten from top to bottom
Er hat uns von oben bis unten gemustert. He looked us up and down.
3 **upstairs**
4 nach oben up, upstairs
Er ist nach oben in sein Zimmer gegangen. He went up to his room.
Geht der Fahrstuhl nach oben? Is the lift going up?
hier oben up here
da oben up there
5 Siehe oben. See above. (on a page)
oben erwähnt above-mentioned
6 oben ohne (informal) topless

der **Ober**, PLURAL die **Ober**
waiter
Herr Ober! Waiter!

oberer, obere, oberes ADJECTIVE
upper, top

die **Oberfläche**, PLURAL die **Oberflächen**
surface

oberflächlich ADJECTIVE
superficial

♟ indicates key words

das **Obergeschoss**, PLURAL die **Obergeschosse**
upper floor

das **Oberhaupt**, PLURAL die **Oberhäupter**
head (of a family, organization)

das **Oberhemd**, PLURAL die **Oberhemden**
shirt

der **Oberlippenbart**, PLURAL die **Oberlippenbärte**
moustache

das **Obers**
(in Southern Germany and Austria) cream

der **Oberschenkel**, PLURAL die **Oberschenkel**
thigh

die **Oberschule**, PLURAL die **Oberschulen**
secondary school

oberster, **oberste**, **oberstes** ADJECTIVE
top

ℰ die **Oberstufe**, PLURAL die **Oberstufen**
sixth form

die **Oberweite**, PLURAL die **Oberweiten**
chest size, bust measurement

das **Objekt**, PLURAL die **Objekte**
object

objektiv ADJECTIVE
objective

das **Objektiv**, PLURAL die **Objektive**
lens

die **Oboe**, PLURAL die **Oboen**
oboe
Sie spielt Oboe. She plays the oboe.

ℰ das **Obst**
fruit

der **Obstbaum**, PLURAL die **Obstbäume**
fruit tree

der **Obstsalat**, PLURAL die **Obstsalate**
fruit salad

die **Obsttorte**, PLURAL die **Obsttorten**
fruit flan

obszön ADJECTIVE
obscene

ℰ **obwohl** CONJUNCTION
although

öde ADJECTIVE
1 desolate
2 dreary, dull

Das ist so ein furchtbar öder Job. It's such a terribly dull job.

ℰ **oder** CONJUNCTION
1 or
2 Du kennst sie doch, oder? You know her, don't you?

der **Ofen**, PLURAL die **Öfen**
1 oven
2 stove
3 heater

ℰ **offen** ADJECTIVE
1 open
Die Geschäfte haben bis sieben Uhr offen. The shops are open until seven o'clock.
Tag der offenen Tür open day
2 honest, frank
3 vacant
eine offene Stelle a vacancy

offen ADVERB
1 openly
2 honestly, frankly
offen gesagt frankly

offenbar ADJECTIVE
obvious

offenbar ADVERB
1 apparently
2 Da hast du dich offenbar geirrt. You seem to have made a mistake.
Sie hat offenbar den Zug verpasst. She must have missed the train.

offenbleiben VERB◇, IMPERFECT **blieb offen**, PERFECT **ist offengeblieben**
to remain unanswered (of a question)

offensichtlich ADJECTIVE
obvious

öffentlich ADJECTIVE
public
öffentliche Verkehrsmittel public transport

die **Öffentlichkeit**
public
in aller Öffentlichkeit in public

offiziell ADJECTIVE
official

der **Offizier**, PLURAL die **Offiziere**
officer

> **WORD TIP** Professions, hobbies, and sports don't take an article in German: Er ist Offizier.

öffnen VERB, PERFECT **hat geöffnet**
to open
jemandem die Tür öffnen to open the door

◇ irregular verb; SEP separable verb; for more help with verbs see centre section

for somebody

der **Öffner**, PLURAL die **Öffner**
opener

die **Öffnung**, PLURAL die **Öffnungen**
opening

die **Öffnungszeiten** PLURAL NOUN
opening times

oft ADVERB
often

öfter, öfters ADVERB
quite often
Früher habe ich ihn öfters mal getroffen.
I used to meet him quite often.

ℓ **ohne** PREPOSITION (+ ACC)
1 without
Ohne mich! Count me out!
2 ohne weiteres easily
3 oben ohne (informal) topless
4 Das ist nicht ohne. (informal) It's quite difficult.

ohne CONJUNCTION
without
ohne zu überlegen without thinking

die **Ohnmacht**
in Ohnmacht fallen to faint

ohnmächtig ADJECTIVE
1 unconscious
2 ohnmächtig werden to faint
Gisela ist ohnmächtig geworden. Gisela fainted.

ℓ das **Ohr**, PLURAL die **Ohren**
ear

ℓ die **Ohrenschmerzen** PLURAL NOUN
earache
Max hat Ohrenschmerzen. Max has earache.

der **Ohrhörer**, PLURAL die **Ohrhörer**
earphone

ℓ der **Ohrring**, PLURAL die **Ohrringe**
earring

oje EXCLAMATION
oh dear!

der **Ökoladen**, PLURAL die **Ökoläden**
health-food shop

die **Ökologie**
ecology

ℓ **ökologisch** ADJECTIVE
ecological

ℓ der **Oktober**
October
im Oktober in October

das **Öl**, PLURAL die **Öle**
oil

die **Ölfarbe**, PLURAL die **Ölfarben**
oil paint

das **Ölgemälde**, PLURAL die **Ölgemälde**
oil painting

ölig ADJECTIVE
oily

die **Olive**, PLURAL die **Oliven**
olive

das **Olivenöl**, PLURAL die **Olivenöle**
olive oil

der **Ölteppich**, PLURAL die **Ölteppiche**
oil slick

die **Olympiade**, PLURAL die **Olympiaden**
Olympic Games
Die Olympiade findet alle vier Jahre statt.
The Olympic Games take place every four years.

olympisch ADJECTIVE
Olympic

ℓ die **Oma**, PLURAL die **Omas**
granny

das **Omelett**, PLURAL die **Omeletts**
omelette

die **Omi**, PLURAL die **Omis**
granny

ℓ der **Onkel**, PLURAL die **Onkel**
uncle

ℓ der **Opa**, PLURAL die **Opas**
grandpa

die **Oper**, PLURAL die **Opern**
opera

die **Operation**, PLURAL die **Operationen**
operation

der **Operationssaal**, PLURAL die **Operationssäle**
operating theatre

operieren VERB, PERFECT **hat operiert**
1 to operate on
sich operieren lassen to have an operation
Sie wurde am Magen operiert. She had a stomach operation.
2 to operate

ℓ indicates key words

das **Opfer**, PLURAL die **Opfer**
1 sacrifice
　Opfer bringen to make sacrifices
2 victim
　Das Erdbeben forderte viele Opfer. The
　earthquake claimed many victims.

der **Optiker**, PLURAL die **Optiker**
optician (male)

WORD TIP Professions, hobbies, and sports
don't take an article in German: Er ist Optiker.

die **Optikerin**, PLURAL die **Optikerinnen**
optician (female)

WORD TIP Professions, hobbies, and sports don't
take an article in German: Sie ist Optikerin.

der **Optimist**, PLURAL die **Optimisten**
optimist

optimistisch ADJECTIVE
optimistic

℗ **orange** ADJECTIVE
orange

℗ die **Orange**, PLURAL die **Orangen**
orange

℗ der **Orangensaft**, PLURAL die **Orangensäfte**
orange juice

℗ das **Orchester**, PLURAL die **Orchester**
orchestra

℗ **ordentlich** ADJECTIVE
1 tidy
2 respectable
3 proper (meal, job, salary)
4 eine ordentliche Tracht Prügel (informal) a
　good hiding
ordentlich ADVERB
1 tidily
　ordentlich schreiben to write neatly
2 respectably
3 properly
4 ordentlich feiern (informal) to have a real
　celebration
5 Wir sind ordentlich nass geworden.
　(informal) We got soaked.

ordinär ADJECTIVE
vulgar

ordnen VERB, PERFECT **hat geordnet**
1 to arrange
2 to put in order

der **Ordner**, PLURAL die **Ordner**
file

℗ die **Ordnung**
1 order

2 tidiness
　Ich muss erst einmal Ordnung machen.
　I have to tidy up first.
3 Mit der Waschmaschine ist etwas nicht in
　Ordnung. There's something wrong with
　the washing machine.
4 etwas in Ordnung bringen to put
　something right
5 In Ordnung! Okay!
6 Er ist in Ordnung. He's all right.

das **Organ**, PLURAL die **Organe**
1 organ
2 (informal) voice

die **Organisation**, PLURAL die **Organisationen**
organization

organisch ADJECTIVE
organic

℗ **organisieren** VERB, PERFECT **hat organisiert**
1 to organize
2 (informal) to get (hold of)

die **Orgel**, PLURAL die **Orgeln**
organ
　Karl spielt Orgel. Karl plays the organ.

orientieren VERB, PERFECT **hat sich orientiert**
1 sich orientieren to get your bearings
2 sich über etwas orientieren to find out
　about something

die **Orientierung**
1 orientation
　Was ist die politische Orientierung dieser
　Zeitung? What is the newspaper's political
　orientation?
2 bearings
　Ich habe die Orientierung verloren. I've
　lost my bearings.
3 zu Ihrer Orientierung for your information

das **Orientierungsjahr**, PLURAL die **Orientierungsjahre**
gap year

der **Orientierungspunkt**, PLURAL die **Orientierungspunkte**
landmark, reference point

das **Orientierungsrennen**, PLURAL die **Orientierungsrennen**
orienteering

der **Orientierungssinn**
sense of direction

originell ADJECTIVE
original

◇ irregular verb; SEP separable verb; for more help with verbs see centre section

der **Orkan**, PLURAL die **Orkane**
hurricane

ℱ der **Ort**, PLURAL die **Orte**
1 place
an Ort und Stelle on the spot
2 (small) town

die **Orthografie**
spelling

örtlich ADJECTIVE
local

die **Ortschaft**, PLURAL die **Ortschaften**
village

das **Ortsgespräch**, PLURAL die
Ortsgespräche
local call

der **Ossi**, PLURAL die **Ossis**
(informal) East German

Ost Berlin NEUTER NOUN
East Berlin

> **OST BERLIN**
> The capital of East Germany (German
> Democratic Republic) from 1949 until 1990.

ℱ der **Osten**
east

das **Osterei**, PLURAL die **Ostereier**
Easter egg

der **Osterhase**, PLURAL die **Osterhasen**
Easter bunny

der **Ostermontag**
Easter Monday

ℱ **Ostern** NEUTER NOUN
Easter

ℱ **Österreich** NEUTER NOUN
Austria

> **ÖSTERREICH**
> Capital: Wien (Vienna). Population: over
> 8 million. Size: 83,872 square km. Official
> language: German. Official currency: euro.

der **Österreicher**, PLURAL die **Österreicher**
Austrian (male)

die **Österreicherin**, PLURAL die
Österreicherinnen
Austrian (female)

österreichisch ADJECTIVE
Austrian

> **WORD TIP** Adjectives never have capitals
> in German, even for regions, countries, or
> nationalities.

östlich ADJECTIVE
1 eastern
2 easterly

östlich ADVERB, PREPOSITION (+ GEN)
östlich der Stadt east of the town
östlich von Wien to the east of Vienna

die **Ostsee**
Baltic (Sea)

oval ADJECTIVE
oval

der **Ozean**, PLURAL die **Ozeane**
ocean

das **Ozon**
ozone

das **Ozonloch**, PLURAL die **Ozonlöcher**
hole in the ozone layer

die **Ozonschicht**, PLURAL die **Ozonschichten**
ozone layer

Pp

ℱ **paar** PRONOUN
ein paar a few
ein paar Mal a few times
alle paar Tage every few days

das **Paar**, PLURAL die **Paare**
1 pair
ein Paar Schuhe a pair of shoes
2 couple
ein junges Paar a young couple

paarweise ADJECTIVE
in pairs
Die Kinder stellten sich paarweise auf. The
children lined up in pairs.

das **Päckchen**, PLURAL die **Päckchen**
1 package, packet
2 (small) parcel

packen VERB, PERFECT **hat gepackt**
1 to pack
Ich muss jetzt meinen Koffer packen. I
have to pack my case now.
2 to grab (hold of)
Er packte mich am Arm. He grabbed my
arm.
Sie waren von Furcht gepackt. They were
gripped with fear.

ℱ die **Packung**, PLURAL die **Packungen**
packet, pack

der **Pädagoge**, PLURAL die **Pädagogen**
1 educationalist *(male)*
2 teacher *(male)*

> **WORD TIP** Professions, hobbies, and sports don't take an article in German: Er ist Pädagoge.

die **Pädagogin**, PLURAL die **Pädagoginnen**
1 educationalist *(female)*
2 teacher *(female)*

> **WORD TIP** Professions, hobbies, and sports don't take an article in German: Sie ist Pädagogin.

pädagogisch ADJECTIVE
educational

das **Paddel**, PLURAL die **Paddel**
paddle

paddeln VERB
1 PERFECT **hat gepaddelt** to paddle *(a canoe)*
2 PERFECT **ist gepaddelt** to paddle *(along a lake, river)*

das **Paket**, PLURAL die **Pakete**
1 parcel
Gabi hat mir ein Paket geschickt. Gabi sent me a parcel.
2 packet
Kaufe bitte ein Paket Waschpulver für mich. Can you please buy me a packet of washing powder?

Pakistan NEUTER NOUN
Pakistan

der **Pakistaner**, PLURAL die **Pakistaner**
Pakistani *(male)*

die **Pakistanerin**, PLURAL die **Pakistanerinnen**
Pakistani *(female)*

pakistanisch ADJECTIVE
Pakistani

> **WORD TIP** Adjectives never have capitals in German, even for regions, countries, or nationalities.

der **Palast**, PLURAL die **Paläste**
palace

die **Palme**, PLURAL die **Palmen**
palm (tree)

die **Pampelmuse**, PLURAL die **Pampelmusen**
grapefruit

die **Panik**
panic
in Panik geraten to panic

♀ die **Panne**, PLURAL die **Pannen**
1 breakdown

Wir haben auf dem Rückweg eine Panne gehabt. We had a breakdown on the way back.
2 mishap
Uns ist eine Panne passiert. We had a mishap.

der **Pantoffel**, PLURAL die **Pantoffeln**
slipper

der **Panzer**, PLURAL die **Panzer**
tank *military*

der **Papa**, PLURAL die **Papas**
dad, daddy

der **Papagei**, PLURAL die **Papageien**
parrot

♀ das **Papier**, PLURAL die **Papiere**
paper

der **Papierkorb**, PLURAL die **Papierkörbe**
waste-paper basket

die **Papiertüte**, PLURAL die **Papiertüten**
paper bag

die **Pappe**, PLURAL die **Pappen**
cardboard

♀ der or die **Paprika**, PLURAL die **Paprikas**
1 pepper
eine rote/grüne Paprika a red/green pepper
2 paprika

die **Paprikaschote**, PLURAL die **Paprikaschoten**
pepper

der **Papst**, PLURAL die **Päpste**
pope

die **Parabolantenne**, PLURAL die **Parabolantennen**
satellite dish

das **Paradies**, PLURAL die **Paradiese**
paradise

der **Paragraf**, PLURAL die **Paragrafen**
1 article *(of a treaty or law)*
2 clause

> **WORD TIP** The German word Paragraf does not mean paragraph in English; the German word for paragraph is Absatz.

parallel ADJECTIVE
parallel

das **Pärchen**, PLURAL die **Pärchen**
couple

das **Parfüm**, PLURAL die **Parfüms**
perfume

◇ irregular verb; SEP separable verb; for more help with verbs see centre section

die **Parfümerie**, *PLURAL* die **Parfümerien**
perfumery

℘ der **Park**, *PLURAL* die **Parks**
park

die **Parkanlage**, *PLURAL* die **Parkanlagen**
park

parken *VERB*, *PERFECT* **hat geparkt**
to park

das **Parkett**, *PLURAL* die **Parkette**
1 parquet floor
2 *(in a theatre)* stalls

das **Parkhaus**, *PLURAL* die **Parkhäuser**
multi-storey car park

die **Parklücke**, *PLURAL* die **Parklücken**
parking space

℘ der **Parkplatz**, *PLURAL* die **Parkplätze**
1 car park
2 parking space

der **Parkschein**, *PLURAL* die **Parkscheine**
car-park ticket

die **Parkuhr**, *PLURAL* die **Parkuhren**
parking meter

das **Parkverbot**
'Parkverbot' 'No parking'
In der Innenstadt ist Parkverbot. You can't
park in the town centre.

das **Parlament**, *PLURAL* die **Parlamente**
parliament

die **Parole**, *PLURAL* die **Parolen**
slogan

die **Partei**, *PLURAL* die **Parteien**
1 (political) party
2 für jemanden Partei ergreifen to side with
somebody

das **Parterre**, *PLURAL* die **Parterres**
ground floor

die **Partie**, *PLURAL* die **Partien**
1 part
2 game *(of tennis, chess)*

℘ der **Partner**, *PLURAL* die **Partner**
partner *(male)*

℘ die **Partnerin**, *PLURAL* die **Partnerinnen**
partner *(female)*

die **Partnerschaft**, *PLURAL* die
Partnerschaften
partnership

die **Partnerstadt**, *PLURAL* die **Partnerstädte**
twin town

℘ die **Party**, *PLURAL* die **Partys**
party
eine Party geben to have a party

der **Pass**, *PLURAL* die **Pässe**
1 passport
2 pass *(in sport or in the mountains)*

die **Passage**, *PLURAL* die **Passagen**
1 shopping arcade
2 passage *(of text)*
3 sequence *(of music, film)*

der **Passagier**, *PLURAL* die **Passagiere**
passenger *(male)*

der **Passant**, *PLURAL* die **Passanten**
passer-by *(male)*

die **Passantin**, *PLURAL* die **Passantinnen**
passer-by *(female)*

℘ **passen**, *PERFECT* **hat gepasst**
1 to fit
jemandem passen to fit somebody
Die Hose passt (mir) gut. The trousers fit
well.
2 to suit
jemandem passen to suit somebody
Freitag passt mir gut. Friday suits me fine.
Samstag passt mir nicht. Saturday's no
good for me.
Seine Art passt mir nicht. I don't like his
manner.
3 zu etwas passen to go with something
Die Jacke passt nicht zu dieser Hose. The
jacket doesn't go with these trousers.
zu jemandem passen to be right for
somebody
Sie passt nicht zu ihm. She's not right for
him.
Die neue Frisur passt nicht zu dir. Your
new hairstyle doesn't suit you.

℘ **passend** *ADJECTIVE*
1 suitable
2 matching

℘ **passieren** *VERB*, *PERFECT* **ist passiert**
to happen
Was ist passiert? What happened?

passiv *ADJECTIVE*
passive

das **Passiv**
passive *(in grammar)*

das **Passivrauchen**
passive smoking

die **Passkontrolle**
passport control

℘ indicates key words

das **Passwort**, *PLURAL* die **Passwörter**
password (in computing)
Geben Sie Ihr Passwort ein. Enter your
password.

die **Paste**, *PLURAL* die **Pasten**
paste

die **Pastete**, *PLURAL* die **Pasteten**
1 pâté
2 pie, pasty

der **Pate**, *PLURAL* die **Paten**
godfather

das **Patenkind**, *PLURAL* die **Patenkinder**
godchild

der **Patenonkel**, *PLURAL* die **Patenonkel**
godfather

patent *ADJECTIVE*
capable, clever

die **Patentante**, *PLURAL* die **Patentanten**
godmother

der **Patient**, *PLURAL* die **Patienten**
patient (male)

die **Patientin**, *PLURAL* die **Patientinnen**
patient (female)

die **Patin**, *PLURAL* die **Patinnen**
godmother

die **Patrone**, *PLURAL* die **Patronen**
cartridge

patschnass *ADJECTIVE*
soaking wet

pauken *VERB*, *PERFECT* **hat gepaukt**
(informal) to swot

pauschal *ADJECTIVE*
all-inclusive

die **Pauschalreise**, *PLURAL* die
Pauschalreisen
package holiday

ℓ die **Pause**, *PLURAL* die **Pausen**
1 break
2 pause
3 interval

der **Pazifik**
der Pazifik the Pacific (Ocean)

der **PC**, *PLURAL* die **PC**, **PCs** *ABBREVIATION*
(=Personal Computer) PC

das **Pech**
1 bad luck
Pech haben to be unlucky
2 pitch (tar)

das **Pedal**, *PLURAL* die **Pedale**
pedal

ℓ **peinlich** *ADJECTIVE*
1 embarrassing
Es war mir sehr peinlich. I felt very
embarrassed about it.
2 awkward
3 meticulous

die **Peitsche**, *PLURAL* die **Peitschen**
whip

die **Pelle**
skin

der **Pelz**, *PLURAL* die **Pelze**
fur

pendeln *VERB*
1 *PERFECT* **ist gependelt** to commute
2 *PERFECT* **hat gependelt** to swing (to and
fro)

der **Pendelverkehr**
1 commuter traffic
2 shuttle service

der **Pendler**, *PLURAL* die **Pendler**
commuter (male)

die **Pendlerin**, *PLURAL* die **Pendlerinnen**
commuter (female)

penetrant *ADJECTIVE*
1 overpowering (odour, perfume)
2 pushy (person)

der **Penis**, *PLURAL* die **Penisse**
penis

pennen *VERB*, *PERFECT* **hat gepennt**
(informal) to sleep, to kip

die **Pension**, *PLURAL* die **Pensionen**
1 guest house
2 volle Pension full board
3 pension
Er hat eine schöne Pension. He gets a
good pension.
in Pension gehen to retire

pensioniert *ADJECTIVE*
retired

per *PREPOSITION* (+ ACC)
by
per Luftpost by airmail

perfekt *ADJECTIVE*
perfect

das **Perfekt**
perfect (in grammar)

◇ irregular verb; *SEP* separable verb; for more help with verbs see centre section

die **Periode**, *PLURAL* die **Perioden**
period

die **Perle**, *PLURAL* die **Perlen**
1 pearl
2 bead

ℙ die **Person**, *PLURAL* die **Personen**
person
für vier Personen for four people
Ich für meine Person bin dagegen.
Personally, I'm against it.

das **Personal**
staff, personnel

der **Personalausweis**, *PLURAL* die
Personalausweise
identity card

der **Personenverkehr**
passenger services

der **Personenzug**, *PLURAL* die **Personenzüge**
passenger train

persönlich *ADJECTIVE*
personal
persönlich *ADVERB*
1 personally
2 in person

ℙ die **Persönlichkeit**, *PLURAL* die
Persönlichkeiten
personality

die **Perücke**, *PLURAL* die **Perücken**
wig

der **Pessimist**, *PLURAL* die **Pessimisten**
pessimist

pessimistisch *ADJECTIVE*
pessimistic

das **Pestizid**, *PLURAL* die **Pestizide**
pesticide

das **Petroleum**
paraffin

der **Pfad**, *PLURAL* die **Pfade**
path

der **Pfadfinder**, *PLURAL* die **Pfadfinder**
(Boy) Scout

die **Pfadfinderin**, *PLURAL* die
Pfadfinderinnen
(Girl) Guide

das **Pfand**, *PLURAL* die **Pfänder**
1 deposit *(on a bottle or can)*
Auf dieser Dose ist 25 Cent Pfand. There's
a deposit of 25 cents on this can.
2 forfeit

3 pledge

ℙ die **Pfandflasche**, *PLURAL* die **Pfandflaschen**
returnable bottle

die **Pfanne**, *PLURAL* die **Pfannen**
(frying) pan

der **Pfannkuchen**, *PLURAL* die **Pfannkuchen**
pancake

der **Pfarrer**, *PLURAL* die **Pfarrer**
1 vicar *(male)*
2 priest *(male)*

die **Pfarrerin**, *PLURAL* die **Pfarrerinnen**
1 vicar *(female)*
2 priest *(female)*

der **Pfau**, *PLURAL* die **Pfauen**
peacock

Pfd. *ABBREVIATION*
(=*Pfund*) pound, half a kilo

der **Pfeffer**
pepper

das **Pfefferkorn**, *PLURAL* die **Pfefferkörner**
peppercorn

der **Pfefferkuchen**
gingerbread

der or das **Pfefferminzbonbon**, *PLURAL* die
Pfefferminzbonbons
mint

die **Pfefferminze**
peppermint

die **Pfeife**, *PLURAL* die **Pfeifen**
1 whistle
2 pipe

pfeifen *VERB*◇, *IMPERFECT* **pfiff**, *PERFECT* **hat
gepfiffen**
to whistle

der **Pfeil**, *PLURAL* die **Pfeile**
arrow

der **Pfeiler**, *PLURAL* die **Pfeiler**
1 pillar
2 support

der **Pfennig**, *PLURAL* die **Pfennige**
pfennig *(one hundredth of a mark in the
former German currency)*
Ich habe keinen Pfennig mehr. I haven't
got a penny left.

ℙ das **Pferd**, *PLURAL* die **Pferde**
horse

A
B
C
D
E
F
G
H
I
J
K
L
M
N
O
P
Q
R
S
T
U
V
W
X
Y
Z

das **Pferderennen**, *PLURAL* die **Pferderennen**
1 horse race
2 horse racing

der **Pferdeschwanz**, *PLURAL* die **Pferdeschwänze**
ponytail

pfiff ▸ SEE **pfeifen**

Pfingsten *NEUTER NOUN*
Whitsun

℗ der **Pfirsich**, *PLURAL* die **Pfirsiche**
peach

℗ die **Pflanze**, *PLURAL* die **Pflanzen**
plant

℗ **pflanzen** *VERB*, *PERFECT* **hat gepflanzt**
to plant
Pflanzt mehr Bäume! Plant more trees!

℗ das **Pflaster**, *PLURAL* die **Pflaster**
1 (sticking) plaster
2 pavement

℗ die **Pflaume**, *PLURAL* die **Pflaumen**
plum

die **Pflege**
1 care
2 nursing care
3 ein Kind in Pflege nehmen to foster a child

die **Pflegeeltern** *PLURAL NOUN*
foster parents

das **Pflegeheim**, *PLURAL* die **Pflegeheime**
nursing home

das **Pflegekind**, *PLURAL* die **Pflegekinder**
foster child

pflegeleicht *ADJECTIVE*
1 easy to look after
2 easy-care *(fabric)*

pflegen *VERB*, *PERFECT* **hat gepflegt**
1 to look after, to care for
eine Freundschaft pflegen to foster a friendship
2 to nurse

der **Pfleger**, *PLURAL* die **Pfleger**
male nurse, care worker *(male)*

WORD TIP Professions, hobbies, and sports don't take an article in German: Er ist Pfleger.

die **Pflegerin**, *PLURAL* die **Pflegerinnen**
nurse, care worker *(female)*

WORD TIP Professions, hobbies, and sports don't take an article in German: Sie ist Pflegerin.

die **Pflicht**, *PLURAL* die **Pflichten**
1 duty
2 Pflicht sein to be compulsory
Eine Fremdsprache ist Pflicht. One foreign language is compulsory.

pflichtbewusst *ADJECTIVE*
conscientious

das **Pflichtfach**, *PLURAL* die **Pflichtfächer**
compulsory subject

pflücken *VERB*, *PERFECT* **hat gepflückt**
to pick

die **Pforte**, *PLURAL* die **Pforten**
gate

der **Pförtner**, *PLURAL* die **Pförtner**
porter, concierge *(male)*

WORD TIP Professions, hobbies, and sports don't take an article in German: Er ist Pförtner.

die **Pförtnerin**, *PLURAL* die **Pförtnerinnen**
porter, concierge *(female)*

WORD TIP Professions, hobbies, and sports don't take an article in German: Sie ist Pförtnerin.

der **Pfosten**, *PLURAL* die **Pfosten**
post, goalpost

die **Pfote**, *PLURAL* die **Pfoten**
paw

pfui *EXCLAMATION*
ugh!

℗ das **Pfund**, *PLURAL* die **Pfund(e)**
1 pound, half a kilo *(in weight)*
2 pound *(money)*

die **Pfütze**, *PLURAL* die **Pfützen**
puddle

der **Philosoph**, *PLURAL* die **Philosophen**
philosopher *(male)*

WORD TIP Professions, hobbies, and sports don't take an article in German: Er ist Philosoph.

die **Philosophie**, *PLURAL* die **Philosophien**
philosophy

die **Philosophin**, *PLURAL* die **Philosophinnen**
philosopher *(female)*

WORD TIP Professions, hobbies, and sports don't take an article in German: Sie ist Philosophin.

die **Phrase**, *PLURAL* die **Phrasen**
1 phrase
2 cliché

ℓ die **Physik**
physics

der **Physiker**, PLURAL die **Physiker**
physicist (male)

> **WORD TIP** Professions, hobbies, and sports don't take an article in German: Er ist Physiker.

die **Physikerin**, PLURAL die **Physikerinnen**
physicist (female)

> **WORD TIP** Professions, hobbies, and sports don't take an article in German: Sie ist Physikerin.

ℓ der **Pickel**, PLURAL die **Pickel**
spot, pimple

> **WORD TIP** The German word Pickel does not mean pickle in English; a German expression for pickle is eingelegtes Gemüse.

ℓ das **Picknick**, PLURAL die **Picknicks**
picnic

das **Piercing**, PLURAL die **Piercings**
piercing

das **Pik**
spades (in cards)

pikant ADJECTIVE
spicy

die **Pille**, PLURAL die **Pillen**
pill

ℓ der **Pilot**, PLURAL die **Piloten**
pilot (male)

> **WORD TIP** Professions, hobbies, and sports don't take an article in German: Er ist Pilot.

ℓ die **Pilotin**, PLURAL die **Pilotinnen**
pilot (female)

> **WORD TIP** Professions, hobbies, and sports don't take an article in German: Sie ist Pilotin.

ℓ der **Pilz**, PLURAL die **Pilze**
1 mushroom
2 fungus

der **Pinguin**, PLURAL die **Pinguine**
penguin

pinkeln VERB, PERFECT **hat gepinkelt**
(informal) to pee

die **Pinnwand**, PLURAL die **Pinnwände**
(pin)board, noticeboard

der **Pinsel**, PLURAL die **Pinsel**
brush

die **Pinzette**, PLURAL die **Pinzetten**
tweezers

der **Pirat**, PLURAL die **Piraten**
pirate (male)

die **Piratin**, PLURAL die **Piratinnen**
pirate (female)

die **Pistazie**, PLURAL die **Pistazien**
pistachio

die **Piste**, PLURAL die **Pisten**
1 run, piste
2 track
3 runway

ℓ die **Pizza**, PLURAL die **Pizzas**
pizza

der **Pkw**, PLURAL die **Pkws** ABBREVIATION
(=Personenkraftwagen) car

plagen VERB, PERFECT **hat geplagt**
1 to bother, to torment
2 to pester
3 sich plagen to struggle
In der Schule hat sie sich geplagt. She struggled at school.
Er muss sich plagen. He has to work hard.

ℓ das **Plakat**, PLURAL die **Plakate**
poster

ℓ der **Plan**, PLURAL die **Pläne**
1 plan
2 map

planen VERB, PERFECT **hat geplant**
to plan

der **Planet**, PLURAL die **Planeten**
planet

die **Planierraupe**, PLURAL die **Planierraupen**
bulldozer

planmäßig ADJECTIVE
scheduled

planmäßig ADVERB
1 according to plan
Alles läuft planmäßig. Everything is going according to plan.
2 on schedule
Der Zug ist planmäßig abgefahren. The train left on schedule.

ℓ das **Plastik**¹
plastic

die **Plastik**², PLURAL die **Plastiken**
sculpture

ℓ die **Plastiktüte**, PLURAL die **Plastiktüten**
plastic bag

das **Platin**
platinum

ℓ indicates key words

platt *ADJECTIVE*
1 flat
2 platt sein *(informal)* to be amazed

plattdeutsch *ADJECTIVE*
Low German

die **Platte**, *PLURAL* die **Platten**
1 plate
2 dish
   kalte Platte cheese and cold meat
3 hotplate
4 record
5 board *(made of wood)*
6 slab *(made of stone)*
7 sheet *(made of metal or glass)*
8 top *(of a table)*

ℓ der **Platz**, *PLURAL* die **Plätze**
1 place
   Sie stellte das Buch an seinen Platz
   zurück. She put the book back in its place.
   Auf die Plätze, fertig, los! On your marks,
   get set, go!
2 room, space
   Hier haben die Tiere viel Platz. The
   animals have plenty of room here.
   Platz lassen to leave room
3 seat
   Nehmen Sie Platz! Take a seat!
4 square *(in a town)*
5 ground, pitch
   einen Spieler vom Platz stellen to send a
   player off
6 court *(for tennis)*
7 course *(for golf)*

das **Plätzchen**, *PLURAL* die **Plätzchen**
1 biscuit
2 spot

platzen *VERB*, *PERFECT* **ist geplatzt**
1 to burst
2 vor Neugier platzen to be bursting with
   curiosity
3 *(informal)* to fall through
   Der Plan ist geplatzt. The plan fell
   through.

die **Platzkarte**, *PLURAL* die **Platzkarten**
seat reservation

plaudern *VERB*, *PERFECT* **hat geplaudert**
to chat

pleite *ADJECTIVE*
(informal) broke

die **Pleite**, *PLURAL* die **Pleiten**
1 bankruptcy
2 *(informal)* flop

die **Plombe**, *PLURAL* die **Plomben**
filling *(in a tooth)*

plombieren *VERB*, *PERFECT* **hat plombiert**
to fill *(a tooth)*

ℓ **plötzlich** *ADJECTIVE*
sudden
plötzlich *ADVERB*
suddenly

plump *ADJECTIVE*
1 plump
2 clumsy

der **Plural**, *PLURAL* die **Plurale**
plural *(in grammar)*

plus *ADVERB*
plus

das **Plus**
1 plus
2 profit
3 advantage

PLZ *ABBREVIATION*
(=Postleitzahl) postcode

der **Po**, *PLURAL* die **Pos**
(informal) bottom, backside

die **Poesie**
poetry

der **Pokal**, *PLURAL* die **Pokale**
1 cup
2 goblet

das **Pokalspiel**, *PLURAL* die **Pokalspiele**
cup tie

der **Pole**, *PLURAL* die **Polen**
Pole *(male)*

ℓ **Polen** *NEUTER NOUN*
Poland

polieren *VERB*, *PERFECT* **hat poliert**
to polish

die **Polin**, *PLURAL* die **Polinnen**
Pole *(female)*

ℓ die **Politik**
1 politics
   Interessierst du dich für Politik? Are you
   interested in politics?
2 policy, policies
   Wie findest du die Politik dieser Partei?
   What do you think of this party's policies?

ℓ der **Politiker**, *PLURAL* die **Politiker**
politician *(male)*

WORD TIP Professions, hobbies, and sports
don't take an article in German: Er ist Politiker.

◇ **irregular verb**; *SEP* **separable verb**; for more help with verbs see centre section

ℓ die **Politikerin**, PLURAL die **Politikerinnen**
politician *(female)*

> **WORD TIP** Professions, hobbies, and sports don't take an article in German: Sie ist Politikerin.

politisch ADJECTIVE
political

die **Politur**, PLURAL die **Polituren**
polish

ℓ die **Polizei**
police

polizeilich ADJECTIVE
police
polizeilich ADVERB
1 by the police
2 sich polizeilich anmelden to register with the police

das **Polizeirevier**, PLURAL die **Polizeireviere**
police station

die **Polizeiwache**, PLURAL die
Polizeiwachen
police station

ℓ der **Polizist**, PLURAL die **Polizisten**
policeman

> **WORD TIP** Professions, hobbies, and sports don't take an article in German: Er ist Polizist.

ℓ die **Polizistin**, PLURAL die **Polizistinnen**
policewoman

> **WORD TIP** Professions, hobbies, and sports don't take an article in German: Sie ist Polizistin.

polnisch ADJECTIVE
Polish

> **WORD TIP** Adjectives never have capitals in German, even for regions, countries, or nationalities.

ℓ die **Pommes frites** PLURAL NOUN
chips, French fries

das **Pony¹**, PLURAL die **Ponys**
pony

der **Pony²**, PLURAL die **Ponys**
fringe

die **Popgruppe**, PLURAL die **Popgruppen**
pop group

das **Popkonzert**, PLURAL die **Popkonzerte**
pop concert

die **Popmusik**
pop music

poppig ADJECTIVE
jazzy
Natalie hat immer poppige Socken an.
Natalie always wears jazzy socks.

der **Popstar**, PLURAL die **Popstars**
pop star

der **Porree**
leek
eine Stange Porree a leek

das **Portemonnaie**, PLURAL die
Portemonnaies
purse

der **Portier**, PLURAL die **Portiers**
porter, doorman

> **WORD TIP** Professions, hobbies, and sports don't take an article in German: Er ist Portier.

ℓ die **Portion**, PLURAL die **Portionen**
portion
Möchtest du eine zweite Portion? Would you like a second helping?

das **Portmonee** ▸ SEE **Portemonnaie**

das **Porto**
postage

das **Porträt**, PLURAL die **Porträts**
portrait

ℓ **Portugal** NEUTER NOUN
Portugal

der **Portugiese**, PLURAL die **Portugiesen**
Portuguese *(male)*

die **Portugiesin**, PLURAL die **Portugiesinnen**
Portuguese *(female)*

portugiesisch ADJECTIVE
Portuguese

> **WORD TIP** Adjectives never have capitals in German, even for regions, countries, or nationalities.

das **Porzellan**
china, porcelain

die **Posaune**, PLURAL die **Posaunen**
trombone
Sam spielt Posaune. Sam plays the trombone.

ℓ die **Post**
1 post
mit der Post by post
2 post office

das **Postamt**, PLURAL die **Postämter**
post office

♂ der **Postbote**, *PLURAL* die **Postboten**
postman

> **WORD TIP** Professions, hobbies, and sports
> don't take an article in German: Er ist Postbote.

♀ die **Postbotin**, *PLURAL* die **Postbotinnen**
postwoman

> **WORD TIP** Professions, hobbies, and sports don't
> take an article in German: Sie ist Postbotin.

♂ das **Poster**, *PLURAL* die **Poster**
poster

das **Postfach**, *PLURAL* die **Postfächer**
1 PO box
2 mailbox *(email)*

♀ die **Postkarte**, *PLURAL* die **Postkarten**
postcard

die **Postleitzahl**, *PLURAL* die **Postleitzahlen**
postcode

die **Pracht**
splendour

prächtig *ADJECTIVE*
splendid

Prag *NEUTER NOUN*
Prague

prahlen *VERB*, *PERFECT* **hat geprahlt**
to boast

das **Praktikum**, *PLURAL* die **Praktika**
work experience
ein Praktikum machen to do work
experience

praktisch *ADJECTIVE*
1 practical
Er hat keine praktische Erfahrung. He has
no practical experience.
2 handy
3 ein praktischer Arzt a general practitioner
praktisch *ADVERB*
1 practically
2 in practice

die **Praline**, *PLURAL* die **Pralinen**
chocolate

die **Präposition**, *PLURAL* die **Präpositionen**
preposition *(in grammar)*

das **Präsens**
present (tense) *(in grammar)*

das **Präservativ**, *PLURAL* die **Präservative**
condom

der **Präsident**, *PLURAL* die **Präsidenten**
president *(male)*

> **WORD TIP** Professions, hobbies, and sports
> don't take an article in German: Er ist Präsident.

die **Präsidentin**, *PLURAL* die **Präsidentinnen**
president *(female)*

> **WORD TIP** Professions, hobbies, and sports don't
> take an article in German: Sie ist Präsidentin.

die **Praxis**, *PLURAL* die **Praxen**
1 practice
2 practical experience
3 surgery

♂ der **Preis**, *PLURAL* die **Preise**
1 price
um keinen Preis not at any price
2 prize

das **Preisausschreiben**, *PLURAL* die
Preisausschreiben
competition

die **Preiselbeere**, *PLURAL* die **Preiselbeeren**
cranberry

♀ **preiswert** *ADJECTIVE*
reasonable, cheap

die **Prellung**, *PLURAL* die **Prellungen**
bruise

der **Premierminister**, *PLURAL* die
Premierminister
prime minister *(male)*

> **WORD TIP** Professions, hobbies, and sports
> don't take an article in German: Er ist
> Premierminister.

die **Premierministerin**, *PLURAL* die
Premierministerinnen
prime minister *(female)*

> **WORD TIP** Professions, hobbies, and sports
> don't take an article in German: Sie ist
> Premierministerin.

die **Presse**
press

der **Priester**, *PLURAL* die **Priester**
priest

> **WORD TIP** Professions, hobbies, and sports
> don't take an article in German: Er ist Priester.

♀ **prima** *ADJECTIVE*
(informal) great, fantastic

der **Prinz**, *PLURAL* die **Prinzen**
prince

◇ irregular verb; *SEP* separable verb; for more help with verbs see centre section

die **Prinzessin**, PLURAL die **Prinzessinnen**
princess

die **Priorität**, PLURAL die **Prioritäten**
priority

die **Prise**, PLURAL die **Prisen**
pinch
eine Prise Salz a pinch of salt

privat ADJECTIVE
private

die **Privatschule**, PLURAL die **Privatschulen**
private school

das **Privileg**, PLURAL die **Privilegien**
privilege

ℙ **pro** PREPOSITION (+ ACC)
per
pro Tag per day

die **Probe**, PLURAL die **Proben**
1 test
jemanden auf die Probe stellen to test
somebody
ein Auto Probe fahren to test drive a car
2 sample
3 rehearsal

ℙ **probieren** VERB, PERFECT **hat probiert**
1 to try
2 to taste

ℙ das **Problem**, PLURAL die **Probleme**
problem

das **Produkt**, PLURAL die **Produkte**
product

der **Produzent**, PLURAL die **Produzenten**
1 maker, manufacturer
2 (film) producer (male)

die **Produzentin**, PLURAL die
Produzentinnen
(film) producer (female)

ℙ **produzieren** VERB, PERFECT **hat produziert**
to produce

der **Profi**, PLURAL die **Profis**
pro, professional

das **Profil**, PLURAL die **Profile**
1 profile
2 tread (of a tyre)

profitieren VERB, PERFECT **hat profitiert**
to profit

ℙ das **Programm**, PLURAL die **Programme**
1 programme
2 program (in computing)
3 channel (on TV)

programmieren VERB, PERFECT **hat
programmiert**
to program

der **Programmierer**, PLURAL die
Programmierer
programmer (male)

WORD TIP Professions, hobbies, and sports don't
take an article in German: Er ist Programmierer.

die **Programmiererin**, PLURAL die
Programmiererinnen
programmer (female)

WORD TIP Professions, hobbies, and sports
don't take an article in German: Sie ist
Programmiererin.

das **Projekt**, PLURAL die **Projekte**
project

der **Projektor**, PLURAL die **Projektoren**
projector

das **Promille**, PLURAL die **Promille**
alcohol level
zu viel Promille haben to be over the limit

der/die **Prominente**, PLURAL die
Prominenten
1 celebrity
2 VIP

das **Pronomen**, PLURAL die **Pronomen**,
Pronomina
pronoun (in grammar)

prosit EXCLAMATION
cheers!
prosit Neujahr! Happy New Year!

der **Prospekt**, PLURAL die **Prospekte**
brochure

WORD TIP The German word Prospekt does not
mean prospect in English; the German word for
prospect is Aussicht.

prost EXCLAMATION
cheers!

das **Protein**, PLURAL die **Proteine**
protein

der **Protest**, PLURAL die **Proteste**
protest

der **Protestant**, PLURAL die **Protestanten**
Protestant (male)

die **Protestantin**, PLURAL die
Protestantinnen
Protestant (female)

ℙ indicates key words

protestantisch ADJECTIVE
Protestant

> **WORD TIP** Adjectives never have capitals in German, even for religions.

protestieren VERB, PERFECT **hat protestiert**
to protest

das Protokoll, PLURAL die **Protokolle**
1 minutes (of a meeting)
2 record (in court)
3 report
4 statement (to the police)
5 protocol

protzen VERB, PERFECT **hat geprotzt**
to show off
Klaus protzt mit seinem neuen Auto.
Klaus is showing off in his new car.

der Proviant
provisions

das Prozent, PLURAL die **Prozente**
1 per cent
zehn Prozent ten per cent
2 Prozente bekommen (informal) to get a discount

der Prozentsatz, PLURAL die **Prozentsätze**
percentage

der Prozess, PLURAL die **Prozesse**
1 court case
Er hat den Prozess gewonnen. He won the case.
2 trial
3 process

die Prozession, PLURAL die **Prozessionen**
procession

prüfen VERB, PERFECT **hat geprüft**
1 to test, to examine (at school)
2 to check
Hast du die Reifen geprüft? Have you checked the tyres?

℘ **die Prüfung**, PLURAL die **Prüfungen**
1 examination, exam
eine Prüfung machen to take an exam
Sie ist durch die Prüfung gefallen. She failed the exam.
Hat er die Prüfung bestanden? Did he pass the exam?
2 check

der Prügel, PLURAL die **Prügel**
1 stick
2 beating
Prügel bekommen to get a beating

die Prügelei, PLURAL die **Prügeleien**
fight

prügeln VERB, PERFECT **hat geprügelt**
1 to beat
2 sich prügeln to fight
sich um etwas prügeln to fight for something

der Psychiater, PLURAL die **Psychiater**
psychiatrist (male)

> **WORD TIP** Professions, hobbies, and sports don't take an article in German: Er ist Psychiater.

die Psychiaterin, PLURAL die **Psychiaterinnen**
psychiatrist (female)

> **WORD TIP** Professions, hobbies, and sports don't take an article in German: Sie ist Psychiaterin.

psychisch ADJECTIVE
psychological

der Psychologe, PLURAL die **Psychologen**
psychologist (male)

> **WORD TIP** Professions, hobbies, and sports don't take an article in German: Er ist Psychologe.

die Psychologie
psychology

die Psychologin, PLURAL die **Psychologinnen**
psychologist (female)

> **WORD TIP** Professions, hobbies, and sports don't take an article in German: Sie ist Psychologin.

das Publikum
1 audience, crowd
2 public

der Pudding, PLURAL die **Puddinge**
blancmange

der Pudel, PLURAL die **Pudel**
poodle

der Puder, PLURAL die **Puder**
powder

der Puffmais
popcorn

der Pulli, PLURAL die **Pullis**
pullover

℘ **der Pullover**, PLURAL die **Pullover**
pullover

der Puls, PLURAL die **Pulse**
pulse

Der Arzt maß meinen Puls. The doctor took my pulse.

das **Pult**, PLURAL die **Pulte**
desk

das **Pulver**, PLURAL die **Pulver**
powder

der **Pulverkaffee**
instant coffee

die **Pumpe**, PLURAL die **Pumpen**
pump

pumpen VERB, PERFECT **hat gepumpt**
1 to pump
2 (informal) to lend
jemandem Geld pumpen to lend somebody money
3 (informal) to borrow
sich etwas pumpen to borrow something

der **Punker**, PLURAL die **Punker**
punk (male)

die **Punkerin**, PLURAL die **Punkerinnen**
punk (female)

⟋ der **Punkt**, PLURAL die **Punkte**
1 dot, spot
Wir treffen uns Punkt sechs Uhr. We'll meet at six on the dot.
2 full stop
3 point
Er siegte nach Punkten. He won on points.

⟋ **pünktlich** ADJECTIVE
punctual

die **Puppe**, PLURAL die **Puppen**
1 doll
2 puppet

pur ADJECTIVE
1 pure
2 neat
Whisky pur neat whisky

der **Purzelbaum**, PLURAL die **Purzelbäume**
somersault

pusten VERB, PERFECT **hat gepustet**
to blow

die **Pute**, PLURAL die **Puten**
turkey

⟋ **putzen** VERB, PERFECT **hat geputzt**
1 to clean
Er hat die ganze Wohnung geputzt. He's cleaned the whole flat.
Putz dir die Zähne! Brush your teeth!
Sie geht putzen, um sich das Studium zu finanzieren. She works as a cleaner to pay

for her university course.
2 sich die Nase putzen to blow your nose

die **Putzfrau**, PLURAL die **Putzfrauen**
cleaner, cleaning lady

WORD TIP Professions, hobbies, and sports don't take an article in German: Sie ist Putzfrau.

putzig ADJECTIVE
cute

der **Putzmann**, PLURAL die **Putzmänner**
cleaner (male)

WORD TIP Professions, hobbies, and sports don't take an article in German: Er ist Putzmann.

das **Puzzle**, PLURAL die **Puzzles**
jigsaw (puzzle)

der **Pyjama**, PLURAL die **Pyjamas**
(pair of) pyjamas

WORD TIP In German, der Pyjama is singular: Der Pyjama ist neu.

die **Pyramide**, PLURAL die **Pyramiden**
pyramid

die **Pyrenäen** (plural noun)
die Pyrenäen the Pyrenees

Qq

das **Quadrat**, PLURAL die **Quadrate**
square

quadratisch ADJECTIVE
square

der **Quadratmeter**, PLURAL die **Quadratmeter**
square metre

quaken VERB, PERFECT **hat gequakt**
1 to quack (of a duck)
2 to croak (of a frog)

die **Qual**, PLURAL die **Qualen**
1 torment
2 agony
Es war eine Qual, das ansehen zu müssen. It was agony to watch.

quälen VERB, PERFECT **hat gequält**
1 to torment
2 to torture
3 to pester
4 sich quälen to suffer
5 sich mit etwas quälen to struggle with something

⟋ indicates key words

Ich habe mich durch das Buch gequält. I struggled (my way) through the book.

der **Quälgeist**, *PLURAL* die **Quälgeister** *(informal)* pest

die **Qualifikation**, *PLURAL* die **Qualifikationen** qualification

qualifizieren *VERB*, *PERFECT* **hat qualifiziert** sich qualifizieren to qualify Sie haben sich für die dritte Runde qualifiziert. They qualified for the third round.

qualifiziert *ADJECTIVE* qualified

die **Qualität**, *PLURAL* die **Qualitäten** quality

die **Qualle**, *PLURAL* die **Quallen** jellyfish

der **Qualm** thick smoke

qualmen *VERB*, *PERFECT* **hat gequalmt**
1 to give off clouds of smoke
2 *(informal)* to smoke
Sie qualmt wie ein Schlot. She smokes like a chimney.

die **Quarantäne** quarantine

der **Quark** curd cheese, quark

das **Quartett**, *PLURAL* die **Quartette** quartet

das **Quartier**, *PLURAL* die **Quartiere**
1 accommodation
2 quarters

quasseln *VERB*, *PERFECT* **hat gequasselt** *(informal)* to natter

ℓ der **Quatsch** *(informal)* rubbish

quatschen *VERB*, *PERFECT* **hat gequatscht** *(informal)* to chat

die **Quelle**, *PLURAL* die **Quellen**
1 source
2 spring

quer *ADVERB*
1 across
2 at right angles
quer zur Straße at right angles to the road
quer gestreift with horizontal stripes
3 quer durch straight through

die **Querflöte**, *PLURAL* die **Querflöten** flute

die **Querstraße**, *PLURAL* die **Querstraßen** side street
Das Geschäft liegt in einer kleinen Querstraße. The shop is in a small side street.
Biegen Sie in die erste Querstraße rechts ein. Take the first turning on the right.

quetschen *VERB*, *PERFECT* **hat gequetscht**
1 to crush
2 to squash
3 sich quetschen to squeeze
Ich habe mich in meine Jeans gequetscht. I squeezed into my jeans.

quietschen *VERB*, *PERFECT* **hat gequietscht** to squeak

quitt *ADJECTIVE* quits
Jetzt bin ich mit ihm quitt. Now I'm quits with him.

ℓ die **Quittung**, *PLURAL* die **Quittungen** receipt

das **Quiz**, *PLURAL* die **Quiz** quiz

Rr

der **Rabatt**, *PLURAL* die **Rabatte** discount

die **Rache** revenge

rächen *VERB*, *PERFECT* **hat gerächt**
1 to avenge
2 sich an jemandem rächen to take revenge on somebody
3 Das wird sich rächen. You'll have to pay for it.

ℓ das **Rad**, *PLURAL* die **Räder**
1 wheel
2 bike
Julia ist mit dem Rad gekommen. Julia came by bike.
3 Rad fahren to cycle

der or das **Radar** radar

die **Radarkontrolle**, *PLURAL* die **Radarkontrollen** (radar-controlled) speed check

◇ **irregular verb;** *SEP* **separable verb; for more help with verbs see centre section**

der **Radarschirm**, PLURAL die **Radarschirme**
radar screen

radeln VERB, PERFECT **ist geradelt**
to cycle
Max ist ins Dorf geradelt. Max cycled into the village.

der **Radfahrer**, PLURAL die **Radfahrer**
cyclist (male)

die **Radfahrerin**, PLURAL die **Radfahrerinnen**
cyclist (female)

ℙ der **Radiergummi**, PLURAL die **Radiergummis**
rubber

das **Radieschen**, PLURAL die **Radieschen**
radish

ℙ das **Radio**, PLURAL die **Radios**
radio

radioaktiv ADJECTIVE
radioactive

die **Radioaktivität**
radioactivity

ℙ der **Radiosender**, PLURAL die **Radiosender**
radio station

ℙ die **Radiosendung**, PLURAL die **Radiosendungen**
radio programme

der **Radler**, PLURAL die **Radler**
cyclist (male)

die **Radlerin**, PLURAL die **Radlerinnen**
cyclist (female)

das **Radrennen**, PLURAL die **Radrennen**
1 cycle race
Maria hat das Radrennen gewonnen. Maria won the cycle race.
2 cycle racing
Radrennen ist Toms Lieblingssport. Cycle racing is Tom's favourite sport.

ℙ die **Radtour**, PLURAL die **Radtouren**
bike ride, cycling tour
Wir machen morgen eine Radtour. We're going on a bike ride tomorrow.

ℙ der **Radweg**, PLURAL die **Radwege**
cycle path, cycle track

raffiniert ADJECTIVE
crafty

der **Rahm**
(used in Southern Germany, Austria, and Switzerland) cream

rahmen VERB, PERFECT **hat gerahmt**
to frame (a picture)

der **Rahmen**, PLURAL die **Rahmen**
1 frame
2 framework
3 limits
im Rahmen des Möglichen within the bounds of possibility

die **Rakete**, PLURAL die **Raketen**
rocket

ran (informal) ▸ SEE **heran**

der **Rand**, PLURAL die **Ränder**
1 edge
Die Kinder sprangen vom Rand des Beckens ins Wasser. The children jumped into the water from the edge of the pool.
2 rim
Der Rand der Tasse war angeschlagen. The rim of the cup was chipped.
3 ring
In der Badewanne war ein schmutziger Rand. There was a dirty ring round the bath.
4 margin (of a page)
Du musst einen Rand für die Korrekturen lassen. You need to leave a margin for the corrections.
5 outskirts (of a town)
6 etwas am Rande erwähnen to mention something in passing
7 am Rande der Pleite sein to be on the verge of bankruptcy
8 außer Rand und Band geraten (informal) to go wild

der **Randstreifen**, PLURAL die **Randstreifen**
hard shoulder

der **Rang**, PLURAL die **Ränge**
1 rank
2 (in a theatre) circle

rannte ▸ SEE **rennen**

der **Rappen**, PLURAL die **Rappen**
centime (one hundredth of a Swiss franc)

rasch ADJECTIVE
quick
rasch ADVERB
quickly

rasen VERB, PERFECT **ist gerast**
1 to tear along, to rush
Sie raste nach Hause. She rushed home.
2 to crash
Er raste gegen eine Mauer. He crashed into a wall.

ℙ indicates key words

ℓ der **Rasen**, PLURAL die **Rasen**
lawn, grass

der **Rasenmäher**, PLURAL die **Rasenmäher**
lawnmower

der **Rasierapparat**, PLURAL die
Rasierapparate
1 shaver
2 razor

die **Rasiercreme**, PLURAL die **Rasiercremes**
shaving cream

rasieren VERB, PERFECT **hat rasiert**
1 to shave
2 sich rasieren to shave

die **Rasierklinge**, PLURAL die **Rasierklingen**
razor blade

das **Rasierwasser**
aftershave

die **Rasse**, PLURAL die **Rassen**
1 race
2 breed
Ich weiß nicht, was für eine Rasse unser
Hund ist. I don't know what breed our
dog is.

der **Rassenhass**
racial hatred

das **Rassenvorurteil**, PLURAL die
Rassenvorurteile
racial prejudice

rassisch ADJECTIVE
racial

der **Rassismus**
racism

der **Rassist**, PLURAL die **Rassisten**
racist *(male)*

die **Rassistin**, PLURAL die **Rassistinnen**
racist *(female)*

rassistisch ADJECTIVE
racist

rasten VERB, PERFECT **hat gerastet**
to rest

das **Rasthaus**, PLURAL die **Rasthäuser**
services *(on a motorway)*

der **Rasthof**, PLURAL die **Rasthöfe**
services *(on a motorway)*

der **Rastplatz**, PLURAL die **Rastplätze**
picnic area

die **Raststätte**, PLURAL die **Raststätten**
services *(on a motorway)*

der **Rat**
1 advice
Er gab mir einen Rat. He gave me a piece
of advice.
Frag doch mal deine Freundin um Rat. Ask
your friend for advice.
2 Ich weiß (mir) keinen Rat. I don't know
what to do.
3 council

ℓ die **Rate**, PLURAL die **Raten**
instalment
Sie zahlen das Auto in monatlichen Raten
ab. They're paying for the car in monthly
instalments.

ℓ **raten** VERB◇, PRESENT **rät**, IMPERFECT **riet**, PERFECT
hat geraten
1 jemandem raten to advise somebody
Sie hat mir geraten, mit meinem Lehrer
darüber zu sprechen. She advised me to
talk to my teacher about it.
Was rätst du mir? What do you advise me
to do?
2 to guess
Du hast richtig geraten. You guessed right.

ℓ das **Ratespiel**, PLURAL die **Ratespiele**
guessing game, quiz

ℓ das **Rathaus**, PLURAL die **Rathäuser**
town hall

rationell ADJECTIVE
efficient

ratlos ADJECTIVE, ADVERB
helpless(ly)
Emma sah mich ratlos an. Emma looked at
me helplessly.
Wir waren ratlos. We didn't know what
to do.

ratsam ADJECTIVE
advisable
Es wäre ratsam, früher zu fahren. It would
be advisable to leave earlier.

der **Ratschlag**, PLURAL die **Ratschläge**
piece of advice, advice
Deine klugen Ratschläge kannst du dir
sparen. You can keep your advice to
yourself.

das **Rätsel**, PLURAL die **Rätsel**
1 puzzle, riddle
2 mystery

rätselhaft ADJECTIVE
mysterious

die **Ratte**, PLURAL die **Ratten**
rat

◇ **irregular verb;** SEP **separable verb; for more help with verbs see centre section**

rau *ADJECTIVE*
1 rough
2 harsh
3 Sie hat eine raue Stimme. She has a husky voice.
4 Ich habe einen rauen Hals. I've got a sore throat.

der **Raub**
robbery

der **Raubdruck**, PLURAL die **Raubdrucke**
pirated edition

der **Räuber**, PLURAL die **Räuber**
robber

der **Rauch**
smoke

ℱ **rauchen** *VERB*, *PERFECT* **hat geraucht**
to smoke
'Rauchen verboten' 'No smoking'

das **Rauchen**
smoking
passives Rauchen passive smoking

der **Raucher**, PLURAL die **Raucher**
smoker *(male)*
Er ist Raucher. He's a smoker.

die **Raucherin**, PLURAL die **Raucherinnen**
smoker *(female)*
Sie ist Raucherin. She's a smoker.

der **Räucherlachs**
smoked salmon

räuchern *VERB*, *PERFECT* **hat geräuchert**
to smoke *(fish, meat)*

das **Rauchverbot**, PLURAL die **Rauchverbote**
smoking ban

rauf
(informal)
▶SEE **herauf, hinauf**

der **Raum**, PLURAL die **Räume**
1 room
Das Haus hat sehr große Räume. The house has very big rooms.
2 space
Wir brauchen mehr Raum. We need more space.
3 Die Rakete ist im Raum explodiert. The rocket exploded in space.
4 area
Sie wohnt im Raum Berlin. She lives in the Berlin area.

räumen *VERB*, *PERFECT* **hat geräumt**
1 to clear
Ich räumte das Geschirr vom Tisch. I cleared away the dishes.
2 to put
Kannst du die Hemden in den Schrank räumen? Can you put the shirts in the cupboard?
Er räumte seine Sachen beiseite. He put his things to one side.
Sie räumte die Akten aus dem Schrank. She took the files out of the cabinet.
3 to vacate
Wir müssen bis zehn Uhr die Zimmer räumen. We have to vacate our rooms by ten o'clock.

die **Raumfahrt**
space travel

das **Raumschiff**, PLURAL die **Raumschiffe**
spaceship

der **Räumungsverkauf**
clearance sale, closing-down sale

die **Raupe**, PLURAL die **Raupen**
caterpillar

raus
(informal)
▶SEE **heraus, hinaus**

das **Rauschgift**, PLURAL die **Rauschgifte**
drug
Rauschgift nehmen to take drugs

der/die **Rauschgiftsüchtige**, PLURAL die **Rauschgiftsüchtigen**
drug addict

rauskriegen *VERB (informal)*, *PERFECT* **hat rausgekriegt**
1 to get out
Ich kriege den Splitter nicht raus. I can't get the splinter out.
2 to find out
Sie hat unser Geheimnis rausgekriegt. She found out our secret.
3 Ich kann die Aufgabe nicht rauskriegen. I can't do the exercise.

räuspern *VERB*, *PERFECT* **hat sich geräuspert**
sich räuspern to clear your throat

reagieren *VERB*, *PERFECT* **hat reagiert**
to react

die **Reaktion**, PLURAL die **Reaktionen**
reaction

realisieren *VERB*, *PERFECT* **hat realisiert**
1 to achieve *(a goal)*
2 to fulfil *(a dream)*
3 to carry out *(a plan)*
4 to realize

231

die **Realityshow**, PLURAL die **Realityshows**
reality show

ℰ die **Realschule**, PLURAL die **Realschulen**
secondary (modern) school (specializing in technical and business subjects)

rebellieren VERB, PERFECT **hat rebelliert**
to rebel

der **Rechen**, PLURAL die **Rechen**
rake

ℰ die **Recherche**, PLURAL die **Recherchen**
1 **investigation**
2 **research**

rechnen VERB, PERFECT **hat gerechnet**
1 **to do arithmetic**
Peter kann gut rechnen. Peter's good at arithmetic.
Ich kann nicht gut rechnen. I'm no good at figures.
2 **to reckon**
mit etwas rechnen to reckon with something
Er wird zu den besten Schauspielern gerechnet. He's reckoned to be one of the best actors.
3 **to count**
Ich rechne dich zu meinen Freunden. I count you as a friend.
4 mit etwas rechnen to expect something
5 auf jemanden rechnen to count on somebody

ℰ der **Rechner**, PLURAL die **Rechner**
1 **calculator**
2 **computer**

ℰ die **Rechnung**, PLURAL die **Rechnungen**
1 **bill**
2 **invoice**
Die Rechnung liegt bei. The invoice is enclosed.
3 **calculation**

recht ADJECTIVE
1 **right**
Er kam im rechten Augenblick. He came at the right moment.
2 jemandem recht sein to be all right with somebody
Wenn es dir recht ist, kommen wir um vier. If it's all right with you, we'll come at four.
3 der/die Rechte the right man/woman
4 das Rechte the right thing
5 etwas Rechtes something proper
Ich habe heute nichts Rechtes gegessen. I haven't had a proper meal today.
etwas Rechtes lernen to learn a proper

trade
6 **real**
Ich habe keine rechte Lust. I don't really feel like it.

recht ADVERB
1 **correctly**
Wenn ich Sie recht verstehe, ... If I understand you correctly, ...
2 **quite**
Das ist recht einfach. It's quite simple.
3 **really**
Ich weiß nicht recht, was ich machen soll. I don't really know what to do.
4 Recht vielen Dank! Many thanks!
5 Das geschieht dir recht! (It) serves you right!
6 es jemandem recht machen to please somebody
Man kann es nicht allen recht machen. You can't please everyone.

ℰ das **Recht**, PLURAL die **Rechte**
1 **law**
Das ist nach deutschem Recht nicht erlaubt. It's illegal under German law.
2 **right**
Er hat ein Recht auf dieses Geld. He's got a right to this money.
Recht haben to be right
im Recht sein to be in the right
Recht bekommen to be proved right
3 jemandem Recht geben to agree with somebody
Da muss ich dir Recht geben. I have to agree with you there.
4 mit Recht rightly
Du hast dich mit Recht beschwert. You were right to complain.

rechte ▸ SEE **rechter**

die **Rechte**
1 **right (side)**
Zu meiner Rechten stand Daniel. Daniel was standing on my right.
2 **right hand**
3 die Rechte the right (in politics)

das **Rechteck**, PLURAL die **Rechtecke**
rectangle

rechteckig ADJECTIVE
rectangular

ℰ **rechter, rechte, rechtes** ADJECTIVE
1 **right**
Sie hat sich den rechten Fuß verstaucht. She sprained her right ankle.
auf der rechten Seite on the right
2 **right-wing**
Rechtspartei right-wing party

◇ irregular verb; SEP separable verb; for more help with verbs see centre section

rechtfertigen *VERB, PERFECT* **hat gerechtfertigt**
1 to justify
2 sich rechtfertigen to justify yourself

rechthaberisch *ADJECTIVE*
self-opinionated

rechtlich *ADJECTIVE*
legal

ℓ **rechts** *ADVERB*
on the right
Nimm die dritte Abzweigung rechts. Take the third turning on the right.
von rechts from the right
rechts abbiegen to turn right

ℓ der **Rechtsanwalt**, *PLURAL* die **Rechtsanwälte**
lawyer *(male)*

> **WORD TIP** Professions, hobbies, and sports don't take an article in German: Er ist Rechtsanwalt.

ℓ die **Rechtsanwältin**, *PLURAL* die **Rechtsanwältinnen**
lawyer *(female)*

> **WORD TIP** Professions, hobbies, and sports don't take an article in German: Sie ist Rechtsanwältin.

die **Rechtschreibprüfung**, *PLURAL* die **Rechtschreibprüfungen**
spellchecker

die **Rechtschreibreform**, *PLURAL* die **Rechtschreibreformen**
spelling reform

⊙ RECHTSCHREIBREFORM

German spelling reform. In 1996 the German-speaking countries signed an agreement on new German spelling rules. These new rules are compulsory only in schools as there is no law relating to orthography. Since then Germany and Austria have made a number of changes to the rules. However, Germany, but not Austria, reversed some of the 1996 changes. As a result, German spelling follows the Duden dictionary, while Austrian school teachers have to consult the Österreichisches Wörterbuch instead. Switzerland has been in a different position from the beginning as there have always been some differences in Swiss German. For example, the letter 'ß' was never used.

die **Rechtschreibung**
spelling

der **Rechtshänder**, *PLURAL* die **Rechtshänder**
Klaus ist Rechtshänder. Klaus is right-handed.

die **Rechtshänderin**, *PLURAL* die **Rechtshänderinnen**
Beate ist Rechtshänderin. Beate is right-handed.

rechtzeitig *ADJECTIVE*
timely, prompt
rechtzeitig *ADVERB*
in time
Wir sind gerade noch rechtzeitig angekommen. We got there just in time.

recyceln *VERB, PERFECT* **hat recycelt**
to recycle

das **Recyclingpapier**
recycled paper

der **Redakteur**, *PLURAL* die **Redakteure**
editor *(male)*

> **WORD TIP** Professions, hobbies, and sports don't take an article in German: Er ist Redakteur.

die **Redakteurin**, *PLURAL* die **Redakteurinnen**
editor *(female)*

> **WORD TIP** Professions, hobbies, and sports don't take an article in German: Sie ist Redakteurin.

die **Rede**, *PLURAL* die **Reden**
1 speech
Er hielt eine kurze Rede. He made a short speech.
2 Es ist nicht der Rede wert. It's not worth mentioning.
3 Davon kann keine Rede sein. It's out of the question.
4 jemanden zur Rede stellen to take somebody to task

ℓ **reden** *VERB, PERFECT* **hat geredet**
1 to talk
Wir haben über die Schule geredet. We talked about school.
Ich möchte mit dir reden. I'd like to talk to you.
2 to speak
Chris redet nicht mehr mit Anna. Chris isn't speaking to Anna any more.
3 to say
Sie hat kein Wort geredet. She didn't say a word.
Mir ist egal, was über mich geredet wird. I don't care what people say about me.

die **Redewendung**, *PLURAL* die **Redewendungen**
idiom, expression

redigieren *VERB, PERFECT* **hat redigiert**
to edit

redlich *ADJECTIVE*
honest

die **Redlichkeit**
honesty

der **Redner**, *PLURAL* die **Redner**
speaker *(male)*

die **Rednerin**, *PLURAL* die **Rednerinnen**
speaker *(female)*

reduzieren *VERB*, *PERFECT* **hat reduziert**
to reduce

reduziert *ADJECTIVE*
reduced

reflexiv *ADJECTIVE*
reflexive *(in grammar)*

das **Reformhaus**, *PLURAL* die **Reformhäuser**
health food shop

⋔ das **Regal**, *PLURAL* die **Regale**
1 shelf
2 shelves, bookcase

⋔ die **Regel**, *PLURAL* die **Regeln**
1 rule
   in der Regel as a rule
2 period *(menstruation)*

⋔ **regelmäßig** *ADJECTIVE*
regular

regeln *VERB*, *PERFECT* **hat geregelt**
1 to regulate
2 to direct *(the traffic)*
3 to settle *(a matter)*
   Wir haben die Sache so geregelt, dass …
   We've arranged things so that …
4 Das wird sich von selbst regeln. It'll sort
   itself out.

die **Regelung**, *PLURAL* die **Regelungen**
1 regulation
2 settlement

⋔ der **Regen**
rain

der **Regenbogen**, *PLURAL* die **Regenbogen**
rainbow

der **Regenmantel**, *PLURAL* die **Regenmäntel**
raincoat

der **Regenschauer**, *PLURAL* die
Regenschauer
shower

⋔ der **Regenschirm**, *PLURAL* die **Regenschirme**
umbrella

der **Regenwald**, *PLURAL* die **Regenwälder**
rain forest

der **Regenwurm**, *PLURAL* die **Regenwürmer**
earthworm

regieren *VERB*, *PERFECT* **hat regiert**
1 to govern
2 to rule, to reign

die **Regierung**, *PLURAL* die **Regierungen**
1 government
2 reign

der **Regisseur**, *PLURAL* die **Regisseure**
director *(film or theatre)* *(male)*

> **WORD TIP** Professions, hobbies, and sports
> don't take an article in German: Er ist Regisseur.

die **Regisseurin**, *PLURAL* die **Regisseurinnen**
director *(film or theatre)* *(female)*

> **WORD TIP** Professions, hobbies, and sports don't
> take an article in German: Sie ist Regisseurin.

das **Register**, *PLURAL* die **Register**
1 index
2 register

⋔ **regnen** *VERB*, *PERFECT* **hat geregnet**
to rain
Es regnet. It's raining.

⋔ **regnerisch** *ADJECTIVE*
rainy

das **Reh**, *PLURAL* die **Rehe**
deer

reiben *VERB*⋔, *IMPERFECT* **rieb**, *PERFECT* **hat
gerieben**
1 to rub
2 to grate

reibungslos *ADJECTIVE*
smooth

⋔ **reich** *ADJECTIVE*
rich

das **Reich**, *PLURAL* die **Reiche**
1 empire
   das Römische Reich the Roman Empire
2 kingdom, realm

reichen *VERB*, *PERFECT* **hat gereicht**
1 to hand, to pass
   Reichen Sie mir bitte das Salz? Could you
   pass me the salt, please?
2 to be enough
   Reicht das Essen für uns alle? Is there
   enough food for all of us?
   Mein Geld reicht nicht für die Fahrkarte. I
   don't have enough money for the ticket.

⋔ irregular verb; *SEP* separable verb; for more help with verbs see centre section

3 bis zu etwas reichen to come up to something
　Er reicht seinem Vater bis zur Schulter. He comes up to his father's shoulder.
　Die Felder reichen bis zum Wald. The fields extend as far as the forest.
4 Mir reichts! *(informal)* I've had enough!

reichlich *ADJECTIVE*
1 large
2 ample *space*
reichlich *ADVERB*
　plenty of

der **Reichstag**
　Reichstag; German parliament (1871–1945)

> ● REICHSTAG
>
> The German parliament, originally built in 1894, was destroyed during the Reichskristallnacht in 1933. It was rebuilt following the reunification of Germany.

der **Reichtum**, *PLURAL* die **Reichtümer**
　wealth

die **Reichweite**
1 reach
　Streichhölzer sollte man außer Reichweite von kleinen Kindern aufbewahren. Matches should be kept out of the reach of small children.
2 range

reif *ADJECTIVE*
1 ripe
2 mature

die **Reife**
1 maturity
2 mittlere Reife exams taken after five years of secondary schooling

ℓ der **Reifen**, *PLURAL* die **Reifen**
1 tyre
2 hoop

der **Reifendruck**
　tyre pressure

ℓ die **Reifenpanne**, *PLURAL* die **Reifenpannen**
　puncture

die **Reihe**, *PLURAL* die **Reihen**
1 row
　Wir saßen in der zweiten Reihe. We sat in the second row.
2 series
　eine Reihe von Ereignissen a series of events
3 der Reihe nach in turn
　außer der Reihe out of turn

　Du bist an der Reihe. It's your turn.

ℓ die **Reihenfolge**, *PLURAL* die **Reihenfolgen**
　order
　Schreib die Zahlen in der richtigen Reihenfolge auf. Write down the numbers in the right order.

ℓ das **Reihenhaus**, *PLURAL* die **Reihenhäuser**
　terraced house

der **Reim**, *PLURAL* die **Reime**
　rhyme

reimen *VERB, PERFECT* **hat gereimt**
1 to rhyme
2 sich reimen to rhyme

rein¹ *ADJECTIVE*
1 pure
2 clean
3 sheer *(madness)*
4 Ich muss den Aufsatz noch ins Reine schreiben. I have to make a fair copy of my essay.
　etwas ins Reine bringen to sort something out
rein *ADVERB*
1 purely
2 absolutely
　Wir haben heute rein gar nichts gelernt. We learned absolutely nothing today.

rein²
　(informal)
　▶ SEE **herein, hinein**

reinigen *VERB, PERFECT* **hat gereinigt**
　to clean

die **Reinigung**, *PLURAL* die **Reinigungen**
1 cleaning
2 (dry) cleaner's

ℓ der **Reis**
　rice

ℓ die **Reise**, *PLURAL* die **Reisen**
1 journey, trip
　Gute Reise! Have a good journey!
2 Reisen travels
　Auf meinen Reisen habe ich schon viel gesehen. I've seen a lot on my travels.
3 voyage

das **Reiseandenken**, *PLURAL* die **Reiseandenken**
　souvenir

ℓ das **Reisebüro**, *PLURAL* die **Reisebüros**
　travel agency

ℓ der **Reisebus**, *PLURAL* die **Reisebusse**
　coach

235

der **Reiseführer**, *PLURAL* die **Reiseführer**
1 guidebook
2 guide, tour leader *(male)*

> **WORD TIP** Professions, hobbies, and sports don't take an article in German: Er ist Reiseführer.

die **Reiseführerin**, *PLURAL* die **Reiseführerinnen**
guide, tour leader *(female)*

> **WORD TIP** Professions, hobbies, and sports don't take an article in German: Sie ist Reiseführerin.

reisekrank *ADJECTIVE*
travel-sick
reisekrank werden to get travel-sick

♀ der **Reiseleiter**, *PLURAL* die **Reiseleiter**
guide, tour leader *(male)*

> **WORD TIP** Professions, hobbies, and sports don't take an article in German: Er ist Reiseleiter.

♀ die **Reiseleiterin**, *PLURAL* die **Reiseleiterinnen**
guide, tour leader *(female)*

> **WORD TIP** Professions, hobbies, and sports don't take an article in German: Sie ist Reiseleiterin.

♀ **reisen** *VERB*, *PERFECT* ist gereist
to travel

der/die **Reisende**, *PLURAL* die **Reisenden**
traveller

der **Reisepass**, *PLURAL* die **Reisepässe**
passport

der **Reisescheck**, *PLURAL* die **Reiseschecks**
traveller's cheque

die **Reisetasche**, *PLURAL* die **Reisetaschen**
holdall

das **Reiseziel**, *PLURAL* die **Reiseziele**
destination

reißen *VERB*◇, *IMPERFECT* riss, *PERFECT* hat gerissen
1 to tear
2 to rip
   Sie hat die Poster von den Wänden gerissen. She ripped the posters off the walls.
3 to pull
   Der Hund riss an der Leine. The dog pulled on the lead.
4 mit sich reißen to sweep away
   Die Lawine hat die Skifahrer mit sich gerissen. The avalanche swept the skiers away.
5 etwas an sich reißen to snatch something
   Der Dieb riss meine Handtasche an sich.

The thief snatched my handbag.
   Die Generäle haben die Macht an sich gerissen. The generals seized power.
6 Witze reißen to crack jokes
7 sich um etwas reißen to fight over something
   Die Leute rissen sich um die Sonderangebote. People were fighting over the bargains.
8 *PERFECT* ist gerissen to tear, to break
   Die Tüte ist gerissen. The bag is torn.
   Das Seil könnte reißen. The rope might break.

der **Reißverschluss**, *PLURAL* die **Reißverschlüsse**
zip

die **Reißzwecke**, *PLURAL* die **Reißzwecken**
drawing pin

♀ **reiten** *VERB*◇, *IMPERFECT* ritt, *PERFECT* hat/ist geritten
to ride

der **Reiter**, *PLURAL* die **Reiter**
rider *(male)*

die **Reiterin**, *PLURAL* die **Reiterinnen**
rider *(female)*

die **Reitschule**, *PLURAL* die **Reitschulen**
riding school

der **Reiz**, *PLURAL* die **Reize**
1 attraction, appeal
2 charm

reizen *VERB*, *PERFECT* hat gereizt
1 to appeal to, to tempt
   Das reizt mich sehr. It's very tempting.
2 to provoke, to tease
   Ihr dürft die Tiere nicht reizen. You mustn't tease the animals.
3 to irritate *(the skin, eyes)*
4 to bid *(when playing cards)*

reizend *ADJECTIVE*
charming

reizvoll *ADJECTIVE*
attractive

♀ die **Reklame**, *PLURAL* die **Reklamen**
1 advertising
   Die privaten Sender werden durch Reklame finanziert. The private stations are funded by advertising.
2 advertisement, advert
   für etwas Reklame machen to advertise something

der **Rekord**, *PLURAL* die **Rekorde**
record

◇ **irregular verb;** *SEP* **separable verb; for more help with verbs see centre section**

der **Rektor**, PLURAL die **Rektoren**
1 **head** (of a school) (male)
2 **vice-chancellor** (of a university) (male)

> **WORD TIP** Professions, hobbies, and sports don't take an article in German: Er ist Rektor.

die **Rektorin**, PLURAL die **Rektorinnen**
1 **head** (of a school) (female)
2 **vice-chancellor** (of a university) (female)

> **WORD TIP** Professions, hobbies, and sports don't take an article in German: Sie ist Rektorin.

relaxen VERB, PERFECT **hat relaxt**
to relax

ℙ die **Religion**, PLURAL die **Religionen**
1 **religion**
2 **religious education** (subject at school)

die **Religionslehre**
religious education (subject at school)

ℙ **religiös** ADJECTIVE
religious

das **Rendezvous**, PLURAL die **Rendezvous**
date

die **Rennbahn**, PLURAL die **Rennbahnen**
racetrack

ℙ **rennen** VERB◇, IMPERFECT **rannte**, PERFECT **ist gerannt**
to run

das **Rennen**, PLURAL die **Rennen**
race

der **Rennfahrer**, PLURAL die **Rennfahrer**
racing driver (male)

> **WORD TIP** Professions, hobbies, and sports don't take an article in German: Er ist Rennfahrer.

die **Rennfahrerin**, PLURAL die **Rennfahrerinnen**
racing driver (female)

> **WORD TIP** Professions, hobbies, and sports don't take an article in German: Sie ist Rennfahrerin.

der **Rennwagen**, PLURAL die **Rennwagen**
racing car

renovieren VERB, PERFECT **hat renoviert**
to renovate, to redecorate

rentabel ADJECTIVE
profitable

die **Rente**, PLURAL die **Renten**
1 **pension**

2 **in Rente gehen** to retire

> **WORD TIP** The German word Rente does not mean rent in English; the German word for rent is Miete.

der **Rentner**, PLURAL die **Rentner**
pensioner (male)
Er ist Rentner. He's a pensioner.

die **Rentnerin**, PLURAL die **Rentnerinnen**
pensioner (female)
Sie ist Rentnerin. She's a pensioner.

die **Reparatur**, PLURAL die **Reparaturen**
repair

die **Reparaturwerkstatt**, PLURAL die **Reparaturwerkstätten**
(repair) workshop, **garage**

ℙ **reparieren** VERB, PERFECT **hat repariert**
to repair

ℙ die **Reportage**, PLURAL die **Reportagen**
1 **report**
2 **live commentary**

ℙ der **Reporter**, PLURAL die **Reporter**
reporter (male)

> **WORD TIP** Professions, hobbies, and sports don't take an article in German: Er ist Reporter.

ℙ die **Reporterin**, PLURAL die **Reporterinnen**
reporter (female)

> **WORD TIP** Professions, hobbies, and sports don't take an article in German: Sie ist Reporterin.

das **Reptil**, PLURAL die **Reptilien**
reptile

die **Republik**, PLURAL die **Republiken**
republic

das **Reservat**, PLURAL die **Reservate**
reservation

das **Reserverad**, PLURAL die **Reserveräder**
spare wheel

ℙ **reservieren** VERB, PERFECT **hat reserviert**
to reserve

ℙ die **Reservierung**, PLURAL die **Reservierungen**
reservation

das **Reservoir**, PLURAL die **Reservoirs**
reservoir

der **Respekt**
respect
Sie haben keinen Respekt vor den Lehrern. They have no respect for the teachers.

ℙ indicates key words

respektieren *VERB*, *PERFECT* **hat respektiert**
to respect

der **Rest**, *PLURAL* die **Reste**
1 rest, remainder
2 Reste leftovers
   Zum Mittagessen gibts die Reste. We're having the leftovers for lunch.
3 Reste remains
   In dem See wurden die Reste einer alten Kultur entdeckt. The remains of an ancient civilization were discovered in the lake.

ℰ das **Restaurant**, *PLURAL* die **Restaurants**
restaurant

restlich *ADJECTIVE*
remaining

restlos *ADJECTIVE*
complete

ℰ das **Resultat**, *PLURAL* die **Resultate**
result

retten *VERB*, *PERFECT* **hat gerettet**
1 to save, to rescue
   Er hat mir das Leben gerettet. He saved my life.
2 sich retten to escape

der **Rettich**, *PLURAL* die **Rettiche**
white radish, mooli

die **Rettung**
1 rescue
2 Du bist meine letzte Rettung. You are my only hope.

das **Rettungsboot**, *PLURAL* die **Rettungsboote**
lifeboat

der **Rettungsring**, *PLURAL* die **Rettungsringe**
lifebelt

der **Rettungsschwimmer**, *PLURAL* die **Rettungsschwimmer**
lifeguard *(male)*
Gibt es einen Rettungsschwimmer im Schwimmbad? Is there a lifeguard at the pool?

WORD TIP Professions, hobbies, and sports don't take an article in German: Er ist Rettungsschwimmer.

die **Rettungsschwimmerin**, *PLURAL* die **Rettungsschwimmerinnen**
lifeguard *(female)*

WORD TIP Professions, hobbies, and sports don't take an article in German: Sie ist Rettungsschwimmerin.

der **Rettungswagen**, *PLURAL* die **Rettungswagen**
ambulance

das **Revier**, *PLURAL* die **Reviere**
1 territory
2 police station

ℰ das **Rezept**, *PLURAL* die **Rezepte**
1 prescription
2 recipe

die **Rezeption**, *PLURAL* die **Rezeptionen**
reception
Bitte geben Sie Ihren Schlüssel an der Rezeption ab. Please leave your key at reception.

das **R-Gespräch**, *PLURAL* die **R-Gespräche**
reverse-charge call

der **Rhabarber**
rhubarb

der **Rhein**
Rhine

das **Rheuma**
rheumatism

der **Rhythmus**, *PLURAL* die **Rhythmen**
rhythm

richten *VERB*, *PERFECT* **hat gerichtet**
1 to direct, to point (a torch, telescope, gun)
2 eine Frage an jemanden richten to put a question to somebody
3 to address (a letter, remarks)
4 to prepare (a meal, room)
5 sich auf etwas richten to be directed at something
   Ihr Blick richtete sich auf die Berge. Her gaze was directed at the mountains.
6 sich nach jemandem richten to fit in with somebody's wishes
   Wir richten uns ganz nach euch. We'll fit in with what you want.
   Ihr müsst euch nach den Vorschriften richten. You have to follow the rules.
7 sich nach etwas richten to depend on something
   Das richtet sich nach dem Wetter. It depends on the weather.

der **Richter**, *PLURAL* die **Richter**
judge *(male)*

WORD TIP Professions, hobbies, and sports don't take an article in German: Er ist Richter.

✧ irregular verb; *SEP* separable verb; for more help with verbs see centre section

die **Richterin**, PLURAL die **Richterinnen**
judge (female)

> **WORD TIP** Professions, hobbies, and sports
> don't take an article in German: Sie ist
> Richterin.

℘ **richtig** ADJECTIVE
1 **right**
Das war die richtige Antwort. That was
the right answer.
2 **das Richtige** the right thing
der/die Richtige the right man/woman
3 **real, proper**
Was ist denn ihr richtiger Name? What's
her real name?
In diesem Jahr gab es keinen richtigen
Sommer. We haven't had a proper summer
this year.

richtig ADVERB
1 **correctly**
Hast du das Formular richtig ausgefüllt?
Have you filled in the form correctly?
2 **really**
Er war richtig wütend. He was really
furious.
3 Ich muss meine Uhr richtig stellen. I have
to set my watch to the right time.
Die Uhr geht richtig. The clock is right.

die **Richtlinie**, PLURAL die **Richtlinien**
guideline

die **Richtung**, PLURAL die **Richtungen**
1 **direction**
2 **trend**

die **Richtungstaste**, PLURAL die
Richtungstasten
direction key

rieb ▸ SEE **reiben**

℘ **riechen** VERB◇, IMPERFECT **roch**, PERFECT **hat
gerochen**
1 **to smell**
2 Ich kann ihn nicht riechen. (informal)
I can't stand him.

rief ▸ SEE **rufen**

der **Riegel**, PLURAL die **Riegel**
1 **bolt**
2 **bar** (of chocolate)

der **Riemen**, PLURAL die **Riemen**
strap

der **Riese**, PLURAL die **Riesen**
giant

riesengroß ADJECTIVE
gigantic

℘ **riesig** ADJECTIVE
gigantic, huge
ein riesiger Lastwagen a huge lorry

die **Riesin**, PLURAL die **Riesinnen**
giantess

riet ▸ SEE **raten**

das **Rind**, PLURAL die **Rinder**
1 **ox**
2 **cow**
Rinder cattle
3 **beef**

die **Rinde**, PLURAL die **Rinden**
1 **bark**
2 **rind**
3 **crust**

℘ der **Rinderbraten**, PLURAL die **Rinderbraten**
roast beef

das **Rindfleisch**
beef

der **Ring**, PLURAL die **Ringe**
ring

das **Ringbuch**, PLURAL die **Ringbücher**
ring binder

das **Ringen**
wrestling

die **Rinne**, PLURAL die **Rinnen**
1 **gutter**
2 **channel**

die **Rippe**, PLURAL die **Rippen**
rib

das **Risiko**, PLURAL die **Risiken**
risk

riskant ADJECTIVE
risky

riskieren VERB, PERFECT **hat riskiert**
to risk, to put at risk

riss ▸ SEE **reißen**

der **Riss**, PLURAL die **Risse**
1 **tear**
2 **crack**

ritt ▸ SEE **reiten**

der **Rivale**, PLURAL die **Rivalen**
rival (male)

die **Rivalin**, PLURAL die **Rivalinnen**
rival (female)

die **Robbe**, PLURAL die **Robben**
seal

℘ **indicates key words**

239

der **Roboter**, PLURAL die **Roboter**
robot

roch ▸SEE **riechen**

♀ der **Rock**, PLURAL die **Röcke**
skirt

rodeln VERB, PERFECT **hat /ist gerodelt**
to go sledging

der **Roggen**
rye

roh ADJECTIVE
1 raw
2 rough
3 brutal

das **Rohr**, PLURAL die **Rohre**
1 pipe
2 reed
3 cane

der **Rohstoff**, PLURAL die **Rohstoffe**
raw material

das **Rollbrett**, PLURAL die **Rollbretter**
skateboard

die **Rolle**, PLURAL die **Rollen**
1 roll
2 reel
3 role, part
4 Es spielt keine Rolle. It doesn't matter.

rollen VERB
1 PERFECT **hat gerollt** to roll
Die Demonstranten haben einen
Betonklotz auf die Straße gerollt. The
protesters rolled a concrete block onto
the road.
2 PERFECT **ist gerollt** to roll
Das Geld ist unters Bett gerollt. The
money rolled under the bed.

der **Roller**, PLURAL die **Roller**
scooter

der **Rollkragen**, PLURAL die **Rollkrägen**
polo neck

der **Rollladen**, PLURAL die **Rollläden**
shutter

der **Rollschuh**, PLURAL die **Rollschuhe**
roller skate
Rollschuh fahren/laufen to roller skate

der **Rollschuhfahrer**, PLURAL die
Rollschuhfahrer
skater (on roller skates) (male)

die **Rollschuhfahrerin**, PLURAL die
Rollschuhfahrerinnen
skater (on roller skates) (female)

das **Rollschuhlaufen**
roller skating

der **Rollstuhl**, PLURAL die **Rollstühle**
wheelchair

die **Rolltreppe**, PLURAL die **Rolltreppen**
escalator

Rom NEUTER NOUN
Rome

♀ der **Roman**, PLURAL die **Romane**
novel

♀ **romantisch** ADJECTIVE
romantic

der **Römer**, PLURAL die **Römer**
Roman (male)

die **Römerin**, PLURAL die **Römerinnen**
Roman (female)

römisch ADJECTIVE
Roman

WORD TIP Adjectives never have capitals
in German, even for regions, countries, or
nationalities.

röntgen VERB, PERFECT **hat geröntgt**
to X-ray

♀ **rosa** ADJECTIVE
pink

die **Rose**, PLURAL die **Rosen**
rose

der **Rosenkohl**
(Brussels) sprouts

der **Rosenmontag**
Monday before Shrove Tuesday

ROSENMONTAG

Rosenmontag is the most important day
during carnival. Schools are closed in some
areas, particularly in the Rhineland. In
Austria it is also called Faschingsmontag. In
Austria Shrove Tuesday (Faschingsdienstag
or Fastnachtsdienstag), the day after
Rosenmontag, is the most important day.

die **Rosine**, PLURAL die **Rosinen**
raisin

der **Rosmarin**
rosemary

die **Rosskastanie**, PLURAL die **Rosskastanien**
horse chestnut, conker

der **Rost**, PLURAL die **Roste**
1 rust
2 grate, grill

⬦ **irregular verb**; SEP **separable verb**; for more help with verbs see centre section

rosten VERB, PERFECT **ist gerostet**
to rust

rösten, PERFECT **hat geröstet**
1 to roast
2 to toast

rostig ADJECTIVE
rusty

die **Röstkartoffeln** PLURAL NOUN
roast potatoes

⚡ **rot** ADJECTIVE
red

die **Röteln** PLURAL NOUN
German measles

rothaarig ADJECTIVE
red-haired

das **Rotkehlchen**, PLURAL die **Rotkehlchen**
robin

der **Rotkohl**
red cabbage

das **Rotkraut**
(used in Austria and Southern Germany)
red cabbage

der **Rotwein**, PLURAL die **Rotweine**
red wine

die **Routine**
routine

rüber ADVERB
(informal) over
Komm zu uns rüber. Come over to us.

die **Rückblende**, PLURAL die **Rückblenden**
flashback

rücken VERB, PERFECT **hat gerückt**
to move
Kannst du ein wenig rücken? Can you
move over a bit?

⚡ der **Rücken**, PLURAL die **Rücken**
1 back
2 spine (of a book)

die **Rückenschmerzen** PLURAL NOUN
backache
Ich hatte Rückenschmerzen. I had
backache.

⚡ die **Rückfahrkarte**, PLURAL die
Rückfahrkarten
return ticket
Eine Rückfahrkarte nach München, bitte.
A return ticket to Munich, please.

die **Rückfahrt**
1 return journey
2 way back
auf der Rückfahrt on the way back

die **Rückgabe**, PLURAL die **Rückgaben**
return

der **Rückgang**, PLURAL die **Rückgänge**
decrease
Im vergangenen Jahr gab es einen
Rückgang in der Anzahl der Unfälle. Last
year, there was a decrease in the number
of accidents.

rückgängig ADJECTIVE
etwas rückgängig machen to cancel
something

die **Rückhand**
backhand (in tennis)

die **Rückkehr**
return

die **Rückreise**
return journey

⚡ der **Rucksack**, PLURAL die **Rucksäcke**
rucksack

die **Rückseite**, PLURAL die **Rückseiten**
back

die **Rücksicht**
consideration

rücksichtslos ADJECTIVE
1 inconsiderate
2 ein rücksichtsloser Fahrer a reckless driver
3 ruthless

rücksichtsvoll ADJECTIVE
considerate

der **Rücksitz**, PLURAL die **Rücksitze**
back seat

rückwärts ADVERB
backwards

der **Rückwärtsgang**, PLURAL die
Rückwärtsgänge
reverse (gear)

der **Rückweg**, PLURAL die **Rückwege**
1 way back
2 return journey

die **Rückzahlung**, PLURAL die
Rückzahlungen
refund, repayment

das **Ruder**, PLURAL die **Ruder**
1 oar
2 rudder

⚡ **indicates key words**

das **Ruderboot**, PLURAL die **Ruderboote**
rowing boat

rudern VERB
1 PERFECT **ist gerudert to row**
Ich bin über den See gerudert. I rowed
across the lake.
Sie rudert gern. She is keen on rowing.
2 PERFECT **hat gerudert to row**
Ich habe Monika über den See gerudert. I
rowed Monika across the lake.

das **Rudern**
rowing
Du bist mit dem Rudern dran. It's your
turn to row.

der **Ruf**, PLURAL die **Rufe**
1 call, shout
2 reputation
3 phone number

♪ **rufen** VERB◇, IMPERFECT **rief**, PERFECT **hat**
gerufen
1 to call out, to shout
Sie rief um Hilfe. She shouted for help.
2 to call
Soll ich einen Arzt rufen? Shall I call a
doctor?

die **Rufnummer**, PLURAL die **Rufnummern**
phone number

die **Ruhe**
1 silence, quiet
Ruhe bitte! Quiet please!
2 rest
3 peace
Ich will in Ruhe essen. I want to have my
meal in peace.
Lass mich in Ruhe! Leave me alone!
in aller Ruhe calmly
4 sich nicht aus der Ruhe bringen lassen to
not get worked up
5 sich zur Ruhe setzen to retire

ruhen VERB, PERFECT **hat geruht**
1 to rest
2 Hier ruht ... Here lies ...

der **Ruhestand**
retirement
im Ruhestand retired
in den Ruhestand gehen to retire

der **Ruhetag**, PLURAL die **Ruhetage**
closing day
'Dienstag Ruhetag' 'Closed on Tuesdays'

♪ **ruhig** ADJECTIVE
1 quiet
Verhaltet euch ruhig. Keep quiet.

2 peaceful
3 calm
Sie blieb ruhig. She remained calm.

ruhig ADVERB
1 quietly
2 calmly
3 Sehen Sie sich ruhig um. You're welcome
to look around.
Du kannst es ihm ruhig sagen. It's OK, you
can tell him.

der **Ruhm**
fame

das **Rührei**
scrambled eggs

rühren VERB, PERFECT **hat gerührt**
1 to stir
2 to move
3 sich rühren to move
4 an etwas rühren to touch, to touch on

die **Ruine**, PLURAL die **Ruinen**
ruin

ruinieren VERB, PERFECT **hat ruiniert**
to ruin

rülpsen VERB, PERFECT **hat gerülpst**
to belch

der **Rum**
rum

der **Rumäne**, PLURAL die **Rumänen**
Romanian (male)

♪ **Rumänien** NEUTER NOUN
Romania

die **Rumänin**, PLURAL die **Rumäninnen**
Romanian (female)

rumänisch ADJECTIVE
Romanian

WORD TIP Adjectives never have capitals
in German, even for regions, countries, or
nationalities.

der **Rummel**
1 hustle and bustle
2 fuss
3 fair

der **Rummelplatz**, PLURAL die
Rummelplätze
fairground

♪ **rund** ADJECTIVE
round

◇ **irregular verb**; SEP **separable verb**; for more help with verbs see centre section

rund *ADVERB*
1 **about**
Die Zugfahrt dauert rund zwei Stunden.
The train journey takes about two hours.
2 **rund um** around
Sie wanderten rund um den See. They
walked around the lake.

die **Runde**, *PLURAL* die **Runden**
1 **round**
2 **lap** *(of a track, etc.)*
3 **circle**, **group**
4 **über die Runden kommen** *(informal)* to
get by

℘ die **Rundfahrt**, *PLURAL* die **Rundfahrten**
tour

die **Rundfrage**, *PLURAL* die **Rundfragen**
survey, **poll**

der **Rundfunk**
radio
im Rundfunk on the radio

der **Rundgang**, *PLURAL* die **Rundgänge**
1 **walk**
2 **tour**
3 **rounds**

rundherum *ADVERB*
all around

der **Rundkurs**, *PLURAL* die **Rundkurse**
(motor racing) circuit

runter *ADVERB (informal)*
▶SEE **herunter**, **hinunter**
Runter da! Get off!

runzlig *ADJECTIVE*
wrinkled

die **Rüsche**, *PLURAL* die **Rüschen**
frill

der **Ruß**
soot

der **Russe**, *PLURAL* die **Russen**
Russian *(male)*

der **Rüssel**, *PLURAL* die **Rüssel**
trunk *(of an elephant)*

die **Russin**, *PLURAL* die **Russinnen**
Russian *(female)*

russisch *ADJECTIVE*
Russian

> **WORD TIP** Adjectives never have capitals
> in German, even for regions, countries, or
> nationalities.

℘ **Russland** *NEUTER NOUN*
Russia

die **Rüstung**, *PLURAL* die **Rüstungen**
1 **armament**
2 **arms**
3 **(suit of) armour**

der **Rutsch**, *PLURAL* die **Rutsche**
slip, **slide**

die **Rutschbahn**, *PLURAL* die **Rutschbahnen**
slide

rutschen *VERB, PERFECT* **ist gerutscht**
1 **to slide**
2 **to slip**
3 **to move over**
Rutsch mal! Move over!

rutschig *ADJECTIVE*
slippery

rütteln *VERB, PERFECT* **hat gerüttelt**
1 **to shake**
2 **am Tor rütteln** to rattle the gate

Ss

Sa. *ABBREVIATION*
(=Samstag, Sonnabend) **Saturday**

der **Saal**, *PLURAL* die **Säle**
hall

die **Saatkrähe**, *PLURAL* die **Saatkrähen**
rook

der **Sabbat**, *PLURAL* die **Sabbate**
Sabbath

℘ die **Sache**, *PLURAL* die **Sachen**
1 **matter**
Das ist eine andere Sache. That's a
different matter.
2 **business**
Das ist seine Sache. That's his business.
3 **thing**
meine Sachen my things *(clothes, etc.)*
Sie räumt nie ihre Sachen weg. She never
puts away her things.
4 **zur Sache kommen** to get to the point
5 Das ist so 'ne Sache. *(informal)* It's a bit
tricky.

die **Sachertorte**, *PLURAL* die **Sachertorten**
Sachertorte *(rich chocolate cake originally*

A
B
C
D
E
F
G
H
I
J
K
L
M
N
O
P
Q
R
S
T
U
V
W
X
Y
Z

243

made in Vienna)

ⓘ SACHERTORTE

The Sacher chocolate cake was created in 1832 by the 16-year-old Franz Sacher. It is the only cake that has ever been the subject of a court case. The legal battle was between the Viennese pastry shop, Demel, and the Sacher Hotel. Both claimed the right to call their chocolate cake a Sachertorte. Sacher won the battle but Demel is still producing a very similar cake, although the official Sachertorte recipe is still a secret.

das **Sachgebiet**, PLURAL die **Sachgebiete**
field, (subject) area

sachlich ADJECTIVE
1 objective
2 factual

sächlich ADJECTIVE
neuter (in grammar)

Sachsen NEUTER NOUN
Saxony

der **Sack**, PLURAL die **Säcke**
1 sack
2 bag

die **Sackgasse**, PLURAL die **Sackgassen**
dead end, cul-de-sac

♀ der **Saft**, PLURAL die **Säfte**
1 juice
2 sap

saftig ADJECTIVE
juicy

die **Säge**, PLURAL die **Sägen**
saw

das **Sägemehl**
sawdust

♀ **sagen** VERB, PERFECT **hat gesagt**
1 to say
Wie sagt man das auf Englisch? How do you say that in English?
Man sagt, dass … It's said that …
Was ich noch sagen wollte, … By the way, …
2 unter uns gesagt between you and me
3 to tell
Er hat mir gesagt, dass er nicht kommen kann. He told me that he can't come.
Ich habe es dir doch gleich gesagt. I told you so.
Sag mal, … Tell me …
4 to think
Was sagen Sie dazu? What do you think

about it?
5 to mean
Das hat nichts zu sagen. It doesn't mean anything.
6 etwas zu jemandem sagen to call somebody something
Das Kind sagt zu unserer Nachbarin Tante. The child calls our neighbour auntie.
7 Ihr Gesicht sagte alles. It was written all over her face.

sägen VERB, PERFECT **hat gesägt**
to saw

sagenhaft ADJECTIVE
1 legendary
2 (informal) brilliant

sah ▸ SEE **sehen**

♀ die **Sahne**
cream

die **Saison**, PLURAL die **Saisons**
season

die **Saite**, PLURAL die **Saiten**
string (of an instrument)

das **Sakko**, PLURAL die **Sakkos**
jacket

die **Salami**, PLURAL die **Salamis**
salami

♀ der **Salat**, PLURAL die **Salate**
1 lettuce
Dazu gab es grünen Salat. It was served with lettuce.
2 salad
Er bestellte einen gemischten Salat. He ordered a mixed salad.

die **Salatsoße**, PLURAL die **Salatsoßen**
salad dressing

♀ die **Salbe**, PLURAL die **Salben**
ointment

der **Salbei**
sage

salopp ADJECTIVE
casual, informal

♀ das **Salz**
salt

salzen VERB, PERFECT **hat gesalzen**
to salt

salzig ADJECTIVE
salty

◇ irregular verb; SEP separable verb; for more help with verbs see centre section

die **Salzkartoffeln** *PLURAL NOUN*
boiled potatoes

das **Salzwasser**
1 salt water
2 salted water *(for cooking)*

der **Samen**, *PLURAL* die **Samen**
1 seed
2 sperm, semen

das **Sammelalbum**, *PLURAL* die **Sammelalben**
scrapbook

ℰ **sammeln** *VERB, PERFECT* **hat gesammelt**
1 to collect
   Martin sammelt Briefmarken. Martin collects stamps.
2 to gather
3 sich sammeln to gather
4 Ich musste meine Gedanken sammeln. I had to gather my thoughts.

der **Sammler**, *PLURAL* die **Sammler**
collector *(male)*

die **Sammlerin**, *PLURAL* die **Sammlerinnen**
collector *(female)*

ℰ die **Sammlung**, *PLURAL* die **Sammlungen**
collection
   Nach dem Konzert wurde eine Sammlung für einen guten Zweck durchgeführt. After the concert there was a collection for charity.

ℰ der **Samstag**, *PLURAL* die **Samstage**
Saturday
   am Samstag on Saturday

samstags *ADVERB*
on Saturdays

samt *PREPOSITION (+ DAT)*
(together) with
   Der Sänger kam samt seiner Band nach Europa. The singer came to Europe together with his band.

der **Samt**, *PLURAL* die **Samte**
velvet

sämtlich *ADJECTIVE*
all
   Ich packte meine sämtlichen Bücher ein. I packed all my books.

der **Sand**
sand

die **Sandale**, *PLURAL* die **Sandalen**
sandal

die **Sandburg**, *PLURAL* die **Sandburgen**
sandcastle

sandig *ADJECTIVE*
sandy

sandte ▸ SEE **senden**

sanft *ADJECTIVE*
1 gentle
2 soft *(voice, colour, music)*

sang ▸ SEE **singen**

ℰ der **Sänger**, *PLURAL* die **Sänger**
singer *(male)*

   WORD TIP Professions, hobbies, and sports don't take an article in German: Er ist Sänger.

ℰ die **Sängerin**, *PLURAL* die **Sängerinnen**
singer *(female)*

   WORD TIP Professions, hobbies, and sports don't take an article in German: Sie ist Sängerin.

sank ▸ SEE **sinken**

die **Sardelle**, *PLURAL* die **Sardellen**
anchovy

die **Sardine**, *PLURAL* die **Sardinen**
sardine

der **Sarg**, *PLURAL* die **Särge**
coffin

der **Sarkasmus**
sarcasm

sarkastisch *ADJECTIVE*
sarcastic

saß ▸ SEE **sitzen**

der **Satellit**, *PLURAL* die **Satelliten**
satellite

das **Satellitenfernsehen**
satellite television

ℰ **satt** *ADJECTIVE*
1 full (up)
   Ich bin satt. I'm full.
   Bist du satt geworden? Have you had enough to eat?
   Die Kinder konnten sich satt essen. The children could eat as much as they wanted.
   Pizza macht satt. Pizza is filling.
2 etwas satt haben *(informal)* to be fed up with something

der **Sattel**, *PLURAL* die **Sättel**
saddle

die **Satteltasche**, *PLURAL* die **Satteltaschen**
saddlebag, pannier

ℓ der **Satz**, PLURAL die **Sätze**
1 sentence
2 set (of things or in tennis)
  ein Satz Reifen a set of tyres
3 movement (in music)
4 rate (of tax, interest)
5 leap, bound

ℓ **sauber** ADJECTIVE
1 clean
2 neat
3 (informal) fine (expressing irony)
4 sauber machen to clean
5 sauber halten to keep clean

die **Sauberkeit**
cleanliness, cleanness

die **Sauce**, PLURAL die **Saucen** ▸ SEE **Soße**

ℓ **sauer** ADJECTIVE
1 sour
2 pickled
3 acid
  saurer Regen acid rain
4 sauer sein (informal) to be annoyed
  Ich bin sauer auf Eva. I'm annoyed with
  Eva.

der **Sauerbraten**, PLURAL die **Sauerbraten**
braised beef (marinaded in vinegar and
spices)

die **Sauerei** (informal) PLURAL die **Sauereien**
1 mess
2 disgrace, scandal
3 obscenity

das **Sauerkraut**
sauerkraut, pickled cabbage

der **Sauerstoff**
oxygen

saufen VERB◇, PRESENT **säuft**, IMPERFECT **soff**,
PERFECT **hat gesoffen**
(informal) to drink, to booze

saugen VERB, PERFECT **hat gesaugt**
1 to suck
2 to vacuum, to hoover

das **Säugetier**, PLURAL die **Säugetiere**
mammal

der **Säugling**, PLURAL die **Säuglinge**
baby, infant

die **Säule**, PLURAL die **Säulen**
column, pillar

der **Saum**, PLURAL die **Säume**
hem

die **Säure**, PLURAL die **Säuren**
acid

das **Saxofon**, PLURAL die **Saxofone**
saxophone
Anna spielt Saxofon. Anna plays the
saxophone.

SB ABBREVIATION
(=Selbstbedienung) self-service

die **S-Bahn**, PLURAL die **S-Bahnen**
city and suburban railway

der **Scanner**, PLURAL die **Scanner**
scanner

schäbig ADJECTIVE
shabby

das **Schach**
1 chess
2 check
  Schach! Check!

das **Schachbrett**, PLURAL die **Schachbretter**
chessboard

die **Schachfigur**, PLURAL die **Schachfiguren**
chess piece

die **Schachtel**, PLURAL die **Schachteln**
box

ℓ **schade** ADJECTIVE
1 schade sein to be a pity
  Es ist schade, dass du schon gehen musst.
  It's a pity that you have to go so soon.
  Schade! (What a) pity!
2 zu schade für jemanden sein to be too
  good for somebody

der **Schädel**, PLURAL die **Schädel**
skull

schaden VERB, PERFECT **hat geschadet**
1 to damage
  Das hat seinem Ruf geschadet. It damaged
  his reputation.
2 jemandem schaden to harm somebody
3 Das schadet nichts. It doesn't matter.

ℓ der **Schaden**, PLURAL die **Schäden**
1 damage
2 disadvantage

schädlich ADJECTIVE
harmful

das **Schaf**, PLURAL die **Schafe**
sheep

der **Schäfer**, PLURAL die **Schäfer**
shepherd (male)

◇ irregular verb; SEP separable verb; for more help with verbs see centre section

der **Schäferhund**, PLURAL die **Schäferhunde**
sheepdog

die **Schäferin**, PLURAL die **Schäferinnen**
shepherdess

schaffen[1] VERB◇, IMPERFECT **schuf**, PERFECT **hat geschaffen**
1 to create
2 to make
Dieses Wörterbuch ist wie geschaffen für die Schule. This dictionary is ideal for school.

ℱ **schaffen**[2] VERB, PERFECT **hat geschafft**
1 to manage
es schaffen, etwas zu tun to manage to do something
Schaffst du es, den Koffer nach oben zu bringen? Can you manage to get the case upstairs?
2 to pass
Sie hat die Prüfung geschafft. She passed the exam.
3 jemandem zu schaffen machen to cause somebody trouble
4 geschafft sein (informal) to be worn out

der **Schaffner**, PLURAL die **Schaffner**
1 conductor (male)
2 (ticket) inspector (male)

WORD TIP Professions, hobbies, and sports don't take an article in German: Er ist Schaffner.

die **Schaffnerin**, PLURAL die **Schaffnerinnen**
1 conductor (female)
2 (ticket) inspector (female)

WORD TIP Professions, hobbies, and sports don't take an article in German: Sie ist Schaffnerin.

der **Schakal**, PLURAL die **Schakale**
jackal

der **Schal**, PLURAL die **Schals**
scarf

die **Schale**, PLURAL die **Schalen**
1 skin (of vegetables, fruit)
2 peel
3 shell
4 dish, bowl
Auf dem Tisch war eine Schale Obst. There was a bowl of fruit on the table.

schälen VERB, PERFECT **hat geschält**
1 to peel
Er hat ihr eine Orange geschält. He peeled an orange for her.
2 sich schälen to peel
Mein Rücken schält sich. My back's peeling.

der **Schall**
sound

die **Schallplatte**, PLURAL die **Schallplatten**
record

schalten VERB, PERFECT **hat geschaltet**
1 to switch, to turn
Schalte die Heizung höher. Turn the heating up.
2 to change gear
3 schnell schalten (informal) to catch on quickly

ℱ der **Schalter**, PLURAL die **Schalter**
1 switch
2 ticket office, counter, desk

das **Schaltjahr**, PLURAL die **Schaltjahre**
leap year

schämen VERB, PERFECT **hat sich geschämt**
sich schämen to be ashamed

die **Schande**
1 disgrace
2 shame

ℱ **scharf** ADJECTIVE
1 sharp
2 hot, spicy (food)
3 biting (wind)
4 fierce (dog)
5 scharf nachdenken to think hard
6 (in photography) scharf sein to be in focus
scharf einstellen to focus
7 scharf schießen to fire live ammunition
8 scharf auf etwas sein (informal) to be really keen on something
Sie ist scharf auf Bernd. (informal) She fancies Bernd.

der or das **Schaschlik**, PLURAL die **Schaschliks**
kebab

der **Schatten**, PLURAL die **Schatten**
1 shadow
2 shade

schattig ADJECTIVE
shady

ℱ der **Schatz**, PLURAL die **Schätze**
1 treasure
2 darling

das **Schätzchen**, PLURAL die **Schätzchen**
darling

schätzen VERB, PERFECT **hat geschätzt**
1 to estimate
2 to value
3 to reckon, to guess

ℱ indicates key words

Schätz mal! Guess!
4 etwas zu schätzen wissen to appreciate something

die **Schau**, *PLURAL* die **Schauen**
show

schauen *VERB*, *PERFECT* **hat geschaut**
1 to look
2 Fernsehen schauen to watch television

der **Schauer**, *PLURAL* die **Schauer**
1 shower
2 shudder

die **Schauergeschichte**, *PLURAL* die **Schauergeschichten**
horror story

die **Schaufel**, *PLURAL* die **Schaufeln**
1 shovel
2 dustpan

das **Schaufenster**, *PLURAL* die **Schaufenster**
shop window

der **Schaufensterbummel**, *PLURAL* die **Schaufensterbummel**
window-shopping
Lass uns einen Schaufensterbummel machen. Let's go window-shopping.

die **Schaukel**, *PLURAL* die **Schaukeln**
swing

schaukeln *VERB*, *PERFECT* **hat geschaukelt**
to swing

der **Schaukelstuhl**, *PLURAL* die **Schaukelstühle**
rocking chair

der **Schaum**
1 foam
2 froth
3 lather

schäumen *VERB*, *PERFECT* **hat geschäumt**
1 to foam
2 to froth (up)

der **Schauplatz**, *PLURAL* die **Schauplätze**
scene

das **Schauspiel**, *PLURAL* die **Schauspiele**
1 play
2 spectacle

ℙ der **Schauspieler**, *PLURAL* die **Schauspieler**
actor

> **WORD TIP** Professions, hobbies, and sports don't take an article in German: Er ist Schauspieler.

ℙ die **Schauspielerin**, *PLURAL* die **Schauspielerinnen**
actress

> **WORD TIP** Professions, hobbies, and sports don't take an article in German: Sie ist Schauspielerin.

die **Schauspielkunst**
dramatic art, acting

der **Scheck**, *PLURAL* die **Schecks**
cheque

ℙ die **Scheibe**, *PLURAL* die **Scheiben**
1 pane *(of a window)*
2 windscreen
3 slice
Sie aß eine Scheibe Schinken. She ate a slice of ham.
Er schnitt die Salami in Scheiben. He sliced the salami.
4 Du könntest dir eine Scheibe von ihr abschneiden. *(informal)* You could take a leaf out of her book.
5 disc

der **Scheibenwischer**, *PLURAL* die **Scheibenwischer**
windscreen wiper

die **Scheide**, *PLURAL* die **Scheiden**
vagina

scheiden *VERB*◊, *IMPERFECT* **schied**, *PERFECT* **hat geschieden**
1 sich scheiden lassen to get divorced
Sie haben sich im Juli scheiden lassen. They got divorced in July.
2 geschieden sein to be divorced
3 to separate

die **Scheidung**, *PLURAL* die **Scheidungen**
divorce

der **Schein**, *PLURAL* die **Scheine**
1 light
Er las beim Schein einer Taschenlampe. He read by the light of a torch.
2 appearance
Der Schein trügt. Appearances are deceptive.
etwas zum Schein machen to pretend to do something
Sie ging zum Schein auf das Angebot ein. She pretended to accept the offer.
3 certificate
4 note *(money)*

scheinbar *ADVERB*
apparently

◊ **irregular verb;** *SEP* **separable verb; for more help with verbs see centre section**

ℒ **scheinen** *VERB*◇, *IMPERFECT* **schien**, *PERFECT* **hat geschienen**
1 **to shine**
2 **to seem**
   Es scheint zu klappen. It seems to be working out.
   Mir scheint, dass ... It seems to me that ...

der **Scheinwerfer**, *PLURAL* die **Scheinwerfer**
1 **headlamp, headlight**
2 **floodlight**
3 **spotlight**

der **Scheitel**, *PLURAL* die **Scheitel**
   parting *(in your hair)*

scheitern *VERB*, *PERFECT* **ist gescheitert**
   to fail

der **Schenkel**, *PLURAL* die **Schenkel**
   thigh

schenken *VERB*, *PERFECT* **hat geschenkt**
1 **to give**
   Ich habe meiner Mutter zu Weihnachten ein Buch geschenkt. I gave my mother a book for Christmas.
   Hast du den Computer geschenkt bekommen? Were you given the computer as a present?
2 sich etwas schenken **to give something a miss**
   Den Film werde ich mir schenken. I'm going to give the film a miss.
3 Das ist ja geschenkt! *(informal)* **It's a bargain!**

ℒ die **Schere**, *PLURAL* die **Scheren**
1 **(pair of) scissors**
2 **(pair of) shears**
3 **claw** *(of a crab)*

   WORD TIP In German, die Schere is singular: Die Schere ist stumpf.

scheren *VERB*, *PERFECT* **hat geschert**
   (informal) **to bother**
   sich nicht um etwas scheren **not to care about something**
   Scher dich um deine eigenen Angelegenheiten! Mind your own business!
   Scher dich zum Teufel! Go to hell!

der **Scherz**, *PLURAL* die **Scherze**
   joke

scheu *ADJECTIVE*
   shy

scheuern *VERB*, *PERFECT* **hat gescheuert**
1 **to scrub**
2 **to rub**

die **Scheune**, *PLURAL* die **Scheunen**
   barn

scheußlich *ADJECTIVE*
   horrible

der **Schi**, *PLURAL* die **Schi(er)** ▶ SEE **Ski**

die **Schicht**, *PLURAL* die **Schichten**
1 **layer**
2 **class, section** *(of the population)*
3 **shift** *(in a factory, etc.)*

ℒ die **Schichtarbeit**
   shift work

schick *ADJECTIVE*
1 **stylish, smart**
2 *(informal)* **great**

ℒ **schicken** *VERB*, *PERFECT* **hat geschickt**
   to send

das **Schicksal**, *PLURAL* die **Schicksale**
   fate

das **Schiebedach**, *PLURAL* die **Schiebedächer**
   sunroof

schieben *VERB*◇, *IMPERFECT* **schob**, *PERFECT* **hat geschoben**
1 **to push**
2 etwas auf jemanden schieben **to blame somebody for something**
   Sie wollen ihre Probleme auf die Lehrer schieben. They want to blame the teachers for their problems.
   die Schuld auf jemanden schieben **to put the blame on somebody**

schied ▶ SEE **scheiden**

der **Schiedsrichter**, *PLURAL* die **Schiedsrichter**
   referee, umpire *(male)*

   WORD TIP Professions, hobbies, and sports don't take an article in German: Er ist Schiedsrichter.

die **Schiedsrichterin**, *PLURAL* die **Schiedsrichterinnen**
   referee, umpire *(female)*

   WORD TIP Professions, hobbies, and sports don't take an article in German: Sie ist Schiedsrichterin.

schief *ADJECTIVE*
1 **crooked**
2 ein schiefer Blick **a funny look**
schief *ADVERB*
   Das Bild hängt schief. The picture is not straight.

der **Schiefer**
   slate

ℒ indicates key words

schiefgehen *VERB*◇, *IMPERFECT* **ging schief**,
PERFECT **ist schiefgegangen**
to go wrong

schielen *VERB*, *PERFECT* **hat geschielt**
to squint

schien ▸ SEE **scheinen**

das **Schienbein**, *PLURAL* die **Schienbeine**
shin

die **Schiene**, *PLURAL* die **Schienen**
1 rail
2 splint

♪ **schießen** *VERB*◇, *IMPERFECT* **schoss**, *PERFECT* **hat
geschossen**
1 to shoot
auf jemanden schießen to shoot at
somebody
ein Tor schießen to score a goal
PERFECT **ist geschossen** to shoot (along)
Andrea ist in die Höhe geschossen.
Andrea's shot up. *(has got a lot taller)*

♪ das **Schiff**, *PLURAL* die **Schiffe**
ship
Das Schiff wurde zu Wasser gelassen. The
ship was launched.

die **Schifffahrt**, *PLURAL* die **Schifffahrten**
1 shipping
2 boat trip

schikanieren *VERB*, *PERFECT* **hat schikaniert**
to bully

das **Schild**[1], *PLURAL* die **Schilder**
1 sign
2 badge
3 label

der **Schild**[2], *PLURAL* die **Schilde**
shield

♪ die **Schildkröte**, *PLURAL* die **Schildkröten**
1 tortoise
2 turtle

der **Schilling**, *PLURAL* die **Schilling(e)**
Schilling *(the currency of Austria until
replaced by the euro)*

der **Schimmel**, *PLURAL* die **Schimmel**
1 mould
2 white horse

der **Schimpanse**, *PLURAL* die **Schimpansen**
chimpanzee

schimpfen *VERB*, *PERFECT* **hat geschimpft**
1 to tell off
2 to grumble

♪ der **Schinken**, *PLURAL* die **Schinken**
ham
Er aß ein Brötchen mit Schinken. He had
a ham roll.

♪ der **Schirm**, *PLURAL* die **Schirme**
1 umbrella
2 sunshade
3 (lamp)shade
4 peak *(of a cap)*

der **Schlaf**
sleep

♪ der **Schlafanzug**, *PLURAL* die **Schlafanzüge**
pyjamas

> **WORD TIP** In German, der Schlafanzug is
> singular: Mein Schlafanzug ist warm.

die **Schlafcouch**, *PLURAL* die **Schlafcouchs**
sofa bed

♪ **schlafen** *VERB*◇, *PRESENT* **schläft**, *IMPERFECT*
schlief, *PERFECT* **hat geschlafen**
1 to sleep
2 to be asleep
Das Baby schläft. The baby's asleep.
3 schlafen gehen to go to bed

schlaff *ADJECTIVE*
1 slack *(rope)*
2 limp *(handshake, body)*
3 lethargic

schläfrig *ADJECTIVE*
sleepy

der **Schlafrock**, *PLURAL* die **Schlafröcke**
dressing gown

der **Schlafsaal**, *PLURAL* die **Schlafsäle**
dormitory

der **Schlafsack**, *PLURAL* die **Schlafsäcke**
sleeping bag

der **Schlafwagen**, *PLURAL* die **Schlafwagen**
sleeper *(on a train)*

♪ das **Schlafzimmer**, *PLURAL* die
Schlafzimmer
bedroom

der **Schlag**, *PLURAL* die **Schläge**
1 blow, punch
Er hat einen Schlag auf den Kopf
bekommen. He received a blow to the
head.
2 Schläge bekommen to get a beating
3 (electric) shock
4 Schlag auf Schlag in quick succession
auf einen Schlag all at once

◇ **irregular verb;** *SEP* **separable verb; for more help with verbs see centre section**

ℊ **schlagen** *VERB*◇, *PRESENT* **schlägt**, *IMPERFECT*
schlug, *PERFECT* **hat geschlagen**

1 to hit
Sie schlug ihm auf die Hand. She hit him
on the hand.
Er schlug einen Nagel in die Wand. He
knocked a nail into the wall.

2 to beat
Deutschland schlug Italien drei zu null.
Germany beat Italy three nil.

3 to bang
Er schlug mit dem Kopf gegen die Wand.
He was banging his head against the wall.

4 to strike *(of a clock)*

5 to whip *(cream)*

6 sich schlagen to fight

7 sich geschlagen geben to admit defeat

der **Schlager**, *PLURAL* die **Schlager**
hit, pop song

der **Schläger**, *PLURAL* die **Schläger**
1 (tennis) racket
2 (baseball) bat
3 (golf) club
4 (hockey) stick
5 thug

die **Schlägerei**, *PLURAL* die **Schlägereien**
fight

die **Schlagsahne**
1 whipping cream
2 whipped cream

> **SCHLAGSAHNE**
> In Austria whipped cream is also called
> Schlagobers or Schlag.

die **Schlagzeile**, *PLURAL* die **Schlagzeilen**
headline

das **Schlagzeug**, *PLURAL* die **Schlagzeuge**
drums
Ich spiele Schlagzeug. I play the drums.

der **Schlagzeuger**, *PLURAL* die **Schlagzeuger**
drummer *(male)*

WORD TIP Professions, hobbies, and sports don't
take an article in German: Er ist Schlagzeuger.

die **Schlagzeugerin**, *PLURAL* die
Schlagzeugerinnen
drummer *(female)*

WORD TIP Professions, hobbies, and sports don't
take an article in German: Sie ist Schlagzeugerin.

der **Schlamm**
mud

schlampen *VERB*, *PERFECT* **hat geschlampt**
to be sloppy, to be careless

die **Schlamperei**, *PLURAL* die **Schlampereien**
1 sloppiness, carelessness
2 mess

schlampig *ADJECTIVE*
1 sloppy, careless
2 scruffy, untidy

ℊ die **Schlange**, *PLURAL* die **Schlangen**
1 snake
2 queue
3 Schlange stehen to queue
Wir mussten stundenlang Schlange
stehen. We had to queue for hours.

ℊ **schlank** *ADJECTIVE*
slim

die **Schlankheitskur**, *PLURAL* die
Schlankheitskuren
diet
Sie macht mal wieder eine
Schlankheitskur. She's on a diet again.

schlapp *ADJECTIVE*
worn out, tired out

schlau *ADJECTIVE*
1 crafty, cunning
2 clever
**3 Ich werde nicht schlau daraus. I can't
make head nor tail of it.**

der **Schlauch**, *PLURAL* die **Schläuche**
1 tube
2 hose

schlauchlos *ADJECTIVE*
tubeless

ℊ **schlecht** *ADJECTIVE*
1 bad
schlechtes Wetter bad weather
schlechter Laune sein to be in a bad mood

2 schlecht werden to go off *(of food)*
Die Sahne ist schlecht geworden. The
cream's gone off.

3 Mir ist schlecht. I feel sick.

**4 jemanden schlecht machen to run
somebody down**

schlecht *ADVERB*
1 badly
Er hat in der Prüfung schlecht
abgeschnitten. He did badly in the exam.
Die Arbeit ist schlecht bezahlt. The work
is badly paid.
Sie ist schlecht gelaunt. She's in a bad
mood.

2 Es geht ihm schlecht. He's not well.

schleichen *VERB*◇, *IMPERFECT* **schlich**, *PERFECT*
ist geschlichen
1 to creep

ℊ indicates key words

A
B
C
D
E
F
G
H
I
J
K
L
M
N
O
P
Q
R
S
T
U
V
W
X
Y
Z

2 to crawl *(in traffic)*
3 sich schleichen to creep

die **Schleife**, PLURAL die **Schleifen**
1 bow
2 loop

der **Schlepper**, PLURAL die **Schlepper**
1 tug
2 tractor

die **Schleuder**, PLURAL die **Schleudern**
1 catapult
2 spin dryer

schleudern VERB, PERFECT **hat geschleudert**
1 to hurl
2 to spin *(washing)*
3 PERFECT **ist geschleudert** to skid
Das Auto geriet ins Schleudern. The car
went into a skid.

schlich ▸ SEE **schleichen**

schlicht ADJECTIVE
plain, simple

schlief ▸ SEE **schlafen**

ℰ**schließen** VERB ◇, IMPERFECT **schloss**, PERFECT
hat geschlossen
1 to close, to shut
2 to close down
3 to lock
4 to conclude
Aus seinem Schweigen schloss ich, dass er
sich schuldig fühlte. I concluded from his
silence that he felt guilty.
5 einen Vertrag schließen to enter into a
contract
6 Freundschaft mit jemandem schließen to
make friends with somebody
7 sich schließen to close

ℰ das **Schließfach**, PLURAL die **Schließfächer**
1 locker
2 deposit box

ℰ**schließlich** ADVERB
1 finally
2 after all
Er hat sie schließlich doch eingeladen. He
has invited her after all.

ℰ**schlimm** ADJECTIVE
bad

schlimmstenfalls ADVERB
if the worst comes to the worst

ℰ der **Schlips**, PLURAL die **Schlipse**
tie

der **Schlitten**, PLURAL die **Schlitten**
sledge

In Österreich gehen wir Schlitten fahren.
In Austria we'll go sledging.

der **Schlittschuh**, PLURAL die **Schlittschuhe**
(ice) skate
Schlittschuh laufen to skate

das **Schlittschuhlaufen**
ice-skating

der **Schlitz**, PLURAL die **Schlitze**
1 slit
2 flies *(in trousers)*
3 slot

schloss ▸ SEE **schließen**

ℰ das **Schloss**, PLURAL die **Schlösser**
1 lock
2 castle, palace

der **Schluck**, PLURAL die **Schlucke**
1 mouthful
2 gulp

der **Schluckauf**
hiccups

schlucken VERB, PERFECT **hat geschluckt**
to swallow

schlug ▸ SEE **schlagen**

der **Schlüpfer**, PLURAL die **Schlüpfer**
(pair of) knickers

der **Schluss**, PLURAL die **Schlüsse**
1 end, ending
2 zum Schluss in the end
3 Schluss machen to stop
4 mit jemandem Schluss machen to finish
with somebody
5 conclusion
zu dem Schluss kommen, dass ... to come
to the conclusion that ...

ℰ der **Schlüssel**, PLURAL die **Schlüssel**
1 key
2 spanner

der **Schlüsselbund**, PLURAL die
Schlüsselbünde
bunch of keys

ℰ das **Schlüsselwort**, PLURAL die
Schlüsselwörter
keyword

ℰ der **Schlussverkauf**
sale

schmackhaft ADJECTIVE
tasty

schmal ADJECTIVE
1 narrow

◇ irregular verb; SEP separable verb; for more help with verbs see centre section

2 thin (hands, wrists, lips)

3 Sie ist schmäler geworden. She's lost weight.

> **WORD TIP** The German word schmal does not mean small in English; the German word for small is klein.

schmecken VERB, PERFECT **hat geschmeckt**
1 to taste
Die Suppe schmeckt gut. The soup tastes good.
Das Eis schmeckt nach Zitrone. The ice cream tastes of lemon.
2 Das schmeckt mir nicht. I don't like it.

schmeicheln VERB, PERFECT **hat geschmeichelt**
to flatter
jemandem schmeicheln to flatter somebody

schmeißen VERB◇, IMPERFECT **schmiss**, PERFECT **hat geschmissen**
(informal) **to chuck, to throw**
Sie schmissen mit Bonbons. They were throwing sweets.

schmelzen VERB◇, PRESENT **schmilzt**, IMPERFECT **schmolz**, PERFECT **ist geschmolzen**
to melt
Der Schnee ist geschmolzen. The snow has melted.)
3 PERFECT **hat geschmolzen to melt** (snow, ice)
Sie haben Schnee geschmolzen, um Wasser zum Trinken zu bekommen. They melted snow to get water for drinking.
4 PERFECT **hat geschmolzen to smelt** (ore)

der Schmerz, PLURAL die **Schmerzen**
1 pain
Schmerzen haben to be in pain
2 grief

schmerzen VERB, PERFECT **hat geschmerzt**
to hurt, to ache
Mein Kopf schmerzt. My head is aching.

schmerzhaft ADJECTIVE
painful

schmerzlos ADJECTIVE
painless

das Schmerzmittel, PLURAL die **Schmerzmittel**
painkiller

die Schmerzschwelle, PLURAL die **Schmerzschwellen**
pain threshold

der Schmetterling, PLURAL die **Schmetterlinge**
butterfly

schmettern VERB, PERFECT **hat geschmettert**
1 to hurl
2 to smash (in tennis)
3 to blare out (music, orders)

schmieren VERB, PERFECT **hat geschmiert**
1 to lubricate
2 to spread (butter, jam)
Sie schmierte Butter auf ihr Brot. She spread butter on her bread.
Brote schmieren to make sandwiches
3 jemandem eine schmieren (informal) to clout somebody
4 to scrawl
5 to smudge

die Schminke
make-up

schminken VERB, PERFECT **hat geschminkt**
1 to make up
2 sich schminken to put on make-up

schmiss ▸SEE **schmeißen**

schmolz ▸SEE **schmelzen**

der Schmuck
1 jewellery
2 decoration

schmücken VERB, PERFECT **hat geschmückt**
to decorate

schmuggeln VERB, PERFECT **hat geschmuggelt**
to smuggle

schmusen VERB, PERFECT **hat geschmust**
to cuddle
Gabi hat mit Max geschmust. Gabi was cuddling Max.

der Schmutz
dirt

schmutzig ADJECTIVE
dirty

die Schmutzigkeit
dirtiness

der Schnabel, PLURAL die **Schnäbel**
beak

die Schnalle, PLURAL die **Schnallen**
buckle

schnallen VERB, PERFECT **hat geschnallt**
1 to fasten

2 to buckle

der **Schnaps**, PLURAL die **Schnäpse**
1 schnapps
2 spirits

schnarchen VERB, PERFECT **hat geschnarcht**
to snore

die **Schnauze**, PLURAL die **Schnauzen**
1 muzzle
Der Hund hat eine kalte Schnauze. The dog has a cold nose.
2 die Schnauze halten (informal) to keep your mouth shut

schnäuzen, PERFECT **hat sich geschnäuzt**
sich schnäuzen to blow your nose

die **Schnecke**, PLURAL die **Schnecken**
snail

♀ der **Schnee**
snow

der **Schneeregen**
sleet

der **Schneesturm**, PLURAL die **Schneestürme**
blizzard

die **Schneewehe**, PLURAL die **Schneewehen**
snowdrift

♀ **schneiden** VERB◇, IMPERFECT **schnitt**, PERFECT **hat geschnitten**
1 to cut
Ich kann dir die Haare schneiden. I can cut your hair.
Laura hat sich die Haare kurz schneiden lassen. Laura's had her hair cut short.
2 in Scheiben schneiden to slice
3 sich schneiden to cut yourself
Ich habe mich geschnitten. I've cut myself.
Ich habe mir in den Finger geschnitten. I've cut my finger.
4 sich schneiden to intersect
5 Gesichter schneiden to pull faces

der **Schneider**, PLURAL die **Schneider**
tailor (male)

WORD TIP Professions, hobbies, and sports don't take an article in German: Er ist Schneider.

die **Schneiderei**, PLURAL die **Schneidereien**
1 tailor's shop
2 dressmaker's shop

die **Schneiderin**, PLURAL die **Schneiderinnen**
dressmaker (female)

WORD TIP Professions, hobbies, and sports don't take an article in German: Sie ist Schneiderin.

♀ **schneien** VERB, PERFECT **hat geschneit**
to snow
Es schneit. It's snowing.

♀ **schnell** ADJECTIVE
quick, fast
schnell ADVERB
quickly
Mach schnell! Hurry up!

die **Schnelligkeit**
speed

♀ der **Schnellimbiss**, PLURAL die **Schnellimbisse**
snack bar

schnellstens ADVERB
as quickly as possible

der **Schnellzug**, PLURAL die **Schnellzüge**
fast train

schnitt ▸ SEE schneiden

der **Schnitt**, PLURAL die **Schnitte**
1 cut
Er hat einen tiefen Schnitt im Finger. He's got a deep cut in his finger.
Das Kostüm hat einen sehr guten Schnitt. The suit is very well cut.
2 average
im Schnitt on average
3 (paper) pattern
4 editing (of a film)

der **Schnittlauch**
chives

das **Schnitzel**, PLURAL die **Schnitzel**
1 escalope
2 scrap

schnitzen VERB, PERFECT **hat geschnitzt**
to carve

der **Schnorchel**, PLURAL die **Schnorchel**
snorkel

schnüffeln VERB, PERFECT **hat geschnüffelt**
1 to sniff
2 to snoop around

der **Schnuller**, PLURAL die **Schnuller**
dummy

♀ der **Schnupfen**, PLURAL die **Schnupfen**
cold
Ich habe Schnupfen. I've got a cold.

die **Schnur**, PLURAL die **Schnüre**
1 (piece of) string
2 flex
3 cord

◇ irregular verb; SEP separable verb; for more help with verbs see centre section

der **Schnurrbart**, *PLURAL* die **Schnurrbärte**
moustache

schnurren *VERB*, *PERFECT* **hat geschnurrt**
to purr

das **Schnurrhaar**, *PLURAL* die **Schnurrhaare**
whisker

der **Schnürsenkel**, *PLURAL* die **Schnürsenkel**
shoelace

schob ▸SEE **schieben**

der **Schock**, *PLURAL* die **Schocks**
shock

schockieren *VERB*, *PERFECT* **hat schockiert**
to shock

℘ die **Schokolade**, *PLURAL* die **Schokoladen**
chocolate

℘ **schon** *ADVERB*
1 already
Er hat schon zweimal angerufen. He's called twice already.
2 (*'schon' is often not translated*)
schon wieder again
schon oft often
Du wirst schon sehen. You'll see.
Ja schon, aber ... Well yes, but ...
Nun geh schon! Go on then!
Du weißt schon ... You know ...
3 yet, ever (*in questions*)
Hast du sie schon gesehen? Have you seen her yet?
Warst du schon einmal in Paris? Have you ever been to Paris?
4 Komm schon! Come on!
5 schon deshalb for that reason alone
6 Das ist schon möglich. That's quite possible.
7 Er war schon mal da. He's been there before.

℘ **schön** *ADJECTIVE*
1 beautiful
2 nice
Schönes Wochenende! Have a nice weekend!
3 good
Na schön. All right then.
4 Schönen Dank! Thank you very much!
Schöne Grüße an deine Mutter! Best wishes to your mother!

schonen *VERB*, *PERFECT* **hat geschont**
1 to look after
2 sich schonen to take things easy

die **Schönheit**, *PLURAL* die **Schönheiten**
beauty

der **Schornstein**, *PLURAL* die **Schornsteine**
1 chimney
2 funnel (*of a ship*)

schoss ▸SEE **schießen**

der **Schoß**, *PLURAL* die **Schöße**
lap

der **Schotte**, *PLURAL* die **Schotten**
Scot, Scotsman
Er ist Schotte. He's a Scot.

die **Schottin**, *PLURAL* die **Schottinnen**
Scot, Scotswoman
Sie ist Schottin. She's a Scot.

schottisch *ADJECTIVE*
Scottish

> **WORD TIP** Adjectives never have capitals in German, even for regions, countries, or nationalities.

℘ **Schottland** *NEUTER NOUN*
Scotland

schräg *ADJECTIVE*
1 diagonal
2 sloping
schräg *ADVERB*
1 diagonally
schräg gegenüber diagonally opposite
2 etwas schräg halten to tilt something
etwas schräg stellen to put something at an angle

der **Schrägstrich**, *PLURAL* die **Schrägstriche**
forward slash

℘ der **Schrank**, *PLURAL* die **Schränke**
1 cupboard
2 wardrobe

die **Schranke**, *PLURAL* die **Schranken**
barrier

die **Schraube**, *PLURAL* die **Schrauben**
screw

schrauben *VERB*, *PERFECT* **hat geschraubt**
to screw

der **Schraubenschlüssel**, *PLURAL* die **Schraubenschlüssel**
spanner

der **Schraubenzieher**, *PLURAL* die **Schraubenzieher**
screwdriver

der **Schreck**
fright
Du hast mir einen Schreck eingejagt. You gave me a fright.
Ich habe einen Schreck bekommen. I got a fright.

℘ **schrecklich** ADJECTIVE
  terrible, awful

der **Schrei**, PLURAL die **Schreie**
1 cry, shout
2 scream
3 der letzte Schrei *(informal)* the latest thing

der **Schreibblock**, PLURAL die **Schreibblöcke**
  writing pad

℘ **schreiben** VERB◇, IMPERFECT **schrieb**, PERFECT
  hat geschrieben
1 to write
  David hat mir einen Brief geschrieben.
  David wrote a letter to me.
  Morgen schreiben wir einen Test. We've
  got a test tomorrow.
2 to spell
  Wie schreibt man das? How is it spelt?
3 to type

die **Schreibmaschine**, PLURAL die
  Schreibmaschinen
  typewriter

das **Schreibpapier**
  writing paper

℘ der **Schreibtisch**, PLURAL die **Schreibtische**
  desk

℘ die **Schreibwaren** PLURAL NOUN
  stationery

das **Schreibwarengeschäft**, PLURAL die
  Schreibwarengeschäfte
  stationery shop

℘ **schreien** VERB◇, IMPERFECT **schrie**, PERFECT **hat
  geschrien**
1 to cry, to shout
  Das Baby schreit. The baby's crying.
2 to scream
  Sie schrien vor Lachen. They screamed
  with laughter.
3 zum Schreien sein *(informal)* to be hilarious

der **Schreiner**, PLURAL die **Schreiner**
  joiner *(male)*

WORD TIP Professions, hobbies, and sports
don't take an article in German: Er ist Schreiner.

die **Schreinerin**, PLURAL die **Schreinerinnen**
  joiner *(female)*

WORD TIP Professions, hobbies, and sports
don't take an article in German: Sie ist
Schreinerin.

schrie ▸ SEE **schreien**

schrieb ▸ SEE **schreiben**

die **Schrift**, PLURAL die **Schriften**
1 writing
2 typeface
3 script

schriftlich ADJECTIVE
  written
schriftlich ADVERB
  in writing
  Das lasse ich mir schriftlich geben. I'll get
  that in writing.
  Er wurde schriftlich eingeladen. He was
  sent a written invitation.

der **Schriftsteller**, PLURAL die **Schriftsteller**
  writer *(male)*

WORD TIP Professions, hobbies, and sports don't
take an article in German: Er ist Schriftsteller.

die **Schriftstellerin**, PLURAL die
  Schriftstellerinnen
  writer *(female)*

WORD TIP Professions, hobbies, and sports don't
take an article in German: Sie ist Schriftstellerin.

der **Schritt**, PLURAL die **Schritte**
1 step
2 footstep

schrumpfen VERB, PERFECT **ist geschrumpft**
1 to shrink
2 to shrivel

die **Schublade**, PLURAL die **Schubladen**
  drawer

schubsen VERB, PERFECT **hat geschubst**
  to shove

℘ **schüchtern** ADJECTIVE
  shy

schuf ▸ SEE **schaffen**

℘ der **Schuh**, PLURAL die **Schuhe**
  shoe

die **Schuhgröße**, PLURAL die **Schuhgrößen**
  shoe size

der **Schulabschluss**, PLURAL die
  Schulabschlüsse
  school-leaving qualification

die **Schularbeit**, PLURAL die **Schularbeiten**
1 Schularbeiten homework
2 *(in Austria)* written test

◇ irregular verb; SEP separable verb; for more help with verbs see centre section

die **Schulaufgaben** *PLURAL NOUN*
homework

die **Schulbildung**
education *(at school)*

das **Schulbuch**, *PLURAL* die **Schulbücher**
(school) textbook

schuld *ADJECTIVE*
schuld sein to be to blame
Du bist schuld daran. It's your fault.

ℓ die **Schuld**
1 **blame**
Du hast Schuld! You're to blame!
Ich gebe den Politikern die Schuld. I blame the politicians.
2 **fault**
Es war seine Schuld. It was his fault.
3 **guilt**
Man konnte ihre Schuld nicht beweisen. Her guilt could not be proved.

schulden *VERB, PERFECT* **hat geschuldet**
to owe

die **Schulden** *PLURAL NOUN*
debt
Schulden haben to be in debt
Schulden machen to get into debt

schuldig *ADJECTIVE*
1 **guilty**
2 jemandem etwas schuldig sein to owe somebody something
Was bin ich Ihnen schuldig? How much do I owe you?

der **Schuldirektor**, *PLURAL* die **Schuldirektoren**
head teacher *(male)*

> **WORD TIP** Professions, hobbies, and sports don't take an article in German: Er ist Schuldirektor.

die **Schuldirektorin**, *PLURAL* die **Schuldirektorinnen**
head teacher *(female)*

> **WORD TIP** Professions, hobbies, and sports don't take an article in German: Sie ist Schuldirektorin.

ℓ die **Schule**, *PLURAL* die **Schulen**
school
Jan ist in der Schule. Jan's at school.
Sie gingen in die Schule. They went to school.

SCHULE

At the age of 10, pupils move from primary school (Grundschule or Volksschule) to one of three types of school in Germany: Hauptschule, Realschule, or Gymnasium. In some areas, there are comprehensive schools (Gesamtschulen). In Austria, pupils move to a Hauptschule or Gymnasium. The Austrian government wants to introduce a new type of school, the 'neue Mittelschule', with some of the features of a comprehensive school. In Switzerland, some cantons have only one type of secondary school, while others divide their pupils up into three types, too. The Hauptschule focuses on more practical subjects, the Gymnasium on more academic subjects. The Realschule is between the two.

schulen *VERB, PERFECT* **hat geschult**
to train

ℓ der **Schüler**, *PLURAL* die **Schüler**
pupil, student *(male)*

ℓ die **Schülerin**, *PLURAL* die **Schülerinnen**
pupil, student *(female)*

schwatzhaft *ADJECTIVE*
talkative

die **Schülermitverwaltung**
school council

die **Schülerzeitung**, *PLURAL* die **Schülerzeitungen**
school magazine

ℓ das **Schulfach**, *PLURAL* die **Schulfächer**
school subject

die **Schulferien** *PLURAL NOUN*
school holidays

schulfrei *ADJECTIVE*
ein schulfreier Tag a day off school
Wir haben heute schulfrei. There's no school today.

der **Schulfreund**, *PLURAL* die **Schulfreunde**
school friend *(male)*

die **Schulfreundin**, *PLURAL* die **Schulfreundinnen**
school friend *(female)*

das **Schulgelände**, *PLURAL* die **Schulgelände**
school grounds

die **Schulgruppe**, *PLURAL* die **Schulgruppen**
school group

das **Schulheft**, *PLURAL* die **Schulhefte**
exercise book

ℓ der **Schulhof**, *PLURAL* die **Schulhöfe**
playground

ℓ **indicates key words**

ℓ das **Schuljahr**, PLURAL die **Schuljahre**
school year

ℓ die **Schulklasse**, PLURAL die **Schulklassen**
class

der **Schulleiter**, PLURAL die **Schulleiter**
headmaster

die **Schulleiterin**, PLURAL die
Schulleiterinnen
headmistress

der **Schulschwänzer**, PLURAL die
Schulschwänzer
truant (male)

die **Schulschwänzerin**, PLURAL die
Schulschwänzerinnen
truant (female)

die **Schulstunde**, PLURAL die **Schulstunden**
period

das **Schulsystem**, PLURAL die **Schulsysteme**
school system

der **Schultag**, PLURAL die **Schultage**
school day

ℓ die **Schultasche**, PLURAL die **Schultaschen**
school bag

die **Schulter**, PLURAL die **Schultern**
shoulder

schummeln VERB, PERFECT **hat geschummelt**
to cheat

die **Schuppe**, PLURAL die **Schuppen**
1 scale (on a fish)
2 Schuppen dandruff
Gabi hat Schuppen. Gabi's got dandruff.

der **Schuppen**, PLURAL die **Schuppen**
shed

die **Schürze**, PLURAL die **Schürzen**
apron

der **Schuss**, PLURAL die **Schüsse**
1 shot
2 dash (of brandy, vinegar)
3 schuss (in skiing)

ℓ die **Schüssel**, PLURAL die **Schüsseln**
bowl, dish

der **Schuster**, PLURAL die **Schuster**
shoemaker, cobbler

WORD TIP Professions, hobbies, and sports
don't take an article in German: Er ist Schuster.

schütteln VERB, PERFECT **hat geschüttelt**
1 to shake
2 sich schütteln to shake yourself

Sie schüttelte sich vor Ekel. She
shuddered.

schütten VERB, PERFECT **hat geschüttet**
1 to pour
Ich schüttete Tee in die Tasse. I poured tea
into the cup.
Es schüttet. (informal) It's pouring (down).
2 to spill
Er schüttete Tee über den Schreibtisch. He
spilled tea on his desk.
3 to tip

der **Schutz**
1 protection
2 shelter
3 conservation

die **Schutzbrille**, PLURAL die **Schutzbrillen**
(pair of) goggles

WORD TIP In German, die Schutzbrille is
singular: Er trägt eine Schutzbrille.

der **Schütze**, PLURAL die **Schützen**
1 marksman
2 Sagittarius
Daniel ist Schütze. Daniel is Sagittarius.

ℓ **schützen** VERB, PERFECT **hat geschützt**
1 to protect
Die meisten Cremes schützen die Haut
gegen Sonnenbrand. Most creams protect
the skin from sunburn.
2 gesetzlich geschützt registered (as a
trademark)

die **Schutzhütte**, PLURAL die **Schutzhütten**
1 mountain refuge
2 shelter

ℓ **schwach** ADJECTIVE
1 weak
2 dim (light)
3 poor (performance, memory)

die **Schwäche**, PLURAL die **Schwächen**
weakness

schwachsinnig ADJECTIVE
idiotic

der **Schwager**, PLURAL die **Schwäger**
brother-in-law

die **Schwägerin**, PLURAL die **Schwägerinnen**
sister-in-law

die **Schwalbe**, PLURAL die **Schwalben**
swallow

schwamm ▶ SEE **schwimmen**

der **Schwamm**, PLURAL die **Schwämme**
sponge

◇ irregular verb; SEP separable verb; for more help with verbs see centre section

der **Schwan**, *PLURAL* die **Schwäne**
swan

schwanger *ADJECTIVE*
pregnant

die **Schwangerschaft**, *PLURAL* die
Schwangerschaften
pregnancy

schwanken *VERB*, *PERFECT* **hat geschwankt**
1 to sway
2 to fluctuate
3 to waver
4 *PERFECT* **ist geschwankt** to stagger

der **Schwanz**, *PLURAL* die **Schwänze**
tail

schwänzen *VERB*, *PERFECT* **hat geschwänzt**
1 to skip, to skive
2 Sie hat die letzte Stunde geschwänzt. She
skived the last lesson.
3 die Schule schwänzen to play truant

der **Schwarm**, *PLURAL* die **Schwärme**
1 swarm
2 Sie ist mein Schwarm. I've got a crush on
her.

schwärmen *VERB*, *PERFECT* **hat geschwärmt**
1 to swarm
2 für jemanden schwärmen to have a crush
on somebody
3 von etwas schwärmen to rave about
something

℘**schwarz** *ADJECTIVE*, *ADVERB*
1 black
Sie waren schwarz gekleidet. They were
dressed in black.
Sie trug ein schwarz gestreiftes Kleid. She
wore a dress with black stripes.
Das habe ich schwarz auf weiß. I have it in
black and white.
2 ins Schwarze treffen to hit the nail on the
head, to score a bull's eye
3 illegally
etwas schwarz machen to do something
illegally

das **Schwarzbrot**, *PLURAL* die **Schwarzbrote**
dark rye bread

der/die **Schwarze**, *PLURAL* die **Schwarzen**
black (man/woman)

schwarzsehen *VERB*◇, *PRESENT* **sieht
schwarz**, *IMPERFECT* **sah schwarz**, *PERFECT*
hat schwarzgesehen
to be pessimistic

der **Schwarzwald**
Black Forest

schwatzen *VERB*, *PERFECT* **hat geschwatzt**
to chatter

der **Schwede**, *PLURAL* die **Schweden**
Swede (male)

℘**Schweden** *NEUTER NOUN*
Sweden

die **Schwedin**, *PLURAL* die **Schwedinnen**
Swede (female)

schwedisch *ADJECTIVE*
Swedish

> **WORD TIP** Adjectives never have capitals
> in German, even for regions, countries, or
> nationalities.

schweigen *VERB*◇, *IMPERFECT* **schwieg**, *PERFECT*
hat geschwiegen
1 to be silent, to say nothing
2 ganz zu schweigen von ... not to
mention ...

℘das **Schwein**, *PLURAL* die **Schweine**
1 pig
2 pork
3 Du Schwein! (informal) You swine!
4 Schwein haben (informal) to be lucky

der **Schweinebraten**
roast pork

das **Schweinefleisch**
pork

das **Schweinekotelett**, *PLURAL* die
Schweinekoteletts
pork chop

der **Schweiß**
sweat

℘die **Schweiz**
die Schweiz Switzerland

> **WORD TIP** This is always used with an article:
> Wir fahren in die Schweiz. Er wohnt in der
> Schweiz.

🔘 **SWITZERLAND**

Capital: Bern. Population: nearly 8 million. Size:
41,285 square km. Main languages: German,
French, Italian, and Romansh (a language
derived from Latin). Official currency: Swiss
franc.

der **Schweizer**, *PLURAL* die **Schweizer**
Swiss (male)

die **Schweizerin**, *PLURAL* die
Schweizerinnen
Swiss (female)

℘ indicates key words

schweizerisch *ADJECTIVE*
Swiss

> **WORD TIP** Adjectives never have capitals
> in German, even for regions, countries, or
> nationalities.

die **Schwelle**, *PLURAL* die **Schwellen**
threshold

die **Schwellung**, *PLURAL* die **Schwellungen**
swelling

_♟_ **schwer** *ADJECTIVE*
1 heavy
 Er trug eine schwere Schultasche. He
 carried a heavy school bag.
 Der Koffer ist zwanzig Kilo schwer. The
 suitcase weighs twenty kilos.
2 difficult
3 serious

schwer *ADVERB*
1 heavily
2 seriously
 Er ist schwer krank. He's seriously ill.
3 Sie müssen schwer arbeiten. They have to
 to work hard.

_♟_ die **Schwerarbeit**
heavy work

schwerfallen *VERB◇*, *PRESENT* **fällt schwer**,
IMPERFECT **fiel schwer**, *PERFECT* **ist**
schwergefallen
jemandem schwerfallen to be hard for
somebody

schwerhörig *ADJECTIVE*
hard of hearing, deaf

das **Schwert**, *PLURAL* die **Schwerter**
sword

schwertun *VERB◇*, *IMPERFECT* **tat sich**
schwer, *PERFECT* **hat sich schwergetan**
sich mit etwas schwertun to have
difficulty with something

_♟_ die **Schwester**, *PLURAL* die **Schwestern**
sister

schwieg ▸SEE **schweigen**

die **Schwiegereltern** *PLURAL NOUN*
parents-in-law

die **Schwiegermutter**, *PLURAL* die
Schwiegermütter
mother-in-law

der **Schwiegersohn**, *PLURAL* die
Schwiegersöhne
son-in-law

die **Schwiegertochter**, *PLURAL* die
Schwiegertöchter
daughter-in-law

der **Schwiegervater**, *PLURAL* die
Schwiegerväter
father-in-law

_♟_ **schwierig** *ADJECTIVE*
difficult

die **Schwierigkeit**, *PLURAL* die
Schwierigkeiten
difficulty

_♟_ das **Schwimmbad**, *PLURAL* die
Schwimmbäder
swimming pool

_♟_ **schwimmen** *VERB◇*, *IMPERFECT* **schwamm**,
PERFECT **ist/hat geschwommen**
1 to swim
2 to float

das **Sekretariat**, *PLURAL* die **Sekretariate**
(secretary's) office

der **Schwimmer**, *PLURAL* die **Schwimmer**
swimmer *(male)*

das **Schwimmerbecken**, *PLURAL* die
Schwimmerbecken
swimmers-only pool, swimming pool *(for
experienced swimmers)*

die **Schwimmerin**, *PLURAL* die
Schwimmerinnen
swimmer *(female)*

die **Schwimmweste**, *PLURAL* die
Schwimmwesten
life jacket

schwindlig *ADJECTIVE*
dizzy
Mir ist schwindlig. I feel dizzy.

der **Schwips**, *PLURAL* die **Schwipse**
einen Schwips haben to be tipsy

schwitzen *VERB*, *PERFECT* **hat geschwitzt**
to sweat

schwören *VERB◇*, *IMPERFECT* **schwor**, *PERFECT*
hat geschworen
to swear

schwul *ADJECTIVE*
gay

schwül *ADJECTIVE*
close *(muggy)*

der **Schwule**, *PLURAL* die **Schwulen**
gay man

◇ **irregular verb;** *SEP* **separable verb; for more help with verbs see centre section**

der **Schwung**, PLURAL die **Schwünge**
1 swing
2 drive
3 Philip brachte die Party in Schwung. Philip got the party going.

die **Science-Fiction**
science fiction

sechs NUMBER
six

ℰ die **Sechs**, PLURAL die **Sechsen**
1 six
2 unsatisfactory (school mark)

> **WORD TIP** Sechs is the worst mark in Germany, but in Austria the worst mark is Fünf.

das **Sechstel**, PLURAL die **Sechstel**
sixth

sechster, sechste, sechstes ADJECTIVE
sixth

ℰ **sechzehn** NUMBER
sixteen

ℰ **sechzig** NUMBER
sixty

ℰ der **See**[1], PLURAL die **Seen**
lake
der Starnberger See Lake Starnberg

ℰ die **See**[2]
1 sea
Die See war stürmisch. The sea was rough.
die irische See the Irish Sea
2 seaside
Wir fahren an die See. We're going to the seaside.
An der See ist es schön. It's nice at the seaside.

> **WORD TIP** The word See has two meanings, depending on the gender. Note that an der See (DAT) belongs to die See.

der **Seehund**, PLURAL die **Seehunde**
seal

seekrank ADJECTIVE
seasick

die **Seekrankheit**
seasickness

das **Seniorenheim**, PLURAL die **Seniorenheime**
old people's home

die **Seele**, PLURAL die **Seelen**
soul

der **Seemann**, PLURAL die **Seeleute**
seaman, sailor

der **Seetang**
seaweed

das **Segel**, PLURAL die **Segel**
sail

das **Segelboot**, PLURAL die **Segelboote**
sailing boat

das **Segelfliegen**
gliding

das **Segelflugzeug**, PLURAL die **Segelflugzeuge**
glider

der **Segellehrer**, PLURAL die **Segellehrer**
sailing instructor (male)

> **WORD TIP** Professions, hobbies, and sports don't take an article in German: Er ist Segellehrer.

die **Segellehrerin**, PLURAL die **Segellehrerinnen**
sailing instructor (female)

> **WORD TIP** Professions, hobbies, and sports don't take an article in German: Sie ist Segellehrerin.

ℰ **segeln** VERB, PERFECT **ist gesegelt**
to sail

sehen VERB◇, PRESENT **sieht**, IMPERFECT **sah**, PERFECT **hat gesehen**
1 to see
Ich habe Lena in der Stadt gesehen. I saw Lena in town.
Mal sehen, ob ... Let's see if ...
2 to look
Sieh mal! Look!
Er sah aus dem Fenster. He was looking out of the window.
3 gut/schlecht sehen to have good/bad eyesight
4 nach jemandem sehen to look after somebody

sehenswert ADJECTIVE
worth seeing

ℰ die **Sehenswürdigkeiten** PLURAL NOUN
sights
Sehenswürdigkeiten besichtigen to go sightseeing

die **Sehnsucht**
longing
Ich habe Sehnsucht nach meiner Schwester. I'm longing to see my sister.

sehnsüchtig ADJECTIVE
longing

A B C D E F G H I J K L M N O P Q R S T U V W X Y Z

ℰ **indicates key words**

sehr *ADVERB*
1 **very**
   sehr gut very good *(also as a school mark)*
2 **Danke sehr.** Thank you very much.
3 **Ich habe Alina sehr gern.** I like Alina a lot.
4 **Sehr geehrte Frau Huber!** Dear Mrs Huber, ... *(in a letter)*

seid ▸ SEE **sein**

die Seide, *PLURAL* **die Seiden**
   silk

die Seife, *PLURAL* **die Seifen**
   soap

die Seifenoper, *PLURAL* **die Seifenopern**
   soap opera

das Seil, *PLURAL* **die Seile**
1 **rope**
2 **cable**

die Seilbahn, *PLURAL* **die Seilbahnen**
   cable railway

sein¹ *VERB◇, PRESENT* **ist**, *IMPERFECT* **war**, *PERFECT* **ist gewesen**
1 **to be**
   Wir sind in der Küche. We're in the kitchen.
   Rosi ist krank. Rosi is ill.
   Mir ist schlecht. I feel sick.
   Mir ist kalt/heiß. I'm cold/hot.
2 **Sie ist Lehrerin.** She's a teacher.
3 **Es ist drei Uhr.** It's three o'clock.
   Karl ist aus München. Karl's from Munich.
   Es war viel zu tun. There was a lot to be done.
4 **aus Seide sein** to be made of silk
5 **etwas sein lassen** to stop something
   Lass das sein! Stop it!
6 **es sei denn, dass ...** unless ...
7 *(used with certain verbs to form past tenses)*
   Ich bin nach Berlin gefahren. I went to Berlin.
   Wir sind kurz vor acht nach Hause gekommen. We got home shortly before eight o'clock.
   Er ist abgeholt worden. He's been collected.

sein² *ADJECTIVE*
1 **his**
   Sein Bruder heißt Kevin. His brother is called Kevin.
2 *(when referring to a thing or animal)* **its**
   Der Hund ist in seiner Hütte. The dog is in its kennel.

3 *(after the pronoun man)* **your, one's**
   Wenn man sich seine Eltern aussuchen könnte, ... If you could choose your parents, ...

seiner, seine, sein(e)s *PRONOUN*
1 **his**
   Das ist nicht meine CD, das ist seine. It's not my CD, it's his.
   Du kannst seins nehmen. You can take his.
2 *(after the pronoun 'man')* **your own, one's own**
   das Seine tun to do your share

seinetwegen *ADVERB*
1 **for his sake**
2 **because of him**
3 **on his account**

seins ▸ SEE **seiner**

seit *PREPOSITION (+ DAT) CONJUNCTION*
1 **since**
   Ich habe ihn seit Sonntag nicht gesehen. I haven't seen him since Sunday.
   Seit du hier wohnst, hast du dich verändert. You've changed since you came to live here.
   Seit wann? Since when?
2 **for**
   Ich bin seit zwei Wochen hier. I've been here for two weeks.
   seit einiger Zeit for some time

seitdem *ADVERB*
   since then
   Ich habe sie seitdem nicht mehr gesehen. I haven't seen her since.

seitdem *CONJUNCTION*
   since

die Seite, *PLURAL* **die Seiten**
1 **side**
   Der Eingang ist auf der rechten Seite. The entrance is on the right side.
2 **page**
   Das steht auf Seite zwanzig. It's on page twenty.
3 **auf der einen Seite ... auf der anderen Seite** on the one hand ... on the other hand

das Seitenstechen
   stitch
   Ich habe Seitenstechen. I've got a stitch.

die Seitenstraße, *PLURAL* **die Seitenstraßen**
   side street

seither *ADVERB*
   since then

◇ **irregular verb;** *SEP* **separable verb; for more help with verbs see centre section**

𝒫 der **Sekretär**, PLURAL die **Sekretäre**
secretary (male)

WORD TIP Professions, hobbies, and sports don't take an article in German: Er ist Sekretär.

𝒫 die **Sekretärin**, PLURAL die **Sekretärinnen**
secretary (female)

WORD TIP Professions, hobbies, and sports don't take an article in German: Sie ist Sekretärin.

der **Sekt**, PLURAL die **Sekte**
sparkling wine

die **Sekte**, PLURAL die **Sekten**
sect

die **Sekunde**, PLURAL die **Sekunden**
second

𝒫 **selbst** PRONOUN
1 ich selbst I myself
er selbst he himself
wir selbst we ourselves
Sie selbst you yourself, you yourselves
2 von selbst by itself
3 Sie schneidet sich die Haare selbst. She cuts her own hair.
4 on your own
Ich kann es selbst machen. I can do it on my own.
5 selbst gemacht home-made

selbst ADVERB
even
Selbst wenn ... Even if ...

die **Selbstbedienung**
self-service

selbstbewusst ADJECTIVE
confident, self-confident

das **Selbstbewusstsein**
confidence, self-confidence

der **Selbstmord**, PLURAL die **Selbstmorde**
suicide
Selbstmord begehen to commit suicide

𝒫 **selbstsicher** ADJECTIVE
confident, self-confident

𝒫 **selbstständig** ADJECTIVE
1 independent
2 self-employed
Er möchte sich selbstständig machen. He wants to set up on his own.

selbstsüchtig ADJECTIVE
selfish

selbstverständlich ADJECTIVE
natural

etwas für selbstverständlich halten to take something for granted
Das ist doch selbstverständlich. It goes without saying.

selbstverständlich ADVERB
naturally, of course
Wir haben ihn selbstverständlich auf die Party eingeladen. Of course we invited him to the party.

𝒫 **selten** ADJECTIVE
rare
selten ADVERB
rarely

seltsam ADJECTIVE
strange, odd

das **Semester**, PLURAL die **Semester**
semester, term

das **Semikolon**, PLURAL die **Semikolons**
semicolon

die **Semmel**, PLURAL die **Semmeln**
(in Southern Germany and Austria)
(bread) roll

𝒫 **senden** VERB, PERFECT **hat gesendet**
1 to send
Bitte senden Sie uns weitere Informationen. Please send further details.
2 to broadcast
Seine Rede wird im ersten Programm gesendet. His speech will be broadcast on channel one.
3 to transmit

der **Sender**, PLURAL die **Sender**
television/radio station, channel

WORD TIP The German word Sender does not mean sender in English; the German word for sender is Absender.

die **Sendereihe**, PLURAL die **Sendereihen**
series (on television or radio)

𝒫 die **Sendung**, PLURAL die **Sendungen**
1 programme
2 consignment

der **Senf**, PLURAL die **Senfe**
mustard

der **Senior**, PLURAL die **Senioren**
1 senior (male)
2 senior citizen (male)

die **Seniorin**, PLURAL die **Seniorinnen**
1 senior (female)
2 senior citizen (female)

simsen VERB, PERFECT **hat gesimst**
to text

𝒫 indicates key words

senkrecht *ADJECTIVE*
vertical

die Sensation, PLURAL **die Sensationen**
sensation, stir

sensationell *ADJECTIVE*
sensational

sensibel *ADJECTIVE*
sensitive

> **WORD TIP** The German word sensibel does not
> mean sensible in English; the German word for
> sensible is vernünftig.

sentimental *ADJECTIVE*
sentimental

℗ der **September**
September
im September in September

die Sequenz, PLURAL **die Sequenzen**
sequence (in a film)

℗ die **Serie**, PLURAL **die Serien**
1 series
2 serial

das **Service¹**, PLURAL **die Service**
set (of china, for example)

der **Service²**
service
Das Essen im Hotel ist gut, aber der
Service ist furchtbar. The food in the hotel
is good but the service is appalling.

die Sitzbank, PLURAL **die Sitzbänke**
bench

servieren *VERB, PERFECT* **hat serviert**
to serve

die Serviette, PLURAL **die Servietten**
napkin, serviette

servus *EXCLAMATION*
1 (used in Southern Germany and Austria)
hello!
2 bye!

der **Sessel**, PLURAL **die Sessel**
armchair

der **Sessellift**, PLURAL **die Sessellifte**
chairlift

℗ **setzen** *VERB, PERFECT* **hat gesetzt**
1 to put
Hier musst du ein Komma setzen. You
have to put a comma here.
Vergiss nicht, deinen Namen auf die Liste
zu setzen. Don't forget to put your name
on the list.

2 to move (a counter in games)
3 auf etwas setzen to bet on something
auf ein Pferd setzen to back a horse
4 sich setzen to sit down
Er setzte sich auf einen Stuhl. He sat down
on a chair.

seufzen *VERB, PERFECT* **hat geseufzt**
to sigh

der **Seufzer**, PLURAL **die Seufzer**
sigh

skateboarden *VERB, PERFECT* **ist
geskateboardet**
to skateboard

der **Sex**
sex
Sex mit jemandem haben to have sex with
somebody

der **Sexismus**
sexism

sexistisch *ADJECTIVE*
sexist

sexuell *ADJECTIVE*
sexual

℗ das **Shampoo**, PLURAL **die Shampoos**
shampoo

die Shorts PLURAL NOUN
shorts

der **Shuttledienst**, PLURAL **die
Shuttledienste**
shuttle service

℗ **sich** *PRONOUN*
1 (with er/sie/es) himself/herself/itself
Sie hat sich eingeschlossen. She locked
herself in.
2 (with plural sie) themselves
3 (with Sie) yourself, yourselves (plural)
4 (with man) yourself, oneself
5 each other, one another
Sie kennen sich. They know each other.
Petra und Werner lieben sich. Petra and
Werner love each other.
6 (not translated with certain verbs)
sich freuen to be pleased
sich wundern to be surprised
7 Anita wäscht sich die Haare. Anita is
washing her hair.
Max hat sich den Arm gebrochen. Max
broke his arm.
8 sich gut verkaufen to sell well
9 von sich aus of your own accord

℗ **sicher** *ADJECTIVE*
1 safe

◇ **irregular verb**; *SEP* **separable verb**; for more help with verbs see centre section

2 certain, sure
Bist du sicher? Are you sure?

sicher _ADVERB_
1 safely
2 certainly, surely
Sicher! Certainly!

die Sicherheit
1 safety
zur Sicherheit for safety's sake
Schnallen Sie sich zu Ihrer eigenen
Sicherheit an. Fasten your seat belt for
your own safety.
etwas in Sicherheit bringen to rescue
something
in Sicherheit sein to be safe
2 security
Die Sicherheit der Arbeitsplätze steht an
erster Stelle. Job security comes first.
3 certainty
Mit Sicherheit! Certainly! _(as a reply)_

der Sicherheitsgurt, _PLURAL_ die
Sicherheitsgurte
seat belt

die Sicherheitsnadel, _PLURAL_ die
Sicherheitsnadeln
safety pin

sicherlich _ADVERB_
definitely, certainly

sichern _VERB_, _PERFECT_ **hat gesichert**
to secure
jemandem etwas sichern to secure
something for somebody

die Sicherung, _PLURAL_ die **Sicherungen**
1 fuse
Die Sicherung ist durchgebrannt. The fuse
has blown.
2 safeguard
Die Gewerkschaft forderte die
Sicherung der Arbeitsplätze. The trade
union demanded that jobs should be
safeguarded.
3 safety catch

die Sicht
1 view
Ich hatte eine gute Sicht auf den See. I had
a good view of the lake.
2 visibility
Die Sicht war gut/schlecht. Visibility was
good/poor.
3 auf lange Sicht in the long term
4 aus meiner Sicht as I see it

sichtbar _ADJECTIVE_
visible

_♪_ **sie** _PRONOUN_
1 she
2 her
Ich kenne sie. I know her.
3 it
So eine hübsche Bluse, war sie teuer?
What a pretty blouse. Was it expensive?
4 they
Sie sind in der Küche. They're in the
kitchen.
5 them
Ich habe sie gestern abgeschickt. I posted
them yesterday.

WORD TIP When referring to a thing, sie is
translated as it.

_♪_ **Sie** _PRONOUN_
you _(polite form singular and plural)_
Kommen Sie herein! Come in!

WORD TIP The word Sie is used when talking to
anybody other than family members, people of
your own age, and close friends.

das Sieb, _PLURAL_ die **Siebe**
1 sieve
2 strainer

_♪_ **sieben** _NUMBER_
seven

_♪_ **die Sieben**, _PLURAL_ die **Siebenen**
seven

das Siebtel, _PLURAL_ die **Siebtel**
seventh

siebter, siebte, siebtes _ADJECTIVE_
seventh

_♪_ **siebzehn** _NUMBER_
seventeen

_♪_ **siebzig** _NUMBER_
seventy

die Siedlung, _PLURAL_ die **Siedlungen**
1 (housing) estate
2 settlement

der Sieg, _PLURAL_ die **Siege**
victory, win

das Siegel, _PLURAL_ die **Siegel**
seal

siegen _VERB_, _PERFECT_ **hat gesiegt**
to win

der Sieger, _PLURAL_ die **Sieger**
winner _(male)_

die Siegerin, _PLURAL_ die **Siegerinnen**
winner _(female)_

265

sieht ▶ SEE sehen

siezen VERB, PERFECT **hat gesiezt**
to call somebody 'Sie'
Sie siezen sich immer, obwohl sie sich schon seit 20 Jahren kennen. They still say 'Sie' to each other, although they've known each other for 20 years.

WORD TIP The word Sie is used when talking to anybody other than family members, people of your own age, and close friends.

die **Silbe**, PLURAL die **Silben**
syllable

ℙ das **Silber**
silver

silbern ADJECTIVE
silver

der or das **Silvester**
New Year's Eve

ℙ der **Silvesterabend**
New Year's Eve

die **Silvesternacht**
night of New Year's Eve

sind ▶ SEE sein

die **Sinfonie**, PLURAL die **Sinfonien**
symphony

ℙ **singen** VERB◇, IMPERFECT **sang**, PERFECT **hat gesungen**
to sing

sinken VERB◇, IMPERFECT **sank**, PERFECT **ist gesunken**
1 to sink
2 to go down

der **Sinn**, PLURAL die **Sinne**
1 sense
2 meaning
3 point
Das hat keinen Sinn. There's no point.

die **Solarenergie**
solar energy

die **Solarzelle**, PLURAL die **Solarzellen**
solar cell

sinnlos ADJECTIVE
pointless

ℙ **sinnvoll** ADJECTIVE
1 sensible
2 meaningful

der **Sirup**, PLURAL die **Sirupe**
(fruit-flavoured) syrup

die **Situation**, PLURAL die **Situationen**
situation

der **Sitz**, PLURAL die **Sitze**
1 seat
2 fit (of clothes)

ℙ **sitzen** VERB◇, IMPERFECT **saß**, PERFECT **hat gesessen**
1 to sit
Wir saßen auf dem Sofa. We were sitting on the sofa.
Bitte bleiben Sie sitzen. Please remain seated.
2 sitzen bleiben to have to repeat a year, to stay down (at school)
3 Er sitzt. (informal) He's in jail.
4 jemanden sitzen lassen (informal) to leave somebody in the lurch
5 to fit (of clothes)
Der Rock sitzt gut. The skirt fits well.

der **Sitzplatz**, PLURAL die **Sitzplätze**
seat

die **Sitzung**, PLURAL die **Sitzungen**
1 meeting
2 session

Sizilien NEUTER NOUN
Sicily

ℙ der **Skandal**, PLURAL die **Skandale**
scandal

Skandinavien NEUTER NOUN
Scandinavia

skandinavisch ADJECTIVE
Scandinavian

WORD TIP Adjectives never have capitals in German, even for regions, countries, or nationalities.

ℙ das **Skateboard**, PLURAL die **Skateboards**
skateboard
Skateboard fahren to skateboard, to go skateboarding

der **Skater**, PLURAL die **Skater**
skateboarder (male)

die **Skaterin**, PLURAL die **Skaterinnen**
skateboarder (female)

das **Skelett**, PLURAL die **Skelette**
skeleton

skeptisch ADJECTIVE
sceptical

ℙ der **Ski**, PLURAL die **Ski(er)**
ski
Ski fahren/laufen to ski, to go skiing

◇ irregular verb; SEP separable verb; for more help with verbs see centre section

der **Skianzug**, *PLURAL* die **Skianzüge**
ski suit

die **Skibrille**, *PLURAL* die **Skibrillen**
ski goggles

> **WORD TIP** In German, die Skibrille is singular:
> Er trägt eine Skibrille.

℗ das **Skifahren**
skiing

der **Skifahrer**, *PLURAL* die **Skifahrer**
skier *(male)*

> **WORD TIP** Professions, hobbies, and sports
> don't take an article in German: Er ist Skifahrer.

die **Skifahrerin**, *PLURAL* die **Skifahrerinnen**
skier *(female)*

> **WORD TIP** Professions, hobbies, and sports don't
> take an article in German: Sie ist Skifahrerin.

das **Skilaufen**
skiing

der **Skiläufer**, *PLURAL* die **Skiläufer**
skier *(male)*

> **WORD TIP** Professions, hobbies, and sports
> don't take an article in German: Er ist Skiläufer.

die **Skiläuferin**, *PLURAL* die **Skiläuferinnen**
skier *(female)*

> **WORD TIP** Professions, hobbies, and sports don't
> take an article in German: Sie ist Skiläuferin.

der **Skilehrer**, *PLURAL* die **Skilehrer**
ski instructor *(male)*

> **WORD TIP** Professions, hobbies, and sports
> don't take an article in German: Er ist Skilehrer.

die **Skilehrerin**, *PLURAL* die **Skilehrerinnen**
ski instructor *(female)*

> **WORD TIP** Professions, hobbies, and sports don't
> take an article in German: Sie ist Skilehrerin.

die **Skizze**, *PLURAL* die **Skizzen**
sketch

der **Skooter**, *PLURAL* die **Skooter**
bumper car, dodgem car

der **Skorpion**, *PLURAL* die **Skorpione**
1 scorpion
2 Scorpio
Julia ist Skorpion. Julia is Scorpio.

die **Skulptur**, *PLURAL* die **Skulpturen**
sculpture

der **Slip**, *PLURAL* die **Slips**
briefs, pants

der **Slowake**, *PLURAL* die **Slowaken**
Slovak *(male)*

℗ die **Slowakei**
die Slowakei Slovakia

> **WORD TIP** This is always used with an article: Wir
> fahren in die Slowakei. Er wohnt in der Slowakei.

die **Slowakin**, *PLURAL* die **Slowakinnen**
Slovak *(female)*

slowakisch *ADJECTIVE*
Slovak

> **WORD TIP** Adjectives never have capitals
> in German, even for regions, countries, or
> nationalities.

der **Slowene**, *PLURAL* die **Slowenen**
Slovene, Slovenian *(male)*

℗ **Slowenien** *NEUTER NOUN*
Slovenia

die **Slowenin**, *PLURAL* die **Sloweninnen**
Slovene, Slovenian *(female)*

slowenisch *ADJECTIVE*
Slovene, Slovenian

> **WORD TIP** Adjectives never have capitals
> in German, even for regions, countries, or
> nationalities.

der **Smoking**, *PLURAL* die **Smokings**
dinner jacket

℗ die **SMS**, *PLURAL* die **SMS** *ABBREVIATION*
(=Short Message Service) **text message**

die **SMV** *ABBREVIATION*
(=Schülermitverwaltung) **school council**

das **Snowboard**, *PLURAL* die **Snowboards**
snowboard
Snowboard fahren to snowboard, to go
snowboarding

℗ **so** *ADVERB*
1 so
nicht so viel not so much
und so weiter and so on
2 like this, like that
so nicht not like that
3 as
Ich rufe so bald wie möglich an. I'll call as
soon as possible.
4 such
Er ist so ein Feigling. He's such a coward.
So ein Zufall! What a coincidence!
5 Das kriegst du so. *(informal)* You get it for
nothing.
6 so um zwanzig Euro *(informal)* about
twenty euros

so CONJUNCTION
so dass so that

so EXCLAMATION
right!, well!
So? Really?

So. ABBREVIATION
(=Sonntag) Sunday

sobald CONJUNCTION
as soon as

♀ die **Socke**, PLURAL die **Socken**
sock

♀ das **Sofa**, PLURAL die **Sofas**
sofa

♀ **sofort** ADVERB
immediately, at once

die **Software**, PLURAL die **Softwares**
software

sogar ADVERB
even

sogleich ADVERB
at once

die **Sohle**, PLURAL die **Sohlen**
sole

der **Sohn**, PLURAL die **Söhne**
son

die **Soja**
soya

solange CONJUNCTION
as long as

solch ADVERB
such
solch einer/eine/eines one like that,
somebody like that

solcher, solche, solches ADJECTIVE, PRONOUN
1 such
Solch einen Quatsch habe ich noch nie
gehört! I've never heard such rubbish.
2 so
Ich habe solche Angst. I'm so frightened.
3 ein solcher Mann a man like that
eine solche Frage a question like that
ein solches Haus a house like that
4 solche (plural) those
solche wie die people like that

♀ der **Soldat**, PLURAL die **Soldaten**
soldier (male)

WORD TIP Professions, hobbies, and sports
don't take an article in German: Er ist Soldat.

♀ die **Soldatin**, PLURAL die **Soldatinnen**
soldier (female)

WORD TIP Professions, hobbies, and sports
don't take an article in German: Sie ist Soldatin.

solide ADJECTIVE
1 solid
2 respectable

der **Solist**, PLURAL die **Solisten**
soloist (male)

WORD TIP Professions, hobbies, and sports
don't take an article in German: Er ist Solist.

die **Solistin**, PLURAL die **Solistinnen**
soloist (female)

WORD TIP Professions, hobbies, and sports
don't take an article in German: Sie ist Solistin.

♀ **sollen** VERB◇, PRESENT **soll**, IMPERFECT
sollte, PERFECT **hat gesollt, hat sollen**
1 should
Sollte es regnen, fällt das Fest aus. If it
should rain, the party will be cancelled.
2 to be supposed to
Was soll das heißen? What's that
supposed to mean?
3 Sagen Sie ihr, sie soll anrufen. Tell her
to ring.
4 shall
Was soll ich machen? What shall I do?
Soll ich? Shall I?
5 Was soll's! So what!

WORD TIP The past participle is gesollt when
sollen is the main verb, and sollen when it is
an auxiliary verb.

sollte, sollten, solltest, solltet ▶ SEE **sollen**

solo ADVERB
solo

♀ der **Sommer**, PLURAL die **Sommer**
summer

die **Sommerferien** PLURAL NOUN
summer holidays

sommerlich ADJECTIVE
summery, summer

der **Sommerschlussverkauf**, PLURAL die
Sommerschlussverkäufe
summer sale

die **Sommersprossen** PLURAL NOUN
freckles

das **Sonderangebot**, PLURAL die **Sonderangebote**
special offer
Erdbeeren sind heute im Sonderangebot.
Strawberries are on special offer today.

sonderbar ADJECTIVE
strange, odd

die **Sonderfahrt**, PLURAL die **Sonderfahrten**
special excursion

ℓ **sondern** CONJUNCTION
but
nicht nur ..., sondern auch ... not only ...,
but also ...

der **Sonderpreis**, PLURAL die **Sonderpreise**
reduced price

der **Song**, PLURAL die **Songs**
song

der **Sonnabend**, PLURAL die **Sonnabende**
Saturday
am Sonnabend on Saturday

sonnabends ADVERB
on Saturdays

ℓ die **Sonne**, PLURAL die **Sonnen**
sun

sonnen VERB, PERFECT **hat sich gesonnt**
sich sonnen to sun yourself, to sunbathe

der **Sonnenaufgang**
sunrise

der **Sonnenbrand**
sunburn

die **Sonnenbräune**
suntan

ℓ die **Sonnenbrille**, PLURAL die **Sonnenbrillen**
sunglasses

> **WORD TIP** In German, die Sonnenbrille is
> singular: Sie trägt eine Sonnenbrille.

die **Sonnencreme**, PLURAL die
Sonnencremes
sun cream

die **Sonnenenergie**
solar energy

die **Sonnenmilch**
suntan lotion

das **Sonnenöl**
suntan oil

der **Sonnenschein**
sunshine

der **Sonnenstich**
sunstroke

ℓ **sonnig** ADJECTIVE
sunny

ℓ der **Sonntag**, PLURAL die **Sonntage**
Sunday
am Sonntag on Sunday

sonntags ADVERB
on Sundays

ℓ **sonst** ADVERB
1 usually
2 else
Wer sonst? Who else?
Was sonst? What else?
3 Sonst noch etwas? Anything else?
Sonst noch jemand? Anybody else?
4 sonst wo somewhere
Es kann sonst wo sein. It could be
anywhere.
5 otherwise
Geh jetzt, sonst verpasst du den Bus. Go
now, otherwise you'll miss the bus.

sonstig ADJECTIVE
other
Sie verkaufen Bücher, Zubehör und
Sonstiges. They sell books, accessories,
and other things.

sooft CONJUNCTION
whenever

ℓ die **Sorge**, PLURAL die **Sorgen**
worry
sich Sorgen machen to worry

sorgen VERB, PERFECT **hat gesorgt**
1 für etwas sorgen to take care of
something
Kannst du für die Musik sorgen? Can you
see to the music?
für jemanden sorgen to look after
somebody
2 dafür sorgen, dass ... to make sure that ...
3 sich sorgen to worry
Ich sorge mich um meine Eltern. I worry
about my parents.

sorgfältig ADJECTIVE
careful

die **Sorte**, PLURAL die **Sorten**
1 kind
2 brand

die **Soße**, PLURAL die **Soßen**
1 sauce
2 gravy
3 dressing

das **Souvenir**, PLURAL die **Souvenirs**
souvenir

soviel CONJUNCTION
as far as
Soviel ich weiß, sind sie weggezogen. As far as I know they've moved away.

soweit CONJUNCTION
as far as
Soweit ich weiß, ist er in den Ferien. As far as I know, he's on holiday.

sowie CONJUNCTION
1 as well as
2 as soon as

sowieso ADVERB
anyway

ℙ**sowohl** ADVERB
sowohl ... als auch ... both ... and ...
Sowohl er als auch sein Freund haben das Rauchen aufgegeben. Both he and his friend have given up smoking.

sozial ADJECTIVE
1 social
soziale Medien social media
2 der soziale Wohnungsbau building of council housing

der **Sozialarbeiter**, PLURAL die **Sozialarbeiter**
social worker (male)

WORD TIP Professions, hobbies, and sports don't take an article in German: Er ist Sozialarbeiter.

die **Sozialarbeiterin**, PLURAL die **Sozialarbeiterinnen**
social worker (female)

WORD TIP Professions, hobbies, and sports don't take an article in German: Sie ist Sozialarbeiterin.

die **Sozialhilfe**
social security

der **Sozialismus**
socialism

sozialistisch ADJECTIVE
socialist

die **Sozialkunde**
social studies

die **Sozialwissenschaft**, PLURAL die **Sozialwissenschaften**
social science

die **Sozialwohnung**, PLURAL die **Sozialwohnungen**
council flat

die **Soziologie**
sociology

sozusagen ADVERB
so to speak

die **Spaghetti** PLURAL NOUN
spaghetti

die **Spalte**, PLURAL die **Spalten**
1 crack
2 column (in text)

spalten VERB, PERFECT **hat gespalten**
to split

ℙ**Spanien** NEUTER NOUN
Spain

ℙ der **Spanier**, PLURAL die **Spanier**
Spaniard (male)

ℙ die **Spanierin**, PLURAL die **Spanierinnen**
Spaniard (female)

spanisch ADJECTIVE
Spanish

WORD TIP Adjectives never have capitals in German, even for regions, countries, or nationalities.

das **Spanisch**
Spanish (language)

spann ▸ SEE **spinnen**

ℙ**spannend** ADJECTIVE
exciting

die **Spannung**, PLURAL die **Spannungen**
1 tension
2 suspense (in a film or novel, for example)
Ich erwarte seine Antwort mit Spannung. I can't wait for his answer.
3 voltage

die **Sparbüchse**, PLURAL die **Sparbüchsen**
money box

ℙ **sparen** VERB, PERFECT **hat gespart**
1 to save
auf etwas sparen to save up for something
2 sich etwas sparen not to bother with something
Das Zähneputzen spare ich mir heute Abend. I won't bother with brushing my teeth tonight.
Spar dir die Mühe! Save yourself the trouble!
3 an etwas sparen to economize on something

der **Spargel**
asparagus

◇ irregular verb; SEP separable verb; for more help with verbs see centre section

ℰ die **Sparkasse**, PLURAL die **Sparkassen**
savings bank

sparsam ADJECTIVE
1 economical
2 thrifty

ℰ das **Sparschwein**, PLURAL die **Sparschweine**
piggy bank

ℰ der **Spaß**, PLURAL die **Späße**
1 fun
   zum/aus Spaß for fun
   Das macht Spaß. It's fun.
   Segeln macht mir keinen Spaß. I don't like sailing.
2 Viel Spaß! Have a good time!
3 joke
   Er macht nur Spaß. He's only joking.

ℰ **spät** ADJECTIVE, ADVERB
1 late
   zu spät kommen to be late
2 Wie spät ist es? What time is it?

der **Spaten**, PLURAL die **Spaten**
spade

ℰ **später** ADJECTIVE
later
   Bis später! See you later!

spätestens ADVERB
at the latest

der **Spatz**, PLURAL die **Spatzen**
sparrow

die **Spätzle** PLURAL NOUN
noodles (South German dish)

ℰ **spazieren** VERB, PERFECT **ist spaziert**
1 to stroll
2 spazieren gehen to go for a walk
   Hast du Lust spazieren zu gehen? Would you like to go for a walk?

ℰ der **Spaziergang**, PLURAL die **Spaziergänge**
walk
   Lass uns einen Spaziergang machen. Let's go for a walk.

der **Speck**
bacon

die **Speiche**, PLURAL die **Speichen**
spoke

der **Speicher**, PLURAL die **Speicher**
1 loft, attic
2 memory (in computing)

die **Speicherkapazität**
storage capacity (on hard disk)

die **Speicherkarte**, PLURAL die **Speicherkarten**
memory card (for computer)

speichern VERB, PERFECT **hat gespeichert**
1 to store
2 to save (in computing)

die **Speise**, PLURAL die **Speisen**
1 food
2 dish

ℰ die **Speisekarte**, PLURAL die **Speisekarten**
menu

der **Speisesaal**, PLURAL die **Speisesäle**
1 dining hall
2 dining room

der **Speisewagen**, PLURAL die **Speisewagen**
dining car

die **Spende**, PLURAL die **Spenden**
donation

spenden VERB, PERFECT **hat gespendet**
1 to donate
2 to give

> **WORD TIP** The German word spenden does not mean spend in English; the German word for spend is ausgeben or verbringen.

die **Spendenaktion**, PLURAL die **Spendenaktionen**
fund-raising campaign

spendieren VERB, PERFECT **hat spendiert**
jemandem etwas spendieren to treat somebody to something

der **Sperling**, PLURAL die **Sperlinge**
sparrow

die **Sperre**, PLURAL die **Sperren**
1 barrier
2 ban

sperren VERB, PERFECT **hat gesperrt**
1 to close
2 to block (an entrance, access)
3 den Strom sperren to cut off the electricity
4 einen Scheck sperren to stop a cheque
5 ein Tier in einen Käfig sperren to shut an animal (up) in a cage

spezialisieren VERB, PERFECT **hat spezialisiert**
sich spezialisieren to specialize

ℰ die **Spezialität**, PLURAL die **Spezialitäten**
speciality

speziell ADJECTIVE
special

A
B
C
D
E
F
G
H
I
J
K
L
M
N
O
P
Q
R
S
T
U
V
W
X
Y
Z

ℰ indicates key words

die **Spezies**, PLURAL die **Spezies**
species

♀ der **Spiegel**, PLURAL die **Spiegel**
mirror

das **Spiegelbild**, PLURAL die **Spiegelbilder**
reflection

das **Spiegelei**, PLURAL die **Spiegeleier**
fried egg

spiegeln VERB, PERFECT **hat gespiegelt**
1 to reflect
2 sich spiegeln to be reflected

♀ das **Spiel**, PLURAL die **Spiele**
1 game
Sollen wir ein Spiel spielen? Shall we play a game?
2 match
Sie haben das Spiel gegen Italien verloren. They lost the match against Italy.
3 pack
Für diesen Zaubertrick brauche ich ein Spiel Karten. I need a pack of cards for this magic trick.
4 Es steht viel auf dem Spiel. There's a lot at stake.

der **Spielautomat**, PLURAL die **Spielautomaten**
gaming machine

♀ **spielen** VERB, PERFECT **hat gespielt**
1 to play
Wir spielen morgen Fußball. We're playing football tomorrow.
Sie spielt Klavier. She plays the piano.
2 to gamble
3 to act
Das Stück war gut gespielt. The play was well acted.
4 Der Film spielt in Rom. The film is set in Rome.

spielend ADVERB
easily

der **Spieler**, PLURAL die **Spieler**
1 player (male)
2 gambler (male)

die **Spielerin**, PLURAL die **Spielerinnen**
1 player (female)
2 gambler (female)

das **Spielfeld**, PLURAL die **Spielfelder**
pitch, field

♀ der **Spielfilm**, PLURAL die **Spielfilme**
feature film

die **Spielhalle**, PLURAL die **Spielhallen**
amusement arcade

die **Spielkonsole**, PLURAL die **Spielkonsolen**
games console

♀ der **Spielplatz**, PLURAL die **Spielplätze**
playground

der **Spielverderber**, PLURAL die **Spielverderber**
spoilsport (male)

die **Spielverderberin**, PLURAL die **Spielverderberinnen**
spoilsport (female)

die **Spielwaren** PLURAL NOUN
toys

♀ das **Spielzeug**
1 toy
2 toys
Sie haben viel Spielzeug. They have a lot of toys.

der **Spinat**
spinach

die **Spinne**, PLURAL die **Spinnen**
spider

spinnen VERB◇, IMPERFECT **spann**, PERFECT **hat gesponnen**
1 to spin
2 Du spinnst! (informal) You're mad!

das **Spinnennetz**, PLURAL die **Spinnennetze**
1 spider's web
2 cobweb

der **Spion**, PLURAL die **Spione**
spy (male)

die **Spionage**
spying, espionage

spionieren VERB, PERFECT **hat spioniert**
to spy

die **Spionin**, PLURAL die **Spioninnen**
spy (female)

die **Spirituosen** PLURAL NOUN
spirits (alcohol)

spitz ADJECTIVE
pointed

die **Spitze**, PLURAL die **Spitzen**
1 point
2 top
an der Spitze der Liste at the top of the list
3 peak
Von hier kann man die schneebedeckten

◇ irregular verb; SEP separable verb; for more help with verbs see centre section

Spitzen sehen. You can see the snow-covered peaks from here.

4 front

an der Spitze liegen to be in the lead

5 lace

6 Spitze sein *(informal)* to be great

Das Hut ist Spitze. *(informal)* The hat is great.

spitzen *VERB, PERFECT* **hat gespitzt**
to sharpen

der **Spitzer**, *PLURAL* die **Spitzer**
sharpener

der **Spitzname**, *PLURAL* die **Spitznamen**
nickname

der **Splitter**, *PLURAL* die **Splitter**
splinter

splittern *VERB, PERFECT* **hat/ist gesplittert**
1 to splinter
2 to shatter

sponsern *VERB, PERFECT* **hat gesponsert**
to sponsor

ℓ der **Sport**
sport
Wir treiben viel Sport. We do a lot of sport.

die **Sportart**, *PLURAL* die **Sportarten**
sport
Welche Sportart machst du am liebsten? Which sport do you like best?

ℓ die **Sportartikel** *PLURAL NOUN*
sports goods

ℓ der **Sportfan**, *PLURAL* die **Sportfans**
sports fan

das **Sportgeschäft**, *PLURAL* die **Sportgeschäfte**
sports shop

ℓ die **Sporthalle**, *PLURAL* die **Sporthallen**
sports hall, gymnasium

der **Sportler**, *PLURAL* die **Sportler**
sportsman

> **WORD TIP** Professions, hobbies, and sports don't take an article in German: Er ist Sportler.

die **Sportlerin**, *PLURAL* die **Sportlerinnen**
sportswoman

> **WORD TIP** Professions, hobbies, and sports don't take an article in German: Sie ist Sportlerin.

ℓ **sportlich** *ADJECTIVE*
1 sporting
2 sporty

der **Sportplatz**, *PLURAL* die **Sportplätze**
sports field, sports ground

der **Sportschuh**, *PLURAL* die **Sportschuhe**
trainer

ℓ die **Sportsendung**, *PLURAL* die **Sportsendungen**
sports programme

das **Sporttauchen**
1 skin diving
2 scuba diving

ℓ der **Sportverein**, *PLURAL* die **Sportvereine**
sports club

der **Sportwagen**, *PLURAL* die **Sportwagen**
1 sports car
2 pushchair

ℓ das **Sportzentrum**, *PLURAL* die **Sportzentren**
sports centre

spotten *VERB, PERFECT* **hat gespottet**
to mock

sprach ▸ SEE **sprechen**

ℓ die **Sprache**, *PLURAL* die **Sprachen**
1 language
2 speech
etwas zur Sprache bringen to bring something up

der **Sprachführer**, *PLURAL* die **Sprachführer**
phrase book

das **Sprachlabor**, *PLURAL* die **Sprachlabors**
language laboratory

sprachlos *ADJECTIVE*
speechless

sprang ▸ SEE **springen**

die **Spraydose**, *PLURAL* die **Spraydosen**
aerosol can

ℓ die **Sprechblase**, *PLURAL* die **Sprechblasen**
speech bubble

> ℓ **sprechen** *VERB◇, PRESENT* **spricht**, *IMPERFECT* **sprach**, *PERFECT* **hat gesprochen**
> **1** to speak
> Sprechen Sie Deutsch? Do you speak German?
> Mit wem spreche ich? Who's speaking? *(on the phone)*
> jemanden sprechen to speak to somebody
> Ich möchte den Geschäftsführer

ℓ indicates key words

sprechen. I'd like to speak to the manager.
2 Frau Hahn ist nicht zu sprechen. Mrs Hahn is not available.
3 to talk
mit jemandem über etwas sprechen to talk to somebody about something
4 to say (a word, sentence)

der **Sprecher**, PLURAL die **Sprecher**
1 spokesman
2 (on TV) announcer (male)
3 (in a film) narrator (male)
4 speaker (male)

die **Sprecherin**, PLURAL die **Sprecherinnen**
1 spokeswoman
2 (on TV) announcer (female)
3 (in a film) narrator (female)
4 speaker (female)

die **Sprechstunde**, PLURAL die **Sprechstunden**
surgery

spricht ▸ SEE sprechen

das **Sprichwort**, PLURAL die **Sprichwörter**
proverb

_P_ **springen** VERB◇, IMPERFECT **sprang**, PERFECT **ist gesprungen**
1 to jump
2 to bounce (of a ball)
3 to dive
4 to crack

die **Spritze**, PLURAL die **Spritzen**
1 syringe
2 injection
3 hose (of a fire extinguisher)

spritzen VERB, PERFECT **hat gespritzt**
1 to inject
2 to splash
Du hast mich nass gespritzt. You've splashed me.
3 to spray
Sie spritzen das Gemüse mit Pestiziden. They spray the vegetables with pesticides.
4 to spit (of fat)
5 PERFECT **ist gespritzt** to splash
Die Farbe ist auf den Boden gespritzt. The paint splashed onto the floor.
6 PERFECT **ist gespritzt** to spurt out (of blood)

der **Sprudel**, PLURAL die **Sprudel**
sparkling mineral water

sprühen VERB, PERFECT **hat gesprüht**
1 to spray

2 to sparkle (of eyes)
3 PERFECT **ist gesprüht** to fly (of sparks)
Die Funken sind in alle Richtungen gesprüht. Sparks flew in all directions.

der **Sprung**, PLURAL die **Sprünge**
1 jump
2 dive
3 crack (in china, glass)

das **Sprungbrett**, PLURAL die **Sprungbretter**
diving board

spucken VERB, PERFECT **hat gespuckt**
to spit

das **Spülbecken**, PLURAL die **Spülbecken**
sink

spülen VERB, PERFECT **hat gespült**
1 to rinse
2 to wash up
3 to flush

_P_ die **Spülmaschine**, PLURAL die **Spülmaschinen**
dishwasher

das **Spülmittel**, PLURAL die **Spülmittel**
washing-up liquid

_P_ die **Spur**, PLURAL die **Spuren**
1 track
Sie sind auf der falschen Spur. You're on the wrong track.
jemandem auf die Spur kommen to get on to somebody
2 lane
Hier muss man in der Spur bleiben. You have to keep in lane here.
3 trail
4 trace

spüren VERB, PERFECT **hat gespürt**
1 to feel
2 to sense

_P_ der **Staat**, PLURAL die **Staaten**
state

staatlich ADJECTIVE
state
Er geht an eine staatliche Schule. He goes to a state school.
staatlich ADVERB
by the state

die **Staatsangehörigkeit**, PLURAL die **Staatsangehörigkeiten**
nationality

stabil ADJECTIVE
1 stable
2 sturdy

◇ irregular verb; SEP separable verb; for more help with verbs see centre section

stach ▸ SEE stechen

der **Stachel**, PLURAL die **Stacheln**
1 spine, thorn
2 spike
3 sting

die **Stachelbeere**, PLURAL die **Stachelbeeren**
gooseberry

der **Stacheldraht**
barbed wire

ℓ das **Stadion**, PLURAL die **Stadien**
stadium

das **Stadium**, PLURAL die **Stadien**
stage

WORD TIP The German word Stadium does not
mean stadium in English; the German word for
stadium is Stadion.

ℓ die **Stadt**, PLURAL die **Städte**
town, city

der **Stadtbummel**, PLURAL die
Stadtbummel
stroll through the town
Wir wollen jetzt einen Stadtbummel
machen. We're going for a stroll through
the town now.

städtisch ADJECTIVE
1 urban
2 municipal

ℓ die **Stadtmitte**
town centre

ℓ der **Stadtplan**, PLURAL die **Stadtpläne**
street map

ℓ der **Stadtrand**
outskirts (of town)
Sie wohnen am Stadtrand von Lübeck.
They live on the outskirts of Lübeck.

der **Stadtrat**, PLURAL die **Stadträte**
1 town council, city council
2 town councillor, city councillor (male)

WORD TIP Professions, hobbies, and sports
don't take an article in German: Er ist Stadtrat.

die **Stadträtin**, PLURAL die **Stadträtinnen**
town councillor, city councillor (female)

WORD TIP Professions, hobbies, and sports
don't take an article in German: Sie ist
Stadträtin.

ℓ die **Stadtrundfahrt**, PLURAL die
Stadtrundfahrten
sightseeing tour (of a town)

der **Stadtteil**, PLURAL die **Stadtteile**
district

das **Stadtviertel**, PLURAL die **Stadtviertel**
district, part of town

das **Stadtwappen**, PLURAL die **Stadtwappen**
municipal coat of arms

das **Stadtzentrum**, PLURAL die **Stadtzentren**
town centre, city centre

stahl ▸ SEE stehlen

der **Stahl**
steel

der **Stall**, PLURAL die **Ställe**
1 stable
2 cowshed
3 pigsty

der **Stamm**, PLURAL die **Stämme**
1 trunk
2 tribe
3 stem (of a word)

ℓ der **Stammbaum**, PLURAL die **Stammbäume**
family tree

stammen VERB, PERFECT **hat gestammt**
aus ... stammen to come from ...

der **Stammgast**, PLURAL die **Stammgäste**
regular customer (in a pub or restaurant)

stand ▸ SEE stehen

der **Stand**, PLURAL die **Stände**
1 state
2 etwas auf den neuesten Stand bringen to
bring something up to date
3 score (in a game)
4 stand (in a fair or market)
5 level (of water, of a river)

ständig ADJECTIVE
constant

der **Standort**, PLURAL die **Standorte**
position, location
Von ihrem Standort aus konnte sie nichts
sehen. She couldn't see anything from
where she was standing.

die **Stange**, PLURAL die **Stangen**
1 bar
2 pole

stank ▸ SEE stinken

starb ▸ SEE sterben

ℓ **stark** ADJECTIVE
1 strong
2 heavy (rain, frost, traffic)

3 bad *(pain)*

4 *(informal)* **great**
Das ist stark! That's great!

die **Stärke**, PLURAL die **Stärken**
1 strength
2 starch

starrsinnig *ADJECTIVE*
obstinate

℗ der **Start**, PLURAL die **Starts**
1 start
2 take-off

die **Startbahn**, PLURAL die **Startbahnen**
runway

starten *VERB*
1 *PERFECT* **ist gestartet to take off** *(of a plane)*
Das Flugzeug ist gerade gestartet. The plane has just taken off.
2 *PERFECT* **hat gestartet to start** *(a motor, race, campaign)*
Sie hat den Motor gestartet. She started the engine.

die **Station**, PLURAL die **Stationen**
1 station
2 stop
Station machen to stop over
3 ward *(in hospital)*

℗ **statt** *CONJUNCTION*, *PREPOSITION (+ GEN)*
instead of
Statt zu arbeiten, gingen sie schwimmen. Instead of working, they went swimming.
Sie ging statt ihrer Schwester. She went instead of her sister.

stattdessen *CONJUNCTION*
instead

stattfinden *VERB◇*, *IMPERFECT* **fand statt**, *PERFECT* **hat stattgefunden**
to take place

der **Stau**, PLURAL die **Staus**
1 congestion
2 traffic jam

der **Staub**
dust

staubig *ADJECTIVE*
dusty

℗ **staubsaugen** *VERB*, *PERFECT* **hat staubgesaugt**
to vacuum, to hoover

der **Staubsauger**, PLURAL die **Staubsauger**
vacuum cleaner, Hoover™

staunen *VERB*, *PERFECT* **hat gestaunt**
to be amazed

das **Steak**, PLURAL die **Steaks**
steak

stechen *VERB◇*, *PRESENT* **sticht**, *IMPERFECT* **stach**, *PERFECT* **hat gestochen**
1 to prick
Ich habe mir in den Finger gestochen. I've pricked my finger.
2 to sting, to bite *(of an insect)*
3 mit etwas in etwas stechen to jab something into something

℗ der **Steckbrief**, PLURAL die **Steckbriefe**
1 description *(of a wanted person)*
2 personal description

die **Steckdose**, PLURAL die **Steckdosen**
socket

℗ **stecken** *VERB*, *PERFECT* **hat gesteckt**
1 to put
Steck die Münze in den Schlitz . Put the coin into the slot.
2 to pin
3 Wo steckt er? Where is he?
4 stecken bleiben to get stuck
5 den Schlüssel stecken lassen to leave the key in the lock

der **Stecker**, PLURAL die **Stecker**
plug

die **Stecknadel**, PLURAL die **Stecknadeln**
pin

die **Steckrübe**, PLURAL die **Steckrüben**
turnip

das **Stehcafé**, PLURAL die **Stehcafés**
stand-up cafe

℗ **stehen** *VERB◇*, *IMPERFECT* **stand** *PERFECT* **hat gestanden**
1 to stand
Wir mussten im Bus stehen. We had to stand on the bus.
2 to be
Es steht zwei zu zwei. The score is two all.
Wie steht's? What's the score?
3 to have stopped *(of a clock or a machine)*
Die Uhr steht. The clock has stopped.
4 Es steht schlecht um ihn. He's in a bad way.
Na, wie steht's? How are you?
5 stehen bleiben to stop
Die Uhr ist stehen geblieben. The clock has stopped.

◇ **irregular verb;** *SEP* **separable verb; for more help with verbs see centre section**

6 to say
In der Zeitung steht, dass ... It says in the paper that ...
7 jemandem (gut) stehen to suit somebody
8 zu jemandem stehen to stand by somebody
9 sich gut stehen to be on good terms
10 zum Stehen kommen to come to a standstill

> **WORD TIP** In Southern Germany, Austria, and Switzerland, the perfect tense is ist gestanden.

ℱ **stehlen** VERB♢, PRESENT **stiehlt**, IMPERFECT **stahl**, PERFECT **hat gestohlen**
to steal

steif ADJECTIVE
stiff

ℱ **steigen** VERB♢, IMPERFECT **stieg**, PERFECT **ist gestiegen**
1 to climb
Er stieg auf die Leiter. He climbed up the ladder.
2 to get
Sie stieg aufs Fahrrad. She got on the bike.
Wir stiegen in den Bus. We got on the bus.
3 to rise

steil ADJECTIVE
steep

ℱ der **Stein**, PLURAL die **Steine**
stone

der **Steinbock**, PLURAL die **Steinböcke**
1 ibex
2 Capricorn
Petra ist Steinbock. Petra is Capricorn.

der **Steinbruch**, PLURAL die **Steinbrüche**
quarry

ℱ die **Stelle**, PLURAL die **Stellen**
1 place, spot
Wir liegen an dritter Stelle. We are in third place.
An deiner Stelle würde ich es nicht tun. If I were you, I wouldn't do it.
2 job
Er sucht eine neue Stelle. He's looking for a new job.
eine freie Stelle a vacancy
3 office
Bei welcher Stelle haben Sie den Antrag gestellt? Which office did you apply to?
4 auf der Stelle immediately

ℱ **stellen** VERB, PERFECT **hat gestellt**
1 to put
2 to set (a watch, task)
3 etwas zur Verfügung stellen to provide something
4 to turn
lauter stellen to turn up
leiser stellen to turn down
Kannst du die Heizung höher stellen? Can you turn the heating up?
5 sich krank stellen to pretend to be ill
6 sich stellen to give yourself up
7 Die Kinder stellten sich an die Wand. The children stood against the wall.

das **Stellenangebot**, PLURAL die **Stellenangebote**
job advertisement

die **Stellenanzeige**, PLURAL die **Stellenanzeigen**
job advertisement

das **Stellengesuch**, PLURAL die **Stellengesuche**
'situation wanted' advertisement
'Stellengesuche' 'situations wanted'

der **Stellplatz**, PLURAL die **Stellplätze**
pitch (for a tent)

die **Stellung**, PLURAL die **Stellungen**
position

stellvertretend ADJECTIVE
1 acting
2 deputy
Er ist der stellvertretende Feuerwehrhauptmann. He's the deputy chief fire officer.

der **Stellvertreter**, PLURAL die **Stellvertreter**
1 deputy (male)
2 representative (male)

die **Stellvertreterin**, PLURAL die **Stellvertreterinnen**
1 deputy (female)
2 representative (female)

der **Stempel**, PLURAL die **Stempel**
1 stamp
2 postmark

stempeln VERB, PERFECT **hat gestempelt**
to stamp

die **Steppdecke**, PLURAL die **Steppdecken**
quilt

ℱ **sterben** VERB♢, PRESENT **stirbt**, IMPERFECT **starb**, PERFECT **ist gestorben**
to die

A B C D E F G H I J K L M N O P Q R S T U V W X Y Z

277

♀ die **Stereoanlage**, PLURAL die
Stereoanlagen
stereo (system)

♂ der **Stern**, PLURAL die **Sterne**
star

das **Sternzeichen**, PLURAL die **Sternzeichen**
star sign
Was ist dein Sternzeichen? What star sign
are you?

das **Steuer**¹, PLURAL die **Steuer**
1 (steering) wheel
2 helm

die **Steuer**², PLURAL die **Steuern**
tax

steuern VERB, PERFECT **hat gesteuert**
1 to steer
2 to control
3 PERFECT **ist gesteuert** to head
Er steuerte nach Westen. He headed west.

der **Steward**, PLURAL die **Stewards**
steward, flight attendant (male)

> **WORD TIP** Professions, hobbies, and sports
> don't take an article in German: Er ist Steward.

die **Stewardess**, PLURAL die **Stewardessen**
stewardess, flight attendant (female)

> **WORD TIP** Professions, hobbies, and sports don't
> take an article in German: Sie ist Stewardess.

der **Stich**, PLURAL die **Stiche**
1 prick
2 stab
3 sting, bite (of an insect)
4 stitch
5 trick (when playing cards)
6 engraving
7 jemanden im Stich lassen to leave
somebody in the lurch

sticht ▸ SEE **stechen**

sticken VERB, PERFECT **hat gestickt**
to embroider

der **Stickstoff**
nitrogen

der **Stiefbruder**, PLURAL die **Stiefbrüder**
stepbrother

der **Stiefel**, PLURAL die **Stiefel**
boot

das **Stiefkind**, PLURAL die **Stiefkinder**
stepchild

♀ die **Stiefmutter**, PLURAL die **Stiefmütter**
stepmother

die **Stiefschwester**, PLURAL die
Stiefschwestern
stepsister

der **Stiefsohn**, PLURAL die **Stiefsöhne**
stepson

die **Stieftochter**, PLURAL die **Stieftöchter**
stepdaughter

♂ der **Stiefvater**, PLURAL die **Stiefväter**
stepfather

stieg ▸ SEE **steigen**

stiehlt ▸ SEE **stehlen**

der **Stiel**, PLURAL die **Stiele**
1 handle
2 stem

der **Stier**, PLURAL die **Stiere**
1 bull
2 Taurus
Andrea ist Stier. Andrea is Taurus.

stieß ▸ SEE **stoßen**

der **Stift**, PLURAL die **Stifte**
1 pencil
2 crayon
3 tack (nail)

der **Stil**, PLURAL die **Stile**
style

still ADJECTIVE
1 quiet
2 still

stillen VERB, PERFECT **hat gestillt**
1 to quench
2 to breastfeed

stillhalten VERB◇, PRESENT **hält still**, IMPERFECT
hielt still, PERFECT **hat stillgehalten**
to keep still

♀ die **Stimme**, PLURAL die **Stimmen**
1 voice
2 vote

♀ **stimmen** VERB, PERFECT **hat gestimmt**
1 to be right
Das stimmt! That's right!
Stimmt das? Is that right?
2 to vote
3 to tune

die **Stimmung**, PLURAL die **Stimmungen**
1 mood
2 atmosphere

stinken VERB◇, IMPERFECT **stank**, PERFECT **hat
gestunken**
to smell, to stink

◇ irregular verb; SEP separable verb; for more help with verbs see centre section

das **Stipendium**, PLURAL die **Stipendien**
1 scholarship
2 grant

stirbt ▸ SEE **sterben**

die **Stirn**, PLURAL die **Stirnen**
forehead

der **Stock**[1], PLURAL die **Stöcke**
stick

℘ der **Stock**[2], PLURAL die **Stock**
floor
Sie wohnen im ersten Stock. They live on
the first floor.

das **Stockwerk**, PLURAL die **Stockwerke**
floor

℘ der **Stoff**, PLURAL die **Stoffe**
1 material, fabric
2 substance

stöhnen VERB, PERFECT **hat gestöhnt**
to groan

stolpern VERB, PERFECT **ist gestolpert**
1 to stumble
2 to trip
Ich bin über einen Stein gestolpert.
I tripped on a stone.

℘ **stolz** ADJECTIVE
proud

der **Stolz**
pride

stoppen VERB, PERFECT **hat gestoppt**
to stop

der **Stöpsel**, PLURAL die **Stöpsel**
1 plug
2 stopper

℘ **stören** VERB, PERFECT **hat gestört**
1 to disturb
Bitte nicht stören! Please do not disturb!
2 to bother
Das stört mich nicht. That doesn't bother
me.
Stört es Sie, wenn ich das Fenster
aufmache? Do you mind if I open the
window?
3 Der Empfang ist gestört. The reception is
bad. (on a TV)

die **Störung**, PLURAL die **Störungen**
1 disturbance, interruption
Entschuldigen Sie die Störung. I'm sorry to
bother you.
2 interference
eine technische Störung a technical fault

der **Stoß**, PLURAL die **Stöße**
1 push
2 pile
Auf dem Regal lag ein Stoß Handtücher.
There was a pile of towels on the shelf.

℘ **stoßen** VERB◇, PRESENT **stößt**, IMPERFECT **stieß**,
PERFECT **hat gestoßen**
1 to push
2 to kick
3 sich stoßen to bump yourself
sich den Kopf stoßen to hit your head
Ich habe mir den Kopf am Balken
gestoßen. I hit my head on the beam.
4 sich an etwas stoßen to object to
something
5 PERFECT **ist gestoßen**
gegen etwas stoßen to bump into
something
6 PERFECT **ist gestoßen**
auf etwas stoßen to come across
something

die **Stoßstange**, PLURAL die **Stoßstangen**
bumper

die **Stoßzeit**, PLURAL die **Stoßzeiten**
rush hour

stottern VERB, PERFECT **hat gestottert**
to stutter

die **Strafarbeit**, PLURAL die **Strafarbeiten**
extra homework (as a punishment)

die **Strafe**, PLURAL die **Strafen**
1 punishment
2 fine
3 penalty

die **Straftat**, PLURAL die **Straftaten**
crime

der **Strahl**, PLURAL die **Strahlen**
1 ray, beam
2 jet

strahlen VERB, PERFECT **hat gestrahlt**
1 to shine
2 to beam

die **Strahlung**, PLURAL die **Strahlungen**
radiation

℘ der **Strand**, PLURAL die **Strände**
beach

der **Strandkorb**, PLURAL die **Strandkörbe**
wicker beach chair

Straßburg NEUTER NOUN
Strasbourg

℘ die **Straße**, PLURAL die **Straßen**
1 street, road

279

℘ indicates key words

In welcher Straße ist der Supermarkt?
Which street is the supermarket in?
Sie gingen über die Straße. They crossed
the road.

2 jemanden auf die Straße setzen *(informal)*
to give somebody the sack

3 Mein Vermieter hat mich einfach auf die
Straße gesetzt. *(informal)* My landlord just
turned me out. *(of a flat or room)*

♀ die **Straßenbahn**, PLURAL die
Straßenbahnen
tram
Wir können mit der Straßenbahn fahren.
We can go by tram.

der **Straßenraub**
1 mugging
2 street robbery

der **Straßenräuber**, PLURAL die
Straßenräuber
mugger

die **Straßenüberführung**, PLURAL die
Straßenüberführungen
1 footbridge
2 roadbridge

die **Straßenunterführung**, PLURAL die
Straßenunterführungen
1 subway
2 underpass

der **Strauch**, PLURAL die **Sträucher**
bush

der **Strauß**[1], PLURAL die **Sträuße**
bunch of flowers, bouquet

der **Strauß**[2], PLURAL die **Strauße**
ostrich

der **Streber**, PLURAL die **Streber**
swot *(male)*

die **Streberin**, PLURAL die **Streberinnen**
swot *(female)*

die **Strecke**, PLURAL die **Strecken**
1 distance
2 route
3 line *(rail)*

strecken VERB, PERFECT **hat gestreckt**
1 to stretch *(your arms, legs)*
2 sich strecken to stretch

der **Streich**, PLURAL die **Streiche**
trick, prank

streicheln VERB, PERFECT **hat gestreichelt**
to stroke

streichen VERB◇, IMPERFECT **strich**, PERFECT **hat
gestrichen**
1 to paint
'Frisch gestrichen' 'Wet paint'
2 to spread *(with butter)*
3 to delete
4 to cancel *(a flight)*
5 jemandem über den Kopf streichen to
stroke somebody's head

das **Streichholz**, PLURAL die **Streichhölzer**
match

der **Streifen**, PLURAL die **Streifen**
1 stripe
2 strip

der **Streik**, PLURAL die **Streiks**
strike

streiken VERB, PERFECT **hat gestreikt**
to strike

♀ der **Streit**, PLURAL die **Streite**
quarrel, argument

♀ **streiten** VERB◇, IMPERFECT **stritt**, PERFECT **hat
gestritten**
1 to quarrel, to argue
2 sich streiten to quarrel, to argue

♀ **streng** ADJECTIVE
strict

der **Stress**
stress

♀ **stressig** ADJECTIVE
stressful

streuen VERB, PERFECT **hat gestreut**
1 to spread
2 to sprinkle
3 die Straßen streuen to grit the roads

strich ▶ SEE **streichen**

der **Strich**, PLURAL die **Striche**
1 line
2 stroke

der **Strichpunkt**, PLURAL die **Strichpunkte**
semicolon

stricken VERB, PERFECT **hat gestrickt**
to knit

die **Strickjacke**, PLURAL die **Strickjacken**
cardigan

stritt ▶ SEE **streiten**

das **Stroh**
straw

◇ **irregular verb**; SEP **separable verb**; for more help with verbs see centre section

der **Strohhalm**, PLURAL die **Strohhalme**
straw (for drinking)

℗ der **Strom**, PLURAL die **Ströme**
1 **electricity**
Der alte Kühlschrank verbraucht viel
Strom. The old fridge uses a lot of
electricity.
2 **river**
3 **stream** (of people or blood)
4 **current**
5 Es regnet in Strömen. It's pouring with
rain.

der **Stromausfall**, PLURAL die **Stromausfälle**
power cut

strömen VERB, PERFECT **ist geströmt**
to stream, to pour

die **Strömung**, PLURAL die **Strömungen**
current

die **Strophe**, PLURAL die **Strophen**
verse

℗ der **Strudel**, PLURAL die **Strudel**
strudel (kind of Austrian cake)

der **Strumpf**, PLURAL die **Strümpfe**
1 **stocking**
2 **sock**

die **Strumpfhose**, PLURAL die **Strumpfhosen**
tights

WORD TIP In German, die Strumpfhose is
singular: Diese Strumpfhose ist mir zu klein.

die **Stube**, PLURAL die **Stuben**
room

℗ das **Stück**, PLURAL die **Stücke**
1 **piece**
Ich nahm ein Stück Kuchen. I took a piece
of cake.
2 das/pro Stück **each**
Sie kosten zwei Euro das Stück. They are
two euros each.
3 **play** (in the theatre)

das **Stückchen**, PLURAL die **Stückchen**
little piece

der **Student**, PLURAL die **Studenten**
student (male)

WORD TIP Professions, hobbies, and sports
don't take an article in German: Er ist Student.

die **Studentin**, PLURAL die **Studentinnen**
student (female)

WORD TIP Professions, hobbies, and sports
don't take an article in German: Sie ist
Studentin.

der **Studienplatz**, PLURAL die **Studienplätze**
place at university

℗ **studieren** VERB, PERFECT **hat studiert**
to study
Katrin studiert Mathematik. Katrin is
studying mathematics.
Er will studieren. He wants to go to
university.

das **Studium**, PLURAL die **Studien**
studies, course

die **Stufe**, PLURAL die **Stufen**
1 **step**
'Vorsicht Stufe' 'Mind the step'
2 **stage** (of development)

℗ der **Stuhl**, PLURAL die **Stühle**
chair

stumm ADJECTIVE
1 **dumb**
2 **silent**

stumpf ADJECTIVE
1 **blunt**
2 **dull**
3 ein stumpfer Winkel an obtuse angle

℗ die **Stunde**, PLURAL die **Stunden**
1 **hour**
2 **lesson**

stundenlang ADVERB
for hours

℗ der **Stundenplan**, PLURAL die **Stundenpläne**
timetable

stündlich ADJECTIVE
hourly

stur ADJECTIVE
stubborn

der **Sturm**, PLURAL die **Stürme**
storm

℗ **stürmisch** ADJECTIVE
stormy

der **Sturz**, PLURAL die **Stürze**
1 **fall**
2 **overthrow**

stürzen VERB, PERFECT **ist gestürzt**
1 **to fall**
2 **to rush** (into a room)
3 PERFECT **hat gestürzt to overthrow**
4 PERFECT **hat sich gestürzt**
Er hat sich aus dem Fenster gestürzt. He
threw himself out of the window.
sich auf jemanden stürzen to pounce on
somebody

℗ **indicates key words**

der **Sturzhelm**, PLURAL die **Sturzhelme**
crash helmet

stützen VERB, PERFECT **hat gestützt**
1 to support
2 sich auf jemanden stützen to lean on
somebody

das **Subjekt**, PLURAL die **Subjekte**
subject (in grammar)

das **Substantiv**, PLURAL die **Substantive**
noun (in grammar)

subtil ADJECTIVE
subtle

die **Subvention**, PLURAL die **Subventionen**
subsidy

subventionieren VERB, PERFECT **hat
subventioniert**
to subsidize

die **Suche**, PLURAL die **Suchen**
search

♀ **suchen** VERB, PERFECT **hat gesucht**
1 to look for
'Zimmer gesucht' 'Room wanted'
2 to search

die **Sucht**, PLURAL die **Suchten**
addiction

süchtig ADJECTIVE
addicted

der/die **Süchtige**, PLURAL die **Süchtigen**
addict

Südafrika NEUTER NOUN
South Africa

Südamerika NEUTER NOUN
South America

♀ der **Süden**
south

südlich ADJECTIVE
1 southern
2 southerly

südlich ADVERB, PREPOSITION (+ GEN)
südlich der Stadt to the south of the town
südlich von Wien south of Vienna

der **Südosten**
south-east

der **Südpol**
South Pole

der **Südwesten**
south-west

die **Summe**, PLURAL die **Summen**
sum

summen VERB, PERFECT **hat gesummt**
1 to hum
2 to buzz

die **Sünde**, PLURAL die **Sünden**
sin

♀ **super** ADJECTIVE
(informal) great

das **Super(benzin)**
4-star petrol

♀ der **Supermarkt**, PLURAL die **Supermärkte**
supermarket

♀ die **Suppe**, PLURAL die **Suppen**
soup

das **Surfbrett**, PLURAL die **Surfbretter**
surfboard

♀ **surfen** VERB, PERFECT **hat gesurft**
to surf (in the sea, on the Internet)
im Internet surfen to surf the Internet

das **Surfen**
surfing

der **Surfer**, PLURAL die **Surfer**
surfer (on the sea and Internet) (male)

die **Surferin**, PLURAL die **Surferinnen**
surfer (on the sea and Internet) (female)

♀ **süß** ADJECTIVE
sweet
Sie isst gern Süßes. She likes sweet things.

♀ die **Süßigkeit**, PLURAL die **Süßigkeiten**
sweet

der **Süßstoff**, PLURAL die **Süßstoffe**
sweetener

die **Süßwaren** PLURAL NOUN
confectionery

der **Süßwarenladen**, PLURAL die
Süßwarenläden
sweetshop

Süßwasser- ADJECTIVE
freshwater

♀ das **Sweatshirt**, PLURAL die **Sweatshirts**
sweatshirt

♀ das **Symbol**, PLURAL die **Symbole**
symbol

symbolisch ADJECTIVE
symbolic

◇ irregular verb; SEP separable verb; for more help with verbs see centre section

𝒫 **sympathisch** *ADJECTIVE*
  likeable
  Sie ist mir sympathisch. I like her.

  WORD TIP The German word sympathisch does
  not mean **sympathetic** in English; the German
  word for **sympathetic** is verständnisvoll.

die **Symphonie**, *PLURAL* die **Symphonien**
  ▶ SEE **Sinfonie**

die **Synagoge**, *PLURAL* die **Synagogen**
  synagogue

synchronisiert *ADJECTIVE*
  dubbed *(film)*

synthetisch *ADJECTIVE*
  synthetic

das **System**, *PLURAL* die **Systeme**
  system

die **Szene**, *PLURAL* die **Szenen**
  scene

Tt

der **Tabak**, *PLURAL* die **Tabake**
  tobacco

die **Tabakwaren** *PLURAL NOUN*
  cigarettes and tobacco

𝒫 die **Tabelle**, *PLURAL* die **Tabellen**
  table, chart

das **Tablett**, *PLURAL* die **Tabletts**
  tray

𝒫 die **Tablette**, *PLURAL* die **Tabletten**
  tablet

𝒫 die **Tafel**, *PLURAL* die **Tafeln**
1 board, blackboard
  Der Lehrer schrieb das Wort an die
  Tafel. The teacher wrote the word on the
  blackboard.
2 eine Tafel Schokolade a bar of chocolate

𝒫 der **Tag**, *PLURAL* die **Tage**
1 day
  Es hat den ganzen Tag geregnet. It rained
  all day.
2 Guten Tag! Hello!
3 daylight, daytime
  Bei Tag sieht man keine Fledermäuse. You
  don't see bats in the daytime.
4 Tag der deutschen Einheit Day of German

Unity

🔵 **TAG DER DEUTSCHEN EINHEIT**
  Der Tag der Deutschen Einheit, 3 October, is
  a national holiday which commemorates the
  reunification of Germany in 1990. Schools are
  closed on this day.

der **Tag der Arbeit**
  Labour Day

𝒫 das **Tagebuch**, *PLURAL* die **Tagebücher**
  diary

tagelang *ADVERB*
  for days

der **Tagesanbruch**
  dawn

𝒫 der **Tagesausflug**, *PLURAL* die **Tagesausflüge**
  day trip

das **Tagesgericht**, *PLURAL* die **Tagesgerichte**
  dish of the day

die **Tageskarte**, *PLURAL* die **Tageskarten**
1 menu (of the day)
2 day ticket

das **Tageslicht**
  daylight

der **Tageslichtprojektor**, *PLURAL* die
  Tageslichtprojektoren
  overhead projector

das **Tagesmenü**, *PLURAL* die **Tagesmenüs**
  set menu (of the day)

die **Tagesmutter**, *PLURAL* die **Tagesmütter**
  childminder

  WORD TIP Professions, hobbies, and sports
  don't take an article in German: Sie ist
  Tagesmutter.

der **Tagesraum**, *PLURAL* die **Tagesräume**
  day room

die **Tagesschau**, *PLURAL* die **Tagesschauen**
  (evening) news *(on television)*

die **Tageszeitung**, *PLURAL* die
  Tageszeitungen
  daily paper

𝒫 **täglich** *ADJECTIVE*
  daily
  im täglichen Leben in daily life
täglich *ADVERB*
  daily, every day
  Das Museum ist täglich außer Montags
  geöffnet. The museum is open every day
  except Mondays.

tagsüber ADVERB
during the day

die **Taille**, PLURAL die **Taillen**
waist

der **Takt**, PLURAL die **Takte**
1 time
Sie klatschten im Takt. They clapped in time to the music
2 rhythm
3 bar (in music)
Er spielte ein paar Takte. He played a few bars.
4 tact

taktlos ADJECTIVE
tactless

taktvoll ADJECTIVE
tactful

℘ das **Tal**, PLURAL die **Täler**
valley

das **Talent**, PLURAL die **Talente**
talent

die **Talkshow**, PLURAL die **Talkshows**
chat show

der **Tampon**, PLURAL die **Tampons**
tampon

der **Tang**
seaweed

der **Tank**, PLURAL die **Tanks**
tank

tanken VERB, PERFECT hat getankt
to fill up (with petrol) to get petrol

der **Tanker**, PLURAL die **Tanker**
tanker (on sea)

℘ die **Tankstelle**, PLURAL die **Tankstellen**
petrol station

der **Tankwagen**, PLURAL die **Tankwagen**
tanker (on road)

der **Tankwart**, PLURAL die **Tankwarte**
petrol-pump attendant

WORD TIP Professions, hobbies, and sports don't take an article in German: Er ist Tankwart.

die **Tanne**, PLURAL die **Tannen**
fir

der **Tannenbaum**, PLURAL die **Tannenbäume**
1 fir tree
2 Christmas tree

℘ die **Tante**, PLURAL die **Tanten**
aunt

der **Tanz**, PLURAL die **Tänze**
dance

℘ **tanzen** VERB, PERFECT hat getanzt
to dance

der **Tänzer**, PLURAL die **Tänzer**
dancer (male)

WORD TIP Professions, hobbies, and sports don't take an article in German: Er ist Tänzer.

die **Tänzerin**, PLURAL die **Tänzerinnen**
dancer (female)

WORD TIP Professions, hobbies, and sports don't take an article in German: Sie ist Tänzerin.

der **Tanzkurs**, PLURAL die **Tanzkurse**
dancing classes

die **Tapete**, PLURAL die **Tapeten**
wallpaper

tapezieren VERB, PERFECT hat tapeziert
to (wall)paper

tapfer ADJECTIVE
brave

die **Tapferkeit**
bravery

der **Tarif**, PLURAL die **Tarife**
1 tariff
2 rate

℘ die **Tasche**, PLURAL die **Taschen**
1 bag
2 pocket
Nimm die Hände aus den Taschen! Take your hands out of your pockets!
Er hat es aus eigener Tasche bezahlt. He paid for it out of his own pocket.
3 Max hat mir fünf Euro aus der Tasche gezogen. (informal) Max wangled five euros out of me.

das **Taschenbuch**, PLURAL die **Taschenbücher**
paperback

der **Taschendieb**, PLURAL die **Taschendiebe**
pickpocket

℘ das **Taschengeld**
pocket money

die **Taschenlampe**, PLURAL die **Taschenlampen**
torch

das **Taschenmesser**, PLURAL die **Taschenmesser**
penknife

◇ **irregular verb**; SEP **separable verb**; for more help with verbs see centre section

der **Taschenrechner**, PLURAL die
Taschenrechner
pocket calculator

ᵖ das **Taschentuch**, PLURAL die **Taschentücher**
handkerchief

ᵖ die **Tasse**, PLURAL die **Tassen**
cup

die **Tastatur**, PLURAL die **Tastaturen**
keyboard

die **Taste**, PLURAL die **Tasten**
1 key (on a keyboard)
2 button (on a phone or a machine)

tasten VERB, PERFECT **hat getastet**
1 to feel
2 sich tasten to feel your way

tat ▸ SEE **tun**

die **Tat**, PLURAL die **Taten**
1 action
2 eine gute Tat a good deed
3 crime
4 in der Tat indeed

der **Täter**, PLURAL die **Täter**
1 culprit (male)
2 offender (male)

die **Täterin**, PLURAL die **Täterinnen**
1 culprit (female)
2 offender (female)

tätig ADJECTIVE
1 active
2 tätig sein to work
Sie ist als Sekretärin tätig. She works as a
secretary.

ᵖ die **Tätigkeit**, PLURAL die **Tätigkeiten**
1 activity
2 job

tätowieren VERB, PERFECT **hat tätowiert**
1 to tattoo
2 sich tätowieren lassen to have a tattoo
done

die **Tätowierung**, PLURAL die
Tätowierungen
tattoo

die **Tatsache**, PLURAL die **Tatsachen**
fact

tatsächlich ADJECTIVE
actual

tatsächlich ADVERB
1 actually
2 really

der **Tau**[1]
dew

das **Tau**[2], PLURAL die **Taue**
rope

taub ADJECTIVE
deaf

die **Taube**, PLURAL die **Tauben**
1 pigeon
2 dove

ᵖ **tauchen** VERB, PERFECT **hat getaucht**
1 to dip
2 PERFECT **hat/ist getaucht** (ist getaucht is
used when movement is described) to dive

der **Taucher**, PLURAL die **Taucher**
diver (male)

> **WORD TIP** Professions, hobbies, and sports
> don't take an article in German: Er ist Taucher.

die **Taucherbrille**, PLURAL die
Taucherbrillen
diving goggles

> **WORD TIP** In German, die Taucherbrille is
> singular: Die Taucherbrille ist teuer.

die **Taucherin**, PLURAL die **Taucherinnen**
diver (female)

> **WORD TIP** Professions, hobbies, and sports
> don't take an article in German: Sie ist
> Taucherin.

tauen VERB, PERFECT **ist getaut**
1 to melt
Der Schne ist getaut. The snow has
melted.
2 PERFECT **hat getaut** to thaw
Es taut. It's thawing.

die **Taufe**, PLURAL die **Taufen**
christening

taufen VERB, PERFECT **hat getauft**
1 to christen
2 to baptize

taugen VERB, PERFECT **hat getaugt**
nichts taugen to be no good

tauschen VERB, PERFECT **hat getauscht**
to exchange, to swap

täuschen VERB, PERFECT **hat getäuscht**
1 to deceive
2 to be deceptive
3 sich täuschen to be wrong

ᵖ **tausend** NUMBER
a thousand

A
B
C
D
E
F
G
H
I
J
K
L
M
N
O
P
Q
R
S
T
U
V
W
X
Y
Z

ᵖ indicates key words

𝒫 das **Taxi**, PLURAL die **Taxis**
taxi

der **Taxifahrer**, PLURAL die **Taxifahrer**
taxi driver (male)

> **WORD TIP** Professions, hobbies, and sports don't take an article in German: Er ist Taxifahrer.

die **Taxifahrerin**, PLURAL die **Taxifahrerinnen**
taxi driver (female)

> **WORD TIP** Professions, hobbies, and sports don't take an article in German: Sie ist Taxifahrerin.

der **Taxistand**, PLURAL die **Taxistände**
taxi rank

die **Technik**, PLURAL die **Techniken**
1 technology
2 technique

der **Techniker**, PLURAL die **Techniker**
technician (male)

> **WORD TIP** Professions, hobbies, and sports don't take an article in German: Er ist Techniker.

die **Technikerin**, PLURAL die **Technikerinnen**
technician (female)

> **WORD TIP** Professions, hobbies, and sports don't take an article in German: Sie ist Technikerin.

technisch ADJECTIVE
1 technical
2 technological

die **Technologie**
technology

technologisch ADJECTIVE
technological

𝒫 der **Teddybär**, PLURAL die **Teddybären**
teddy bear

𝒫 der **Tee**, PLURAL die **Tee(s)**
tea
Einen Tee mit Zitrone, bitte. One lemon tea, please.
Ich trinke meinen Tee mit Milch. I have milk in my tea.

der **Teebeutel**, PLURAL die **Teebeutel**
tea bag

die **Teekanne**, PLURAL die **Teekannen**
teapot

der **Teelöffel**, PLURAL die **Teelöffel**
teaspoon

der **Teenager**, PLURAL die **Teenager**
teenager

der **Teich**, PLURAL die **Teiche**
pond

der **Teig**, PLURAL die **Teige**
1 dough
2 pastry
3 mixture

die **Teigwaren** PLURAL NOUN
pasta

𝒫 der **Teil**¹, PLURAL die **Teile**
1 part
Wie gefiel dir der zweite Teil der Serie? How did you like the second episode?
2 zum Teil partly
3 zum größten Teil mostly, mainly
4 share
Sie bekamen ihren Teil am Gewinn. They received their share of the profit.

das **Teil**², PLURAL die **Teile**
1 spare part
2 part (of a car, machine)
3 unit (of furniture)

𝒫 **teilen** VERB, PERFECT **hat geteilt**
1 to divide
2 to share
sich etwas mit jemandem teilen to share something with somebody

teilentrahmt ADJECTIVE
semi-skimmed

teilnehmen VERB◇, PRESENT **nimmt teil**, IMPERFECT **nahm teil**, PERFECT **hat teilgenommen**
an etwas teilnehmen to take part in something

𝒫 der **Teilnehmer**, PLURAL die **Teilnehmer**
1 participant (male)
2 competitor (male)

𝒫 die **Teilnehmerin**, PLURAL die **Teilnehmerinnen**
1 participant (female)
2 competitor (female)

teils ADVERB
partly

die **Teilung**, PLURAL die **Teilungen**
division

die **Teilzeitarbeit**
part-time work

der **Teilzeitjob**, PLURAL die **Teilzeitjobs**
part-time job

◇ **irregular verb**; SEP **separable verb**; for more help with verbs see centre section

_ℓ_ das **Telefon,** _PLURAL_ die **Telefone**
telephone

der **Telefonanruf,** _PLURAL_ die **Telefonanrufe**
phone call

das **Telefonat,** _PLURAL_ die **Telefonate**
phone call

das **Telefonbuch,** _PLURAL_ die **Telefonbücher**
telephone directory, phone book

das **Telefongespräch,** _PLURAL_ die
Telefongespräche
phone call, phone conversation

der **Telefonhörer,** _PLURAL_ die **Telefonhörer**
receiver

telefonieren _VERB_, _PERFECT_ **hat telefoniert**
to telephone, to make a phone call

telefonisch _ADJECTIVE_
telephone
telefonisch _ADVERB_
by phone
Er ist telefonisch nicht erreichbar. He can't
be contacted by phone.

_ℓ_ die **Telefonkarte,** _PLURAL_ die **Telefonkarten**
phonecard

die **Telefonnummer,** _PLURAL_ die
Telefonnummern
phone number

_ℓ_ die **Telefonzelle,** _PLURAL_ die **Telefonzellen**
phone box, call box

das **Teleskop,** _PLURAL_ die **Teleskope**
telescope

_ℓ_ der **Teller,** _PLURAL_ die **Teller**
plate

die **Temperatur,** _PLURAL_ die **Temperaturen**
temperature

das **Tempo¹,** _PLURAL_ die **Tempos**
speed
Tempo, Tempo! _(informal)_ Hurry up!

das **Tempo™²,** _PLURAL_ die **Tempos™**
tissue, paper handkerchief
Kannst du mir ein Tempo-Taschentuch
geben? Could you give me a tissue?

die **Tendenz,** _PLURAL_ die **Tendenzen**
1 trend
2 tendency

tendieren _VERB_, _PERFECT_ **hat tendiert**
zu etwas tendieren to tend towards
something

das **Tennis**
tennis

der **Tennisplatz,** _PLURAL_ die **Tennisplätze**
tennis court

_ℓ_ der **Tennisschläger,** _PLURAL_ die
Tennisschläger
tennis racket

der **Tennisspieler,** _PLURAL_ die **Tennisspieler**
tennis player _(male)_

WORD TIP Professions, hobbies, and sports don't
take an article in German: Er ist Tennisspieler.

die **Tennisspielerin,** _PLURAL_ die
Tennisspielerinnen
tennis player _(female)_

WORD TIP Professions, hobbies, and sports don't
take an article in German: Sie ist Tennisspielerin.

_ℓ_ der **Teppich,** _PLURAL_ die **Teppiche**
1 carpet
2 rug

der **Teppichboden,** _PLURAL_ die
Teppichböden
fitted carpet

der **Termin,** _PLURAL_ die **Termine**
1 date
Sollen wir gleich einen Termin
vereinbaren? Shall we fix a date now?
2 appointment
Ich habe einen Termin beim Zahnarzt.
I have a dental appointment.
3 der letzte Termin the deadline

der or das **Terminal¹,** _PLURAL_ die **Terminals**
terminal _(at airport)_

das **Terminal²,** _PLURAL_ die **Terminals**
(computer) terminal

_ℓ_ der **Terminkalender,** _PLURAL_ die
Terminkalender
diary

_ℓ_ die **Terrasse,** _PLURAL_ die **Terrassen**
terrace

der **Terror**
terror

der **Terrorismus**
terrorism

der **Terrorist,** _PLURAL_ die **Terroristen**
terrorist _(male)_

die **Terroristin,** _PLURAL_ die **Terroristinnen**
terrorist _(female)_

der **Tesafilm**™
Sellotape™

der **Test**, PLURAL die **Tests**
test
Wir schreiben Freitag einen Test. We've got a test on Friday.

testen VERB, PERFECT **hat getestet**
to test

ℰ **teuer** ADJECTIVE
1 expensive
2 Wie teuer war es? How much was it?

der **Teufel**, PLURAL die **Teufel**
devil

ℰ der **Text**, PLURAL die **Texte**
1 text
2 lyrics
3 caption

die **Textverarbeitung**
word processing

ℰ das **Theater**, PLURAL die **Theater**
1 theatre
Sie gehen morgen ins Theater. They are going to the theatre tomorrow.
2 (informal) fuss
Mach nicht so ein Theater! Don't make such a fuss!

das **Theaterstück**, PLURAL die **Theaterstücke**
play

die **Theke**, PLURAL die **Theken**
1 bar
2 counter

ℰ das **Thema**, PLURAL die **Themen**
subject, topic

der **Themenpark**, PLURAL die **Themenparks**
theme park

die **Themse**
Thames

theoretisch ADJECTIVE
theoretical

theoretisch ADVERB
in theory

die **Theorie**, PLURAL die **Theorien**
theory

die **Therapie**, PLURAL die **Therapien**
therapy

das **Thermometer**, PLURAL die **Thermometer**
thermometer

der **Thron**, PLURAL die **Throne**
throne

der **Thunfisch**, PLURAL die **Thunfische**
tuna

ℰ **tief** ADJECTIVE
1 deep (hole, water, voice)
2 low (note, temperature, level)

das **Tief**, PLURAL die **Tiefs**
low

der **Tiefdruck**
low pressure

die **Tiefe**, PLURAL die **Tiefen**
depth

die **Tiefgarage**, PLURAL die **Tiefgaragen**
underground car park

das **Tiefkühlfach**, PLURAL die **Tiefkühlfächer**
freezer compartment

die **Tiefkühlkost**
frozen food

der **Tiefkühlschrank**, PLURAL die **Tiefkühlschränke**
freezer

die **Tiefkühltruhe**, PLURAL die **Tiefkühltruhen**
(chest) freezer

die **Tiefsttemperatur**, PLURAL die **Tiefsttemperaturen**
minimum temperature

der **Tiefstwert**, PLURAL die **Tiefstwerte**
minimum temperature

ℰ das **Tier**, PLURAL die **Tiere**
animal

die **Tierart**, PLURAL die **Tierarten**
species

ℰ der **Tierarzt**, PLURAL die **Tierärzte**
vet (male)

> **WORD TIP** Professions, hobbies, and sports don't take an article in German: Er ist Tierarzt.

ℰ die **Tierärztin**, PLURAL die **Tierärztinnen**
vet (female)

> **WORD TIP** Professions, hobbies, and sports don't take an article in German: Sie ist Tierärztin.

der **Tierfreund**, PLURAL die **Tierfreunde**
animal lover (male)

ℰ die **Tierfreundin**, PLURAL die **Tierfreundinnen**
animal lover (female)

der **Tiergarten**, *PLURAL* die **Tiergärten**
zoo

das **Tierheim**, *PLURAL* die **Tierheime**
animal shelter

der **Tierkreis**
zodiac

das **Tierkreiszeichen**, *PLURAL* die
Tierkreiszeichen
sign of the zodiac

der **Tierpark**, *PLURAL* die **Tierparks**
zoo

der **Tiger**, *PLURAL* die **Tiger**
tiger

die **Tinte**, *PLURAL* die **Tinten**
ink

der **Tintenfisch**, *PLURAL* die **Tintenfische**
1 octopus
2 squid

ℰ der **Tipp**, *PLURAL* die **Tipps**
tip, piece of advice

tippen *VERB*, *PERFECT* **hat getippt**
1 to type
2 to tap
3 auf etwas tippen to bet on something
Ich tippe auf ihn. I'm tipping him to win.
Tippst du im Lotto? Do you do the lottery?

der **Tippfehler**, *PLURAL* die **Tippfehler**
typing mistake

ℰ der **Tisch**, *PLURAL* die **Tische**
1 table
Decke bitte den Tisch. Please lay the table.
2 nach Tisch after the meal, after lunch/
dinner

die **Tischdecke**, *PLURAL* die **Tischdecken**
tablecloth

der **Tischler**, *PLURAL* die **Tischler**
carpenter, joiner *(male)*

WORD TIP Professions, hobbies, and sports
don't take an article in German: Er ist Tischler.

die **Tischlerin**, *PLURAL* die **Tischlerinnen**
carpenter, joiner *(female)*

WORD TIP Professions, hobbies, and sports don't
take an article in German: Sie ist Tischlerin.

ℰ das **Tischtennis**
table tennis

das **Tischtuch**, *PLURAL* die **Tischtücher**
tablecloth

der **Titel**, *PLURAL* die **Titel**
title

der **Toast**, *PLURAL* die **Toasts**
toast

toben *VERB*, *PERFECT* **hat getobt**
1 to rage
2 to go wild
3 to charge about

ℰ die **Tochter**, *PLURAL* die **Töchter**
daughter

der **Tod**, *PLURAL* die **Tode**
death

die **Todesstrafe**
death penalty

tödlich *ADJECTIVE*
1 fatal
2 deadly

todmüde *ADJECTIVE*
(informal) dead tired

todschick *ADJECTIVE*
(informal) trendy

ℰ die **Toilette**, *PLURAL* die **Toiletten**
toilet
Ich muss zur Toilette. I have to go to
the toilet.

das **Toilettenpapier**
toilet paper

tolerant *ADJECTIVE*
tolerant

ℰ **toll** *ADJECTIVE*
(informal) brilliant, great, fantastic

die **Tollwut**
rabies

ℰ die **Tomate**, *PLURAL* die **Tomaten**
tomato

das **Tomatenmark**
tomato purée

die **Tomatensoße**, *PLURAL* die
Tomatensoßen
tomato sauce

der **Ton**[1], *PLURAL* die **Töne**
1 sound
Er hat keinen Ton gesagt. He didn't say a
word.
2 große Töne spucken *(informal)* to talk big
3 tone (of voice)
Sprich nicht in diesem Ton mit mir. Don't
speak to me in that tone of voice.
4 note

289

Du hast einen falschen Ton gespielt. You played a wrong note.
5 **shade** *(of colour)*
6 **stress** *(in pronunciation)*

der **Ton²**
clay

das **Tonband**, PLURAL die **Tonbänder**
tape

das **Tonbandgerät**, PLURAL die **Tonbandgeräte**
tape recorder

die **Tonne**, PLURAL die **Tonnen**
1 **barrel**
2 **bin** *(for rubbish)*
3 **tonne, ton**

der **Topf**, PLURAL die **Töpfe**
1 **pot**
2 **pan**

die **Töpferei**, PLURAL die **Töpfereien**
pottery

⚲ das **Tor**, PLURAL die **Tore**
1 **gate**
2 **goal**
Wir haben mit 3 zu 2 Toren gewonnen.
We won by 3 goals to 2.

⚲ die **Torte**, PLURAL die **Torten**
1 **gateau**
2 **cake**

der **Torwart**, PLURAL die **Torwarte**
goalkeeper *(male)*

> **WORD TIP** Professions, hobbies, and sports don't take an article in German: Er ist Torwart.

die **Torwartin**, PLURAL die **Torwartinnen**
goalkeeper *(female)*

> **WORD TIP** Professions, hobbies, and sports don't take an article in German: Sie ist Torwartin.

⚲ **tot** ADJECTIVE
dead

⚲ **total** ADJECTIVE
complete
total ADVERB
1 **completely, totally**
Du bist total verrückt! You're completely mad!
2 *(informal)* **really**
Es war total gut. It was really good.

der/die **Tote**, PLURAL die **Toten**
1 **dead man/woman**
die Toten the dead

2 **fatality**

töten VERB, PERFECT **hat getötet**
to kill

totlachen VERB, PERFECT **hat sich totgelacht**
(informal) sich totlachen to kill yourself laughing

der **Touchscreen**, PLURAL die **Touchscreens**
touchscreen

die **Tour**, PLURAL die **Touren**
1 **tour**
2 **trip**
3 auf diese Tour *(informal)* in this way

der **Tourismus**
tourism

der **Tourist**, PLURAL die **Touristen**
tourist *(male)*

die **Touristeninformation**, PLURAL die **Touristeninformationen**
1 **tourist information office**
2 **tourist information**

die **Touristin**, PLURAL die **Touristinnen**
tourist *(female)*

die **Tournee**, PLURAL die **Tournees**
tour

traben VERB, PERFECT **ist getrabt**
to trot

die **Tradition**, PLURAL die **Traditionen**
tradition

traditionell ADJECTIVE
traditional

traf ► SEE **treffen**

tragbar ADJECTIVE
1 **portable**
2 **wearable**

⚲ **tragen** VERB◇, PRESENT **trägt**, IMPERFECT **trug**, PERFECT **hat getragen**
1 **to carry**
2 **to wear** *(clothes, glasses)*
Sie trug ein weißes Kleid. She was wearing a white dress.
Man trägt wieder kurz. Short skirts are in fashion again.
3 **to bear** *(hairstyle, name, title)*
4 **to bear** *(cost, risk, responsibility)*
Er trägt die Schuld. He's to blame.
5 **to support**
Die Organisation trägt sich selbst. The organization is self-supporting.

der **Träger**, PLURAL die **Träger**
1 **porter**

◇ **irregular verb;** SEP **separable verb; for more help with verbs see centre section**

2 **bearer** *(of a name, title)*

3 **strap** *(of a dress)*

4 **girder**

die **Tragetasche**, PLURAL die **Tragetaschen**
carrier bag

tragisch ADJECTIVE
tragic

die **Tragödie**, PLURAL die **Tragödien**
tragedy

ℙ der **Trainer**, PLURAL die **Trainer**
coach, trainer *(male)*

> **WORD TIP** Professions, hobbies, and sports
> don't take an article in German: Er ist Trainer.

ℙ die **Trainerin**, PLURAL die **Trainerinnen**
coach, trainer *(female)*

> **WORD TIP** Professions, hobbies, and sports
> don't take an article in German: Sie ist Trainerin.

trainieren VERB, PERFECT **hat trainiert**

1 to coach

2 to train

das **Training**
training

ℙ der **Trainingsanzug**, PLURAL die
Trainingsanzüge
tracksuit

das **Trainingslager**, PLURAL die
Trainingslager
training camp

der **Trainingsschuh**, PLURAL die
Trainingsschuhe
trainer *(shoe)*

der **Traktor**, PLURAL die **Traktoren**
tractor

trampen VERB, PERFECT **ist getrampt**
to hitchhike

das **Trampen**
hitchhiking

der **Tramper**, PLURAL die **Tramper**
hitchhiker *(male)*

die **Tramperin**, PLURAL die **Tramperinnen**
hitchhiker *(female)*

das **Trampolin**, PLURAL die **Trampoline**
trampoline

das **Trampolinspringen**
trampolining

die **Träne**, PLURAL die **Tränen**
tear

trank ▸SEE **trinken**

die **Transplantation**, PLURAL die
Transplantationen
transplant

der **Transport**, PLURAL die **Transporte**

1 transport

2 consignment

transportieren VERB, PERFECT **hat
transportiert**
to transport

trat ▸SEE **treten**

die **Traube**, PLURAL die **Trauben**

1 grape

2 bunch of grapes

trauen VERB, PERFECT **hat getraut**

1 to trust
Ich traue ihm nicht. I don't trust him.

2 sich trauen to dare
Ich trau mich nicht. I don't dare to.

3 to marry

die **Trauer**

1 grief

2 mourning

trauern VERB, PERFECT **hat getrauert**

1 to grieve

2 to mourn

ℙ der **Traum**, PLURAL die **Träume**
dream

träumen VERB, PERFECT **hat geträumt**
to dream

traumhaft ADJECTIVE
fabulous

ℙ **traurig** ADJECTIVE
sad

die **Traurigkeit**
sadness

die **Trauung**, PLURAL die **Trauungen**
wedding

der **Trauzeuge**, PLURAL die **Trauzeugen**
witness *(at a wedding ceremony) (male)*

die **Trauzeugin**, PLURAL die **Trauzeuginnen**
witness *(at a wedding ceremony) (female)*

ℙ **treffen** VERB◇, PRESENT **trifft**, IMPERFECT **traf**,
PERFECT **hat getroffen**

1 to hit

2 to meet
sich mit jemandem treffen to meet
somebody

3 to hurt

A
B
C
D
E
F
G
H
I
J
K
L
M
N
O
P
Q
R
S
T
U
V
W
X
Y
Z

Die Kritik hat ihn getroffen. He was hurt by the criticism.
4 **to make** (arrangements, a decision)
5 Das trifft sich gut! That's lucky!
6 PERFECT **ist getroffen**
auf etwas treffen to meet with (resistance, difficulties, approval)

das **Treffen**, PLURAL die **Treffen**
meeting

der **Treffer**, PLURAL die **Treffer**
1 **hit**
2 **winner**
3 **goal**

♪ der **Treffpunkt**, PLURAL die **Treffpunkte**
meeting place

treiben VERB♦, IMPERFECT **trieb**, PERFECT **hat getrieben**
1 **to drive**
Die gestiegene Nachfrage trieb die Preise in die Höhe. The increased demand drove prices up.
2 **to do**
Wir treiben viel Sport. We do a lot of sport.
Handel treiben to trade
3 jemanden zur Eile treiben to hurry somebody up
4 Unsinn treiben to mess about
5 PERFECT **ist getrieben to drift**

das **Treibhaus**, PLURAL die **Treibhäuser**
hothouse

der **Treibhauseffekt**
greenhouse effect

der **Treibstoff**, PLURAL die **Treibstoffe**
fuel

trennbar ADJECTIVE
separable (in grammar)

♪ **trennen** VERB, PERFECT **hat getrennt**
1 **to separate**
2 **to divide** (words, parts of a room)
3 sich trennen to separate
Wir haben uns getrennt. We've separated.
Jutta hat sich von ihm getrennt. Jutta has left him.
4 sich von etwas trennen to part with something
Ich kann mich von den alten Fotos nicht trennen. I can't bear to part with the old photos.

die **Trennung**, PLURAL die **Trennungen**
1 **separation**
2 **division**

♪ die **Treppe**, PLURAL die **Treppen**
stairs
eine Treppe a flight of stairs

das **Treppenhaus**
stairwell
Ich habe ihn zufällig im Treppenhaus getroffen. I bumped into him on the stairs.

treten VERB♦, PRESENT **tritt**, IMPERFECT **trat**, PERFECT **ist getreten**
1 **to step**
2 **to tread**
Du bist mir auf den Fuß getreten! You trod on my foot!
3 mit jemandem in Verbindung treten to get in touch with somebody
4 PERFECT **hat getreten to kick**
Sie hat mich getreten! She kicked me!
Er trat gegen die Tür. He kicked the door.

treu ADJECTIVE
1 **faithful**
2 **loyal**

die **Treue**
loyalty

die **Treuekarte**, PLURAL die **Treuekarten**
loyalty card

die **Tribüne**, PLURAL die **Tribünen**
1 **stand** (in a stadium)
2 **platform**

der **Trick**, PLURAL die **Tricks**
trick

♪ der **Trickfilm**, PLURAL die **Trickfilme**
cartoon

trieb ▸ SEE **treiben**

trifft ▸ SEE **treffen**

das **Trimester**, PLURAL die **Trimester**
term

der **Trimm-dich-Pfad**, PLURAL die **Trimm-dich-Pfade**
fitness trail

trimmen VERB, PERFECT **hat getrimmt**
1 **to trim**
2 sich trimmen to keep fit

trinkbar ADJECTIVE
drinkable

♪ **trinken** VERB♦, IMPERFECT **trank**, PERFECT **hat getrunken**
to drink

das **Trinkgeld**, PLURAL die **Trinkgelder**
tip

♦ irregular verb; SEP separable verb; for more help with verbs see centre section

die **Trinkhalle**, PLURAL die **Trinkhallen**
(refreshment) kiosk

die **Trinkschokolade**
drinking chocolate

das **Trinkwasser**
drinking water

tritt ▸ SEE **treten**

der **Tritt**, PLURAL die **Tritte**
1 step
2 kick

der **Triumph**, PLURAL die **Triumphe**
triumph

℘ **trocken** ADJECTIVE
dry

trockenlegen VERB, PERFECT **hat
trockengelegt**
to drain (a marsh, a pond)

trocknen VERB, PERFECT **hat getrocknet**
to dry

der **Trockner**, PLURAL die **Trockner**
drier

der **Trödel**
(informal) junk

der **Trödelmarkt**, PLURAL die **Trödelmärkte**
flea market

die **Trommel**, PLURAL die **Trommeln**
drum
Er spielt Trommel. He plays the drum.

trommeln VERB, PERFECT **hat getrommelt**
to drum

die **Trompete**, PLURAL die **Trompeten**
trumpet
Sie spielt Trompete. She plays the
trumpet.

℘ die **Tropen** PLURAL NOUN
die Tropen the tropics

tropfen VERB, PERFECT **hat getropft**
to drip

der **Tropfen**, PLURAL die **Tropfen**
drop

die **Trophäe**, PLURAL die **Trophäen**
trophy

tropisch ADJECTIVE
tropical

trösten VERB, PERFECT **hat getröstet**
to console, to comfort

℘ **trotz** PREPOSITION (+ GEN)
despite, in spite of

℘ **trotzdem** ADVERB
nevertheless

trüb ADJECTIVE
1 dull, dismal
2 cloudy (liquid)

trübsinnig ADJECTIVE
gloomy

trug ▸ SEE **tragen**

die **Truhe**, PLURAL die **Truhen**
chest (box)

die **Trümmer** PLURAL NOUN
ruins

der **Trumpf**, PLURAL die **Trümpfe**
1 trump (card)
2 trumps

die **Trunkenheit**
drunkenness
Trunkenheit am Steuer drink-driving

die **Truppen** PLURAL NOUN
troops

der **Truthahn**, PLURAL die **Truthähne**
turkey

der **Tscheche**, PLURAL die **Tschechen**
Czech (male)

die **Tschechin**, PLURAL die **Tschechinnen**
Czech (female)

tschechisch ADJECTIVE
Czech

WORD TIP Adjectives never have capitals
in German, even for regions, countries, or
nationalities.

℘ die **Tschechische Republik**
Czech Republic

℘ **tschüs, tschüss** EXCLAMATION
bye!

℘ das **T-Shirt**, PLURAL die **T-Shirts**
T-shirt

die **Tube**, PLURAL die **Tuben**
tube

die **Tuberkulose**
tuberculosis

das **Tuch**, PLURAL die **Tücher**
1 cloth
2 scarf

℘ **indicates key words**

tüchtig ADJECTIVE
1 efficient, hard-working
2 competent, capable

die Tüchtigkeit
1 efficiency
2 competence

die Tulpe, PLURAL **die Tulpen**
tulip

der Tumor, PLURAL **die Tumoren**
tumour

℘ **tun** VERB◇, PRESENT **tut**, IMPERFECT **tat**, PERFECT **hat getan**
1 to do
Das tut man nicht. You don't do that.
Das tut's. (informal) That'll do.
2 to put
Tu die Butter in den Kühlschrank. Put the butter in the fridge.
3 to pretend
Er tut nur so. He's only pretending.
4 to act
Sie tut immer so freundlich. She always acts so friendly.
5 jemandem etwas tun to hurt somebody
6 mit jemandem etwas zu tun haben to have dealings with somebody
7 Das hat nichts damit zu tun. It's got nothing to do with it.
8 Das tut nichts zur Sache. It doesn't matter.
9 Es hat sich viel getan. A lot has happened.

Tunesien NEUTER NOUN
Tunisia

der Tunfisch, PLURAL **die Tunfische**
tuna

der Tunnel, PLURAL **die Tunnel**
tunnel

tupfen VERB, PERFECT **hat getupft**
to dab

der Tupfen, PLURAL **die Tupfen**
dot

℘ **die Tür**, PLURAL **die Türen**
door

der Türke, PLURAL **die Türken**
Turk (male)

🔵 **TÜRKE**

Turks are one of the largest ethnic groups in Germany (3% of the population) and Austria (also 3%). Many Turks arrived as Gastarbeiter (guest-workers) in the years following the Second World War.

---

die Türkei
die Türkei Turkey

WORD TIP This is always used with an article: Wir fahren in die Türkei. Er wohnt in der Türkei.

die Türkin, PLURAL **die Türkinnen**
Turk (female)

türkis ADJECTIVE
turquoise

türkisch ADJECTIVE
Turkish

WORD TIP Adjectives never have capitals in German, even for regions, countries, or nationalities.

der Turm, PLURAL **die Türme**
1 tower
2 steeple
3 rook, castle (in chess)

der Turnanzug, PLURAL **die Turnanzüge**
leotard

℘ **turnen** VERB, PERFECT **hat geturnt**
to do gymnastics

das Turnen
1 gymnastics
2 physical education, PE

℘ **die Turnhalle**, PLURAL **die Turnhallen**
gymnasium, gym

das Turnier, PLURAL **die Turniere**
tournament

℘ **der Turnschuh**, PLURAL **die Turnschuhe**
1 trainer
2 gym shoe

der Turnverein, PLURAL **die Turnvereine**
gymnastics club, gym club

tuscheln VERB, PERFECT **hat getuschelt**
to whisper

tut ▸ SEE **tun**

℘ **die Tüte**, PLURAL **die Tüten**
bag

der Typ, PLURAL **die Typen**
1 type of person
2 (informal) bloke

typisch ADJECTIVE
typical

Uu

u.a. ABBREVIATION
(=unter anderem) **among other things**

ℓ die **U-Bahn**, PLURAL die **U-Bahnen**
underground

die **U-Bahn-Station**, PLURAL die **U-Bahn-Stationen**
underground station

übel ADJECTIVE
1 **bad**
2 Mir ist übel. **I feel sick.**
3 etwas übel nehmen **to take offence at something**
Bitte nimm es mir nicht übel, wenn ich … **Please don't be offended if I …**

die **Übelkeit**
nausea

ℓ **üben** VERB, PERFECT **hat geübt**
to practise

ℓ **über** PREPOSITION (+ DAT or + ACC)
1 (the dative is used when talking about position; the accusative shows movement or a change of place) **over**
Er sprang über den Zaun. (ACC) **He jumped over the fence.**
Sie trug eine Jacke über dem Kleid. (DAT) **She wore a jacket over her dress.**
Wir fahren über Weihnachten weg. (ACC) **We're going away over Christmas.**
2 **above**
Er wohnt über uns. (DAT) **He lives above us.**
Es ist fünf Grad über null. (DAT) **It's five degrees above zero.**
3 **about**
Sie schrieb über ihre Ferien. (ACC) **She wrote about her holidays.**
4 **for**
Hier ist ein Scheck über hundert Euro. (ACC) **Here's a cheque for one hundred euros.**
5 **across** (a field, the street)
Sie ruderte über den See. (ACC) **She rowed across the lake.**
Ich ging über die Straße. (ACC) **I crossed the road.**
6 **via**
Sie fahren über Frankfurt. (ACC) **They're**

going via Frankfurt.

WORD TIP über + dem gives überm; über + das gives übers

über ADVERB
1 über und über **over and over**
2 etwas über haben (informal) **to be fed up with something**
Nudeln habe ich über. **I'm getting fed up with pasta.**
3 über sein (informal) **to be left over**
Ein Stück ist noch über. **There's one piece left over.**

ℓ **überall** ADVERB
everywhere

überarbeiten VERB, PERFECT **hat überarbeitet**
to revise (a text)

überbevölkert ADJECTIVE
overpopulated

der **Überblick**, PLURAL die **Überblicke**
1 **view**
Wir hatten einen guten Überblick über die Bühne. **We had a good view of the stage.**
2 **overview, summary**
Die Broschüre bietet einen Überblick über das Kursangebot. **The leaflet gives an overview of the courses available.**
3 **overall picture**
Sie versuchte, sich einen Überblick über die Lage zu verschaffen. **She tried to get an overall picture of the situation.**
4 den Überblick verlieren **to lose track of things**

überblicken VERB, PERFECT **hat überblickt**
1 **to overlook**
2 **to assess**

die **Überdosis**, PLURAL die **Überdosen**
overdose

der **Überdruss**
bis zum Überdruss **ad nauseam**

übereinander ADVERB
1 **one on top of the other**
2 Sie sprechen nicht übereinander. **They don't talk about each other.**

übereinstimmen VERB, PERFECT **hat übereingestimmt**
to agree

überempfindlich ADJECTIVE
hypersensitive

ℓ indicates key words

überfahren VERB◇, PRESENT **überfährt**, IMPERFECT **überfuhr**, PERFECT **hat überfahren**
to run over
Das Kind ist von einem Auto überfahren worden. The child was run over by a car.

die **Überfahrt**, PLURAL die **Überfahrten**
crossing

der **Überfall**, PLURAL die **Überfälle**
1 attack
2 raid

überfallen VERB◇, PRESENT **überfällt**, IMPERFECT **überfiel**, PERFECT **hat überfallen**
1 to attack, to mug
2 to raid
3 Sie überfielen ihn mit Fragen. They bombarded him with questions.

überfällig ADJECTIVE
overdue

überflüssig ADJECTIVE
superfluous

die **Überführung**, PLURAL die **Überführungen**
1 transfer
2 flyover
3 footbridge

überfüllt ADJECTIVE
1 crowded
2 oversubscribed

der **Übergang**, PLURAL die **Übergänge**
1 crossing
2 transition

übergeben VERB◇, PRESENT **übergibt**, IMPERFECT **übergab**, PERFECT **hat übergeben**
1 to hand over
2 sich übergeben to be sick

übergewichtig ADJECTIVE
overweight

♪**überhaupt** ADVERB
1 in general
2 anyway
Was will er überhaupt? What does he want anyway?
3 at all
überhaupt nicht not at all
überhaupt nichts nothing at all
Ich habe überhaupt keine Zeit. I have no time at all.

überholen VERB, PERFECT **hat überholt**
1 to overtake
2 to overhaul

überholt ADJECTIVE
outdated

überlassen VERB◇, PRESENT **überlässt**, IMPERFECT **überließ**, PERFECT **hat überlassen**
1 jemandem etwas überlassen to let somebody have something
2 etwas jemandem überlassen to leave something (up) to somebody
Ich überlasse dir die Entscheidung. I'm leaving the decision to you.
Das bleibt dir überlassen. It's up to you.

überlaufen VERB◇, PRESENT **läuft über**, IMPERFECT **lief über**, PERFECT **ist übergelaufen**
to overflow

überleben VERB, PERFECT **hat überlebt**
to survive

überlegen¹ VERB, PERFECT **hat überlegt**
1 to think
Ich muss es mir überlegen. I'll have to think about it.
Ohne zu überlegen sagte er zu. He accepted without thinking.
2 Ich habe es mir anders überlegt. I've changed my mind.

überlegen² ADJECTIVE
1 superior
jemandem überlegen sein to be superior to somebody
In Mathe ist sie mir weit überlegen. She's far better than me at maths.
2 convincing (victory)

überm ▸ SEE über dem

übermäßig ADJECTIVE
excessive

übermorgen ADVERB
the day after tomorrow

übernächster, **übernächste**, **übernächstes** ADJECTIVE
next but one
übernächstes Jahr the year after next

übernachten VERB, PERFECT **hat übernachtet**
to stay the night
Ich habe bei Alex übernachtet. I stayed the night at Alex's house.

die **Übernachtung**, PLURAL die **Übernachtungen**
1 overnight stay
2 Übernachtung mit Frühstück bed and breakfast

◇ irregular verb; SEP separable verb; for more help with verbs see centre section

übernehmen *VERB*◇, *PRESENT* **übernimmt**, *IMPERFECT* **übernahm**, *PERFECT* **hat übernommen**
1 to take over
2 to take on
3 sich übernehmen to take on too much

überqueren *VERB*, *PERFECT* **hat überquert**
to cross

überraschen *VERB*, *PERFECT* **hat überrascht**
to surprise

♪ die **Überraschung**, *PLURAL* die **Überraschungen**
surprise

überreden *VERB*, *PERFECT* **hat überredet**
to persuade

übers ▶ SEE über das

überschreiten *VERB*◇, *IMPERFECT* **überschritt**, *PERFECT* **hat überschritten**
1 to cross
2 to exceed

♪ die **Überschrift**, *PLURAL* die **Überschriften**
heading

überschüssig *ADJECTIVE*
surplus

überschütten *VERB*, *PERFECT* **hat überschüttet**
jemanden mit etwas überschütten to shower somebody with something

die **Überschwemmung**, *PLURAL* die **Überschwemmungen**
flood

übersehen *VERB*◇, *PRESENT* **übersieht**, *IMPERFECT* **übersah**, *PERFECT* **hat übersehen**
1 to overlook, to miss
Der Lehrer hat einen Fehler übersehen. The teacher missed a mistake.
2 to assess *(consequences, damages)*

♪ **übersetzen** *VERB*, *PERFECT* **hat übersetzt**
to translate

der **Übersetzer**, *PLURAL* die **Übersetzer**
translator *(male)*

> **WORD TIP** Professions, hobbies, and sports don't take an article in German: Er ist Übersetzer.

die **Übersetzerin**, *PLURAL* die **Übersetzerinnen**
translator *(female)*

> **WORD TIP** Professions, hobbies, and sports don't take an article in German: Sie ist Übersetzerin.

die **Übersetzung**, *PLURAL* die **Übersetzungen**
translation

die **Übersicht**
1 overview
2 summary

überspringen *VERB*◇, *IMPERFECT* **übersprang**, *PERFECT* **hat übersprungen**
1 to jump (over)
2 to skip *(a chapter, etc.)*

überstehen *VERB*◇, *IMPERFECT* **überstand**, *PERFECT* **hat überstanden**
1 to get over
2 to survive

die **Überstunden** *PLURAL NOUN*
overtime
Sie mussten Überstunden machen. They had to work overtime.

übertragen *VERB*◇, *PRESENT* **überträgt**, *IMPERFECT* **übertrug**, *PERFECT* **hat übertragen**
1 to transfer
2 to transmit
3 to broadcast
4 to copy
Er übertrug die neuen Vokabeln in sein Heft. He copied the new words into his exercise book.
5 sich auf jemanden übertragen to spread to somebody
Ihre Begeisterung übertrug sich auf die Schüler. She passed her enthusiasm on to her students.

die **Übertragung**, *PLURAL* die **Übertragungen**
1 broadcast
2 transmission

übertreiben *VERB*◇, *IMPERFECT* **übertrieb**, *PERFECT* **hat übertrieben**
1 to exaggerate
2 to overdo

die **Übertreibung**, *PLURAL* die **Übertreibungen**
exaggeration

überwältigend *ADJECTIVE*
overwhelming

überweisen *VERB*◇, *IMPERFECT* **überwies**, *PERFECT* **hat überwiesen**
1 to transfer
2 to refer *(a patient)*

♪ indicates key words

überwinden VERB◇, IMPERFECT **überwand**, PERFECT **hat überwunden**
1 **to overcome**
2 **sich überwinden** to force yourself

überzeugen VERB, PERFECT **hat überzeugt**
1 **to convince**
2 **sich selbst überzeugen** to satisfy yourself

überzeugend ADJECTIVE
convincing

die **Überzeugung**, PLURAL die **Überzeugungen**
conviction

überziehen¹ VERB◇, IMPERFECT **zog über**, PERFECT **hat übergezogen**
to put on (a cardigan, jacket)

überziehen² VERB◇, IMPERFECT **überzog**, PERFECT **hat überzogen**
1 **to overdraw**
Ich habe mein Konto überzogen. I'm overdrawn.
2 **to cover** (with icing, for example)

üblich ADJECTIVE
usual

das **U-Boot**, PLURAL die **U-Boote**
submarine

übrig ADJECTIVE
1 **remaining**
2 **übrig sein** to be left over
3 **etwas übrig lassen** to leave something (over)
4 **Uns blieb nichts anderes übrig.** We had no other choice.
5 **alles Übrige** the rest
die Übrigen the others
6 **im Übrigen** besides

übrigens ADVERB
by the way

♀ die **Übung**, PLURAL die **Übungen**
1 **exercise**
2 **practice**
Ich bin aus der Übung. I'm out of practice.

das **Ufer**, PLURAL die **Ufer**
1 **bank** (of a river)
2 **shore**

♀ die **Uhr**, PLURAL die **Uhren**
1 **clock**
2 **watch**
3 (in time phrases)
Wie viel Uhr ist es? What's the time?
Es ist ein Uhr. It's one o'clock.
Sie kommen um sechzehn Uhr an.

They are arriving at four o'clock (in the afternoon).

der **Uhrzeiger**, PLURAL die **Uhrzeiger**
hand (of a clock or watch)

der **Uhrzeigersinn**
im Uhrzeigersinn clockwise
entgegen dem Uhrzeigersinn anticlockwise

♀ die **Uhrzeit**
time
Er fragte mich nach der Uhrzeit. He asked me the time.

ulkig ADJECTIVE
funny

ultraviolett ADJECTIVE
ultraviolet

♀ **um** PREPOSITION (+ ACC)
1 **round, around**
Sie rannten um das Haus herum. They ran around the house.
2 **at**
Er ist um fünf Uhr gegangen. He left at five o'clock.
Um wie viel Uhr musst du ins Bett? What time do you have to go to bed?
3 **about, around**
Es hat um die dreihundert Euro herum gekostet. It cost about three hundred euros.
Die Hochsaison ist um Weihnachten. The high season is around Christmas.
4 **for**
um etwas bitten to ask for something
um seinetwillen for his sake
5 **sich um jemanden sorgen** to worry about somebody
6 **by** (indicating difference)
Die Preise sind um zehn Prozent gestiegen. Prices have gone up by ten per cent.
7 ▸ SEE **umso**

WORD TIP um + das gives ums

um ADVERB
um sein (informal) to be over
Die Ferien sind schon um. The holidays are over already.
Die Zeit ist um. The time's up.

um CONJUNCTION
um zu (in order) to
Er ist noch zu klein, um in die Schule zu gehen. He's too young to go to school.

umarmen VERB, PERFECT **hat umarmt**
to hug

der **Umbau**, *PLURAL* die **Umbauten**
1 renovation
2 conversion

umbinden *VERB* ◇, *IMPERFECT* **band um**, *PERFECT* **hat umgebunden**
to put on

umblättern *VERB*, *PERFECT* **hat umgeblättert**
to turn over

umbringen *VERB* ◇, *IMPERFECT* **brachte um**, *PERFECT* **hat umgebracht**
to kill

umdrehen *VERB*, *PERFECT* **hat umgedreht**
1 to turn (round/over)
2 sich umdrehen to turn round, to turn over

umfallen *VERB* ◇, *PRESENT* **fällt um**, *IMPERFECT* **fiel um**, *PERFECT* **ist umgefallen**
to fall down, to fall over

ℰ die **Umfrage**, *PLURAL* die **Umfragen**
survey

umgänglich *ADJECTIVE*
sociable

die **Umgangsformen** *PLURAL NOUN*
manners

die **Umgangssprache**
colloquial language

umgeben *VERB* ◇, *PRESENT* **umgibt**, *IMPERFECT* **umgab**, *PERFECT* **hat umgeben**
to surround

die **Umgebung**, *PLURAL* die **Umgebungen**
1 surroundings
2 neighbourhood

umgehen¹ *VERB* ◇, *IMPERFECT* **ging um**, *PERFECT* **ist umgegangen**
1 to go round (of a rumour, an illness)
2 Sie geht mit den Kindern sehr streng um. She's very strict with the children.
3 Er kann mit Geld nicht umgehen. He's not good with money.
Bitte geh mit deinen Sachen sorgfältig um. Please be careful with your things.

umgehen² *VERB* ◇, *IMPERFECT* **umging**, *PERFECT* **hat umgangen**
to avoid

die **Umgehungsstraße**, *PLURAL* die **Umgehungsstraßen**
bypass

umgekehrt *ADJECTIVE*
1 opposite
2 reverse (order)

3 Es war umgekehrt. It was the other way round.

umgekehrt *ADVERB*
1 ... und umgekehrt ... and vice versa
2 the other way round
Warum machst du es nicht umgekehrt? Why don't you do it the other way round?

umkehren *VERB*, *PERFECT* **ist umgekehrt**
to turn back
Nach zehn Minuten sind wir wieder umgekehrt. Ten minutes later we turned back again.

ℰ die **Umkleidekabine**, *PLURAL* die **Umkleidekabinen**
changing cubicle

der **Umkleideraum**, *PLURAL* die **Umkleideräume**
changing room

umkommen *VERB* ◇, *IMPERFECT* **kam um**, *PERFECT* **ist umgekommen**
to be killed

der **Umlaut**, *PLURAL* die **Umlaute**
umlaut

umlegen *VERB*, *PERFECT* **hat umgelegt**
1 to put on (a scarf)
2 to transfer (a patient, call)
3 jemanden umlegen (informal) to bump somebody off

die **Umleitung**, *PLURAL* die **Umleitungen**
diversion

umrechnen *VERB*, *PERFECT* **hat umgerechnet**
to convert

die **Umrechnung**
conversion

der **Umrechnungskurs**
exchange rate

der **Umriss**, *PLURAL* die **Umrisse**
outline

umrühren *VERB*, *PERFECT* **hat umgerührt**
to stir

ums ▸ SEE um das

umschalten *VERB*, *PERFECT* **hat umgeschaltet**
1 to switch over
Kannst du mal vom ersten aufs zweite Programm umschalten? Can you to switch from channel one to channel two?
2 Die Ampel schaltete auf Rot um. The traffic light changed to red.

der **Umschlag**, *PLURAL* die **Umschläge**
1 envelope
2 cover

ℰ indicates key words

umsehen *VERB*◇, *PRESENT* **sieht sich um**, *IMPERFECT* **sah sich um**, *PERFECT* **hat sich umgesehen**
sich umsehen to look round

umso *ADVERB*
all the ...
Jetzt ist es umso wichtiger, dass ... Now it's all the more important that ...
Umso besser! So much the better!

umsonst *ADVERB*
1 in vain
2 free, for nothing

der **Umstand**, *PLURAL* die **Umstände**
1 circumstance
Unter diesen Umständen bleibt mir nichts anderes übrig. Under the circumstances I have no other choice.
2 unter Umständen possibly
3 jemandem Umstände machen to put somebody to trouble
Das macht gar keine Umstände! It's no trouble at all!
4 in anderen Umständen sein to be pregnant

umständlich *ADJECTIVE*
1 laborious, slow
2 complicated

ℰ **umsteigen** *VERB*◇, *IMPERFECT* **stieg um**, *PERFECT* **ist umgestiegen**
to change (trains, buses)

umstellen[1] *VERB*, *PERFECT* **hat umgestellt**
1 to rearrange
2 to reset
3 to change over
4 sich umstellen to adjust

umstellen[2] *VERB*, *PERFECT* **hat umstellt**
to surround

der **Umtausch**
exchange

umtauschen *VERB*, *PERFECT* **hat umgetauscht**
to change, to exchange

der **Umweg**, *PLURAL* die **Umwege**
detour

ℰ die **Umwelt**
environment

umweltbewusst *ADJECTIVE*
concerned about the environment, green

ℰ **umweltfeindlich** *ADJECTIVE*
harmful to the environment

ℰ **umweltfreundlich** *ADJECTIVE*
environmentally friendly

ℰ die **Umweltorganisation**, *PLURAL* die **Umweltorganisationen**
environmental agency

der **Umweltschutz**
environmental protection

der **Umweltschützer**, *PLURAL* die **Umweltschützer**
environmentalist, conservationist (male)

WORD TIP Professions, hobbies, and sports don't take an article in German: Er ist Umweltschützer.

die **Umweltschützerin**, *PLURAL* die **Umweltschützerinnen**
environmentalist, conservationist (female)

WORD TIP Professions, hobbies, and sports don't take an article in German: Sie ist Umweltschützerin.

ℰ die **Umweltverschmutzung**
pollution

umwerfen *VERB*◇, *PRESENT* **wirft um**, *IMPERFECT* **warf um**, *PERFECT* **hat umgeworfen**
1 to knock over
2 to upset (a plan)
3 Das hat mich umgeworfen. It's thrown me.

umwerfend *ADJECTIVE*
fantastic

ℰ **umziehen** *VERB*◇, *IMPERFECT* **zog um**, *PERFECT* **ist umgezogen**
1 to move
Sie ziehen nächste Woche nach Leipzig um. They're moving to Leizpig next week.
2 *PERFECT* **hat umgezogen** to change
Sie zog das Baby um. She changed the baby's clothes.
3 *PERFECT* **hat sich umgezogen**
sich umziehen to get changed
Ich muss mich noch umziehen. I have to get changed.

ℰ der **Umzug**, *PLURAL* die **Umzüge**
1 move
2 procession

unabhängig *ADJECTIVE*
independent

die **Unabhängigkeit**
independence

unangenehm *ADJECTIVE*
1 unpleasant
2 embarrassing (question, situation)

◇ irregular verb; *SEP* separable verb; for more help with verbs see centre section

unartig *ADJECTIVE*
naughty

unbedeutend *ADJECTIVE*
insignificant

unbedeutend *ADVERB*
slightly

unbedingt *ADJECTIVE*
absolute

unbedingt *ADVERB*
really
Ich muss ihn unbedingt sprechen. I really must talk to him.
nicht unbedingt not necessarily

unbefriedigend *ADJECTIVE*
unsatisfactory

unbefriedigt *ADJECTIVE*
unsatisfied

unbegrenzt *ADJECTIVE*
unlimited

unbehaglich *ADJECTIVE*
1 uncomfortable
2 uneasy

ℙ **unbekannt** *ADJECTIVE*
unknown

ℙ **unbeliebt** *ADJECTIVE*
unpopular

ℙ **unbequem** *ADJECTIVE*
uncomfortable

unbesetzt *ADJECTIVE*
vacant

unbestimmt *ADJECTIVE*
1 indefinite *(also in grammar)*
Sie sind auf unbestimmte Zeit verreist.
They went away for an indefinite period.
2 vague

unbewusst *ADJECTIVE*
unconscious

ℙ **und** *CONJUNCTION*
and
und so weiter and so on
Na und? So what?

undankbar *ADJECTIVE*
ungrateful

undeutlich *ADJECTIVE*
unclear

undicht *ADJECTIVE*
leaking, leaky
Im Dach ist eine undichte Stelle. The roof has a leak.

uneben *ADJECTIVE*
uneven

ℙ **unehrlich** *ADJECTIVE*
dishonest

unempfindlich *ADJECTIVE*
1 hard-wearing
2 immune
Sie ist unempfindlich gegen Kälte. She doesn't feel the cold.

unentbehrlich *ADJECTIVE*
indispensable

ℙ **unentschieden** *ADJECTIVE*
1 undecided
2 Das Spiel endete unentschieden. The match ended in a draw.

unerträglich *ADJECTIVE*
unbearable

unerwartet *ADJECTIVE*
unexpected

unfähig *ADJECTIVE*
1 incompetent
2 unfähig sein, etwas zu tun to be incapable of doing something

unfair *ADJECTIVE*
unfair

ℙ der **Unfall**, *PLURAL* die **Unfälle**
accident

unfit *ADJECTIVE*
unfit

ℙ **unfreundlich** *ADJECTIVE*
unfriendly

der **Unfug**
1 nonsense
2 mischief
Die Jungen machen den ganzen Tag nur Unfug. The boys get up to mischief all day.

der **Ungar**, *PLURAL* die **Ungarn**
Hungarian *(male)*

die **Ungarin**, *PLURAL* die **Ungarinnen**
Hungarian *(female)*

ungarisch *ADJECTIVE*
Hungarian

> **WORD TIP** Adjectives never have capitals in German, even for regions, countries, or nationalities.

ℙ **Ungarn** *NEUTER NOUN*
Hungary

ℙ **indicates key words**

die **Ungeduld**
impatience

ℓ **ungeduldig** *ADJECTIVE*
impatient

ungeeignet *ADJECTIVE*
unsuitable

ℓ **ungefähr** *ADJECTIVE*
approximate, rough

ungefähr *ADVERB*
approximately, about

ungefährlich *ADJECTIVE*
safe, harmless

ungeheuer *ADJECTIVE*
enormous

das **Ungeheuer**, *PLURAL* die **Ungeheuer**
monster

ungehorsam *ADJECTIVE*
disobedient

ungelegen *ADJECTIVE*
inconvenient

ungemütlich *ADJECTIVE*
uncomfortable

ungenau *ADJECTIVE*
1 inaccurate
2 vague

ungenießbar *ADJECTIVE*
1 inedible
2 undrinkable
3 *(informal)* unbearable
Ben ist heute ziemlich ungenießbar. Ben is
being quite unbearable today.

ℓ **ungenügend** *ADJECTIVE*
1 insufficient, inadequate
2 unsatisfactory *(also as a school mark)*

ungerade *ADJECTIVE*
eine ungerade Zahl an odd number

ℓ **ungerecht** *ADJECTIVE*
unjust, unfair

ungern *ADVERB*
reluctantly

ungeschickt *ADJECTIVE*
clumsy

ℓ **ungesund** *ADJECTIVE*
unhealthy

ungewöhnlich *ADJECTIVE*
unusual

das **Ungeziefer**
vermin

ungezwungen *ADJECTIVE*
1 informal

2 natural

ℓ **unglaublich** *ADJECTIVE*
incredible, unbelievable

das **Unglück**, *PLURAL* die **Unglücke**
1 accident
2 misfortune
3 bad luck
Das bringt Unglück. That's unlucky.

ℓ **unglücklich** *ADJECTIVE*
1 unhappy
2 unfortunate

unglücklicherweise *ADVERB*
unfortunately

unheilbar *ADJECTIVE*
incurable

unheimlich *ADJECTIVE*
eerie

unheimlich *ADVERB*
1 eerily
2 *(informal)* incredibly
Sie haben unheimlich viel gegessen. They
ate an incredible amount.

unhöflich *ADJECTIVE*
rude

die **Uni**, *PLURAL* die **Unis**
(informal) university, uni

ℓ die **Uniform**, *PLURAL* die **Uniformen**
uniform

uninteressant *ADJECTIVE*
1 not interesting
2 irrelevant

ℓ die **Universität**, *PLURAL* die **Universitäten**
university

die **Unkenntnis**
ignorance

unklar *ADJECTIVE*
unclear

die **Unkosten** *PLURAL NOUN*
expenses

das **Unkraut**
weed

unleserlich *ADJECTIVE*
illegible

unlogisch *ADJECTIVE*
illogical

unmittelbar *ADJECTIVE*
immediate, direct

◇ irregular verb; *SEP* separable verb; for more help with verbs see centre section

unmodern *ADJECTIVE*
old-fashioned

unmöglich *ADJECTIVE*
impossible

die **Unmöglichkeit**
impossibility

unnötig *ADJECTIVE*
unnecessary

ᵽ **unordentlich** *ADJECTIVE*
untidy

die **Unordnung**
1 untidiness
2 mess

unpraktisch *ADJECTIVE*
impractical

unpünktlich *ADJECTIVE, ADVERB*
late
Sie ist immer unpünktlich. She's always
late.

unrecht *ADJECTIVE*
1 wrong
2 jemandem unrecht tun to do somebody
an injustice

das **Unrecht**
wrong
zu Unrecht wrongly
Unrecht haben, im Unrecht sein to be
wrong

unregelmäßig *ADJECTIVE*
irregular

unreif *ADJECTIVE*
1 unripe
2 immature

die **Unruhe**, *PLURAL* die **Unruhen**
1 restlessness
2 concern, anxiety
3 Unruhen unrest

der **Unruhestifter**, *PLURAL* die **Unruhestifter**
troublemaker

unruhig *ADJECTIVE*
1 restless
2 worried, anxious

ᵽ **uns** *PRONOUN*
1 us
Sie kommen mit uns. They're coming
with us.
2 to us
Gib es uns. Give it to us.
3 ourselves
Wir sahen uns im Spiegel an. We looked

at ourselves in the mirror.
Wir waschen uns die Hände. We are
washing our hands.
4 each other
Wir kennen uns. We know each other.

unscharf *ADJECTIVE*
blurred, indistinct

unschuldig *ADJECTIVE*
innocent

ᵽ **unser** *ADJECTIVE*
our

unserer, unsere, unser(e)s *PRONOUN*
ours

unseretwegen *ADVERB*
1 for our sake
2 because of us
3 as far as we're concerned

unsicher *ADJECTIVE*
1 uncertain
2 insecure
3 dangerous

unsicher *ADVERB*
unsteadily

unsichtbar *ADJECTIVE*
invisible

der **Unsinn**
nonsense

unsrer ▸ SEE unserer

ᵽ **unsympathisch** *ADJECTIVE*
unpleasant
Tobias ist mir unsympathisch. I don't like
Tobias.

> **WORD TIP** The German word unsympathisch
> does not mean unsympathetic in English; a
> German expression for **unsympathetic** is ohne
> Mitgefühl.

ᵽ **unten** *ADVERB*
1 at the bottom
2 below
Siehe unten. See below.
3 downstairs
hier unten down here
nach unten down

> ᵽ **unter** *PREPOSITION (+ DAT or + ACC)*
> 1 *(the dative is used generally and when
> talking about position; the accusative
> shows movement or a change of place)*
> under, below
> Wir saßen unter einem Baum. *(DAT)* We
> were sitting under a tree.

> Sie legten die Decke unter einen Baum. (ACC) They put the rug under a tree.
> **2** among
> unter anderem among other things
> **3** Sie waren unter sich. They were by themselves.
> unter uns gesagt between ourselves
> **4** unter der Woche during the week
>
> **WORD TIP** unter + dem gives unterm; unter + das gives unters

das **Unterbewusstsein**
subconscious

unterbrechen VERB◇, PRESENT **unterbricht**, IMPERFECT **unterbrach**, PERFECT **hat unterbrochen**
to interrupt

die **Unterbrechung**, PLURAL die **Unterbrechungen**
interruption

unterbringen VERB◇, IMPERFECT **brachte unter**, PERFECT **hat untergebracht**
1 to put
2 to put up (a guest)

untere ▸SEE **unterer**

untereinander ADVERB
1 among ourselves/yourselves/themselves
2 one below the other

unterer, untere, unteres ADJECTIVE
lower

die **Unterführung**, PLURAL die **Unterführungen**
subway

der **Untergang**, PLURAL die **Untergänge**
1 sinking (of a ship)
2 setting (of the sun)

untergehen VERB◇, IMPERFECT **ging unter**, PERFECT **ist untergegangen**
1 to sink, to drown
2 to set (of the sun)
3 to come to an end (of the world)

das **Untergeschoss**, PLURAL die **Untergeschosse**
basement

die **Untergrundbahn**, PLURAL die **Untergrundbahnen**
underground

unterhalb PREPOSITION (+ GEN)
below

unterhalten VERB◇, PRESENT **unterhält**, IMPERFECT **unterhielt**, PERFECT **hat unterhalten**
1 to support
2 to run (a hotel, leisure centre)
3 to entertain
4 sich unterhalten to talk
Sie unterhielten sich über die Schule. They talked about school.
5 sich gut unterhalten to enjoy yourself

unterhaltsam ADJECTIVE
entertaining

die **Unterhaltung**, PLURAL die **Unterhaltungen**
1 conversation
2 entertainment

das **Unterhemd**, PLURAL die **Unterhemden**
vest

die **Unterhose**, PLURAL die **Unterhosen**
underpants

die **Unterkunft**, PLURAL die **Unterkünfte**
accommodation

die **Unterlagen** PLURAL NOUN
documents, papers

unterm ▸SEE **unter dem**

der **Untermieter**, PLURAL die **Untermieter**
lodger (male)

die **Untermieterin**, PLURAL die **Untermieterinnen**
lodger (female)

unternehmen VERB◇, PRESENT **unternimmt**, IMPERFECT **unternahm**, PERFECT **hat unternommen**
1 to do
Was unternehmt ihr heute? What are you doing today?
Warum haben Sie nichts dagegen unternommen? Why didn't you do something about it?
2 to make (a journey, an attempt)

das **Unternehmen**, PLURAL die **Unternehmen**
1 enterprise
2 concern

unternehmungslustig ADJECTIVE
active

♪ der **Unterricht**
1 lessons, classes
Heute haben wir keinen Unterricht. We've got no lessons today.
im Unterricht in class

◇ **irregular verb;** SEP **separable verb; for more help with verbs see centre section**

2 teaching

unterrichten VERB, PERFECT **hat unterrichtet**
1 to teach
2 to inform

das **Unterrichtsfach**, PLURAL die **Unterrichtsfächer**
subject

der **Unterrock**, PLURAL die **Unterröcke**
slip

unters ▸SEE **unter das**

unterscheiden VERB◇, IMPERFECT **unterschied**, PERFECT **hat unterschieden**
1 to distinguish, to tell apart
2 sich unterscheiden to differ, to be different

℘ der **Unterschied**, PLURAL die **Unterschiede**
difference

unterschiedlich ADJECTIVE
1 different
2 varying
Das ist unterschiedlich. It varies.

unterschreiben VERB◇, IMPERFECT **unterschrieb**, PERFECT **hat unterschrieben**
to sign

℘ die **Unterschrift**, PLURAL die **Unterschriften**
signature

Unterseeboot, PLURAL die **Unterseeboote**
submarine

unterster, unterste, unterstes ADJECTIVE
bottom, lowest

unterstreichen VERB◇, IMPERFECT **unterstrich**, PERFECT **hat unterstrichen**
to underline

unterstützen VERB, PERFECT **hat unterstützt**
to support

die **Unterstützung**
support

untersuchen VERB, PERFECT **hat untersucht**
1 to examine
2 to investigate

die **Untersuchung**, PLURAL die **Untersuchungen**
1 examination, check-up
2 investigation

die **Untertasse**, PLURAL die **Untertassen**
saucer

der **Untertitel**, PLURAL die **Untertitel**
subtitle

die **Unterwäsche**
underwear

unterwegs ADVERB
1 out
Ich war den ganzen Tag unterwegs. I've been out all day.
2 on the way
Unterwegs trafen wir Jan. We met Jan on the way.

untreu ADJECTIVE
1 unfaithful
2 disloyal

untrinkbar ADJECTIVE
undrinkable

untüchtig ADJECTIVE
1 inefficient
2 incompetent

ununterbrochen ADJECTIVE
uninterrupted

unverbleit ADJECTIVE
unleaded

℘ **unvergesslich** ADJECTIVE
unforgettable

unvergleichlich ADJECTIVE
incomparable

unverheiratet ADJECTIVE
unmarried

unverkäuflich ADJECTIVE
1 not for sale
2 ein unverkäufliches Muster a free sample

unverschämt ADJECTIVE
outrageous, rude

unverständlich ADJECTIVE
incomprehensible

unverzüglich ADJECTIVE
promptly
Bitte antworten Sie unverzüglich. Please reply promptly.

unvorsichtig ADJECTIVE
careless

unvorstellbar ADJECTIVE
unimaginable

unwahr ADJECTIVE
untrue

unwahrscheinlich ADJECTIVE
1 unlikely
2 incredible
unwahrscheinlich ADVERB
(informal) incredibly

Es war unwahrscheinlich schön. It was incredibly beautiful.

das **Unwetter**, PLURAL die **Unwetter**
storm

unwichtig ADJECTIVE
unimportant

unzählig ADJECTIVE
countless

unzerbrechlich ADJECTIVE
unbreakable

unzertrennlich ADJECTIVE
inseparable

unzufrieden ADJECTIVE
dissatisfied

uploaden VERB, PERFECT **hat upgeloadet**
to upload

üppig ADJECTIVE
lavish

uralt ADJECTIVE
ancient

der **Urenkel**, PLURAL die **Urenkel**
1 great-grandson
2 die Urenkel *(plural)* the great-grandchildren

die **Urenkelin**, PLURAL die **Urenkelinnen**
great-granddaughter

die **Urkunde**, PLURAL die **Urkunden**
certificate

ℐ der **Urlaub**, PLURAL die **Urlaube**
holiday
auf/im Urlaub on holiday
Herr Meier hat Urlaub. Mr Meier has on holiday.

der **Urlauber**, PLURAL die **Urlauber**
holidaymaker *(male)*

die **Urlauberin**, PLURAL die **Urlauberinnen**
holidaymaker *(female)*

die **Ursache**, PLURAL die **Ursachen**
1 cause
2 Keine Ursache! Don't mention it!

der **Ursprung**, PLURAL die **Ursprünge**
origin

ursprünglich ADJECTIVE
original

ursprünglich ADVERB
originally

das **Urteil**, PLURAL die **Urteile**
1 judgement
2 opinion

3 verdict

urteilen VERB, PERFECT **hat geurteilt**
to judge

der **Urwald**, PLURAL die **Urwälder**
jungle

die **USA** PLURAL NOUN
die USA the USA

> **WORD TIP** This is always used with an article: Wir fahren in die USA. Er wohnt in den USA.

ℐ **usw.** ABBREVIATION
(=und so weiter) etc.

Vv

Vaduz NEUTER NOUN
Vaduz

> ⬤ **VADUZ**
>
> Vaduz is the capital city of Liechtenstein.

vage ADJECTIVE
vague

die **Vagina**, PLURAL die **Vaginen**
vagina

die **Valentinskarte**, PLURAL die **Valentinskarten**
valentine card

der **Valentinstag**
Valentine's Day

der **Vandalismus**
vandalism

die **Vanille**
vanilla

das **Vanilleeis**
vanilla ice cream

ℐ **Variante** DIE, PLURAL die **Varianten**
1 variety
2 version

die **Vase**, PLURAL die **Vasen**
vase

ℐ der **Vater**, PLURAL die **Väter**
father

das **Vaterunser**
Lord's Prayer

der **Vati**, PLURAL die **Vatis**
dad

⬦ irregular verb; *SEP* separable verb; for more help with verbs see centre section

der **Veganer**, PLURAL die **Veganer**
vegan (male)

> **WORD TIP** Professions, hobbies, and sports
> don't take an article in German: Er ist Veganer.

die **Veganerin**, PLURAL die **Veganerinnen**
vegan (female)

> **WORD TIP** Professions, hobbies, and sports don't
> take an article in German: Sie ist Veganerin.

𝄐 der **Vegetarier**, PLURAL die **Vegetarier**
vegetarian (male)

> **WORD TIP** Professions, hobbies, and sports don't
> take an article in German: Er ist Vegetarier.

𝄐 die **Vegetarierin**, PLURAL die
Vegetarierinnen
vegetarian (female)

> **WORD TIP** Professions, hobbies, and sports don't
> take an article in German: Sie ist Vegetarierin.

𝄐 **vegetarisch** ADJECTIVE
vegetarian

das **Veilchen**, PLURAL die **Veilchen**
violet

die **Vene**, PLURAL die **Venen**
vein

Venedig NEUTER NOUN
Venice

das **Ventil**, PLURAL die **Ventile**
valve

der **Ventilator**, PLURAL die **Ventilatoren**
fan

verabreden VERB, PERFECT **hat verabredet**
1 to arrange, to agree
   Was habt ihr verabredet? What did you
   arrange?
2 sich mit jemandem verabreden to arrange
   to meet somebody
   Ich habe mich mit Oliver zum Tennis
   verabredet. I've arranged to play tennis
   with Oliver.
3 mit jemandem verabredet sein to have
   arranged to meet somebody
   Ich bin um drei mit den anderen
   verabredet. I've arranged to meet the
   others at three.
   Laura ist mit Frank verabredet. Laura has a
   date with Frank.

die **Verabredung**, PLURAL die
Verabredungen
1 appointment
2 date
3 arrangement

verabschieden VERB, PERFECT **hat**
verabschiedet
1 jemanden verabschieden to say goodbye
   to somebody
2 sich verabschieden to say goodbye

die **Verachtung**
contempt

verallgemeinern VERB, PERFECT **hat**
verallgemeinert
to generalize

die **Verallgemeinerung**, PLURAL die
Verallgemeinerungen
generalization

veralten VERB, PERFECT **ist veraltet**
to become obsolete

veränderlich ADJECTIVE
changeable

𝄐 **verändern** VERB, PERFECT **hat verändert**
1 to change
2 sich verändern to change

die **Veränderung**, PLURAL die
Veränderungen
change

veranstalten VERB, PERFECT **hat veranstaltet**
to organize

der **Veranstalter**, PLURAL die **Veranstalter**
organizer

die **Veranstaltung**, PLURAL die
Veranstaltungen
event

verantwortlich ADJECTIVE
responsible

die **Verantwortlichkeit**
responsibility

die **Verantwortung**
responsibility

verantwortungsbewusst ADJECTIVE
responsible

das **Verantwortungsbewusstsein**
sense of responsibility

verantwortungslos ADJECTIVE
irresponsible

verarbeiten VERB, PERFECT **hat verarbeitet**
1 to process
   etwas zu etwas verarbeiten to make
   something into something
2 to digest (food, information)

𝄐 indicates key words

die **Verarbeitung**
1 use
2 digestion
3 processing of data

verärgern *VERB, PERFECT* **hat verärgert**
to annoy

das **Verb**, *PLURAL* die **Verben**
verb *(in grammar)*

verband ▸ SEE **verbinden**

ℰ der **Verband**, *PLURAL* die **Verbände**
1 association
Die Betriebe schlossen sich zu einem Verband zusammen. The businesses formed an association.
2 bandage, dressing
Die Krankenschwester legte einen neuen Verband an. The nurse applied a new dressing.

verbergen *VERB◇, PRESENT* **verbirgt**, *IMPERFECT* **verbarg**, *PERFECT* **hat verborgen**
1 to hide
2 sich verbergen to hide

verbessern *VERB, PERFECT* **hat verbessert**
1 to improve
2 to correct
3 sich verbessern to improve

die **Verbesserung**, *PLURAL* die **Verbesserungen**
1 improvement
2 correction

verbiegen *VERB◇, IMPERFECT* **verbog**, *PERFECT* **hat verbogen**
1 to bend
2 sich verbiegen to bend

ℰ **verbieten** *VERB◇, IMPERFECT* **verbot**, *PERFECT* **hat verboten**
1 to forbid
Sie hat ihm verboten, das Haus zu betreten. She forbade him to enter the house.
Meine Eltern verbieten mir, am Abend wegzugehen. My parents don't allow me to go out in the evening.
2 to ban

verbilligt *ADJECTIVE*
reduced *(price)*

verbinden *VERB◇, IMPERFECT* **verband**, *PERFECT* **hat verbunden**
1 to connect, to join
2 to combine
3 to bandage, to dress *(a wound)*
jemandem die Augen verbinden to

blindfold somebody
4 jemanden verbinden to put somebody through *(on the phone)*
Ich verbinde. I'm putting you through.

verbindlich *ADJECTIVE*
1 friendly
2 binding *(agreement, decision)*

ℰ die **Verbindung**, *PLURAL* die **Verbindungen**
1 connection, link
Die Universität hat gute Verbindungen zu Firmen im Ausland. The university has close links with companies abroad.
2 touch
sich mit jemandem in Verbindung setzen to get in touch with somebody
3 combination
Ihre Werke sind eine Verbindung von Kunst und Wissenschaft. Her works are a combination of art and science.
4 line
Wir hatten eine schlechte Verbindung. It was a bad line.
5 compound *(in chemistry)*

verbirgt ▸ SEE **verbergen**

verbleit *ADJECTIVE*
leaded

verblüffen *VERB, PERFECT* **hat verblüfft**
to amaze

verblüfft *ADJECTIVE*
astonished

verbog ▸ SEE **verbiegen**

verborgen *ADJECTIVE*
hidden

verbot ▸ SEE **verbieten**

das **Verbot**, *PLURAL* die **Verbote**
ban

ℰ **verboten** *ADJECTIVE*
forbidden
'Parken verboten' 'No parking'

verbracht, **verbrachte** ▸ SEE **verbringen**

verbrannt, **verbrannte** ▸ SEE **verbrennen**

der **Verbrauch**
consumption

verbrauchen *VERB, PERFECT* **hat verbraucht**
to use, to use (up)
Die Waschmaschine verbraucht nicht viel Strom. The washing machine doesn't use much electricity.

der **Verbraucher**, *PLURAL* die **Verbraucher**
consumer

◇ irregular verb; *SEP* separable verb; for more help with verbs see centre section

der **Verbrauchermarkt**, *PLURAL* die
Verbrauchermärkte
supermarket

das **Verbrechen**, *PLURAL* die **Verbrechen**
crime

der **Verbrecher**, *PLURAL* die **Verbrecher**
criminal

verbreiten *VERB*, *PERFECT* **hat verbreitet**
1 to spread
Die Krankheit wird durch Zecken
verbreitet. The disease is spread by ticks.
2 sich verbreiten to spread
Die Neuigkeit hat sich schnell verbreitet.
The news spread quickly.
3 to broadcast
Die Warnungen wurden durch den
Rundfunk verbreitet. The warnings were
broadcast on the radio.

verbreitet *ADJECTIVE*
widespread

verbrennen *VERB◇*, *IMPERFECT* **verbrannte**,
PERFECT **hat verbrannt**
1 to burn *(rubbish, leaves)*
2 to cremate
3 sich verbrennen to burn yourself
Ich habe mir die Hand verbrannt. I burnt
my hand.
4 *PERFECT* **ist verbrannt** to burn
Der Kuchen ist verbrannt. The cake got
burnt.

℘ **verbringen** *VERB◇*, *IMPERFECT* **verbrachte**,
PERFECT **hat verbracht**
to spend
Wir haben schöne Ferien in Bayern
verbracht. We had a lovely holiday in
Bavaria.

verbunden ▸ SEE **verbinden**

der **Verdacht**
suspicion

verdächtig *ADJECTIVE*
suspicious

verdächtigen *VERB*, *PERFECT* **hat verdächtigt**
to suspect

verdammt *ADJECTIVE*, *ADVERB*
(informal) damned
Verdammt! Damn!

verdarb ▸ SEE **verderben**

verdauen *VERB*, *PERFECT* **hat verdaut**
to digest

die **Verdauung**
digestion

verderben *VERB◇*, *PRESENT* **verdirbt**, *IMPERFECT*
verdarb, *PERFECT* **hat verdorben**
1 to spoil, to ruin
Das hat mir den Abend verdorben. It
ruined the evening for me.
Ich habe mir den Magen verdorben. I've
got an upset stomach.
2 es sich mit jemandem verderben to get
into somebody's bad books
Er hat es sich mit ihr verdorben. He has
got into her bad books.
3 *PERFECT* **ist verdorben** to go off
Die Milch verdirbt, wenn du sie nicht in
den Kühlschrank stellst. The milk will go
off if you don't put it in the fridge.

℘ **verdienen** *VERB*, *PERFECT* **hat verdient**
1 to earn
2 to deserve

der **Verdienst**, *PLURAL* die **Verdienste**
1 salary
2 achievement

verdirbt ▸ SEE **verderben**

verdoppeln *VERB*, *PERFECT* **hat verdoppelt**
1 to double
2 sich verdoppeln to double

verdorben ▸ SEE **verderben**

verdünnen *VERB*, *PERFECT* **hat verdünnt**
to dilute

verehren *VERB*, *PERFECT* **hat verehrt**
to worship

der **Verehrer**, *PLURAL* die **Verehrer**
admirer *(male)*

die **Verehrerin**, *PLURAL* die **Verehrerinnen**
admirer *(female)*

℘ der **Verein**, *PLURAL* die **Vereine**
1 society, club
2 organization

vereinbaren *VERB*, *PERFECT* **hat vereinbart**
1 to agree
2 to arrange

die **Vereinbarung**, *PLURAL* die
Vereinbarungen
1 agreement
2 arrangement

vereinfachen *VERB*, *PERFECT* **hat vereinfacht**
to simplify

vereinigen *VERB*, *PERFECT* **hat vereinigt**
to unite

℘ das **Vereinigte Königreich**
United Kingdom

℘ indicates key words

die **Vereinigten Staaten** *PLURAL NOUN*
United States

WORD TIP This is always used with an article:
Wir fahren in die Vereinigten Staaten. Er
wohnt in den Vereinigten Staaten.

die **Vereinigung**, *PLURAL* die **Vereinigungen**
1 unification
2 organization

verfahren *VERB*◇, *PRESENT* **verfährt**, *IMPERFECT*
verfuhr, *PERFECT* **ist verfahren**
1 to proceed
2 *PERFECT* **hat sich verfahren**
sich verfahren to get lost
Ich habe mich verfahren. I'm lost.

verfallen *VERB*◇, *PRESENT* **verfällt**, *IMPERFECT*
verfiel, *PERFECT* **ist verfallen**
1 to decay
2 to expire *(of a passport or ticket)*

das **Verfallsdatum**, *PLURAL* die
Verfallsdaten
expiry date, use-by date

die **Verfassung**, *PLURAL* die **Verfassungen**
1 constitution
2 state *(of a person)*

verfaulen *VERB*, *PERFECT* **ist verfault**
to rot

verfiel ▸ SEE **verfallen**

verflixt *ADJECTIVE*
(informal) flipping, damn

verfolgen *VERB*, *PERFECT* **hat verfolgt**
1 to follow
2 to persecute

die **Verfolgung**, *PLURAL* die **Verfolgungen**
1 pursuit, hunt
2 persecution

verfügbar *ADJECTIVE*
available

die **Verfügung**
jemandem etwas zur Verfügung stellen to
put something at somebody's disposal
jemandem zur Verfügung stehen to be at
somebody's disposal

verfuhr ▸ SEE **verfahren**

verführen *VERB*, *PERFECT* **hat verführt**
1 to tempt
2 to seduce

die **Verführung**, *PLURAL* die **Verführungen**
1 temptation
2 seduction

vergab ▸ SEE **vergeben**

vergangen[1] *VERB* ▸ SEE **vergehen**

vergangen[2] *ADJECTIVE*
last
Es war im vergangenen Jahr. It happened
last year.

♫ die **Vergangenheit**
1 past
2 past tense *(in grammar)*

vergaß ▸ SEE **vergessen**

vergeben *VERB*◇, *PRESENT* **vergibt**, *IMPERFECT*
vergab, *PERFECT* **hat vergeben**
1 to forgive
Das werde ich ihm nie vergeben. I'll never
forgive him for that.
2 to give away, to award
3 vergeben sein to be taken
Das Zimmer ist schon vergeben. The
room's already taken.

vergeblich *ADVERB*
in vain

vergehen *VERB*◇, *IMPERFECT* **verging**, *PERFECT*
ist vergangen
to pass

♫ **vergessen** *VERB*◇, *PRESENT* **vergisst**, *IMPERFECT*
vergaß, *PERFECT* **hat vergessen**
to forget

vergesslich *ADJECTIVE*
forgetful

vergewaltigen *VERB*, *PERFECT* **hat**
vergewaltigt
to rape

die **Vergewaltigung**, *PLURAL* die
Vergewaltigungen
rape

vergibt ▸ SEE **vergeben**

vergiften *VERB*, *PERFECT* **hat vergiftet**
to poison

verging ▸ SEE **vergehen**

vergisst ▸ SEE **vergessen**

der **Vergleich**, *PLURAL* die **Vergleiche**
comparison

vergleichen *VERB*◇, *IMPERFECT* **verglich**,
PERFECT **hat verglichen**
to compare

vergnügen *VERB*, *PERFECT* **hat sich vergnügt**
sich vergnügen to have fun

◇ irregular verb; *SEP* separable verb; for more help with verbs see centre section

ₚ das **Vergnügen**, *PLURAL* die **Vergnügen**
pleasure
Viel Vergnügen! Have fun!

vergnügt *ADJECTIVE*
cheerful, happy

vergrößern *VERB, PERFECT* **hat vergrößert**
1 to enlarge
2 to increase
3 to magnify
4 to extend *(a room, building)*
5 sich vergrößern to expand, to grow bigger

die **Vergrößerung**, *PLURAL* die
Vergrößerungen
1 expansion
2 enlargement *(of a photograph)*

verhaften *VERB, PERFECT* **hat verhaftet**
to arrest
Er ist verhaftet worden. He was arrested.

verhalten *VERB*◇, *PRESENT* **verhält sich**,
IMPERFECT **verhielt sich**, *PERFECT* **hat sich
verhalten**
sich verhalten to behave

das **Verhalten**
behaviour

das **Verhältnis**, *PLURAL* die **Verhältnisse**
1 relationship
Sie hat ein gutes Verhältnis zu ihren
Eltern. She has a good relationship with
her parents.
2 affair
Gabi hat ein Verhältnis mit einem
verheirateten Mann. Gabi is having an
affair with a married man.
3 ratio *(in maths)*
4 proportion
in keinem Verhältnis zu etwas stehen to
be out of all proportion to something
5 Verhältnisse conditions
Sie leben in schlimmen Verhältnissen.
They are living in terrible conditions.
6 Verhältnisse background
Er kommt aus einfachen Verhältnissen. He
comes from a poor background.
7 über seine Verhältnisse leben to live
beyond your means

verhältnismäßig *ADVERB*
relatively

verhandeln *VERB, PERFECT* **hat verhandelt**
to negotiate
über etwas verhandeln to negotiate
something

die **Verhandlung**, *PLURAL* die
Verhandlungen
1 negotiation
2 hearing, trial

verhauen *VERB, PERFECT* **hat verhauen**
1 to beat up
2 Ich habe die Prüfung verhauen. *(informal)*
I made a mess of the exam.

verheimlichen *VERB, PERFECT* **hat
verheimlicht**
to keep secret

ₚ **verheiratet** *ADJECTIVE*
married

verhext *ADJECTIVE*
bewitched

verhielt ▸ SEE **verhalten**

verhindern *VERB, PERFECT* **hat verhindert**
1 to prevent
2 verhindert sein to be unable to make it
Petra ist verhindert. Petra won't be able
to make it.

verhungern *VERB, PERFECT* **ist verhungert**
to starve

das **Verhütungsmittel**, *PLURAL* die
Verhütungsmittel
contraceptive

verirren *VERB, PERFECT* **hat sich verirrt**
sich verirren to get lost

verkam ▸ SEE **verkommen**

der **Verkauf**, *PLURAL* die **Verkäufe**
sale
Das Haus steht zum Verkauf. The house is
for sale.

ₚ **verkaufen** *VERB, PERFECT* **hat verkauft**
to sell
Ist es zu verkaufen? Is it for sale?

ₚ der **Verkäufer**, *PLURAL* die **Verkäufer**
1 seller, vendor *(male)*
2 sales assistant *(male)*

> **WORD TIP** Professions, hobbies, and sports
> don't take an article in German: Er ist Verkäufer.

ₚ die **Verkäuferin**, *PLURAL* die
Verkäuferinnen
1 seller, vendor *(female)*
2 sales assistant *(female)*

> **WORD TIP** Professions, hobbies, and sports don't
> take an article in German: Sie ist Verkäuferin.

der **Verkaufsautomat,** *PLURAL* die
  Verkaufsautomaten
  vending machine

♪ der **Verkehr**
  traffic

die **Verkehrsampel,** *PLURAL* die
  Verkehrsampeln
  traffic lights

♪ das **Verkehrsamt,** *PLURAL* die
  Verkehrsämter
  tourist office

die **Verkehrsinsel,** *PLURAL* die
  Verkehrsinseln
  traffic island

♪ das **Verkehrsmittel,** *PLURAL* die
  Verkehrsmittel
  1 means of transport
  2 öffentliche Verkehrsmittel public
    transport
    Sie fahren mit öffentlichen
    Verkehrsmitteln zur Schule. They go to
    school by public transport.

der **Verkehrsunfall,** *PLURAL* die
  Verkehrsunfälle
  road accident

das **Verkehrszeichen,** *PLURAL* die
  Verkehrszeichen
  traffic sign, road sign

verkehrt *ADJECTIVE*
1 wrong
2 verkehrt herum back to front, the wrong
    way round

verklagen *VERB, PERFECT* **hat verklagt**
  to sue

verkleiden *VERB, PERFECT* **hat sich verkleidet**
  sich verkleiden to dress up
  Er hat sich als Cowboy verkleidet. He
  dressed up as a cowboy.

die **Verkleidung,** *PLURAL* die **Verkleidungen**
  disguise, fancy dress

verkommen *VERB◇, IMPERFECT* **verkam,**
  PERFECT **ist verkommen**
1 to go off *(of food)*
2 to become dilapidated *(of a house)*
3 to go to the bad

verkratzt *ADJECTIVE*
  scratched

der **Verlag,** *PLURAL* die **Verlage**
  publisher *(company)*

verlangen *VERB, PERFECT* **hat verlangt**
1 to ask for, to require
  Wir verlangten die Rechnung. We asked
  for the bill.
  Sie werden am Telefon verlangt. You are
  wanted on the phone.
2 to demand
3 to charge

verlängern *VERB, PERFECT* **hat verlängert**
1 to extend
2 to lengthen
3 to renew *(a passport, driving licence)*

die **Verlängerung,** *PLURAL* die
  Verlängerungen
1 extension
2 renewal
3 extra time *(in sport)*

♪ **verlassen¹** *VERB◇, PRESENT* **verlässt,** *IMPERFECT*
  verließ, *PERFECT* **hat verlassen**
1 to leave
  Er hat seine Frau verlassen. He left his
  wife.
2 sich auf jemanden/etwas verlassen to rely
  on somebody/something
  Du kannst dich auf ihn verlassen. You can
  rely on him.

verlassen² *ADJECTIVE*
  deserted

verlaufen *VERB◇, PRESENT* **verläuft,** *IMPERFECT*
  verlief, *PERFECT* **ist verlaufen**
1 to go
  Die Operation ist gut verlaufen. The
  operation went well.
2 *PERFECT* **hat sich verlaufen**
  sich verlaufen to lose your way
3 *PERFECT* **hat sich verlaufen** to disperse
  Die Menge verlief sich schnell. The crowd
  quickly dispersed.

verlegen¹ *ADJECTIVE*
  embarrassed

verlegen² *VERB, PERFECT* **hat verlegt**
1 to mislay
2 to postpone
3 to publish
4 to lay *(a carpet, cable)*

die **Verlegenheit**
  embarrassment

der **Verleih,** *PLURAL* die **Verleihe**
1 renting out, hire
2 rental firm, hire shop

verleihen *VERB◇, IMPERFECT* **verlieh,** *PERFECT*
  hat verliehen
1 to hire out

◇ irregular verb; *SEP* separable verb; for more help with verbs see centre section

2 to lend
3 to award

verlernen VERB, PERFECT **hat verlernt**
to forget

verletzen VERB, PERFECT **hat verletzt**
1 to injure
2 to hurt
3 to violate *(a law)*
4 sich verletzen to hurt yourself

ℓ **verletzt** ADJECTIVE
injured

ℓ **der/die Verletzte**, PLURAL die **Verletzten**
1 injured person
die Verletzten the injured
2 casualty

die Verletzung, PLURAL die **Verletzungen**
injury

verlieben VERB, PERFECT **hat sich verliebt**
sich verlieben to fall in love

verliebt ADJECTIVE
in love
Er ist in Nina verliebt. He's in love with Nina.

verlief ▸ SEE verlaufen

verlieh ▸ SEE verleihen

ℓ **verlieren** VERB◇, IMPERFECT **verlor**, PERFECT **hat verloren**
to lose

verließ ▸ SEE verlassen

verloben VERB, PERFECT **hat sich verlobt**
sich verloben to get engaged

verlobt ADJECTIVE
engaged

der Verlobte[1], PLURAL die **Verlobten**
1 fiancé
Er ist ihr Verlobter. He's her fiancé.
2 die Verlobten *plural* the engaged couple

die Verlobte[2], PLURAL die **Verlobten**
fiancée
Sie ist seine Verlobte. She's his fiancée.

die Verlobung, PLURAL die **Verlobungen**
engagement

verlocken VERB, PERFECT **hat verlockt**
to tempt, to entice

verlor, verloren ▸ SEE verlieren

die Verlosung, PLURAL die **Verlosungen**
prize draw, raffle

ℓ **der Verlust**, PLURAL die **Verluste**
loss

vermeiden VERB◇, IMPERFECT **vermied**, PERFECT **hat vermieden**
to avoid

vermieten VERB, PERFECT **hat vermietet**
1 to rent out, to hire out
2 to let
'Zimmer zu vermieten' 'Rooms to let'

der Vermieter, PLURAL die **Vermieter**
landlord

die Vermieterin, PLURAL die **Vermieterinnen**
landlady

die Vermietung
1 renting out, hiring out
2 letting

ℓ **vermischen** VERB, PERFECT **hat vermischt**
to mix

ℓ **vermissen** VERB, PERFECT **hat vermisst**
to miss

die Vermittlung, PLURAL die **Vermittlungen**
1 arrangement
2 agency
3 switchboard
4 telephone exchange
5 mediation

das Vermögen, PLURAL die **Vermögen**
fortune
Er hat an der Börse ein Vermögen gemacht. He made a fortune on the stock market.

vermuten VERB, PERFECT **hat vermutet**
to suspect

vermutlich ADJECTIVE
probable
vermutlich ADVERB
probably

vernachlässigen VERB, PERFECT **hat vernachlässigt**
to neglect

vernichten VERB, PERFECT **hat vernichtet**
1 to destroy
2 to exterminate

die Vernunft
reason

ℓ **vernünftig** ADJECTIVE
sensible

313

ℓ indicates key words

verpacken *VERB, PERFECT* **hat verpackt**
1 to pack
2 to wrap up

ℓ die **Verpackung**, *PLURAL* die **Verpackungen**
  packaging

ℓ **verpassen** *VERB, PERFECT* **hat verpasst**
  to miss

ℓ **verpesten** *VERB, PERFECT* **hat verpestet**
  to pollute

die **Verpflegung**
  food
  Unterkunft und Verpflegung board and
  lodging

verpflichten *VERB, PERFECT* **hat verpflichtet**
1 sich verpflichten to promise
2 sich vertraglich verpflichten to sign a
   contract
3 verpflichtet sein, etwas zu tun to be
   obliged to do something
   jemandem zu Dank verpflichtet sein to be
   obliged to somebody

verpflichtend *ADJECTIVE*
  binding

die **Verpflichtung**, *PLURAL* die
   Verpflichtungen
1 obligation
2 commitment

verprügeln *VERB, PERFECT* **hat verprügelt**
  to beat up

verraten *VERB⬦, PRESENT* **verrät**, *IMPERFECT*
   verriet, *PERFECT* **hat verraten**
1 to betray
2 to give away
3 to tell
4 sich verraten to give yourself away

verrechnen *VERB, PERFECT* **hat sich
   verrechnet**
   sich verrechnen to make a mistake, to
   miscalculate

verregnet *ADJECTIVE*
  rainy

verreisen *VERB, PERFECT* **ist verreist**
  to go away
  verreist sein to be away

verriet ▸ SEE **verraten**

verrosten *VERB, PERFECT* **ist verrostet**
  to rust

verrostet *ADJECTIVE*
  rusty

ℓ **verrückt** *ADJECTIVE*
  mad, crazy

der/die **Verrückte**, *PLURAL* die **Verrückten**
  maniac

versagen *VERB, PERFECT* **hat versagt**
  to fail

versammeln *VERB, PERFECT* **hat versammelt**
1 to assemble
2 sich versammeln to assemble

die **Versammlung**, *PLURAL* die
   Versammlungen
   meeting

versäumen *VERB, PERFECT* **hat versäumt**
  to miss
  es versäumen, etwas zu tun to fail to do
  something

verschenken *VERB, PERFECT* **hat verschenkt**
  to give away

verschieben *VERB⬦, IMPERFECT* **verschob**,
   PERFECT **hat verschoben**
  to postpone

ℓ **verschieden** *ADJECTIVE*
1 different
2 various

verschlafen *VERB⬦, PRESENT* **verschläft**,
   IMPERFECT **verschlief**, *PERFECT* **hat
   verschlafen**
1 to oversleep
2 to sleep through *(the day)*
3 to miss *(a date, the train)*

verschlechtern *VERB, PERFECT* **hat
   verschlechtert**
1 to make worse
2 sich verschlechtern to get worse

verschlief ▸ SEE **verschlafen**

verschließen *VERB⬦, IMPERFECT* **verschloss**,
   PERFECT **hat verschlossen**
1 to close *(a tin, package)*
2 to lock *(a door, drawer)*

verschlimmern *VERB, PERFECT* **hat
   verschlimmert**
1 to make worse
2 sich verschlimmern to get worse

verschloss ▸ SEE **verschließen**

verschlucken *VERB, PERFECT* **hat verschluckt**
1 to swallow
2 sich an etwas verschlucken to choke on
   something

⬦ irregular verb; *SEP* separable verb; for more help with verbs see centre section

der **Verschluss**, *PLURAL* die **Verschlüsse**
1 fastener, clasp
2 top *(of a bottle)*

verschmutzen *VERB, PERFECT* **hat verschmutzt**
1 to pollute *(the air, water, environment)*
2 to dirty

die **Verschmutzung**
pollution

verschob ▶ SEE **verschieben**

verschreiben *VERB◇, IMPERFECT* **verschrieb**, *PERFECT* **hat verschrieben**
1 to prescribe
2 sich verschreiben to make a mistake

verschütten *VERB, PERFECT* **hat verschüttet**
to spill

verschwand ▶ SEE **verschwinden**

ℒ **verschwenden** *VERB, PERFECT* **hat verschwendet**
to waste

die **Verschwendung**
waste

verschwinden *VERB◇, IMPERFECT* **verschwand**, *PERFECT* **ist verschwunden**
to disappear

verschwommen *ADJECTIVE*
blurred

das **Versehen**, *PLURAL* die **Versehen**
oversight
Es war ein Versehen. It was an oversight.
aus Versehen by mistake

versehentlich *ADVERB*
by mistake

versetzen *VERB, PERFECT* **hat versetzt**
1 to move, to transfer *(a person)*
2 to move up *(into the next class at school)*
Philip wird nicht versetzt. Philip will not move up into the next class.
3 jemanden versetzen to stand somebody up
4 jemandem einen Schreck versetzen to give somebody a fright
5 jemandem einen Tritt versetzen to kick somebody
6 sich in jemandes Lage versetzen to put yourself in somebody's position

verseuchen *VERB, PERFECT* **hat verseucht**
to contaminate

die **Verseuchung**, *PLURAL* die **Verseuchungen**
contamination

versichern *VERB, PERFECT* **hat versichert**
1 to insure
2 to assert
3 jemandem versichern, dass ... to assure somebody that ...

die **Versicherung**, *PLURAL* die **Versicherungen**
1 insurance
2 assurance

die **Versicherungsgesellschaft**, *PLURAL* die **Versicherungsgesellschaften**
insurance company

der **Versicherungsschein**, *PLURAL* die **Versicherungsscheine**
insurance policy document

versöhnen *VERB, PERFECT* **hat sich versöhnt**
sich versöhnen to make up
sich mit jemandem versöhnen to make it up with somebody

versorgen *VERB, PERFECT* **hat versorgt**
1 to supply
2 to provide for
3 to look after

verspäten *VERB, PERFECT* **hat sich verspätet**
sich verspäten to be late

die **Verspätung**
delay
Der Zug hatte Verspätung. The train was late.

ℒ **versprechen** *VERB◇, PRESENT* **verspricht**, *IMPERFECT* **versprach**, *PERFECT* **hat versprochen**
1 to promise
2 sich etwas von etwas versprechen to expect something of something
Ich hatte mir mehr davon versprochen. I expected more from it.
3 sich versprechen to make a slip of the tongue

ℒ das **Versprechen**, *PLURAL* die **Versprechen**
promise

verstand ▶ SEE **verstehen**

der **Verstand**
1 mind
Hast du den Verstand verloren? Have you gone out of your mind?
2 reason

A
B
C
D
E
F
G
H
I
J
K
L
M
N
O
P
Q
R
S
T
U
V
W
X
Y
Z

316

verstanden ▸SEE **verstehen**

verständigen VERB, PERFECT **hat verständigt**
1 to notify
2 sich verständigen to communicate, to make yourself understood
3 sich über etwas verständigen to agree on something

die **Verständigung**
1 communication
2 notification

verständlich ADJECTIVE
1 understandable
2 jemandem etwas verständlich machen to make something clear to somebody
3 comprehensible, easy to understand

das **Verständnis**, PLURAL die **Verständnisse**
1 comprehension
2 understanding

verständnisvoll ADJECTIVE
understanding

der **Verstärker**, PLURAL die **Verstärker**
amplifier

verstauchen VERB, PERFECT **hat verstaucht**
to sprain
Sandra hat sich den Fuß verstaucht.
Sandra has sprained her ankle.

das **Versteck**, PLURAL die **Verstecke**
hiding place

verstecken VERB, PERFECT **hat versteckt**
1 to hide
2 sich verstecken to hide

ℰ **verstehen** VERB◇, IMPERFECT **verstand**, PERFECT **hat verstanden**
1 to understand
Ich verstehe nicht. I don't understand.
etwas falsch verstehen to misunderstand something
2 sich verstehen to get on
Lisa und Sara verstehen sich gut. Lisa and Sara get on well.
3 Das versteht sich von selbst. That goes without saying.

verstellbar ADJECTIVE
adjustable

verstellen VERB, PERFECT **hat verstellt**
1 to adjust
2 to block
3 to disguise
4 sich verstellen to pretend

verstimmt ADJECTIVE
1 out of tune

2 annoyed
3 ein verstimmter Magen an upset stomach

verstopft ADJECTIVE
1 blocked
2 constipated

die **Verstopfung**, PLURAL die **Verstopfungen**
1 blockage
2 constipation

der **Versuch**, PLURAL die **Versuche**
1 attempt
2 experiment

ℰ **versuchen** VERB, PERFECT **hat versucht**
to try

verteidigen VERB, PERFECT **hat verteidigt**
to defend

der **Verteidiger**, PLURAL die **Verteidiger**
1 defender (male)
2 defence counsel (male)

WORD TIP Professions, hobbies, and sports don't take an article in German: Er ist Verteidiger.

die **Verteidigerin**, PLURAL die **Verteidigerinnen**
1 defender (female)
2 defence counsel (female)

WORD TIP Professions, hobbies, and sports don't take an article in German: Sie ist Verteidigerin.

die **Verteidigung**
defence

verteilen VERB, PERFECT **hat verteilt**
to distribute

der **Vertrag**, PLURAL die **Verträge**
1 contract
2 treaty

vertragen VERB◇, PRESENT **verträgt**, IMPERFECT **vertrug**, PERFECT **hat vertragen**
1 to be able to take
Sie verträgt keine Kritik. She can't take criticism.
Ich vertrage keinen Kaffee. Coffee disagrees with me.
2 sich vertragen to get on
Anna und Julia vertragen sich nicht. Anna and Julia don't get on.
sich wieder vertragen to make it up

vertrat ▸SEE **vertreten**

vertrauen VERB, PERFECT **hat vertraut**
to trust

das **Vertrauen**
trust, confidence

◇ irregular verb; SEP separable verb; for more help with verbs see centre section

Sie hat mir im Vertrauen erzählt, dass ...
She told me in confidence that ...

vertraulich *ADJECTIVE*
1 confidential
2 familiar

vertreiben *VERB◇, IMPERFECT* **vertrieb**, *PERFECT*
hat vertrieben
to drive out

vertreten *VERB◇, PRESENT* **vertritt**, *IMPERFECT*
vertrat, *PERFECT* **hat vertreten**
1 to stand in for
2 to represent
3 eine Meinung vertreten to hold an opinion
4 sich die Beine vertreten to stretch your
legs

der **Vertreter**, *PLURAL* die **Vertreter**
1 representative *(male)*
2 deputy *(male)*

> **WORD TIP** Professions, hobbies, and sports
> don't take an article in German: Er ist Vertreter.

die **Vertreterin**, *PLURAL* die **Vertreterinnen**
1 representative *(female)*
2 deputy *(female)*

> **WORD TIP** Professions, hobbies, and sports don't
> take an article in German: Sie ist Vertreterin.

vertritt ▸ SEE **vertreten**

vertrug ▸ SEE **vertragen**

verunglücken *VERB, PERFECT* **ist verunglückt**
to have an accident

verursachen *VERB, PERFECT* **hat verursacht**
to cause

verurteilen *VERB, PERFECT* **hat verurteilt**
1 to sentence
2 to condemn

die **Verwaltung**, *PLURAL* die **Verwaltungen**
administration

verwandt *ADJECTIVE*
related

♪ der/die **Verwandte**, *PLURAL* die **Verwandten**
relative

die **Verwandtschaft**
relatives

verwechseln *VERB, PERFECT* **hat verwechselt**
1 to mix up, to confuse
2 jemanden mit jemandem verwechseln to
mistake somebody for somebody
Ich verwechsele ihn immer mit seinem
Bruder. I always get him mixed up with his
brother.

♪ **verwenden** *VERB, PERFECT* **hat verwendet**
to use

die **Verwendung**
use

verwickelt *ADJECTIVE*
complicated

verwirren *VERB, PERFECT* **hat verwirrt**
1 to confuse
2 to tangle up

verwirrt *ADJECTIVE*
confused

verwöhnen *VERB, PERFECT* **hat verwöhnt**
to spoil

verwunden *VERB, PERFECT* **hat verwundet**
to wound

der/die **Verwundete**, *PLURAL* die
Verwundeten
casualty, injured person
die Verwundeten the injured

die **Verwundung**, *PLURAL* die
Verwundungen
injury, wound

verzählen *VERB, PERFECT* **hat sich verzählt**
sich verzählen to miscount

das **Verzeichnis**, *PLURAL* die **Verzeichnisse**
1 list
2 index

♪ **verzeihen** *VERB, IMPERFECT* **verzieh**, *PERFECT* **hat**
verziehen
to forgive
Das werde ich ihr nie verzeihen. I'll never
forgive her for that.
Verzeihen Sie, können Sie mir sagen ...?
Excuse me, could you tell me ...?

die **Verzeihung**
forgiveness
jemanden um Verzeihung bitten to
apologize to somebody
Verzeihung! Sorry!

verzichten *VERB, PERFECT* **hat verzichtet**
1 auf jemanden/etwas verzichten to do
without somebody/something
Ich verzichte auf deine Hilfe. I can do
without your help.
Auf Frau Meier können wir nicht
verzichten. We couldn't manage without
Frau Meier.
2 auf etwas verzichten to give up something
Er verzichtete auf seinen Anspruch. He
gave up his claim.

♪ indicates key words

verzieh, verziehen ▸SEE verzeihen

verzögern VERB, PERFECT **hat verzögert**
1 to delay
2 sich verzögern to be delayed

die Verzögerung, PLURAL die
Verzögerungen
delay

verzollen VERB, PERFECT **hat verzollt**
to pay duty on
Muss ich die Zigaretten verzollen?
Do I have to pay duty on the
cigarettes?
Haben Sie etwas zu verzollen? Have you
anything to declare?

verzweifeln VERB, PERFECT **ist verzweifelt**
to despair

verzweifelt ADJECTIVE
desperate

die Verzweiflung
despair, desperation

der Vetter, PLURAL die **Vettern**
cousin (male)

ℰ **das Video,** PLURAL die **Videos**
video

das Videogerät, PLURAL die **Videogeräte**
video recorder

die Videokamera, PLURAL die
Videokameras
video camera

das Videospiel, PLURAL die **Videospiele**
video game

das Vieh
cattle

ℰ **viel** ADJECTIVE, PRONOUN
1 a lot of
Lena hat viel Arbeit. Lena's got a lot of
work.
2 viele (plural) many, a lot of
Es waren nicht viele Leute da. There
weren't many people there.
3 much, a lot
Wie viel? How much?, How many?
zu viel too much
Ich habe zu viel gegessen. I've eaten too
much.
4 Vielen Dank! Thank you very much!
Viel Spaß! Have fun!
Viel Glück/Erfolg! Good luck!

5 das viele Geld all that money

viel ADVERB
1 much, a lot
viel weniger much less
so viel wie möglich as much as possible
Sie redet viel. She talks a lot.
2 viel zu ... far too ..., much too ...
Die Schuhe sind viel zu groß. The shoes
are far too big.
Das dauert viel zu lange. It'll take far too
long.

ℰ **vielleicht** ADVERB
perhaps

vielmals ADVERB
Danke vielmals. Many thanks.

ℰ **vier** NUMBER
four

die Vier, PLURAL die **Vieren**
1 four
2 adequate (school mark)

das Viereck, PLURAL die **Vierecke**
1 rectangle
2 square

viereckig ADJECTIVE
1 rectangular
2 square

vierte ▸SEE vierter

viertel ADJECTIVE
quarter (used in time phrases in
Southern Germany, Austria,
and Switzerland)
Wir treffen uns um viertel acht. We'll
meet at quarter past seven.
Sie kommen um drei viertel acht. They are
coming at quarter to eight.

ℰ **das Viertel,** PLURAL die **Viertel**
quarter
Es ist Viertel vor acht. It's quarter to
eight.

das Viertelfinale, PLURAL die **Viertelfinale**
quarter-final

die Viertelstunde, PLURAL die
Viertelstunden
quarter of an hour

vierter, vierte, viertes ADJECTIVE
fourth

ℰ **vierzehn** NUMBER
fourteen

◇ irregular verb; SEP separable verb; for more help with verbs see centre section

_ℓ_ **vierzehn** NUMBER
fourteen

_ℓ_ **vierzig** NUMBER
forty

die **Vignette**, PLURAL die **Vignetten**
sticker *(usually displayed on windscreen to show you have paid to drive on motorways)*
▸SEE **Maut**

die **Villa**, PLURAL die **Villen**
villa

die **Violine**, PLURAL die **Violinen**
violin

virtuell ADJECTIVE
virtual
die virtuelle Realität virtual reality

das or der **Virus**, PLURAL die **Viren**
virus

visuell ADJECTIVE
visual

das **Visum**, PLURAL die **Visa**, **Visen**
visa

das **Vitamin**, PLURAL die **Vitamine**
vitamin

vitaminarm ADJECTIVE
low in vitamins

vitaminreich ADJECTIVE
high in vitamins

_ℓ_ der **Vogel**, PLURAL die **Vögel**
1 bird
2 character
3 einen Vogel haben *(informal)* to have a screw loose

der **Vogelbeobachter**, PLURAL die
Vogelbeobachter
birdwatcher *(male)*

WORD TIP Professions, hobbies, and sports don't take an article in German: Er ist Vogelbeobachter.

die **Vogelbeobachterin**, PLURAL die
Vogelbeobachterinnen
birdwatcher *(female)*

WORD TIP Professions, hobbies, and sports don't take an article in German: Sie ist Vogelbeobachterin.

die **Vogelscheuche**, PLURAL die
Vogelscheuchen
scarecrow

_ℓ_ die **Vokabel**, PLURAL die **Vokabeln**
word

Vokabeln vocabulary

das **Vokabular**, PLURAL die **Vokabulare**
vocabulary

der **Vokal**, PLURAL die **Vokale**
vowel

das **Volk**, PLURAL die **Völker**
people

die **Volkshochschule**
adult education centre
Sie besucht einen Kurs an der Volkshochschule. She goes to an adult education class.

das **Volkslied**, PLURAL die **Volkslieder**
folk song

die **Volksmusik**
folk music

die **Volkswirtschaft**
economics

_ℓ_ **voll** ADJECTIVE
1 full
Sie trug einen Korb voll Äpfel. She was carrying a basket full of apples.
2 whole
Du hast mir nicht die volle Wahrheit gesagt. You didn't tell me the whole truth.
3 crowded
Es war unheimlich voll. It was really crowded.
voll ADVERB
1 fully, completely
voll und ganz completely
2 jemanden nicht für voll nehmen *(informal)* not to take somebody seriously

_ℓ_ der **Volleyball**
volleyball

völlig ADJECTIVE
complete
völlig ADVERB
completely

volljährig ADJECTIVE
of age

vollkommen ADJECTIVE
1 perfect
2 complete
vollkommen ADVERB
completely

das **Vollkornbrot**
wholemeal bread

vollmachen, PERFECT **hat vollgemacht**
to fill up

319

die **Vollmilch**
full-cream milk

♀ die **Vollpension**
full board

vollständig ADJECTIVE
complete

volltanken, PERFECT **hat vollgetankt**
to fill up with petrol

die **Vollzeitarbeit**
full-time work

vom ▸ SEE **von dem**

♀ **von** PREPOSITION (+ DAT)
1 **from**
von heute an from today
Wir sind von hier bis zum Kino gelaufen.
We walked from here to the cinema.
2 **of**
Sie ist eine Freundin von mir. She's a
friend of mine.
3 **about**
Peter hat mir von dem neuen Haus
erzählt. Peter told me about the new
house.
4 **by**
Wir lesen gerade ein Theaterstück von
Brecht. We're reading a play by Brecht.
5 von mir aus I don't mind

WORD TIP von + dem gives vom

---

voneinander ADVERB
from each other
Sie haben es voneinander gelernt. They
learned it from each other.
Sie sind voneinander abhängig. They
depend on each other.

♀ **vor** PREPOSITION (+ DAT or + ACC)
1 (the dative is used generally and when
talking about position; the accusative shows
movement or a change of place) **in front of**
Die Mülltonne steht vor dem Haus. (DAT)
The dustbin is in front of the house.
Stellst du die Mülltonne vor das Haus?
(ACC) Would you put the dustbin in front of
the house?
2 **before**
Max war vor euch da. (DAT) Max arrived
before you.
3 **with**
Ich zitterte vor Angst. (DAT) I was shaking
with fear.
4 **to** (with times)
Es ist zehn vor fünf. It's ten to five.

5 **ago**
vor zwei Jahren two years ago
6 sich vor jemandem fürchten to be
frightened of somebody
7 vor allen Dingen above all
8 vor sich hin summen to hum to yourself

WORD TIP vor + dem gives vorm; vor + das
gives vors

vor ADVERB
forward
vor und zurück backwards and forwards

♀ **voraus** ADVERB
1 **ahead**
2 im Voraus in advance

vorausgehen VERB◇, IMPERFECT **ging voraus**,
PERFECT **ist vorausgegangen**
1 to go on ahead
2 to precede

voraussetzen VERB, PERFECT **hat
vorausgesetzt**
1 to take for granted
2 to require
3 vorausgesetzt, dass ... provided that ...

die **Voraussetzung**, PLURAL die
Voraussetzungen
1 condition
2 assumption

♀ **vorbei** ADVERB
1 **past**
Er ging einfach an uns vorbei. He walked
straight past us.
2 **over**
Die Ferien sind vorbei. The holidays are
over.

vorbeifahren VERB◇, PRESENT **fährt
vorbei**, IMPERFECT **fuhr vorbei**, PERFECT **ist
vorbeigefahren**
to drive past, to pass

vorbeigehen VERB◇, IMPERFECT **ging vorbei**,
PERFECT **ist vorbeigegangen**
1 to go past, to pass
Er ging an uns vorbei. He went past us.
2 to drop in
Ich gehe bei Anne vorbei. I'll drop in on
Anne.

vorbeikommen VERB◇, IMPERFECT **kam
vorbei**, PERFECT **ist vorbeigekommen**
1 to pass
2 to get past
3 to drop in

♀ **vorbereiten** VERB, PERFECT **hat vorbereitet**
1 to prepare
2 sich vorbereiten to prepare

◇ **irregular verb**; SEP **separable verb**; for more help with verbs see centre section

die **Vorbereitung**, PLURAL die **Vorbereitungen**
preparation

vorbeugen VERB, PERFECT **hat vorgebeugt**
1 to prevent
2 sich vorbeugen to lean forward

die **Vorbeugung**
prevention

das **Vorbild**, PLURAL die **Vorbilder**
example

vorderer, vordere, vorderes ADJECTIVE
front

der **Vordergrund**
foreground
im Vordergrund in the foreground

die **Vorderseite**
front

vorderster, vorderste, vorderstes
ADJECTIVE
front

der **Vorfahr**, PLURAL die **Vorfahren**
ancestor

die **Vorfahrt**
right of way
Wer hat hier Vorfahrt? Whose right of way is it?
'Vorfahrt beachten/gewähren' 'Give way'

der **Vorfall**, PLURAL die **Vorfälle**
incident

vorführen VERB, PERFECT **hat vorgeführt**
1 to show
2 to perform
3 to demonstrate

die **Vorführung**, PLURAL die **Vorführungen**
1 performance
2 demonstration

der **Vorgänger**, PLURAL die **Vorgänger**
predecessor (male)

die **Vorgängerin**, PLURAL die **Vorgängerinnen**
predecessor (female)

vorgehen VERB◇, IMPERFECT **ging vor**, PERFECT **ist vorgegangen**
1 to go on ahead
2 to go forward
3 to proceed
4 Die Uhr geht vor. The clock is fast.
5 Was geht hier vor? What's going on here?

ℓ **vorgestern** ADVERB
the day before yesterday

vorhaben VERB◇, PRESENT **hat vor**, IMPERFECT **hatte vor**, PERFECT **hat vorgehabt**
1 to intend
Sie haben vor, nach Italien zu fahren. They intend to go to Italy.
2 etwas vorhaben to have something planned
Ich habe heute noch nichts vor. I've got nothing planned for today.

der **Vorhang**, PLURAL die **Vorhänge**
curtain

das **Vorhängeschloss**, PLURAL die **Vorhängeschlösser**
padlock

ℓ **vorher** ADVERB
beforehand, before

die **Vorhersage**, PLURAL die **Vorhersagen**
1 forecast
2 prediction

vorhin ADVERB
just now

voriger, vorige, voriges ADJECTIVE
last

vorkommen VERB◇, IMPERFECT **kam vor**, PERFECT **ist vorgekommen**
1 to happen
2 to occur
3 to come forward
4 to come out (from behind somewhere)
5 to seem
jemandem bekannt vorkommen to seem familiar to somebody
6 sich ... vorkommen to feel ...
Ich kam mir ziemlich dumm vor. I felt rather stupid.

der **Vorlauf**
fast forward (on video)

vorläufig ADJECTIVE
temporary

vorlesen VERB◇, PRESENT **liest vor**, IMPERFECT **las vor**, PERFECT **hat vorgelesen**
1 to read (out)
2 jemandem vorlesen to read to somebody

vorletzter, vorletzte, vorletztes ADJECTIVE
last but one
vorletztes Jahr the year before last

vorm ▸ SEE vor dem

ℓ der **Vormittag**, PLURAL die **Vormittage**
morning

ℓ indicates key words

vormittags ADVERB
in the morning(s)

vorn ADVERB
1 at the front, in front
nach vorn to the front
2 von vorn from the beginning
Wir mussten wieder von vorn anfangen.
We had to start again at the beginning.
3 da vorn over there

♭ der **Vorname**, PLURAL die **Vornamen**
first name

vorne ▸ SEE vorn

vornehm ADJECTIVE
1 exclusive, smart
2 distinguished

vornehmen VERB◇, PRESENT **nimmt
vor**, IMPERFECT **nahm vor**, PERFECT **hat
vorgenommen**
1 to carry out
2 sich vornehmen, etwas zu tun to plan to
do something

♭ der **Vorort**, PLURAL die **Vororte**
suburb

der **Vorrat**, PLURAL die **Vorräte**
supply, stock

vors ▸ SEE vor das

der **Vorsatz**, PLURAL die **Vorsätze**
intention

die **Vorschau**, PLURAL die **Vorschauen**
1 preview
2 trailer (of a film)

der **Vorschlag**, PLURAL die **Vorschläge**
suggestion

♭ **vorschlagen** VERB◇, PRESENT **schlägt
vor**, IMPERFECT **schlug vor**, PERFECT **hat
vorgeschlagen**
to suggest

die **Vorschrift**, PLURAL die **Vorschriften**
1 regulation
2 instruction

die **Vorschule**, PLURAL die **Vorschulen**
nursery school

vorsehen VERB◇, PRESENT **sieht sich vor**,
IMPERFECT **sah sich vor**, PERFECT **hat sich
vorgesehen**
sich vorsehen to be careful

♭ die **Vorsicht**
care, caution
Vorsicht! Be careful!

Vorsicht Stufe! Mind the step!

♭ **vorsichtig** ADJECTIVE
careful

vorsichtshalber ADVERB
to be on the safe side

die **Vorsichtsmaßnahme**, PLURAL die
Vorsichtsmaßnahmen
precaution
Vorsichtsmaßnahmen gegen etwas
ergreifen to take precautions against
something

♭ die **Vorspeise**, PLURAL die **Vorspeisen**
starter, first course

der **Vorsprung**, PLURAL die **Vorsprünge**
1 ledge (of a rock)
2 lead (over somebody)

die **Vorstadt**, PLURAL die **Vorstädte**
suburb

♭ **vorstellen** VERB, PERFECT **hat vorgestellt**
1 to introduce
Darf ich Ihnen Herrn Schulz vorstellen?
May I introduce Mr Schulz?
2 sich vorstellen to introduce yourself
3 Er musste sich beim Personalchef
vorstellen. He had to go for an interview
with the personnel manager.
4 sich etwas vorstellen to imagine
something
Stell dir vor! Just imagine!
5 die Uhr vorstellen to put the clocks
forward

♭ die **Vorstellung**, PLURAL die **Vorstellungen**
1 performance
2 introduction
3 interview (for a job)
4 idea
5 imagination

♭ das **Vorstellungsgespräch**, PLURAL die
Vorstellungsgespräche
interview (for a job)

♭ der **Vorteil**, PLURAL die **Vorteile**
advantage

der **Vortrag**, PLURAL die **Vorträge**
talk, lecture

vorüber ADVERB
over
Die Krise ist vorüber. The crisis is over.

vorübergehend ADJECTIVE
temporary
vorübergehend ADVERB
temporarily

das **Vorurteil**, PLURAL die **Vorurteile**
prejudice

ℙ die **Vorwahl**, PLURAL die **Vorwahlen**
(dialling) code
Wählen Sie die Vorwahl 00 44 für
Großbritannien. Dial 00 44 for Britain.

die **Vorwahlnummer**, PLURAL die
Vorwahlnummern
(dialling) code

vorwärts ADVERB
forward(s)

vorwiegend ADVERB
predominantly

der **Vorwurf**, PLURAL die **Vorwürfe**
reproach
jemandem Vorwürfe machen to reproach
somebody

vorzeigen VERB, PERFECT **hat vorgezeigt**
to show

ℙ **vorziehen** VERB◇, PRESENT **zieht vor**, IMPERFECT
zog vor, PERFECT **hat vorgezogen**
1 to prefer
2 to pull up (a chair)
3 die Vorhänge vorziehen to draw the
curtains

vorzüglich ADJECTIVE
excellent

vulgär ADJECTIVE
vulgar

der **Vulkan**, PLURAL die **Vulkane**
volcano

Ww

die **Waage**, PLURAL die **Waagen**
1 scales
2 Libra
Max ist Waage. Max is Libra.

waagerecht, **waagrecht** ADJECTIVE
horizontal

wach ADJECTIVE
awake
wach sein to be awake
wach werden to wake up

die **Wache**, PLURAL die **Wachen**
1 guard
2 (police) station

der **Wachhund**, PLURAL die **Wachhunde**
guard dog

das **Wachs**
wax

ℙ **wachsen** VERB◇, PRESENT **wächst**, IMPERFECT
wuchs, PERFECT **ist gewachsen**
to grow

das **Wachstum**
growth

wackelig ADJECTIVE
wobbly

wackeln VERB, PERFECT **hat gewackelt**
to wobble

die **Wade**, PLURAL die **Waden**
calf

die **Waffe**, PLURAL die **Waffen**
weapon

die **Waffel**, PLURAL die **Waffeln**
waffle

der **Waffenhandel**
arms trade

wagen VERB, PERFECT **hat gewagt**
1 to risk
2 es wagen, etwas zu tun to dare to do
something
Er wagte sich nicht nach draußen. He
didn't dare go outside.

ℙ der **Wagen**, PLURAL die **Wagen**
1 car
Nimmst du den Wagen? Are you going
by car?
2 carriage (of a train)
3 cart

der **Wagenheber**, PLURAL die **Wagenheber**
jack

ℙ die **Wahl**, PLURAL die **Wahlen**
1 choice
Er hat die Wahl. It's his choice.
2 election
Die nächsten Wahlen sind im Herbst. The
next election is in autumn.

ℙ **wählen** VERB, PERFECT **hat gewählt**
1 to choose
Wir können zwischen zwei Möglichkeiten
wählen. We can choose between two
options.
2 Haben Sie schon gewählt? Are you ready
to order? (in a restaurant)
3 to elect
4 to vote, to vote for
Sie wählt immer grün. She always votes
green.

A
B
C
D
E
F
G
H
I
J
K
L
M
N
O
P
Q
R
S
T
U
V
W
X
Y
Z

ℙ indicates key words

Wen hast du gewählt? Who did you vote for?
5 to dial
Ich muss die falsche Nummer gewählt haben. I must have dialled the wrong number.

das **Wahlfach**, PLURAL die **Wahlfächer**
optional subject, option

der **Wahnsinn**
madness

wahnsinnig ADJECTIVE
1 mad
wahnsinnig werden to go mad
2 terrible
Ich hatte wahnsinnige Kopfschmerzen. I had a terrible headache.

wahnsinnig ADVERB
incredibly, terribly
Der Film war wahnsinnig gut. The film was incredibly good.

ℓ **wahr** ADJECTIVE
1 true
2 ..., nicht wahr? ..., isn't he/she/it, etc.?
Du kommst doch, nicht wahr? You're coming, aren't you?

ℓ **während** PREPOSITION (+ GEN)
during
während CONJUNCTION
1 while
2 whereas

ℓ die **Wahrheit**, PLURAL die **Wahrheiten**
truth

der **Wahrsager**, PLURAL die **Wahrsager**
fortune teller (male)

die **Wahrsagerin**, PLURAL die **Wahrsagerinnen**
fortune teller (female)

ℓ **wahrscheinlich** ADJECTIVE
probable, likely
wahrscheinlich ADVERB
probably

die **Währung**, PLURAL die **Währungen**
currency

die **Waise**, PLURAL die **Waisen**
orphan
Er ist Waise. He's an orphan.

der **Wal**, PLURAL die **Wale**
whale

ℓ der **Wald**, PLURAL die **Wälder**
wood, forest

der **Waliser**, PLURAL die **Waliser**
Welshman
Er ist Waliser. He's Welsh.

die **Waliserin**, PLURAL die **Waliserinnen**
Welshwoman
Sie ist Waliserin. She's Welsh.

walisisch ADJECTIVE
Welsh

WORD TIP Adjectives never have capitals in German, even for regions, countries, or nationalities.

die **Walnuss**, PLURAL die **Walnüsse**
walnut

ℓ die **Wand**, PLURAL die **Wände**
wall

der **Wanderer**, PLURAL die **Wanderer**
hiker, rambler (male)

die **Wanderin**, PLURAL die **Wanderinnen**
hiker, rambler (female)

ℓ **wandern** VERB, PERFECT **ist gewandert**
to hike, to go walking

das **Wandern**
hiking

ℓ die **Wanderung**, PLURAL die **Wanderungen**
walk, hike

ℓ **wann** ADVERB
when

die **Wanne**, PLURAL die **Wannen**
1 tub
2 bath

war ▶ SEE **sein**

warb ▶ SEE **werben**

die **Ware**, PLURAL die **Waren**
1 article
2 Waren goods

waren ▶ SEE **sein**

das **Warenhaus**, PLURAL die **Warenhäuser**
department store

WORD TIP The German word Warenhaus does not mean warehouse in English; the German word for warehouse is Lager.

warf ▶ SEE **werfen**

ℓ **warm** ADJECTIVE
warm
eine warme Mahlzeit a hot meal
Er machte das Essen warm. He heated up the food.

◇ irregular verb; SEP separable verb; for more help with verbs see centre section

die **Wärme**
warmth

wärmen *VERB*, *PERFECT* **hat gewärmt**
to warm, to heat

warmherzig *ADJECTIVE*
warm-hearted

das **Warndreieck**, *PLURAL* die
Warndreiecke
warning triangle

warnen *VERB*, *PERFECT* **hat gewarnt**
to warn
jemanden vor etwas warnen to warn
somebody of something

die **Warnung**, *PLURAL* die **Warnungen**
warning

Warschau *NEUTER NOUN*
Warsaw

warst, wart ▶ SEE **sein**

die **Warteliste**, *PLURAL* die **Wartelisten**
waiting list

ℰ **warten** *VERB*, *PERFECT* **hat gewartet**
1 to wait
auf jemanden warten to wait for
somebody
2 lange auf sich warten lassen to be a long
time coming

der **Wärter**, *PLURAL* die **Wärter**
1 keeper *(male)*
2 attendant *(male)*
3 warder *(male)*

der **Warteraum**, *PLURAL* die **Warteräume**
waiting room

die **Wärterin**, *PLURAL* die **Wärterinnen**
1 keeper *(female)*
2 attendant *(female)*
3 warder *(female)*

der **Wartesaal**, *PLURAL* die **Wartesäle**
waiting room *(in a station)*

die **Wartezeit**, *PLURAL* die **Wartezeiten**
wait
Nach einer Stunde Wartezeit kam endlich
unser Essen. After an hour's wait, our food
finally arrived.

das **Wartezimmer**, *PLURAL* die
Wartezimmer
waiting room

ℰ **warum** *ADVERB*
why

die **Warze**, *PLURAL* die **Warzen**
wart

ℰ **was** *PRONOUN*
1 what
Was für ein/eine ...? What kind of ...?
Was für ein Fahrrad hast du? What kind of
bike do you have?
Was für ein Glück! What luck!
Was kostet das? How much is it?
2 that
Wir haben alles, was wir brauchen. We
have all (that) we need.
Du bekommst alles, was du willst. You can
have everything you want.
3 *(short for etwas)* something
Heute gibts was Gutes im Fernsehen.
There's something good on television
today.
4 *(short for etwas in questions and negatives)*
anything
Hast du was für mich? Have you got
anything for me?

das **Waschbecken**, *PLURAL* die
Waschbecken
washbasin

ℰ die **Wäsche**
1 washing
2 underwear

ℰ **waschen** *VERB*◇, *PRESENT* **wäscht**, *IMPERFECT*
wusch, *PERFECT* **hat gewaschen**
1 to wash
2 sich waschen to have a wash
sich die Hände waschen to wash your
hands

die **Wäscherei**, *PLURAL* die **Wäschereien**
laundry

der **Waschlappen**, *PLURAL* die **Waschlappen**
flannel

ℰ die **Waschmaschine**, *PLURAL* die
Waschmaschinen
washing machine

das **Waschpulver**, *PLURAL* die **Waschpulver**
washing powder

der **Waschraum**, *PLURAL* die **Waschräume**
washroom

der **Waschsalon**, *PLURAL* die **Waschsalons**
launderette

ℰ das **Wasser**
water

wasserdicht *ADJECTIVE*
waterproof

der **Wasserfall**, PLURAL die **Wasserfälle**
waterfall

die **Wasserfarbe**, PLURAL die **Wasserfarben**
watercolour

der **Wasserhahn**, PLURAL die **Wasserhähne**
tap

die **Wasserkraft**
hydroelectric power

der **Wassermann**
Aquarius
Lisa ist Wassermann. Lisa is Aquarius.

die **Wassermelone**, PLURAL die **Wassermelonen**
watermelon

das **Wasserskifahren**
waterskiing

der **Wassersport**
water sport

die **Wassertiefe**
depth (of water)
'Wassertiefe: 2 Meter' 'Depth: 2 metres'

die **Watte**
cotton wool

wattiert ADJECTIVE
padded

das **WC**, PLURAL die **WCs**
WC, toilet

die **Webcam**, PLURAL die **Webcams**
webcam

weben VERB, PERFECT **hat gewebt**
to weave

ρ die **Webseite**, PLURAL die **Webseiten**
web page

die **Website**, PLURAL die **Websites**
website

wechselhaft ADJECTIVE
changeable

ρ der **Wechselkurs**, PLURAL die **Wechselkurse**
exchange rate

ρ **wechseln** VERB, PERFECT **hat gewechselt**
1 to change
Kannst du mir zehn Euro wechseln? Have you got change for ten euros?
2 to exchange (glances, letters)

die **Wechselstube**, PLURAL die **Wechselstuben**
bureau de change

ρ **wecken** VERB, PERFECT **hat geweckt**
to wake (up)

ρ der **Wecker**, PLURAL die **Wecker**
alarm clock
Max geht mir auf den Wecker. (informal)
Max gets on my nerves.

ρ **weder** CONJUNCTION
weder ... noch neither ... nor

ρ **weg** ADVERB
1 away
Geh weg! Go away!
Hände weg! Hands off!
2 gone
Der Ring ist weg. The ring's gone.
Heidi ist schon weg. Heidi's already gone.

ρ der **Weg**, PLURAL die **Wege**
1 way
Auf dem Weg nach Hause traf ich Gabi. I met Gabi on the way home.
2 path
3 sich auf den Weg machen to set off
4 im Weg sein to be in the way

ρ **wegen** PREPOSITION (+ GEN)
because of

wegfahren VERB◇, PRESENT **fährt weg**, IMPERFECT **fuhr weg**, PERFECT **ist weggefahren**
1 to leave
Sie fahren gerade weg. They are just leaving.
2 PERFECT **hat weggefahren** to move (a car), to take away (things)

weggehen VERB◇, IMPERFECT **ging weg**, PERFECT **ist weggegangen**
1 to go away
2 to leave
3 to go out
Wir gehen heute Abend weg. We're going out tonight.
4 to come out (of a stain)

weglassen VERB◇, PRESENT **lässt weg**, IMPERFECT **ließ weg**, PERFECT **hat weggelassen**
1 to let go
2 to leave out

weglaufen VERB◇, PRESENT **läuft weg**, IMPERFECT **lief weg**, PERFECT **ist weggelaufen**
to run away

weglegen VERB, PERFECT **hat weggelegt**
1 to put down
2 to put away

◇ irregular verb; SEP separable verb; for more help with verbs see centre section

wegmachen *VERB*, *PERFECT* **hat weggemacht**
(informal) **to get rid of** *(a stain or wart, for example)*

wegmüssen *VERB◇*, *PRESENT* **muss weg**, *IMPERFECT* **musste weg**, *PERFECT* **hat weggemusst**
(informal) **to have to go**

wegnehmen *VERB◇*, *PRESENT* **nimmt weg**, *IMPERFECT* **nahm weg**, *PERFECT* **hat weggenommen**
to take away

wegräumen *VERB*, *PERFECT* **hat weggeräumt**
to clear away

wegschicken *VERB*, *PERFECT* **hat weggeschickt**
1 **to send away**
2 **to send off**

wegtun *VERB◇*, *IMPERFECT* **tat weg**, *PERFECT* **hat weggetan**
to put away

der **Wegweiser**, *PLURAL* die **Wegweiser**
signpost

⌁ **wegwerfen** *VERB◇*, *PRESENT* **wirft weg**, *IMPERFECT* **warf weg**, *PERFECT* **hat weggeworfen**
to throw away

weh *ADJECTIVE*
1 **sore**
2 **Oh weh!** Oh dear!
3 ►SEE **wehtun**

wehen *VERB*, *PERFECT* **hat geweht**
to blow

der **Wehrdienst**
military service

wehren *VERB*, *PERFECT* **hat sich gewehrt**
sich wehren to defend yourself

wehrlos *ADJECTIVE*
defenceless

⌁ **wehtun** *VERB◇*, *PRESENT* **tut weh**, *IMPERFECT* **tat weh**, *PERFECT* **hat wehgetan**
1 **to hurt**
Mein Arm tut weh. My arm hurts.
Er hat mir wehgetan. He hurt me.
2 **sich wehtun to hurt yourself**
Hast du dir wehgetan? Have you hurt yourself?

das **Weibchen**, *PLURAL* die **Weibchen**
female *(animal)*

weiblich *ADJECTIVE*
1 **female**

2 **feminine** *(in grammar)*

⌁ **weich** *ADJECTIVE*
soft

die **Weide**, *PLURAL* die **Weiden**
1 **willow**
2 **pasture**

weigern *VERB*, *PERFECT* **hat sich geweigert**
sich weigern to refuse

⌁ **Weihnachten** *NEUTER NOUN*, *PLURAL* die **Weihnachten**
Christmas
Frohe Weihnachten! Merry Christmas!

die **Weihnachtskrippe**, *PLURAL* die **Weihnachtskrippen**
(Christmas) crib

das **Weihnachtslied**, *PLURAL* die **Weihnachtslieder**
Christmas carol

⌁ der **Weihnachtsmann**, *PLURAL* die **Weihnachtsmänner**
Father Christmas

der **Weihnachtstag**, *PLURAL* die **Weihnachtstage**
der erste Weihnachtstag Christmas Day
der zweite Weihnachtstag Boxing Day

⌁ **weil** *CONJUNCTION*
because

> **WORD TIP** The German word weil does not mean while in English; the German word for while is während or Weile.

die **Weile**
while

⌁ der **Wein**, *PLURAL* die **Weine**
wine

der **Weinberg**, *PLURAL* die **Weinberge**
vineyard

die **Weinbergschnecke**, *PLURAL* die **Weinbergschnecken**
snail

der **Weinbrand**, *PLURAL* die **Weinbrände**
brandy

⌁ **weinen** *VERB*, *PERFECT* **hat geweint**
to cry

die **Weinkarte**, *PLURAL* die **Weinkarten**
wine list

der **Weinkeller**, *PLURAL* die **Weinkeller**
wine cellar

⌁ indicates key words

die **Weinprobe**, PLURAL die **Weinproben**
wine tasting

die **Weinstube**, PLURAL die **Weinstuben**
wine bar

die **Weintraube**, PLURAL die **Weintrauben**
1 grape
2 bunch of grapes

weise ADJECTIVE
wise

die **Weise**, PLURAL die **Weisen**
way
auf diese Weise in this way

die **Weisheit**, PLURAL die **Weisheiten**
wisdom

weiß[1] ▸ SEE **wissen**

ℰ **weiß**[2] ADJECTIVE
white

der **Weißwein**, PLURAL die **Weißweine**
white wine

ℰ **weit** ADJECTIVE, ADVERB
1 wide, loose (clothes)
2 long
Es ist eine weite Reise. It's a long journey.
3 far
Wie weit ist es? How far is it?
Ist es noch weit? Is it much further?
4 so weit wie möglich as far as possible
5 bei weitem by far
6 zu weit gehen to go too far
7 von weitem from a distance
8 Ich bin so weit. I'm ready.
9 weit verbreitet widespread

weiten VERB, PERFECT **hat sich geweitet**
sich weiten to stretch

ℰ **weiter** ADVERB
1 further
2 in addition
3 etwas weiter tun to go on doing
something
Wenn du weiter so wenig isst, wirst du
noch krank. If you go on eating so little
you'll get ill.
4 else
weiter nichts nothing else
weiter niemand nobody else
5 und so weiter and so on

weiterbilden VERB, PERFECT **hat
weitergebildet**
sich weiterbilden to continue your
education, to do further training

die **Weiterbildung**
further education

weiterer, weitere, weiteres ADJECTIVE
1 further
2 ohne Weiteres just like that, easily
3 bis auf Weiteres for the time being

weiterfahren VERB◇, PRESENT **fährt
weiter**, IMPERFECT **fuhr weiter**, PERFECT **ist
weitergefahren**
to go on

ℰ **weitergehen** VERB◇, IMPERFECT **ging weiter**,
PERFECT **ist weitergegangen**
to go on, to continue

weiterhin ADVERB
1 still
2 in future
3 etwas weiterhin tun to go on doing
something

weitermachen VERB, PERFECT **hat
weitergemacht**
to carry on

der **Weitsprung**
long jump

der **Weizen**
wheat

ℰ **welcher, welche, welches** ADJECTIVE
which
Welches Kleid soll ich anziehen? Which
dress shall I wear?
Um welche Zeit ist der Film zu Ende? What
time does the film finish?

welcher welche welches PRONOUN
1 which (one)
2 some
Brauchst du Briefmarken? Ich habe
welche. Do you need stamps? I've got
some.
3 any
Hast du welche? Have you got any?

die **Welle**, PLURAL die **Wellen**
wave

ℰ der **Wellensittich**, PLURAL die
Wellensittiche
budgerigar, budgie

wellig ADJECTIVE
wavy

ℰ die **Welt**, PLURAL die **Welten**
world
auf der ganzen Welt in the whole world

das **Weltall**
universe

◇ **irregular verb;** SEP **separable verb; for more help with verbs see centre section**

der **Weltkrieg**, *PLURAL* die **Weltkriege**
world war
der Erste/Zweite Weltkrieg the First/
Second World War

ℰ der **Weltmeister**, *PLURAL* die **Weltmeister**
world champion *(male)*

ℰ die **Weltmeisterin**, *PLURAL* die
Weltmeisterinnen
world champion *(female)*

die **Weltmeisterschaft**, *PLURAL* die
Weltmeisterschaften
1 **world championship**
2 die Weltmeisterschaft *(football)* the World
Cup

der **Weltraum**
space

Weltreise *DIE*, *PLURAL* die **Weltreisen**
world tour

ℰ **weltweit** *ADJECTIVE*
worldwide

ℰ **wem** *PRONOUN*
to whom, who ... to
Wem hat er das Geld gegeben? Who did
he give the money to?

ℰ **wen** *PRONOUN*
whom, who
Wen hast du eingeladen? Who did you
invite?

ℰ die **Wende**
1 **change**
2 **reunification** *(of Germany)*

ℰ **wenig** *PRONOUN, ADJECTIVE*
1 **little**
zu wenig too little, not enough
2 **wenige few**
in wenigen Wochen in a few weeks
wenig *ADVERB*
little
so wenig wie möglich as little as possible

ℰ **weniger** *PRONOUN, ADJECTIVE, ADVERB*
1 **less, fewer**
Er sollte weniger reden und mehr
zuhören. He should talk less and listen
more.
Sie hat weniger Geschenke bekommen.
She got fewer presents.
immer weniger Geld less and less money
immer weniger Häuser fewer and fewer
houses
2 **minus**
Zehn weniger vier ist sechs. Ten minus
four is six.

wenigste ▸ SEE **wenigster**

ℰ **wenigstens** *ADVERB*
at least
Du könntest dich wenigstens bedanken.
You could at least say thank you.

wenigster, wenigste, wenigstes *ADJECTIVE,*
PRONOUN
least
am wenigsten least
Das letzte Lied hat mir am wenigsten
gefallen. I liked the last song least.

ℰ **wenn** *CONJUNCTION*
1 **if**
Wenn es regnet, bleiben wir hier. If it
rains, we'll stay here.
2 **when**
Wenn ich in München bin, schreibe ich dir.
I'll write to you when I'm in Munich.
3 immer wenn whenever
Immer wenn ich frage, schweigt sie.
Whenever I ask she says nothing.
4 selbst wenn, auch wenn even if
5 außer wenn unless

ℰ **wer** *PRONOUN*
who

die **Werbeagentur**, *PLURAL* die
Werbeagenturen
advertising agency

werben *VERB◇*, *PRESENT* **wirbt**, *IMPERFECT*
warb, *PERFECT* **hat geworben**
1 **to advertise**
2 **to recruit** *(members, staff)*

ℰ der **Werbespot**, *PLURAL* die **Werbespots**
commercial, advert

ℰ die **Werbung**, *PLURAL* die **Werbungen**
1 **advertisement, advert**
Im Fernsehen kommt viel Werbung. There
are many adverts on television.
Werbung für etwas machen to advertise
something
2 **advertising**
Er möchte in der Werbung arbeiten. He
wants to work in advertising.

ℰ **werden** *VERB◇*, *PRESENT* **wird**, *IMPERFECT*
wurde, *PERFECT* **ist geworden**
1 **to become**
Sie wurden Freunde. They became
friends.
Er will Arzt werden. He wants to be a
doctor.
2 **to get**
müde werden to get tired

329

ℰ indicates key words

alt werden to get old
Mir wird kalt. I'm getting cold.
3 Mir wurde schlecht. I felt sick.
Sie wurde blass. She turned pale.
4 wach werden to wake up
5 *(used to form the future tense)* **will**, **shall**
Sie wird anrufen. She'll ring.
Er wird gleich da sein. He'll be here in a minute.
6 *(used to form the passive)* **to be**
Der Flug wurde ausgerufen. The flight was called.
Der Briefkasten wird täglich geleert. The postbox is emptied daily.
7 *(used to form the conditional)*
Sie würde kommen. She would come.
Ich würde gern kommen, aber ... I'd like to come but ...

ℙ **werfen** VERB◇, PRESENT **wirft**, IMPERFECT **warf**, PERFECT **hat geworfen**
to throw

das **Werk**, PLURAL die **Werke**
1 work
2 works *(a factory)*

ℙ das **Werken**
handicraft, design and technology

die **Werkstatt**, PLURAL die **Werkstätten**
1 workshop
2 garage *(for repairs)*

der **Werktag**, PLURAL die **Werktage**
weekday

werktags ADVERB
on weekdays

das **Werkzeug**, PLURAL die **Werkzeuge**
tool

wert ADJECTIVE
viel wert sein to be worth a lot
nichts wert sein to be worthless

der **Wert**, PLURAL die **Werte**
1 value
Sie gewann einen Gutschein im Wert von hundert Euro. She won a voucher worth one hundred euros.
2 auf etwas Wert legen to attach importance to something
3 Es hat doch keinen Wert. There's no point.

wertlos ADJECTIVE
worthless

wertvoll ADJECTIVE
valuable

das **Wesen**, PLURAL die **Wesen**
1 nature, manner
2 creature

wesentlich ADJECTIVE
essential
im Wesentlichen essentially

wesentlich ADVERB
considerably

weshalb ADVERB
why

die **Wespe**, PLURAL die **Wespen**
wasp

ℙ **wessen** PRONOUN
whose

der **Wessi**, PLURAL die **Wessis**
(informal) West German

die **Weste**, PLURAL die **Westen**
waistcoat

ℙ der **Westen**
west

der **Western**, PLURAL die **Western**
western *(film)*

der **Westinder**, PLURAL die **Westinder**
West Indian *(male)*

die **Westinderin**, PLURAL die **Westinderinnen**
West Indian *(female)*

westlich ADJECTIVE
1 western
2 westerly

westlich ADVERB, PREPOSITION (+ GEN)
westlich der Stadt to the west of the city
westlich von Wien west of Vienna

weswegen ADVERB
why

ℙ der **Wettbewerb**, PLURAL die **Wettbewerbe**
competition, contest

die **Wette**, PLURAL die **Wetten**
bet
mit jemandem um die Wette laufen to race somebody

wetten VERB, PERFECT **hat gewettet**
to bet
mit jemandem um etwas wetten to bet somebody something

ℙ das **Wetter**
weather

◇ **irregular verb**; SEP **separable verb**; for more help with verbs see centre section

ₚ der **Wetterbericht**, *PLURAL* die
　Wetterberichte
　weather forecast

die **Wetterlage**, *PLURAL* die **Wetterlagen**
　weather situation

die **Wettervorhersage**
　weather forecast

der **Wettkampf**, *PLURAL* die **Wettkämpfe**
　contest, competition

der **Wettlauf**, *PLURAL* die **Wettläufe**
　race

ₚ **wichtig** *ADJECTIVE*
　important
　Das wichtigste Exportgut ist Wolle. The
　most important export is wool.

wickeln *VERB, PERFECT* **hat gewickelt**
1　to wind
2　ein Kind wickeln to change a baby's nappy

der **Widder**, *PLURAL* die **Widder**
1　ram
2　Aries
　Jan ist Widder. Jan is Aries.

widerlich *ADJECTIVE*
　disgusting

widersprechen *VERB◇, PRESENT*
　widerspricht, *IMPERFECT* **widersprach**,
　PERFECT **hat widersprochen**
　to contradict

der **Widerspruch**, *PLURAL* die
　Widersprüche
　contradiction

der **Widerstand**
　resistance

widerstehen *VERB◇, IMPERFECT* **widerstand**,
　PERFECT **hat widerstanden**
　to resist

widmen *VERB, PERFECT* **hat gewidmet**
1　to dedicate
2　to devote
3　sich einer Sache widmen to devote
　yourself to something

ₚ **wie** *ADVERB*
1　how
　Wie geht's? How are you?
　Wie viel? How much?, How many?
　Wie viele Leute waren da? How many
　people were there?
2　what
　Wie ist Ihr Name? What is your name?
　Wie ist das Wetter? What's the weather
　like?

　Wie heißt er? What's he called?
　Um wie viel Uhr kommst du? (At) what
　time are you coming?
3　Wie bitte? Sorry?

wie *CONJUNCTION*
1　as
　so schnell wie möglich as quickly as possible
2　like
　Er ist genau wie du. He's just like you.
3　wie zum Beispiel such as

ₚ **wieder** *ADVERB*
　again
　Sie ist wieder da. She's back again.

wiederbekommen *VERB◇, IMPERFECT* **bekam**
　wieder, *PERFECT* **hat wiederbekommen**
　to get back

wiederbeleben *VERB, PERFECT* **hat**
　wiederbelebt
　to revive

wiedererkennen *VERB◇, IMPERFECT* **erkannte**
　wieder, *PERFECT* **hat wiedererkannt**
　to recognize

wiederfinden *VERB◇, IMPERFECT* **fand**
　wieder, *PERFECT* **hat wiedergefunden**
　to find (again)

ₚ **wiederholen** *VERB, PERFECT* **hat wiederholt**
1　to repeat
2　to bring back
3　to revise (schoolwork)
4　sich wiederholen to recur
5　Er hat sich ständig wiederholt. He kept
　repeating himself.

ₚ die **Wiederholung**, *PLURAL* die
　Wiederholungen
1　repetition
2　repeat performance
3　replay
4　revision (at school)

das **Wiederhören**
　Auf Wiederhören! (said on the phone)
　Goodbye!

wiederkommen *VERB◇, IMPERFECT* **kam**
　wieder, *PERFECT* **ist wiedergekommen**
1　to come back
2　to come again

wiedersehen *VERB◇, PRESENT* **sieht wieder**,
　IMPERFECT **sah wieder**, *PERFECT* **hat**
　wiedergesehen
　to see again

ₚ das **Wiedersehen**, *PLURAL* die **Wiedersehen**
1　reunion
2　Auf Wiedersehen! Goodbye!

wiedervereinigen VERB, PERFECT **hat wiedervereinigt**
to reunify

die **Wiedervereinigung**
reunification

wiederverwerten VERB, PERFECT **hat wiederverwertet**
to recycle

die **Wiederverwertung**
recycling

die **Wiege**, PLURAL die **Wiegen**
cradle

wiegen VERB◇, IMPERFECT **wog**, PERFECT **hat gewogen**
to weigh

das **Wiegenlied**, PLURAL die **Wiegenlieder**
lullaby

Wien NEUTER NOUN
Vienna

die **Wiener**, PLURAL die **Wiener**
type of sausage (like a frankfurter)

WORD TIP The German word Wiener can refer to residents of Vienna as well as the food.

das **Wiener Schnitzel**, PLURAL die **Wiener Schnitzel**
slice of pork or veal breaded and fried

WIENER SCHNITZEL OR SCHNITZEL

A speciality in Austria and some parts of Germany. Originally from Turkey and brought via Milan to Vienna: it is a slice of veal (or sometimes pork) fried in breadcrumbs and often served with potatoes and a mixed salad.

ℓ die **Wiese**, PLURAL die **Wiesen**
meadow

wieso ADVERB
why

wievielmal ADVERB
how often

wievielter, wievielte, wieviltes ADJECTIVE
1 which
2 Die wievielte Querstraße ist das von hier aus? How many roads do you cross to get there from here?
Der Wievielte ist heute? What's the date today?

ℓ **wild** ADJECTIVE
wild

das **Wildleder**
suede

der **Wildpark**, PLURAL die **Wildparks**
wildlife park

das **Wildschwein**, PLURAL die **Wildschweine**
wild boar

will ▸SEE **wollen**

der **Wille**
will
Er will immer seinen Willen durchsetzen. He always wants to get his own way.

ℓ **willkommen** ADJECTIVE
welcome
jemanden willkommen heißen to welcome somebody
Herzlich willkommen! Welcome!

willst ▸SEE **wollen**

Wilna NEUTER NOUN
Vilnius

die **Wimper**, PLURAL die **Wimpern**
eyelash

die **Wimperntusche**, PLURAL die **Wimperntuschen**
mascara

ℓ der **Wind**, PLURAL die **Winde**
wind

die **Windel**, PLURAL die **Windeln**
nappy

der **Windhund**, PLURAL die **Windhunde**
greyhound

ℓ **windig** ADJECTIVE
windy

die **Windmühle**, PLURAL die **Windmühlen**
windmill

der **Windpark**, PLURAL die **Windparks**
wind farm

die **Windpocken** PLURAL NOUN
chickenpox

die **Windschutzscheibe**, PLURAL die **Windschutzscheiben**
windscreen

das **Windsurfen**
windsurfing
Wir wollen Windsurfen gehen. We want to go windsurfing.

der **Windsurfer**, PLURAL die **Windsurfer**
windsurfer (male)

◇ irregular verb; SEP separable verb; for more help with verbs see centre section

der **Windsurferin**, *PLURAL* die
Windsurferinnen
windsurfer *(female)*

der **Winkel**, *PLURAL* die **Winkel**
1 angle
2 corner

ℰ **winken** *VERB*, *PERFECT* **hat gewinkt**
to wave

ℰ der **Winter**, *PLURAL* die **Winter**
winter

der **Wintergarten**, *PLURAL* die
Wintergärten
conservatory

der **Wintersport**
winter sports

winzig *ADJECTIVE*
tiny

die **Wippe**, *PLURAL* die **Wippen**
seesaw

ℰ **wir** *PRONOUN*
we
Wir sind fertig. We are ready.
Wir sind es. It's us.
Wir alle gehen hin. All of us are going.

der **Wirbel**, *PLURAL* die **Wirbel**
1 whirl
2 whirlwind
3 whirlpool
4 commotion

die **Wirbelsäule**, *PLURAL* die **Wirbelsäulen**
spine *of the back*

wirbt ▸ SEE **werben**

wird ▸ SEE **werden**

wirft ▸ SEE **werfen**

wirken *VERB*, *PERFECT* **hat gewirkt**
1 to have an effect
2 gegen etwas wirken to be effective against something
3 to seem *(sad, happy)*

ℰ **wirklich** *ADJECTIVE*
real
wirklich *ADVERB*
really

die **Wirklichkeit**
reality

wirksam *ADJECTIVE*
effective

die **Wirkung**, *PLURAL* die **Wirkungen**
effect

wirst ▸ SEE **werden**

der **Wirt**, *PLURAL* die **Wirte**
landlord

die **Wirtin**, *PLURAL* die **Wirtinnen**
landlady

ℰ die **Wirtschaft**, *PLURAL* die **Wirtschaften**
1 economy
2 pub

wirtschaftlich *ADJECTIVE*
economic

die **Wirtschaftslehre**
business studies

die **Wirtschaftswissenschaften** *PLURAL NOUN*
economics

das **Wirtshaus**, *PLURAL* die **Wirtshäuser**
pub

wischen *VERB*, *PERFECT* **hat gewischt**
to wipe

ℰ **wissen** *VERB*◇, *PRESENT* **weiß**, *IMPERFECT* **wusste**, *PERFECT* **hat gewusst**
to know
Das weiß ich nicht. I don't know.
Ich weiß, dass er in London wohnt. I know he lives in London.
Ich wüsste gern ... I'd like to know ...
Davon weiß ich nichts. I don't know anything about that.
Weißt du was? You know what?

das **Wissen**
knowledge

die **Wissenschaft**, *PLURAL* die **Wissenschaften**
science

der **Wissenschaftler**, *PLURAL* die **Wissenschaftler**
scientist *(male)*

WORD TIP Professions, hobbies, and sports don't take an article in German: Er ist Wissenschaftler.

die **Wissenschaftlerin**, *PLURAL* die **Wissenschaftlerinnen**
scientist *(female)*

WORD TIP Professions, hobbies, and sports don't take an article in German: Sie ist Wissenschaftlerin.

wissenschaftlich *ADJECTIVE*
scientific

ℰ indicates key words

wissenschaftlich ADVERB
scientifically

ℰ die **Witwe**, PLURAL die **Witwen**
widow
Sie ist Witwe. She's a widow.

ℰ der **Witwer**, PLURAL die **Witwer**
widower
Er ist Witwer. He's a widower.

ℰ der **Witz**, PLURAL die **Witze**
joke

ℰ **witzig** ADJECTIVE
funny, witty

das **WLAN** ABBREVIATION
(=wireless local area network) WiFi

ℰ **wo** ADVERB
where
Wo seid ihr gewesen? Where have you
been?
Wir fahren nach München, wo Markus
seit einem Jahr lebt. We're going to
Munich, where Markus has been living for
a year.
wo immer wherever

wo CONJUNCTION
1 seeing that
2 although
Jetzt ist sie mir böse, wo ich doch so nett
zu ihr war. Now she's angry with me,
although I've been so nice to her.

woanders ADVERB
elsewhere

ℰ die **Woche**, PLURAL die **Wochen**
week

ℰ das **Wochenende**, PLURAL die
Wochenenden
weekend

wochenlang ADVERB
for weeks

ℰ der **Wochentag**, PLURAL die **Wochentage**
weekday

wochentags ADVERB
on weekdays

ℰ **wöchentlich** ADJECTIVE, ADVERB
weekly

ℰ **wofür** ADVERB
what ... for
Wofür brauchst du das Geld? What do you
need the money for?

wog ▸SEE **wiegen**

ℰ **woher** ADVERB
where ... from
Woher ist er? Where does he come from?
Woher weißt du das? How do you know?

ℰ **wohin** ADVERB
where ... (to)
Wohin geht ihr? Where are you going?

wohl ADVERB
1 probably
Er hat den Zug wohl verpasst. He's
probably missed the train.
Du bist wohl verrückt! You must be mad!
2 well
Das mag wohl sein. That may well be true.
Das weiß sie sehr wohl. She knows that
perfectly well.
3 wohl kaum hardly

das **Wohl**
1 welfare, well-being
2 benefit
Es ist zu eurem Wohl. It's for your benefit.
3 Zum Wohl! Cheers!

wohlfühlen VERB, PERFECT **hat sich
wohlgefühlt**
1 sich wohlfühlen to feel well
Ich fühle mich heute nicht wohl. I don't
feel well today.
2 sich wohlfühlen to be happy
Anne fühlt sich in London wohl. Anne is
happy in London.

wohlhabend ADJECTIVE
well off

der **Wohltätigkeitsverein**, PLURAL die
Wohltätigkeitsvereine
charity

wohltun VERB◇, PRESENT **tut wohl**, IMPERFECT
tat wohl, PERFECT **hat wohlgetan**
jemandem wohltun to do somebody good

der **Wohnblock**, PLURAL die **Wohnblöcke**
block of flats

ℰ **wohnen** VERB, PERFECT **hat gewohnt**
1 to live
2 to stay (for a short time)

die **Wohngemeinschaft**, PLURAL die
Wohngemeinschaften
people sharing a flat/house
Wir wohnen in einer Wohngemeinschaft.
We share a flat.

wohnhaft ADJECTIVE
resident

◇ irregular verb; SEP separable verb; for more help with verbs see centre section

das **Wohnheim**, PLURAL die **Wohnheime**
1 hostel
2 home *(for old people)*
3 hall of residence *(for students)*

ℰ das **Wohnmobil**, PLURAL die **Wohnmobile**
camper van

ℰ der **Wohnort**, PLURAL die **Wohnorte**
place of residence

ℰ die **Wohnsiedlung**, PLURAL die
Wohnsiedlungen
housing estate

der **Wohnsitz**, PLURAL die **Wohnsitze**
address, place of residence

ℰ die **Wohnung**, PLURAL die **Wohnungen**
flat, apartment

ℰ der **Wohnwagen**, PLURAL die **Wohnwagen**
caravan

ℰ das **Wohnzimmer**, PLURAL die
Wohnzimmer
living room

der **Wolf**, PLURAL die **Wölfe**
wolf

die **Wolke**, PLURAL die **Wolken**
cloud

der **Wolkenkratzer**, PLURAL die
Wolkenkratzer
skyscraper

wolkenlos ADJECTIVE
cloudless

ℰ **wolkig** ADJECTIVE
cloudy

die **Wolldecke**, PLURAL die **Wolldecken**
blanket

die **Wolle**
wool

ℰ **wollen** VERB◊, PRESENT **will**, IMPERFECT
wollte, PERFECT **hat gewollt**, **hat
wollen**
1 to want
Anne will einen Hund. Anne wants a
dog.
Ich will nach Hause. I want to go home.
Sie will ins Kino gehen. She wants to go
to the cinema.
2 Sie wollte gerade gehen. She was just
about to go.

3 ganz wie du willst just as you like

WORD TIP The past participle is gewollt when
wollen is the main verb, and wollen when it is
an auxiliary verb.

die **Wolljacke**, PLURAL die **Wolljacken**
cardigan

womit ADVERB
1 what ... with
Womit hast du das gewaschen? What did
you wash it with?
2 with which

womöglich ADVERB
possibly

wonach ADVERB
1 what ... for
Wonach suchst du? What are you looking
for?
Wonach riecht es? What does it smell of?
2 after which, according to which
Es gibt eine neue Regelung, wonach wir
eine Stunde mehr arbeiten müssen. There
is a new rule according to which we have to
work an extra hour.

woran ADVERB
1 what ... of
Woran denkst du? What are you thinking
of?
2 Woran hast du ihn erkannt? How did you
recognize him?
3 on which, of which
Hier gibt es nichts, woran man sich
verletzen könnte. There's nothing here
you could hurt yourself on.

worauf ADVERB
1 what ... on, what ... for
Worauf hast du die Vase gestellt? What
did you put the vase on?
Worauf wartet ihr? What are you waiting
for?
2 on which, for which
Es ist das Regal, worauf die Anlage steht.
It's the shelf the stereo is on.
Die Ferien sind das Einzige, worauf ich
mich freue. The holidays are the only thing
I'm looking forward to.

woraus ADVERB
1 what ... from, what ... of
Woraus ist das? What's it made of?
2 from which
Es gibt nichts, woraus wir trinken können.
There isn't anything we can drink out of.

worin ADVERB
1 **what ... in, in what**
Worin soll ich es verpacken? What shall I wrap it in?
2 **in which**
Es gibt nur wenige Punkte, worin ich mit dir übereinstimme. There are only a few points I agree with you on.

℘ das **Wort**, PLURAL die **Worte/Wörter**
word
Mir fehlen die Worte. I'm lost for words.
Ich habe heute zwanzig neue Wörter gelernt. I've learnt twenty new words today.

WORD TIP Worte is the plural when the meaning is 'speech' or 'writing'. Wörter is the plural when the meaning is 'individual words'.

℘ das **Wörterbuch**, PLURAL die **Wörterbücher**
dictionary

wörtlich ADJECTIVE
1 **word for word**
2 **literal**
wörtlich ADVERB
1 **word for word**
2 **literally**

℘ der **Wortschatz**
vocabulary

das **Wortspiel**, PLURAL die **Wortspiele**
pun

℘ die **Wortstellung**
word order

worüber ADVERB
1 **what ... over, what ... about**
Worüber lacht ihr? What are you laughing about?
2 **over which, about which**

worum ADVERB
1 **about what, what ... for**
Worum geht es? What's it about?
Worum hat sie dich gebeten? What did she ask you for?
2 **for which**
3 **round which**

wovon ADVERB
1 **what ... from, what ... about**
Wovon redet ihr? What are you talking about?
2 **from which, about which**
der Geruch, wovon mir schlecht geworden ist the smell which made me feel sick

wovor ADVERB
1 **what ... of**
Wovor hast du Angst? What are you afraid of?
2 **in front of what**
3 **of which**
4 **in front of which**
der Turm, wovor wir stehen the tower we are standing in front of

wozu ADVERB
1 **what ... for, why**
Wozu brauchst du das? What do you need it for?
Wozu? What for?
2 **to which, for which**
Ich weiß nicht, wozu ich dir raten würde. I don't know what I would advise you to do.

das **Wrack**, PLURAL die **Wracks**
wreck

wuchs ▸ SEE **wachsen**

der **Wuchs**
growth

wund ADJECTIVE
sore

die **Wunde**, PLURAL die **Wunden**
wound

das **Wunder**, PLURAL die **Wunder**
miracle
Kein Wunder! No wonder!

wunderbar ADJECTIVE
wonderful

wundern VERB, PERFECT **hat sich gewundert**
sich wundern to be surprised

wunderschön ADJECTIVE
beautiful

wundervoll ADJECTIVE
wonderful

der **Wundschorf**, PLURAL die **Wundschorfe**
scab

der **Wunsch**, PLURAL die **Wünsche**
1 **wish**
2 **request**
auf Wunsch on request
Haben Sie sonst noch einen Wunsch? Will there be anything else?

℘ **wünschen** VERB, PERFECT **hat gewünscht**
1 **to wish**
Ich wünschte ihr alles Gute zum Geburtstag. I wished her a happy birthday.
Ich wünschte, ich könnte ... I wish I could ...

336

Was wünschen Sie? Can I help you?

2 sich etwas wünschen to want something
Was wünschst du dir zu Weihnachten?
What do you want for Christmas?

wünschenswert *ADJECTIVE*
desirable, desired *(effect, result)*

wurde, würde, wurden, würden,
wurdest, würdest, wurdet, würdet
▸SEE **werden**

der **Wurf**, *PLURAL* die **Würfe**
throw

der **Würfel**, *PLURAL* die **Würfel**
1 dice *(in games)*
2 cube

würfeln *VERB*, *PERFECT* **hat gewürfelt**
1 to play dice
2 to throw
Er hat eine Sechs gewürfelt. He's thrown
a six.

ℓ das **Würfelspiel**, *PLURAL* die **Würfelspiele**
game of dice

der **Wurm**, *PLURAL* die **Würmer**
worm

ℓ die **Wurst**, *PLURAL* die **Würste**
1 sausage
2 salami
3 Das ist mir Wurst. *(informal)* I couldn't
care less.

die **Wurstbude**, *PLURAL* die **Wurstbuden**
sausage stand

das **Würstchen**, *PLURAL* die **Würstchen**
sausage

die **Wurzel**, *PLURAL* die **Wurzeln**
root

würzen *VERB*, *PERFECT* **hat gewürzt**
to season

würzig *ADJECTIVE*
spicy

wusch ▸SEE **waschen**

wusste ▸SEE **wissen**

die **Wüste**, *PLURAL* die **Wüsten**
desert

die **Wut**
rage
eine Wut auf jemanden haben to be
furious with somebody

wütend *ADJECTIVE*
furious

Xx

x-beliebig *ADJECTIVE*
(informal) **any**
Nimm eine x-beliebige Zahl. Take any
number (you like).

x-mal *ADVERB*
(informal) **umpteen times**
Ich habe es dir schon x-mal erklärt. I've
explained it to you umpteen times.

das **Xylophon**, *PLURAL* die **Xylophone**
xylophone
Sie spielt Xylophon. She plays the
xylophone.

Yy

das **Yoga**
yoga
Yoga machen to do yoga

das **Ypsilon**, *PLURAL* die **Ypsilons**
Y

Zz

zaghaft *ADJECTIVE*
1 timid
2 tentative

zäh *ADJECTIVE*
tough

ℓ die **Zahl**, *PLURAL* die **Zahlen**
1 number
2 figure

ℓ **zahlen** *VERB*, *PERFECT* **hat gezahlt**
1 to pay
Hast du schon gezahlt? Have you paid?
2 to pay for
Ich zahle die Getränke. I'll pay for the
drinks.
Zahlen, bitte! Can I have the bill please!

ℓ **zählen** *VERB*, *PERFECT* **hat gezählt**
1 to count
auf jemanden zählen to count on
somebody
jemanden zu seinen Freunden zählen to
count somebody among your friends
2 zählen zu to be one of
Goethe zählt zu den bekanntesten

deutschen Schriftstellern. Goethe is one of the most famous German authors.

der **Zähler**, PLURAL die **Zähler**
meter

zahlreich ADJECTIVE
numerous

die **Zahlung**, PLURAL die **Zahlungen**
payment

die **Zählung**, PLURAL die **Zählungen**
1 count
2 census

zahm ADJECTIVE
tame

ℓ der **Zahn**, PLURAL die **Zähne**
tooth
Hast du dir die Zähne geputzt? Have you cleaned your teeth?

ℓ der **Zahnarzt**, PLURAL die **Zahnärzte**
dentist (male)

> **WORD TIP** Professions, hobbies, and sports don't take an article in German: Er ist Zahnarzt.

ℓ die **Zahnärztin**, PLURAL die **Zahnärztinnen**
dentist (female)

> **WORD TIP** Professions, hobbies, and sports don't take an article in German: Sie ist Zahnärztin.

die **Zahnbürste**, PLURAL die **Zahnbürsten**
toothbrush

die **Zahncreme**, PLURAL die **Zahncremes**
toothpaste

das **Zahnfleisch**
gums

ℓ die **Zahnpasta**, PLURAL die **Zahnpasten**
toothpaste

ℓ die **Zahnschmerzen** PLURAL NOUN
toothache
Ich habe Zahnschmerzen. I've got toothache.

die **Zahnspange**, PLURAL die **Zahnspangen**
brace

die **Zange**, PLURAL die **Zangen**
(pair of) pliers

> **WORD TIP** In German, die Zange is singular: Ich brauche eine Zange.

zanken VERB, PERFECT **hat sich gezankt**
sich zanken to squabble

der **Zapfen**, PLURAL die **Zapfen**
1 cone
2 icicle

zappeln VERB, PERFECT **hat gezappelt**
1 to wriggle
2 to fidget

zart ADJECTIVE
1 delicate, soft
2 gentle
3 tender

zärtlich ADJECTIVE
affectionate, tender

der **Zauber**
1 magic
2 spell

der **Zauberer**, PLURAL die **Zauberer**
1 magician, conjurer (male)
2 wizard

zauberhaft ADJECTIVE
enchanting

die **Zauberin**, PLURAL die **Zauberinnen**
magician, conjurer (female)

zaubern VERB, PERFECT **hat gezaubert**
to do magic

das **Zaumzeug**, PLURAL die **Zaumzeuge**
bridle

der **Zaun**, PLURAL die **Zäune**
fence

ℓ **z. B.** ABBREVIATION
(=zum Beispiel) e.g.

das **ZDF** ABBREVIATION
(=Zweites Deutsches Fernsehen) (a German public TV channel)

das **Zebra**, PLURAL die **Zebras**
zebra

der **Zebrastreifen**, PLURAL die **Zebrastreifen**
zebra crossing

die **Zecke**, PLURAL die **Zecken**
tick insect

ℓ der **Zeh**, PLURAL die **Zehen**
toe

die **Zehe**, PLURAL die **Zehen**
1 toe
2 clove (of garlic)

die **Zehenspitze**, PLURAL die **Zehenspitzen**
tip of the toe
auf Zehenspitzen on tiptoe

ℓ **zehn** NUMBER
ten

die **Zehn**, PLURAL die **Zehnen**
ten

338

das **Zehntel**, PLURAL die **Zehntel**
tenth

zehnter, **zehnte**, **zehntes** ADJECTIVE
tenth

das **Zeichen**, PLURAL die **Zeichen**
1 sign
2 signal

ℓ der **Zeichentrickfilm**, PLURAL die
Zeichentrickfilme
cartoon (film)

ℓ **zeichnen** VERB, PERFECT **hat gezeichnet**
to draw

die **Zeichnung**, PLURAL die **Zeichnungen**
drawing

der **Zeigefinger**, PLURAL die **Zeigefinger**
index finger

ℓ **zeigen** VERB, PERFECT **hat gezeigt**
1 to show
Peter hat uns sein neues Auto gezeigt.
Peter showed us his new car.
2 to point
auf jemanden zeigen to point at somebody
3 sich zeigen to appear
4 Es hat sich gezeigt, dass ... It has become
clear that ...
Es wird sich zeigen. Time will tell.

der **Zeiger**, PLURAL die **Zeiger**
hand (on a watch, clock)

ℓ **ziehen** VERB◇, IMPERFECT **zog**, PERFECT **hat
gezogen**
1 to pull an etwas ziehen to pull on
something einen Zahn ziehen to take a
tooth out
2 to draw einen Strich ziehen to draw a line
eine Niete ziehen to draw a blank
3 to grow (vegetables, flowers)
4 sich ziehen to run (of a path, road)
5 PERFECT ist gezogen
6 to move Sie sind nach Berlin gezogen.
They've moved to Berlin.

die **Zeile**, PLURAL die **Zeilen**
line

ℓ die **Zeit**, PLURAL die **Zeiten**
1 time
sich Zeit lassen to take your time
Ich habe keine Zeit mehr. I haven't got any
more time.
eine Zeit lang for a time
2 Es hat Zeit. There's no hurry.
3 die erste Zeit at first
4 in nächster Zeit in the near future
5 tense (in grammar)

das **Zeitalter**, PLURAL die **Zeitalter**
age

die **Zeitlupe**
slow motion
Das Tor wurde noch einmal in Zeitlupe
gezeigt. The goal was shown again in slow
motion.

der **Zeitraum**, PLURAL die **Zeiträume**
period

ℓ die **Zeitschrift**, PLURAL die **Zeitschriften**
magazine

ℓ die **Zeitung**, PLURAL die **Zeitungen**
newspaper

der **Zeitungshändler**, PLURAL die
Zeitungshändler
newsagent

der **Zeitungskiosk**, PLURAL die
Zeitungskioske
newspaper kiosk

der **Zeitungsstand**, PLURAL die
Zeitungsstände
news-stand

die **Zeitverschwendung**
waste of time

zeitweise ADVERB
at times

die **Zelle**, PLURAL die **Zellen**
1 cell
2 booth

ℓ das **Zelt**, PLURAL die **Zelte**
tent

ℓ **zelten** VERB, PERFECT **hat gezeltet**
to camp

der **Zeltplatz**, PLURAL die **Zeltplätze**
campsite

der **Zement**
cement

der **Zentimeter**, PLURAL die **Zentimeter**
centimetre

das **Zentimetermaß**, PLURAL die
Zentimetermaße
tape measure

zentral ADJECTIVE
central

die **Zentrale**, PLURAL die **Zentralen**
1 central office, head office
2 headquarters
3 (telephone) exchange, switchboard

die **Zentralheizung**
central heating

339

das **Zentrum**, PLURAL die **Zentren**
centre

ℓ **zerbrechen** VERB◇, PRESENT **zerbricht**, IMPERFECT **zerbrach**, PERFECT **hat zerbrochen**
1 to break
Ben hat meine Brille zerbrochen. Ben broke my glasses.
2 PERFECT **ist zerbrochen** to break
Die Untertasse ist zerbrochen. The saucer broke into pieces.

zerbrechlich ADJECTIVE
fragile

die **Zerbrechlichkeit**
fragility

die **Zeremonie**, PLURAL die **Zeremonien**
ceremony

zerfallen VERB◇, PRESENT **zerfällt**, IMPERFECT **zerfiel**, PERFECT **ist zerfallen**
to disintegrate, to decay

zerreißen VERB◇, IMPERFECT **zerriss**, PERFECT **hat zerrissen**
1 to tear
Sie hat sich das Kleid zerrissen. She tore her dress.
2 to tear up
Anna hat seinen Brief zerrissen. Anna tore up his letter.
3 PERFECT **ist zerrissen** to tear
Das Hemd ist in der Wäsche zerrissen. The shirt got torn in the washing.

zerschlagen VERB◇, PRESENT **zerschlägt**, IMPERFECT **zerschlug**, PERFECT **hat zerschlagen**
1 to smash, to smash up
2 sich zerschlagen to fall through (of plans)
Meine Hoffnungen haben sich zerschlagen. My hopes were dashed.

ℓ **zerschneiden** VERB◇, IMPERFECT **zerschnitt**, PERFECT **hat zerschnitten**
to cut up, to cut to pieces

ℓ **zerstören** VERB, PERFECT **hat zerstört**
to destroy

die **Zerstörung**
destruction

zerstreuen VERB, PERFECT **hat zerstreut**
1 to scatter
2 jemanden zerstreuen to entertain somebody
3 sich zerstreuen to take your mind off things
4 Die Menge hat sich zerstreut. The crowd dispersed.

zerstreut ADJECTIVE
absent-minded

die **Zerstreutheit**
absent-mindedness

ℓ der **Zettel**, PLURAL die **Zettel**
1 piece of paper
2 note
3 leaflet

ℓ das **Zeug** (informal)
1 stuff
2 things, gear
3 dummes Zeug nonsense

der **Zeuge**, PLURAL die **Zeugen**
witness (male)

die **Zeugin**, PLURAL die **Zeuginnen**
witness (female)

ℓ das **Zeugnis**, PLURAL die **Zeugnisse**
1 certificate
2 report (at school)

der **Zickzack**, PLURAL die **Zickzacke**
zigzag
im Zickzack laufen to zigzag

die **Ziege**, PLURAL die **Ziegen**
goat

der **Ziegel**, PLURAL die **Ziegel**
1 brick
2 tile

ℓ **ziehen** VERB◇, IMPERFECT **zog**, PERFECT **hat gezogen**
1 to pull
an etwas ziehen to pull on something
einen Zahn ziehen to take a tooth out
2 to draw
einen Strich ziehen to draw a line
eine Niete ziehen to draw a blank
3 to grow (vegetables, flowers)
4 sich ziehen to run (of a path, road)
5 PERFECT **ist gezogen** to move
Sie sind nach Berlin gezogen. They've moved to Berlin.

ℓ das **Ziel**, PLURAL die **Ziele**
1 destination
2 goal, aim
3 finish, finishing line (in sport)

zielen VERB, PERFECT **hat gezielt**
to aim
auf etwas zielen to aim at something

die **Zielscheibe**, PLURAL die **Zielscheiben**
target

zielstrebig ADJECTIVE
determined, purposeful

◇ irregular verb; SEP separable verb; for more help with verbs see centre section

♀ ziemlich ADVERB
1 quite, rather
ziemlich viel quite a lot
2 fairly, pretty
Das Haus ist ziemlich groß. The house is
pretty big.
ziemlich ADJECTIVE
Das war ein ziemlicher Schock. It was
quite a shock.

zierlich ADJECTIVE
dainty, delicate

die Ziffer, PLURAL die **Ziffern**
1 figure
2 number, numeral
römische Ziffern Roman numerals

das Zifferblatt, PLURAL die **Zifferblätter**
face, dial

zig ADJECTIVE
(informal) umpteen

♀ die Zigarette, PLURAL die **Zigaretten**
cigarette

die Zigarre, PLURAL die **Zigarren**
cigar

der Zigeuner, PLURAL die **Zigeuner**
gypsy (male)

die Zigeunerin, PLURAL die **Zigeunerinnen**
gypsy (female)

♀ das Zimmer, PLURAL die **Zimmer**
room
Zimmer mit Frühstück bed and breakfast
'Zimmer frei' 'Vacancies'

das Zimmermädchen, PLURAL die
Zimmermädchen
chambermaid

> **WORD TIP** Professions, hobbies, and sports don't
> take an article in German: Sie ist Zimmermädchen.

der Zimt
cinnamon

das Zink
zinc

zirka ADVERB
about

der Zirkel, PLURAL die **Zirkel**
pair of compasses

> **WORD TIP** In German, der Zirkel is singular: Wo
> ist mein Zirkel?

der Zirkus, PLURAL die **Zirkusse**
circus

zischen VERB, PERFECT **hat gezischt**
to hiss

das Zitat, PLURAL die **Zitate**
quotation

zitieren VERB, PERFECT **hat zitiert**
to quote

♀ die Zitrone, PLURAL die **Zitronen**
lemon

der Zitronensaft, PLURAL die **Zitronensäfte**
lemon juice

zittern VERB, PERFECT **hat gezittert**
to tremble
Er zitterte vor Angst. He was trembling
with fear.
Ich zitterte vor Kälte. I was shivering.

zivil ADJECTIVE
civil
zivile Partnerschaft civil partnership

der Zivildienst
community service (as an alternative to
military service)

der Zivildienstleistende, PLURAL die
Zivildienstleistenden
a young man doing community service
(as an alternative to military service)

die Zivilisation, PLURAL die **Zivilisationen**
civilization

zog ▶ SEE **ziehen**

zögern VERB, PERFECT **hat gezögert**
to hesitate

der Zoll, PLURAL die **Zölle**
1 customs
Es gab lange Schlangen am Zoll. There
were long queues at customs.
2 duty
Muss man auf Zigaretten Zoll bezahlen?
Do you have to pay duty on cigarettes?

der Zollbeamte, PLURAL die **Zollbeamten**
customs officer (male)

> **WORD TIP** Professions, hobbies, and sports don't
> take an article in German: Er ist Zollbeamter.

die Zollbeamtin, PLURAL die
Zollbeamtinnen
customs officer (female)

> **WORD TIP** Professions, hobbies, and sports don't
> take an article in German: Sie ist Zollbeamtin.

zollfrei ADJECTIVE
duty-free

A
B
C
D
E
F
G
H
I
J
K
L
M
N
O
P
Q
R
S
T
U
V
W
X
Y
Z

♀ indicates key words

die **Zollkontrolle**, PLURAL die **Zollkontrollen**
customs check

die **Zone**, PLURAL die **Zonen**
zone

♀ der **Zoo**, PLURAL die **Zoos**
zoo

das **Zoomobjektiv**, PLURAL die
Zoomobjektive
zoom lens

der **Zopf**, PLURAL die **Zöpfe**
plait

der **Zorn**
anger

zornig ADJECTIVE
angry

♀ **zu** PREPOSITION (+ DAT)
1 **to**
Ich gehe zum Arzt. I'm going to the
doctor's.
Wir sind zu einer Party eingeladen. We
are invited to a party.
2 **with**
Das passt nicht zu meinem Mantel. It
doesn't go with my coat.
Es gab Wein zum Käse. There was wine
with the cheese.
3 **at**
zu Hause at home
zu Weihnachten at Christmas
4 **zu etwas werden** to turn into something
Das Wasser wurde zu Eis. The water
turned into ice.
5 **for**
zum Spaß for fun
zu diesem Zweck for this purpose
zum ersten Mal for the first time
Was schenkst du Karin zum Geburtstag?
What are you giving Karin for her birthday?
Ich brauche Papier zum Schreiben. I need
paper to write on.
6 **sich zu etwas äußern** to comment on
something
7 **nett zu jemandem sein** to be nice to
somebody
8 Sie waren zu zweit. There were two of
them.
9 eine Marke zu achtzig Cent an 80-cent
stamp
10 Es steht drei zu zwei. The score is 3–2.
11 **zu Fuß** on foot

WORD TIP zu + dem gives zum; zu + der
gives zur

zu ADVERB
1 **too**
Es ist zu groß. It's too big.
2 **closed**
Heute haben wir zu. We're closed today.
Alle Läden sind zu gewesen. The shops
were all closed.
Tür zu! (informal) Shut the door!
3 **towards** (indicating direction)
4 Mach zu! (informal) Hurry up!

zu CONJUNCTION
to
Es gab nichts zu essen. There was nothing
to eat.
Das Haus ist zu verkaufen. The house is
for sale.

zuallererst ADVERB
first of all

zuallerletzt ADVERB
last of all

das **Zubehör**
accessories, attachments

zubereiten VERB, PERFECT **hat zubereitet**
to prepare
Er bereitet das Essen zu. He's preparing
the meal.

zubinden VERB◇, IMPERFECT **band zu**, PERFECT
hat zugebunden
to tie, to tie up

zubringen VERB◇, IMPERFECT **brachte zu**,
PERFECT **hat zugebracht**
to spend
Sie bringt viel Zeit bei ihrem Freund
zu. She spends a lot of time with her
boyfriend.

die **Zucchini**, PLURAL die **Zucchini**
courgette

die **Zucht**, PLURAL die **Zuchten**
1 **breed, species**
2 **breeding** (of animals)
3 **stud, kennels** (for horses)

züchten VERB, PERFECT **hat gezüchtet**
to breed

zucken VERB, PERFECT **hat gezuckt**
to twitch

♀ der **Zucker**
sugar

der **Zuckerguss**
icing

◇ irregular verb; SEP separable verb; for more help with verbs see centre section

zuckerkrank ADJECTIVE
  diabetic

die **Zuckerkrankheit**
  diabetes

zudecken VERB, PERFECT **hat zugedeckt**
1 to cover up, to cover
2 to tuck up (in bed)

zueinander ADVERB
1 to each other
  lieb zueinander sein to be nice to each
  other
2 together
  zueinander passen to go together
  zueinander halten to stick together

ℐ **zuerst** ADVERB
1 first
2 at first

die **Zufahrt**, PLURAL die **Zufahrten**
1 access
2 drive(way)

ℐ der **Zufall**, PLURAL die **Zufälle**
1 chance
  durch Zufall by chance
2 coincidence
  So ein komischer Zufall! What a strange
  coincidence!
  Per Zufall traf ich ihn in der U-Bahn. I
  bumped into him in the tube.

zufällig ADJECTIVE
  chance
  ein zufälliges Zusammentreffen a chance
  meeting
  Das war rein zufällig. It was pure chance.

zufällig ADVERB
  by chance
  Kannst du mir zufällig zehn Euro leihen?
  Could you lend me ten euros by any
  chance?

zufrieden ADJECTIVE
1 content
2 satisfied
  mit etwas zufrieden sein to be satisfied
  with something

zufriedenstellen VERB, PERFECT **hat
  zufriedengestellt**
  to satisfy

ℐ der **Zug**, PLURAL die **Züge**
1 train
2 procession
3 characteristic, trait
4 move (in games)
5 swig (when drinking)
6 drag (when smoking)

7 in einem Zug in one go

die **Zugabe**, PLURAL die **Zugaben**
1 free gift
2 encore

der **Zugang**, PLURAL die **Zugänge**
  access

zugeben VERB◇, PRESENT **gibt zu**, IMPERFECT
  gab zu, PERFECT **hat zugegeben**
1 to add
2 to admit

zugehen VERB◇, IMPERFECT **ging zu**, PERFECT **ist
  zugegangen**
1 to close, to shut
  Die Tür geht nicht zu. The door won't shut.
2 auf etwas zugehen to go towards
  something
  auf jemanden zugehen to walk up to
  somebody
3 Auf der Party ging es lustig zu. The party
  was good fun.
4 dem Ende zugehen to be nearing the end

der **Zugführer**, PLURAL die **Zugführer**
  guard

zügig ADJECTIVE
  quick

zugreifen VERB◇, IMPERFECT **griff zu**, PERFECT
  hat zugegriffen
1 to grab it/them
2 to help yourself
3 to lend a hand

zugunsten PREPOSITION (+ GEN)
  in favour of

ℐ das **Zuhause**
  home

ℐ **zuhören** VERB, PERFECT **hat zugehört**
  to listen

der **Zuhörer**, PLURAL die **Zuhörer**
  listener (male)

die **Zuhörerin**, PLURAL die **Zuhörerinnen**
  listener (female)

zukleben VERB, PERFECT **hat zugeklebt**
  to seal an envelope

zukommen VERB◇, IMPERFECT **kam zu**, PERFECT
  ist zugekommen
1 auf jemanden zukommen to come up to
  somebody
  Nächstes Jahr kommt eine Menge Arbeit
  auf mich zu. I'm in for a lot of work next
  year.
2 jemandem etwas zukommen lassen to
  give somebody something

ℐ indicates key words

3 etwas auf sich zukommen lassen to take things as they come

🔑 die **Zukunft**
future

zukünftig ADJECTIVE
future

die **Zukunftspläne** PLURAL NOUN
plans for the future

zulassen VERB◇, PRESENT **lässt zu**, IMPERFECT **ließ zu**, PERFECT **hat zugelassen**
1 to allow
2 to register (a car)
3 to leave closed

die **Zulassung**, PLURAL die **Zulassungen**
1 registration
2 admission

zuletzt ADVERB
1 last
2 in the end

zum ▸ SEE **zu dem**
1 Hast du etwas zum Lesen? Have you got something to read?
2 Ich muss den Aufsatz bis spätestens zum fünften März abgeben. I have to hand in my essay by 5 March at the latest.
3 Er hat es zum Fenster hinausgeworfen. He threw it out of the window.

🔑 **zumachen** VERB, PERFECT **hat zugemacht**
1 to close, to shut
2 to fasten

zumindest ADVERB
at least

zunächst ADVERB
1 first (of all)
2 at first

die **Zunahme**, PLURAL die **Zunahmen**
increase

der **Zuname**, PLURAL die **Zunamen**
surname

zunehmen VERB◇, PRESENT **nimmt zu**, IMPERFECT **nahm zu**, PERFECT **hat zugenommen**
1 to increase
2 to put on weight

🔑 die **Zunge**, PLURAL die **Zungen**
tongue

zur ▸ SEE **zu der**

zurechtkommen VERB◇, IMPERFECT **kam zurecht**, PERFECT **ist zurechtgekommen**
to cope, to manage

zurechtlegen VERB, PERFECT **hat zurechtgelegt**
1 to put out ready
2 sich eine Ausrede zurechtlegen to think up an excuse

Zürich NEUTER NOUN
Zurich

🔑 **zurück** ADVERB
1 back
2 Hamburg, hin und zurück, bitte. A return to Hamburg, please.

zurückbekommen VERB◇, IMPERFECT **bekam zurück**, PERFECT **hat zurückbekommen**
to get back
Ich bekam zehn Cent zurück. I got ten cents change.

🔑 **zurückbringen** VERB◇, IMPERFECT **brachte zurück**, PERFECT **hat zurückgebracht**
1 to bring back
2 to take back

🔑 **zurückfahren** VERB◇, PRESENT **fährt zurück**, IMPERFECT **fuhr zurück**, PERFECT **ist zurückgefahren**
1 to go back
2 to drive back, to travel back
3 PERFECT **hat zurückgefahren** to drive back
Mein Vater fährt uns zurück. My father will drive us back.

🔑 **zurückgeben** VERB◇, PRESENT **gibt zurück**, IMPERFECT **gab zurück**, PERFECT **hat zurückgegeben**
to give back

🔑 **zurückgehen** VERB◇, IMPERFECT **ging zurück**, PERFECT **ist zurückgegangen**
1 to go back
zurückgehen auf to go back to
2 to go down
3 to decrease

zurückhalten VERB◇, PRESENT **hält zurück**, IMPERFECT **hielt zurück**, PERFECT **hat zurückgehalten**
1 to hold back
2 sich zurückhalten to restrain yourself

zurückkehren VERB, PERFECT **ist zurückgekehrt**
to return

🔑 **zurückkommen** VERB◇, IMPERFECT **kam zurück**, PERFECT **ist zurückgekommen**
1 to get back, to return
2 to come back
auf etwas zurückkommen to come back to something

zurücklassen VERB◇, PRESENT **lässt zurück**, IMPERFECT **ließ zurück**, PERFECT **hat zurückgelassen**
to leave behind

zurücklegen VERB, PERFECT **hat zurückgelegt**
1 to put back
2 to keep, to put aside
3 Geld für etwas zurücklegen to put money by for something
4 to cover (a distance)
5 sich zurücklegen to lie back

zurücknehmen VERB◇, PRESENT **nimmt zurück**, IMPERFECT **nahm zurück**, PERFECT **hat zurückgenommen**
to take back

℘ **zurückrufen** VERB◇, IMPERFECT **rief zurück**, PERFECT **hat zurückgerufen**
to call back

zurückstellen VERB, PERFECT **hat zurückgestellt**
to put back

zurücktreten VERB◇, PRESENT **tritt zurück**, IMPERFECT **trat zurück**, PERFECT **ist zurückgetreten**
1 to step back
2 to resign

℘ **zurückzahlen** VERB, PERFECT **hat zurückgezahlt**
to pay back

zurückziehen VERB◇, IMPERFECT **zog zurück**, PERFECT **hat zurückgezogen**
1 to draw back
2 to withdraw (an offer)
3 sich zurückziehen to withdraw, to retire

℘ **zurzeit** ADVERB
at the moment, at present

die **Zusage**, PLURAL die **Zusagen**
acceptance

℘ **zusammen** ADVERB
1 together
zusammen sein to be together
2 altogether

die **Zusammenarbeit**
cooperation

zusammenarbeiten VERB, PERFECT **hat zusammengearbeitet**
to cooperate

℘ **zusammenbleiben** VERB◇, IMPERFECT **blieb zusammen**, PERFECT **ist zusammengeblieben**
to stay together

zusammenbrechen VERB◇, PRESENT **bricht zusammen**, IMPERFECT **brach zusammen**, PERFECT **ist zusammengebrochen**
to collapse

zusammenfassen VERB, PERFECT **hat zusammengefasst**
to summarize

℘ die **Zusammenfassung**, PLURAL die **Zusammenfassungen**
summary

zusammenhalten VERB◇, PRESENT **hält zusammen**, IMPERFECT **hielt zusammen**, PERFECT **hat zusammengehalten**
1 to hold together
2 to keep together
3 Die Kinder haben zusammengehalten. The children stuck together.

der **Zusammenhang**, PLURAL die **Zusammenhänge**
1 context
2 connection

zusammenkommen VERB◇, IMPERFECT **kam zusammen**, PERFECT **ist zusammengekommen**
1 to meet
2 to accumulate

die **Zusammenkunft**, PLURAL die **Zusammenkünfte**
meeting

zusammenlegen VERB, PERFECT **hat zusammengelegt**
1 to put together
2 to fold up
3 to club together

zusammennehmen VERB◇, PRESENT **nimmt zusammen**, IMPERFECT **nahm zusammen**, PERFECT **hat zusammengenommen**
1 to gather up
2 to summon up, to collect
3 sich zusammennehmen to pull yourself together

℘ **zusammenpassen** VERB, PERFECT **hat zusammengepasst**
1 to match
2 to be well matched (of people)
3 to fit together

das **Zusammensein**
get-together

der **Zusammenstoß**, PLURAL die **Zusammenstöße**
collision, crash

zusammenstoßen VERB◇, PRESENT **stößt zusammen**, IMPERFECT **stieß zusammen**, PERFECT **ist zusammengestoßen**
to collide, to crash

zusammenzählen VERB, PERFECT **hat zusammengezählt**
to add up

zusätzlich ADJECTIVE
additional, extra
zusätzlich ADVERB
in addition, extra

zuschauen VERB, PERFECT **hat zugeschaut**
to watch

♀ der **Zuschauer**, PLURAL die **Zuschauer**
1 spectator (male)
2 viewer (male)
3 die Zuschauer the audience

♀ die **Zuschauerin**, PLURAL die **Zuschauerinnen**
1 spectator (female)
2 viewer (female)

der **Zuschlag**, PLURAL die **Zuschläge**
1 surcharge
2 supplement

zuschlagpflichtig ADJECTIVE
subject to a supplement

der **Zuschuss**, PLURAL die **Zuschüsse**
1 contribution
2 grant

zusehen VERB◇, PRESENT **sieht zu**, IMPERFECT **sah zu**, PERFECT **hat zugesehen**
1 to watch
2 zusehen, dass ... to see (to it) that ...

zusenden VERB, PERFECT **hat zugesendet**
to send
jemandem etwas zusenden to send something to somebody

♀ der **Zustand**, PLURAL die **Zustände**
1 condition
2 state

zustande ADVERB
zustande bringen to bring about
zustande kommen to come about

zuständig ADJECTIVE
responsible

die **Zustellung**, PLURAL die **Zustellungen**
delivery

zustimmen VERB, PERFECT **hat zugestimmt**
to agree

die **Zustimmung**, PLURAL die **Zustimmungen**
1 agreement
2 approval

zustoßen VERB◇, PRESENT **stößt zu**, IMPERFECT **stieß zu**, PERFECT **ist zugestoßen**
to happen

die **Zutat**, PLURAL die **Zutaten**
ingredient

zutreffen VERB◇, PRESENT **trifft zu**, IMPERFECT **traf zu**, PERFECT **hat zugetroffen**
auf etwas zutreffen to apply to something

der **Zutritt**
entry
Zutritt haben to have access

♀ **zuverlässig** ADJECTIVE
reliable

zuversichtlich ADJECTIVE
confident, optimistic

die **Zuversichtlichkeit**
confidence

zuvor ADVERB
1 before
der Tag zuvor the day before
2 first

zuzahlen VERB, PERFECT **hat zugezahlt**
to pay extra

zuziehen VERB◇, IMPERFECT **zog zu**, PERFECT **hat zugezogen**
1 to pull tight
2 to draw (curtains)
3 to call in (an expert etc.)
4 PERFECT ist zugezogen to move into an area
5 sich eine Verletzung zuziehen to sustain an injury
sich eine Erkältung zuziehen to catch a cold

zuzüglich PREPOSITION (+ GEN)
plus

zwang ▸ SEE **zwingen**

der **Zwang**, PLURAL die **Zwänge**
1 compulsion
2 urge
3 obligation

zwängen VERB, PERFECT **hat gezwängt**
to squeeze

◇ **irregular verb;** SEP **separable verb; for more help with verbs see centre section**

zwanglos ADJECTIVE
casual, informal

ℰ **zwanzig** NUMBER
twenty

zwar ADVERB
1 admittedly
2 (often not translated) Ich war zwar dabei, habe aber nichts gesehen. I was there, but I didn't see anything.
3 und zwar to be exact

der **Zweck**, PLURAL die **Zwecke**
1 purpose
2 point
Es hat keinen Zweck. There's no point.

zwecklos ADJECTIVE
pointless

ℰ **zwei** NUMBER
two

die **Zwei**, PLURAL die **Zweien**
1 two
2 good (school mark)

das **Zweibettzimmer**, PLURAL die **Zweibettzimmer**
twin room

zweideutig ADJECTIVE
ambiguous

zweifach ADJECTIVE
twice, double

der **Zweifel**, PLURAL die **Zweifel**
doubt
ohne Zweifel no doubt

zweifelhaft ADJECTIVE
1 doubtful
2 dubious

zweifellos ADVERB
undoubtedly

zweifeln VERB, PERFECT hat gezweifelt
to doubt
an etwas zweifeln to doubt something

der **Zweig**, PLURAL die **Zweige**
1 branch
2 twig

zweihundert NUMBER
two hundred

ℰ **zweimal** ADVERB
twice
Sie treffen sich zweimal im Monat. They meet twice a month.

zweisprachig ADJECTIVE
bilingual

zweispurig ADJECTIVE
two-track (railway, recording, road)
eine zweispurige Straße a dual carriageway

zweit ADVERB
zu zweit in twos
Wir sind zu zweit. There are two of us.

zweite ▸ SEE **zweiter**

zweitens ADVERB
secondly

ℰ **zweiter, zweite, zweites** ADJECTIVE
second
Mario kam als Zweiter. Mario was the second to arrive.

der **Zwerg**, PLURAL die **Zwerge**
dwarf

ℰ die **Zwiebel**, PLURAL die **Zwiebeln**
1 onion
2 bulb

ℰ der **Zwilling**, PLURAL die **Zwillinge**
1 twin
2 Zwillinge Gemini
Markus ist Zwilling. Markus is Gemini.

zwingen VERB◇, IMPERFECT **zwang**, PERFECT **hat gezwungen**
1 to force
2 sich zwingen to force yourself

zwinkern VERB, PERFECT **hat gezwinkert**
to wink

ℰ **zwischen** PREPOSITION (+ DAT or + ACC)
1 (the dative is used when talking about position; the accusative shows movement or a change of place) (in) between
Ich saß zwischen meinem Vater und meiner Mutter. (DAT) I was sitting between my father and my mother.
Er setzte sich zwischen die beiden Mädchen. (ACC) He sat down between the two girls.
2 among (a crowd)

zwischendurch ADVERB
1 in between
2 now and again

der **Zwischenfall**, PLURAL die **Zwischenfälle**
incident

ℰ indicates key words

die **Zwischenlandung**, *PLURAL* die
Zwischenlandungen
stopover

der **Zwischenraum**, *PLURAL* die
Zwischenräume
gap, space

die **Zwischenzeit**
in der Zwischenzeit in the meantime

zwo *NUMBER*
(informal) two

ℓ **zwölf** *NUMBER*
twelve

zwoter, zwote, zwotes *ADJECTIVE*
(informal) second

Zypern *NEUTER NOUN*
Cyprus

◇ **irregular verb;** *SEP* **separable verb; for more help with verbs see centre section**

Using your German

Important words and phrases

When does it happen?

gewöhnlich usually

normalerweise normally

im Allgemeinen generally

meistens most of the time

jeden Tag every day

oft often

manchmal sometimes

ab und zu from time to time

immer always

einmal in der Woche once a week

zweimal im Jahr twice a year

selten rarely

nie never

Formal or informal?

Speaking to a friend

Kannst du mir bitte helfen?
Can you help me, please?

Willst du ins Kino gehen?
Do you want to go to the cinema?

Darf ich heute Abend weggehen?
Can I go out tonight?

Keine Ursache. Don't mention it.

Entschuldige bitte die Störung.
Sorry for disturbing you.

Ich möchte mit dir sprechen.
I'd like to see you.

Speaking to an adult

Können Sie mir bitte helfen?
Can you help me, please?

Wollen Sie mich sprechen?
Do you want to see me?

Nichts zu danken. Don't mention it.

Entschuldigen Sie bitte die Störung.
Sorry for disturbing you.

Ich würde Ihnen gern(e) helfen.
I'd like to help you.

Können Sie mir sagen … ?
Could you tell me … ?

Agreeing and disagreeing

Ich bin völlig deiner Meinung.
I completely agree.

Genau! Exactly!

Ich bin für … I'm in favour of …

Du hast recht. You are right.

Ich bin derselben Meinung. I'm of the
same opinion.

Das stimmt wahrscheinlich. That's
probably true.

Dem stimme ich überhaupt nicht zu.
I don't agree at all.

Auf keinen Fall! Certainly not!

ich bin gegen I'm against

Du irrst dich. You're wrong.

Ich bin anderer Meinung. I don't share
your opinion.

Das stimmt überhaupt nicht. That's not
true at all.

Opinions

meiner Meinung nach in my opinion

ich glaube, dass … I believe that …

ich bin davon überzeugt, dass …
I'm convinced that …

ich interessiere mich für …
I'm interested in …

ich hasse I hate

Ich kann … nicht leiden. I can't stand …

Das interessiert mich nicht.
That doesn't interest me.

weil es … ist because it is …

lustig fun, amusing

spannend exciting

interessant interesting

angenehm pleasant

langweilig boring

schrecklich awful

eine Zeitverschwendung a waste of
time

Questions

Wo gehst du heute Abend hin?
Where are you going tonight?

Mit wem? Who with?

Um wieviel Uhr fängt der Unterricht an?
What time do lessons start?

Welchen Sport magst du gern?
What kind of sports do you prefer?

Wann fährst du in Urlaub? When are
you going on holiday?

Experiences

ich habe angefangen, zu I began to
ich habe mich entschlossen, zu
I decided to
ich habe es geschafft, zu I managed to
ich habe mich geweigert, zu I refused to
ich habe versucht, zu I tried to
ich bin gegangen I went
ich habe viel Spaß gehabt I had a good
time

ich werde/werde nicht I'm going/
not going to
ich möchte I'd like to
ich will nicht I don't want to
ich habe vor I intend to
ich hoffe I hope to
ich träume davon I dream of

Connectives

wenn when, if, whether
außerdem what's more
weil because
seit since, for
da as, because of
wie like
während whereas
also so, therefore
wo where
während while
auch also
sobald as soon as

Role play phrases

Ich habe ... vergessen. I've forgotten ...
Ich habe ... verloren. I've lost ...
Ich suche ... I'm looking for ...
Was ist los? What's the matter?
Können Sie mir sagen ... ? Can you tell
me ... ?
Ich brauche I need
Wie komme ich ins Stadtzentrum?
How do I get to the town centre?
Wie schreibt man das? How do you
spell that?
Was ist passiert? What's happened?

Prepositions

mit/ohne with/without
trotz in spite of
außer except
wegen because of
neben next to
gegenüber opposite
vor in front of
hinter behind
links von to the left of
rechts von to the right of
in der Mitte in the middle
hinten at the back
vorne at the front
zwischen between

Letters, emails and social media

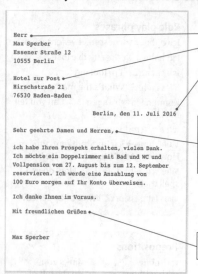

Formal letters

The sender's name and address go on the left.

The name and the address the letter is being sent to.

The name of the town and the date the letter is being written go on the right before the text of the letter.

Sehr geehrte Frau ... *(to a woman)*
Sehr geehrter Herr ... *(to a man)*
Sehr geehrte Damen und Herren *(if you do not know the name)*

It is polite to write Du, Dir, etc. with a capital, unless you are writing informal emails or messages.

Mit freundlichen Grüßen
Yours faithfully/Yours sincerely

Emails

eine E-Mail an email
eine E-Mail-Adresse an email address
ein Posteingangsordner an inbox
das Thema the subject
eine E-Mail schicken to send an email
eine E-Mail bekommen to receive an email
ein Anhang an attachment
beifügen/anhängen to attach
ein At-Zeichen (ein Klammeraffe) an @ sign
eine Webseite a website
(an)klicken to click (on)

To a whole family or group

Hallo zusammen Hello everyone/Dear all
Liebe Freunde Dear friends
Bis (ganz) bald See you (very) soon
Grüße und Küsse Love and kisses
Ich schicke dir einen dicken Kuss. I send you a big kiss.
Herzliche Grüße/Ganz herzliche Grüße Best wishes/Very best wishes
Mit herzlichen Grüßen With best wishes

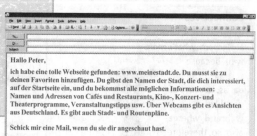

Film und Fernsehen
Films and television

Es gibt ... There's ...

- ein Sportprogramm. a sports programme.
- eine Dokumentarsendung. a documentary.
- eine Seifenoper. a soap.
- eine Spielshow. a game show.
- die Nachrichten. the news.

Meine Lieblingsserie ist ...
My favourite series is ...

ins Kino gehen to go to the cinema

Dort läuft ... They're showing ...

- ein Krimi. a detective film.
- ein Zeichentrickfilm. a cartoon.
- ein Drama/eine Komödie. a drama/ a comedy.
- ein Horrorfilm. a horror film.

Was denkst du?
What do you think?

Handys sind praktisch in Notsituationen.
Mobiles are practical for emergencies.

Meine Handyrechnung ist sehr hoch.
My mobile bill is very high.

Bestimmte Klingeltöne nerven mich.
Certain ringtones annoy me.

Man kann Videos und Spiele herunterladen. You can download videos and games.

Internetbetrug ist ein großes Problem.
Internet fraud is a big problem.

Die Jugendlichen werden immer passiver. Young people are becoming too passive.

Sie verbringen zu viel Zeit vor einem Bildschirm. They spend too much time in front of a screen.

Cybermobbing beunruhigt mich.
Cyberbullying concerns me.

Telefonieren
On the telephone

Hallo! Hello!
Kann ich ... sprechen? Can I speak to ... ?
Wer ist am Apparat? Who's calling?
Einen Moment, bitte. Hold on please.
Kann ich eine Nachricht hinterlassen? Can I leave a message?
Ich rufe später zurück. I'll call back later.
Ich verbinde Sie. I'll put you through.

Mit meinem Computer ...
On my computer ...

- surfe ich im Netz. I surf the web.
- downloade ich Musik, Videos und Spiele. I download music, videos and games.
- maile ich Freunden. I email friends.
- mache ich Hausaufgaben. I do homework.

Als Informationsquelle ist das Internet unentbehrlich. The Internet is indispensible for finding information.

- ein Laptop a laptop
- ein Chatraum a chatroom
- ein soziales Netzwerk a social network
- das/der Blog a blog
- die Webcam a webcam

Careers and future plans

```
Lebenslauf

Persönliche Daten

Lucy Belmont
34, Darlington Street
London NW4 5RT
Tel: +44 (0)203 5687
Email: llib@email.com
geboren am 30.7.1995 in London
britische Staatsangehörigkeit

Schule

seit 2016:          Owen's Sixth Form Centre; Vorbereitung auf
                    die A-levels (auf das Abitur)
Wahlfächer:         Englisch, Französisch, Deutsch, Musik

09/2010-06/2016:    Ashworth Secondary School
                    (Gesamtschule)
Pflichtfächer:      Mathematik, Englisch, Naturwissenschaften,
                    Geschichte, Deutsch
Wahlfächer:         Musik, Erdkunde, Theater

Praktika und berufliche Erfahrung

07/2015             Ferienjob: Praktikum bei einer
                    Lokalzeitung
08/2014             Ferienjob: Verkäuferin
2014                Babysitten

Zusatzqualifikationen

Sprachkenntnisse: Französisch (gute Kenntnisse in Wort
und Schrift), Deutsch (gute Kenntnisse), Spanisch
(Grundkenntnisse)

EDV-Kenntnisse: Microsoft Office (gute Kenntnisse)
Hobbys und Interessen: Reisen, Sprachen, Lesen, Musik, Kino
Mitglied des Schulorchesters und der Theatergruppe

Unterschrift.......................... Datum ..........
```

Writing a CV

Check your spelling and grammar.

In Germany, you need to attach a passport-sized photo of yourself to your CV when applying for a job.

Always write a covering letter.

Don't forget to sign and date your CV.

Was denkst du?
What do you think?

Bei der Stellensuche ist eine Berufsausbildung nützlich. Vocational training is useful for finding a job.

Ich will eine gut bezahlte Stelle finden. I want to find a well-paid job.

Ich will viel reisen. I want to travel a lot.

Ich will nicht in einem Büro arbeiten. I don't want to work in an office.

Die Arbeit ist mir zu eintönig. I find the work too monotonous.

Ich arbeite lieber im Freien. I prefer to work in the open air.

Ich wollte Ärztin werden, aber ich kann kein Blut sehen. I wanted to be a doctor but I'm afraid of blood.

Ich will Lehrerin werden, weil ich Kinder mag. I want to become a teacher because I like children.

Der Kontakt mit der Öffentlichkeit ist mir wichtig. Contact with the public is important to me.

Haben Sie Berufserfahrung?
Have you done any work experience?

Ich habe schon einmal in ... gearbeitet. I've already worked in ...

- einem Büro an office
- einer Fabrik a factory
- einer Tankstelle a filling-station
- einem Supermarkt a supermarket
- eine Woche/ein Monat/ein Jahr. for a week/month/a year.

Letztes Jahr habe ich in einer Grundschule in der Nähe meiner Wohnung gearbeitet. Ich fand die Arbeit sehr anstrengend. Ich habe den Kindern bei ihren Aufgaben geholfen, was mir viel Spaß gemacht hat.
Last year I worked in a primary school near where I live. I found the work very tiring. I helped the children with their work which I enjoyed a lot.

Nach der Schule möchte ich ...
After school I want ...

- eine Lehre/Ausbildung machen. to do an apprenticeship.
- einen Job finden. to find a job.
- studieren. to go to university.
- ein Jahr Auszeit nehmen. to have a gap year.
- einen Ferienjob finden. to find a holiday job.
- eine Teilzeitstelle finden. to find a part-time job.

Mein Ziel ist es, ...
My ambition is ...

- Buchhalter/Buch-halterin zu werden.
  to be an accountant.

- Friseur/Friseurin zu werden.
  to be a hairdresser.

- ins Ausland zu gehen.
  to go abroad.

- in einem Geschäft zu arbeiten.
  to work in a shop.

- Obdachlosen zu helfen.
  to help the homeless.

Ich will Mechaniker werden, weil ich mich für Autos interessiere. I want to become a mechanic because I am interested in cars.

Mein Traum ist es, Arzt zu werden, weil ich anderen helfen will. I dream of working as a doctor because I want to help others.

Ich arbeite ehrenamtlich, um älteren Menschen zu helfen. I do voluntary work to help the elderly.

Ich möchte ehrenamtlich tätig sein, aber ich habe keine Zeit. I want to do voluntary work but I don't have the time.

Wir müssen die Chancengleichheit fördern. We must promote equal opportunities.

Wir müssen die Armut bekämpfen. We must fight poverty.

Meiner Meinung nach sind Tierrechte wichtig. Animal rights are important, in my opinion.

➤ **Was sieht man auf dem Foto?**
What's in the photo?

Da ist eine Frau, die in einer Autowerkstatt arbeitet. Sie repariert ein Auto. Ich glaube, sie ist Mechanikerin. Sie trägt einen Overall und benutzt außerdem einen Laptop. There is a woman who is working in a garage. She is repairing a car. I think she is a mechanic. She's wearing overalls and is using a laptop to help her.

➤ **Was für eine Arbeit würdest du gerne machen und warum?** **What sort of job interests you and why?**

Das weiß ich noch nicht. Erst einmal habe ich vor zu studieren und dann ein Jahr Auszeit zu nehmen, weil ich ein bisschen reisen will. Danach werde ich eine gut bezahlte Stelle suchen. I don't know yet. First of all I intend to go to university and then to have a gap year because I want to travel a little. Afterwards I will look for a well-paid job.

Family

In meiner Familie gibt es ...
In my family there are ...

- meine Eltern. my parents.
- meinen Vater/meine Mutter. my father/my mother.
- meinen Stiefvater/meine Stiefmutter. my stepfather/my stepmother.

Er/Sie hat ... He/She has ...

- Kinder. children.
- einen Sohn/eine Tochter. a son/a daughter.

Ich habe ... I have ...

- einen Bruder/eine Schwester. a brother/a sister.
- einen Halbbruder/eine Halbschwester. a half-brother/a half-sister.
- einen Stiefbruder/eine Stiefschwester. a stepbrother/stepsister.
- einen Zwilling/einen Zwillingsbruder/eine Zwillingsschwester. a twin/twin brother/twin sister.

Ich bin (ein) Einzelkind. I'm an only child.

Ich komme mit ... gut/nicht gut aus. I get on well/I don't get on well with ...

- meinem Cousin/meiner Cousine my cousin.

Er/Sie ist ... He/She is ...

- ledig. single.
- verlobt. engaged.
- verheiratet. married.
- geschieden. divorced.
- tot. dead.

- groß. tall.
- klein. short.
- blond. blond.
- dunkelhaarig. dark-haired.
- sehr nett. really nice.

Er/Sie lebt getrennt von seiner Frau/ihrem Mann. He/She is separated from his wife/her husband.

Was denkst du?
What do you think?

Ich verstehe mich mit meinen Eltern gut, weil sie mir zuhören und mir vertrauen. I get on well with my parents because they listen to me and trust me.

Ich verstehe mich nicht mit meinen Eltern, weil sie streng sind und mich wie ein Kind behandeln. I don't get on with my parents because they are strict and treat me like a child.

Mein Bruder/Meine Schwester nervt mich, wir streiten uns ständig. My brother/My sister annoys me, we argue all the time.

Meine Freunde sind mir wichtig, ich kann mich immer auf sie verlassen. My friends are important for me, I can always count on them.

356

Shopping and eating out

At the restaurant/cafe

Ich möchte einen Tisch für vier Personen reservieren. I'd like to reserve a table for four people.

Was darf es sein? What would you like?

Ich möchte ... I'd like ...

- einen Kaffee. a coffee.
- eine Tasse Tee. a cup of tea.
- einen Orangensaft. an orange juice.

Zahlen, bitte.
The bill, please.

Ich gehe ... einkaufen.
I go shopping (for food) ...

- im Supermarkt.
  at the supermarket.
- im Feinkostgeschäft.
  at the delicatessen.
- im Internet.
  on the Internet.
- beim Lebensmittelhändler.
  at the grocer's.
- in der Konditorei.
  at the cake shop.
- beim Bäcker
  at the baker's.
- beim Metzger/Schlachter.
  at the butcher's.
- auf dem Markt
  at the market.

> ➤ Was sieht man auf dem Foto?
> What's in the photo?

Es ist eine Familie, die gerade Maiskolben, Ananas und Wassermelonen isst. Die Mutter ist auf der linken Seite und der Vater auf der rechten. Zwischen den Eltern sind zwei Kinder. Sie essen im Freien und alle lächeln. It's a family eating corn, pineapple and watermelon. The mother is on the left and the father on the right. Between the parents there are two children. They are eating outside and they are having a very good time.

> ➤ Was hast du letztes Wochenende mit deiner Familie gemacht? What did you do with your family last weekend?

Wir sind in ein italienisches Restaurant gegangen, um den Geburtstag meiner Schwester zu feiern. Es hat sehr gut geschmeckt und die Bedienung war sehr zuvorkommend. Wir hatten viel Spaß. We went to an Italian restaurant to celebrate my sister's birthday. We ate very well and the service was excellent. We had a good laugh.

357

Healthy living

Ich esse zweimal am Tag Obst.
I eat fruit twice a day.

Ich habe Hunger. I'm hungry.

Ich habe Durst. I'm thirsty.

Ich bin müde. I'm tired.

Ich habe Kopfschmerzen. I have a headache.

Ich habe eine Allergie. I have an allergy.

Um gesund zu bleiben, muss man ...
To stay healthy, you have to ...

* sich ausgewogen mit Obst und Gemüse ernähren. eat a balanced diet which includes fruit and vegetables.
* früh aufstehen. get up early.
* früh ins Bett gehen. not go to bed late.
* Sport machen. get exercise.
* zu Fuß gehen. walk.

Was denkst du?
What do you think?

Passivrauchen ist für Nichtraucher sehr gefährlich. Passive smoking is very dangerous for non-smokers.

Alkohol kann zu Gewalttätigkeit führen und ist schlecht für die Leber. Alcohol can lead to violence and is bad for the liver.

Gruppenzwang führt dazu, dass Jugendliche Drogen nehmen. Young people take drugs because of peer pressure.

Es ist gesund. It's healthy.

Du solltest Alkohol/Koffein vermeiden.
You should avoid alcohol/caffeine.

Du solltest nicht rauchen.
You mustn't smoke.

Mein Lieblingssport ist ...
My favourite sport is ...

* Fußball spielen. playing football.
* Tennis spielen. playing tennis.
* Volleyball spielen. playing volleyball.
* Leichtathletik. athletics.
* Mountainbiken. mountain biking.
* Bergsteigen. mountaineering.
* Tauchen. scuba diving.
* Surfen. surfing.
* Rad fahren. cycling.
* Skaten/Skateboarden. skateboarding.
* Eislaufen/Inlineskaten. skating/ice skating/inline skating.

Ich treibe gerne/nicht gerne Sport.
I like/don't like playing sport.

Ich bin/Er/Sie ist ...
I am/He/She is ...

* sportlich. sporty.
* aktiv. active.
* bei guter Gesundheit. in good health.

Ich halte mich gern fit. I like to keep fit.

➤ **Was sieht man auf dem Foto?**
What's in the photo?

Wollen wir in den Park gehen? Shall we go to the park?

Treffen wir uns doch im Fitnesszentrum! Let's meet up at the leisure centre!

Ich würde lieber ins Fußball-Stadion gehen. I'd rather go to the football stadium.

Ich treffe dich dann …
See you …

- im Kino! at the cinema!
- in der Disco! at the disco!
- beim Wettkampf!/ beim Match! at the competition!/at the match!
- im Freizeitzentrum! at the leisure centre!
- auf der Party! at the party!

Es ist eine Gruppe Jugendlicher, die einen Film im Kino ansehen. Sie trinken Softdrinks und essen Popcorn. Es ist wohl ein Horrorfilm, weil sie erschrocken wirken und das Popcorn fallen lassen. It's a group of young people who are watching a film at the cinema. They are drinking fizzy drinks and eating popcorn. It may be a horror film because they look scared and are dropping the popcorn.

➤ **Was für Filme siehst du besonders gerne?**
What kind of films do you prefer?

Ich mag besonders Komödien, weil ich gerne mit meinen Freunden so richtig lache. Ich mag auch Abenteuerfilme, die spannend sind. Aber Science-Fiction-Filme kann ich nicht ausstehen. Ich finde sie langweilig. I prefer comedy films because I like a good laugh with my friends. I also like adventure films which are exciting. However, I can't stand science fiction films which I find boring.

➤ **Erzähl mir von deinem letzten Kinobesuch.** Tell me about your last visit to the cinema.

Vor zwei Wochen war ich mit meiner besten Freundin im Kino. Wir haben einen Liebesfilm gesehen. Wir haben etwas zu essen gekauft, aber es war teuer. Der Film war nicht besonders gut, weil die Handlung nicht so interessant war und die Schauspieler durchschnittlich waren. Two weeks ago, I went to the cinema with my best friend to see a romantic film. We bought something to eat but it was expensive. The film wasn't too good because the plot wasn't interesting and the actors were average.

Meine Lieblingsbeschäftigung ist …
My favourite pastime is …

- mit Freunden ausgehen. going out with friends.
- in die Stadt gehen. going into town.
- einkaufen/shoppen gehen. going shopping.
- in Konzerte gehen. going to concerts.
- lesen. reading.
- Musik hören. listening to music.
- fernsehen. watching TV.
- an einer Spielkonsole spielen. playing on a games console.
- auf Partys gehen. going to parties.

Environment

der Ökotourismus ecotourism

die Umwelt the environment

umweltfreundlich environmentally friendly

der Naturschutz conservation

die Erde retten saving the planet

sich umweltfreundlich verhalten 'going green'

die globale Erderwärmung global warming

die Umweltverschmutzung pollution

recyceln to recycle

Was denkst du?
What do you think?

Wir müssen mehr Fußgängerzonen und Radwege bauen.
We must create more pedestrian zones and cycle lanes.

Wir müssen mehr Bäume pflanzen, um für saubere Luft zu sorgen.
We must plant more trees to make the air cleaner.

Die Supermärkte verwenden zu viel Verpackungen. Supermarkets use too much packaging.

➤ **Was sieht man auf dem Foto?**
What's in the photo?

Man sieht sechs Windkraftanlagen, die Energie aus Wind gewinnen – das ist gut für die Umwelt. Das Foto wurde entweder bei Sonnenauf- oder Sonnenuntergang gemacht. There are six wind turbines which produce energy from the wind. This is good for the environment. The photo was taken either at sunrise or sunset.

➤ **Was hast du in letzter Zeit gemacht, um den Planeten zu schützen?**
What have you done recently to protect the planet?

Ich habe Altglas und Altpapier recycelt, und um Wasser zu sparen, habe ich geduscht, statt zu baden. Letzte Woche bin ich zu Fuß in die Schule gegangen. I have recycled glass and paper and I have taken showers rather than baths to save water. Last week I went to school on foot.

➤ **Was für Umweltprobleme gibt es in deiner Gegend? What are the envoironmental problems in your area?**

Leider lassen die Leute ihren Abfall liegen, und es gibt zu viel Verkehr, so dass die Luft verschmutzt ist. Unfortunately, people drop litter on the ground and there is too much traffic so the air is polluted.

➤ **Was wirst du in Zukunft tun, um die Umwelt zu schützen? What are you going to do in the future to protect the environment?**

Ich werde keine Plastiktüten verwenden, weil sie umweltschädlich sind und Tiere töten können. Ich werde Gartenabfälle kompostieren. I won't use plastic bags because they cause environmental damage and can kill animals. I am going to use garden waste to make compost.

Travel

Ich möchte ...
I'd like ...

- eine einfache Fahrt/eine Rückfahrkarte nach Berlin, bitte. a single/a return to Berlin, please.
- eine Fahrkarte kaufen. to buy a ticket.
- einen Sitzplatz reservieren. to reserve a seat.
- im Fahrplan nachsehen. to check the timetable.

Ich fahre mit ...
I'm going ...

- dem Zug.
  by train.

- dem Motorrad.
  on a motorbike.

- dem (Fahr)Rad.
  by bike.

- dem Auto.
  by car.

- dem Bus.
  by bus.

- dem (Reise)Bus.
  by coach.

- dem Schiff.
  by ship.

- dem Taxi.
  by taxi.

- dem Flugzeug.
  by plane.

Sollen wir uns ... treffen?
Shall we meet ... ?

- am Flughafen at the airport
- am Hafen at the port
- am Bahnhof at the station
- am Busbahnhof at the bus station

Wir müssen die Menschen dazu bringen, ihre Autos stehen zu lassen. We must encourage people to give up their cars.

Es gibt zu viele (Verkehrs)Staus in den Stoßzeiten. There are too many traffic jams at rush hour.

Von welchem Bahnsteig fährt der Zug ab?
What platform does the train leave from?

Wo ist die Bushaltestelle?
Where is the bus stop?

Die U-Bahn-Station ist ganz in der Nähe.
The underground station is close by.

Wie lang ist der Flug? How long is the flight?

Wir sind mit dem (Reise)Bus gefahren.
We travelled by coach.

Ich bin noch nie im Ausland gewesen.
I have never been abroad.

Tourismus ist schlecht für die Umwelt und kann die Kultur eines Landes bedrohen.
Tourism is bad for the environment and can threaten the local culture of a country.

School and home

Mein Lieblingsfach ist ...
My favourite subject is ...

- Kunst.
  art.

- Naturwissenschaften.
  science.

- Deutsch.
  German.

- Erdkunde.
  geography.

- Musik.
  music.

- Sport.
  PE.

- Geschichte.
  history.

- Englisch.
  English.

- Informatik.
  computing.

- Mathematik.
  mathematics.

$$+ 1 \div$$
$$3 - 2$$

Ich gehe zu Fuß zur Schule. I walk to school.

In meiner Klasse sind 25 Schüler. There are 25 pupils in my class.

Eine Unterrichtsstunde dauert 45 Minuten. A lesson lasts 45 minutes.

Mittags esse ich in der Schulkantine. At lunchtime, I have lunch in the canteen.

Wir haben viele Hausaufgaben. We have a lot of homework.

Ich bin in ... gut. I am good at ...

Ich bin in ... nicht sehr gut. I am not very good at ...

➤ **Was sieht man auf dem Foto?**
What's in the photo?

Das Wetter ist gut. Die Szene findet auf einem Fußballplatz statt. Ein Junge, der Torwarthandschuhe trägt, hat den Ball gefangen. It's fine weather. The scene takes place on a football pitch. A boy who is wearing goalkeeper gloves has caught the ball.

➤ **Was ist dein Lieblingsfach und warum?**
What is your favourite subject and why?

Ich mag Englisch sehr, weil ich mich für Sprachen interessiere, und die Lehrerin sehr lustig und freundlich ist. Ich bin ziemlich gut in Englisch. I like English a lot because I'm interested in languages and the teacher is very funny and pleasant. I'm quite good at English.

➤ **Beschreibe einen Schulausflug/ Klassenausflug, an dem du teilgenommen hast.** Talk about a school trip you've taken part in.

Letztes Jahr war ich mit meiner Klasse/ mit meinen Klassenkameraden in Öesterreich. Wir sind mit der Fähre und dem Bus hingefahren, was ich anstrengend und langweilig fand. Wir haben vier Tage in Wien verbracht. Während unseres Aufenthalts haben wir alle berühmten Sehenswürdigkeiten besucht und viel Spaß gehabt. Eines Tages möchte ich wieder hinfahren. Last year, I went to Austria with my classmates. We went there by ferry and coach which I found tiring and boring. We spent four days in Vienna. During our stay we visited all the famous monuments and we had a good time. I'd like to go back one day.

Wohnst du ...
Do you live ...

- im Stadtzentrum? in the city centre?
- in einem Vorort? in the suburbs?
- auf dem Land? in the country?
- am Meer? at the seaside?
- in den Bergen? in the mountains?

Ich wohne im Norden/Süden/Osten/Westen/im Zentrum von ... I live in the north/south/east/west/centre of ...

Es ist eine Industriestadt/eine moderne Stadt/eine Stadt voller Leben. It's an industrial/a modern/a lively town.

Ich wohne auf dem Land/in einem ruhigen Dorf. I live in the country/a quiet village.

Was denkst du?
What do you think?

Mir gefällt mein Haus, weil es nicht weit von den Geschäften liegt, was praktisch ist. I like my house because it is situated near the shops which is practical.

Ich wohne seit fünf Jahren in meinem Haus, aber im Moment teile ich ein Zimmer mit meinem Bruder. Ich hätte gerne ein eigenes Zimmer. I've lived in my house for five years but at the moment I share my room with my brother. I would like my own bedroom.

In meiner Stadt werden viele Konzerte und Veranstaltungen angeboten und man kann immer etwas unternehmen. In my town, there's a lot of concerts and events and there is always something to do.

Ich wohne in ...
I live in ...

- einem Haus. a house.
- einer Wohnung im zweiten Stock. a flat on the second floor.

Meine Wohnung /Mein Haus ist klein/groß/modern/ein Altbau. My flat/house is small/big/modern/old.

Mein Haus/Meine Wohnung hat ...
In my house/flat there is ...

- ein Wohnzimmer. a lounge/a living room.
- ein Schlafzimmer. a bedroom.
- eine Küche. a kitchen.
- eine Toilette. a toilet.
- ein Esszimmer. a dining room.
- ein Badezimmer. a bathroom.
- ein Arbeitszimmer. an office/a study.
- eine Garage. a garage.
- einen Garten. a garden.

363

Holidays and festivals

➤ **Was sieht man auf dem Foto?**
What's in the photo?

Ich mag ... /
Ich mag ... nicht.
I like/don't like ...

- **das Wetter**
  the weather.
- **das Essen**
  the food.
- **die Musik**
  the music.
- **die Kultur**
  the culture.

Die Szene zeigt ein Musikfestival. Links und rechts kann man Zelte sehen und es gibt viele Fahnen/Flaggen in verschiedenen Farben. Leider ist der Himmel grau und es könnte vielleicht zu regnen anfangen. The scene takes place at a music festival. To the left and right, you can see tents and there are a lot of flags in different colours. Unfortunately, the sky is grey and it's perhaps going to rain.

➤ **Warst du schon mal auf einem Musikfestival?** Have you ever been to a music festival?

Nein, ich war noch nie auf einem Festival, aber nächstes Jahr will ich auf eins gehen. Ich muss Geld sparen, weil die Eintrittspreise sehr hoch sind. Wir werden zelten und Spaß haben, auch wenn es regnet. No, I've never been to a festival but next year I hope to go to one. I must save money because the price of tickets is very expensive. We will go camping and have a good time even if it rains.

Was denkst du?
What do you think?

Was für eine Art der Unterkunft ist dir am liebsten und warum? What sort of accommodation do you prefer and why?

Zelten ist nicht so angenehm, wenn es kalt ist. Ich übernachte lieber in einer Ferienwohnung/einem Ferienhaus, weil es billiger ist und man unabhängiger ist. Camping is not pleasant when it's cold. I prefer to stay in a holiday home because it's cheaper than a hotel and you have more freedom.

Im Urlaub kann man neue Freundschaften schließen und neue Orte erkunden. On holiday, you can make new friends and see new places.

Ich würde gerne mit meinen Freunden Urlaub machen, weil es mehr Spaß machen würde. Meine Eltern sind ein bisschen streng. I'd like to go on holiday with my friends because it would be more fun. My parents are a bit strict.

In den Ferien ...
During the holidays ...

- **wohne ich in einem Hotel.**
  I stay in a hotel.
- **wohne ich in einer Jugendherberge.**
  I stay in a youth hostel.
- **wohne ich in einem Ferienhaus.**
  I stay in a holiday home.
- **fahre ich ans Meer.** I stay by the sea.
- **fahre ich in die Berge.** I stay in the mountains.
- **fahre ich aufs Land.** I stay in the country.

Jeden Sommer fahre ich nach Italien. Every summer, I go to Italy.

Nächsten Sommer fahre ich nach Zürich. Next summer, I'll be going to Zurich.

Numbers

NUMBERS

One can be eins, ein or eine in German depending on the context. It's eins for the mathematical number, for example, but if you want to use the indefinite article for a German noun it's either ein or eine depending on the gender of that noun, e.g. ein Buntstift (*MASCULINE*), eine Schere (*FEMININE*) or ein Auto (*NEUTER*).

Ordinal numbers use a full stop after the number, e.g. 3rd is 3., 20th is 20., 101st is 101., etc.

In a decimal number a comma is used, e.g. 1.6 is 1,6.

0	null				
1	eins, ein, eine	1st	1.	erste
2	zwei	2nd	2.	zweite
3	drei	3rd	3.	dritte
4	vier	4th	4.	vierte
5	fünf	5th	5.	fünfte
6	sechs	6th	6.	sechste
7	sieben	7th	7.	siebte
8	acht	8th	8.	achte
9	neun	9th	9.	neunte
10	zehn	10th	10.	zehnte
11	elf	11th	11.	elfte
12	zwölf	12th	12.	zwölfte
13	dreizehn	13th	13.	dreizehnte
14	vierzehn	14th	14.	vierzehnte
15	fünfzehn	15th	15.	fünfzehnte
16	sechzehn	16th	16.	sechzehnte
17	siebzehn	17th	17.	siebzehnte
18	achtzehn	18th	18.	achtzehnte
19	neunzehn	19th	19.	neunzehnte
20	zwanzig	20th	20.	zwanzigste
21	einundzwanzig	21st	21.	einundzwanzigste
22	zweiundzwanzig	22nd	22.	zweiundzwanzigste
30	dreißig	30th	30.	dreißigste
40	vierzig	40th	40.	vierzigste
50	fünfzig	50th	50.	fünfzigste
60	sechzig	60th	60.	sechzigste
70	siebzig	70th	70.	siebzigste
71	einundsiebzig	71st	71.	einundsiebzigste
80	achtzig	80th	80.	achtzigste
81	einundachtzig	81st	81.	einundachtzigste
82	zweiundachtzig	82nd	82.	zweiundachtzigste
90	neunzig	90th	90.	neunzigste
91	einundneunzig	91st	91.	einundneunzigste
92	zweiundneunzig	92nd	92.	zweiundneunzigste
99	neunundneunzig	99th	99.	neunundneunzigste
100	hundert	100th	100.	hundertste
101	hunderteins	101st	101.	hundertunderste
102	hundertzwei	102nd	102.	hundertundzweite
200	zweihundert	200th	200.	zweihundertste
201	zweihunderteins	201st	201.	zweihundertunderste
202	zweihundertzwei	202nd	202.	zweihundertundzweite

For larger numbers, German uses a space or, for sums of money, a full stop instead of a comma, e.g. 1 000 or 12.000. Telephone numbers are grouped differently.

1 000	tausend	1000th	1000.	tausendste
1 001	tausendeins	1001st	1001.	tausenderste
1 002	tausendzwei	1002nd	1002.	tausendzweite
2 000	zweitausend	2000th	2000.	zweitausendste
1 000 000	eine Million	1 000000th	1 000 000.	millionste

365

Time

Months

Januar *(Jänner in Austria)* January
Februar February
März March
April April
Mai May
Juni June
Juli July
August August
September September
Oktober October
November November
Dezember December

Ich habe im Februar Geburtstag.
My birthday is in February.
Sie ist im März gegangen.
She left in March.
Wir kommen am 11. November
an. We're arriving on 11th
November.
Richard wurde am 2. August
geboren. Richard was born on
2nd August.
2010 in 2010
1999 in 1999

Days of the week

Montag Monday
Dienstag Tuesday
Mittwoch Wednesday
Donnerstag Thursday
Freitag Friday
Samstag Saturday
Sonntag Sunday

Seasons

der Frühling spring
der Sommer summer
der Herbst autumn
der Winter winter

Time

Wie spät ist es?
What time is it?
Es ist ein Uhr morgens.
It is one o'clock in the morning.
Es ist 13 Uhr.
It is one o'clock in the afternoon.
Es ist halb fünf.
It's half past four.
Es ist Viertel nach sechs.
It's quarter past six.
Es ist Viertel vor sechs.
It's quarter to six.
Es ist zehn nach neun.
It's ten past nine.
Es ist zehn vor neun.
It's ten to nine.
Es ist 12 Uhr mittags.
It's midday.
Es ist Mitternacht.
It's midnight.
Es ist 19 Uhr.
It's 7p.m. (19.00).
Es ist dreizehn Uhr fünfzehn.
It's 1.15p.m. (13.15).

ein Uhr
one o'clock

halb fünf
half past four

Viertel nach sechs
quarter past six

Viertel vor sechs
quarter to six

zehn nach neun
ten past nine

zehn vor neun
ten to nine

7 Uhr abends/
19 Uhr
7p.m. (19.00)

1 Uhr 15 nachmittags
(13.15 Uhr)
1.15p.m. (13.15)

12 Uhr mittags
midday

Mitternacht
midnight

Verb tables

In this section you will find a list of common German verbs and verb forms and the English translations. The important verbs haben and sein are given at the beginning. They are followed by the regular German verbs arbeiten and machen and then the forms for all the main irregular verbs in alphabetical order: bleiben, dürfen, essen, fahren, geben, gehen, kommen, können, mögen, müssen, nehmen, sehen, sollen, sprechen, trinken, werden, wissen and wollen. The forms for a reflexive verb sich waschen are given after the irregular verbs.

There is also a list of the main forms of other irregular verbs. Note that the forms for separable verbs such as aufstehen are not given as they can be looked up under the base form, for example, stehen.

Guide to the verb tables
Personal pronouns

ich = I	wir = we
du = you *(singular)*	ihr = you *(plural)*
er/sie/es = he/she/it	Sie = you *(polite form/singular and plural)*
	sie = they

Perfect and Imperfect tense
In German, both these tenses are past tenses. The Perfect tense is usually used in spoken German or informal letters. The Imperfect tense is usually used when writing formal letters or stories. When you are translating sentences with 'already' or 'yet' in them (German schon), the English Perfect tense should be translated with the German Perfect tense, not the Imperfect. For example:

I saw the film yesterday.	Ich **habe** den Film gestern **gesehen** *or* Ich **sah** den Film gestern.
I have seen the film <u>already</u>.	Ich **habe** den Film <u>schon</u> **gesehen**.

Translation of Perfect and Imperfect tense
Both German past tenses can sometimes be translated into English with the 'I was doing' form of the verb. For example:

Wir spielten Tischtennis, als er ankam./ Wir haben Tischtennis gespielt, als er ankam.	We were playing table tennis when he arrived.

Imperative
The Imperative form does not make sense with all verbs. Therefore it has only been given where it makes sense. For example:

Frag!	Ask!	*(to one friend)*
Fragen wir!	Let's ask!	*(to yourself and others)*
Fragt!	Ask!	*(to two or more friends)*
Fragen Sie!	Ask!	*(polite form)*

haben
to have

Past participle

gehabt — had

Imperfect

ich hatte	I had
du hattest	you had
er/sie/es hatte	he/she/it had
wir hatten	we had
ihr hattet	you had
Sie/sie hatten	you/they had

Present

ich habe	I have
du hast	you have
er/sie/es hat	he/she/it has
wir haben	we have
ihr habt	you have
Sie/sie haben	you/they have

Imperfect subjunctive

ich hätte*	I would have
du hättest	you would have
er/sie/es hätte	he/she/it would have
wir hätten	we would have
ihr hättet	you would have
Sie/sie hätten	you/they would have

*'Ich hätte' *can also be translated as 'I had'* e.g. Wenn ich viel Geld hätte ... *If I had lots of money ...*

Perfect

ich habe gehabt	I had
du hast gehabt	you had
er/sie/es hat gehabt	he/she/it had
wir haben gehabt	we had
ihr habt gehabt	you had
Sie/sie haben gehabt	you/they had

Conditional

ich würde haben	I would have
du würdest haben	you would have
er/sie/es würde haben	he/she/it would have
wir würden haben	we would have
ihr würdet haben	you would have
Sie/sie würden haben	you/they would have

Future

ich werde haben	I will have
du wirst haben	you will have
er/sie/es wird haben	he/she/it will have
wir werden haben	we will have
ihr werdet haben	you will have
Sie/sie werden haben	you/they will have

Imperative

Hab/Habe!	Have!
Haben wir!	Let's have!
Habt!	Have!
Haben Sie!	Have!

sein
to be

Past participle

gewesen   been

Imperfect

ich war	I was
du warst	you were
er/sie/es war	he/she/it was
wir waren	we were
ihr wart	you were
Sie/sie waren	you/they were

Present

ich bin	I am
du bist	you are
er/sie/es ist	he/she/it is
wir sind	we are
ihr seid	you are
Sie/sie sind	you/they are

Imperfect subjunctive

ich wäre*	I would be
du wärst/wärest	you would be
er/sie/es wäre	he/she/it would be
wir wären	we would be
ihr wärt/wäret	you would be
Sie/sie wären	you/they would be

*'Ich wäre' can also be translated as 'I were'
e.g. Wenn ich du wäre ... If I were you ...

Perfect

ich bin gewesen	I was
du bist gewesen	you were
er/sie/es ist gewesen	he/she/it was
wir sind gewesen	we were
ihr seid gewesen	you were
Sie/sie sind gewesen	you/they were

Conditional

ich würde sein	I would be
du würdest sein	you would be
er/sie/es würde sein	he/she/it would be
wir würden sein	we would be
ihr würdet sein	you would be
Sie/sie würden sein	you/they would be

Future

ich werde sein	I will be
du wirst sein	you will be
er/sie/es wird sein	he/she/it will be
wir werden sein	we will be
ihr werdet sein	you will be
Sie/sie werden sein	you/they will be

Imperative

Sei!	Be!
Seien wir!	Let's be!
Seid!	Be!
Seien Sie!	Be!

arbeiten
to work

Past participle
gearbeitet worked

Present
ich arbeite	I work
du arbeitest	you work
er/sie/es arbeitet	he/she/it works
wir arbeiten	we work
ihr arbeitet	you work
Sie/sie arbeiten	you/they work

Imperfect
ich arbeitete	I worked
du arbeitetest	you worked
er/sie/es arbeitete	he/she/it worked
wir arbeiteten	we worked
ihr arbeitetet	you worked
Sie/sie arbeiteten	you/they worked

Perfect
ich habe gearbeitet	I worked
du hast gearbeitet	you worked
er/sie/es hat gearbeitet	he/she/it worked
wir haben gearbeitet	we worked
ihr habt gearbeitet	you worked
Sie/sie haben gearbeitet	you/they worked

Conditional
ich würde arbeiten	I would work
du würdest arbeiten	you would work
er/sie/es würde arbeiten	he/she/it would work
wir würden arbeiten	we would work
ihr würdet arbeiten	you would work
Sie/sie würden arbeiten	you/they would work

Future
ich werde arbeiten	I will work
du wirst arbeiten	you will work
er/sie/es wird arbeiten	he/she/it will work
wir werden arbeiten	we will work
ihr werdet arbeiten	you will work
Sie/sie werden arbeiten	you/they will work

Imperative
Arbeite!	Work!
Arbeiten wir!	Let's work!
Arbeitet!	Work!
Arbeiten Sie!	Work!

machen
to do *or* to make

Past participle

gemacht — done/made

Present

ich mache	I do/make
du machst	you do/make
er/sie/es macht	he/she/it does/makes
wir machen	we do/make
ihr macht	you do/make
Sie/sie machen	you/they do/make

Imperfect

ich machte	I did/made
du machtest	you did/made
er/sie/es machte	he/she/it did/made
wir machten	we did/made
ihr machtet	you did/made
Sie/sie machten	you/they did/made

Perfect

ich habe gemacht	I did/made
du hast gemacht	you did/made
er/sie/es hat gemacht	he/she/it did/made
wir haben gemacht	we did/made
ihr habt gemacht	you did/made
Sie/sie haben gemacht	you/they did/made

Conditional

ich würde machen	I would do/make
du würdest machen	you would do/make
er/sie/es würde machen	he/she/it would do/make
wir würden machen	we would do/make
ihr würdet machen	you would do/make
Sie/sie würden machen	you/they would do/make

Future

ich werde machen	I will do/make
du wirst machen	you will do/make
er/sie/es wird machen	he/she/it will do/make
wir werden machen	we will do/make
ihr werdet machen	you will do/make
Sie/sie werden machen	you/they will do/make

Imperative

Mach!	Do/Make!
Machen wir!	Let's do/make!
Macht!	Do/Make!
Machen Sie!	Do/Make!

bleiben
to stay

Past participle
geblieben   stayed

Present
ich bleibe	I stay
du bleibst	you stay
er/sie/es bleibt	he/she/it stays
wir bleiben	we stay
ihr bleibt	you stay
Sie/sie bleiben	you/they stay

Imperfect
ich blieb	I stayed
du bliebst	you stayed
er/sie/es blieb	he/she/it stayed
wir blieben	we stayed
ihr bliebt	you stayed
Sie/sie blieben	you/they stayed

Perfect
ich bin geblieben	I stayed
du bist geblieben	you stayed
er/sie/es ist geblieben	he/she/it stayed
wir sind geblieben	we stayed
ihr seid geblieben	you stayed
Sie/sie sind geblieben	you/they stayed

Conditional
ich würde bleiben	I would stay
du würdest bleiben	you would stay
er/sie/es würde bleiben	he/she/it would stay
wir würden bleiben	we would stay
ihr würdet bleiben	you would stay
Sie/sie würden bleiben	you/they would stay

Future
ich werde bleiben	I will stay
du wirst bleiben	you will stay
er/sie/es wird bleiben	he/she/it will stay
wir werden bleiben	we will stay
ihr werdet bleiben	you will stay
Sie/sie werden bleiben	you/they will stay

Imperative
Bleib!	Stay!
Bleiben wir!	Let's stay!
Bleibt!	Stay!
Bleiben Sie!	Stay!

dürfen
to be allowed

Past participle

gedurft   allowed

Present

ich darf	I am allowed
du darfst	you are allowed
er/sie/es darf	he/she/it is allowed
wir dürfen	we are allowed
ihr dürft	you are allowed
Sie/sie dürfen	you/they are allowed

Imperfect

ich durfte	I was allowed
du durftest	you were allowed
er/sie/es durfte	he/she/it was allowed
wir durften	we were allowed
ihr durftet	you were allowed
Sie/sie durften	you/they were allowed

Perfect

ich habe gedurft	I was allowed
du hast gedurft	you were allowed
er/sie/es hat gedurft	he/she/it was allowed
wir haben gedurft	we were allowed
ihr habt gedurft	you were allowed
Sie/sie haben gedurft	you/they were allowed

Conditional

ich würde dürfen	I would be allowed
du würdest dürfen	you would be allowed
er/sie/es würde dürfen	he/she/it would be allowed
wir würden dürfen	we would be allowed
ihr würdet dürfen	you would be allowed
Sie/sie würden dürfen	you/they would be allowed

Future

ich werde dürfen	I will be allowed
du wirst dürfen	you will be allowed
er/sie/es wird dürfen	he/she/it will be allowed
wir werden dürfen	we will be allowed
ihr werdet dürfen	you will be allowed
Sie/sie werden dürfen	you/they will be allowed

essen
to eat

Past participle

gegessen   eaten

Present

ich esse	I eat
du isst	you eat
er/sie/es isst	he/she/it eats
wir essen	we eat
ihr esst	you eat
Sie/sie essen	you/they eat

Imperfect

ich aß	I ate
du aßest	you ate
er/sie/es aß	he/she/it ate
wir aßen	we ate
ihr aßt	you ate
Sie/sie aßen	you/they ate

Perfect

ich habe gegessen	I ate
du hast gegessen	you ate
er/sie/es hat gegessen	he/she/it ate
wir haben gegessen	we ate
ihr habt gegessen	you ate
Sie/sie haben gegessen	you/they ate

Conditional

ich würde essen	I would eat
du würdest essen	you would eat
er/sie/es würde essen	he/she/it would eat
wir würden essen	we would eat
ihr würdet essen	you would eat
Sie/sie würden essen	you/they would eat

Future

ich werde essen	I will eat
du wirst essen	you will eat
er/sie/es wird essen	he/she/it will eat
wir werden essen	we will eat
ihr werdet essen	you will eat
Sie/sie werden essen	you/they will eat

Imperative

Iss!	Eat!
Essen wir!	Let's eat!
Esst!	Eat!
Essen Sie!	Eat!

fahren
to drive *or* to go

Past participle

gefahren   driven/gone

Present

ich fahre	I drive/go
du fährst	you drive/go
er/sie/es fährt	he/she/it drives/goes
wir fahren	we drive/go
ihr fahrt	you drive/go
Sie/sie fahren	you/they drive/go

Imperfect

ich fuhr	I drove/went
du fuhrst	you drove/went
er/sie/es fuhr	he/she/it drove/went
wir fuhren	we drove/went
ihr fuhrt	you drove/went
Sie/sie fuhren	you/they drove/went

Perfect

ich bin gefahren	I drove/went
du bist gefahren	you drove/went
er/sie/es ist gefahren	he/she/it drove/went
wir sind gefahren	we drove/went
ihr seid gefahren	you drove/went
Sie/sie sind gefahren	you/they drove/went

Conditional

ich würde fahren	I would drive/go
du würdest fahren	you would drive/go
er/sie/es würde fahren	he/she/it would drive/go
wir würden fahren	we would drive/go
ihr würdet fahren	you would drive/go
Sie/sie würden fahren	you/they would drive/go

Future

ich werde fahren	I will drive/go
du wirst fahren	you will drive/go
er/sie/es wird fahren	he/she/it will drive/go
wir werden fahren	we will drive/go
ihr werdet fahren	you will drive/go
Sie/sie werden fahren	you/they will drive/go

Imperative

Fahr!	Drive/Go!
Fahren wir!	Let's drive/go!
Fahrt!	Drive/Go!
Fahren Sie!	Drive/Go!

geben
to give

Past participle
gegeben   given

Present
ich gebe	I give
du gibst	you give
er/sie/es gibt	he/she/it gives
wir geben	we give
ihr gebt	you give
Sie/sie geben	you/they give

Imperfect
ich gab	I gave
du gabst	you gave
er/sie/es gab	he/she/it gave
wir gaben	we gave
ihr gabt	you gave
Sie/sie gaben	you/they gave

Perfect
ich habe gegeben	I gave
du hast gegeben	you gave
er/sie/es hat gegeben	he/she/it gave
wir haben gegeben	we gave
ihr habt gegeben	you gave
Sie/sie haben gegeben	you/they gave

Conditional
ich würde geben	I would give
du würdest geben	you would give
er/sie/es würde geben	he/she/it would give
wir würden geben	we would give
ihr würdet geben	you would give
Sie/sie würden geben	you/they would give

Future
ich werde geben	I will give
du wirst geben	you will give
er/sie/es wird geben	he/she/it will give
wir werden geben	we will give
ihr werdet geben	you will give
Sie/sie werden geben	you/they will give

Imperative
Gib!	Give!
Geben wir!	Let's give!
Gebt!	Give!
Geben Sie!	Give!

gehen
to go *or* to leave

Past participle
gegangen   gone/went

Present
ich gehe	I go/leave
du gehst	you go/leave
er/sie/es geht	he/she/it goes/leaves
wir gehen	we go/leave
ihr geht	you go/leave
Sie/sie gehen	you/they go/leave

Imperfect
ich ging	I went/left
du gingst	you went/left
er/sie/es ging	he/she/it went/left
wir gingen	we went/left
ihr gingt	you went/left
Sie/sie gingen	you/they went/left

Perfect
ich bin gegangen	I went/left
du bist gegangen	you went/left
er/sie/es ist gegangen	he/she/it went/left
wir sind gegangen	we went/left
ihr seid gegangen	you went/left
Sie/sie sind gegangen	you/they went/left

Conditional
ich würde gehen	I would go/leave
du würdest gehen	you would go/leave
er/sie/es würde gehen	he/she/it would go/leave
wir würden gehen	we would go/leave
ihr würdet gehen	you would go/leave
Sie/sie würden gehen	you/they would go/leave

Future
ich werde gehen	I will go/leave
du wirst gehen	you will go/leave
er/sie/es wird gehen	he/she/it will go/leave
wir werden gehen	we will go/leave
ihr werdet gehen	you will go/leave
Sie/sie werden gehen	you/they will go/leave

Imperative
Geh!	Go/Leave!
Gehen wir!	Let's go/leave!
Geht!	Go/Leave!
Gehen Sie!	Go/Leave!

kommen
to come

Past participle
gekommen   came

Present
ich komme	I come
du kommst	you come
er/sie/es kommt	he/she/it comes
wir kommen	we come
ihr kommt	you come
Sie/sie kommen	you/they come

Imperfect
ich kam	I came
du kamst	you came
er/sie/es kam	he/she/it came
wir kamen	we came
ihr kamt	you came
Sie/sie kamen	you/they came

Perfect
ich bin gekommen	I came
du bist gekommen	you came
er/sie/es ist gekommen	he/she/it came
wir sind gekommen	we came
ihr seid gekommen	you came
Sie/sie sind gekommen	you/they came

Conditional
ich würde kommen	I would come
du würdest kommen	you would come
er/sie/es würde kommen	he/she/it would come
wir würden kommen	we would come
ihr würdet kommen	you would come
Sie/sie würden kommen	you/they would come

Future
ich werde kommen	I will come
du wirst kommen	you will come
er/sie/es wird kommen	he/she/it will come
wir werden kommen	we will come
ihr werdet kommen	you will come
Sie/sie werden kommen	you/they will come

Imperative
Komm!	Come!
Kommen wir!	Let's come!
Kommt!	Come!
Kommen Sie!	Come!

können
can *or* to be able to

Past participle
gekonnt	could/been able to
können	could/been able to

Present
ich kann	I can/am able to
du kannst	you can/are able to
er/sie/es kann	he/she/it can/is able to
wir können	we can/are able to
ihr könnt	you can/are able to
Sie/sie können	you/they can/are able to

Imperfect
ich konnte	I could/was able to
du konntest	you could/were able to
er/sie/es konnte	he/she/it could/was able to
wir konnten	we could/were able to
ihr konntet	you could/were able to
Sie/sie konnten	you/they could/were able to

Perfect
ich habe gekonnt	I could/was able to
du hast gekonnt	you could/were able to
er/sie/es hat gekonnt	he/she/it could/was able to
wir haben gekonnt	we could/were able to
ihr habt gekonnt	you could/were able to
Sie/sie haben gekonnt	you/they could/were able to

Imperfect subjunctive
ich könnte	I could/would be able to
du könntest	you could/would be able to
er/sie/es könnte	he/she/it could/would be able to
wir könnten	we could/would be able to
ihr könntet	you could/would be able to
Sie/sie könnten	you/they could/would be able to

Future
ich werde können	I will be able to
du wirst können	you will be able to
er/sie/es wird können	he/she/it will be able to
wir werden können	we will be able to
ihr werdet können	you will be able to
Sie/sie werden können	you/they will be able to

Conditional
ich würde können	I could/would be able to
du würdest können	you could/would be able to
er/sie/es würde können	he/she/it could/would be able to
wir würden können	you could/would be able to
ihr würdet können	we could/would be able to
Sie/sie würden können	you/they could/would be able to

mögen
to like

Past participle

gemocht · liked

Present

ich mag	I like
du magst	you like
er/sie/es mag	he/she/it likes
wir mögen	we like
ihr mögt	you like
Sie/sie mögen	you/they like

Imperfect

ich mochte	I liked
du mochtest	you liked
er/sie/es mochte	he/she/it liked
wir mochten	we liked
ihr mochtet	you liked
Sie/sie mochten	you/they liked

Perfect

ich habe gemocht	I liked
du hast gemocht	you liked
er/sie/es hat gemocht	he/she/it liked
wir haben gemocht	we liked
ihr habt gemocht	you liked
Sie/sie haben gemocht	you/they liked

Imperfect subjunctive

ich möchte	I would like
du möchtest	you would like
er/sie/es möchte	he/she/it would like
wir möchten	we would like
ihr möchtet	you would like
Sie/sie möchten	you/they would like

Future

ich werde mögen	I will like
du wirst mögen	you will like
er/sie/es wird mögen	he/she/it will like
wir werden mögen	we will like
ihr werdet mögen	you will like
Sie/sie werden mögen	you/they will like

Conditional

ich würde mögen	I would like
du würdest mögen	you would like
er/sie/es würde mögen	he/she/it would like
wir würden mögen	we would like
ihr würdet mögen	you would like
Sie/sie würden mögen	you/they would like

müssen
must *or* to have to

Past participle
gemusst   had
müssen   had

Present
ich muss	I must/have to
du musst	you must/have to
er/sie/es muss	he/she/it must/ has to
wir müssen	we must/have to
ihr müsst	you must/have to
Sie/sie müssen	you/they must/ have to

Imperfect
ich musste	I had to
du musstest	you had to
er/sie/es musste	he/she/it had to
wir mussten	we had to
ihr musstet	you had to
Sie/sie mussten	you/they had to

Perfect
ich habe gemusst	I had to
du hast gemusst	you had to
er/sie/es hat gemusst	he/she/it had to
wir haben gemusst	we had to
ihr habt gemusst	you had to
Sie/sie haben gemusst	you/they had to

Conditional
ich würde müssen	I would have to
du würdest müssen	you would have to
er/sie/es würde müssen	he/she/it would have to
wir würden müssen	we would have to
ihr würdet müssen	you would have to
Sie/sie würden müssen	you/they would have to

Future
ich werde müssen	I will have to
du wirst müssen	you will have to
er/sie/es wird müssen	he/she/it will have to
wir werden müssen	we will have to
ihr werdet müssen	you will have to
Sie/sie werden müssen	you/they will have to

nehmen
to take

Past participle

genommen   taken

Present

ich nehme	I take
du nimmst	you take
er/sie/es nimmt	he/she/it takes
wir nehmen	we take
ihr nehmt	you take
Sie/sie nehmen	you/they take

Imperfect

ich nahm	I took
du nahmst	you took
er/sie/es nahm	he/she/it took
wir nahmen	we took
ihr nahmt	you took
Sie/sie nahmen	you/they took

Perfect

ich habe genommen	I took
du hast genommen	you took
er/sie/es hat genommen	he/she/it took
wir haben genommen	we took
ihr habt genommen	you took
Sie/sie haben genommen	you/they took

Conditional

ich würde nehmen	I would take
du würdest nehmen	you would take
er/sie/es würde nehmen	he/she/it would take
wir würden nehmen	we would take
ihr würdet nehmen	you would take
Sie/sie würden nehmen	you/they would take

Future

ich werde nehmen	I will take
du wirst nehmen	you will take
er/sie/es wird nehmen	he/she/it will take
wir werden nehmen	we will take
ihr werdet nehmen	you will take
Sie/sie werden nehmen	you/they will take

Imperative

Nimm!	Take!
Nehmen wir!	Let's take!
Nehmt!	Take!
Nehmen Sie!	Take!

sehen
to see

Past participle
gesehen   seen

Present
ich sehe	I see
du siehst	you see
er/sie/es sieht	he/she/it sees
wir sehen	we see
ihr seht	you see
Sie/sie sehen	you/they see

Imperfect
ich sah	I saw
du sahst	you saw
er/sie/es sah	he/she/it saw
wir sahen	we saw
ihr saht	you saw
Sie/sie sahen	you/they saw

Perfect
ich habe gesehen	I saw
du hast gesehen	you saw
er/sie/es hat gesehen	he/she/it saw
wir haben gesehen	we saw
ihr habt gesehen	you saw
Sie/sie haben gesehen	you/they saw

Conditional
ich würde sehen	I would see
du würdest sehen	you would see
er/sie/es würde sehen	he/she/it would see
wir würden sehen	we would see
ihr würdet sehen	you would see
Sie/sie würden sehen	you/they would see

Future
ich werde sehen	I will see
du wirst sehen	you will see
er/sie/es wird sehen	he/she/it will see
wir werden sehen	we will see
ihr werdet sehen	you will see
Sie/sie werden sehen	you/they will see

Imperative
Sieh!	See!
Sehen wir!	Let's see!
Seht!	See!
Sehen Sie!	See!

sollen
should *or* to have to

Past participle

gesollt · should/have to

sollen · should/have to

Present

ich soll	I should/have to
du sollst	you should/have to
er/sie/es soll	he/she/it should/have to
wir sollen	we should/have to
ihr sollt	you should/have to
Sie/sie sollen	you/they should/have to

Imperfect

ich sollte	I had to
du solltest	you had to
er/sie/es sollte	he/she/it had to
wir sollten	we had to
ihr solltet	you had to
Sie/sie sollten	you/they had to

Perfect

ich habe gesollt	I had to
du hast gesollt	you had to
er/sie/es hat gesollt	he/she/it had to
wir haben gesollt	we had to
ihr habt gesollt	you had to
Sie/sie haben gesollt	you/they had to

Imperfect subjunctive

ich sollte	I should
du solltest	you should
er/sie/es sollte	he/she/it should
wir sollten	we should
ihr solltet	you should
Sie/sie sollten	you/they should

Future

ich werde sollen	I will have to
du wirst sollen	you will have to
er/sie/es wird sollen	he/she/it will have to
wir werden sollen	we will have to
ihr werdet sollen	you will have to
Sie/sie werden sollen	you/they will have to

Conditional

ich würde sollen	I would have to
du würdest sollen	you would have to
er/sie/es würde sollen	he/she/it would have to
wir würden sollen	we would have to
ihr würdet sollen	you would have to
Sie/sie würden sollen	you/they would have to

sprechen
to speak

Past participle

gesprochen   spoken

Present

ich spreche	I speak
du sprichst	you speak
er/sie/es spricht	he/she/it speaks
wir sprechen	we speak
ihr sprecht	you speak
Sie/sie sprechen	you/they speak

Imperfect

ich sprach	I spoke
du sprachst	you spoke
er/sie/es sprach	he/she/it spoke
wir sprachen	we spoke
ihr spracht	you spoke
Sie/sie sprachen	you/they spoke

Perfect

ich habe gesprochen	I spoke
du hast gesprochen	you spoke
er/sie/es hat gesprochen	he/she/it spoke
wir haben gesprochen	we spoke
ihr habt gesprochen	you spoke
Sie/sie haben gesprochen	you/they spoke

Conditional

ich würde sprechen	I would speak
du würdest sprechen	you would speak
er/sie/es würde sprechen	he/she/it would speak
wir würden sprechen	we would speak
ihr würdet sprechen	you would speak
Sie/sie würden sprechen	you/they would speak

Future

ich werde sprechen	I will speak
du wirst sprechen	you will speak
er/sie/es wird sprechen	he/she/it will speak
wir werden sprechen	we will speak
ihr werdet sprechen	you will speak
Sie/sie werden sprechen	you/they will speak

Imperative

Sprich!	Speak!
Sprechen wir!	Let's speak!
Sprecht!	Speak!
Sprechen Sie!	Speak!

trinken
to drink

Past participle
getrunken   drunk

Present
ich trinke	I drink
du trinkst	you drink
er/sie/es trinkt	he/she/it drinks
wir trinken	we drink
ihr trinkt	you drink
Sie/sie trinken	you/they drink

Imperfect
ich trank	I drank
du trankst	you drank
er/sie/es trank	he/she/it drank
wir tranken	we drank
ihr trankt	you drank
Sie/sie tranken	you/they drank

Perfect
ich habe getrunken	I drank
du hast getrunken	you drank
er/sie/es hat getrunken	he/she/it drank
wir haben getrunken	we drank
ihr habt getrunken	you drank
Sie/sie haben getrunken	you/they drank

Conditional
ich würde trinken	I would drink
du würdest trinken	you would drink
er/sie/es würde trinken	he/she/it would drink
wir würden trinken	we would drink
ihr würdet trinken	you would drink
Sie/sie würden trinken	you/they would drink

Future
ich werde trinken	I will drink
du wirst trinken	you will drink
er/sie/es wird trinken	he/she/it will drink
wir werden trinken	we will drink
ihr werdet trinken	you will drink
Sie/sie werden trinken	you/they will drink

Imperative
Trink!	Drink!
Trinken wir!	Let's drink!
Trinkt!	Drink!
Trinken Sie!	Drink!

werden
to become

Past participle

geworden   become

Present

ich werde	I become
du wirst	you become
er/sie/es wird	he/she/it becomes
wir werden	we become
ihr werdet	you become
Sie/sie werden	you/they become

Imperfect

ich wurde	I became
du wurdest	you became
er/sie/es wurde	he/she/it became
wir wurden	we became
ihr wurdet	you became
Sie/sie wurden	you/they became

Perfect

ich bin geworden	I became
du bist geworden	you became
er/sie/es ist geworden	he/she/it became
wir sind geworden	we became
ihr seid geworden	you became
Sie/sie sind geworden	you/they became

Conditional

ich würde werden	I would become
du würdest werden	you would become
er/sie/es würde werden	he/she/it would become
wir würden werden	we would become
ihr würdet werden	you would become
Sie/sie würden werden	you/they would become

Future

ich werde werden	I will become
du wirst werden	you will become
er/sie/es wird werden	he/she/it will become
wir werden werden	we will become
ihr werdet werden	you will become
Sie/sie werden werden	you/they will become

wissen
to know

Past participle
gewusst   known

Present
ich weiß	I know
du weißt	you know
er/sie/es weiß	he/she/it knows
wir wissen	we know
ihr wisst	you know
Sie/sie wissen	you/they know

Imperfect
ich wusste	I knew
du wusstest	you knew
er/sie/es wusste	he/she/it knew
wir wussten	we knew
ihr wusstet	you knew
Sie/sie wussten	you/they knew

Perfect
ich habe gewusst	I knew
du hast gewusst	you knew
er/sie/es hat gewusst	he/she/it knew
wir haben gewusst	we knew
ihr habt gewusst	you knew
Sie/sie haben gewusst	you/they knew

Conditional
ich würde wissen	I would know
du würdest wissen	you would know
er/sie/es würde wissen	he/she/it would know
wir würden wissen	we would know
ihr würdet wissen	you would know
Sie/sie würden wissen	you/they would know

Future
ich werde wissen	I will know
du wirst wissen	you will know
er/sie/es wird wissen	he/she/it will know
wir werden wissen	we will know
ihr werdet wissen	you will know
Sie/sie werden wissen	they will know

wollen
to want

Past participle
gewollt   wanted

Present
ich will	I want
du willst	you want
er/sie/es will	he/she/it wants
wir wollen	we want
ihr wollt	you want
Sie/sie wollen	you/they want

Imperfect
ich wollte	I wanted
du wolltest	you wanted
er/sie/es wollte	he/she/it wanted
wir wollten	we wanted
ihr wolltet	you wanted
Sie/sie wollten	you/they wanted

Perfect
ich habe gewollt	I wanted
du hast gewollt	you wanted
er/sie/es hat gewollt	he/she/it wanted
wir haben gewollt	we wanted
ihr habt gewollt	you wanted
Sie/sie haben gewollt	you/they wanted

Conditional
ich würde wollen	I would want
du würdest wollen	you would want
er/sie/es würde wollen	he/she/it would want
wir würden wollen	we would want
ihr würdet wollen	you would want
Sie/sie würden wollen	you/they would want

Future
ich werde wollen	I will want
du wirst wollen	you will want
er/sie/es wird wollen	he/she/it will want
wir werden wollen	we will want
ihr werdet wollen	you will want
Sie/sie werden wollen	you/they will want

sich waschen
to wash (yourself)

Past participle

gewaschen	washed

Present

ich wasche mich	I wash
du wäschst dich	you wash
er/sie/es wäscht sich	he/she/it washes
wir waschen uns	we wash
ihr wascht euch	you wash
Sie/sie waschen sich	you/they wash

Imperfect

ich wusch mich	I washed
du wuschst dich	you washed
er/sie/es wusch sich	he/she/it washed
wir wuschen uns	we washed
ihr wuscht euch	you washed
Sie/sie wuschen sich	you/they washed

Perfect

ich habe mich gewaschen	I washed
du hast dich gewaschen	you washed
er/sie/es hat sich gewaschen	he/she/it washed
wir haben uns gewaschen	we washed
ihr habt euch gewaschen	you washed
Sie/sie haben sich gewaschen	you/they washed

Conditional

ich würde mich waschen	I would wash
du würdest dich waschen	you would wash
er/sie/es würde sich waschen	he/she/it would wash
wir würden uns waschen	we would wash
ihr würdet euch waschen	you would wash
Sie/sie würden sich waschen	you/they would wash

Future

ich werde mich waschen	I will wash
du wirst dich waschen	you will wash
er/sie/es wird sich waschen	he/she/it will wash
wir werden uns waschen	we will wash
ihr werdet euch waschen	you will wash
Sie/sie werden sich waschen	you/they will wash

Imperative

Wasch dich!	Wash!
Waschen wir uns!	Let's wash!
Wascht euch!	Wash!
Waschen Sie sich!	Wash!

Infinitive	Present ich, du, er/sie/es	Imperfect er/sie/es	Perfect er/sie/es
befehlen	befehle, befiehlst, befiehlt	befahl	hat befohlen
beginnen	beginne, beginnst, beginnt	begann	hat begonnen
beißen	beiße, beißt, beißt	biss	hat gebissen
bekommen	bekomme, bekommst, bekommt	bekam	hat bekommen
bergen	berge, birgst, birgt	barg	hat geborgen
besitzen	besitze, besitzt, besitzt	besaß	hat besessen
betrügen	betrüge, betrügst, betrügt	betrog	hat betrogen
biegen	biege, biegst, biegt	bog	hat *or* ist gebogen
bieten	biete, bietest, bietet	bot	hat geboten
binden	binde, bindest, bindet	band	hat gebunden
bitten	bitte, bittest, bittet	bat	hat gebeten
blasen	blase, bläst, bläst	blies	hat geblasen
bleiben	bleibe, bleibst, bleibt	blieb	ist geblieben
braten	brate, brätst, brät	briet	hat gebraten
brechen	breche, brichst, bricht	brach	hat *or* ist gebrochen
brennen	brenne, brennst, brennt	brannte	hat gebrannt
bringen	bringe, bringst, bringt	brachte	hat gebracht
denken	denke, denkst, denkt	dachte	hat gedacht
dürfen	darf, darfst, darf	durfte	hat gedurft
einladen	lade ein, lädst ein, lädt ein	lud ein	hat eingeladen
empfangen	empfange, empfängst, empfängt	empfing	hat empfangen
empfehlen	empfehle, empfiehlst, empfiehlt	empfahl	hat empfohlen
entscheiden	entscheide, entscheidest, entscheidet	entschied	hat entschieden
erfahren	erfahre, erfährst, erfährt	erfuhr	hat erfahren
erfinden	erfinde, erfindest, erfindet	erfand	hat erfunden
erschrecken	erschrecke, erschrickst, erschrickt	erschrak	ist erschrocken
ertrinken	ertrinke, ertrinkst, ertrinkt	ertrank	ist ertrunken
essen	esse, isst, isst	aß	hat gegessen
fahren	fahre, fährst, fährt	fuhr	ist *or* hat gefahren
fallen	falle, fällst, fällt	fiel	ist gefallen
fangen	fange, fängst, fängt	fing	hat gefangen
fechten	fechte, fichtst, ficht	focht	hat gefochten
finden	finde, findest, findet	fand	hat gefunden
fliegen	fliege, fliegst, fliegt	flog	ist *or* hat geflogen
fliehen	fliehe, fliehst, flieht	floh	ist geflohen
fließen	fließe, fließt, fließt	floss	ist geflossen
fressen	fresse, frisst, frisst	fraß	hat gefressen
frieren	friere, frierst, friert	fror	hat *or* ist gefroren

Infinitive	Present	Imperfect	Perfect
geben	gebe, gibst, gibt	gab	hat gegeben
gefallen	gefalle, gefällst, gefällt	gefiel	hat gefallen
gehen	gehe, gehst, geht	ging	ist gegangen
gelingen	es gelingt mir, dir, ihm/ihr/ihm	gelang	ist gelungen
gelten	gelte, giltst, gilt	galt	hat gegolten
genießen	genieße, genießt, genießt	genoss	hat genossen
geraten	gerate, gerätst, gerät	geriet	ist geraten
geschehen	es geschieht	geschah	ist geschehen
gewinnen	gewinne, gewinnst, gewinnt	gewann	hat gewonnen
gießen	gieße, gießt, gießt	goss	hat gegossen
gleichen	gleiche, gleichst, gleicht	glich	hat geglichen
graben	grabe, gräbst, gräbt	grub	hat gegraben
greifen	greife, greifst, greift	griff	hat gegriffen
haben	habe, hast, hat	hatte	hat gehabt
halten	halte, hältst, hält	hielt	hat gehalten
heißen	heiße, heißt, heißt	hieß	hat geheißen
helfen	helfe, hilfst, hilft	half	hat geholfen
hinweisen	weise hin, weist hin, weist hin	wies hin	hat hingewiesen
kennen	kenne, kennst, kennt	kannte	hat gekannt
klingen	klinge, klingst, klingt	klang	hat geklungen
kneifen	kneife, kneifst, kneift	kniff	hat gekniffen
kommen	komme, kommst, kommt	kam	ist gekommen
können	kann, kannst, kann	konnte	hat gekonnt
kriechen	krieche, kriechst, kriecht	kroch	ist gekrochen
lassen	lasse, lässt, lässt	ließ	hat gelassen
laufen	laufe, läufst, läuft	lief	ist gelaufen
leiden	leide, leidest, leidet	litt	hat gelitten
leihen	leihe, leihst, leiht	lieh	hat geliehen
lesen	lese, liest, liest	las	hat gelesen
liegen	liege, liegst, liegt	lag	hat gelegen
lügen	lüge, lügst, lügt	log	hat gelogen
mahlen	mahle, mahlst, mahlt	mahlte	hat gemahlen
meiden	meide, meidest, meidet	mied	hat gemieden
messen	messe, misst, misst	maß	hat gemessen
misslingen	es misslingt mir, dir, ihm/ihr/ihm	misslang	ist misslungen
mögen	mag, magst, mag	mochte	hat gemocht
müssen	muss, musst, muss	musste	hat gemusst
nehmen	nehme, nimmst, nimmt	nahm	hat genommen
nennen	nenne, nennst, nennt	nannte	hat genannt

Infinitive	Present	Imperfect	Perfect
pfeifen	pfeife, pfeifst, pfeift	pfiff	hat gepfiffen
raten	rate, rätst, rät	riet	hat geraten
reiben	reibe, reibst, reibt	rieb	hat gerieben
reißen	reiße, reißt, reißt	riss	hat or ist gerissen
reiten	reite, reitest, reitet	ritt	hat or ist geritten
rennen	renne, rennst, rennt	rannte	ist gerannt
riechen	rieche, riechst, riecht	roch	hat gerochen
rufen	rufe, rufst, ruft	rief	hat gerufen
saufen	saufe, säufst, säuft	soff	hat gesoffen
schaffen	schaffe, schaffst, schafft	schuf	hat geschaffen
scheiden	scheide, scheidest, scheidet	schied	hat or ist geschieden
scheinen	scheine, scheinst, scheint	schien	hat geschienen
schieben	schiebe, schiebst, schiebt	schob	hat geschoben
schießen	schieße, schießt, schießt	schoss	hat or ist geschossen
schlafen	schlafe, schläfst, schläft	schlief	hat geschlafen
schlagen	schlage, schlägst, schlägt	schlug	hat geschlagen
schleichen	schleiche, schleichst, schleicht	schlich	ist geschlichen
schließen	schließe, schließt, schließt	schloss	hat geschlossen
schmeißen	schmeiße, schmeißt, schmeißt	schmiss	hat geschmissen
schmelzen	schmelze, schmilzt, schmilzt	schmolz	ist geschmolzen
schneiden	schneide, schneidest, schneidet	schnitt	hat geschnitten
schreiben	schreibe, schreibst, schreibt	schrieb	hat geschrieben
schreien	schreie, schreist, schreit	schrie	hat geschrien
schweigen	schweige, schweigst, schweigt	schwieg	hat geschwiegen
schwimmen	schwimme, schwimmst, schwimmt	schwamm	ist or hat geschwommen
schwören	schwöre, schwörst, schwört	schwor	hat geschworen
sehen	sehe, siehst, sieht	sah	hat gesehen
sein	bin, bist, ist	war	ist gewesen
singen	singe, singst, singt	sang	hat gesungen
sinken	sinke, sinkst, sinkt	sank	ist gesunken
sitzen	sitze, sitzt, sitzt	saß	hat gesessen
sollen	soll, sollst, soll	sollte	hat gesollt
spinnen	spinne, spinnst, spinnt	spann	hat gesponnen
sprechen	spreche, sprichst, spricht	sprach	hat gesprochen
springen	springe, springst, springt	sprang	ist gesprungen
stechen	steche, stichst, sticht	stach	hat gestochen
stehen	stehe, stehst, steht	stand	hat or ist gestanden
stehlen	stehle, stiehlst, stiehlt	stahl	hat gestohlen
steigen	steige, steigst, steigt	stieg	ist gestiegen
sterben	sterbe, stirbst, stirbt	starb	ist gestorben
stinken	stinke, stinkst, stinkt	stank	hat gestunken

Infinitive	Present	Imperfect	Perfect
stoßen	stoße, stößt, stößt	stieß	hat or ist gestoßen
streichen	streiche, streichst, streicht	strich	hat gestrichen
streiten	streite, streitest, streitet	stritt	hat gestritten
tragen	trage, trägst, trägt	trug	hat getragen
treffen	treffe, triffst, trifft	traf	hat getroffen
treiben	treibe, treibst, treibt	trieb	hat getrieben
treten	trete, trittst, tritt	trat	hat or ist getreten
trinken	trinke, trinkst, trinkt	trank	hat getrunken
tun	tue, tust, tut	tat	hat getan
überweisen	überweise, überweist, überweist	überwies	hat überwiesen
umziehen	ziehe um, ziehst um, zieht um	zog um	ist or hat umgezogen
verbieten	verbiete, verbietest, verbietet	verbot	hat verboten
verderben	verderbe, verdirbst, verdirbt	verdarb	hat or ist verdorben
vergessen	vergesse, vergisst, vergisst	vergaß	hat vergessen
verlieren	verliere, verlierst, verliert	verlor	hat verloren
verschwinden	verschwinde, verschwindest, verschwindet	verschwand	ist verschwunden
verzeihen	verzeihe, verzeihst, verzeiht	verzieh	hat verziehen
verstehen	verstehe, verstehst, versteht	verstand	hat verstanden
wachsen	wachse, wächst, wächst	wuchs	ist gewachsen
waschen	wasche, wäschst, wäscht	wusch	hat gewaschen
werben	werbe, wirbst, wirbt	warb	hat geworben
werden	werde, wirst, wird	wurde	ist geworden
werfen	werfe, wirfst, wirft	warf	hat geworfen
wiegen	wiege, wiegst, wiegt	wog	hat gewogen
wissen	weiß, weißt, weiß	wusste	hat gewusst
wollen	will, willst, will	wollte	hat gewollt
ziehen	ziehe, ziehst, zieht	zog	hat or ist gezogen
zwingen	zwinge, zwingst, zwingt	zwang	hat gezwungen

Aa

_ρ_ **a** DETERMINER
1 (before a noun which is masculine in German) **ein**
    a tree ein Baum
2 (before a noun which is feminine in German) **eine**
    a story eine Geschichte
3 (before a noun which is neuter in German) **ein**
    a dress ein Kleid
4 **not a** kein
    The party was not a success. Die Party war kein Erfolg.
    He didn't say a word. Er hat kein Wort gesagt.
5 **ten euros a metre** zehn Euro der Meter
6 **fifty kilometres an hour** fünfzig Stundenkilometer
7 **three times a day** dreimal täglich

A & E NOUN
    die Notaufnahme

to **abandon** VERB
1 **aufgeben**◇ SEP
    They abandoned the plan. Sie gaben den Plan auf.
2 **verlassen**◇
    They abandoned the city. Sie verließen die Stadt.

abbey NOUN
    die Abtei (PL die Abteien)

abbreviation NOUN
    die Abkürzung (PL die Abkürzungen)

ability NOUN
    die Fähigkeit (PL die Fähigkeiten)
    to have the ability to do something etwas tun können◇

_ρ_ **able** ADJECTIVE
    fähig
    to be able to do something etwas tun können◇
    She wasn't able to come. Sie konnte nicht kommen.

to **abolish** VERB
    abschaffen SEP

abortion NOUN
    die Abtreibung (PL die Abtreibungen)

_ρ_ **about** PREPOSITION
1 **über** (+ACC)
    a film about space ein Film über den Weltraum
    to talk about something/somebody über etwas/jemanden reden
    What is she talking about? Worüber redet sie?
2 **um** (+ACC)
    to be about something um etwas gehen
    What's it about? Worum geht es?
3 **to know about something** von etwas (DAT) wissen
    She didn't know about the party. Sie wusste nichts von der Party.
    He knows nothing about it. Er weiß nichts davon.
4 **to think about something/somebody** an etwas/jemanden (ACC) denken
    I'm thinking about you. Ich denke an dich.

about ADVERB
1 (approximately) **ungefähr**
    about sixty people ungefähr sechzig Leute
    in about a week in ungefähr einer Woche
2 (when talking about time) **gegen**
    about three o'clock gegen drei Uhr
3 **to be about to do something** gerade etwas tun wollen
    I was (just) about to leave. Ich wollte gerade gehen.

_ρ_ **above** PREPOSITION
1 **über** (+DAT)
    the light above the table die Lampe über dem Tisch
2 **above all** vor allem

_ρ_ **abroad** ADVERB
    im Ausland
    to live abroad im Ausland leben
    to go abroad ins Ausland fahren

abscess NOUN
    der Abszess (PL die Abszesse)

abseiling NOUN
    das Abseilen

_ρ_ **absent** ADJECTIVE
    abwesend
    to be absent from school in der Schule fehlen

absent-minded ADJECTIVE
    zerstreut

absolute ADJECTIVE
    absolut
    an absolute disaster eine absolute Katastrophe

_ρ_ **absolutely** ADVERB
1 wirklich
    It's absolutely dreadful. Das ist wirklich

furchtbar.
2 **völlig**
You're absolutely right. Du hast völlig
Recht.
absolutely nothing überhaupt nichts

abuse NOUN
1 der **Missbrauch**
drug abuse der Drogenmissbrauch
2 (insults) die **Beschimpfungen** (PLURAL)

to **abuse** VERB
1 **to abuse somebody** jemanden
missbrauchen
2 (insult) beschimpfen

to **accelerate** VERB
beschleunigen

accelerator NOUN
das **Gaspedal** (PL die **Gaspedale**)

ℓ **accent** NOUN
der **Akzent** (PL die **Akzente**)
to speak with a German accent mit
deutschem Akzent sprechen

to **accept** VERB
annehmen◇ SEP
He accepted the invitation. Er nahm die
Einladung an.

acceptable ADJECTIVE
annehmbar

access NOUN
der **Zugang**

to **access** VERB
to access data auf Daten zugreifen

accessory NOUN
1 das **Zubehörteil**
accessories das Zubehör
2 (fashion items) die **Accessoires**
(PLURAL)

ℓ **accident** NOUN
1 der **Unfall** (PL die **Unfälle**)
to have an accident einen Unfall haben
road accident der Verkehrsunfall
car accident der Autounfall
2 der **Zufall** (PL die **Zufälle**)
by accident zufällig
I found it by accident. Ich habe es zufällig
gefunden.

accident & emergency NOUN
die **Notaufnahme**

accidental ADJECTIVE
zufällig
an accidental discovery eine zufällige
Entdeckung

ℓ **accidentally** ADVERB
1 (without meaning to) versehentlich
I accidentally threw it away. Ich habe es
versehentlich weggeworfen.
2 (by chance) zufällig
I accidentally discovered that ... Ich habe
zufällig herausgefunden, dass ...

ℓ **accommodation** NOUN
die **Unterkunft**
Accommodation is free. Unterkunft ist
kostenlos.
I'm looking for accommodation. (when
looking for a room) Ich suche ein Zimmer.

ℓ to **accompany** VERB
begleiten
to accompany somebody jemanden
begleiten

ℓ **according** IN PHRASE
according to laut (+DAT)
according to Sophie laut Sophie

accordion NOUN
das **Akkordeon** (PL die **Akkordeons**)
He plays the accordion. Er spielt
Akkordeon.

WORD TIP Don't use the article when you talk
about playing an instrument.

ℓ **account** NOUN
1 (in a bank, shop, or post office) das **Konto**
(PL die **Konten**)
bank account das Bankkonto
to open an account ein Konto eröffnen
I have fifty pounds in my account. Ich habe
fünfzig Pfund auf meinem Konto.
2 (an explanation) die **Darstellung** (PL die
Darstellungen)
**I want to hear his account of what
happened.** Ich möchte seine Darstellung
der Ereignisse hören.
3 **on account of** wegen (+GEN)
4 **to take something into account** etwas
berücksichtigen

ℓ **accountant** NOUN
der **Buchhalter** (PL die **Buchhalter**) die
Buchhalterin (PL die **Buchhalterinnen**)

WORD TIP Professions, hobbies, and sports don't
take an article in German: Sie ist Buchhalterin.
---

accurate ADJECTIVE
genau

accurately ADVERB
genau

ℓ to **accuse** VERB
beschuldigen

◇ **irregular verb;** SEP **separable verb; for more help with verbs see centre section**

She accused me of stealing her pen. Sie beschuldigte mich, ihren Stift gestohlen zu haben.

ace NOUN
das Ass (PL die Asse)
the ace of hearts das Herzass

ace ADJECTIVE
klasse (informal)
He's an ace drummer. Er spielt klasse Schlagzeug.

℗ **to ache** VERB
schmerzen, wehtun◇ SEP
My head aches. Mein Kopf tut weh.

to achieve VERB
1 leisten
She's achieved a great deal. Sie hat eine Menge geleistet.
2 erreichen (an aim)
He achieved what he wanted. Er hat erreicht, was er wollte.

achievement NOUN
die Leistung (PL die Leistungen)
It's a great achievement. Das ist eine große Leistung.

acid NOUN
die Säure (PL die Säuren)

acne NOUN
die Akne

℗ **across** PREPOSITION
1 (over to the other side of) über (+ACC)
to run across the road über die Straße laufen
We walked across the park. Wir sind durch den Park gegangen.
2 (on the other side of) auf der anderen Seite (+GEN)
He lives across the river. Er wohnt auf der anderen Seite des Flusses.
3 **They live across the street.** Sie wohnen gegenüber.

℗ **act** NOUN
(deed) die Tat (PL die Taten)

to act VERB
(in a play or film) spielen
to act the part of the hero die Rolle des Helden spielen

action NOUN
1 die Handlung (PL die Handlungen)
2 **to take action** etwas unternehmen◇

action replay NOUN
die Wiederholung (PL die Wiederholungen)

active NOUN
(in grammar) das Aktiv

active ADJECTIVE
aktiv

℗ **activity** NOUN
die Aktivität (PL die Aktivitäten)

℗ **actor** NOUN
der Schauspieler (PL die Schauspieler)

> **WORD TIP** Professions, hobbies, and sports don't take an article in German: Er ist Schauspieler.

℗ **actress** NOUN
die Schauspielerin (PL die Schauspielerinnen)

> **WORD TIP** Professions, hobbies, and sports don't take an article in German: Sie ist Schauspielerin.

actual ADJECTIVE
What were his actual words? Was genau hat er gesagt?
in actual fact eigentlich

> **WORD TIP** Do not translate the English word actual with the German aktuell.

℗ **actually** ADVERB
1 (in fact, as it happens) eigentlich
Actually, I'm relieved. Eigentlich bin ich erleichtert.
2 (really and truly) wirklich
Did she actually say that? Hat sie das wirklich gesagt?

℗ **ad** NOUN
1 (on TV) der Werbespot (PL die Werbespots)
2 (in a newspaper) die Anzeige (PL die Anzeigen)
to put an ad in the paper eine Anzeige in die Zeitung setzen
the small ads die Kleinanzeigen

AD ABBREVIATION
(Anno Domini) n. Chr., (nach Christus)
in 400 AD 400 n. Chr.

to adapt VERB
1 **to adapt something** (a book or film) etwas bearbeiten
2 **to adapt to** sich anpassen SEP (+DAT)
She's adapted to her new surroundings. Sie hat sich der neuen Umgebung angepasst.

adaptor NOUN
1 der Adapter (PL die Adapter)
2 (for two plugs) der Doppelstecker (PL die Doppelstecker)

℗ **to add** VERB
1 hinzufügen SEP
to add an introduction to something

℗ indicates key words

etwas *(DAT)* eine Einleitung hinzufügen
2 *dazugeben*◇ *SEP*
Add three eggs. Geben Sie drei dazu.
• **to add up**
zusammenzählen *SEP*

addict NOUN
1 *(drug addict)* der/die **Süchtige** (PL die Süchtigen)
2 **She's a telly addict.** Sie ist fernsehsüchtig.
He's a football addict. Er ist ein Fußballnarr.

addicted ADJECTIVE
1 **to become addicted to drugs**
drogensüchtig werden
2 **He's addicted to football.** Fußball ist bei ihm zur Sucht geworden.
3 **I'm addicted to sweets.** Ich bin nach Süßigkeiten süchtig.

ℓ **addition** NOUN
1 *(adding up)* die **Addition**
2 **in addition** außerdem
3 **in addition to** zusätzlich zu *(+DAT)*

ℓ **additional** ADJECTIVE
zusätzlich

additive NOUN
der **Zusatz** (PL die Zusätze)

ℓ **address** NOUN
die **Adresse** (PL die Adressen)
Do you know his address? Weißt du seine Adresse?
to change address die Adresse wechseln

address book NOUN
das **Adressbuch** (PL die Adressbücher)

adequate ADJECTIVE
angemessen

adhesive NOUN
der **Klebstoff**

adhesive ADJECTIVE
adhesive tape der Klebstreifen

adjective NOUN
das **Adjektiv** (PL die Adjektive) *(in grammar)*

to adjust VERB
1 **to adjust something** etwas einstellen *SEP*
He adjusted the set. Er stellte das Gerät ein.
to adjust the distance auf die (richtige) Entfernung einstellen
2 **to adjust to something** sich an etwas *(ACC)* gewöhnen

adjustable ADJECTIVE
verstellbar

administration NOUN
die **Verwaltung**

admiration NOUN
die **Bewunderung**

ℓ **to admire** VERB
bewundern

admission NOUN
der **Eintritt**
'Admission free' 'Eintritt frei'

ℓ **to admit** VERB
1 *(confess, concede)* zugeben◇ *SEP*
She admits she lied. Sie gibt zu, dass sie gelogen hat.
2 *(allow to enter)* hereinlassen◇ *SEP*
Children not admitted. Kinder haben keinen Zutritt.
3 **to be admitted to hospital** ins Krankenhaus eingeliefert werden

adolescence NOUN
die **Pubertät**

ℓ **adolescent** NOUN
der/die **Jugendliche** (PL die Jugendlichen)

to adopt VERB
adoptieren

adopted ADJECTIVE
adoptiert

adoption NOUN
die **Adoption** (PL die Adoptionen)

to adore VERB
lieben

ℓ **adult** NOUN
der/die **Erwachsene** (PL die Erwachsenen)

adult ADJECTIVE
the adult population Erwachsene *(PLURAL)*

advance NOUN
der **Fortschritt** (PL die Fortschritte)
advances in technology technologische Fortschritte

to advance VERB
1 *(make progress)* Fortschritte machen
2 *(move forward)* *(of a group or an army)* vorrücken *SEP* *(PERF sein)*

advanced ADJECTIVE
fortgeschritten *(student, age)*

ℓ **advantage** NOUN
1 der **Vorteil** (PL die Vorteile)
There are several advantages. Es gibt verschiedene Vorteile.
2 **to take advantage of something** etwas ausnutzen *SEP*
I always take advantage of the sales to buy myself some shoes. Ich warte immer

◇ **irregular verb;** *SEP* **separable verb; for more help with verbs see centre section**

bis zum Schlussverkauf, um mir Schuhe zu kaufen.

3 to take advantage of somebody *(unfairly)* jemanden ausnutzen *SEP*

Advent *NOUN*
der Advent

adventure *NOUN*
das Abenteuer (*PL* die Abenteuer)

adverb *NOUN*
das Adverb (*PL* die Adverbien) *(in grammar)*

ℙ **advert**, **advertisement** *NOUN*
1 *(at the cinema or on television)* der Werbespot (*PL* die Werbespots)
2 *(in a newspaper for a job, article for sale, etc.)* die Anzeige (*PL* die Anzeigen)
She answered a job advertisement. Sie meldete sich auf eine Stellenanzeige.

ℙ to **advertise** *VERB*
to advertise something in the newspaper *(in the small ads)* etwas in der Zeitung inserieren
I saw a bike advertised in the paper. Ich habe ein Rad in der Zeitung inseriert gesehen.

ℙ **advertising** *NOUN*
die Werbung

ℙ **advice** *NOUN*
der Rat
to ask somebody's advice jemanden um Rat fragen
a piece of advice ein Ratschlag

ℙ to **advise** *VERB*
raten◊ *(+DAT)*
to advise somebody to do something jemandem raten, etwas zu tun
I advised him to stop. Ich riet ihm aufzuhören.
I advised her not to buy the car. Ich habe ihr geraten, das Auto nicht zu kaufen.

aerial *NOUN*
die Antenne (*PL* die Antennen)

aerobics *NOUN*
das Aerobic
to do aerobics Aerobic machen

ℙ **aeroplane** *NOUN*
das Flugzeug (*PL* die Flugzeuge)

aerosol *NOUN*
an aerosol can eine Spraydose

affair *NOUN*
1 die Angelegenheit (*PL* die Angelegenheiten)
international affairs internationale

Angelegenheiten
current affairs die Tagespolitik
2 love affair das Liebesverhältnis (*PL* die Affäre)

ℙ to **affect** *VERB*
beeinflussen
That will not affect my decision. Das wird meine Entscheidung nicht beeinflussen.

affectionate *ADJECTIVE*
liebevoll

ℙ to **afford** *VERB*
to be able to afford something sich *(DAT)* etwas leisten können
We can't afford to go out much. Wir können es uns nicht leisten, oft auszugehen.
I can't afford a new bike. Ich kann mir kein neues Rad leisten.

ℙ **afraid** *ADJECTIVE*
1 to be afraid of something Angst vor etwas *(DAT)* haben
She's afraid of dogs. Sie hat Angst vor Hunden.
2 I'm afraid I can't help you. Ich kann dir leider nicht helfen.
I'm afraid so. Leider ja.
I'm afraid not. Leider nicht.

Africa *NOUN*
Afrika *(NEUTER)*
to Africa nach Afrika

African *NOUN*
der Afrikaner (*PL* die Afrikaner die Afrikanerin) (*PL* die Afrikanerinnen)

African *ADJECTIVE*
afrikanisch
the African countries die afrikanischen Länder
He's African. Er ist Afrikaner.
She's African. Sie ist Afrikanerin.

WORD TIP Adjectives never have capitals in German, even for regions, countries, or nationalities.

ℙ **after** *PREPOSITION, ADVERB*
1 nach *(+DAT)*
after ten o'clock nach zehn Uhr
after lunch nach dem Mittagessen
after school nach der Schule
2 the day after tomorrow übermorgen
soon after kurz danach
3 to run after somebody jemandem hinterherlaufen◊ *SEP*

after *CONJUNCTION*
nachdem
after I'd finished my homework nachdem ich meine Hausaufgaben gemacht hatte

ℙ indicates key words

after all ADVERB
schließlich
After all, she's only six. Sie ist schließlich erst sechs.

ℓ **afternoon** NOUN
1 der **Nachmittag** (PL die **Nachmittage**)
  in the afternoon am Nachmittag
  every afternoon jeden Nachmittag
2 **this afternoon** heute Nachmittag
  on Sunday afternoon am Sonntagnachmittag
3 **on Saturday afternoons** samstags nachmittags
  at four o' clock in the afternoon um vier Uhr nachmittags

aftershave NOUN
das **Rasierwasser** (PL die **Rasierwasser**)

afterwards ADVERB
danach
shortly afterwards kurz danach

ℓ **again** ADVERB
1 wieder
  She's ill again. Sie ist wieder krank.
2 **I saw her again yesterday.** Ich habe sie gestern wieder gesehen.
3 **Never again!** Nie wieder!
  again and again immer wieder
4 (one more time) noch einmal
  Try again. Versuche es noch einmal.
  You should ask her again. Du solltest sie noch einmal fragen.

ℓ **against** PREPOSITION
gegen (+ACC)
against the wall gegen die Wand
to lean against the wall sich gegen die Wand lehnen
I'm against the idea. Ich bin gegen die Idee.

ℓ **age** NOUN
1 das **Alter**
  at the age of fifty im Alter von fünfzig
  She's the same age as me. Sie ist genauso alt wie ich.
  to be under age minderjährig sein
2 **I haven't seen Johnny for ages.** Ich habe Johnny schon ewig nicht mehr gesehen.
  I haven't been to London for ages. Ich bin schon ewig nicht mehr in London gewesen.

ℓ **aged** ADJECTIVE
alt
aged six sechs Jahre alt
a woman aged thirty eine dreißigjährige Frau

age limit NOUN
die **Altersgrenze** (PL die **Altersgrenzen**)

agent NOUN
der **Vertreter** (PL die **Vertreter**), die **Vertreterin** (PL die **Vertreterinnen**)
an estate agent ein Immobilienmakler
a travel agent's ein Reisebüro

aggressive ADJECTIVE
aggressiv

ℓ **ago** ADVERB
vor (+DAT)
an hour ago vor einer Stunde
three days ago vor drei Tagen
a long time ago vor langer Zeit
not long ago vor kurzem
How long ago was it? Wie lange ist das her?

ℓ **to agree** VERB
1 **to agree with somebody** mit jemandem gleicher Meinung sein
  I agree with Laura. Ich stimme Laura zu.
2 **I agree.** Ich bin der gleichen Meinung.
  I don't agree. Ich bin anderer Meinung.
3 **to agree that** zugeben ◇ SEP, dass
  I agree that it's too late now. Ich gebe zu, dass es jetzt zu spät ist.
4 **to agree to something** mit etwas einverstanden sein
  Steve's agreed to help me. Steve hat sich einverstanden erklärt, mir zu helfen.
5 **Coffee doesn't agree with me.** Kaffee bekommt mir nicht.

ℓ **agreement** NOUN
1 (when sharing an opinion) die **Übereinstimmung**
2 (contract) das **Abkommen** (PL die **Abkommen**)

agriculture NOUN
die **Landwirtschaft**

ℓ **ahead** ADVERB
1 **Go ahead!** Bitte!
2 **straight ahead** geradeaus
  Keep going straight ahead until you get to the crossroads. Gehen Sie immer geradeaus bis zur Kreuzung.
3 **Our team was ten points ahead.** Unsere Mannschaft hatte zehn Punkte Vorsprung.
4 **ahead of time** früher als geplant
5 **the people ahead of me** die Leute vor mir

aid NOUN
1 die **Hilfe**
  aid to developing countries die Entwicklungshilfe
2 **in aid of** zugunsten (+GEN)

400

in aid of the homeless zugunsten der
Obdachlosen

_ℓ_ **Aids** NOUN
das Aids
to have Aids Aids haben

aim NOUN
das Ziel (PL die Ziele)
Their aim is to control pollution. Ihr Ziel
ist es (PL die Umweltverschmutzung unter
Kontrolle zu bringen.)

to **aim** VERB
1 **to aim to do something** beabsichtigen,
etwas zu tun
We're aiming to finish it today. Wir
beabsichtigen, es heute fertig zu machen.
2 **The campaign is aimed at young people.**
Die Kampagne zielt auf junge Leute ab.

_ℓ_ **air** NOUN
1 die Luft
in the open air im Freien
to go out for a breath of air frische Luft
schöpfen gehen
2 **to travel by air** fliegen◇ (PERF sein)

airbag NOUN
der Airbag (PL die Airbags)

air-conditioned ADJECTIVE
klimatisiert

air conditioning NOUN
die Klimaanlage (PL die Klimaanlagen)

air force NOUN
die Luftwaffe

air hostess NOUN
die Stewardess (PL die Stewardessen)

> **WORD TIP** Professions, hobbies, and sports don't
> take an article in German: Sie ist Stewardess.

airline NOUN
die Fluggesellschaft (PL die
Fluggesellschaften)

airmail NOUN
by airmail per Luftpost

air pollution NOUN
die Luftverschmutzung

_ℓ_ **airport** NOUN
der Flughafen (PL die Flughäfen)
We'll pick you up from the airport. Wir
werden dich vom Flughafen abholen.

alarm NOUN
der Alarm (PL die Alarme)
fire alarm der Feuermelder
burglar alarm die Alarmanlage

alarm clock NOUN
der Wecker (PL die Wecker)

album NOUN
das Album (PL die Alben)

alcohol NOUN
der Alkohol

alcoholic NOUN
der Alkoholiker (PL die Alkoholiker), die
Alkoholikerin (PL die Alkoholikerinnen)

alcoholic ADJECTIVE
alkoholisch

A levels NOUN
das Abitur (_Students take 'Abitur' at about
19 years of age. You can explain A levels
briefly as follows: Diese Prüfungen werden
in zwei Schritten abgelegt: AS und A2.
AS Prüfungen finden nach einjähriger
Vorbereitungszeit statt und umfassen
normalerweise vier bis fünf Fächer. A2
Prüfungen macht man in weniger Fächern
als man für die AS Prüfungen belegt hatte.
AS und A2 Prüfungen werden benotet von A
(beste Note) bis U (nicht bestanden). A levels
stellen eine Zugangsberechtigung für die
Universität dar._)
▶ SEE **Abitur**
▶ SEE **Matura** (in Austria)

algebra NOUN
die Algebra

alien NOUN
1 (_foreigner_) der Ausländer (PL die
Ausländer), die Ausländerin (PL die
Ausländerinnen)
2 (_from outer space_) der/die Außerirdische
(PL die Außerirdischen)

alike ADJECTIVE
1 gleich
2 **They're all alike.** Sie sind alle gleich.
3 **to look alike** sich (DAT) ähnlich sehen◇
The two brothers look alike. Die beiden
Brüder sehen sich ähnlich.

_ℓ_ **alive** ADJECTIVE
1 **to be alive** leben
to stay alive am Leben bleiben
2 (_lively_) lebendig

_ℓ_ **all** ADJECTIVE
1 (_with a singular noun_) ganz
all the time die ganze Zeit
all day den ganzen Tag
2 (_with a plural noun_) alle
all the knives alle Messer

all our friends alle unsere Freunde

WORD TIP Do not translate the English expression **all day** with the German **alle Tage**.

all PRONOUN
1 *(everything)* alles
They've eaten it all. Sie haben alles aufgegessen.
2 *(everybody)* alle
all of us wir alle
They're all there. Sie sind alle da.
3 not at all gar nicht

all ADVERB
1 ganz
all alone ganz allein
2 three all drei beide

all along ADVERB
die ganze Zeit
I knew it all along. Ich habe es die ganze Zeit gewusst.

allergic ADJECTIVE
allergisch
to be allergic to something gegen etwas *(ACC)* allergisch sein

allergy NOUN
die Allergie *(PL* die Allergien)
a peanut allergy eine Erdnussallergie

ℓ **to allow** VERB
1 to allow somebody to do something jemandem erlauben, etwas zu tun
The teacher allowed them to go home. Der Lehrer erlaubte ihnen, nach Hause zu gehen.
2 to be allowed to dürfen◇
I'm not allowed to go to the cinema during the week. Ich darf während der Woche nicht ins Kino gehen.

ℓ **all right** ADVERB
1 *(yes)* ist gut, okay *(informal)*
'Come round to my house around six.' – 'All right.' 'Komm um sechs bei mir vorbei.' – 'Okay.'
2 *(fine)* in Ordnung, okay *(informal)*
Is everything all right? Ist alles okay?
She's all right again. Es geht ihr wieder gut.
It's all right by me. Das geht in Ordnung.
Is it all right if I come later? Ist es in Ordnung, wenn ich später komme?
3 *(not bad)* gut, okay *(informal)*
The meal was all right. Das Essen war okay.
4 'How are you?' – 'I'm all right.' 'Wie geht's dir?' – 'Mir geht's gut.'

almost ADVERB
fast

almost every day fast jeden Tag
almost everybody fast alle

ℓ **alone** ADJECTIVE
1 allein
He lives alone. Er lebt allein.
2 Leave me alone! Lass mich in Ruhe!

ℓ **along** PREPOSITION
1 entlang *(+ACC OR +DAT)*
There are trees all along the river. Am Fluss entlang stehen Bäume.
They walked along the road. Sie gingen die Straße entlang. *(ACC)*
2 *(there is often no direct translation for along, so the sentence has to be expressed differently)*
She lives along the road from me. Sie wohnt in der gleichen Straße wie ich.
I'll bring it along. Ich bringe es mit.

aloud ADVERB
laut
to read something aloud etwas vorlesen◇ *SEP*

ℓ **alphabet** NOUN
das Alphabet *(PL* die Alphabete)

Alps PLURAL NOUN
the Alps die Alpen

🔘 **THE ALPS**

The Alps cover much of Austria and Switzerland, and stretch along the southern border of Germany. They are a popular holiday area in both summer and winter. The highest peaks in the three countries are: Großglockner 3798m (Austria), Monte Rosa 4634m (Switzerland), Zugspitze 2964m (Germany).

ℓ **already** ADVERB
schon
They've already left. Sie sind schon weggegangen.
It's six o'clock already. Es ist schon sechs Uhr.

alright ADVERB ▸ SEE **all right**

Alsatian NOUN
der Schäferhund *(PL* die Schäferhunde)

ℓ **also** ADVERB
auch
I've also invited Karen. Ich habe Karen auch eingeladen.

WORD TIP Do not translate the English word **also** with the German **also**.

to alter VERB
1 ändern *(a report, a dress)*
2 *(change)* sich verändern

◇ **irregular verb**; *SEP* **separable verb**; for more help with verbs see centre section

alternative NOUN
1 die Alternative (PL die Alternativen)
  There are several alternatives. Es gibt
  mehrere Alternativen.
2 **We have no alternative.** Wir haben keine
  andere Wahl.

alternative ADJECTIVE
  anderer/andere/anderes (masculine/
  feminine/neuter)
  to find an alternative solution eine andere
  Lösung finden

alternative medicine NOUN
  die Alternativmedizin

although CONJUNCTION
  obwohl
  Although she's ill, she wants to help us.
  Obwohl sie krank ist, will sie uns helfen.

altogether ADVERB
1 insgesamt
  I've spent thirty pounds altogether.
  Insgesamt habe ich dreißig Pfund
  ausgegeben.
2 (completely) ganz
  I'm not altogether convinced. Ich bin nicht
  ganz überzeugt.

ℱ **always** ADVERB
  immer
  I always leave at five. Ich gehe immer um
  fünf (weg).

am VERB ► SEE **be**

ℱ **a.m.** ABBREVIATION
  vormittags, morgens
  at 8 a.m. um acht Uhr morgens

amateur NOUN
1 der Amateur (PL die Amateure), die
  Amateurin (PL die Amateurinnen)
2 **amateur dramatics** das Laientheater

to amaze VERB
  erstaunen
  What amazes me is ... Was mich erstaunt,
  ist ...

amazed ADJECTIVE
  erstaunt
  I was amazed to see her. Ich war erstaunt,
  sie zu sehen.

amazing ADJECTIVE
1 (terrific) fantastisch
  They've got an amazing house. Sie haben
  ein fantastisches Haus.
2 (extraordinary) erstaunlich
  She has an amazing number of friends. Sie
  hat erstaunlich viele Freunde.

ambassador NOUN
  der Botschafter (PL die Botschafter) die
  Botschafterin (die Botschafterinnen)

> **WORD TIP** Professions, hobbies, and sports don't
> take an article in German: Er ist Botschafter.

ℱ **ambition** NOUN
  der Ehrgeiz

ambitious ADJECTIVE
  ehrgeizig

ℱ **ambulance** NOUN
  der Krankenwagen (PL die
  Krankenwagen), das Rettungsauto (PL die
  Rettungsautos) (in Austria)

America NOUN
  Amerika (NEUTER)
  in America in Amerika
  to America nach Amerika

American NOUN
  der Amerikaner (PL die Amerikaner), die
  Amerikanerin (PL die Amerikanerinnen)

American ADJECTIVE
  amerikanisch
  the American flag die amerikanische
  Flagge
  He's American. Er ist Amerikaner.
  She's American. Sie ist Amerikanerin.

> **WORD TIP** Adjectives never have capitals
> in German, even for regions, countries, or
> nationalities.

amnesty NOUN
  die Amnestie (PL die Amnestien)

ℱ **among**, **amongst** PREPOSITION
1 unter (+DAT)
  I found it amongst my books. Ich habe das
  unter meinen Büchern gefunden.
  amongst other things unter anderem
2 (between)
  among yourselves untereinander

amount NOUN
1 die Menge (PL die Mengen)
  a huge amount of work eine Menge Arbeit
2 (of money) der Betrag (PL die Beträge)
  a large amount of money ein sehr hoher
  Betrag

to amount VERB
  to amount to sich belaufen◇ auf (+ACC)
  The bill amounts to five hundred euros.
  Die Rechnung beläuft sich auf fünfhundert
  Euro.

amp NOUN
1 (amplifier) der Verstärker (PL die Verstärker)
2 (in electricity) das Ampere (PL die Ampere)

amplifier | **answer**

amplifier NOUN
der Verstärker (PL die Verstärker)

to **amuse** VERB
amüsieren

amusement arcade NOUN
die Spielhalle (PL die Spielhallen)

ℰ **amusing** ADJECTIVE
amüsant

an ARTICLE ▶ SEE **a**

anaesthetic NOUN
die Narkose (PL die Narkosen)

to **analyse** VERB
analysieren

ancestor NOUN
der Vorfahr (PL die Vorfahren)

anchovy NOUN
die Sardelle (PL die Sardellen)

ancient ADJECTIVE
1 alt
ancient Greece das alte Griechenland
2 (very old) uralt
an ancient pair of jeans uralte Jeans

ℰ **and** CONJUNCTION
1 und
Rosie and I Rosie und ich
girls and boys Mädchen und Jungen
2 **louder and louder** immer lauter
3 **Try and come.** Versuche zu kommen.

angel NOUN
der Engel (PL die Engel)

anger NOUN
der Zorn

angle NOUN
der Winkel (PL die Winkel)

angrily ADVERB
wütend

ℰ **angry** ADJECTIVE
to be angry böse sein
She was angry with me. Sie war böse auf mich.
to get angry böse werden

ℰ **animal** NOUN
das Tier (PL die Tiere)

animal rights PLURAL NOUN
die Tierrechte (PLURAL)

animal shelter NOUN
das Tierheim (PL die Tierheime)

ankle NOUN
der Knöchel (PL die Knöchel)

ℰ **anniversary** NOUN
1 der Jahrestag (PL die Jahrestage)
2 **our wedding anniversary** unser Hochzeitstag

to **announce** VERB
bekannt geben✧
She announced her engagement. Sie gab ihre Verlobung bekannt.

announcement NOUN
1 die Ankündigung (PL die Ankündigungen)
2 (over a loudspeaker) die Durchsage (PL die Durchsagen)
to make an announcement eine Durchsage machen

to **annoy** VERB
ärgern
It really annoys me. Es ärgert mich sehr.
to be annoyed verärgert sein
to get annoyed with somebody sich über jemanden ärgern
She got annoyed about it. Sie hat sich darüber geärgert.

ℰ **annoying** ADJECTIVE
ärgerlich

annual ADJECTIVE
jährlich

anorak NOUN
der Anorak (PL die Anoraks)

anorexia NOUN
die Magersucht

anorexic ADJECTIVE
magersüchtig
She's anorexic. Sie ist magersüchtig.

ℰ **another** ADJECTIVE
1 (additional) noch ein/noch eine/noch ein
Would you like another cup of tea? Möchtest du noch eine Tasse Tee?
We need another three chairs. Wir brauchen noch drei Stühle.
2 (different) ein anderer/eine andere/ein anderes
We saw another film. Wir haben einen anderen Film gesehen.
3 **in another two years** in zwei weiteren Jahren

ℰ **answer** NOUN
1 die Antwort (PL die Antworten)
the right answer die richtige Antwort
the wrong answer die falsche Antwort
2 **the answer to a problem** die Lösung eines

✧ irregular verb; SEP separable verb; for more help with verbs see centre section

Problems

to answer VERB
1 antworten *(+DAT)*
Why don't you answer him? Warum antwortest du ihm nicht?
2 beantworten *(a letter, a question)*
He hasn't answered our letter. Er hat unseren Brief nicht beantwortet.

answering machine NOUN
der Anrufbeantworter *(PL die Anrufbeantworter)*

ant NOUN
die Ameise *(PL die Ameisen)*

Antarctic NOUN
the Antarctic die Antarktis

anthem NOUN
the national anthem die Nationalhymne

antibiotic NOUN
das Antibiotikum *(PL die Antibiotika)*
to be on antibiotics Antibiotika nehmen

antique NOUN
antiques die Antiquitäten *(PLURAL)*

antique ADJECTIVE
antik
an antique table ein antiker Tisch

antique shop NOUN
das Antiquitätengeschäft *(PL die Antiquitätengeschäfte)*

antiseptic NOUN
das Antiseptikum *(PL die Antiseptika)*

ℓ **anxious** ADJECTIVE
1 *(worried)* besorgt
2 *(keen)*
She was anxious to see him. Sie wollte ihn unbedingt sehen.

anxiously ADVERB
ängstlich

ℓ **any** DETERMINER
1 irgendein
If they had any plan, ... Wenn sie irgendeinen Plan hätten, ...
2 *(with plural nouns)* irgendwelche
If they had any plans, ... Wenn sie irgendwelche Pläne hätten, ...
3 *(in questions 'any' is often not translated)*
Have you got any stamps? Haben Sie Briefmarken?
Have we got any milk? Haben wir Milch?
4 not any kein
They haven't made any plans. Sie haben nichts geplant.

We haven't got any milk. Wir haben keine Milch.
5 *(no matter which)* jeder beliebige/jede beliebige/jedes beliebige
You can have any colour. Du kannst jede beliebige Farbe haben.

any PRONOUN
1 *(in questions, replacing the noun)* welcher/welche/welches, *(replacing a plural noun)* welche
I need some flour, have you got any? Ich brauche Mehl, hast du welches?
2 not any keiner/keine/kein(e)s, *(replacing a plural noun)* keine
I don't want any. Ich will keins haben.
There aren't any. Es gibt keine.
3 *(no matter which one)* irgendein
'Which chair can I take?' – 'Take any of them.' 'Welchen Stuhl kann ich nehmen?' – 'Nimm irgendeinen.'

any ADVERB
1 *(in questions)* noch
Would you like any more? Möchtest du noch etwas?
2 *(with negatives)*
I can't see him any more. Ich kann ihn nicht mehr sehen.

ℓ **anybody**, **anyone** PRONOUN
1 *(in questions)* jemand
Does anybody want some tea? Möchte jemand Tee?
Is anybody in? Ist irgendjemand da?
2 not anybody niemand
There isn't anybody in the office. Niemand ist im Büro.
3 *(absolutely anybody)* jeder
Anybody can do it. Das kann jeder.

anyhow ADVERB ▶ SEE **anyway**

anyone PRONOUN ▶ SEE **anybody**

ℓ **anything** PRONOUN
1 *(in questions)* irgendetwas
Is there anything I can do? Kann ich irgendetwas tun?
2 not anything nichts
There isn't anything on the table. Auf dem Tisch liegt nichts.
3 *(anything at all)* alles
I'll do anything to help him. Ich werde alles tun, um ihm zu helfen.

anyway, **anyhow** ADVERB
1 jedenfalls
Anyway, I'll ring you before I leave. Jedenfalls ruf ich dich an, bevor ich fahre.
2 sowieso
Anyway, it's too late now. Jetzt ist es

ℓ indicates key words

sowieso schon zu spät.

℘ **anywhere** ADVERB
1 (in questions) **irgendwo**
   Have you seen my keys anywhere? Hast du
   meine Schlüssel irgendwo gesehen?
2 not anywhere **nirgends**
   I can't find my keys anywhere. Ich kann
   meine Schlüssel nirgends finden.
3 (to any place) **irgendwohin**
   Are you going anywhere tomorrow?
   Fährst du morgen irgendwohin?
   Put your cases down anywhere. Stell deine
   Koffer irgendwohin.
4 (in any place) **überall**
   You can get that anywhere. Das kann man
   überall kriegen.

apart ADJECTIVE, ADVERB
1 (separate) **auseinander**
   They've been apart for some time. Sie sind
   schon lange auseinander.
2 to be two metres apart **zwei Meter
   auseinander liegen**
3 apart from **außer** (+DAT)
   **Apart from my brother everybody was
   there.** Außer meinem Bruder waren alle da.

℘ **apartment** NOUN
   die **Wohnung** (PL die **Wohnungen**)
   We rented an apartment in Spain. Wir
   haben eine Wohnung in Spanien gemietet.

℘ to **apologize** VERB
   sich entschuldigen
   He apologized for his mistake. Er
   enschuldigte sich für seinen Fehler.
   He apologized to Sam. Er hat sich bei Sam
   entschuldigt.

apology NOUN
   die **Entschuldigung** (PL die
   Entschuldigungen)

apostrophe NOUN
   der **Apostroph** (PL die **Apostrophe**)

app NOUN
   (application) die **App** (PL die **Apps**)

apparent ADJECTIVE
   offensichtlich

apparently ADVERB
   offensichtlich

appeal NOUN
   der **Appell** (PL die **Appelle**)
to **appeal** VERB
1 to appeal for something um etwas (ACC)
   bitten◇
2 to appeal to somebody **sich an jemanden
   wenden**◇

3 **Horror films don't appeal to me.**
   Horrorfilme sind nicht mein Geschmack.

to **appear** VERB
1 **erscheinen**◇ (PERF sein)
   Mick appeared at breakfast. Mick erschien
   zum Frühstück.
2 **to appear on television** im Fernsehen
   auftreten◇ SEP (PERF sein)
3 (seem) **scheinen**◇
   **It appears that somebody has stolen the
   key.** Es scheint, dass jemand den Schlüssel
   gestohlen hat.

appendicitis NOUN
   die **Blinddarmentzündung**

appetite NOUN
   der **Appetit**
   It'll spoil your appetite. Das verdirbt dir
   den Appetit.

to **applaud** VERB
   Beifall klatschen

applause NOUN
   der **Beifall**

℘ **apple** NOUN
   der **Apfel** (PL die **Äpfel**)

apple juice NOUN
   der **Apfelsaft** (PL die **Apfelsäfte**)

apple tree NOUN
   der **Apfelbaum** (PL die **Apfelbäume**)

applicant NOUN
   der **Bewerber** (PL die **Bewerber**), die
   Bewerberin (PL die **Bewerberinnen**)

application NOUN
1 (for job) die **Bewerbung** (PL die
   Bewerbungen)
2 (on mobile device) die **Anwendung** (PL die
   Anwendungen)

application form NOUN
   (for a job) das **Bewerbungsformular** (PL die
   Bewerbungsformulare)

to **apply** VERB
1 to apply for a job sich um eine Stelle
   bewerben◇
2 to apply for university sich um einen
   Studienplatz **bewerben**◇
3 to apply for a passport einen Pass
   beantragen
4 to apply to **zutreffen**◇ SEP auf (+ACC)
   That doesn't apply to students. Das trifft
   nicht auf Studenten zu.

℘ **appointment** NOUN
   der **Termin** (PL die **Termine**)

◇ irregular verb; SEP separable verb; for more help with verbs see centre section

to make a dental appointment einen
Zahnarzttermin vereinbaren
I've got a hair appointment at four. Ich
habe um vier einen Friseurtermin.

℘ to appreciate VERB
I appreciate your advice. Ich bin dir für
deinen Rat dankbar.
I'd appreciate it if you could tidy up
afterwards. Es wäre nett von dir, wenn du
danach aufräumen würdest.

apprentice NOUN
der Lehrling (PL die Lehrlinge)

apprenticeship NOUN
die Lehre (PL die Lehren)

to approach VERB
sich nähern (+DAT) (PERF sein)
We were approaching the village. Wir
näherten uns dem Dorf.

to approve VERB
to approve of something mit etwas (DAT)
einverstanden sein
They don't approve of her friends. Sie
lehnen ihre Freunde ab.

approximate ADJECTIVE
ungefähr

approximately ADVERB
ungefähr
approximately fifty people ungefähr
fünfzig Personen

℘ apricot NOUN
die Aprikose (PL die Aprikosen)

℘ April NOUN
der April
in April im April

April Fool NOUN
(trick) der Aprilscherz (PL die Aprilscherze)
April fool! April, April!

April Fool's Day NOUN
der erste April

apron NOUN
die Schürze (PL die Schürzen)

aquarium NOUN
das Aquarium (PL die Aquarien)

Aquarius NOUN
der Wassermann
Sharon is Aquarius. Sharon ist
Wassermann.

Arab NOUN
der Araber (PL die Araber), die Araberin
(PL die Araberinnen)

Arab ADJECTIVE
arabisch
the Arab countries die arabischen Länder

WORD TIP Adjectives never have capitals
in German, even for regions, countries, or
nationalities.

Arabic NOUN
das Arabisch
They speak Arabic. Sie sprechen Arabisch.

arch NOUN
der Bogen (PL die Bögen)

archaeologist NOUN
der Archäologe (PL die Archäologen), die
Archäologin (PL die Archäologinnen)

WORD TIP Professions, hobbies, and sports don't
take an article in German: Sie ist Archäologin.

archaeology NOUN
die Archäologie

archery NOUN
das Bogenschießen

architect NOUN
der Architekt (PL die Architekten), die
Architektin (PL die Architektinnen)

WORD TIP Professions, hobbies, and sports
don't take an article in German: Er ist Architekt.

architecture NOUN
die Architektur

Arctic NOUN
the Arctic die Arktis

are VERB ▸ SEE **be**

℘ area NOUN
1 (part of a town, a region) die Gegend (PL die
Gegenden
a nice area eine nette Gegend
in the Leeds area in der Gegend von Leeds
2 picnic area der Picknickplatz

℘ to argue VERB
sich streiten◊
to argue about something sich über etwas
(ACC) streiten
They're arguing about the result. Sie
streiten sich über das Ergebnis.

argument NOUN
1 der Streit (PL die Streite)
to get into an argument with somebody
mit jemandem in Streit geraten◊
to have an argument sich streiten◊
2 (point) das Argument (PL die Argumente)

Aries NOUN
der Widder

Pauline is Aries. Pauline ist Widder.

arithmetic NOUN
die **Arithmetik**, das **Rechnen**

♀ **arm** NOUN
der **Arm** (PL die **Arme**)
arm in arm Arm in Arm
to break your arm sich (DAT) den Arm
brechen

armchair NOUN
der **Sessel** (PL die **Sessel**)

armed ADJECTIVE
bewaffnet

army NOUN
1 die **Armee** (PL die **Armeen**), das **Heer**
(PL die **Heere**)
2 (profession) das **Militär**
to join the army zum Militär gehen

♀ **around** PREPOSITION, ADVERB
1 (with time of day) **gegen** (+ACC)
We'll be there around ten. Wir werden
gegen zehn da sein.
2 (with ages or amounts) **etwa**
She's around fifteen. Sie ist etwa fünfzehn.
We need around six kilos. Wir brauchen
etwa sechs Kilo.
3 (with dates) **um** (+ACC) ... **herum**
around 10 August um den 10. August
herum
4 (surrounding) **um** (+ACC) ... **herum**
the countryside around Edinburgh die
Landschaft um Edinburgh herum
5 (near) **Is there a post office around here?**
Gibt es hier in der Gegend eine Post?
Is Phil around? Ist Phil da?

♀ to **arrange** VERB
to arrange something etwas vereinbaren
**We've arranged to go to the cinema
on Saturday.** Wir haben vereinbart, am
Samstag ins Kino zu gehen.

arrest NOUN
to be under arrest verhaftet sein
to **arrest** VERB
verhaften

arrival NOUN
die **Ankunft** (PL die **Ankünfte**)

♀ to **arrive** VERB
ankommen◇ SEP (PERF sein)
They arrived at 3 p.m. Sie kamen um
fünfzehn Uhr an.

arrow NOUN
der **Pfeil** (PL die **Pfeile**)

art NOUN
1 die **Kunst** (PL die **Künste**)
modern art moderne Kunst
2 (school subject) die **Kunsterziehung**

artery NOUN
die **Arterie** (PL die **Arterien**)

art gallery NOUN
die **Kunstgalerie** (PL die **Kunstgalerien**)

artichoke NOUN
die **Artischocke** (PL die **Artischocken**)

♀ **article** NOUN
1 (in a newspaper or magazine) der **Artikel**
(PL die **Artikel**)
2 (object) das **Stück** (PL die **Stücke**)

artificial ADJECTIVE
künstlich

artist NOUN
der **Künstler** (PL die **Künstler**), die
Künstlerin (PL die **Künstlerinnen**)

WORD TIP Professions, hobbies, and sports
don't take an article in German: Er ist Künstler.

artistic ADJECTIVE
künstlerisch

art school NOUN
die **Kunsthochschule** (PL die
Kunsthochschulen)

♀ **as** CONJUNCTION, ADVERB
1 **wie**
as you know wie du weißt
as usual wie üblich
as I told you wie ich dir gesagt habe
2 (because) **da**
As there was no bus, we took a taxi. Da es
keinen Bus gab, nahmen wir ein Taxi.
3 **as ... as** so ... wie
He's as tall as his brother. Er ist so groß wie
sein Bruder.
Come as quickly as possible. Komm so
schnell wie möglich.
4 **as much ... as** so viel ... wie
You have as much time as I do. Du hast so
viel Zeit wie ich.
5 **as many ... as** so viele ... wie
We have as many problems as he does.
Wir haben genauso viele Probleme wie er.
6 **as long as** vorausgesetzt
**We'll go tomorrow, as long as it's a nice
day.** Wir gehen morgen, vorausgesetzt es
ist schönes Wetter.
7 **for as long as** solange
You can stay for as long as you like. Du
kannst bleiben, solange du willst.

◇ irregular verb; SEP separable verb; for more help with verbs see centre section

8 as soon as possible so bald wie möglich
9 to work as arbeiten als
    He works as a waiter in the evenings.
    Abends arbeitet er als Kellner.
10 as well auch

ash NOUN
1 die Asche (PL die Aschen)
2 (tree) die Esche (PL die Eschen)

ashamed ADJECTIVE
    to be ashamed of something sich wegen
    etwas (DAT) schämen
    You should be ashamed of yourself! Du
    solltest dich schämen!

ashtray NOUN
    der Aschenbecher (PL die Aschenbecher)

Asia NOUN
    das Asien
    in Asia in Asien

Asian NOUN
    der Asiate (PL die Asiaten), die Asiatin
    (PL die Asiatinnen)

Asian ADJECTIVE
    asiatisch

> **WORD TIP** Adjectives never have capitals
> in German, even for regions, countries, or
> nationalities.

ℰ **to ask** VERB
1 fragen
    to ask somebody something jemanden
    nach etwas (DAT) fragen
    I asked him the way. Ich fragte ihn nach
    dem Weg.
2 **to ask something** um etwas (ACC) bitten◇
    to ask somebody a favour jemanden um
    einen Gefallen bitten
    to ask somebody to do something
    jemanden bitten, etwas zu tun
    Ask Danny to give you a hand. Bitte Danny,
    dir zu helfen.
3 **to ask somebody a question** jemandem
    eine Frage stellen
    I asked him a few questions. Ich habe ihm
    ein paar Fragen gestellt.
4 einladen◇ SEP
    They've asked us to a party. Sie haben uns
    auf eine Party eingeladen.
    Paul's asked Janie out on Friday. Paul hat
    Janie Freitag eingeladen.
5 **to ask for** verlangen
    How much are they asking for the car?
    Wie viel verlangen sie für das Auto?

ℰ **asleep** ADJECTIVE
    to be asleep schlafen◇
    The baby is asleep. Das Baby schläft.

to fall asleep einschlafen◇ SEP (PERF sein)

asparagus NOUN
    der Spargel (PL die Spargel)

ℰ **aspirin** NOUN
    das Aspirin

assembly NOUN
    (at school) die morgendliche
    Versammlung (PL die morgendlichen
    Versammlungen)

to assess VERB
    beurteilen

assignment NOUN
    (at school) die Aufgabe (PL die Aufgaben)

to assist VERB
    helfen◇ (+DAT)

assistance NOUN
    die Hilfe

assistant NOUN
1 der Helfer (PL die Helfer), die Helferin
    (PL die Helferinnen)
2 (in school) der Assistent (PL die
    Assistenten), die Assistentin (PL die
    Assistentinnen)
3 **shop assistant** der Verkäufer (PL die
    Verkäuferin)

association NOUN
    der Verband (PL die Verbände)

assorted ADJECTIVE
    gemischt

assortment NOUN
    die Auswahl

to assume VERB
    annehmen◇ SEP
    I assume that ... Ich nehme an, dass ...

asterisk NOUN
    das Sternchen (PL die Sternchen)

asthma NOUN
    das Asthma

astrology NOUN
    die Astrologie

astronaut NOUN
    der Astronaut (PL die Astronauten), die
    Astronautin (PL die Astronautinnen)

> **WORD TIP** Professions, hobbies, and sports
> don't take an article in German: Er ist Astronaut.

astronomy NOUN
    die Astronomie

asylum NOUN
    das Asyl

ℰ indicates key words

asylum seeker NOUN
der **Asylbewerber** (PL die **Asylbewerber**),
die **Asylbewerberin** (PL die
Asylbewerberinnen)
He's an asylum seeker. Er ist Asylbewerber.

℘at PREPOSITION
1 **in** (+DAT)
at school in der Schule
at my office in meinem Büro
at the supermarket im Supermarkt
2 **an** (+DAT)
at the station am Bahnhof
at the bus stop an der Bushaltestelle
3 **bei** (+DAT)
at the dentist beim Zahnarzt
at Emma's bei Emma
at the hairdresser's beim Friseur
She's at her brother's this evening. Sie ist
heute Abend bei ihrem Bruder.
4 **at a party** auf einer Party
5 **at home** zu Hause
6 (talking about the time) **um**
at eight o'clock um acht Uhr
7 **at night** nachts
at Christmas zu Weihnachten
at the weekend am Wochenende
8 (in email addresses) der **Klammeraffe**
(informal)
9 **at last** endlich
She's found a job at last. Sie hat endlich
einen Job gefunden.

athlete NOUN
der **Sportler** (PL die **Sportler**), die
Sportlerin (PL die **Sportlerinnen**), der
Athlet (PL die **Athleten**), die **Athletin** (PL die
Athletinnen)

WORD TIP Professions, hobbies, and sports
don't take an article in German: Er ist Sportler.

athletic ADJECTIVE
sportlich

℘athletics NOUN
die **Leichtathletik**

Atlantic NOUN
the Atlantic (Ocean) der Atlantik

atlas NOUN
der **Atlas** (PL die **Atlanten**)

atmosphere NOUN
die **Atmosphäre** (PL die **Atmosphären**)

atom NOUN
das **Atom** (PL die **Atome**)

atomic ADJECTIVE
Atom-
an atomic bomb eine Atombombe

at-sign NOUN
das **At-Zeichen** (PL die **At-Zeichen**)

℘to attach VERB
befestigen

attached ADJECTIVE
(emotionally)
to be attached to somebody/something an
jemandem/etwas (DAT) hängen◊

attachment NOUN
1 (in a letter) die **Anlage** (PL die **Anlagen**)
2 (in an email) der **Anhang** (PL die **Anhänge**)

attack NOUN
der **Angriff** (PL die **Angriffe**)

to attack VERB
1 **angreifen**◊ SEP
2 (mug or raid) **überfallen**◊

attempt NOUN
der **Versuch** (PL die **Versuche**)
at the first attempt beim ersten Versuch

to attempt VERB
to attempt to do something versuchen,
etwas zu tun

to attend VERB
teilnehmen◊ SEP **an** (+DAT)
to attend a meeting an einer Besprechung
teilnehmen
to attend an evening class einen
Abendkurs besuchen

attendance NOUN
die **Anwesenheit**

℘attention NOUN
1 die **Aufmerksamkeit**
to pay attention aufpassen SEP
I wasn't paying attention. Ich habe nicht
aufgepasst.
2 **He wasn't paying attention to the teacher.**
Er hörte dem Lehrer nicht zu.

attic NOUN
der **Dachboden** (PL die **Dachböden**)
in the attic auf dem Dachboden

attitude NOUN
1 (way of thinking) die **Einstellung**
2 (way of acting) die **Haltung**

to attract VERB
anziehen◊ SEP

attraction NOUN
1 die **Anziehung**
2 (a thing that attracts) die **Attraktion** (PL die
Attraktionen)
The whale was a big attraction. Der Wal
war eine große Attraktion.

◊ **irregular verb**; SEP **separable verb**; for more help with verbs see centre section

attractive ADJECTIVE
attraktiv

aubergine NOUN
die Aubergine (PL die Auberginen)

auction NOUN
die Auktion (PL die Auktionen)

ℰ **audience** NOUN
das Publikum
the television audience die
Fernsehzuschauer (PLURAL)

audition NOUN
(singing) das Vorsingen, (acting) das
Vorsprechen

ℰ **August** NOUN
der August
in August im August

ℰ **aunt, auntie** NOUN
die Tante (PL die Tanten)

au pair NOUN
das Au-pair-Mädchen (PL die Au-pair-
Mädchen)
I'm looking for a job as an au pair. Ich
suche eine Au-pair-Stelle.

Australia NOUN
Australien (NEUTER)
to Australia nach Australien

Australian NOUN
der Australier (PL die Australier), die
Australierin (PL die Australierinnen)

Australian ADJECTIVE
australisch
the Australian government die australische
Regierung
He's Australian. Er ist Australier.
She's Australian. Sie ist Australierin.

WORD TIP Adjectives never have capitals
in German, even for regions, countries, or
nationalities.

Austria NOUN
Österreich (NEUTER)
in Austria in Österreich

🅞 **AUSTRIA**

Capital: Wien (Vienna). Population: over
8 million. Size: 83,872 square km. Official
language: German. Official currency: euro.

Austrian NOUN
der Österreicher (PL die Österreicher), die
Österreicherin (PL die Österreicherinnen)

Austrian ADJECTIVE
österreichisch
Austrian cuisine die österreichische Küche

He's Austrian. Er ist Österreicher.
She's Austrian. Sie ist Österreicherin.

WORD TIP Adjectives never have capitals
in German, even for regions, countries, or
nationalities.

ℰ **author** NOUN
der Autor (PL die Autoren), die Autorin
(PL die Autorinnen)

WORD TIP Professions, hobbies, and sports
don't take an article in German: Sie ist Autorin.

autobiography NOUN
die Autobiografie (PL die Autobiografien)

autograph NOUN
das Autogramm (PL die Autogramme)

automatic ADJECTIVE
automatisch

automatically ADVERB
automatisch

ℰ **autumn** NOUN
der Herbst (PL die Herbste)
in autumn im Herbst

available ADJECTIVE
(on sale) erhältlich

avalanche NOUN
die Lawine (PL die Lawinen)

ℰ **average** NOUN
der Durchschnitt (PL die Durchschnitte)
on average im Durchschnitt
above average über dem Durchschnitt

average ADJECTIVE
durchschnittlich
the average height die durchschnittliche
Größe

avocado NOUN
die Avocado (PL die Avocados)

to **avoid** VERB
1 vermeiden◇
to avoid doing something es vermeiden,
etwas zu tun
I avoid speaking to him. Ich vermeide es,
mit ihm zu reden.
2 (keep away from somebody or a place)
meiden◇
She's avoiding me. Sie meidet mich.

awake ADJECTIVE
to be awake wach sein
Are you still awake? Bist du noch wach?

award NOUN
der Preis (PL die Preise)
to win an award einen Preis gewinnen

ℰ indicates key words

aware ADJECTIVE
  to be aware of a problem sich (DAT) eines
  Problems bewusst sein
  I'm aware of the danger. Ich bin mir der
  Gefahr bewusst.
  as far as I'm aware soweit ich weiß

ℓ **away** ADVERB
  1 **to be away** nicht da sein◇ (PERF **sein**)
     I'll be away next week. Ich bin nächste
     Woche nicht da.
  2 **to go away** verreisen (PERF **sein**)
     Laura's gone away for a week. Laura ist für
     eine Woche verreist.
     Go away! Geh weg!
  3 **to run away** weglaufen◇ SEP (PERF **sein**)
     The thieves ran away. Die Diebe liefen weg.
  4 **The school is two kilometres away.** Die
     Schule ist zwei Kilometer entfernt.
     How far away is it? Wie weit entfernt ist
     es?
     not far away nicht weit entfernt
  5 **to put something away** etwas wegräumen
     SEP
     I'm just putting my books away. Ich räume
     gerade meine Bücher weg.
  6 **to give something away** etwas
     weggeben◇ SEP, (as a present) etwas
     verschenken
     She's given away all her cassettes. Sie hat
     alle ihre Kassetten verschenkt.

away match NOUN
  das **Auswärtsspiel** (PL die **Auswärtsspiele**)

ℓ **awful** ADJECTIVE
  furchtbar
  The film was awful. Der Film war furchtbar.
  I feel awful. (ill) Ich fühle mich furchtbar.
  I feel awful about it. Es ist mir furchtbar
  unangenehm.
  an awful lot of mistakes furchtbar viele
  Fehler

awkward ADJECTIVE
  1 schwierig
     It's an awkward situation. Das ist eine
     schwierige Situation.
     It's a bit awkward. Das ist ein bisschen
     schwierig.
     an awkward child ein schwieriges Kind
  2 **an awkward question** eine peinliche Frage

axe NOUN
  die **Axt** (PL die **Äxte**)

Bb

ℓ **baby** NOUN
  das **Baby** (PL die **Babys**)

to **babysit** VERB
  babysitten

babysitter NOUN
  der **Babysitter** (PL die **Babysitter**), die
  Babysitterin (PL die **Babysitterinnen**)

babysitting NOUN
  das **Babysitten**

bachelor NOUN
  der **Junggeselle** (PL die **Junggesellen**)
  Andy is a bachelor. Andy ist Junggeselle.

ℓ **back** NOUN
  1 (of a person or animal) der **Rücken** (PL die
     Rücken)
     He did it behind my back. Er hat es hinter
     meinem Rücken getan.
  2 (of a piece of paper, cheque, or building) die
     Rückseite (PL die **Rückseiten**)
     on the back auf der Rückseite
  3 **the back of your hand** der Handrücken
  4 **at the back** hinten
     at the back of the room hinten im Zimmer
     We sat at the back. Wir saßen hinten.
     a garden at the back of the house ein
     Garten hinter dem Haus
  5 (of a chair or sofa) die **Rückenlehne** (PL die
     Rückenlehnen)
  6 (in football or hockey) der **Verteidiger** (PL
     die **Verteidiger**), die **Verteidigerin** (PL die
     Verteidigerinnen)
     left back der Linksverteidiger

back ADJECTIVE
  the back door die Hintertür
  the back garden der Garten hinter dem
  Haus

back ADVERB
  1 zurück
     there and back hin und zurück
     to go back (on foot) zurückgehen◇ SEP (PERF
     sein), (in a vehicle) zurückfahren◇ SEP (PERF
     sein)
  2 **to come back** zurückkommen◇ SEP (PERF
     sein)
     They've come back from Italy. Sie sind aus
     Italien zurückgekommen.
     I'll be back at eight o'clock. Ich bin um acht
     Uhr zurück.
     Sue's not back yet. Sue ist noch nicht
     zurück.
  3 **to phone back** zurückrufen◇ SEP

◇ **irregular verb;** SEP **separable verb; for more help with verbs see centre section**

I'll ring back later. Ich rufe dich später zurück.
4 **to give something back to somebody** jemandem etwas zurückgeben◇ *SEP*
Give it back! Gib es zurück!

to **back** *VERB*
(bet on) setzen auf (+*ACC*)
• **to back up** *(computing)* sichern
to back up a file eine Sicherungskopie machen
• **to back somebody up** jemanden unterstützen

backache *NOUN*
die **Rückenschmerzen** (*PLURAL*)
I had backache. Ich hatte Rückenschmerzen.

background *NOUN*
1 *(of a person)* die **Verhältnisse** (*PLURAL*)
She comes from a poor background. Sie kommt aus ärmlichen Verhältnissen.
2 *(in a picture, view, or situation)* der **Hintergrund** (*PL* die **Hintergründe**)
background noise die Hintergrundgeräusche (*PLURAL*)
3 *(to events or problems)* die **Hintergründe** (*PLURAL*)

backhand *NOUN*
die **Rückhand**

backing *NOUN*
1 *(moral support)* die **Unterstützung**
2 *(in music)* die **Begleitung**
a backing group eine Begleitband

backpack *NOUN*
der **Rucksack** (*PL* die **Rucksäcke**)

backpacking *NOUN*
to go backpacking als Rucksacktourist unterwegs sein◇ (*PERF* sein)

back seat *NOUN*
der **Rücksitz** (*PL* die **Rücksitze**)

backstroke *NOUN*
das **Rückenschwimmen**

back to front *ADVERB*
verkehrt herum
Your jumper is back to front. Du hast deinen Pullover verkehrt herum an.

backup *NOUN*
1 *(support)* die **Unterstützung**
2 *(in computing)* die **Sicherungskopie** (*PL* die **Sicherungskopien**)
a backup disk eine Sicherungsdiskette

backwards *ADVERB*
1 rückwärts
2 **to lean backwards** sich nach hinten lehnen
to fall backwards nach hinten fallen

bacon *NOUN*
der **Speck**
bacon and eggs Eier mit Speck

ℰ **bad** *ADJECTIVE*
1 *(not good)* schlecht
a bad idea eine schlechte Idee
a bad meal ein schlechtes Essen
His new film's not bad. Sein neuer Film ist nicht schlecht.
It's bad for your health. Das ist ungesund.
I'm bad at physics. Ich bin schlecht in Physik.
2 *(serious)* schlimm
a bad mistake ein schlimmer Fehler
a bad cold eine schlimme Erkältung
3 **a bad accident** ein schwerer Unfall
4 *(rotten)* schlecht
to go bad schlecht werden
5 **a bad apple** ein fauler Apfel
6 **bad language** die Kraftausdrücke (*PLURAL*)
7 **Too bad!** Schade!, So ein Pech!

badge *NOUN*
das **Abzeichen** (*PL* die **Abzeichen**)
a name badge ein Namensschild

ℰ **badly** *ADVERB*
1 *(poorly)* schlecht
He writes badly. Er schreibt schlecht.
I slept badly. Ich habe schlecht geschlafen.
2 *(seriously)* schwer
They were badly injured. Sie waren schwer verletzt.
3 *(very much)* dringend
to need something badly etwas dringend brauchen

bad-mannered *ADJECTIVE*
to be bad-mannered schlechte Manieren haben

badminton *NOUN*
das **Badminton**

bad-tempered *ADJECTIVE*
schlecht gelaunt
a bad-tempered old man ein schlecht gelaunter alter Mann

ℰ **bag** *NOUN*
1 die **Tasche** (*PL* die **Taschen**)
2 *(made of paper or plastic)* die **Tüte** (*PL* die **Tüten**)

baggage *NOUN*
das **Gepäck**

ℰ indicates key words

bagpipes PLURAL NOUN
der Dudelsack (PL die Dudelsäcke)

bags PLURAL NOUN
das Gepäck
to pack your bags (seine Sachen) packen
to have bags under your eyes Ringe unter den Augen haben (informal)

to bake VERB
1 backen
to bake a cake einen Kuchen backen
2 **I'm baking.** Mir ist furchtbar heiß.

baked ADJECTIVE
1 (fish or fruit) überbacken
baked apples Bratäpfel
2 **baked potatoes** Ofenkartoffeln

baked beans PLURAL NOUN
Bohnen in Tomatensoße

baker NOUN
der Bäcker (PL die Bäcker)
to go to the baker's zum Bäcker gehen
at the baker's beim Bäcker

WORD TIP Professions, hobbies, and sports don't take an article in German: Er ist Bäcker.

bakery NOUN
die Bäckerei (PL die Bäckereien)

balance NOUN
1 das Gleichgewicht
to lose your balance das Gleichgewicht verlieren◇
2 (in a bank account) der Kontostand

balanced ADJECTIVE
ausgeglichen

balcony NOUN
der Balkon (PL die Balkons)

bald ADJECTIVE
1 kahl
2 (of a person) kahlköpfig
to go bald eine Glatze bekommen

WORD TIP Do not translate the English word bald with the German bald.

ball NOUN
1 (for tennis, football, or golf) der Ball (PL die Bälle)
2 (for billiards, croquet) die Kugel (PL die Kugeln)
3 (of string or wool) das Knäuel (PL die Knäuel)

ballet NOUN
das Ballett (PL die Ballette)

ballet dancer NOUN
der Balletttänzer (PL die Balletttänzer), die

Balletttänzerin (PL die Balletttänzerinnen)

WORD TIP Professions, hobbies, and sports don't take an article in German: Sie ist Balletttänzerin.

balloon NOUN
1 der Luftballon (PL die Luftballons)
2 (hot-air) der Ballon (PL die Ballons)

ballpoint (pen) NOUN
der Kugelschreiber (PL die Kugelschreiber)

ban NOUN
das Verbot (PL die Verbote)
a ban on smoking ein Rauchverbot

to ban VERB
verbieten◇
to ban someone from smoking jemandem verbieten zu rauchen

banana NOUN
1 die Banane (PL die Bananen)
2 **a banana yoghurt** ein Bananenjoghurt

band NOUN
1 (playing music) die Band (PL die Bands)
rock band die Rockband
brass band die Blaskapelle
2 **rubber band** das Gummiband

bandage NOUN
der Verband (PL die Verbände)

to bandage VERB
verbinden◇

bang NOUN
(noise) der Knall (PL die Knalle)

to bang VERB
1 (hit, knock) schlagen◇
He banged his fist on the table. Er schlug mit der Faust auf den Tisch.
to bang on the door gegen die Tür schlagen
2 **I banged my head on the door.** Ich habe mir den Kopf an der Tür gestoßen.
3 **to bang into something** gegen etwas (ACC) knallen
4 (shut loudly) zuknallen SEP
He banged the door. Er knallte die Tür zu.

bang EXCLAMATION
peng!

bank NOUN
1 (for money) die Bank (PL die Banken)
I'm going to the bank. Ich gehe auf die Bank.
2 (of a river or lake) das Ufer (PL die Ufer)

bank account NOUN
das Bankkonto (PL die Bankkonten)

◇ irregular verb; SEP separable verb; for more help with verbs see centre section

bank balance NOUN
der **Kontostand** (PL die **Kontostände**)

bank holiday NOUN
der **gesetzliche Feiertag** (PL die **gesetzlichen Feiertage**)

banknote NOUN
der **Geldschein** (PL die **Geldscheine**)

bank statement NOUN
der **Kontoauszug** (PL die **Kontoauszüge**)

ℙ **bar** NOUN
1 (selling drinks) die **Bar** (PL die **Bars**)
Janet works in a bar. Janet arbeitet in einer Bar.
2 (counter) die **Theke** (PL die **Theken**)
on the bar auf der Theke
3 **a bar of chocolate** eine Tafel Schokolade
4 **a bar of soap** ein Stück Seife
5 (made of wood or metal) die **Stange** (PL die **Stangen**)
an iron bar eine Eisenstange
6 (in music) der **Takt** (PL die **Takte**)

barbecue NOUN
1 (apparatus) der **Grill** (PL die **Grills**)
2 (party) das **Grillfest** (PL die **Grillfeste**)

to **barbecue** VERB
to barbecue a chicken ein Hühnchen grillen
barbecued chicken gegrilltes Hühnchen

bare ADJECTIVE
nackt

barefoot ADJECTIVE
to be barefoot barfuß sein
to walk barefoot barfuß gehen

bargain NOUN
(a good buy) der **gute Kauf** (PL die **guten Käufe**)
I got a bargain. Ich habe einen guten Kauf gemacht.
It's a bargain! Das ist ein Schnäppchen!

barge NOUN
der **Kahn** (PL die **Kähne**)

bark NOUN
1 (of a tree) die **Rinde** (PL die **Rinden**)
2 (of a dog) das **Bellen**

to **bark** VERB
bellen

barn NOUN
die **Scheune** (PL die **Scheunen**)

barrel NOUN
das **Fass** (PL die **Fässer**)

barrier NOUN
die **Absperrung** (PL die **Absperrungen**)

base NOUN
(bottom part) der **Fuß** (PL die **Füße**)

baseball NOUN
der **Baseball**

based ADJECTIVE
1 **to be based on** basieren auf (+DAT)
The film is based on a true story. Der Film basiert auf einer wahren Geschichte.
2 **to be based in** wohnen in (+DAT)
He's based in Bristol. Er wohnt in Bristol.

ℙ **basement** NOUN
das **Kellergeschoss** (PL die **Kellergeschosse**)

bash NOUN
1 der **Schlag** (PL die **Schläge**)
2 **I'll have a bash.** Ich probier's mal.

to **bash** VERB
I bashed my head. Ich habe mir den Kopf angestoßen.

basic ADJECTIVE
1 grundlegend, Grund-
basic knowledge die Grundkenntnisse (PLURAL)
her basic salary ihr Grundgehalt
2 **the basic problem** das Hauptproblem
3 (not luxurious) einfach

basically ADVERB
1 grundsätzlich
It's basically all right. Grundsätzlich ist es okay.
2 **Basically, I don't want to come.** Eigentlich will ich nicht kommen.

basics PLURAL NOUN
the basics das Wesentliche

basin NOUN
das **Becken** (PL die **Becken**)

basis NOUN
1 die **Basis**
2 **on a regular basis** regelmäßig

ℙ **basket** NOUN
der **Korb** (PL die **Körbe**)
a basket of apples ein Korb Äpfel
waste-paper basket der Papierkorb

basketball NOUN
der **Basketball**

bass NOUN
1 der **Bass** (PL die **Bässe**)
2 **double bass** der Kontrabass

bass guitar NOUN
die **Bassgitarre** (PL die **Bassgitarren**)

bassoon NOUN
das **Fagott** (PL die **Fagotte**)
He plays the bassoon. Er spielt Fagott.

WORD TIP Don't use the article when you talk about playing an instrument.

bat NOUN
1 (for games) der **Schläger** (PL die **Schläger**)
2 (animal) die **Fledermaus** (PL die **Fledermäuse**)

ℰ **bath** NOUN
1 das **Bad** (PL die **Bäder**)
to have a bath baden
2 (tub) die **Badewanne** (PL die **Badewannen**)

ℰ **bathroom** NOUN
das **Badezimmer** (PL die **Badezimmer**)

baths PLURAL NOUN
die **Badeanstalt** (PL die **Badeanstalten**)

bath towel NOUN
das **Badetuch** (PL die **Badetücher**)

batter NOUN
der **Teig** (PL die **Teige**)
fish in batter ausgebackener Fisch

battery NOUN
die **Batterie** (PL die **Batterien**)

battle NOUN
1 (in war) die **Schlacht** (PL die **Schlachten**)
2 (contest) der **Kampf** (PL die **Kämpfe**)

Bavaria NOUN
Bayern (NEUTER)

bay NOUN
1 (on coast) die **Bucht** (PL die **Buchten**)
2 (in bus station) die **Haltebucht** (PL die **Haltebuchten**)

BC ABBREVIATION
(before Christ) v. Chr., (vor Christus)

ℰ to **be** VERB
1 sein◇ (PERF sein)
Melanie is in the kitchen. Melanie ist in der Küche.
Where is the butter? Wo ist die Butter?
I'm tired. Ich bin müde.
when we were in Germany als wir in Deutschland waren
2 (with jobs and professions) sein◇ (PERF sein)
She's a teacher. Sie ist Lehrerin.
He's a taxi driver. Er ist Taxifahrer.
3 (in clock times, days of the week, dates, and age) sein◇ (PERF sein)

It's three o'clock. Es ist drei Uhr.
It's half past five. Es ist halb sechs.
What day is it today? Welcher Tag ist heute?
It's Tuesday today. Heute ist Dienstag.
It's the twentieth of May. Heute ist der zwanzigste Mai.
What's the date today? Der Wievielte ist heute?
How old are you? Wie alt bist du?
I'm fifteen. Ich bin fünfzehn.
4 (cold, hot, ill) sein◇ (PERF sein)
to be ill krank sein
I'm hot. Mir ist heiß.
I'm cold. Mir ist kalt.
5 (weather) sein◇ (PERF sein)
It's cold today. Heute ist es kalt.
It's a nice day. Es ist schönes Wetter.
It's raining. Es regnet.
6 **I'm hungry.** Ich habe Hunger.
She's thirsty. Sie hat Durst.
7 (saying how much something costs) kosten
How much are the bananas? Wie viel kosten die Bananen?
8 (go, come, or visit) sein◇ (PERF sein)
I've never been to Berlin. Ich war noch nie in Berlin.
Have you been to England before? Warst du schon einmal in England?
Has the postman been? War der Briefträger schon da?
9 (forming the passive) werden◇ (PERF sein)
to be loved geliebt werden
He has been promoted. Er ist befördert worden.
10 **there is/are** es gibt
Is there a bank near here? Gibt es hier in der Nähe eine Bank?

ℰ **beach** NOUN
der **Strand** (PL die **Strände**)
to go to the beach zum Strand gehen
on the beach am Strand

bead NOUN
die **Perle** (PL die **Perlen**)

beak NOUN
der **Schnabel** (PL die **Schnäbel**)

beam NOUN
1 (of light) der **Strahl** (PL die **Strahlen**)
2 (for a roof) der **Balken** (PL die **Balken**)

bean NOUN
die **Bohne** (PL die **Bohnen**)
green beans grüne Bohnen

bear NOUN
der **Bär** (PL die **Bären**)

◇ **irregular verb**; SEP **separable verb**; for more help with verbs see centre section

to bear VERB
1 ertragen◇
   I can't bear the idea. Ich kann den Gedanken nicht ertragen.
2 **to bear something in mind** an etwas (ACC) denken◇
   I'll bear it in mind. Ich denke daran.

beard NOUN
der Bart (PL die Bärte)

bearded ADJECTIVE
bärtig

beast NOUN
1 (animal) das Tier (PL die Tiere)
2 **You beast!** Du Biest!

beat NOUN
(in music) der Takt

to beat VERB
1 (defeat) schlagen◇
   We beat them! Wir haben sie geschlagen!
2 **You can't beat a good meal.** Es geht doch nichts über ein gutes Essen.
• **to beat somebody up**
  jemanden verprügeln

beautician NOUN
die Kosmetikerin (PL die Kosmetikerinnen)

WORD TIP Professions, hobbies, and sports don't take an article in German: Sie ist Kosmetikerin.

℘ **beautiful** ADJECTIVE
schön

beauty NOUN
1 die Schönheit (PL die Schönheiten)
2 **The beauty of it is that...** Das Schöne daran ist, dass...

℘ **because** CONJUNCTION
1 weil
   because it's cold weil es kalt ist
2 **because of** wegen (+GEN)
   because of the accident wegen des Unfalls
   because of you deinetwegen

to become VERB
werden◇ (PERF sein)
She's become a painter. Sie ist Malerin geworden.

WORD TIP Do not translate the English word become with the German bekommen.

℘ **bed** NOUN
1 das Bett (PL die Betten)
   double bed das Doppelbett
   in bed im Bett
   to go to bed ins Bett gehen
2 (flower bed) das Beet (PL die Beete)

bedclothes PLURAL NOUN
das Bettzeug (SINGULAR)

bedding NOUN
das Bettzeug

℘ **bedroom** NOUN
das Schlafzimmer (PL die Schlafzimmer)
bedroom furniture die Schlafzimmermöbel (PLURAL)
my bedroom window mein Schlafzimmerfenster

bedside table NOUN
der Nachttisch (PL die Nachttische)

bedsit, bedsitter NOUN
das möblierte Zimmer (PL die möblierten Zimmer)

bedspread NOUN
die Tagesdecke (PL die Tagesdecken)

bedtime NOUN
die Schlafenszeit
at bedtime vor dem Schlafengehen

bee NOUN
die Biene (PL die Bienen)

beech NOUN
die Buche (PL die Buchen)

℘ **beef** NOUN
das Rindfleisch
We had roast beef. Wir haben Rinderbraten gegessen.

beefburger NOUN
der Hamburger (PL die Hamburger)

℘ **beer** NOUN
das Bier (PL die Biere)
Two beers please. Zwei Bier bitte.
beer can die Bierdose
beer bottle die Bierflasche

beetle NOUN
der Käfer (PL die Käfer)

beetroot NOUN
die Rote Bete

℘ **before** PREPOSITION
1 vor (+DAT)
   before Monday vor Montag
   He left before me. Er ist vor mir gegangen.
   the day before the wedding am Tag vor der Hochzeit
2 **the day before** am Tag zuvor
   the day before yesterday vorgestern
   the week before in der Woche zuvor
3 (already) schon einmal
   I've seen him before somewhere. Ich habe

℘ indicates key words

ihn schon einmal irgendwo gesehen.
I had seen the film before. Ich hatte den
Film schon einmal gesehen.

before CONJUNCTION
bevor
**I closed the windows before leaving
(or before I left).** Ich habe die Fenster
zugemacht, bevor ich wegging.
before the train leaves bevor der Zug
abfährt
Oh, before I forget ... Oh, bevor ich es
vergesse ...

beforehand ADVERB
(ahead of time) vorher
Phone beforehand. Rufe vorher an.

to **beg** VERB
1 betteln
to beg for money um Geld betteln
2 *(ask)* bitten◇
He begged her not to say anything. Er bat
sie, nichts zu sagen.
3 **I beg your pardon.** Entschuldigen Sie bitte.

ℰ to **begin** VERB
anfangen◇ SEP, beginnen◇
The meeting begins at ten. Die
Besprechung fängt um zehn an.
the words beginning with P die Wörter (PL
die mit P anfangen)
to begin to do something anfangen, etwas
zu tun
I'm beginning to understand why ... Jetzt
verstehe ich langsam, warum ...

beginner NOUN
der Anfänger (PL die Anfänger), die
Anfängerin (PL die Anfängerinnen)

beginning NOUN
der Anfang (PL die Anfänge)
at the beginning am Anfang
at the beginning of the holidays am
Anfang der Ferien

ℰ **behalf** NOUN
on behalf of im Namen von (+DAT)
on behalf of Mr and Mrs Smith im Namen
von Herrn und Frau Smith

ℰ to **behave** VERB
1 sich benehmen◇
He behaved badly. Er hat sich schlecht
benommen.
2 **to behave yourself** sich benehmen◇
Behave yourself! Benimm dich!

ℰ **behaviour** NOUN
das Benehmen

ℰ **behind** NOUN
der Hintern *(informal)* die Hintern

behind PREPOSITION, ADVERB
1 hinter *(+DAT, or, with movement towards a
place, +ACC)*
behind the sofa hinter dem Sofa
behind them hinter ihnen
the car behind das Auto hinter ihnen/uns
2 **to leave something behind** *(belongings)*
etwas vergessen◇

beige ADJECTIVE
beige

ℰ **Belgian** NOUN
der Belgier (PL die Belgier), die Belgierin
(PL die Belgierinnen)

Belgian ADJECTIVE
belgisch
Belgian chocolates belgische Pralinen
He's Belgian. Er ist Belgier.
She's Belgian. Sie ist Belgierin.

WORD TIP Adjectives never have capitals
in German, even for regions, countries, or
nationalities.

ℰ **Belgium** NOUN
Belgien *(NEUTER)*
to Belgium nach Belgien

belief NOUN
der Glaube (PL die Glauben)
his political beliefs seine politische
Überzeugung *(SINGULAR)*

ℰ to **believe** VERB
1 glauben
I believe so. Ich glaube schon.
They believed what I said. Sie glaubten,
was ich sagte.
I don't believe you. Das glaube ich dir nicht.
2 **to believe in something** an etwas (ACC)
glauben
to believe in God an Gott glauben

bell NOUN
1 *(in a church)* die Glocke (PL die Glocken)
2 *(on a door)* die Klingel (PL die Klingeln)
to ring the bell klingeln
3 *(for a cat or toy)* das Glöckchen (PL die
Glöckchen)
4 **That name rings a bell.** Der Name sagt mir
etwas. *(literally: says something to me)*

ℰ to **belong** VERB
1 **to belong to** gehören (+DAT)
That belongs to my mother. Das gehört
meiner Mutter.
2 **to belong to a club** einem Klub angehören
3 *(go)* gehören
Where does this vase belong? Wo gehört

◇ **irregular verb;** SEP **separable verb; for more help with verbs see centre section**

diese Vase hin?

belongings PLURAL NOUN
die **Sachen** (PLURAL)
all my belongings alle meine Sachen

ℱ **below** PREPOSITION
unter (+DAT, or, with movement towards a place, +ACC)
below the window unter dem Fenster
the flat below yours die Wohnung unter dir

below ADVERB
1 (further down) **unten**
He called from below. Er rief von unten herauf.
2 **the flat below** die Wohnung darunter

ℱ **belt** NOUN
der **Gürtel** (PL die **Gürtel**)

bench NOUN
die **Bank** (PL die **Bänke**)

bend NOUN
1 (in a road) die **Kurve** (PL die **Kurven**)
2 (in a river) die **Biegung** (PL die **Biegungen**)
to **bend** VERB
1 (make a bend in) **biegen**◇ (a pipe or wire)
beugen (your knee, arm, or head)
2 (curve) eine **Biegung machen**
3 **to bend down** sich **bücken**

beneath PREPOSITION
unter (+DAT)

benefit NOUN
1 der **Vorteil** (PL die **Vorteile**)
2 **unemployment benefit** die **Arbeitslosenunterstützung**

bent ADJECTIVE
verbogen

beret NOUN
die **Baskenmütze** (PL die **Baskenmützen**)

Berlin NOUN
Berlin (NEUTER)
to Berlin nach Berlin

🔵 **BERLIN**
Berlin is the capital city of Germany.

ℱ **beside** PREPOSITION
1 (next to) **neben** (+DAT, or, with movement towards a place, +ACC)
She was sitting beside me. Sie saß neben mir. (DAT)
She sat down beside me. Sie hat sich neben mich gesetzt. (ACC)
2 **That's beside the point.** Das hat nichts damit zu tun.

besides ADVERB
(anyway) **außerdem**
Besides, it's too late. Außerdem ist es zu spät.
(as well) **four dogs, and six cats besides** vier Hunde und außerdem sechs Katzen

ℱ **best** ADJECTIVE
1 **bester/beste/bestes**
She's my best friend. Sie ist meine beste Freundin.
2 **She's the best at tennis.** Im Tennis ist sie die Beste.
It's best to wait. Das Beste ist zu warten.

best ADVERB
am besten
He plays best. Er spielt am besten.
I like Munich best. München gefällt mir am besten.
best of all am allerbesten
I like grapes best. Ich mag Weintrauben am liebsten.
All the best! Alles Gute!
to make the best of it das Beste daraus machen
to do your best sein Bestes tun
I did my best to help her. Ich habe mein Bestes getan, um ihr zu helfen.

best-before date NOUN
das **Mindesthaltbarkeitsdatum** (PL die **Mindesthaltbarkeitsdaten**)

best man NOUN
der **Trauzeuge** (PL die **Trauzeugen**)

bet NOUN
die **Wette** (PL die **Wetten**)
to **bet** VERB
wetten
to bet on a horse auf ein Pferd wetten
I bet you he'll forget it. Ich wette mit dir, dass er es vergisst.

ℱ **better** ADJECTIVE, ADVERB
1 **besser**
She's found a better flat. Sie hat eine bessere Wohnung gefunden.
2 **It works better than the other one.** Dieser geht besser als der andere.
even better noch besser
It's even better than before. Das ist noch besser als vorher.
3 (less ill)
I'm better. Es geht mir besser.
He's a bit better today. Es geht ihm heute ein bisschen besser.
I feel better. Ich fühle mich besser.
4 **to get better** besser werden
My German is getting better. Mein

Deutsch wird besser.
5 **so much the better** umso besser
the sooner the better je eher, desto besser
6 *(to say you must do something)*
It's better to phone at once. Es wäre besser, sofort anzurufen.
He'd better not go. Er sollte besser nicht gehen.
I'd better go now. Ich gehe jetzt besser.

better off *ADJECTIVE*
1 *(richer)* besser gestellt
They're better off than us. Sie sind besser gestellt als wir.
2 *(more comfortable)*
to be better off besser dran sein
You'd be better off in bed. Im Bett wärst du besser aufgehoben.

℘ **between** *PREPOSITION*
1 zwischen *(+DAT, or, with movement towards a place, +ACC)*
between London and Dover zwischen London und Dover
between Monday and Friday zwischen Montag und Freitag
2 *(sharing)* unter *(+DAT)*
between ourselves unter uns
between the two of them unter sich

beyond *PREPOSITION*
1 *(in space)* jenseits *(+GEN)*
beyond the border jenseits der Grenze
2 *(in time)* nach *(+DAT)*
beyond midnight nach Mitternacht
3 **It's beyond me!** Das ist mir unverständlich.

Bible *NOUN*
the Bible die Bibel

℘ **bicycle** *NOUN*
das Fahrrad (*PL* die Fahrräder)
She rides a bicycle. Sie fährt Rad.

℘ **big** *ADJECTIVE*
groß
a big house ein großes Haus
my big sister meine große Schwester
a big mistake ein großer Fehler
It's too big for me. Das ist mir zu groß.

big toe *NOUN*
die große Zehe (*PL* die großen Zehen)

℘ **bike** *NOUN*
1 *(with pedals)* das Rad (*PL* die Räder)
by bike mit dem Rad
2 *(with engine)* das Motorrad (*PL* die Motorräder)

bikini *NOUN*
der Bikini (*PL* die Bikinis)

bilingual *ADJECTIVE*
zweisprachig

℘ **bill** *NOUN*
die Rechnung (*PL* die Rechnungen)
Can we have the bill, please? Die Rechnung bitte./Zahlen bitte.

billiards *NOUN*
das Billard
to play billiards Billard spielen

billion *NOUN*
die Milliarde (*PL* die Milliarden)
two billion euros zwei Milliarden Euro

WORD TIP Do not translate the English word billion with the German Billion.

bin *NOUN*
der Mülleimer (*PL* die Mülleimer)

℘ **binoculars** *PLURAL NOUN*
das Fernglas (*PL* die Ferngläser)

WORD TIP In German, das Fernglas is singular.

biochemistry *NOUN*
die Biochemie

biofuel *NOUN*
der Biokraftstoff (*PL* die Biokraftstoffe)

biography *NOUN*
die Biografie (*PL* die Biografien)

biologist *NOUN*
der Biologe (*PL* die Biologen), die Biologin (*PL* die Biologinnen)

WORD TIP Professions, hobbies, and sports don't take an article in German: Er ist Biologe.

℘ **biology** *NOUN*
die Biologie

℘ **bird** *NOUN*
der Vogel (*PL* die Vögel)

bird flu *NOUN*
die Vogelgrippe

bird sanctuary *NOUN*
das Vogelschutzgebiet (*PL* die Vogelschutzgebiete)

birdwatching *NOUN*
das Beobachten von Vögeln
to go birdwatching Vögel beobachten

Biro® *NOUN*
der Kugelschreiber (*PL* die Kugelschreiber), der Kuli (*PL* die Kulis)

℘ **birth** *NOUN*
die Geburt (*PL* die Geburten)

◇ irregular verb; *SEP* separable verb; for more help with verbs see centre section

birth certificate NOUN
die **Geburtsurkunde** (PL die **Geburtsurkunden**)

ℐ **birthday** NOUN
der **Geburtstag** (PL die **Geburtstage**)
Happy birthday! Herzlichen Glückwunsch zum Geburtstag!

ℐ **birthday party** NOUN
die **Geburtstagsfeier** (PL die **Geburtstagsfeiern**)

ℐ **biscuit** NOUN
der **Keks** (PL die **Kekse**)

bishop NOUN
1 (churchman) der **Bischof** (PL die **Bischöfe**)
2 (in chess) der **Läufer** (PL die **Läufer**)

ℐ **bit** NOUN
1 (piece) das **Stückchen** (PL die **Stückchen**)
a bit of chocolate ein Stückchen Schokolade
2 (a small amount)
a bit of ein bisschen
a bit of sugar ein bisschen Zucker
with a bit of luck mit ein bisschen Glück
3 (in a book, film, etc.) der **Teil** (PL die **Teile**)
This bit is brilliant. Dieser Teil ist hervorragend.
4 **a bit** ein bisschen
a bit too early ein bisschen zu früh
Wait a bit! Warte ein bisschen!
5 **He's a bit of a show-off.** Er ist ein ziemlicher Angeber.
6 **bit by bit** nach und nach

ℐ **bite** NOUN
1 (snack) der **Happen** (PL die **Happen**)
We'll just have a bite before we go. Wir essen noch einen kleinen Happen, bevor wir gehen.
2 (from an insect) der **Stich** (PL die **Stiche**)
mosquito bite der Mückenstich
3 (from a dog) der **Biss** (PL die **Bisse**)
to **bite** VERB
1 (person or dog) **beißen**⬦
2 (insect) **stechen**⬦

bitter ADJECTIVE
(taste) bitter

ℐ **black** ADJECTIVE
1 **schwarz**
my black jacket meine schwarze Jacke
2 **a black man** ein Schwarzer
a black woman eine Schwarze

blackberry NOUN
die **Brombeere** (PL die **Brombeeren**)

blackbird NOUN
die **Amsel** (PL die **Amseln**)

blackboard NOUN
die **Tafel** (PL die **Tafeln**)

blackcurrant NOUN
die **Schwarze Johannisbeere** (PL die **Schwarzen Johannisbeeren**)

black eye NOUN
das **blaue Auge** (PL die **blauen Augen**)

black pudding NOUN
die **Blutwurst** (PL die **Blutwürste**)

blade NOUN
die **Klinge** (PL die **Klingen**)

blame NOUN
die **Schuld**
to take the blame for something die Schuld für etwas (ACC) auf sich (ACC) nehmen
to put the blame on somebody die Schuld auf jemanden schieben
to **blame** VERB
to blame somebody for something jemandem die Schuld an etwas (DAT) geben
They blamed him for the accident. Sie haben ihm die Schuld an dem Unfall gegeben.
She is to blame for it. Sie ist daran schuld.
I blame the parents. Ich gebe den Eltern Schuld.
I don't blame you. Ich kann es dir nicht verdenken.

blank NOUN
die **Lücke** (PL die **Lücken**)
blank ADJECTIVE
1 (page) leer, (screen) schwarz
2 (tape or disk) unbespielt
3 **blank cheque** der Blankoscheck

ℐ **blanket** NOUN
die **Decke** (PL die **Decken**)

blast NOUN
die **Explosion** (PL die **Explosionen**)

blaze NOUN
das **Feuer** (PL die **Feuer**)
to **blaze** VERB
brennen⬦

bleach NOUN
das **Bleichmittel** (PL die **Bleichmittel**)

to **bleed** VERB
bluten
My nose is bleeding. Meine Nase blutet.

A
B
C
D
E
F
G
H
I
J
K
L
M
N
O
P
Q
R
S
T
U
V
W
X
Y
Z

ℐ indicates key words

to **blend** *VERB*
mischen

blender *NOUN*
der **Mixer** (*PL* die **Mixer**)

to **bless** *VERB*
segnen
Bless you! (*after a sneeze*) Gesundheit!

blind *NOUN*
(*in a window*) das **Rollo** (*PL* die **Rollos**)

blind *ADJECTIVE*
blind

to **blink** *VERB*
(mit den Augen) blinzeln

blister *NOUN*
die **Blase** (*PL* die **Blasen**)

blizzard *NOUN*
der **Schneesturm** (*PL* die **Schneestürme**)

♂**block** *NOUN*
(*a building or buildings*) der **Block** (*PL* die **Blocks**)
block of flats der Wohnblock
office block das Bürohaus
to drive round the block um den Block fahren

to **block** *VERB*
1 sperren (*an exit or a road*)
2 **The sink is blocked.** Das Spülbecken ist verstopft.

blog *NOUN*
das or der **Blog** (*PL* die **Blogs**)

♂**blonde** *ADJECTIVE*
blond

♂**blood** *NOUN*
das **Blut**

blood test *NOUN*
die **Blutprobe** (*PL* die **Blutproben**)

bloody *ADJECTIVE*
blutig

♂**blouse** *NOUN*
die **Bluse** (*PL* die **Blusen**)

♂**blow** *NOUN*
der **Schlag** (*PL* die **Schläge**)

to **blow** *VERB*
1 (*a person*) blasen◊
2 (*the wind*) wehen
3 **The bomb blew the bridge to pieces.** Die Bombe hat die Brücke in die Luft gesprengt.
4 **to blow your nose** sich (*DAT*) die Nase putzen

• **to blow something out** etwas ausblasen◊ *SEP*
• **to blow up** (*explode*) explodieren (*PERF* sein)
• **to blow something up** (*a tyre or balloon*) etwas aufblasen◊ *SEP*, (*with explosives*) etwas sprengen

blow-dry *NOUN*
das **Föhnen**
a cut and blow-dry Schneiden und Föhnen

♂**blue** *ADJECTIVE*
blau
blue eyes blaue Augen

blunder *NOUN*
der **Fehler** (*PL* die **Fehler**)

blunt *ADJECTIVE*
1 (*a knife, pencil, or scissors*) stumpf
2 (*a person or question*) direkt

blurred *ADJECTIVE*
1 (*not distinct*) verschwommen
2 (*photo*) unscharf

to **blush** *VERB*
erröten (*PERF* sein)

board *NOUN*
1 (*plank, noticeboard, game*) das **Brett** (*PL* die **Bretter**)
chess board das Schachbrett
2 (*in a classroom*) die **Tafel** (*PL* die **Tafeln**)
3 (*accommodation in a hotel*)
full board die Vollpension
half board die Halbpension
board and lodging Unterkunft und Verpflegung
4 **on board** an Bord

boarder *NOUN*
(*in a school*) der **Internatsschüler** (*PL* die **Internatsschüler**), die **Internatsschülerin** (*PL* die **Internatsschülerinnen**)

board game *NOUN*
das **Brettspiel** (*PL* die **Brettspiele**)

boarding *NOUN*
(*on a plane, train*) das **Einsteigen**

boarding card *NOUN*
die **Bordkarte** (*PL* die **Bordkarten**)

boarding school *NOUN*
das **Internat** (*PL* die **Internate**)

to **boast** *VERB*
prahlen
He was boasting about his new bike. Er prahlte mit seinem neuen Rad.

◊ **irregular verb;** *SEP* **separable verb; for more help with verbs see centre section**

℘ **boat** NOUN
1 das **Boot** (PL die **Boote**)
   rowing boat das Ruderboot
2 (larger boat) das **Schiff** (PL die **Schiffe**)
   to go by boat mit dem Schiff fahren

℘ **body** NOUN
1 der **Körper** (PL die **Körper**)
2 (corpse) die **Leiche** (PL die **Leichen**)

bodybuilding NOUN
das **Bodybuilding**

bodyguard NOUN
der **Leibwächter** (PL die **Leibwächter**), die
Leibwächterin (PL die **Leibwächterinnen**)

WORD TIP Professions, hobbies, and sports
don't take an article in German: Er ist
Leibwächter.

body odour NOUN
der **Körpergeruch** (PL die **Körpergerüche**)

℘ **boil** NOUN
1 **to bring the water to the boil** das Wasser
   zum Kochen bringen
2 (swelling) der **Furunkel** (PL die **Furunkel**)
to **boil** VERB
1 **kochen**
   The water is boiling. Das Wasser kocht.
   to boil vegetables Gemüse kochen
2 (put the kettle on)
   to boil some water Wasser aufsetzen SEP
• **to boil over**
   überkochen SEP (PERF **sein**)

boiled egg NOUN
das **gekochte Ei** (PL die **gekochten Eier**)

boiled potato NOUN
die **Salzkartoffel** (PL die **Salzkartoffeln**)

boiler NOUN
(for central heating) der **Heizkessel** (PL die
Heizkessel)

boiling ADJECTIVE
1 (water) **kochend**
2 **It's boiling hot today.** Heute ist es
   wahnsinnig heiß.

bolt NOUN
(on a door) der **Riegel** (PL die **Riegel**)
to **bolt** VERB
1 (lock) **verriegeln**
2 (gobble down) **runterschlingen**◇ SEP
   (informal)

bomb NOUN
die **Bombe** (PL die **Bomben**)
to **bomb** VERB
bombardieren

bombing NOUN
1 (in war) die **Bombardierung** (PL die
   Bombardierungen)
2 (a terrorist attack) das **Bombenattentat**
   (PL die **Bombenattentate**)

bone NOUN
1 der **Knochen** (PL die **Knochen**)
2 (of a fish) die **Gräte** (PL die **Gräten**)

bonfire NOUN
das **Feuer** (PL die **Feuer**)

Bonn NOUN
Bonn (NEUTER)
to Bonn nach Bonn

BONN
Bonn was the capital of West Germany (BRD)
from 1949 to 1990.

bonnet NOUN
1 (of a car) die **Kühlerhaube** (PL die
   Kühlerhauben)
2 (clothing) die **Haube** (PL die **Hauben**)

to **boo** VERB
ausbuhen SEP
The crowd booed the referee. Die Menge
buhte den Schiedsrichter aus.

℘ **book** NOUN
1 das **Buch** (PL die **Bücher**)
   a book about dinosaurs ein Buch über
   Dinosaurier
   my biology book mein Biologiebuch
   cheque book das Scheckbuch
2 (of stamps, tickets) das **Heft** (PL die **Hefte**)
3 **exercise book** das Heft
to **book** VERB
1 **buchen** (holiday, flight)
2 **bestellen** (a table, theatre, or cinema
   tickets)
   I booked a table for 8 p.m. Ich habe einen
   Tisch für zwanzig Uhr bestellt.

bookcase NOUN
das **Bücherregal** (PL die **Bücherregale**)

℘ **booking** NOUN
(for a flight or a holiday, for example) die
Buchung (PL die **Buchungen**)

booking office NOUN
1 (at a train station) der **Fahrkartenschalter**
   (PL die **Fahrkartenschalter**)
2 (in a theatre or cinema) die **Kasse** (PL die
   Kassen)

℘ **booklet** NOUN
die **Broschüre** (PL die **Broschüren**)

bookshelf NOUN
das **Bücherregal** (PL die **Bücherregale**)

ℰ**bookshop** NOUN
die **Buchhandlung** (PL die **Buchhandlungen**)

ℰ**boot** NOUN
1 der **Stiefel** (PL die **Stiefel**)
2 (for football, walking, climbing, or skiing) der **Schuh** (PL die **Schuhe**)
football boots Fußballschuhe
3 (of a car) der **Kofferraum** (PL die **Kofferräume**)

border NOUN
(between countries) die **Grenze** (PL die **Grenzen**)
at the border an der Grenze

bore NOUN
1 (a boring person) der **langweilige Mensch** (PL die **langweiligen Menschen**)
2 (a nuisance)
What a bore! Wie ärgerlich!

bored ADJECTIVE
to be bored sich langweilen
I'm bored. Ich langweile mich.

ℰ**boring** ADJECTIVE
langweilig

ℰ**born** ADJECTIVE
geboren
to be born geboren werden
She was born in Germany. Sie ist in Deutschland geboren.

to **borrow** VERB
sich (DAT) **leihen**◇
Can I borrow your bike? Kann ich mir dein Rad leihen?
to borrow something from somebody sich etwas von jemandem leihen
I borrowed some money from Dad. Ich habe mir Geld von Vati geliehen.

ℰ**boss** NOUN
der **Chef** (PL die **Chefs**) die **Chefin** (PL die **Chefinnen**)

bossy ADJECTIVE
herrisch

both PRONOUN
beide
They both came. Sie kamen beide.
Both my sisters were there. Meine beiden Schwestern waren da.
both of us wir beide
They are both sold. Beide sind verkauft.

both ADVERB
both at home and at school sowohl zu Hause als auch in der Schule

both in summer and in winter sowohl im Sommer als auch im Winter

ℰ**bother** NOUN
1 (minor trouble) der **Ärger**
I've had a lot of bother with the car. Ich hatte viel Ärger mit dem Auto.
2 if it isn't too much bother wenn es nicht zu viel Mühe macht
It's no bother. Das ist kein Problem.
The children were no bother. Die Kinder waren kein Problem.
without any bother ohne irgendwelche Schwierigkeiten

to **bother** VERB
1 (disturb) stören
I'm sorry to bother you. Es tut mir leid, dich zu stören.
2 (worry) stören
What's bothering you? Was stört dich?
It doesn't bother me at all. Das stört mich überhaupt nicht.
3 (take trouble)
Don't bother to write. Du brauchst nicht zu schreiben.
She didn't even bother to wait. Sie hat nicht einmal gewartet.
Don't bother! Lass es! (informal)
I can't be bothered. Ich habe keine Lust.

ℰ**bottle** NOUN
die **Flasche** (PL die **Flaschen**)

bottle bank NOUN
der **Altglascontainer** (PL die **Altglascontainer**)

bottle opener NOUN
der **Flaschenöffner** (PL die **Flaschenöffner**)

ℰ**bottom** NOUN
1 (of a bag, bottle, hole, or stretch of water) der **Boden** (PL die **Böden**)
at the bottom of the lake am Boden des Sees
at the bottom of the well auf dem Grund des Brunnens
2 (of a hill or building) der **Fuß** (PL die **Füße**)
at the bottom of the tower am Fuß des Turms
3 (of a garden, street, list) das **Ende** (PL die **Enden**)
at the bottom of the street am Ende der Straße
4 at the bottom of the page unten auf der Seite
5 (buttocks) der **Hintern** (informal) (PL die **Hintern**)

bottom ADJECTIVE
1 unterster/unterste/unterstes

◇ irregular verb; SEP separable verb; for more help with verbs see centre section

the **bottom shelf** das unterste Regalbrett
2 the **bottom flat** die Wohnung im
  Erdgeschoss

to **bounce** VERB
  (jump) springen◇ (PERF sein)

bouncer NOUN
  der Rausschmeißer (PL die
  Rausschmeißer), der Türsteher (PL die
  Türsteher)

  WORD TIP Professions, hobbies, and sports
  don't take an article in German: Er ist Türsteher.

bound ADJECTIVE
  (certain)
  He's bound to be late. Er kommt ganz
  bestimmt zu spät.
  That was bound to happen. Das musste ja
  kommen.

boundary NOUN
  die Grenze (PL die Grenzen)

bow NOUN
1 (in a shoelace or ribbon) die Schleife (PL die
  Schleifen)
2 (for a violin or with arrows) der Bogen
  (PL die Bögen)
  with a bow and arrow mit Pfeil und Bogen

ℬ **bowl** NOUN
1 (large, for salad, mixing, or washing up) die
  Schüssel (PL die Schüsseln)
2 (smaller) die Schale (PL die Schalen)

bowler NOUN
  (in cricket) der Werfer (PL die Werfer),
  (PL die Werferin (PL die Werferinnen)

bowling NOUN
  (tenpin) das Bowling
  to go bowling Bowling spielen

bow tie NOUN
  die Fliege (PL die Fliegen)

ℬ **box** NOUN
1 die Schachtel (PL die Schachteln)
  a box of chocolates eine Schachtel Pralinen
2 **cardboard box** der Karton
3 (on a form) das Kästchen (PL die Kästchen)

boxer NOUN
  der Boxer (PL die Boxer)

  WORD TIP Professions, hobbies, and sports
  don't take an article in German: Er ist Boxer.

boxer shorts PLURAL NOUN
  die Boxershorts (PLURAL)

boxing NOUN
1 das Boxen
2 **boxing match** der Boxkampf

Boxing Day NOUN
  der zweite Weihnachtstag

box office NOUN
  die Kasse (PL die Kassen)

ℬ **boy** NOUN
  der Junge (PL die Jungen)
  a little boy ein kleiner Junge

ℬ **boyfriend** NOUN
  der Freund (PL die Freunde)

bra NOUN
  der BH (PL die BHs)

brace NOUN
  (for teeth) die Zahnspange (PL die
  Zahnspangen)

bracelet NOUN
  das Armband (PL die Armbänder)

bracket NOUN
  die Klammer (PL die Klammern)
  in brackets in Klammern
  round/square brackets runde/eckige
  Klammern

brain NOUN
  das Gehirn (PL die Gehirne)

brainwave NOUN
  der Geistesblitz (PL die Geistesblitze)

ℬ **brake** NOUN
  die Bremse (PL die Bremsen)

to **brake** VERB
  bremsen

branch NOUN
1 (of a tree) der Ast (PL die Äste)
2 (of a shop) die Filiale (PL die Filialen)
3 (of a bank) die Zweigstelle (PL die
  Zweigstellen)

ℬ **brand** NOUN
  die Marke (PL die Marken)

brand new ADJECTIVE
  nagelneu

brandy NOUN
  der Weinbrand (PL die Weinbrände)

brass NOUN
1 (metal) das Messing
2 (in an orchestra)
  the brass die Blechbläser (PLURAL)

brass band NOUN
  die Blaskapelle (PL die Blaskapellen)

ℬ indicates key words

brave ADJECTIVE
tapfer

> **WORD TIP** Do not translate the English word brave with the German brav.

bravery NOUN
die **Tapferkeit**

Brazil NOUN
Brasilien (NEUTER)

Brazilian NOUN
der **Brasilianer** (PL die **Brasilianer**), die
Brasilianerin (PL die **Brasilianerinnen**)

Brazilian ADJECTIVE
brasilianisch

> **WORD TIP** Adjectives never have capitals
> in German, even for regions, countries, or
> nationalities.

ℓ **bread** NOUN
das **Brot** (PL die **Brote**)
a slice of bread eine Scheibe Brot
a loaf of bread ein (Laib) Brot
a piece of bread and butter ein Butterbrot

ℓ **break** NOUN
1 (a short rest or at school) die **Pause** (PL die
Pausen)
ten minutes' break eine Pause von zehn
Minuten
to take a break Pause machen
at break in der Pause
2 the Christmas break die Weihnachtsferien
(PLURAL)

to **break** VERB
1 zerbrechen◇, kaputtmachen SEP
(informal)
He broke a glass. Er hat ein Glas
zerbrochen.
Don't break the doll. Mach die Puppe nicht
kaputt.
2 (get damaged) zerbrechen◇ (PERF sein),
kaputtgehen◇ SEP (informal) (PERF sein)
The glass broke. Das Glas zerbrach.
The eggs broke. Die Eier sind
kaputtgegangen.
3 to break your arm sich (DAT) den Arm
brechen◇
4 brechen◇ (rules, promise)
to break your promise sein Versprechen
brechen
5 to break the record den Rekord brechen◇
6 to break the news that ... melden, dass ...
• to **break down**
1 (car) eine Panne haben
The car broke down. Das Auto hatte eine
Panne.

2 (talks, negotiations) scheitern (PERF sein)
• to **break in**
einbrechen◇ SEP (PERF sein)
• to **break up**
1 (couple) sich trennen
2 (crowd) sich auflösen SEP
3 We break up on Thursday. Die Ferien
fangen am Donnerstag an.

ℓ **breakdown** NOUN
1 (of a vehicle) die **Panne** (PL die **Pannen**)
We had a breakdown on the motorway.
Wir hatten eine Panne auf der Autobahn.
2 (in talks or negotiations) das **Scheitern**
3 (a nervous collapse) der **Zusammenbruch**
(PL die **Zusammenbrüche**)
to have a nervous breakdown einen
Nervenzusammenbruch haben

breakdown truck NOUN
der **Abschleppwagen** (PL die
Abschleppwagen)

ℓ **breakfast** NOUN
das **Frühstück** (PL die **Frühstücke**)
We have breakfast at eight. Wir
frühstücken um acht Uhr.

break-in NOUN
der **Einbruch** (PL die **Einbrüche**)

breast NOUN
die **Brust** (PL die **Brüste**)

breaststroke NOUN
das **Brustschwimmen**

breath NOUN
1 der **Atem**
out of breath außer Atem
to hold your breath den Atem anhalten
to get your breath back wieder zu Atem
kommen
to take a deep breath tief einatmen
2 to have bad breath Mundgeruch haben

to **breathe** VERB
atmen
• to **breathe in**
einatmen SEP

breathing NOUN
das **Atmen**

breed NOUN
(of animal) die **Rasse** (PL die **Rassen**)

breeze NOUN
die **Brise** (PL die **Brisen**)

to **brew** VERB
1 brauen beer
2 aufbrühen SEP (tea)
The tea's brewing. Der Tee zieht noch.

◇ **irregular verb**; SEP **separable verb**; for more help with verbs see centre section

brewery NOUN
die Brauerei (PL die Brauereien)

brick NOUN
der Ziegel (PL die Ziegel)
a brick wall eine Ziegelmauer

ℰ **bride** NOUN
die Braut (PL die Bräute)
the bride and groom das Brautpaar

ℰ **bridegroom** NOUN
der Bräutigam (PL die Bräutigame)

bridesmaid NOUN
die Brautjungfer (PL die Brautjungfern)

ℰ **bridge** NOUN
1 (over a river) die Brücke (PL die Brücken)
2 (card game) das Bridge
to play bridge Bridge spielen

bridle NOUN
das Zaumzeug (PL die Zaumzeuge)

brief ADJECTIVE
kurz

briefcase NOUN
die Aktentasche (PL die Aktentaschen)

briefly ADVERB
kurz

briefs PLURAL NOUN
der Slip (PL die Slips)

bright ADJECTIVE
1 (colour) leuchtend
bright green socks leuchtend grüne Socken
2 (eyes, sunshine) strahlend
3 (light) hell
4 (clever) intelligent
She's not very bright. Sie ist nicht sehr
intelligent.
5 to look on the bright side die Dinge positiv
sehen (literally: to see things positively)

brilliant ADJECTIVE
1 (very clever) glänzend
He's a brilliant surgeon. Er ist ein
glänzender Chirurg.
2 (wonderful) toll
The party was brilliant! Die Party war toll!

ℰ to **bring** VERB
1 mitbringen◇ SEP
He brought a present. Er brachte ein
Geschenk mit.
Bring your camera. Bring deinen
Fotoapparat mit.
2 (to a place) bringen◇
She's bringing the children home. Sie
bringt die Kinder nach Hause.

• to bring somebody up
jemanden großziehen◇ SEP
He was brought up by his aunt. Er wurde
von seiner Tante großgezogen.

ℰ **Britain**, **Great Britain** NOUN
Großbritannien (NEUTER)
to Britain nach Großbritannien

ℰ **British** PLURAL NOUN
the British die Briten

British ADJECTIVE
1 britisch
British politicians britische Politiker
the British Isles die Britischen Inseln
2 He's British. Er ist Brite.
She's British. Sie ist Britin.

> **WORD TIP** Adjectives never have capitals
> in German, even for regions, countries, or
> nationalities. Names like die Britischen Inseln
> are an exception.

broad ADJECTIVE
1 (wide) breit
2 (extensive) weit

broadband NOUN
das Breitband

broad bean NOUN
die dicke Bohne (PL die dicken Bohnen)

ℰ **broadcast** NOUN
die Sendung (PL die Sendungen)
to **broadcast** VERB
senden

broccoli NOUN
der Brokkoli

ℰ **brochure** NOUN
die Broschüre (PL die Broschüren)

broke ADJECTIVE
to be broke pleite sein (informal)

broken ADJECTIVE
zerbrochen, kaputt (informal)
The window's broken. Das Fenster ist
kaputt.
to have a broken leg ein gebrochenes Bein
haben

bronchitis NOUN
die Bronchitis

brooch NOUN
die Brosche (PL die Broschen)

broom NOUN
der Besen (PL die Besen)

ℰ **brother** NOUN
der Bruder (PL die Brüder)

A
B
C
D
E
F
G
H
I
J
K
L
M
N
O
P
Q
R
S
T
U
V
W
X
Y
Z

ℰ indicates key words

A
B
C
D
E
F
G
H
I
J
K
L
M
N
O
P
Q
R
S
T
U
V
W
X
Y
Z

my mother's brother der Bruder meiner Mutter

brother-in-law NOUN
der Schwager (PL die Schwäger)

ℓ **brown** ADJECTIVE
braun
my brown shoes meine braunen Schuhe
light brown hellbraun
dark brown dunkelbraun
to go brown (suntanned) braun werden

brown bread NOUN
das Mischbrot (PL die Mischbrote)

bruise NOUN
1 (on a person) der blaue Fleck (PL die blauen Flecken)
2 (on fruit) die Druckstelle (PL die Druckstellen)

ℓ **brush** NOUN
1 (for your hair, clothes, nails, or shoes) die Bürste (PL die Bürsten)
2 (for sweeping) der Besen (PL die Besen)
3 (for paint) der Pinsel (PL die Pinsel)

to **brush** VERB
1 bürsten
to brush your hair sich (DAT) die Haare bürsten
I brushed my hair. Ich habe mir die Haare gebürstet.
2 to brush your teeth sich (DAT) die Zähne putzen

Brussels NOUN
Brüssel NEUTER

Brussels sprout NOUN
der Rosenkohl
He likes Brussels sprouts. Er mag Rosenkohl.

bubble NOUN
die Blase (PL die Blasen)

bucket NOUN
der Eimer (PL die Eimer)

buckle NOUN
die Schnalle (PL die Schnallen)

Buddhism NOUN
der Buddhismus

Buddhist NOUN
der Buddhist (PL die Buddhisten), die Buddhistin (PL die Buddhistinnen)

budget NOUN
das Budget (PL die Budgets)

budgie NOUN
der Wellensittich (PL die Wellensittiche)

ℓ **buffet** NOUN
das Büffet (PL die Büffets)

buffet car NOUN
der Speisewagen (PL die Speisewagen)

bug NOUN
1 (insect) das Insekt (PL die Insekten)
2 (germ) der Bazillus (PL die Bazillen)
a stomach bug eine Magengrippe
3 a computer bug ein Programmierfehler

to **build** VERB
bauen

builder NOUN
der Bauarbeiter (PL die Bauarbeiter), die Bauarbeiterin (PL die Bauarbeiterinnen)

WORD TIP Professions, hobbies, and sports don't take an article in German: Er ist Bauarbeiter.

ℓ **building** NOUN
das Gebäude (PL die Gebäude)

building site NOUN
die Baustelle (PL die Baustellen)

building society NOUN
die Bausparkasse (PL die Bausparkassen)

built-up ADJECTIVE
1 bebaut
2 built-up area das Wohngebiet

bulb NOUN
1 (light bulb) die Glühbirne (PL die Glühbirnen)
2 (flower bulb) die Blumenzwiebel (PL die Blumenzwiebeln)

bull NOUN
der Bulle (PL die Bullen)

bulldozer NOUN
die Planierraupe (PL die Planierraupen)

ℓ **bullet** NOUN
die Kugel (PL die Kugeln)

bulletin NOUN
1 (written) das Bulletin (PL die Bulletins)
2 (on TV, radio)
news bulletin die Kurzmeldung

bully NOUN
1 (in school) der Rabauke (PL die Rabauken)
2 (adult) der Tyrann (PL die Tyrannen)
to **bully** VERB
schikanieren, mobben

bum NOUN
der Hintern (informal) (PL die Hintern)

bump NOUN
1 (on a surface) die Unebenheit (PL die

428

Unebenheiten)
There are lots of bumps in the road. Die
Straße ist sehr uneben.

2 *(swelling)* die **Beule** (PL die **Beulen**)
a bump on the head eine Beule am Kopf

3 *(jolt)* der **Stoß** (PL die **Stöße**)

4 *(noise)* der **Bums** (PL die **Bumse**)

to **bump** VERB

1 *(bang)* **stoßen**◇
I bumped my head. Ich habe mir den Kopf
gestoßen.
to bump into something gegen etwas *(ACC)*
stoßen

2 **to bump into somebody** *(meet by chance)*
jemanden zufällig treffen◇

bumper NOUN
die **Stoßstange** (PL die **Stoßstangen**)

bumpy ADJECTIVE
holperig
a bumpy flight ein unruhiger Flug

bun NOUN

1 *(for a burger)* das **Brötchen** PL die **Brötchen**,
die **Semmel** (PL die **Semmeln**)

2 *(sweet)* das **süße Brötchen** (PL die **süßen
Brötchen**)

bunch NOUN

1 *(of flowers)* der **Strauß** (PL die **Sträuße**)

2 *(of carrots, radishes)* das **Bund** (PL die
Bunde)
a bunch of keys ein Schlüsselbund

3 **a bunch of grapes** eine ganze Weintraube

bundle NOUN
das **Bündel** (PL die **Bündel**)

bungalow NOUN
der **Bungalow** (PL die **Bungalows**)

bunk NOUN

1 *(on a boat)* die **Koje** (PL die **Kojen**)

2 *(on a train)* das **Bett** (PL die **Betten**)

bunk bed NOUN
das **Etagenbett** (PL die **Etagenbetten**)

burger NOUN
der **Hamburger** (PL die **Hamburger**)

burglar NOUN
der **Einbrecher** (PL die **Einbrecher**), die
Einbrecherin (PL die **Einbrecherinnen**)

burglar alarm NOUN
die **Alarmanlage** (PL die **Alarmanlagen**)

ℱ **burglary** NOUN
der **Einbruch** (PL die **Einbrüche**)

ℱ **burn** NOUN

1 *(on the skin)* die **Verbrennung** (PL die
Verbrennungen)

2 *(on fabric, object)* die **Brandstelle** (PL die
Brandstellen)

to **burn** VERB

1 **verbrennen**◇
She burnt his letters. Sie hat seine Briefe
verbrannt.

2 *(fire, candle)* **brennen**◇

3 *(injure)* **verbrennen**◇
to burn yourself sich verbrennen
You'll burn your fingers! Du verbrennst dir
die Finger!

4 *(cake, meat, etc.)* **anbrennen lassen**◇
Mum has burnt the cake. Mutti hat den
Kuchen anbrennen lassen.

burnt ADJECTIVE

1 *(papers, rubbish)* **verbrannt**

2 *(cake, meat, etc.)* **angebrannt**

ℱ to **burst** VERB

1 **platzen lassen** *(a balloon)*
He burst the balloon. Er ließ den Ballon
platzen.

2 **platzen** *(PERF* sein*)* *(of a balloon, a tyre)*
The tyre has burst. Der Reifen ist geplatzt.

3 **to burst out laughing** in Lachen
ausbrechen◇ SEP *(PERF* sein*)*
to burst into tears in Tränen ausbrechen◇
SEP *(PERF* sein*)*

4 **to burst into flames** in Flammen
aufgehen◇ SEP *(PERF* sein*)*

to **bury** VERB

1 **begraben**◇ *(a dead person)*

2 **vergraben**◇ *(treasure or a bone)*

ℱ **bus** NOUN
der **Bus** (PL die **Busse**)
on the bus im Bus
by bus mit dem Bus

bus driver NOUN
der **Busfahrer** (PL die **Busfahrer**), die
Busfahrerin (PL die **Busfahrerinnen**)

WORD TIP Professions, hobbies, and sports
don't take an article in German: Er ist Busfahrer.

bush NOUN
der **Busch** (PL die **Büsche**)

ℱ **business** NOUN

1 *(commercial dealings)* die **Geschäfte** *(PLURAL)*
Business is bad. Die Geschäfte gehen
schlecht.
He's in Leeds on business. Er ist
geschäftlich in Leeds.

2 *(a line of business or profession)* die **Branche**
(PL die **Branchen**)
He's in the insurance business. Er ist in der
Versicherungsbranche.

ℱ indicates key words

3 *(firm or company)* der **Betrieb** (PL die
Betriebe)
small businesses kleine Betriebe
4 *(personal concern)* die **Angelegenheit** (PL
die **Angelegenheiten**)
Mind your own business! Kümmere dich
um deine eigenen Angelegenheiten!

businessman NOUN
der **Geschäftsmann** (PL die **Geschäftsleute**)

> **WORD TIP** Professions, hobbies, and sports don't
> take an article in German: Er ist Geschäftsmann.

business trip NOUN
die **Geschäftsreise** (PL die **Geschäftsreisen**)

businesswoman NOUN
die **Geschäftsfrau** (PL die **Geschäftsfrauen**)

> **WORD TIP** Professions, hobbies, and sports don't
> take an article in German: Sie ist Geschäftsfrau.

bus lane NOUN
die **Busspur** (PL die **Busspuren**)

bus pass NOUN
(weekly, etc.) die **Zeitkarte** (PL die **Zeitkarten**)

bus route NOUN
die **Buslinie** (PL die **Buslinien**)

bus shelter NOUN
das **Wartehäuschen** (PL die
Wartehäuschen)

bus station NOUN
der **Busbahnhof** (PL die **Busbahnhöfe**)

bus stop NOUN
die **Bushaltestelle** (PL die **Bushaltestellen**)

bus ticket NOUN
die **Busfahrkarte** (PL die **Busfahrkarten**)

ℐ **busy** ADJECTIVE
1 **beschäftigt**
He's busy. Er ist beschäftigt.
She was busy packing. Sie war mit dem
Packen beschäftigt.
2 **to have a busy day** viel zu tun haben
3 **The shops were busy.** In den Läden war
sehr viel los.
4 *(phone)* besetzt

ℐ **but** CONJUNCTION
1 **aber**
small but strong klein aber stark
2 *(after a negative statement)* **sondern**
not Thursday but Friday nicht Donnerstag,
sondern Freitag
not only ... but also nicht nur ... sondern
auch

but PREPOSITION
1 **außer** (+DAT)
everyone but Winston alle außer Winston

Anything but that! Nur das nicht!
2 **the last but one** der/die/das Vorletzte

ℐ **butcher** NOUN
1 der **Fleischer** (PL die **Fleischer**), die
Fleischerin (PL die **Fleischerinnen**), der
Metzger (PL die **Metzger**), die **Metzgerin**
(PL die **Metzgerinnen**)
2 **the butcher's** die Fleischerei (PL die
Metzgerei)

> **WORD TIP** Professions, hobbies, and sports
> don't take an article in German: Er ist Metzger.

ℐ **butter** NOUN
die **Butter**

to **butter** VERB
buttern

butterfly NOUN
der **Schmetterling** (PL die **Schmetterlinge**)

ℐ **button** NOUN
1 der **Knopf** (PL die **Knöpfe**)
2 die **Taste** (PL die **Tasten**)
the record button die Aufnahmetaste

buttonhole NOUN
das **Knopfloch** (PL die **Knopflöcher**)

ℐ **buy** NOUN
der **Kauf** (PL die **Käufe**)
a bad buy ein schlechter Kauf

to **buy** VERB
kaufen
I bought the tickets. Ich habe die Karten
gekauft.
to buy something for somebody
jemandem etwas kaufen
Sarah bought him a sweater. Sarah hat ihm
einen Pullover gekauft.

to **buzz** VERB
(a fly or bee) summen

buzzer NOUN
der **Summer** (PL die **Summer**)

ℐ **by** PREPOSITION
1 **von** (+DAT)
I was bitten by a dog. Ich bin von einem
Hund gebissen worden.
by Mozart von Mozart
2 **by mistake** versehentlich
3 *(travel)* **mit** (+DAT)
to come by bus mit dem Bus kommen
to go by train mit dem Zug fahren
by bike mit dem Rad
4 *(near)* **an** (+DAT)
by the sea am Meer
the stop by the school die Haltestelle an
der Schule
5 *(before)* bis

◇ **irregular verb**; SEP **separable verb**; for more help with verbs see centre section

It'll be ready by Monday. Es wird bis Montag fertig sein.
I'll be back by four. Ich bin bis vier Uhr zurück.
6 **by now** inzwischen
7 **by yourself** ganz allein
I was by myself in the house. Ich war ganz allein im Haus.
She did it by herself. Sie hat es ganz allein gemacht.
8 **by the way** übrigens
9 **to go by** vorbeigehen◇ *(SEP) (PERF* **sein)**

bye *EXCLAMATION*
tschüs! *(informal)*

bypass *NOUN*
die **Umgehungsstraße** *(PL die* **Umgehungsstraßen)**

Cc

cab *NOUN*
1 das **Taxi** *(PL die* **Taxis)**
to call a cab ein Taxi rufen
2 *(on a lorry)* das **Führerhaus** *(PL die* **Führerhäuser)**

ℓ **cabbage** *NOUN*
der **Kohl** *(in Southern Germany and Austria)*
das **Kraut**

cabin *NOUN*
die **Kabine** *(PL die* **Kabinen)**

ℓ **cable** *NOUN*
das **Kabel** *(PL die* **Kabel)**

ℓ **cafe** *NOUN*
das **Café** *(PL die* **Cafés)**

> **CAFE**
> This is not only a place to drink your coffee, tea or hot chocolate and enjoy a piece of cake; it is also a place to relax, to read newspapers, to meet friends. There is a real Kaffeehaus culture in cities such as Vienna. One of the most famous coffee houses in Vienna is the Landtmann opposite the town hall (Rathaus).

cage *NOUN*
der **Käfig** *(PL die* **Käfige)**

cagoule *NOUN*
der **Anorak** *(PL die* **Anoraks)**

ℓ **cake** *NOUN*
der **Kuchen** *(PL die* **Kuchen)**
Would you like a piece of cake? Möchtest du ein Stück Kuchen?

to **calculate** *VERB*
berechnen

calculation *NOUN*
die **Rechnung** *(PL die* **Rechnungen)**

calculator *NOUN*
der **Taschenrechner** *(PL die* **Taschenrechner)**

calendar *NOUN*
der **Kalender** *(PL die* **Kalender)**

ℓ **calf** *NOUN*
1 *(animal)* das **Kalb** *(PL die* **Kälber)**
2 *(of your leg)* die **Wade** *(PL die* **Waden)**

ℓ **call** *NOUN*
(telephone) der **Anruf** *(PL die* **Anrufe)**
I had several calls this morning. Ich erhielt heute Morgen mehrere Anrufe.
Thank you for your call. Danke für deinen Anruf.
a phone call ein Telefonanruf

to **call** *VERB*
1 rufen◇
to call a taxi ein Taxi rufen
to call the doctor einen Arzt rufen
They called the police. Sie riefen die Polizei.
2 *(phone)* anrufen◇ *SEP*
Call me later. Ruf mich später an.
Thank you for calling. Danke für deinen Anruf.
I'll call you back later. Ich rufe dich später zurück.
3 nennen◇
They've called the baby Julie. Sie haben das Baby Julie genannt.
4 **to be called** heißen◇
Her brother is called Dan. Ihr Bruder heißt Dan.
What's he called? Wie heißt er?

call box *NOUN*
die **Telefonzelle** *(PL die* **Telefonzellen)**

ℓ **calm** *ADJECTIVE*
ruhig

to **calm** *VERB*
beruhigen
• **to calm down**
sich beruhigen
He's calmed down a bit. Er hat sich etwas beruhigt.
• **to calm somebody down**
jemanden beruhigen
I tried to calm her down. Ich habe versucht, sie zu beruhigen.

calmly *ADVERB*
ruhig

calorie NOUN
die **Kalorie** (PL die **Kalorien**)

camcorder NOUN
der **Camcorder** (PL die **Camcorder**)

camel NOUN
das **Kamel** (PL die **Kamele**)

camera NOUN
1 (for photos) der **Fotoapparat** (PL die **Fotoapparate**)
2 (for film) die **Kamera** (PL die **Kameras**)

ℓ **camp** NOUN
das **Lager** (PL die **Lager**)

to **camp** VERB
campen, zelten

campaign NOUN
die **Kampagne** (PL die **Kampagnen**)

ℓ **camper** NOUN
1 (person) der **Camper** (PL die **Camper**), die **Camperin** (PL die **Camperinnen**)
2 (vehicle) der **Campingbus** (PL die **Campingbusse**)

ℓ **camper van** NOUN
das **Wohnmobil** (PL die **Wohnmobile**)

campfire NOUN
das **Lagerfeuer** (PL die **Lagerfeuer**)

ℓ **camping** NOUN
das **Camping**
to go camping zelten
We're going camping in Bavaria this summer. Diesen Sommer zelten wir in Bayern.

ℓ **campsite** NOUN
der **Campingplatz** (PL die **Campingplätze**)

ℓ **can** NOUN
1 die **Dose** (PL die **Dosen**)
a can of tomatoes eine Dose Tomaten
2 (for petrol or oil) der **Kanister** (PL die **Kanister**)

can VERB
1 können◇
I can't be there before ten. Ich kann vor zehn Uhr nicht da sein.
Can you open the door, please? Kannst du bitte die Tür aufmachen?
Can I help you? Kann ich Ihnen helfen?
They couldn't come. Sie konnten nicht kommen.
You could have told me. Das hättest du mir wirklich sagen können.
I can't see him. Ich kann ihn nicht sehen.
I can't remember it. Ich kann mich nicht daran erinnern.

She can't drive. Sie kann nicht Auto fahren.
2 (be allowed) dürfen◇
You can't smoke here. Sie dürfen hier nicht rauchen.

Canada NOUN
Kanada (NEUTER)
to Canada nach Kanada

ℓ **Canadian** NOUN
der **Kanadier** (PL die **Kanadier**), die **Kanadierin** (PL die **Kanadierinnen**)

Canadian ADJECTIVE
kanadisch
the Canadian coast die kanadische Küste
He is Canadian. Er ist Kanadier.
She is Canadian. Sie ist Kanadierin.

WORD TIP Adjectives never have capitals in German, even for regions, countries, or nationalities.

canal NOUN
der **Kanal** (PL die **Kanäle**)

to **cancel** VERB
absagen SEP
The concert has been cancelled. Das Konzert ist abgesagt worden.

cancer NOUN
der **Krebs**
to have lung cancer Lungenkrebs haben

Cancer NOUN
der **Krebs** (PL die **Krebse**)
I'm Cancer. Ich bin Krebs.

candidate NOUN
der **Kandidat** (PL die **Kandidaten**), die **Kandidatin** (PL die **Kandidatinnen**)

candle NOUN
die **Kerze** (PL die **Kerzen**)

candlestick NOUN
der **Kerzenständer** (PL die **Kerzenständer**)

canned ADJECTIVE
in Dosen
canned tomatoes Tomaten in Dosen

ℓ **cannot**, **can't** VERB ▶ SEE can

canoe NOUN
das **Kanu** (PL die **Kanus**)

canoeing NOUN
to go canoeing Kanu fahren◇ (PERF sein)
I like canoeing. Ich fahre gerne Kanu.

can-opener NOUN
der **Dosenöffner** (PL die **Dosenöffner**)

ℓ **canteen** NOUN
die **Kantine** (PL die **Kantinen**)

◇ irregular verb; SEP separable verb; for more help with verbs see centre section

canvas NOUN
1 (of a tent or bag) das **Segeltuch**
2 (for painting on) die **Leinwand**

cap NOUN
1 (hat) die **Kappe** (PL die **Kappen**)
   baseball cap die Baseballkappe
2 (on a bottle or tube) der **Verschluss** (PL die **Verschlüsse**)

capable ADJECTIVE
   fähig
   to be capable of doing something etwas tun können

capital NOUN
1 (city) die **Hauptstadt** (PL die **Hauptstädte**)
   Berlin is the capital of Germany. Berlin ist die Hauptstadt von Deutschland.
2 (letter) der **Großbuchstabe** (PL die **Großbuchstaben**)
   in capitals mit Großbuchstaben

capitalism NOUN
   der **Kapitalismus**

Capricorn NOUN
   der **Steinbock** (PL die **Steinböcke**)
   Linda is Capricorn. Linda ist Steinbock.

captain NOUN
   der **Kapitän** (PL die **Kapitäne**)

> **WORD TIP** Professions, hobbies, and sports don't take an article in German: Er ist Kapitän.

to **capture** VERB
   festnehmen◇ SEP

ℱ **car** NOUN
   das **Auto** (PL die **Autos**)
   to park the car das Auto einparken
   We're going by car. Wir fahren mit dem Auto.
   car crash der Autounfall

caramel NOUN
   der **Karamell** (PL die **Karamells**)

ℱ **caravan** NOUN
   der **Wohnwagen** (PL die **Wohnwagen**)

carbon NOUN
   der **Kohlenstoff**

ℱ **card** NOUN
   die **Karte** (PL die **Karten**)
   card game das Kartenspiel
   to have a game of cards Karten spielen

cardboard NOUN
   die **Pappe**
   cardboard box der Pappkarton

cardigan NOUN
   die **Strickjacke** (PL die **Strickjacken**)

cardphone NOUN
   das **Kartentelefon** (PL die **Kartentelefone**)

ℱ **care** NOUN
1 die **Vorsicht**
   to take care crossing the road beim Überqueren der Straße vorsichtig sein
   Take care! (be careful) Sei vorsichtig!, (when saying goodbye) Mach's gut!
2 **to take care to do something** darauf achten, dass man etwas tut
3 **to take care of somebody** auf jemanden aufpassen

to **care** VERB
1 **to care about something** sich für etwas (ACC) interessieren
   She cares about the environment. Die Umwelt liegt ihr am Herzen.
2 **She doesn't care.** Es ist ihr egal.
   I couldn't care less! Das ist mir völlig egal!

career NOUN
   die **Karriere** (PL die **Karrieren**)

ℱ **careful** ADJECTIVE
   vorsichtig
   a careful driver ein vorsichtiger Fahrer, eine vorsichtige Fahrerin
   Be careful! Sei vorsichtig!

carefully ADVERB
1 **sorgfältig**
   to read the instructions carefully die Anweisungen sorgfältig lesen
2 **vorsichtig**
   She put the vase down carefully. Sie stellte die Vase vorsichtig hin.
   Drive carefully! Fahr vorsichtig!
3 **Listen carefully!** Hören Sie gut zu!

careless ADJECTIVE
1 **He's very careless.** Er ist sehr nachlässig.
   This is careless work. Das ist eine schlampige Arbeit.
2 **a careless mistake** ein Flüchtigkeitsfehler
3 **a careless driver** ein leichtsinniger Fahrer

ℱ **caretaker** NOUN
   der **Hausmeister** (PL die **Hausmeister**), die **Hausmeisterin** (PL die **Hausmeisterinnen**)

> **WORD TIP** Professions, hobbies, and sports don't take an article in German: Er ist Hausmeister.

car ferry NOUN
   die **Autofähre** (PL die **Autofähren**)

car hire NOUN
   die **Autovermietung**

ℱ indicates key words

Caribbean NOUN
the Caribbean (islands) die Karibik (SINGULAR)
to go to the Caribbean in die Karibik fahren

carnation NOUN
die Nelke (PL die Nelken)

carnival NOUN
der Karneval (PL die Karnevale) der Fasching

ℰ **car park** NOUN
der Parkplatz (PL die Parkplätze), (multi-storey) das Parkhaus (PL die Parkhäuser)

ℰ **carpenter** NOUN
der Tischler (PL die Tischler), die Tischlerin (PL die Tischlerinnen)

> **WORD TIP** Professions, hobbies, and sports don't take an article in German: Er ist Tischler.

carpentry NOUN
das Tischlerhandwerk

carpet NOUN
der Teppich (PL die Teppiche)

car phone NOUN
das Autotelefon (PL die Autotelefone)

car radio NOUN
das Autoradio (PL die Autoradios)

carriage NOUN
(of a train) das Abteil (PL die Abteile)

carrier bag NOUN
die Tragetasche (PL die Tragetaschen)

ℰ **carrot** NOUN
die Karotte (PL die Karotten), die Möhre (PL die Möhren), die Mohrrübe (PL die Mohrrüben)

ℰ to **carry** VERB
tragen◇
She was carrying a case. Sie trug einen Koffer.

• to **carry on**
weitermachen SEP
They carried on working. Sie arbeiteten weiter.

carrycot NOUN
die Babytragetasche (PL die Babytragetaschen)

carsick ADJECTIVE
He gets carsick. Ihm wird beim Autofahren schlecht.

carton NOUN
1 (of cream or yoghurt) der Becher (PL die Becher)

2 (of milk or juice) die Packung (PL die Packungen)

ℰ **cartoon** NOUN
1 (a film) der Zeichentrickfilm (PL die Zeichentrickfilme)
2 (a comic strip) der Cartoon (PL die Cartoons)
3 (a drawing) die Karikatur (PL die Karikaturen)

cartridge NOUN
(for a pen) die Patrone (PL die Patronen)

case[1] NOUN
1 (suitcase) der Koffer (PL die Koffer)
to pack a case einen Koffer packen
2 (a large wooden box) die Kiste (PL die Kisten)
3 (for spectacles or small things) das Etui (PL die Etuis)

case[2] NOUN
1 (situation) der Fall (PL die Fälle)
in that case in dem Fall
That's not the case. Das ist nicht der Fall.
in case of fire bei Feuer
2 in case falls
in case he comes falls er kommt
3 just in case für alle Fälle
4 in any case sowieso
In any case, it's too late. Es ist sowieso zu spät.

cash NOUN
1 (money in general) das Geld
I haven't any cash on me. Ich habe kein Geld dabei.
2 (money rather than a cheque) das Bargeld
to pay in cash bar zahlen
£50 in cash fünfzig Pfund in bar

cash card NOUN
die Bankkarte (PL die Bankkarten)

cash desk NOUN
die Kasse (PL die Kassen)
to pay at the cash desk an der Kasse zahlen

cash dispenser NOUN
der Geldautomat (PL die Geldautomaten), (in Austria) der Bankomat (PL die Bankomaten)

cashier NOUN
der Kassierer (PL die Kassierer), die Kassiererin (PL die Kassiererinnen)

cash point NOUN
der Geldautomat (PL die Geldautomaten), (in Austria) der Bankomat (PL die Bankomaten)

◇ irregular verb; SEP separable verb; for more help with verbs see centre section

cassette NOUN
die **Kassette** (PL die **Kassetten**)

cast NOUN
(of a play) die **Besetzung**

♟ **castle** NOUN
1 die **Burg** (PL die **Burgen**)
2 (in chess) der **Turm** (PL die **Türme**)

casual ADJECTIVE
zwanglos

casualty NOUN
1 (in an accident) der/die **Verletzte** (PL die **Verletzten**)
2 (hospital department) die **Unfallstation** (PL die **Unfallstationen**)
He's in casualty. Er ist auf der Unfallstation.

♟ **cat** NOUN
1 die **Katze** (PL die **Katzen**), (tomcat) der **Kater** (PL die **Kater**)
2 It's raining cats and dogs. Es regnet in Strömen. (literally: it's raining in streams)

catalogue NOUN
der **Katalog** (PL die **Kataloge**)

catastrophe NOUN
die **Katastrophe** (PL die **Katastrophen**)

♟ **catch** NOUN
1 (on a door) der **Schnappriegel** (PL die **Schnappriegel**)
2 (a drawback) der **Haken** (PL die **Haken**)
Where's the catch? Wo ist der Haken?

to **catch** VERB
1 fangen◇
Tom caught the ball. Tom hat den Ball gefangen.
She caught a fish. Sie hat einen Fisch gefangen.
Catch me! Fang mich!
2 to catch somebody doing something jemanden bei etwas (DAT) erwischen
He was caught stealing money. Er wurde beim Geldstehlen erwischt.
3 (be in time for) noch erreichen
Did Tim catch his plane? Hat Tim sein Flugzeug noch erreicht?
4 (become ill with) bekommen◇
She's caught chickenpox. Sie hat die Windpocken bekommen.
5 verstehen◇ (what somebody says)
I didn't catch your name. Ich habe Ihren Namen nicht verstanden.
• to catch up with somebody
jemanden einholen SEP

category NOUN
die **Kategorie** (PL die **Kategorien**)

catering NOUN
1 (trade) die **Gastronomie**
2 Who's doing the catering? Wer liefert das Essen und die Getränke?

caterpillar NOUN
die **Raupe** (PL die **Raupen**)

♟ **cathedral** NOUN
die **Kathedrale** die Kathedralen, der **Dom** (PL die **Dome**)
Cologne cathedral der Kölner Dom

Catholic NOUN
der **Katholik** (PL die **Katholiken**), die **Katholikin** (PL die **Katholikinnen**)
He's a Catholic. Er ist Katholik.

Catholic ADJECTIVE
katholisch

WORD TIP Adjectives never have capitals in German, even for religions.

cattle PLURAL NOUN
das **Vieh** SINGULAR

♟ **cauliflower** NOUN
der **Blumenkohl**
cauliflower cheese mit Käse überbackener Blumenkohl

♟ **cause** NOUN
1 die **Ursache** (PL die **Ursachen**)
the cause of the accident die Unfallursache
2 for a good cause für eine gute Sache

to **cause** VERB
verursachen
to cause difficulties Schwierigkeiten verursachen

cave NOUN
die **Höhle** (PL die **Höhlen**)

caving NOUN
die **Höhlenforschung**
to go caving auf Höhlenforschung gehen

♟ **CD** NOUN
die **CD** (PL die **CDs**)

♟ **ceiling** NOUN
die **Decke** (PL die **Decken**)
on the ceiling an der Decke

to **celebrate** VERB
feiern
He's celebrating his birthday. Er feiert seinen Geburtstag.

♟ indicates key words

celebrity NOUN
(person) der/die **Prominente** (PL die **Prominenten**)

celery NOUN
der **Sellerie**

cell NOUN
die **Zelle** (PL die **Zellen**)

ℓ **cellar** NOUN
der **Keller** (PL die **Keller**)

cello NOUN
das **Cello** (PL die **Cellos**)
He plays the cello. Er spielt Cello.

WORD TIP Don't use the article when you talk about playing an instrument.

cement NOUN
der **Zement**

cemetery NOUN
der **Friedhof** (PL die **Friedhöfe**)

ℓ **cent** NOUN
1 *(in euro system)* der **Eurocent** (PL die **Eurocent**), der **Cent** (PL die **Cent**)
50 cents 50 (Euro)cent
2 *(in dollar system)* der **Cent** (PL die **Cent**)
25 cents 25 Cent

centigrade ADJECTIVE
Celsius
ten degrees centigrade zehn Grad Celsius

ℓ **centimetre** NOUN
der **Zentimeter** (PL die **Zentimeter**)

ℓ **central** ADJECTIVE
1 **zentral**
The office is very central. Das Büro ist sehr zentral gelegen.
2 **in central London** im Zentrum von London

Central Europe NOUN
Mitteleuropa NEUTER

ℓ **central heating** NOUN
die **Zentralheizung**

ℓ **centre** NOUN
das **Zentrum** (PL die **Zentren**)
in the centre of im Zentrum von (+DAT)
in the town centre im Stadtzentrum
a shopping centre ein Einkaufszentrum

ℓ **century** NOUN
das **Jahrhundert** (PL die **Jahrhunderte**)
in the twentieth century im zwanzigsten Jahrhundert

cereal NOUN
breakfast cereal die Frühstücksflocken (PLURAL)

ceremony NOUN
die **Zeremonie** (PL die **Zeremonien**)

ℓ **certain** ADJECTIVE
1 *(definite)* **bestimmt**
a certain number of eine bestimmte Zahl von (+DAT)
2 *(confident)* **sicher**
to be certain sich *(DAT)* sicher sein
Are you certain of the address? Bist du sicher, dass das die richtige Adresse ist?
I'm absolutely certain. Ich bin mir ganz sicher.
to be certain that sicher sein, dass
3 **Nobody knows for certain.** Niemand weiß es genau.

ℓ **certainly** ADVERB
bestimmt
certainly not bestimmt nicht

ℓ **certificate** NOUN
1 die **Bescheinigung** (PL die **Bescheinigungen**)
2 **birth certificate** die Geburtsurkunde
3 *(at school)* das **Zeugnis** (PL die **Zeugnisse**)

CFC NOUN
(chlorofluorocarbon) das **FCKW** (PL die **FCKWs**)

ℓ **chain** NOUN
die **Kette** (PL die **Ketten**)

ℓ **chair** NOUN
1 *(upright)* der **Stuhl** (PL die **Stühle**)
a kitchen chair ein Küchenstuhl
2 *(with arms)* der **Sessel** (PL die **Sessel**)

chair lift NOUN
der **Sessellift** (PL die **Sessellifte**)

chalet NOUN
1 *(in the mountains)* das **Chalet** (PL die **Chalets**)
2 *(in a holiday camp)* das **Ferienhaus** (PL die **Ferienhäuser**)

chalk NOUN
die **Kreide** (PL die **Kreiden**)

challenge NOUN
die **Herausforderung** (PL die **Herausforderungen**)

champagne NOUN
der **Champagner** (PL die **Champagner**)

ℓ **champion** NOUN
der **Meister** (PL die **Meister**), die **Meisterin** (PL die **Meisterinnen**)
the world slalom champion der Weltmeister im Slalom (PL die Weltmeisterin im Slalom

◇ **irregular verb;** *SEP* **separable verb; for more help with verbs see centre section**

ℐ **chance** NOUN
1 *(opportunity)* die **Gelegenheit** (PL die **Gelegenheiten**)
 to have the chance to do something die Gelegenheit haben, etwas zu tun
 if you have the chance to go to New York wenn du die Gelegenheit hast, nach New York zu fahren
 I had no chance to speak to him. Ich hatte keine Gelegenheit, mit ihm zu reden.
2 *(likelihood)* die **Aussicht** (PL die **Aussichten**)
 He's got no chance of winning. Er hat keine Aussicht zu gewinnen.
3 *(luck)* der **Zufall**
 by chance zufällig
 Do you know her address, by any chance? Hast du zufällig ihre Adresse?

ℐ **change** NOUN
1 *(from one thing to another)* die **Änderung** (PL die **Änderungen**)
 a change of address eine Adressenänderung
 There's been a change of plan. Der Plan ist geändert worden.
2 *(alteration)* die **Veränderung** (PL die **Veränderungen**)
 They've made some changes to the house. Sie haben im Haus ein paar Veränderungen vorgenommen.
 a change in the weather ein Wetterumschwung
3 *(for the sake of variety)*
 For a change, we could go to a restaurant. Zur Abwechslung könnten wir in ein Restaurant gehen.
 It makes a change from hamburgers. Das ist mal etwas anderes als Hamburger.
 a change of clothes etwas anderes zum Anziehen
4 *(from a larger amount)* das **Wechselgeld**
 I haven't any change. Ich habe kein Wechselgeld.
5 *(coins)* das **Kleingeld**

to change VERB
1 *(make different)* **ändern**
 You can't change her. Du kannst sie nicht ändern.
 to change your address seine Adresse ändern
2 *(become different)* **sich verändern**
 Liz has changed a lot. Liz hat sich sehr verändert.
3 *(transform completely)* **verwandeln**
 The prince changed into a frog. Der Prinz verwandelte sich in einen Frosch.
4 *(exchange in a shop)* **umtauschen** SEP
 Just change it for a different size. Tauschen

Sie es einfach gegen eine andere Größe um.
5 *(change clothes)* **sich umziehen**◇ SEP
 Mike's just changing. Mike zieht sich gerade um.
6 *(switch from one train or bus to another)* **umsteigen**◇ (PERF **sein**)
 We changed trains at Glasgow. Wir stiegen in Glasgow um.
7 *(switch one thing for another)* **wechseln**
 I want to change my job. Ich möchte meine Stelle wechseln.
 They changed places. Sie haben die Plätze gewechselt.
 to change some money Geld wechseln
8 **to change your mind** sich anders entschließen◇

changing room NOUN
 der **Umkleideraum** (PL die **Umkleideräume**)

ℐ **channel** NOUN
1 *(on TV)* der **Kanal** (PL die **Kanäle**)
 to change channels auf einen anderen Kanal umschalten
2 **the Channel** der **Ärmelkanal**

Channel Tunnel NOUN
 der **Eurotunnel**

chaos NOUN
 das **Chaos**
 It was chaos! Das war ein Chaos!

chapel NOUN
 die **Kapelle** (PL die **Kapellen**)

chapter NOUN
 das **Kapitel** (PL die **Kapitel**)
 in chapter two im zweiten Kapitel

character NOUN
1 *(personality)* der **Charakter**
2 *(somebody in a book, play, or film)* der **Figur** (PL die **Figuren**)
3 **the main character** die Hauptfigur

characteristic NOUN
 die **Charaktereigenschaft** (PL die **Charaktereigenschaften**)

charcoal NOUN
1 *(for burning)* die **Holzkohle**
2 *(for drawing)* die **Kohle**

ℐ **charge** NOUN
1 *(what you pay)* die **Gebühr** (PL die **Gebühren**)
 a booking charge eine Buchungsgebühr
 an extra or additional charge eine zusätzliche Gebühr
 There's no charge. Das ist kostenlos.
2 **to be in charge of something** für etwas (ACC) verantwortlich sein

ℐ indicates key words

Who's in charge of the children? Wer ist für die Kinder verantwortlich?

3 **to be on a charge of theft** wegen Diebstahls angeklagt sein

to **charge** VERB

1 (ask to pay) berechnen
They charge us fifteen pounds an hour. Sie berechnen uns fünfzehn Pfund pro Stunde.
They didn't charge for delivery. Sie haben die Lieferung nicht berechnet.
We won't charge you for it. Wir berechnen Ihnen nichts dafür.

2 **to charge somebody with something** jemanden wegen etwas (GEN) anklagen SEP

charity NOUN

1 die Wohlfahrt
to give money to charity Geld für wohltätige Zwecke spenden

2 die Wohlfahrtsorganisation (PL die Wohlfahrtsorganisationen)

ℓ **charming** ADJECTIVE
reizend

chart NOUN

1 (table) die Tabelle (PL die Tabellen)
2 **the weather chart** die Wetterkarte
3 **the charts** die Hitparade (SINGULAR)

charter flight NOUN
der Charterflug (PL die Charterflüge)

chase NOUN
die Verfolgungsjagd (PL die Verfolgungsjagden)
a car chase eine Verfolgungsjagd mit dem Auto

to **chase** VERB
jagen

ℓ **chat** NOUN
die Plauderei (PL die Plaudereien)
to have a chat with somebody mit jemandem plaudern

to **chat** VERB
plaudern, (on the Internet) chatten

chatroom NOUN
der Chatroom (PL die Chatrooms)

chat show NOUN
die Talkshow (PL die Talkshows)

to **chatter** VERB

1 (talk) schwatzen
2 **My teeth were chattering.** Ich klapperte mit den Zähnen.

ℓ **cheap** ADJECTIVE
billig
cheap shoes billige Schuhe
That's very cheap. Das ist sehr billig.

cheaply ADVERB
billig
to eat cheaply billig essen

cheap-rate ADJECTIVE
verbilligt
a cheap-rate phone call ein Gespräch zum Billigtarif

cheat NOUN

1 der Betrüger (PL die Betrüger), die Betrügerin (PL die Betrügerinnen)
2 (in games) der Mogler (PL die Mogler), die Moglerin (PL die Moglerinnen)

to **cheat** VERB

1 betrügen◇
2 (in a game, exam) mogeln, schummeln

ℓ **check** NOUN

1 (in a factory or at a border control) die Kontrolle (PL die Kontrollen)
passport check die Passkontrolle
2 (in chess)
Check! Schach!

to **check** VERB

1 (make sure) prüfen
He checked their statements. Er prüfte ihre Aussagen.
2 (make sure by looking) nachsehen◇ SEP
to check the time auf die Uhr sehen
Check they're all back. Sieh nach, ob alle wieder da sind.
3 (inspect) kontrollieren
to check the tickets die Fahrkarten kontrollieren

• **to check in**
sich anmelden SEP
to check in at the airport am Flughafen einchecken

• **to check out**
abreisen◇ SEP (PERF sein)
to check out of the hotel das Hotel verlassen◇

ℓ **check-in** NOUN
der Abfertigungsschalter (PL die Abfertigungsschalter)

ℓ **checkout** NOUN
die Kasse (PL die Kassen)
at the checkout an der Kasse

check-up NOUN
die Untersuchung (PL die Untersuchungen)

cheek NOUN

1 (part of face) die Backe (PL die Backen)
2 (nerve) die Frechheit
What a cheek! So eine Frechheit!

◇ irregular verb; SEP separable verb; for more help with verbs see centre section

cheeky ADJECTIVE
frech

ℱ **cheer** NOUN
1 Three cheers for Tom! Ein dreifaches Hoch auf Tom!
2 *(when drinking)*
Cheers! Prost!

to **cheer** VERB
(shout hurray) Hurra schreien◇
• to cheer somebody up
jemanden aufmuntern SEP
Your visits always cheer me up. Deine Besuche muntern mich immer auf.
Cheer up! Kopf hoch!

cheerful ADJECTIVE
fröhlich

ℱ **cheese** NOUN
der Käse
a cheese sandwich ein Käsebrot

ℱ **chef** NOUN
der Koch (PL die Köche), die Köchin (PL die Köchinnen)

> **WORD TIP** Do not translate the English word chef with the German Chef. Professions, hobbies, and sports don't take an article in German: Er ist Koch.

chemical NOUN
die Chemikalie (PL die Chemikalien)

ℱ **chemist** NOUN
1 *(in a pharmacy)* der Apotheker (PL die Apotheker), die Apothekerin (PL die Apothekerinnen)
2 chemist's *(pharmacy)* die Apotheke (PL die Apotheken), *(shop)* die Drogerie (PL die Drogerien)
at the chemist's in der Apotheke/Drogerie
3 *(scientist)* der Chemiker (PL die Chemiker), die Chemikerin (PL die Chemikerinnen)

> **WORD TIP** Professions, hobbies, and sports don't take an article in German: Er ist Apotheker.

ℱ **chemistry** NOUN
die Chemie

ℱ **cheque** NOUN
der Scheck (PL die Schecks)
to pay by cheque mit Scheck bezahlen
to write a cheque einen Scheck ausstellen

ℱ **cherry** NOUN
die Kirsche (PL die Kirschen)

ℱ **chess** NOUN
das Schach
to play chess Schach spielen

chessboard NOUN
das Schachbrett (PL die Schachbretter)

ℱ **chest** NOUN
1 *(part of the body)* die Brust (PL die Brüste)
2 *(box)* die Truhe (PL die Truhen)
3 chest of drawers die Kommode

ℱ **chestnut** NOUN
die Esskastanie (PL die Esskastanien)

chestnut tree NOUN
1 *(horse chestnut)* die Rosskastanie (PL die Rosskastanien)
2 *(sweet chestnut)* die Edelkastanie (PL die Edelkastanien)

to **chew** VERB
kauen

chewing gum NOUN
der Kaugummi (PL die Kaugummis)

ℱ **chicken** NOUN
das Huhn (PL die Hühner)
roast chicken das Brathähnchen
chicken breast die Hühnerbrust

chickenpox NOUN
die Windpocken (PLURAL)

ℱ **child** NOUN
das Kind (PL die Kinder)
When I was a child ... Als Kind ...

childish ADJECTIVE
kindisch

childminder NOUN
die Tagesmutter (PL die Tagesmütter)

chill NOUN
1 die Kälte
2 to have a chill eine Erkältung haben

chilled ADJECTIVE
gekühlt

chilli NOUN
der Chili

to **chill out** VERB
sich entspannen

chilly ADJECTIVE
kühl

chimney NOUN
der Schornstein (PL die Schornsteine)

chimpanzee NOUN
der Schimpanse (PL die Schimpansen)

ℱ **chin** NOUN
das Kinn (PL die Kinne)

ℱ indicates key words

china NOUN
das **Porzellan**
china bowl die **Porzellanschüssel**

China NOUN
China NEUTER

Chinese NOUN
1 **the Chinese** (people) die **Chinesen**
2 (language) das **Chinesisch**

Chinese ADJECTIVE
1 **chinesisch**
Chinese culture die **chinesische Kultur**
a Chinese man ein **Chinese**
a Chinese woman eine **Chinesin**
2 **to have a Chinese meal** chinesisch essen

> **WORD TIP** Adjectives never have capitals
> in German, even for regions, countries, or
> nationalities.

ℰ **chip** NOUN
1 (fried potato)
chips die **Pommes frites** (PLURAL)
fish and chips ausgebackener Fisch mit
Pommes frites
2 (microchip) der **Chip** (PL die **Chips**)
3 (in glass or china) die **angeschlagene Stelle**
(PL die **angeschlagenen Stellen**)

> **WORD TIP** Do not translate the English word
> chips with the German Chips.

chipped ADJECTIVE
angeschlagen

chocolate NOUN
1 die **Schokolade**
a bar of chocolate eine **Tafel Schokolade**
chocolate ice cream das **Schokoladeneis**
2 die **Praline** (PL die **Pralinen**)
a box of chocolates eine **Schachtel Pralinen**
3 **a cup of hot chocolate** eine **Tasse heiße**
Schokolade

ℰ **choice** NOUN
1 die **Wahl** (PL die **Wahlen**)
to make a good choice eine gute Wahl
treffen
2 (variety) die **Auswahl**
You have a choice of two flights. Du hast
zwei Flüge zur Auswahl.

choir NOUN
der **Chor** (PL die **Chöre**)

choke NOUN
(on a car) der **Choke** (PL die **Chokes**)

to choke VERB
(on food or drink) sich **verschlucken**
She choked on a bone. Sie hat sich an einer
Gräte verschluckt.

ℰ **to choose** VERB
1 **wählen**
You chose well. Du hast gut gewählt.
It's hard to choose from all these colours.
Es ist schwer, unter allen diesen Farben zu
wählen.
2 (select from a group of things) sich (DAT)
aussuchen SEP
Cathy chose the red skirt. Cathy suchte
sich den roten Rock aus.

chop NOUN
das **Kotelett** (PL die **Koteletts**)
a pork chop ein Schweinekotelett

to chop VERB
hacken

chord NOUN
der **Akkord** (PL die **Akkorde**)

chorus NOUN
1 (when you all join in the song) der **Refrain**
(PL die **Refrains**)
2 (a group of singers) der **Chor** (PL die **Chöre**)

Christ NOUN
der **Christus**

christening NOUN
die **Taufe** (PL die **Taufen**)

Christian NOUN
der **Christ** (PL die **Christen**), die **Christin**
(PL die **Christinnen**)
He's a Christian. Er ist Christ.

Christian ADJECTIVE
christlich

> **WORD TIP** Adjectives never have capitals in
> German, even for religions.

Christianity NOUN
das **Christentum**

Christian name NOUN
der **Vorname** (PL die **Vornamen**)

ℰ **Christmas** NOUN
Weihnachten NEUTER die **Weihnachten**
at Christmas zu Weihnachten
What did you get for Christmas? Was hast
du zu Weihnachten bekommen?
Happy Christmas! Frohe Weihnachten!

Christmas card NOUN
die **Weihnachtskarte** (PL die
Weihnachtskarten)

Christmas carol NOUN
das **Weihnachtslied** (PL die
Weihnachtslieder)

Christmas cracker NOUN
der or das **Knallbonbon** (PL die
Knallbonbons)

Christmas Day NOUN
der erste Weihnachtstag

Christmas Eve NOUN
der **Heiligabend**, der **Heilige Abend**
on Christmas Eve Heiligabend

Christmas present NOUN
das **Weihnachtsgeschenk** (PL die
Weihnachtsgeschenke)

Christmas tree NOUN
der **Weihnachtsbaum** (PL die
Weihnachtsbäume)

ℓ **church** NOUN
die **Kirche** (PL die **Kirchen**)
to go to church in die Kirche gehen

chute NOUN
(in a swimming pool or playground) die
Rutsche (PL die **Rutschen**)

ℓ **cider** NOUN
der **Apfelwein** (PL die **Apfelweine**)

cigar NOUN
die **Zigarre** (PL die **Zigarren**)

ℓ **cigarette** NOUN
die **Zigarette** (PL die **Zigaretten**)

ℓ **cinema** NOUN
das **Kino** (PL die **Kinos**)
to go to the cinema ins Kino gehen

ℓ **circle** NOUN
der **Kreis** (PL die **Kreise**)
to sit in a circle im Kreis sitzen
to go round in circles sich im Kreis drehen

circuit NOUN
1 (for athletes) die **Bahn** (PL die **Bahnen**)
2 (for cars) die **Rennbahn** (PL die
Rennbahnen)

circumference NOUN
der **Umfang**

circumstances PLURAL NOUN
die **Umstände** (PLURAL)
under these circumstances unter diesen
Umständen

ℓ **circus** NOUN
der **Zirkus** (PL die **Zirkusse**)

citizen NOUN
der **Bürger** (PL die **Bürger**) die **Bürgerin**
(PL die **Bürgerinnen**)

city NOUN
die **Stadt** (PL die **Städte**)
the city of Berlin die Stadt Berlin

city centre NOUN
das **Stadtzentrum** (PL die **Stadtzentren**)

in the city centre im Stadtzentrum, in der
Innenstadt

civilization NOUN
die **Zivilisation** (PL die **Zivilisationen**)

civil partnership NOUN
die **zivile Partnerschaft** (PL die **zivilen
Partnerschaften**)

ℓ **civil servant** NOUN
der **Beamte** (PL die **Beamten**), die **Beamtin**
(PL die **Beamtinnen**)

> **WORD TIP** Professions, hobbies, and sports
> don't take an article in German: Sie ist Beamtin.

civil war NOUN
der **Bürgerkrieg** (PL die **Bürgerkriege**)

claim NOUN
1 (statement) die **Behauptung** (PL die
Behauptungen)
2 (for compensation) der **Anspruch** (PL die
Ansprüche)
to make a claim on insurance seine
Versicherungsansprüche geltend machen

to **claim** VERB
1 behaupten
He claims to know who ... Er behauptet zu
wissen, wer ...
2 fordern
She claimed compensation. Sie forderte
Schadensersatz.

to **clap** VERB
1 klatschen
Everyone clapped. Alle klatschten.
2 to clap your hands in die Hände klatschen

clarinet NOUN
die **Klarinette** (PL die **Klarinetten**)
I play the clarinet. Ich spiele Klarinette.

> **WORD TIP** Don't use the article when you talk
> about playing an instrument.

clash NOUN
(between two groups) der **Zusammenstoß**
(PL die **Zusammenstöße**)

to **clash** VERB
1 (rival groups) zusammenstoßen◇ SEP
2 (colours) sich beißen◇
Avoid colours that clash. Vermeiden Sie
Farben (PL die sich beißen.
The jumper clashes with the skirt. Der
Pullover passt nicht zum Rock.

ℓ **class** NOUN
1 (a group of students or pupils) die **Klasse**
(PL die **Klassen**)
She's in my class. Sie geht in meine Klasse.

ℓ indicates key words

2 *(a lesson)* die **Stunde** (PL die **Stunden**)
history class die Geschichtsstunde
in class im Unterricht

3 *(category)* die **Klasse** (PL die **Klassen**)

4 **social class** die Gesellschaftsschicht

classic ADJECTIVE
klassisch

classical ADJECTIVE
klassisch
He likes classical music. Er mag klassische Musik.

ℓ **classroom** NOUN
das **Klassenzimmer** (PL die **Klassenzimmer**)

clay NOUN
der **Ton**

ℓ **clean** ADJECTIVE
sauber
a clean shirt ein sauberes Hemd
My hands are clean. Ich habe saubere Hände.
clean towels frische Handtücher
clean water reines Wasser

to **clean** VERB

1 putzen
I cleaned the windows. Ich habe die Fenster geputzt.

2 **to clean your teeth** sich (DAT) die Zähne putzen
I'm going to clean my teeth. Ich putze mir jetzt die Zähne.

cleaner NOUN

1 *(cleaning lady)* die **Putzfrau** (PL die **Putzfrauen**)

2 *(in a public place)* die **Reinigungskraft** (PL die **Reinigungskräfte**)

3 **dry cleaner's** die (chemische) Reinigung

WORD TIP Professions, hobbies, and sports don't take an article in German: Sie ist Putzfrau.

ℓ **cleaning** NOUN
to do the cleaning putzen

cleanser NOUN

1 *(for your face)* die **Reinigungsmilch**

2 *(for the house)* das **Reinigungsmittel** (PL die **Reinigungsmittel**)

ℓ **clear** ADJECTIVE
klar
clear water klares Wasser
clear instructions klare Anweisungen
Is that clear? Ist das klar? *(informal)*
to make something clear etwas klarmachen SEP

to **clear** VERB

1 räumen

Have you cleared your stuff out of your room? Hast du deine Sachen aus deinem Zimmer geräumt?

2 **Can I clear the table?** Kann ich den Tisch abräumen? SEP

3 **to clear your throat** sich räuspern

• **to clear up**

1 *(tidy up)* aufräumen SEP

2 *(the weather)* sich aufklären SEP
The weather is clearing up a bit. Das Wetter klärt sich ein bisschen auf.

clearly ADVERB

1 *(to think, speak, or hear)* deutlich

2 *(obviously)* eindeutig
She was clearly better. Sie war eindeutig besser.

clementine NOUN
die **Klementine** (PL die **Klementinen**)

ℓ **clever** ADJECTIVE

1 klug
Their children are all very clever. Ihre Kinder sind alle sehr klug.

2 *(ingenious)* clever
a clever idea eine clevere Idee

click NOUN

1 *(noise)* das **Klicken**

2 *(with a mouse)* der **Klick** (PL die **Klicks**)
a double click ein Doppelklick

to **click** VERB
(with a mouse)
to click on something etwas anklicken SEP
Click on the icon. Klicken Sie auf das Symbol.

ℓ **client** NOUN
der **Klient** (PL die **Klienten**) die **Klientin** (PL die **Klientinnen**)

cliff NOUN
die **Klippe** (PL die **Klippen**)

ℓ **climate** NOUN
das **Klima** (PL die **Klimas**)

to **climb** VERB

1 *(the stairs, a hill)* hinaufgehen◇ SEP (PERF sein)
to climb a mountain einen Berg besteigen◇ (PERF sein)

2 *(a wall, tree, or rock)* klettern (PERF sein) auf (+ACC)
to climb a tree auf einen Baum klettern

climber NOUN
der **Bergsteiger** (PL die **Bergsteiger**), die **Bergsteigerin** (PL die **Bergsteigerinnen**)

WORD TIP Professions, hobbies, and sports don't take an article in German: Er ist Bergsteiger.

◇ **irregular verb;** SEP **separable verb; for more help with verbs see centre section**

A
B
C
D
E
F
G
H
I
J
K
L
M
N
O
P
Q
R
S
T
U
V
W
X
Y
Z

ℓ **climbing** *NOUN*
das **Bergsteigen**
They go climbing in Italy. Sie gehen in
Italien bergsteigen.

clinic *NOUN*
die **Klinik** (*PL* die **Kliniken**)

clip *NOUN*
1 *(from a film)* der **Ausschnitt** (*PL* die
Ausschnitte)
2 *(for your hair)* die **Klammer** (*PL* die
Klammern)

cloakroom *NOUN*
(for coats) die **Garderobe** (*PL* die
Garderoben)

ℓ **clock** *NOUN*
1 die **Uhr** (*PL* die **Uhren**)
to put the clocks forward an hour die Uhr
eine Stunde vorstellen *SEP*
to put the clocks back die Uhr
zurückstellen *SEP*
2 **an alarm clock** ein Wecker

ℓ **close¹** *ADJECTIVE, ADVERB*
1 *(result)* **knapp**
2 *(friend, connection)* **eng**
3 *(relation or acquaintance)* **nahe**
4 *(near)* **in der Nähe**
The station's very close. Der Bahnhof ist
ganz in der Nähe.
She lives close by. Sie wohnt in der Nähe.
5 **close to** nahe, nah *(informal)* (*+DAT*)
close to the cinema nahe am Kino
not very close nicht sehr nah

ℓ **close²** *NOUN*
das **Ende**
at the close am Ende

to **close** *VERB*
zumachen *SEP*, **schließen**◇
Close your eyes! Mach die Augen zu!
She closed the door. Sie machte die Tür zu.
The post office closes at six. Die Post macht
um sechs zu./Die Post schließt um sechs.

ℓ **closed** *ADJECTIVE*
geschlossen
'Closed on Mondays' 'Montags
geschlossen'

closely *ADVERB*
1 *(in distance)* **eng**
2 *(carefully)* **genau**
to look at something closely sich etwas
genau ansehen◇ *SEP*

closing date *NOUN*
the closing date for entries *(for a
competition)* der Einsendeschluss, *(for a
sporting event)* der Meldeschluss

ℓ **closing time** *NOUN*
1 der **Ladenschluss**
2 *(of a pub)* die **Polizeistunde**

cloth *NOUN*
1 *(for drying up and polishing)* das **Tuch** (*PL* die
Tücher)
2 *(for the floor)* der **Lappen** (*PL* die **Lappen**)
3 *(fabric)* der **Stoff** (*PL* die **Stoffe**)

ℓ **clothes** *PLURAL NOUN*
1 die **Kleider** (*PLURAL*)
2 **to put your clothes on** sich anziehen◇ *SEP*
to take your clothes off sich ausziehen◇ *SEP*
to change your clothes sich umziehen◇ *SEP*

clothes peg *NOUN*
die **Wäscheklammer** (*PL* die
Wäscheklammern)

clothing *NOUN*
die **Kleidung**

ℓ **cloud** *NOUN*
die **Wolke** (*PL* die **Wolken**)

ℓ **cloudy** *ADJECTIVE*
bewölkt

clown *NOUN*
der **Clown** (*PL* die **Clowns**)

ℓ **club** *NOUN*
1 der **Klub** (*PL* die **Klubs**), *(for footballers)* der
Verein (*PL* die **Vereine**)
a youth club ein Jugendklub
a football club ein Fußballverein
2 *(in cards)* das **Kreuz** (*PL* die **Kreuze**)
the four of clubs die Kreuz-Vier
3 *(in golf)* der **Schläger** (*PL* die **Schläger**)

to **club** *VERB*
to go clubbing in die Disco gehen◇

clue *NOUN*
1 der **Anhaltspunkt** (*PL* die **Anhaltspunkte**)
They have a few clues. Sie haben ein paar
Anhaltspunkte.
I haven't a clue. Ich habe keine Ahnung.
Give me a clue. Gib mir einen Hinweis.
2 *(in a crossword)* die **Frage** (*PL* die **Fragen**)

clumsy *ADJECTIVE*
ungeschickt

clutch *NOUN*
(in a car) die **Kupplung** (*PL* die **Kupplungen**)

to **clutch** *VERB*
to clutch something etwas festhalten◇ *SEP*

ℓ **coach** *NOUN*
1 *(bus)* der **Bus** (*PL* die **Busse**), der **Reisebus**
(*PL* die **Reisebusse**)
on the coach im Bus

ℓ indicates key words

to travel by coach mit dem Bus fahren
2 *(sports trainer)* der **Trainer** (PL die **Trainer**), die **Trainerin** (PL die **Trainerinnen**)
3 *(railway carriage)* der **Wagen** (PL die **Wagen**)

coach station NOUN
der **Busbahnhof** (PL die **Busbahnhöfe**)

coach trip NOUN
der **Busausflug** (PL die **Busausflüge**)
to go on a coach trip einen Busausflug machen

coal NOUN
die **Kohle** (PL die **Kohlen**)

coarse ADJECTIVE
grob

coast NOUN
die **Küste** (PL die **Küsten**)
on the east coast an der Ostküste

ℓ **coat** NOUN
1 der **Mantel** (PL die **Mäntel**)
2 **coat of paint** der Anstrich

coat hanger NOUN
der **Kleiderbügel** (PL die **Kleiderbügel**)

cobweb NOUN
das **Spinnennetz** (PL die **Spinnennetze**)

cocaine NOUN
das **Kokain**

cock NOUN
der **Hahn** (PL die **Hähne**)

cocoa NOUN
der **Kakao**

coconut NOUN
die **Kokosnuss** (PL die **Kokosnüsse**)

cod NOUN
der **Kabeljau** (PL die **Kabeljaue**)

code NOUN
1 *(in law)* das **Gesetzbuch**
the highway code die Straßenverkehrsordnung
2 **the dialling code for Hull** die Vorwahl für Hull

ℓ **coffee** NOUN
der **Kaffee** (PL die **Kaffees**)
a cup of coffee eine Tasse Kaffee
A black coffee, please. Einen Kaffee ohne Milch bitte.
A white coffee, please. Einen Kaffee mit Milch bitte.

coffee break NOUN
die **Kaffeepause** (PL die **Kaffeepausen**)

coffee cup NOUN
die **Kaffeetasse** (PL die **Kaffeetassen**)

coffee machine NOUN
die **Kaffeemaschine** (PL die **Kaffeemaschinen**)

coffin NOUN
der **Sarg** (PL die **Särge**)

ℓ **coin** NOUN
1 die **Münze** (PL die **Münzen**)
She collects old coins. Sie sammelt alte Münzen.
2 **a pound coin** ein Einpfundstück

coincidence NOUN
der **Zufall** (PL die **Zufälle**)

Coke® NOUN
das *or* die **Cola**®
Two Cokes, please. Zwei Cola bitte.

ℓ **cold** NOUN
1 *(cold weather)* die **Kälte**
to be out in the cold draußen in der Kälte sein
2 *(illness)* der **Schnupfen** (PL die **Schnupfen**), die **Erkältung** (PL die **Erkältungen**)
to have a cold Schnupfen haben
Carol's got a cold. Carol hat Schnupfen.
a bad cold eine schlimme Erkältung

cold ADJECTIVE
1 **kalt**
Your hands are cold. Du hast kalte Hände.
cold milk kalte Milch
2 *(weather, temperature)*
It's cold today. Heute ist es kalt.
3 *(feeling)*
I'm cold. Mir ist kalt.

to collapse VERB
1 *(a roof or wall)* einstürzen SEP (PERF sein)
2 *(a person)* zusammenbrechen◇ SEP (PERF sein)
He collapsed in his office. Er brach in seinem Büro zusammen.

collar NOUN
1 *(on a garment)* der **Kragen** (PL die **Kragen**)
2 *(for an animal)* das **Halsband** (PL die **Halsbänder**)

colleague NOUN
der **Kollege** (PL die **Kollegen**), die **Kollegin** (PL die **Kolleginnen**)

ℓ **to collect** VERB
1 *(as a hobby)* sammeln
Do you collect stamps? Sammelst du Briefmarken?
2 *(fetch)* abholen SEP
She collects the children from school. Sie

◇ **irregular verb**; SEP **separable verb**; **for more help with verbs see centre section**

holt die Kinder von der Schule ab.
3 to collect up the exercise books die Hefte
einsammeln *SEP*

collection *NOUN*
(of stamps, money, etc.) die **Sammlung**
(*PL* die **Sammlungen**)

collector *NOUN*
der **Sammler** (*PL* die **Sammler**), die
Sammlerin (*PL* die **Sammlerinnen**)

college *NOUN*
1 (for higher education) die **Hochschule**
(*PL* die **Hochschulen**)
to go to college studieren
2 (a school) das **College** (*PL* die **Colleges**)

Cologne *NOUN*
(city in Germany) **Köln** (*NEUTER*)

ℙ **colour** *NOUN*
die **Farbe** (*PL* die **Farben**)
What colour is it? Welche Farbe hat es?
Do you have it in a different colour? Haben
Sie es in einer anderen Farbe?

to colour *VERB*
1 (with paints or crayons) anmalen *SEP*
to colour something red etwas rot
anmalen
2 (with dye) färben

colour blind *ADJECTIVE*
farbenblind

colourful *ADJECTIVE*
bunt

column *NOUN*
1 (of a building) die **Säule** (*PL* die **Säulen**)
2 (on a page) die **Spalte** (*PL* die **Spalten**)

ℙ **comb** *NOUN*
der **Kamm** (*PL* die **Kämme**)

to comb *VERB*
kämmen
to comb your hair sich (*DAT*) die Haare
kämmen
I'll just comb my hair. Ich kämme mir nur
die Haare.

ℙ **to come** *VERB*
kommen◇ (*PERF* sein)
Come quick! Komm schnell!
Come here! Komm mal her!
Come on!/Come along! Komm schon!
Nick came by car. Nick kam mit dem Auto.
Can you come over for a coffee? Kannst du
auf eine Tasse Kaffee kommen?
Did Jess come to school yesterday? War
Jess gestern in der Schule?
Coming! Ich komme schon!

The bus is coming. Der Bus kommt gerade.
• **to come back**
zurückkommen◇ *SEP* (*PERF* sein)
He's coming back to collect us. Er kommt
zurück, um uns abzuholen.
• **to come down**
herunterkommen◇ *SEP* (*PERF* sein)
• **to come for somebody** (collect)
jemanden abholen *SEP*
My father's coming for me. Mein Vater holt
mich ab.
• **to come in**
hereinkommen◇ *SEP* (*PERF* sein)
Come in! Herein!
• **to come off** (a button)
abgehen◇ *SEP* (*PERF* sein)
• **to come out**
herauskommen◇ *SEP* (*PERF* sein)
They came out when I called. Als ich rief,
kamen sie heraus.
The new song is coming out soon. Die
neue Lied kommt bald heraus.
• **to come up**
heraufkommen◇ *SEP* (*PERF* sein)
Can you come up a moment? Kannst du
eine Sekunde heraufkommen?
• **to come up to somebody**
auf jemanden zukommen◇ *SEP* (*PERF* sein)

comedian *NOUN*
der **Komiker** (*PL* die **Komiker**), die
Komikerin (*PL* die **Komikerinnen**)

> **WORD TIP** Professions, hobbies, and sports
> don't take an article in German: Er ist Komiker.

comedy *NOUN*
die **Komödie**

ℙ **comfortable** *ADJECTIVE*
1 bequem
This chair's really comfortable. Dieser
Sessel ist wirklich bequem.
2 to feel comfortable (a person) sich
wohlfühlen *SEP*

comfortably *ADVERB*
bequem

ℙ **comic** *NOUN*
(magazine) das **Comicheft** (*PL* die
Comichefte

comic strip *NOUN*
der **Comic** (*PL* die **Comics**)

comma *NOUN*
das **Komma** (*PL* die **Kommas**)

command *NOUN*
der **Befehl** (*PL* die **Befehle**)

ℙ indicates key words

comment NOUN
(remark) die **Bemerkung** (PL die Bemerkungen)
He made some rude comments about my friends. Er hat ein paar unhöfliche Bemerkungen über meine Freunde gemacht.

commentary NOUN
die **Reportage** (PL die Reportagen)
the commentary on the soccer match die Reportage über das Fußballspiel

commentator NOUN
der **Reporter** (PL die Reporter), die **Reporterin** (PL die Reporterinnen)
sports commentator der Sportreporter

commercial NOUN
der **Werbespot** (PL die Werbespots)

commercial ADJECTIVE
kommerziell

to **commit** VERB
1 **begehen**◇ (a crime or suicide)
2 **to commit yourself to** sich festlegen SEP auf (+ACC)

committee NOUN
der **Ausschuss** (PL die Ausschüsse)

common ADJECTIVE
1 **häufig**
It's a common problem. Das Problem kommt häufig vor.
2 **in common gemeinsam**
They have nothing in common. Sie haben nichts gemeinsam.

common sense NOUN
der **gesunde Menschenverstand**

to **communicate** VERB
kommunizieren

communication NOUN
die **Verständigung** (PL die Kommunikation)

communion NOUN
(in a Catholic church) die **Kommunion**, (in a Protestant church) das **Abendmahl**

communism NOUN
der **Kommunismus**

community NOUN
die **Gemeinschaft** (PL die Gemeinschaften)

to **commute** VERB
pendeln (PERF sein)
to commute between Oxford and London zwischen Oxford und London pendeln

commuter NOUN
der **Pendler** (PL die Pendler), die **Pendlerin** (PL die Pendlerinnen)

company NOUN
1 (business) die **Gesellschaft** (PL die Gesellschaften), die **Firma** (PL die Firmen)
an airline company eine Fluggesellschaft
She's set up a company. Sie hat eine Firma gegründet.
2 (group) die **Truppe** (PL die Truppen)
a theatre company eine Theatertruppe
3 **to keep somebody company** jemandem Gesellschaft leisten
The dog keeps me company. Der Hund leistet mir Gesellschaft.

℘to **compare** VERB
vergleichen◇
if you compare the German phrase with the English wenn man den deutschen mit dem englischen Ausdruck vergleicht
Our house is small compared with yours. Verglichen mit eurem ist unser Haus klein.

℘**compartment** NOUN
das **Abteil** (PL die Abteile)

compass NOUN
der **Kompass** (PL die Kompasse)

compatible ADJECTIVE
1 **zueinander passend**
2 (in computing) **kompatibel**

to **compete** VERB
1 **to compete in something** (race, event) an etwas (DAT) teilnehmen◇ SEP
2 **to compete with each other** miteinander konkurrieren
3 **to compete for something** um etwas (ACC) kämpfen
Thirty people are competing for one job. Dreißig Leute kämpfen um eine Stelle.

competent ADJECTIVE
fähig

competition NOUN
1 (a contest) der **Wettbewerb** (PL die Wettbewerbe)
2 (in a magazine, etc.) das **Preisausschreiben** (PL die Preisausschreiben)

competitor NOUN
der **Konkurrent** (PL die Konkurrenten), die **Konkurrentin** (PL die Konkurrentinnen)

to **complain** VERB
sich beschweren
We complained about the meals. Wir haben uns über das Essen beschwert.

◇ **irregular verb;** SEP **separable verb; for more help with verbs see centre section**

complaint NOUN
die **Beschwerde** (PL die **Beschwerden**)
to make a complaint sich beschweren
She made a complaint to the manager about the poor service. Sie beschwerte sich bei dem Geschäftsführer über den schlechten Service.

ℐ **complete** ADJECTIVE
1 (whole) **vollständig**
the complete collection die vollständige Sammlung
2 (absolute) **völlig**
a complete idiot ein völliger Idiot (informal)

to **complete** VERB
(finish) **beenden**

ℐ **completely** ADVERB
völlig

complexion NOUN
der **Teint** (PL die **Teints**)

complicated ADJECTIVE
kompliziert

compliment NOUN
das **Kompliment** (PL die **Komplimente**)
to pay somebody a compliment jemandem ein Kompliment machen

composer NOUN
der **Komponist** (PL die **Komponisten**), die **Komponistin** (PL die **Komponistinnen**)

compost NOUN
der **Kompost**

to **compost** VERB
kompostieren

comprehension NOUN
das **Verständnis**
a comprehension test ein Test zum Textverständnis

comprehensive school NOUN
die **Gesamtschule** (PL die **Gesamtschulen**)

ℐ **compulsory** ADJECTIVE
1 **obligatorisch**
2 (at school)
compulsory subject das Pflichtfach

ℐ **computer** NOUN
der **Computer** (PL die **Computer**)
to work on a computer am Computer arbeiten
to play on the computer am Computer spielen
to have something on computer etwas im Computer gespeichert haben

computer engineer NOUN
der **Computertechniker** (PL die **Computertechniker**), die **Computertechnikerin** (PL die **Computertechnikerinnen**)

computer game NOUN
das **Computerspiel** (PL die **Computerspiele**)

computer program NOUN
das **Computerprogramm** (PL die **Computerprogramme**)

computer programmer NOUN
der **Programmierer** (PL die **Programmierer**), die **Programmiererin** (PL die **Programmiererinnen**)

computer science NOUN
die **Informatik**

ℐ **computing** NOUN
die **Informatik**

to **concentrate** VERB
sich konzentrieren
I can't concentrate. Ich kann mich nicht konzentrieren.
I was concentrating on the film. Ich konzentrierte mich auf den Film.

concentration NOUN
die **Konzentration**

to **concern** VERB
(affect) **betreffen**◇
This doesn't concern you. Das betrifft Sie nicht.
as far as I'm concerned was mich betrifft

ℐ **concert** NOUN
das **Konzert** (PL die **Konzerte**)
to go to a concert ins Konzert gehen
concert ticket die Konzertkarte

conclusion NOUN
der **Schluss** (PL die **Schlüsse**)

concrete NOUN
der **Beton**
concrete floor der Betonboden

to **condemn** VERB
verurteilen
to condemn somebody to death jemanden zum Tode verurteilen

ℐ **condition** NOUN
1 der **Zustand** (PL die **Zustände**)
in good condition in gutem Zustand
weather conditions die Wetterlage
2 (something you insist on) die **Bedingung** (PL die **Bedingungen**)

ℐ **indicates key words**

on condition that you let me pay unter der Bedingung, dass du mich zahlen lässt

conditional NOUN
(in grammar) das **Konditional**

conditioner NOUN
(for your hair) die **Spülung** (PL die **Spülungen**)

condom NOUN
das **Kondom** (PL die **Kondome**)

conduct NOUN
das **Benehmen**

to **conduct** VERB
dirigieren (an orchestra or a piece of music)

conductor NOUN
(of an orchestra) der **Dirigent** (PL die **Dirigenten**), die **Dirigentin** (PL die **Dirigentinnen**)

WORD TIP Professions, hobbies, and sports don't take an article in German: Er ist Dirigent.

cone NOUN
1 (for ice cream) die **Eistüte** (PL die **Eistüten**)
2 (for traffic) der **Leitkegel** (PL die **Leitkegel**)

conference NOUN
die **Konferenz** (PL die **Konferenzen**)

to **confess** VERB
gestehen◇

confession NOUN
das **Geständnis** (PL die **Geständnisse**)

confidence NOUN
1 (self-confidence) das **Selbstvertrauen**
to be lacking in confidence kein Selbstvertrauen haben
2 (faith in somebody else) das **Vertrauen**
to have confidence in somebody jemandem vertrauen

ℓ **confident** ADJECTIVE
1 (sure of yourself) **selbstbewusst**
2 (sure that something will happen) **zuversichtlich**

to **confirm** VERB
bestätigen
He confirmed the date. Er bestätigte das Datum.

ℓ to **confuse** VERB
1 **verwirren** (a person)
2 to confuse someone with somebody else jemanden mit jemand anderem **verwechseln**
I always confuse him with his brother. Ich verwechsle ihn immer mit seinem Bruder.

ℓ **confused** ADJECTIVE
1 **wirr**
a confused story eine wirre Geschichte
2 **verwirrt**
Now I'm completely confused. Jetzt bin ich völlig verwirrt.
I'm confused about the holiday plans. Ich bin mit den Ferienplänen durcheinander.

confusing ADJECTIVE
verwirrend
The instructions are confusing. Die Anweisungen sind verwirrend.

confusion NOUN
die **Verwirrung**

to **congratulate** VERB
gratulieren
I congratulated Tim on passing his exam. Ich gratulierte Tim zur bestandenen Prüfung.

ℓ **congratulations** PLURAL NOUN
Congratulations! Herzlichen Glückwunsch!

to **connect** VERB
(plug in to the mains) **anschließen**◇ SEP (a dishwasher or TV, for example)

connection NOUN
1 (between two ideas or events) der **Zusammenhang** (PL die **Zusammenhänge**)
There's no connection between his letter and my decision. Es besteht kein Zusammenhang zwischen seinem Brief und meiner Entscheidung.
2 (between trains, planes, on phone, and electrical) der **Anschluss** (PL die **Anschlüsse**)
Sally missed her connection. Sally hat ihren Anschluss verpasst.
an Internet connection ein Internetanschluss

conscience NOUN
das **Gewissen**
to have a guilty conscience ein schlechtes Gewissen haben

conscious ADJECTIVE
to be conscious bei Bewusstsein sein◇
She is not fully conscious yet. Sie ist noch nicht wieder bei vollem Bewusstsein.
I was conscious that he was a policeman. Es war mir bewusst, dass er Polizist war.

conservation NOUN
(of nature) der **Schutz**
environmental conservation der Umweltschutz
a nature conservation programme ein Naturschutzprojekt

◇ **irregular verb;** SEP **separable verb; for more help with verbs see centre section**

conservative *NOUN*
der/die **Konservative** (*PL* die **Konservativen**)

conservative *ADJECTIVE*
konservativ

conservatory *NOUN*
der **Wintergarten** (*PL* die **Wintergärten**)

to **consider** *VERB*
1 sich (*DAT*) **überlegen** (*a suggestion or idea*)
all things considered alles in allem
2 (*think about (doing)*) **erwägen**◇
They are considering buying a flat. Sie erwägen, eine Wohnung zu kaufen.

considerate *ADJECTIVE*
rücksichtsvoll

considering *PREPOSITION*
wenn man bedenkt
considering her age wenn man ihr Alter bedenkt
considering he did it all himself wenn man bedenkt, dass er es ganz allein gemacht hat

to **consist** *VERB*
to consist of bestehen◇ aus (*+DAT*)

consonant *NOUN*
der **Konsonant** (*PL* die **Konsonanten**)

constant *ADJECTIVE*
ständig

constipated *ADJECTIVE*
verstopft

to **construct** *VERB*
bauen

construction *NOUN*
1 (*building*) das **Gebäude** (*PL* die **Gebäude**)
a construction site eine Baustelle
2 (*in grammar*) die **Konstruktion** (*PL* die **Konstruktionen**)

consul *NOUN*
der **Konsul** (*PL* die **Konsuln**)

consulate *NOUN*
das **Konsulat** (*PL* die **Konsulate**)

to **consult** *VERB*
konsultieren

consumer *NOUN*
der **Verbraucher** (*PL* die **Verbraucher**), die **Verbraucherin** (*PL* die **Verbraucherinnen**)

contact *NOUN*
der **Kontakt** (*PL* die **Kontakte**)
to be in contact with somebody mit jemandem in Kontakt sein

We've lost contact. Wir haben den Kontakt verloren.
Rob has contacts in the music business.
Rob hat Kontakte zur Musikindustrie.

to **contact** *VERB*
sich in Verbindung setzen mit (*+DAT*)
I'll contact you tomorrow. Ich setze mich morgen mit dir in Verbindung.

contact lens *NOUN*
die **Kontaktlinse** (*PL* die **Kontaktlinsen**)

to **contain** *VERB*
enthalten◇

container *NOUN*
der **Behälter** (*PL* die **Behälter**)

to **contaminate** *VERB*
verseuchen

contemporary *ADJECTIVE*
1 (*belonging to the same time*) zeitgenössisch
2 (*modern*) modern

contents *PLURAL NOUN*
der **Inhalt**
the contents of my suitcase der Inhalt meines Koffers

contest *NOUN*
der **Wettbewerb** (*PL* die **Wettbewerbe**)

contestant *NOUN*
der **Teilnehmer** (*PL* die **Teilnehmer**), die **Teilnehmerin** (*PL* die **Teilnehmerinnen**)

continent *NOUN*
der **Kontinent** (*PL* die **Kontinente**)

ℰ to **continue** *VERB*
1 fortsetzen *SEP*
We continued (with) our journey. Wir setzten unsere Reise fort.
2 **to continue to do something** etwas weiter tun
Jill continued talking. Jill redete weiter.
3 'To be continued.' 'Fortsetzung folgt.'

continuous *ADJECTIVE*
ununterbrochen

contraception *NOUN*
die **Verhütung**

contraceptive *NOUN*
das **Verhütungsmittel** (*PL* die **Verhütungsmittel**)

contract *NOUN*
der **Vertrag** (*PL* die **Verträge**)

to **contradict** *VERB*
widersprechen◇ (*+DAT*)

449

ℰ indicates key words

contradiction   **cool**

contradiction NOUN
der **Widerspruch** (PL die **Widersprüche**)

contrary NOUN
das **Gegenteil**
on the contrary im Gegenteil

contrast NOUN
der **Kontrast** (PL die **Kontraste**)

to **contribute** VERB
1 beitragen ◇ SEP
2 (to charity or an appeal) spenden

contribution NOUN
1 der **Beitrag** (PL die **Beiträge**)
2 (to charity or an appeal) die **Spende** (PL die **Spenden**)

control NOUN
(of a crowd or animals) die **Kontrolle**
The police are in control of the situation.
Die Polizei hat die Situation unter Kontrolle.
Keep your dogs under control. Halten Sie Ihre Hunde unter Kontrolle.
Everything's under control. Alles ist unter Kontrolle.
to get out of control außer Kontrolle geraten

to **control** VERB
1 kontrollieren
2 **to control yourself** sich beherrschen

ℰ **convenient** ADJECTIVE
1 praktisch
Frozen food is very convenient.
Tiefkühlkost ist sehr praktisch.
2 **to be convenient for somebody** jemandem passen
Whenever is convenient for you. Wann immer es dir passt.

conventional ADJECTIVE
konventionell

conversation NOUN
das **Gespräch** (PL die **Gespräche**)

to **convert** VERB
1 umwandeln SEP
2 (adapt a building) umbauen SEP
We're going to convert the garage into a workshop. Wir wollen die Garage zu einer Werkstatt umbauen.

to **convince** VERB
überzeugen
I'm convinced he's wrong. Ich bin davon überzeugt, dass er sich irrt.

convincing ADJECTIVE
überzeugend

ℰ to **cook** VERB
1 kochen
Who's cooking tonight? Wer kocht heute Abend?
I like cooking. Ich koche gern.
to cook vegetables and pasta Gemüse und Nudeln kochen
Cook the cabbage for five minutes. Lass den Kohl fünf Minuten kochen.
2 (prepare food or a meal) machen
Fran is busy cooking supper. Fran macht gerade Abendessen.
How do you cook duck? Wie macht man Ente?
3 (boil) kochen, (fry or roast) braten ◇
The potatoes are cooking. Die Kartoffeln kochen.
The sausages are cooking. Die Würstchen braten.

cook NOUN
der **Koch** (PL die **Köche**), die **Köchin** (PL die **Köchinnen**)

WORD TIP Professions, hobbies, and sports don't take an article in German: Er ist Koch.

ℰ **cooker** NOUN
der **Herd** (PL die **Herde**)
electric cooker der Elektroherd
gas cooker der Gasherd

cookery NOUN
das **Kochen**

cookery book NOUN
das **Kochbuch** (PL die **Kochbücher**)

ℰ **cooking** NOUN
1 (preparing food) das **Kochen**
Cooking is fun. Kochen macht Spaß.
Who's doing the cooking? Wer kocht?
2 (food) die **Küche**
Italian cooking die italienische Küche

ℰ **cool** NOUN
1 (coldness) die **Kühle**
2 (calm)
to lose your cool durchdrehen SEP (PERF sein) (informal)
Don't lose your cool! Dreh nicht durch!
He kept his cool. Er blieb gelassen.

cool ADJECTIVE
1 (cold) kühl
It's cool inside. Drinnen ist es kühl.
2 (laid back) gelassen
to stay cool gelassen bleiben ◇ (PERF sein)
3 (great) cool
That's cool! Das ist cool!

to **cool** VERB
abkühlen SEP (PERF sein)

to **cooperate** VERB
zusammenarbeiten SEP

ℙ **cop** NOUN
der **Polizist** (PL die **Polizisten**)

> **WORD TIP** Professions, hobbies, and sports don't take an article in German: Er ist Polizist.

to **cope** VERB
zurechtkommen◇ SEP (PERF sein)
She copes well. Sie kommt gut zurecht.
to cope with the children mit den Kindern zurechtkommen
She's had a lot to cope with. Sie musste mit viel fertig werden.

copy NOUN
1 (photocopy) die **Kopie** (PL die **Kopien**)
2 (of a book) das **Exemplar** (PL die **Exemplare**)

to **copy** VERB
1 **kopieren**
2 (in writing) **abschreiben**◇ SEP
I copied (down) the address. Ich habe die Adresse abgeschrieben.
(in an exam) **to copy from somebody** bei jemandem abschreiben

cord NOUN
(for a blind, for example) die **Schnur** (PL die **Schnüre**)

cordless phone NOUN
das **schnurlose Telefon** (PL die **schnurlosen Telefone**)

core NOUN
(of an apple or a pear) das **Kerngehäuse** (PL die **Kerngehäuse**)

cork NOUN
1 (in a bottle) der **Korken** (PL die **Korken**)
2 (material) der **Kork**

corkscrew NOUN
der **Korkenzieher** (PL die **Korkenzieher**)

corn NOUN
1 (wheat) das **Korn**, das **Getreide**
2 (sweetcorn) der **Mais**

ℙ **corner** NOUN
1 die **Ecke** (PL die **Ecken**)
at the corner of the street an der Straßenecke
It's just round the corner. Es ist gleich um die Ecke.
2 (of mouth) der **Mundwinkel** (PL die **Mundwinkel**)
3 (of eye) der **Augenwinkel** (PL die **Augenwinkel**)
out of the corner of your eye aus den Augenwinkeln heraus
4 (bend in the road) die **Kurve** (PL die **Kurven**)
5 (in football) der **Eckball** (PL die **Eckbälle**)

cornflakes PLURAL NOUN
die **Cornflakes** (PLURAL)

corpse NOUN
die **Leiche** (PL die **Leichen**)

ℙ **correct** ADJECTIVE
1 **richtig**
the correct answer die richtige Antwort
2 **Yes, that's correct.** Ja, das stimmt.

to **correct** VERB
1 **verbessern**
2 (teacher) **korrigieren**
The teacher has already corrected our homework. Der Lehrer hat unsere Hausaufgaben schon korrigiert.

correction NOUN
die **Verbesserung** (PL die **Verbesserungen**)

correctly ADVERB
richtig
Have you filled in the form correctly? Hast du das Formular richtig ausgefüllt?

corridor NOUN
der **Gang** (PL die **Gänge**) der **Flur** (PL die **Flure**)

cosmetics PLURAL NOUN
die **Kosmetik** (SINGULAR)

ℙ **cost** NOUN
der **Preis** (PL die **Kosten** (PLURAL))
the cost of a new computer der Preis für einen neuen Computer
the cost of living die Lebenshaltungskosten (PLURAL)

to **cost** VERB
kosten
How much does it cost? Was kostet es?
The tickets cost £10. Die Karten kosten zehn Pfund.
It costs too much. Das ist zu teuer.

ℙ **costume** NOUN
das **Kostüm** (PL die **Kostüme**)

cosy ADJECTIVE
(a room) **gemütlich**

cot NOUN
das **Kinderbett** (PL die **Kinderbetten**)

cottage NOUN
das **Häuschen** (PL die **Häuschen**)

ℙ **cotton** NOUN
1 (fabric) die **Baumwolle**
cotton shirt das Baumwollhemd

2 *(thread)* das **Nähgarn** (*PL* die **Nähgarne**)

cotton wool *NOUN*
die **Watte**

couch *NOUN*
die **Couch** (*PL* die **Couchs**)

cough *NOUN*
der **Husten**
a nasty cough ein schlimmer Husten
to have a cough Husten haben

to **cough** *VERB*
husten

⌀ **could** *VERB*
1 *(the past tense of können is used to translate the meaning 'was able to')*
I couldn't open it. Ich konnte es nicht aufmachen.
They couldn't come. Sie konnten nicht kommen.
She did all she could. Sie hat getan, was sie konnte.
He couldn't drive. Er konnte nicht Auto fahren.
She couldn't see anything. Sie konnte nichts sehen.
2 *(the past tense of dürfen is used to translate the meaning 'was allowed to')*
They couldn't smoke there. Sie durften dort nicht rauchen.
3 *(might) (the subjunctive of können is used to translate a wish or suggestion)*
Could I speak to David? Könnte ich mit David sprechen?
You could try phoning. Du könntest versuchen anzurufen.
if he could pay wenn er zahlen könnte
He could be right. Er könnte recht haben.

⌀ **council** *NOUN*
der **Stadtrat** (*PL* die **Stadträte**)

⌀ to **count** *VERB*
1 *(reckon up)* zählen
I counted my money. Ich habe mein Geld gezählt.
2 *(include)* mitzählen *SEP*
thirty-five not counting the children fünfunddreißig (*PL* die Kinder nicht mitgezählt)

counter *NOUN*
1 *(in a shop)* der **Ladentisch** (*PL* die **Ladentische**)
2 *(in a post office or bank)* der **Schalter** (*PL* die **Schalter**)
3 *(in a bar or cafe)* die **Theke** (*PL* die **Theken**)
4 *(for board games)* die **Spielmarke** (*PL* die **Spielmarken**)

⌀ **country** *NOUN*
1 *(Germany, etc.)* das **Land** (*PL* die **Länder**)
a foreign country ein fremdes Land
from another country aus einem anderen Land
2 *(not town)* das **Land**
in the country auf dem Land
country road die Landstraße

country dancing *NOUN*
der **Volkstanz**

countryside *NOUN*
1 *(not town)* das **Land**
2 *(scenery)* die **Landschaft**

county *NOUN*
die **Grafschaft** (*PL* die **Grafschaften**)

⌀ **couple** *NOUN*
1 *(a pair)* das **Paar** (*PL* die **Paare**)
2 **a couple of** ein paar
a couple of times ein paar Mal
I've got a couple of things to do. Ich habe ein paar Sachen zu tun.

courage *NOUN*
der **Mut**

courgette *NOUN*
die **Zucchini** (*PL* die **Zucchini**)

courier *NOUN*
1 *(for tourist group)* der **Reiseleiter** (*PL* die **Reiseleiter**), die **Reiseleiterin** (*PL* die **Reiseleiterinnen**)
2 *(delivery person)* der **Kurier** (*PL* die **Kuriere**)
It will be delivered by courier. Es wird mit Kurierdienst gebracht.

⌀ **course** *NOUN*
1 *(lessons)* der **Kurs** (*PL* die **Kurse**)
computer course der Computerkurs
to go on a course einen Kurs machen
2 *(part of a meal)* der **Gang** (*PL* die **Gänge**)
the main course der Hauptgang
3 **golf course** der Golfplatz
4 **of course** natürlich
Yes, of course! Ja, natürlich!
He's forgotten, of course. Er hat es natürlich vergessen.

court *NOUN*
1 *(for playing sports)* der **Platz** (*PL* die **Plätze**)
2 *(law court)* das **Gericht**
to go to court vor Gericht gehen

⌀ **cousin** *NOUN*
der **Cousin** (*PL* die **Cousins**), die **Kusine** (*PL* die **Kusinen**)
my cousin Sonia meine Kusine Sonia

ℙ cover NOUN
1 *(of a book)* der **Einband** (PL die **Einbände**)
2 *(for a duvet or cushion)* der **Bezug** (PL die **Bezüge**)
3 *(of a song)* die **Cover-Version** (PL die **Cover-Versionen**)

to cover VERB
1 *(cover up)* **zudecken** SEP
   He covered her with a blanket. Er hat sie mit einer Decke zugedeckt.
2 **He was covered in spots.** Er war mit Pickeln übersät.
   The room was covered in dust. Das Zimmer war völlig verstaubt.
3 *(with leaves, snow, or for protection)* **bedecken**
   The ground was covered with snow. Der Boden war mit Schnee bedeckt.
4 *(with fabric)* **beziehen**◇

ℙ cow NOUN
   die **Kuh** (PL die **Kühe**)
   mad cow disease der Rinderwahn

coward NOUN
   der **Feigling** (PL die **Feiglinge**)

cowboy NOUN
   der **Cowboy** (PL die **Cowboys**)

crab NOUN
   die **Krabbe** (PL die **Krabben**)

crack NOUN
1 *(in a glass or cup)* der **Sprung** (PL die **Sprünge**)
2 *(in wood or a wall)* der **Riss** (PL die **Risse**)
3 *(a cracking noise)* der **Knacks** (PL die **Knackse**)

to crack VERB
1 *(make a crack in)* **anschlagen**◇ SEP
2 *(break)* **zerbrechen**◇
3 *(make a noise) (a twig)* **knacken**

cracker NOUN
1 *(biscuit)* der **Cracker** (PL die **Cracker**)
2 *(Christmas cracker)* der or das **Knallbonbon** (PL die **Knallbonbons**)

craft NOUN
   (at school) das **Werken**

cramp NOUN
   der **Krampf** (PL die **Krämpfe**)
   to have cramp in your leg einen Krampf im Bein haben

crane NOUN
1 *(machine)* der **Kran** (PL die **Kräne**)
2 *(bird)* der **Kranich** (PL die **Kraniche**)

crash NOUN
1 *(an accident)* der **Unfall** (PL die **Unfälle**)
   car crash der Autounfall

2 *(a noise)* das **Krachen**

to crash VERB
1 *(a plane, a computer)* **abstürzen** SEP (PERF sein)
   The plane crashed. Das Flugzeug ist abgestürzt.
2 *(have a collision in a car)* **einen Unfall haben**
3 **to crash into something** gegen etwas (ACC) **krachen** (PERF sein)
   The car crashed into a tree. Das Auto krachte gegen einen Baum.

crash course NOUN
   der **Schnellkurs** (PL die **Schnellkurse**)

crash helmet NOUN
   der **Sturzhelm** (PL die **Sturzhelme**)

ℙ crate NOUN
   die **Kiste** (PL die **Kisten**)

crawl NOUN
   (in swimming) das **Kraulen**

to crawl VERB
1 *(a person)* **kriechen**◇ (PERF sein), *(a baby)* **krabbeln** (PERF sein)
2 *(cars in a jam)* im Schneckentempo **fahren**◇ (PERF sein)
   We were crawling along. Wir fuhren im Schneckentempo.

crayon NOUN
1 *(wax)* der **Wachsmalstift** (PL die **Wachsmalstifte**)
2 *(coloured pencil)* der **Buntstift** (PL die **Buntstifte**)

craze NOUN
   die **Mode** (PL die **Moden**)
   the latest craze among teenagers die neuste Mode bei Teenagern
   the fitness craze die Fitnesswelle

ℙ crazy ADJECTIVE
   verrückt
   to go crazy verrückt werden◇
   to be crazy for something verrückt auf etwas (ACC) sein

ℙ cream NOUN
   die **Sahne**
   strawberries and cream Erdbeeren mit Sahne

cream cheese NOUN
   der **Frischkäse**

creased ADJECTIVE
   zerknittert

453

to **create** VERB
(er)schaffen◇

creative ADJECTIVE
kreativ

creature NOUN
das Geschöpf (PL die Geschöpfe)

crèche NOUN
die Kinderkrippe (PL die Kinderkrippen)

credit NOUN
der Kredit
to buy something on credit etwas auf Kredit kaufen

credit card NOUN
die Kreditkarte (PL die Kreditkarten)

creepy ADJECTIVE
unheimlich

cress NOUN
die Kresse

crew NOUN
1 (on a ship or plane) die Besatzung (PL die Besatzungen)
2 das Team (PL die Teams)
camera crew das Kamerateam
3 (in rowing) die Mannschaft (PL die Mannschaften)

crew cut NOUN
der Bürstenschnitt (PL die Bürstenschnitte)

cricket NOUN
1 (game) das Kricket
to play cricket Kricket spielen
2 (insect) die Grille (PL die Grillen)

cricket bat NOUN
der Kricketschläger (PL die Kricketschläger)

crime NOUN
1 das Verbrechen (PL die Verbrechen)
Theft is a crime. Diebstahl ist ein Verbrechen.
2 (criminality) die Kriminalität
to fight crime die Kriminalität bekämpfen

criminal NOUN
der/die Kriminelle (PL die Kriminellen)

criminal ADJECTIVE
kriminell

crisis NOUN
die Krise (PL die Krisen)

ℓ**crisp** NOUN
der Chip (PL die Chips)
a packet of potato crisps eine Tüte Kartoffelchips

crisp ADJECTIVE
1 (biscuit) knusprig
2 (apple) knackig

critical ADJECTIVE
1 kritisch
2 entscheidend (moment)

criticism NOUN
die Kritik

to **criticize** VERB
kritisieren

crocodile NOUN
das Krokodil (PL die Krokodile)

crook NOUN
(criminal) der Gauner (PL die Gauner), die Gaunerin (PL die Gaunerinnen)

crooked ADJECTIVE
krumm, schief
The picture was crooked. Das Bild hing schief.

crop NOUN
die Ernte

ℓ**cross** NOUN
das Kreuz (PL die Kreuze)

cross ADJECTIVE
ärgerlich
She was very cross. Sie war sehr ärgerlich.
I'm cross with you. Ich bin sehr ärgerlich auf dich.

to **cross** VERB
1 (cross over) überqueren
to cross the road die Straße überqueren
2 to cross your legs die Beine übereinanderschlagen◇ SEP
3 (cross each other) sich kreuzen
The two roads cross here. Die beiden Straßen kreuzen sich hier.
• to cross something out etwas durchstreichen◇ SEP

cross-Channel ADJECTIVE
a cross-Channel ferry eine Fähre über den Ärmelkanal

cross-country NOUN
1 der Querfeldeinlauf
2 cross-country skiing der Langlauf

ℓ**crossing** NOUN
1 (from one place to another) die Überquerung (PL die Überquerungen)
2 (a sea journey) die Überfahrt (PL die Überfahrten)
Channel crossing die Überfahrt über den Ärmelkanal

3 pedestrian crossing der Fußgängerübergang
level crossing der Bahnübergang

ℓ **crossroads** NOUN
die **Kreuzung** (PL die **Kreuzungen**)
at the crossroads an der Kreuzung

crossword NOUN
das **Kreuzworträtsel** (PL die Kreuzworträtsel)
to do a crossword ein Kreuzworträtsel machen

crow NOUN
die **Krähe** (PL die **Krähen**)

to crow VERB
(a cock) krähen

ℓ **crowd** NOUN
1 die **Menschenmenge** (PL die Menschenmengen)
in the crowd in der Menschenmenge
2 *(spectators)*
a crowd of five thousand fünftausend Zuschauer *(PLURAL)*

to crowd VERB
to crowd into or onto something sich in etwas *(ACC)* drängen
We all crowded into the train. Wir drängten uns alle in den Zug.

crowded ADJECTIVE
überfüllt

crown NOUN
die **Krone** (PL die **Kronen**)

crude ADJECTIVE
1 *(rough and ready)* primitiv
2 *(vulgar)* ordinär

cruel ADJECTIVE
grausam

cruise NOUN
die **Kreuzfahrt** (PL die **Kreuzfahrten**)
to go on a cruise eine Kreuzfahrt machen

crumb NOUN
der **Krümel** (PL die **Krümel**)

crumpled ADJECTIVE
zerknittert

crunchy ADJECTIVE
knusprig

to crush VERB
zerquetschen

crust NOUN
die **Kruste** (PL die **Krusten**)

crusty ADJECTIVE
knusprig

crutch NOUN
die **Krücke** (PL die **Krücken**)
to be on crutches an Krücken gehen

ℓ **cry** NOUN
der **Schrei** (PL die **Schreie**)

to cry VERB
1 *(weep)* weinen
2 *(call out)* schreien◇

cub NOUN
1 *(animal)* das **Junge** (PL die **Jungen**)
2 *(boy scout)* der **Wölfling** (PL die **Wölflinge**)

cube NOUN
der **Würfel** (PL die **Würfel**)
ice cube der Eiswürfel

cubic ADJECTIVE
(in measurements) Kubik-
three cubic metres drei Kubikmeter

cubicle NOUN
1 *(in a changing room)* die **Kabine** (PL die **Kabinen**)
2 *(in a public lavatory)* die **Toilette** (PL die **Toiletten**)

cuckoo NOUN
der **Kuckuck** (PL die **Kuckucke**)

cucumber NOUN
die **Gurke** (PL die **Gurken**)

cuddle NOUN
to give somebody a cuddle jemanden in den Arm nehmen◇

to cuddle VERB
schmusen

cue NOUN
(billiards, pool, snooker) das **Queue** (PL die **Queues**)

cuff NOUN
(on a shirt) die **Manschette** (PL die **Manschetten**)

cul-de-sac NOUN
die **Sackgasse** (PL die **Sackgassen**)

culture NOUN
die **Kultur** (PL die **Kulturen**)

cunning ADJECTIVE
listig

ℓ **cup** NOUN
1 *(for drinking)* die **Tasse** (PL die **Tassen**)
a cup of tea eine Tasse Tee
2 *(a trophy)* der **Pokal** (PL die **Pokale**)

ℓ indicates key words

cupboard   **cutlery**

♂ **cupboard** NOUN
  der **Schrank** (PL die **Schränke**)
  in the kitchen cupboard im Küchenschrank

cup final NOUN
  das **Pokalendspiel** (PL die **Pokalendspiele**)
  das **Pokalfinale** (PL die **Pokalfinale**)

cup tie NOUN
  das **Pokalspiel** (PL die **Pokalspiele**)

cure NOUN
  das **Heilmittel** (PL die **Heilmittel**)

to **cure** VERB
  heilen

curiosity NOUN
  die **Neugier**

curious ADJECTIVE
  neugierig

curl NOUN
  die **Locke** (PL die **Locken**)

to **curl** VERB
1 **locken** (hair)
2 (of hair) **sich locken**

curly ADJECTIVE
  lockig
  curly hair lockiges Haar

currant NOUN
  die **Korinthe** (PL die **Korinthen**)

♂ **currency** NOUN
  die **Währung** (PL die **Währungen**)
  the Japanese currency die japanische
  Währung
  foreign currencies die Devisen (PLURAL)

current NOUN
1 (electricity) der **Strom**
2 (in water or air) die **Strömung** (PL die
  Strömungen)

current ADJECTIVE
  aktuell

current affairs NOUN
  die **Tagespolitik**

curriculum NOUN
  der **Lehrplan** (PL die **Lehrpläne**)

curry NOUN
  das **Curry**
  vegetable curry das Gemüse in Currysoße

♂ **cursor** NOUN
  der **Cursor** (PL die **Cursors**)

♂ **curtain** NOUN
  der **Vorhang** (PL die **Vorhänge**)

cushion NOUN
  das **Kissen** (PL die **Kissen**)

custard NOUN
  die **Vanillesoße** (PL die **Vanillesoßen**)

custom NOUN
  der **Brauch** (PL die **Bräuche**)

♂ **customer** NOUN
  der **Kunde** (PL die **Kunden**), die **Kundin**
  (PL die **Kundinnen**)
  customer services der Kundendienst

♂ **customs** PLURAL NOUN
  der **Zoll**
  to go through customs durch den Zoll
  gehen

customs hall NOUN
  die **Zollabfertigung**

customs officer NOUN
  der **Zollbeamte** (PL die **Zollbeamten**), die
  Zollbeamtin (PL die **Zollbeamtinnen**)

♂ **cut** NOUN
1 (injury) die **Schnittwunde** (PL die
  Schnittwunden)
2 (haircut) der **Schnitt** (PL die **Schnitte**)

to **cut** VERB
1 **schneiden**◇
  Can you cut the bread please? Kannst du
  bitte das Brot schneiden?
  You'll cut yourself! Du schneidest dich!
  Kevin's cut his finger. Kevin hat sich in den
  Finger geschnitten.
2 **to cut the grass** den Rasen mähen
3 **to get your hair cut** sich (DAT) die Haare
  schneiden lassen
  I had my hair cut. Ich habe mir die Haare
  schneiden lassen.
4 **to cut prices** die Preise senken
5 (on the computer) **ausschneiden**◇ SEP
  to cut and paste ausschneiden und
  einfügen
• **to cut down**
1 **fällen** (a tree)
2 **to cut down on cigarettes** seinen
  Zigarettenkonsum einschränken SEP
• **to cut out something**
1 etwas **ausschneiden**◇ SEP (a shape, a
  newspaper article)
2 etwas **streichen**◇ (sugar, fatty food,
  holidays, for example)
• **to cut something up**
  etwas klein **schneiden**◇ (food)

cutlery NOUN
  das **Besteck** (PL die **Bestecke**)

CV NOUN
der **Lebenslauf** (PL die **Lebensläufe**)

cyberbullying NOUN
das **Internet-Mobbing**

cycle NOUN
(bike) das **Rad** (PL die **Räder**)

to **cycle** VERB
Rad fahren✧ (PERF **sein**)
Do you like cycling? Fährst du gerne Rad?
We cycle to school. Wir fahren mit dem Rad zur Schule.

cycle lane NOUN
der **Fahrradweg** (PL die **Fahrradwege**)

cycle race NOUN
das **Radrennen** (PL die **Radrennen**)

ℱ **cycling** NOUN
das **Radfahren**

cycling shorts NOUN
die **Radlerhose** (PL die **Radlerhosen**)

ℱ **cyclist** NOUN
der **Radfahrer** (PL die **Radfahrer**), die **Radfahrerin** (PL die **Radfahrerinnen**)

Dd

ℱ **dad** NOUN
1 der **Vater** (PL die **Väter**)
 Tim's dad Tims Vater
2 (as a name) der **Papa** (PL die **Papas**), der **Vati** (PL die **Vatis**)
 Bye, Dad! Tschüs, Papa!

daffodil NOUN
die **Osterglocke** (PL die **Osterglocken**)

daily ADJECTIVE
täglich
his daily visit sein täglicher Besuch
a daily paper eine Tageszeitung

daily ADVERB
täglich
She visits him daily. Sie besucht ihn täglich.

dairy products PLURAL NOUN
die **Milchprodukte** (PLURAL)

daisy NOUN
das **Gänseblümchen** (PL die **Gänseblümchen**)

dam NOUN
der **Damm** (PL die **Dämme**)

ℱ **damage** NOUN
der **Schaden** (PL die **Schäden**)

to do a lot of damage großen Schaden anrichten

to **damage** VERB
beschädigen

damn NOUN
I don't give a damn. Das ist mir piepegal. (informal)

damn EXCLAMATION
Damn! Verdammt!

damp ADJECTIVE
feucht

damp NOUN
die **Feuchtigkeit**

dance NOUN
der **Tanz** (PL die **Tänze**)
a folk dance ein Volkstanz

to **dance** VERB
tanzen
I like dancing. Ich tanze gerne.

dancer NOUN
der **Tänzer** (PL die **Tänzer**), die **Tänzerin** (PL die **Tänzerinnen**)

> **WORD TIP** Professions, hobbies, and sports don't take an article in German: Er ist Tänzer.

dancing NOUN
das **Tanzen**

dancing class NOUN
die **Tanzstunde** (PL die **Tanzstunden**)
to go to dancing classes in die Tanzstunde gehen

dandruff NOUN
die **Schuppen** (PLURAL)

danger NOUN
die **Gefahr** (PL die **Gefahren**)
to be in danger in Gefahr sein

ℱ **dangerous** ADJECTIVE
gefährlich
It's dangerous to drive so fast. Es ist gefährlich, so schnell zu fahren.

Danish NOUN
das **Dänisch**

Danish ADJECTIVE
dänisch
the Danish coast die dänische Küste
He's Danish. Er ist Däne.
She's Danish. Sie ist Dänin.

> **WORD TIP** Adjectives never have capitals in German, even for regions, countries, or nationalities.

A B C D E F G H I J K L M N O P Q R S T U V W X Y Z

457

to dare *VERB*
1 **wagen**
 to dare to do something es wagen, etwas
 zu tun
 I didn't dare suggest it. Ich habe es nicht
 gewagt, das vorzuschlagen.
2 **Don't you dare tell her I'm here!** Untersteh
 dich, ihr zu sagen, dass ich hier bin!
3 **I dare you!** Du traust dich doch nicht!
 I dare you to tell him! Sag's ihm doch,
 wenn du dich traust!

daring *ADJECTIVE*
 gewagt
 That was a bit daring. Das war etwas
 gewagt.

dark *NOUN*
 in the dark im Dunkeln
 after dark nach Einbruch der Dunkelheit
 to be afraid of the dark Angst im Dunkeln
 haben

dark *ADJECTIVE*
1 *(colour)* **dunkel**
 a dark colour eine dunkle Farbe
 It gets dark around five. Es wird gegen fünf
 dunkel.
 It's dark in here. Hier drinnen ist es dunkel.
2 **a dark blue skirt** ein dunkelblauer Rock
 She has dark brown hair. Sie hat
 dunkelbraune Haare.

 WORD TIP German adjectives ending in -el drop
 the e when followed by a vowel, which means
 that dunkel becomes dunkler/dunkle/dunkles.

darkness *NOUN*
 die **Dunkelheit**
 in darkness in der Dunkelheit

darling *NOUN*
 der **Liebling** (*PL* die **Lieblinge**)
 See you later, darling! Bis später, Liebling!

dart *NOUN*
1 der **Wurfpfeil** (*PL* die **Wurfpfeile**)
2 *(game)* **darts** Darts (*NEUTER*)
 to play darts Darts spielen

data *PLURAL NOUN*
 die **Daten** (*PLURAL*)

database *NOUN*
 die **Datenbank** (*PL* die **Datenbanken**)

℘ **date** *NOUN*
1 das **Datum** (*PL* die **Daten**)
 What's the date today? Welches Datum
 haben wir heute?
 the date of the meeting das Datum für das
 Treffen
 What date is he coming? Wann kommt er?

2 der **Termin** (*PL* die **Termine**)
 the last date for payment der letzte
 Zahlungstermin
3 **out of date** ungültig
 My passport's out of date. Mein Pass ist
 ungültig.
4 **up to date** modern
 The equipment is completely up to date.
 Die Ausstattung ist ganz modern.
5 *(appointment)* die **Verabredung** (*PL* die
 Verabredungen)
 Laura's got a date with Frank. Laura ist mit
 Frank verabredet.
6 *(fruit)* die **Dattel** (*PL* die **Datteln**)

date of birth *NOUN*
 das **Geburtsdatum** (*PL* die **Geburtsdaten**)

℘ **daughter** *NOUN*
 die **Tochter** (*PL* die **Töchter**)
 Tina's daughter Tinas Tochter

daughter-in-law *NOUN*
 die **Schwiegertochter** (*PL* die
 Schwiegertöchter)

dawn *NOUN*
 die **Morgendämmerung** (*PL* die
 Morgendämmerungen)

℘ **day** *NOUN*
1 der **Tag** (*PL* die **Tage**)
 three days later drei Tage später
 a few days ago vor ein paar Tagen
 the day I went to London an dem Tag, an
 dem ich nach London gefahren bin
 We spent the day in London. Wir haben
 den Tag in London verbracht.
 It rained all day. Es hat den ganzen Tag
 geregnet.
 the day after am Tag danach
 the day after the wedding am Tag nach der
 Hochzeit
 the day before am Tag davor
 the day before the wedding am Tag vor der
 Hochzeit
2 **another day** ein anderes Mal
 We can go there another day. Wir können
 ein anderes Mal hingehen.
3 **one day** einmal, eines Tages
 One day I want to go to America. Ich
 möchte einmal nach Amerika.
4 **the other day** neulich
 I saw him the other day. Ich habe ihn
 neulich gesehen.
5 **the day after tomorrow** übermorgen
 **My sister's arriving the day after
 tomorrow.** Meine Schwester kommt
 übermorgen an.
6 **the day before yesterday** vorgestern

◈ **irregular verb**; *SEP* **separable verb**; for more help with verbs see centre section

My brother arrived the day before yesterday. Mein Bruder kam vorgestern an.
7 **during the day** tagsüber
8 **a day off** ein freier Tag
We've got a day off next week. Wir haben nächste Woche einen freien Tag.

ℓ **dead** ADJECTIVE
tot
Her father's dead. Ihr Vater ist tot.

dead ADVERB
(really) **irre** (informal)
He's dead nice. Er ist irre nett.
It was dead easy. Es war kinderleicht.
You're dead right. Du hast völlig recht.
She arrived dead on time. Sie kam auf die Minute pünktlich an.

dead end NOUN
die **Sackgasse** (PL die **Sackgassen**)

deadline NOUN
der **letzte Termin** (PL die **letzten Termine**)

ℓ **deaf** ADJECTIVE
taub

deafening ADJECTIVE
ohrenbetäubend

deal NOUN
1 (involving money) das **Geschäft** (PL die **Geschäfte**)
It's a good deal. Das ist ein gutes Geschäft.
2 (agreement) die **Vereinbarung** (PL die **Vereinbarungen**)
to make a deal with somebody mit jemandem eine Vereinbarung treffen◇
It's a deal! Abgemacht!
3 **a great deal of** viel
I don't have a great deal of time. Ich habe nicht viel Zeit.

to deal VERB
(in cards) **geben**◇
It's you to deal. Du gibst.
• **to deal with something**
sich um etwas (ACC) kümmern
Linda deals with the accounts. Linda kümmert sich um die Buchführung.
I'll deal with it as soon as possible. Ich kümmere mich so schnell wie möglich darum.

ℓ **dear** ADJECTIVE
1 **lieb**
Dear Franz Lieber Franz
Dear Monika Liebe Monika
Dear Mr Smith Sehr geehrter Herr Smith
Dear Sir or Madam Sehr geehrte Damen und Herren
2 (expensive) **teuer**

death NOUN
der **Tod**
after his father's death nach dem Tod seines Vaters
three deaths drei Todesfälle
I was bored to death. Ich habe mich zu Tode gelangweilt.
I'm sick to death of it. Ich habe es gründlich satt.

death penalty NOUN
die **Todesstrafe**
to abolish the death penalty die Todesstrafe abschaffen

debate NOUN
die **Debatte** (PL die **Debatten**)

to debate VERB
debattieren

debt NOUN
(money owed) die **Schulden** (PLURAL)
to get into debt in Schulden geraten
to be in debt Schulden haben

decade NOUN
das **Jahrzehnt** (PL die **Jahrzehnte**)

decaffeinated ADJECTIVE
koffeinfrei

to deceive VERB
betrügen◇

ℓ **December** NOUN
der **Dezember** (PL die **Dezember**)
in December im Dezember

decent ADJECTIVE
anständig
a decent salary ein anständiges Gehalt
a decent meal ein anständiges Essen

ℓ **to decide** VERB
1 **sich entscheiden**◇
I haven't decided yet. Ich habe mich noch nicht entschieden.
to decide on something sich für etwas (ACC) entscheiden
He's decided against buying a new car. Er hat sich entschieden, kein neues Auto zu kaufen.
2 **to decide to do something** sich entschließen◇, etwas zu tun
They've decided to buy a house. Sie haben sich entschlossen, ein Haus zu kaufen.

decimal ADJECTIVE
Dezimal-
decimal number die Dezimalzahl

decimal point NOUN
das Komma (PL die Kommas)

> **WORD TIP** In German, decimals are written with a comma: 2,7 (zwei Komma sieben).

decision NOUN
die Entscheidung (PL die Entscheidungen)
to make a decision eine Entscheidung treffen
It was the right decision. Es war die richtige Entscheidung.

deck NOUN
das Deck (PL die Decks)
on deck an Deck

deckchair NOUN
der Liegestuhl (PL die Liegestühle)

to declare VERB
1 erklären
2 (at customs)
nothing to declare nichts zu verzollen

to decorate VERB
1 schmücken
to decorate the Christmas tree den Weihnachtsbaum schmücken
2 (with paint) streichen◇, (with wallpaper) tapezieren
We're decorating the kitchen this weekend. Wir streichen dieses Wochenende die Küche.

decoration NOUN
die Verzierung (PL die Verzierungen)
Christmas decorations der Weihnachtsschmuck

decrease NOUN
der Rückgang (PL die Rückgänge)
a decrease in the number of accidents ein Rückgang in der Anzahl der Unfälle

to decrease VERB
zurückgehen◇ SEP (PERF sein)
The population is decreasing. Die Bevölkerung geht zurück.

deep ADJECTIVE
tief
a deep feeling of gratitude ein tiefes Dankbarkeitsgefühl
How deep is the swimming pool? Wie tief ist das Schwimmbecken?
a hole two metres deep ein zwei Meter tiefes Loch

deep end NOUN
das Schwimmbecken (PL die Schwimmbecken)
'Deep end: 2 metres' 'Wassertiefe: 2 Meter'

deep freeze NOUN
die Tiefkühltruhe (PL die Tiefkühltruhen), (upright) der Gefrierschrank (PL die Gefrierschränke)

deeply ADVERB
tief

deer NOUN
1 der Hirsch (PL die Hirsche)
2 (roe deer) das Reh (PL die Rehe)

defeat NOUN
die Niederlage (PL die Niederlagen)

to defeat VERB
schlagen◇

defence NOUN
die Verteidigung

to defend VERB
verteidigen

defender NOUN
der Verteidiger (PL die Verteidiger), die Verteidigerin (PL die Verteidigerinnen)

definite ADJECTIVE
1 eindeutig
a definite improvement eine eindeutige Besserung
2 (certain) sicher
It's not definite yet. Es ist noch nicht sicher.
3 (exact) klar
a definite answer eine klare Antwort

definite article NOUN
(in grammar) der **bestimmte Artikel**

definitely ADVERB
1 (when giving your opinion about something) eindeutig
Your German is definitely better than mine. Dein Deutsch ist eindeutig besser als meins.
2 (without doubt) bestimmt
She's definitely going to be there. Sie wird bestimmt dort sein.
I'm definitely not coming. Ich komme ganz bestimmt nicht.
3 'Are you sure you like this one better?' – 'Definitely!' 'Gefällt dir diese wirklich besser?' – 'Auf jeden Fall!'

definition NOUN
die Definition (PL die Definitionen)

♂ **degree** NOUN
1 der Grad (PL die Grade)
thirty degrees dreißig Grad
2 **a university degree** ein akademischer Grad
Has she got a degree? Hat sie einen Universitätsabschluss?

◇ irregular verb; SEP separable verb; for more help with verbs see centre section

My brother is doing a physics degree.
Mein Bruder studiert Physik.

ℓ **delay** NOUN
die Verspätung (PL die Verspätungen)
a two-hour delay eine zweistündige
Verspätung

to **delay** VERB
1 (hold up) aufhalten◇ SEP
She was delayed in the office. Sie ist im
Büro aufgehalten worden.
2 (train, plane)
to be delayed Verspätung haben
The flight was delayed by bad weather.
Der Flug hatte wegen des schlechten
Wetters Verspätung.
3 (postpone) aufschieben◇ SEP
**The decision has been delayed until
Thursday.** Die Entscheidung wurde bis
Donnerstag aufgeschoben.

to **delete** VERB
1 streichen◇
2 (in computing) löschen

deliberate ADJECTIVE
absichtlich

deliberately ADVERB
absichtlich
She did it deliberately. Sie hat es
absichtlich getan.

delicate ADJECTIVE
1 (fabric, health) zart
2 (situation, question) heikel
3 (taste, smell) fein

> **WORD TIP** German adjectives ending in -el drop
> the e when followed by a vowel, which means
> that heikel becomes heikler/heikle/heikles.

delicatessen NOUN
das Feinkostgeschäft (PL die
Feinkostgeschäfte)

ℓ **delicious** ADJECTIVE
köstlich

ℓ **delighted** ADJECTIVE
hocherfreut
to be delighted begeistert sein
They're delighted with their new flat. Sie
sind von ihrer neuen Wohnung begeistert.
I'm delighted that you can come. Ich freue
mich sehr, dass ihr kommen könnt.

to **deliver** VERB
1 liefern
**They're delivering the washing machine
tomorrow.** Die Waschmaschine wird
morgen geliefert.

2 (mail, newspapers) zustellen SEP

delivery NOUN
1 die Lieferung (PL die Lieferungen)
delivery van der Lieferwagen
2 (of mail, newspapers) die Zustellung (PL die
Zustellungen)

demand NOUN
die Nachfrage
much in demand sehr gefragt

to **demand** VERB
verlangen

demo NOUN
(protest) die Demo (informal) (PL die Demos)

democracy NOUN
die Demokratie (PL die Demokratien)
parliamentary democracy die
parlamentarische Demokratie

democratic ADJECTIVE
demokratisch

to **demolish** VERB
(a building) abreißen◇ SEP

to **demonstrate** VERB
1 (a machine, product, or technique)
vorführen SEP
2 (protest) demonstrieren
to demonstrate against something gegen
etwas (ACC) demonstrieren

demonstration NOUN
1 (of a machine, product, or technique) die
Vorführung (PL die Vorführungen)
2 (protest) die Demonstration (PL die
Demonstrationen)

demonstrator NOUN
der Demonstrant (PL die Demonstranten),
die Demonstrantin (PL die
Demonstrantinnen)

denim NOUN
der Jeansstoff
a denim jacket eine Jeansjacke

Denmark NOUN
Dänemark (NEUTER)

dental ADJECTIVE
1 Zahn-
dental floss die Zahnseide
dental hygiene die Zahnpflege
2 **to have a dental appointment** einen
Zahnarzttermin haben

ℓ **dentist** NOUN
der Zahnarzt (PL die Zahnärzte), die

Zahnärztin (PL die **Zahnärztinnen**)

WORD TIP Professions, hobbies, and sports don't take an article in German: Sie ist Zahnärztin.

to **deny** VERB
  bestreiten◇
  She denied having said it. Sie bestritt, dass sie es gesagt habe.

deodorant NOUN
  das Deodorant (PL die **Deodorants**)

to **depart** VERB
1 (set out on a journey) abreisen SEP (PERF sein)
2 (train, coach) abfahren◇ SEP (PERF sein)
3 (plane) abfliegen◇ SEP (PERF sein)

℘ **department** NOUN
1 (in a shop, firm, or hospital) die Abteilung (PL die **Abteilungen**)
  the men's department die Herrenabteilung
2 (of a university) das Seminar (PL die **Seminare**)
  the history department das Seminar für Geschichte
3 (in school) der Fachbereich (PL die **Fachbereiche**)

department store NOUN
  das Kaufhaus (PL die **Kaufhäuser**)

℘ **departure** NOUN
1 (of a person) die Abreise
2 (of a car, train) die Abfahrt
3 (of a plane) der Abflug

departure lounge NOUN
  die Abflughalle (PL die **Abflughallen**)

to **depend** VERB
1 **to depend on** abhängen◇ SEP von (+DAT)
  It depends on the price. Das hängt vom Preis ab.
  It depends on what you want. Das hängt davon ab, was du willst.
2 **It depends.** Es kommt darauf an.

dependent ADJECTIVE
  to be dependent on abhängig sein◇ von (+DAT)

℘ **deposit** NOUN
1 (when renting or hiring) die Kaution (PL die **Kautionen**)
2 (when booking a holiday or hotel room) die Anzahlung (PL die **Anzahlungen**)
  to pay a deposit eine Anzahlung leisten
3 (on a bottle) das Pfand (PL die **Pfänder**)

depressed ADJECTIVE
  deprimiert

depressing ADJECTIVE
  deprimierend

depth NOUN
  die Tiefe

deputy NOUN
1 der Stellvertreter (PL die **Stellvertreter**), die Stellvertreterin (PL die **Stellvertreterinnen**)
2 **the deputy headteacher** der Konrektor (PL die **Konrektoren**), die Konrektorin (PL die **Konrektorinnen**)

℘ to **describe** VERB
  beschreiben◇

℘ **description** NOUN
  die Beschreibung (PL die **Beschreibungen**)

desert NOUN
  die Wüste (PL die **Wüsten**)

desert island NOUN
  die einsame Insel (PL die **einsamen Inseln**)

to **deserve** VERB
  verdienen

design NOUN
1 die Konstruktion (PL die **Konstruktionen**)
  the design of the plane die Flugzeugkonstruktion
2 (artistic design) das Design
  modern design modernes Design
3 (pattern) das Muster (PL die **Muster**)
  a floral design ein Blumenmuster
4 (sketch) der Entwurf (PL die **Entwürfe**)

to **design** VERB
1 konstruieren (a machine, plane, system)
2 entwerfen◇ (costumes, fabric, scenery)

designer NOUN
  der Designer (PL die **Designer**), die Designerin (PL die **Designerinnen**)

WORD TIP Professions, hobbies, and sports don't take an article in German: Er ist Designer.

℘ **desk** NOUN
1 (in an office or at home) der Schreibtisch (PL die **Schreibtische**)
2 (in school) das Pult (PL die **Pulte**)
3 **reception desk** die Rezeption
  information desk die Auskunft

despair NOUN
  die Verzweiflung
  We were in despair. Wir waren verzweifelt.

to **despair** VERB
  to despair of doing something alle Hoffnung aufgeben◇ SEP, etwas zu tun

◇ **irregular verb;** SEP **separable verb; for more help with verbs see centre section**

desperate *ADJECTIVE*
1 verzweifelt
   a desperate attempt ein verzweifelter Versuch
2 **to be desperate to do something** etwas dringend tun müssen
   I'm desperate to speak to you. Ich muss dich dringend sprechen.
   to be desperate for something etwas dringend brauchen

ℱ **dessert** *NOUN*
der Nachtisch (*PL* die Nachtische)
What's for dessert? Was gibt es zum Nachtisch?

ℱ **destination** *NOUN*
das Ziel (*PL* die Ziele)

to **destroy** *VERB*
zerstören

destruction *NOUN*
die Zerstörung

detached house *NOUN*
das Einfamilienhaus (*PL* die Einfamilienhäuser)

detail *NOUN*
die Einzelheit (*PL* die Einzelheiten)

detailed *ADJECTIVE*
ausführlich

ℱ **detective** *NOUN*
1 (*in the police*) der Kriminalbeamte (*PL* die Kriminalbeamten), die Kriminalbeamtin (*PL* die Kriminalbeamtinnen)
2 **private detective** der Detektiv (*PL* die Detektivin)

   WORD TIP Professions, hobbies, and sports don't take an article in German: Sie ist Kriminalbeamtin.

detective story *NOUN*
die Detektivgeschichte (*PL* die Detektivgeschichten)

detention *NOUN*
1 (*at school*) das Nachsitzen
   I got a detention. Ich musste nachsitzen.
2 (*in prison*) die Haft

detergent *NOUN*
das Waschmittel (*PL* die Waschmittel)

determined *ADJECTIVE*
entschlossen
He's determined to leave. Er ist fest entschlossen zu gehen.

detour *NOUN*
der Umweg (*PL* die Umwege)

to **develop** *VERB*
1 entwickeln
2 sich entwickeln
   how children develop wie Kinder sich entwickeln

developing country *NOUN*
das Entwicklungsland (*PL* die Entwicklungsländer)

development *NOUN*
die Entwicklung (*PL* die Entwicklungen)

devil *NOUN*
der Teufel (*PL* die Teufel)

devoted *ADJECTIVE*
treu

diabetes *NOUN*
die Zuckerkrankheit
My father has diabetes. Mein Vater ist Diabetiker.

diabetic *NOUN*
der Diabetiker (*PL* die Diabetiker), die Diabetikerin (*PL* die Diabetikerinnen)
She's a diabetic. Sie ist Diabetikerin.

diabetic *ADJECTIVE*
zuckerkrank
to be diabetic zuckerkrank sein

diagnosis *NOUN*
die Diagnose (*PL* die Diagnosen)

diagonal *ADJECTIVE*
diagonal

diagram *NOUN*
das Diagramm (*PL* die Diagramme)

to **dial** *VERB*
wählen
I dialled the wrong number. Ich habe die falsche Nummer gewählt.
Dial 00 49 for Germany. Wählen Sie die Vorwahl 00 49 für Deutschland.

dialling tone *NOUN*
das Freizeichen

dialogue *NOUN*
der Dialog (*PL* die Dialoge)

diameter *NOUN*
der Durchmesser (*PL* die Durchmesser)

diamond *NOUN*
1 der Diamant (*PL* die Diamanten), (*gemstone*) der Brillant (*PL* die Brillanten) (*diamond ring*) der Diamantring
2 (*in cards*) das Karo
   (*the jack of diamonds*) der Karobube
3 (*shape*) die Raute (*PL* die Rauten)

ℱ indicates key words

diarrhoea NOUN
der Durchfall

diary NOUN
1 *(of what you do every day)* das Tagebuch (PL die Tagebücher)
to keep a diary ein Tagebuch führen
2 *(for appointments)* der Terminkalender (PL die Terminkalender)

dice NOUN
der Würfel (PL die Würfel)
to throw the dice würfeln

dictation NOUN
das Diktat (PL die Diktate)

dictionary NOUN
das Wörterbuch (PL die Wörterbücher)

did VERB ▸ SEE do

to die VERB
1 sterben◇ *(PERF sein)*
My granny died in January. Meine Oma starb im Januar.
2 to be dying to do something darauf brennen◇, etwas zu tun
I'm dying to meet her. Ich brenne darauf, sie kennenzulernen.
• to die out
aussterben◇ SEP

diesel NOUN
1 *(fuel)* der Diesel(kraftstoff)
2 *(car)* der Diesel (PL die Diesel), das Dieselauto (PL die Dieselautos)
Our car is a diesel. Unser Auto ist ein Diesel.
Diesel cars are more expensive. Dieselautos sind teurer.
3 diesel engine der Dieselmotor

℘ diet NOUN
1 die Ernährung
a healthy diet eine gesunde Ernährung
2 *(slimming or special)* die Diät (PL die Diäten)
Have you tried this new diet? Hast du diese neue Diät schon ausprobiert?
to be on a diet eine Schlankheitskur machen
No thanks, I'm on a diet. Nein danke, ich will abnehmen.

℘ difference NOUN
1 der Unterschied (PL die Unterschiede)
I can't see any difference between the two. Ich erkenne keinen Unterschied zwischen den beiden.
What's the difference between ...? Was ist der Unterschied zwischen ...?
2 It makes no difference. Es ist egal.

It makes no difference what I say. Es ist egal, was ich sage.
Does it make a difference? Macht es etwas aus?

℘ different ADJECTIVE
1 verschieden
The two sisters are very different. Die beiden Schwestern sind sehr verschieden.
2 to be different from anders sein als
She's very different from her sister. Sie ist ganz anders als ihre Schwester.
3 *(separate)* anderer/andere/anderes
She reads a different book every day. Sie liest jeden Tag ein anderes Buch.

℘ difficult ADJECTIVE
schwer
It's really difficult. Es ist sehr schwer.
He finds it difficult. Es fällt ihm schwer.
I find German quite difficult. Ich finde Deutsch ziemlich schwer.

difficulty NOUN
die Schwierigkeit (PL die Schwierigkeiten)
to have difficulty doing something Schwierigkeiten haben, etwas zu tun
I had difficulty finding your house. Ich hatte Schwierigkeiten, dein Haus zu finden.

to dig VERB
graben◇
to dig a hole ein Loch graben

digestion NOUN
die Verdauung

digital ADJECTIVE
digital
digital camera die Digitalkamera
digital recording die Digitalaufnahme

dim ADJECTIVE
1 schwach
a dim light ein schwaches Licht
2 beschränkt
She's a bit dim. Sie ist ein bisschen beschränkt.

din NOUN
der Lärm
Stop making such a din! Hör auf, so einen Lärm zu machen!

dinghy NOUN
1 *(sailing dinghy)* das Dingi
2 *(rubber dinghy)* das Schlauchboot

℘ dining room NOUN
das Esszimmer (PL die Esszimmer)
in the dining room im Esszimmer

464

◇ irregular verb; SEP separable verb; for more help with verbs see centre section

_ρ_ **dinner** NOUN
1 *(evening)* das **Abendessen** (PL die **Abendessen**)
   to invite somebody to dinner jemanden zum Abendessen einladen
2 *(midday)* das **Mittagessen** (PL die **Mittagessen**)
   to have school dinners in der Schulkantine zu Mittag essen

dinner time NOUN
die **Essenszeit**

dinosaur NOUN
der **Dinosaurier** (PL die **Dinosaurier**)

_ρ_ **diploma** NOUN
das **Diplom** (PL die **Diplome**)

_ρ_ **direct** ADJECTIVE
direkt
a direct flight ein Direktflug

direct ADVERB
direkt
The bus goes direct to the airport. Der Bus fährt direkt zum Flughafen.

to **direct** VERB
1 **to direct a film or a play** bei einem Film oder einem Theaterstück Regie führen
2 regeln *(traffic)*

_ρ_ **direction** NOUN
1 die **Richtung** (PL die **Richtungen**)
   to go in the other direction in die andere Richtung gehen
2 **to ask somebody for directions** jemanden nach dem Weg fragen
3 **directions for use** die Gebrauchsanweisung *(SINGULAR)*

directly ADVERB
direkt
directly afterwards gleich danach

_ρ_ **director** NOUN
1 *(of a company)* der **Direktor** (PL die **Direktoren**), die **Direktorin** (PL die **Direktorinnen**)
2 *(of a play, film)* der **Regisseur** (PL die **Regisseure**), die **Regisseurin** (PL die **Regisseurinnen**)

_ρ_ **directory** NOUN
das **Telefonbuch** (PL die **Telefonbücher**)
He's ex-directory. Seine Nummer steht nicht im Telefonbuch.

dirt NOUN
der **Schmutz**

_ρ_ **dirty** ADJECTIVE
schmutzig
My hands are dirty. Ich habe schmutzige

Hände.
to get something dirty etwas schmutzig machen
You'll get your dress dirty. Du machst dir das Kleid schmutzig.
to get dirty schmutzig werden ◇

disability NOUN
die **Behinderung** (PL die **Behinderungen**)
Does he have a disability? Ist er behindert?

disabled ADJECTIVE
behindert
disabled people Behinderte *(PLURAL)*

disadvantage NOUN
1 der **Nachteil** (PL die **Nachteile**)
2 **to be at a disadvantage** im Nachteil sein

disadvantaged ADJECTIVE
benachteiligt

to **disagree** VERB
1 **I disagree.** Ich bin anderer Meinung.
2 **to disagree with somebody** mit jemandem nicht übereinstimmen SEP
   I disagree with James. Ich stimme mit James nicht überein.

to **disappear** VERB
verschwinden ◇ *(PERF sein)*

disappearance NOUN
das **Verschwinden**

_ρ_ **disappointed** ADJECTIVE
enttäuscht
I'm disappointed with my marks. Ich bin über meine Noten enttäuscht.

disappointment NOUN
die **Enttäuschung** (PL die **Enttäuschungen**)

disaster NOUN
die **Katastrophe** (PL die **Katastrophen**)
It was a complete disaster. Es war eine komplette Katastrophe.

disastrous ADJECTIVE
katastrophal

disc NOUN
1 **compact disc** die CD
2 **tax disc** *(for a vehicle)* die Steuerplakette
3 **slipped disc** der Bandscheibenvorfall

discipline NOUN
die **Disziplin**

disc jockey NOUN
der **Diskjockey** (PL die **Diskjockeys**)

> **WORD TIP** Professions, hobbies, and sports don't take an article in German: Er ist Diskjockey.

_ρ_ indicates key words

ℰ disco NOUN
die Disko (PL die Diskos)
They're having a disco. Sie veranstalten
eine Disko.
to go to a disco in eine Disko gehen

discount NOUN
der Rabatt (PL die Rabatte)

to discourage VERB
**to discourage somebody from doing
something** jemanden davon abhalten◊,
etwas zu tun
**His parents discouraged him from
becoming an actor.** Seine Eltern hielten ihn
davon ab, Schauspieler zu werden.

to discover VERB
entdecken

discovery NOUN
die Entdeckung (PL die Entdeckungen)

discreet ADJECTIVE
diskret

discrimination NOUN
die Diskriminierung
discrimination against women die
Diskriminierung von Frauen
racial discrimination die
Rassendiskriminierung

ℰ to discuss VERB
to discuss something etwas besprechen◊
We'll discuss the problem tomorrow. Wir
besprechen das Problem morgen.
I'm going to discuss it with Phil. Ich werde
es mit Phil besprechen.

discussion NOUN
das Gespräch (PL die Gespräche), (debate)
die Diskussion (PL die Diskussionen)

disease NOUN
die Krankheit (PL die Krankheiten)

disgraceful ADJECTIVE
schändlich
It's disgraceful that ... Es ist eine Schande,
dass ...

disguise NOUN
die Verkleidung (PL die Verkleidungen)
to be in disguise verkleidet sein

to disguise VERB
verkleiden
disguised as a woman als Frau verkleidet

disgust NOUN
der Ekel

disgusted ADJECTIVE
1 (filled with indignation) empört

2 (nauseated) angeekelt

ℰ disgusting ADJECTIVE
eklig

ℰ dish NOUN
1 die Schüssel (PL die Schüsseln)
a large white dish eine große weiße
Schüssel
satellite dish die Satellitenschüssel
2 (type of food) das Gericht (PL die Gerichte)
Risotto is my favourite dish. Risotto ist
mein Lieblingsgericht.
dish of the day das Tagesgericht
3 (crockery) **the dishes** das Geschirr
to do the dishes Geschirr spülen

dishonest ADJECTIVE
unehrlich

dishonesty NOUN
die Unehrlichkeit

ℰ dishwasher NOUN
die Geschirrspülmaschine (PL die
Geschirrspülmaschinen)

to disinfect VERB
desinfizieren

disinfectant NOUN
das Desinfektionsmittel

ℰ disk NOUN
die Diskette (PL die Disketten)

disk drive NOUN
das Diskettenlaufwerk (PL die
Diskettenlaufwerke)

to dislike VERB
nicht mögen◊
I really dislike people like that. Solche
Leute mag ich überhaupt nicht.

to dismiss VERB
entlassen◊ (an employee)

disobedient ADJECTIVE
ungehorsam

to disobey VERB
nicht gehorchen

display NOUN
1 die Ausstellung (PL die Ausstellungen)
handicrafts display die
Handarbeitsausstellung
to be on display ausgestellt sein
2 **window display** die Auslage
3 **firework display** das Feuerwerk

to display VERB
ausstellen SEP

◊ **irregular verb;** SEP **separable verb; for more help with verbs see centre section**

disposable ADJECTIVE
Wegwerf-
disposable towel das Wegwerfhandtuch

to disqualify VERB
disqualifizieren

to disrupt VERB
stören

to dissolve VERB
auflösen SEP

ℙ **distance** NOUN
die Entfernung (PL die Entfernungen)
from this distance aus dieser Entfernung
from a distance von weitem
in the distance in der Ferne
It's within walking distance. Es ist zu Fuß
erreichbar.

distant ADJECTIVE
fern

distinct ADJECTIVE
deutlich

distinctly ADVERB
1 deutlich
2 It's distinctly odd. Es ist äußerst komisch.

to distract VERB
ablenken SEP

to distribute VERB
verteilen

district NOUN
1 (of a town) der Stadtteil (PL die Stadtteile)
a poor district of Berlin ein ärmlicher
Stadtteil von Berlin
2 (in the country) das Gebiet (PL die Gebiete)

to disturb VERB
stören
Sorry to disturb you. Entschuldigung, dass
ich störe.

dive NOUN
der Kopfsprung (PL die Kopfsprünge)

to dive VERB
1 einen Kopfsprung machen
2 (swim underwater) tauchen (PERF sein)

diver NOUN
1 (underwater) der Taucher (PL die Taucher),
die Taucherin (PL die Taucherinnen)
2 (from a diving board) der Kunstspringer
(PL die Kunstspringer), die
Kunstspringerin (PL die
Kunstspringerinnen)

WORD TIP Professions, hobbies, and sports
don't take an article in German: Er ist Taucher.

ℙ **diversion** NOUN
(of traffic) die Umleitung (PL die
Umleitungen)

to divide VERB
teilen
to divide something in half etwas
halbieren

diving NOUN
1 (underwater) das Tauchen
2 (from a diving board) das Kunstspringen

diving board NOUN
das Sprungbrett (PL die Sprungbretter)

division NOUN
1 (dividing something) die Teilung (PL die
Teilungen)
2 (in maths) die Division (PL die Divisionen)
3 (sports league) die Liga (PL die Ligen)

divorce NOUN
die Scheidung (PL die Scheidungen)

to divorce VERB
sich scheiden lassen◇
He divorced her. Er ließ sich von ihr
scheiden.
They divorced in May. Sie haben sich im
Mai scheiden lassen.

ℙ **divorced** ADJECTIVE
geschieden

ℙ **DIY** NOUN
1 das Heimwerken
2 to do DIY heimwerken
3 a DIY shop ein Baumarkt

dizzy ADJECTIVE
I feel dizzy. Mir ist schwindlig.

DJ NOUN
der DJ (PL die DJs)

ℙ **to do** VERB
1 tun◇, machen
What are you doing? Was machst du?
I'm doing my homework. Ich mache meine
Hausaufgaben.
What have you done with the hammer?
Was hast du mit dem Hammer gemacht?
Can you do me a favour? Kannst du mir
einen Gefallen tun?
Do as I say. Tu, was ich sage.
2 She's doing the cleaning. Sie putzt.
I'll do the washing up. Ich wasche ab.
I must do the shopping. Ich muss
einkaufen gehen.
3 (in questions)
Do you like it? Gefällt es dir?
When does the film start? Wann fängt der
Film an?

How do you open the door? Wie macht man die Tür auf?
Do you know him? Kennst du ihn?
4 *(in negative sentences)*
I don't like mushrooms. Ich mag keine Pilze.
Rosie doesn't like spinach. Rosie mag keinen Spinat.
You didn't shut the door. Du hast die Tür nicht zugemacht.
It doesn't matter. Das macht nichts.
5 *(when it refers back to another verb, 'do' is not translated)*
'Do you live here?' – 'Yes, I do' 'Wohnst du hier?' – 'Ja.'
She has more money than I do. Sie hat mehr Geld als ich.
'I live in Oxford.' – 'So do I.' 'Ich wohne in Oxford.' – 'Ich auch.'
'I didn't phone Gemma.' – 'Neither did I.' 'Ich habe Gemma nicht angerufen.' – 'Ich auch nicht.'
6 **..., don't you? ..., doesn't he?** ..., nicht wahr?
You know Helen, don't you? Du kennst Helen, nicht wahr?
She left on Thursday, didn't she? Sie ist Donnerstag abgefahren, nicht wahr?
7 **That'll do.** Das reicht.
It'll do like that. Das geht so.
• **to do something up**
1 etwas zubinden◇ *SEP (shoes)*
2 etwas zumachen *SEP (a coat, jacket)*
3 etwas renovieren *(a house)*
• **to do without something**
ohne etwas *(ACC)* auskommen◇ *SEP (PERF sein)*
We can do without knives. Wir können ohne Messer auskommen.

ℰ **doctor** NOUN
der **Arzt** (*PL* die **Ärzte**) die **Ärztin** (*PL* die **Ärztinnen**)

WORD TIP Professions, hobbies, and sports don't take an article in German: Sie ist Ärztin.

document NOUN
das **Dokument** (*PL* die **Dokumente**)

documentary NOUN
der **Dokumentarfilm** (*PL* die **Dokumentarfilme**)

dodgems PLURAL NOUN
to go on the dodgems Autoskooter fahren

ℰ **dog** NOUN
der **Hund** (*PL* die **Hunde**)

do-it-yourself NOUN
das **Heimwerken**

dole NOUN
das **Arbeitslosengeld**
to be on the dole arbeitslos sein

ℰ **doll** NOUN
die **Puppe** (*PL* die **Puppen**)

dollar NOUN
der **Dollar** (*PL* die **Dollars**)

dolphin NOUN
der **Delfin** (*PL* die **Delfine**)

dome NOUN
die **Kuppel** (*PL* die **Kuppeln**)

WORD TIP Do not translate the English word dome with the German Dom.

domino NOUN
1 der **Dominostein** (*PL* die **Dominosteine**)
2 *(game)*
dominoes das Domino
to play dominoes Domino spielen

to donate VERB
spenden

donation NOUN
die **Spende** (*PL* die **Spenden**)
to make a donation eine Spende geben

donkey NOUN
der **Esel** (*PL* die **Esel**)

don't VERB ▸ SEE **do**

ℰ **door** NOUN
die **Tür** (*PL* die **Türen**)
to open the door die Tür aufmachen *SEP*
to shut the door die Tür zumachen *SEP*

doorbell NOUN
die **Türklingel** (*PL* die **Türklingeln**)
to ring the doorbell klingeln

ℰ **dormitory** NOUN
der **Schlafsaal** (*PL* die **Schlafsäle**)

dot NOUN
1 der **Punkt** (*PL* die **Punkte**)
at ten on the dot Punkt zehn Uhr
2 *(small dot on fabric)* das **Pünktchen** (*PL* die **Pünktchen**)

ℰ **double** ADJECTIVE, ADVERB
1 doppelt
a double helping eine doppelte Portion
double the size doppelt so groß
double the time doppelt so viel Zeit
at double the price zum doppelten Preis
2 **double room** das Doppelzimmer

468

3 double bed das Doppelbett

double bass NOUN
der **Kontrabass** (PL die **Kontrabässe**)
He plays the double bass. Er spielt Kontrabass.

WORD TIP Don't use the article when you talk about playing an instrument.

double-decker bus NOUN
der **Doppeldeckerbus** (PL die **Doppeldeckerbusse**)

doubles NOUN
(in tennis) das **Doppel** (PL die **Doppel**)

doubt NOUN
der **Zweifel** (PL die **Zweifel**)
no doubt ohne Zweifel
I have my doubts. Ich habe gewisse Zweifel.
There's no doubt about it. Es besteht kein Zweifel daran.

to **doubt** VERB
to doubt something etwas bezweifeln
I doubt it. Das bezweifle ich.
I doubt that … Ich bezweifle, dass …
I doubt they'll buy it. Ich bezweifle, dass sie es kaufen.

doubtful ADJECTIVE
1 fraglich
It's doubtful. Es ist fraglich.
2 to be doubtful about doing something Bedenken haben, ob man etwas tun soll
I'm doubtful about inviting them together. Ich habe Bedenken, ob ich sie zusammen einladen soll.

dough NOUN
der **Teig**

doughnut NOUN
der **Berliner** (PL die **Berliner**), der **Krapfen** (PL die **Krapfen**)

_ℓ_ **down** ADVERB, PREPOSITION
1 unten
He's down in the cellar. Er ist unten im Keller.
It's down there. Es ist da unten.
2 down the road (nearby) in der Nähe
There's a chemist's just down the road. Eine Apotheke ist ganz in der Nähe.
3 to go down nach unten gehen
I went down to open the door. Ich ging nach unten, um die Tür aufzumachen.
to walk down the street die Straße entlanggehen◇ SEP (PERF sein)
to run down the stairs die Treppe runterrennen SEP (PERF sein) (informal)

4 to come down herunterkommen◇ SEP (PERF sein)
She came down into the kitchen. Sie kam in die Küche herunter.
5 to sit down sich setzen
She sat down on the chair. Sie setzte sich auf den Stuhl.
6 to write something down etwas aufschreiben◇ SEP

downhill ADVERB
bergab

to **download** VERB
herunterladen◇ SEP
I downloaded it from the Internet. Ich habe es aus dem Internet heruntergeladen.

_ℓ_ **downstairs** ADVERB
1 unten
She's downstairs. Sie ist unten.
2 (with movement) nach unten
to go downstairs nach unten gehen
3 im Erdgeschoss
the flat downstairs die Wohnung im Erdgeschoss

to **doze** VERB
dösen

dozen NOUN
das **Dutzend** (PL die **Dutzende**)

drag NOUN
1 What a drag! So'n Mist! (informal)
2 She's such a drag! Mann, ist die langweilig! (informal)

to **drag** VERB
schleppen

dragon NOUN
der **Drache** (PL die **Drachen**)

drain NOUN
1 (outlet pipe) das Abflussrohr (PL die **Abflussrohre**)
2 the drains die Kanalisation (SINGULAR)

to **drain** VERB
1 abgießen◇ SEP (vegetables)
2 trockenlegen SEP (fields, land)

drama NOUN
das **Drama** (PL die **Dramen**)
He made a big drama out of it. Er hat ein großes Drama daraus gemacht. (informal)

dramatic ADJECTIVE
dramatisch

draught NOUN
der **Luftzug**
There's a draught in here. Hier zieht es.

draughts NOUN
das Damespiel
to play draughts Dame spielen

℘ **draw** NOUN
1 (in a match) das Unentschieden
to end in a draw mit einem Unentschieden enden
2 (lottery) die Ziehung (PL die Ziehungen)

to **draw** VERB
1 zeichnen
She can draw really well. Sie kann wirklich sehr gut zeichnen.
2 **to draw the curtains** (open) die Vorhänge aufziehen ◇ SEP, (close) die Vorhänge zuziehen ◇ SEP
3 (in a match) unentschieden spielen
We drew three all. Wir haben drei zu drei unentschieden gespielt.

drawer NOUN
die Schublade (PL die Schubladen)

℘ **drawing** NOUN
die Zeichnung (PL die Zeichnungen)

drawing pin NOUN
die Reißzwecke (PL die Reißzwecken)

dreadful ADJECTIVE
furchtbar

dreadfully ADVERB
furchtbar
I'm dreadfully late. Ich habe mich furchtbar verspätet.
I'm dreadfully sorry. Es tut mir furchtbar leid.

dream NOUN
der Traum (PL die Träume)
to have a dream einen Traum haben

to **dream** VERB
träumen
to dream about something von etwas (DAT) träumen

℘ **dress** NOUN
das Kleid (PL die Kleider)

to **dress** VERB
to dress a child ein Kind anziehen ◇ SEP
• **to dress up**
sich verkleiden
to dress up as a vampire sich als Vampir verkleiden

℘ **dressed** ADJECTIVE
1 angezogen
Is Tom dressed yet? Ist Tom schon angezogen?
2 **She was dressed in black trousers and a**

yellow shirt. Sie trug eine schwarze Hose und eine gelbe Bluse.
3 **to get dressed** sich anziehen ◇ SEP
I got dressed quickly. Ich zog mich schnell an.

dressing gown NOUN
der Morgenrock (PL die Morgenröcke)

drill NOUN
der Bohrer (PL die Bohrer)

℘ **drink** NOUN
1 das Getränk (PL die Getränke)
to have a drink etwas trinken ◇
Would you like a drink of water? Möchtest du etwas Wasser trinken?
2 (an alcoholic drink) der Drink (PL die Drinks)
They've invited my parents round for drinks. Sie haben meine Eltern auf einen Drink eingeladen.
Let's have a drink! Trinken wir einen! (informal)

> **DRINK**
>
> Apple juice with sparkling water is called Apfelschorle in Germany and Apfelsaft gespritzt in Austria. Other special drinks are: Almdudler®, a popular Austrian soft drink made from Alpine herbs, Holundersaft, elderflower juice, and Radler, lemonade shandy.

to **drink** VERB
trinken ◇
He drank a glass of water. Er trank ein Glas Wasser.

℘ **drive** NOUN
1 **to go for a drive** eine Autofahrt machen
2 (in front of a house) die Einfahrt (PL die Einfahrten)

to **drive** VERB
1 fahren ◇ (PERF sein)
She drives very fast. Sie fährt sehr schnell.
to drive a car Auto fahren
Can you drive? Kannst du Auto fahren?
She doesn't drive. Sie hat keinen Führerschein.
My brother is learning to drive. Mein Bruder macht seinen Führerschein.
2 **We drove to Berlin.** Wir sind mit dem Auto nach Berlin gefahren.
3 **to drive somebody (to a place)** jemanden (irgendwohin) fahren (PERF haben)
Mum drove me to the station. Mutti hat mich zum Bahnhof gefahren.
to drive somebody home jemanden nach Hause fahren
4 **She drives me mad!** Sie macht mich verrückt!

◇ irregular verb; SEP separable verb; for more help with verbs see centre section

ρ **driver** NOUN
1 der **Fahrer** (PL die **Fahrer**), die **Fahrerin**
(PL die **Fahrerinnen**)
2 (of a locomotive) der **Lokomotivführer**
(PL die **Lokomotivführer**), die
Lokomotivführerin (PL die
Lokomotivführerinnen)

WORD TIP Professions, hobbies, and sports don't
take an article in German: Er ist Lokomotivführer.

driving instructor NOUN
der **Fahrlehrer** (PL die **Fahrlehrer**), die
Fahrlehrerin (PL die **Fahrlehrerinnen**)

WORD TIP Professions, hobbies, and sports don't
take an article in German: Sie ist Fahrlehrerin.

driving lesson NOUN
die **Fahrstunde** (PL die **Fahrstunden**)

ρ **driving licence** NOUN
der **Führerschein** (PL die **Führerscheine**)

driving school NOUN
die **Fahrschule** (PL die **Fahrschulen**)

driving test NOUN
die **Fahrprüfung**
to take your driving test die Fahrprüfung
machen
Jenny's passed her driving test. Jenny hat
die Fahrprüfung bestanden.

ρ **drop** NOUN
der **Tropfen** (PL die **Tropfen**)

to **drop** VERB
1 to drop something etwas fallen lassen◇
I dropped my glasses. Ich habe meine Brille
fallen lassen.
2 Drop it! Lass das!
3 I'm going to drop history next year.
Nächstes Jahr wähle ich Geschichte ab.
4 absetzen SEP (a person)
Could you drop me at the station?
Könntest du mich am Bahnhof absetzen?

ρ **drought** NOUN
die **Dürre** (PL die **Dürren**)

ρ to **drown** VERB
ertrinken◇ (PERF sein)
She drowned in the lake. Sie ist im See
ertrunken.

ρ **drug** NOUN
1 (medicine) das **Medikament** (PL die
Medikamente)
2 (illegal)
drugs die **Drogen** (PLURAL)

drug abuse NOUN
der **Drogenmissbrauch**

drug addict NOUN
der/die **Drogenabhängige** (PL die
Drogenabhängigen)
She's a drug addict. Sie ist
drogenabhängig.

drug addiction NOUN
die **Drogenabhängigkeit**

drum NOUN
1 die **Trommel** (PL die **Trommeln**)
2 drums das **Schlagzeug**
to play the drums Schlagzeug spielen

WORD TIP Don't use the article when you talk
about playing an instrument.

drummer NOUN
der **Schlagzeuger** (PL die **Schlagzeuger**),
die **Schlagerzeugerin** (PL die
Schlagzeugerinnen)

WORD TIP Professions, hobbies, and sports
don't take an article in German: Er ist
Schlagzeuger.

drunk NOUN
der/die **Betrunkene** (PL die **Betrunkenen**)

drunk ADJECTIVE
betrunken
to get drunk sich betrinken◇

ρ **dry** ADJECTIVE
trocken

to **dry** VERB
1 trocknen
to let something dry etwas trocknen
lassen◇
to dry your hair sich (DAT) die Haare
trocknen
to dry the washing die Wäsche trocknen
2 to dry your hands sich (DAT) die Hände
abtrocknen SEP
I dried my feet. Ich trocknete mir die Füße
ab.
to dry the dishes das Geschirr abtrocknen
• to dry up
abtrocknen SEP
You wash and I'll dry up. Du spülst und ich
trockne ab.

dry cleaner's NOUN
die **chemische Reinigung**

dual carriageway NOUN
die **zweispurige Straße** (PL die
zweispurigen Straßen)

dubbed ADJECTIVE
a dubbed film ein synchronisierter Film

ρ **duck** NOUN
die **Ente** (PL die **Enten**)

471

ρ indicates key words

due dyed

due ADJECTIVE
1 **When is the bus due?** Wann soll der Bus kommen?
The essay is due in on Monday. Ich muss den Aufsatz am Montag abgeben.
Paul's due back soon. Paul muss bald zurück sein.
We're due to leave on Thursday. Wir müssen Donnerstag abfahren.
2 **due to** wegen (+GEN)
due to bad weather wegen schlechten Wetters

dull ADJECTIVE
1 **dull weather** trübes Wetter
It's a dull day today. Heute ist ein trüber Tag.
2 (boring) langweilig

dumb ADJECTIVE
1 stumm
2 (stupid) dumm
He asked some dumb questions. Er hat ein paar dumme Fragen gestellt.

to **dump** VERB
1 abladen◇ SEP (rubbish)
2 (put down) hinwerfen◇ SEP
He dumped it on the floor. Er warf es auf den Boden.
3 Schluss machen mit (a person)
She's dumped her boyfriend. Sie hat mit ihrem Freund Schluss gemacht.

dune NOUN
die Düne (PL die Dünen)

dungarees PLURAL NOUN
die Latzhose (PL die Latzhosen)
a pair of dungarees eine Latzhose
She was wearing dungarees. Sie trug eine Latzhose.

♪ **during** PREPOSITION
während (+GEN)
during the night während der Nacht
I saw her during the holidays. Ich habe sie während der Ferien gesehen.

dusk NOUN
die Dämmerung
at dusk bei Einbruch der Dunkelheit

dust NOUN
der Staub

to **dust** VERB
1 abstauben SEP (furniture, objects)
2 (in a room) Staub wischen
She's dusting. Sie wischt Staub.

♪ **dustbin** NOUN
die Mülltonne (PL die Mülltonnen)

dustman NOUN
der Müllmann (PL die Müllmänner)

> **WORD TIP** Professions, hobbies, and sports don't take an article in German: Er ist Müllmann.

dusty ADJECTIVE
staubig

Dutch NOUN
1 (language) das Holländisch
2 **the Dutch people** die Holländer
Dutch ADJECTIVE
holländisch
the Dutch border die holländische Grenze
He's Dutch. Er ist Holländer.
She's Dutch. Sie ist Holländerin.

> **WORD TIP** Adjectives never have capitals in German, even for regions, countries, or nationalities.

duty NOUN
1 die Pflicht (PL die Pflichten)
to have a duty to do something die Pflicht haben, etwas zu tun
You have a duty to inform us. Sie sind verpflichtet, uns zu benachrichtigen.
2 **to be on duty** Dienst haben
to be on night duty Nachtdienst haben
I'm off duty tonight. Ich habe heute Abend keinen Dienst.

duty-free ADJECTIVE
zollfrei
duty-free shop der Duty-free-Shop
duty-free goods zollfreie Waren (PLURAL)

duvet NOUN
die Bettdecke (PL die Bettdecken)

duvet cover NOUN
der Bettbezug (PL die Bettbezüge)

DVD NOUN
die DVD (PL die DVDs)

dwarf NOUN
der Zwerg (PL die Zwerge)

dye NOUN
das Färbemittel (PL die Färbemittel)
to **dye** VERB
färben
to dye your hair sich (DAT) die Haare färben
I'm going to dye my hair black. Ich werde mir die Haare schwarz färben.
I'm going to have my hair dyed pink. Ich lasse mir die Haare rosa färben.

dyed ADJECTIVE
gefärbt

dynamic *ADJECTIVE*
dynamisch

dyslexia *NOUN*
die **Legasthenie**

dyslexic *ADJECTIVE*
legasthenisch
to be dyslexic Legastheniker sein,
Legasthenikerin sein

Ee

ℙ **each** *DETERMINER, PRONOUN*
1 jeder/jede/jedes
each Sunday jeden Sonntag
each time jedes Mal
at the beginning of each year am Anfang
jedes Jahres
We each have an invitation. Jeder von uns
hat eine Einladung.
My sisters each have a computer. Jede
meiner Schwestern hat einen Computer.
She gave us an apple each. Sie hat jedem
von uns einen Apfel gegeben.
each of you jeder von euch/jede von euch
We each got a present. Jeder Einzelne von
uns hat ein Geschenk bekommen.
2 The tickets cost ten pounds each. Die
Karten kosten je zehn Pfund.
£5 each *(per person)* fünf Pfund pro Person,
(per item) fünf Pfund pro Stück

each other *PRONOUN*
*('each other' is usually translated using a
reflexive pronoun)*
They love each other. Sie lieben sich.
We know each other. Wir kennen uns.
Do you see each other often? Seht ihr euch
oft?

eagle *NOUN*
der **Adler** (*PL* die **Adler**)

ℙ **ear** *NOUN*
das **Ohr** (*PL* die **Ohren**)

earache *NOUN*
to have earache Ohrenschmerzen haben

earlier *ADVERB*
1 *(not as late)* früher
We should have started earlier. Wir hätten
früher anfangen sollen.
2 *(a while ago)* vor kurzem
Your brother phoned earlier. Dein Bruder
hat vor kurzem angerufen.

ℙ **early** *ADVERB*
1 *(in the morning)* früh
to get up early früh aufstehen
It's too early. Es ist zu früh.
2 *(for an appointment)*
to be early (zu) früh dran sein
We're early; the train doesn't leave until
ten. Wir sind früh dran; der Zug fährt erst
um zehn Uhr ab.

early *ADJECTIVE*
1 früh
in the early afternoon am frühen
Nachmittag
in the early hours in den frühen
Morgenstunden
I'm getting the early train. Ich nehme den
Frühzug.
2 *(one of the first)*
in the early months während der ersten
Monate
3 to have an early lunch früh zu Mittag essen
Jan's having an early night. Jan geht früh
zu Bett.

to **earn** *VERB*
verdienen
Richard earns seven pounds an hour.
Richard verdient sieben Pfund die Stunde.

earphones *PLURAL NOUN*
der **Kopfhörer** (*PL* die **Kopfhörer**)

earring *NOUN*
der **Ohrring** (*PL* die **Ohrringe**)

earth *NOUN*
die **Erde**
life on earth das Leben auf der Erde
What on earth are you doing? Was in aller
Welt machst du da?

earthquake *NOUN*
das **Erdbeben** (*PL* die **Erdbeben**)

easily *ADVERB*
leicht
He's easily the best. Er ist mit Abstand der
Beste.

ℙ **east** *NOUN*
der **Osten**
in the east im Osten

east *ADJECTIVE*
östlich, Ost-
the east side die Ostseite
an east wind ein Ostwind

east *ADVERB*
1 *(towards the east)* nach Osten
to travel east nach Osten fahren
2 east of Munich östlich von München

ℙ indicates key words

Easter NOUN
Ostern (NEUTER)
They're coming at Easter. Sie kommen zu Ostern.
Happy Easter! Frohe Ostern!

Easter Day NOUN
der Ostersonntag (PL die Ostersonntage)

Easter egg NOUN
das Osterei (PL die Ostereier)

Easter Monday NOUN
der Ostermontag

ᵱ **eastern** ADJECTIVE
östlich, Ost-
on the eastern side of the mountain an der Ostseite des Berges

Eastern Europe NOUN
Osteuropa (NEUTER)

ᵱ **easy** ADJECTIVE
leicht
It's easy! Das ist leicht!
It was easy to find. Es war leicht zu finden.
It was easy to decide. Die Entscheidung fiel uns leicht.

ᵱ **to eat** VERB
1 essen◇
He was eating a banana. Er aß eine Banane.
We're going to have something to eat. Wir essen jetzt etwas.
2 (of animals) fressen◇
The dog ate all the meat. Der Hund hat das ganze Fleisch gefressen.
3 to eat your breakfast frühstücken

EC NOUN
die EG Europäische Gemeinschaft

echo NOUN
das Echo (PL die Echos)

to echo VERB
1 (reverberate) hallen
2 (repeat) wiederholen

eclipse NOUN
die Finsternis (PL die Finsternisse)
an eclipse of the moon eine Mondfinsternis
an eclipse of the sun eine Sonnenfinsternis

ecological ADJECTIVE
ökologisch

ecology NOUN
die Ökologie

economic ADJECTIVE
wirtschaftlich
the economic situation die Wirtschaftslage

economical ADJECTIVE
sparsam

economics NOUN
die Wirtschaftswissenschaften (PLURAL)

economy NOUN
die Wirtschaft

eczema NOUN
das Ekzem

ᵱ **edge** NOUN
1 die Kante (PL die Kanten)
the edge of the table die Tischkante
2 (of a road, sheet of paper, or cliff) der Rand (PL die Ränder)
at the edge of the forest am Waldrand

edible ADJECTIVE
essbar

to edit VERB
redigieren

editor NOUN
1 (of a newspaper or magazine) der Chefredakteur (PL die Chefredakteure), die Chefredakteurin (PL die Chefredakteurinnen)
2 (of a book) der Redakteur (PL die Redakteure), die Redakteurin (PL die Redakteurinnen)

WORD TIP Professions, hobbies, and sports don't take an article in German: Er ist Redakteur.

to educate VERB
erziehen◇

education NOUN
die Ausbildung

effect NOUN
1 die Wirkung (PL die Wirkungen)
The effect of the explosion was horrific. Die Wirkung der Explosion war entsetzlich.
2 to have an effect on something eine Auswirkung auf etwas (ACC) haben
It had a good effect on the whole family. Es hatte eine gute Auswirkung auf die ganze Familie.
3 (in a film) der Effekt (PL die Effekte)
special effects die Spezialeffekte

effective ADJECTIVE
effektiv

efficient ADJECTIVE
1 (person) tüchtig
2 (machine or organization) leistungsfähig

effort NOUN
1 die Mühe (PL die Mühen)

◇ irregular verb; SEP separable verb; for more help with verbs see centre section

2 to make an effort sich bemühen
Toya made an effort to help us. Toya hat sich bemüht, uns zu helfen.
He didn't even make the effort to apologize. Er hat sich nicht einmal die Mühe gemacht, sich zu entschuldigen.

e.g. *ABBREVIATION*
z.B. (zum Beispiel)

ℓ**egg** *NOUN*
das Ei (*PL* die Eier)
a fried egg ein Spiegelei
a hard-boiled egg ein hart gekochtes Ei
scrambled egg das Rührei

egg cup *NOUN*
der Eierbecher (*PL* die Eierbecher)

eggshell *NOUN*
die Eierschale (*PL* die Eierschalen)

egg white *NOUN*
das Eiweiß (*PL* die Eiweiße)

egg yolk *NOUN*
das Eigelb (*PL* die Eigelbe)

ℓ**eight** *NUMBER*
acht
Maya's eight. Maya ist acht.
at eight o'clock um acht Uhr

ℓ**eighteen** *NUMBER*
achtzehn
Jason's eighteen. Jason ist achtzehn.

eighteenth *NUMBER*
achtzehnter/achtzehnte/achtzehntes

ℓ**eighth** *NUMBER*
achter/achte/achtes
on the eighth of July am achten Juli

eightieth *NUMBER*
achtzigster/achtzigste/achtzigstes

ℓ**eighty** *NUMBER*
achtzig
eighty-five fünfundachtzig

ℓ**either** *PRONOUN*
1 *(one or the other)* einer von beiden/eine von beiden/eins von beiden
Take either (of them). Nimm einen von beiden/eine von beiden/eins von beiden.
I don't like either (of them). Ich mag keinen von beiden/keine von beiden/keins von beiden.
You can ask either of us. Du kannst einen von uns beiden fragen.
2 *(both)* beide *(PLURAL)*
Either is possible. Beide sind möglich.
on either side auf beiden Seiten

either *CONJUNCTION*
1 **either ... or** entweder ... oder
either Susie or Judy entweder Susie oder Judy
2 *(with a negative)*
either ... or weder ... noch
He didn't ring either Sam or Emma. Er hat weder Sam noch Emma angerufen.
3 **I don't know them either.** Ich kenne sie auch nicht.
'I can't do this question.' 'I can't either.' 'Ich kann diese Frage nicht beantworten.' 'Ich auch nicht.'

elastic *NOUN*
das Gummiband (*PL* die Gummibänder)

elastic band *NOUN*
das Gummiband (*PL* die Gummibänder)

ℓ**elbow** *NOUN*
der Ellbogen (*PL* die Ellbogen)

ℓ**elder** *ADJECTIVE*
ältere/ältere/älteres
her elder brother ihr älterer Bruder

ℓ**elderly** *ADJECTIVE*
alt
the elderly ältere Menschen *(PLURAL)*

ℓ**eldest** *ADJECTIVE*
ältester/älteste/ältestes
her eldest brother ihr ältester Bruder

to **elect** *VERB*
wählen
She has been elected. Sie ist gewählt worden.

ℓ**election** *NOUN*
die Wahl (*PL* die Wahlen)
in the election bei den Wahlen
to call an election allgemeine Wahlen ausrufen

electric *ADJECTIVE*
elektrisch

electrical *ADJECTIVE*
elektrisch, Elektro-
electrical equipment die Elektrogeräte *(PLURAL)*

electrician *NOUN*
der Elektriker (*PL* die Elektriker), die Elektrikerin (*PL* die Elektrikerinnen)

WORD TIP Professions, hobbies, and sports don't take an article in German: Er ist Elektriker.

ℓ**electricity** *NOUN*
der Strom

ℓ **indicates key words**

electronic ADJECTIVE
elektronisch

electronics NOUN
die Elektronik

⚘ **elegant** ADJECTIVE
elegant

elephant NOUN
der Elefant (PL die Elefanten)

⚘ **eleven** NUMBER
elf
Josh is eleven. Josh ist elf.
at eleven o'clock um elf Uhr
a football eleven eine Fußballelf

⚘ **eleventh** NUMBER
elfter/elfte/elftes
the eleventh of September der elfte September
on the eleventh floor im elften Stock

else ADVERB
1 (in addition) sonst
Who else? Wer sonst?
Did you see anyone else? Hast du sonst noch jemanden gesehen?
nothing else sonst nichts
I don't want anything else. Ich will sonst nichts.
2 **Would you like something else?** Möchten Sie sonst noch etwas?
3 (instead or different) anderer/andere/ anderes
somewhere else irgendwo anders
everyone else alle anderen
somebody else jemand anders
something else etwas anderes
4 or else sonst
Hurry up, or else we'll be late. Beeil dich, sonst kommen wir zu spät.

⚘ **email** NOUN
die E-Mail (PL die E-Mails), die Mail (PL die Mails)
I sent Dan an email. Ich habe Dan eine Mail geschickt.
I contacted them by email. Ich habe sie per E-Mail kontaktiert.
What is your email address? Was ist deine E-Mail-Adresse?

to **email** VERB
mailen
I'll email you. Ich maile dir.
Can you email me the details? Kannst du mir die Einzelheiten mailen?

embarrassed ADJECTIVE
verlegen

He was very embarrassed. Er war ganz verlegen.

embarrassing ADJECTIVE
peinlich

embassy NOUN
die Botschaft (PL die Botschaften)
the German Embassy die Deutsche Botschaft

⚘ **emergency** NOUN
der Notfall (PL die Notfälle)

emergency exit NOUN
der Notausgang (PL die Notausgänge)

emotion NOUN
das Gefühl (PL die Gefühle)

emotional ADJECTIVE
1 (person) emotional
2 (speech or occasion) emotionsgeladen

emperor NOUN
der Kaiser (PL die Kaiser)

to **emphasize** VERB
betonen
He emphasized that it was voluntary. Er betonte, dass es freiwillig war.

empire NOUN
das Reich (PL die Reiche)
the Roman Empire das Römische Reich

to **employ** VERB
1 (have working for you) beschäftigen
2 (take on a worker) einstellen SEP

⚘ **employee** NOUN
der/die Angestellte (PL die Angestellten)

WORD TIP Professions, hobbies, and sports don't take an article in German: Er ist Angestellter.

employer NOUN
der Arbeitgeber (PL die Arbeitgeber), die Arbeitgeberin (PL die Arbeitgeberinnen)

employment NOUN
die Arbeit

⚘ **empty** ADJECTIVE
leer
an empty bottle eine leere Flasche

to **empty** VERB
1 (empty out) ausleeren SEP
2 (pour) schütten

to **enclose** VERB
(in a letter) beilegen SEP
Please find enclosed a cheque. Ein Scheck liegt bei.

to **encourage** VERB
ermutigen

⬦ **irregular verb;** SEP **separable verb; for more help with verbs see centre section**

to encourage somebody to do something
jemanden (dazu) ermutigen, etwas zu tun
Mum encouraged me to try again. Mutti
hat mich dazu ermutigt, es noch einmal zu
versuchen.

encouragement NOUN
die **Ermutigung** (PL die **Ermutigungen**)

encouraging ADJECTIVE
ermutigend

encyclopedia NOUN
das **Lexikon** (PL die **Lexika**)

℘ **end** NOUN
1 das **Ende** (PL die **Enden**)
'The End' 'Ende'
at the end of the film am Ende des Films
by the end of the lesson als die Stunde zu
Ende war
In the end I went home. Schließlich bin ich
nach Hause gegangen.
Sally's coming at the end of June. Sally
kommt Ende Juni.
I read to the end of the page. Ich habe die
Seite zu Ende gelesen.
Hold the other end. Halte das andere Ende
fest.
at the end of the street am Ende der Straße
2 (in sports) die **Spielfeldhälfte** (PL die
Spielfeldhälften)
to change ends die Seiten wechseln

to **end** VERB
1 (put an end to) **beenden**
They've ended the strike. Sie haben den
Streik beendet.
2 (come to an end) **enden**
The day ended with a meal. Der Tag endete
mit einem Essen.
The match ended in a draw. Das Spiel
endete unentschieden.
• **to end up**
1 **to end up doing something** am Ende etwas
tun
We ended up taking a taxi. Am Ende haben
wir ein Taxi genommen.
2 **to end up somewhere** irgendwo landen
(PERF **sein**) (informal)
Rob ended up in Berlin. Rob landete
schließlich in Berlin.

endangered ADJECTIVE
gefährdet
an endangered species eine von
Aussterben bedrohte Art

ending NOUN
1 das **Ende** (PL die **Enden**)
2 (in grammar) die **Endung** (PL die **Endungen**)

endless ADJECTIVE
endlos (day or journey, for example)

enemy NOUN
der **Feind** (PL die **Feinde**)
to make enemies sich (DAT) Feinde machen

energetic ADJECTIVE
energiegeladen

energy NOUN
die **Energie**

℘ **engaged** ADJECTIVE
1 (to be married) **verlobt**
They're engaged. Sie sind verlobt.
to get engaged sich verloben
2 (a phone or toilet) **besetzt**
It's engaged, I'll ring later. Es ist besetzt,
ich rufe später an.

engagement NOUN
(to marry) die **Verlobung** (PL die
Verlobungen)

engagement ring NOUN
der **Verlobungsring** (PL die
Verlobungsringe)

℘ **engine** NOUN
1 (in a car) der **Motor** (PL die **Motoren**)
2 (pulling a train) die **Lokomotive** (PL die
Lokomotiven)

℘ **engineer** NOUN
1 (who comes for repairs) der **Techniker** (PL
die **Techniker**), die **Technikerin** (PL die
Technikerinnen)
2 (who builds roads and bridges) der
Ingenieur (PL die **Ingenieure**), die
Ingenieurin (PL die **Ingenieurinnen**)

WORD TIP Professions, hobbies, and sports
don't take an article in German: Er ist Ingenieur.

---

engineering NOUN
das **Ingenieurwesen**
He's doing engineering at university. Er
studiert Ingenieurwesen.

℘ **England** NOUN
England (NEUTER)
I'm from England. Ich bin Engländer./Ich
bin Engländerin.

℘ **English** NOUN
1 (the language) das **Englisch**
Do you speak English? Sprechen Sie
Englisch?
He answered in English. Er hat auf Englisch
geantwortet.
2 (the people)
the English die Engländer

English ADJECTIVE
1 *(of or from England)* **englisch**
the English team die englische Mannschaft
He's English. Er ist Engländer.
She's English. Sie ist Engländerin.
2 an English lesson eine Englischstunde
our English teacher unser Englischlehrer/
unsere Englischlehrerin

> **WORD TIP** Adjectives never have capitals in German, even for regions, countries, or nationalities.

English Channel NOUN
the English Channel der Ärmelkanal

Englishman NOUN
der Engländer (PL die Engländer)
He's an Englishman. Er ist Engländer.

Englishwoman NOUN
die Engländerin (PL die Engländerinnen)
She's an Englishwoman. Sie ist
Engländerin.

ℒ **to enjoy** VERB
1 Did you enjoy the party? Hat dir die Party gefallen?
We really enjoyed the concert. Das Konzert hat uns wirklich gut gefallen.
2 to enjoy doing something etwas gerne tun◇
I enjoy reading. Ich lese gerne.
Do you enjoy living in York? Wohnst du gerne in York?
3 to enjoy yourself sich gut amüsieren
Did you enjoy yourself? Hast du dich gut amüsiert?
We really enjoyed ourselves. Wir haben uns richtig gut amüsiert.
Enjoy yourselves! Viel Vergnügen!

enjoyable ADJECTIVE
nett

enormous ADJECTIVE
riesig

ℒ **enough** ADVERB, ADJECTIVE, PRONOUN
1 genug
There's enough for everyone. Es gibt genug für alle.
big enough groß genug
Have we got enough bread? Haben wir genug Brot?
2 That's enough. Das reicht.

to enquire VERB
to enquire about sich erkundigen nach (+DAT)
I'm going to enquire about the trains. Ich werde mich nach den Zügen erkundigen.

to enrol VERB
sich anmelden SEP
I want to enrol on the course. Ich möchte mich zu dem Kurs anmelden.

ℒ **to enter** VERB
1 *(go inside)* gehen◇ *(PERF sein)* in *(+ACC)* *(a room or a building)*
We all entered the church. Wir gingen alle in die Kirche hinein.
2 *(in computing)* eingeben◇ SEP
3 to enter for sich anmelden SEP zu *(+DAT)* *(an exam or a race)*
I entered for the marathon. Ich habe mich zum Marathon angemeldet.
to enter for a competition an einem Preisausschreiben teilnehmen◇ SEP

to entertain VERB
1 *(keep amused)* unterhalten◇
2 *(have people round)* Gäste haben◇
They don't entertain much. Sie haben selten Gäste.

entertainment NOUN
(fun) die Unterhaltung
There wasn't much entertainment in the evenings. Abends war wenig Unterhaltung geboten.

enthusiasm NOUN
die Begeisterung

enthusiast NOUN
1 der Enthusiast (PL die Enthusiasten), die Enthusiastin (PL die Enthusiastinnen)
2 *(for sports)* der Fan (PL die Fans)
He's a rugby enthusiast. Er ist ein Rugbyfan.

enthusiastic ADJECTIVE
begeistert

entire ADJECTIVE
ganz
the entire class die ganze Klasse

entirely ADVERB
ganz

entrance NOUN
1 *(fee)* der Eintritt
2 *(way in)* der Eingang (PL die Eingänge)

entrance exam NOUN
die Aufnahmeprüfung (PL die Aufnahmeprüfungen)

entry NOUN
1 *(way in)* der Eingang (PL die Eingänge), *(for cars)* die Einfahrt (PL die Einfahrten)
2 'No entry' 'Zutritt verboten', *(to cars)* 'Einfahrt verboten'

entryphone *NOUN*
die **Sprechanlage** (PL die **Sprechanlagen**)

envelope *NOUN*
der **Briefumschlag** (PL die **Briefumschläge**)

envious *ADJECTIVE*
neidisch
I was very envious of them. Ich war sehr neidisch auf sie.

environment *NOUN*
die **Umwelt**

environmental *ADJECTIVE*
Umwelt-
environmental pollution die Umweltverschmutzung

environmentally friendly *ADJECTIVE*
umweltfreundlich

epidemic *NOUN*
die **Epidemie** (PL die **Epidemien**)

epileptic *ADJECTIVE*
epileptisch

episode *NOUN*
1 (an event) die **Episode** (PL die **Episoden**)
2 (on TV or radio) die **Folge** (PL die **Folgen**)

equal *ADJECTIVE*
gleich
milk and water in equal quantities gleich viel Milch und Wasser
equal opportunities die Chancengleichheit (SINGULAR)

to **equal** *VERB*
gleich sein◇
Two plus two equals four. Zwei plus zwei ist gleich vier.

equality *NOUN*
die **Gleichberechtigung**

to **equalize** *VERB*
ausgleichen ◇ SEP
They equalized in the last minute. Sie haben in der letzten Minute ausgeglichen.

equally *ADVERB*
(to share) gleichmäßig
We divided it equally. Wir haben es gleichmäßig verteilt.

equator *NOUN*
der **Äquator**

to **equip** *VERB*
ausrüsten SEP
well equipped for the hike für die Wanderung gut ausgerüstet
equipped with rucksacks mit Rucksäcken ausgerüstet

equipment *NOUN*
1 (for sport) die **Ausrüstung** (PL die **Ausrüstungen**)
2 die **Ausstattung** (PL die **Ausstattungen**)
laboratory equipment die Laborausstattung
3 (something needed for an activity) die **Geräte** (PLURAL)
recording equipment Aufnahmegeräte
a useful piece of equipment ein nützliches Gerät

equivalent *ADJECTIVE*
gleichwertig
to be equivalent to etwas (DAT) entsprechen◇
A litre is equivalent to about 1.75 pints. Ein Liter entspricht ungefähr 1,75 Pints.

error *NOUN*
1 (in spelling, typing, on a computer, or in maths) der **Fehler** (PL die **Fehler**)
spelling error der Rechtschreibfehler
2 (wrong opinion) der **Irrtum** (PL die **Irrtümer**)

error message *NOUN*
die **Fehlermeldung** (PL die **Fehlermeldungen**)

escalator *NOUN*
die **Rolltreppe** (PL die **Rolltreppen**)

escape *NOUN*
(from prison) der **Ausbruch** (PL die **Ausbrüche**)

to **escape** *VERB*
1 (from prison) ausbrechen◇ SEP (PERF sein)
2 entkommen◇ (PERF sein)
to escape from somebody jemandem entkommen

ᵱ **especially** *ADVERB*
besonders

essay *NOUN*
der **Aufsatz** (PL die **Aufsätze**)
an essay on German reunification ein Aufsatz über die deutsche Wiedervereinigung

essential *ADJECTIVE*
unbedingt erforderlich
It's essential to reply quickly. Es ist unbedingt erforderlich, sofort zu antworten.

estate *NOUN*
1 (a housing estate) die **Wohnsiedlung** (PL die **Wohnsiedlungen**)
2 (a big house and grounds) der **Landsitz** (PL die **Landsitze**)

estate agent NOUN
der **Immobilienmakler** (PL
die **Immobilienmakler**), die
Immobilienmaklerin (PL die
Immobilienmaklerinnen)

WORD TIP Professions, hobbies, and sports
don't take an article in German: Er ist
Immobilienmakler.

estate car NOUN
der **Kombiwagen** (PL die **Kombiwagen**)

estimate NOUN
1 (a quote for work) der **Kostenvoranschlag**
(PL die **Kostenvoranschläge**)
2 (a rough guess) die **Schätzung** (PL die
Schätzungen)
to **estimate** VERB
schätzen

etc. ABBREVIATION
usw. und so weiter

ethnic ADJECTIVE
ethnisch
an ethnic minority eine ethnische
Minderheit

EU NOUN
die **EU** Europäische Union

♀**euro** NOUN
der **Euro** (PL die **Euro**)
The euro is divided into 100 cents. Ein Euro
hat 100 Cent.

Europe NOUN
Europa (NEUTER)

♀**European** NOUN
der **Europäer** (PL die **Europäer**), die
Europäerin (PL die **Europäerinnen**)

European ADJECTIVE
europäisch

WORD TIP Adjectives never have capitals
in German, even for regions, countries, or
nationalities.

European Union NOUN
die **Europäische Union**

Eurozone NOUN
das **Euroland**

♀**even** ADVERB
1 sogar
Even Lisa is coming. Sogar Lisa kommt.
2 not even nicht einmal
I don't like animals, not even dogs. Ich
mag keine Tiere, nicht einmal Hunde.
She didn't even read the letter. Sie hat den
Brief noch nicht einmal gelesen.
3 without even asking ohne wenigstens zu

fragen
4 even if selbst wenn
even if they arrive late selbst wenn sie spät
ankommen
5 (with a comparison) (sogar) noch
even bigger sogar noch größer
even faster noch schneller
even better than sogar noch besser als
The song is even better than their last
one. Das Lied ist sogar noch besser als ihr
letztes.
6 even so trotzdem
Even so, we had a good time. Trotzdem
haben wir uns gut amüsiert.

even ADJECTIVE
1 (surface or layer) eben
2 (number) gerade
Six is an even number. Sechs ist eine
gerade Zahl.
3 (equal) gleich distance, value
The score is even. Die Punktzahl ist gleich.
4 to get even with somebody es jemandem
heimzahlen SEP

♀**evening** NOUN
1 der **Abend** (PL die **Abende**)
in the evening am Abend
this evening heute Abend
tomorrow evening morgen Abend
on Monday evening am Montagabend
every Thursday evening jeden
Donnerstagabend
the evening before am Abend zuvor
the evening meal das Abendessen
2 at six o'clock in the evening um sechs Uhr
abends
the other evening neulich abends
I work in the evening(s). Ich arbeite
abends.

evening class NOUN
der **Abendkurs** (PL die **Abendkurse**)

♀**event** NOUN
1 (a happening) das **Ereignis** (PL die
Ereignisse)
2 (in athletics) die **Disziplin** (PL die
Disziplinen)

eventually ADVERB
schließlich

WORD TIP Do not translate the English word
eventually with the German eventuell.

♀**ever** ADVERB
1 (at any time) je
Have you ever noticed that? Hast du das je
bemerkt?
more than ever mehr denn je

colder than ever kälter denn je
He drove more slowly than ever. Er fuhr langsamer als je zuvor.
Have you ever been to Spain? Bist du schon einmal in Spanien gewesen?
Have you ever played hockey? Hast du schon einmal Hockey gespielt?

2 *not ever* nie
Nobody ever came. Es kam nie jemand.
hardly ever fast nie

3 bloß
How ever did you do that? Wie hast du das bloß gemacht?

4 *(always)* immer
as cheerful as ever so vergnügt wie immer
the same as ever so wie immer

5 ever since seitdem
and it's been raining ever since und seitdem regnet es

6 ever so unheimlich *(informal)*
She's ever so nice. Sie ist unheimlich nett.

℘ **every** *ADJECTIVE*

1 jeder/jede/jedes
Every house has a garden. Jedes Haus hat einen Garten.
every day jeden Tag
every Monday jeden Montag
every time jedes Mal

2 every few days alle paar Tage
every ten kilometres alle zehn Kilometer

3 every one jeder Einzelne/jede Einzelne/ jedes Einzelne
I've seen every one of his films. Ich habe jeden Einzelnen seiner Filme gesehen.

4 every now and then ab und zu

℘ **everybody, everyone** *PRONOUN*

1 alle *(PLURAL)*
Everybody knows that ... Alle wissen, dass ...
everyone else alle anderen ...

2 *(each one)* jeder
Not everybody can afford it. Das kann sich nicht jeder leisten.

℘ **everything** *PRONOUN*
alles
Everything is ready. Es ist alles fertig.
Everything's fine. Es ist alles okay. *(informal)*
everything else alles andere
He gets everything he wants. Er bekommt alles, was er will.

℘ **everywhere** *ADVERB*

1 überall
There was dirt everywhere. Überall war Dreck.
She went everywhere. Sie ist überall

hingegangen.
everywhere else sonst überall

2 everywhere she went wohin sie auch ging

evidently *ADVERB*
offensichtlich

evil *NOUN*
das Böse
to fight against evil gegen das Böse kämpfen

evil *ADJECTIVE*
böse

exact *ADJECTIVE*
genau
the exact fare das genaue Fahrgeld
It's the exact opposite. Das ist das genaue Gegenteil.

exactly *ADVERB*
genau
They're exactly the right age. Sie sind genau im richtigen Alter.
Yes, exactly! Ja, genau!
It's not exactly cheap. Es ist nicht gerade billig.

to **exaggerate** *VERB*
übertreiben◇

exaggeration *NOUN*
die Übertreibung (PL die Übertreibungen)

℘ **exam** *NOUN*
die Prüfung (PL die Prüfungen)
history exam die Geschichtsprüfung
to sit an exam eine Prüfung machen
to pass an exam eine Prüfung bestehen◇
to fail an exam durch eine Prüfung fallen◇

examination *NOUN*
die Prüfung (PL die Prüfungen)

to **examine** *VERB*

1 *(at school or university)* prüfen

2 *(at the doctor's)* untersuchen

examiner *NOUN*
der Prüfer (PL die Prüfer), die Prüferin (PL die Prüferinnen)

℘ **example** *NOUN*
das Beispiel (PL die Beispiele)
for example zum Beispiel
to set a good example ein gutes Beispiel geben◇

to **exceed** *VERB*

1 *(amount)* übersteigen◇

2 *(limit)* überschreiten◇

℘ **excellent** *ADJECTIVE*
ausgezeichnet

℘ indicates key words

except PREPOSITION
1 außer (+DAT)
every day except Tuesday täglich außer Dienstag
We play except when it rains. Wir spielen, außer wenn es regnet.
except in March außer (im) März
2 except for außer (+DAT)
except for the children außer den Kindern

exception NOUN
die Ausnahme (PL die Ausnahmen)
without exception ohne Ausnahme
with the exception of mit Ausnahme von (+DAT)

exchange NOUN
der Austausch
I'm going on the German exchange.
Ich nehme an dem Austausch mit der deutschen Schule teil.
The students are coming to London on an exchange. Die Schüler kommen auf einen Schüleraustausch nach London.
exchange student der Austauschschüler (PL die Austauschschülerin)
3 in exchange for his help für seine Hilfe

to **exchange** VERB
umtauschen SEP
Can I exchange this shirt for a smaller one?
Kann ich dieses Hemd gegen ein kleineres umtauschen?

exchange rate NOUN
der Wechselkurs (PL die Wechselkurse)

to **excite** VERB
1 (thrill) begeistern
2 (agitate) aufregen SEP

excited ADJECTIVE
1 aufgeregt
The children are excited. Die Kinder sind aufgeregt.
The dogs get excited when they hear the car. Die Hunde geraten in Aufregung, wenn sie das Auto hören.
2 (annoyed or angry)
to get excited sich aufregen SEP

excitement NOUN
die Aufregung

exciting ADJECTIVE
aufregend
a very exciting film ein sehr aufregender Film

exclamation mark NOUN
das Ausrufezeichen (PL die Ausrufezeichen)

excursion NOUN
der Ausflug (PL die Ausflüge)

excuse NOUN
die Entschuldigung (PL die Entschuldigungen)

to **excuse** VERB
(apologizing)
Excuse me! Entschuldigung!

exercise NOUN
1 die Übung (PL die Übungen)
a maths exercise eine Matheübung
2 physical exercise körperliche Bewegung
to get exercise sich Bewegung verschaffen

exercise bike NOUN
der Heimtrainer (PL die Heimtrainer)

exercise book NOUN
das Heft (PL die Hefte)
my German exercise book mein Deutschheft

exhaust (pipe) NOUN
der Auspuff (PL die Auspuffe)

exhausted ADJECTIVE
erschöpft

exhaust fumes PLURAL NOUN
die Abgase (PLURAL)

exhibition NOUN
die Ausstellung (PL die Ausstellungen)
the Dürer exhibition die Dürer-Ausstellung

to **exist** VERB
existieren

exit NOUN
1 der Ausgang (PL die Ausgänge)
2 (for a car) die Ausfahrt (PL die Ausfahrten)
Leave the motorway at exit 20. Fahren Sie bei der Ausfahrt 20 von der Autobahn ab.

to **expect** VERB
1 erwarten (visitors or a baby)
We're expecting thirty visitors. Wir erwarten dreißig Besucher.
2 (require something)
to expect somebody to do something von jemandem erwarten, dass er etwas tut
3 rechnen mit (+DAT) (something to happen)
I didn't expect that. Damit habe ich nicht gerechnet.
I didn't expect it at all. Damit habe ich überhaupt nicht gerechnet.
4 (suppose) annehmen ◇ SEP
I expect she'll bring her boyfriend. Ich nehme an, sie bringt ihren Freund mit.
Yes, I expect so. Ich glaube ja.

◇ irregular verb; SEP separable verb; for more help with verbs see centre section

expedition NOUN
  die Expedition (PL die Expeditionen)

to expel VERB
  to be expelled (from school) von der Schule
  verwiesen werden

ℱ **expensive** ADJECTIVE
  teuer
  Those shoes are too expensive for me.
  Diese Schuhe sind mir zu teuer.
  the most expensive clothes die teuersten
  Kleidung

experience NOUN
1 die Erfahrung (PL die Erfahrungen)
2 (an event) das Erlebnis (PL die Erlebnisse)

experienced ADJECTIVE
  erfahren

experiment NOUN
  das Experiment (PL die Experimente)
  to do an experiment ein Experiment
  machen
  experiments on animals Tierversuche

expert NOUN
  der Experte (PL die Experten), die Expertin
  (PL die Expertinnen)
  He's a computer expert. Er ist ein
  Computerexperte.

to expire VERB
  ablaufen◇ SEP (PERF sein)

expiry date NOUN
  das Verfallsdatum (PL die Verfallsdaten)

ℱ **to explain** VERB
  erklären

ℱ **explanation** NOUN
  die Erklärung (PL die Erklärungen)

to explode VERB
  explodieren (PERF sein)

to explore VERB
  erforschen

explosion NOUN
  die Explosion (PL die Explosionen)

export NOUN
  der Export (PL die Exporte)
  The chief export is wool. Das wichtigste
  Exportgut ist Wolle.

to export VERB
  exportieren
  Russia exports a lot of oil and timber.
  Russland exportiert viel Öl und Holz.

ℱ **to express** VERB
1 ausdrücken SEP
2 **to express yourself** sich ausdrücken

expression NOUN
  der Ausdruck (PL die Ausdrücke)

to extend VERB
1 verlängern
2 ausbauen SEP (a house)

extension NOUN
1 (to a house) der Anbau (PL die Anbauten)
2 (telephone) der Apparat (PL die Apparate)
  Can I have extension 2347 please? Bitte
  verbinden Sie mich mit Apparat 2347. (note
  that in spoken German telephone numbers
  are usually broken down into groups of two
  figures)
3 (electrical) die Verlängerung (PL die
  Verlängerungen)

extension number NOUN
  die Durchwahl (PL die Durchwahlen)

exterior ADJECTIVE
  äußerer/äußere/äußeres

extinct ADJECTIVE
1 (animal) ausgestorben
2 (volcano) erloschen

to extinguish VERB
1 löschen a fire
2 **to extinguish a cigarette** eine Zigarette
  ausmachen SEP

extinguisher NOUN
  der Feuerlöscher (PL die Feuerlöscher)

extra ADJECTIVE
1 zusätzlich, extra (informal)
  extra homework zusätzliche Hausaufgaben
  Wine is extra. Wein kostet extra.
  You have to pay extra. Das wird extra
  berechnet.
2 **at no extra charge** ohne Aufschlag

extra ADVERB
1 besonders
  He was extra careful. Er war besonders
  vorsichtig.
2 **extra large** extragroß

  WORD TIP The German adjective extra never
  has an ending.

ℱ **extraordinary** ADJECTIVE
  außerordentlich

extra time NOUN
  (in football) die Verlängerung (PL die
  Verlängerungen)
  to go into extra time in die Verlängerung
  gehen

ℱ indicates key words

extravagant *ADJECTIVE*
verschwenderisch *(person)*

extreme *NOUN*
das Extrem (*PL* die Extreme)
to go from one extreme to another von
einem Extrem ins andere fallen

extreme *ADJECTIVE*
extrem
extreme sports der Extremsport

ℐ **extremely** *ADVERB*
äußerst
extremely fast äußerst schnell

ℐ **eye** *NOUN*
das Auge (*PL* die Augen)
a girl with blue eyes ein Mädchen mit
blauen Augen
Shut your eyes! Mach die Augen zu!
to keep an eye on something auf etwas
(ACC) aufpassen *SEP*

eyebrow *NOUN*
die Augenbraue (*PL* die Augenbrauen)

eyelash *NOUN*
die Augenwimper (*PL* die Augenwimpern)

eyelid *NOUN*
das Augenlid (*PL* die Augenlider)

eyeliner *NOUN*
der Eyeliner (*PL* die Eyeliner)

eye shadow *NOUN*
der Lidschatten (*PL* die Lidschatten)

eyesight *NOUN*
to have good eyesight gute Augen haben
to have bad eyesight schlechte Augen
haben

Ff

fabric *NOUN*
(cloth) der Stoff (*PL* die Stoffe)

> **WORD TIP** Do not translate the English word
> fabric with the German Fabrik.

ℐ **fabulous** *ADJECTIVE*
fantastisch

ℐ **face** *NOUN*
1 *(of a person)* das Gesicht (*PL* die Gesichter)
to pull a face eine Grimasse schneiden
2 *(of a clock or watch)* das Zifferblatt (*PL* die
Zifferblätter)

to **face** *VERB*
1 gegenüberstehen◇ *SEP* *(PERF* sein*)* *(+DAT)*
She was facing him. Sie stand ihm
gegenüber.
2 The house faces the park. Das Haus
befindet sich gegenüber dem Park.
3 stehen vor *(DAT)* *(a problem or a decision)*
4 *(stand the idea of)* fertigbringen◇ *SEP*
I can't face going back. Ich bringe es nicht
fertig zurückzugehen.
5 to face up to something sich etwas *(DAT)*
stellen

facilities *PLURAL NOUN*
1 The school has good sports facilities. Die
Schule hat gute Sportanlagen.
2 The flat has no cooking facilities. Die
Wohnung hat keine Kochgelegenheit.

fact *NOUN*
die Tatsache (*PL* die Tatsachen)
The fact is that ... Tatsache ist, dass ...
in fact tatsächlich
Is that a fact? Tatsache?

ℐ **factory** *NOUN*
die Fabrik (*PL* die Fabriken)

to **fade** *VERB*
1 *(fabric)* ausbleichen◇ *SEP* *(PERF* sein*)*
faded jeans ausgeblichene Jeans
2 *(a colour or memory)* verblassen *(PERF* sein*)*
The colours have faded. Die Farben sind
verblasst.

ℐ to **fail** *VERB*
1 nicht bestehen◇ a test or an exam
I failed my driving test. Ich habe meine
Fahrprüfung nicht bestanden.
2 *(in a test or an exam)* durchfallen◇ *SEP* *(PERF*
sein*)*
Three students failed. Drei Studenten sind
durchgefallen.
3 to fail to do something etwas nicht tun
He failed to inform us. Er hat uns nicht
benachrichtigt.
without fail auf jeden Fall
Ring me without fail. Ruf mich auf jeden
Fall an.

failure *NOUN*
1 der Misserfolg (*PL* die Misserfolge)
It was a terrible failure. Es war ein
schrecklicher Misserfolg.
2 *(of equipment)* der Ausfall (*PL* die Ausfälle)
a power failure ein Stromausfall

ℐ **faint** *ADJECTIVE*
1 *(slight)* leicht
a faint smell of gas ein leichter Gasgeruch
2 *(voice or sound)* leise

◇ irregular verb; *SEP* separable verb; for more help with verbs see centre section

3 I haven't the faintest idea. Ich habe nicht die leiseste Ahnung. *(informal)*

to faint VERB
ohnmächtig werden◇
Lisa fainted. Lisa wurde ohnmächtig.

ᵖ**fair** NOUN
der **Jahrmarkt** (PL die **Jahrmärkte**)

fair ADJECTIVE
1 *(not unfair)* gerecht
2 *(hair)* blond
He's fair-haired. Er ist blond.
3 *(skin)* hell
fair-skinned hellhäutig
4 *(fairly good)* ganz gut *(chance, condition, or performance)*
5 *(weather)* schön
If it's fair tomorrow, ... Wenn es morgen schön ist, ...

fairground NOUN
der **Jahrmarkt** (PL die **Jahrmärkte**)

fairly ADVERB
1 *(quite)* ziemlich
2 *(not unfairly)* gerecht

fairy NOUN
die **Fee** (PL die **Feen**)

fairy story, **fairy tale** NOUN
das **Märchen** (PL die **Märchen**)

faith NOUN
1 *(trust)* das **Vertrauen**
to have faith in somebody Vertrauen zu jemandem haben
2 *(religious belief)* der **Glaube** (PL die **Glauben**)

faithful ADJECTIVE
treu
to be faithful to somebody jemandem treu sein

faithfully ADVERB
Yours faithfully Hochachtungsvoll

fake NOUN
1 die **Imitation** (PL die **Imitationen**)
The diamonds were fakes. Die Brillanten waren eine Imitation.
2 *(a painting or money)* die **Fälschung** (PL die **Fälschungen**)

fake ADJECTIVE
gefälscht
a fake passport ein gefälschter Pass

ᵖ**fall** NOUN
to have a fall stürzen *(PERF sein)*

to fall VERB
1 fallen◇ *(PERF sein)*
Mind you don't fall. Pass auf, dass du

nicht hinfällst.
Tony fell off his bike. Tony ist vom Rad gefallen.
She fell down the stairs. Sie ist die Treppe hinuntergefallen.
2 *(of temperature, prices)* sinken◇ *(PERF sein)*

ᵖ**false** ADJECTIVE
falsch
a false alarm ein falscher Alarm

fame NOUN
der **Ruhm**

familiar ADJECTIVE
bekannt
His face is familiar. Sein Gesicht kommt mir bekannt vor.

ᵖ**family** NOUN
die **Familie** (PL die **Familien**)
a family of six eine sechsköpfige Familie
Ben's one of the family. Ben gehört zur Familie.
the Morris family Familie Morris
My family are all tall. In meiner Familie sind alle groß.
All the family live in London. Die ganze Familie wohnt in London.

famine NOUN
die **Hungersnot**

famous ADJECTIVE
berühmt

fan NOUN
1 *(a supporter)* der **Fan** (PL die **Fans**)
Will's a Chelsea fan. Will ist ein Fan von Chelsea.
2 *(electric, for cooling)* der **Ventilator** (PL die **Ventilatoren**)
3 *(hand-held)* der **Fächer** (PL die **Fächer**)

fanatic NOUN
der **Fanatiker** (PL die **Fanatiker**), die **Fanatikerin** (PL die **Fanatikerinnen**)

fancy NOUN
to take somebody's fancy jemandem gefallen◇
The picture took his fancy. Das Bild gefiel ihm.

fancy ADJECTIVE
(equipment) ausgefallen

to fancy VERB
1 *(want)*
(Do you) fancy a coffee? Hast du Lust auf einen Kaffee?
Do you fancy going to the cinema? Hast du Lust, ins Kino zu gehen?

2 I really fancy him. Ich stehe total auf ihn.
(informal)
3 (Just) fancy that! Stell dir vor!
Fancy you being here! Na so was, dich hier
zu treffen!

fancy dress NOUN
in fancy dress verkleidet
fancy dress party das Kostümfest

ℰ **fantastic** ADJECTIVE
fantastisch
Really? That's fantastic! Wirklich? Das ist ja
fantastisch!
a fantastic holiday fantastische Ferien

ℰ **far** ADVERB, ADJECTIVE
1 weit
It's not far. Es ist nicht weit.
Is it far to Carlisle? Ist es weit nach Carlisle?
How far is it to Bristol? Wie weit ist es bis
nach Bristol?
Do you live far from Berlin? Wohnen Sie
weit von Berlin entfernt?
2 He took us as far as Newport. Er hat uns bis
Newport mitgenommen.
3 by far bei weitem
the prettiest by far bei weitem das
hübscheste
4 (much) viel
far better viel besser
far faster viel schneller
far too many people viel zu viele Leute
5 so far bis jetzt
So far everything's going well. Bis jetzt
läuft alles gut.
6 as far as I know soweit ich weiß

ℰ **fare** NOUN
1 (on a bus, train, or the underground) der
Fahrpreis (PL die **Fahrpreise**)
half fare der halbe Fahrpreis
full fare der volle Fahrpreis
2 (on a plane) der **Flugpreis** (PL die
Flugpreise)

Far East NOUN
the Far East der Ferne Osten, Fernost

ℰ **farm** NOUN
der **Bauernhof** (PL die **Bauernhöfe**)

ℰ **farmer** NOUN
der **Bauer** (PL die **Bauern**), die **Bäuerin**
(PL die **Bäuerinnen**)

WORD TIP Professions, hobbies, and sports
don't take an article in German: Er ist Bauer.

farmhouse NOUN
das **Bauernhaus** (PL die **Bauernhäuser**)

farming NOUN
die **Landwirtschaft**

fascinating ADJECTIVE
faszinierend

fashion NOUN
die **Mode** (PL die **Moden**)
in fashion in Mode
to go out of fashion aus der Mode kommen

fashionable ADJECTIVE
modisch

fashion designer NOUN
der **Modeschöpfer** (PL die **Modeschöpfer**),
die **Modeschöpferin** (PL die
Modeschöpferinnen)

fashion show NOUN
die **Modenschau** (PL die **Modenschauen**)

ℰ **fast** ADJECTIVE
1 schnell
a fast car ein schnelles Auto
2 of a clock or watch to be fast vorgehen◇
SEP (PERF **sein**)
My watch is fast. Meine Uhr geht vor.
You're ten minutes fast. Deine Uhr geht
zehn Minuten vor.

fast ADVERB
1 schnell
He swims fast. Er schwimmt schnell.
2 to be fast asleep fest schlafen

WORD TIP Do not translate the English word
fast with the German fast.

fast food NOUN
das **Fast Food**

fast forward NOUN
der **Vorlauf**

ℰ **fat** NOUN
das **Fett** (PL die **Fette**)

fat ADJECTIVE
1 (meat) fett
2 (person) dick, fett *(informal)*
a fat man ein dicker Mann
to get fat fett werden *(informal)*

fatal ADJECTIVE
tödlich

ℰ **father** NOUN
der **Vater** (PL die **Väter**)
my father's office das Büro von meinem
Vater

Father Christmas NOUN
der **Weihnachtsmann**

father-in-law NOUN
der **Schwiegervater** (PL die
Schwiegerväter)

◇ **irregular verb;** SEP **separable verb; for more help with verbs see centre section**

Father's Day NOUN
  der **Vatertag**

ℱ **fault** NOUN
  1 *(when you are responsible)* die **Schuld**
    It's Stephen's fault. Stephen ist schuld.
    It's not my fault. Es ist nicht meine Schuld.
  2 *(in tennis)* der **Fehler** (PL die **Fehler**)
    double fault der Doppelfehler

ℱ **favour** NOUN
  1 *(a kindness)* der **Gefallen** (PL die **Gefallen**)
    to do somebody a favour jemandem einen
    Gefallen tun◇
    Can you do me a favour? Kannst du mir
    einen Gefallen tun?
    to ask a favour of somebody jemanden um
    einen Gefallen bitten
  2 **to be in favour of something** für etwas
    (ACC) sein

ℱ **favourite** ADJECTIVE
  Lieblings-
  my favourite band meine Lieblingsband

ℱ **fear** NOUN
  die **Angst** (PL die **Ängste**)
to **fear** VERB
  fürchten

feather NOUN
  die **Feder** (PL die **Federn**)

feature NOUN
  1 *(of your face)* der **Gesichtszug** (PL die
    Gesichtszüge)
    to have delicate features feine
    Gesichtszüge haben
  2 *(of a car or a machine)* das **Merkmal** (PL die
    Merkmale)

ℱ **February** NOUN
  der **Februar**
  in February im Februar

ℱ **fed up** ADJECTIVE
  1 **I'm fed up.** Ich habe die Nase voll. *(informal)*
    He's fed up with her. Er hat die Nase voll
    von ihr.
  2 **to be fed up with something** etwas *(ACC)*
    satt haben *(informal)*
    I'm fed up with working every day. Ich
    habe es satt, jeden Tag zu arbeiten.

to **feed** VERB
  füttern
  Have you fed the dog? Hast du den Hund
  gefüttert?

to **feel** VERB
  1 **sich fühlen**
    I don't feel well. Ich fühle mich nicht gut.

  2 **spüren**
    I didn't feel a thing. Ich habe nichts
    gespürt.
  3 **I feel tired.** Ich bin müde.
    I feel cold. Mir ist kalt.
  4 **to feel afraid** Angst haben
    to feel thirsty Durst haben
  5 **to feel like doing something** Lust haben,
    etwas zu tun
    I feel like going to the cinema. Ich habe
    Lust, ins Kino zu gehen.
  6 *(touch)* **fühlen**
  7 *(to the touch)* **sich anfühlen** SEP
    to feel soft sich weich anfühlen

feeling NOUN
  1 das **Gefühl** (PL die **Gefühle**)
    to show your feelings seine Gefühle zeigen
    a dizzy feeling ein Schwindelgefühl
    I have the feeling James doesn't like me.
    Ich habe das Gefühl, dass James mich nicht
    mag.
  2 **to hurt somebody's feelings** jemanden
    verletzen

felt-tip (pen) NOUN
  der **Filzstift** (PL die **Filzstifte**)

female NOUN
  (animal) das **Weibchen** (PL die **Weibchen**)

female ADJECTIVE
  weiblich

feminine ADJECTIVE
  weiblich

feminist NOUN
  die **Feministin** (PL die **Feministinnen**),
  der **Feminist** (PL die **Feministen**)

feminist ADJECTIVE
  feministisch

fence NOUN
  der **Zaun** (PL die **Zäune**)

ferry NOUN
  die **Fähre** (PL die **Fähren**)

fertilizer NOUN
  das **Düngemittel**

festival NOUN
  1 *(of pop music, jazz, etc.)* das **Festival** (PL die
    Festivals)
  2 *(of films, theatre, or classical music)* die
    Festspiele (PLURAL)

to **fetch** VERB
  1 *(collect)* **abholen** SEP
    Tom's fetching the children. Tom holt die
    Kinder ab.
  2 **holen**

ℱ indicates key words

Fetch me the other knife. Hol mir das andere Messer.

fever NOUN
das Fieber

ℓ **few** ADJECTIVE, PRONOUN
1 wenige
Few people know that ... Wenige Leute wissen, dass ...
2 a few (several) ein paar
a few weeks ein paar Wochen
in a few minutes in ein paar Minuten
Have you got any tomatoes? We want a few for the salad. Haben Sie Tomaten? Wir brauchen ein paar für den Salat.
3 quite a few eine ganze Menge
There were quite a few questions. Es gab eine ganze Menge Fragen

WORD TIP The German expression ein paar never has an ending.

ℓ **fewer** ADJECTIVE
weniger
There are fewer mosquitoes this year. Dieses Jahr gibt es weniger Mücken.

ℓ **fiancé** NOUN
der Verlobte (PL die Verlobten)

ℓ **fiancée** NOUN
die Verlobte (PL die Verlobten)

fiction NOUN
die Romane (PLURAL)

ℓ **field** NOUN
1 (with grass or crops) das Feld (PL die Felder)
a field of wheat ein Kornfeld
2 (for sport) das Spielfeld (PL die Spielfelder)

fierce ADJECTIVE
1 wild (animal or person)
2 heftig (storm or battle)

ℓ **fifteen** NUMBER
fünfzehn

ℓ **fifth** NUMBER
fünfter/fünfte/fünftes
the fifth of January der fünfte Januar
on the fifth floor im fünften Stock

ℓ **fifty** NUMBER
fünfzig

fig NOUN
die Feige (PL die Feigen)

fight NOUN
1 (a scuffle) die Schlägerei (PL die Schlägereien)
2 (in boxing or against illness) der Kampf

(PL die Kämpfe)

to **fight** VERB
1 (have a fight) sich prügeln
They were fighting. Sie haben sich geprügelt.
2 (quarrel) sich streiten◇
They're always fighting. Sie streiten sich immer.
3 (struggle against) kämpfen gegen (+ACC) (poverty or a disease)

figure NOUN
1 (number) die Zahl (PL die Zahlen)
a four-figure number eine vierstellige Zahl
2 (body shape) die Figur
good for your figure gut für die Figur
3 (a person) die Gestalt (PL die Gestalten)

to **figure** VERB
to figure something out etwas herausfinden◇ SEP the answer or reason

file NOUN
1 (for records of a person or case) die Akte (PL die Akten)
2 (ring binder or folder) der Ordner (PL die Ordner)
3 (on a computer) die Datei (PL die Dateien)
4 a nail file eine Nagelfeile

to **file** VERB
1 ablegen SEP (documents)
2 to file your nails sich (DAT) die Nägel feilen

ℓ to **fill** VERB
1 füllen (a container)
She filled my glass. Sie füllte mein Glas.
2 to be filled with people voller Menschen sein
filled with smoke voller Rauch
• to fill in
ausfüllen SEP (a form)

filling NOUN
(of a pie, in a tooth) die Füllung (PL die Füllungen)

ℓ **film** NOUN
(in a cinema and for a camera) der Film (PL die Filme)
Shall we go and see the new Batman film? Wollen wir uns den neuen Batman-Film ansehen?
a film about sharks ein Film über Haie
to make a film einen Film drehen
a 24-exposure colour film ein Farbfilm mit 24 Aufnahmen

film star NOUN
der Filmstar (PL die Filmstars)

◇ irregular verb; SEP separable verb; for more help with verbs see centre section

filter *NOUN*
der **Filter** (PL die **Filter**)

ℙ **filthy** *ADJECTIVE*
dreckig

final *NOUN*
(in sport) das **Endspiel** (PL die **Endspiele**)

final *ADJECTIVE*
letzter/letzte/letztes
the final instalment die letzte Folge
the final result das Endergebnis

ℙ **finally** *ADVERB*
schließlich

ℙ **to find** *VERB*
finden◇
Did you find your passport? Hast du deinen Pass gefunden?
I can't find my keys. Ich kann meine Schlüssel nicht finden.
• **to find out**
1 *(enquire)* sich informieren
I don't know. I'll find out. Das weiß ich nicht. Ich werde mich informieren.
2 **to find something out** etwas *(ACC)* herausfinden◇ *SEP (the facts or an answer)*
when she found out the truth als sie die Wahrheit herausfand

fine *NOUN*
das **Bußgeld** (PL die **Bußgelder**) *(for parking or speeding)*

fine *ADJECTIVE*
1 *(in good health)* gut
'How are you?' – 'Fine, thanks.' 'Wie gehts?' – 'Danke, gut.'
I'm fine. Mir geht es gut.
2 *(convenient)* in Ordnung
Ten o'clock? Yes, that's fine! Zehn Uhr? Ja, in Ordnung!
Friday will be fine. Freitag geht in Ordnung.
3 *(sunny)* schön *(weather or day)*
If it's fine, ... Wenn es schön ist, ...
in fine weather bei schönem Wetter
4 *(not coarse or thick)* fein

finely *ADVERB*
fein *(chopped or grated)*

ℙ **finger** *NOUN*
der **Finger** (PL die **Finger**)
I'll keep my fingers crossed for you. Ich drücke dir die Daumen.

fingernail *NOUN*
der **Fingernagel** (PL die **Fingernägel**)

ℙ **finish** *NOUN*
1 *(end)* der **Schluss** (PL die **Schlüsse**)

2 *(in a race)* das **Ziel** (PL die **Ziele**)

to finish *VERB*
1 beenden *(a conversation or quarrel)*
to finish a discussion ein Gespräch beenden
to be finished with something mit etwas *(DAT)* fertig sein *(work or a project)*
Have you finished your homework? Bist du mit den Hausaufgaben fertig?
Wait, I haven't finished! Warte, ich bin noch nicht fertig!
2 *(finish off)*
to finish doing something etwas beenden
Have you finished (reading) the letter? Hast du den Brief zu Ende gelesen?
He hasn't yet finished (writing) the report. Er hat den Bericht noch nicht zu Ende geschrieben.
3 *(come to an end)* zu Ende sein, aus sein *(informal) (a meeting or performance)*
The film finishes at ten o'clock. Der Film ist um zehn Uhr zu Ende.
When does school finish? Wann ist die Schule aus?
• **to finish with**
(complete your use of) nicht mehr brauchen
When you've finished with these clothes, give them back to me. Wenn du die Sachen nicht mehr brauchst, gib sie mir zurück.
Have you finished with the computer? Brauchen Sie den Computer noch?

Finland *NOUN*
Finnland *(NEUTER)*

Finnish *NOUN*
(the language) das **Finnisch**

Finnish *ADJECTIVE*
finnisch
the Finnish coast die finnische Küste
He's Finnish. Er ist Finne.
She's Finnish. Sie ist Finnin.

> **WORD TIP** Adjectives never have capitals in German, even for regions, countries, or nationalities.

ℙ **fire** *NOUN*
1 *(in a grate)* das **Kaminfeuer** (PL die **Kaminfeuer**)
to light the fire das Feuer im Kamin anmachen *SEP*
2 *(accidental)* das **Feuer** (PL die **Feuer**)
to catch fire *(fabric, furnishings)* Feuer fangen◇
3 *(in a building or forest)* der **Brand** (PL die **Brände**)
to set fire to a factory eine Fabrik in Brand stecken
4 **to be on fire** brennen◇

ℙ indicates key words

to fire VERB
1 *(with a gun)* schießen◇
   to fire at somebody auf jemanden schießen
2 abfeuern SEP a gun

fire alarm NOUN
   der Feuermelder (PL die Feuermelder)

fire brigade NOUN
   die Feuerwehr

fire engine NOUN
   das Feuerwehrauto (PL die Feuerwehrautos)

fire escape NOUN
   die Feuertreppe (PL die Feuertreppen)

fire extinguisher NOUN
   der Feuerlöscher (PL die Feuerlöscher)

firefighter NOUN
   der Feuerwehrmann (PL die Feuerwehrleute), die Feuerwehrfrau (PL die Feuerwehrfrauen)

> **WORD TIP** Professions, hobbies, and sports don't take an article in German: Er ist Feuerwehrmann.

fireplace NOUN
   der Kamin (PL die Kamine)

fire station NOUN
   die Feuerwache (PL die Feuerwachen)

firework NOUN
   der Feuerwerkskörper (PL die Feuerwerkskörper)
   firework display das Feuerwerk

firm NOUN
   (business) die Firma (PL die Firmen)

firm ADJECTIVE
1 fest
2 *(strict)* streng

𝒫**first** ADJECTIVE
   erster/erste/erstes
   the first of May der erste Mai
   for the first time zum ersten Mal
   I was the first to arrive. Ich kam als Erster/Erste an.
   Susan was first. Susan war die Erste.
   to come first in the 100 metres beim Hundertmeterlauf Erster/Erste werden

first ADVERB
1 *(to begin with)* zuerst
   First, I'm going to make some tea. Zuerst mache ich Tee.
2 **at first** zuerst
   At first he was shy. Er war zuerst schüchtern.

3 *(for the first time)* zum ersten Mal
   I first went to Germany in 2006. Ich bin 2006 zum ersten Mal nach Deutschland gefahren.

first aid NOUN
   die erste Hilfe

first class ADJECTIVE
   (ticket, carriage, or hotel) erster Klasse *(goes after the noun)*
   a first-class hotel ein Hotel erster Klasse
   He always travels first class. Er reist immer erster Klasse.
   a first-class compartment ein Erste-Klasse-Abteil

first floor NOUN
   der erste Stock
   on the first floor im ersten Stock

firstly ADVERB
   zunächst

𝒫**first name** NOUN
   der Vorname (PL die Vornamen)

fir tree NOUN
   die Tanne (PL die Tannen)

𝒫**fish** NOUN
   der Fisch (PL die Fische)

to fish VERB
   fischen, *(with a rod)* angeln

fish and chips NOUN
   ausgebackener Fisch mit Pommes frites

𝒫**fisherman** NOUN
   der Fischer (PL die Fischer)

> **WORD TIP** Professions, hobbies, and sports don't take an article in German: Er ist Fischer.

fish finger NOUN
   das Fischstäbchen (PL die Fischstäbchen)

𝒫**fishing** NOUN
   das Fischen, *(with a rod)* das Angeln
   to go fishing fischen/angeln gehen

fishing rod NOUN
   die Angel (PL die Angeln)

fishing tackle NOUN
   die Angelausrüstung

𝒫**fist** NOUN
   die Faust (PL die Fäuste)

𝒫**fit** NOUN
   der Anfall (PL die Anfälle)
   an epileptic fit ein epileptischer Anfall
   Your dad'll have a fit when he sees your hair. Dein Vater kriegt bestimmt einen Anfall, wenn er deine Haare sieht.

◇ irregular verb; SEP separable verb; for more help with verbs see centre section

fit ADJECTIVE
(healthy) **fit**
I feel really fit. Ich fühle mich richtig fit.
to keep fit fit bleiben

to **fit** VERB
1 (be the right size for) (of shoes or clothes)
passen (+DAT)
This skirt doesn't fit me. Der Rock passt mir nicht.
2 (be able to be put into) **passen in** (+ACC)
Will my cases all fit in the car? Passen meine Koffer alle in das Auto?
The key doesn't fit in the lock. Der Schlüssel passt nicht ins Schloss.
3 (install) **einbauen** SEP

fitted carpet NOUN
der **Teppichboden** (PL die **Teppichböden**)

fitted kitchen NOUN
die **Einbauküche** (PL die **Einbauküchen**)

fitting room NOUN
die **Umkleidekabine** (PL die **Umkleidekabinen**)

⅁ **five** NUMBER
fünf
It's five o'clock. Es ist fünf Uhr.

to **fix** VERB
1 (repair) **reparieren**
Mum's fixed the computer. Mutti hat den Computer repariert.
2 (decide on) **festlegen** SEP
to fix a date einen Termin festlegen
3 **machen** (a meal)
I'll fix supper. Ich mache Abendessen.

fizzy ADJECTIVE
sprudelnd
fizzy water das Sprudelwasser

flag NOUN
die **Fahne** (PL die **Fahnen**)

flame NOUN
die **Flamme** (PL die **Flammen**)

flan NOUN
der **Kuchen** (PL die **Kuchen**)
fruit flan der Obstkuchen

to **flap** VERB
of a bird to flap its wings mit den Flügeln schlagen◇

flash NOUN
(on a camera) der **Blitz** (PL die **Blitze**)
flash of lightning der Blitz

to **flash** VERB
1 (a light) **aufleuchten** SEP, (repeatedly)
blinken

2 to flash by or past **vorbeiflitzen** SEP
(informal)

flashback NOUN
die **Rückblende** (PL die **Rückblenden**)

⅁ **flat** NOUN
die **Wohnung** (PL die **Wohnungen**)
a third-floor flat eine Wohnung im dritten Stock

flat ADJECTIVE
1 **flach**
flat shoes flache Schuhe
a flat landscape eine flache Landschaft
2 a flat tyre ein platter Reifen

flatmate NOUN
der **Mitbewohner** (PL die **Mitbewohner**) die **Mitbewohnerin**, (PL die **Mitbewohnerinnen**)

flatter NOUN
schmeicheln (+DAT)

⅁ **flavour** NOUN
1 der **Geschmack** (PL die **Geschmäcke**)
The sauce has a bitter flavour. Die Soße hat einen bitteren Geschmack.
strawberry flavour der Erdbeergeschmack
2 (of drinks, coffee, or tea) das **Aroma** (PL die **Aromen**)

to **flavour** VERB
würzen
vanilla-flavoured mit Vanillegeschmack

flea NOUN
der **Floh** (PL die **Flöhe**)

flesh NOUN
das **Fleisch**

flex NOUN
das **Kabel** (PL die **Kabel**)

⅁ **flight** NOUN
1 der **Flug** (PL die **Flüge**)
The flight was delayed. Der Flug hatte Verspätung.
charter flight der Charterflug
The flight from Munich to London takes an hour and a half. Die Flugzeit von München nach London beträgt eineinhalb Stunden.
2 flight of stairs die Treppe

flight attendant NOUN
der **Flugbegleiter** (PL die **Flugbegleiter**), die **Flugbegleiterin** (PL die **Flugbegleiterinnen**)

WORD TIP Professions, hobbies, and sports don't take an article in German: Er ist Flugbegleiter.

flipper NOUN
die **Flosse** (PL die **Flossen**)

⅁ indicates key words

to **flirt** VERB
flirten

to **float** VERB
1 (on water) **treiben**◇
2 (in the air) **schweben**

flood NOUN
1 (of water) die **Überschwemmung** (PL die Überschwemmungen)
2 to be in floods of tears in Tränen aufgelöst sein
3 (of letters or complaints) die **Flut**

to **flood** VERB
überschwemmen

floodlight NOUN
das **Flutlicht**

ℙ**floor** NOUN
1 der **Boden** (PL die Böden)
Your glasses are on the floor. Deine Brille liegt auf dem Boden.
2 to sweep the floor **fegen**
to sweep the kitchen floor die Küche fegen
3 (a storey) der **Stock** (PL die Stock)
on the second floor im zweiten Stock

WORD TIP Do not translate the English word floor with the German Flur.

florist NOUN
der **Blumenhändler** (PL die Blumenhändler), die **Blumenhändlerin** (PL die Blumenhändlerinnen)

WORD TIP Professions, hobbies, and sports don't take an article in German: Sie ist Blumenhändlerin.

flour NOUN
das **Mehl**

to **flow** VERB
fließen◇ (PERF sein)

ℙ**flower** NOUN
die **Blume** (PL die Blumen)
bunch of flowers der Blumenstrauß

to **flower** VERB
blühen

ℙ**flu** NOUN
die **Grippe** (PL die Grippen)
to have flu (die) Grippe haben

fluent ADJECTIVE
She speaks fluent Italian. Sie spricht fließend Italienisch.

fluently ADVERB
fließend

to **flush** VERB
spülen

I couldn't flush the toilet. Ich konnte die Toilette nicht spülen.
The toilet wouldn't flush. Die Toilettenspülung funktionierte nicht.

flute NOUN
die **Flöte** (PL die Flöten)
I play the flute. Ich spiele Flöte.

WORD TIP Don't use the article when you talk about playing an instrument.

ℙ**fly** NOUN
die **Fliege** (PL die Fliegen)

to **fly** VERB
1 **fliegen**◇ (PERF sein)
We flew to Berlin. Wir sind nach Berlin geflogen.
2 **steigen lassen**◇ (a kite)
3 **fliegen**◇ (PERF haben) (a plane or helicopter)
Who flew the plane? Wer hat das Flugzeug geflogen?
4 (pass quickly) **schnell vergehen**◇ (PERF sein)

foam NOUN
1 (foam rubber) der **Schaumgummi**
foam mattress die Schaumgummimatratze
2 (on a drink) der **Schaum**

focus NOUN
der **Brennpunkt** (PL die Brennpunkte)
to be in focus scharf sein
to be out of focus unscharf sein

to **focus** VERB
scharf stellen (a camera)

ℙ**fog** NOUN
der **Nebel**

foggy ADJECTIVE
neblig

foil NOUN
(kitchen foil) die **Alufolie**

fold NOUN
1 (in fabric or skin) die **Falte** (PL die Falten)
2 (in paper) der **Falz** (PL die Falze)

to **fold** VERB
falten
to fold something up etwas **zusammenfalten** SEP

folder NOUN
die **Mappe** (PL die Mappen)

folk music NOUN
die **Volksmusik**

to **follow** VERB
1 **folgen** (PERF sein) (+DAT)
Follow me! Folgen Sie mir!
2 **verstehen**◇

◇ irregular verb; SEP separable verb; for more help with verbs see centre section

Do you follow me? Verstehst du, was ich meine?

following ADJECTIVE
folgend
the following evening am folgenden Abend

fond ADJECTIVE
to be fond of somebody jemanden gern haben
I'm very fond of him. Ich habe ihn sehr gern.

ℰ**food** NOUN
1 das Essen
I have to buy some food. Ich muss noch etwas zu essen einkaufen.
2 I like German food. Ich mag die deutsche Küche.
3 (stocks) die Lebensmittel (PLURAL)
We bought food for the holiday. Wir haben Lebensmittel für die Ferien eingekauft.

food poisoning NOUN
die Lebensmittelvergiftung
I got food poisoning. Ich hatte eine Lebensmittelvergiftung.

fool NOUN
der Dummkopf (PL die Dummköpfe)

ℰ**foot** NOUN
der Fuß (PL die Füße)
Lucy came on foot. Lucy ist zu Fuß gekommen.

ℰ**football** NOUN
der Fußball (PL die Fußbälle)
to play football Fußball spielen

footballer NOUN
der Fußballspieler (PL die Fußballspieler), die Fußballspielerin (PL die Fußballspielerinnen)

WORD TIP Professions, hobbies, and sports don't take an article in German: Er ist Fußballspieler.

footpath NOUN
der Fußweg (PL die Fußwege)

footprint NOUN
der Fußabdruck (PL die Fußabdrücke)

footstep NOUN
der Schritt (PL die Schritte)

ℰ**for** PREPOSITION
1 für (+ACC)
a present for my mother ein Geschenk für meine Mutter
What's it for? Wofür ist das?
2 (for a particular occasion or event) zu (+DAT)
sausages for lunch Würstchen zum

Mittagessen
Sam got a bike for Christmas. Sam hat zu Weihnachten ein Rad bekommen.
What for? Wozu?
3 (time expressions in the past but continuing in the present) seit (+DAT)
I've been waiting here for an hour. (and I'm still waiting) Ich warte hier seit einer Stunde.
My brother's been living in Berlin for three years. (and he still lives there) Mein Bruder wohnt seit drei Jahren in Berlin.
4 (time expressions in the past or the future)
I studied French for six years. but I no longer do Ich habe sechs Jahre lang Französisch gelernt.
I'll be away for four days. Ich werde vier Tage nicht da sein.
5 (with a price) für (+ACC)
I sold my bike for fifty pounds. Ich habe mein Rad für fünfzig Pfund verkauft.
6 What's the German for 'bee'? Wie heißt 'bee' auf Deutsch?

to **forbid** VERB
verbieten⬦
to forbid somebody to do something jemandem verbieten, etwas zu tun

ℰ**forbidden** ADJECTIVE
verboten

force NOUN
die Kraft (PL die Kräfte)
to **force** VERB
zwingen⬦
to force somebody to do something jemanden zwingen, etwas zu tun

forecast NOUN
die Vorhersage (PL die Vorhersagen)

foreground NOUN
der Vordergrund
in the foreground im Vordergrund

forehead NOUN
die Stirn (PL die Stirnen)

foreign ADJECTIVE
1 ausländisch
in a foreign country im Ausland
from a foreign country aus dem Ausland
2 foreign language die Fremdsprache

ℰ**foreigner** NOUN
der Ausländer (PL die Ausländer), die Ausländerin (PL die Ausländerinnen)
He's a foreigner. Er ist Ausländer.

ℰ**forest** NOUN
der Wald (PL die Wälder)

ℰ indicates key words

forever ADVERB
1 **immer**
I'd like to stay here forever. Ich möchte für immer hier bleiben.
2 *(non-stop)* **ständig**
He's forever asking questions. Er fragt ständig.

ᵽ to **forget** VERB
vergessen◇
to forget about something etwas vergessen
We've forgotten the bread. Wir haben das Brot vergessen.
to forget to do something vergessen, etwas zu tun
I forgot to phone. Ich habe vergessen anzurufen.

to **forgive** VERB
verzeihen◇ *(+DAT)*
to forgive somebody jemandem verzeihen
I forgave him. Ich habe ihm verziehen.
to forgive somebody for doing something jemandem verzeihen, dass er/sie etwas getan hat
I forgave her for losing my ring. Ich habe ihr verziehen, dass sie meinen Ring verloren hat.

ᵽ **fork** NOUN
die **Gabel** (PL die **Gabeln**)

ᵽ **form** NOUN
1 das **Formular** (PL die **Formulare**)
to fill in a form ein Formular ausfüllen
2 *(shape or kind)* die **Form** (PL die **Formen**)
in the form of in Form von
to be on form gut in Form sein
3 *(in school)* die **Klasse** (PL die **Klassen**)
to **form** VERB
bilden

formal ADJECTIVE
formell *(invitation, event)*

format NOUN
das **Format** (PL die **Formate**)

ᵽ **former** ADJECTIVE
ehemalig
a former pupil ein ehemaliger Schüler/eine ehemalige Schülerin

fortnight NOUN
vierzehn Tage *(PLURAL)*
We're going to Spain for a fortnight. Wir fahren vierzehn Tage nach Spanien.

fortunately ADVERB
glücklicherweise

fortune NOUN
das **Vermögen** (PL die **Vermögen**)
to make a fortune ein Vermögen machen

ᵽ **forty** NUMBER
vierzig

forward NOUN
(in sport) der **Stürmer** (PL die **Stürmer**)
forward ADVERB
(to the front) **nach vorn**
to move forward vorrücken SEP (PERF sein)
a seat further forward ein Platz weiter vorn

forward slash NOUN
der **Schrägstrich** (PL die **Schrägstriche**)

foster child NOUN
das **Pflegekind** (PL die **Pflegekinder**)

foul NOUN
(in sport) das **Foul** (PL die **Fouls**)
foul ADJECTIVE
scheußlich
The weather's foul. Das Wetter ist scheußlich.

ᵽ **fountain** NOUN
der **Brunnen** (PL die **Brunnen**)

fountain pen NOUN
der **Füllfederhalter** (PL die **Füllfederhalter**)

ᵽ **four** NUMBER
vier
It's four o'clock. Es ist vier Uhr.
on all fours auf allen vieren

ᵽ **fourteen** NUMBER
vierzehn

fourteenth NUMBER
vierzehnter/vierzehnte/vierzehntes

ᵽ **fourth** NUMBER
vierter/vierte/viertes
the fourth of July der vierte Juli
on the fourth floor im vierten Stock

fox NOUN
der **Fuchs** (PL die **Füchse**)

ᵽ **fragile** ADJECTIVE
zerbrechlich

frame NOUN
1 der **Rahmen** (PL die **Rahmen**)
2 *(of spectacles)* das **Gestell** (PL die **Gestelle**)

ᵽ **franc** NOUN
1 *(Swiss)* der **Franken** (PL die **Franken**)
a fifty-franc note ein Fünfzig-Franken-Schein
2 *(former French and Belgian currencies)* der

◇ irregular verb; SEP separable verb; for more help with verbs see centre section

Franc (PL die Francs)

ℓ **France** NOUN
Frankreich (NEUTER)
to France nach Frankreich

frantic ADJECTIVE
1 (very upset)
to be frantic außer sich (DAT) sein
I was frantic with worry. Ich war außer mir
vor Sorge.
2 (desperate) fieberhaft (effort or search)

freckle NOUN
die Sommersprosse (PL die
Sommersprossen)

ℓ **free** ADJECTIVE
1 (when you don't pay) kostenlos
a free ride eine kostenlose Fahrt
a free ticket eine Freikarte
2 (without charge) umsonst
to do something for free etwas umsonst
machen
3 (not occupied) frei
Are you free on Thursday? Haben Sie am
Donnerstag Zeit?
We don't get much free time. Wir haben
nicht viel Freizeit.
4 sugar-free ohne Zucker
lead-free bleifrei

to **free** VERB
befreien

freedom NOUN
die Freiheit

free gift NOUN
das Werbegeschenk (PL die
Werbegeschenke)

free kick NOUN
der Freistoß (PL die Freistöße)

ℓ to **freeze** VERB
1 (in a freezer) einfrieren◇ SEP
to freeze raspberries Himbeeren einfrieren
2 (in cold weather) frieren◇
It's freezing. Es friert.
to freeze to death erfrieren◇
3 (become covered with ice) zufrieren◇ SEP
(PERF sein)
The pond is frozen. Der Teich ist
zugefroren.

ℓ **freezer** NOUN
die Tiefkühltruhe (PL die Tiefkühltruhen),
(upright) der Gefrierschrank (PL die
Gefrierschränke)

freezing NOUN
below freezing unter Null

three degrees above freezing drei Grad
über Null

freezing ADJECTIVE
1 I'm freezing. Ich friere sehr.
2 It's freezing outside. Es ist eiskalt draußen.

ℓ **French** NOUN
1 (the language) das Französisch
2 (the people)
the French die Franzosen

French ADJECTIVE
1 französisch
the French coast die französische Küste
He is French. Er ist Franzose.
She is French. Sie ist Französin.
2 (teacher or lesson) Französisch-
the French class der Französischunterricht

> **WORD TIP** Adjectives never have capitals
> in German, even for regions, countries, or
> nationalities.

French bean NOUN
die grüne Bohne (PL die grünen Bohnen)

French dressing NOUN
die Vinaigrette

French fries PLURAL NOUN
die Pommes frites (PLURAL)

Frenchman NOUN
der Franzose (PL die Franzosen)

French window NOUN
die Terrassentür (PL die Terrassentüren)

Frenchwoman NOUN
die Französin (PL die Französinnen)

frequent ADJECTIVE
häufig

ℓ **fresh** ADJECTIVE
frisch
fresh eggs frische Eier
I'm going out for some fresh air. Ich gehe
ein bisschen frische Luft schnappen.

freshwater ADJECTIVE
Süßwasser-

ℓ **Friday** NOUN
1 der Freitag (PL die Freitage)
next Friday nächsten Freitag
last Friday letzten Freitag
on Friday (am) Freitag
I'll phone you on Friday evening. Ich rufe
dich Freitagabend an.
every Friday jeden Freitag
Good Friday Karfreitag
2 on Fridays freitags
closed on Fridays freitags geschlossen

A
B
C
D
E
F
G
H
I
J
K
L
M
N
O
P
Q
R
S
T
U
V
W
X
Y
Z

ℓ indicates key words

ℰ **fridge** NOUN
  der **Kühlschrank** (PL die **Kühlschränke**)
  Put it in the fridge. Stell es in den
  Kühlschrank.

ℰ **friend** NOUN
  1 der **Freund** (PL die **Freunde**), die **Freundin**
  (PL die **Freundinnen**)
  a friend of mine ein Freund von mir/eine
  Freundin von mir
  2 to make friends sich anfreunden
  He made friends with Danny. Er hat sich
  mit Danny angefreundet.
  He is friends with Danny. Er ist mit Danny
  befreundet.

friendly ADJECTIVE
  freundlich

friendship NOUN
  die **Freundschaft** (PL die **Freundschaften**)

fries PLURAL NOUN
  die **Pommes frites** (PLURAL)

fright NOUN
  1 der **Schreck** (PL die **Schrecke**)
  to have or get a fright einen Schreck
  bekommen◇
  2 You gave me a fright! Du hast mich
  erschreckt!

to **frighten** VERB
  1 (of an explosion or shot) erschrecken
  2 (scare or threaten)
  to frighten somebody jemandem Angst
  machen

ℰ **frightened** ADJECTIVE
  to be frightened Angst haben
  Martin's frightened of snakes. Martin hat
  Angst vor Schlangen.

frightening ADJECTIVE
  beängstigend

fringe NOUN
  1 (hairstyle) der **Pony** (PL die **Ponys**)
  2 (on clothes or a curtain) die **Fransen** (PLURAL)

frog NOUN
  der **Frosch** (PL die **Frösche**)

ℰ **from** PREPOSITION
  1 von (+DAT)
  ten metres from the cinema zehn Meter
  vom Kino
  a letter from Tom ein Brief von Tom
  from Monday to Friday von Montag bis
  Freitag
  from now on von jetzt an
  2 aus (+DAT)
  He comes from Dublin. Er kommt aus

Dublin.
  Where do you come from? Woher
  kommen Sie?
  the train from London der Zug aus London
  Paper is made from wood. Papier wird aus
  Holz hergestellt.
  3 from seven o'clock onwards ab sieben Uhr
  from then on von da ab

ℰ **front** NOUN
  1 (of a cupboard, card, or envelope) die
  Vorderseite (PL die **Vorderseiten**)
  (of a building) die **Vorderfront** (PL die
  Vorderfronten)
  2 (of a garment or in an interior) das
  Vorderteil (PL die **Vorderteile**)
  3 (at the seaside) die **Strandpromenade**
  (PL die **Strandpromenaden**)
  4 (of a car)
  to sit in (the) front vorne sitzen
  5 (of a train or queue) das **vordere Ende**
  6 (of a procession or in a race) die **Spitze**
  7 in/at the front vorne
  in/at the front of vorne in (+DAT, or, with
  movement towards a place, +ACC)
  **There are still seats at the front of the
  train.** Es gibt noch Plätze vorne im Zug.
  (DAT)
  We got on at the front of the train. Wir
  sind vorne in den Zug eingestiegen. (ACC)
  8 in front of vor (+DAT, or, with movement
  towards a place, +ACC)
  They were sitting in front of the TV. Sie
  saßen vor dem Fernseher. (DAT)
  He sat down in front of me. Er setzte sich
  vor mich. (ACC)

front ADJECTIVE
  1 vorderer/vordere/vorderes
  in the front rows in den vorderen Reihen
  2 Vorder-
  front seat of a car der Vordersitz
  front wheel das Vorderrad

front door NOUN
  die **Haustür** (PL die **Haustüren**)

frontier NOUN
  die **Grenze** (PL die **Grenzen**)

frost NOUN
  der **Frost**

frosty ADJECTIVE
  frostig

to **frown** VERB
  die **Stirn runzeln**
  He frowned at us. Er blickte uns mit
  gerunzelter Stirn an.

◇ **irregular verb**; SEP **separable verb**; for more help with verbs see centre section

frozen ADJECTIVE
(in a freezer) tiefgekühlt
a frozen pizza eine Tiefkühlpizza

ℱ **fruit** NOUN
1 (fruit in general) das Obst
We bought cheese and fruit. Wir haben Käse und Obst gekauft.
I like all types of fruit. Ich mag alle Obstsorten.
2 (a single fruit) die Frucht (PL die Früchte)
tropical fruits die Südfrüchte (PLURAL)

fruit juice NOUN
der Fruchtsaft (PL die Fruchtsäfte)

fruit machine NOUN
der Spielautomat (PL die Spielautomaten)

fruit salad NOUN
der Obstsalat (PL die Obstsalate)

frustrated ADJECTIVE
frustriert

to **fry** VERB
braten◇
We fried fish. Wir haben Fisch gebraten.
fried potatoes die Bratkartoffeln (PLURAL)
fried egg das Spiegelei

frying pan NOUN
die Bratpfanne (PL die Bratpfannen)

fuel NOUN
1 der Brennstoff
2 (for a car) der Kraftstoff

ℱ **full** ADJECTIVE
1 voll
The glass is full. Das Glas ist voll.
full-cream milk die Vollmilch
2 (not hungry) satt
I'm full. Ich bin satt.
3 full of voller (+GEN)
The train was full of tourists. Der Zug war voller Touristen.
4 at full speed in voller Fahrt
5 to write something out in full etwas voll ausschreiben

full stop NOUN
der Punkt (PL die Punkte)

full-time ADJECTIVE
a full-time job eine Ganztagsstelle
full-time work die Vollzeitarbeit

fully ADVERB
voll

fun NOUN
1 der Spaß
Have fun! Viel Spaß!

We had fun catching the ponies. Die Ponys einzufangen machte uns Spaß.
Skiing is fun. Skifahren macht Spaß.
I do it for fun. Ich mache es aus Spaß.
2 to have fun sich amüsieren
3 to make fun of somebody sich über jemanden lustig machen

funds PLURAL NOUN
die Geldmittel (PLURAL)

funeral NOUN
die Beerdigung (PL die Beerdigungen)

funfair NOUN
der Jahrmarkt (PL die Jahrmärkte)

ℱ **funny** ADJECTIVE
1 (amusing) lustig
a funny story eine lustige Geschichte
He's so funny. Er ist so witzig.
2 (strange) komisch
a funny noise ein komisches Geräusch
That's funny, I'm sure I paid. Das ist komisch, ich bin mir sicher, dass ich gezahlt habe.

fur NOUN
1 (on an animal) das Fell (PL die Felle)
2 (for a coat) der Pelz (PL die Pelze)
fur coat der Pelzmantel

furious ADJECTIVE
wütend
She was furious with Steve. Sie war wütend auf Steve.

ℱ **furniture** NOUN
die Möbel (PLURAL)
to buy some furniture Möbel kaufen
piece of furniture das Möbelstück

further ADVERB
weiter
further than the station weiter als der Bahnhof
ten kilometres further on zehn Kilometer weiter
further off weiter entfernt
further forward weiter vorn
further back weiter hinten

fuse NOUN
die Sicherung (PL die Sicherungen)

fuss NOUN
das Theater
to make a fuss ein Theater machen
to make a big fuss about the bill ein großes Theater um die Rechnung machen

fussy ADJECTIVE
to be fussy about something wählerisch in etwas (DAT) sein (food, for example)

future NOUN
die **Zukunft**
in future in Zukunft

Gg

gadget NOUN
das **Gerät** (PL die **Geräte**)

to **gain** VERB
1 **gewinnen**◇
in order to gain time um Zeit zu gewinnen
2 **profitieren**
to gain by something von etwas profitieren

gale NOUN
der **Sturm** (PL die **Stürme**)

gallery NOUN
die **Galerie** (PL die **Galerien**)

to **gamble** VERB
spielen (for money)

gambling NOUN
das **Glücksspiel**

game NOUN
1 das **Spiel** (PL die **Spiele**)
game of chance das Glücksspiel
board game das Brettspiel
2 **to have a game of cards** eine Partie Karten spielen
3 **to have a game of football** Fußball spielen
4 **games** (at school) der **Sport**

games console NOUN
die **Spielkonsole** (PL die **Spielkonsolen**)

gaming NOUN
(playing computer games) das **Spielen am Computer**

gang NOUN
die **Bande** (PL die **Banden**)
All the gang were there. Die ganze Bande war da.

gangster NOUN
der **Gangster** (PL die **Gangster**)

gap NOUN
1 (hole) die **Lücke** (PL die **Lücken**)
2 (in time) die **Pause** (PL die **Pausen**)
a two-hour gap eine zweistündige Pause
3 **age gap** der Altersunterschied

gap year NOUN
das **Orientierungsjahr** (PL die **Orientierungsjahre**)

garage NOUN
1 (for keeping your car in) die **Garage** (PL die **Garagen**)
2 (for repairing cars) die **Autowerkstatt** (PL die **Autowerkstätten**)
3 (for petrol) die **Tankstelle** (PL die **Tankstellen**)

garden NOUN
der **Garten** (PL die **Gärten**)

gardener NOUN
der **Gärtner** (PL die **Gärtner**) die **Gärtnerin** (PL die **Gärtnerinnen**)

WORD TIP Professions, hobbies, and sports don't take an article in German: Er ist Gärtner.

gardening NOUN
die **Gartenarbeit**
My mother's hobby is gardening. Das Hobby meiner Mutter ist die Gartenarbeit.

garlic NOUN
der **Knoblauch**

garment NOUN
das **Kleidungsstück** (PL die **Kleidungsstücke**)

gas NOUN
das **Gas**

gas cooker NOUN
der **Gasherd** (PL die **Gasherde**)

gas fire NOUN
der **Gasofen** (PL die **Gasöfen**)

gas meter NOUN
der **Gaszähler** (PL die **Gaszähler**)

gate NOUN
1 das **Tor** (PL die **Tore**)
2 (in field) das **Gatter** (PL die **Gatter**)
3 (at an airport) der **Flugsteig** (PL die **Flugsteige**)

to **gather** VERB
1 (of people) sich **versammeln**
2 **sammeln** (fruit, vegetables, flowers)
3 **as far as I can gather** soweit ich weiß

gay ADJECTIVE
(homosexual) **schwul** (informal)

to **gaze** VERB
to gaze at something etwas anstarren SEP

◇ irregular verb; SEP separable verb; for more help with verbs see centre section

GCSEs NOUN PLURAL (*You can explain GCSEs briefly as follows: Dies sind Prüfungen, die im Alter von ca 16 Jahren in bis zu 12 Fächern abgelegt werden. Sie werden von A*◇ *(beste Note) bis U (nicht bestanden) benotet. Viele Schüler und Schülerinnen machen nach den GCSEs weiter und legen die A-level Prüfungen ab.*) ▸ SEE **A levels**

gear NOUN
1 (*in a car*) der **Gang** (PL die **Gänge**)
to change gear schalten
2 (*equipment*) die **Ausrüstung**
camping gear die Campingausrüstung
3 (*things*) die **Sachen** (PLURAL)
I've left all my gear at Gary's. Ich habe alle meine Sachen bei Gary gelassen.

gear lever NOUN
der **Schalthebel** (PL die **Schalthebel**)

gel NOUN
das **Gel** (PL die **Gele**)

Gemini NOUN
Zwillinge (PLURAL)
Steph is Gemini. Steph ist Zwilling.

gender NOUN
(*of a word*) das **Geschlecht** (PL die **Geschlechter**)
What is the gender of 'Haus'? Welches Geschlecht hat 'Haus'?

ℓ **general** NOUN
der **General** (PL die **Generäle**)
general ADJECTIVE
allgemein
in general im Allgemeinen
the general election die allgemeinen Wahlen

general knowledge NOUN
das **Allgemeinwissen**

ℓ **generally** ADVERB
im Allgemeinen

generation NOUN
die **Generation** (PL die **Generationen**)

generator NOUN
der **Generator** (PL die **Generatoren**)

generous ADJECTIVE
großzügig

genetic ADJECTIVE
genetisch
genetic engineering die Gentechnik

genetically ADVERB
genetisch
genetically modified genmanipuliert

genetics NOUN
die **Genetik**

Geneva NOUN
Genf (NEUTER)
Lake Geneva der Genfer See

genius NOUN
das **Genie** (PL die **Genies**)
Lisa, you're a genius! Lisa, du bist ein Genie!

ℓ **gentle** ADJECTIVE
sanft

ℓ **gentleman** NOUN
der **Herr** (PL die **Herren**)
Ladies and gentlemen! Meine Damen und Herren!

ℓ **gently** ADVERB
sanft

ℓ **gents** NOUN
(*lavatory*) die **Herrentoilette** (PL die **Herrentoiletten**)
(*on a sign*) 'Gents' 'Herren'
Where's the gents? Wo ist die Herrentoilette?

genuine ADJECTIVE
1 (*real, authentic*) **echt**
a genuine diamond ein echter Brillant
2 **aufrichtig** person
She's very genuine. Sie ist sehr aufrichtig.

ℓ **geography** NOUN
die **Geografie/Geographie**, (*at school*) die **Erdkunde**

germ NOUN
1 der **Keim** (PL die **Keime**)
2 (*causing a cold*)
germs die Bazillen (PLURAL)

German NOUN
1 (*person*) der/die **Deutsche** (PL die **Deutschen**)
2 (*language*) das **Deutsch**
in German auf Deutsch
German ADJECTIVE
deutsch
the German coast die deutsche Küste
He is German. Er ist Deutscher.
She is German. Sie ist Deutsche.
our German teacher unser Deutschlehrer/unsere Deutschlehrerin

WORD TIP Adjectives never have capitals in German, even for regions, countries, or nationalities.

Germany NOUN
Deutschland (NEUTER)
to Germany nach Deutschland

ℓ indicates key words

from Germany aus Deutschland

> **GERMANY**
>
> Capital: Berlin. Population: over 82 million. Size: 357,021 square km. Official language: German. Official currency: euro.

𝄞 to **get** VERB

1 (obtain, receive) **bekommen**◇, **kriegen** (informal)
I got a bike for my birthday. Ich habe ein Rad zum Geburtstag bekommen.
Fred got the job. Fred hat die Stelle bekommen.
She got a shock. Sie hat einen Schreck gekriegt.
I got a good mark for my German homework. Ich habe für meine Deutschhausaufgaben eine gute Note bekommen.

2 **He's got lots of money.** Er hat viel Geld.
She's got long hair. Sie hat lange Haare.
I've got a headache. Ich habe Kopfschmerzen.

3 (fetch) **holen**
I'll get some bread. Ich hole Brot.
I'll get your bag for you. Ich hole dir deine Tasche.

4 **to have got to do something** etwas tun müssen◇
I've got to phone before midday. Ich muss vor Mittag anrufen.

5 **to get (to) somewhere** irgendwo ankommen◇ SEP (PERF **sein**)
when I got to London als ich in London ankam
We got here this morning. Wir sind heute Morgen angekommen.
What time did they get there? Wann sind sie angekommen?

6 (become) **werden**◇ (PERF **sein**)
It's getting late. Es wird spät.
It's getting dark. Es wird dunkel.

7 **to get something done** etwas machen lassen◇
I'm getting my hair cut today. Ich lasse mir heute die Haare schneiden.

• **to get back**
zurückkommen◇ SEP (PERF **sein**)
Mum gets back at six. Mutti kommt um sechs zurück.

• **to get something back**
etwas zurückbekommen◇ SEP, etwas zurückkriegen SEP (informal)
Did you get your books back? Hast du deine Bücher zurückbekommen?

• **to get into something**
(a vehicle) in etwas (ACC) einsteigen◇ SEP

He got into the car. Er ist ins Auto eingestiegen.

• **to get off something**
(a vehicle) aus etwas (DAT) aussteigen◇ SEP (PERF **sein**)
I got off the train at Banbury. Ich bin in Banbury aus dem Zug ausgestiegen.

• **to get on**
How's Amanda getting on? Wie geht's Amanda?

• **to get on something**
(a vehicle) in etwas (ACC) einsteigen◇ SEP (PERF **sein**)
She got on the train at Reading. Sie ist in Reading in den Zug eingestiegen.

• **to get on with somebody**
sich mit jemandem verstehen◇
She doesn't get on with her brother. Sie versteht sich nicht mit ihrem Bruder.

• **to get out of something**
(a vehicle) aus etwas (DAT) aussteigen◇ SEP (PERF **sein**)
Laura got out of the car. Laura ist aus dem Auto ausgestiegen.

• **to get together**
sich treffen◇
We must get together soon. Wir müssen uns bald mal treffen.

• **to get up**
aufstehen◇ SEP (PERF **sein**)
I get up at seven. Ich stehe um sieben auf.

ghost NOUN
der **Geist** (PL die **Geister**)

giant NOUN
der **Riese** (PL die **Riesen**)

giant ADJECTIVE
riesig
a giant lorry ein riesiger Lastwagen

𝄞 **gift** NOUN

1 das **Geschenk** (PL die **Geschenke**)
a Christmas gift ein Weihnachtsgeschenk

2 die **Begabung**
to have a gift for something für etwas (ACC) begabt sein
Jo has a real gift for languages. Jo ist wirklich sprachbegabt.

WORD TIP Do not translate the English word **gift** with the German **Gift**.

gifted ADJECTIVE
begabt
gifted children begabte Kinder

gig NOUN
das **Konzert** (PL die **Konzerte**), der **Gig**

◇ **irregular verb**; SEP **separable verb**; for more help with verbs see centre section

(*PL* die **Gigs**) *(informal)*
We went to a gig at the weekend. Wir waren am Wochenende bei einem Konzert.

gigabyte *NOUN*
das **Gigabyte** (*PL* die **Gigabytes**)
a fifty gigabyte hard disk eine Festplatte mit fünfzig Gigabyte Speicherkapazität

gigantic *ADJECTIVE*
riesig

gin *NOUN*
der **Gin** (*PL* die **Gins**)

ginger *NOUN*
der **Ingwer**

gipsy *NOUN*
der **Zigeuner** (*PL* die **Zigeuner**), die **Zigeunerin** (*PL* die **Zigeunerinnen**)

giraffe *NOUN*
die **Giraffe** (*PL* die **Giraffen**)

ℓ **girl** *NOUN*
das **Mädchen** (*PL* die **Mädchen**)
three boys and four girls drei Jungen und vier Mädchen
When I was a little girl I had ... Als kleines Mädchen hatte ich ...

ℓ **girlfriend** *NOUN*
die **Freundin** (*PL* die **Freundinnen**)

ℓ to **give** *VERB*
1 geben◇
   to give something to somebody jemandem etwas geben
   I'll give you my address. Ich gebe dir meine Adresse.
   Give me the key. Gib mir den Schlüssel.
   Yasmin's dad gave her the money. Yasmins Vater hat ihr das Geld gegeben.
2 *(give as a gift)* schenken
   to give somebody a present jemandem etwas schenken
 • **to give something away** etwas weggeben◇ *SEP*
   She's given away all her books. Sie hat alle ihre Bücher weggegeben.
 • **to give something back to somebody** jemandem etwas zurückgeben◇ *SEP*
   I gave her back the keys. Ich habe ihr die Schlüssel zurückgegeben.
 • **to give in** nachgeben◇ *SEP*
   My mum said no but she gave in in the end. Meine Mutti hat nein gesagt, aber schließlich hat sie nachgegeben.
 • **to give up** aufgeben◇ *SEP*

 • **to give up doing something** etwas aufgeben◇ *SEP*
   She's given up smoking. Sie hat das Rauchen aufgegeben.

ℓ **glad** *ADJECTIVE*
froh
I'm glad to hear he's better. Ich bin froh, dass es ihm besser geht.
I'm glad to be back. Ich bin froh, dass ich wieder zurück bin.
We would be glad to see you. Wir würden uns freuen, dich zu sehen.

ℓ **glass** *NOUN*
das **Glas** (*PL* die **Gläser**)
a glass of water ein Glas Wasser
a glass table ein Glastisch

ℓ **glasses** *PLURAL NOUN*
die **Brille** (*PL* die **Brillen**)
to wear glasses eine Brille tragen
a new pair of glasses eine neue Brille

WORD TIP In German die Brille is singular.

glider *NOUN*
das **Segelflugzeug** (*PL* die **Segelflugzeuge**)

global warming *NOUN*
die **globale Erwärmung**

glove *NOUN*
der **Handschuh** (*PL* die **Handschuhe**)
a pair of gloves ein Paar Handschuhe

glue *NOUN*
der **Klebstoff** (*PL* die **Klebstoffe**)

ℓ **go** *NOUN*
1 *(in a game)*
   Whose go is it? Wer ist dran?
   It's my go. Ich bin dran.
2 **to have a go at doing something** versuchen, etwas zu tun
   I'll have a go at mending it. Ich versuche, es zu reparieren.

to **go** *VERB*
1 *(on foot)* gehen◇ *(PERF* sein)
   to go to school in die Schule gehen
   Mark's gone to the dentist's. Mark ist zum Zahnarzt gegangen.
   to go shopping einkaufen gehen
2 *(in a vehicle)* fahren◇ *(PERF* sein)
   We're going to London. Wir fahren nach London.
   We're planning to go early. Wir wollen früh losfahren.
   to go on holiday in die Ferien fahren
3 *(by plane)* fliegen◇ *(PERF* sein)

ℓ indicates key words

A B C D E F G H I J K L M N O P Q R S T U V W X Y Z

4 **to go for a walk** spazieren gehen◇ *(PERF* sein)

5 *(with another verb)*
I'm going to do it. Ich werde es tun.
I'm going to make some tea. Ich mache Tee.
He was going to phone you. Er wollte dich anrufen.

6 *(leave)* gehen◇*(PERF* sein)
Pauline's already gone. Pauline ist schon gegangen.

7 *(on a journey)* abfahren◇ *SEP (PERF* sein)
When does the train go? Wann fährt der Zug ab?

8 *(turn out)* verlaufen◇ *(PERF* sein) event
How did your evening go? Wie ist dein Abend verlaufen?
The party went well. Die Party war gut.

• **to go away**
1 weggehen◇ *SEP (PERF* sein)
Go away! Geh weg!
2 *(on holiday)* verreisen *(PERF* sein)

• **to go back**
1 zurückgehen◇ *SEP (PERF* sein)
I'm not going back there again! Ich gehe nicht wieder dorthin zurück!
I'm going back to Germany in March. Ich werde im März nach Deutschland zurückkehren.
2 **I went back home.** Ich bin nach Hause gegangen.

• **to go down**
1 hinuntergehen◇ *SEP (PERF* sein)
She's gone down to the kitchen. Sie ist in die Küche hinuntergegangen.
to go down the stairs die Treppe hinuntergehen
2 *(price, temperature)* fallen◇ *(PERF* sein)
3 *(tyre, balloon, airbed)* Luft verlieren◇

• **to go in**
hineingehen◇ *SEP (PERF* sein)
He went in and shut the door. Er ist hineingegangen und hat die Tür zugemacht.

• **to go into**
1 *(person)* gehen in *(+ACC) (PERF* sein)
Fran went into the kitchen. Fran ging in die Küche.
2 *(object)* passen in *(+ACC)*
This book won't go into my bag. Dieses Buch passt nicht in meine Tasche.

• **to go off**
1 *(bomb)* explodieren*(PERF* sein)
2 *(alarm clock)* klingeln
My alarm clock went off at six. Mein Wecker hat um sechs geklingelt.
3 *(fire or burglar alarm)* losgehen◇ *SEP*

(PERF sein)
The fire alarm went off. Der Feuermelder ging los.

• **to go on**
1 **What's going on?** Was ist los?
2 **to go on doing something** weiter etwas tun
She went on talking. Sie hat weitergeredet.
3 **to go on about something** stundenlang von etwas *(DAT)* reden
He's always going on about his dog. Er redet stundenlang von seinem Hund.

• **to go out**
1 *(for an evening)* ausgehen◇ *SEP*, weggehen◇ *SEP (PERF* sein) *(informal)*
We're going out tonight. Wir gehen heute Abend aus.
2 *(leave)*
She went out of the kitchen. Sie ist aus der Küche gegangen.
3 **to be going out with somebody** mit jemandem gehen◇ *(PERF* sein) *(informal)*
She's going out with my brother. Sie geht mit meinem Bruder.
4 *(light, fire)* ausgehen◇ *SEP (PERF* sein)
The light went out. Das Licht ist ausgegangen.

• **to go past something**
an etwas *(DAT)* vorbeigehen◇ *SEP (PERF* sein)
We went past your house. Wir sind an eurem Haus vorbeigegangen.

• **to go round**
to go round to somebody's house jemanden besuchen
We went round to Fred's last night. Wir haben gestern Abend Fred besucht.

• **to go round something**
besichtigen **museum, monument**

• **to go through**
1 **The train goes through Cologne.** Der Zug fährt durch Köln.
2 **to go through a room** durch ein Zimmer gehen
3 *(search)* durchsuchen

• **to go up**
1 *(person)* hinaufgehen◇ *SEP (PERF* sein)
She's gone up to her room. Sie ist in ihr Zimmer hinaufgegangen.
to go up the stairs die Treppe hinaufgehen
2 *(prices)* steigen◇ *(PERF* sein)
The price of petrol has gone up. Die Benzinpreise sind gestiegen.

goal *NOUN*
das **Tor** *(PL* die **Tore**)
to score a goal ein Tor schießen◇
to win by 3 goals to 2 mit 3 zu 2 Toren gewinnen◇

◇ **irregular verb;** *SEP* **separable verb; for more help with verbs see centre section**

goalkeeper *NOUN*
der **Torwart** (*PL* die **Torwarte**), die **Torfrau**
(*PL* die **Torfrauen**)

goat *NOUN*
die **Ziege** (*PL* die **Ziegen**)

god *NOUN*
der **Gott** (*PL* die **Götter**)

God *NOUN*
der **Gott**
to believe in God an Gott glauben

godchild *NOUN*
das **Patenkind** (*PL* die **Patenkinder**)

goddaughter *NOUN*
die **Patentochter** (*PL* die **Patentöchter**)

goddess *NOUN*
die **Göttin** (*PL* die **Göttinnen**)

godfather *NOUN*
der **Pate** (*PL* die **Paten**)

godmother *NOUN*
die **Patin** (*PL* die **Patinnen**)

godson *NOUN*
der **Patensohn** (*PL* die **Patensöhne**)

goggles *PLURAL NOUN*
die **Schutzbrille** (*PL* die **Schutzbrillen**)
swimming goggles die Schwimmbrille
skiing goggles die Skibrille
a pair of goggles eine Schwimmbrille/
Skibrille

WORD TIP In German die Brille is singular.

go-karting *NOUN*
das **Gokartfahren**

gold *NOUN*
das **Gold**
a gold bracelet ein Goldarmband

goldfish *NOUN*
der **Goldfisch** (*PL* die **Goldfische**)

golf *NOUN*
das **Golf**
to play golf Golf spielen

golf club *NOUN*
1 *(place)* der **Golfklub** (*PL* die **Golfklubs**)
2 *(iron)* der **Golfschläger** (*PL* die
Golfschläger)

golf course *NOUN*
der **Golfplatz** (*PL* die **Golfplätze**)

golfer *NOUN*
der **Golfspieler** (*PL* die **Golfspieler**), die

Golfspielerin (*PL* die **Golfspielerinnen**)

WORD TIP Professions, hobbies, and sports don't take an article in German: Er ist Golfspieler.

♪ **good** *ADJECTIVE*
1 gut
She's a good teacher. Sie ist eine gute
Lehrerin.
The cherries are very good. Die Kirschen
sind sehr gut.
2 to be good for you gesund sein
Tomatoes are good for you. Tomaten sind
gesund.
3 good at gut in (*+DAT*)
She's good at maths. Sie ist gut in Mathe.
He's good at drawing. Er kann gut
zeichnen.
4 *(well-behaved)* brav
Be good! Sei brav!
5 *(kind)* nett
She's been very good to me. Sie ist sehr
nett zu mir gewesen.
6 for good endgültig
He's stopped smoking for good. Er hat das
Rauchen endgültig aufgegeben.

good afternoon *EXCLAMATION*
guten Tag!

goodbye *EXCLAMATION*
auf Wiedersehen!

good evening *EXCLAMATION*
guten Abend!

Good Friday *NOUN*
der **Karfreitag** (*PL* die **Karfreitage**)

good-looking *ADJECTIVE*
gut aussehend

good luck *EXCLAMATION*
viel Glück!

good morning *EXCLAMATION*
guten Morgen!

goodnight *EXCLAMATION*
gute Nacht!

goods *PLURAL NOUN*
die **Waren** (*PLURAL*)

goods train *NOUN*
der **Güterzug** (*PL* die **Güterzüge**)

goose *NOUN*
die **Gans** (*PL* die **Gänse**)

gorgeous *ADJECTIVE*
herrlich
It's a gorgeous day. Es ist ein herrlicher
Tag.

gorilla NOUN
der **Gorilla** (PL die **Gorillas**)

gosh EXCLAMATION
Mensch!

gossip NOUN
1 (person) die **Klatschbase** (PL die **Klatschbasen**)
2 (scandal) der **Klatsch**

to **gossip** VERB
klatschen

government NOUN
die **Regierung** (PL die **Regierungen**)

to **grab** VERB
1 **packen**
She grabbed my arm. Sie packte mich am Arm.
2 **to grab something from somebody** jemandem etwas (ACC) entreißen◇
He grabbed the book from me. Er hat mir das Buch entrissen.

grade NOUN
(mark) die **Note** (PL die **Noten**)
to get good grades gute Noten bekommen

gradual ADJECTIVE
allmählich

gradually ADVERB
allmählich
The weather got gradually better. Das Wetter wurde allmählich besser.

graffiti PLURAL NOUN
die **Graffiti** (PLURAL)

grain NOUN
das **Korn** (PL die **Körner**)

ℙ **gram** NOUN
das **Gramm**
100 grams of salami hundert Gramm Salami

grammar NOUN
die **Grammatik**

grammar school NOUN
das **Gymnasium** (PL die **Gymnasien**)

grammatical ADJECTIVE
grammatikalisch
a grammatical error eine Grammatikfehler

gran NOUN
die **Oma** (PL die **Omas**)

ℙ **grandchildren** PLURAL NOUN
die **Enkelkinder** (PLURAL)

granddad NOUN
der **Opa** (PL die **Opas**)

ℙ **granddaughter** NOUN
die **Enkelin** (PL die **Enkelinnen**)

ℙ **grandfather** NOUN
der **Großvater** (PL die **Großväter**)

grandma NOUN
die **Oma** (PL die **Omas**)

ℙ **grandmother** NOUN
die **Großmutter** (PL die **Großmütter**)

grandpa NOUN
der **Opa** (PL die **Opas**)

ℙ **grandparents** PLURAL NOUN
die **Großeltern** (PLURAL)

ℙ **grandson** NOUN
der **Enkel** (PL die **Enkel**)

granny NOUN
die **Omi** (PL die **Omis**)

ℙ **grape** NOUN
die **Weintraube** (PL die **Weintrauben**)
a grape eine Weintraube
to buy some grapes Weintrauben kaufen
Do you like grapes? Magst du Weintrauben?
a bunch of grapes eine ganze Weintraube

grapefruit NOUN
die **Grapefruit** (PL die **Grapefruits**)

graph NOUN
das **Diagramm** (PL die **Diagramme**)

graphic designer NOUN
der **Grafikdesigner** (PL die **Grafikdesigner**), die **Grafikdesignerin** (PL die **Grafikdesignerinnen**)

WORD TIP Professions, hobbies, and sports don't take an article in German: Er ist Grafikdesigner.

graphics NOUN
die **Grafik**

to **grasp** VERB
festhalten◇ SEP

ℙ **grass** NOUN
1 das **Gras**
to lie on the grass im Gras liegen
2 (lawn) der **Rasen** (PL die **Rasen**)
to cut the grass den Rasen mähen

grasshopper NOUN
die **Heuschrecke** (PL die **Heuschrecken**)

to **grate** VERB
reiben◇
grated cheese geriebener Käse

◇ **irregular verb;** SEP **separable verb; for more help with verbs see centre section**

grateful *ADJECTIVE*
dankbar
to be grateful to somebody jemandem
dankbar sein

grater *NOUN*
die Reibe (PL die Reiben)

grave *NOUN*
das Grab (PL die Gräber)

graveyard *NOUN*
der Friedhof (PL die Friedhöfe)

gravy *NOUN*
die Soße (PL die Soßen)

grease *NOUN*
das Fett

ℙ **greasy** *ADJECTIVE*
1 fettig
to have greasy skin fettige Haut haben
2 (food) fett

ℙ **great** *ADJECTIVE*
1 groß
a great poet ein großer Dichter
2 (terrific) großartig
It was a great party. Das war eine
großartige Party.
Great! Großartig!, Prima! (informal)
3 **a great deal of** sehr viel
a great many sehr viele

Great Britain *NOUN*
Großbritannien (NEUTER)

Greece *NOUN*
Griechenland (NEUTER)

greedy *ADJECTIVE*
gierig, (with food) gefräßig

Greek *NOUN*
1 (person) der Grieche (PL die Griechen), die
Griechin (PL die Griechinnen)
2 (language) das Griechisch

Greek *ADJECTIVE*
griechisch
the Greek islands die griechischen Inseln
He's Greek. Er ist Grieche.
She's Greek. Sie ist Griechin.

WORD TIP Adjectives never have capitals
in German, even for regions, countries, or
nationalities.

ℙ **green** *NOUN*
1 (colour) das Grün
a pale green ein Hellgrün
2 **the Greens** (ecologists) die Grünen (PLURAL)

green *ADJECTIVE*
1 grün
a green door eine grüne Tür

2 **the Green Party** die Grünen (PLURAL)

greengrocer *NOUN*
der Obst- und Gemüsehändler (PL die
Obst- und Gemüsehändler)

WORD TIP Professions, hobbies, and sports
don't take an article in German: Er ist Obst- und
Gemüsehändler.

greenhouse *NOUN*
das Gewächshaus (PL die Gewächshäuser)

greenhouse effect *NOUN*
der Treibhauseffekt

greetings *PLURAL NOUN*
die Grüße (PLURAL)
Season's Greetings Fröhliche Weihnachten
und ein glückliches neues Jahr

greetings card *NOUN*
die Glückwunschkarte (PL die
Glückwunschkarten)

ℙ **grey** *ADJECTIVE*
grau

greyhound *NOUN*
der Windhund (PL die Windhunde)

grid *NOUN*
1 (grating) das Gitter (PL die Gitter)
2 (network) das Netz (PL die Netze)

grief *NOUN*
die Trauer

ℙ **grill** *NOUN*
der Grill (PL die Grills)

to grill *VERB*
grillen
I'm going to grill the sausages. Ich grille
die Würstchen.

grim *ADJECTIVE*
grauenvoll

to grin *VERB*
grinsen

to grind *VERB*
mahlen

to grip *VERB*
(hold on to) festhalten ◊ SEP

groan *NOUN*
das Stöhnen

to groan *VERB*
stöhnen

ℙ **grocer** *NOUN*
der Lebensmittelhändler

ℙ indicates key words

(PL die **Lebensmittelhändler**)

WORD TIP Professions, hobbies, and sports don't take an article in German: Er ist Lebensmittelhändler.

groceries PLURAL NOUN
die **Lebensmittel** (PLURAL)

grocer's NOUN
das **Lebensmittelgeschäft** (PL die **Lebensmittelgeschäfte**)

groom NOUN
der **Bräutigam** (PL die **Bräutigame**)
the bride and groom das Brautpaar

gross ADJECTIVE
1 **a gross injustice** eine schreiende Ungerechtigkeit
2 **grob**
   a gross error ein grober Fehler
3 (disgusting) **ekelhaft**
   The food was gross! Das Essen war ekelhaft!

ground NOUN
1 der **Boden**
   to sit on the ground auf dem Boden sitzen
2 (for sport) der **Sportplatz** (PL die **Sportplätze**)
   football ground der Fußballplatz

ground ADJECTIVE
gemahlen
ground coffee gemahlener Kaffee

ground floor NOUN
das **Erdgeschoss**
They live on the ground floor. Sie wohnen im Erdgeschoss.

group NOUN
die **Gruppe** (PL die **Gruppen**)

to grow VERB
1 (get bigger or longer) **wachsen**◇ (PERF sein)
   My little sister's grown quite a bit this year. Meine kleine Schwester ist dieses Jahr ein ganzes Stück gewachsen.
   The number of students is still growing. Die Zahl der Studenten wächst noch.
   Your hair grows very quickly. Deine Haare wachsen sehr schnell.
2 **anbauen** SEP (fruit, vegetables)
3 **to grow a beard** sich (DAT) einen Bart wachsen lassen
4 (become) **werden**◇ (PERF sein)
   to grow old alt werden
• **to grow up**
1 **erwachsen werden**◇ (PERF sein)
   The children are growing up. Die Kinder werden erwachsen.
2 **aufwachsen**◇ SEP (PERF sein)

She grew up in Scotland. Sie ist in Schottland aufgewachsen.

to growl VERB
knurren

grown-up NOUN
der/die **Erwachsene** (PL die **Erwachsenen**)

growth NOUN
das **Wachstum**

grudge NOUN
to bear a grudge against somebody etwas gegen jemanden haben
She bears me a grudge. Sie hat etwas gegen mich.

gruesome ADJECTIVE
furchtbar

to grumble VERB
1 **murren**
   He's always grumbling. Er murrt immer.
2 **to grumble about something** sich über etwas (ACC) beklagen
   What's she grumbling about? Worüber beklagt sie sich?

guarantee NOUN
die **Garantie** (PL die **Garantien**)
a year's guarantee ein Jahr Garantie

to guarantee VERB
garantieren

guard NOUN
1 **prison guard** der **Gefängniswärter** (PL die **Gefängniswärterin**)
2 (on a train) der **Zugführer** (PL die **Zugführer**), die **Zugführerin** (PL die **Zugführerinnen**)
3 **security guard** der **Wächter** (PL die **Wächterin**)

to guard VERB
bewachen

WORD TIP Professions, hobbies, and sports don't take an article in German: Er ist Gefängniswärter.

guard dog NOUN
der **Wachhund** (PL die **Wachhunde**)

guess NOUN
Have a guess! Rate mal!
It's a good guess. Gut geraten.

to guess VERB
1 **raten**◇
   Guess who I saw last night. Rate mal, wen ich gestern Abend gesehen habe.
2 (guess something correctly) es **erraten**◇
   You'll never guess! Du errätst es nie!

guest NOUN
der **Gast** (PL die **Gäste**)
We've got guests coming tonight. Wir haben heute Abend Gäste.

◇ **irregular verb**; SEP **separable verb**; for more help with verbs see centre section

a paying guest ein zahlender Gast

guest house NOUN
die **Pension** (PL die **Pensionen**)
We stayed at a guest house. Wir haben in einer Pension gewohnt.

ᵖ **guide** NOUN
1 (person) der **Führer** (PL die **Führer**), die **Führerin** (PL die **Führerinnen**)
2 (book) der **Reiseführer** (PL die **Reiseführer**)
3 (girl guide) die **Pfadfinderin** (PL die **Pfadfinderinnen**)

> **WORD TIP** Professions, hobbies, and sports don't take an article in German: Sie ist Pfadfinderin.

guidebook NOUN
1 der **Reiseführer** (PL die **Reiseführer**)
2 (to a museum or monument) das **Handbuch** (PL die **Handbücher**)

guide dog NOUN
der **Blindenhund** (PL die **Blindenhunde**)

guideline NOUN
die **Richtlinie** (PL die **Richtlinien**)

guilty ADJECTIVE
1 **schuldig**
2 **to feel guilty** ein schlechtes Gewissen haben
I felt guilty about the noise. Ich hatte ein schlechtes Gewissen wegen des Lärms.

guinea pig NOUN
1 (pet) das **Meerschweinchen** (PL die **Meerschweinchen**)
2 (in an experiment) das **Versuchskaninchen** (PL die **Versuchskaninchen**)

guitar NOUN
die **Gitarre** (PL die **Gitarren**)
Pete plays the guitar. Pete spielt Gitarre.

> **WORD TIP** Don't use the article when you talk about playing an instrument.

guitarist NOUN
der **Gitarrist** (PL die **Gitarristen**), die **Gitarristin** (PL die **Gitarristinnen**)

> **WORD TIP** Professions, hobbies, and sports don't take an article in German: Sie ist Gitarristin.

gum NOUN
1 (chewing gum) der **Kaugummi** (PL die **Kaugummi**)
2 **gums** (in your mouth) das **Zahnfleisch**

> **WORD TIP** In German, das Zahnfleisch is singular.

gun NOUN
1 die **Pistole** (PL die **Pistolen**)
2 (rifle) das **Gewehr** (PL die **Gewehre**)

gutter NOUN
1 (in the street) der **Rinnstein** (PL die **Rinnsteine**)
2 (on roof edge) die **Dachrinne** (PL die **Dachrinnen**)

guy NOUN
der **Typ** (PL die **Typen**) (informal)
He's a nice guy. Er ist ein netter Typ.
that guy from Newcastle der Typ aus Newcastle
What do you guys want to eat? Was wollt ihr essen, Leute?

ᵖ **gym** NOUN
1 (school lesson) das **Turnen**
2 (building) die **Turnhalle** (PL die **Turnhallen**)
3 (health club) das **Fitnesszentrum** (PL die **Fitnesszentren**)
to go to the gym ins Fitnesszentrum gehen

ᵖ **gymnasium** NOUN
die **Turnhalle** (PL die **Turnhallen**)

> **WORD TIP** Do not translate the English word gymnasium with the German Gymnasium.

gymnast NOUN
der **Turner** (PL die **Turner**), die **Turnerin** (PL die **Turnerinnen**)

> **WORD TIP** Professions, hobbies, and sports don't take an article in German: Sie ist Turnerin.

gymnastics NOUN
das **Turnen**

gym shoe NOUN
der **Turnschuh** (PL die **Turnschuhe**)

Hh

ᵖ **habit** NOUN
die **Gewohnheit** (PL die **Gewohnheiten**)
It's a bad habit. Es ist eine schlechte Gewohnheit.

haddock NOUN
der **Schellfisch**
smoked haddock geräucherter Schellfisch

hail NOUN
der **Hagel**
to hail VERB
hageln
It's hailing. Es hagelt.

ᵖ indicates key words

hailstone NOUN
    das **Hagelkorn** (PL die **Hagelkörner**)

hailstorm NOUN
    der **Hagelschauer** (PL die **Hagelschauer**)

♪ **hair** NOUN
1 die **Haare** (PLURAL)
    He's got long hair. Er hat lange Haare.
    to comb your hair sich (DAT) die Haare
    kämmen
    to wash your hair sich (DAT) die Haare
    waschen◇
    to have your hair cut sich (DAT) die Haare
    schneiden lassen◇
    She's had her hair cut. Sie hat sich die
    Haare schneiden lassen.
2 das **Haar** (PL die **Haare**)
    There's a hair in my soup. In meiner Suppe
    ist ein Haar.

hairbrush NOUN
    die **Haarbürste** (PL die **Haarbürsten**)

haircut NOUN
1 der **Haarschnitt** (PL die **Haarschnitte**)
2 **to have a haircut** sich (DAT) die Haare
    schneiden lassen◇

♪ **hairdresser** NOUN
    der **Friseur** (PL die **Friseure**), die **Friseurin**
    (PL die **Friseurinnen**)
    at the hairdresser's beim Friseur

> **WORD TIP** Professions, hobbies, and sports
> don't take an article in German: Er ist Friseur.

hairdryer NOUN
    der **Föhn** (PL die **Föhne**)

hair gel NOUN
    das **Haargel** (PL die **Haargele**)

hairgrip NOUN
    die **Haarklemme** (PL die **Haarklemmen**)

hairslide NOUN
    die **Haarspange** (PL die **Haarspangen**)

hairspray NOUN
    das **Haarspray** (PL die **Haarsprays**)

hairstyle NOUN
    die **Frisur** (PL die **Frisuren**)

hairy ADJECTIVE
    behaart

♪ **half** NOUN
1 die **Hälfte** (PL die **Hälften**)
    half of die Hälfte von (+DAT)
    I gave him half of the money. Ich habe ihm
    die Hälfte von dem Geld gegeben.
    half of it die Hälfte davon
2 **half an apple** ein halber Apfel
3 **to cut something in half** etwas halbieren

4 *(as a fraction)* **halb**
    three and a half dreieinhalb
5 *(in time)* **halb**
    half an hour eine halbe Stunde
    an hour and a half anderthalb Stunden
    It's half past three. Es ist halb vier. *(literally:
    half on the way to four)*
6 *(in weights and measures)* **halb**
    half a litre ein halber Liter

half hour NOUN
    die **halbe Stunde**
    every half hour jede halbe Stunde

half-price ADJECTIVE, ADVERB
    zum **halben Preis**
    half-price CDs CDs zum halben Preis

half-time NOUN
    die **Halbzeit**
    At half-time the score is 0-0. Zur Halbzeit
    steht es null zu null.

halfway ADVERB
1 auf **halbem Weg**
    halfway to Frankfurt auf halbem Weg nach
    Frankfurt
2 **to be halfway through doing something**
    mit etwas halb fertig sein
    I'm halfway through my homework. Ich
    bin mit meinen Hausaufgaben halb fertig.

♪ **hall** NOUN
1 *(in a house)* die **Diele** (PL die **Dielen**)
2 *(public)* der **Saal** (PL die **Säle**)
    village hall der Gemeindesaal
    concert hall der Konzertsaal

Hallowe'en NOUN
    der **Tag vor Allerheiligen**

♪ **ham** NOUN
    der **Schinken**
    a ham sandwich ein Schinkenbrot

hamburger NOUN
    der **Hamburger** (PL die **Hamburger**)

> **WORD TIP** The German word Hamburger can
> refer to a resident of Hamburg as well as to the
> food.

hammer NOUN
    der **Hammer** (PL die **Hammer**)

hamster NOUN
    der **Hamster** (PL die **Hamster**)

♪ **hand** NOUN
1 die **Hand** (PL die **Hände**)
    to have something in your hand etwas in
    der Hand haben
    to hold somebody's hand jemandes Hand
    halten

◇ **irregular verb;** SEP **separable verb; for more help with verbs see centre section**

2 to give somebody a hand jemandem
helfen⬦
**Can you give me a hand to move the table
into the corner?** Kannst du mir helfen, den
Tisch in die Ecke zu rücken?
Do you need a hand? Kann ich dir helfen?
3 On the other hand ... Andererseits ...
4 *(of a watch or clock)* der **Zeiger** (*PL* die
Zeiger)
the hour hand der Stundenzeiger

to **hand** *VERB*
to hand something to somebody
jemandem etwas geben⬦
I handed him the keys. Ich gab ihm die
Schlüssel.
• **to hand something in**
etwas abgeben⬦ *SEP*
Hand in your homework. Gebt eure
Hausaufgaben ab.
• **to hand something out**
etwas austeilen *SEP*

handbag *NOUN*
die **Handtasche** (*PL* die **Handtaschen**)

handcuffs *PLURAL NOUN*
die **Handschellen** (*PLURAL*)

handful *NOUN*
a handful of eine Handvoll

handicapped *ADJECTIVE*
behindert

ℓ **handkerchief** *NOUN*
das **Taschentuch** (*PL* die **Taschentücher**)

ℓ **handle** *NOUN*
1 *(of a door, drawer, bag, or knife)* der **Griff**
(*PL* die **Griffe**)
2 *(on a cup, jug, or basket)* der **Henkel** (*PL* die
Henkel)
3 *(of a frying pan or broom)* der **Stiel** (*PL* die
Stiele)

to **handle** *VERB*
1 erledigen
Gina handles the correspondence. Gina
erledigt die Korrespondenz.
2 umgehen⬦ *SEP* (*PERF* sein) mit
She's good at handling people. Sie kann
gut mit Menschen umgehen.
3 fertig werden⬦ (*PERF* sein) mit
He can't handle problems. Er kann mit
Problemen nicht fertig werden.

handlebars *PLURAL NOUN*
die **Lenkstange** (*PL* die **Lenkstangen**)

hand luggage *NOUN*
das **Handgepäck**

handmade *ADJECTIVE*
handgemacht

ℓ **handsome** *ADJECTIVE*
gut aussehend
He's a handsome guy. Er ist ein gut
aussehender Typ.

handwriting *NOUN*
die **Handschrift** (*PL* die **Handschriften**)

ℓ **handy** *ADJECTIVE*
1 praktisch
This little knife is very handy. Dieses kleine
Messer ist sehr praktisch.
2 griffbereit
I always keep a notebook handy. Ich habe
immer ein kleines Notizbuch griffbereit.

WORD TIP Do not translate the English word
handy with the German Handy.

ℓ to **hang** *VERB*
1 hängen⬦
There was a mirror hanging on the wall.
An der Wand hing ein Spiegel.
2 aufhängen *SEP*
to hang a mirror on the wall einen Spiegel
an der Wand aufhängen
• **to hang around**
rumhängen⬦ *SEP* (*PERF* sein) (*informal*)
**We were hanging around outside
the cinema.** Wir haben vor dem Kino
rumgehangen.
• **to hang on**
warten
Hang on a second! Warten Sie einen
Moment!
• **to hang up**
(on the phone) auflegen *SEP*
She hung up on me. Sie hat einfach
aufgelegt.
• **to hang something up**
etwas aufhängen *SEP*

hang-gliding *NOUN*
das **Drachenfliegen**
to go hang-gliding Drachenfliegen gehen

hangover *NOUN*
der **Kater** (*PL* die **Kater**)

to **happen** *VERB*
1 passieren (*PERF* sein)
What happened? Was ist passiert?
It happened in June. Es ist im Juni passiert.
2 What's happening? Was ist los?
What's happened to Jill? Was ist mit Jill los?
3 What's happened to the can-opener? Wo
ist der Dosenöffner?
4 if you happen to see him wenn du ihn
zufällig triffst
Leila happened to be there. Leila war
zufällig da.

happily ADVERB
1 glücklich
2 (willingly) gerne
I'll happily do it for you. Ich tu es gerne für dich.

happiness NOUN
das Glück

♫ happy ADJECTIVE
glücklich
a happy child ein glückliches Kind
Happy Birthday! Herzlichen Glückwunsch zum Geburtstag!

♫ harbour NOUN
der Hafen (PL die Häfen)

♫ hard ADJECTIVE
1 hart
2 (difficult) schwer
a hard question eine schwere Frage
It's hard to say. Es ist schwer zu sagen.

hard ADVERB
1 **to work hard** hart arbeiten
2 **to try hard** sich sehr bemühen

hard disk NOUN
die Festplatte (PL die Festplatten)

hardly ADVERB
1 kaum
I can hardly hear him. Ich kann ihn kaum hören.
There was hardly anybody there. Es war kaum jemand da.
We've got hardly any milk. Wir haben kaum Milch.
hardly anything kaum etwas
He ate hardly anything. Er hat kaum etwas gegessen.
2 **hardly ever** fast nie
I hardly ever see him. Ich sehe ihn fast nie.

hard up ADJECTIVE
to be hard up knapp bei Kasse sein

hare NOUN
der Hase (PL die Hasen)

harm NOUN
It won't do any harm. Es kann nicht schaden.

to harm VERB
1 **to harm somebody** jemandem etwas tun◊
They didn't harm him. Sie haben ihm nichts getan.
2 schaden (+DAT) (health, environment, reputation)
A cup of coffee won't harm you. Eine Tasse Kaffee schadet nicht.

harmful ADJECTIVE
schädlich

harmless ADJECTIVE
1 unschädlich
2 (joke, etc.) harmlos

harvest NOUN
die Ernte (PL die Ernten)
to get the harvest in die Ernte einbringen

♫ hat NOUN
der Hut (PL die Hüte)
a woolly hat eine Mütze

♫ to hate VERB
hassen
I hate geography. Ich hasse Erdkunde.

hatred NOUN
der Hass

♫ to have VERB
1 haben◊
Anna has three brothers. Anna hat drei Brüder.
How many sisters do you have? Wie viele Schwestern hast du?
2 **What have you got in your hand?** Was hast du in der Hand?
He has (got) flu. Er hat die Grippe.
3 (to form past tenses, some verbs in German take 'haben' and others 'sein')
I've finished. Ich bin fertig.
Have you seen the film? Hast du den Film gesehen?
Rosie hasn't arrived yet. Rosie ist noch nicht angekommen.
4 **to have to do something** etwas tun müssen◊
I have to phone my mum. Ich muss meine Mutter anrufen.
5 ('have' is often translated by a more specific German verb)
We had a coffee. Wir haben einen Kaffee getrunken.
What will you have? Was nehmen Sie?
I'll have an omelette. Ich nehme ein Omelett.
I'm going to have a shower. Ich dusche jetzt.
to have lunch zu Mittag essen
to have dinner (in the evening) zu Abend essen
6 (get) bekommen◊
Emma had a letter from Sam yesterday. Gestern bekam Emma einen Brief von Sam.
She had a baby. Sie hat ein Baby bekommen.
7 **to have something done** etwas machen

◊ irregular verb; SEP separable verb; for more help with verbs see centre section

lassen◇
I'm going to have my hair cut. Ich lasse mir die Haare schneiden.

8 **to have on** *(be wearing)* anhaben◇ *SEP*
to have nothing on nichts anhaben

hawk *NOUN*
der Habicht (*PL* die Habichte)

hay *NOUN*
das Heu

hay fever *NOUN*
der Heuschnupfen

hazelnut *NOUN*
die Haselnuss (*PL* die Haselnüsse)

🔑 **he** *PRONOUN*
er
He lives in Manchester. Er wohnt in Manchester.

🔑 **head** *NOUN*
1 der Kopf (*PL* die Köpfe)
He shook his head. Er schüttelte den Kopf.
head first mit dem Kopf zuerst
2 *(of a school)* der Direktor (*PL* die Direktoren), die Direktorin (*PL* die Direktorinnen)
3 *(of a firm)* der Chef (*PL* die Chefs), die Chefin (*PL* die Chefinnen)
4 *(when tossing a coin)*
'**Heads or tails?**' 'Kopf oder Zahl?'

to head *VERB*
to head for something auf etwas (*ACC*) zusteuern *SEP* *(PERF sein)*
Liz headed for the door. Liz steuerte auf die Tür zu.

🔑 **headache** *NOUN*
die Kopfschmerzen (*PLURAL*)
I've got a headache. Ich habe Kopfschmerzen.

headlight *NOUN*
der Scheinwerfer (*PL* die Scheinwerfer)

headline *NOUN*
die Schlagzeile (*PL* die Schlagzeilen)

headmaster *NOUN*
der Direktor (*PL* die Direktoren)

WORD TIP Professions, hobbies, and sports don't take an article in German: Er ist Direktor.

headmistress *NOUN*
die Direktorin (*PL* die Direktorinnen)

WORD TIP Professions, hobbies, and sports don't take an article in German: Sie ist Direktorin.

headphones *PLURAL NOUN*
der Kopfhörer (*PL* die Kopfhörer)

headquarters *PLURAL NOUN*
(of a company) der Hauptsitz (*PL* die Hauptsitze)

🔑 **headteacher** *NOUN*
der Direktor (*PL* die Direktoren), die Direktorin (*PL* die Direktorinnen)

WORD TIP Professions, hobbies, and sports don't take an article in German: Er ist Direktor.

🔑 **health** *NOUN*
die Gesundheit

health centre *NOUN*
das Ärztezentrum (*PL* die Ärztezentren)

healthy *ADJECTIVE*
gesund

heap *NOUN*
der Haufen (*PL* die Haufen)
I've got heaps of work. Ich habe einen Haufen Arbeit. *(informal)*

🔑 **to hear** *VERB*
hören
I can hear somebody. Ich kann jemanden hören.
I can't hear anything. Ich kann überhaupt nichts hören.
I hear you've bought a dog. Ich habe gehört, dass ihr einen Hund gekauft habt.
• **to hear about something**
von etwas (*DAT*) hören
Have you heard about the concert? Hast du von dem Konzert gehört?
• **to hear from somebody**
von jemandem hören

hearing aid *NOUN*
das Hörgerät (*PL* die Hörgeräte)

heart *NOUN*
1 das Herz (*PL* die Herzen)
2 **to learn something by heart** etwas auswendig lernen
3 *(in cards)* das Herz
the jack of hearts der Herzbube

heart attack *NOUN*
der Herzinfarkt (*PL* die Herzinfarkte), der Herzanfall (*PL* die Herzanfälle)

🔑 **heat** *NOUN*
die Hitze

to heat *VERB*
1 **to heat something** etwas heiß machen
I'll go and heat the soup. Ich mache die Suppe heiß.
2 heizen a room

511

🔑 indicates key words

A B C D E F G H I J K L M N O P Q R S T U V W X Y Z

- **to heat something up**
  etwas aufwärmen SEP
  I'm heating the sauce up. Ich wärme die Soße auf.

heater NOUN
das Heizgerät (PL die Heizgeräte)

heather NOUN
das Heidekraut

ℓ **heating** NOUN
die Heizung

heatwave NOUN
die Hitzewelle (PL die Hitzewellen)

heaven NOUN
der Himmel
to go to heaven in den Himmel kommen

ℓ **heavy** ADJECTIVE
1 schwer
My rucksack's really heavy. Mein Rucksack ist sehr schwer.
2 (busy)
I've got a heavy day tomorrow. Ich habe morgen viel zu tun.
3 (in quantity) stark
heavy rain starker Regen

hectic ADJECTIVE
hektisch
a hectic day ein hektischer Tag

hedge NOUN
die Hecke (PL die Hecken)

hedgehog NOUN
der Igel (PL die Igel)

ℓ **heel** NOUN
1 (of foot or sock) die Ferse (PL die Fersen)
2 (of a shoe) der Absatz (PL die Absätze)

ℓ **height** NOUN
1 (of a person) die Größe
What height are you? Wie groß bist du?
2 (of a building, mountain) die Höhe
What height is it? Wie hoch ist es?

helicopter NOUN
der Hubschrauber (PL die Hubschrauber)

hell NOUN
die Hölle
to go to hell in die Hölle kommen
Hell! Verdammt! (informal)

ℓ **hello** EXCLAMATION
1 (polite) guten Tag!
2 (informal, and on the phone) hallo!

helmet NOUN
der Helm (PL die Helme)

a crash helmet ein Sturzhelm

ℓ **help** NOUN
die Hilfe
Do you need any help? Kann ich dir helfen?, (in a shop) Kann ich Ihnen behilflich sein?

to **help** VERB
1 helfen◇ (+DAT)
to help somebody (to) do something jemandem helfen, etwas zu tun
Can you help me lay the table? Kannst du mir helfen, den Tisch zu decken?
2 **to help yourself to something** sich (DAT) etwas nehmen◇
Help yourself to vegetables. Nimm dir Gemüse.
Help yourself! Greif zu!
3 **Help!** Hilfe!
4 **He can't help it.** Er kann nichts dafür.

helper NOUN
der Helfer (PL die Helfer), die Helferin (PL die Helferinnen)

helpful ADJECTIVE
(person) hilfsbereit

helping NOUN
die Portion (PL die Portionen)
Would you like a second helping? Möchtest du eine zweite Portion?

hem NOUN
der Saum (PL die Säume)

ℓ **hen** NOUN
die Henne (PL die Hennen)

ℓ **her** PRONOUN (in German this pronoun changes according to the function it has in the sentence or the preposition it follows)
1 (as a direct object in the accusative) sie
I know her. Ich kenne sie.
I saw her last week. Ich habe sie letzte Woche gesehen.
2 (after prepositions +ACC) sie
without her ohne sie
We've heard a lot about her. Wir haben viel über sie gehört.
3 (as an indirect object or after verbs that take the dative) ihr
I gave her my address. Ich habe ihr meine Adresse gegeben.
We helped her. Wir haben ihr geholfen.
4 (after prepositions +DAT) ihr
with her mit ihr
5 (in comparisons) sie
He's older than her. Er ist älter als sie.
6 (in the nominative) sie
It was her. Sie war es.

◇ irregular verb; SEP separable verb; for more help with verbs see centre section

her *ADJECTIVE*
1 *(before a masculine noun)* **ihr**
  her brother ihr Bruder
2 *(before a feminine noun)* **ihre**
  her sister ihre Schwester
3 *(before a neuter noun)* **ihr**
  her house ihr Haus
4 *(before a plural noun)* **ihre**
  her children ihre Kinder
5 *(with parts of the body)* **der/die/das** (*PL* **die**)
  (PLURAL)
  She had a glass in her hand. Sie hatte ein Glas in der Hand.
  She's washing her hands. Sie wäscht sich die Hände.

ℱ **herb** *NOUN*
  das **Kraut** (*PL* die **Kräuter**)

herd *NOUN*
  (of cattle, goats) die **Herde** (*PL* die **Herden**)

ℱ **here** *ADVERB*
1 *(in or at this place)* **hier**
  not far from here nicht weit von hier
  Here's my address. Hier ist meine Adresse.
  I want to stay here. Ich möchte hier bleiben.
2 *(to this place)* **hierher**
  when Peter came here als Peter hierher kam
  Come here. Komm her.
3 **Here they are!** Da sind sie!
  Tom isn't here at the moment. Tom ist im Moment nicht da.
4 **Here you are. This is the cake you wanted.** Bitte schön. Dies ist die Kuchen (*PL* die Sie haben wollten.)

hero *NOUN*
  der **Held** (*PL* die **Helden**)

heroin *NOUN*
  das **Heroin**

heroine *NOUN*
  die **Heldin** (*PL* die **Heldinnen**)

herring *NOUN*
  der **Hering** (*PL* die **Heringe**)

ℱ **hers** *PRONOUN*
1 *(for a masculine noun)* **ihrer**
  My coat is blue and hers is red. Mein Mantel ist blau und ihrer ist rot.
  I took my umbrella and she took hers. Ich nahm meinen Schirm und sie nahm ihren.
2 *(for a feminine noun)* **ihre**
  I gave Ann my address and she gave me hers. Ich habe Ann meine Adresse gegeben und sie hat mir ihre gegeben.

3 *(for a neuter noun)* **ihr(e)s**
  My bike is new but hers is old. Mein Rad ist neu, aber ihrs ist alt.
4 *(for masculine/ feminine/neuter plural nouns)* **ihre**
  I showed Emma my photos and she showed me hers. Ich habe Emma meine Fotos gezeigt und sie hat mir ihre gezeigt.
5 **The CDs are hers.** Die CDs gehören ihr.
  It's hers. Das gehört ihr.

herself *PRONOUN*
1 *(reflexive)* **sich**
  She's hurt herself. Sie hat sich wehgetan.
2 *(stressing something)* **selbst**
  She said it herself. Sie hat es selbst gesagt.
3 **She did it by herself.** Sie hat es ganz allein gemacht.

to **hesitate** *VERB*
  zögern

heterosexual *ADJECTIVE*
  heterosexuell

heterosexual *NOUN*
  der/die **Heterosexuelle** (*PL* die **Heterosexuellen**)

ℱ **hi** *EXCLAMATION*
  hallo!

hiccups *PLURAL NOUN*
  to have the hiccups einen Schluckauf haben

hidden *ADJECTIVE*
  verborgen

to **hide** *VERB*
1 **sich verstecken**
  She hid behind the door. Sie hat sich hinter der Tür versteckt.
2 **to hide something** etwas verstecken

hi-fi *NOUN*
  die **Hi-Fi-Anlage** (*PL* die **Hi-Fi-Anlagen**)

ℱ **high** *ADJECTIVE, ADVERB*
1 **hoch**
  How high is the wall? Wie hoch ist die Mauer?
  The wall is two metres high. Die Mauer ist zwei Meter hoch.
  The shelf is too high. Das Regal ist zu hoch.
  I can't jump any higher. Ich kann nicht höher springen.
  a high tower ein hoher Turm
  a high wall eine hohe Mauer
  at high speed mit hoher Geschwindigkeit
  a high voice eine hohe Stimme
2 **high winds** starker Wind

ℱ indicates key words

3 *(on drugs)* **high**

> **WORD TIP** The German adjective hoch loses its c when it has an ending, becoming hoher/hohe/hohes.

higher education NOUN
die **Hochschulbildung**

Highers, Advanced Highers PLURAL NOUN
das **Abitur** *(Students take Abitur at about 19 years of age. You can explain Highers briefly as follows: Highers werden in Schottland im vorletzten Jahr der Sekundarstufe in bis zu fünf Fächern abgelegt. Manche Schüler legen zusätzlich Advanced Highers in ihrem letzten Schuljahr ab. Advanced Highers werden in bis zu drei Fächern, die bereits für Highers belegt wurden, abgelegt. Beide Qualifikationen werden von A bis U benotet und sind Hochschulzugangsberechtigungen.)*
▶ SEE **Abitur, Matura** *(in Austria)*

high-heeled ADJECTIVE
hochhackig

high jump NOUN
der **Hochsprung**

to **hijack** VERB
to hijack a plane ein Flugzeug entführen

hijacker NOUN
der **Entführer** (PL die **Entführer**), die **Entführerin** (PL die **Entführerinnen**)

hijacking NOUN
die **Entführung** (PL die **Entführungen**)

hike NOUN
die **Wanderung** (PL die **Wanderungen**)
to go on a hike eine Wanderung machen

hiker NOUN
der **Wanderer** (PL die **Wanderer**), die **Wanderin** (PL die **Wanderinnen**)

hiking NOUN
das **Wandern**
to go hiking wandern gehen

hilarious ADJECTIVE
sehr lustig

hill NOUN
1 *(large hill)* der **Berg** (PL die **Berge**)
You can see the hills. Man kann die Berge sehen.
2 *(smaller)* der **Hügel** (PL die **Hügel**)
to walk up the hill den Hügel hinaufgehen
3 *(hillside)* der **Hang** (PL die **Hänge**)
the house on the hill das Haus am Hang

him PRONOUN *(in German this pronoun changes according to the function it has in the sentence or the preposition it follows)*
1 *(as a direct object in the accusative)* **ihn**
I know him. Ich kenne ihn.
I saw him last week. Ich habe ihn letzte Woche gesehen.
2 *(after prepositions +ACC)* **ihn**
He fought against him. Er hat gegen ihn gekämpft.
without him ohne ihn
3 *(as an indirect object or after verbs that take the dative)* **ihm**
I gave him my address. Ich habe ihm meine Adresse gegeben.
You must help him. Du musst ihm helfen.
4 *(after prepositions +DAT)* **ihm**
with him mit ihm
5 *(in comparisons)* **er**
She's older than him. Sie ist älter als er.
6 *(in the nominative)* **er**
It was him. Er war es.

himself PRONOUN
1 *(reflexive)* **sich**
He's hurt himself. Er hat sich wehgetan.
2 *(stressing something)* **selbst**
He said it himself. Er hat es selbst gesagt.
3 **He did it by himself.** Er hat es ganz allein gemacht.

Hindu NOUN
der/die **Hindu** (PL die **Hindus**)
He's a Hindu. Er ist Hindu.
She's a Hindu. Sie ist Hindu.

Hindu ADJECTIVE
hinduistisch
Hindu customs hinduistische Bräuche
a Hindu temple ein Hindutempel

> **WORD TIP** Adjectives never have capitals in German, even for religions.

hip NOUN
die **Hüfte** (PL die **Hüften**)

hippie NOUN
der **Hippie** (PL die **Hippies**)

hippopotamus NOUN
das **Nilpferd** (PL die **Nilpferde**)

hire NOUN
1 die **Vermietung**
car hire die Autovermietung
2 **for hire** zu vermieten

to **hire** VERB
mieten

his ADJECTIVE
1 *(before a masculine noun)* **sein**

◇ irregular verb; SEP separable verb; for more help with verbs see centre section

his brother sein Bruder
2 *(before a feminine noun)* seine
his sister seine Schwester
3 *(before a neuter noun)* sein
his house sein Haus
4 *(before a plural noun)* seine
his children seine Kinder
5 *(with parts of the body)* der/die/das *(PL die (PLURAL))*
He had a glass in his hand. Er hatte ein Glas in der Hand.
He's washing his hands. Er wäscht sich *(DAT)* die Hände.

his PRONOUN
1 *(for a masculine noun)* seiner
My coat is red and his is blue. Mein Mantel ist rot und seiner ist blau.
2 *(for a feminine noun)* seine
I gave him my address and he gave me his. Ich habe ihm meine Adresse gegeben und er hat mir seine gegeben.
3 *(for a neuter noun)* sein(e)s
My book is new but his is old. Mein Buch ist neu, aber seins ist alt.
4 *(for masculine/feminine/neuter plural nouns)* seine
I've invited my parents and Steve's invited his. Ich habe meine Eltern eingeladen und Steve hat seine eingeladen.
5 The green car is his. Das grüne Auto gehört ihm.
It's his. Das gehört ihm.

historic ADJECTIVE
historisch

ℙ **history** NOUN
die Geschichte

ℙ **hit** NOUN
1 *(song)* der Hit *(PL die Hits)*
their latest hit ihr neuester Hit
2 *(success)* der Erfolg *(PL die Erfolge)*
The film is a huge hit. Der Film ist ein großer Erfolg.

to **hit** VERB
1 schlagen◇
He hit me in the face. Er hat mich ins Gesicht geschlagen.
2 treffen◇ *(a ball, target)*
to hit the ball den Ball treffen
3 to hit your head on something sich *(DAT)* den Kopf an etwas *(DAT)* stoßen◇
I hit my head on the door. Ich habe mir den Kopf an der Tür gestoßen.
4 prallen gegen *(+ACC)* *(PERF sein)*
The car hit a wall. Das Auto ist gegen eine Mauer geprallt.
5 to be hit by a car von einem Auto

angefahren werden

hitch NOUN
das Problem *(PL die Probleme)*
There's been a slight hitch. Ein kleines Problem ist aufgetaucht.

to **hitch** VERB
to hitch a lift per Anhalter fahren◇ *(PERF sein)*

ℙ to **hitchhike** VERB
per Anhalter fahren◇ *(PERF sein)*
We hitchhiked to Heidelberg. Wir sind per Anhalter nach Heidelberg gefahren.

ℙ **hitchhiker** NOUN
der Anhalter *(PL die Anhalter)*, die Anhalterin *(PL die Anhalterinnen)*

ℙ **hitchhiking** NOUN
das Trampen

HIV-negative ADJECTIVE
HIV-negativ

HIV-positive ADJECTIVE
HIV-positiv

ℙ **hobby** NOUN
das Hobby *(PL die Hobbys)*

hockey NOUN
das Hockey

hockey stick NOUN
der Hockeyschläger *(PL die Hockeyschläger)*

to **hold** VERB
1 halten◇
to hold something in your hand etwas in der Hand halten
Can you hold the torch? Kannst du die Taschenlampe halten?
2 *(be able to contain)* fassen
The jug holds a litre. Der Krug fasst einen Liter.
3 to hold a meeting eine Versammlung abhalten◇ SEP
4 Can you hold the line, please? Bleiben Sie bitte am Apparat.
5 Hold on! *(wait)* Warten Sie!, *(on the phone)* Bleiben Sie am Apparat!
• to hold on to something
(stop yourself from falling) sich an etwas *(DAT)* festhalten◇ SEP
• to hold somebody up
(delay) jemanden aufhalten◇ SEP
I was held up at the dentist's. Ich bin beim Zahnarzt aufgehalten worden.
• to hold something up
(raise) etwas hochhalten◇ SEP

ℙ indicates key words

hold-up NOUN
1 die **Verzögerung** (PL die **Verzögerungen**)
2 (traffic jam) der **Stau** (PL die **Staus**)
3 (robbery) der **Überfall** (PL die **Überfälle**)

hole NOUN
das **Loch** (PL die **Löcher**)

ℰ **holiday** NOUN
1 die **Ferien** (PLURAL), der **Urlaub**
Where are you going for your holiday? Wo fahrt ihr in den Ferien hin?
Have a good holiday! Schöne Ferien!/ Schönen Urlaub!
to be away on holiday auf Urlaub sein/in den Ferien sein
to go on holiday in Urlaub fahren/in die Ferien fahren
the school holidays die Schulferien
2 (day off work) der **freie Tag** (PL die **freien Tage**)
I'm taking two days' holiday next week. Ich nehme mir nächste Woche zwei Tage frei.
3 **bank/public holiday** der Feiertag
Monday's a bank holiday. Montag ist ein Feiertag.

> **WORD TIP** Students, schoolchildren, and families usually have Ferien; people in paid employment usually have Urlaub.

holiday home NOUN
das **Ferienhaus** (PL die **Ferienhäuser**)

holiday job NOUN
der **Ferienjob** (PL die **Ferienjobs**)

Holland NOUN
Holland (NEUTER)

hollow ADJECTIVE
hohl

holy ADJECTIVE
heilig

ℰ **home** NOUN
1 **I was at home.** Ich war zu Hause.
to stay at home zu Hause bleiben
He left home at seventeen. Er ist mit siebzehn von zu Hause ausgezogen.
2 **Make yourself at home.** Mach es dir bequem.

home ADVERB
1 (to home) nach Hause
Susie's gone home. Susie ist nach Hause gegangen.
on my way home auf dem Weg nach Hause
to get home nach Hause kommen
We got home at midnight. Wir sind um Mitternacht nach Hause gekommen.
2 (at home) zu Hause

I'll be home in the afternoon. Ich bin am Nachmittag zu Hause.

home game/match NOUN
das **Heimspiel** (PL die **Heimspiele**)

ℰ **homeless** ADJECTIVE
obdachlos
the homeless die Obdachlosen

home-made ADJECTIVE
selbst gemacht
home-made biscuits selbst gebackene Kekse

homeopathic ADJECTIVE
homöopathisch

homesick ADJECTIVE
to be homesick Heimweh haben

ℰ **homework** NOUN
die **Hausaufgaben** (PLURAL)
I did my homework. Ich habe meine Hausaufgaben gemacht.
my German homework meine Deutschhausaufgaben
We have a lot of homework. Wir haben viele Hausaufgaben auf.

homosexual ADJECTIVE
homosexuell

homosexual NOUN
der/die **Homosexuelle** (PL die **Homosexuellen**)

ℰ **honest** ADJECTIVE
ehrlich

honestly ADVERB
ehrlich

honesty NOUN
die **Ehrlichkeit**

honey NOUN
der **Honig**

honeymoon NOUN
die **Flitterwochen** (PLURAL)
They're going to Italy for their honeymoon. Sie fahren in den Flitterwochen nach Italien.

honour NOUN
die **Ehre**

hood NOUN
1 die **Kapuze** (PL die **Kapuzen**)
2 (on a car) das **Verdeck** (PL die **Verdecke**)

hook NOUN
1 der **Haken** (PL die **Haken**)
2 **to take the phone off the hook** das Telefon aushängen SEP

◇ **irregular verb;** SEP **separable verb; for more help with verbs see centre section**

hooligan NOUN
der Hooligan (PL die Hooligans)

hooray EXCLAMATION
hurra!

to **hoover** VERB
saugen
I did the hoovering. Ich habe gesaugt.
I hoovered my bedroom. Ich habe mein
Schlafzimmer gesaugt.

Hoover® NOUN
der Staubsauger (PL die Staubsauger)

𝒫 **hope** NOUN
die Hoffnung (PL die Hoffnungen)
to give up hope die Hoffnung aufgeben◇
SEP

to **hope** VERB
1 hoffen
We hope you'll be able to come. Wir
hoffen, ihr könnt kommen.
I'm hoping to see you on Friday. Ich hoffe,
dich am Freitag zu sehen.
2 **I hope so.** Hoffentlich.
I hope not. Hoffentlich nicht.

hopefully ADVERB
hoffentlich
Hopefully, the film won't have started.
Hoffentlich hat der Film noch nicht
angefangen.

hopeless ADJECTIVE
hoffnungslos
I'm hopeless at physics. Ich bin ein
hoffnungsloser Fall in Physik.

horizontal ADJECTIVE
horizontal, waagrecht
The flag has three horizontal bars. Die
Flagge hat drei waagrechte Streifen.

horn NOUN
1 (of an animal, instrument) das Horn (PL die
Hörner)
2 (of a car) die Hupe (PL die Hupen)

horoscope NOUN
das Horoskop (PL die Horoskope)

𝒫 **horrible** ADJECTIVE
1 furchtbar
The weather was horrible. Das Wetter war
furchtbar.
2 (person) gemein
He was really horrible to me. Er war richtig
gemein zu mir.

horror NOUN
das Entsetzen

horror film NOUN
der Horrorfilm (PL die Horrorfilme)

𝒫 **horse** NOUN
das Pferd (PL die Pferde)

horse chestnut NOUN
(tree and nut) die Rosskastanie (PL die
Rosskastanien)

horse racing NOUN
das Pferderennen

horseshoe NOUN
das Hufeisen (PL die Hufeisen)

hose NOUN
der Schlauch (PL die Schläuche)

hosepipe NOUN
der Schlauch (PL die Schläuche)

𝒫 **hospital** NOUN
das Krankenhaus (PL die Krankenhäuser)
in hospital im Krankenhaus
to be taken into hospital ins Krankenhaus
kommen

hospitality NOUN
die Gastfreundschaft

host NOUN
1 der Gastgeber (PL die Gastgeber)
2 (on a TV programme) der Moderator (PL die
Moderatoren)

hostage NOUN
die Geisel (PL die Geiseln)

hostel NOUN
das Wohnheim (PL die Wohnheime)
youth hostel die Jugendherberge

hostess NOUN
1 die Gastgeberin (PL die Gastgeberinnen)
2 (on a TV programme) die Moderatorin
(PL die Moderatorinnen)
3 air hostess die Stewardess

> **WORD TIP** Professions, hobbies, and sports
> don't take an article in German: Sie ist
> Stewardess.

𝒫 **hot** ADJECTIVE
1 heiß
Be careful, the plates are hot. Sei
vorsichtig (PL die Teller sind heiß.)
It's hot today. Heute ist es heiß.
2 person
I'm very hot. Mir ist sehr heiß.
3 (spicy) scharf
The curry's too hot for me. Das Curry ist
mir zu scharf.
4 **a hot meal** ein warmes Essen

𝒫 indicates key words

hot dog NOUN
das or der **Hotdog** (PL die **Hotdogs**)

ℐ **hotel** NOUN
das **Hotel** (PL die **Hotels**)
to stay the night in a hotel in einem Hotel übernachten

ℐ **hour** NOUN
1 die **Stunde** (PL die **Stunden**)
two hours later zwei Stunden später
We waited for two hours. Wir haben zwei Stunden lang gewartet.
I've been waiting for hours. Ich warte schon seit Stunden.
two hours ago vor zwei Stunden
to be paid by the hour pro Stunde bezahlt werden
every hour jede Stunde
half an hour eine halbe Stunde
a quarter of an hour eine Viertelstunde
an hour and a half anderthalb Stunden
2 **the opening hours of the museum** die Öffnungszeiten des Museums

ℐ **house** NOUN
1 das **Haus** (PL die **Häuser**)
2 **at somebody's house** bei jemandem
I'm at Judy's house. Ich bin bei Judy.
I'm going to Sid's house tonight. Ich gehe heute Abend zu Sid.
I phoned from Jill's house. Ich habe von Jill aus angerufen.

housewife NOUN
die **Hausfrau** (PL die **Hausfrauen**)

ℐ **housework** NOUN
die **Hausarbeit**
Housework is boring. Hausarbeit ist langweilig.
He does all the housework. Er macht den Haushalt.

hovercraft NOUN
das **Luftkissenfahrzeug** (PL die **Luftkissenfahrzeuge**)

ℐ **how** ADVERB
1 **wie**
How did you do it? Wie hast du das gemacht?
How are you? Wie geht es dir?
How many? Wie viele?
How many brothers do you have? Wie viele Brüder hast du?
How old are you? Wie alt bist du?
How far is it? Wie weit ist es?
How far is it to York? Wie weit ist es bis York?
How long will it take? Wie lange dauert es?

How long have you known her? Wie lange kennst du sie?
2 **How much?** Wie viel?
How much money do you have? Wie viel Geld hast du?
How much is it? Wie viel kostet das?
3 **How about ...?** Wie wäre es mit ...?
How about going to the cinema? Wie wäre es mit Kino?
I'm not going. How about you? Ich gehe nicht hin. Und du?

however ADVERB
1 **jedoch**
2 *(in questions)*
However did she do it? Wie hat sie das nur gemacht?
3 **however famous he is** wie berühmt er auch sein mag

hug NOUN
to give somebody a hug jemanden umarmen
She gave me a hug. Sie hat mich umarmt.

to hug VERB
umarmen

huge ADJECTIVE
riesig

to hum VERB
summen

human ADJECTIVE
menschlich

human being NOUN
der **Mensch** (PL die **Menschen**)

human right NOUN
das **Menschenrecht** (PL die **Menschenrechte**)

humour NOUN
der **Humor**
to have a sense of humour Humor haben

humourless ADJECTIVE
humorlos

ℐ **hundred** NUMBER
hundert
two hundred zweihundert
two hundred and ten zweihundertzehn
a hundred people hundert Menschen
about a hundred um die hundert
hundreds of people Hunderte von Menschen

Hungary NOUN
Ungarn *(NEUTER)*

hunger NOUN
der **Hunger**

◇ irregular verb; SEP separable verb; for more help with verbs see centre section

ℓ **hungry** *ADJECTIVE*
  to be hungry Hunger haben
  I'm hungry. Ich habe Hunger.
  I'm not hungry. Ich habe keinen Hunger.

to **hunt** *VERB*
1 jagen *(an animal)*
2 suchen *(a person)*

hunting *NOUN*
  die Jagd
  fox-hunting die Fuchsjagd

hurricane *NOUN*
  der Orkan *(PL die Orkane)*

ℓ **hurry** *NOUN*
  to be in a hurry es eilig haben
  I'm in a hurry. Ich habe es eilig.
  There's no hurry. Es eilt nicht.

to **hurry** *VERB*
1 sich beeilen
  I must hurry. Ich muss mich beeilen.
  Hurry up! Beeil dich!
2 He hurried home. Er ging schnell nach
  Hause.

ℓ to **hurt** *VERB*
1 to hurt somebody jemandem wehtun◇ *SEP*
  You're hurting me! Du tust mir weh!
  That hurts! Das tut weh!
2 My arm hurts. Der Arm tut mir weh.
3 to hurt yourself sich *(DAT)* wehtun◇ *SEP*
  Did you hurt yourself? Hast du dir
  wehgetan?

hurt *ADJECTIVE*
1 *(in an accident)* verletzt
  Three people were hurt. Drei Menschen
  wurden verletzt.
2 *(in feelings)* gekränkt
  She felt hurt. Sie fühlte sich gekränkt.

ℓ **husband** *NOUN*
  der Ehemann *(PL die Ehemänner)*, der
  Mann *(PL die Männer)*
  her husband ihr Mann

hydroelectric power *NOUN*
  die Wasserkraft

hygienic *ADJECTIVE*
  hygienisch

hymn *NOUN*
  das Kirchenlied *(PL die Kirchenlieder)*

ℓ **hypermarket** *NOUN*
  der Großmarkt *(PL die Großmärkte)*

hyphen *NOUN*
  der Bindestrich *(PL die Bindestriche)*

Ii

ℓ **I** *PRONOUN*
  ich
  I have two sisters. Ich habe zwei
  Schwestern.

ℓ **ice** *NOUN*
  das Eis

ℓ **ice cream** *NOUN*
  das Eis *(PL die Eis)*
  two chocolate ice creams zwei
  Schokoladeneis

ice hockey *NOUN*
  das Eishockey

ℓ **ice rink** *NOUN*
  die Eisbahn *(PL die Eisbahnen)*

ice skating *NOUN*
  to go ice skating Schlittschuh laufen◇ *(PERF
  sein)*

icon *NOUN*
  (on a computer screen) das Symbol *(PL die
  Symbole)*

icy *ADJECTIVE*
1 vereist road
2 *(very cold)* eiskalt

ℓ **idea** *NOUN*
1 die Idee *(PL die Ideen)*
  What a good idea! Was für eine gute Idee!
2 I've no idea. Ich habe keine Ahnung.

ideal *ADJECTIVE*
  ideal

identical *ADJECTIVE*
1 identisch
2 *(twins)* eineiig

ℓ **identification** *NOUN*
1 die Identifizierung
2 *(proof of identity)* die Ausweispapiere
  (PLURAL)

ℓ **identity card** *NOUN*
  der Personalausweis *(PL die
  Personalausweise)*

ℓ **idiot** *NOUN*
  der Idiot *(PL die Idioten)*

idiotic *ADJECTIVE*
  idiotisch

i.e. *ABBREVIATION*
  d. h. das heißt

ℓ indicates key words

if CONJUNCTION
1 wenn
 if it rains wenn es regnet
 if I won the lottery wenn ich im Lotto
 gewinnen sollte
 if not wenn nicht
 if only wenn nur
 If only you'd told me! Wenn du mir das nur
 gesagt hättest!
2 *(even if)* selbst wenn
 even if it snows selbst wenn es schneit
3 **if I were you** an deiner Stelle
4 *(whether)* ob
 I wonder if he'll come. Ich bin gespannt, ob
 er kommt.
 as if als ob

to **ignore** VERB
 ignorieren

ill ADJECTIVE
 krank
 to be ill krank sein
 to fall ill/to be taken ill krank werden
 I feel ill. Ich fühle mich krank.
 seriously ill schwer krank

illegal ADJECTIVE
 illegal

illness NOUN
 die Krankheit (PL die Krankheiten)

illusion NOUN
 die Illusion (PL die Illusionen)

illustration NOUN
 die Illustration (PL die Illustrationen)

image NOUN
 das Bild (PL die Bilder)
 He's the spitting image of his father. Er ist
 das Ebenbild seines Vaters.

imagination NOUN
 die Fantasie

imaginative ADJECTIVE
 fantasievoll

to **imagine** VERB
 sich (DAT) vorstellen SEP
 Imagine that you're very rich. Stell dir vor,
 du bist sehr reich.
 You can't imagine how hard it was. Du
 kannst dir nicht vorstellen, wie schwer es
 war.

to **imitate** VERB
 nachahmen SEP

immediate ADJECTIVE
1 *(without delay)* unmittelbar

2 **the immediate family** die engste Familie

immediately ADVERB
1 sofort
 I rang them immediately. Ich habe sie
 sofort angerufen.
2 **immediately before** unmittelbar davor
 immediately after unmittelbar danach

immigrant NOUN
 der Einwanderer (PL die Einwanderer), die
 Einwanderin (PL die Einwanderinnen)

immigration NOUN
 die Einwanderung

impatience NOUN
 die Ungeduld

impatient ADJECTIVE
1 ungeduldig
2 **to be impatient with somebody**
 ungeduldig mit jemandem sein

impatiently ADVERB
 ungeduldig

imperfect NOUN
 (verb tense) das Imperfekt
 'Ich schlug' is in the imperfect. 'Ich schlug'
 steht im Imperfekt.

import NOUN
 der Import (PL die Importe)
to **import** VERB
 importieren

importance NOUN
 die Wichtigkeit

important ADJECTIVE
 wichtig
 an important decision eine wichtige
 Entscheidung
 The important thing is to keep fit. Das
 Wichtige ist, dass man fit bleibt.

impossible ADJECTIVE
 unmöglich
 It's impossible to find a telephone. Es ist
 unmöglich, ein Telefon zu finden.

impressed ADJECTIVE
 beeindruckt
 to be impressed by something von etwas
 (DAT) beeindruckt sein

impression NOUN
 der Eindruck (PL die Eindrücke)
 to make a good impression on somebody
 einen guten Eindruck auf jemanden
 machen
 **I got the impression he was hiding
 something.** Ich hatte den Eindruck, dass er

etwas verheimlichte.

impressive ADJECTIVE
eindrucksvoll

ℱ to **improve** VERB
1 to improve something etwas verbessern
2 (get better) besser werden◇
The weather is improving. Das Wetter wird besser.

improvement NOUN
die Verbesserung (PL die Verbesserungen)

ℱ **in** PREPOSITION
1 in (+DAT or, with movement into, +ACC)
It is in my pocket. Es ist in meiner Tasche. (DAT)
(with movement) He put it in his pocket. Er hat es in die Tasche gesteckt. (ACC)
She sat in the sun. Sie saß in der Sonne. (DAT)
I read it in the newspaper. Ich habe es in der Zeitung gelesen. (DAT)
in Oxford in Oxford
in Germany in Deutschland
2 the biggest city in the world die größte Stadt der Welt
a house in the country ein Haus auf dem Land
in the street auf der Straße
3 (wearing and with colours) in (+DAT)
the girl in the pink shirt das Mädchen im rosa Hemd
the woman in black die Frau in Schwarz
4 in German auf Deutsch
5 (time expressions) in (+DAT)
in May im Mai
in 2008 (im Jahre) 2008
in winter im Winter
in summer im Sommer
in the night in der Nacht
I'll phone you in ten minutes. Ich rufe dich in zehn Minuten an.
She was ready in five minutes. Sie war in fünf Minuten fertig.
6 (some time expressions use different German prepositions)
in the morning am Morgen
in the afternoon am Nachmittag
at eight in the morning um acht Uhr morgens
at four in the afternoom um vier Uhr nachmittags
7 (among people or in literature) bei (+DAT)
It's rare in children. Das ist bei Kindern selten.
in Shakespeare bei Shakespeare
in the army beim Militär

8 in time rechtzeitig

in ADVERB
1 (inside) hinein-, herein-, rein- (informal)
(Herein-, hinein-, and rein- form prefixes to separable verbs. 'Herein-' is used with verbs like kommen, which have the sense of moving towards the speaker. 'Hinein-' is used with verbs like gehen, which have the sense of going away from the speaker. The informal 'rein-' can be used with either movement.)
to come in hereinkommen◇ SEP (PERF sein)
to go in hineingehen◇ SEP (PERF sein)
He was not allowed to go into the room. Er durfte nicht ins Zimmer reingehen.
to run in reinlaufen◇ SEP (PERF sein) (informal)
2 to be in da sein
Mick's not in at the moment. Mick ist im Moment nicht da.
My maths homework needs to be in on Monday. Ich muss meine Mathehausaufgabe am Montag abgeben.
3 (at home) zu Hause
4 (indoors) drinnen
in here hier drinnen
in there da drinnen

ℱ to **include** VERB
einschließen◇ SEP
Service is included in the price. Die Bedienung ist im Preis inbegriffen.

ℱ **including** PREPOSITION
1 einschließlich (+GEN)
everyone, including the children alle, einschließlich der Kinder
£50 including postage fünfzig Pfund einschließlich Porto
including Sundays einschließlich sonntags
2 not including Sundays außer sonntags

income NOUN
das Einkommen (PL die Einkommen)

income tax NOUN
die Einkommenssteuer

ℱ **increase** NOUN
die Erhöhung (PL die Erhöhungen) (in price, for example)
to **increase** VERB
1 (go up) steigen◇ (PERF sein)
The price has increased by £10. Der Preis ist um zehn Pfund gestiegen.
2 (put up) erhöhen

incredible ADJECTIVE
unglaublich

incredibly ADVERB
(very) **unglaublich**
The film's incredibly boring. Der Film ist
unglaublich langweilig.

indeed ADVERB
1 (to emphasize) **wirklich**
She's very pleased indeed. Sie hat sich
wirklich sehr gefreut.
2 Thank you very much indeed. Vielen
herzlichen Dank.

indefinite article NOUN
(in grammar) der **unbestimmte Artikel**

independence NOUN
die **Unabhängigkeit**

independent ADJECTIVE
unabhängig
independent school die Privatschule

index NOUN
das **Register** (PL die **Register**)

India NOUN
Indien (NEUTER)

Indian NOUN
1 der **Inder** (PL die **Inder**), die **Inderin** (PL die
Inderinnen)
2 (a Native American) der **Indianer**
(PL die **Indianer**), die **Indianerin**
(PL die **Indianerinnen**)
cowboys and Indians Cowboys und
Indianer

Indian ADJECTIVE
1 **indisch**
Indian cooking die indische Küche
He's Indian. Er ist Inder.
She's Indian. Sie ist Inderin.
2 (Native American) **indianisch**
Indian culture die indianische Kultur

WORD TIP Adjectives never have capitals
in German, even for regions, countries, or
nationalities.

to **indicate** VERB
1 (point at) **zeigen auf** (+ACC) (a person or a
thing)
2 (of a car or driver) **blinken**

indigestion NOUN
die **Magenverstimmung** (PL die
Magenverstimmungen)
I've got indigestion. Ich habe eine
Magenverstimmung.

individual NOUN
der/die **Einzelne** (PL die **Einzelnen**)

individual ADJECTIVE
1 **einzeln** (serving, contribution)
2 individual tuition der Einzelunterricht

indoor ADJECTIVE
an indoor swimming pool ein Hallenbad
indoor games Spiele im Haus, (in sports)
Hallenspiele

indoors ADVERB
drinnen
It's cooler indoors. Drinnen ist es kühler.
to go indoors ins Haus gehen

industrial ADJECTIVE
industriell

industrial estate NOUN
das **Industriegebiet** (PL die
Industriegebiete)

ℰ **industry** NOUN
die **Industrie** (PL die **Industrien**)
the car industry die Autoindustrie

inefficient ADJECTIVE
uneffektiv

inevitable ADJECTIVE
unvermeidlich

inevitably ADVERB
zwangsläufig

inexperienced ADJECTIVE
unerfahren

infant school NOUN
die **Vorschule** (PL die **Vorschulen**)

infection NOUN
die **Infektion** (PL die **Infektionen**)
eye infection die Augeninfektion
throat infection die Halsentzündung

infectious ADJECTIVE
ansteckend

infinitive NOUN
(in grammar) der **Infinitiv** (PL die **Infinitive**)

inflammable ADJECTIVE
leicht entflammbar

inflatable ADJECTIVE
inflatable mattress die Luftmatratze
inflatable boat das Schlauchboot

to **inflate** VERB
aufblasen ◇ SEP (a mattress or boat)

inflation NOUN
die **Inflation**

influence NOUN
der **Einfluss** (PL die **Einflüsse**)
to be a good influence on somebody einen
guten Einfluss auf jemanden haben

to **influence** VERB
beeinflussen

◇ **irregular verb;** SEP **separable verb; for more help with verbs see centre section**

A
B
C
D
E
F
G
H
I
J
K
L
M
N
O
P
Q
R
S
T
U
V
W
X
Y
Z

to **inform** VERB
informieren
to inform somebody of something
jemanden über etwas (ACC) informieren

informal ADJECTIVE
1 **zwanglos** (meal or event)
2 **ungezwungen** (language, tone)

℘**information** NOUN
die **Auskunft**
Where can I get information about flights to Berlin? Wo kann ich Auskunft über Flüge nach Berlin bekommen?

information desk NOUN
die **Auskunft** (PL die **Auskünfte**)

information office NOUN
das **Informationsbüro** (PL die **Informationsbüros**)

information technology NOUN
die **Informatik**

informative ADJECTIVE
aufschlussreich, lehrreich

ingredient NOUN
die **Zutat** (PL die **Zutaten**)

inhabitant NOUN
der **Einwohner** (PL die **Einwohner**), die **Einwohnerin** (PL die **Einwohnerinnen**)

inhaler NOUN
der **Inhalator** (PL die **Inhalatoren**)

initials PLURAL NOUN
die **Initialen** (PLURAL)

initiative NOUN
die **Initiative** (PL die **Initiativen**)
You must use your initiative. Du musst Initiative zeigen.

injection NOUN
die **Spritze** (PL die **Spritzen**)

℘to **injure** VERB
verletzen

injury NOUN
die **Verletzung** (PL die **Verletzungen**)
a serious injury eine schwere Verletzung

ink NOUN
die **Tinte** (PL die **Tinten**)

in-laws NOUN
die **Schwiegereltern** (PLURAL)

inner ADJECTIVE
innerer/innere/inneres

innocent ADJECTIVE
unschuldig

insane ADJECTIVE
1 **geisteskrank**
2 (foolish) **wahnsinnig**

℘**insect** NOUN
das **Insekt** (PL die **Insekten**)
insect bite der Insektenstich

insect repellent NOUN
das **Insektenschutzmittel**

℘**inside** NOUN
on the inside innen
The inside of the oven is black. Innen ist der Herd schwarz.

inside PREPOSITION
in (+DAT, or, with movement towards a place, +ACC)
inside the cinema im Kino (DAT)
to go inside (the house) ins Haus gehen (ACC)

inside ADVERB
drinnen
She's inside, I think. Ich glaube, sie ist drinnen.

inside out ADVERB
(clothing) auf links
I had my sweater on inside out. Ich hatte meinen Pullover auf links an.

to **insist** VERB
darauf bestehen◇
if you insist wenn du darauf bestehst
to insist on doing something darauf bestehen, etwas zu tun
He insists on paying. Er besteht darauf zu zahlen.
to insist that ... darauf bestehen, dass ...
Ruth insisted I was wrong. Ruth bestand darauf, dass ich unrecht hatte.

inspector NOUN
1 (on a bus or train) der **Kontrolleur** (PL die **Kontrolleure**), die **Kontrolleurin** (PL die **Kontrolleurinnen**)
2 (in the police) der **Kommissar** (PL die **Kommissare**), die **Kommissarin** (PL die **Kommissarinnen**)

> **WORD TIP** Professions, hobbies, and sports don't take an article in German: Er ist Kontrolleur.

to **install** VERB
installieren

instalment NOUN
(of a story or serial) die **Folge** (PL die **Folgen**)

℘ indicates key words

instance NOUN
for instance zum Beispiel

instant NOUN
der Augenblick (PL die Augenblicke)
Come here this instant! Komm sofort her!

instant ADJECTIVE
1 Instant- (coffee, tea)
2 (immediate) sofortig

instantly ADVERB
sofort

ᵖ **instead** ADVERB
1 Ted couldn't come, so I came instead (of him). Ted konnte nicht kommen, also bin ich an seiner Stelle gekommen.
2 instead of statt (+GEN OR +DAT)
He bought a bike instead of a car. Statt eines Autos hat er ein Fahrrad gekauft.
Instead of cake I had cheese. Statt Kuchen habe ich Käse genommen.
Instead of playing tennis we went swimming. Statt Tennis zu spielen, sind wir schwimmen gegangen.

instinct NOUN
der Instinkt (PL die Instinkte)

institute NOUN
das Institut (PL die Institute)

ᵖ **instructions** PLURAL NOUN
die Anweisung (PL die Anweisungen)
Follow the instructions on the packet. Befolgen Sie die Anweisung auf der Packung.
'Instructions for use' 'Gebrauchsanweisung'

instructor NOUN
der Lehrer (PL die Lehrer), die Lehrerin (PL die Lehrerinnen)
my skiing instructor mein Skilehrer
his driving instructor sein Fahrlehrer

WORD TIP Professions, hobbies, and sports don't take an article in German: Er ist Lehrer.

ᵖ **instrument** NOUN
das Instrument (PL die Instrumente)
to play an instrument ein Instrument spielen

insulin NOUN
das Insulin

insult NOUN
die Beleidigung (PL die Beleidigungen)
to **insult** VERB
beleidigen

insurance NOUN
die Versicherung (PL die Versicherungen)
travel insurance die Reiseversicherung
Do you have insurance? Bist du versichert?

intelligence NOUN
die Intelligenz

ᵖ **intelligent** ADJECTIVE
intelligent

to **intend** VERB
beabsichtigen
as I intended wie beabsichtigt
to intend to do something beabsichtigen, etwas zu tun
We intend to spend the night in Rome. Wir beabsichtigen, in Rom zu übernachten.

intensive care NOUN
1 die Intensivpflege
2 (hospital ward) die Intensivstation
He's now in intensive care. Er ist jetzt auf der Intensivstation.

intention NOUN
die Absicht (PL die Absichten)
I have no intention of paying. Ich habe nicht die Absicht zu zahlen.

ᵖ **interest** NOUN
1 das Interesse (PL die Interessen)
to have lots of interests viele Interessen haben
2 (financial) die Zinsen (PLURAL)
to **interest** VERB
interessieren
That doesn't interest me. Das interessiert mich nicht.

interested ADJECTIVE
to be interested in something sich für etwas (ACC) interessieren
Sean's interested in cooking. Sean interessiert sich für Kochen.

ᵖ **interesting** ADJECTIVE
interessant

to **interfere** VERB
1 to interfere with something (fiddle with it) sich (DAT) an etwas (DAT) zu schaffen machen
Don't interfere with my computer! Mach dir nicht an meinem Computer zu schaffen!
2 to interfere in something sich in etwas (ACC) einmischen SEP (somebody else's affairs)
Stop interfering! Misch dich nicht immer ein!

interior designer NOUN
der Innenarchitekt (PL die Innenarchitektenv) die Innenarchitektin

◇ irregular verb; SEP separable verb; for more help with verbs see centre section

(PL die **Innenarchitektinnen**)

WORD TIP Professions, hobbies, and sports don't take an article in German: Er ist Innenarchitekt.

℘ **international** ADJECTIVE
international

Internet NOUN
das **Internet**
on the Internet im Internet
I downloaded it from the Internet. Ich habe es aus dem Internet heruntergeladen.

to **interpret** VERB
(act as an interpreter) dolmetschen

interpreter NOUN
der **Dolmetscher** (PL die **Dolmetscher**), die **Dolmetscherin** (PL die **Dolmetscherinnen**)

WORD TIP Professions, hobbies, and sports don't take an article in German: Sie ist Dolmetscherin.

to **interrupt** VERB
unterbrechen◇

interruption NOUN
die **Unterbrechung** (PL die **Unterbrechungen**)

interval NOUN
(in a play or concert) die **Pause** (PL die **Pausen**)

℘ **interview** NOUN
1 (for a job) das **Vorstellungsgespräch** (PL die **Vorstellungsgespräche**)
to go for an interview sich vorstellen SEP
2 (in a newspaper, on TV, or radio) das **Interview** (PL die **Interviews**)

to **interview** VERB
interviewen (on TV, radio)

interviewer NOUN
der **Interviewer** (PL die **Interviewer**), die **Interviewerin** (PL die **Interviewerinnen**)

℘ **into** PREPOSITION
1 in (+ACC)
He's gone into the garden. Er ist in den Garten gegangen.
I put the ball into the bag. Ich habe den Ball in die Tasche getan.
We all got into the car. Wir sind alle ins Auto gestiegen.
to go into town in die Stadt gehen
to get into bed ins Bett gehen
to translate into German ins Deutsche übersetzen
to change pounds into euros Pfund in Euro

wechseln
2 (against) gegen (+ACC)
He drove into the wall. Er ist gegen die Mauer gefahren.
3 **to be into jazz** auf Jazz abfahren◇ SEP (PERF sein) (informal)

to **introduce** VERB
1 vorstellen SEP
She introduced me to her brother. Sie hat mich ihrem Bruder vorgestellt.
She introduced her brother to me. Sie hat mir ihren Bruder vorgestellt.
Can I introduce you to my mother? Darf ich Sie meiner Mutter vorstellen?
2 (programme on radio, TV) moderieren

introduction NOUN
(in a book) die **Einleitung** (PL die **Einleitungen**)

to **invade** VERB
einfallen◇ SEP (PERF sein) in (+ACC)

invalid NOUN
der/die **Kranke** (PL die **Kranken**)

to **invent** VERB
erfinden◇

invention NOUN
die **Erfindung** (PL die **Erfindungen**)

inverted commas PLURAL NOUN
die **Anführungszeichen** (PLURAL)
in inverted commas in Anführungszeichen

investigation NOUN
die **Untersuchung** (PL die **Untersuchungen**)
an investigation into the incident eine Untersuchung des Vorfalls

invisible ADJECTIVE
unsichtbar

invitation NOUN
die **Einladung** (PL die **Einladungen**)
an invitation to a party eine Einladung zu einer Party

℘ to **invite** VERB
einladen◇ SEP
Kirsty invited me to lunch. Kirsty hat mich zum Mittagessen eingeladen.
He's invited me out on Tuesday. Er hat mich eingeladen, Dienstag mit ihm auszugehen.
They invited us round. Sie haben uns zu sich eingeladen.

inviting ADJECTIVE
verlockend

A
B
C
D
E
F
G
H
I
J
K
L
M
N
O
P
Q
R
S
T
U
V
W
X
Y
Z

℘ indicates key words

to **involve** VERB
1 erfordern
It involves a lot of time. Es erfordert viel Zeit.
2 (include) einbeziehen◇ SEP
Try to involve everybody in the game. Versuchen Sie, alle in das Spiel einzubeziehen.
to be involved in something an etwas (DAT) beteiligt sein
I am involved in the new project. Ich bin an dem neuen Projekt beteiligt.
3 (implicate) verwickeln
to get involved in something in etwas (ACC) verwickelt werden
Two cars were involved in the accident. Zwei Autos waren in den Unfall verwickelt.
4 to get involved with somebody sich mit jemandem einlassen◇ SEP

Iran NOUN
der Iran

WORD TIP In German, this is always used with the article: Sie fahren in den Iran. Er wohnt im Iran.

Iraq NOUN
der Irak

WORD TIP In German, this is always used with the article: Sie fahren in den Irak. Er wohnt im Irak.

♀**Ireland** NOUN
Irland (NEUTER)
the Republic of Ireland die Republik Irland

♀**Irish** NOUN
1 (the language) das Irisch
2 (the people)
the Irish die Iren

Irish ADJECTIVE
irisch
the Irish coast die irische Küste
He's Irish. Er ist Ire.
She's Irish. Sie ist Irin.

WORD TIP Adjectives never have capitals in German, even for regions, countries, or nationalities.

Irishman NOUN
der Ire (PL die Iren)

Irish Sea NOUN
die Irische See

Irishwoman NOUN
die Irin (PL die Irinnen)

iron NOUN
1 (for clothes) das Bügeleisen (PL die Bügeleisen)
2 (the metal) das Eisen

to **iron** VERB
bügeln

ironing NOUN
das Bügeln
to do the ironing bügeln

ironing board NOUN
das Bügelbrett (PL die Bügelbretter)

ironmonger's NOUN
das Haushaltswarengeschäft (PL die Haushaltswarengeschäfte)

irregular ADJECTIVE
unregelmäßig

irritable ADJECTIVE
reizbar

to **irritate** VERB
ärgern

irritating ADJECTIVE
ärgerlich

Islam NOUN
der Islam

Islamic ADJECTIVE
islamisch

WORD TIP Adjectives never have capitals in German, even for religions.

island NOUN
die Insel (PL die Inseln)

isolated ADJECTIVE
1 (remote) abgelegen
2 (single) einzeln
isolated cases Einzelfälle

Israel NOUN
Israel (NEUTER)

Israeli NOUN
der/die Israeli (PL die Israelis)

Israeli ADJECTIVE
israelisch

WORD TIP Adjectives never have capitals in German, even for regions, countries, or nationalities.

issue NOUN
1 (something you discuss) die Frage (PL die Fragen)
a political issue eine politische Frage
2 (of a magazine) die Ausgabe (PL die Ausgaben)
3 (problem) das Problem (PL die Probleme)

to **issue** VERB
(hand out) ausgeben◇ SEP

♀**it** PRONOUN
1 (as the subject) er (standing for a masculine noun), sie (standing for a feminine noun), es

◇ irregular verb; SEP separable verb; for more help with verbs see centre section

(standing for a neuter noun)
'Where's my key?' – 'It's in the kitchen.'
'Wo ist mein Schlüssel?' – 'Er ist in der Küche.'
'Where's my bag?' – 'It's in the living room.' 'Wo ist meine Tasche?' – 'Sie ist im Wohnzimmer.'
'How old is your car?' – 'It's five years old.' 'Wie alt ist dein Auto?' – 'Es ist fünf Jahre alt.'
2 *(as the direct object, in the accusative)* **ihn** *(standing for a masculine noun)*, **sie** *(standing for a feminine noun)*, **es** *(standing for a neuter noun)*
'Where's your umbrella?' – 'I've lost it.' 'Wo ist dein Regenschirm?' – 'Ich habe ihn verloren.'
'Have you seen my bag?' – 'I saw it in the kitchen.' 'Hast du meine Tasche gesehen?' – 'Ich habe sie in der Küche gesehen.'
'Have you read his new book?' – 'I've just bought it.' 'Hast du sein neues Buch gelesen?' – 'Ich habe es gerade gekauft.'
3 to it ihm *(masculine)*, ihr *(feminine)*, ihm *(neuter)*
4 Yes, it's true. Ja, das stimmt.
It doesn't matter. Das macht nichts.
5 Who is it? Wer ist da?
It's me. Ich bin's.
What is it? Was ist los?
6 It's raining. Es regnet.
It's Monday. Es ist Montag.
It's two o'clock. Es ist zwei Uhr.
7 of it davon
8 out of it daraus

ℓ **IT** *NOUN*
die **Informatik**
She works in IT. Sie ist Informatikerin.

Italian *NOUN*
1 *(the language)* das **Italienisch**
2 *(person)* der **Italiener** *(PL die Italiener)*, die **Italienerin** *(PL die Italienerinnen)*
Italian *ADJECTIVE*
1 italienisch
Italian food die italienische Küche
He's Italian. Er ist Italiener.
She's Italian. Sie ist Italienerin.
2 my Italian class mein Italienischunterricht

> **WORD TIP** Adjectives never have capitals in German, even for regions, countries, or nationalities.

italics *PLURAL NOUN*
die **Kursivschrift**
in italics kursiv

Italy *NOUN*
Italien *(NEUTER)*

to itch *VERB*
1 My back's itching. Mein Rücken juckt.
2 This jumper itches. Dieser Pullover kratzt.

item *NOUN*
1 der **Gegenstand** *(PL die Gegenstände)*
2 *(for sale in a shop)* der **Artikel** *(PL die Artikel)*

its *ADJECTIVE*
1 sein *(for a masculine noun)*, **ihr** *(for a feminine noun)*, **sein** *(for a neuter noun)*
The dog has lost its collar. Der Hund hat sein Halsband verloren.
The cat is in its basket. Die Katze ist in ihrem Korb.
The horse is brown and its mane is black. Das Pferd ist braun und seine Mähne ist schwarz.
2 *(with plural nouns, use seine when 'its' refers back to a masculine or neuter noun and ihre when 'its' refers back to a feminine noun)*
The dog has eaten its biscuits. Der Hund hat seine Hundekuchen gefressen.
The cat is washing its paws. Die Katze putzt ihre Pfoten.
The horse has won all its races. Das Pferd hat alle seine Rennen gewonnen.

itself *PRONOUN*
1 *(reflexive)* **sich**
The cat's washing itself. Die Katze putzt sich.
2 He left the dog by itself. Er hat den Hund allein gelassen.

ivy *NOUN*
der **Efeu**

Jj

jack *NOUN*
1 *(in cards)* der **Bube** *(PL die Buben)*
the jack of clubs der Kreuzbube
2 *(for a car)* der **Wagenheber** *(PL die Wagenheber)*

ℓ **jacket** *NOUN*
die **Jacke** *(PL die Jacken)*

jacket potato *NOUN*
die **in der Schale gebackene Kartoffel**

jackpot *NOUN*
der **Jackpot** *(PL die Jackpots)*
to win the jackpot den Jackpot gewinnen
to hit the jackpot das große Los ziehen

jam | join

jam NOUN
1 die **Marmelade** (*PL* die **Marmeladen**)
   raspberry jam die Himbeermarmelade
2 **traffic jam** der Stau

January NOUN
der **Januar**
in January im Januar

Japan NOUN
Japan (*NEUTER*)

Japanese NOUN
1 (*the language*) das **Japanisch**
2 (*person*) der **Japaner** (*PL* die **Japaner**), die **Japanerin** (*PL* die **Japanerinnen**)
   the Japanese die Japaner

Japanese ADJECTIVE
japanisch
Japanese art japanische Kunst
He's Japanese. Er ist Japaner.
She's Japanese. Sie ist Japanerin.

WORD TIP Adjectives never have capitals in German, even for regions, countries, or nationalities.

jar NOUN
1 (*small*) das **Glas** (*PL* die **Gläser**)
   a jar of jam ein Glas Marmelade
2 (*large*) der **Topf** (*PL* die **Töpfe**)

javelin NOUN
der **Speer** (*PL* die **Speere**)

jaw NOUN
der **Kiefer** (*PL* die **Kiefer**)

jazz NOUN
der **Jazz**

jealous ADJECTIVE
eifersüchtig
to be jealous of somebody eifersüchtig auf jemanden sein

jeans PLURAL NOUN
die **Jeans**
my jeans meine Jeans
a pair of jeans ein Paar Jeans
These jeans are too tight. Diese Jeans ist zu eng.

WORD TIP In German die Jeans is singular.

jelly NOUN
1 das **Gelee** (*PL* die **Gelees**)
2 (*dessert*) die **Götterspeise** (*PL* die **Götterspeisen**)

jellyfish NOUN
die **Qualle** (*PL* die **Quallen**)

jersey NOUN
1 (*jumper*) der **Pullover** (*PL* die **Pullover**)
2 (*for football*) das **Trikot** (*PL* die **Trikots**)

Jesus NOUN
der **Jesus**
Jesus Christ Jesus Christus

jet NOUN
(*a plane*) der **Jet** (*PL* die **Jets**)

jet lag NOUN
der **Jetlag**

Jew NOUN
der **Jude** (*PL* die **Juden**), die **Jüdin** (*PL* die **Jüdinnen**)
He's a Jew. Er ist Jude.

jewel NOUN
der **Edelstein** (*PL* die **Edelsteine**)

jeweller NOUN
der **Juwelier** (*PL* die **Juweliere**)

jeweller's NOUN
das **Juweliergeschäft**

jewellery NOUN
der **Schmuck**

Jewish ADJECTIVE
jüdisch

WORD TIP Adjectives never have capitals in German, even for religions.

jigsaw NOUN
das **Puzzlespiel** (*PL* die **Puzzlespiele**)

job NOUN
1 (*paid work*) die **Stelle** (*PL* die **Stellen**), der **Job** (*PL* die **Jobs**) (*informal*)
   a job as a secretary eine Stelle als Sekretärin
2 (*a task*) die **Arbeit** (*PL* die **Arbeiten**)
   It's not an easy job. Das ist keine leichte Arbeit.
3 **She made a good job of it.** Sie hat es gut gemacht.

jobless ADJECTIVE
arbeitslos

to jog VERB
joggen (*PERF* sein)

to join VERB
1 (*become a member of*) **beitreten**◇ *SEP* (+*DAT*) (*PERF* sein)
   I've joined the tennis club. Ich bin dem Tennisklub beigetreten.
2 (*meet up with*) **treffen**◇
   I'll join you later. Ich treffe euch später.
• **to join in**
1 **mitmachen** *SEP*
   Kylie never joins in. Kylie macht nie mit.
2 **to join in something** bei etwas (*DAT*)

◇ **irregular verb;** *SEP* **separable verb; for more help with verbs see centre section**

mitmachen *SEP*
Won't you join in the game? Willst du bei dem Spiel nicht mitmachen?

joint *NOUN*
1 *(of meat)* der **Braten** (*PL* die **Braten**)
  a joint of beef ein Rinderbraten
2 *(in your body)* das **Gelenk** (*PL* die **Gelenke**)

joke *NOUN*
der **Witz** (*PL* die **Witze**)
to tell a joke einen Witz erzählen

to **joke** *VERB*
Witze machen
You must be joking! Du machst wohl Witze!

joker *NOUN*
(in cards) der **Joker** (*PL* die **Joker**)

journalism *NOUN*
der **Journalismus**

ℒ **journalist** *NOUN*
der **Journalist** (*PL* die **Journalisten**), die **Journalistin** (*PL* die **Journalistinnen**)

> **WORD TIP** Professions, hobbies, and sports don't take an article in German: Sie ist Journalistin.

ℒ **journey** *NOUN*
1 *(a long one)* die **Reise** (*PL* die **Reisen**)
  on our journey to Italy auf unserer Reise nach Italien
2 *(shorter; to work or school)* die **Fahrt** (*PL* die **Fahrten**)
  bus journey die Busfahrt

joy *NOUN*
die **Freude** (*PL* die **Freuden**)

joystick *NOUN*
(for computer games) der **Joystick** (*PL* die **Joysticks**)

Judaism *NOUN*
das **Judentum**

judge *NOUN*
1 *(in court)* der **Richter** (*PL* die **Richter**)
2 *(in sporting events)* der **Schiedsrichter** (*PL* die **Schiedsrichter**)
3 *(in a competition)* der **Preisrichter** (*PL* die **Preisrichter**)

> **WORD TIP** Professions, hobbies, and sports don't take an article in German: Er ist Richter.

to **judge** *VERB*
1 beurteilen
2 schätzen *(time or distance)*

judo *NOUN*
das **Judo**

He does judo. Er macht Judo.

jug *NOUN*
der **Krug** (*PL* die **Krüge**)

ℒ **juice** *NOUN*
der **Saft**
Two orange juices, please. Zwei Orangensaft bitte.

juicy *ADJECTIVE*
saftig

jukebox *NOUN*
die **Jukebox** (*PL* die **Jukeboxes**)

ℒ **July** *NOUN*
der **Juli**
in July im Juli

jumble sale *NOUN*
der **Flohmarkt** (*PL* die **Flohmärkte**)

ℒ **jump** *NOUN*
der **Sprung** (*PL* die **Sprünge**)
parachute jump der Fallschirmsprung

to **jump** *VERB*
springen◇ *(PERF* sein*)*

ℒ **jumper** *NOUN*
der **Pullover** (*PL* die **Pullover**)

junction *NOUN*
1 *(of roads)* die **Kreuzung** (*PL* die **Kreuzungen**)
2 *(bigger)* der **Knotenpunkt** (*PL* die **Knotenpunkte**) *(on motorways)*, die **Anschlussstelle** (*PL* die **Anschlussstellen**)

ℒ **June** *NOUN*
der **Juni**
in June im Juni

jungle *NOUN*
der **Dschungel**

ℒ **junior** *ADJECTIVE*
jünger
junior school die Grundschule
the juniors *(at primary school)* die Grundschüler (*PL* die Grundschülerinnen)

junk *NOUN*
der **Trödel**

junk food *NOUN*
das **ungesunde Essen**

just *ADVERB*
1 gerade
  to have just done something gerade etwas getan haben
  Tom has just arrived. Tom ist gerade angekommen.
  I was only just in time. Ich kam gerade noch rechtzeitig.

ℒ indicates key words

2 to be just doing something gerade dabei sein, etwas zu tun
I'm just doing the food. Ich bin gerade dabei, Essen zu machen.

3 just before midday kurz vor Mittag
just after 4 o'clock kurz nach vier Uhr

4 *(only)* nur
just for fun nur zum Vergnügen
He's just a child. Er ist doch nur ein Kind.
Just me and Sam are coming. Nur ich und Sam kommen.

5 Just a minute! Einen Moment!

6 Just coming! Ich komme schon!

7 *(exactly)*
just as genauso wie
He's got just as many friends. Er hat genauso viele Freunde.

justice NOUN
die **Gerechtigkeit**

Kk

kangaroo NOUN
das **Känguru** (PL die **Kängurus**)

karate NOUN
das **Karate**
I do karate. Ich mache Karate.

karting NOUN
das **Kartfahren**
to go karting Kartfahren gehen

kebab NOUN
der **Kebab** (PL die **Kebabs**)

keen ADJECTIVE
1 *(enthusiastic or committed)* begeistert
He's a keen photographer. Er ist ein begeisterter Fotograf.
You don't seem too keen. Du scheinst nicht gerade begeistert zu sein.

2 to be keen on mögen◇
I'm not keen on fish. Ich mag Fisch nicht.

3 to be keen on doing (or to do) something etwas gerne tun

ᴩ to **keep** VERB
1 behalten◇
You can keep the book. Du kannst das Buch behalten.
to keep a secret ein Geheimnis für sich behalten

2 Will you keep my seat? Können Sie meinen Platz freihalten?

3 to keep somebody waiting jemanden warten lassen

4 *(store)* aufbewahren SEP
Can I keep my watch in your desk? Kann ich meine Uhr in deinem Schreibtisch aufbewahren?
Where do you keep saucepans? Wo sind die Töpfe?

5 *(not throw away)* aufheben◇ SEP
I kept all his letters. Ich habe alle seine Briefe aufgehoben.

6 to keep on doing something etwas weiter tun
She kept on talking. Sie hat weitergeredet.
to keep straight on weiter geradeaus gehen

7 to keep on doing something *(time after time)* dauernd etwas tun
He keeps on ringing me up. Er ruft mich dauernd an.

8 *(maintain)* halten◇
to keep the food warm das Essen warm halten
to keep a promise ein Versprechen halten

9 *(stay)* bleiben◇ (PERF sein)
to keep calm ruhig bleiben
to keep out of the sun im Schatten bleiben

• **to keep up**
mithalten◇ SEP
I couldn't keep up with them. Ich konnte nicht mit ihnen mithalten.

kennel NOUN
1 *(for one dog)* die **Hundehütte** (PL die **Hundehütten**)
2 *(for boarding)*
kennels die Hundepension

kerb NOUN
der **Randstein**

ketchup NOUN
der or das **Ketchup**

kettle NOUN
der **Kessel** (PL die **Kessel**)
to put the kettle on Wasser aufsetzen

ᴩ **key** NOUN
1 *(for a lock)* der **Schlüssel** (PL die **Schlüssel**)
bunch of keys der Schlüsselbund
2 *(on a piano or keyboard)* die **Taste**

keyboard NOUN
1 *(for a computer)* die **Tastatur** (PL die **Tastaturen**)
2 *(musical instrument)* das **Keyboard** (PL die **Keyboards**)
Tom plays the keyboard. Tom spielt Keyboard.

WORD TIP Don't use the article when you talk about playing an instrument.

◇ **irregular verb;** SEP **separable verb; for more help with verbs see centre section**

key ring NOUN
der **Schlüsselring** (PL die **Schlüsselringe**)

ℐ**kick** NOUN
1 *(from a person or a horse)* der **Tritt** (PL die **Tritte**)
 to give somebody a kick jemandem einen Tritt geben
2 *(in football)* der **Schuss** (PL die **Schüsse**)
3 **to get a kick out of doing something** etwas leidenschaftlich gerne tun

to **kick** VERB
1 **to kick somebody** jemandem einen Tritt geben◇
2 **to kick the ball** den Ball schießen◇
• **to kick off**
 anstoßen◇ SEP

kick-off NOUN
der **Anstoß**

ℐ**kid** NOUN
 (child) das **Kind** (PL die **Kinder**)
 He's looking after the kids. Er passt auf die Kinder auf.

to **kidnap** VERB
 entführen

kidnapper NOUN
der **Entführer** (PL die **Entführer**), die **Entführerin** (PL die **Entführerinnen**)

kidney NOUN
die **Niere** (PL die **Nieren**)

ℐto **kill** VERB
1 töten *(an animal)*
2 *(murder)* umbringen◇ SEP
 He killed the girl. Er brachte das Mädchen um.
3 **She was killed in a car accident.** Sie kam bei einem Autounfall ums Leben.

killer NOUN
der **Mörder** (PL die **Mörder**), die **Mörderin** (PL die **Mörderinnen**)

ℐ**kilo** NOUN
das **Kilo** (PL die **Kilo**)
 a kilo of sugar ein Kilo Zucker
 two euros a kilo zwei Euro das Kilo

kilogram NOUN
das **Kilogramm** (PL die **Kilogramm**)

ℐ**kilometre** NOUN
der **Kilometer** (PL die **Kilometer**)

kilt NOUN
der **Kilt** (PL die **Kilts**)

ℐ**kind** NOUN
1 die **Art** (PL die **Arten**)

this kind of book diese Art Buch
 all kinds of people alle möglichen Leute
2 *(brand)* die **Sorte** (PL die **Sorten**)

kind ADJECTIVE
 nett
 She was very kind to me. Sie war sehr nett zu mir.

kindness NOUN
die **Freundlichkeit**

king NOUN
der **König** (PL die **Könige**)
 the king of hearts der Herzkönig

kingdom NOUN
das **Königreich** (PL die **Königreiche**)
 the United Kingdom das Vereinigte Königreich

ℐ**kiosk** NOUN
1 *(for newspapers or snacks)* der **Kiosk** (PL die **Kioske**)
2 *(for a phone)* die **Telefonzelle** (PL die **Telefonzellen**)

kipper NOUN
der **Räucherhering** (PL die **Räucherheringe**)

ℐ**kiss** NOUN
der **Kuss** (PL die **Küsse**)
 to give somebody a kiss jemandem einen Kuss geben

to **kiss** VERB
 küssen
 Kiss me! Küss mich!
 We kissed each other. Wir haben uns geküsst.
 They were kissing. Sie küssten sich.

kit NOUN
1 *(set of tools)* das **Werkzeug**
2 *(in a box)* **a tool kit** ein Werkzeugkasten
3 *(clothes)* die **Sachen** (PLURAL)
 Where's my football kit? Wo sind meine Fußballsachen?
4 *(for making a model, a piece of furniture, etc.)* der **Bausatz** (PL die **Bausätze**)

ℐ**kitchen** NOUN
die **Küche** (PL die **Küchen**)
 the kitchen table der Küchentisch

kitchen foil NOUN
die **Alufolie**

kitchen roll NOUN
die **Küchenrolle** (PL die **Küchenrollen**)

kite NOUN
der **Drachen** (PL die **Drachen**)
 to fly a kite einen Drachen steigen lassen

ℐ indicates key words

kitten NOUN
das Kätzchen (PL die Kätzchen)

kiwi fruit NOUN
die Kiwi (PL die Kiwis)

♀**knee** NOUN
das Knie (PL die Knie)
on (your) hands and knees auf allen vieren

to **kneel** VERB
knien
to kneel (down) sich hinknien SEP

♀**knickers** PLURAL NOUN
der Schlüpfer (PL die Schlüpfer)
a pair of knickers ein Schlüpfer

WORD TIP In German, der Schlüpfer is singular.

♀**knife** NOUN
das Messer (PL die Messer)

to **knife** VERB
einstechen◇ SEP auf (+ACC) (kill)
erstechen◇

knight NOUN
1 (on horse) der Ritter (PL die Ritter)
2 (in chess) der Springer (PL die Springer)

to **knit** VERB
stricken

knitting NOUN
das Stricken

knob NOUN
1 (on a door or walking stick) der Knauf (PL die Knäufe)
2 (control on a radio or machine) der Knopf (PL die Knöpfe)
3 **knob of butter** das kleine Stückchen Butter

knock NOUN
1 der Schlag (PL die Schläge)
a knock on the head ein Schlag auf den Kopf
2 **a knock at the door** ein Klopfen an der Tür

to **knock** VERB
1 (bang) stoßen◇
I knocked my arm on the table. Ich habe mir den Arm am Tisch gestoßen.
2 **to knock on something** an etwas (ACC) klopfen
• **to knock down**
1 (in a traffic accident) anfahren◇ SEP (a person)
2 (demolish) abreißen◇ SEP (an old building)
• **to knock out**
1 (make unconscious) bewusstlos schlagen◇
2 (in sport, to eliminate) k.o. schlagen◇

knot NOUN
der Knoten (PL die Knoten)
to tie a knot einen Knoten machen

♀to **know** VERB
1 (know a fact) wissen◇
Do you know where Tim is? Weißt du, wo Tim ist?
I know they've moved house. Ich weiß, dass sie umgezogen sind.
Yes, I know. Ja, weiß ich.
I don't know. Ich weiß es nicht.
You never know! Man kann nie wissen!
I know how to get to town. Ich weiß, wie man in die Stadt kommt.
2 **to let somebody know** jemandem Bescheid sagen
I'll let you know as soon as possible. Ich sage Ihnen so bald wie möglich Bescheid.
3 (be personally acquainted with) kennen◇
Do you know the Jacksons? Kennst du die Jacksons?
all the people I know alle Leute (PL die ich kenne)
I don't know his mother. Ich kenne seine Mutter nicht.
4 **to know how to do something** wissen, wie man etwas macht
Steve knows how to make potato salad. Steve weiß, wie man Kartoffelsalat macht.
Liz knows how to mend it. Liz kann es reparieren.
5 **to know about** Bescheid wissen über (+ACC)
items in the news
6 **to know about** sich auskennen◇ SEP mit
machines, cars, etc.
Lindy knows about computers. Lindy kennt sich mit Computern aus.
7 **to get to know somebody** jemanden kennenlernen SEP

knowledge NOUN
das Wissen

Koran NOUN
der Koran

kosher ADJECTIVE
koscher

Ll

lab NOUN
das Labor (PL die Labors)

label NOUN
das Etikett (PL die Etikette)

◇ irregular verb; SEP separable verb; for more help with verbs see centre section

laboratory NOUN
das Labor (PL die Labors)

lace NOUN
1 (for a shoe) der Schnürsenkel (PL die Schnürsenkel)
   to tie your laces sich (DAT) die Schnürsenkel binden◇
2 (fabric or trimming) die Spitze

ladder NOUN
1 (for climbing) die Leiter (PL die Leitern)
2 (in your tights) die Laufmasche (PL die Laufmaschen)

ladies NOUN
(lavatory) die Damentoilette (PL die Damentoiletten)
(on a sign) 'Ladies' 'Damen'

ℓ **lady** NOUN
die Dame (PL die Damen)
ladies and gentlemen meine Damen und Herren

ladybird NOUN
der Marienkäfer (PL die Marienkäfer)

lager NOUN
das helle Bier (PL die hellen Biere), das Helle (PL die Hellen) (informal)
A lager, please. Ein Helles bitte.

laid-back ADJECTIVE
gelassen

ℓ **lake** NOUN
der See (PL die Seen)
Lake Geneva der Genfer See

lamb NOUN
1 (young sheep) das Lamm (PL die Lämmer)
2 (meat) das Lamm, das Lammfleisch

landlady NOUN
1 (of a house or room) die Vermieterin (PL die Vermieterinnen)
2 (of a pub) die Gastwirtin (PL die Gastwirtinnen)

landline NOUN
die Festnetzleitung (PL die Festnetzleitungen)
I'll call you on the landline. Ich rufe dich über das Festnetz an.

landlord NOUN
1 (of a house or room) der Vermieter (PL die Vermieter)
2 (of a pub) der Gastwirt (PL die Gastwirte)

lane NOUN
1 (small road) der Weg (PL die Wege)
2 (of a motorway) die Spur (PL die Spuren)

3 (in sport) die Bahn (PL die Bahnen)

ℓ **language** NOUN
1 (German, Italian, etc.) die Sprache (PL die Sprachen)
   foreign language die Fremdsprache
2 (way of speaking) die Ausdrucksweise
   bad language die Kraftausdrücke (PLURAL)

> 🔵 **LANGUAGE**
>
> More people in the European Union have German as their mother tongue than English, French, or Spanish.

lap NOUN
1 der Schoß (PL die Schöße)
2 (in races) die Runde (PL die Runden)

laptop NOUN
der Laptop (PL die Laptops)

ℓ **large** ADJECTIVE
groß

laser NOUN
der Laser (PL die Laser)

laser printer NOUN
der Laserdrucker (PL die Laserdrucker)

ℓ **last** ADJECTIVE
letzter/letzte/letztes
last week letzte Woche
for the last time zum letzten Mal
last night gestern Nacht
He was the last to leave. Er ging als Letzter.

last ADVERB
1 (in final position) als Letzter/als Letzte/als Letztes
   Rob arrived last. Rob kam als Letzter an.
2 **At last!** Endlich!
3 (most recently) zuletzt
   I last saw him in May. Ich habe ihn zuletzt im Mai gesehen.

to last VERB
dauern
The film lasted two hours. Der Film dauerte zwei Stunden.

ℓ **late** ADJECTIVE, ADVERB
1 spät
   I'm late. Ich bin spät dran.
   We were five minutes late. Wir kamen fünf Minuten zu spät.
   They arrived late. Sie sind zu spät angekommen.
   to be late for something zu spät zu etwas (DAT) kommen
   We were late for the party. Wir kamen zu spät zur Party.
2 **to be late** (of a bus or train) Verspätung haben

533

ℓ indicates key words

The train was an hour late. Der Zug hatte eine Stunde Verspätung.

3 *(late in the day)* spät
We got up late. Wir sind spät aufgestanden.
The chemist is open late. Die Apotheke hat bis spät auf.
late last night gestern spät in der Nacht
Too late! Zu spät!

lately ADVERB
in letzter Zeit

ℰ **later** ADVERB
später
I'll explain later. Ich erkläre es später.
See you later! Bis später!

latest ADJECTIVE
1 neuester/neueste/neuestes
the latest news die neuesten Nachrichten
the latest in audio equipment das Neueste an Audioausrüstung
2 at the latest spätestens

Latin NOUN
das Latein

ℰ **laugh** NOUN
das Lachen
to do something for a laugh etwas aus Spaß machen

to **laugh** VERB
1 lachen
Everybody laughed. Alle haben gelacht.
to laugh about something über etwas (ACC) lachen
It makes me laugh. Es bringt mich zum Lachen.
2 to laugh at somebody jemanden auslachen SEP
They'll laugh at me. Sie werden mich auslachen.

launch NOUN
1 *(of a ship)* der Stapellauf
2 *(of a product)* die Einführung
3 *(of a spacecraft)* der Abschuss

to **launch** VERB
1 zu Wasser lassen◇ *(a ship)*
2 auf den Markt bringen◇ *(a product)*
3 ins All schießen◇ *(a spacecraft)*

launderette NOUN
der Waschsalon (PL die Waschsalons)

lavatory NOUN
die Toilette (PL die Toiletten)
to go to the lavatory auf die Toilette gehen

law NOUN
1 das Gesetz (PL die Gesetze)
to break the law gegen das Gesetz verstoßen
2 It's against the law. Das ist verboten.
3 *(subject of study)* Jura
to study law Jura studieren

ℰ **lawn** NOUN
der Rasen (PL die Rasen)

lawnmower NOUN
der Rasenmäher (PL die Rasenmäher)

lawyer NOUN
der Rechtsanwalt (PL die Rechtsanwälte)
die Rechtsanwältin (PL die Rechtsanwältinnen)

WORD TIP Professions, hobbies, and sports don't take an article in German: Er ist Rechtsanwalt.

ℰ to **lay** VERB
1 *(put)* legen
She laid the cards on the table. Sie legte die Karten auf den Tisch.
2 to lay the table den Tisch decken

lay-by NOUN
die Haltebucht (PL die Haltebuchten)

layer NOUN
die Schicht (PL die Schichten)

ℰ **lazy** ADJECTIVE
faul

lead[1] NOUN
1 *(when you are ahead)* die Führung
to be in the lead in Führung liegen◇
Baxter's in the lead. Baxter liegt in Führung.
to take the lead in Führung gehen◇
2 *(electric)* das Kabel (PL die Kabel)
3 *(for a dog)* die Leine (PL die Leinen)
Dogs must be kept on a lead. Hunde an der Leine führen.
4 *(role)* die Hauptrolle (PL die Hauptrollen)
5 *(an actor)* der Hauptdarsteller (PL die Hauptdarsteller), die Hauptdarstellerin (PL die Hauptdarstellerinnen)

to **lead** VERB
1 führen
The path leads to the sea. Der Weg führt zum Meer.
to lead by three points mit drei Punkten führen
2 to lead the way vorangehen◇ SEP (PERF sein)
3 to lead to something zu etwas (DAT) führen *(an accident or problems, for example)*

lead[2] NOUN
(metal) das Blei

◇ irregular verb; SEP separable verb; for more help with verbs see centre section

ℓ **leader** NOUN
1 *(of a political party)* der/die **Vorsitzende**
   (PL die **Vorsitzenden**)
2 *(of an expedition or group)* der **Leiter** (PL die
   Leiter), die **Leiterin** (PL die **Leiterinnen**)
3 *(in a competition)* der/die **Erste** (PL die
   Ersten)
   the league leader der Tabellenführer
4 *(of a gang)* der **Anführer** (PL die **Anführer**)
   (PL die **Anführerin** (PL die **Anführerinnen**)

lead singer NOUN
   der **Leadsänger** (PL die **Leadsänger**), die
   Leadsängerin (PL die **Leadsängerinnen**)

leaf NOUN
   das **Blatt** (PL die **Blätter**)

ℓ **leaflet** NOUN
1 *(with instructions)* das **Merkblatt** (PL die
   Merkblätter)
2 *(for advertising)* das **Reklameblatt** (PL die
   Reklameblätter)

league NOUN
   die **Liga** (PL die **Ligen**)
   League 1 die erste Liga

leak NOUN
1 *(in a roof, tent)* die **undichte Stelle** (PL die
   undichten Stellen)
2 **gas leak** der Gasaustritt
   There's a gas leak. Irgendwo tritt Gas aus.
3 *(in a boat)* das **Leck** (PL die **Lecks**)
to leak VERB
   (bottle or roof) **undicht sein**

lean ADJECTIVE
   (meat) **mager**
to lean VERB
1 **to lean on something** sich an etwas *(ACC)*
   lehnen
   He leaned against the door. Er hat sich
   gegen die Tür gelehnt.
2 **sich lehnen**
   She was leaning out of the window. Sie
   lehnte sich aus dem Fenster.
3 **to lean forward** sich vorbeugen SEP

leap year NOUN
   das **Schaltjahr** (PL die **Schaltjahre**)

ℓ **to learn** VERB
   lernen
   to learn German Deutsch lernen
   to learn (how) to drive Autofahren lernen

learner NOUN
1 der **Lerner** (PL die **Lerner**)
   to be a fast learner schnell lernen
2 *(beginner)* der **Anfänger** (PL die **Anfänger**),
   die **Anfängerin** (PL die **Anfängerinnen**)

ℓ **least** ADJECTIVE, PRONOUN
1 **wenigster/wenigste/wenigstes**
   to have least time am wenigsten Zeit
   haben
   Tony has the least money. Tony hat das
   wenigste Geld.
2 *(the slightest)* **geringster/geringste/**
   geringstes
   I haven't the least idea. Ich habe nicht die
   geringste Ahnung.

least ADVERB
1 **am wenigsten**
   I like the blue shirt least. Ich mag das blaue
   Hemd am wenigsten.
2 **the least expensive hotel** das billigste
   Hotel
3 **at least** *(at a minimum)* **mindestens**
   at least twenty people mindestens
   zwanzig Leute
4 **at least** *(at any rate)* **wenigstens**
   She's a teacher, at least I think she is. Sie
   ist Lehrerin, glaube ich wenigstens.

ℓ **leather** NOUN
   das **Leder**
   leather jacket die Lederjacke
   It's made of leather. Es ist aus Leder.

ℓ **leave** NOUN
   der **Urlaub**
   three days' leave drei Tage Urlaub
to leave VERB
1 *(go away)* **gehen**◇ *(PERF* sein), *(by car)*
   fahren◇ SEP *(PERF* sein), *(a train or bus)*
   abfahren◇ SEP *(PERF* sein)
   We left at six. Wir sind um sechs Uhr
   gegangen.
   They're leaving tomorrow evening. Sie
   fahren morgen Abend.
   The train leaves Munich at ten. Der Zug
   fährt um zehn Uhr von München ab.
2 *(go away from or go out of)* **verlassen**◇
   I left the office at five. Ich habe das Büro
   um fünf verlassen.
   He left his wife. Er hat seine Frau verlassen.
3 *(deposit or allow to remain in the same state)*
   lassen◇
   You can leave your coats in the hall. Sie
   können Ihre Mäntel in der Diele lassen.
   to leave the door open die Tür offen lassen
   Leave it until tomorrow. Lass es bis morgen.
4 **to leave somebody something** jemandem
   etwas **hinterlassen**◇ *(a message or money)*
   He didn't leave a message. Er hat keine
   Nachricht hinterlassen.
5 *(not do)* **stehen lassen**◇
   Leave the washing up. Lass den Abwasch
   stehen.

535

ℓ *indicates key words*

lecture
less

6 *(forget)* **vergessen**◇
He left his umbrella on the train. Er hat seinen Regenschirm im Zug vergessen.

7 **to be left** übrig sein *(PERF sein)*
There are two pancakes left. Zwei Pfannkuchen sind noch übrig.
I don't have any money left. Ich habe kein Geld mehr übrig.
We have ten minutes left. Wir haben noch zehn Minuten Zeit.

• **to leave alone**
in Ruhe lassen◇
Just leave me alone! Lass mich in Ruhe!

• **to leave out**
1 **to leave somebody out** jemanden ausschließen◇ *SEP*
2 **to leave something out** etwas auslassen◇ *SEP*

lecture *NOUN*
1 *(at university)* die **Vorlesung** (*PL* die **Vorlesungen**)
2 *(public)* der **Vortrag** (*PL* die **Vorträge**)

leek *NOUN*
der **Lauch**

ℓ left *NOUN*
on the left links
to drive on the left links fahren
on my left links von mir

left *ADVERB*
links
Turn left at the church. An der Kirche links abbiegen.

left *ADJECTIVE*
linker/linke/linkes
his left foot sein linker Fuß

left-click *NOUN*
der **Klick mit der linken Maustaste**

to left-click *VERB*
Left-click (on) the icon. Das Symbol mit der linken Maustaste anklicken.

left-hand *ADJECTIVE*
the left-hand side die linke Seite

left-handed *ADJECTIVE*
linkshändig
I'm left-handed. Ich bin Linkshänder.

ℓ left-luggage office *NOUN*
die **Gepäckaufbewahrung** (*PL* die **Gepäckaufbewahrungen**)

ℓ leg *NOUN*
1 das **Bein** (*PL* die **Beine**)
my left leg mein linkes Bein
to break your leg sich (*DAT*) das Bein brechen◇

2 *(in cooking)* die **Keule** (*PL* die **Keulen**)
leg of lamb die Lammkeule
to pull somebody's leg jemanden auf den Arm nehmen◇

legal *ADJECTIVE*
gesetzlich

leggings *PLURAL NOUN*
die **Leggings** (*PLURAL*)

ℓ leisure *NOUN*
die **Freizeit**
in my leisure time in meiner Freizeit

ℓ lemon *NOUN*
die **Zitrone** (*PL* die **Zitronen**)

ℓ lemonade *NOUN*
die **Limonade** (*PL* die **Limonaden**)

lemon juice *NOUN*
der **Zitronensaft**

ℓ to lend *VERB*
leihen◇
to lend something to somebody
jemandem etwas leihen
I lent Judy my bike. Ich habe Judy mein Rad geliehen.
Will you lend it to me? Kannst du es mir leihen?

length *NOUN*
die **Länge** (*PL* die **Längen**)

ℓ lens *NOUN*
1 *(in a camera)* das **Objektiv** (*PL* die **Objektive**)
2 *(in spectacles)* das **Brillenglas** (*PL* die **Brillengläser**)
3 **contact lenses** die Kontaktlinsen (*PLURAL*)

Lent *NOUN*
die **Fastenzeit**

lentil *NOUN*
die **Linse** (*PL* die **Linsen**)

Leo *NOUN*
der **Löwe** (*PL* die **Löwen**)
I'm a Leo. Ich bin Löwe.

leotard *NOUN*
der **Turnanzug** (*PL* die **Turnanzüge**)

lesbian *NOUN*
die **Lesbe** (*PL* die **Lesben**)

lesbian *ADJECTIVE*
lesbisch

ℓ less *PRONOUN, ADJECTIVE, ADVERB*
weniger *('weniger' never changes)*
Ben eats less. Ben isst weniger.
less time weniger Zeit

◇ **irregular verb;** *SEP* **separable verb; for more help with verbs see centre section**

less than weniger als
less than three hours weniger als drei Stunden
You spent less than me. Du hast weniger als ich ausgegeben.
less and less immer weniger

𝒫 **lesson** NOUN
(class) die **Stunde** (PL die **Stunden**)
German lesson die Deutschstunde
driving lesson die Fahrstunde

𝒫 **to let¹** VERB
1 *(allow)* **lassen**◇
to let somebody do something jemanden etwas tun lassen
She lets me drive her car. Sie lässt mich mit ihrem Auto fahren.
The police let us through. Die Polizei hat uns durchgelassen.
Let me in. Lass mich hinein.
2 *(as a suggestion or a command)*
Let's go! Gehen wir!
Let's not talk about it. Reden wir nicht mehr darüber.
Let's eat out. Lasst uns essen gehen.
• **to let go**
loslassen◇ SEP
• **to let somebody down**
jemanden enttäuschen
• **to let off**
1 abfeuern SEP *(fireworks)*
2 *(excuse from)* befreien von (+DAT) *(homework)*

to let² VERB
(rent out) **vermieten**
'Flat to let' 'Wohnung zu vermieten'

𝒫 **letter** NOUN
1 der **Brief** (PL die **Briefe**)
a letter for you from Delia ein Brief für dich von Delia
2 *(of the alphabet)* der **Buchstabe** (PL die **Buchstaben**)

letter box NOUN
der **Briefkasten** (PL die **Briefkästen**)

lettuce NOUN
der **Salat**
two lettuces zwei Salatköpfe

leukaemia NOUN
die **Leukämie**

level NOUN
die **Höhe** (PL die **Höhen**)
at eye level in Augenhöhe

level ADJECTIVE
1 **eben** *(ground or floor)*

2 *(horizontal)* **waagerecht** shelf
3 *(at the same height)* **auf gleicher Höhe**
to be level with the ground auf gleicher Höhe mit dem Boden sein

level crossing NOUN
der **Bahnübergang** (PL die **Bahnübergänge**)

lever NOUN
der **Hebel** (PL die **Hebel**)

liar NOUN
der **Lügner** (PL die **Lügner** die **Lügnerin** (PL die **Lügnerinnen**)

liberal ADJECTIVE
1 **tolerant**
2 *(in politics)* **liberal**
the Liberal Democrats die Liberaldemokraten

Libra NOUN
die **Waage**
Sean is Libra. Sean ist Waage.

librarian NOUN
der **Bibliothekar** (PL die **Bibliothekare**), die **Bibliothekarin** (PL die **Bibliothekarinnen**)

> **WORD TIP** Professions, hobbies, and sports don't take an article in German: Sie ist Bibliothekarin.

𝒫 **library** NOUN
die **Bibliothek** (PL die **Bibliotheken**)
public library die öffentliche Bücherei
the school library die Schulbibliothek

𝒫 **licence** NOUN
1 *(for a TV)* die **Genehmigung** (PL die **Genehmigungen**)
2 *(driving licence)* der **Führerschein** (PL die **Führerscheine**)

to lick VERB
lecken

lid NOUN
der **Deckel** (PL die **Deckel**)

𝒫 **lie** NOUN
die **Lüge** (PL die **Lügen**)
to tell a lie (or lies) **lügen**◇

to lie VERB
1 *(be stretched out)* **liegen**◇
He's lying on the sofa. Er liegt auf dem Sofa.
My coat lay on the bed. Mein Mantel lag auf dem Bett.
2 **to lie down** *(for a rest)* **sich hinlegen** SEP
I'm going to lie down for a little. Ich lege mich ein bisschen hin.
3 *(tell lies)* **lügen**◇

537

𝒫 indicates key words

lie-in NOUN
to have a lie-in ausschlafen◇ SEP

ℒ **life** NOUN
das Leben (PL die Leben)
all her life ihr ganzes Leben lang
full of life voller Leben
That's life! So ist das Leben!

lifeboat NOUN
das Rettungsboot (PL die Rettungsboote)

lifeguard NOUN
1 der Rettungsschwimmer
(PL die Rettungsschwimmer), die
Rettungsschwimmerin (PL die
Rettungsschwimmerinnen)
2 (at a swimming pool) der Bademeister
(PL die Bademeister), die Bademeisterin
(PL die Bademeisterinnen)
Is there a lifeguard at the pool? Gibt es
einen Bademeister im Schwimmbad?

WORD TIP Professions, hobbies, and sports don't
take an article in German: Er ist Bademeister.

life jacket NOUN
die Schwimmweste (PL die
Schwimmwesten)

lifestyle NOUN
der Lebensstil (PL die Lebensstile)

ℒ **lift** NOUN
1 der Aufzug (PL die Aufzüge)
Let's take the lift. Fahren wir mit dem
Aufzug.
2 (a ride)
to give somebody a lift to the station
jemanden zum Bahnhof mitnehmen◇ SEP
Khaled's giving me a lift. Khaled nimmt
mich mit.
Would you like a lift? Möchtest du
mitfahren?

to **lift** VERB
hochheben◇ SEP
He lifted the box. Er hob die Kiste hoch.

ℒ **light** NOUN
1 das Licht
Will you turn the light on? Kannst du das
Licht anmachen?
to turn off the light das Licht ausmachen
Are your lights on? Hast du das Licht an?
2 (in the street) die Straßenlampe (PL die
Straßenlampen)
3 (a lamp) die Lampe (PL die Lampen)
4 traffic lights die Ampel (SINGULAR)
The lights are green. Die Ampel ist grün.
5 (for a cigarette)
Have you got a light? Hast du Feuer?

light ADJECTIVE
1 (not dark) hell
It gets light at six. Es wird um sechs hell.
a light blue dress ein hellblaues Kleid
2 (not heavy) leicht
a light coat ein leichter Mantel
a light breeze eine leichte Brise

to **light** VERB
1 anzünden SEP (the fire, a match, the gas)
We lit a fire. Wir zündeten ein Feuer an.
2 to light a cigarette sich (DAT) eine Zigarette
anzünden

light bulb NOUN
die Glühbirne (PL die Glühbirnen)

lighter NOUN
das Feuerzeug (PL die Feuerzeuge)

lighthouse NOUN
der Leuchtturm (PL die Leuchttürme)

ℒ **lightning** NOUN
der Blitz
flash of lightning der Blitz
to be struck by lightning vom Blitz
getroffen werden

ℒ **like¹** PREPOSITION, CONJUNCTION
1 wie
like me wie ich
like a duck wie eine Ente
like I said wie gesagt
What's it like? Wie ist es?
What was the weather like? Wie war das
Wetter?
2 like this/that so
Do it like this. Mach es so.
3 ähnlich (+DAT)
to look like somebody jemandem ähnlich
sehen◇
Cindy looks like her father. Cindy sieht
ihrem Vater ähnlich.

ℒ to **like²** VERB
1 mögen◇
I like vegetables. Ich mag Gemüse.
I don't like meat. Ich mag kein Fleisch.
I like Dürer best. Ich mag Dürer am
liebsten.
2 to like doing something etwas gerne tun
Mum likes reading. Mutti liest gerne.
3 I would like ... Ich möchte gerne ...
Would you like a coffee? Möchten Sie einen
Kaffee?
What would you like to eat? Was möchten
Sie essen?
Yes, if you like. Ja, wenn du willst.
4 I like the dress. Das Kleid gefällt mir.
How do you like it? Wie gefällt es dir?

◇ irregular verb; SEP separable verb; for more help with verbs see centre section

likely ADJECTIVE
wahrscheinlich
She's likely to phone. Wahrscheinlich ruft sie an.

lime NOUN
1 der Kalk
2 (fruit) die Limone (PL die Limonen)

limit NOUN
die Grenze (PL die Grenzen)
speed limit die Geschwindigkeitsbeschränkung
to exceed the speed limit das Tempolimit überschreiten

limp NOUN
to have a limp hinken

℘ **line** NOUN
1 die Linie (PL die Linien)
a straight line eine gerade Linie
to draw a line eine Linie ziehen
2 (in writing) die Zeile (PL die Zeilen)
six lines of text sechs Zeilen Text
3 (railway) die Bahnlinie (PL die Bahnlinien) (from one place to another)
Take the Victoria line. Nimm die Victoria-Linie.
on the line (the track) auf den Gleisen
4 (a queue of people or cars) die Schlange (PL die Schlangen)
to stand in line Schlange stehen
5 (telephone) die Leitung (PL die Leitungen)
The line's bad. Die Verbindung ist schlecht.
Hold the line, please. Bitte bleiben Sie am Apparat.

to **line** VERB
füttern (a coat)

℘ **linen** NOUN
das Leinen
a linen jacket eine Leinenjacke

lining NOUN
das Futter (PL die Futter)

link NOUN
1 die Verbindung (PL die Verbindungen)
What's the link between the two? Was für eine Verbindung besteht zwischen den beiden?
2 (to a website) der Link (PL die Links)

to **link** VERB
verbinden◇ (two places)
The two towns are linked by a railway line. Die beiden Städte sind durch eine Bahnlinie miteinander verbunden.

lion NOUN
der Löwe (PL die Löwen)

lip NOUN
die Lippe (PL die Lippen)

to **lip-read** VERB
von den Lippen lesen◇

lipstick NOUN
der Lippenstift (PL die Lippenstifte)

liquid NOUN
die Flüssigkeit (PL die Flüssigkeiten)

liquid ADJECTIVE
flüssig

liquidizer NOUN
der Mixer (PL die Mixer)

list NOUN
die Liste (PL die Listen)

℘ to **listen** VERB
1 zuhören SEP
I wasn't listening. Ich habe nicht zugehört.
to listen to somebody jemandem zuhören
You're not listening to me. Du hörst mir nicht zu.
2 to listen to something etwas (ACC) hören
to listen to the radio Radio hören

listener NOUN
(to the radio) der Hörer (PL die Hörer), die Hörerin (PL die Hörerinnen)

literature NOUN
die Literatur

℘ **litre** NOUN
der Liter (PL die Liter)
a litre of milk ein Liter Milch

litter NOUN
(rubbish) der Abfall

litter bin NOUN
der Abfalleimer (PL die Abfalleimer)

℘ **little** ADJECTIVE, PRONOUN
1 (small) klein
a little boy ein kleiner Junge
a little break eine kleine Pause
2 (not much) wenig
We have very little time. Wir haben sehr wenig Zeit.
3 a little ein bisschen
Just a little, please. Nur ein bisschen, bitte.
It's a little late. Es ist ein bisschen spät.
a little more ein bisschen mehr
a little less ein bisschen weniger
We have a little left. Wir haben ein bisschen übrig.
little by little nach und nach

little finger NOUN
der kleine Finger (PL die kleinen Finger)

℘ indicates key words

A B C D E F G H I J K L M N O P Q R S T U V W X Y Z

𝔓 to **live¹** *VERB*
1 *(in a house or town)* **wohnen**
   She lives in York. Sie wohnt in York.
   We live in a flat. Wir wohnen in einer
   Wohnung.
2 *(be or stay alive, spend one's life)* **leben**
   We're living in the country now. Wir leben
   jetzt auf dem Land.
   They live on fruit. Sie leben von Obst.
   They live apart. Sie leben getrennt.

live² *ADJECTIVE, ADVERB*
1 live *(broadcast)*
   a live programme eine Livesendung
   live music die Livemusik
   a broadcast live from Wembley eine
   Liveübertragung aus Wembley
   to broadcast a concert live ein Konzert live
   senden
2 *(alive)* **lebend**

lively *ADJECTIVE*
   lebhaft

liver *NOUN*
   die **Leber** (*PL* die **Lebern**)

𝔓 **living** *NOUN*
   der **Lebensunterhalt**
   to earn a living sich (*DAT*) seinen
   Lebensunterhalt verdienen

living room *NOUN*
   das **Wohnzimmer** (*PL* die **Wohnzimmer**)

lizard *NOUN*
   die **Eidechse** (*PL* die **Eidechsen**)

𝔓 **load** *NOUN*
1 *(on a lorry)* die **Ladung** (*PL* die **Ladungen**)
   a (lorry) load of bricks eine Ladung
   Ziegelsteine
2 **a bus load of tourists** ein Bus voll Touristen
3 **loads of** massenhaft *(informal)*
   loads of tourists massenhaft Touristen
   They've got loads of money. Sie haben
   einen Haufen Geld. *(informal)*

to **load** *VERB*
   beladen◇ *(a vehicle)*

loaf *NOUN*
   das **Brot** (*PL* die **Brote**)
   a loaf of white bread ein Weißbrot

loan *NOUN*
1 *(from a person)* die **Leihgabe** (*PL* die
   Leihgaben)
2 *(from a bank)* der **Kredit** (*PL* die **Kredite**)

to **loan** *VERB*
   leihen◇

to **loathe** *VERB*
   hassen
   I loathe getting up early. Ich hasse es, früh
   aufzustehen.

local *NOUN*
1 *(a pub)* die **Stammkneipe** (*PL* die
   Stammkneipen)
2 **the locals** *(people)* die **Einheimischen**

local *ADJECTIVE*
1 **hiesig**
   the local library die hiesige Bücherei
2 **local newspaper** die Lokalzeitung
3 **local time** die Ortszeit

lock *NOUN*
   das **Schloss** (*PL* die **Schlösser**)

to **lock** *VERB*
   abschließen◇ *SEP (a door, room, or bicycle)*
   Have you locked the door? Hast du
   abgeschlossen?

locker *NOUN*
   das **Schließfach** (*PL* die **Schließfächer**)

lodger *NOUN*
   der **Untermieter** (*PL* die **Untermieter**), die
   Untermieterin (*PL* die **Untermieterinnen**)

loft *NOUN*
   der **Dachboden** (*PL* die **Dachböden**)

log *NOUN*
1 der **Baumstamm** (*PL* die **Baumstämme**)
2 *(as firewood)* das **Holzscheit** (*PL* die
   Holzscheite)
   a log fire ein offenes Feuer

lollipop *NOUN*
   der **Lutscher** (*PL* die **Lutscher**)

London *NOUN*
   London *(NEUTER)*

Londoner *NOUN*
   der **Londoner** (*PL* die **Londoner**), die
   Londonerin (*PL* die **Londonerinnen**)
   He's a Londoner. Er ist Londoner.

𝔓 **lonely** *ADJECTIVE*
   einsam
   to feel lonely sich einsam fühlen

𝔓 **long** *ADJECTIVE, ADVERB*
1 **lang**
   a long film ein langer Film
   a long day ein langer Tag
   It's five metres long. Es ist fünf Meter lang.
   The film is an hour long. Der Film dauert
   eine Stunde.
2 **a long time** lange
   He stayed for a long time. Er ist lange
   geblieben.
   I've been here for a long time. Ich bin

◇ **irregular verb;** *SEP* **separable verb; for more help with verbs see centre section**

schon lange hier.

long ago, a long time ago vor langer Zeit
This won't take long. Das dauert nicht
lange.
How long? Wie lange?
How long have you been here? Wie lange
sind Sie schon hier?

3 **a long way** weit
It's a long way to the cinema. Bis zum Kino
ist es weit.

4 **all night long** die ganze Nacht

5 **no longer** nicht mehr
He doesn't work here any longer. Er
arbeitet nicht mehr hier.

to **long** VERB
to long to do something sich danach
sehnen, etwas zu tun
I'm longing to see you. Ich sehne mich
danach, dich zu sehen.

long-distance call NOUN
(within the country) das **Ferngespräch**
(PL die **Ferngespräche**)

long jump NOUN
der **Weitsprung**

longlife milk NOUN
die **H-Milch**

loo NOUN
das **Klo** (PL die **Klos**) (informal)
to go to the loo aufs Klo gehen

ℒ **look** NOUN
1 (a glance) der **Blick** (PL die **Blicke**)
to take a look at somebody einen Blick auf
jemanden werfen◇

2 (a tour)
to have a look at the school sich (DAT) die
Schule ansehen◇
to have a look round the town sich (DAT)
die Stadt ansehen

3 **to have a look for** suchen

to **look** VERB
1 sehen◇
to look out of the window aus dem Fenster
sehen
I wasn't looking. Ich habe nicht
hingesehen.

2 **to look at** ansehen◇ SEP
He looked at the girl. Er sah das Mädchen
an.
to look at something sich (DAT) etwas
ansehen
I'm looking at the photos. Ich sehe mir die
Fotos an.

3 (seem) aussehen◇ SEP
She looks sad. Sie sieht traurig aus.
The salad looks delicious. Der Salat sieht

köstlich aus.
to look like aussehen wie
What does the house look like? Wie sieht
das Haus aus?

4 (resemble)
to look like somebody jemandem ähnlich
sehen
She looks like her aunt. Sie sieht ihrer
Tante ähnlich.
They look like each other. Sie sehen sich
ähnlich.

• **to look after**
1 sich kümmern um (+ACC)
He's looking after the children. Er
kümmert sich um die Kinder.

2 aufpassen SEP auf (+ACC) (luggage, etc.)

• **to look for**
suchen
I'm looking for my keys. Ich suche meine
Schlüssel.

• **to look forward to**
sich freuen auf (+ACC) (a party or a trip, for
example)
I'm looking foward to the game. Ich freue
mich auf das Spiel.

• **to look out**
(be careful) aufpassen SEP
Look out, it's hot! Pass auf, das ist heiß!

• **to look up**◇
1 nachschlagen◇ SEP (in a dictionary or
directory)
He's looking it up in the dictionary. Er
schlägt es im Wörterbuch nach.

2 nachsehen◇ SEP (on the Internet)
**I'll look up the opening times on the
Internet.** Ich sehe die Öffnungszeiten im
Internet nach.

loose ADJECTIVE
1 (screw or knot) locker
2 (garment) weit
3 **loose change** das Kleingeld
4 **I'm at a loose end.** Ich habe nichts zu tun.

ℒ **lorry** NOUN
der **Lastkraftwagen** (PL die
Lastkraftwagen)

lorry driver NOUN
der **Lastkraftwagenfahrer**
(PL die **Lastkraftwagenfahrer**), die
Lastkraftwagenfahrerin (PL die
Lastkraftwagenfahrerinnen)

WORD TIP Professions, hobbies, and sports
don't take an article in German: Er ist
Lastkraftwagenfahrer.

ℒ to **lose** VERB
1 verlieren◇

We lost. Wir haben verloren.
We lost the match. Wir haben das Spiel verloren.
Sam's lost his watch. Sam hat seine Uhr verloren.
2 **to get lost** sich verlaufen◇
We got lost in the woods. Wir haben uns im Wald verlaufen.
3 **to lose weight** abnehmen◇ SEP

loser NOUN
1 der **Verlierer** (PL die **Verlierer**), die **Verliererin** (PL die **Verliererinnen**)
2 (unsuccessful person) der **Versager** (PL die **Versager**), die **Versagerin** (PL die **Versagerinnen**)

loss NOUN
der **Verlust** (PL die **Verluste**)

ℓ **lost property** NOUN
die **Fundsachen** (PLURAL)

ℓ **lot** NOUN
1 **a lot** viel
Wilbur eats a lot. Wilbur isst viel.
I spent a lot. Ich habe viel ausgegeben.
He's a lot better. Es geht ihm viel besser.
a lot of viel
a lot of coffee viel Kaffee
2 (many) **a lot of** viele
a lot of books viele Bücher
3 **lots of** eine Menge (informal)
lots of people eine Menge Leute

lottery NOUN
die **Lotterie** (PL die **Lotterien**) (on TV) das **Lotto** (PL die **Lottos**)
to win the lottery im Lotto gewinnen

ℓ **loud** ADJECTIVE
1 **laut**
in a loud voice mit lauter Stimme
2 **to say something out loud** etwas laut sagen

loudly ADVERB
laut

loudspeaker NOUN
der **Lautsprecher** (PL die **Lautsprecher**)

lounge NOUN
1 (in a house) das **Wohnzimmer** (PL die **Wohnzimmer**)
2 (in an airport) die **Halle** (PL die **Hallen**)
departure lounge die Abflughalle

love NOUN
1 die **Liebe**
for love aus Liebe
2 **to be in love with somebody** in jemanden

verliebt sein
She's in love with Jake. Sie ist in Jake verliebt.
3 **Gina sends her love.** Gina lässt grüßen.
With love from Charlie. Herzliche Grüße von Charlie.
4 (in tennis) **null**

to **love** VERB
1 **lieben** (a person)
I love you. Ich liebe dich.
2 **sehr gerne mögen**◇ (a place or food)
She loves London. Sie mag London sehr gerne.
Wayne loves chocolate. Wayne mag Schokolade sehr gerne.
3 **to love doing something** etwas sehr gerne tun
I love dancing. Ich tanze sehr gerne.
4 **I'd love to come.** Ich würde sehr gerne kommen.

ℓ **lovely** ADJECTIVE
schön
a lovely dress ein schönes Kleid
We had lovely weather. Wir hatten schönes Wetter.
We had a lovely day. Der Tag war sehr schön.

ℓ **low** ADJECTIVE
1 **niedrig**
a low table ein niedriger Tisch
at a low price zu einem niedrigen Preis
2 (not loud) **leise**
in a low voice mit leiser Stimme

lower ADJECTIVE
(not as high) **tiefer**

to **lower** VERB
senken

loyalty NOUN
die **Loyalität** (PL die **Loyalitäten**)

loyalty card NOUN
die **Treuekarte** (PL die **Treuekarten**)

ℓ **luck** NOUN
1 (good) **luck** das **Glück**
with a bit of luck wenn wir Glück haben
I had some good luck. Ich hatte Glück.
Good luck! Viel Glück!
2 **bad luck** das **Pech**
Bad luck! So ein Pech!

🔵 LUCK

Black cats and Friday the 13th are said to bring bad luck in German speaking countries.

luckily ADVERB
zum Glück

◇ **irregular verb;** SEP **separable verb; for more help with verbs see centre section**

    luckily for them zu ihrem Glück

_ℓ_ **lucky** ADJECTIVE
1 **to be lucky** Glück haben
  We were lucky. Wir haben Glück gehabt.
2 **to be lucky** (bringing luck) Glück bringen
  It's supposed to be lucky. Es soll Glück
  bringen.
  my lucky number meine Glückszahl

_ℓ_ **luggage** NOUN
  das **Gepäck**
  My luggage is in the boot. Mein Gepäck ist
  im Kofferraum.
  two pieces of luggage zwei Gepäckstücke

lump NOUN
1 der **Klumpen** (PL die **Klumpen**)
2 (of sugar or butter) das **Stück** (PL die **Stücke**)
3 (in the body) die **Geschwulst** (PL die
  Geschwülste)

_ℓ_ **lunch** NOUN
  das **Mittagessen** (PL die **Mittagessen**)
  to have lunch zu Mittag essen◇
  We had lunch in Oxford. Wir haben in
  Oxford zu Mittag gegessen.

lunch break NOUN
  die **Mittagspause** (PL die **Mittagspausen**)

lunch hour, **lunch time** NOUN
  die **Mittagszeit**

lung NOUN
  der **Lungenflügel**
  lungs die Lunge (SINGULAR)

luxurious ADJECTIVE
  luxuriös

luxury NOUN
  der **Luxus**
  They couldn't afford luxuries. Sie konnten
  sich keinen Luxus leisten.

lyrics PLURAL NOUN
  der **Text** (SINGULAR)

Mm

mac NOUN
  der **Regenmantel** (PL die **Regenmäntel**)

macaroni NOUN
  die **Makkaroni** (PLURAL)

machine NOUN
1 die **Maschine** (PL die **Maschinen**)
2 (slot machine) der **Automat** (PL die
  Automaten)

machinery NOUN
  die **Maschinen** (PLURAL)

_ℓ_ **mad** ADJECTIVE
1 verrückt
  She's completely mad! Sie ist total
  verrückt!
2 (angry) wütend
  to be mad at somebody wütend auf
  jemanden sein
3 **to be mad about something** ganz verrückt
  auf etwas (ACC) sein
  She's mad about horses. Sie ist ganz
  verrückt auf Pferde.

_ℓ_ **madman** NOUN
  der **Verrückte** (PL die **Verrückten**)

madness NOUN
  der **Wahnsinn**

madwoman NOUN
  die **Verrückte** (PL die **Verrückten**)

_ℓ_ **magazine** NOUN
  die **Zeitschrift** (PL die **Zeitschriften**)
  (with mostly photos) das **Magazin** (PL die
  Magazine)

magic NOUN
  der **Zauber**, (conjuring tricks) PL die
  Zauberei

magic ADJECTIVE
1 Zauber-
  magic wand der Zauberstab
2 (great) super (informal)

magician NOUN
1 (wizard) der **Zauberer** (PL die **Zauberer**)
2 (conjurer) der **Zauberkünstler** (PL die
  Zauberkünstler)

magnificent ADJECTIVE
  wundervoll

magnifying glass NOUN
  die **Lupe** (PL die **Lupen**)

maiden name NOUN
  der **Mädchenname** (PL die
  Mädchennamen)

_ℓ_ **mail** NOUN
  die **Post**

mailbox NOUN
  (for e-mails) die **Mailbox** (PL die **Mailboxen**),
  das **Postfach** (PL die **Postfächer**)

mail order NOUN
  die **Bestellung per Post**
  to buy something by mail order etwas bei
  einem Versandhaus bestellen
  mail order catalogue der
  Versandhauskatalog

_ℓ_ indicates key words

p **main** ADJECTIVE
Haupt-
main entrance der Haupteingang

main course NOUN
das **Hauptgericht** (PL die **Hauptgerichte**)

mainly ADVERB
hauptsächlich

main road NOUN
die **Hauptstraße** (PL die **Hauptstraßen**)

maize NOUN
der **Mais**

major ADJECTIVE
1 (important) groß
2 (serious) schwer
a major accident ein schwerer Unfall

Majorca NOUN
Mallorca (NEUTER)

majority NOUN
die **Mehrheit**

p **make** NOUN
die **Marke** (PL die **Marken**)
Which make of car does he drive? Welche
Automarke fährt er?

to **make** VERB
1 machen
to make a meal Essen machen
I made breakfast. Ich habe Frühstück
gemacht.
She made her bed. Sie hat ihr Bett
gemacht.
to make somebody happy jemanden
glücklich machen
It makes you tired. Das macht einen müde.
2 (produce) herstellen SEP
They make computers. Sie stellen
Computer her.
'Made in Germany.' 'In Deutschland
hergestellt.'
3 He made me wait. Er ließ mich warten.
She makes me laugh. Sie bringt mich zum
Lachen.
4 (earn) verdienen
He makes forty pounds a day. Er verdient
vierzig Pfund pro Tag.
to make a living seinen Lebensunterhalt
verdienen
5 (force) zwingen◇
to make somebody do something
jemanden zwingen, etwas zu tun
She made him give the money back.
Sie hat ihn gezwungen, das Geld
zurückzugeben.
6 (the verb 'make' is often translated by a more

specific verb)
to make a cake einen Kuchen backen
to make a phone call telefonieren
to make a dress ein Kleid nähen
7 to make friends with somebody sich mit
jemandem anfreunden SEP
8 I can't make it tonight. Ich kann heute
Abend nicht kommen.
9 Two and three make five. Zwei und drei
ist fünf.
• to make something up
1 etwas erfinden◇
She made up an excuse. Sie hat eine
Ausrede erfunden.
2 to make it up (after a quarrel) sich
versöhnen
They've made it up again. Sie haben sich
wieder versöhnt.

p **make-up** NOUN
1 das **Make-up**
I don't wear make-up. Ich trage kein
Make-up.
2 to put on your make-up sich schminken
Jo's putting on her make-up. Jo schminkt
sich.

male ADJECTIVE
1 männlich
male voice die Männerstimme
2 male animal das Männchen
male rat das Rattenmännchen
3 male student der Student

male chauvinist NOUN
der **Chauvinist** (PL die **Chauvinisten**)

mall NOUN
das **Einkaufszentrum** (PL die
Einkaufszentren)
a shopping mall ein Einkaufszentrum

mammal NOUN
das **Säugetier** (PL die **Säugetiere**)

p **man** NOUN
1 der **Mann** (PL die **Männer**)
an old man ein alter Mann
2 (the human race) der **Mensch** (PL die
Menschen)
man and the animals der Mensch und die
Tiere
All men are equal. Alle Menschen sind
gleich.

to **manage** VERB
1 leiten (a business, team)
She manages a travel agency. Sie leitet ein
Reisebüro.
2 (cope) zurechtkommen◇ SEP (PERF sein)
I can manage. Ich komme schon zurecht.
3 to manage to do something es schaffen,

etwas zu tun
He managed to push the door open. Er hat
es geschafft (PL die Tür aufzustoßen.)
I didn't manage to get in touch with her.
Ich habe es nicht geschafft, sie zu erreichen.

management NOUN
1 das Management
   management course der Managementkurs
2 (people) die Leitung

ℓ **manager** NOUN
1 (of a company or bank) der Direktor (PL
   die Direktoren), die Direktorin (PL die
   Direktorinnen)
2 (of a shop or restaurant) der
   Geschäftsführer (PL die Geschäftsführer),
   die Geschäftsführerin (PL die
   Geschäftsführerinnen)
3 (in football) der Trainer (PL die Trainer), die
   Trainerin (PL die Trainerinnen)
4 (in entertainment) der Manager (PL
   die Manager), die Managerin (PL die
   Managerinnen)

   WORD TIP Professions, hobbies, and sports
   don't take an article in German: Er ist Trainer.

manageress NOUN
   (of a shop or restaurant) die
   Geschäftsführerin (PL die
   Geschäftsführerinnen)

   WORD TIP Professions, hobbies, and sports
   don't take an article in German: Sie ist
   Geschäftsführerin.

managing director NOUN
   der Geschäftsführer (PL die
   Geschäftsführer), die Geschäftsführerin
   (PL die Geschäftsführerinnen)

   WORD TIP Professions, hobbies, and sports don't
   take an article in German: Er ist Geschäftsführer.

mania NOUN
   die Manie (PL die Manien)

maniac NOUN
   der/die Wahnsinnige (PL die
   Wahnsinnigen)
   She drives like a maniac. Sie fährt wie eine
   Wahnsinnige.

man-made ADJECTIVE
   man-made fibre die Kunstfaser

manner NOUN
1 **in a manner of speaking** mehr oder
   weniger
2 **manners** die Manieren (PLURAL)
   to have good manners gute Manieren
   haben
   It's bad manners to talk like that. Es

gehört sich nicht, so zu reden.

mantelpiece NOUN
   der Kaminsims (PL die Kaminsimse)

manual NOUN
   das Handbuch (PL die Handbücher)

to **manufacture** VERB
   herstellen SEP

manufacturer NOUN
   der Hersteller (PL die Hersteller)

ℓ **many** DETERMINER, PRONOUN
1 viele
   Does she have many friends? Hat sie viele
   Freunde?
   We didn't see many people. Wir haben
   nicht viele Leute gesehen.
   not many nicht viele
   Many of them forgot. Viele haben es
   vergessen.
   There were too many people. Es waren zu
   viele (Leute) da.
   How many? Wie viele?
   How many were there? Wie viele waren
   da?
   How many sisters have you got? Wie viele
   Schwestern hast du?
   How many are there left? Wie viele sind
   übrig geblieben?
   I've never had so many presents. Ich habe
   noch nie so viele Geschenke bekommen.
   I have so many things to do. Ich habe so
   viel zu tun.
2 (as much as)
   as many as so viel wie
   Take as many as you like. Nimm so viel wie
   du willst.
3 (too much)
   That's far too many. Das ist viel zu viel.

ℓ **map** NOUN
1 die Karte (PL die Karten)
2 (of a town) der Stadtplan (PL die
   Stadtpläne)

   WORD TIP Do not translate the English word
   map with the German Mappe.

marathon NOUN
   der Marathonlauf (PL die Marathonläufe)

marble NOUN
1 der Marmor
2 (for playing) die Murmel (PL die Murmeln)
   to play marbles Murmeln spielen

march NOUN
   der Marsch (PL die Märsche)

to **march** VERB
   marschieren (PERF sein)

A
B
C
D
E
F
G
H
I
J
K
L
M
N
O
P
Q
R
S
T
U
V
W
X
Y
Z

ℓ indicates key words

ℰ **March** NOUN
der März
in March im März

mare NOUN
die Stute (PL die Stuten)

margarine NOUN
die Margarine

margin NOUN
(of a page, or of society) der Rand (PL die Ränder)

marijuana NOUN
das Marihuana

ℰ **mark** NOUN
1 (at school) die Note (PL die Noten)
I got a good mark in German. Ich habe eine gute Note in Deutsch bekommen.
2 (stain) der Fleck (PL die Flecke)
3 (German currency until replaced by the euro) die Mark (PL die Mark)

to **mark** VERB
1 korrigieren
The teacher marks our homework. Die Lehrerin korrigiert unsere Hausaufgaben.
2 (in sports) decken

> 🟢 **MARK**
>
> In Germany, the best mark is 1, the worst is 6.
> In Austria, the best mark is 1, the worst is 5. In
> Switzerland, the best mark is 6, the worst is 1.
> In Switzerland Halbnoten such as 3.5 or 5.5
> may also be given. These marks mean that the
> pupil's performance in a particular subject is
> between two marks.

ℰ **market** NOUN
der Markt (PL die Märkte)

marketing NOUN
das Marketing

marmalade NOUN
die Orangenmarmelade

maroon ADJECTIVE
kastanienbraun

ℰ **marriage** NOUN
1 die Ehe (PL die Ehen)
2 (wedding) die Hochzeit (PL die Hochzeiten)

ℰ **married** ADJECTIVE
1 verheiratet
They've been married for twenty years.
Sie sind seit zwanzig Jahren verheiratet.
2 **married couple** das Ehepaar

ℰ to **marry** VERB
1 **to marry somebody** jemanden heiraten
She married a Frenchman. Sie hat einen

Franzosen geheiratet.
2 **to get married** heiraten
They got married in July. Sie haben im Juli geheiratet.

martial art NOUN
die Kampfsportart (PL die Kampfsportarten)

ℰ **marvellous** ADJECTIVE
wunderbar

marzipan NOUN
das Marzipan

mascara NOUN
die Wimperntusche

mascot NOUN
das Maskottchen (PL die Maskottchen)

ℰ **masculine** NOUN
männlich

to **mash** VERB
stampfen

mashed potatoes PLURAL NOUN
der Kartoffelbrei (SINGULAR)

mask NOUN
die Maske (PL die Masken)

mass NOUN
1 **a mass of** eine Menge
a mass of people eine Menschenmenge
2 **masses of** massenhaft (informal)
They've got masses of money. Sie haben massenhaft Geld.
There's masses left over. Es ist massenhaft übrig geblieben.
3 (religious) die Messe (PL die Messen)
to go to mass zur Messe gehen

massage NOUN
die Massage (PL die Massagen)

massive ADJECTIVE
riesig

to **master** VERB
1 meistern
2 **to master a language** eine Sprache beherrschen

masterpiece NOUN
das Meisterwerk (PL die Meisterwerke)

mat NOUN
1 (doormat) die Matte (PL die Matten)
2 (to put under a hot dish) der Untersetzer (PL die Untersetzer)
3 **table mat** das Platzdeckchen

ℰ **match** NOUN
1 (for lighting) das Streichholz (PL die

◇ irregular verb; SEP separable verb; for more help with verbs see centre section

    Streichhölzer)
    box of matches die Streichholzschachtel
2 *(in sports)* das **Spiel** (PL die **Spiele**)
    football match das Fußballspiel
    to watch the match das Spiel sehen
    to win the match das Spiel gewinnen
    to lose the match das Spiel verlieren
to **match** VERB
    passen zu (+DAT)
    The jacket matches the skirt. Die Jacke
    passt zum Rock.

ℓ **mate** NOUN
    der **Freund** (PL die **Freunde**)
    I'm going to the match with my mates. Ich
    gehe mit meinen Freunden zum Spiel.

material NOUN
1 *(fabric, also information)* der **Stoff** (PL die
    Stoffe)
2 *(substance)* das **Material** (PL die
    Materialien)
    raw materials die Rohstoffe (PLURAL)

ℓ **mathematics** NOUN
    die **Mathematik**

ℓ **maths** NOUN
    Mathe (NEUTER) (informal)
    I like maths. Ich mag Mathe gerne.
    Anna's good at maths. Anna ist gut in
    Mathe.

ℓ **matter** NOUN
1 die **Angelegenheit**
    a serious matter eine ernste Angelegenheit
2 **What's the matter?** Was ist los?
    There's something the matter with the
    computer. Mit dem Computer stimmt
    etwas nicht.
to **matter** VERB
1 **wichtig sein**◇ (PERF **sein**)
    That's what matters most. Das ist am
    wichtigsten.
    It matters a lot to me. Es ist mir sehr
    wichtig.
    Does it really matter? Ist das wirklich so
    wichtig?
2 **It doesn't matter.** Es macht nichts.
    It doesn't matter if it rains. Es macht
    nichts, wenn es regnet.
3 **You can write it in German or English; it**
    doesn't matter. Du kannst es auf Deutsch
    oder Englisch schreiben, das ist egal.
4 **to matter to somebody** jemandem etwas
    ausmachen SEP
    Does it matter to you if I leave earlier?
    Macht es dir etwas aus, wenn ich früher
    gehe?

mattress NOUN
    die **Matratze** (PL die **Matratzen**)

maximum NOUN
    das **Maximum** (PL die **Maxima**)

maximum ADJECTIVE
    Höchst-, maximal
    the maximum temperature die
    Höchsttemperatur
    She got the maximum points. Sie erreichte
    die maximale Punktzahl.

may VERB
1 **She may be ill.** Vielleicht ist sie krank.
    We may go to Spain. Wir fahren vielleicht
    nach Spanien.
2 *(expressing permission)* **dürfen**◇
    May I close the door? Darf ich die Tür
    zumachen?

ℓ **May** NOUN
    der **Mai**
    in May im Mai

ℓ **maybe** ADVERB
    vielleicht
    Maybe they've got lost. Vielleicht haben
    sie sich verlaufen.

May Day NOUN
    der **Erste Mai**

mayonnaise NOUN
    die **Mayonnaise** (PL die **Majonäse**)

mayor NOUN
    der **Bürgermeister** (PL die **Bürgermeister**),
    die **Bürgermeisterin** (PL die
    Bürgermeisterinnen)

ℓ **me** PRONOUN *(in German this pronoun changes*
    according to the function it has in the
    sentence or the preposition it follows)
1 *(as a direct object in the accusative)* **mich**
    She knows me. Sie kennt mich.
2 *(after a preposition that takes the accusative)*
    mich
    They left without me. Sie sind ohne mich
    losgefahren.
    Wait for me! Warte auf mich!
3 *(as an indirect object or following a verb that*
    takes the dative) **mir**
    Can you give me your address? Kannst du
    mir deine Adresse geben?
    He helped me. Er hat mir geholfen.
4 *(after a preposition that takes the dative)* **mir**
    She never talks to me. Sie redet nie mit
    mir.
5 *(in comparisons)*
    than me als ich
    She's older than me. Sie ist älter als ich.
6 *(in the nominative)* **ich**

ℓ **indicates key words**

It's me. Ich bin's.
Not me. Ich nicht.

meadow NOUN
die Wiese (PL die Wiesen)

ℰ **meal** NOUN
1 das Essen (PL die Essen)
   She cooked the meal. Sie hat das Essen
   gekocht.
2 **to go for a meal** essen gehen
3 **three meals a day** drei Mahlzeiten am Tag

ℰ **to mean** VERB
1 (signify) bedeuten
   What does that mean? Was bedeutet das?
2 (intend to say) meinen
   What do you mean? Was meinst du?
   That's not what I meant. Das habe ich nicht
   gemeint.
3 **to mean to do something** etwas tun
   wollen⬦
   I meant to phone my mother. Ich wollte
   meine Mutter anrufen.
4 **to be meant to do something** etwas tun
   sollen⬦
   She was meant to be here at six. Sie sollte
   um sechs hier sein.

mean ADJECTIVE
1 (with money) geizig
2 (unkind) gemein
   She's really mean to her brother. Sie ist
   richtig gemein zu ihrem Bruder.
   What a mean thing to do! Das ist gemein!

meaning NOUN
die Bedeutung (PL die Bedeutungen)

ℰ **means** NOUN
1 das Mittel (PL die Mittel)
   means of transport das Verkehrsmittel
2 **a means of** eine Möglichkeit
   a means of earning money eine
   Möglichkeit, Geld zu verdienen
3 **by means of** mit Hilfe (+GEN)
4 **By all means!** Selbstverständlich!

meantime NOUN
in the meantime in der Zwischenzeit
for the meantime vorübergehend

meanwhile ADVERB
inzwischen
Meanwhile she was waiting at the station.
Inzwischen wartete sie am Bahnhof.

measles NOUN
die Masern (PLURAL)

to measure VERB
messen⬦

measurements PLURAL NOUN
die Maße (PLURAL)
the measurements of the room die Maße
des Zimmers
my measurements meine Maße

ℰ **meat** NOUN
das Fleisch
I don't like meat. Ich mag kein Fleisch.

meatball NOUN
das Fleischbällchen (PL die
Fleischbällchen)

ℰ **mechanic** NOUN
der Mechaniker (PL die Mechaniker), die
Mechanikerin (PL die Mechanikerinnen)

   WORD TIP Professions, hobbies, and sports don't
   take an article in German: Er ist Mechaniker.

mechanical ADJECTIVE
mechanisch

medal NOUN
die Medaille (PL die Medaillen)
the gold medal die Goldmedaille

media NOUN
the media die Medien (PLURAL)

media studies NOUN
die Medienwissenschaft

medical NOUN
1 die ärztliche Untersuchung (PL die
   ärztlichen Untersuchungen)
2 **to have a medical** sich untersuchen lassen

medical ADJECTIVE
1 medizinisch
2 ärztlich (examination, treatment)

ℰ **medicine** NOUN
1 (drug) das Medikament (PL die
   Medikamente)
   I forgot to take my medicine. Ich
   habe vergessen, mein Medikament
   einzunehmen.
2 (subject of study) die Medizin
   She's studying medicine. Sie studiert
   Medizin.
3 **alternative medicine** die Alternativmedizin

medieval ADJECTIVE
mittelalterlich

Mediterranean NOUN
the Mediterranean (Sea) das Mittelmeer

ℰ **medium** ADJECTIVE
mittlerer/mittlere/mittleres

medium-sized ADJECTIVE
mittelgroß

⬦ irregular verb; SEP separable verb; for more help with verbs see centre section

to **meet** VERB

1 *(by chance)* **treffen**◇
   I met Rosie at the baker's. Ich habe Rosie beim Bäcker getroffen.
2 *(by appointment)* **sich treffen mit** (+DAT)
   I'll meet you outside the cinema. Ich treffe mich mit dir vor dem Kino.
3 **sich treffen**
   We're meeting at six. Wir treffen uns um sechs.
4 *(get to know)* **kennenlernen** SEP
   I met a German girl last week. Ich habe letzte Woche eine Deutsche kennengelernt.
5 **I've never met Oskar.** Ich kenne Oskar nicht.
6 *(off a train or bus, for example)* **abholen** SEP
   My dad's meeting me at the station. Mein Vater holt mich vom Bahnhof ab.

℘ **meeting** NOUN

1 *(by arrangement)* das **Treffen** (PL die **Treffen**)
2 *(in business)* die **Besprechung** (PL die **Besprechungen**)
   She's in a meeting. Sie ist in einer Besprechung.
3 *(by chance or in sports)* die **Begegnung** (PL die **Begegnungen**)

megabyte NOUN

das **Megabyte** (PL die **Megabytes**)

℘ **melon** NOUN

die **Melone** (PL die **Melonen**)

to **melt** VERB

1 **schmelzen**◇ (PERF sein)
   The snow has melted. Der Schnee ist geschmolzen.
2 *(in cookery)* **zerlassen**◇ *(butter, fat)*
   Melt the butter in a saucepan. Die Butter im Topf zerlassen.

member NOUN

das **Mitglied** (PL die **Mitglieder**)
member of staff der Mitarbeiter/die Mitarbeiterin, *(in a school)* der Lehrer/die Lehrerin

Member of Parliament NOUN

der/die **Abgeordnete** (PL die **Abgeordneten**)

> **WORD TIP** Professions, hobbies, and sports don't take an article in German: Er ist Abgeordneter.

membership NOUN

die **Mitgliedschaft**

membership card NOUN

die **Mitgliedskarte** (PL die **Mitgliedskarten**)

membership fee NOUN

der **Mitgliedsbeitrag** (PL die **Mitgliedsbeiträge**)

memorial NOUN

das **Denkmal** (PL die **Denkmäler**)
a war memorial ein Kriegsdenkmal

to **memorize** VERB

to memorize something etwas auswendig lernen

memory NOUN

1 *(of a person)* das **Gedächtnis**
   You have a good memory. Du hast ein gutes Gedächtnis.
2 *(of the past)* die **Erinnerung** (PL die **Erinnerungen**)
   I have good memories of our stay in Italy. Ich habe schöne Erinnerungen an unseren Urlaub in Italien.
3 *(of a computer)* der **Speicher** (PL die **Speicher**)

memory card NOUN

die **Speicherkarte** (PL die **Speicherkarten**)

to **mend** VERB

1 **reparieren**
2 *(by sewing)* **ausbessern** SEP

meningitis NOUN

die **Hirnhautentzündung**

mental ADJECTIVE

1 **geistig**
2 **mental illness** die Geisteskrankheit
   mental hospital die psychiatrische Klinik

to **mention** VERB

erwähnen
'Thanks for your help.' 'Don't mention it.' 'Danke für Ihre Hilfe.' 'Gern geschehen.'

℘ **menu** NOUN

1 *(in a restaurant)* die **Speisekarte** (PL die **Speisekarten**)
   Is there a set menu? Gibt es ein Menü?
2 *(in computing)* das **Menü** (PL die **Menüs**)

meringue NOUN

das **Baiser** (PL die **Baisers**)

merit NOUN

1 *(good feature or advantage)* der **Vorzug** (PL die **Vorzüge**)
2 *(special award)* die **Auszeichnung (für besonders gute Leistungen)**
3 **She got the job on merit.** Sie bekam die Stelle aufgrund ihrer Leistungen.

merry ADJECTIVE

1 **fröhlich**
   Merry Christmas! Fröhliche Weihnachten!
2 *(from drinking)* **angeheitert**

merry-go-round NOUN
das **Karussell** (PL die **Karussells**)

mess NOUN
1 das **Durcheinander**
My papers are in a complete mess.
Meine Unterlagen sind ein einziges
Durcheinander.
What a mess! Was für ein Durcheinander!
2 **to make a mess** Unordnung machen
3 **to clear up the mess** aufräumen SEP

to mess VERB
• **to mess about**
herumalbern SEP
Stop messing about! Hört auf
herumzualbern!
• **to mess about with something**
mit etwas (DAT) herumspielen SEP
**It's dangerous to mess about with
matches.** Es ist gefährlich, mit
Streichhölzern herumzuspielen.
• **to mess something up**
1 etwas durcheinander bringen◇
You've messed up all my papers. Sie haben
meine Unterlagen völlig durcheinander
gebracht.
2 (make dirty) etwas schmutzig machen
3 (botch) etwas verpfuschen

message NOUN
1 die **Nachricht** (PL die **Nachrichten**)
She left a message for you. Sie hat dir eine
Nachricht hinterlassen.
text message die SMS
I deleted all my messages. Ich habe alle
SMS gelöscht.
2 **to give somebody a message** jemandem
etwas ausrichten SEP
Can I take a message? Kann ich etwas
ausrichten?

message board NOUN
die **elektronische Anschlagtafel** (PL die
elektronischen Anschlagtafeln)

messy ADJECTIVE
1 (dirty)
It's a messy job. Das ist eine schmutzige
Arbeit.
2 **He's a messy eater.** Er bekleckert sich beim
Essen.
3 **Her writing's really messy.** Sie hat eine
furchtbare Schrift.
4 (untidy)
She's very messy. Sie ist sehr unordentlich.

metal NOUN
das **Metall** (PL die **Metalle**)

meter NOUN
1 (electricity, gas, taxi) der **Zähler** (PL die
Zähler)
to read the meter den Zähler ablesen◇ SEP
2 **parking meter** die Parkuhr

method NOUN
die **Methode** (PL die **Methoden**)

Methodist NOUN
der **Methodist** (PL die **Methodisten**), die
Methodistin (PL die **Methodistinnen**)
He's a Methodist. Er ist Methodist.

ℓ **metre** NOUN
der **Meter** (PL die **Meter**)

metric ADJECTIVE
metrisch

microchip NOUN
der **Mikrochip** (PL die **Mikrochips**)

microphone NOUN
das **Mikrofon** (PL die **Mikrofone**)

microscope NOUN
das **Mikroskop** (PL die **Mikroskope**)

microwave (oven) NOUN
der **Mikrowellenherd** (PL die
Mikrowellenherde)

ℓ **midday** NOUN
der **Mittag**
at midday mittags

ℓ **middle** NOUN
1 die **Mitte**
in the middle of the room in der Mitte des
Zimmers
in the middle of June Mitte Juni
in the middle of the night mitten in der
Nacht
2 **to be in the middle of doing something**
gerade dabei sein, etwas zu tun
**When she phoned I was in the middle of
washing my hair.** Als sie anrief, war ich
gerade dabei, mir die Haare zu waschen.

middle ADJECTIVE
mittlerer/mittlere/mittleres
I like the middle one best. Ich mag das
mittlere am liebsten.

middle-aged ADJECTIVE
mittleren Alters
a middle-aged lady eine Dame mittleren
Alters

middle-class ADJECTIVE
a middle-class family eine Familie der
Mittelschicht
They are middle-class. Sie gehören zur
Mittelschicht.

Middle East NOUN
the Middle East der Nahe Osten

middle school NOUN
Schule für Kinder von 9 bis 13

midge NOUN
die **Mücke** (PL die **Mücken**)

ℐ **midnight** NOUN
die **Mitternacht**
at midnight um Mitternacht

Midsummer's Day NOUN
die **Sommersonnenwende**

midwife NOUN
die **Hebamme** (PL die **Hebammen**)

WORD TIP Professions, hobbies, and sports don't take an article in German: Sie ist Hebamme.

might VERB
1 'Are you going to phone him?' – 'I might.'
'Rufst du ihn an?' – 'Vielleicht.'
I might invite Jo. Vielleicht lade ich Jo ein.
He might have forgotten. Vielleicht hat er
es vergessen.
I might not come. Vielleicht komme ich
nicht.
2 She might be right. Sie könnte Recht
haben.

migraine NOUN
die **Migräne**

mike NOUN
(microphone) das **Mikro** (PL die **Mikros**)
(informal)

mild ADJECTIVE
mild

mile NOUN
1 die **Meile** (PL die **Meilen**) (Germans use
kilometres for distances; to convert miles to
kilometres, multiply by 8 and divide by 5.)
It's ten miles to Oxford. Es sind sechzehn
Kilometer bis Oxford.
We've walked miles already. Wir sind
schon kilometerweit gelaufen.
2 It's miles better. Das ist viel besser.

military ADJECTIVE
militärisch

ℐ **milk** NOUN
die **Milch**
full-cream milk die Vollmilch
skimmed milk die Magermilch
semi-skimmed milk die fettarme Milch
to **milk** VERB
melken◇

milk chocolate NOUN
die **Milchschokolade**

milkman NOUN
der **Milchmann** (PL die **Milchmänner**)

WORD TIP Professions, hobbies, and sports
don't take an article in German: Er ist
Milchmann.

milk shake NOUN
der **Milchshake** (PL die **Milchshakes**)

millennium NOUN
das **Jahrtausend** (PL die **Jahrtausende**)

millimetre NOUN
der **Millimeter** (PL die **Millimeter**)

million NOUN
1 die **Million** (PL die **Millionen**)
a million people eine Million Menschen
two million people zwei Millionen
Menschen
2 (very many)
There were millions of people there. Es
waren wahnsinnig viele Leute da.

millionaire NOUN
der **Millionär** (PL die **Millionäre**), die
Millionärin (PL die **Millionärinnen**)

WORD TIP Professions, hobbies, and sports
don't take an article in German: Er ist Millionär.

to **mimic** VERB
nachmachen SEP

mince NOUN
das **Hackfleisch**

ℐ **mind** NOUN
1 der **Sinn**
It never crossed my mind to ask them for
help. Es kam mir überhaupt nicht in den
Sinn, sie um Hilfe zu bitten.
2 die **Meinung**
to change your mind seine Meinung
ändern
I've changed my mind. Ich habe meine
Meinung geändert.
3 to make up your mind to do something
sich entschließen◇, etwas zu tun
I can't make up my mind which dress to
wear. Ich kann mich nicht entschließen,
welches Kleid ich anziehe.
4 I've made up my mind. Ich habe mich
entschieden.
to **mind** VERB
1 aufpassen SEP auf (+ACC)
Can you mind my bag for me? Können Sie
auf meine Tasche aufpassen?
Could you mind the baby for ten minutes?

ℐ indicates key words

Könntest du zehn Minuten auf das Baby aufpassen?

2 Do you mind closing the door? Würden Sie bitte die Tür zumachen?

3 Do you mind if ...? Würde es Ihnen etwas ausmachen, wenn ...?
Do you mind if I open the window? Würde es Ihnen etwas ausmachen, wenn ich das Fenster aufmache?
I don't mind. Es macht mir nichts aus.
I don't mind the heat. Die Hitze macht mir nichts aus.

4 Never mind. Macht nichts.

5 *(in warnings)*
Mind you don't slip. Pass auf, dass du nicht ausrutschst.
Mind the step! Vorsicht, Stufe!
Mind out! Vorsicht!

mine[1] *NOUN*
das **Bergwerk** (*PL* die **Bergwerke**)
coal mine das Kohlenbergwerk

ℐ **mine**[2] *PRONOUN*
1 *(for a masculine noun)* **mein**
She took her coat and I took mine. Sie hat ihren Mantel genommen und ich habe meinen genommen.

2 *(for a feminine noun)* **meine**
She gave me her address and I gave her mine. Sie hat mir ihre Adresse gegeben und ich habe ihr meine gegeben.

3 *(for a neuter noun)* **meins**
Her T-shirt is red and mine is blue. Ihr T-Shirt ist rot und meins ist blau.

4 *(for masculine/ feminine/neuter plural nouns)* **meine**
She showed me her photos and I showed her mine. Sie hat mir ihre Fotos gezeigt und ich habe ihr meine gezeigt.

5 a friend of mine ein Freund von mir
It's mine. Das gehört mir.

miner *NOUN*
der **Bergarbeiter** (*PL* die **Bergarbeiter**)

WORD TIP Professions, hobbies, and sports don't take an article in German: Er ist Bergarbeiter.

ℐ **mineral water** *NOUN*
das **Mineralwasser**

miniature *NOUN*
die **Miniatur** (*PL* die **Miniaturen**)

miniature *ADJECTIVE*
Miniatur-
miniature model das Miniaturmodell

minibus *NOUN*
der **Kleinbus** (*PL* die **Kleinbusse**)

minimum *NOUN*
das **Minimum**
a minimum of ein Minimum von

minimum *ADJECTIVE*
Mindest-
the minimum age das Mindestalter
minimum wage der Mindestlohn

miniskirt *NOUN*
der **Minirock** (*PL* die **Miniröcke**)

minister *NOUN*
1 *(in government)* de **Minister** (*PL* die **Minister**), die **Ministerin** (*PL* die **Ministerinnen**)

2 *(of a church)* der/die **Geistliche** (*PL* die **Geistlichen**)

WORD TIP Professions, hobbies, and sports don't take an article in German: Sie ist Ministerin.

ministry *NOUN*
das **Ministerium** (*PL* die **Ministerien**)

minor *ADJECTIVE*
kleiner

minority *NOUN*
die **Minderheit** (*PL* die **Minderheiten**)

mint *NOUN*
1 *(herb)* die **Minze**
2 *(sweet)* der or das **Pfefferminzbonbon** (*PL* die **Pfefferminzbonbons**)

minus *PREPOSITION*
minus *(+GEN)*
Seven minus three is four. Sieben minus drei ist vier.
It was minus ten this morning. Heute Morgen war es minus zehn Grad.

ℐ **minute**[1] *NOUN*
1 die **Minute** (*PL* die **Minuten**)
I'll be ready in two minutes. Ich bin in zwei Minuten fertig.
It's five minutes' walk from here. Es ist fünf Minuten zu Fuß von hier.

2 der **Moment**
Just a minute! Einen Moment bitte!

3 In a minute. Gleich.

minute[2] *ADJECTIVE*
winzig
The bedrooms are minute. Die Schlafzimmer sind winzig.

miracle *NOUN*
das **Wunder** (*PL* die **Wunder**)

ℐ **mirror** *NOUN*
der **Spiegel** (*PL* die **Spiegel**)
He looked at himself in the mirror. Er hat

◇ **irregular verb;** *SEP* **separable verb; for more help with verbs see centre section**

sich im Spiegel betrachtet.

to **misbehave** VERB
sich schlecht benehmen◇

miserable ADJECTIVE
1 elend
He was miserable without her. Ohne sie
fühlte er sich elend.
I feel really miserable today. Ich fühle mich
heute richtig elend.
2 mies
It's miserable weather. Das Wetter ist
mies.
She gets paid a miserable salary. Sie
bekommt ein mieses Gehalt.

ℰ to **miss** VERB
1 verpassen
She missed her train. Sie hat ihren Zug
verpasst.
I missed the film. Ich habe den Film
verpasst.
to miss an opportunity eine Gelegenheit
verpassen
2 (not hit or go into) nicht treffen◇
The stone missed me. Der Stein hat mich
nicht getroffen.
The ball missed the goal. Der Schuss ging
am Tor vorbei.
Missed! Nicht getroffen!
3 (not go to) versäumen
He's missed his classes. Er hat den
Unterricht versäumt.
4 vermissen (a person or thing)
I miss you. Ich vermisse dich.
She's missing her sister. Sie vermisst ihre
Schwester.
I miss England. Ich vermisse England.
• to miss out
auslassen◇SEP
You missed out an important point. Du
hast einen wichtigen Punkt ausgelassen.

ℰ **Miss** NOUN
das Fräulein
Miss Jones Fräulein Jones, Frau Jones

WORD TIP Adult women are usually addressed
as Frau, whether or not they are married.

missing ADJECTIVE
1 fehlend
She's found the missing pieces. Sie hat die
fehlenden Teile gefunden.
the missing link das fehlende Glied
2 to be missing fehlen
There's a plate missing. Ein Teller fehlt.
There are three forks missing. Drei Gabeln
fehlen.

3 to go missing verschwinden◇ (PERF sein)
Several things have gone missing
lately. Mehrere Sachen sind kürzlich
verschwunden.
4 Three children are missing. Drei Kinder
werden vermisst.

missionary NOUN
der Missionar (PL die Missionare), die
Missionarin (PL die Missionarinnen)

WORD TIP Professions, hobbies, and sports
don't take an article in German: Er ist Missionar.

mist NOUN
der Nebel

WORD TIP Do not translate the English word
mist with the German Mist.

ℰ **mistake** NOUN
1 der Fehler (PL die Fehler)
spelling mistake der Rechtschreibfehler
You've made lots of mistakes. Du hast viele
Fehler gemacht.
2 to make a mistake (be mistaken) sich irren
Sorry, I made a mistake. Entschuldigung,
ich habe mich geirrt.
3 by mistake aus Versehen

to **mistake** VERB
I mistook you for your brother. Ich habe
dich mit deinem Bruder verwechselt.

mistaken ADJECTIVE
to be mistaken sich täuschen
You're mistaken. Du täuschst dich.

mistletoe NOUN
die Mistel

misty ADJECTIVE
dunstig
a misty morning ein dunstiger Morgen

to **misunderstand** VERB
missverstehen◇
I misunderstood. Ich habe es
missverstanden.

misunderstanding NOUN
das Missverständnis (PL die
Missverständnisse)
There's been a misunderstanding. Da liegt
ein Missverständnis vor.

ℰ **mix** NOUN
die Mischung (PL die Mischungen)
a good mix eine gute Mischung
cake mix die Backmischung

to **mix** VERB
1 vermischen
Mix the ingredients together. Die Zutaten

vermischen.

Mix the cream into the sauce. Die Sahne in die Soße rühren.

2 **to mix with** verkehren mit *(+DAT)*
She mixes with lots of interesting people. Sie verkehrt mit vielen interessanten Leuten.

• **to mix up**

1 durcheinander bringen ◇
You've mixed up all the papers. Du hast alle Unterlagen durcheinander gebracht.
You've got it all mixed up. Du hast alles durcheinander gebracht.

2 *(confuse)* verwechseln
I get him mixed up with his brother. Ich verwechsele ihn mit seinem Bruder.

ℓ **mixed** *ADJECTIVE*

1 bunt
a mixed programme ein buntes Programm

2 gemischt
a mixed salad ein gemischter Salat

mixture *NOUN*
die Mischung (PL die Mischungen)
It's a mixture of jazz and rock. Es ist eine Mischung aus Jazz und Rock.

to **moan** *VERB*
(complain) jammern
Stop moaning! Hör auf zu jammern!

mobile (phone) *NOUN*
das Handy (PL die Handys)
I called him on my mobile. Ich habe ihn auf dem Handy angerufen.

mobile home *NOUN*
der Wohnwagen (PL die Wohnwagen)

mock *NOUN*
(mock exam) die Übungsprüfung (PL die Übungsprüfungen)

to **mock** *VERB*
sich lustig machen über *(+ACC)*
Stop mocking me. Hör auf, dich über mich lustig zu machen.

model *NOUN*

1 das Modell (PL die Modelle)
His car is the latest model. Sein Auto ist das neueste Modell.
a model of Westminster Abbey ein Modell von der Westminsterabtei

2 *(fashion model)* das Mannequin (PL die Mannequins), *(in photos)* das Fotomodell (PL die Fotomodelle)

WORD TIP Professions, hobbies, and sports don't take an article in German: Sie ist Fotomodell.

model aeroplane *NOUN*
das Modellflugzeug (PL die Modellflugzeuge)

model railway *NOUN*
die Modelleisenbahn (PL die Modelleisenbahnen)

ℓ **modem** *NOUN*
der Modem (PL die Modems)

ℓ **modern** *ADJECTIVE*
modern

to **modernize** *VERB*
modernisieren

modern languages *NOUN*
moderne Fremdsprachen (PLURAL)

modest *ADJECTIVE*
bescheiden

to **modify** *VERB*
abändern *SEP*

moisture *NOUN*
die Feuchtigkeit

moisturizer *NOUN*
die Feuchtigkeitscreme

mole *NOUN*

1 *(animal)* der Maulwurf (PL die Maulwürfe)

2 *(on the skin)* der Leberfleck (PL die Leberflecke)

molecule *NOUN*
das Molekül (PL die Moleküle)

ℓ **moment** *NOUN*

1 der Moment (PL die Momente)
at any moment jeden Moment
at the moment im Moment, im Augenblick
at the right moment im richtigen Moment

2 der Augenblick (PL die Augenblicke)
Wait a moment! Einen Augenblick!

3 **He'll be ready in a moment.** Er ist gleich fertig.

ℓ **monarchy** *NOUN*
die Monarchie

monastery *NOUN*
das Kloster (PL die Klöster)

ℓ **Monday** *NOUN*

1 der Montag
on Monday am Montag
I'm going to see him on Monday. Ich sehe ihn am Montag.
See you on Monday! Bis Montag!
every Monday jeden Montag
last Monday letzten Montag
next Monday nächsten Montag

Monday morning Montagmorgen
Monday afternoon Montagnachmittag
Monday evening Montagabend
2 **on Mondays** montags
The museum is closed on Mondays. Das
Museum ist montags geschlossen.

ℓ**money** NOUN
das Geld
I don't have enough money. Ich habe nicht
genug Geld.
to make money Geld verdienen

money box NOUN
die Sparbüchse (PL die Sparbüchsen)

mongrel NOUN
der Mischling (PL die Mischlinge)
Our dog is a mongrel. Unser Hund ist ein
Mischling.

monitor NOUN
(of a computer) der Monitor (PL die
Monitoren)

monk NOUN
der Mönch (PL die Mönche)

> **WORD TIP** Professions, hobbies, and sports
> don't take an article in German: Er ist Mönch.

monkey NOUN
der Affe (PL die Affen)

monotonous ADJECTIVE
eintönig

monster NOUN
das Ungeheuer (PL die Ungeheuer)

ℓ**month** NOUN
der Monat
in the month of May im Mai
this month diesen Monat
next month nächsten Monat
last month letzten Monat
for three months drei Monate lang
every month jeden Monat
every three months alle drei Monate
in two months' time in zwei Monaten
at the end of the month am Monatsende

monthly ADJECTIVE
monatlich
monthly payment die monatliche Zahlung
monthly ticket die Monatskarte

ℓ**monument** NOUN
das Denkmal (PL die Denkmäler)

ℓ**mood** NOUN
1 die Laune (PL die Launen)
to be in a good mood gute Laune haben
to be in a (bad) mood schlechte Laune
haben

2 **I'm not in the mood.** Ich habe keine Lust
dazu.
I'm not in the mood for working. Ich habe
keine Lust zum Arbeiten.

ℓ**moon** NOUN
der Mond (PL die Monde)
by the light of the moon im Mondschein
to be over the moon im siebten Himmel
sein (literally: to be in seventh heaven)

moonlight NOUN
der Mondschein
by moonlight im Mondschein

moped NOUN
das Moped (PL die Mopeds)

moral NOUN
die Moral
the moral of the story die Moral der
Geschichte

moral ADJECTIVE
moralisch

morals NOUN
die Moral

ℓ**more** ADJECTIVE, PRONOUN
1 **mehr** ('mehr' never changes)
more friends mehr Freunde
more than mehr als
They have more money than we do. Sie
haben mehr Geld als wir.
He eats more than me. Er isst mehr als ich.
2 **more and more** immer mehr
It takes more and more time. Es
beansprucht immer mehr Zeit.
3 **no more** kein
There's no more milk. Es ist keine Milch
mehr da.
No more, thank you. Nichts mehr, danke.
4 (of something you have already) **noch**
Would you like some more cake? Möchtest
du noch etwas Kuchen?
a few more glasses noch ein paar Gläser
We need three more. Wir brauchen noch
drei.
Any more? Noch etwas?

more ADVERB
1 (followed by an adjective) (In German, the
ending '-er' is added to the adjective to show
the comparative. Don't use 'mehr' for the
comparative.)
more interesting interessanter
The book's more interesting than the film.
Das Buch ist interessanter als der Film.
more difficult schwieriger
more slowly langsamer
more easily einfacher

Books are getting more and more
expensive. Bücher werden immer teurer.

2 not any more *(no longer)* nicht mehr
She doesn't live here any more. Sie wohnt
nicht mehr hier.

3 more or less mehr oder weniger
It's more or less finished. Es ist mehr oder
weniger fertig.

⚲ **morning** NOUN
1 der Morgen (PL die Morgen)
in the morning am Morgen
this morning heute Morgen
tomorrow morning morgen früh
yesterday morning gestern Morgen
on Friday morning am Freitagmorgen

2 in the morning *(regularly)* morgens
She doesn't work in the morning. Sie
arbeitet morgens nicht.
on Friday mornings freitagmorgens
at six o'clock in the morning um sechs Uhr
morgens

3 *(as opposed to afternoon)* der Vormittag
(PL die Vormittage)
I spent the whole morning waiting for
him. Ich habe den ganzen Vormittag auf
ihn gewartet.

4 Good morning! Guten Morgen!

mortgage NOUN
die Hypothek (PL die Hypotheken)

Moscow NOUN
Moskau *(NEUTER)*

mosque NOUN
die Moschee (PL die Moscheen)

mosquito NOUN
die Mücke (PL die Mücken)
mosquito bite der Mückenstich

⚲ **most** DETERMINER, PRONOUN
1 *(followed by a plural noun)* die meisten
Most children like chocolate. Die meisten
Kinder mögen Schokolade.
most of my friends die meisten meiner
Freunde

2 *(followed by a singular noun)* der meiste/
die meiste/das meiste
They've eaten most ice cream. Sie haben
das meiste Eis gegessen.
I've written most of the essay. Ich habe das
meiste von dem Aufsatz geschrieben.

3 the most *(followed by a noun or a verb)* am
meisten
I've got the most time. Ich habe am
meisten Zeit.

4 most of the time die meiste Zeit
most of them die meisten

most ADVERB
1 *(followed by an adjective)* *(In German, the
ending '-(e)st' is added to the adjective to
show the superlative.)*
the most interesting film der
interessanteste Film
the most exciting story die spannendste
Geschichte
the most boring book das langweiligste
Buch

2 am meisten
The noise bothers me most. Der Lärm stört
mich am meisten.

3 *(very)* höchst
It's most unlikely. Es ist höchst
unwahrscheinlich.

moth NOUN
1 der Nachtfalter (PL die Nachtfalter)
2 *(clothes moth)* die Motte (PL die Motten)

⚲ **mother** NOUN
die Mutter (PL die Mütter)
Kate's mother Kates Mutter

⚲ **mother-in-law** NOUN
die Schwiegermutter (PL die
Schwiegermütter)

Mother's Day NOUN
der Muttertag (PL die Muttertage)

motivated ADJECTIVE
motiviert
I wasn't feeling very motivated. Ich fühlte
mich nicht sehr motiviert.

motivation NOUN
die Motivation

⚲ **motor** NOUN
der Motor (PL die Motoren)

⚲ **motorbike** NOUN
das Motorrad (PL die Motorräder)
She rides a motorbike. Sie fährt Motorrad.

motorcyclist NOUN
der Motorradfahrer (PL die
Motorradfahrer), die Motorradfahrerin
(PL die Motorradfahrerinnen)

motorist NOUN
der Autofahrer (PL die Autofahrer), die
Autofahrerin (PL die Autofahrerinnen)

motor racing NOUN
der Autorennsport

⚲ **motorway** NOUN
die Autobahn (PL die Autobahnen)
We went on the motorway. Wir sind über
die Autobahn gefahren.

a crash on the motorway ein Unfall auf der Autobahn

mouldy ADJECTIVE
schimmelig

ℰ **mountain** NOUN
der Berg (PL die Berge)
in the mountains in den Bergen

> 🄲 **MOUNTAIN**
>
> The highest mountains in the German-speaking countries are: the Großglockner 3798m (Austria), the Zugspitze 2964m (Germany), the Monte Rosa 4634m (Switzerland). The most famous Swiss mountain, the Matterhorn, at 4478m is only the second highest mountain in the country.

mountain bike NOUN
das Mountainbike (PL die Mountainbikes)

mountaineer NOUN
der Bergsteiger (PL die Bergsteiger), die Bergsteigerin (PL die Bergsteigerinnen)

> **WORD TIP** Professions, hobbies, and sports don't take an article in German: Er ist Bergsteiger.

mountaineering NOUN
das Bergsteigen
to go mountaineering Bergsteigen gehen◇

mountainous ADJECTIVE
gebirgig

ℰ **mouse** NOUN
die Maus (PL die Mäuse) (also for a computer)

mousse NOUN
die Mousse (PL die Mousses)

moustache NOUN
der Schnurrbart (PL die Schnurrbärte)

ℰ **mouth** NOUN
1 (of a person) der Mund (PL die Münder)
2 (of an animal) das Maul (PL die Mäuler)
3 (of a river) die Mündung (PL die Mündungen)

mouthful NOUN
(food) der Bissen (PL die Bissen) (informal)

mouth organ NOUN
die Mundharmonika (PL die Mundharmonikas)
She plays the mouth organ. Sie spielt Mundharmonika.

> **WORD TIP** Don't use the article when you talk about playing an instrument.

ℰ **move** NOUN
1 (to a different house) der Umzug (PL die Umzüge)
2 (in a game) der Zug (PL die Züge)
Your move! Du bist am Zug!

to **move** VERB
1 sich bewegen
She didn't move. Sie hat sich nicht bewegt.
2 to move over/up (sideways) rücken (PERF sein)
Move over a bit! Rück mal ein Stück!
3 wegnehmen◇ SEP
Can you move your bag, please? Können Sie Ihre Tasche bitte wegnehmen?
4 to move something somewhere else etwas woandershin stellen
I've moved the chest into the cellar. Ich habe die Truhe in den Keller gestellt.
5 (car) fahren◇ (PERF sein)
The car was moving fast. Das Auto fuhr schnell.
6 (traffic) vorwärtskommen◇ SEP (PERF sein)
The traffic was not moving. Der Verkehr kam nicht vorwärts.
7 (driver) wegfahren◇ SEP
Could you move your car, please? Würden Sie bitte Ihr Auto wegfahren?
8 to move forward (person) vorrücken SEP (PERF sein) (vehicle) vorwärts fahren◇ (PERF sein)
9 (move house) umziehen◇ SEP (PERF sein)
We're moving on Tuesday. Wir ziehen am Dienstag um.
They've moved to London. Sie sind nach London umgezogen.
• to move away
wegziehen◇ SEP (PERF sein)
• to move in
einziehen◇ SEP (PERF sein)
She's moving in with friends. Sie zieht bei Freunden ein.
• to move out
ausziehen◇ SEP (PERF sein)
We're moving out next week. Wir ziehen nächste Woche aus.

movement NOUN
die Bewegung (PL die Bewegungen)

movie NOUN
der Film (PL die Filme)
to go to the movies ins Kino gehen◇

moving ADJECTIVE
1 fahrend
a moving car ein fahrendes Auto
2 (emotionally) ergreifend

to **mow** VERB
mähen

mower NOUN
der **Rasenmäher** (PL die **Rasenmäher**)

MP NOUN
der/die **Abgeordnete** (PL die **Abgeordneten**)

WORD TIP Professions, hobbies, and sports don't take an article in German: Er ist Abgeordneter.

MP3 player NOUN
der **MP3-Spieler** (PL die **MP3-Spieler**)

⚲**Mr** NOUN
Herr
(in an address) **Mr Angus Brown** Herrn Angus Brown
(in a letter) **Dear Mr Brown** Sehr geehrter Herr Brown

⚲**Mrs** NOUN
Frau
Mrs Mary Hendry Frau Mary Hendry
(in a letter) **Dear Mrs Hendry** Sehr geehrte Frau Hendry

⚲**Ms** NOUN
Frau
Ms Taylor Frau Taylor

WORD TIP There is no direct equivalent to 'Ms' in German, but Frau may be used whether the woman is married or not.

⚲**much** ADJECTIVE, ADVERB, PRONOUN
1 **viel**
She doesn't eat much for breakfast. Sie isst nicht viel zum Frühstück.
much more viel mehr
much quicker viel schneller
We don't have much time. Wir haben nicht viel Zeit.
2 **not much** nicht viel
'Do you have a lot of work?' – 'No, not much.' 'Hast du viel Arbeit?' – ' Nein, nicht viel.'
3 **so much** so viel
I have so much to do. Ich habe so viel zu tun.
You shouldn't have given me so much. Du hättest mir nicht so viel geben sollen.
4 **as much as** so viel
Take as much as you like. Nimm so viel du willst.
5 **too much** zu viel
She gets too much money from her parents. Sie bekommt zu viel Geld von ihren Eltern.
That's far too much. Das ist viel zu viel.
6 **How much?** Wie viel?
How much is it? Wie viel kostet es?
How much do you want? Wie viel möchten

Sie?
How much money do you need? Wie viel Geld brauchst du?
7 (greatly) **sehr**
He loved her very much. Er hat sie sehr geliebt.
too much zu sehr
so much (so) sehr
We liked it so much. Es hat uns sehr gefallen.
8 (often) **oft**
I don't watch television much. Ich sehe nicht oft fern.
We don't go out much. Wir gehen nicht oft aus.
9 **Thank you very much.** Vielen Dank.

mud NOUN
der **Schlamm**

muddle NOUN
1 das **Durcheinander**
2 **to be in a muddle** durcheinander sein

mug NOUN
der **Becher** (PL die **Becher**)
a mug of milk ein Becher Milch

to **mug** VERB
to mug somebody jemanden überfallen◇
to be mugged überfallen werden

mugging NOUN
der **Straßenraub** (PL die **Straßenraube**)

multicultural ADJECTIVE
multikulturell

multiplication NOUN
die **Multiplikation**

to **multiply** VERB
multiplizieren
six multiplied by four sechs multipliziert mit vier

⚲**mum** NOUN
1 die **Mutter** (PL die **Mütter**)
Tom's mum Toms Mutter
I'll ask my mum. Ich frage meine Mutter.
2 (as a name) die **Mama** (PL die **Mamas**), die **Mutti** (PL die **Muttis**)
Bye, Mum! Tschüs, Mama!

mumps NOUN
der **Mumps**

Munich NOUN
München (NEUTER)

murder NOUN
der **Mord** (PL die **Morde**)

◇ **irregular verb;** SEP **separable verb; for more help with verbs see centre section**

to murder VERB
ermorden

> **WORD TIP** Do not translate the English word murder with the German Mörder.

murderer NOUN
der Mörder (PL die Mörder), die Mörderin (PL die Mörderinnen)

muscle NOUN
der Muskel (PL die Muskeln)

muscular ADJECTIVE
muskulös

ℱ **museum** NOUN
das Museum (PL die Museen)
to go to the museum ins Museum gehen

ℱ **mushroom** NOUN
der Pilz (PL die Pilze), der Champignon (PL die Champignons)
mushroom salad der Champignonsalat

ℱ **music** NOUN
die Musik
pop music die Popmusik
classical music die klassische Musik

musical NOUN
das Musical (PL die Musicals)

musical ADJECTIVE
1 musikalisch
They're a very musical family. Sie sind eine sehr musikalische Familie.
2 **musical instrument** das Musikinstrument

musician NOUN
der Musiker (PL die Musiker), die Musikerin (PL die Musikerinnen)

> **WORD TIP** Professions, hobbies, and sports don't take an article in German: Sie ist Musikerin.

Muslim NOUN
der Muslim (PL die Muslime or Muslims)
die Muslimin (PL die Musliminnen)
He's a Muslim. Er ist Muslim.

Muslim ADJECTIVE
muslimisch

> **WORD TIP** Adjectives never have capitals in German, even for religions.

mussel NOUN
die Muschel (PL die Muscheln)

ℱ **must** VERB
1 müssen◇
We must leave now. Wir müssen jetzt gehen.
You must learn the vocabulary. Du musst die Vokabeln lernen.

2 (with a negative)
must not nicht dürfen◇
You mustn't do that. Das darfst du nicht tun.
3 (expressing probability) müssen◇
You must be tired. Ihr müsst müde sein.
It must be five o'clock. Es muss fünf Uhr sein.
He must have forgotten. Er muss es vergessen haben.

ℱ **mustard** NOUN
der Senf (PL die Senfe)

to mutter VERB
murmeln

ℱ **my** ADJECTIVE
1 (before a masculine noun) mein
my brother mein Bruder
They don't like my dog. Sie mögen meinen Hund nicht.
2 (before a feminine noun) meine
my sister meine Schwester
3 (before a neuter noun) mein
That's my new car. Das ist mein neues Auto.
We can go in my car. Wir können mit meinem Auto fahren.
4 (before masculine/feminine/neuter plural nouns) meine
my friends meine Freunde
5 (with parts of the body) der/die/das
I had a glass in my hand. Ich hatte ein Glas in der Hand.
I'm washing my hands. Ich wasche mir die Hände.

myself PRONOUN
1 (reflexive and after a preposition taking the accusative) mich
I've cut myself. Ich habe mich geschnitten.
I've addressed the letter to myself. Ich habe den Brief an mich adressiert.
2 (reflexive and after a preposition taking the dative) mir
I've hurt myself. Ich habe mir wehgetan.
I said to myself ... Ich habe mir gesagt, ...
3 (stressing something) selbst
I said it myself. Ich habe es selbst gesagt.
4 **by myself** allein

ℱ **mysterious** ADJECTIVE
rätselhaft

mystery NOUN
1 das Rätsel (PL die Rätsel)
2 (book) der Krimi (PL die Krimis) (informal)

myth NOUN
der Mythos (PL die Mythen)

ℱ indicates key words

mythology NOUN
die Mythologie (PL die Mythologien)

Nn

nail NOUN
(on your finger or toe, also metal) der Nagel
(PL die Nägel)

to **nail** VERB
nageln

nail brush NOUN
die Nagelbürste (PL die Nagelbürsten)

nail file NOUN
die Nagelfeile (PL die Nagelfeilen)

nail polish NOUN
der Nagellack

nail polish remover NOUN
der Nagellackentferner

nail scissors PLURAL NOUN
die Nagelschere (PL die Nagelscheren)

naked ADJECTIVE
nackt

ℒ **name** NOUN
1 der Name (PL die Namen)
I've forgotten her name. Ich habe ihren
Namen vergessen.
What's your name? Wie heißt du?
My name's Joy. Ich heiße Joy.
user name der Benutzername
file name der Dateiname
2 (of a book or film) der Titel (PL die Titel)

ℒ **napkin** NOUN
die Serviette (PL die Servietten)

nappy NOUN
die Windel (PL die Windeln)

ℒ **narrow** ADJECTIVE
1 schmal
a narrow street eine schmale Straße
2 knapp
a narrow majority eine knappe Mehrheit
I had a narrow escape. Ich kam mit
knapper Not davon.

ℒ **nasty** ADJECTIVE
1 (mean) gemein
That was a nasty thing to do. Das war
gemein.
2 (unpleasant, bad) scheußlich
That's a nasty job. Das ist eine scheußliche
Arbeit.

a nasty smell ein scheußlicher Geruch

nation NOUN
die Nation (PL die Nationen)

national ADJECTIVE
national

national anthem NOUN
die Nationalhymne (PL die
Nationalhymnen)

nationality NOUN
die Nationalität (PL die Nationalitäten)

national park NOUN
der Nationalpark (PL die Nationalparks)

native ADJECTIVE
Heimat-
native country das Heimatland
French is his native language. Französisch
ist seine Muttersprache.

Native American NOUN
der Indianer (PL die Indianer), die
Indianerin (PL die Indianerinnen)

ℒ **natural** ADJECTIVE
natürlich

naturally ADVERB
natürlich

natural resources PLURAL NOUN
die Naturschätze (PLURAL)

ℒ **nature** NOUN
die Natur
in nature in der Natur

nature reserve NOUN
das Naturschutzgebiet (PL die
Naturschutzgebiete)

ℒ **naughty** ADJECTIVE
unartig

navy NOUN
die Marine
My uncle's in the navy. Mein Onkel ist bei
der Marine.

navy blue ADJECTIVE
marineblau

ℒ **near** ADJECTIVE
1 nah(e)
2 (the superlative of nah(e) is der/die/das
nächste)
the nearest park der nächste Park
the nearest bank die nächste Bank
the nearest shop das nächste Geschäft

near PREPOSITION
nahe an (+DAT)
near (to) the station nahe am Bahnhof
I want to sit near the window. Ich möchte

✧ irregular verb; SEP separable verb; for more help with verbs see centre section

am Fenster sitzen.

near ADVERB
1 **nah(e)** (in spoken German 'nah' is more common)
   They live quite near. Sie wohnen ganz nah.
2 **to come nearer** näher kommen

ℰ **nearby** ADVERB
   nahe gelegen
   There's a park nearby. In der Nähe ist ein Park.

ℰ **nearly** ADVERB
   fast
   nearly empty fast leer

ℰ **neat** ADJECTIVE
1 (well organized, tidy) **ordentlich**
   a neat room ein ordentliches Zimmer
2 **adrett** (clothes or the way you look)

necessarily ADVERB
   not necessarily nicht unbedingt

ℰ **necessary** ADJECTIVE
   nötig
   if necessary falls nötig

ℰ **neck** NOUN
1 (of a person) **der Hals** (PL die **Hälse**)
2 (of a garment) **der Kragen** (PL die **Kragen**)

necklace NOUN
   die Halskette (PL die **Halsketten**)

ℰ **need** NOUN
   There's no need, I've already done it. Das ist nicht nötig, ich habe es schon gemacht.
   There's no need to wait. Du brauchst nicht zu warten.

to need VERB
1 **brauchen**
   We need bread. Wir brauchen Brot.
   everything you need alles, was man braucht
2 (have to) **müssen**◇
   I need to go to the bank. Ich muss zur Bank gehen.
3 (with a negative)
   You needn't wait. Du brauchst nicht zu warten.

needle NOUN
   die Nadel (PL die **Nadeln**)

needy ADJECTIVE
   bedürftig

negative NOUN
1 (of a photo) **das Negativ** (PL die **Negative**)
2 (in grammar) **die Verneinung**
   The sentence is in the negative. Der Satz ist verneint.

neglected ADJECTIVE
   vernachlässigt

ℰ **neighbour** NOUN
   der Nachbar (PL die **Nachbarn**), die **Nachbarin** (PL die **Nachbarinnen**)
   We're going round to the neighbours'. Wir besuchen die Nachbarn.

ℰ **neighbourhood** NOUN
   die Nachbarschaft
   in our neighbourhood in unserer Nachbarschaft

ℰ **neither** CONJUNCTION
1 **neither ... nor ...** weder ... noch ...
   I have neither the time nor the money. Ich habe weder die Zeit noch das Geld.
2 **Neither do I.** Ich auch nicht.
   'I don't like fish.' – 'Neither do I.' 'Ich mag keinen Fisch.' – 'Ich auch nicht.'
   'I didn't like the film.' – 'Neither did Kirsty.' 'Mir hat der Film nicht gefallen.' – 'Kirsty hat er auch nicht gefallen.'

neither PRONOUN
   keiner von beiden/keine von beiden/ keins von beiden
   'Which do you like?' – 'Neither.' 'Welches gefällt dir?' – 'Keins von beiden.'

ℰ **nephew** NOUN
   der Neffe (PL die **Neffen**)

ℰ **nerve** NOUN
1 **der Nerv** (PL die **Nerven**)
2 **to lose your nerve** die Nerven verlieren
   You've got a nerve! Du hast Nerven! (informal)
3 **What a nerve!** So eine Frechheit!
4 **He gets on my nerves.** Er geht mir auf die Nerven. (informal)

nervous ADJECTIVE
1 (afraid) **ängstlich**
   to feel nervous about something Angst vor etwas (DAT) haben
2 (highly strung) **nervös** (person)

nest NOUN
   das Nest (PL die **Nester**)

ℰ **net** NOUN
   das Netz (PL die **Netze**)

netball NOUN
   der Korbball

Netherlands PLURAL NOUN
   the Netherlands die Niederlande (PLURAL)
   in the Netherlands in den Niederlanden

nettle NOUN
   die Nessel (PL die **Nesseln**)

ℰ indicates key words

network NOUN
das **Netzwerk** (PL die **Netzwerke**)

neutral NOUN
(neutral gear) der **Leerlauf**
to be in neutral im Leerlauf sein

neutral ADJECTIVE
neutral

♀ **never** ADVERB
1 **nie**
Ben never smokes. Ben raucht nie.
I've never told him. Ich habe es ihm nie
gesagt.
never again nie wieder
2 **noch nie**
'Have you ever been to Spain?' – 'No,
never.' 'Warst du schon mal in Spanien?' –
'Nein, noch nie.'
3 **Never mind.** Macht nichts.

♀ **new** ADJECTIVE
neu
Have you seen their new house? Hast du
ihr neues Haus gesehen?

♀ **news** NOUN
1 (new information) die **Nachricht** (PL die
Nachrichten)
I've got good news. Ich habe gute
Nachrichten.
2 a piece of news eine Neuigkeit
Any news? Was gibt es Neues?
3 (on TV or the radio) die **Nachrichten** (PLURAL)
We saw it on the news. Wir haben es in
den Nachrichten gesehen.

♀ **newsagent** NOUN
der **Zeitungshändler** (PL die
Zeitungshändler)

WORD TIP Professions, hobbies, and sports don't
take an article in German: Er ist Zeitungshändler.

♀ **newspaper** NOUN
die **Zeitung** (PL die **Zeitungen**)

newsreader NOUN
der **Nachrichtensprecher** (PL
die **Nachrichtensprecher**), die
Nachrichtensprecherin (PL die
Nachrichtensprecherinnen)

WORD TIP Professions, hobbies, and sports
don't take an article in German: Sie ist
Nachrichtensprecherin.

♀ **New Year** NOUN
das **Neujahr**
Happy New Year! Ein gutes neues Jahr!

New Year's Day NOUN
das **Neujahr**, der **Neujahrstag**

New Year's Eve NOUN
der or das **Silvester**
on New Year's Eve an Silvester

New Zealand NOUN
Neuseeland (NEUTER)

♀ **next** ADJECTIVE
1 **nächster/nächste/nächstes**
The next train leaves at ten. Der nächste
Zug fährt um zehn ab.
next week nächste Woche
next Thursday nächsten Donnerstag
next year nächstes Jahr
next time I see you nächstes Mal, wenn ich
dich sehe
2 (following)
Next please! Der Nächste bitte!/Die
Nächste bitte!
the next thing das Nächste
the next day am nächsten Tag
The letter arrived the next day. Der Brief
kam am nächsten Tag an.
3 the week after next übernächste Woche
4 (next door) nebenan
I'm in the next room. Ich bin nebenan.

next ADVERB
1 (afterwards) danach
What did he say next? Was hat er danach
gesagt?
2 (now) als Nächstes
What shall we do next? Was machen wir
als Nächstes?
3 next to neben (+DAT, or with movement
towards a place +ACC)
the house next to the baker's das Haus
neben dem Bäcker (DAT)
I sat down next to her. Ich habe mich
neben sie gesetzt. (ACC)

next door ADVERB
nebenan
They live next door. Sie wohnen nebenan.
the girl next door das Mädchen von
nebenan

♀ **nice** ADJECTIVE
1 (pleasant) schön
We had a nice evening. Wir haben einen
schönen Abend verbracht.
Brighton's a nice town. Brighton ist eine
schöne Stadt.
We had nice weather. Wir hatten schönes
Wetter.
It's nice and warm here. Hier ist es schön
warm.
2 We had a nice time. Wir haben uns gut
amüsiert.
Have a nice time! Viel Spaß!

◇ irregular verb; SEP separable verb; for more help with verbs see centre section

3 *(attractive to look at)* **hübsch**
That's a nice dress. Das ist ein hübsches Kleid.

4 *(kind, friendly)* **nett** person
She's really nice. Sie ist wirklich nett.

5 **to be nice to somebody** nett zu jemandem sein
She's been very nice to me. Sie war sehr nett zu mir.

6 *(tasting good)* **gut**
It tastes nice. Es schmeckt gut.

nickname NOUN
der **Spitzname** (PL die **Spitznamen**)

℘ **niece** NOUN
die **Nichte** (PL die **Nichten**)

℘ **night** NOUN
1 *(after bedtime)* die **Nacht** (PL die **Nächte**)
during the night während der Nacht
Sunday night Sonntag Nacht
It's cold at night. Nachts ist es kalt.
to stay the night über Nacht bleiben
I stayed the night at Emma's. Ich habe bei Emma übernachtet.

2 *(before you go to bed)* der **Abend** (PL die **Abende**)
one night eines Abends
tomorrow night morgen Abend
I met Greg last night. Ich habe Greg gestern Abend getroffen.
on Friday night am Freitagabend

night club NOUN
der **Nachtklub** (PL die **Nachtklubs**)

nightie NOUN
das **Nachthemd** (PL die **Nachthemden**)

nightmare NOUN
der **Albtraum** (PL die **Albträume**)

nil NOUN
(in sport) **null**
They won four-nil. Sie haben vier zu null gewonnen.

℘ **nine** NUMBER
neun

℘ **nineteen** NUMBER
neunzehn

℘ **ninety** NUMBER
neunzig

ninth NUMBER
neunter/neunte/neuntes
on the ninth floor im neunten Stock
on the ninth of June am neunten Juni

℘ **no** ADVERB
nein
I said no. Ich habe nein gesagt.
No thank you. Nein danke.

no ADJECTIVE
1 **kein**
We've got no bread. Wir haben kein Brot.
No problem! Kein Problem!

2 *(on a notice)*
'No smoking' 'Rauchen verboten'
'No parking' 'Parken verboten'

℘ **nobody** PRONOUN
niemand
'Who's there?' – 'Nobody.' 'Wer ist da?' – 'Niemand.'
There's nobody in the kitchen. Es ist niemand in der Küche.
Nobody was at home. Niemand war zu Hause.

to nod VERB
nicken
He nodded in agreement. Er hat zustimmend genickt.

℘ **noise** NOUN
der **Lärm**
to make a noise Lärm machen

noise pollution NOUN
die **Lärmbelästigung**

℘ **noisy** ADJECTIVE
laut

℘ **none** PRONOUN
1 *(not one)* **keiner/keine/keins**
none of us keiner von uns/keine von uns
'How many students failed the exam?' – 'None.' 'Wie viele Schüler sind durch die Prüfung gefallen?' – 'Keine.'
None of the boys knows him. Keiner der Jungen kennt ihn.

2 There's none left. Es ist nichts mehr übrig.

nonsense NOUN
der **Unsinn**
to talk nonsense Unsinn reden
Nonsense! Unsinn!

℘ **non-smoker** NOUN
der **Nichtraucher** (PL die **Nichtraucher**), die **Nichtraucherin** (PL die **Nichtraucherinnen**)

non-stop ADJECTIVE
durchgehend *(train)* **Nonstop-** flight

non-stop ADVERB
ununterbrochen
She talks non-stop. Sie redet ununterbrochen.

℘ indicates key words

noodles PLURAL NOUN
die Nudeln (PLURAL)

℗ **noon** NOUN
der Mittag
at (twelve) noon um zwölf (Uhr mittags)

℗ **no one** PRONOUN
niemand
'Who's there?' – 'No one.' 'Wer ist da?' –
'Niemand.'
There's no one in the kitchen. Es ist
niemand in der Küche.
No one was at home. Niemand war zu
Hause.

℗ **nor** CONJUNCTION
1 neither ... nor ... weder ... noch ...
I have neither the time nor the money. Ich
habe weder die Zeit noch das Geld.
2 **Nor do I.** Ich auch nicht.
'I don't like fish.' – 'Nor do I.' 'Ich mag
keinen Fisch.' – 'Ich auch nicht.'
Nor do we. Wir auch nicht.

℗ **normal** ADJECTIVE
normal

normally ADVERB
1 (usually) normalerweise
2 (in a normal way) normal

℗ **north** NOUN
der Norden
in the north im Norden

north ADJECTIVE
nördlich, Nord-
the north side die Nordseite
north wind der Nordwind

north ADVERB
1 (towards the north) nach Norden
to travel north nach Norden fahren
2 **north of London** nördlich von London

North America NOUN
Nordamerika (NEUTER)

North American NOUN
der Nordamerikaner (PL die
Nordamerikaner), die Nordamerikanerin
(PL die Nordamerikanerinnen)

North American ADJECTIVE
nordamerikanisch

WORD TIP Adjectives never have capitals
in German, even for regions, countries, or
nationalities.

north-east NOUN
der Nordosten

north-east ADJECTIVE
in north-east England in Nordostengland

northern ADJECTIVE
nördlich, Nord-
on the northern side of the mountain an
der Nordseite des Berges

℗ **Northern Ireland** NOUN
Nordirland (NEUTER)

℗ **Northern Irish** ADJECTIVE
nordirisch
the Northern Irish coast die nordirische
Küste
He's Northern Irish. Er ist Nordire.
She's Northern Irish. Sie ist Nordirin.

WORD TIP Adjectives never have capitals
in German, even for regions, countries, or
nationalities.

North Pole NOUN
der Nordpol

North Sea NOUN
the North Sea die Nordsee

north-west NOUN
der Nordwesten

north-west ADJECTIVE
in north-west England in Nordwestengland

Norway NOUN
Norwegen (NEUTER)

Norwegian NOUN
1 (person) der Norweger (PL die
Norweger) (PL die Norwegerin (PL die
Norwegerinnen)
2 (language) das Norwegisch

Norwegian ADJECTIVE
norwegisch
the Norwegian coast die norwegische
Küste
He's Norwegian. Er ist Norweger.
She's Norwegian. Sie ist Norwegerin.

WORD TIP Adjectives never have capitals
in German, even for regions, countries, or
nationalities.

℗ **nose** NOUN
die Nase (PL die Nasen)
to blow your nose sich (DAT) die Nase
putzen

℗ **not** ADVERB
1 nicht
not on Sundays sonntags nicht
Not all alone! Nicht ganz allein!
not bad nicht schlecht
not at all überhaupt nicht
not yet noch nicht
Sam didn't phone. Sam hat nicht
angerufen.
I hope not. Hoffentlich nicht.

◇ **irregular verb;** SEP **separable verb; for more help with verbs see centre section**

2 not a kein/keine
He's not a specialist. Er ist kein Fachmann.
not a bit kein bisschen

ℓ **note** NOUN
1 *(a letter)* der **kurze Brief** (PL die **kurzen**)
Briefe *(short message on a piece of paper)*
der **Zettel** (PL die **Zettel**)
She put a note on the door. Sie hängte
einen Zettel an die Tür.
2 *(for the teacher, from parents)* die
Entschuldigung (PL die **Entschuldigungen**)
3 **to make a note of something** sich (DAT)
etwas aufschreiben◇ SEP
4 *(in class, etc.)*
notes die **Notizen** (PLURAL)
to take notes sich (DAT) Notizen machen
5 *(a banknote)* der **Schein** (PL die **Scheine**)
a ten-pound note ein Zehnpfundschein
6 *(in music)* die **Note** (PL die **Noten**)

notebook NOUN
das **Notizbuch** (PL die **Notizbücher**)

notepad NOUN
der **Notizblock** (PL die **Notizblöcke**)

ℓ **nothing** PRONOUN
nichts
'What did you say?' – 'Nothing.' 'Was hast
du gesagt?' – 'Nichts.'
nothing special nichts Besonderes
nothing new nichts Neues
I saw nothing. Ich habe nichts gesehen.
There's nothing left. Es ist nichts mehr
übrig.

ℓ **notice** NOUN
1 *(a sign)* das **Schild** (PL die **Schilder**)
2 *(an advertisement)* die **Anzeige** (PL die
Anzeigen)
3 *(advance warning)* die **Ankündigung**
4 **Don't take any notice of her.** Nimm keine
Notiz von ihr.
5 **at short notice** kurzfristig
to notice VERB
bemerken
I didn't notice anything. Ich habe nichts
bemerkt.

noticeboard NOUN
das **Anschlagbrett** (PL die
Anschlagbretter)

ℓ **nought** NOUN
die **Null** (PL die **Nullen**)
nought NUMBER
null
nought point three (0.3) null Komma drei
(0,3)

ℓ **noun** NOUN
das **Substantiv** (PL die **Substantive**)

ℓ **novel** NOUN
der **Roman** (PL die **Romane**)

novelist NOUN
der **Romanautor** (PL die **Romanautoren**),
die **Romanautorin** (PL die
Romanautorinnen)

ℓ **November** NOUN
der **November**
in November im November

ℓ **now** ADVERB
1 **jetzt**
Where is he now? Wo ist er jetzt?
from now on von jetzt an
2 He left just now. Er ist gerade eben
gegangen.
I saw her just now in the corridor. Ich habe
sie gerade eben im Gang gesehen.
3 Do it right now! Mach es sofort!
4 **now and then** hin und wieder

ℓ **nowadays** ADVERB
heutzutage
Nowadays they are quite common.
Heutzutage sind sie ziemlich häufig.

nowhere ADVERB
nirgends
There's nowhere to park. Man kann
nirgends parken.

nuclear ADJECTIVE
Kern-
nuclear power die Kernenergie
nuclear power station das Kernkraftwerk

nude NOUN
in the nude nackt
nude ADJECTIVE
nackt

nuisance NOUN
It's a nuisance. Das ist ärgerlich.
What a nuisance! Wie ärgerlich!

numb ADJECTIVE
(with cold) gefühllos

ℓ **number** NOUN
1 *(of a house, telephone, or account)* die
Nummer (PL die **Nummern**)
I live at number five. Ich wohne in der
Nummer fünf.
my new phone number meine neue
Telefonnummer
2 *(a written figure)* die **Zahl** (PL die **Zahlen**)
3 *(amount)* die **Anzahl**
the number of visitors die Anzahl der

ℓ indicates key words

ENGLISH—GERMAN

Besucher

number plate NOUN
das Nummernschild (PL die Nummernschilder)

nun NOUN
die Nonne (PL die Nonnen)

WORD TIP Professions, hobbies, and sports don't take an article in German: Sie ist Nonne.

♀ **nurse** NOUN
1 (female) die Krankenschwester (PL die Krankenschwestern)
2 (male) der Krankenpfleger (PL die Krankenpfleger)

WORD TIP Professions, hobbies, and sports don't take an article in German: Sie ist Krankenschwester.

nursery NOUN
1 (for children) die Kindertagesstätte (PL die Kindertagesstätten)
2 (for plants) die Gärtnerei (PL die Gärtnereien)

nursery school NOUN
der Kindergarten (PL die Kindergärten)

nut NOUN
1 die Nuss (PL die Nüsse)
2 (for a bolt) die Mutter (PL die Muttern)

♀ **nylon** NOUN
das Nylon®

Oo

oak NOUN
die Eiche (PL die Eichen)

oar NOUN
das Ruder (PL die Ruder)

oats PLURAL NOUN
der Hafer
porridge oats die Haferflocken (PLURAL)

obedient ADJECTIVE
gehorsam

obese ADJECTIVE
fettleibig

to **obey** VERB
1 gehorchen (+DAT)
to obey somebody jemandem gehorchen
2 **to obey the rules** sich an die Vorschriften halten◇

object NOUN
1 (thing) der Gegenstand (PL die

Gegenstände)
2 (aim) der Zweck (PL die Zwecke)
3 (in grammar) das Objekt (PL die Objekte)

to **object** VERB
etwas dagegen haben◇
if you don't object wenn Sie nichts dagegen haben

objection NOUN
der Einwand (PL die Einwände)

oboe NOUN
die Oboe (PL die Oboen)
I play the oboe. Ich spiele Oboe.

WORD TIP Don't use the article when you talk about playing an instrument.

obscene ADJECTIVE
obszön

to **observe** VERB
beobachten

obsessed ADJECTIVE
besessen
She's really obsessed with her diet. Sie ist von ihrer Schlankheitskur ganz besessen.

obstacle NOUN
das Hindernis (PL die Hindernisse)

obstinate ADJECTIVE
starrsinnig

to **obtain** VERB
erhalten◇

obvious ADJECTIVE
eindeutig

obviously ADVERB
1 (of course) natürlich
2 (looking at something) offensichtlich
The house is obviously empty. Das Haus steht offensichtlich leer.

occasion NOUN
die Gelegenheit (PL die Gelegenheiten)
on special occasions zu besonderen Gelegenheiten

occasionally ADVERB
gelegentlich

occupation NOUN
der Beruf (PL die Berufe)

occupied ADJECTIVE
1 (taken) besetzt
The seat is occupied. Der Platz ist besetzt.
2 (lived in) bewohnt

to **occur** VERB
1 **to occur to somebody** jemandem

◇ **irregular verb;** SEP **separable verb; for more help with verbs see centre section**

einfallen◇ *SEP (PERF* **sein)**
It occurs to me that ... Mir fällt ein, dass ...
2 **It never occurred to me.** Darauf wäre ich
nie gekommen.
3 *(happen)* sich ereignen

ocean *NOUN*
der Ozean (*PL* die Ozeane)

o'clock *ADVERB*
at ten o'clock um zehn Uhr
It's three o'clock. Es ist drei Uhr.

ℱ **October** *NOUN*
der Oktober
in October im Oktober

octopus *NOUN*
der Tintenfisch (*PL* die Tintenfische)

ℱ **odd** *ADJECTIVE*
1 *(strange)* komisch
That's odd, I'm sure I heard the bell. Das
ist komisch, ich habe es bestimmt klingeln
gehört.
2 *(number)* ungerade
Three is an odd number. Drei ist eine
ungerade Zahl.
3 **the odd one out** die Ausnahme

odds and ends *PLURAL NOUN*
der Kleinkram (*SINGULAR*)

ℱ **of** *PREPOSITION*
1 **von** (*+DAT*)
*(instead of translating 'of' with 'von', the
genitive case can be used)* **the parents of the
children** die Eltern von den Kindern (*PL* die
Eltern der Kinder)
the name of the flower der Name der
Blume
It's very kind of you. Das ist sehr nett von
Ihnen.
2 *(with quantities 'of' is not translated)*
a kilo of tomatoes ein Kilo Tomaten
a bottle of milk eine Flasche Milch
the three of us wir drei
3 **of it/them** davon *(things)*
of them von ihnen *(people)*
**Ray has four cars but he's selling three of
them.** Ray hat vier Autos, aber er verkauft
drei davon.
half of it die Hälfte davon
We ate a lot of it. Wir haben viel davon
gegessen.
How many of them didn't pay? Wie viele
von ihnen haben nicht gezahlt?
4 **the sixth of June** der sechste Juni
5 **made of** aus
a bracelet made of silver ein Armband aus
Silber

ℱ **off** *ADVERB, ADJECTIVE, PREPOSITION*
1 *(switched off)* aus
Is the telly off? Ist der Fernseher aus?
to turn off the lights das Licht ausmachen
SEP
2 *(electricity, water, gas)* abgestellt
The gas and electricity were off. Gas und
Strom waren abgestellt.
to turn off the tap den Wasserhahn
zudrehen *SEP*
3 **to be off** *(leave)* gehen◇ *(PERF* **sein)**, *(in a
vehicle)* fahren◇ *(PERF* **sein)**
I must be off. Ich muss gehen.
4 **on my day off** an meinem freien Tag
to take three days off work sich (*DAT*) drei
Tage freinehmen◇ *SEP*
We were given two days off school. Wir
hatten zwei Tage schulfrei.
to be off sick wegen Krankheit fehlen
Maya's off school today. Maya fehlt heute
in der Schule.
5 *(cancelled)* abgesagt
The match is off. Das Spiel ist abgesagt
worden.
6 **'20% off shoes'** 'Schuhe 20% reduziert'

offence *NOUN*
1 *(crime)* die Straftat (*PL* die Straftaten)
2 **to take offence** beleidigt sein
He takes offence easily. Er ist schnell
beleidigt.

offer *NOUN*
1 das Angebot (*PL* die Angebote)
job offer das Stellenangebot
2 **on special offer** im Sonderangebot

to offer *VERB*
anbieten◇ *SEP (a present, a reward, or a job)*
He offered her a chair. Er bot ihr einen
Stuhl an.
to offer to do something anbieten, etwas
zu tun
He offered to drive me to the station.
Er hat angeboten, mich zum Bahnhof zu
fahren.

ℱ **office** *NOUN*
das Büro (*PL* die Büros)
He's still at the office. Er ist noch im Büro.

office block *NOUN*
das Bürohaus (*PL* die Bürohäuser)

officer *NOUN*
der Offizier (*PL* die Offiziere)

> **WORD TIP** Professions, hobbies, and sports
> don't take an article in German: Er ist Offizier.

official *ADJECTIVE*
offiziell

off-licence NOUN
die **Wein- und Spirituosenhandlung** (PL die **Wein- und Spirituosenhandlungen**)

offside ADJECTIVE
im **Abseits**
He was offside! Er war im Abseits!

ℓ **often** ADVERB
1 oft
He's often late. Er kommt oft zu spät.
How often? Wie oft?
2 **more often** öfter
Couldn't you come more often? Könntest du nicht öfter kommen?

ℓ **oil** NOUN
1 (crude oil) das **Öl**
2 **olive oil** das Olivenöl
suntan oil das Sonnenöl

oil slick NOUN
der **Ölteppich** (PL die **Ölteppiche**)

ointment NOUN
die **Salbe** (PL die **Salben**)

okay ADJECTIVE
1 okay (informal)
Tomorrow at ten, okay? Morgen um zehn, okay?
Is it okay if I don't come till Friday? Ist es okay, wenn ich erst Freitag komme?
2 (person) in Ordnung
Daisy's okay. Daisy ist in Ordnung.
3 (nothing special, not ill) ganz gut
The film was okay. Der Film war ganz gut.
I've been ill but I'm okay now. Ich war krank, aber jetzt geht es mir ganz gut.
'**How are you?' – 'Okay.'** 'Wie geht's?' – 'Ganz gut.'
4 **It's okay by me.** Mir ist es recht.

ℓ **old** ADJECTIVE
1 (not young, not new, previous) alt
an old man ein alter Mann
an old lady eine alte Dame
an old tree ein alter Baum
old people alte Leute
Bring some old clothes. Bring ein paar alte Sachen mit.
I've only got their old address. Ich habe nur ihre alte Adresse.
2 (talking about age)
How old are you? Wie alt bist du?
James is ten years old. James ist zehn Jahre alt.
3 **a two-year-old child** ein zweijähriges Kind
4 **my older sister** meine ältere Schwester
She's older than me. Sie ist älter als ich.
He's a year older than me. Er ist ein Jahr

älter als ich.

old age NOUN
das **Alter**

old age pensioner NOUN
der **Rentner** (PL die **Rentner**), die **Rentnerin** (PL die **Rentnerinnen**)

old-fashioned NOUN
altmodisch

old people's home NOUN
das **Altenheim** (PL die **Altenheime**)

olive NOUN
die **Olive** (PL die **Oliven**)

olive oil NOUN
das **Olivenöl** (PL die **Olivenöle**)

Olympic Games, **Olympics** PLURAL NOUN
die **Olympischen Spiele** (PLURAL)

omelette NOUN
das **Omelett** (PL die **Omeletts**)
a cheese omelette ein Käseomelett

ℓ **on** PREPOSITION
1 auf (+DAT, or, with movement towards a place, +ACC)
It's on the desk. Es ist auf dem Schreibtisch. (DAT)
Put it on the desk. Lege es auf den Schreibtisch. (ACC)
2 (attached to) an (+DAT, or, with movement towards a place, +ACC)
It's on the wall. Es hängt an der Wand. (DAT)
Hang it on the wall. Hänge es an die Wand. (ACC)
3 **on the beach** am Strand
on the right/left rechts/links
4 (in expressions of time)
on March 21st am 21. März
He's arriving on Tuesday. Er kommt am Dienstag an.
It's shut on Sundays. Es ist sonntags geschlossen.
on rainy days an Regentagen
5 (for buses, trains, etc.)
to go on the bus/train mit dem Bus/Zug fahren
I met Jackie on the train. Ich habe Jackie im Zug getroffen.
Let's go on our bikes. Fahren wir mit dem Rad.
6 **on TV** im Fernsehen
on the radio im Radio
7 **on holiday** in den Ferien

on ADJECTIVE
1 (switched on)

568

to be on an sein
The lights are on. Das Licht ist an.
Is the radio on? Ist das Radio an?
2 *(happening)*
What's on TV? Was gibts im Fernsehen?
What's on this week at the cinema? Was läuft diese Woche im Kino?

℘ **once** ADVERB
1 **einmal**
I've tried once already. Ich habe es schon einmal versucht.
Try once more. Versuch es noch einmal.
once a day einmal täglich
Once upon a time there was … Es war einmal …
2 **more than once** mehrmals
3 **at once** *(immediately)* sofort
The doctor came at once. Der Arzt kam sofort.
4 **at once** *(at the same time)* gleichzeitig
I can't do two things at once. Ich kann nicht zwei Sachen gleichzeitig machen.

℘ **one** NUMBER
(when counting) **eins**, *(with a noun)* **ein**
one, two, three eins, zwei, drei
one son ein Sohn
one cat eine Katze
one house ein Haus
at one o'clock um ein Uhr

one PRONOUN
1 **einer/eine/eins**
I saw the photos, can I have one of them? Ich habe die Fotos gesehen, kann ich eins davon haben?
If you want a biro I've got one. Falls du einen Kugelschreiber brauchst, habe ich einen.
2 **this one** dieser/diese/dieses
I'd prefer that bike, but this one's cheaper. Ich würde lieber das Rad haben, aber dieses ist billiger.
3 **that one** der da/die da/das da
'Which photo?' – 'That one.' 'Welches Foto?' – 'Das da.'
4 **Which one?** Welcher/welche/welches?
'My foot's hurting.' – 'Which one?' 'Mir tut der Fuß weh.' – 'Welcher?'
'She borrowed a skirt from me.' – 'Which one?' 'Sie hat sich einen Rock von mir geliehen.' – 'Welchen?'
5 *(you)* **man**
One never knows. Man kann nie wissen.

one's ADJECTIVE
sein/seine/sein
One pays for one's car. Man zahlt für sein Auto.

oneself PRONOUN
1 *(reflexive)* **sich**
to wash oneself sich waschen
2 *(stressing something)* **selbst**
One has to do everything oneself. Man muss alles selbst machen.

℘ **one-way street** NOUN
die **Einbahnstraße** (PL die **Einbahnstraßen**)

℘ **onion** NOUN
die **Zwiebel** (PL die **Zwiebeln**)

online ADJECTIVE, ADVERB
online
You have to be online to download it. Man muss online sein, um es herunterzuladen.
I ordered the book online. Ich habe das Buch online bestellt.

℘ **only** ADJECTIVE
1 **einziger/einzige/einziges**
the only free seat der einzige freie Platz
the only thing you could do das Einzige, was du machen könntest
2 **an only child** ein Einzelkind

only ADVERB, CONJUNCTION
1 **nur**
They've only got two bedrooms. Sie haben nur zwei Schlafzimmer.
Anne's only free on Fridays. Anne hat nur freitags Zeit.
There are only three left. Es sind nur noch drei übrig.
I'd walk, only it's raining. Ich würde zu Fuß gehen, nur regnet es.
2 *(very recently)*
only just gerade erst
He's only just got the message. Er hat die Nachricht gerade erst bekommen.
3 *(barely)*
only just gerade noch
We've only just made it on time. Wir sind gerade noch rechtzeitig angekommen.
4 *(not until)* **erst**
They only arrived at ten. Sie kamen erst um zehn.

onto PREPOSITION
auf (+ACC)

℘ **open** NOUN
in the open im Freien

open ADJECTIVE
1 **offen**
The door's open. Die Tür ist offen.
The baker's is not open. Die Bäckerei ist nicht geöffnet.
2 **in the open air** im Freien

to **open** VERB
1 aufmachen SEP
  Can you open the door for me? Kannst du
  mir die Tür aufmachen?
  The bank opens at nine. Die Bank macht
  um neun auf.
2 *(open up)* sich öffnen
  The door opened slowly. Die Tür öffnete
  sich langsam.

open-air swimming pool NOUN
  das Freibad (PL die Freibäder)

opera NOUN
  die Oper (PL die Opern)
  to go to the opera in die Oper gehen

to **operate** VERB
1 *(medically)* operieren
  Will they have to operate (on him/her)?
  Werden sie ihn/sie operieren müssen?
2 bedienen *(a machine)*

operating system NOUN
  das Betriebssystem (PL die
  Betriebssysteme)

operation NOUN
1 die Operation (PL die Operationen)
2 **to have an operation** operiert werden

ℓ **opinion** NOUN
  die Meinung (PL die Meinungen)
  in my opinion meiner Meinung nach

opinion poll NOUN
  die Meinungsumfrage (PL die
  Meinungsumfragen)

opponent NOUN
  der Gegner (PL die Gegner), die Gegnerin
  (PL die Gegnerinnen)

opportunity NOUN
  die Gelegenheit (PL die Gelegenheiten)
  **to have the opportunity of doing
  something** die Gelegenheit haben, etwas
  zu tun
  equal opportunities die Chancengleichheit
  (SINGULAR)

ℓ **opposite** NOUN
  das Gegenteil (PL die Gegenteile)
  No, quite the opposite. Nein, ganz im
  Gegenteil.

opposite ADJECTIVE
1 entgegengesetzt *(direction)*
  She went off in the opposite direction. Sie
  ging in die entgegengesetzte Richtung.
2 *(facing)* gegenüberliegend
  in the house opposite im
  gegenüberliegenden Haus

opposite ADVERB
  gegenüber
  They live opposite. Sie wohnen gegenüber.

opposite PREPOSITION
  gegenüber *(+DAT)*
  opposite the station gegenüber dem
  Bahnhof

ℓ **optician** NOUN
  der Optiker (PL die Optiker), die Optikerin
  (PL die Optikerinnen)

  WORD TIP Professions, hobbies, and sports
  don't take an article in German: Er ist Optiker.

optimistic ADJECTIVE
  zuversichtlich, optimistisch

option NOUN
  die Wahl
  We have no option. Wir haben keine
  andere Wahl.

optional ADJECTIVE
  auf Wunsch erhältlich
  optional subject das Wahlfach

ℓ **or** CONJUNCTION
1 oder
  English or German? Englisch oder Deutsch?
  Today or Tuesday? Heute oder Dienstag?
2 *(in negatives)* noch
  I don't have a cat or a dog. Ich habe weder
  eine Katze noch einen Hund.
  Not in June or July. Weder im Juni noch
  im Juli.
3 *(or else)* sonst
  Phone Mum, or she'll worry. Ruf Mutti an,
  sonst macht sie sich Sorgen.

ℓ **oral** NOUN
  (an exam) das Mündliche *(informal)*
  my German oral meine mündliche
  Deutschprüfung

ℓ **orange** NOUN
  (the fruit) die Orange (PL die Orangen)
  orange juice der Orangensaft

orange ADJECTIVE
  orange *('orange' never changes)*
  my orange socks meine orange Socken

ℓ **orchestra** NOUN
  das Orchester (PL die Orchester)

ℓ **order** NOUN
1 *(sequence)* die Reihenfolge (PL die
  Reihenfolgen)
  in the right order in der richtigen
  Reihenfolge
  in the wrong order in der falschen
  Reihenfolge

⬦ **irregular verb;** SEP **separable verb; for more help with verbs see centre section**

in alphabetical order in alphabetischer Reihenfolge

2 *(in a restaurant, cafe, or shop)* die **Bestellung** (*PL* die **Bestellungen**)

3 **'Out of order'** 'Außer Betrieb'

4 **in order to do something** um etwas zu tun

to **order** *VERB*

1 *(in a restaurant or a shop)* **bestellen**
We ordered soup. Wir haben Suppe bestellt.
Have you ordered? Haben Sie schon bestellt?

2 **bestellen** *(a taxi)*

3 **to order somebody to do something** jemandem befehlen◇, etwas zu tun

ℓ **ordinary** *ADJECTIVE*
normal

organ *NOUN*

1 *(the instrument)* die **Orgel** (*PL* die **Orgeln**)
Tom plays the organ. Tom spielt Orgel.

2 *(of the body)* das **Organ** (*PL* die **Organe**)

> **WORD TIP** Don't use the article when you talk about playing an instrument.

organic *ADJECTIVE*
Bio- food
organic food die **Biokost**

organic waste *NOUN*
der **Biomüll**

organization *NOUN*
die **Organisation** (*PL* die **Organisationen**)

to **organize** *VERB*

1 **organisieren**

2 **veranstalten** *(a conference or festival)*

orienteering *NOUN*
der **Orientierungslauf**

original *ADJECTIVE*

1 **ursprünglich**
The original plan was better. Der ursprüngliche Plan war besser.

2 *(new and interesting)* **originell**
It's a really original novel. Das ist ein wirklich origineller Roman.

originally *ADVERB*
ursprünglich
Originally we wanted to go by car. Ursprünglich wollten wir mit dem Auto fahren.

orphan *NOUN*
die **Waise** (*PL* die **Waisen**)
He is an orphan. Er ist Waise.

ostrich *NOUN*
der **Strauß** (*PL* die **Strauße**)

ℓ **other** *ADJECTIVE, PRONOUN*

1 **anderer/andere/anderes**
We took the other road. Wir haben die andere Straße genommen.
Where are the others? Wo sind die anderen?
the other two cars die anderen beiden Autos

2 **Give me the other one.** Gib mir den anderen/die andere/das andere. *(The translation of 'the other one' depends on the gender of the noun it refers to.)*

3 **the other day** neulich

4 **every other week** jede zweite Woche

5 **somebody or other** irgendjemand
something or other irgendetwas
somewhere or other irgendwo

6 **Any other questions?** Sonst noch Fragen?

otherwise *ADVERB, CONJUNCTION*
sonst

ℓ **ought** *VERB* ('ought' is usually translated by the subjunctive of 'sollen')
I ought to go. Ich sollte eigentlich gehen.
They ought to have known the address. Sie hätten die Adresse kennen sollen.
You oughtn't to have any problems. Du solltest keine Probleme haben.

ℓ **our** *ADJECTIVE*

1 *(before a masculine noun)* **unser**
our father unser Vater

2 *(before a feminine noun)* **unsere**
our mother unsere Mutter

3 *(before a neuter noun)* **unser**
our house unser Haus

4 *(before masculine/feminine/neuter plural nouns)* **unsere**
our parents unsere Eltern

5 *(with parts of the body)* **der/die/das** (*PL* die (PLURAL))
We'll go and wash our hands. Wir waschen uns die Hände.

ours *PRONOUN*

1 *(for a masculine noun)* **unserer**
Their garden is bigger than ours. Ihr Garten ist größer als unserer.

2 *(for a feminine noun)* **unsere**
Their kitchen is smaller than ours. Ihre Küche ist kleiner als unsere.

3 *(for a neuter noun)* **unseres**
Their child is younger than ours. Ihr Kind ist jünger als unseres.

4 *(for plural nouns)* **unsere**
They've invited their friends and we've

ℓ **indicates key words**

invited ours. Sie haben ihre Freunde
eingeladen und wir haben unsere
eingeladen.

5 **The green car is ours.** Das grüne Auto
gehört uns.
It's ours. Es gehört uns.
a friend of ours ein Freund von uns

ourselves PRONOUN

1 (reflexive) uns
We introduced ourselves. Wir haben uns
vorgestellt.

2 (for emphasis) selbst
In the end we did it ourselves. Schließlich
haben wir es selbst gemacht.

3 **by ourselves** allein

𝓟 **out** ADVERB

1 (outside) draußen
It's cold out there. Es ist kalt da draußen.
They're out in the garden. Sie sind draußen
im Garten.

2 **to go out** hinausgehen◇ SEP (PERF sein),
rausgehen◇ SEP (PERF sein) (informal)
to go out shopping einkaufen gehen◇ (PERF
sein)

3 **Get out!** Raus! (informal)

4 **The ball is out.** Der Ball ist aus.

5 (absent)
to be out nicht da sein
Mr Barnes is out. Herr Barnes ist nicht da.

6 **to go out** (for an evening, or to the theatre
or cinema) ausgehen◇ SEP (PERF sein),
weggehen◇ SEP (PERF sein) (informal)
Are you going out this evening? Gehst du
heute Abend weg?

7 **to be going out with somebody** mit
jemandem gehen◇ (PERF sein)
Alison's going out with Danny now. Alison
geht jetzt mit Danny.

8 **to ask somebody out** jemanden einladen◇
SEP
He's asked me out. Er hat mich eingeladen.

9 (light, fire) aus
Are all the lights out? Ist das Licht aus?

out PREPOSITION
out of aus (+DAT)
to go out of the room aus dem Zimmer
gehen◇ (PERF sein)
He threw it out of the window. Er hat es
aus dem Fenster geworfen.
to drink out of a glass aus einem Glas
trinken◇
She took the photo out of her bag. Sie hat
das Foto aus der Tasche genommen.

outdoor ADJECTIVE
(activity or sport) im Freien ('im Freien'
comes after the noun)

outdoor games Spiele im Freien

outdoors ADVERB
draußen
to go outdoors nach draußen gehen

outing NOUN
der Ausflug (PL die Ausflüge)
to go on an outing einen Ausflug machen

outline NOUN
(of an object) der Umriss (PL die Umrisse)

out of date ADJECTIVE

1 (no longer valid) ungültig
My passport is out of date. Mein Pass ist
ungültig.

2 (old-fashioned) altmodisch (clothes, music)

𝓟 **outside** NOUN
die Außenseite
It's blue on the outside. Außen ist es blau.

outside ADJECTIVE
Außen-

outside ADVERB
draußen
It's cold outside. Es ist kalt draußen.

outside PREPOSITION
vor (+DAT)
I'll meet you outside the cinema. Ich treffe
mich vor dem Kino mit dir.

outskirts PLURAL NOUN
der Stadtrand
on the outskirts of Lübeck am Stadtrand
von Lübeck

oven NOUN
der Ofen (PL die Öfen)
to put something in the oven etwas in den
Ofen tun

𝓟 **over** PREPOSITION

1 (above) über (+DAT)
There's a mirror over the sink. Über dem
Waschbecken hängt ein Spiegel.

2 (involving movement) über (+ACC)
He threw the ball over the wall. Er hat den
Ball über die Mauer geworfen.

3 **over here** hier drüben
The food is over here. Das Essen ist hier
drüben.

4 **over there** da drüben
She's over there. Sie ist da drüben.

5 (more than) über
It will cost over a hundred pounds. Es wird
über hundert Pfund kosten.
He's over sixty. Er ist über sechzig.

6 (during) über (+ACC)
over Christmas über Weihnachten
over the weekend übers Wochenende

◇ irregular verb; SEP separable verb; for more help with verbs see centre section

7 *(finished)* zu Ende
when the meeting's over wenn die Besprechung zu Ende ist
It's all over. Es ist vorbei.

8 **over the phone** am Telefon
to ask someone over jemanden einladen◇ SEP
to come over herüberkommen◇ SEP *(PERF* sein)
Come over on Saturday. Komm am Samstag zu uns herüber.

9 **all over the place** überall
I've been looking for it all over. Ich habe überall danach gesucht.

overcrowded ADJECTIVE
überfüllt

overdose NOUN
die Überdosis *(PL die Überdosen)*

overpopulated ADJECTIVE
überbevölkert

to oversleep VERB
verschlafen◇

⋔ **to overtake** VERB
überholen

⋔ **overtime** NOUN
to work overtime Überstunden machen

overweight ADJECTIVE
to be overweight Übergewicht haben

⋔ **to owe** VERB
schulden
I owe him ten pounds. Ich schulde ihm zehn Pfund.

owing ADJECTIVE
1 *(outstanding)* ausstehend
There's five pounds owing. Fünf Pfund stehen aus.
2 **owing to** wegen *(+GEN)*
owing to the snow wegen des Schnees

⋔ **owl** NOUN
die Eule *(PL die Eulen)*

⋔ **own** ADJECTIVE
1 eigen
my own computer mein eigener Computer
I've got my own room. Ich habe mein eigenes Zimmer.
My brother wants a room of his own. Mein Bruder will sein eigenes Zimmer haben.
2 **on your own** allein
Annie did it on her own. Annie hat es allein gemacht.
He lives on his own. Er lebt allein.

to own VERB
besitzen◇

owner NOUN
der Besitzer *(PL die Besitzer)*, die Besitzerin *(PL die Besitzerinnen)*

oxygen NOUN
der Sauerstoff

ozone layer NOUN
die Ozonschicht
the hole in the ozone layer das Ozonloch

Pp

pace NOUN
1 *(a step)* der Schritt *(PL die Schritte)*
2 *(the speed you walk at)* das Tempo

Pacific NOUN
the Pacific (Ocean) der Pazifik

⋔ **pack** NOUN
1 die Packung *(PL die Packungen)*
2 **pack of cards** das Kartenspiel

to pack VERB
1 packen your case
I haven't packed yet. Ich habe noch nicht gepackt.
I'll pack my case tonight. Ich packe meinen Koffer heute Abend.
2 einpacken SEP *(clothes, shoes, etc.)*
Have you packed my red shirt? Hast du mein rotes Hemd eingepackt?

⋔ **package** NOUN
das Paket *(PL die Pakete)*

package holiday NOUN
der Pauschalurlaub *(PL die Pauschalurlaube)*

packed lunch NOUN
das Lunchpaket *(PL die Lunchpakete)*

⋔ **packet** NOUN
1 das Päckchen *(PL die Päckchen)*
a packet of tea ein Päckchen Tee
2 *(box)* die Schachtel *(PL die Schachteln)*
3 *(bag)* die Tüte *(PL die Tüten)*
a packet of crisps eine Tüte Chips

packing NOUN
das Packen
I have to do my packing. Ich muss packen.

pad NOUN
(of paper) der Block *(PL die Blöcke)*

paddle NOUN
(for a canoe) das Paddel *(PL die Paddel)*

⋔ indicates key words

A
B
C
D
E
F
G
H
I
J
K
L
M
N
O
P
Q
R
S
T
U
V
W
X
Y
Z

to **paddle** VERB
1 *(at the seaside)* planschen *(PERF sein)*
  to go paddling planschen gehen◇
2 *(a canoe)* paddeln

padlock NOUN
  das Vorhängeschloss *(PL die
  Vorhängeschlösser)*

page NOUN
  die Seite *(PL die Seiten)*
  on page seven auf Seite sieben

ℰ **pain** NOUN
1 der Schmerz *(PL die Schmerzen)*
  to be in pain Schmerzen haben
  I've got a pain in my leg. Ich habe
  Schmerzen im Bein.
2 **Eric's a real pain (in the neck).** Eric geht
  einem richtig auf den Wecker. *(informal)*

painful ADJECTIVE
  schmerzhaft

painkiller NOUN
  das Schmerzmittel *(PL die Schmerzmittel)*

paint NOUN
  die Farbe *(PL die Farben)*
  'Wet paint' 'Frisch gestrichen'

to **paint** VERB
  malen *(a picture)*, streichen◇ *(a room)*
  to paint a room pink ein Zimmer rosa
  streichen

paintbrush NOUN
  der Pinsel *(PL die Pinsel)*

painter NOUN
1 *(paints pictures)* der Maler *(PL die Maler)*,
  die Malerin *(PL die Malerinnen)*
2 *(paints walls)* der Anstreicher *(PL die
  Anstreicher)*, die Anstreicherin *(PL die
  Anstreicherinnen)*

  WORD TIP Professions, hobbies, and sports
  don't take an article in German: Er ist Maler.

ℰ **painting** NOUN
  (picture) das Gemälde *(PL die Gemälde)*
  a painting by Picasso ein Gemälde von
  Picasso

ℰ **pair** NOUN
1 das Paar *(PL die Paare)*
  a pair of socks ein Paar Socken
2 **a pair of scissors** eine Schere
3 **a pair of trousers** eine Hose
  a pair of knickers eine Unterhose
4 **to work in pairs** paarweise arbeiten

Pakistan NOUN
  Pakistan *(NEUTER)*

palace NOUN
  der Palast *(PL die Paläste)*

ℰ **pale** ADJECTIVE
  blass
  to turn pale blass werden◇ *(PERF sein)*
  pale green zartgrün

palm NOUN
1 *(of your hand)* die Handfläche *(PL die
  Handflächen)*
2 *(a palm tree)* die Palme *(PL die Palmen)*

ℰ **pan** NOUN
1 *(saucepan)* der Topf *(PL die Töpfe)*
  a pan of water ein Topf Wasser
2 *(frying pan)* die Pfanne *(PL die Pfannen)*

ℰ **pancake** NOUN
  der Pfannkuchen *(PL die Pfannkuchen)*

Pancake Day NOUN
  der Faschingsdienstag

panel NOUN
1 *(for a discussion)* die Diskussionsrunde *(PL
  die Diskussionsrunden)*, *(for a quiz)* das
  Rateteam *(PL die Rateteams)*
2 *(a piece of wood)* die Tafel *(PL die Tafeln)*

panic NOUN
  die Panik

to **panic** VERB
  in Panik geraten◇ *(PERF sein)*
  Don't panic! Keine Panik!

pantomime NOUN
  die lustige Märchenvorstellung zu
  Weihnachten

pants PLURAL NOUN
  die Unterhose *(PL die Unterhosen)*
  a pair of pants eine Unterhose

  WORD TIP In German die Unterhose is
  singular.

ℰ **paper** NOUN
1 das Papier
  a sheet of paper ein Blatt Papier
2 **paper hanky** das Papiertaschentuch
3 **paper cup** der Pappbecher
4 *(newspaper)* die Zeitung *(PL die Zeitungen)*
  It was in the paper. Es stand in der Zeitung.
5 **papers** *(documents)* die Unterlagen *(PLURAL)*

paperback NOUN
  das Taschenbuch *(PL die Taschenbücher)*

paper boy NOUN
  der Zeitungsjunge *(PL die Zeitungsjungen)*

paper clip NOUN
  die Büroklammer *(PL die Büroklammern)*

◇ irregular verb; SEP separable verb; for more help with verbs see centre section

paper girl *NOUN*
das **Zeitungsmädchen** (*PL* die **Zeitungsmädchen**)

paper towel *NOUN*
das **Papierhandtuch** (*PL* die **Papierhandtücher**)

parachute *NOUN*
der **Fallschirm** (*PL* die **Fallschirme**)

parachuting *NOUN*
das **Fallschirmspringen**

parade *NOUN*
der **Umzug** (*PL* die **Umzüge**)

paraffin *NOUN*
das **Petroleum**

paragliding *NOUN*
das **Gleitschirmfliegen**

paragraph *NOUN*
der **Absatz**
'New paragraph' 'Absatz'

> **WORD TIP** Do not translate the English word paragraph with the German Paragraf.

parallel *ADJECTIVE*
parallel

Paralympics, Paralympic Games *PLURAL NOUN*
die **Paralympics** (*PLURAL*)

paralysed *ADJECTIVE*
gelähmt

℘ **parcel** *NOUN*
das **Paket** (*PL* die **Pakete**)

℘ **pardon** *NOUN*
I beg your pardon (*as an apology*)
Entschuldigung!
Pardon? Wie bitte?

℘ **parent** *NOUN*
der **Elternteil**
parents die **Eltern** (*PLURAL*)
My parents live in Germany. Meine Eltern
wohnen in Deutschland.
parents' evening der **Elternsprechabend**

℘ **park** *NOUN*
1 der **Park** (*PL* die **Parks**)
theme park der **Themenpark**, der
Freizeitpark
2 car park der **Parkplatz**
to **park** *VERB*
1 **parken**
You can park outside the house. Du kannst
vor dem Haus parken.

2 to find somewhere to park einen Parkplatz
finden◇

℘ **parking** *NOUN*
das **Parken**
'No parking' 'Parken verboten'

parking meter *NOUN*
die **Parkuhr** (*PL* die **Parkuhren**)

parking space *NOUN*
die **Parklücke** (*PL* die **Parklücken**)

parking ticket *NOUN*
der **Strafzettel** (*PL* die **Strafzettel**)

parliament *NOUN*
das **Parlament** (*PL* die **Parlamente**)

parrot *NOUN*
der **Papagei** (*PL* die **Papageien**)

℘ **part** *NOUN*
1 der **Teil** (*PL* die **Teile**)
part of the garden Teil des Gartens
the last part of the book der letzte Teil des
Buches
2 That's part of your job. Das gehört zu
deiner Arbeit dazu.
3 to take part in something an etwas (*DAT*)
teilnehmen◇ *SEP*
4 (*spare part*) das **Teil** (*PL* die **Teile** (*for a
machine or an engine*)
5 (*a role in a play*) die **Rolle** (*PL* die **Rollen**)

particular *ADJECTIVE*
besonderer/besondere/besonderes
nothing in particular nichts Besonderes

particularly *ADVERB*
besonders
not particularly interesting nicht
besonders interessant

parting *NOUN*
1 (*in your hair*) der **Scheitel** (*PL* die **Scheitel**)
2 (*departure*) der **Abschied** (*PL* die **Abschiede**)

partly *ADVERB*
teilweise

partner *NOUN*
der **Partner** (*PL* die **Partner**), die **Partnerin**
(*PL* die **Partnerinnen**)

partnership *NOUN*
die **Partnerschaft** (*PL* die **Partnerschaft**)

part-time *ADJECTIVE*
Teilzeit-
part-time work die **Teilzeitarbeit**

part-time *ADVERB*
to work part-time Teilzeit arbeiten

𝒫 **party** NOUN
1 die **Party** (PL die **Partys**), die **Feier** (PL die **Feiern**)
 to have a birthday party eine Geburtstagsparty machen
 a Christmas party eine Weihnachtsfeier
2 (group) die **Gruppe** (PL die **Gruppen**)
 a party of schoolchildren eine Gruppe Schulkinder
3 (in politics) die **Partei** (PL die **Parteien**)

𝒫 **pass** NOUN
1 (to let you in) der **Ausweis** (PL die **Ausweise**)
2 **bus pass** die Buskarte
3 (over the mountains) der **Pass** (PL die **Pässe**)
4 (in an exam)
 to get a pass in maths die Mathematikprüfung bestehen

to pass VERB
1 (walk past) **vorbeigehen**◇ SEP (PERF **sein**) **an** (+DAT) (a place or building)
 We passed your house. Wir sind an deinem Haus vorbeigegangen.
2 (drive past) **vorbeifahren**◇ SEP (PERF **sein**) **an** (+DAT) (a place or building)
3 (overtake) **überholen** (a car)
4 (give) **reichen**
 Could you pass me the sugar please? Könnten Sie mir bitte den Zucker reichen?
5 (time) **vergehen**◇ (PERF **sein**)
 The time passed slowly. Die Zeit verging langsam.
6 **bestehen**◇ (an exam)
 to pass an exam eine Prüfung bestehen
 Did you pass in German? Hast du die Deutschprüfung bestanden?

passage NOUN
1 (corridor) der **Gang** (PL die **Gänge**)
2 (a piece of text) die **Passage** (PL die **Passagen**)

𝒫 **passenger** NOUN
1 (in a plane or ship) der **Passagier** (PL die **Passagiere**)
2 (in a train or bus) der **Fahrgast** (PL die **Fahrgäste**)
3 (in a car) der **Mitfahrer** (PL die **Mitfahrer**)

passive NOUN
(in grammar) das **Passiv**

passive ADJECTIVE
passiv

Passover NOUN
das **Passah**

𝒫 **passport** NOUN
der **Reisepass** (PL die **Reisepässe**), der **Pass** (PL die **Pässe**)

password NOUN
1 (to gain entry) das **Kennwort** (PL die **Kennwörter**)
2 (for access to data) das **Passwort** (PL die **Passwörter**)
 to enter your password das Passwort eingeben

𝒫 **past** NOUN
die **Vergangenheit**
 in the past in der Vergangenheit

past ADJECTIVE
1 (recent) **letzter/letzte/letztes**
 in the past few weeks in den letzten paar Wochen
2 (over) **vorbei**
 Winter is past. Der Winter ist vorbei.

past PREPOSITION, ADVERB
1 **to walk past something** an etwas (DAT) **vorbeigehen**◇ SEP (PERF **sein**)
 We went past the school. Wir sind an der Schule vorbeigegangen.
 to go past **vorbeifahren**◇ SEP (PERF **sein**)
2 (after) **nach** (+DAT)
 It's just past the post office. Es ist kurz nach der Post.
3 (talking about time)
 ten past six zehn nach sechs
 half past four halb fünf
 a quarter past two Viertel nach zwei

𝒫 **pasta** NOUN
die **Nudeln** (PLURAL)
 I don't like pasta. Ich mag keine Nudeln.

pastry NOUN
1 (for baking) der **Teig**
2 (a small cake) das **Gebäckstück**

patch NOUN
1 (for mending) der **Flicken** (PL die **Flicken**)
2 (of snow or ice) die **Stelle** (PL die **Stellen**)
3 (of blue sky) das **Stückchen** (PL die **Stückchen**)

𝒫 **path** NOUN
der **Weg** (PL die **Wege**), (very narrow) der **Pfad** (PL die **Pfade**)

pathetic ADJECTIVE
(useless, hopeless) **jämmerlich**

patience NOUN
1 die **Geduld**
2 (card game) die **Patience**

𝒫 **patient** NOUN
der **Patient** (PL die **Patienten**), die **Patientin** (PL die **Patientinnen**)

patient ADJECTIVE
geduldig

patiently ADVERB
geduldig

patio NOUN
die Terrasse (PL die Terrassen)

pattern NOUN
1 (on wallpaper or fabric) das Muster (PL die Muster)
2 (dressmaking, knitting) der Schnitt (PL die Schnitte)

pause NOUN
die Pause (PL die Pausen)

ℰ **pavement** NOUN
der Bürgersteig (PL die Bürgersteige)
on the pavement auf dem Bürgersteig

paw NOUN
die Pfote (PL die Pfoten)

pawn NOUN
(in chess) der Bauer (PL die Bauern)

ℰ **pay** NOUN
(wage) der Lohn (PL die Löhne), (salary) das Gehalt (PL die Gehälter)

to **pay** VERB
1 zahlen
I'm paying. Ich zahle.
to pay cash bar zahlen
to pay by credit card mit Kreditkarte zahlen
They pay £8 an hour. Sie zahlen acht Pfund die Stunde.
to pay by cheque mit Scheck zahlen
2 bezahlen (bezahlen is used when you pay a person, a bill or for something)
to pay for something etwas bezahlen
Tony paid for the drinks. Tony hat die Getränke bezahlt.
It's all paid for. Es ist alles bezahlt.
3 to pay somebody back (money) jemandem Geld zurückzahlen SEP
4 to pay attention aufpassen SEP
5 to pay a visit to somebody jemanden besuchen

payment NOUN
1 die Bezahlung (of sum, bill, debt, or fine)
2 die Zahlung (PL die Zahlungen) (of interest, tax, or fee)

pay phone NOUN
der Münzfernsprecher (PL die Münzfernsprecher)

PC NOUN
(computer) der PC (PL die PC)

ℰ **pea** NOUN
die Erbse (PL die Erbsen)

ℰ **peace** NOUN
der Frieden
to hope for peace auf den Frieden hoffen

peaceful ADJECTIVE
friedlich

ℰ **peach** NOUN
der Pfirsich (PL die Pfirsiche)

peacock NOUN
der Pfau (PL die Pfauen)

peak period NOUN
(for holidays) die Hauptferienzeit (PL die Hauptferienzeiten)

peak rate NOUN
(for phoning) der Höchsttarif (PL die Höchsttarife)

peak time NOUN
(for traffic) die Stoßzeit (PL die Stoßzeiten)

ℰ **peanut** NOUN
die Erdnuss (PL die Erdnüsse)

peanut butter NOUN
die Erdnussbutter

ℰ **pear** NOUN
die Birne (PL die Birnen)

pearl NOUN
die Perle (PL die Perlen)

pebble NOUN
der Kieselstein (PL die Kieselsteine)
a pebble beach ein Kieselstrand

peculiar ADJECTIVE
komisch

pedal NOUN
das Pedal (PL die Pedale)

to **pedal** VERB
(on a bike) to pedal off (mit dem Rad) wegfahren◇ SEP (PERF sein)
I had to pedal hard. Ich musste ordentlich in die Pedale treten.

ℰ **pedestrian** NOUN
der Fußgänger (PL die Fußgänger), die Fußgängerin (PL die Fußgängerinnen)

pedestrian crossing NOUN
der Fußgängerüberweg (PL die Fußgängerüberwege)

pedestrian precinct NOUN
die Fußgängerzone (PL die Fußgängerzonen)

pee NOUN
to have a pee pinkeln (informal)

ℰ indicates key words

P **peel** NOUN
die Schale (PL die Schalen)

to **peel** VERB
schälen (fruit, vegetables)

peg NOUN
1 (hook) der Haken (PL die Haken)
2 clothes peg die Wäscheklammer (PL die Wäscheklammern)
3 (for a tent) der Hering (PL die Heringe)

P **pen** NOUN
(ballpoint) der Kugelschreiber (PL die Kugelschreiber)
felt pen der Filzstift

penalty NOUN
1 (a fine) die Geldstrafe (PL die Geldstrafen)
2 (in football) der Elfmeter (PL die Elfmeter)
3 (in some other sports) der Strafstoß (PL die Strafstöße)

pence PLURAL NOUN
die Pence (PLURAL)

P **pencil** NOUN
der Bleistift (PL die Bleistifte)
to write in pencil mit Bleistift schreiben◇

pencil case NOUN
das Federmäppchen (PL die Federmäppchen)

pencil sharpener NOUN
der Bleistiftanspitzer (PL die Bleistiftanspitzer)

P **penfriend** NOUN
der Brieffreund (PL die Brieffreunde), die Brieffreundin (PL die Brieffreundinnen)
My German penfriend is called Heidi.
Meine deutsche Brieffreundin heißt Heidi.

penguin NOUN
der Pinguin (PL die Pinguine)

penis NOUN
der Penis (PL die Penisse)

penknife NOUN
das Taschenmesser (PL die Taschenmesser)

penny NOUN
der Penny (PL die Pence)

P **pension** NOUN
die Rente (PL die Renten)

pensioner NOUN
der Rentner (PL die Rentner), die Rentnerin (PL die Rentnerinnen)

P **people** PLURAL NOUN
1 die Leute (PLURAL) die Menschen (PLURAL) ('Menschen' is used in a more formal context)

most people round here die meisten Leute hier
several people verschiedene Leute
nice people nette Leute
all the people in the world alle Menschen auf der Welt
a crowd of people eine Menschenmenge
2 (when you're counting them) die Personen (PLURAL)
for ten people für zehn Personen
How many people have you invited? Wie viele Personen hast du eingeladen?
3 People say that ... Man sagt, dass ...

P **pepper** NOUN
1 (spice) der Pfeffer
2 (vegetable) die Paprikaschote (PL die Paprikaschoten)

peppermint NOUN
1 (plant) die Pfefferminze
peppermint tea der Pfefferminztee
2 (sweet) der or das Pfefferminzbonbon (PL die Pfefferminzbonbons)

per PREPOSITION
pro (+ACC)
ten pounds per person zehn Pfund pro Person

per cent ADVERB
das Prozent
sixty per cent of students sechzig Prozent der Studenten

percentage NOUN
der Prozentsatz (PL die Prozentsätze)

percussion NOUN
das Schlagzeug
Max plays percussion. Max spielt Schlagzeug.

WORD TIP Don't use the article when you talk about playing an instrument.

P **perfect** ADJECTIVE
1 perfekt
She speaks perfect English. Sie spricht perfekt Englisch.
2 (ideal) herrlich (day or weather)

perfectly ADVERB
1 (absolutely) vollkommen
2 (faultlessly) perfekt

to **perform** VERB
1 spielen (a piece of music or a part)
2 singen◇ (a song)
3 to perform a play ein Theaterstück aufführen SEP

578

◇ irregular verb; SEP separable verb; for more help with verbs see centre section

ℒ **performance** NOUN
1 (playing or acting) die **Darstellung** (PL die Darstellungen)
   his performance as Hamlet seine Darstellung des Hamlet
2 (show or film) die **Vorstellung** (PL die Vorstellungen)
   The performance starts at eight. Die Vorstellung fängt um acht Uhr an.
3 (by a band) der **Auftritt** (PL die Auftritte)
   a live performance by the band ein Liveauftritt der Band
4 (of a play or opera) die **Aufführung** (PL die Aufführungen)

ℒ **perfume** NOUN
   das **Parfüm** (PL die Parfüme)

ℒ **perhaps** ADVERB
   vielleicht
   Perhaps he's missed the train. Vielleicht hat er den Zug verpasst.

ℒ **period** NOUN
1 (length of time) die **Zeit** (PL die Zeiten)
   trial period die Probezeit
2 (a portion of time) der **Zeitraum** (PL die Zeiträume)
   a two-year period ein Zeitraum von zwei Jahren
3 (in school) die **Stunde** (PL die Stunden)
4 (menstruation) die **Periode** (PL die Perioden)
   I've got my period. Ich habe meine Periode.

perm NOUN
   die **Dauerwelle** (PL die Dauerwellen)

permanent ADJECTIVE
1 **ständig**
2 **fest** (job or address, for example)

permanently ADVERB
1 **dauernd**
2 **to be permanently employed** fest angestellt sein

permission NOUN
   die **Erlaubnis**
   to get permission to do something Erlaubnis zu etwas (DAT) erhalten◇

permit NOUN
   die **Genehmigung** (PL die Genehmigungen)

to **permit** VERB
1 **erlauben**
   to permit somebody to do something jemandem erlauben, etwas zu tun
   Smoking is not permitted. Rauchen ist nicht gestattet.
2 **weather permitting** bei entsprechendem Wetter

ℒ **person** NOUN
1 die **Person** (PL die Personen)
   There's still room for one more person. Wir haben noch Platz für eine Person.
2 **in person** persönlich

personal ADJECTIVE
   persönlich

personality NOUN
   die **Persönlichkeit** (PL die Persönlichkeiten)

personally ADVERB
   persönlich
   Personally, I'm against it. Ich persönlich bin dagegen.

perspiration NOUN
   der **Schweiß**

ℒ to **persuade** VERB
   überreden
   to persuade somebody to come jemanden überreden zu kommen

pessimistic ADJECTIVE
   pessimistisch

pest NOUN
1 (greenfly, for example) der **Schädling** (PL die Schädlinge)
2 (annoying person) die **Nervensäge** (PL die Nervensägen) (informal)

ℒ **pet** NOUN
1 das **Haustier** (PL die Haustiere)
   Do you have a pet? Habt ihr Haustiere?
   a pet dog ein Hund
2 **Julie is teacher's pet.** Julie ist der Liebling des Lehrers.

pet name NOUN
   der **Kosename** (PL die Kosenamen)

ℒ **petrol** NOUN
   das **Benzin** (PL die Benzine)
   to fill up with petrol tanken
   to run out of petrol kein Benzin mehr haben

petrol station NOUN
   die **Tankstelle** (PL die Tankstellen)

pharmacist NOUN
   der **Apotheker** (PL die Apotheker), die **Apothekerin** (PL die Apothekerinnen)

   WORD TIP Professions, hobbies, and sports don't take an article in German: Sie ist Apothekerin.

pharmacy NOUN
   die **Apotheke** (PL die Apotheken)

ℒ indicates key words

philosophy NOUN
die Philosophie (PL die Philosophien)

ℐ **phone** NOUN
das Telefon (PL die Telefone), *(mobile)* das
Handy (PL die Handys)
She's on the phone. Sie telefoniert.
I was on the phone to Sophie. Ich habe mit
Sophie telefoniert.
You can book by phone. Du kannst
telefonisch buchen.
My phone just rang. Mein Handy hat
gerade geklingelt.
His phone is switched off. Sein Handy ist
ausgeschaltet.

to **phone** VERB
1 telefonieren
while I was phoning während ich
telefonierte
2 **to phone somebody** jemanden anrufen◇
SEP
I'll phone you tonight. Ich rufe dich heute
Abend an.

ℐ **phone book** NOUN
das Telefonbuch (PL die Telefonbücher)

ℐ **phone box** NOUN
die Telefonzelle (PL die Telefonzellen)

ℐ **phone call** NOUN
1 der Anruf (PL die Anrufe)
to get a phone call einen Anruf erhalten◇
2 **to make a phone call** ein Telefongespräch
führen
Phone calls are free. Telefongespräche sind
gebührenfrei.

ℐ **phone number** NOUN
die Telefonnummer (PL die
Telefonnummern)

ℐ **photo** NOUN
das Foto (PL die Fotos)
to take a photo ein Foto machen
to take a photo of somebody ein Foto von
jemandem machen

photocopier NOUN
das Fotokopiergerät (PL die
Fotokopiergeräte)

photocopy NOUN
die Fotokopie (PL die Fotokopien)
to **photocopy** VERB
fotokopieren

photograph NOUN
die Fotografie (PL die Fotografien)
to take a photograph ein Foto machen
to **photograph** VERB
fotografieren

photographer NOUN
der Fotograf (PL die Fotografen), die
Fotografin (PL die Fotografinnen)

WORD TIP Professions, hobbies, and sports
don't take an article in German: Er ist Fotograf.

photography NOUN
die Fotografie

ℐ **phrase** NOUN
die Phrase (PL die Phrasen)
an idiomatic phrase eine Redewendung

phrase book NOUN
der Sprachführer (PL die Sprachführer)

physical ADJECTIVE
körperlich

ℐ **physics** NOUN
die Physik

physiotherapist NOUN
der Physiotherapeut (PL die
Physiotherapeuten), die
Physiotherapeutin (PL die
Physiotherapeutinnen)

WORD TIP Professions, hobbies, and sports
don't take an article in German: Sie ist
Physiotherapeutin.

physiotherapy NOUN
die Physiotherapie

ℐ **piano** NOUN
das Klavier (PL die Klaviere)
piano lesson die Klavierstunde
Anne plays the piano. Anne spielt Klavier.

WORD TIP Don't use the article when you talk
about playing an instrument.

ℐ **pick** NOUN
to take your pick sich (DAT) etwas
aussuchen SEP

to **pick** VERB
1 *(select)* wählen
He picked his words carefully. Er wählte
seine Worte mit Bedacht.
2 *(choose for oneself)* sich (DAT) aussuchen SEP
Pick any book. Such dir irgendein Buch aus.
3 **to pick a team** eine Mannschaft aufstellen
SEP
4 pflücken *(fruit)*
to pick strawberries Erdbeeren pflücken
• **to pick up**
1 *(lift)* (in die Hand) nehmen◇
He picked up the papers. Er nahm die
Unterlagen.
2 *(collect)* abholen SEP
I'll pick you up at six. Ich hole dich um
sechs Uhr ab.

◇ irregular verb; SEP separable verb; for more help with verbs see centre section

I'll pick up the keys tomorrow. Ich hole die Schlüssel morgen ab.

pickpocket NOUN
der Taschendieb (PL die Taschendiebe)

picnic NOUN
das Picknick (PL die Picknicke)
to have a picnic ein Picknick machen

℘ **picture** NOUN
1 das Bild (PL die Bilder)
2 **to go to the pictures** (the cinema) ins Kino gehen

pie NOUN
1 (sweet) der Kuchen (PL die Kuchen)
apple pie der Apfelkuchen
2 (savoury) die Pastete (PL die Pasteten)

℘ **piece** NOUN
1 (a bit) das Stück (PL die Stücke)
a big piece of cheese ein großes Stück Käse
2 (that you fit together) das Teil (PL die Teile)
the pieces of a jigsaw die Teile von einem Puzzle
to take something to pieces etwas in seine Einzelteile zerlegen
3 **piece of furniture** das Möbelstück
a piece of information eine Information
a piece of luck ein Glücksfall
4 (coin) das Stück (PL die Stücke)
a five-pence piece ein Fünf-Pence-Stück

to pierce VERB
1 durchstechen◇ SEP
She had her ears pierced. Sie hat sich Ohrlöcher stechen lassen.
2 **to have pierced ears** Löcher in den Ohrläppchen haben

piercing NOUN
das Piercing (PL die Piercings)
She's got two piercings. Sie hat zwei Piercings.

℘ **pig** NOUN
das Schwein (PL die Schweine)

pigeon NOUN
die Taube (PL die Tauben)

piggy bank NOUN
das Sparschwein (PL die Sparschweine)

pigtail NOUN
der Zopf (PL die Zöpfe)

℘ **pile** NOUN
1 (a neat stack) der Stapel (PL die Stapel)
a pile of plates ein Stapel Teller
2 (a heap) der Haufen (PL die Haufen)

to pile VERB
• **to pile something up**
(neatly) etwas aufstapeln SEP, (in a heap) etwas auftürmen SEP

℘ **pill** NOUN
die Pille (PL die Pillen)

pillar NOUN
die Säule (PL die Säulen)

pillow NOUN
das Kopfkissen (PL die Kopfkissen)

pilot NOUN
der Pilot (PL die Piloten), die Pilotin (PL die Pilotinnen)

WORD TIP Professions, hobbies, and sports don't take an article in German: Er ist Pilot.

pimple NOUN
der Pickel (PL die Pickel)

pin NOUN
1 (for sewing) die Stecknadel (PL die Stecknadeln)
2 **a three-pin plug** ein dreipoliger Stecker

to pin VERB
• **to pin up**
anschlagen◇ SEP a notice
I pinned it up on the noticeboard. Ich habe es ans Anschlagbrett gehängt.

PIN NOUN
(personal identification number) die Geheimnummer (PL die Geheimnummern)

pinball NOUN
das Flippern
to play pinball flippern
pinball machine der Flipper

pinch NOUN
(of salt, for example) die Prise (PL die Prisen)

to pinch VERB
1 kneifen◇
She pinched my arm. Sie hat mich in den Arm gekniffen.
2 (to steal) klauen (informal)
Somebody's pinched my bike. Jemand hat mein Rad geklaut.

pine NOUN
die Kiefer (PL die Kiefern)
pine furniture die Kiefernmöbel (PLURAL)

℘ **pineapple** NOUN
die Ananas (PL die Ananas)

ping-pong NOUN
das Tischtennis
to play ping-pong Tischtennis spielen

ℓ **pink** *ADJECTIVE*
rosa ('rosa' never changes)
pink hats rosa Hüte

pip *NOUN*
(in a fruit) der Kern (PL die Kerne)

pipe *NOUN*
1 (for gas or water) das Rohr (PL die Rohre)
2 (for smoking) die Pfeife (PL die Pfeifen)
He smokes a pipe. Er raucht Pfeife.

pirate *NOUN*
der Pirat (PL die Piraten)

Pisces *NOUN*
Fische (PLURAL)
Amanda is Pisces. Amanda ist Fisch.

pistachio *NOUN*
die Pistazie (PL die Pistazien)

ℓ **pitch** *NOUN*
der Platz (PL die Plätze)
football pitch der Fußballplatz

to **pitch** *VERB*
to pitch a tent ein Zelt aufstellen *SEP*

ℓ **pity** *NOUN*
1 (feeling sorry for somebody) das Mitleid
2 What a pity! Wie schade!
It would be a pity to miss the beginning.
Es wäre schade, den Anfang zu verpassen.

to **pity** *VERB*
to pity somebody jemanden bemitleiden

ℓ **pizza** *NOUN*
die Pizza (PL die Pizzas)

ℓ **place** *NOUN*
1 der Ort (PL die Orte)
Salzburg is a wonderful place. Salzburg ist
ein sehr schöner Ort.
in place an Ort und Stelle
place of birth der Geburtsort
2 all over the place überall
3 (a space) der Platz (PL die Plätze)
a place for the car ein Platz für das Auto
Is there a place for me? Ist Platz für mich?
Will you keep my place? Kannst du mir den
Platz freihalten?
to change places die Plätze tauschen
4 (spot) die Stelle (PL die Stellen)
This is a good place to stop. Das ist eine
gute Stelle zum Halten.
5 (in a race or competition) der Platz (PL die
Plätze)
to gain first place den ersten Platz belegen
6 at your place bei dir
We'll go round to Zafir's place. Wir gehen
zu Zafir.

7 to take place stattfinden◇ *SEP*
The competition will take place at four.
Der Wettbewerb findet um vier Uhr statt.

to **place** *VERB*
(upright) stellen, (lying flat) legen

ℓ **plain** *NOUN*
die Ebene (PL die Ebenen)

plain *ADJECTIVE*
1 einfach
plain food einfaches Essen
2 (unflavoured) Natur-
plain yoghurt der Naturjoghurt
3 (not patterned) einfarbig
plain curtains einfarbige Vorhänge

plait *NOUN*
der Zopf (PL die Zöpfe)

ℓ **plan** *NOUN*
der Plan (PL die Pläne)
We've made plans for the summer. Wir
haben Pläne für den Sommer gemacht.
to go according to plan nach Plan gehen◇
Everything went according to plan. Alles
ging nach Plan.

to **plan** *VERB*
1 to plan to do something etwas vorhaben◇
SEP
We're planning to leave at eight. Wir
haben vor, um acht abzufahren.
2 (make plans for, organize, design) planen
She's planning a trip to Italy. Sie plant eine
Reise nach Italien.

ℓ **plane** *NOUN*
das Flugzeug (PL die Flugzeuge)
We went by plane. Wir sind geflogen.

planet *NOUN*
der Planet (PL die Planeten)

ℓ **plant** *NOUN*
die Pflanze (PL die Pflanzen)
a house plant eine Zimmerpflanze

to **plant** *VERB*
pflanzen

ℓ **plaster** *NOUN*
1 (sticking plaster) das Pflaster (PL die
Pflaster)
2 (for walls) der Verputz
3 der Gips
to have your leg in plaster das Bein in Gips
haben

plastic *NOUN*
das Plastik
plastic bag die Plastiktüte

ℓ **plate** *NOUN*
der Teller (PL die Teller)

582

◇ **irregular verb;** *SEP* **separable verb; for more help with verbs see centre section**

ℰ **platform** NOUN
1 *(in a station)* der **Bahnsteig** (PL die **Bahnsteige**)
I was standing on the platform. Ich stand auf dem Bahnsteig.
2 *(when you say the number of the platform)* das **Gleis** (PL die **Gleise**)
The train is arriving at platform six. Der Zug fährt auf Gleis sechs ein.
3 *(for lecturing or performing)* das **Podium** (PL die **Podien**)

ℰ **play** NOUN
(in the theatre) das **Stück** (PL die **Stücke**)
television play das **Fernsehspiel**
We are putting on a play by Brecht at school. Wir führen ein Stück von Brecht in der Schule auf.

to **play** VERB
1 **spielen**
The children are playing with a ball. Die Kinder spielen Ball.
They play the piano and the guitar. Sie spielen Klavier und Gitarre.
Who's playing Hamlet? Wer spielt Hamlet?
to play tennis Tennis spielen
They were playing cards. Sie haben Karten gespielt.
2 *(in sport)*
to play somebody gegen jemanden spielen
Italy are playing Germany. Italien spielt gegen Deutschland.
3 **spielen** *(a DVD, etc.)*

ℰ **player** NOUN
1 der **Spieler** (PL die **Spieler**), die **Spielerin** (PL die **Spielerinnen**)
football player der **Fußballspieler**
2 *(in the theatre)* der **Schauspieler** (PL die **Schauspieler**), die **Schauspielerin** (PL die **Schauspielerinnen**)

playground NOUN
der **Spielplatz** (PL die **Spielplätze**)
school playground der **Schulhof**

playing field NOUN
der **Sportplatz** (PL die **Sportplätze**)

ℰ **pleasant** ADJECTIVE
angenehm

ℰ **please** ADVERB
bitte
Two coffees, please. Zwei Kaffee bitte.
Could you turn the TV off, please? Könntest du bitte den Fernseher ausmachen?

ℰ **pleased** ADJECTIVE
1 **erfreut**

I'm really pleased! Das freut mich wirklich!
2 She was pleased with her present. Sie hat sich über ihr Geschenk gefreut.
3 Pleased to meet you! Freut mich!

ℰ **pleasure** NOUN
1 *(amusement)* das **Vergnügen**
2 *(joy)* die **Freude**
to get a lot of pleasure out of something viel Freude an etwas (DAT) haben

ℰ **plenty** PRONOUN
1 *(lots)* **viel**
He's got plenty of money. Er hat viel Geld.
2 *(enough)* **genug**
That's plenty! Das ist genug!
We've got plenty of time left. Wir haben noch genug Zeit.

plot NOUN
(of a film or novel) die **Handlung**

plug NOUN
1 *(electrical)* der **Stecker** (PL die **Stecker**)
2 *(in a bath or sink)* der **Stöpsel** (PL die **Stöpsel**)
to pull out the plug den Stöpsel herausziehen

ℰ **plum** NOUN
die **Pflaume** (PL die **Pflaumen**)
plum tart der **Pflaumenkuchen**

plumber NOUN
der **Installateur** (PL die **Installateure**), die **Installateurin** (PL die **Installateurinnen**)

WORD TIP Professions, hobbies, and sports don't take an article in German: Er ist Installateur.

plural NOUN
(in grammar) die **Mehrzahl**, der **Plural**
in the plural in der Mehrzahl, im Plural

plus PREPOSITION
plus (+DAT)
four plus two vier plus zwei
three children plus a baby drei Kinder und ein Baby

p.m. ABBREVIATION
nachmittags *(for times up to 6 p.m.)*
abends *(for times after 6 p.m.)*
at two p.m. um zwei Uhr nachmittags, um vierzehn Uhr
at nine p.m. um neun Uhr abends, um einundzwanzig Uhr

WORD TIP In German you usually express times after midday in terms of the 24-hour clock.

pneumonia NOUN
die **Lungenentzündung**
He had pneumonia. Er hatte eine Lungenentzündung.

ℐ **pocket** NOUN
die Tasche (PL die Taschen)

ℐ **pocket money** NOUN
das Taschengeld

poem NOUN
das Gedicht (PL die Gedichte)

poet NOUN
der Dichter (PL die Dichter), die Dichterin
(PL die Dichterinnen)

WORD TIP Professions, hobbies, and sports
don't take an article in German: Er ist Dichter.

poetry NOUN
die Dichtung

ℐ **point** NOUN
1 (tip) die Spitze (PL die Spitzen)
the point of a nail die Spitze eines Nagels
2 (a tiny mark or dot) der Punkt (PL die
Punkte)
3 (in time) der Zeitpunkt (PL die Zeitpunkte)
at that point zu diesem Zeitpunkt
to be on the point of doing something
gerade etwas tun wollen◇
4 That's not the point. Darum geht es nicht.
There's no point phoning, he's out. Es hat
keinen Sinn anzurufen, er ist nicht da.
What's the point? Wozu?
5 That's a good point! Das stimmt!
The point is ... Es geht darum ...
6 point of view der Standpunkt
from my point of view von meinem
Standpunkt aus
7 her strong point ihre Stärke
8 (in scoring) der Punkt (PL die Punkte)
to win by fifteen points mit fünfzehn
Punkten Vorsprung gewinnen
9 (in decimals)
decimal point das Komma
6 point 4 (6.4) sechs Komma vier (6,4)

WORD TIP In German, decimals are written with
a comma.

to **point** VERB
1 hinweisen◇ SEP auf (+ACC)
a notice pointing to the station ein Schild,
das in Richtung Bahnhof zeigt
2 (with your finger) zeigen auf (+ACC)
He pointed at Tom. Er zeigte auf Tom.

ℐ **pointless** ADJECTIVE
sinnlos
It's pointless to keep on ringing. Es ist
sinnlos, dauernd anzurufen.

poison NOUN
das Gift (PL die Gifte)

to **poison** VERB
vergiften

poisonous ADJECTIVE
giftig

Poland NOUN
Polen (NEUTER)

polar bear NOUN
der Eisbär (PL die Eisbären)

pole NOUN
1 (for a tent) die Stange (PL die Stangen)
2 (for skiing) der Stock (PL die Stöcke)
3 the North/South Pole der Nordpol/Südpol

Pole NOUN
(a Polish person) der Pole (PL die Polen), die
Polin (PL die Polinnen)

ℐ **police** NOUN
the police die Polizei (SINGULAR)
The police are coming. Die Polizei kommt.

police car NOUN
der Streifenwagen (PL die Streifenwagen)

policeman NOUN
der Polizist (PL die Polizisten)

WORD TIP Professions, hobbies, and sports
don't take an article in German: Er ist Polizist.

police officer NOUN
der Polizist (PL die Polizisten), die Polizistin
(PL die Polizistinnen)

WORD TIP Professions, hobbies, and sports
don't take an article in German: Er ist Polizist.

police station NOUN
die Polizeiwache (PL die Polizeiwachen)

policewoman NOUN
die Polizistin (PL die Polizistinnen)

WORD TIP Professions, hobbies, and sports
don't take an article in German: Sie ist Polizistin.

policy NOUN
1 (plan of action) die Politik
the policy on immigration die
Einwanderungspolitik
2 (insurance document) der
Versicherungsschein (PL die
Versicherungsscheine)

polish NOUN
1 (for furniture) die Politur
2 (for shoes) die Schuhcreme
3 (for the floor) das Bohnerwachs
to **polish** VERB
1 polieren (furniture, silver)
2 to polish your shoes seine Schuhe putzen

◇ irregular verb; SEP separable verb; for more help with verbs see centre section

Polish NOUN
(language) das **Polnisch**

Polish ADJECTIVE
polnisch
the Polish coast die polnische Küste
He's Polish. Er ist Pole.
She's Polish. Sie ist Polin.

> **WORD TIP** Adjectives never have capitals in German, even for regions, countries, or nationalities.

ℙ **polite** ADJECTIVE
höflich
to be polite to somebody höflich zu jemandem sein

political ADJECTIVE
politisch

politician NOUN
der **Politiker** (PL die **Politiker**),)die **Politikerin** (PL die **Politikerinnen**)

> **WORD TIP** Professions, hobbies, and sports don't take an article in German: Er ist Politiker.

politics NOUN
die **Politik**
I'm not interested in politics. Ich interessiere mich nicht für Politik.

pollen NOUN
der **Pollen**
The pollen count for today is ... Die Pollenzahl heute ist ...

ℙ **polluted** ADJECTIVE
verschmutzt

ℙ **pollution** NOUN
die **Umweltverschmutzung**

polo-necked ADJECTIVE
Rollkragen-
a polo-necked sweater ein Rollkragenpullover

ℙ **pond** NOUN
der **Teich** (PL die **Teiche**)

pony NOUN
das **Pony** (PL die **Ponys**)

ponytail NOUN
der **Pferdeschwanz** (PL die **Pferdeschwänze**)

poodle NOUN
der **Pudel** (PL die **Pudel**)

pool NOUN
1 (swimming pool) das **Schwimmbecken** (PL die **Schwimmbecken**)
an indoor pool ein Hallenbad

an open-air/outdoor pool ein Freibad
2 (pond) der **Tümpel** (PL die **Tümpel**)
3 (puddle) die **Lache** (PL die **Lachen**)
4 (game) das **Poolbillard**
5 **the football pools** das **Toto**
to do the pools Toto spielen

ℙ **poor** ADJECTIVE
1 arm
a poor country ein armes Land
a poor family eine arme Familie
2 **Poor Tanya's failed her exam.** Die arme Tanya ist durch die Prüfung gefallen.
3 (bad) schlecht
That's a poor result. Das ist ein schlechtes Ergebnis.
The weather was pretty poor. Das Wetter war ziemlich schlecht.

pop NOUN
die **Popmusik**
pop concert das Popkonzert
pop star der Popstar
pop song der Popsong

to pop VERB
1 (go somewhere) gehen◇ (PERF sein)
I'm just popping to the bank. Ich gehe kurz auf die Bank.
2 (put something somewhere) tun◇
Pop the books on the table. Tu die Bücher auf den Tisch.
• **to pop in** vorbeikommen◇ SEP (PERF sein)

popcorn NOUN
das **Popcorn**

pope NOUN
der **Papst** (PL die **Päpste**)

poppy NOUN
die **Mohnblume** (PL die **Mohnblumen**)

popular ADJECTIVE
beliebt

ℙ **population** NOUN
die **Bevölkerung**

porch NOUN
der **Vorbau** (PL die **Vorbauten**)

ℙ **pork** NOUN
das **Schweinefleisch**
pork chop das Schweinekotelett
roast pork der Schweinebraten

porridge NOUN
der **Haferbrei**

ℙ **port** NOUN
1 der **Hafen** (PL die **Häfen**)
2 (wine) der **Portwein** (PL die **Portweine**)

ℙ **indicates key words**

porter NOUN
1 (at a station or an airport) der Gepäckträger (PL die Gepäckträger)
2 (in a hotel) der Portier (PL die Portiers)

WORD TIP Professions, hobbies, and sports don't take an article in German: Er ist Portier.

portion NOUN
(of food) die Portion (PL die Portionen)

portrait NOUN
das Porträt (PL die Porträts)

Portugal NOUN
Portugal (NEUTER)

Portuguese NOUN
1 (language) das Portugiesisch
2 (a person) der Portugiese (PL die Portugiesen), die Portugiesin (PL die Portugiesinnen)

Portuguese ADJECTIVE
portugiesisch
the Portuguese coast die portugiesische Küste
He's Portuguese. Er ist Portugiese.
She's Portuguese. Sie ist Portugiesin.

WORD TIP Adjectives never have capitals in German, even for regions, countries, or nationalities.

posh ADJECTIVE
vornehm
a posh area eine vornehme Gegend

position NOUN
1 der Platz (PL die Plätze)
2 (situation) die Lage (PL die Lagen)
What would you do in my position? Was würdest du an meiner Stelle tun?
3 (status, job) die Stellung (PL die Stellungen)

℘ positive ADJECTIVE
1 (sure) sicher
I'm positive he's left. Ich bin mir sicher, dass er gegangen ist.
2 (enthusiastic) positiv
Her reaction was very positive. Ihre Reaktion war sehr positiv.

to possess VERB
besitzen◇

℘ possessions PLURAL NOUN
die Sachen (PLURAL)
All my possessions are in the flat. Alle meine Sachen sind in der Wohnung.

possibility NOUN
die Möglichkeit (PL die Möglichkeiten)

℘ possible ADJECTIVE
möglich

It's possible. Es ist gut möglich.
if possible wenn möglich
as quickly as possible so schnell wie möglich

possibly ADVERB
1 (maybe) möglicherweise
'Will you be at home at midday?' – 'Possibly.' 'Bist du mittags zu Hause?' – 'Möglicherweise.'
2 How can you possibly believe that? Wie kannst du das nur glauben?
I can't possibly arrive before Thursday. Ich kann unmöglich vor Donnerstag ankommen.

℘ post NOUN
1 die Post
to send something by post etwas per Post schicken
(letters) Is there any post for me? Ist Post für mich gekommen?
2 (a pole) der Pfosten (PL die Pfosten)
3 (a job) die Stelle (PL die Stellen)

to post VERB
to post a letter einen Brief abschicken SEP

postage NOUN
das Porto
How much is the postage to Germany? Was kostet das Porto nach Deutschland?

postbox NOUN
der Briefkasten (PL die Briefkästen)

℘ postcard NOUN
die Postkarte (PL die Postkarten)

postcode NOUN
die Postleitzahl (PL die Postleitzahlen)

℘ poster NOUN
1 (for decoration) das Poster (PL die Poster)
I put some posters on my walls. Ich habe ein paar Poster aufgehängt.
2 (advertising) das Plakat (PL die Plakate)
I saw a poster for the concert. Ich habe ein Plakat für das Konzert gesehen.

℘ postman NOUN
der Briefträger (PL die Briefträger)

WORD TIP Professions, hobbies, and sports don't take an article in German: Er ist Briefträger.

℘ post office NOUN
die Post
The post office is on the right. Die Post ist auf der rechten Seite.

to postpone VERB
verschieben◇

586

We've postponed the meeting until next week. Wir haben die Besprechung auf nächste Woche verschoben.

postwoman NOUN
die **Briefträgerin** (PL die **Briefträgerinnen**)

WORD TIP Professions, hobbies, and sports don't take an article in German: Sie ist Briefträgerin.

pot NOUN
1 (jar) der **Topf** (PL die **Töpfe**)
  a pot of honey ein Topf Honig
2 (teapot) die **Kanne** (PL die **Kannen**)
3 **the pots and pans** die Töpfe und Pfannen

ℙ **potato** NOUN
  die **Kartoffel** (PL die **Kartoffeln**)
  fried potatoes die Bratkartoffeln (PLURAL)
  mashed potatoes der Kartoffelbrei (SINGULAR)

potato crisps PLURAL NOUN
  die **Kartoffelchips** (PLURAL)

pottery NOUN
1 (craft) die **Töpferei**
2 (objects) die **Töpferwaren** (PLURAL)

ℙ **pound** NOUN
1 (money) das **Pfund** (PL die **Pfund**)
  fourteen pounds vierzehn Pfund
  1.2 euros to the pound 1,2 Euro für ein Pfund
  a five-pound note ein Fünfpfundschein
2 (in weight) das **Pfund** (PL die **Pfund**)
  two pounds of apples zwei Pfund Äpfel

ℙ to **pour** VERB
1 gießen◇ (liquid)
  He poured milk into the pan. Er hat Milch in den Topf gegossen.
2 eingießen◇ SEP (a drink)
  to pour the tea den Tee eingießen
  I poured him a drink. Ich habe ihm etwas zu trinken eingeschenkt.
3 (with rain)
  It's pouring. Es gießt.

ℙ **poverty** NOUN
  die **Armut**

ℙ **powder** NOUN
1 das **Pulver** (PL die **Pulver**)
  washing powder das Waschpulver
2 (for face or body) der **Puder** (PL die **Puder**)

power NOUN
1 (electricity) der **Strom**
  a power cut eine Stromsperre
2 (energy) die **Energie**
  nuclear power die Kernenergie
3 (strength) die **Kraft**

4 (over other people) die **Macht**
  to be in power an der Macht sein

powerful ADJECTIVE
  (strong) stark, (influential) mächtig

power point NOUN
  die **Steckdose** (PL die **Steckdosen**)

power station NOUN
  das **Kraftwerk** (PL die **Kraftwerke**)

practical ADJECTIVE
  praktisch

practically ADVERB
  fast

ℙ **practice** NOUN
1 (for sport) das **Training**
  hockey practice das Hockeytraining
2 die **Übung**
  to do your piano practice Klavier üben
  to be out of practice aus der Übung sein

ℙ to **practise** VERB
1 üben (an instrument, exercise, or skill)
  to practise the piano Klavier üben
2 anwenden SEP (a language)
  a week in Berlin to practise my German eine Woche in Berlin, um mein Deutsch anzuwenden
3 (in sport) trainieren
  The team practises on Wednesday. Die Mannschaft trainiert mittwochs.

ℙ to **praise** VERB
  loben
  to praise somebody for something jemanden für etwas (ACC) loben

pram NOUN
  der **Kinderwagen** (PL die **Kinderwagen**)

ℙ **prawn** NOUN
  die **Garnele** (PL die **Garnelen**)

to **pray** VERB
  beten

prayer NOUN
  das **Gebet** (PL die **Gebete**)

precaution NOUN
  die **Vorsichtsmaßnahme** (PL die **Vorsichtsmaßnahmen**)
  to take precautions against something Vorsichtsmaßnahmen gegen etwas (ACC) ergreifen◇

precinct NOUN
  shopping precinct das Einkaufszentrum
  pedestrian precinct die Fußgängerzone

ℙ **indicates key words**

precisely ADVERB
genau
at eleven o'clock precisely um genau elf Uhr

ℓ to **prefer** VERB
1 vorziehen◇ SEP
I prefer Anna to her sister. Ich mag Anna lieber als ihre Schwester.
2 **to prefer to do something** etwas lieber tun
I prefer to stay at home. Ich bleibe lieber zu Hause.

pregnancy NOUN
die Schwangerschaft (PL die Schwangerschaften)

pregnant ADJECTIVE
schwanger

prejudice NOUN
das Vorurteil (PL die Vorurteile)
to fight against racial prejudice gegen Rassenvorurteile kämpfen

prejudiced ADJECTIVE
to be prejudiced voreingenommen sein

preparation NOUN
die Vorbereitung (PL die Vorbereitungen)
in preparation for something in Vorbereitung auf etwas (ACC)
our preparations for Christmas unsere Weihnachtsvorbereitungen

ℓ to **prepare** VERB
1 vorbereiten SEP
to prepare somebody for something jemanden auf etwas (ACC) vorbereiten
2 **to be prepared for the worst** sich auf das Schlimmste gefasst machen

prepared ADJECTIVE
bereit
I'm prepared to pay half. Ich bin bereit (PL die Hälfte zu zahlen.)

preposition NOUN
die Präposition (PL die Präpositionen)

prep school NOUN
die private Grundschule

prescription NOUN
das Rezept (PL die Rezepte)
on prescription auf Rezept

presence NOUN
die Anwesenheit
He admitted it in my presence. Er gab es in meiner Anwesenheit zu.

ℓ **present**
1 (a gift) das Geschenk (PL die Geschenke)
to give somebody a present jemandem ein Geschenk machen
2 (the time now) die Gegenwart
3 (in grammar)
the present (tense) das Präsens
in the present tense im Präsens

present ADJECTIVE
1 (attending) anwesend
Mr Jones is not present. Herr Jones ist nicht anwesend.
to be present at something bei etwas (DAT) anwesend sein
Fifty people were present at the funeral. Fünfzig Personen waren bei der Beerdigung anwesend.
2 (existing now) gegenwärtig
the present situation die gegenwärtige Lage
3 **at the present time** zur Zeit

to **present** VERB
1 überreichen (a prize)
2 (on TV, radio) moderieren (a programme)

presenter NOUN
(on TV) der Moderator (PL die Moderatoren), die Moderatorin (PL die Moderatorinnen)

> **WORD TIP** Professions, hobbies, and sports don't take an article in German: Er ist Moderator.

presently ADVERB
1 (now) momentan
2 (soon) bald

ℓ **president** NOUN
der Präsident (PL die Präsidenten), die Präsidentin (PL die Präsidentinnen)

> **WORD TIP** Professions, hobbies, and sports don't take an article in German: Er ist Präsident.

ℓ **press** NOUN
the press die Presse

to **press** VERB
1 (push) drücken
Press here! Hier drücken!
2 drücken auf (+ACC) (a button or switch)
She pressed the button. Sie hat auf den Knopf gedrückt.

press conference NOUN
die Pressekonferenz (PL die Pressekonferenzen)

pressure NOUN
der Druck
to put pressure on somebody jemanden unter Druck setzen

pressure group NOUN
die Interessengruppe (PL die Interessengruppen)

◇ irregular verb; SEP separable verb; for more help with verbs see centre section

ℐ **to pretend** VERB
    to pretend that ... so tun◇, als ob ...
    He's pretending not to hear. Er tut so, als
    ob er nichts hört.

ℐ **pretty** ADJECTIVE
    hübsch
    a pretty dress ein hübsches Kleid

    pretty ADVERB
    ziemlich
    It was pretty silly. Das war ziemlich blöd.

ℐ **to prevent** VERB
    **to prevent somebody from doing
    something** jemanden daran hindern, etwas
    zu tun
    **There's nothing to prevent you from
    leaving.** Niemand kann dich daran hindern
    zu gehen.

    previous ADJECTIVE
    1 (earlier) früher (years, opportunity, or job)
    2 (immediately preceding) vorig
    on the previous Tuesday am vorigen
    Dienstag

    previously ADVERB
    früher

ℐ **price** NOUN
    der Preis (PL die Preise)
    the price per kilo der Preis pro Kilo
    Trainers have gone up in price. Die
    Turnschuhe sind im Preis gestiegen.
    What is the price of petrol now? Was
    kostet Benzin jetzt?

    price list NOUN
    die Preisliste (PL die Preislisten)

    to prick VERB
    stechen◇
    to prick your finger sich (DAT) in den Finger
    stechen

    pride NOUN
    der Stolz

    priest NOUN
    der Priester (PL die Priester)

    WORD TIP Professions, hobbies, and sports
    don't take an article in German: Er ist Priester.

ℐ **primary (school) teacher** NOUN
    der Grundschullehrer
    (PL die Grundschullehrer), die
    Grundschullehrerin (PL die
    Grundschullehrerinnen)

    WORD TIP Professions, hobbies, and sports
    don't take an article in German: Sie ist
    Grundschullehrerin.

ℐ **primary school** NOUN
    die Grundschule (PL die Grundschulen)

ℐ **prime minister** NOUN
    der Premierminister (PL die
    Premierminister), die Premierministerin
    (PL die Premierministerinnen)

    WORD TIP Professions, hobbies, and sports
    don't take an article in German: Er ist
    Premierminister.

    prince NOUN
    der Prinz (PL die Prinzen)

    princess NOUN
    die Prinzessin (PL die Prinzessinnen)

ℐ **principal** ADJECTIVE
    (main) Haupt-

    principal NOUN
    (of a college) der Direktor (PL die
    Direktoren), die Direktorin (PL die
    Direktorinnen)

    WORD TIP Professions, hobbies, and sports
    don't take an article in German: Er ist Direktor.

    principle NOUN
    das Prinzip (PL die Prinzipien)
    on principle aus Prinzip
    That's true in principle. Im Prinzip stimmt
    das.

    print NOUN
    1 (letters) der Druck
    in small print klein gedruckt
    2 (a photo) der Abzug (PL die Abzüge)
    colour print der Farbabzug

    to print VERB
    drucken
    to print something out etwas ausdrucken
    SEP

ℐ **printer** NOUN
    (for a computer) der Drucker (PL die
    Drucker)

    printout NOUN
    der Ausdruck (PL die Ausdrucke)

    priority NOUN
    die Priorität (PL die Prioritäten)

    prison NOUN
    das Gefängnis (PL die Gefängnisse)
    in prison im Gefängnis

    prisoner NOUN
    der/die Gefangene (PL die Gefangenen)

ℐ **private** ADJECTIVE
    1 Privat-, privat
    private school die Privatschule
    private property das Privateigentum

ENGLISH—GERMAN

to have private lessons Privatstunden nehmen

2 in private privat

privately ADVERB
privat

ℰ **prize** NOUN
der Preis (PL die Preise)
to win a prize einen Preis gewinnen ◇

prize-giving NOUN
die Preisverleihung (PL die Preisverleihungen)

prizewinner NOUN
der Gewinner (PL die Gewinner), die Gewinnerin (PL die Gewinnerinnen)

ℰ **probable** ADJECTIVE
wahrscheinlich

probably ADVERB
wahrscheinlich

ℰ **problem** NOUN
das Problem (PL die Probleme)
It's a serious problem. Das ist ein ernstes Problem.
No problem! Kein Problem!

process NOUN
1 der Prozess (PL die Prozesse)
the peace process der Friedensprozess
2 to be in the process of doing something dabei sein, etwas zu tun

procession NOUN
1 (in parade) der Umzug (PL die Umzüge)
2 (at religious festival) die Prozession (PL die Prozessionen)

produce NOUN
(food) die Erzeugnisse (PLURAL)
local produce Erzeugnisse aus der Region

to **produce** VERB
1 herstellen SEP (goods, food)
2 vorzeigen SEP (a ticket, document)
I produced my passport. Ich habe meinen Pass vorgezeigt.
3 (create) erzeugen (interest, tension, heat, etc.)
It produces heat. Es erzeugt Wärme.
4 to produce a film einen Film produzieren
5 to produce a play ein Theaterstück inszenieren

producer NOUN
(of a film or programme) der Produzent (PL die Produzenten), die Produzentin (PL die Produzentinnen)

WORD TIP Professions, hobbies, and sports don't take an article in German: Er ist Produzent.

ℰ **product** NOUN
das Produkt (PL die Produkte)

production NOUN
1 (of a film or an opera) die Produktion (PL die Produktionen)
2 (of a play) die Inszenierung (PL die Inszenierungen)
a new production of Hamlet eine neue Inszenierung von Hamlet
3 (by a factory) die Produktion

profession NOUN
der Beruf (PL die Berufe)

professional NOUN
1 (a trained person) der Fachmann (PL die Fachleute)
2 (in sport) der Profi (PL die Profis)

professional ADJECTIVE
1 professionell
Her work looks very professional. Ihre Arbeit sieht sehr professionell aus.
2 Berufs-, Profi-
He's a professional footballer. Er ist Profifußballer.

professor NOUN
der Professor (PL die Professoren), die Professorin (PL die Professorinnen)

WORD TIP Professions, hobbies, and sports don't take an article in German: Er ist Professor.

profile NOUN
das Profil (PL die Profile)

profit NOUN
der Gewinn (PL die Gewinne)

profitable ADJECTIVE
rentabel

ℰ **program** NOUN
das Programm (PL die Programme)

ℰ **programme** NOUN
1 (for a play or an event) das Programm (PL die Programme)
2 (on TV or radio) die Sendung (PL die Sendungen)

programmer NOUN
der Programmierer (PL die Programmierer), die Programmiererin (PL die Programmiererinnen)

WORD TIP Professions, hobbies, and sports don't take an article in German: Er ist Programmierer.

ℰ **progress** NOUN
1 der Fortschritt (PL die Fortschritte)
to make progress Fortschritte machen
2 to be in progress im Gange sein

◇ **irregular verb;** SEP **separable verb; for more help with verbs see centre section**

ℓ **project** NOUN
  das **Projekt** (PL die **Projekte**)
  a project to build a bridge ein
  Brückenbauprojekt
  a project on volcanoes ein Projekt über
  Vulkane

projector NOUN
  der **Projektor** (PL die **Projektoren**)

ℓ **promise** NOUN
  das **Versprechen** (PL die **Versprechen**)
  to make somebody a promise jemandem
  ein Versprechen geben◇
  to keep a promise ein Versprechen halten◇
  It's a promise! Versprochen!

to **promise** VERB
  to promise something etwas versprechen◇
  I've promised to ring my mother. Ich habe
  versprochen, meine Mutter anzurufen.

to **promote** VERB
  to be promoted (in football) aufsteigen◇
  SEP (PERF sein), (at work) befördert werden◇
  (PERF sein)

ℓ **promotion** NOUN
  1 die **Beförderung**
  2 (in football) der **Aufstieg**
  3 (in advertising) die **Werbung**

promptly ADVERB
  1 (at once) **sofort**
    He promptly fell off again. Er fiel sofort
    wieder herunter.
  2 (quickly) **schnell**
    Please reply promptly. Bitte antworten Sie
    unverzüglich.
  3 (punctually) **pünktlich**
    They left promptly at five o'clock. Sie
    fuhren pünktlich um 5 Uhr ab.

pronoun NOUN
  (in grammar) das **Pronomen** (PL die
  Pronomen)

ℓ to **pronounce** VERB
  aussprechen◇ SEP
  You don't pronounce the 'c'. Das 'c' spricht
  man nicht aus.

pronunciation NOUN
  die **Aussprache**

ℓ **proof** NOUN
  der **Beweis** (PL die **Beweise**)
  There's no proof that ... Es gibt keine
  Beweise dafür, dass ...

propaganda NOUN
  die **Propaganda**

propeller NOUN
  der **Propeller** (PL die **Propeller**)

ℓ **proper** ADJECTIVE
  richtig
  the proper answer die richtige Antwort
  He's not a proper doctor. Er ist kein
  richtiger Arzt.
  Put the book back in its proper place. Stell
  das Buch an den richtigen Ort zurück.
  I need a proper meal. Ich brauche etwas
  Richtiges zu essen.

ℓ **properly** ADVERB
  richtig

property NOUN
  1 (your belongings) das **Eigentum**
  2 (land, premises) der **Besitz**
    'Private property' 'Privatbesitz'
  3 (house) das **Haus** (PL die **Häuser**)

to **propose** VERB
  1 (suggest) **vorschlagen**◇ SEP
  2 (marriage)
    He proposed to her. Er hat ihr einen
    Heiratsantrag gemacht.

ℓ to **protect** VERB
  schützen
  to protect somebody from something
  jemanden vor etwas (DAT) schützen

protection NOUN
  der **Schutz**

protein NOUN
  das **Protein** (PL die **Proteine**)

ℓ **protest** NOUN
  der **Protest** (PL die **Proteste**)
  in protest against something aus Protest
  gegen etwas (ACC)

to **protest** VERB
  protestieren
  to protest about something gegen etwas
  (ACC) protestieren

Protestant NOUN
  der **Protestant** (PL die **Protestanten**), die
  Protestantin (PL die **Protestantinnen**)
  He's a Protestant. Er ist Protestant.

Protestant ADJECTIVE
  protestantisch

  WORD TIP Adjectives never have capitals in
  German, even for religions.

protest march NOUN
  der **Protestmarsch** (PL die
  Protestmärsche)

ℓ **proud** ADJECTIVE
  stolz
  to be proud of somebody/something stolz

auf jemanden/etwas *(ACC)* sein
I was proud of my sister. Ich war stolz auf meine Schwester.

ℰ **to prove** *VERB*
beweisen◇

proverb *NOUN*
das Sprichwort (*PL* die Sprichwörter)

to provide *VERB*
zur Verfügung stellen

ℰ **provided, providing** *CONJUNCTION*
vorausgesetzt
provided it doesn't rain vorausgesetzt, es regnet nicht

prune *NOUN*
die Backpflaume (*PL* die Backpflaumen)

PS *ABBREVIATION*
PS

psychiatrist *NOUN*
der Psychiater (*PL* die Psychiater), die Psychiaterin (*PL* die Psychiaterinnen)

WORD TIP Professions, hobbies, and sports don't take an article in German: Sie ist Psychiaterin.

psychological *ADJECTIVE*
psychologisch

psychologist *NOUN*
der Psychologe (*PL* die Psychologen), die Psychologin (*PL* die Psychologinnen)

WORD TIP Professions, hobbies, and sports don't take an article in German: Sie ist Psychologin.

psychology *NOUN*
die Psychologie

PTO *ABBREVIATION*
b.w. bitte wenden

pub *NOUN*
die Kneipe (*PL* die Kneipen) *(informal)*

ℰ **public** *NOUN*
the public die Öffentlichkeit
It's not open to the public. Es ist für die Öffentlichkeit nicht zugänglich.
in public in aller Öffentlichkeit

public *ADJECTIVE*
öffentlich

ℰ **public holiday** *NOUN*
der gesetzliche Feiertag (*PL* die gesetzlichen Feiertage)
January 1st is a public holiday. Der erste Januar ist ein gesetzlicher Feiertag.

publicity *NOUN*
1 die Publicity
2 *(advertising)* die Werbung

public school *NOUN*
die Privatschule (*PL* die Privatschulen)

public transport *NOUN*
die öffentlichen Verkehrsmittel *(PLURAL)*

to publish *VERB*
veröffentlichen

publisher *NOUN*
1 der Verleger (*PL* die Verleger), die Verlegerin (*PL* die Verlegerinnen)
2 *(company)* der Verlag (*PL* die Verlage)

WORD TIP Professions, hobbies, and sports don't take an article in German: Er ist Verleger.

ℰ **pudding** *NOUN*
(dessert) der Nachtisch (*PL* die Nachtische)
For pudding we've got strawberries. Zum Nachtisch gibt es Erdbeeren.

puddle *NOUN*
die Pfütze (*PL* die Pfützen)

puff *NOUN*
(of smoke) das Wölkchen (*PL* die Wölkchen)

ℰ **to pull** *VERB*
1 ziehen◇
to pull a cart einen Wagen ziehen
He pulled a letter out of his pocket. Er zog einen Brief aus der Tasche.
2 ziehen◇ an *(+DAT)*
to pull a rope an einem Seil ziehen
She pulled my hair. Sie hat mich an den Haaren gezogen.
3 **He's pulling your leg!** Er nimmt dich auf den Arm. *(literally: He's picking you up in his arms.)*
• **to pull down**
1 herunterziehen◇ *SEP*
2 *(demolish)* abreißen◇ *SEP (a building)*
• **to pull in**
(at the roadside) an den Straßenrand fahren◇ *(PERF sein)*
• **to pull yourself together**
sich zusammenreißen◇ *SEP*

ℰ **pullover** *NOUN*
der Pullover (*PL* die Pullover)

pulse *NOUN*
der Puls
The doctor took my pulse. Der Arzt fühlte meinen Puls.

pump *NOUN*
die Pumpe (*PL* die Pumpen)

◇ **irregular verb;** *SEP* **separable verb; for more help with verbs see centre section**

bicycle pump die Fahrradpumpe

to **pump** VERB
pumpen
• to **pump up**
aufpumpen SEP

pumpkin NOUN
der Kürbis (PL die Kürbisse)

punch NOUN
1 (in boxing) der Faustschlag (PL die Faustschläge)
2 (drink) die Bowle (PL die Bowlen)

to **punch** VERB
1 He punched me in the stomach. Er hat mich in den Magen geboxt.
2 lochen (a ticket)

punctual ADJECTIVE
pünktlich

punctually ADVERB
pünktlich

punctuation NOUN
die Zeichensetzung

punctuation mark NOUN
das Satzzeichen (PL die Satzzeichen)

puncture NOUN
(flat tyre) die Reifenpanne (PL die Reifenpannen)
I've got a puncture. Ich habe eine Reifenpanne.

to **punish** VERB
bestrafen

punishment NOUN
die Strafe (PL die Strafen)

ᵱ **pupil** NOUN
der Schüler (PL die Schüler) die Schülerin (PL die Schülerinnen)

puppet NOUN
die Marionette (PL die Marionetten)

puppy NOUN
der junge Hund (PL die jungen Hunde)
a boxer puppy ein junger Boxer

pure ADJECTIVE
rein

ᵱ **purple** ADJECTIVE
lila ('lila' never changes)

ᵱ **purpose** NOUN
1 der Zweck (PL die Zwecke)
What's the purpose of it? Was hat das für einen Zweck?
2 on purpose absichtlich

She did it on purpose. Das hat sie absichtlich getan.
He closed the door on purpose. Er hat die Tür absichtlich zugemacht.

to **purr** VERB
schnurren

ᵱ **purse** NOUN
das Portemonnaie (PL die Portemonnaies)

ᵱ **push** NOUN
to give something a push etwas schieben◇

to **push** VERB
1 schubsen
He pushed me. Er hat mich geschubst.
2 (press) drücken auf (+ACC) (a bell or button)
to push somebody to do something jemanden zu etwas drängen
His teacher is pushing him to sit the exam. Sein Lehrer drängt ihn (PL die Prüfung zu machen.)
3 to push your way through the crowd sich durch die Menge drängeln
• to push something away
etwas wegschieben◇ SEP
She pushed her plate away. Sie schob ihren Teller weg.

pushchair NOUN
der Sportwagen (PL die Sportwagen)

ᵱ to **put** VERB
1 (place generally) tun◇
Put some milk in your tea. Tu etwas Milch in den Tee.
You can put the butter in the fridge. Du kannst die Butter in den Kühlschrank tun.
2 (lay flat) legen
She put the pencil on the desk. Sie hat den Bleistift auf den Schreibtisch gelegt.
3 (place upright) stellen
Where did you put my bag? Wo hast du meine Tasche hingestellt?
4 (write) schreiben◇
Put your address here. Schreiben Sie Ihre Adresse hierhin.
• to put away
wegräumen SEP
Put away your things. Räume deine Sachen weg.
• to put back
1 zurücktun◇ SEP, zurücklegen SEP, zurückstellen SEP (the translation of 'put back' depends on the way it is done: if it's placed lying down, use 'zurücklegen', if placed upright use 'zurückstellen' and if it could be either, use 'zurücktun')
I put it back in the drawer. Ich habe es in die Schublade zurückgetan.

2 (postpone) verschieben◇
**The meeting has been put back until
Thursday.** Die Besprechung ist auf
Donnerstag verschoben worden.

• **to put down**
(lying down) hinlegen SEP, (upright)
hinstellen SEP
Where can I put the vase down? Wo kann
ich die Vase hinstellen?

• **to put off**
1 (postpone) verschieben◇
He's put off my lesson till Thursday. Er hat
meine Stunde auf Donnerstag verschoben.
2 (turn off) ausmachen SEP
Don't forget to put off the lights. Vergiss
nicht, das Licht auszumachen.
3 **to put somebody off something** jemandem
die Lust an etwas (DAT) verderben◇
It really put me off my food. Das hat mir
wirklich den Appetit verdorben.
4 **to put somebody off doing something**
jemanden davon abbringen◇ SEP, etwas
zu tun
Don't be put off. Lass dich nicht davon
abbringen.

• **to put on**
1 anziehen◇ SEP (clothes)
I'll just put my shoes on. Ich ziehe nur
schnell meine Schuhe an.
2 auflegen SEP (a record)
I'm putting on Oasis. Ich lege Oasis auf.
3 (switch on) anmachen SEP (a light or the
heating)
Could you put the lamp on? Kannst du die
Lampe anmachen?

• **to put out**
1 (put outside) nach draußen tun◇, raustun◇
SEP (informal)
Have you put the rubbish out? Hast du den
Müll rausgebracht?
2 ausmachen SEP (a light or cigarette)
I've put the lights out. Ich habe das Licht
ausgemacht.
3 **to put out your hand** die Hand ausstrecken
SEP

• **to put up**
1 heben◇ (your hand)
2 aufhängen SEP (a picture or poster)
I've put up some posters in my room. Ich
habe ein paar Poster in meinem Zimmer
aufgehängt.
3 anschlagen◇ SEP (a notice)
4 erhöhen (the price)
They've put up the fare. Sie haben den
Fahrpreis erhöht.
5 (for the night)
Friends put me up. Ich habe bei Freunden

übernachtet.
Can you put me up on Friday? Kann ich
Freitag bei euch übernachten?

• **to put up with something**
etwas aushalten◇ SEP
I don't know how she puts up with it. Ich
weiß nicht, wie sie das aushält.

puzzle NOUN
(jigsaw) das Puzzle (PL die Puzzles)

puzzled ADJECTIVE
verdutzt

pyjamas PLURAL NOUN
der Schlafanzug (PL die Schlafanzüge)
a pair of pyjamas ein Schlafanzug
Where are my pyjamas? Wo ist mein
Schlafanzug?

WORD TIP In German, der Schlafanzug is
singular.

Qq

qualification NOUN
1 (ability, experience) die Qualifikation (PL die
Qualifikationen)
vocational qualifications berufliche
Qualifikationen
He did not have any qualifications. Er hatte
keinen Abschluss.
2 (on paper) das Zeugnis (PL die Zeugnisse)
I showed them my qualifications. Ich
zeigte ihnen meine Zeugnisse.

qualified ADJECTIVE
1 ausgebildet
She's a qualified ski instructor. Sie ist
ausgebildete Skilehrerin.
2 (having a degree or a diploma) Diplom-
a qualified engineer ein Diplomingenieur

to qualify VERB
1 (be eligible) berechtigt sein
We don't qualify for a reduction. Wir
bekommen keine Ermäßigung.
2 (in sport) sich qualifizieren
They qualified for the third round. Sie
haben sich für die dritte Runde qualifiziert.

quality NOUN
die Qualität
good quality products Waren von guter
Qualität

quantity NOUN
die Menge (PL die Mengen)

◇ irregular verb; SEP separable verb; for more help with verbs see centre section

quarrel NOUN
der Streit (PL die Streite)
to have a quarrel Streit haben

to **quarrel** VERB
sich streiten◇
They're always quarrelling. Sie streiten sich dauernd.

quarry NOUN
der Steinbruch (PL die Steinbrüche)

quarter NOUN
1 das Viertel (PL die Viertel)
a quarter of the price ein Viertel des Preises
three quarters of the class drei Viertel der Klasse
It's a quarter past ten. Es ist Viertel nach zehn.
It's a quarter to ten. Es ist Viertel vor zehn.
2 We meet at quarter to eight. Wir treffen uns um Viertel vor acht.
3 a quarter of an hour eine Viertelstunde
4 three quarters of an hour eine Dreiviertelstunde
5 an hour and a quarter eineinviertel Stunden

quarter finals PLURAL NOUN
das Viertelfinale (PL die Viertelfinale)
They are in the quarter finals. Sie sind im Viertelfinale.

quay NOUN
der Kai (PL die Kais)

ℙ **queen** NOUN
1 die Königin (PL die Königinnen)
2 (in chess, cards) die Dame (PL die Damen)

query NOUN
die Frage (PL die Fragen)
Are there any queries? Gibt es irgendwelche Fragen?

ℙ **question** NOUN
die Frage (PL die Fragen)
to ask somebody a question jemandem eine Frage stellen
I asked her a question. Ich habe ihr eine Frage gestellt.
It's out of the question. Das kommt nicht in Frage.

to **question** VERB
befragen (a person)

question mark NOUN
das Fragezeichen (PL die Fragezeichen)

questionnaire NOUN
der Fragebogen (PL die Fragebögen)

to fill in a questionnaire einen Fragebogen ausfüllen

queue NOUN
(of people, cars) die Schlange (PL die Schlangen)
to stand in a queue Schlange stehen◇
a queue of cars eine Autoschlange

to **queue** VERB
Schlange stehen◇
We had to queue for an hour. Wir mussten eine Stunde Schlange stehen.

ℙ **quick** ADJECTIVE
schnell
to have a quick lunch schnell etwas zu Mittag essen
It's quicker on the motorway. Auf der Autobahn geht es schneller.
to have a quick look at something sich (DAT) schnell etwas ansehen
Be quick! Mach schnell!

ℙ **quickly** ADVERB
schnell
I'll just quickly phone my mother. Ich rufe nur schnell meine Mutter an.

ℙ **quiet** ADJECTIVE
1 (silent) still
to keep quiet still sein
Please keep quiet. Sei bitte still.
2 (not loud) leise
The children are very quiet. Die Kinder sind ganz leise.
in a quiet voice mit leiser Stimme
3 (peaceful) ruhig
a quiet street eine ruhige Straße

ℙ **quietly** ADVERB
1 (speak, move) leise
He got up quietly. Er ist leise aufgestanden.
2 (read or play) ruhig
to sit quietly ruhig sitzen

ℙ **quilt** NOUN
die Steppdecke (PL die Steppdecken)

ℙ to **quit** VERB
1 aufhören SEP mit (smoking, for example)
2 (on computer) abbrechen◇ SEP

ℙ **quite** ADVERB
1 (fairly) ziemlich
It's quite cold outside. Es ist ziemlich kalt draußen.
quite often ziemlich oft
quite a few ziemlich viele
Quite a few of our friends came. Ziemlich viele unserer Freunde sind gekommen.
quite a few people ziemlich viele Leute

That's quite a good idea. Das ist eine ganz
gute Idee.

2 *(completely)* **ganz**
not quite nicht ganz
She's not quite ready. Sie ist noch nicht
ganz fertig.
It was quite amazing. Es war einfach
fantastisch.

3 **genau**
I don't quite know what he wants. Ich
weiß nicht genau, was er will.
Quite! Genau!

quiz NOUN
das Quiz (PL die Quiz)

quotation NOUN
(from a book) das Zitat (PL die Zitate)

quotation marks PLURAL NOUN
die Anführungszeichen *(PLURAL)*
in quotation marks in Anführungszeichen

quote NOUN
1 *(from a book)* das Zitat (PL die Zitate)
2 *(estimate)* der Kostenvoranschlag (PL die
Kostenvoranschläge)

to **quote** VERB
zitieren

Rr

rabbi NOUN
der Rabbiner (PL die Rabbiner), die
Rabbinerin (PL die Rabbinerinnen)

WORD TIP Professions, hobbies, and sports
don't take an article in German: Er ist Rabbiner.

rabbit NOUN
das Kaninchen (PL die Kaninchen)

rabies NOUN
die Tollwut

ℰ **race** NOUN
1 *(a sports event)* das Rennen (PL die Rennen)
cycle race das Radrennen
2 **to have a race** *(running)* um die Wette
laufen◇ *(PERF sein)*, *(swimming)* um die
Wette schwimmen◇ *(PERF sein)*
3 *(an ethnic group)* die Rasse (PL die Rassen)

racecourse NOUN
die Pferderennbahn (PL die
Pferderennbahnen)

racetrack NOUN
(for cars) die Rennbahn (PL die
Rennbahnen)

racial ADJECTIVE
rassisch, Rassen-
racial discrimination die
Rassendiskriminierung

racing NOUN
1 **horse racing** der Pferderennsport
2 **motor racing** der Autorennsport

racing car NOUN
der Rennwagen (PL die Rennwagen)

racing driver NOUN
der Rennfahrer (PL die Rennfahrer)die
Rennfahrerin (PL die Rennfahrerinnen)

WORD TIP Professions, hobbies, and sports don't
take an article in German: Er ist Rennfahrer.

racism NOUN
der Rassismus

racist NOUN
der Rassist (PL die Rassisten), die Rassistin
(PL die Rassistinnen)

racist ADJECTIVE
rassistisch

racket NOUN
1 *(for tennis)* der Schläger (PL die Schläger)
my tennis racket mein Tennisschläger
2 *(noise)* der Krach

radiation NOUN
die Strahlung (PL die Strahlungen)

radiator NOUN
der Heizkörper (PL die Heizkörper)

ℰ **radio** NOUN
das Radio (PL die Radios)
to listen to the radio Radio hören
I heard it on the radio. Ich habe es im Radio
gehört.

radioactive ADJECTIVE
radioaktiv

radio-controlled ADJECTIVE
ferngesteuert

radio station NOUN
die Rundfunkstation (PL die
Rundfunkstationen)

radish NOUN
das Radieschen (PL die Radieschen)

rag NOUN
der Lumpen (PL die Lumpen)

rage NOUN
die Wut
to fly into a rage in Wut geraten◇ *(PERF
sein)*

◇ irregular verb; SEP separable verb; for more help with verbs see centre section

She's in a rage. Sie ist wütend.
It's all the rage. Das ist der letzte Schrei.
(literally: it's the last scream)

rail NOUN
1 *(for a train)* die **Schiene** (PL die **Schienen**)
2 *(the railway)*
to go by rail mit der Bahn fahren
3 *(on a balcony, bridge, or stairs)* das **Geländer**
(PL die **Geländer**)

railcard NOUN
der **Bahnpass** (PL die **Bahnpässe**)

railing(s) NOUN
das **Geländer** (PL die **Geländer**)

ℱ**railway** NOUN
1 *(the system)* die **Bahn**
the railways die **Bahn** (SINGULAR)
2 **railway line** *(from one place to another)* die
Bahnlinie
3 **on the railway line** *(the track)* auf den
Gleisen

ℱ**railway station** NOUN
der **Bahnhof** (PL die **Bahnhöfe**)

ℱ**rain** NOUN
der **Regen**
in the rain im Regen
to rain VERB
regnen
It's raining. Es regnet.
It's going to rain. Es wird regnen.

rainbow NOUN
der **Regenbogen** (PL die **Regenbogen**)

raincoat NOUN
der **Regenmantel** (PL die **Regenmäntel**)

ℱ**rainy** ADJECTIVE
regnerisch

to raise VERB
1 *(lift up)* hochheben⬦ SEP
2 *(increase)* erhöhen *(prices)*
3 **to raise money for something** Geld für
etwas sammeln

raisin NOUN
die **Rosine** (PL die **Rosinen**)

rake NOUN
der **Rechen** (PL die **Rechen**)

rally NOUN
1 *(a meeting)* die **Versammlung** (PL die
Versammlungen)
2 *(for cars)* die **Rallye** (PL die **Rallyes**)
3 *(in tennis)* der **Ballwechsel** (PL die
Ballwechsel)

rambler NOUN
der **Wanderer** (PL die **Wanderer**), die
Wanderin (PL die **Wanderinnen**)

rambling NOUN
das **Wandern**

range NOUN
1 *(a choice)* die **Auswahl**
a wide range of travel brochures eine
große Auswahl an Reiseprospekten
2 **a range of subjects** verschiedene Fächer
in a range of colours in verschiedenen
Farben
3 **a computer in this price range** ein
Computer in dieser Preislage
That's out of my price range. Das kann ich
mir nicht leisten.

rap NOUN
der **Rap** *(music)*

rape NOUN
die **Vergewaltigung** (PL die
Vergewaltigungen)
to rape VERB
vergewaltigen

ℱ**rare** ADJECTIVE
1 selten
2 englisch gebraten *steak*
I like my steak rare. Ich mag mein Steak
englisch gebraten.

rarely ADVERB
selten

rash NOUN
der **Ausschlag** (PL die **Ausschläge**)
rash ADJECTIVE
voreilig

ℱ**raspberry** NOUN
die **Himbeere** (PL die **Himbeeren**)
raspberry jam die Himbeermarmelade

rat NOUN
die **Ratte** (PL die **Ratten**)

ℱ**rate** NOUN
1 *(a charge)* die **Gebühren** (PLURAL)
postage rates Postgebühren
2 **Are there special rates for children?** Gibt es
Sonderpreise für Kinder?
at reduced rates zu ermäßigten Preisen
3 **rate of exchange** der Wechselkurs
4 **rate of pay** die Bezahlung
5 *(a level)* die **Rate** (PL die **Raten**)
a high cancellation rate eine hohe
Absagerate
6 **at any rate** auf jeden Fall

ℱ indicates key words

rather ADVERB
1 lieber
I'd rather wait. Ich warte lieber.
I'd rather you didn't go. Es wäre mir lieber, wenn du nicht gingest.
2 ziemlich
I'm rather busy. Ich habe ziemlich viel zu tun.
I've got rather a lot of shopping to do. Ich muss noch ziemlich viel einkaufen.
3 **rather than** eher als
in summer rather than winter eher im Sommer als im Winter

raw ADJECTIVE
roh

razor NOUN
der Rasierapparat (PL die Rasierapparate)

razor blade NOUN
die Rasierklinge (PL die Rasierklingen)

RE NOUN
der Religionsunterricht

ℰ **reach** NOUN
die Reichweite
out of reach außer Reichweite
within reach leicht erreichbar
to be within easy reach of Munich von München aus leicht erreichbar sein

to **reach** VERB
1 ankommen◇ SEP (PERF sein) an (+DAT) (a place or point), ankommen◇ SEP (PERF sein) in (+DAT) (a town or country)
when you reach the station wenn du am Bahnhof ankommst
when you reach York wenn du in York ankommst
2 kommen◇ (PERF sein) zu (+DAT) (an agreement, a conclusion)
to reach a decision zu einer Entscheidung kommen
3 **to reach for something** nach etwas (DAT) greifen◇

to **react** VERB
reagieren

reaction NOUN
die Reaktion (PL die Reaktionen)

ℰ to **read** VERB
1 lesen◇
What are you reading at the moment? Was liest du zur Zeit?
I'm reading a detective novel. Ich lese einen Krimi.
2 **to read out** vorlesen◇ SEP
He read out the list to the students. Er hat

die Liste den Studenten vorgelesen.

ℰ **reading** NOUN
1 (action) das Lesen
2 (reading matter) die Lektüre
some easy reading for the holidays eine leichte Lektüre für die Ferien

ℰ **ready** ADJECTIVE
1 fertig
Supper's not ready yet. Das Essen ist noch nicht fertig.
We are not quite ready. Wir sind noch nicht ganz fertig.
Are you ready to leave? Seid ihr fertig? (on a journey) Seid ihr reisefertig?
to get ready sich fertig machen
I'm getting ready to play tennis. Ich mache mich zum Tennisspielen fertig.
I was getting ready for bed. Ich war gerade dabei, ins Bett zu gehen.
2 **to get something ready** etwas vorbereiten SEP
I'll get your room ready. Ich bereite dein Zimmer vor.
I'm getting the lunch ready. Ich mache das Mittagessen.

ℰ **real** ADJECTIVE
1 (genuine) echt
It's a real diamond. Das ist ein echter Brillant.
He's a real coward. Er ist ein echter Feigling.
2 (true) richtig
Is that her real name? Ist das ihr richtiger Name?
3 (not imagined) wirklich
It's a real pity you can't come. Es ist wirklich schade, dass du nicht kommen kannst.

realistic ADJECTIVE
realistisch

reality NOUN
die Wirklichkeit
a reality show eine Reality-Show

ℰ to **realize** VERB
1 wissen◇
I hadn't realized. Das hatte ich nicht gewusst.
I didn't realize he was French. Ich wusste nicht, dass er Franzose ist.
Do you realize what time it is? Weißt du, wie viel Uhr es ist?
2 (become aware) merken
I realized that he was joking. Ich merkte, dass er Witze machte.

◇ irregular verb; SEP separable verb; for more help with verbs see centre section

℘ **really** ADVERB
1 **wirklich**
The film was really good. Der Film war
wirklich gut.
Really? Wirklich?
2 **not really** eigentlich nicht

℘ **reason** NOUN
der **Grund** (PL die **Gründe**)
for that reason aus diesem Grund
the reason why I phoned der Grund meines
Anrufs

reasonable ADJECTIVE
(sensible) **vernünftig**

℘ **receipt** NOUN
die **Quittung** (PL die **Quittungen**)

℘ to **receive** VERB
erhalten◇

℘ **receiver** NOUN
der **Hörer** (PL die **Hörer**)
to pick up the receiver den Hörer
abnehmen◇ SEP

℘ **recent** ADJECTIVE
1 **kürzlich erfolgter/kürzlich erfolgte/
kürzlich erfolgtes**
the recent closure die kürzlich erfolgte
Schließung
2 **in recent years** in den letzten Jahren

recently ADVERB
1 (at a time not long ago) **kürzlich**
I saw her recently. Ich habe sie kürzlich
gesehen.
2 (over the recent period) **in letzter Zeit**
Prices have been going up recently. Die
Preise sind in letzter Zeit gestiegen.

reception NOUN
1 die **Rezeption** (PL die **Rezeptionen**)
He's waiting at reception. Er wartet an der
Rezeption.
2 der **Empfang** (PL die **Empfänge**)
a big wedding reception ein großer
Hochzeitsempfang
3 **to get a good reception** gut aufgenommen
werden

receptionist NOUN
1 der **Empfangschef** (PL die **Empfangschefs**),
die **Empfangsdame** (PL die
Empfangsdamen)
2 (in a doctor's surgery) die
Sprechstundenhilfe (PL die
Sprechstundenhilfen)

WORD TIP Professions, hobbies, and sports
don't take an article in German: Sie ist
Sprechstundenhilfe.

℘ **recipe** NOUN
das **Rezept** (PL die **Rezepte**)

to **reckon** VERB
glauben
I reckon it's a good idea. Ich glaube, das ist
eine gute Idee.

℘ to **recognize** VERB
erkennen◇

℘ to **recommend** VERB
empfehlen◇
Can you recommend a dentist? Kannst du
mir einen Zahnarzt empfehlen?
I recommend the fish soup. Ich empfehle
die Fischsuppe.

recommendation NOUN
die **Empfehlung** (PL die **Empfehlungen**)

℘ **record** NOUN
1 der **Rekord** (PL die **Rekorde**)
It's a world record. Das ist ein Weltrekord.
record sales Verkaufsrekorde
He broke the record. Er hat den Rekord
gebrochen.
the record holder der Rekordhalter
2 (of events) die **Aufzeichnung** (PL die
Aufzeichnungen)
on record aufgezeichnet
to keep a record of something über etwas
(ACC) Buch führen
3 (music) die **Platte** (PL die **Platten**)
a Miles Davis record eine Platte von Miles
Davis
4 **records** (office files) die **Unterlagen** (PLURAL)
I'll just check your records. Ich prüfe nur
Ihre Unterlagen.

to **record** VERB
aufnehmen◇ SEP
I'm recording it. Ich nehme es auf.

recorder NOUN
1 die **Blockflöte** (PL die **Blockflöten**)
Helen plays the recorder. Helen spielt
Blockflöte.

WORD TIP Don't use the article when you talk
about playing an instrument.

℘ **recording** NOUN
die **Aufnahme** (PL die **Aufnahmen**)

to **recover** VERB
(get better) **sich erholen**
She's recovered now. Sie hat sich wieder
erholt.

recovery NOUN
(from an illness) die **Erholung**
to make a good recovery sich gut erholen

℘ indicates key words

rectangle NOUN
das Rechteck (PL die Rechtecke)

rectangular ADJECTIVE
rechteckig

to recycle VERB
recyceln

recycling NOUN
das Recycling (PL die Wiederverwertung)

ℛ **red** ADJECTIVE
rot
a red car ein rotes Auto
to go red rot werden
to have red hair rote Haare haben

Red Cross NOUN
the Red Cross das Rote Kreuz

redcurrant NOUN
die Rote Johannisbeere (PL die Roten Johannisbeeren)

to redecorate VERB
(with paint) neu streichen◇, (with wallpaper) neu tapezieren
They've redecorated the kitchen. Sie haben die Küche neu gestrichen.

to redo VERB
noch einmal machen

ℛ **to reduce** VERB
1 **to reduce prices** die Preise herabsetzen SEP
2 **to reduce speed** die Geschwindigkeit verringern

ℛ **reduction** NOUN
1 (in price) die Ermäßigung (PL die Ermäßigungen)
2 (in speed or number) die Reduzierung

redundant ADJECTIVE
to be made redundant entlassen werden◇

referee NOUN
(in sport) der Schiedsrichter (PL die Schiedsrichter), die Schiedsrichterin (PL die Schiedsrichterinnen)

> **WORD TIP** Professions, hobbies, and sports don't take an article in German: Er ist Schiedsrichter.

reference NOUN
die Referenz (PL die Referenzen) (for a job)
She gave me a good reference. Sie hat mir eine gute Referenz gegeben.

reference book NOUN
das Nachschlagewerk (PL die Nachschlagewerke)

to refill VERB
nachfüllen SEP

to reflect VERB
spiegeln
to be reflected sich spiegeln

reflection NOUN
1 (in a mirror or on water) die Spiegelung (PL die Spiegelungen)
to see your reflection in the mirror sich im Spiegel sehen
2 (thought) die Überlegung
on reflection nach nochmaliger Überlegung

reflexive ADJECTIVE
(in grammar)
a reflexive verb ein reflexives Verb

refreshing ADJECTIVE
erfrischend

refreshment NOUN
die Erfrischung (PL die Erfrischungen)

refrigerator NOUN
der Kühlschrank (PL die Kühlschränke)

refugee NOUN
der Flüchtling (PL die Flüchtlinge)

refund NOUN
die Rückzahlung (PL die Rückzahlungen)

to refund VERB
zurückerstatten SEP

refusal NOUN
1 die Weigerung (PL die Weigerungen)
2 (for a job) die Absage (PL die Absagen)
to get a refusal eine Absage bekommen◇

refuse NOUN
(rubbish) der Abfall

to refuse VERB
sich weigern
I refused. Ich habe mich geweigert.
He refuses to help. Er weigert sich zu helfen.

regards PLURAL NOUN
die Grüße (PLURAL)
Regards to your parents. Viele Grüße an deine Eltern.
Nat sends his regards. Nat lässt grüßen.

reggae NOUN
der Reggae

ℛ **region** NOUN
das Gebiet (PL die Gebiete)

regional ADJECTIVE
regional

ℰ **register** NOUN
(in school) die **Anwesenheitsliste** (PL die **Anwesenheitslisten**)

to **register** VERB
sich anmelden SEP, **sich einschreiben**◇ SEP (for a course)
I registered for the course. Ich habe mich für den Kurs eingeschrieben.

registered letter NOUN
das **Einschreiben** (PL die **Einschreiben**)

registered post NOUN
to send something by registered post etwas per Einschreiben schicken

registration number NOUN
das **polizeiliche Kennzeichen** (PL die **polizeilichen Kennzeichen**)

to **regret** VERB
bedauern

regular ADJECTIVE
regelmäßig
regular visits regelmäßige Besuche

regularly ADVERB
regelmäßig

ℰ **regulation** NOUN
die **Vorschrift** (PL die **Vorschriften**)

rehearsal NOUN
die **Probe** (PL die **Proben**)

to **rehearse** VERB
proben

to **reheat** VERB
aufwärmen SEP

reindeer NOUN
das **Rentier** (PL die **Rentiere**)

to **reject** VERB
ablehnen SEP

related ADJECTIVE
verwandt
We're not related. Wir sind nicht verwandt.

ℰ **relation** NOUN
der/die **Verwandte** (PL die **Verwandten**)

relationship NOUN
die **Beziehung** (PL die **Beziehungen**)
I have a good relationship with my parents. Ich habe eine gute Beziehung zu meinen Eltern.

relative NOUN
der/die **Verwandte** (PL die **Verwandten**)

relatively ADVERB
relativ

ℰ to **relax** VERB
sich entspannen
I'm going to relax and watch telly tonight.
Heute Abend entspanne ich mich und sehe fern.

relaxation NOUN
die **Entspannung**
There wasn't much time for relaxation. Es gab nicht viel Zeit zur Entspannung.

relaxed ADJECTIVE
entspannt

relaxing ADJECTIVE
entspannend

relay race NOUN
die **Staffel** (PL die **Staffeln**)

release NOUN
1 (a film or book) die **Neuerscheinung** (PL die **Neuerscheinungen**)
2 (of a prisoner or hostage) die **Freilassung** (PL die **Freilassungen**)

to **release** VERB
1 **herausbringen**◇ SEP (a film or book)
2 **freilassen**◇ SEP (a person)

ℰ **reliable** ADJECTIVE
zuverlässig

relief NOUN
die **Erleichterung**
What a relief! Da bin ich aber erleichtert!

to **relieve** VERB
lindern pain

relieved ADJECTIVE
erleichtert
I was relieved to hear you'd arrived.
Ich war erleichtert zu hören, dass du angekommen bist.

religion NOUN
die **Religion** (PL die **Religionen**)

religious ADJECTIVE
religiös

ℰ to **rely** VERB
1 (trust)
to rely on somebody sich auf jemanden verlassen◇
I'm relying on your help for Saturday.
Ich verlasse mich darauf, dass du mir am Samstag hilfst.
2 (be dependent on) **to rely on** angewiesen sein auf (+ACC)

ℰ indicates key words

ℓ to **remain** *VERB*
1 *(be left over)* übrig bleiben◇ *(PERF sein)*
2 *(stay)* bleiben◇ *(PERF sein)*
  She remained absolutely still. Sie blieb ganz still.

remark *NOUN*
  die Bemerkung *(PL die Bemerkungen)*
  to make remarks about something
  Bemerkungen über etwas *(ACC)* machen

remarkable *ADJECTIVE*
  bemerkenswert

remarkably *ADVERB*
  bemerkenswert

ℓ to **remember** *VERB*
1 sich erinnern an *(+ACC) (a person or an occasion)*
  I don't remember. Daran kann ich mich nicht erinnern.
  Do you remember the holiday in Italy? Erinnerst du dich noch an die Ferien in Italien?
2 **I can't remember his number.** Seine Nummer fällt mir nicht ein.
3 **to remember to do something** daran denken◇, etwas zu tun
  Remember to lock the door. Denk daran abzuschließen.
  I remembered to bring the cake. Ich habe daran gedacht *(PL die kuchen mitzubringen).*

ℓ to **remind** *VERB*
1 erinnern
  to remind somebody to do something jemanden daran erinnern, etwas zu tun
  Remind your mother to pick me up. Erinnere deine Mutter daran, mich abzuholen.
  He reminds me of my brother. Er erinnert mich an meinen Bruder.
2 **Oh, that reminds me, ...** Dabei fällt mir ein, ...

remote *ADJECTIVE*
  abgelegen

remote control *NOUN*
1 *(for a car or plane)* die Fernsteuerung *(PL die Fernsteuerungen)*
2 *(for TV)* die Fernbedienung *(PL die Fernbedienungen)*

to **remove** *VERB*
1 entfernen *(a stain, mark, or obstacle)*
2 ausziehen◇ *SEP (clothes)*

to **renew** *VERB*
  verlängern *(a passport or licence)*

ℓ **rent** *NOUN*
  die Miete *(PL die Mieten)*
to **rent** *VERB*
  mieten
  Simon's rented a flat. Simon hat eine Wohnung gemietet.

  WORD TIP Do not translate the English word rent with the German Rente.

to **reorganize** *VERB*
  umorganisieren

ℓ **repair** *NOUN*
  die Reparatur *(PL die Reparaturen)*
to **repair** *VERB*
  reparieren
  to get something repaired etwas reparieren lassen◇
  We've had the television repaired. Wir haben unseren Fernseher reparieren lassen.

to **repay** *VERB*
  zurückzahlen *SEP*

ℓ **repeat** *NOUN*
  die Wiederholung *(PL die Wiederholungen)*
to **repeat** *VERB*
  wiederholen

repetitive *ADJECTIVE*
  eintönig

ℓ to **replace** *VERB*
  ersetzen

ℓ **reply** *NOUN*
  die Antwort *(PL die Antworten)*
  I didn't get a reply to my letter. Ich habe keine Antwort auf meinen Brief bekommen.
  There's no reply. Niemand antwortet.
to **reply** *VERB*
  antworten
  I still haven't replied to the letter. Ich habe immer noch nicht auf den Brief geantwortet.

ℓ **report** *NOUN*
1 *(of an event)* der Bericht *(PL die Berichte)*
2 *(school report)* das Zeugnis *(PL die Zeugnisse)*
to **report** *VERB*
1 melden *(a problem or an accident)*
  We've reported the theft. Wir haben den Diebstahl gemeldet.
2 sich melden
  I had to report to reception. Ich musste mich an der Rezeption melden.
3 *(in the news)* berichten

◇ irregular verb; *SEP* separable verb; for more help with verbs see centre section

to report on the strike über den Streik berichten

reporter NOUN
der **Reporter** (PL die **Reporter**), die **Reporterin** (PL die **Reporterinnen**)

> **WORD TIP** Professions, hobbies, and sports don't take an article in German: Er ist Reporter.

to **represent** VERB
1 **darstellen** SEP (a word, a thing, an idea)
2 **vertreten**◇ (a group or company)

representative NOUN
der **Vertreter** (PL die **Vertreter**), die **Vertreterin** (PL die **Vertreterinnen**)

reproduction NOUN
1 (process) die **Fortpflanzung** (PL die **Fortpflanzungen**)
2 (of sound etc) die **Wiedergabe**
3 (copy) die **Reproduktion** (PL die **Reproduktionen**)

reptile NOUN
das **Reptil** (PL die **Reptilien**)

republic NOUN
die **Republik** (PL die **Republiken**)

reputation NOUN
1 der **Ruf**
to have a good reputation einen guten Ruf haben
2 **She has a reputation for honesty.** Sie gilt als ehrlich.

request NOUN
die **Bitte** (PL die **Bitten**)
at my mother's request auf Bitte meiner Mutter

to **request** VERB
bitten◇
to request something um etwas (ACC) bitten

rescue NOUN
die **Rettung**
rescue operation die Rettungsaktion
to come to somebody's rescue jemandem zu Hilfe kommen

to **rescue** VERB
retten
They rescued the dog. Sie haben den Hund gerettet.

rescue party NOUN
die **Rettungsmannschaft** (PL die **Rettungsmannschaften**)

research NOUN
1 die **Forschung**
for research into Aids für die Aidsforschung

2 **to do research** forschen

to **research** VERB
to research (into) something etwas erforschen

resemblance NOUN
die **Ähnlichkeit** (PL die **Ähnlichkeiten**)

reservation NOUN
(a booking) die **Reservierung** (PL die **Reservierungen**)
to make a reservation (for a room) (ein Zimmer) reservieren lassen◇

reserve NOUN
1 die **Reserve** (PL die **Reserven**)
We have a few in reserve. Wir haben ein paar in Reserve.
2 **nature reserve** das Naturschutzgebiet
3 (for a match) der **Reservespieler** (PL die **Reservespieler**), die **Reservespielerin** (PL die **Reservespielerinnen**)

to **reserve** VERB
reservieren
This table is reserved. Dieser Tisch ist reserviert.

reservoir NOUN
das **Reservoir** (PL die **Reservoirs**)

resident NOUN
der **Bewohner** (PL die **Bewohner**), die **Bewohnerin** (PL die **Bewohnerinnen**)

residential ADJECTIVE
Wohn-
a residential area eine Wohngegend

to **resign** VERB
1 (from your job) **kündigen**
2 (from an official post) **zurücktreten**◇ SEP

resignation NOUN
1 die **Kündigung** (PL die **Kündigungen**)
2 (from an official post) der **Rücktritt** (PL die **Rücktritte**)

to **resist** VERB
widerstehen◇ (+DAT) (an offer or temptation)

to **resit** VERB
wiederholen (an exam)

resort NOUN
1 (for holidays)
holiday resort der Urlaubsort
ski resort der Wintersportort
seaside resort das Seebad
2 **as a last resort** als letzter Ausweg

respect NOUN
der **Respekt**

to respect *VERB*
respektieren

respectable *ADJECTIVE*
anständig

responsibility *NOUN*
die **Verantwortung** (*PL* die
Verantwortungen)

ℰ **responsible** *ADJECTIVE*
1 verantwortlich
He was responsible for the accident. Er
war für den Unfall verantwortlich.
I'm responsible for booking the rooms.
Ich bin für die Zimmerreservierung
verantwortlich.
2 (*reliable*) verantwortungsbewusst
He's not very responsible. Er ist nicht sehr
verantwortungsbewusst.

ℰ **rest** *NOUN*
1 the rest der Rest
the rest of the day der Rest des Tages
the rest of the bread der Brotrest, der Rest
von dem Brot
2 (*the others*) **the rest** die Übrigen
The rest have gone home. Die Übrigen sind
nach Hause gegangen.
3 die Erholung
He's going to the mountains for a rest. Er
fährt zur Erholung ins Gebirge.
ten days' rest zehn Tage Erholung
to have a rest sich ausruhen *SEP*
4 (*a short break*) die Pause (*PL* die **Pausen**)
to stop for a rest eine Pause machen

to rest *VERB*
(*have a rest*) sich ausruhen *SEP*

ℰ **restaurant** *NOUN*
das **Restaurant** (*PL* die **Restaurants**)

restless *ADJECTIVE*
unruhig

to restrain *VERB*
zurückhalten◇ *SEP*

ℰ **result** *NOUN*
1 das **Ergebnis** (*PL* die **Ergebnisse**)
the exam results die Prüfungsergebnisse
2 **as a result** infolgedessen
As a result we missed the train.
Infolgedessen haben wir den Zug verpasst.

to retire *VERB*
1 (*from work*) in den Ruhestand gehen◇
(*PERF* sein), (*civil servant, teacher, soldier*) in
Pension gehen◇ (*PERF* sein)
She retires in June. Sie geht im Juni in
Pension.
2 **to be retired** im Ruhestand sein◇

retirement *NOUN*
der Ruhestand
since his retirement seitdem er in den
Ruhestand gegangen ist

ℰ **return** *NOUN*
1 (*coming back*) die **Rückkehr**
the return journey die Rückreise
2 **by return of post** postwendend
3 **in return for** für
in return for his help für seine Hilfe
4 **Many happy returns!** Herzlichen
Glückwunsch zum Geburtstag!
5 (*on train or bus*) die **Rückfahrkarte** (*PL* die
Rückfahrkarten)

to return *VERB*
1 (*come back*) zurückkommen◇ *SEP* (*PERF*
sein)
He returned ten minutes later. Er kam zehn
Minuten später zurück.
to return from holiday aus den Ferien
zurückkommen
2 (*go back*) zurückgehen◇ *SEP* (*PERF* sein),
(*drive*) zurückfahren◇ *SEP* (*PERF* sein)
We are planning to return in the evening.
Wir wollen am Abend zurückfahren.
3 (*give back*) zurückgeben◇ *SEP*
Gemma's never returned the dress.
Gemma hat das Kleid nie zurückgegeben.

return fare *NOUN*
der Preis für eine Rückfahrkarte (*for a
flight*) der Preis für einen Rückflugschein

return ticket *NOUN*
die **Rückfahrkarte** (*PL* die **Rückfahrkarten**)
(*for a flight*) das **Rückflugticket** (*PL* die
Rückflugtickets)

reunion *NOUN*
das **Treffen** (*PL* die **Treffen**)
We had a class reunion. Wir hatten ein
Klassentreffen.

to reveal *VERB*
enthüllen

to reverse *VERB*
1 (*in a car*) rückwärts fahren◇ (*PERF* sein)
2 **to reverse the charges** ein R-Gespräch
führen

review *NOUN*
(*of a book, play, or film*) die **Kritik** (*PL* die
Kritiken)

to review *VERB*
rezensieren (*a book, play, or film*)

to revise *VERB*
1 lernen (*for an exam*)
Tessa's revising for her exams. Tessa lernt

◇ **irregular verb;** *SEP* **separable verb; for more help with verbs see centre section**

für ihre Prüfung.

2 wiederholen
to revise maths Mathe wiederholen

revision NOUN
die **Wiederholung**

to **revive** VERB
1 (a person) **wiederbeleben** SEP
2 (recover) **sich erholen**

revolting ADJECTIVE
eklig

revolution NOUN
die **Revolution** (PL die **Revolutionen**)

revolving door NOUN
die **Drehtür** (PL die **Drehtüren**)

ℛ **reward** NOUN
die **Belohnung** (PL die **Belohnungen**)

to **reward** VERB
belohnen

rhinoceros NOUN
das **Nashorn** (PL die **Nashörner**)

rhubarb NOUN
der **Rhabarber**

rhyme NOUN
der **Reim** (PL die **Reime**)

rhythm NOUN
der **Rhythmus** (PL die **Rhythmen**)

rib NOUN
die **Rippe** (PL die **Rippen**)

ribbon NOUN
das **Band** (PL die **Bänder**)

ℛ **rice** NOUN
der **Reis**
rice pudding der **Milchreis**

ℛ **rich** ADJECTIVE
1 reich
They are very rich. Sie sind sehr reich.
2 the rich die **Reichen**

ℛ **rid** ADJECTIVE
to get rid of something etwas **loswerden**◇
SEP (PERF **sein**)
We got rid of the car. Wir sind das Auto
losgeworden.

riddle NOUN
das **Rätsel** (PL die **Rätsel**)

ℛ **ride** NOUN
die **Fahrt** (PL die **Fahrten**)
to go for a ride (on a bike) eine Fahrt (mit
dem Fahrrad) machen

to go for a ride (on a horse) reiten gehen◇
(PERF **sein**)
He took me for a ride in his new car. Er hat
mich in seinem neuen Auto mitgenommen.

to **ride** VERB
1 to ride a bike Rad fahren◇ (PERF **sein**)
Can you ride a bike? Kannst du Rad fahren?
I've never ridden a bike. Ich bin noch nie
Rad gefahren.
2 to ride (a horse) reiten◇ (PERF **sein**)
I've never ridden a horse. Ich bin noch nie
auf einem Pferd geritten.

rider NOUN
1 (on a horse) der **Reiter** (PL die **Reiter**), die
Reiterin (PL die **Reiterinnen**)
2 (on a bike) der **Radfahrer** (PL die **Radfahrer**),
die **Radfahrerin** (PL die **Radfahrerinnen**)
3 (on a motorbike) der **Fahrer** (PL die **Fahrer**),
die **Fahrerin** (PL die **Fahrerinnen**)

ridiculous ADJECTIVE
lächerlich

ℛ **riding** NOUN
das **Reiten**
to go riding reiten gehen◇ (PERF **sein**)

riding school NOUN
die **Reitschule** (PL die **Reitschulen**)

rifle NOUN
das **Gewehr** (PL die **Gewehre**)

ℛ **right** NOUN
1 (not left) die **rechte Seite**
on the right auf der rechten Seite
on my right rechts von mir
2 (to do something) das **Recht** (PL die **Rechte**)
to have the right to something ein Recht
auf etwas (ACC) haben
the right to work das Recht auf Arbeit
You have no right to say that. Du hast kein
Recht, das zu sagen.

right ADJECTIVE
1 (not left) **rechter/rechte/rechtes**
my right hand meine rechte Hand
2 (correct) **richtig**
the right answer die richtige Antwort
Is this the right address? Ist das die richtige
Adresse?
3 to be right (of a person) Recht haben
You see, I was right. Siehst du, ich hatte
Recht.
4 You were right not to say anything. Du
hattest Recht, nichts zu sagen.
5 The clock is right. Die Uhr geht richtig.
6 Yes, that's right. Ja, das stimmt.
Is that right? Stimmt das?

right ADVERB
1 (direction) rechts
Turn right at the lights. Biege an der Ampel rechts ab.
2 (correctly) richtig
You're not doing it right. Du machst das nicht richtig.
3 (completely) ganz
right at the bottom ganz unten
right at the beginning ganz am Anfang
4 (exactly) genau
right in the middle genau in der Mitte
5 **right now** sofort
6 (okay) gut
Right, let's go. Gut, gehen wir.

right-click NOUN
der Klick mit der rechten Maustaste

to **right-click** VERB
Right-click (on) the icon. Das Symbol mit der rechten Maustaste anklicken.

right-hand ADJECTIVE
on the right-hand side rechts

right-handed ADJECTIVE
rechtshändig
I'm right-handed. Ich bin Rechtshänder.

♪ **ring** NOUN
1 (on the phone)
to give somebody a ring jemanden anrufen✧ SEP
2 (for your finger) der Ring (PL die Ringe)
3 (circle) der Kreis (PL die Kreise)
4 **There was a ring at the door.** Es hat geklingelt.

to **ring** VERB
1 (a bell or phone) klingeln
The phone rang. Das Telefon klingelte.
2 (phone) anrufen✧ SEP
I'll ring you tomorrow. Ich rufe dich morgen an.
3 **to ring for a taxi** ein Taxi rufen✧
• **to ring back**
zurückrufen✧ SEP
I'll ring you back later. Ich rufe dich später zurück.
• **to ring off**
auflegen SEP

ring road NOUN
die Ringstraße (PL die Ringstraßen)

ringtone NOUN
der Klingelton (PL die Klingeltöne)

to **rinse** VERB
spülen

riot NOUN
der Aufstand (PL die Aufstände)

rioting NOUN
die Unruhen (PLURAL)

to **rip** VERB
zerreißen✧

ripe ADJECTIVE
reif
Are the tomatoes ripe? Sind die Tomaten reif?

rip-off NOUN
It's a rip-off. Das ist Nepp. (informal)

♪ **rise** NOUN
1 der Anstieg
a rise in temperature ein Temperaturanstieg
2 **pay rise** die Gehaltserhöhung

to **rise** VERB
1 (the sun) aufgehen✧ SEP (PERF sein)
2 (prices) steigen✧ (PERF sein)

♪ **risk** NOUN
das Risiko (PL die Risiken)
to take a risk ein Risiko eingehen✧ SEP (PERF sein)

to **risk** VERB
riskieren
He risks losing his job. Er riskiert es, seine Stelle zu verlieren.

rival NOUN
der Rivale (PL die Rivalen), die Rivalin (PL die Rivalinnen)

♪ **river** NOUN
der Fluss (PL die Flüsse)
There were boats on the river. Auf dem Fluss waren Boote.
a house on the river ein Haus am Fluss

♪ **road** NOUN
1 die Straße (PL die Straßen)
the road to London die Straße nach London
2 **The baker's is on the other side of the road.** Die Bäckerei ist auf der anderen Straßenseite.
3 **across the road** gegenüber
They live across the road from us. Sie wohnen bei uns gegenüber.

road accident NOUN
der Verkehrsunfall (PL die Verkehrsunfälle)

road map NOUN
die Straßenkarte (PL die Straßenkarten)

roadside NOUN
by the roadside am Straßenrand

✧ irregular verb; SEP separable verb; for more help with verbs see centre section

⚑ **road sign** NOUN
das Straßenschild (PL die Straßenschilder)

roadworks PLURAL NOUN
die Straßenarbeiten (PLURAL)

⚑ **roast** NOUN
der Braten (PL die Braten)

roast ADJECTIVE
gebraten
roast potatoes Bratkartoffeln
roast beef der Rinderbraten

to **rob** VERB
1 berauben (a person)
2 ausrauben SEP (a bank)

robber NOUN
der Räuber (PL die Räuber)

robbery NOUN
der Raub (PL die Raube)
bank robbery der Bankraub

robot NOUN
der Roboter (PL die Roboter)

rock NOUN
1 (a big stone) der Felsen (PL die Felsen)
2 (the material) der Fels
3 (music) der Rock
rock band die Rockband
to dance rock and roll Rock 'n' Roll tanzen

rock climbing NOUN
das Klettern
to go rock climbing (zum) Klettern gehen◇
(PERF sein)

rocket NOUN
die Rakete (PL die Raketen)

rock music NOUN
die Rockmusik

rock star NOUN
der Rockstar (PL die Rockstars)

rocky ADJECTIVE
felsig

rod NOUN
a fishing rod eine Angel

role NOUN
die Rolle (PL die Rollen)
to play the role of Hamlet die Rolle des
Hamlet spielen

⚑ **roll** NOUN
1 die Rolle (PL die Rollen)
a toilet roll eine Rolle Toilettenpapier
2 **bread roll** das Brötchen (PL die Semmel) (in
Southern Germany and Austria)

to **roll** VERB
1 rollen
They rolled the barrel across the yard. Sie
haben das Fass über den Hof gerollt.
2 rollen (PERF sein)
The money rolled under the bed. Das Geld
ist unters Bett gerollt.

roller NOUN
1 (for hair) der Lockenwickler (PL die
Lockenwickler)
2 (for paint) die Rolle (PL die Rollen)

to **Rollerblade** VERB
inlineskaten

Rollerblades® PLURAL NOUN
die Inlineskates (PLURAL) die Inliners (PLURAL)

roller coaster NOUN
die Achterbahn (PL die Achterbahnen)

to **roller skate** VERB
Rollschuh laufen◇ (PERF sein)

roller skates PLURAL NOUN
die Rollschuhe (PLURAL)

Roman Catholic ADJECTIVE
römisch-katholisch

> **WORD TIP** Adjectives never have capitals in
> German, even for religions.

⚑ **romantic** ADJECTIVE
romantisch

roof NOUN
das Dach (PL die Dächer)

roof rack NOUN
der Dachgepäckträger (PL die
Dachgepäckträger)

rook NOUN
1 (in chess) der Turm (PL die Türme)
2 (bird) die Saatkrähe (PL die Saatkrähen)

⚑ **room** NOUN
1 das Zimmer (PL die Zimmer)
She's in the other room. Sie ist im anderen
Zimmer.
a three-room flat eine
Dreizimmerwohnung
2 (space) der Platz
enough room for two genug Platz für zwei
very little room wenig Platz
to make room Platz machen

root NOUN
die Wurzel (PL die Wurzeln)

rope NOUN
das Seil (PL die Seile)

rose NOUN
die Rose (PL die Rosen)

to **rot** VERB
verfaulen (PERF sein)

rotten ADJECTIVE
verfault

rough ADJECTIVE
1 (scratchy) rau
2 (vague) grob (plan or estimate)
3 a rough idea eine vage Vorstellung
4 (stormy) stürmisch
  a rough sea eine stürmische See
5 (difficult)
  to have a rough time es schwer haben
6 to sleep rough auf der Straße leben

roughly ADVERB
(approximately) ungefähr
roughly ten per cent ungefähr zehn Prozent
It takes roughly three hours. Es dauert ungefähr drei Stunden.

round NOUN
die Runde (PL die Runden)
a round of talks eine Gesprächsrunde
a round of drinks eine Runde

round ADJECTIVE
rund
a round table ein runder Tisch

round PREPOSITION
1 um (+ACC)
  round the city um die Stadt
  round my arm um meinen Arm
  They were sitting round the table. Sie haben um den Tisch gesessen.
  It's just round the corner. Es ist gleich um die Ecke.
  They showed us round the town. Sie haben uns die Stadt gezeigt.
2 to go round a museum ein Museum besuchen
3 to look round the shops sich in den Geschäften umsehen SEP

round ADVERB
1 to go round to somebody's house jemanden besuchen
2 to invite somebody round jemanden zu sich (DAT) einladen SEP
  We invited Sally round for lunch. Wir haben Sally zum Mittagessen eingeladen.
3 to pass something round etwas herumgehen lassen
4 all the year round das ganze Jahr hindurch

roundabout NOUN
1 (for traffic) der Kreisverkehr
2 (in a fairground) das Karussell (PL die Karussells)

route NOUN
1 (that you plan) die Route (PL die Routen)
  The best route is via Calais. Die beste Route führt über Calais.
2 bus route die Buslinie

routine NOUN
die Routine (PL die Routinen)

row[1] NOUN
1 (a quarrel) der Krach (informal) (PL die Kräche)
  to have a row Krach haben
  I had a row with my parents. Ich habe Krach mit meinen Eltern gehabt.
2 (noise) der Krach
  They were making a terrible row. Sie haben einen furchtbaren Krach gemacht.

row[2] NOUN
1 die Reihe (PL die Reihen)
  in the front row in der ersten Reihe
  in the back row in der letzten Reihe
2 in a row hintereinander
  four times in a row viermal hintereinander

to **row** VERB
1 (in a boat) rudern (PERF sein)
  We rowed across the lake. Wir sind über den See gerudert.
2 (a boat, a person) rudern
  He rowed us across the lake. Er hat uns über den See gerudert.

rowing NOUN
das Rudern
to go rowing rudern gehen (PERF sein)

rowing boat NOUN
das Ruderboot (PL die Ruderboote)

royal ADJECTIVE
königlich
the royal family die königliche Familie

to **rub** VERB
reiben
to rub your eyes sich (DAT) die Augen reiben
• to rub something out etwas ausradieren SEP

rubber NOUN
1 (an eraser) der Radiergummi (PL die Radiergummis)
2 (material) der Gummi
  rubber soles Gummisohlen

rubbish NOUN
1 (for the bin) der Müll
2 (nonsense) der Quatsch (informal)
  You're talking rubbish! Du redest Quatsch!

◇ irregular verb; SEP separable verb; for more help with verbs see centre section

rubbish *ADJECTIVE*
schlecht
The film was rubbish. Der Film war schlecht.
They're a rubbish band. Sie sind eine lausige Band. *(informal)*

rubbish bin *NOUN*
der **Mülleimer** (*PL* die **Mülleimer**)

ℓ **rucksack** *NOUN*
der **Rucksack** (*PL* die **Rucksäcke**)

rude *ADJECTIVE*
1 unhöflich
That's rude. Das ist unhöflich.
2 unanständig
a rude joke ein unanständiger Witz

rug *NOUN*
1 der **Teppich** (*PL* die **Teppiche**)
2 *(a blanket)* die **Decke** (*PL* die **Decken**)

rugby *NOUN*
das **Rugby**

ruin *NOUN*
(remains) die **Ruine** (*PL* die **Ruinen**)
in ruins in Trümmern

to **ruin** *VERB*
1 ruinieren
You'll ruin your jacket. Du ruinierst dir die Jacke.
2 verderben◇ *(day, holiday)*
It ruined my evening. Das hat mir den Abend verdorben.

ℓ **rule** *NOUN*
1 die **Regel** (*PL* die **Regeln**)
the rules of the game die Spielregeln
as a rule in der Regel
2 *(administrative)* die **Vorschrift** (*PL* die **Vorschriften**)
according to the school rules nach den Schulvorschriften

ruler *NOUN*
das **Lineal** (*PL* die **Lineale**)
I've lost my ruler. Ich habe mein Lineal verloren.

rum *NOUN*
der **Rum**

rumour *NOUN*
das **Gerücht** (*PL* die **Gerüchte**)

ℓ **run** *NOUN*
1 *(in games, sport, and for fitness)* der **Lauf** (*PL* die **Läufe**)
to go for a run laufen gehen◇ *(PERF sein)*, joggen gehen◇ *(PERF sein)*
2 *(of a play)* die **Laufzeit**

3 *(in skiing)* die **Abfahrt** (*PL* die **Abfahrten**)
4 **in the long run** auf lange Sicht

to **run** *VERB*
1 laufen◇ *(PERF sein)*
I ran ten kilometres. Ich bin zehn Kilometer gelaufen.
He ran across the pitch. Er ist über das Spielfeld gelaufen.
2 *(run fast)* rennen◇ *(PERF sein)*
Kitty ran for the bus. Kitty rannte, um den Bus zu kriegen.
3 *(drive)* fahren◇
I'll run you home later. Ich fahre dich später nach Hause.
4 *(organize)* veranstalten *(a course or competition)*
Who's running this competition? Wer veranstaltet diesen Wettbewerb?
5 *(manage)* leiten *(a business)*
She's been running the firm for years. Sie leitet die Firma schon seit Jahren.
to run a shop ein Geschäft leiten
6 *(a train or a bus)* fahren◇ *(PERF sein)*
The buses don't run on Sundays. Sonntags fahren keine Busse.
7 *(water or tears)* fließen◇ *(PERF sein)*
Tears ran down her cheeks. Tränen flossen ihr über die Wangen.
8 **to run a bath** ein Bad einlaufen lassen◇
• **to run away**
weglaufen◇ *SEP (PERF sein)*
• **to run into something**
gegen etwas *(ACC)* fahren◇ *(PERF sein)*
The car ran into a tree. Das Auto ist gegen einen Baum gefahren.
• **to run out of something**
We've run out of bread. Wir haben kein Brot mehr.
I'm running out of money. Ich habe kaum noch Geld.
• **to run somebody over**
jemanden überfahren◇
He nearly got run over. Er ist beinahe überfahren worden.

runner *NOUN*
der **Läufer** (*PL* die **Läufer**), die **Läuferin** (*PL* die **Läuferinnen**)

runner-up *NOUN*
der/die **Zweite** (*PL* die **Zweiten**)

running *NOUN*
(for exercise) das **Laufen**, das **Jogging**
running *ADJECTIVE*
1 **running water** fließendes Wasser
2 **three days running** drei Tage hintereinander
to win three times running dreimal

ℓ **indicates key words**

hintereinander gewinnen

runway NOUN

1 *(for take-off)* die **Startbahn** (PL die **Startbahnen**)

2 *(for landing)* die **Landebahn** (PL die **Landebahnen**)

rush NOUN
(a hurry)
to be in a rush in Eile sein
Sorry, I'm in a rush. Entschuldigung, ich bin in Eile.

to rush VERB

1 *(hurry)* sich **beeilen**
I must rush! Ich muss mich beeilen!

2 *(run)* **stürmen**(PERF sein)
She rushed out. Sie stürmte raus. *(informal)*

3 **Louise was rushed to hospital.** Louise ist schnellstens ins Krankenhaus gebracht worden.

rush hour NOUN
die **Stoßzeit** (PL die **Stoßzeiten**)
in the rush hour während der Stoßzeit

Russia NOUN
Russland *(NEUTER)*

Russian NOUN

1 *(a person)* der **Russe** (PL die **Russen**), die **Russin** (PL die **Russinnen**)

2 *(the language)* das **Russisch**

Russian ADJECTIVE
russisch
Russian music russische Musik
He's Russian. Er ist Russe.
She's Russian. Sie ist Russin.

> **WORD TIP** Adjectives never have capitals in German, even for regions, countries, or nationalities.

rust NOUN
der **Rost**

rusty ADJECTIVE
rostig

rye NOUN
der **Roggen**

Ss

Sabbath NOUN

1 *(Jewish)* der **Sabbat** (PL die **Sabbate**)

2 *(Christian)* der **Sonntag** (PL die **Sonntage**)

sack NOUN

1 der **Sack** (PL die **Säcke**)

2 **to get the sack** rausgeschmissen

werden◇ *(PERF* **sein**) *(informal)*

to sack VERB
to sack somebody jemanden rausschmeißen◇ SEP *(informal)*

♪ **sad** ADJECTIVE
traurig

saddle NOUN
der **Sattel** (PL die **Sättel**)

saddlebag NOUN
die **Satteltasche** (PL die **Satteltaschen**)

sadly ADVERB

1 **traurig**
She looked at me sadly. Sie hat mich traurig angesehen.

2 *(unfortunately)* **leider**

♪ **safe** ADJECTIVE

1 *(out of danger)* **sicher**
to feel safe from something sich vor etwas *(DAT)* sicher fühlen

2 **She's safe.** Sie ist in Sicherheit.

3 *(not dangerous)* **ungefährlich**
The path is safe. Der Weg ist ungefährlich.
It's not safe. Das ist gefährlich.

safety NOUN
die **Sicherheit**

safety belt NOUN
der **Sicherheitsgurt** (PL die **Sicherheitsgurte**)

safety pin NOUN
die **Sicherheitsnadel** (PL die **Sicherheitsnadeln**)

Sagittarius NOUN
der **Schütze**
Kylie is Sagittarius. Kylie ist Schütze.

sail NOUN
das **Segel** (PL die **Segel**)

to sail VERB
segeln *(PERF* **sein**)

sailing NOUN
das **Segeln**
to go sailing segeln gehen◇ *(PERF* **sein**)

sailing boat NOUN
das **Segelboot** (PL die **Segelboote**)

sailor NOUN
der **Seemann** (PL die **Seeleute**)

> **WORD TIP** Professions, hobbies, and sports don't take an article in German: Er ist Seemann.

saint NOUN
der/die **Heilige** (PL die **Heiligen**)

◇ **irregular verb;** SEP **separable verb; for more help with verbs see centre section**

sake NOUN
1 **for your mother's sake** deiner Mutter zuliebe
2 **For heaven's sake!** Um Gottes willen!

𝒫**salad** NOUN
der Salat (PL die Salate)
tomato salad der Tomatensalat

salad dressing NOUN
die Salatsoße (PL die Salatsoßen)

𝒫**salami** NOUN
die Salami (PL die Salamis)

salary NOUN
das Gehalt (PL die Gehälter)

𝒫**sale** NOUN
1 (selling) der Verkauf (PL die Verkäufe)
the sale of the house der Verkauf des Hauses
'For sale' 'Zu verkaufen'
2 **the sales** der Ausverkauf (SINGULAR)
I bought it in the sales. Ich habe es im Ausverkauf gekauft.

𝒫**sales assistant** NOUN
der Verkäufer (PL die Verkäufer), die Verkäuferin (PL die Verkäuferinnen)

> **WORD TIP** Professions, hobbies, and sports don't take an article in German: Sie ist Verkäuferin.

𝒫**salesman** NOUN
der Verkäufer (PL die Verkäufer)

> **WORD TIP** Professions, hobbies, and sports don't take an article in German: Er ist Verkäufer.

𝒫**saleswoman** NOUN
die Verkäuferin (PL die Verkäuferinnen)

> **WORD TIP** Professions, hobbies, and sports don't take an article in German: Sie ist Verkäuferin.

salmon NOUN
der Lachs (PL die Lachse)

𝒫**salt** NOUN
das Salz

𝒫**salty** ADJECTIVE
salzig

𝒫**same** ADJECTIVE
1 **the same** der gleiche/die gleiche/das gleiche
She said the same thing. Sie hat das gleiche gesagt.
Her birthday's the same day as mine. Sie hat am gleichen Tag Geburtstag wie ich.
at the same time zur gleichen Zeit
Their car's the same as ours. Sie haben das

gleiche Auto wie wir.
2 (identical)
the same derselbe/dieselbe/dasselbe
She comes from the same town as me. Sie kommt aus derselben Stadt wie ich.
I'll wear the same clothes again tomorrow. Ich ziehe morgen dieselben Sachen wieder an.

same ADVERB
1 **the same** gleich
The two bikes look the same. Die beiden Fahrräder sehen gleich aus.
2 **all the same** trotzdem

same-sex ADJECTIVE
gleichgeschlechtlich

sample NOUN
das Muster (PL die Muster)
a free sample ein unverkäufliches Muster, eine Warenprobe

sand NOUN
der Sand

𝒫**sandal** NOUN
die Sandale (PL die Sandalen)
a pair of sandals ein Paar Sandalen

𝒫**sandwich** NOUN
das Sandwich (PL die Sandwichs), das belegte Brot (PL die belegten Brote)
ham sandwich das Schinkenbrot

sandy ADJECTIVE
sandig
a sandy beach ein Sandstrand

sanitary towel NOUN
die Damenbinde (PL die Damenbinden)

Santa Claus NOUN
der Weihnachtsmann

sarcastic ADJECTIVE
sarkastisch

sardine NOUN
die Sardine (PL die Sardinen)

𝒫**satellite** NOUN
der Satellit (PL die Satelliten)

satellite dish NOUN
die Satellitenschüssel (PL die Satellitenschüsseln)

satellite television NOUN
das Satellitenfernsehen

satisfactory ADJECTIVE
befriedigend

𝒫**satisfied** ADJECTIVE
zufrieden

A
B
C
D
E
F
G
H
I
J
K
L
M
N
O
P
Q
R
S
T
U
V
W
X
Y
Z

𝒫 **indicates key words**

to **satisfy** VERB
befriedigen

satisfying ADJECTIVE
1 befriedigend
2 a satisfying meal ein sättigendes Essen

ℰ **Saturday** NOUN
1 der Samstag (PL die Samstage), der Sonnabend (North German) (PL die Sonnabende)
on Saturday am Samstag/am Sonnabend
I'm going out on Saturday. Ich gehe Samstag/Sonnabend aus.
See you on Saturday! Bis Samstag/Sonnabend!
every Saturday jeden Samstag/Sonnabend
last Saturday vorigen Samstag/Sonnabend
next Saturday nächsten Samstag/Sonnabend
2 on Saturdays samstags, sonnabends (North German)
The museum is closed on Saturdays. Das Museum ist samstags/sonnabends geschlossen.
to have a Saturday job samstags/sonnabends arbeiten

sauce NOUN
die Soße (PL die Soßen)

saucepan NOUN
der Kochtopf (PL die Kochtöpfe)

ℰ **saucer** NOUN
die Untertasse (PL die Untertassen)

ℰ **sausage** NOUN
die Wurst (PL die Würste)

ℰ to **save** VERB
1 retten (life)
to save somebody's life jemandem das Leben retten
The doctors saved his life. Die Ärzte haben ihm das Leben gerettet.
2 sparen (money)
I've saved £60. Ich habe sechzig Pfund gespart.
I cycle to school to save money. Ich fahre mit dem Rad zur Schule, um Geld zu sparen.
We'll take a taxi to save time. Um Zeit zu sparen, nehmen wir ein Taxi.
3 (on a computer) speichern
4 (stop) abwehren SEP (a shot)
to save a penalty einen Elfmeter abwehren
• to save up
sparen
I'm saving up for a car. Ich spare auf ein Auto.

savings PLURAL NOUN
die Ersparnisse (PLURAL)

ℰ **savoury** ADJECTIVE
(not sweet) pikant

saw NOUN
die Säge (PL die Sägen)

sax NOUN
das Saxophon (PL die Saxophone)

WORD TIP Don't use the article when you talk about playing an instrument.

saxophone NOUN
das Saxophon (PL die Saxophone)
Rachel plays the saxophone. Rachel spielt Saxophon.

WORD TIP Don't use the article when you talk about playing an instrument.

ℰ to **say** VERB
1 sagen
to say something to somebody jemandem etwas sagen
What did you say? Was hast du gesagt?
She says she's tired. Sie sagt, dass sie müde ist.
He said to wait here. Er hat gesagt, wir sollen hier warten.
they say, ... man sagt, ...
2 to say something again etwas wiederholen
3 that's to say das heißt

saying NOUN
die Redensart (PL die Redensarten)
It's just a saying. Das ist so eine Redensart.
as the saying goes wie man so sagt

scab NOUN
der Wundschorf (PL die Wundschorfe)

scale NOUN
1 (of a map or model) der Maßstab (PL die Maßstäbe)
2 (extent) das Ausmaß (PL die Ausmaße)
the scale of the disaster das Ausmaß der Katastrophe
3 (in music) die Tonleiter (PL die Tonleitern)

scales PLURAL NOUN
die Waage (PL die Waagen)
bathroom scales die Personenwaage

WORD TIP In German die Waage is singular.

scandal NOUN
1 der Skandal (PL die Skandale)
2 (gossip) der Klatsch (informal)

Scandinavia NOUN
Skandinavien (NEUTER)

✧ irregular verb; SEP separable verb; for more help with verbs see centre section

Scandinavian _ADJECTIVE_
  skandinavisch
  the Scandinavian countries die
  skandinavischen Länder

> **WORD TIP** Adjectives never have capitals
> in German, even for regions, countries, or
> nationalities.

scanner _NOUN_
  der Scanner (_PL_ die Scanner)

scar _NOUN_
  die Narbe (_PL_ die Narben)

_ℰ_ **scarce** _ADJECTIVE_
  knapp

_ℰ_ **scare** _NOUN_
  1 der Schrecken (_PL_ die Schrecken)
  to give somebody a scare jemandem einen
  Schrecken einjagen _SEP_
  2 (_general alarm_) die Panik (_PL_ die Paniken)
  to cause a scare eine Panik auslösen
  3 **bomb scare** die Bombendrohung

to **scare** _VERB_
  to scare somebody jemanden erschrecken
  You scared me! Du hast mich erschreckt!

scarecrow _NOUN_
  die Vogelscheuche (_PL_ die
  Vogelscheuchen)

_ℰ_ **scared** _ADJECTIVE_
  1 **to be scared** Angst haben
  I'm scared. Ich habe Angst.
  to be scared of something vor etwas (_DAT_)
  Angst haben
  He's scared of dogs. Er hat vor Hunden
  Angst.
  2 **to be scared of doing something** sich nicht
  trauen, etwas zu tun
  I'm scared of telling him the truth. Ich
  traue mich nicht, ihm die Wahrheit zu
  sagen.

scarf _NOUN_
  1 (_silky_) das Tuch (_PL_ die Tücher)
  2 (_long, warm_) der Schal (_PL_ die Schals)

scary _ADJECTIVE_
  unheimlich

_ℰ_ **scene** _NOUN_
  1 (_of an incident or event_) der Schauplatz
  (_PL_ die Schauplätze)
  to be on the scene am Schauplatz sein
  the scene of the crime der Tatort
  2 (_world_)
  the music scene die Musikszene
  on the fashion scene in der Modewelt
  3 (_argument_) die Szene (_PL_ die Szenen)
  to make a scene eine Szene machen

scenery _NOUN_
  1 (_landscape_) die Landschaft
  2 (_in the theatre_) das Bühnenbild

_ℰ_ **schedule** _NOUN_
  das Programm (_PL_ die Programme)

scheduled flight _NOUN_
  der Linienflug (_PL_ die Linienflüge)

scheme _NOUN_
  das Projekt (_PL_ die Projekte)

scholarship _NOUN_
  das Stipendium (_PL_ die Stipendien)

_ℰ_ **school** _NOUN_
  die Schule (_PL_ die Schulen)
  at school in der Schule
  to go to school zur Schule gehen
  Children start school at 5 in Britain. In
  Großbritannien kommen die Kinder mit 5
  in die Schule.
  You can leave school at 16. Man kann mit
  16 von der Schule gehen.
  School starts at 9 and finishes at 3.30. Die
  Schule fängt um 9 an und ist um 15.30 zu
  Ende.

> **SCHOOL**
> At the age of 10, pupils move from primary
> school (Grundschule or Volksschule) to
> one of three types of school in Germany:
> Hauptschule, Realschule, or Gymnasium. In
> some areas, there are comprehensive schools
> (Gesamtschulen). In Austria, pupils move to
> a Hauptschule or Gymnasium. The Austrian
> government wants to introduce a new type
> of school, the 'neue Mittelschule', with some
> of the features of a comprehensive school.
> In Switzerland, some cantons have only
> one type of secondary school, while others
> divide their pupils up into three types, too.
> The Hauptschule focuses on more practical
> subjects, the Gymnasium on more academic
> subjects. The Realschule is between the two.

school bag _NOUN_
  die Schultasche (_PL_ die Schultaschen)

schoolbook _NOUN_
  das Schulbuch (_PL_ die Schulbücher)

schoolboy _NOUN_
  der Schüler (_PL_ die Schüler)

schoolchildren _PLURAL NOUN_
  die Schulkinder (_PLURAL_)

school friend _NOUN_
  der Schulfreund (_PL_ die Schulfreunde), die
  Schulfreundin (_PL_ die Schulfreundinnen)

schoolgirl _NOUN_
  die Schülerin (_PL_ die Schülerinnen)

_ℰ_ indicates key words

school group NOUN
die Schulgruppe (PL die Schulgruppen)

school magazine NOUN
die Schulzeitung (PL die Schulzeitungen)

♪ **science** NOUN
1 die Wissenschaft (PL die Wissenschaften)
2 (biology, chemistry, physics)
die Naturwissenschaft (PL die Naturwissenschaften)
3 (as a school subject) die Naturwissenschaften (PLURAL)

science fiction NOUN
die Science-Fiction

scientific ADJECTIVE
wissenschaftlich

scientist NOUN
der Wissenschaftler (PL die Wissenschaftler), die Wissenschaftlerin (PL die Wissenschaftlerinnen)

WORD TIP Professions, hobbies, and sports don't take an article in German: Sie ist Wissenschaftlerin.

♪ **scissors** PLURAL NOUN
die Schere (PL die Scheren)
a pair of scissors eine Schere

WORD TIP In German die Schere is singular.

scoop NOUN
1 (ice cream) die Eiskugel (PL die Eiskugeln)
How many scoops would you like? Wie viele Kugeln Eis möchtest du?
2 (in journalism) der Knüller (PL die Knüller)

scooter NOUN
1 (motor scooter) der Motorroller (PL die Motorroller)
to ride a scooter Motorroller fahren◊ (PERF sein)
2 (for a child) der Roller (PL die Roller)

♪ **score** NOUN
der Spielstand (PL die Spielstände)
The score was three two. Es stand drei zu zwei.

to **score** VERB
1 to score a goal ein Tor schießen◊
2 to score three points drei Punkte erzielen
3 (keep score) zählen

Scorpio NOUN
der Skorpion
Neil is Scorpio. Neil ist Skorpion.

♪ **Scot** NOUN
der Schotte (PL die Schotten), die Schottin (PL die Schottinnen)

He's a Scot. Er ist Schotte.
the Scots die Schotten

♪ **Scotland** NOUN
Schottland (NEUTER)
from Scotland aus Schottland
Pauline's from Scotland. Pauline kommt aus Schottland.
to Scotland nach Schottland

Scots ADJECTIVE
schottisch

WORD TIP Adjectives never have capitals in German, even for regions, countries, or nationalities.

Scotsman NOUN
der Schotte (PL die Schotten)

Scotswoman NOUN
die Schottin (PL die Schottinnen)

♪ **Scottish** ADJECTIVE
schottisch
the Scottish mountains die schottischen Berge
He's Scottish. Er ist Schotte.
She's Scottish. Sie ist Schottin.

WORD TIP Adjectives never have capitals in German, even for regions, countries, or nationalities.

scout NOUN
der Pfadfinder (PL die Pfadfinder)

scrambled eggs NOUN
das Rührei

scrap NOUN
das Stück (PL die Stücke)
a scrap of paper ein Stück Papier

scrapbook NOUN
das Sammelalbum (PL die Sammelalben)

to **scrape** VERB
1 schaben (potatoes or carrots)
2 (remove dirt or paint) abkratzen SEP
3 (damage) schrammen

scratch NOUN
1 (on your skin or a surface) der Kratzer (PL die Kratzer)
2 to start from scratch von vorn anfangen◊ SEP

to **scratch** VERB
(scratch yourself) sich kratzen
to scratch your head sich am Kopf kratzen

♪ **scream** NOUN
der Schrei (PL die Schreie)

to **scream** VERB
schreien◊

ℰ screen NOUN
1 der **Bildschirm** (PL die **Bildschirme**) (of a TV or computer)
   on the screen auf dem Bildschirm
2 (in the cinema) die **Leinwand** (PL die **Leinwände**)

screw NOUN
die **Schraube** (PL die **Schrauben**)

to screw VERB
schrauben

screwdriver NOUN
der **Schraubenzieher** (PL die **Schraubenzieher**)

to scribble VERB
kritzeln

to scrub VERB
1 scheuern (a saucepan or the floor)
2 **to scrub your nails** sich (DAT) die Nägel bürsten

scuba diving NOUN
das **Gerätetauchen**

sculptor NOUN
der **Bildhauer** (PL die **Bildhauer**), die **Bildhauerin** (PL die **Bildhauerinnen**)

> **WORD TIP** Professions, hobbies, and sports don't take an article in German: Sie ist Bildhauerin.

sculpture NOUN
die **Skulptur** (PL die **Skulpturen**)

ℰ sea NOUN
das **Meer** (PL die **Meere**), die **See**
by the sea am Meer, an der See
We went to the sea for the day. Wir sind einen Tag ans Meer gefahren.

ℰ seafood NOUN
die **Meeresfrüchte** (PLURAL)
I love seafood. Ich esse Meeresfrüchte sehr gern.

seagull NOUN
die **Möwe** (PL die **Möwen**)

seal NOUN
(animal) die **Robbe** (PL die **Robben**), der **Seehund** (PL die **Seehunde**)

to seal VERB
zukleben SEP (an envelope)

ℰ to search VERB
1 absuchen SEP
   I've searched my desk but I can't find the letter. Ich habe meinen Schreibtisch abgesucht, aber ich kann den Brief nicht finden.
2 durchsuchen
   They searched the building for him. Sie haben das Gebäude nach ihm durchsucht.
3 suchen
   to search for something nach etwas (DAT) suchen
   I've been searching everywhere for my scissors. Ich habe überall nach meiner Schere gesucht.

seashell NOUN
die **Muschel** (PL die **Muscheln**)

seasick ADJECTIVE
to be seasick seekrank sein

seaside NOUN
at the seaside am Meer
We went to the seaside for the day. Wir sind einen Tag ans Meer gefahren.

ℰ season NOUN
1 die **Jahreszeit** (PL die **Jahreszeiten**)
   the four seasons die vier Jahreszeiten
2 (period of social or sporting activity) die **Saison** (PL die **Saisons**)
   the tennis season die Tennissaison
   off-season prices Preise außerhalb der Saison
3 **the strawberry season** die Erdbeerzeit
   Strawberries are not in season at the moment. Jetzt ist nicht die richtige Zeit für Erdbeeren.

season ticket NOUN
die **Dauerkarte** (PL die **Dauerkarten**)

seat NOUN
1 der **Sitz** (PL die **Sitze**)
   the front seat (in a car) der Vordersitz
   the back seat der Rücksitz
   Take a seat. Nehmen Sie Platz. (formal), Setz dich. (informal)
2 (on a bus, in the theatre, etc.) der **Platz** (PL die **Plätze**)
   to book a seat einen Platz reservieren
   Can you keep my seat? Kannst du mir meinen Platz freihalten?

seatbelt NOUN
der **Sicherheitsgurt** (PL die **Sicherheitsgurte**)

seaweed NOUN
der **Tang**

ℰ second NOUN
die **Sekunde** (PL die **Sekunden**)
Can you wait a second? Kannst du eine Sekunde warten?

second ADJECTIVE
1 zweiter/zweite/zweites
   for the second time zum zweiten Mal

2 **the second of July** der zweite Juli

_ℓ_ **secondary school** NOUN
  1 die **weiterführende Schule** (PL die **weiterführenden Schulen**) (Germans define the type of secondary school)
  2 das **Gymnasium** (PL die **Gymnasien**) (grammar school, from age 10 to 18 when Abitur is taken)
  3 die **Realschule** (PL die **Realschulen**) (from age 10 to 16, less academic than a Gymnasium)

_ℓ_ **second-hand** ADJECTIVE, ADVERB
  gebraucht
  a second-hand bike ein gebrauchtes Fahrrad
  second-hand car der Gebrauchtwagen
  I bought it second-hand. Ich habe es gebraucht gekauft.

secondly ADVERB
  zweitens

_ℓ_ **secret** NOUN
  das **Geheimnis** (PL die **Geheimnisse**)
  to tell somebody a secret jemandem ein Geheimnis verraten◇
  in secret heimlich

secret ADJECTIVE
  geheim
  a secret plan ein geheimer Plan
  to keep something secret etwas geheim halten◇

_ℓ_ **secretary** NOUN
  der **Sekretär** (PL die **Sekretäre**), die **Sekretärin** (PL die **Sekretärinnen**)
  the secretary's office das Sekretariat

  WORD TIP Professions, hobbies, and sports don't take an article in German: Sie ist Sekretärin.

secretly ADVERB
  heimlich

sect NOUN
  die **Sekte** (PL die **Sekten**)

_ℓ_ **section** NOUN
  der **Teil** (PL die **Teile**)

security NOUN
  die **Sicherheit**

security guard NOUN
  der **Wächter** (PL die **Wächter**), die **Wächterin** (PL die **Wächterinnen**)

  WORD TIP Professions, hobbies, and sports don't take an article in German: Er ist Wächter.

_ℓ_ **to see** VERB
  1 sehen◇

I saw Lindy yesterday. Ich habe Lindy gestern gesehen.
  Have you seen the film? Hast du den Film gesehen?
  I can't see anything. Ich kann überhaupt nichts sehen.
  2 **to go and see** nachsehen◇ SEP
  I'll go and see. Ich sehe mal nach.
  3 (visit) besuchen
  Why don't you come and see us in the summer? Warum besucht ihr uns nicht im Sommer?
  4 (understand) verstehen◇
  I don't see what you mean. Ich verstehe nicht, was Sie meinen.
  5 (accept) einsehen◇SEP
  She doesn't see why she should go. Sie sieht nicht ein, warum sie gehen soll.
  6 **to see somebody home** jemanden nach Hause begleiten
  7 **See you!** Tschüs! (informal)
  See you on Saturday! Bis Samstag!
  See you soon! Bis bald!
  • **to see to something**
  sich um etwas (ACC) kümmern
  Jo's seeing to the drinks. Jo kümmert sich um die Getränke.

seed NOUN
  der **Samen** (PL die **Samen**)

_ℓ_ **to seem** VERB
  1 scheinen◇
  He seems shy. Er scheint schüchtern zu sein.
  The museum seems to be closed. Das Museum scheint geschlossen zu sein.
  His story seems odd to me. Seine Geschichte kommt mir komisch vor.
  2 **It seems (that) ...** Anscheinend ...
  It seems he's left. Anscheinend ist er weggegangen.
  It seems that there are problems. Anscheinend gibt es Probleme.

see-saw NOUN
  die **Wippe** (PL die **Wippen**)

to select VERB
  auswählen SEP

self-confidence NOUN
  das **Selbstbewusstsein**
  She doesn't have much self-confidence. Sie hat sehr wenig Selbstbewusstsein.

self-confident ADJECTIVE
  selbstsicher, selbstbewusst

self-conscious ADJECTIVE
  gehemmt

◇ **irregular verb;** SEP **separable verb; for more help with verbs see centre section**

self-employed ADJECTIVE
  to be self-employed selbstständig sein
  My parents are self-employed. Meine
  Eltern sind selbstständig.

selfish ADJECTIVE
  egoistisch

℘ **self-service** ADJECTIVE
  a self-service restaurant ein
  Selbstbedienungsrestaurant

℘ to **sell** VERB
1 verkaufen
   to sell something to somebody jemandem
   etwas verkaufen
   I sold him my bike. Ich habe ihm mein Rad
   verkauft.
   The house sold for a million. Das Haus
   wurde für eine Million verkauft.
2 The concert's sold out. Das Konzert ist
   ausverkauft.
   The tickets sold out very quickly. Die
   Karten waren schnell ausverkauft.

sell-by date NOUN
  das Verfallsdatum (PL die Verfallsdaten)

Sellotape® NOUN
  der Tesafilm®

to **sellotape** VERB
  to sellotape something etwas mit Tesafilm
  kleben

℘ **semi** NOUN
  die Doppelhaushälfte (PL die
  Doppelhaushälften)

semicircle NOUN
  der Halbkreis (PL die Halbkreise)

semicolon NOUN
  der Strichpunkt (PL die Strichpunkte)

semi-detached house NOUN
  die Doppelhaushälfte (PL die
  Doppelhaushälften)

semi-final NOUN
  das Halbfinale (PL die Halbfinale)

semi-skimmed ADJECTIVE
  teilentrahmt

℘ to **send** VERB
1 schicken
   to send something to somebody
   jemandem etwas schicken
   I sent her a present for her birthday. Ich
   habe ihr zum Geburtstag ein Geschenk
   geschickt.
2 Send Marcus my love. Grüße Marcus von
   mir.

• to send somebody back
  jemanden zurückschicken SEP
• to send something back
  etwas zurückschicken SEP

sender NOUN
  der Absender (PL die Absender)

> **WORD TIP** Do not translate the English word
> sender with the German Sender.

senior citizen NOUN
  der Senior (PL die Senioren), die Seniorin
  (PL die Seniorinnen)

sensation NOUN
1 (feeling) das Gefühl
2 (impact) die Sensation (PL die Sensationen)
   She caused a sensation. Sie erregte viel
   Aufsehen.

sensational ADJECTIVE
  sensationell

℘ **sense** NOUN
1 (common sense) der Verstand
2 (faculty) der Sinn (PL die Sinne)
   sense of smell der Geruchssinn
   sense of touch der Tastsinn
   to have a sense of humour Humor haben
   She has no sense of humour. Sie hat keinen
   Sinn für Humor.
3 (meaning) der Sinn
   This sentence makes no sense. Dieser Satz
   ergibt keinen Sinn.
   It doesn't make sense to do that. Es ist
   Unsinn, das zu machen.
   It makes sense to collect her first. Es ist
   sinnvoll, sie erst abzuholen.

℘ **sensible** ADJECTIVE
  vernünftig
  Be sensible. Sei vernünftig.
  That's a sensible suggestion. Das ist ein
  vernünftiger Vorschlag.

> **WORD TIP** Do not translate the English word
> sensible with the German sensibel.

℘ **sensitive** ADJECTIVE
  empfindlich
  for sensitive skin für empfindliche Haut

℘ **sentence** NOUN
1 (words) der Satz (PL die Sätze)
2 (prison) die Strafe (PL die Strafen)
   the death sentence die Todesstrafe

to **sentence** VERB
  verurteilen
  to be sentenced to death zum Tode
  verurteilt werden
  to sentence somebody to a year in

℘ indicates key words

prison jemanden zu einem Jahr Gefängnis verurteilen

sentimental _ADJECTIVE_
sentimental

_ℰ_ **separate** _ADJECTIVE_
1 extra _(extra never has an ending)_
a separate pile ein extra Stapel
The drinks are separate. Die Getränke gehen extra.
She wrote it on a separate sheet of paper. Sie hat es auf ein anderes Blatt Papier geschrieben.
2 _(different)_ verschieden
two separate problems zwei verschiedene Probleme
3 They have separate rooms. Sie haben getrennte Zimmer.

to **separate** _VERB_
1 trennen
2 _(a couple)_ sich trennen

separately _ADVERB_
1 extra
You must pay for the food separately. Sie müssen das Essen extra bezahlen.
2 getrennt
They live separately. Sie leben getrennt.

separation _NOUN_
die Trennung (_PL_ die Trennungen)

_ℰ_ **September** _NOUN_
der September
in September im September

sequel _NOUN_
die Folge (_PL_ die Folgen)

sequence _NOUN_
1 _(series)_ die Reihe (_PL_ die Reihen)
a sequence of events eine Reihe von Ereignissen
in sequence in der richtigen Reihenfolge
2 _(in a film)_ die Sequenz (_PL_ die Sequenzen)

sergeant _NOUN_
1 _(in the police)_ der Polizeimeister (_PL_ die Polizeimeister), die Polizeimeisterin (_PL_ die Polizeimeisterinnen)
2 _(in the army)_ der Feldwebel (_PL_ die Feldwebel)

WORD TIP Professions, hobbies, and sports don't take an article in German: Er ist Polizeimeister.

_ℰ_ **serial** _NOUN_
1 die Fortsetzungsgeschichte (_PL_ die Fortsetzungsgeschichten)
2 _(on TV or radio)_ die Serie (_PL_ die Serien)

series _NOUN_
die Serie (_PL_ die Serien)
television series die Fernsehserie

_ℰ_ **serious** _ADJECTIVE_
1 ernst
a serious discussion eine ernste Unterhaltung
to be serious about something etwas ernst nehmen◇
Are you serious? Ist das dein Ernst?
2 schwer _(accident or mistake)_

_ℰ_ **seriously** _ADVERB_
1 im Ernst
Seriously, I have to go now. Im Ernst, ich muss jetzt gehen.
Seriously? Im Ernst?
2 to take somebody seriously jemanden ernst nehmen◇
3 _(gravely)_ schwer
She is seriously ill. Sie ist schwer krank.

servant _NOUN_
der/die Bedienstete (_PL_ die Bediensteten)

WORD TIP Professions, hobbies, and sports don't take an article in German: Er ist Bediensteter.

serve _NOUN_
(in tennis) der Aufschlag (_PL_ die Aufschläge)
It's my serve. Ich habe Aufschlag.

to **serve** _VERB_
1 _(in tennis)_ aufschlagen◇ _SEP_
Nadal is serving. Nadal schlägt auf.
2 servieren
Can you serve the vegetables, please? Können Sie bitte das Gemüse servieren?
3 It serves him right. Das geschieht ihm recht.

_ℰ_ **service** _NOUN_
1 _(in a restaurant, shop, etc.)_ die Bedienung
Service is included. Inklusive Bedienung.
2 _(from a company or firm to a customer)_ der Service
3 the emergency services der Notdienst
4 _(church service)_ der Gottesdienst (_PL_ die Gottesdienste)
5 _(of a car or machine)_ die Wartung (_PL_ die Wartungen)

service area _NOUN_
die Raststätte (_PL_ die Raststätten)

service charge _NOUN_
die Bedienung
There is no service charge. Die Bedienung wird nicht extra berechnet.

◇ **irregular verb;** _SEP_ **separable verb; for more help with verbs see centre section**

ℰ**service station** NOUN
die **Tankstelle** (PL die **Tankstellen**)

serviette NOUN
die **Serviette** (PL die **Servietten**)

ℰ**session** NOUN
die **Sitzung** (PL die **Sitzungen**)

ℰ**set** NOUN
1 (for playing a game) das **Spiel** (PL die **Spiele**)
   chess set das **Schachspiel**
2 **train set** die **Spielzeugeisenbahn**
3 (in tennis) der **Satz** (PL die **Sätze**)

set ADJECTIVE
1 **fest** (hours, habits)
   a set date ein festes Datum
   at a set time zu einer festgesetzten Zeit
2 **set menu** das **Menü**

to **set** VERB
1 **festlegen** SEP (a date, time)
2 **aufstellen** SEP (a record)
3 **to set the table** den Tisch decken
4 **to set an alarm clock** einen Wecker stellen
   I've set my alarm for seven. Ich habe
   meinen Wecker auf sieben gestellt.
   to set your watch seine Uhr richtig stellen
5 (sun) **untergehen**◇ SEP (PERF **sein**)
• **to set off**
   aufbrechen◇ SEP (PERF **sein**)
   We're setting off at ten. Wir brechen um
   zehn auf.
   They set off for Vienna yesterday. Sie sind
   gestern nach Wien aufgebrochen.
• **to set off something**
1 etwas **auslösen** SEP (an alarm, reaction)
2 etwas **abbrennen**◇ SEP (a firework)
3 etwas **explodieren lassen**◇ (a bomb)
• **to set out**
   aufbrechen◇ SEP (PERF **sein**)
   They set out for Hamburg at ten. Sie sind
   um zehn nach Hamburg aufgebrochen.

ℰ**settee** NOUN
das **Sofa** (PL die **Sofas**)

ℰto **settle** VERB
1 **bezahlen** (a bill)
2 **lösen** (a problem)
3 **beilegen** SEP (an argument)

ℰ**seven** NUMBER
sieben
Rosie's seven. Rosie ist sieben.

ℰ**seventeen** NUMBER
siebzehn
I'm seventeen. Ich bin siebzehn.

ℰ**seventh** ADJECTIVE
siebter/siebte/siebtes

on the seventh floor im siebten Stock
the seventh of July der siebte Juli

seventies PLURAL NOUN
the seventies die Siebzigerjahre
in the seventies in den Siebzigerjahren

seventieth ADJECTIVE
siebzigster/siebzigste/siebzigstes
It's her seventieth birthday. Es ist ihr
siebzigster Geburtstag.

ℰ**seventy** NUMBER
siebzig
My granny's seventy. Meine Oma ist
siebzig.

ℰ**several** DETERMINER, PRONOUN
1 **mehrere**
   I've read several of her novels. Ich habe
   mehrere ihrer Romane gelesen.
2 **I've seen her several times.** Ich habe sie
   mehrmals gesehen.

to **sew** VERB
nähen

sewing NOUN
das **Nähen**
I like sewing. Ich nähe gern.

sex NOUN
1 (gender) das **Geschlecht** (PL die
   Geschlechter)
2 (intercourse) der **Sex**
   to have sex with someone mit jemandem
   Sex haben

sex education NOUN
der **Aufklärungsunterricht**

sexism NOUN
der **Sexismus**

sexist ADJECTIVE
sexistisch
sexist remarks sexistische Bemerkungen

sexual ADJECTIVE
sexuell

sexual harassment NOUN
die **sexuelle Belästigung**

sexuality NOUN
die **Sexualität**

sexy ADJECTIVE
sexy

shabby ADJECTIVE
schäbig

shade NOUN
1 der **Ton** (PL die **Töne**)
   a shade of green ein Grünton

2 der **Schatten**
in the shade im Schatten

shadow NOUN
der **Schatten** (PL die **Schatten**)

♭to **shake** VERB
1 (tremble) **zittern**
I was shaking with fear. Ich zitterte vor Angst.
2 **to shake something** etwas **schütteln**
to shake your head (meaning no) den Kopf schütteln
3 **to shake hands with somebody** jemandem die Hand geben◇
She shook hands with me. Sie hat mir die Hand gegeben.
We shook hands. Wir gaben uns die Hand.

shaken ADJECTIVE
erschüttert
I was shaken by the news. Die Nachricht hat mich erschüttert.

♭**shall** VERB
1 **sollen**
Shall I come with you? Soll ich mitkommen?
Shall we stop now? Sollen wir jetzt aufhören?
2 (will) **werden**
I shall see him tomorrow. Ich werde ihn morgen sehen.
We shan't arrive before 7. Wir werden nicht vor 7 ankommen.

shallow ADJECTIVE
flach
Stay in the shallow end of the pool. Bleib am flachen Ende des Beckens.

shambles NOUN
das **Chaos**
It was a total shambles! Es war ein völliges Chaos!

♭**shame** NOUN
1 die **Schande**
The shame of it! Was für eine Schande!
2 **What a shame!** Wie schade!
It's a shame she can't come. Schade, dass sie nicht kommen kann.

♭**shampoo** NOUN
das **Shampoo** (PL die **Shampoos**)
I bought some shampoo. Ich habe Shampoo gekauft.

shamrock NOUN
der **Klee**

shandy NOUN
der **Radler** (PL die **Radler**) (South German), das **Alsterwasser** (PL die **Alsterwasser**) (North German)

shape NOUN
die **Form** (PL die **Formen**)

♭**share** NOUN
1 der **Anteil** (PL die **Anteile**)
your share of the money dein Anteil am Geld
He paid his share. Er hat seinen Anteil gezahlt.
2 (in a company) die **Aktie** (PL die **Aktien**)
to share VERB
teilen
I'm sharing a room with Lucy. Ich teile ein Zimmer mit Lucy.

shark NOUN
der **Hai** (PL die **Haie**)

♭**sharp** ADJECTIVE
1 (knife) **scharf**
This knife isn't very sharp. Dieses Messer ist nicht sehr scharf.
2 (pointed) **spitz**
a sharp pencil ein spitzer Bleistift
3 **a sharp bend** eine scharfe Kurve
4 (clever) **clever**

to shave VERB
1 (have a shave) **sich rasieren**
2 **to shave your legs** sich (DAT) die Beine rasieren
3 **to shave off your beard** den Bart abrasieren SEP

shaver NOUN
der **Rasierapparat** (PL die **Rasierapparate**)
electric shaver der Elektrorasierer

shaving cream NOUN
die **Rasiercreme** (PL die **Rasiercremes**)

shaving foam NOUN
der **Rasierschaum**

♭**she** PRONOUN
sie
She's a student. Sie ist Studentin.
She's a very good teacher. Sie ist eine sehr gute Lehrerin.

shed NOUN
der **Schuppen** (PL die **Schuppen**)

♭**sheep** NOUN
das **Schaf** (PL die **Schafe**)

sheepdog NOUN
der **Schäferhund** (PL die **Schäferhunde**)

◇ irregular verb; SEP separable verb; for more help with verbs see centre section

sheer ADJECTIVE
rein
It's sheer stupidity. Das ist reine Dummheit.

ℐ **sheet** NOUN
1 *(for a bed)* das Laken (PL die Laken)
2 a sheet of paper ein Blatt Papier
a blank sheet ein leeres Blatt
3 *(of glass or metal)* die Platte (PL die Platten)
4 to be as white as a sheet leichenblass sein

ℐ **shelf** NOUN
1 *(in the home or a shop)* das Regal (PL die Regale)
a set of shelves ein Regal
2 *(in an oven)* die Schiene (PL die Schienen)
Cook the pizza on the top shelf. Die Pizza auf der obersten Schiene backen.

shell NOUN
1 *(of an egg or a nut)* die Schale (PL die Schalen)
2 *(seashell)* die Muschel (PL die Muscheln)

shellfish NOUN
1 das Schalentier (PL die Schalentiere)
2 *(in cookery)* die Meeresfrüchte (PLURAL)

ℐ **shelter** NOUN
der Schutz
in the shelter of im Schutz (+GEN)
to take shelter from the rain sich unterstellen SEP

shepherd NOUN
der Schäfer (PL die Schäfer)

WORD TIP Professions, hobbies, and sports don't take an article in German: Er ist Schäfer.

Shetland Islands NOUN
die Shetlandinseln (PLURAL)

shield NOUN
der Schild (PL die Schilde)

shift NOUN
die Schicht (PL die Schichten)
the night shift die Nachtschicht
to be on night shift Nachtschicht haben
to **shift** VERB
to shift something etwas verrücken

shifty ADJECTIVE
verschlagen
He looks shifty. Er sieht verschlagen aus.
a shifty-looking guy ein verschlagener Typ

shin NOUN
das Schienbein (PL die Schienbeine)

ℐ to **shine** VERB
scheinen◇

The sun is shining. Die Sonne scheint.

shiny ADJECTIVE
glänzend

ℐ **ship** NOUN
das Schiff (PL die Schiffe)

shipyard NOUN
die Werft (PL die Werften)

ℐ **shirt** NOUN
1 *(man's)* das Hemd (PL die Hemden)
2 *(woman's)* die Bluse (PL die Blusen)

ℐ to **shiver** VERB
zittern

ℐ **shock** NOUN
1 der Schock (PL die Schocks)
to get a shock einen Schock bekommen◇
It gave me a shock. Das hat mir einen Schock versetzt.
2 electric shock der elektrische Schlag
to **shock** VERB
(upset) erschüttern, *(cause scandal)* schockieren

shocked ADJECTIVE
schockiert

shocking ADJECTIVE
schockierend

ℐ **shoe** NOUN
der Schuh (PL die Schuhe)
a pair of shoes ein Paar Schuhe

shoelace NOUN
der Schnürsenkel (PL die Schnürsenkel)

shoe polish NOUN
die Schuhcreme (PL die Schuhcremes)

shoe shop NOUN
das Schuhgeschäft (PL die Schuhgeschäfte)

ℐ to **shoot** VERB
1 *(fire)* schießen◇
to shoot at somebody auf jemanden schießen
She shot him in the leg. Sie hat ihm ins Bein geschossen.
He was shot in the arm. Er wurde am Arm getroffen.
2 *(kill, execute)* erschießen◇
He was shot by terrorists. Er wurde von Terroristen erschossen.
3 *(in football, hockey)* schießen◇
4 to shoot a film einen Film drehen

ℐ **shop** NOUN
das Geschäft (PL die Geschäfte), der Laden (PL die Läden)

ℐ indicates key words

shoe shop das Schuhgeschäft
to go round the shops einen
Einkaufsbummel machen

♪ **shop assistant** NOUN
der Verkäufer (PL die Verkäufer), die
Verkäuferin (PL die Verkäuferinnen)

WORD TIP Professions, hobbies, and sports don't
take an article in German: Sie ist Verkäuferin.

♪ **shopkeeper** NOUN
der Ladenbesitzer (PL die Ladenbesitzer),
die Ladenbesitzerin (PL die
Ladenbesitzerinnen)

WORD TIP Professions, hobbies, and sports don't
take an article in German: Er ist Ladenbesitzer.

shoplifter NOUN
der Ladendieb (PL die Ladendiebe), die
Ladendiebin (PL die Ladendiebinnen)

shoplifting NOUN
der Ladendiebstahl

shopping NOUN
1 die Einkäufe (PLURAL)
Can you put the shopping away? Kannst
du die Einkäufe wegräumen?
2 (activity) das Einkaufen
Shopping is fun. Einkaufen macht Spaß.
to go shopping einkaufen gehen ⬦ (PERF
sein)

shopping bag NOUN
die Einkaufstasche (PL die
Einkaufstaschen)

shopping centre, shopping mall NOUN
das Einkaufszentrum (PL die
Einkaufszentren)

shopping trolley NOUN
der Einkaufswagen (PL die
Einkaufswagen)

♪ **shop window** NOUN
das Schaufenster (PL die Schaufenster)

♪ **short** ADJECTIVE
1 kurz
a short dress ein kurzes Kleid
She has short hair. Sie hat kurze Haare.
2 a short break eine kurze Pause
to go for a short walk einen kurzen
Spaziergang machen
It's a short walk from the bus stop. Es ist
nicht weit zu Fuß von der Bushaltestelle.
3 We're short of milk. Wir haben nicht mehr
viel Milch.
We're a bit short of money at the
moment. Wir sind im Moment etwas knapp
bei Kasse.

We're getting short of time. Die Zeit wird
uns knapp.

shortage NOUN
der Mangel

shortbread NOUN
das Buttergebäck

short cut NOUN
die Abkürzung (PL die Abkürzungen)

to **shorten** VERB
kürzen
I had to shorten the skirt. Ich musste den
Rock kürzen.

shortly ADVERB
1 kurz
shortly before I left kurz bevor ich ging
shortly after kurz danach
2 gleich
We'll be ready shortly. Wir sind gleich
fertig.

♪ **shorts** PLURAL NOUN
die Shorts (PLURAL)
a pair of shorts ein Paar Shorts
my red shorts meine roten Shorts

short-sighted ADJECTIVE
kurzsichtig
I'm short-sighted. Ich bin kurzsichtig.

short story NOUN
die Kurzgeschichte (PL die
Kurzgeschichten)

shot NOUN
1 (from a gun) der Schuss (PL die Schüsse)
2 (a photo) die Aufnahme (PL die
Aufnahmen)

♪ **should** VERB
1 sollen ⬦ ('should' is usually translated by the
imperfect subjunctive of sollen)
You should ask Simon. Du solltest Simon
fragen.
The potatoes should be ready now. Die
Kartoffeln sollten jetzt fertig sein.
2 ('should have' is translated by hätte sollen)
You should have told me. Du hättest es mir
sagen sollen.
I shouldn't have stayed. Ich hätte nicht
bleiben sollen.
You shouldn't have said that. Das hättest
du nicht sagen sollen.
3 ('should' meaning 'would' is translated by
würde)
I should forget it if I were you. An deiner
Stelle würde ich es vergessen.
4 I should think ich würde sagen
I should think he's forgotten. Ich würde
sagen, er hat's vergessen.

⬦ irregular verb; SEP separable verb; for more help with verbs see centre section

5 This should be enough. Das müsste eigentlich reichen.

ℱ**shoulder** NOUN
die Schulter (PL die Schultern)

shoulder bag NOUN
die Umhängetasche (PL die Umhängetaschen)

ℱ**shout** NOUN
der Schrei (PL die Schreie)

to **shout** VERB
1 schreien◇
Stop shouting! Hör auf zu schreien!
2 (call) rufen◇
He shouted at us to come back. Er rief uns zu, wir sollten zurückkommen.

shovel NOUN
die Schaufel (PL die Schaufeln)

ℱ**show** NOUN
1 (on stage) die Show (PL die Shows)
We went to see a show. Wir haben eine Show gesehen.
2 (on TV, radio) die Sendung (PL die Sendungen)
3 (exhibition) die Ausstellung (PL die Ausstellungen)
fashion show die Modenschau

to **show** VERB
1 zeigen
to show something to somebody jemandem etwas zeigen
I'll show you my photos. Ich zeige dir meine Fotos.
to show somebody how something works jemandem zeigen, wie etwas funktioniert
He showed me how to make pancakes. Er hat mir gezeigt, wie man Pfannkuchen macht.
2 It shows! Das sieht man!
• to show off
angeben◇ SEP
Stop showing off! Hör auf so anzugeben!

ℱ**shower** NOUN
1 (in a bathroom) die Dusche (PL die Duschen)
to have a shower duschen
2 (of rain) der Schauer (PL die Schauer)

showjumping NOUN
das Springreiten

show-off NOUN
der Angeber (PL die Angeber), die Angeberin (PL die Angeberinnen)

to **shriek** VERB
kreischen

shrimp NOUN
die Krabbe (PL die Krabben)

to **shrink** VERB
1 schrumpfen (PERF sein)
2 (clothes) einlaufen◇ SEP (PERF sein)
My sweater has shrunk. Mein Pullover ist eingelaufen.

Shrove Tuesday NOUN
der Fastnachtsdienstag

to **shrug** VERB
to shrug your shoulders mit den Achseln zucken

to **shuffle** VERB
to shuffle the cards die Karten mischen

ℱ**shut** ADJECTIVE
zu
The shops are shut. Die Geschäfte haben zu.

to **shut** VERB
zumachen SEP
Can you shut the door please? Kannst du die Tür bitte zumachen?
The shops shut at six. Die Geschäfte machen um sechs zu.
• to shut up
den Mund halten◇ (informal)
Shut up! Halt den Mund!

shuttlecock NOUN
der Federball (PL die Federbälle)

shuttle service NOUN
der Shuttledienst
There's a shuttle service from the airport. Es gibt einen Shuttledienst vom Flughafen.

ℱ**shy** ADJECTIVE
schüchtern

shyness NOUN
die Schüchternheit

Sicily NOUN
Sizilien (NEUTER)

ℱ**sick** ADJECTIVE
1 (ill) krank
2 to be sick (vomit) sich übergeben◇
I was sick several times. Ich habe mich mehrmals übergeben.
3 I feel sick. Mir ist schlecht.
4 übel
a sick joke ein übler Witz
5 to be sick of something etwas satt haben
I'm sick of staying at home every day. Ich habe es satt, jeden Tag zu Hause zu sitzen.

sickness NOUN
die Krankheit (PL die Krankheiten)

ℱ indicates key words

side NOUN
1 die **Seite** (PL die **Seiten**)
   on the other side of the street auf der anderen Straßenseite
   on the wrong side auf der falschen Seite
   I'm on your side. (I agree with you) Ich bin auf deiner Seite.
2 (edge) der **Rand** (PL die **Ränder**) (of a pool, river)
   at the side of the road am Straßenrand
3 (team) die **Mannschaft** (PL die **Mannschaften**)
   the winning side die siegreiche Mannschaft
   She plays on our side. Sie spielt bei uns mit.
4 **to take sides** Partei ergreifen◇
   He always takes sides against her. Er ergreift immer gegen sie Partei.
5 **side by side** nebeneinander

side effect NOUN
die **Nebenwirkung** (PL die **Nebenwirkungen**)

side street NOUN
die **Seitenstraße** (PL die **Seitenstraßen**)

sieve NOUN
das **Sieb** (PL die **Siebe**)

sigh NOUN
der **Seufzer** (PL die **Seufzer**)

to **sigh** VERB
seufzen

sight NOUN
1 der **Anblick**
   It was a marvellous sight. Es war ein herrlicher Anblick.
2 **at first sight** auf den ersten Blick
3 (eyesight)
   to have poor sight schlechte Augen haben
4 **to know somebody by sight** jemanden vom Sehen kennen◇
   out of sight außer Sicht
   to lose sight of somebody jemanden aus den Augen verlieren◇
5 **the sights** die Sehenswürdigkeiten
   to see the sights die Sehenswürdigkeiten besichtigen

sightseeing NOUN
das **Sightseeing**
   to go sightseeing Sightseeing machen
   to do some sightseeing einige Sehenswürdigkeiten besichtigen

sign NOUN
1 (notice) das **Schild** (PL die **Schilder**)
   There's a sign on the door. An der Tür ist ein Schild.
2 (trace, indication) das **Zeichen** (PL die **Zeichen**)
3 (of the zodiac) das **Sternzeichen** (PL die Sternzeichen)
   What sign are you? Was für ein Sternzeichen bist du?

to **sign** VERB
1 unterschreiben◇
   to sign a letter einen Brief unterschreiben
2 (using sign language) sich durch Zeichensprache verständigen

signal NOUN
das **Signal** (PL die **Signale**)

signature NOUN
die **Unterschrift** (PL die **Unterschriften**)

significant ADJECTIVE
bedeutend

sign language NOUN
die **Zeichensprache**

signpost NOUN
der **Wegweiser** (PL die **Wegweiser**)

silence NOUN
die **Stille**

silent ADJECTIVE
still

silk NOUN
die **Seide**

silk ADJECTIVE
Seiden-
   a silk blouse eine Seidenbluse

silky ADJECTIVE
seidig

silly ADJECTIVE
dumm
   It was a really silly thing to do. Das war wirklich dumm.

silver NOUN
das **Silber**

silver ADJECTIVE
Silber-
   a silver medal eine Silbermedaille

SIM card NOUN
die **SIM-Karte** (PL die **SIM-Karten**)

similar ADJECTIVE
ähnlich
   It looks similar to my old bike. Es sieht so ähnlich wie mein altes Rad aus.

similarity NOUN
die **Ähnlichkeit** (PL die **Ähnlichkeiten**)

simple ADJECTIVE
einfach

simply ADVERB
einfach

◇ irregular verb; SEP separable verb; for more help with verbs see centre section

sin NOUN
die **Sünde** (PL die **Sünden**)

ℙ **since** PREPOSITION
1 **seit** (+DAT) *(notice that German uses the present tense for an action starting in the past and still going on in the present)*
I have been in Berlin since Saturday. Ich bin seit Samstag in Berlin.
Since when? Seit wann?
2 *(with a negative the perfect tense is used)*
I haven't seen her since Monday. Ich habe sie seit Montag nicht gesehen.

since CONJUNCTION
1 **seit**
since I have known him seit ich ihn kenne
since I've been learning German seitdem ich Deutsch lerne
2 *(because)* **da**
Since it was raining, the match was cancelled. Da es regnete, wurde das Spiel abgesagt.

since ADVERB
seitdem
I haven't seen him since. Ich habe ihn seitdem nicht mehr gesehen.

sincere ADJECTIVE
aufrichtig

sincerely ADVERB
Yours sincerely Mit freundlichen Grüßen

ℙ to **sing** VERB
singen◇

ℙ **singer** NOUN
der **Sänger** (PL die **Sänger**), die **Sängerin** (PL die **Sängerinnen**)

WORD TIP Professions, hobbies, and sports don't take an article in German: Sie ist Sängerin.

ℙ **singing** NOUN
1 das **Singen**
a singing lesson eine Singstunde
2 **I like singing.** Ich singe gern.

ℙ **single** NOUN
1 *(ticket)* die **einfache Fahrkarte** (PL die **einfachen Fahrkarten**)
A single to Munich, please. Eine einfache Fahrkarte nach München bitte.
2 *(Music)* die **Single** (PL die **Singles**)

single ADJECTIVE
1 *(not married)* **alleinstehend**, *(on forms)* **ledig**
a single woman eine alleinstehende Frau
2 *(just one)* **einzig**
I haven't had a single reply. Ich habe keine einzige Antwort bekommen.

3 **not a single one** kein Einziger/keine Einzige/kein Einziges
4 **single room** das Einzelzimmer
single bed das Einzelbett

single parent NOUN
der/die **Alleinerziehende** (PL die **Alleinerziehenden**)
She's a single parent. Sie ist alleinerziehende Mutter.
a single-parent family eine Einelternfamilie

singles PLURAL NOUN
(in tennis) das **Einzel** (PL die **Einzel**)
the women's singles das Dameneinzel
the men's singles das Herreneinzel

singular NOUN
(in grammar) die **Einzahl**, der **Singular**
in the singular in der Einzahl, im Singular

ℙ **sink** NOUN
das **Spülbecken** (PL die **Spülbecken**)

to **sink** VERB
sinken◇ *(PERF* **sein**)

ℙ **sir** NOUN
der **Herr** (PL die **Herren**)
(in German,' Sir' is usually not translated)
Would you like another one, sir? Möchten Sie noch eins?
Yes, sir. Ja, mein Herr.

ℙ **sister** NOUN
die **Schwester** (PL die **Schwestern**)
My sister's ten. Meine Schwester ist zehn.

ℙ **sister-in-law** NOUN
die **Schwägerin** (PL die **Schwägerinnen**)

ℙ to **sit** VERB
1 *(sit down)* **sich setzen**
You can sit on the sofa. Du kannst dich aufs Sofa setzen.
Sit on the floor. Setz dich auf den Boden.
2 *(be sitting)* **sitzen**◇
Leila was sitting on the sofa. Leila saß auf dem Sofa.
to sit on the floor auf dem Boden sitzen
3 **to sit an exam** eine Prüfung machen
• **to sit down**
sich setzen
He sat down on the chair. Er setzte sich auf den Stuhl.
Do sit down. Setzen Sie sich.

sitcom NOUN
die **Situationskomödie** (PL die **Situationskomödien**)

ℙ **site** NOUN
1 **building site** die Baustelle

2 camping site der Campingplatz

3 archaeolological site die archäologische Stätte

ℰ **sitting room** NOUN
das Wohnzimmer (PL die Wohnzimmer)

ℰ **situated** ADJECTIVE
to be situated sich befinden◇
The house is situated in a small village. Das Haus befindet sich in einem kleinen Dorf.

situation NOUN
1 (location) die Lage (PL die Lagen)
2 (circumstances) die Situation (PL die Situationen)

ℰ **six** NUMBER
sechs
Harry's six. Harry ist sechs.

ℰ **sixteen** NUMBER
sechzehn
Alice is sixteen. Alice ist sechzehn.

ℰ **sixth** ADJECTIVE
sechster/sechste/sechstes
on the sixth floor im sechsten Stock
on the sixth of July am sechsten Juli

ℰ **sixty** NUMBER
sechzig
She's sixty. Sie ist sechzig.

ℰ **size** NOUN
1 die Größe (PL die Größen)
It depends on the size of the house. Es kommt auf die Größe des Hauses an.
2 What size is the window? Wie groß ist das Fenster?
3 (in clothes) die Größe (PL die Größen)
What size do you take? Welche Größe haben Sie?
4 (of shoes) die Schuhgröße (PL die Schuhgrößen)
I take a size thirty-eight. Ich habe Schuhgröße achtunddreißig.

skate NOUN
1 (an ice skate) der Schlittschuh (PL die Schlittschuhe)
2 (a roller skate) der Rollschuh (PL die Rollschuhe)

to **skate** VERB
1 (ice-skate) Schlittschuh laufen◇ (PERF sein)
2 (roller-skate) Rollschuh laufen◇ (PERF sein)

skateboard NOUN
das Skateboard (PL die Skateboards)

skateboarding NOUN
das Skateboardfahren
to go skateboarding Skateboard fahren◇ (PERF sein)

skater NOUN
1 (on ice) der Eisläufer (PL die Eisläufer), die Eisläuferin (PL die Eisläuferinnen)
2 (on roller skates) der Rollschuhfahrer (PL die Rollschuhfahrer), die Rollschuhfahrerin (PL die Rollschuhfahrerinnen)
3 (on a skateboard) der Skater (PL die Skater)

skating NOUN
1 (on ice) das Schlittschuhlaufen
to go skating Schlittschuh laufen◇ (PERF sein)
2 (roller-skating) das Rollschuhlaufen
to go roller-skating Rollschuh laufen◇ (PERF sein)

ℰ **skating rink** NOUN
1 (ice rink) die Eisbahn (PL die Eisbahnen)
2 (for roller-skating) die Rollschuhbahn (PL die Rollschuhbahnen)

skeleton NOUN
das Skelett (PL die Skelette)

sketch NOUN
1 die Skizze (PL die Skizzen)
2 (comedy routine) der Sketch (PL die Sketche)

ski NOUN
der Ski (PL die Skier)

to **ski** VERB
Ski fahren◇ (PERF sein)
He can ski. Er kann Ski fahren.

ski boot NOUN
der Skistiefel (PL die Skistiefel)

to **skid** VERB
schleudern (PERF sein)
The car skidded. Das Auto kam ins Schleudern.

skier NOUN
der Skifahrer (PL die Skifahrer), die Skifahrerin (PL die Skifahrerinnen)

> **WORD TIP** Professions, hobbies, and sports don't take an article in German: Er ist Skifahrer.

ℰ **skiing** NOUN
das Skifahren
to go skiing Ski fahren◇ (PERF sein)

ski lift NOUN
der Skilift (PL die Skilifte)

skimmed milk NOUN
die Magermilch

ℰ **skin** NOUN
die Haut (PL die Häute)

◇ irregular verb; SEP separable verb; for more help with verbs see centre section

skinhead NOUN
der **Skinhead** (PL die **Skinheads**)

skinny ADJECTIVE
dünn

skip NOUN
(for rubbish) der **Container** (PL die **Container**)

to **skip** VERB
1 **auslassen**◇ SEP (a meal, part of a book)
I skipped a few chapters. Ich ließ ein paar Kapitel aus.
2 **to skip a lesson** ein Stunde schwänzen (informal)
3 (with a rope) **Seil springen**◇ (PERF sein)

ℓ **skirt** NOUN
der **Rock** (PL die **Röcke**)
a long skirt ein langer Rock
a tight skirt ein enger Rock
a miniskirt ein Minirock

ski suit NOUN
der **Skianzug** (PL die **Skianzüge**)

skittles PLURAL NOUN
das **Kegeln**
to play skittles kegeln

skull NOUN
der **Schädel** (PL die **Schädel**)

ℓ **sky** NOUN
der **Himmel** (PL die **Himmel**)
in the sky am Himmel

skyscraper NOUN
der **Wolkenkratzer** (PL die **Wolkenkratzer**)

to **slam** VERB
1 **zuknallen** SEP
She slammed the door. Sie hat die Tür zugeknallt.
2 **zuknallen** SEP (PERF sein)
The door slammed. Die Tür ist zugeknallt.

slang NOUN
der **Slang**

slap NOUN
der **Klaps** (PL die **Klapse**), (in the face) die **Ohrfeige** (PL die **Ohrfeigen**)

to **slap** VERB
to slap somebody (across the face) jemanden ohrfeigen (on the bottom) jemandem einen Klaps geben

sledge NOUN
der **Schlitten** (PL die **Schlitten**)

sledging NOUN
to go sledging Schlitten fahren◇ (PERF sein)

ℓ **sleep** NOUN
der **Schlaf**
You need more sleep. Du brauchst mehr Schlaf.
I had a good sleep. Ich habe gut geschlafen.
to go to sleep einschlafen◇ SEP (PERF sein)
He's gone back to sleep. Er ist wieder eingeschlafen.

to **sleep** VERB
schlafen◇
She's sleeping. Sie schläft.

ℓ **sleeping bag** NOUN
der **Schlafsack** (PL die **Schlafsäcke**)

ℓ **sleepy** ADJECTIVE
to be sleepy schläfrig sein
He was getting sleepy. Er wurde schläfrig.

sleet NOUN
der **Schneeregen**

sleeve NOUN
der **Ärmel** (PL die **Ärmel**)
a long-sleeved jumper ein Pullover mit langen Ärmeln
a short-sleeved shirt ein Hemd mit kurzen Ärmeln
to roll up your sleeves die Ärmel hochkrempeln SEP

ℓ **slice** NOUN
die **Scheibe** (PL die **Scheiben**)
a slice of bread eine Scheibe Brot

to **slice** VERB
to slice something etwas in Scheiben schneiden◇

ℓ **slide** NOUN
1 (hairslide) die **Haarspange** (PL die **Haarspangen**)
2 (for sliding down) die **Rutschbahn** (PL die **Rutschbahnen**)
to go down the slide rutschen (PERF sein)
3 (photo) das **Dia** (PL die **Dias**)

ℓ **slight** ADJECTIVE
klein
There is a slight problem. Es gibt ein kleines Problem.

slightly ADVERB
etwas

slim ADJECTIVE
schlank

to **slim** VERB
abnehmen◇ SEP
I'm slimming. Ich mache eine Schlankheitskur.

ℓ indicates key words

sling *NOUN*
die **Schlinge** (*PL* die **Schlingen**)
to have your arm in a sling den Arm in der Schlinge haben

ᵖ**slip** *NOUN*
1 *(mistake)* der **Fehler** (*PL* die **Fehler**)
2 *(petticoat)* der **Unterrock** (*PL* die **Unterröcke**)

to slip *VERB*
1 *(slide)* **ausrutschen** *SEP* (*PERF* **sein**)
2 **It slipped my mind.** Es ist mir entfallen.
• **to slip up**
einen Fehler machen

slipper *NOUN*
der **Hausschuh** (*PL* die **Hausschuhe**)

slippery *ADJECTIVE*
glatt

slope *NOUN*
der **Hang** (*PL* die **Hänge**)

slot *NOUN*
der **Schlitz** (*PL* die **Schlitze**)

slot machine *NOUN*
1 *(vending machine)* der **Automat** (*PL* die **Automaten**)
2 *(games machine)* der **Spielautomat** (*PL* die **Spielautomaten**)

ᵖ**slow** *ADJECTIVE*
1 **langsam**
The service is a bit slow. Die Bedienung ist etwas langsam.
2 *(of a clock or watch)*
to be slow nachgehen◇ *SEP* (*PERF* **sein**)
My watch is slow. Meine Uhr geht nach.
• **to slow down**
langsamer werden◇ (*PERF* **sein**)

ᵖ**slowly** *ADVERB*
langsam
He got up slowly. Er ist langsam aufgestanden.
Can you speak more slowly, please? Können Sie bitte etwas langsamer sprechen?

slug *NOUN*
die **Nacktschnecke** (*PL* die **Nacktschnecken**)

slum *NOUN*
der **Slum** (*PL* die **Slums**)
They lived in the slums on the edge of the city. Sie wohnten in den Slums am Stadtrand.

sly *ADJECTIVE*
gerissen *(a person)*

on the sly heimlich

smack *NOUN*
der **Klaps** (*PL* die **Klapse**)

to smack *VERB*
to smack somebody jemandem einen Klaps geben◇

ᵖ**small** *ADJECTIVE*
klein
a small dog ein kleiner Hund

> **WORD TIP** Do not translate the English word **small** with the German schmal.

ᵖ**smart** *ADJECTIVE*
1 *(well dressed, posh)* **elegant**
a smart restaurant ein elegantes Restaurant
2 *(clever)* **clever**

smash *NOUN*
(collision) der **Zusammenstoß** (*PL* die **Zusammenstöße**)

to smash *VERB*
1 *(break)* **zerschlagen**◇
They smashed a windowpane. Sie haben eine Fensterscheibe zerschlagen.
2 *(get broken)* **zerbrechen**◇ (*PERF* **sein**)
The plate smashed. Der Teller ist zerbrochen.

smashing *ADJECTIVE*
klasse *(informal)*

ᵖ**smell** *NOUN*
der **Geruch** (*PL* die **Gerüche**)
a nasty smell ein scheußlicher Geruch
a smell of gas ein Gasgeruch

to smell *VERB*
1 **riechen**◇
I can't smell anything. Ich kann nichts riechen.
to smell of perfume nach Parfüm riechen
That smells good! Das riecht gut!
2 *(smell bad)* **stinken**◇
The drains smell. Der Abfluss stinkt.

smelly *ADJECTIVE*
1 **stinkend**
her smelly dog ihr stinkender Hund
2 **to be smelly** stinken◇

ᵖ**smile** *NOUN*
das **Lächeln**

to smile *VERB*
lächeln
to smile at somebody jemanden anlächeln *SEP*

ᵖ**smoke** *NOUN*
der **Rauch**

◇ irregular verb; *SEP* separable verb; for more help with verbs see centre section

smoke

to smoke VERB
rauchen
She doesn't smoke. Sie raucht nicht.

smoked ADJECTIVE
geräuchert
smoked salmon der Räucherlachs

smoker NOUN
der Raucher (PL die Raucher), die
Raucherin (PL die Raucherinnen)

smoking NOUN
'No smoking' 'Rauchen verboten'
to give up smoking mit dem Rauchen
aufhören

♀**smooth** ADJECTIVE
1 glatt
a smooth surface eine glatte Oberfläche
2 (person) aalglatt

smug ADJECTIVE
selbstgefällig

to smuggle VERB
to smuggle something etwas schmuggeln

smuggler NOUN
1 der Schmuggler (PL die Schmuggler), die
Schmugglerin (PL die Schmugglerinnen)
2 **drugs smuggler** der Drogenschmuggler

snack NOUN
der Snack (PL die Snacks)
We had a snack at one o'clock. Wir haben
um ein Uhr einen Snack zu uns genommen.

♀**snail** NOUN
die Schnecke (PL die Schnecken)

snake NOUN
die Schlange (PL die Schlangen)

snap NOUN
(card game) das Schnippschnapp

to snap VERB
1 (break) brechen◇ (PERF sein)
2 **to snap something** etwas zerbrechen◇
3 **to snap your fingers** mit den Fingern
schnalzen

snapshot NOUN
der Schnappschuss (PL die
Schnappschüsse)

to snarl VERB
knurren

to snatch VERB
1 entreißen◇
to snatch something from somebody
jemandem etwas entreißen
She had her bag snatched. Man hat ihr die

---

so

Handtasche entrissen.
2 **He snatched it out of my hand.** Er hat es
mir aus der Hand gerissen.

to sneak VERB
to sneak in sich hineinschleichen◇ SEP
to sneak out sich hinausschleichen◇ SEP

to sneeze VERB
niesen

to sniff VERB
schnüffeln

snob NOUN
der Snob (PL die Snobs)

snobbery NOUN
der Snobismus

snooker NOUN
das Snooker

snooze NOUN
das Nickerchen (PL die Nickerchen)
to have a snooze ein Nickerchen machen

to snooze VERB
ein Nickerchen machen

to snore VERB
schnarchen

♀**snow** NOUN
der Schnee

to snow VERB
schneien
It's snowing. Es schneit.

snowball NOUN
der Schneeball (PL die Schneebälle)

snowboard NOUN
das Snowboard (PL die Snowboards)

snowboarding NOUN
snowboarden
to go snowboarding snowboarden gehen◇
(PERF sein)

snowdrift NOUN
die Schneewehe (PL die Schneewehen)

snowman NOUN
der Schneemann (PL die Schneemänner)

♀**so** ADVERB, CONJUNCTION
1 so
He's so lazy. Er ist so faul.
**Our house is a bit like yours, but not so
big.** Unser Haus ist so ähnlich wie eures,
aber nicht so groß.
2 **so much** so sehr
I hate it so much. Ich hasse es so sehr.
3 **so much** so viel

629

♀ indicates key words

ENGLISH—GERMAN

I have so much work. Ich habe so viel Arbeit.
Not so much! Nicht so viel!

4 **so many** so viele
   We've got so many problems. Wir haben so viele Probleme.

5 *(therefore)* also
   He got up late, so he missed his train. Er ist zu spät aufgestanden und hat deshalb den Zug verpasst.
   So what shall we do? Also, was machen wir?

6 **So what?** Na und?

7 *(also)*
   so do I, so did I ich auch
   'I live in Leeds.' – 'So do I.' 'Ich wohne in Leeds.' – 'Ich auch.'
   I liked the film and so did he. Ich fand den Film gut und er auch.
   so am I ich auch
   so do we wir auch

8 **I think so.** Ich glaube schon.

9 **I hope so.** Hoffentlich.

to **soak** *VERB*
   einweichen *SEP*

soaked *ADJECTIVE*
   patschnass
   to be soaked to the skin patschnass sein

♭ **soap** *NOUN*
1 die Seife (*PL* die Seifen)
2 *(soap opera)* die Seifenoper (*PL* die Seifenopern)

sober *ADJECTIVE*
   nüchtern

to **sober** *VERB*
• **to sober up**
   nüchtern werden◇ (*PERF* **sein**)

♭ **soccer** *NOUN*
   der Fußball

social *ADJECTIVE*
1 sozial
   social problems soziale Probleme
2 gesellschaftlich *(engagement, ambition)*
   social engagements gesellschaftliche Verpflichtungen
   social class die gesellschaftliche Schicht
3 *(sociable)* gesellig *(evening, person)*

socialism *NOUN*
   der Sozialismus

socialist *NOUN*
   der Sozialist (*PL* die Sozialisten), die Sozialistin (*PL* die Sozialistinnen)
   He's a socialist. Er ist Sozialist.

social media *NOUN*
   soziale Medien (*PLURAL*)

social security *NOUN*
1 die Sozialhilfe
   to be on social security Sozialhilfe bekommen
2 *(national insurance system)* die Sozialversicherung

social worker *NOUN*
   der Sozialarbeiter (*PL* die Sozialarbeiter), die Sozialarbeiterin (*PL* die Sozialarbeiterinnen)

WORD TIP Professions, hobbies, and sports don't take an article in German: Sie ist Sozialarbeiterin.

society *NOUN*
   die Gesellschaft (*PL* die Gesellschaften)
   They want to change society. Sie wollen die Gesellschaft verändern.

sociology *NOUN*
   die Soziologie

♭ **sock** *NOUN*
   die Socke (*PL* die Socken)
   a pair of socks ein Paar Socken

socket *NOUN*
   (power point) die Steckdose (*PL* die Steckdosen)

♭ **sofa** *NOUN*
   das Sofa (*PL* die Sofas)

sofa bed *NOUN*
   die Schlafcouch (*PL* die Schlafcouchs)

♭ **soft** *ADJECTIVE*
1 weich
2 **a soft option** eine bequeme Lösung
3 **to have a soft spot for somebody** eine Schwäche für jemanden haben

soft drink *NOUN*
   das alkoholfreie Getränk (*PL* die alkoholfreien Getränke)

soft toy *NOUN*
   das Stofftier (*PL* die Stofftiere)

software *NOUN*
   die Software

soil *NOUN*
   die Erde

solar cell *NOUN*
   die Solarzelle (*PL* die Solarzellen)

solar energy *NOUN*
   die Sonnenenergie

soldier *NOUN*
   der Soldat (*PL* die Soldaten), die Soldatin

◇ **irregular verb;** *SEP* **separable verb; for more help with verbs see centre section**

(PL die **Soldatinnen**)

> **WORD TIP** Professions, hobbies, and sports don't take an article in German: Er ist Soldat.

solicitor NOUN
1 (dealing with lawsuits) der **Rechtsanwalt** (PL die **Rechtsanwälte**), die **Rechtsanwältin** (PL die **Rechtsanwältinnen**)
2 (dealing with property or documents) der **Notar** (PL die **Notare**), die **Notarin** (PL die **Notarinnen**)

> **WORD TIP** Professions, hobbies, and sports don't take an article in German: Er ist Rechtsanwalt.

solid ADJECTIVE
1 (not flimsy) **stabil**
a solid structure ein stabiler Bau
2 **massiv**
a table made of solid oak ein Tisch aus massiver Eiche
solid silver massives Silber

solo NOUN
das **Solo** (PL die **Solos**)
guitar solo das Gitarrensolo

solo ADJECTIVE
Solo-
a solo act eine Solonummer

solo ADVERB
solo

soloist NOUN
der **Solist** (PL die **Solisten**), die **Solistin** (PL die **Solistinnen**)

> **WORD TIP** Professions, hobbies, and sports don't take an article in German: Er ist Solist.

solution NOUN
die **Lösung** (PL die **Lösungen**)
the solution to the problem die Lösung des Problems

to **solve** VERB
lösen

ℰ **some** DETERMINER, ADVERB
1 (followed by a singular noun) **etwas** (etwas does not change)
Would you like some salad? Möchtest du etwas Salat?
Can you lend me some money? Kannst du mir etwas Geld leihen?
Have you got some bread? (some is often not translated) Hast du Brot?
2 (followed by a plural noun) (a few) **ein paar** (ein paar does not change)
I've bought some apples. Ich habe ein paar Äpfel gekauft.
3 (followed by a plural noun) (a certain number

but not all) **einige**
Some of his films are too violent. Einige von seinen Filmen sind zu brutal.
4 (referring to something that has been mentioned)
'Would you like tea?' – 'Thanks, I've got some.' 'Möchten Sie Tee?' – 'Nein danke, ich habe schon welchen.'
He's eaten some of it. Er hat etwas davon gegessen.
I'd like some. Ich möchte etwas. (with a plural noun) Ich möchte welche.
5 (certain people or things) **manche**
Some people think he's right. Manche Leute glauben, dass er Recht hat.
6 **some day** eines Tages

ℰ **somebody**, **someone** PRONOUN
jemand
There's somebody in the garden. Da ist jemand im Garten.
I saw somebody in the garden. Ich habe jemanden im Garten gesehen.
Give it to someone else. Gib es jemand anderem.

ℰ **somehow** ADVERB
irgendwie
I've got to finish this essay somehow. Ich muss diesen Aufsatz irgendwie fertig schreiben.

ℰ **something** PRONOUN
1 **etwas**
There's something I've got to tell you. Ich muss dir etwas erzählen.
something new etwas Neues
something interesting etwas Interessantes
There's something wrong. Irgendetwas stimmt nicht.
2 Their house is really something! Ihr Haus ist einfach Klasse!

sometime ADVERB
irgendwann
Give me a ring sometime next week. Ruf mich irgendwann nächste Woche an.

ℰ **sometimes** ADVERB
manchmal
I sometimes take the train. Manchmal fahre ich mit der Bahn.

ℰ **somewhere** ADVERB
1 (in a place) **irgendwo**
I've left my bag somewhere here. Ich habe meine Tasche hier irgendwo liegen lassen.
2 (to a place) **irgendwohin**
I'd like to go somewhere warm. Ich möchte irgendwohin fahren, wo es warm ist.

ℰ indicates key words

son | **south**

℗ **son** NOUN
der **Sohn** (PL die **Söhne**)

℗ **song** NOUN
das **Lied** (PL die **Lieder**)

son-in-law NOUN
der **Schwiegersohn** (PL die
Schwiegersöhne)

℗ **soon** ADVERB
1 **bald**
We'll soon be on holiday. Wir haben bald
Ferien.
See you soon! Bis bald!
2 **as soon as she arrives** sobald sie ankommt
as soon as possible so bald wie möglich
3 **It's too soon.** Es ist zu früh.

sooner ADVERB
1 **früher**
We should have started sooner. Wir hätten
früher anfangen sollen.
sooner or later früher oder später
2 *(rather)* **lieber**
I'd sooner wait. Ich würde lieber warten.

soprano NOUN
der **Sopran** (PL die **Soprane**)

℗ **sore** NOUN
die **wunde Stelle** (PL die **wunden Stellen**)

sore ADJECTIVE
1 *(inflamed)* **wund**
His feet were sore after the walk. Nach der
Wanderung hatte er wunde Füße.
to have a sore throat Halsschmerzen haben
2 **My arm's sore.** Mir tut der Arm weh.
3 **It's a sore point.** Das ist ein wunder Punkt.

℗ **sorry** ADJECTIVE
1 **I'm really sorry.** Es tut mir wirklich leid.
Sorry to disturb you. Es tut mir leid, dass
ich dich störe.
I'm sorry I forgot your birthday. Es tut mir
leid, dass ich deinen Geburtstag vergessen
habe.
I'm sorry, we're closing. Es tut mir leid,
aber wir machen jetzt zu.
2 **Sorry!** Entschuldigung!
3 **Sorry?** Wie bitte?
4 **I feel sorry for him.** Er tut mir leid.

℗ **sort** NOUN
die **Art** (PL die **Arten**)
a sort of dance music eine Art Tanzmusik
What sort of car have you got? Was für ein
Auto hast du?
all sorts of people alle möglichen Leute
for all sorts of reasons aus allen möglichen
Gründen

to **sort** VERB
sortieren
• **to sort something out**
1 **Ordnung schaffen◇** in etwas (DAT) *(papers,
desk, room, possessions)*
I must sort out my room tonight. Ich muss
heute Abend in meinem Zimmer Ordnung
schaffen.
2 **etwas klären** *(a problem, arrangement)*
Liz is sorting it out. Liz klärt es.

so-so ADJECTIVE
so lala *(informal)*
'How was the film?' – 'So-so.' 'Wie war der
Film?' – 'So lala.'

soul NOUN
1 die **Seele** (PL die **Seelen**)
2 *(music)* der **Soul**

℗ **sound** NOUN
1 *(noise)* das **Geräusch** (PL die **Geräusche**)
2 *(of voices, laughter, bell)* der **Klang**
the sound of her voice der Klang ihrer
Stimme
I can hear the sound of voices. Ich kann
Stimmen hören.
3 **without a sound** lautlos
4 *(volume)* die **Lautstärke**
Could you turn the sound down? Kannst
du es leiser stellen?

to **sound** VERB
1 **It sounds easy.** Es hört sich einfach an.
2 **It sounds as if she's happy.** Sie scheint
glücklich zu sein.

sound asleep ADVERB
to be sound asleep fest schlafen◇

sound effect NOUN
der **Geräuscheffekt** (PL die
Geräuscheffekte)

soundtrack NOUN
der **Soundtrack** (PL die **Soundtracks**)

℗ **soup** NOUN
die **Suppe** (PL die **Suppen**)
mushroom soup die Pilzsuppe

sour ADJECTIVE
sauer

℗ **south** NOUN
der **Süden**
in the south im Süden

south ADJECTIVE
südlich, Süd-
the south side die Südseite
south wind der Südwind

south ADVERB
1 *(towards the south)* **nach Süden**
to travel south nach Süden fahren

632

2 **south of Berlin** südlich von Berlin

South Africa NOUN
Südafrika (NEUTER)

South America NOUN
Südamerika (NEUTER)

south-east NOUN
der Südosten

south-east ADJECTIVE
in south-east England in Südostengland

southern ADJECTIVE
südlich, Süd-
on the southern side of the mountain an
der Südseite des Berges

South Pole NOUN
der Südpol

south-west NOUN
der Südwesten

south-west ADJECTIVE
in south-west England in Südwestengland

souvenir NOUN
das Souvenir (PL die Souvenirs)

soya NOUN
die Soja

spa NOUN
1 (town) der Kurort (PL die Kurorte), der
Badeort (PL die Badeorte)
2 (in a hotel, etc.) der Wellnessbereich (PL die
Wellnessbereiche)

℘**space** NOUN
1 (room) der Platz
There's enough space. Es ist genug Platz.
We've got enough space for two. Wir
haben genug Platz für zwei.
2 (gap) der Zwischenraum (PL die
Zwischenräume)
to leave a large space between lines viel
Platz zwischen den Zeilen lassen
3 (parking) space die Parklücke
4 (outer space) der Weltraum
in space im Weltraum

spaceship NOUN
das Raumschiff (PL die Raumschiffe)

spade NOUN
1 der Spaten (PL die Spaten)
2 (in cards) das Pik
the queen of spades die Pikdame

℘**Spain** NOUN
Spanien (NEUTER)
from Spain aus Spanien
to Spain nach Spanien

℘**Spaniard** NOUN
der Spanier (PL die Spanier), die Spanierin
(PL die Spanierinnen)

℘**Spanish** NOUN
1 (language) das Spanisch
I'm learning Spanish. Ich lerne Spanisch.
2 the Spanish (people) die Spanier

Spanish ADJECTIVE
spanisch
the Spanish coast die spanische Küste
He is Spanish. Er ist Spanier.
She is Spanish. Sie ist Spanierin.

WORD TIP Adjectives never have capitals
in German, even for regions, countries, or
nationalities.

spanner NOUN
der Schraubenschlüssel (PL die
Schraubenschlüssel)

℘**spare** ADJECTIVE
Ersatz-
Have you got a spare key? Hast du einen
Ersatzschlüssel?
We have a spare ticket. Wir haben eine
Karte übrig.

to **spare** VERB
to have time to spare Zeit haben
Can you spare a moment? Hast du einen
Moment Zeit?

spare part NOUN
das Ersatzteil (PL die Ersatzteile)

spare room NOUN
das Gästezimmer (PL die Gästezimmer)

℘**spare time** NOUN
die Freizeit
in my spare time in meiner Freizeit

spare wheel NOUN
das Reserverad (PL die Reserveräder)

sparkling ADJECTIVE
sparkling mineral water Mineralwasser mit
Kohlensäure
sparkling wine der Schaumwein

sparrow NOUN
der Spatz (PL die Spatzen)

℘to **speak** VERB
1 sprechen◇
Do you speak Spanish? Sprechen Sie
Spanisch?
spoken German gesprochenes Deutsch
to speak to somebody about something
mit jemandem über etwas (ACC) sprechen
She's speaking to Mike about it. Sie spricht

℘ indicates key words

mit Mike darüber.

2 Who's speaking? *(on the phone)* Wer ist am Apparat?

speaker *NOUN*
1 *(on a music system)* der **Lautsprecher** (PL die **Lautsprecher**)
2 *(at a public lecture)* der **Redner** (PL die **Redner**), die **Rednerin** (PL die **Rednerinnen**)

ℓ **special** *ADJECTIVE*
1 besonderer/besondere/besonderes
on special occasions bei besonderen Anlässen
2 special offer das Sonderangebot

specialist *NOUN*
1 *(expert)* der **Fachmann** (PL die **Fachleute**), die **Fachfrau** (PL die **Fachfrauen**)
2 *(doctor)* der **Facharzt** (PL die **Fachärzte**), die **Fachärztin** (PL die **Fachärztinnen**)

WORD TIP Professions, hobbies, and sports don't take an article in German: Er ist Facharzt.

to **specialize** *VERB*
to specialize in sich spezialisieren auf *(+ACC)*
I'm specializing in business studies. Ich spezialisiere mich auf Wirtschaftswissenschaften.

ℓ **specially** *ADVERB*
1 besonders
not specially nicht besonders
It's specially good for babies. Es ist besonders gut für Babys.
2 *(specifically)* speziell
I made this cake specially for you. Ich habe diesen Kuchen speziell für dich gebacken.

special needs *PLURAL NOUN*
children with special needs lernbehinderte Kinder
a special needs teacher ein Sonderschullehrer

species *NOUN*
die **Art** (PL die **Arten**)

spectacles *PLURAL NOUN*
die **Brille** (PL die **Brillen**)
a pair of spectacles eine Brille

WORD TIP In German die Brille is singular.

spectacular *ADJECTIVE*
spektakulär

ℓ **spectator** *NOUN*
der **Zuschauer** (PL die **Zuschauer**), die **Zuschauerin** (PL die **Zuschauerinnen**)

634

speech *NOUN*
die **Rede** (PL die **Reden**)
to make a speech eine Rede halten◇

speechless *ADJECTIVE*
sprachlos
She was speechless with rage. Sie war sprachlos vor Wut.

ℓ **speed** *NOUN*
1 die **Geschwindigkeit** (PL die **Geschwindigkeiten**)
at top speed mit Höchstgeschwindigkeit
What speed was he doing? Wie schnell ist er gefahren?
2 *(gear)* der **Gang** (PL die **Gänge**)
a twelve-speed bike ein Rad mit zwölf Gängen

to **speed** *VERB*
• to speed up
1 beschleunigen *(a car)*
2 *(of a person, car)* schneller werden◇ *(PERF sein)*

speeding *NOUN*
zu schnelles Fahren
He was fined for speeding. Er hat wegen zu schnellen Fahrens ein Bußgeld bekommen.

speed limit *NOUN*
die **Geschwindigkeitsbegrenzung**
to exceed the speed limit das Tempolimit überschreiten◇

ℓ **spell** *NOUN*
1 *(of time)* die **Weile**
for a spell eine Weile
2 cold spell die Kälteperiode
sunny spells sonnige Abschnitte

to **spell** *VERB*
1 *(in writing)* schreiben◇
How do you spell it? Wie schreibt man das?
How do you spell your surname? Wie schreibt man Ihren Nachnamen?
2 *(out loud)* buchstabieren
Shall I spell it for you? Soll ich es dir buchstabieren?

spellchecker *NOUN*
die **Rechtschreibprüfung** (PL die **Rechtschreibprüfungen**)

spelling *NOUN*
die **Rechtschreibung**
spelling mistake der Rechtschreibfehler

ℓ to **spend** *VERB*
1 ausgeben◇ SEP *(money)*
I've spent all my money. Ich habe mein ganzes Geld ausgegeben.
2 verbringen◇ *(time)*

We spent three days in Munich. Wir haben drei Tage in München verbracht.
She spends her time reading. Sie verbringt ihre Zeit mit Lesen.

WORD TIP Do not translate the English word spend with the German spenden.

spice NOUN
das Gewürz (PL die Gewürze)

spicy ADJECTIVE
scharf
He doesn't like spicy food. Er mag kein scharfes Essen.

spider NOUN
die Spinne (PL die Spinnen)

ℰ **to spill** VERB
verschütten
I've spilled my coffee on the carpet. Ich habe meinen Kaffee auf dem Teppich verschüttet.

spinach NOUN
der Spinat

spine NOUN
(bones in the back) die Wirbelsäule (PL die Wirbelsäulen)

spire NOUN
die Turmspitze (PL die Turmspitzen)

spirit NOUN
1 (energy) die Energie
2 **in the right spirit** mit der richtigen Einstellung

spirits NOUN
1 (alcohol) die Spirituosen (PLURAL)
2 **to be in good spirits** guter Laune sein

to spit VERB
1 spucken
2 **to spit something out** etwas ausspucken SEP
Spit it out! Spuck es aus!

spite NOUN
1 **in spite of** trotz (+GEN)
We decided to go in spite of the rain. Wir beschlossen trotz des Regens zu gehen.
2 (nastiness) die Boshaftigkeit
to do something out of spite etwas aus Boshaftigkeit tun

spiteful ADJECTIVE
gehässig

splash NOUN
1 (noise) der Platsch
2 **splash of colour** der Farbfleck

to splash VERB
to splash somebody (with water) jemanden bespritzen

ℰ **splendid** ADJECTIVE
herrlich

splinter NOUN
der Splitter (PL die Splitter)

ℰ **to split** VERB
1 (with an axe or a knife) spalten
to split wood Holz spalten
2 (come apart) zerreißen◇ (PERF sein)
The lining has split. Das Futter ist zerrissen.
3 (divide up) teilen
They split the money between them. Sie haben das Geld untereinander geteilt.
• **to split up**
1 (a group or crowd) sich auflösen SEP
2 (a couple) sich trennen
She's split up with her husband. Sie hat sich von ihrem Mann getrennt.
She's split up with Sam. Sie hat mit Sam Schluss gemacht.

to spoil VERB
1 verderben◇
It completely spoiled our evening. Das hat uns den Abend völlig verdorben.
to spoil somebody's fun jemandem den Spaß verderben
2 (children, animals) verwöhnen
They spoil their dogs. Sie verwöhnen ihre Hunde.

spoiled ADJECTIVE
verwöhnt
a spoiled child ein verwöhntes Kind

spoilsport NOUN
der Spielverderber (PL die Spielverderber), die Spielverderberin (PL die Spielverderberinnen)

spoke NOUN
(of a wheel) die Speiche (PL die Speichen)

spokesman NOUN
der Sprecher (PL die Sprecher)

spokeswoman NOUN
die Sprecherin (PL die Sprecherinnen)

sponge NOUN
1 der Schwamm (PL die Schwämme)
2 (cake) der Biskuitkuchen (PL die Biskuitkuchen), der Rührkuchen (PL die Rührkuchen)

sponsor NOUN
der Sponsor (PL die Sponsoren), die Sponsorin (PL die Sponsorinnen)

ℰ indicates key words

to **sponsor** VERB
sponsern
sponsored walk der Sponsorenlauf

spooky ADJECTIVE
gruselig
a spooky story eine gruselige Geschichte

♂ **spoon** NOUN
der Löffel (PL die Löffel)
a spoon of sugar ein Löffel Zucker
soup spoon der Suppenlöffel
teaspoon der Teelöffel

spoonful NOUN
der Löffel (PL die Löffel)
two spoonfuls of sugar zwei Löffel Zucker

♂ **sport** NOUN
1 der Sport
to be good at sport gut im Sport sein
my favourite sport mein Lieblingssport
2 (in games)
to be a good sport ein guter Verlierer sein

sports bag NOUN
die Sporttasche (PL die Sporttaschen)

sports car NOUN
der Sportwagen (PL die Sportwagen)

sports centre NOUN
das Sportzentrum (PL die Sportzentren)

sports club NOUN
der Sportverein (PL die Sportvereine)

♂ **sportsman** NOUN
der Sportler (PL die Sportler)

> **WORD TIP** Professions, hobbies, and sports don't take an article in German: Er ist Sportler.

sportswear NOUN
die Sportbekleidung

♂ **sportswoman** NOUN
die Sportlerin (PL die Sportlerinnen)

> **WORD TIP** Professions, hobbies, and sports don't take an article in German: Sie ist Sportlerin.

♂ **sporty** ADJECTIVE
sportlich
She's very sporty. Sie ist sehr sportlich.

♂ **spot** NOUN
1 (pattern in fabric) der Punkt (PL die Punkte)
a red shirt with black spots ein rotes Hemd mit schwarzen Punkten
2 (on your skin) der Pickel (PL die Pickel)
I've got spots. Ich habe Pickel.
to be covered in spots völlig verpickelt sein
3 (stain) der Fleck (PL die Flecke)

You've got a spot on your shirt. Du hast einen Fleck auf dem Hemd.
4 **on the spot** (immediately) sofort
We'll do it for you on the spot. Wir machen es sofort für Sie.
5 **on the spot** (at hand) zur Stelle
An ambulance was on the spot in five minutes. Ein Rettungswagen war in fünf Minuten zur Stelle.

to **spot** VERB
entdecken
He spotted his friend in the crowd. Er entdeckte seinen Freund in der Menge.

spotlight NOUN
1 der Scheinwerfer (PL die Scheinwerfer)
2 (in the home) der Spot (PL die Spots)

spotty ADJECTIVE
(pimply) pickelig

spouse NOUN
1 (male) der Ehemann (PL die Ehemänner)
2 (female) die Ehefrau (PL die Ehefrauen)

sprain NOUN
die Verstauchung (PL die Verstauchungen)

to **sprain** VERB
to sprain your ankle sich (DAT) den Fuß verstauchen

spray NOUN
(spray can) das Spray (PL die Sprays)

to **spray** VERB
sprühen

♂ **spread** NOUN
der Brotaufstrich
cheese spread der Streichkäse

to **spread** VERB
1 (of news or a disease) sich verbreiten
2 streichen◇ (butter, jam, glue)

spreadsheet NOUN
(on a computer) die Tabellenkalkulation

♂ **spring** NOUN
1 (the season) der Frühling (PL die Frühlinge)
in the spring im Frühling
spring flowers Frühlingsblumen
2 (made of metal) die Feder (PL die Federn)
3 (providing water) die Quelle (PL die Quellen)

springtime NOUN
das Frühjahr
in springtime im Frühjahr

sprint NOUN
der Sprint (PL die Sprints)

to **sprint** VERB
sprinten (PERF sein)

◇ irregular verb; SEP separable verb; for more help with verbs see centre section

sprinter NOUN
der **Sprinter** (PL die **Sprinter**), die
Sprinterin (PL die **Sprinterinnen**)

sprout NOUN
(Brussels sprout) der **Rosenkohl**
He likes sprouts. Er mag Rosenkohl.

spy NOUN
der **Spion** (PL die **Spione**) die **Spionin** (PL die
Spioninnen)

> **WORD TIP** Professions, hobbies, and sports
> don't take an article in German: Er ist Spion.

to **spy** VERB
to spy on somebody jemandem
nachspionieren SEP
He's spying on me. Er spioniert mir nach.

to **squabble** VERB
sich zanken

ℱ **square** NOUN
1 (shape) das **Quadrat** (PL die **Quadrate**)
2 (in a town or village) der **Platz** (PL die **Plätze**)
the village square der Dorfplatz
3 to go back to square one noch einmal von
vorn anfangen

square ADJECTIVE
quadratisch
a square box eine quadratische Schachtel
three square metres drei Quadratmeter
The room is four metres square. Das
Zimmer ist vier mal vier Meter.

squash NOUN
1 (drink) das **Fruchtsaftgetränk**
orange squash das Orangensaftgetränk
2 (sport) das **Squash**
3 It was a squash in the car. Es war ziemlich
eng im Auto.

to **squash** VERB
zerquetschen

to **squeak** VERB
1 (door, hinge) quietschen
2 (person, animal) quieken

to **squeeze** VERB
1 drücken
to squeeze somebody's hand jemandem
die Hand drücken
2 pressen (lemon, orange)
3 sich quetschen
We all squeezed into the car. Wir
quetschten uns alle ins Auto.

squirrel NOUN
das **Eichhörnchen** (PL die **Eichhörnchen**)

to **stab** VERB
stechen◇

to stab somebody (kill) jemanden
erstechen◇

stable NOUN
der **Stall** (PL die **Ställe**)

stable ADJECTIVE
stabil

stack NOUN
1 der **Stapel** (PL die **Stapel**)
2 stacks of ein Haufen
She's got stacks of old CDs. Sie hat einen
Haufen Alten CDs.

ℱ **stadium** NOUN
das **Stadion** (PL die **Stadien**)

> **WORD TIP** Do not translate the English word
> stadium with the German Stadium.

staff NOUN
1 (of a company) das **Personal**
2 (in a school) die **Lehrkräfte** (PLURAL)

ℱ **stage** NOUN
1 (for a performance) die **Bühne** (PL die
Bühnen)
on stage auf der Bühne
2 (phase) die **Phase** (PL die **Phasen**)
at this stage of the project in dieser Phase
des Projekts
At this stage it's hard to say. Im Augenblick
ist es schwer zu sagen.

staggered ADJECTIVE
(amazed) verblüfft

stain NOUN
der **Fleck** (PL die **Flecke**)

to **stain** VERB
beflecken

stainless steel NOUN
der **Edelstahl**
a stainless steel sink ein Spülbecken aus
Edelstahl

ℱ **stair** NOUN
1 (step) die **Stufe** (PL die **Stufen**)
2 the stairs die **Treppe** (SINGULAR)
I met her on the stairs. Ich habe sie auf der
Treppe getroffen.

ℱ **staircase** NOUN
die **Treppe** (PL die **Treppen**)

stale ADJECTIVE
alt

stalemate NOUN
(in chess) das **Patt** (PL die **Patts**)

stall NOUN
1 (at a market or fair) der **Stand** (PL die
Stände)
2 (in a theatre) the stalls das Parkett

stammer NOUN
to have a stammer stottern

ℰ **stamp** NOUN
die Briefmarke (PL die Briefmarken)

to **stamp** VERB
1 frankieren (a letter)
2 to stamp your foot mit dem Fuß
aufstampfen SEP

stamp album NOUN
das Briefmarkenalbum (PL die
Briefmarkenalben)

stamp collection NOUN
die Briefmarkensammlung (PL die
Briefmarkensammlungen)

ℰ **stand** NOUN
1 (in a stadium) die Tribüne (PL die Tribünen)
2 (in a fair) der Stand (PL die Stände)

to **stand** VERB
1 stehen◇
Several people were standing. Viele Leute
standen.
We stood outside the cinema. Wir haben
vor dem Kino gestanden.
2 (bear) ausstehen◇ SEP
I can't stand her. Ich kann sie nicht
ausstehen.
I can't stand waiting. Ich kann es nicht
ausstehen, wenn ich warten muss.
3 (keep going) aushalten◇ SEP
I can't stand it any longer. Ich halte es nicht
mehr aus.

stand
• to stand for something
(be short for) etwas bedeuten
UN stands for United Nations. UN bedeutet
United Nations.
• to stand up
aufstehen◇ SEP (PERF sein)
Everybody stood up. Alle standen auf.

standard NOUN
1 (level) das Niveau
of high standard von hohem Niveau
2 standard of living der Lebensstandard
3 She sets herself high standards. Sie stellt
hohe Ansprüche an sich selbst.

standard ADJECTIVE
normal
the standard size die Normalgröße

Standard Grades NOUN PLURAL (You can
explain Standard Grades as follows: Diese
Prüfungen werden in Schottland im Alter
von ca 16 Jahren in sechs oder sieben
Fächern abgelegt. Sie werden von 1 (beste
Note) bis 7 (Kurs abgeschlossen) benotet.
Viele Schüler machen nach Standard Grades
weiter und legen Highers und Advanced
Highers ab.) ▸ SEE **Highers**

staple NOUN
die Heftklammer (PL die Heftklammern)

to **staple** VERB
heften
to staple the pages together die Seiten
zusammenheften

stapler NOUN
der Hefter (PL die Hefter)

ℰ **star** NOUN
1 (in the sky) der Stern (PL die Sterne)
2 (person) der Star (PL die Stars)
She's a film star. Sie ist ein Filmstar.

to **star** VERB
to star in a film in einem Film die
Hauptrolle spielen
starring in der Hauptrolle

to **stare** VERB
1 starren
What are you staring at? Was starrst du
so?
2 to stare at somebody/something
jemanden/etwas (ACC) anstarren SEP
He's staring at the wall. Er starrt die Wand
an.

ℰ **star sign** NOUN
das Sternzeichen (PL die Sternzeichen)
What star sign are you? Welches
Sternzeichen bist du?

ℰ **start** NOUN
1 der Anfang
at the start am Anfang
at the start of the film am Anfang des Films
from the start von Anfang an
We knew from the start that it was
dangerous. Wir wussten von Anfang an,
dass es gefährlich war.
2 to make a start on something mit etwas
(DAT) anfangen◇ SEP
I've made a start on my homework.
Ich habe mit meinen Hausaufgaben
angefangen.
3 (of a race) der Start (PL die Starts)

to **start** VERB
1 anfangen◇ SEP
The film starts at eight. Der Film fängt um

◇ irregular verb; SEP separable verb; for more help with verbs see centre section

acht an.
I've started the book. Ich habe das Buch
angefangen.
to start doing something anfangen, etwas
zu tun
I've started learning Spanish. Ich habe
angefangen, Spanisch zu lernen.
to start crying anfangen zu weinen
2 **to start a business** ein Geschäft gründen
3 **to start a car** ein Auto starten
She started the car. Sie hat das Auto
gestartet.
4 **The car won't start.** Das Auto springt nicht
an.

ℰ **starter** NOUN
(first course) die **Vorspeise** (PL die
Vorspeisen)

to starve VERB
verhungern
I'm starving! Ich bin schon am Verhungern!

ℰ **state** NOUN
1 der **Zustand** (PL die **Zustände**)
The house is in a very bad state. Das Haus
ist in einem sehr schlechten Zustand.
2 *(country)* der **Staat** (PL die **Staaten**)
the state der Staat
3 **the States** *(USA)* die Staaten
They live in the States. Sie leben in den
Staaten.

to state VERB
1 erklären *(intention, reason)*
2 angeben◇ SEP *(an address, income, a
reason)*

stately home NOUN
das **herrschaftliche Anwesen** (PL die
herrschaftlichen Anwesen)

statement NOUN
die **Erklärung** (PL die **Erklärungen**)

state school NOUN
die **staatliche Schule** (PL die **staatlichen
Schulen**)

ℰ **station** NOUN
1 der **Bahnhof** (PL die **Bahnhöfe**)
at the railway station am Bahnhof
bus station der Busbahnhof
2 **police station** die Polizeiwache
3 **radio station** der Rundfunksender

stationer's NOUN
das **Schreibwarengeschäft** (PL die
Schreibwarengeschäfte)

stationery NOUN
die **Schreibwaren** *(PLURAL)*
a stationery shop ein
Schreibwarengeschäft

statistics NOUN
1 *(subject)* die **Statistik** *(SINGULAR)*
He's studying statistics. Er studiert
Statistik.
2 **the statistics** *(figures)* die Statistiken
(PLURAL)
The statistics are difficult to analyse. Die
Statistiken sind schwer zu analysieren.

statue NOUN
die **Statue** (PL die **Statuen**)

ℰ **stay** NOUN
der **Aufenthalt** (PL die **Aufenthalte**)
our stay in Cologne unser Aufenthalt in
Köln
Enjoy your stay! Einen schönen Aufenthalt!

to stay VERB
1 bleiben◇ *(PERF sein)*
I'll stay here. Ich bleibe hier.
How long are you staying? Wie lange
bleibst du?
2 *(spend the night)*
You can stay with us. Du kannst bei uns
übernachten.
to stay the night with friends bei Freunden
übernachten
3 *(live temporarily)* wohnen
Where are you staying? Wo wohnst du?
I'm staying in a hotel. Ich wohne im Hotel.
4 *(be on a visit)*
sein◇ *(PERF sein)*
**I'm going to stay with my sister this
weekend.** Ich bin am Wochenende bei
meiner Schwester.
I stayed in Munich for a couple of days. Ich
war ein paar Tage in München.
• **to stay in**
zu Hause bleiben◇ *(PERF sein)*
I'm staying in tonight. Heute Abend bleibe
ich zu Hause.
• **to stay up**
aufbleiben◇ SEP *(PERF sein)*

ℰ **steady** ADJECTIVE
1 fest
a steady job eine feste Stelle
2 gleichmäßig
at a steady pace mit gleichmäßiger
Geschwindigkeit
3 *(hand, voice)* ruhig
to hold something steady etwas ruhig
halten
4 *(dependable)* zuverlässig

ℰ **steak** NOUN
das **Steak** (PL die **Steaks**)
steak and chips Steak mit Pommes frites

ℰ to **steal** VERB
stehlen◇

ℰ **steam** NOUN
der Dampf

steamed ADJECTIVE
gedämpft, gedünstet

steel NOUN
der Stahl

steep ADJECTIVE
steil
a steep slope ein steiler Hang

steeple NOUN
(spire) der Kirchturm (PL die Kirchtürme)

steering wheel NOUN
das Lenkrad (PL die Lenkräder)

ℰ **step** NOUN
1 der Schritt (PL die Schritte)
to take a step forwards einen Schritt nach
vorn machen
to take a step backwards einen Schritt
zurück machen
2 (stair) die Stufe (PL die Stufen)
to **step** VERB
• to step back
zurücktreten◇ SEP (PERF sein)
• to step forward
vortreten◇ SEP (PERF sein)

stepbrother NOUN
der Stiefbruder (PL die Stiefbrüder)

stepdaughter NOUN
die Stieftochter (PL die Stieftöchter)

ℰ **stepfather** NOUN
der Stiefvater (PL die Stiefväter)

stepladder NOUN
die Trittleiter (PL die Trittleitern)

ℰ **stepmother** NOUN
die Stiefmutter (PL die Stiefmütter)

stepsister NOUN
die Stiefschwester (PL die
Stiefschwestern)

stepson NOUN
der Stiefsohn (PL die Stiefsöhne)

ℰ **stereo** NOUN
die Stereoanlage (PL die Stereoanlagen)

sterling NOUN
der Sterling
in sterling in Pfund (Sterling)

stew NOUN
der Eintopf (PL die Eintöpfe)

steward NOUN
der Steward (PL die Stewards)

WORD TIP Professions, hobbies, and sports
don't take an article in German: Er ist Steward.

stewardess NOUN
die Stewardess (PL die Stewardessen)

WORD TIP Professions, hobbies, and sports don't
take an article in German: Sie ist Stewardess.

ℰ **stick** NOUN
1 der Stock (PL die Stöcke)
2 hockey stick der Hockeyschläger
to **stick** VERB
1 (with glue) kleben
2 (put) tun◇
Stick them on my desk. Tu sie auf meinen
Schreibtisch.

sticker NOUN
der Aufkleber (PL die Aufkleber)

sticky ADJECTIVE
1 klebrig
I've got sticky hands. Ich habe klebrige
Hände.
2 a sticky label ein Aufkleber

sticky tape NOUN
der Klebestreifen

ℰ **stiff** ADJECTIVE
1 steif
to feel stiff steif sein, (after exercise)
Muskelkater haben
to have a stiff neck einen steifen Hals
haben
2 to be bored stiff sich zu Tode langweilen
3 to be scared stiff furchtbare Angst haben

ℰ **still** ADJECTIVE
1 Sit still! Sitz still!
Keep still! Halt still!
2 still mineral water Mineralwasser ohne
Kohlensäure

still ADVERB
1 noch
Do you still live in London? Wohnst du
noch in London?
I've still not finished. Ich bin immer noch
nicht fertig.
He's still working. Er arbeitet noch.
2 (nevertheless) trotzdem
I told her not to, but she still did it. Ich
habe es ihr verboten, aber sie hat es
trotzdem gemacht.
3 better still noch besser

ℰ **sting** NOUN
der Stich (PL die Stiche)

◇ irregular verb; SEP separable verb; for more help with verbs see centre section

to **sting** VERB
  stechen◇

stink NOUN
  der **Gestank**

to **stink** VERB
  stinken◇
  It stinks of fish in here. Es stinkt hier nach Fisch.

ℬ to **stir** VERB
  rühren

stitch NOUN
1 (in sewing, surgical) der **Stich** (PL die **Stiche**)
2 (in knitting) die **Masche** (PL die **Maschen**)
3 (pain) das **Seitenstechen**

stock NOUN
1 (in a shop) der **Warenbestand**
  to have something in stock etwas auf Lager haben
  to be out of stock ausverkauft sein
2 (supply) der **Vorrat** (PL die **Vorräte**)
  I always have a stock of pencils. Ich habe immer einen Bleistiftvorrat.
3 (for cooking) die **Brühe**
  chicken stock die Hühnerbrühe

to **stock** VERB
  (in a shop) **führen**
  They don't stock books. Sie führen keine Bücher.

stock cube NOUN
  der **Brühwürfel** (PL die **Brühwürfel**)

stock exchange NOUN
  die **Börse** (PL die **Börsen**)

stocking NOUN
  der **Strumpf** (PL die **Strümpfe**)

ℬ **stomach** NOUN
  der **Magen** (PL die **Mägen**)

ℬ **stomach ache** NOUN
  die **Magenschmerzen** (PLURAL)
  to have stomach ache Magenschmerzen haben

ℬ **stone** NOUN
  der **Stein** (PL die **Steine**)
  stone wall die Steinmauer

stool NOUN
  der **Hocker** (PL die **Hocker**)

ℬ **stop** NOUN
  die **Haltestelle** (PL die **Haltestellen**)
  bus stop die Bushaltestelle

to **stop** VERB
1 **halten**◇
  Does the train stop in Stuttgart? Hält der Zug in Stuttgart?
2 **to stop somebody/something** jemanden/ etwas anhalten◇ SEP
  The police stopped the car. Die Polizei hielt den Wagen an.
3 (cease) **aufhören** SEP
  The noise has stopped. Der Lärm hat aufgehört.
  to stop doing something aufhören, etwas zu tun
  He's stopped smoking. Er hat aufgehört zu rauchen.
  She never stops asking questions. Sie hört nie auf, Fragen zu stellen.
  Stop it! Hör auf!
4 **to stop somebody doing something** jemanden daran hindern, etwas zu tun
  I can't stop her ringing him. Ich kann sie nicht daran hindern, ihn anzurufen.
5 (prevent) **verhindern** (an accident, a crime)

stopwatch NOUN
  die **Stoppuhr** (PL die **Stoppuhren**)

store NOUN
  (shop) das **Geschäft** (PL die **Geschäfte**)
  department store das Kaufhaus

to **store** VERB
1 **aufbewahren** SEP, (in a warehouse) **lagern**
2 (on a computer) **speichern**

ℬ **storey** NOUN
  das **Stockwerk** (PL die **Stockwerke**)
  a four-storey house ein vierstöckiges Haus

ℬ **storm** NOUN
1 der **Sturm** (PL die **Stürme**)
2 (thunderstorm) das **Gewitter** (PL die **Gewitter**)

stormy ADJECTIVE
  stürmisch

ℬ **story** NOUN
  die **Geschichte** (PL die **Geschichten**)
  to tell a story eine Geschichte erzählen

stove NOUN
  (cooker) der **Herd** (PL die **Herde**)

ℬ **straight** ADJECTIVE
1 gerade
  a straight line eine gerade Linie
2 **to have straight hair** glatte Haare haben

straight ADVERB
1 (in direction)
  straight ahead geradeaus
  to go straight ahead geradeaus gehen
2 (immediately, directly) sofort
  He went straight to the doctor's. Er ging sofort zum Arzt.
  straight away sofort

ℬ **indicates key words**

straightforward ADJECTIVE
einfach

strain NOUN
der Stress
the strain of the last few weeks der Stress in den letzten Wochen
to be a strain anstrengend sein

to **strain** VERB
1 zerren (a muscle)
She's strained a muscle. Sie hat sich (DAT) einen Muskel gezerrt.
2 verrenken (your arm, back)
He's strained his back. Er hat sich (DAT) den Rücken verrenkt.

♪ **strange** ADJECTIVE
seltsam
his strange behaviour sein seltsames Verhalten

♪ **stranger** NOUN
der/die **Fremde** (PL die **Fremden**)
I'm a stranger here. Ich bin hier fremd.

to **strangle** VERB
erwürgen

strap NOUN
1 (on a case, bag, camera) der **Riemen** (PL die **Riemen**)
2 (on a garment) der **Träger** (PL die **Träger**)
3 (of a watch) das **Armband** (PL die **Armbänder**)

strapless ADJECTIVE
trägerlos

straw NOUN
1 (for drinking) der **Strohhalm** (PL die **Strohhalme**)
2 (the material) das **Stroh**
straw hat der Strohhut

♪ **strawberry** NOUN
die **Erdbeere** (PL die **Erdbeeren**)
strawberry jam die Erdbeermarmelade

stray ADJECTIVE
a stray dog ein streunender Hund

stream NOUN
der **Bach** (PL die **Bäche**)

♪ **street** NOUN
die **Straße** (PL die **Straßen**)
I met Simon in the street. Ich habe Simon auf der Straße getroffen.

street lamp NOUN
die **Straßenlaterne** (PL die **Straßenlaternen**)

street map NOUN
der **Stadtplan** (PL die **Stadtpläne**)

streetwise ADJECTIVE
gewieft

♪ **strength** NOUN
die **Kraft** (PL die **Kräfte**)

stress NOUN
der **Stress**

to **stress** VERB
betonen
to stress the importance of something die Wichtigkeit von etwas betonen

♪ to **stretch** VERB
1 (garment, shoes) sich dehnen
This jumper has stretched. Der Pullover hat sich gedehnt.
2 **to stretch your legs** sich (DAT) die Beine vertreten◇

stretcher NOUN
die **Trage** (PL die **Tragen**)

stretchy ADJECTIVE
elastisch

strict ADJECTIVE
streng

♪ **strike** NOUN
der **Streik** (PL die **Streiks**)
to go on strike in den Streik treten◇ (PERF sein)
to be on strike streiken

to **strike** VERB
1 (hit) schlagen◇
The clock struck six. Die Uhr schlug sechs.
2 (be on strike) streiken

striker NOUN
1 (in football) der **Stürmer** (PL die **Stürmer**), die **Stürmerin** (PL die **Stürmerinnen**)
2 (person on strike) der/die **Streikende** (PL die **Streikenden**)

WORD TIP Professions, hobbies, and sports don't take an article in German: Er ist Stürmer.

string NOUN
1 (for tying) die **Schnur** (PL die **Schnüre**)
2 (on a musical instrument) die **Saite** (PL die **Saiten**)

strip NOUN
der **Streifen** (PL die **Streifen**)

to **strip** VERB
1 (undress) sich ausziehen◇ SEP
2 (remove paint from) abbeizen SEP

strip cartoon NOUN
der **Comicstrip** (PL die **Comicstrips**)

◇ **irregular verb;** SEP **separable verb; for more help with verbs see centre section**

stripe *NOUN*
der **Streifen** (*PL* die **Streifen**)

striped *ADJECTIVE*
gestreift

stroke *NOUN*
1 *(style of swimming)* der **Schwimmstil** (*PL* die **Schwimmstile**)
2 *(medical)* der **Schlaganfall** (*PL* die **Schlaganfälle**)
to have a stroke einen Schlaganfall bekommen◇
3 a stroke of luck ein Glücksfall
to have a stroke of luck Glück haben

to **stroke** *VERB*
streicheln

℘ **strong** *ADJECTIVE*
1 *(person, drink, feeling)* stark
2 *(sturdy)* stabil *(furniture)*
strong shoes feste Schuhe

strongly *ADVERB*
1 *(believe, oppose)* fest
2 *(support)* nachdrücklich
3 *(advise, recommend)* dringend
4 She smelt strongly of garlic. Sie hat stark nach Knoblauch gerochen.

struggle *NOUN*
der **Kampf** (*PL* die **Kämpfe**)
the struggle for freedom der Kampf für die Freiheit
It's been a struggle. Es war ein Kampf.

to **struggle** *VERB*
1 *(to obtain something)* kämpfen
to struggle to do something kämpfen, um etwas zu tun
She struggled for a place. Sie kämpfte um einen Platz.
2 *(physically)* sich wehren
I struggled and screamed for help. Ich wehrte mich und rief um Hilfe.
3 *(have difficulty in doing something)* sich abmühen *SEP*
They are struggling to pay the rent. Sie mühen sich ab, ihre Miete zu zahlen.
He's struggling with his homework. Er müht sich mit seinen Hausaufgaben ab.

stub *NOUN*
cigarette stub die Kippe

to **stub** *VERB*
• to stub out
ausdrücken *SEP*

stubborn *ADJECTIVE*
stur

stuck *ADJECTIVE*
1 *(jammed)*
It's stuck. Es klemmt.
The drawer's stuck. Die Schublade klemmt.
2 to get stuck person stecken bleiben◇ *(PERF sein) (in a lift, traffic jam, or place)*
3 I'm stuck on exercise 2. Bei Übung 2 komme ich nicht weiter.

stud *NOUN*
1 *(on clothes)* die **Niete** (*PL* die **Nieten**)
2 *(on a boot)* der **Stollen** (*PL* die **Stollen**)
3 *(earring)* der **Ohrstecker** (*PL* die **Ohrstecker**)

℘ **student** *NOUN*
1 *(at college or university)* der **Student** (*PL* die **Studenten**), die **Studentin** (*PL* die **Studentinnen**)
He's a student. Er ist Student.
2 *(at school)* der **Schüler** (*PL* die **Schüler**), die **Schülerin** (*PL* die **Schülerinnen**)

studio *NOUN*
1 *(film, TV)* das **Studio** (*PL* die **Studios**)
2 *(artist's)* das **Atelier** (*PL* die **Ateliers**)

℘ to **study** *VERB*
1 lernen
He's busy studying for his exams. Er lernt fleißig für seine Prüfung.
2 studieren
She's studying medicine. Sie studiert Medizin.

study *NOUN*
(room) das **Arbeitszimmer** (*PL* die **Arbeitszimmer**)

study group *NOUN*
die **Arbeitsgemeinschaft** (*PL* die **Arbeitsgemeinschaften**)

stuff *NOUN*
1 *(things, personal belongings)* das **Zeug** *(informal)*
We can put all that stuff in the attic. Wir können das ganze Zeug auf den Dachboden bringen.
You can leave your stuff at my house. Du kannst dein Zeug bei mir lassen.
2 I like pasta and pizza and stuff like that. Ich mag Nudeln und Pizza und so was.

to **stuff** *VERB*
1 *(shove)* stopfen
She stuffed some things into a suitcase. Sie hat ein paar Sachen in einen Koffer gestopft.
2 füllen *(vegetables, turkey)*
stuffed peppers gefüllte Paprikaschoten

℘ indicates key words

stuffing NOUN
(in cooking) die Füllung (PL die Füllungen)

stuffy ADJECTIVE
(airless) stickig

to **stumble** VERB
stolpern (PERF sein)

stunned ADJECTIVE
sprachlos

stunning ADJECTIVE
toll (informal)

stunt NOUN
(in a film) der Stunt (PL die Stunts)

stuntman NOUN
der Stuntman (PL die Stuntmen)

> **WORD TIP** Professions, hobbies, and sports
> don't take an article in German: Er ist Stuntman.

ℐ **stupid** ADJECTIVE
dumm
That was really stupid. Das war wirklich
dumm.
I did something stupid. Ich habe etwas
Blödes gemacht.

stutter NOUN
to have a stutter stottern

to **stutter** VERB
stottern

ℐ **style** NOUN
1 der Stil (PL die Stile)
style of living der Lebensstil
He has his own style. Er hat seinen eigenen
Stil.
2 (fashion) die Mode
It's the latest style. Das ist die neueste
Mode.

ℐ **subject** NOUN
1 das Thema (PL die Themen)
the subject of my talk das Thema meines
Vortrags
2 (at school) das Fach (PL die Fächer)
My favourite subject is biology. Mein
Lieblingsfach ist Biologie.

submarine NOUN
das Unterseeboot (PL die Unterseeboote),
das U-Boot (PL die U-Boote)

subscription NOUN
das Abonnement (PL die Abonnements)
to take out a subscription to a magazine
eine Zeitschrift abonnieren

to **subsidize** VERB
subventionieren

subsidy NOUN
die Subvention (PL die Subventionen)

substance NOUN
die Substanz (PL die Substanzen)

substitute NOUN
(in sport) der Ersatzspieler (PL die
Ersatzspieler), die Ersatzspielerin (PL die
Ersatzspielerinnen)

to **substitute** VERB
ersetzen

ℐ **subtitled** ADJECTIVE
mit Untertiteln

ℐ **subtitles** PLURAL NOUN
die Untertitel (PLURAL)

subtle ADJECTIVE
subtil

to **subtract** VERB
abziehen◇ SEP

ℐ **suburb** NOUN
der Vorort (PL die Vororte)
a suburb of Edinburgh ein Vorort von
Edinburgh
in the suburbs of London in den Londoner
Vororten

suburban ADJECTIVE
Vorort-
a suburban train ein Vorortzug

subway NOUN
(underpass) die Unterführung (PL die
Unterführungen)

ℐ to **succeed** VERB
gelingen◇ (PERF sein)
We've succeeded in contacting her. Es ist
uns gelungen, sie zu erreichen.

ℐ **success** NOUN
der Erfolg (PL die Erfolge)
a great success ein großer Erfolg

successful ADJECTIVE
1 erfolgreich
He's a successful writer. Er ist ein
erfolgreicher Schriftsteller.
2 **to be successful in doing something** etwas
mit Erfolg tun◇

successfully ADVERB
mit Erfolg

ℐ **such** ADJECTIVE, ADVERB
1 so
They're such nice people. Das sind so nette
Leute.
I've had such a busy day. Ich habe so einen

◇ irregular verb; SEP separable verb; for more help with verbs see centre section

hektischen Tag gehabt.
It's such a long way. Es ist so weit.
It's such a pity. Es ist so schade.

2 such a lot of *(followed by a singular noun)*
so viel
They've got such a lot of money. Sie haben
so viel Geld.

3 such a lot of *(followed by a plural noun)* so
viele
She's got such a lot of problems. Sie hat so
viele Probleme.

4 such as wie
in big cities such as Glasgow in großen
Städten wie Glasgow

5 There's no such thing. So etwas gibt es
nicht.

to suck *VERB*
lutschen
to suck your thumb am Daumen lutschen

℘ **sudden** *ADJECTIVE*
plötzlich
all of a sudden plötzlich

℘ **suddenly** *ADVERB*
plötzlich
He suddenly started to laugh. Plötzlich hat
er angefangen zu lachen.
Suddenly the light went out. Plötzlich ging
das Licht aus.

suede *NOUN*
das **Wildleder**
suede jacket die Wildlederjacke

to suffer *VERB*
leiden◊
to suffer from asthma an Asthma leiden

sufficiently *ADVERB*
genug

℘ **sugar** *NOUN*
der **Zucker**
Do you take sugar? Nimmst du Zucker?
Two sugars, please. Zwei Löffel Zucker
bitte.

℘ **to suggest** *VERB*
vorschlagen◊ *SEP*
**He suggested I should speak to you about
it.** Er hat vorgeschlagen, dass ich mit Ihnen
darüber sprechen soll.

suggestion *NOUN*
der **Vorschlag** (*PL* die **Vorschläge**)
to make a suggestion einen Vorschlag
machen

suicide *NOUN*
der **Selbstmord** (*PL* die **Selbstmorde**)

to commit suicide Selbstmord begehen◊

℘ **suit** *NOUN*
1 *(man's)* der **Anzug** (*PL* die **Anzüge**)
2 *(woman's)* das **Kostüm** (*PL* die **Kostüme**)

to suit *VERB*
1 *(be convenient)* passen (*+DAT*)
Does Monday suit you? Passt Ihnen
Montag?
2 *(look good on)* stehen◊ (*+DAT*)
Hats suit her. Ihr stehen Hüte.

℘ **suitable** *ADJECTIVE*
1 geeignet
to be suitable for something für etwas
geeignet sein
It's suitable for children. Es ist für Kinder
geeignet.
2 *(convenient)* passend
at a suitable time zur passenden Zeit
Saturday is the most suitable day for me.
Samstag passt mir am besten.
3 *(for a social occasion)* angemessen *(clothes)*

℘ **suitcase** *NOUN*
der **Koffer** (*PL* die **Koffer**)

to sulk *VERB*
schmollen

sum *NOUN*
1 die **Summe** (*PL* die **Summen**)
a sum of money eine Geldsumme
2 *(calculation)* die **Rechenaufgabe** (*PL* die
Rechenaufgaben)

to sum *VERB*
• **to sum up**
zusammenfassen *SEP*

to summarize *VERB*
zusammenfassen *SEP*

summary *NOUN*
die **Zusammenfassung** (*PL* die
Zusammenfassungen)

℘ **summer** *NOUN*
der **Sommer** (*PL* die **Sommer**)
in summer im Sommer
summer clothes die Sommerkleidung
the summer holidays die Sommerferien

summertime *NOUN*
der **Sommer**
in summertime im Sommer

summit *NOUN*
der **Gipfel** (*PL* die **Gipfel**)

℘ **sun** *NOUN*
die **Sonne** (*PL* die **Sonnen**)
in the sun in der Sonne

℘ **indicates key words**

to **sunbathe** VERB
sich sonnen

sunblock NOUN
der Sunblocker (PL die Sunblocker)

ℰ **sunburn** NOUN
der Sonnenbrand (PL die Sonnenbrände)

sunburned ADJECTIVE
to get sunburned einen Sonnenbrand
bekommen◇

ℰ **Sunday** NOUN
1 der Sonntag (PL die Sonntage)
on Sunday am Sonntag
I'm going to the cinema on Sunday. Ich
gehe (am) Sonntag ins Kino.
See you on Sunday! Bis Sonntag!
every Sunday jeden Sonntag
last Sunday vorigen Sonntag
next Sunday nächsten Sonntag
2 on Sundays sonntags
The museum is closed on Sundays. Das
Museum ist sonntags geschlossen.

sunflower NOUN
die Sonnenblume (PL die Sonnenblumen)
sunflower oil das Sonnenblumenöl

sunglasses PLURAL NOUN
die Sonnenbrille (PL die Sonnenbrillen)
a pair of sunglasses eine Sonnenbrille

WORD TIP In German die Sonnenbrille is singular.

sunlight NOUN
das Sonnenlicht

sunny ADJECTIVE
sonnig
a sunny day ein sonniger Tag
sunny intervals sonnige Abschnitte

sunrise NOUN
der Sonnenaufgang (PL die
Sonnenaufgänge)

sunroof NOUN
das Schiebedach (PL die Schiebedächer)

sunscreen NOUN
das Sonnenschutzmittel (PL die
Sonnenschutzmittel)

sunset NOUN
der Sonnenuntergang (PL die
Sonnenuntergänge)

sunshine NOUN
der Sonnenschein

sunstroke NOUN
der Sonnenstich (PL die Sonnenstiche)
to get sunstroke einen Sonnenstich
bekommen◇

ℰ **suntan** NOUN
die Bräune
to have a suntan braun sein
to get a suntan braun werden◇ (PERF sein)

suntan lotion NOUN
die Sonnenmilch

suntan oil NOUN
das Sonnenöl

super ADJECTIVE
klasse (informal) ('klasse' never changes)
We had a super time. Es war wirklich
klasse.

ℰ **supermarket** NOUN
der Supermarkt (PL die Supermärkte)

supernatural ADJECTIVE
übernatürlich

superstitious ADJECTIVE
abergläubisch

superstore NOUN
der Großmarkt (PL die Großmärkte)

to **supervise** VERB
beaufsichtigen

supervisor NOUN
der Aufseher (PL die Aufseher), die
Aufseherin (PL die Aufseherinnen)

WORD TIP Professions, hobbies, and sports
don't take an article in German: Er ist Aufseher.

ℰ **supper** NOUN
das Abendessen (PL die Abendessen)
I had supper at Sandy's. Ich war bei Sandy
zum Abendessen.

ℰ **supplement** NOUN
1 (to newspaper) die Beilage (PL die Beilagen)
2 (to fare) der Zuschlag (PL die Zuschläge)

ℰ **supply** NOUN
1 (stock) der Vorrat (PL die Vorräte)
2 to be in short supply knapp sein
to **supply** VERB
1 stellen
The school supplies the books. Die Schule
stellt die Bücher.
2 (deliver) liefern
to supply somebody with something
jemandem etwas liefern

supply teacher NOUN
der Aushilfslehrer (PL die Aushilfslehrer),
die Aushilfslehrerin (PL die

◇ irregular verb; SEP separable verb; for more help with verbs see centre section

Aushilfslehrerinnen)

WORD TIP Professions, hobbies, and sports don't take an article in German: Sie ist Aushilfslehrerin.

𝒫 **support** NOUN
die **Unterstützung**
in support zur Unterstützung

to **support** VERB
1 (back up) **unterstützen**
Her teachers have really supported her. Die Lehrer haben sie sehr unterstützt.
to support somebody financially jemanden finanziell unterstützen
2 Will supports Chelsea. Will ist ein Chelsea-Fan.
What team do you support? Für welche Mannschaft bist du?
3 (keep, provide for) **ernähren**
to support a family eine Familie ernähren

supporter NOUN
1 der **Fan** (PL die **Fans**)
She's a Manchester United supporter. Sie ist ein Manchester-United-Fan.
2 (of a party or cause) der **Anhänger** (PL die **Anhänger**), die **Anhängerin** (PL die **Anhängerinnen**)

to **suppose** VERB
annehmen◇ SEP
I suppose she's forgotten. Ich nehme an, sie hat es vergessen.

𝒫 **supposed** ADJECTIVE
to be supposed to do something etwas tun sollen◇
You were supposed to be here at six. Du solltest um sechs hier sein.

𝒫 **sure** ADJECTIVE
1 **sicher**
Are you sure? Bist du sicher?
Are you sure you saw her? Bist du sicher, dass du sie gesehen hast?
2 Sure! Klar!
3 Make sure you are home by 11. Sorge dafür, dass du um 11 wieder zu Hause bist.
I'll check again to make sure. Ich sehe nochmal nach, um mich zu vergewissern.

surely ADVERB
doch sicherlich
Surely she hasn't forgotten. Sie hat es doch sicherlich nicht vergessen.

𝒫 **surf** NOUN
das **Surfen**

to **surf** VERB
to surf the Net/Web im Internet surfen

surface NOUN
die **Oberfläche** (PL die **Oberflächen**)

surfboard NOUN
das **Surfbrett** (PL die **Surfbretter**)

surfer NOUN
(on the sea and Internet) der **Surfer** (PL die **Surfer**), die **Surferin** (PL die **Surferinnen**)

WORD TIP Professions, hobbies, and sports don't take an article in German: Er ist Surfer.

surfing NOUN
das **Surfen**

surgeon NOUN
der **Chirurg** (PL die **Chirurgen**), die **Chirurgin** (PL die **Chirurginnen**)

WORD TIP Professions, hobbies, and sports don't take an article in German: Sie ist Chirurgin.

surgery NOUN
1 **to have surgery** operiert werden◇ (PERF sein)
2 (doctor's) die **Praxis** (PL die **Praxen**)
the dentist's surgery die Zahnarztpraxis
3 (surgery hours) die **Sprechstunde**

𝒫 **surname** NOUN
der **Nachname** (PL die **Nachnamen**)

𝒫 **surprise** NOUN
die **Überraschung** (PL die **Überraschungen**)
What a surprise! Was für eine Überraschung!

surprised ADJECTIVE
überrascht
I was surprised to see her. Ich war überrascht, sie zu sehen.

𝒫 **surprising** ADJECTIVE
überraschend

𝒫 to **surround** VERB
umgeben
surrounded by umgeben von (+DAT)
She was surrounded by friends. Sie war von Freunden umgeben.

𝒫 **survey** NOUN
die **Umfrage** (PL die **Umfragen**)

to **survive** VERB
überleben

survivor NOUN
der/die **Überlebende** (PL die **Überlebenden**)

suspect NOUN
der/die **Verdächtige** (PL die **Verdächtigen**)

to **suspect** VERB
verdächtigen

to suspend VERB
1 **to be suspended** *(from school)* vom Unterricht ausgeschlossen werden◇ *(PERF sein)*
2 *(from a team)* **sperren**
   to suspend a player for four weeks einen Spieler für vier Wochen sperren

suspense NOUN
die **Spannung**

ℐ **suspicious** ADJECTIVE
1 **misstrauisch**
   to be suspicious of somebody jemandem misstrauen
2 *(suspicious looking)* **verdächtig**

swallow NOUN
(bird) die **Schwalbe** (PL die **Schwalben**)

to swallow VERB
schlucken

swan NOUN
der **Schwan** (PL die **Schwäne**)

ℐ **to swap** VERB
tauschen
   Do you want to swap? Willst du tauschen?
   He swapped his bike for a computer. Er hat sein Rad gegen einen Computer getauscht.
   We swapped seats. Wir tauschten die Plätze.

to swear VERB
(use bad language) **fluchen**

swearword NOUN
der **Kraftausdruck** (PL die **Kraftausdrücke**)

sweat NOUN
der **Schweiß**

to sweat VERB
schwitzen

ℐ **sweater** NOUN
der **Pullover** (PL die **Pullover**)

sweatshirt NOUN
das **Sweatshirt** (PL die **Sweatshirts**)

swede NOUN
die **Kohlrübe** (PL die **Kohlrüben**)
   I don't like swede. Ich mag keine Kohlrüben.

Swede NOUN
der **Schwede** (PL die **Schweden**), die **Schwedin** (PL die **Schwedinnen**)

Sweden NOUN
Schweden *(NEUTER)*
   from Sweden aus Schweden
   to Sweden nach Schweden

Swedish NOUN
(the language) das **Schwedisch**

Swedish ADJECTIVE
schwedisch
   the Swedish coast die schwedische Küste
   He's Swedish. Er ist Schwede.
   She's Swedish. Sie ist Schwedin.

WORD TIP Adjectives never have capitals in German, even for regions, countries, or nationalities.

to sweep VERB
fegen

ℐ **sweet** NOUN
1 der **Bonbon** (PL die **Bonbons**)
2 *(dessert)* der **Nachtisch** (PL die **Nachtische**)

sweet ADJECTIVE
1 **süß**
   I try not to eat sweet things. Ich versuche nichts Süßes zu essen.
   She looks really sweet in that hat. Mit dem Hut sieht sie richtig süß aus.
2 *(kind)* **lieb**
   She's a really sweet person. Sie ist wirklich ein sehr lieber Mensch.
   How sweet of him. Wie lieb von ihm.

sweetcorn NOUN
der **Mais**

to swell VERB
(part of the body) **anschwellen**◇ SEP *(PERF sein)*

swelling NOUN
die **Schwellung** (PL die **Schwellungen**)

ℐ **swim** NOUN
to go for a swim schwimmen gehen◇ *(PERF sein)*

to swim VERB
schwimmen◇ *(PERF sein)*
   Can he swim? Kann er schwimmen?
   to swim across a lake über einen See schwimmen

swimmer NOUN
der **Schwimmer** (PL die **Schwimmer**), die **Schwimmerin** (die **Schwimmerinnen**)
   She's a strong swimmer. Sie ist eine gute Schwimmerin.

ℐ **swimming** NOUN
das **Schwimmen**
   to go swimming schwimmen gehen◇ *(PERF sein)*

swimming cap NOUN
die **Badekappe** (PL die **Badekappen**)

◇ **irregular verb;** SEP **separable verb; for more help with verbs see centre section**

swimming costume NOUN
der **Badeanzug** (PL die **Badeanzüge**)

swimming pool NOUN
1 das **Schwimmbecken** (PL die **Schwimmbecken**)
2 (building) das **Schwimmbad** (PL die **Schwimmbäder**)

swimming trunks NOUN
die **Badehose** (PL die **Badehosen**)
a pair of swimming trunks eine Badehose

WORD TIP In German die Badehose is singular.

ℙ **swimsuit** NOUN
der **Badeanzug** (PL die **Badeanzüge**)

swindle NOUN
der **Betrug** (PL die **Betrüge**)
What a swindle! Was für ein Betrug!

to **swindle** VERB
betrügen◇

swing NOUN
die **Schaukel** (PL die **Schaukeln**)

Swiss NOUN
(person) der **Schweizer** (PL die **Schweizer**),
die **Schweizerin** (PL die **Schweizerinnen**)
the Swiss die Schweizer

Swiss ADJECTIVE
schweizerisch
the Swiss railways die schweizerischen Eisenbahnen
He is Swiss. Er ist Schweizer.
She is Swiss. Sie ist Schweizerin.

WORD TIP Adjectives never have capitals in German, even for regions, countries, or nationalities.

ℙ **switch** NOUN
(for a light, radio, etc.) der **Schalter** (PL die **Schalter**)

to **switch** VERB
(change) **wechseln**
to switch places die Plätze wechseln
• **to switch something off**
etwas ausschalten SEP
• **to switch something on**
etwas anschalten SEP

Switzerland NOUN
die **Schweiz**
from Switzerland aus der Schweiz
in Switzerland in der Schweiz

to Switzerland in die Schweiz

WORD TIP In German, this is always used with the article.

🔵 **SWITZERLAND**

Capital: Bern. Population: nearly 8 million. Size: 41,285 square km. Main languages: German, French, Italian, and Romansh (a language derived from Latin). Official currency: Swiss franc.

swollen ADJECTIVE
geschwollen

to **swop** VERB ▶ SEE **swap**

sword NOUN
das **Schwert** (PL die **Schwerter**)

ℙ **syllabus** NOUN
der **Lehrplan** (PL die **Lehrpläne**)
to be on the syllabus auf dem Lehrplan stehen◇

symbol NOUN
das **Symbol** (PL die **Symbole**)

symbolic ADJECTIVE
symbolisch

sympathetic ADJECTIVE
verständnisvoll

WORD TIP Do not translate the English word sympathetic with the German sympathisch.

to **sympathize** VERB
to sympathize with somebody mit jemandem mitfühlen SEP
I sympathize with you. Ich kann mit Ihnen mitfühlen.

sympathy NOUN
das **Mitleid**

symphony NOUN
die **Sinfonie** (PL die **Sinfonien**)

symptom NOUN
das **Symptom** (PL die **Symptome**)

synagogue NOUN
die **Synagoge** (PL die **Synagogen**)

synthesizer NOUN
der **Synthesizer** (PL die **Synthesizer**)

synthetic ADJECTIVE
synthetisch

syringe NOUN
die **Spritze** (PL die **Spritzen**)

system NOUN
das **System** (PL die **Systeme**)
the German school system das deutsche Schulsystem

ℙ indicates key words

Tt

table NOUN
der **Tisch** (PL die **Tische**)
to lay the table den Tisch decken
to clear the table den Tisch abräumen SEP

tablecloth NOUN
die **Tischdecke** (PL die **Tischdecken**)

tablespoon NOUN
der **Esslöffel** (PL die **Esslöffel**)
a tablespoon of flour ein Esslöffel Mehl

tablet NOUN
die **Tablette** (PL die **Tabletten**)

table tennis NOUN
das **Tischtennis**

tackle NOUN
der **Angriff** (PL die **Angriffe**)
to tackle VERB
1 (in football or hockey) **angreifen**◇ SEP
2 **angehen**◇ SEP (PERF **sein**) (a job or a problem)

tact NOUN
der **Takt**

tactful ADJECTIVE
taktvoll
That wasn't very tactful. Das war nicht sehr taktvoll.

tadpole NOUN
die **Kaulquappe** (PL die **Kaulquappen**)

tail NOUN
1 der **Schwanz** (PL die **Schwänze**)
2 'Heads or tails?' – 'Tails.' 'Kopf oder Zahl?' – 'Zahl.'

to take VERB
1 **nehmen**◇
He took a sweet. Er nahm einen Bonbon.
Take my hand. Nimm meine Hand.
I took the bus. Ich habe den Bus genommen.
Do you take sugar? Nimmst du Zucker?
Do you take credit cards? Nehmen Sie Kreditkarten?
2 (with time) **dauern**
It takes two hours. Es dauert zwei Stunden.
3 (react to) **aufnehmen**◇ SEP
He took the news calmly. Er hat die Nachricht gelassen aufgenommen.
4 (take to a place) **bringen**◇
I'm taking Jake to my parents. Ich bringe Jake zu meinen Eltern.
He took the car to the garage. Er brachte

das Auto in die Werkstatt.
to take somebody home jemanden nach Hause bringen
5 **to take something up(stairs)** etwas nach oben bringen◇
Could you take the towels up? Könntest du die Handtücher nach oben bringen?
6 **to take something down(stairs)** etwas nach unten bringen◇
Cheryl's taken the cups down. Cheryl hat die Tassen nach unten gebracht.
7 (carry with you) **mitnehmen**◇ SEP
She's taken the files home. Sie hat die Akten mit nach Hause genommen.
I'm taking my swimsuit. Ich nehme meinen Badeanzug mit.
I'll take him next time. Nächstes Mal nehme ich ihn mit.
8 **machen** (an exam, a holiday, or a photo)
She's taking her driving test tomorrow. Sie macht morgen ihre Fahrprüfung.
to take a holiday Ferien machen
9 (need) **brauchen**
It takes a lot of courage. Dazu braucht man viel Mut.
It took me at least two hours to read it. Ich habe mindestens zwei Stunden gebraucht, um es zu lesen.
10 **haben**◇ (clothes size)
What size do you take? Welche Größe haben Sie?
• **to take something apart**
etwas auseinandernehmen◇ SEP
• **to take something back**
etwas zurückbringen◇ SEP
• **to take off**
1 (plane) **abfliegen**◇ SEP (PERF **sein**)
2 **ausziehen**◇ SEP (clothes, shoes)
Take your jacket off. Zieh die Jacke aus.
to take your clothes off sich ausziehen
3 **abziehen**◇ SEP (money)
He took five pounds off the price. Er hat fünf Pfund vom Preis abgezogen.
• **to take out something**
(from a bag or pocket) etwas herausnehmen◇ SEP
Eric took out his wallet. Eric nahm seine Brieftasche heraus.
• **to take somebody out**
jemanden ausführen SEP
to take somebody out for a meal jemanden zum Essen in ein Restaurant einladen◇ SEP

takeaway NOUN
1 (meal) das **Essen zum Mitnehmen** (PL die **Essen zum Mitnehmen**)
an Indian takeaway ein indisches Essen

◇ **irregular verb**; SEP **separable verb**; for more help with verbs see centre section

zum Mitnehmen
Let's get a Chinese takeaway. Lass uns etwas beim Chinesen holen.

2 *(where you buy it)* das **Restaurant mit Straßenverkauf** (PL die **Restaurants mit Straßenverkauf**)

take-off NOUN
(of a plane) der **Abflug** (PL die **Abflüge**)

talent NOUN
das **Talent** (PL die **Talente**)
to have a talent for painting ein Talent zum Malen haben

talented ADJECTIVE
talentiert
He's really talented. Er ist wirklich talentiert.

♭ **talk** NOUN
1 *(a chat)* das **Gespräch** (PL die **Gespräche**)
We had a serious talk about it. Wir hatten ein ernstes Gespräch darüber.
2 *(in public)* der **Vortrag** (PL die **Vorträge**)
She's giving a talk on Hungary. Sie hält einen Vortrag über Ungarn.

to **talk** VERB
1 reden
to talk to somebody mit jemandem reden
We talked about football. Wir haben über Fußball geredet.
What's he talking about? Wovon redet er?
We'll talk about it later. Darüber reden wir später.
They're always talking. Sie reden immer.
2 **to talk to somebody on the phone** mit jemandem telefonieren

talkative ADJECTIVE
schwatzhaft

♭ **tall** ADJECTIVE
1 groß
She's very tall. Sie ist sehr groß.
I'm 1.7 metres tall. Ich bin ein Meter siebzig groß.
2 hoch *(building or tree)*

tame ADJECTIVE
zahm

tampon NOUN
der **Tampon** (PL die **Tampons**)

♭ **tan** NOUN
die **Bräune**
to have a tan braun sein
to get a tan braun werden◇ (PERF **sein**)

tank NOUN
1 *(for petrol or water)* der **Tank** (PL die **Tanks**)

2 *(for fish)* das **Aquarium** (PL die **Aquarien**)
3 *(military)* der **Panzer** (PL die **Panzer**)

tanker NOUN
1 *(on sea)* der **Tanker** (PL die **Tanker**)
2 *(on the road)* der **Tankwagen** (PL die **Tankwagen**)

tanned ADJECTIVE
braun

♭ **tap** NOUN
der **Wasserhahn** (PL die **Wasserhähne**)
to turn on the tap den Wasserhahn aufdrehen SEP
to turn off the tap den Wasserhahn zudrehen SEP
the hot tap der Warmwasserhahn

to **tap** VERB
klopfen
to tap on the door an die Tür klopfen

tap-dancing NOUN
das **Stepptanzen**

♭ **tape** NOUN
1 die **Kassette** (PL die **Kassetten**)
my tape of the Stones meine Kassette von den Stones
I've got it on tape. Ich habe es auf Kassette.
2 **sticky tape** der Klebestreifen

to **tape** VERB
aufnehmen◇ SEP

tape measure NOUN
das **Metermaß** (PL die **Metermaße**)

tape recorder NOUN
das **Tonbandgerät** (PL die **Tonbandgeräte**)

target NOUN
das **Ziel** (PL die **Ziele**)

♭ **tart** NOUN
der **Kuchen** (PL die **Kuchen**)
apple tart der Apfelkuchen

tartan ADJECTIVE
Schotten-
a tartan skirt ein Schottenrock

task NOUN
die **Aufgabe** (PL die **Aufgaben**)

♭ **taste** NOUN
1 der **Geschmack** (PL die **Geschmäcke**)
a taste of onions ein Zwiebelgeschmack
She's got no taste. Sie hat keinen Geschmack.
2 **in bad taste** geschmacklos

♭ indicates key words

to **taste** VERB
1 schmecken
   The soup tastes horrible. Die Suppe
   schmeckt furchtbar.
2 **to taste of something** nach etwas (DAT)
   schmecken
   It tastes of garlic. Es schmeckt nach
   Knoblauch.
3 (try a little) probieren
   Do you want to taste? Möchtest du mal
   probieren?

tasty ADJECTIVE
   schmackhaft

tattoo NOUN
   die Tätowierung (PL die Tätowierungen)
   He's got a tattoo on his arm. Er hat eine
   Tätowierung am Arm.

Taurus NOUN
   der Stier
   Jo is Taurus. Jo ist Stier.

tax NOUN
   die Steuer (PL die Steuern) (on goods,
   income)

taxi NOUN
   das Taxi (PL die Taxis)
   to go by taxi mit dem Taxi fahren◇ (PERF
   sein)
   to take a taxi ein Taxi nehmen◇

taxi driver NOUN
   der Taxifahrer (PL die Taxifahrer), die
   Taxifahrerin (PL die Taxifahrerinnen)

   WORD TIP Professions, hobbies, and sports
   don't take an article in German: Er ist Taxifahrer.

taxi rank NOUN
   der Taxistand (PL die Taxistände)

ℓ **tea** NOUN
1 der Tee (PL die Tees)
   a cup of tea eine Tasse Tee
   to have tea Tee trinken◇
2 (evening meal) das Abendessen (PL die
   Abendessen)

tea bag NOUN
   der Teebeutel (PL die Teebeutel)

ℓ to **teach** VERB
1 beibringen◇ SEP
   She's teaching me to drive. Sie bringt mir
   das Autofahren bei.
2 **to teach yourself something** sich (DAT)
   etwas beibringen◇ SEP
   I taught myself Italian. Ich habe mir
   Italienisch beigebracht.
3 **That'll teach you!** Das wird dir eine Lehre
   sein!

4 unterrichten
   Her mum teaches maths. Ihre Mutter
   unterrichtet Mathematik.

ℓ **teacher** NOUN
   der Lehrer (PL die Lehrer) die Lehrerin
   (PL die Lehrerinnen)

   WORD TIP Professions, hobbies, and sports
   don't take an article in German: Er ist Lehrer.

teaching NOUN
   das Unterrichten

ℓ **team** NOUN
   die Mannschaft (PL die Mannschaften)
   football team die Fußballmannschaft
   The team are playing well. Die Mannschaft
   spielt gut.

teapot NOUN
   die Teekanne (PL die Teekannen)

tear[1] NOUN
   (a rip) der Riss (PL die Risse)

to **tear** VERB
1 zerreißen◇
   She tore up my letter. Sie hat meinen Brief
   zerrissen.
2 reißen◇ (PERF sein)
   The net has torn. Das Netz ist gerissen.
   Be careful, it tears easily. Sei vorsichtig, es
   reißt leicht.

tear[2] NOUN
   (when you cry) die Träne (PL die Tränen)
   to be in tears in Tränen aufgelöst sein
   to burst into tears in Tränen ausbrechen◇
   (PERF sein)

to **tease** VERB
1 necken (a person)
2 quälen (an animal)

teaspoon NOUN
   der Teelöffel (PL die Teelöffel)
   a teaspoon of vinegar ein Teelöffel Essig

ℓ **teatime** NOUN
   (evening meal) die Abendessenszeit
   It's teatime! Es gibt Abendessen!

tea towel NOUN
   das Geschirrtuch (PL die Geschirrtücher)

technical ADJECTIVE
   technisch

technical college NOUN
   die technische Fachschule (PL die
   technischen Fachschulen)

technician NOUN
   der Techniker (PL die Techniker), die

◇ irregular verb; SEP separable verb; for more help with verbs see centre section

Technikerin (PL die **Technikerinnen**)

WORD TIP Professions, hobbies, and sports don't take an article in German: Er ist Techniker.

technique NOUN
die Technik (PL die **Techniken**)

techno NOUN
(music) der **Techno**

technological ADJECTIVE
technologisch

technology NOUN
1 die **Technologie**
2 information technology die **Informatik**

teddy bear NOUN
der Teddybär (PL die **Teddybären**)

ℓ **teenage** ADJECTIVE
1 Teenage-
2 They have a teenage son. Sie haben einen Sohn im Teenageralter.
3 (films, magazines, etc.) für Teenager
a teenage magazine eine Jugendzeitschrift

ℓ **teenager** NOUN
der Teenager (PL die **Teenager**)
a group of teenagers eine Gruppe von Teenagern

teens PLURAL NOUN
the teens die Teenagerjahre
He's in his teens. Er ist ein Teenager.

ℓ **tee shirt** NOUN
das T-Shirt (PL die **T-Shirts**)

ℓ **telephone** NOUN
das Telefon (PL die **Telefone**)
on the telephone am Telefon

to **telephone** VERB
anrufen◇ SEP
I'll telephone the bank. Ich rufe die Bank an.

telephone box NOUN
die Telefonzelle (PL die **Telefonzellen**)

telephone call NOUN
das Telefongespräch (PL die **Telefongespräche**)

telephone directory NOUN
das Telefonbuch (PL die **Telefonbücher**)

telephone number NOUN
die Telefonnummer (PL die **Telefonnummern**)

telescope NOUN
das Fernrohr (PL die **Fernrohre**), das Teleskop (PL die **Teleskope**)

to **televise** VERB
im Fernsehen übertragen◇
They're televising the match. Sie übertragen das Spiel im Fernsehen.

ℓ **television** NOUN
1 (set) der Fernseher (PL die **Fernseher**)
We've got a new television. Wir haben einen neuen Fernseher.
2 das Fernsehen
I saw it on television. Ich habe es im Fernsehen gesehen.
3 to watch television fernsehen◇ SEP
I'm watching television. Ich sehe fern.

television programme NOUN
die Fernsehsendung (PL die **Fernsehsendungen**)

ℓ to **tell** VERB
1 sagen
to tell somebody something jemandem etwas sagen
If she asks, tell her. Sag's ihr, wenn sie fragt.
Tell me what to do. Sag mir, was ich machen soll.
2 to tell somebody to do something jemandem sagen, er/sie soll etwas tun
He told me to do it myself. Er hat mir gesagt, ich soll es selbst machen.
She told me not to wait. Sie sagte, ich solle nicht warten.
3 (explain) Can you tell me how to do it? Kannst du mir sagen, wie man das macht?
4 erzählen (a story)
Tell me about your holiday. Erzähl mir von deinen Ferien.
5 (see) sehen◇
You can tell it's old. Man sieht, dass es alt ist.
I can't tell them apart. Ich kann sie nicht unterscheiden.
6 I told you so. Das habe ich dir ja gleich gesagt.

telly NOUN
1 (set) der Fernseher (PL die **Fernseher**)
2 to watch telly fernsehen◇ SEP
I saw her on telly. Ich habe sie im Fernsehen gesehen.

temp NOUN
die Aushilfskraft (PL die **Aushilfskräfte**)

temper NOUN
to lose your temper wütend werden◇ (PERF sein)

ℓ **temperature** NOUN
1 die Temperatur (PL die **Temperaturen**)

ℓ indicates key words

high temperatures hohe Temperaturen
What is the temperature? Wie viel Grad
sind es?
2 to have a temperature Fieber haben

temple NOUN
der Tempel (PL die Tempel)

temporary ADJECTIVE
vorübergehend

temptation NOUN
die Versuchung (PL die Versuchungen)

tempted ADJECTIVE
versucht
I'm really tempted to come. Ich würde am
liebsten kommen.

tempting ADJECTIVE
verlockend

♂ **ten** NUMBER
zehn
Harry's ten. Harry ist zehn.

to **tend** VERB
to tend to do something dazu neigen,
etwas zu tun

tender ADJECTIVE
1 (loving) zärtlich
2 (painful) empfindlich

tennis NOUN
das Tennis
to play tennis Tennis spielen

tennis ball NOUN
der Tennisball (PL die Tennisbälle)

tennis court NOUN
der Tennisplatz (PL die Tennisplätze)

tennis player NOUN
der Tennisspieler (PL die Tennisspieler), die
Tennisspielerin (PL die Tennisspielerinnen)

WORD TIP Professions, hobbies, and sports
don't take an article in German: Sie ist
Tennisspielerin.

tennis racket NOUN
der Tennisschläger (PL die Tennisschläger)

tenor NOUN
der Tenor (PL die Tenöre)

tenpin bowling NOUN
das Bowling

tense NOUN
(in grammar) die Zeit
the present tense das Präsens
in the future tense im Futur

tense ADJECTIVE
gespannt

♂ **tent** NOUN
das Zelt (PL die Zelte)
to put up a tent ein Zelt aufbauen SEP

♂ **tenth** NUMBER
zehnter/zehnte/zehntes
on the tenth floor im zehnten Stock
the tenth of April der zehnte April

♂ **term** NOUN
(in school) das Halbjahr (PL die Halbjahre)
(at university) das Semester (PL die
Semester)

terminal NOUN
1 (at an airport) der Terminal (PL die
Terminals)
2 bus terminal die Endstation
3 (computer terminal) das Terminal (PL die
Terminals)

terrace NOUN
1 (outside a house) die Terrasse (PL die
Terrassen)
2 (row of houses) die Häuserreihe (PL die
Häuserreihen)
3 the terraces (at a stadium) die Ränge
(PLURAL)

♂ **terrible** ADJECTIVE
furchtbar

terribly ADVERB
1 (very) sehr
not terribly clean nicht sehr sauber
2 (badly) furchtbar
I played terribly. Ich habe furchtbar
gespielt.

terrific ADJECTIVE
1 irre (informal)
a terrific amount eine irre Menge
2 Terrific! Super! (informal)

terrified ADJECTIVE
to be terrified furchtbare Angst haben

terrorism NOUN
der Terrorismus

terrorist NOUN
der Terrorist (PL die Terroristen), die
Terroristin (PL die Terroristinnen)

♂ **test** NOUN
1 (in school) die Klassenarbeit (PL die
Klassenarbeiten)
We've got a maths test tomorrow. Wir
schreiben morgen eine Mathearbeit.
2 (medical check, trial) der Test (PL die Tests)
eye test der Sehtest
blood test die Blutprobe

◇ **irregular verb;** SEP **separable verb; for more help with verbs see centre section**

3 driving test die Fahrprüfung
She's taking her driving test on Friday. Sie macht am Freitag ihre Fahrprüfung.
He passed his driving test. Er hat seine Fahrprüfung bestanden.

to test VERB
testen, *(orally)* **abfragen** SEP
Can you test me? Kannst du mich abfragen?

test tube NOUN
das **Reagenzglas** (PL die **Reagenzgläser**)

ℓ **text** NOUN
1 der **Text** (PL die **Texte**)
2 *(text message)* die **SMS** (PL die **SMS**)

to text VERB
eine SMS schicken
Text me this evening. Schick mir heute Abend eine SMS.
I texted him the results. Ich habe ihm die Ergebnisse per SMS geschickt.

textbook NOUN
das **Lehrbuch** (PL die **Lehrbücher**)

text message NOUN
die **SMS** (PL die **SMS**)

Thames NOUN
the Thames die Themse

ℓ **than** CONJUNCTION
als
They have more money than we do. Sie haben mehr Geld als wir.
more than forty mehr als vierzig
more than thirty years mehr als dreißig Jahre

to thank VERB
1 **to thank somebody for something** sich bei jemandem für etwas (ACC) bedanken
2 **Thank you.** Danke.
Thank you for looking after my bike. Danke, dass du auf mein Rad aufgepasst hast.

ℓ **thanks** PLURAL NOUN
1 der **Dank** (SINGULAR)
Thanks a lot! Vielen Dank!
Many thanks. Vielen Dank.
2 **No thanks.** Nein danke.
Thanks for your letter. Danke für deinen Brief.
3 **thanks to** dank (+DAT)
It was thanks to him that we made it. Dank ihm haben wir es geschafft.

ℓ **thank you** ADVERB
danke

No thank you. Nein danke.
Thank you very much for the money. Herzlichen Dank für das Geld.
a thank-you letter ein Dankbrief

ℓ **that** DETERMINER
1 dieser/diese/dieses
that boy dieser Junge
that woman diese Frau
that house dieses Haus
2 **that one** der da/die da/das da
'Which cake would you like?' – 'That one, please.' 'Welchen Kuchen möchten Sie?' – 'Den da, bitte.'
I like all the dresses but I'm going to buy that one. Mir gefallen alle Kleider, aber ich kaufe das da.

that ADVERB
so
It's not that easy. Es ist nicht so einfach.

that PRONOUN
1 das
What's that? Was ist das?
Who's that? Wer ist das?
Where's that? Wo ist das?
Is that Mandy? Ist das Mandy?
2 das
Did you see that? Hast du das gesehen?
That's my bedroom. Das ist mein Schlafzimmer.
3 *(in relative clauses)* der/die/das *(depending on the gender of the noun 'that' refers to)* *(plural)* die
the train that's leaving now der Zug, der jetzt abfährt
the flower that I picked die Blume (PL die ich gepflückt habe
the car that's red das Auto, das rot ist

that CONJUNCTION
dass
I knew that he was lying. Ich wußte, dass er log.

ℓ **the** DETERMINER
1 der/die/das *(the article changes according to the gender of the noun)*
(before a masculine noun) **the dog** der Hund
(before a feminine noun) **the cat** die Katze
(before a neuter noun) **the car** das Auto
2 *(before all plural nouns)* die
the windows die Fenster

ℓ **theatre** NOUN
das **Theater** (PL die **Theater**)
to go to the theatre ins Theater gehen◊ *(PERF* sein)

ℓ **theft** NOUN
der **Diebstahl** (PL die **Diebstähle**)

A B C D E F G H I J K L M N O P Q R S T U V W X Y Z

655

ℰ **their** DETERMINER

ihr *(PLURAL)* ihre
their son ihr Sohn
their daughter ihre Tochter
their car ihr Auto
their presents ihre Geschenke

ℰ **theirs** PRONOUN

1 ihrer *(when standing for a masculine noun)*
Our garden's smaller than theirs. Unser Garten ist kleiner als ihrer.

2 ihre *(when standing for a feminine noun)*
Your flat is bigger than theirs. Deine Wohnung ist größer als ihre.

3 ihrs *(when standing for a neuter noun)*
Our car was cheaper than theirs. Unser Auto war billiger als ihrs.

4 ihre *(when standing for a plural noun)*
Our children are older than theirs. Unsere Kinder sind älter als ihre.

5 **The yellow car is theirs.** Das gelbe Auto gehört ihnen.
It's theirs. Das gehört ihnen.

ℰ **them** PRONOUN

1 *(as a direct object in the accusative)* sie
I know them. Ich kenne sie.
I don't know them. Ich kenne sie nicht.

2 *(after prepositions +ACC)* sie
It's for them. Das ist für sie.

3 *(as an indirect object or following a verb that takes the dative)* ihnen
I told them a story. Ich habe ihnen eine Geschichte erzählt.

4 *(to them)* ihnen
I gave them my address. Ich habe ihnen meine Adresse gegeben.

5 *(after prepositions +DAT)* ihnen
I'll go with them. Ich gehe mit ihnen mit.

6 *(in comparisons)* **He's older than them.** Er ist älter als sie.

theme NOUN

das Thema *(PL die Themen)*

theme park NOUN

der Themenpark *(PL die Themenparks)*

themselves PRONOUN

1 sich
They enjoyed themselves. Sie haben sich amüsiert.

2 *(for emphasis)* selbst
The boys can do it themselves. Die Jungen können es selbst machen.

ℰ **then** ADVERB

1 *(next)* dann
I get up and then I make the bed. Ich stehe auf und dann mache ich das Bett.

I went to the post office and then the bank. Ich bin zur Post und dann auf die Bank gegangen.

2 *(at that time)* damals
We were living in York then. Wir haben damals in York gewohnt.

3 *(in that case)* dann
Then why worry? Warum machst du dir dann Sorgen?

4 **since then** seitdem

5 **from then on** von da an

theory NOUN

1 die Theorie *(PL die Theorien)*

2 **in theory** theoretisch

ℰ **there** ADVERB

1 *(in a fixed location)* da
up there da oben
down there da unten
in there da drin
Stay there! Bleib da!

2 **over there** da drüben
She's over there with Mark. Sie ist da drüben mit Mark.

3 *(with movement to a place)* dahin
Put it there. Leg es dahin.
We're going there on Tuesday. Wir fahren am Dienstag dahin.

4 *(further away)* dort
I've seen photos of Oxford but I've never been there. Ich habe Fotos von Oxford gesehen, aber ich war noch nie dort.

5 **there is** *(there is at this moment)* da ist, es ist
There's a cat in the garden. Da ist eine Katze im Garten.
There's enough bread. Es ist genug Brot da.
No, there's not enough. Nein, es ist nicht genug da.

6 **there is** *(there exists)* es gibt
There's only one hospital in this town. In dieser Stadt gibt es nur ein Krankenhaus.

7 **there are** *(there are at this moment)* da sind, es sind
There were lots of people in town. Es waren viele Leute in der Stadt.

8 **there are** *(there exist)* es gibt
There are lots of museums here. Es gibt hier viele Museen.

9 *(when drawing attention)* da
There they are! Da sind sie!
There's the bus coming! Da kommt der Bus!

ℰ **therefore** ADVERB

deshalb

◇ **irregular verb;** SEP **separable verb; for more help with verbs see centre section**

thermometer NOUN
das **Thermometer** (PL die **Thermometer**)

these ADJECTIVE
diese
these glasses diese Gläser

these PRONOUN
die
These are cheaper. Die sind billiger.

ℙ they PRONOUN
1 sie
'Where are the knives?' – 'They're in the drawer.' 'Wo sind die Messer?' – 'Sie sind in der Schublade.'
2 man
they say man sagt

ℙ thick ADJECTIVE
dick
a thick layer of butter eine dicke Schicht Butter

ℙ thief NOUN
der **Dieb** (PL die **Diebe**), die **Diebin** (PL die **Diebinnen**)

thigh NOUN
der **Oberschenkel** (PL die **Oberschenkel**)

ℙ thin ADJECTIVE
dünn

ℙ thing NOUN
1 (an object) das **Ding** (PL die **Dinge**)
They have lots of nice things. Sie haben viele schöne Dinge.
She told me some strange things. Sie hat mir ein paar seltsame Dinge erzählt.
that thing next to the hammer das Ding da neben dem Hammer
2 **things** (belongings) die **Sachen** (PLURAL)
You can leave your things in my room. Du kannst deine Sachen in meinem Zimmer lassen.
3 **The best thing to do is …** Am besten wäre es …
It was a good thing that you asked. Es war gut, dass du gefragt hast.
4 (subject, affair) die **Sache** (PL die **Sachen**)
The thing is, I've lost her address. Die Sache ist die, ich habe ihre Adresse verloren.
5 **How are things?** Wie geht's?

ℙ to think VERB
1 (believe) **glauben**
Do you think they'll come? Glaubst du, sie kommen?
No, I don't think so. Nein, ich glaube nicht.
I think so. Ich glaube schon.

I think he's already paid. Ich glaube, er hat schon gezahlt.
2 **denken**◇
I'm thinking about you. Ich denke an dich.
What are you thinking about? Woran denkst du?
3 **What do you think of that?** Was halten Sie davon?
I don't think much of her proposal. Ich halte nicht viel von ihrem Vorschlag.
4 **What do you think of my new jacket?** Wie findest du meine neue Jacke?
5 (remember)
to think to do something daran denken, etwas zu tun
He didn't think of locking the door. Er hat nicht daran gedacht (PL die Tür abzuschließen.)
6 (think carefully) **nachdenken**◇ SEP
He thought for a moment. Er hat einen Moment lang nachgedacht.
Think about it! Denk darüber nach!
7 **I've thought it over carefully.** Ich habe es mir genau überlegt.
8 (imagine) **sich** (DAT) **vorstellen** SEP
Just think, we'll soon be in Spain! Stell dir nur vor, bald sind wir in Spanien!
I never thought it would be like this. So habe ich es mir nie vorgestellt.

ℙ third NOUN
das **Drittel** (PL die **Drittel**)
a third of the population ein Drittel der Bevölkerung

third ADJECTIVE
dritter/dritte/drittes
on the third floor im dritten Stock
on the third of March am dritten März

thirdly ADVERB
drittens

ℙ Third World NOUN
die **Dritte Welt**

thirst NOUN
der **Durst**

ℙ thirsty ADJECTIVE
durstig
to be thirsty Durst haben
I'm thirsty. Ich habe Durst.
We were all thirsty. Wir hatten alle Durst.

ℙ thirteen NUMBER
dreizehn
Ahmed's thirteen. Ahmed ist dreizehn.

ℙ thirty NUMBER
dreißig

ℓ this DETERMINER
1 **dieser/diese/dieses**
this boy dieser Junge
this flower diese Blume
this car dieses Auto
at the end of this week Ende dieser Woche
2 **this morning** heute Morgen
this evening heute Abend
this afternoon heute Nachmittag
3 **this one** der/die/das (with more emphasis)
dieser/diese/dieses
If you need a pen you can have this one.
Wenn du einen Kugelschreiber brauchst,
kannst du den haben.
I'll take this one. Ich nehme diesen.

this PRONOUN
1 **das**
Can you hold this? Kannst du das
festhalten?
What's this? Was ist das?
2 **This is my sister Carla.** (in introductions)
Das ist meine Schwester Carla.
3 **This is Tracy speaking.** (on the phone) Hier
spricht Tracy.

thistle NOUN
die **Distel** (PL die **Disteln**)

thorn NOUN
der **Dorn** (PL die **Dornen**)

ℓ those DETERMINER
diese
those books diese Bücher

those PRONOUN
die da
If you need more pens you can take those.
Wenn du mehr Stifte brauchst, kannst du
die da nehmen.

though CONJUNCTION
obwohl
though it's cold obwohl es kalt ist
though ADVERB
dennoch
It was a good idea, though. Es war
dennoch eine gute Idee.

thought NOUN
der **Gedanke** (PL die **Gedanken**)

ℓ thousand NUMBER
1 **tausend**
a thousand eintausend
three thousand dreitausend
2 **thousands of** Tausende von
There were thousands of tourists in
Venice. Tausende von Touristen waren in
Venedig.

thread NOUN
der **Faden** (PL die **Fäden**)
to thread VERB
einfädeln (a needle)

threat NOUN
die **Drohung** (PL die **Drohungen**)
Is that a threat? Soll das eine Drohung sein?

to threaten VERB
drohen (+DAT)
He threatened her. Er hat ihr gedroht.
to threaten to do something damit
drohen, etwas zu tun

ℓ three NUMBER
drei
Oskar's three. Oskar ist drei.

ℓ three quarters NOUN
drei Viertel
three quarters of an hour eine Dreiviertelstunde
three-quarters ADVERB
three-quarters full drei viertel voll

thrilled ADJECTIVE
to be thrilled sich wahnsinnig freuen

thriller NOUN
der **Thriller** (PL die **Thriller**)

thrilling ADJECTIVE
spannend

ℓ throat NOUN
der **Hals** (PL die **Hälse**)
to have a sore throat Halsschmerzen haben

ℓ through PREPOSITION
1 (across, via) **durch** (+ACC)
through the forest durch den Wald
through the window durch das Fenster
The train goes through Leeds. Der Zug
fährt durch Leeds.
2 **to let somebody through** jemanden
durchlassen◇ SEP
The police let us through. Die Polizei ließ
uns durch.
3 **I know them through my cousin.** Ich kenne
sie über meinen Vetter.

ℓ to throw VERB
1 **werfen**◇
I threw the letter in the bin. Ich habe den
Brief in den Mülleimer geworfen.
2 **to throw something to somebody**
jemandem etwas zuwerfen◇ SEP
Throw me the ball. Wirf mir den Ball zu.
3 **to throw something at somebody** etwas
nach jemandem werfen◇

◇ **irregular verb;** SEP **separable verb; for more help with verbs see centre section**

thumb

tighten

ENGLISH—GERMAN

- **to throw something away**
  etwas wegwerfen◇ SEP
  I'm throwing away the old newspapers.
  Ich werfe die alten Zeitungen weg.
- **to throw somebody out**
  jemanden rauswerfen◇ SEP
- **to throw something out**
  etwas wegwerfen◇ SEP (rubbish)

thumb NOUN
der Daumen (PL die Daumen)

to thumb VERB
schlagen◇ auf (+ACC)
He thumped the radio to see if it would work. Er schlug auf das Radio, um zu sehen, ob es dann funktionierte.

thunder NOUN
der Donner
peal of thunder der Donnerschlag

to thunder VERB
donnern
It's thundering. Es donnert.

thunderstorm NOUN
das Gewitter (PL die Gewitter)

thundery ADJECTIVE
gewittrig

ℱ**Thursday** NOUN
1 der Donnerstag (PL die Donnerstage)
  on Thursday (am) Donnerstag
  I'm leaving on Thursday. Ich fahre am Donnerstag ab.
  See you on Thursday. Bis Donnerstag.
  every Thursday jeden Donnerstag
  last Thursday vorigen Donnerstag
  next Thursday nächsten Donnerstag
2 **on Thursdays** donnerstags
  The museum is closed on Thursdays. Das Museum ist donnerstags geschlossen.

to tick VERB
1 (clock, watch) ticken
2 (on a list) abhaken SEP
3 ankreuzen SEP (a box)

ℱ**ticket** NOUN
1 (for an exhibition, theatre, or cinema) die Karte (PL die Karten)
  two tickets for the concert zwei Karten für das Konzert
2 (for the underground, a bus, or a train) die Fahrkarte (PL die Fahrkarten)
  a plane ticket ein Flugschein, ein Ticket
3 (for left luggage, parking) der Zettel (PL die Zettel)
  parking ticket der Strafzettel
4 (for a lottery or raffle) das Los (PL die Lose)

ticket inspector NOUN
der Schaffner (PL die Schaffner), die Schaffnerin (PL die Schaffnerinnen)

WORD TIP Professions, hobbies, and sports don't take an article in German: Er ist Schaffner.

ℱ**ticket office** NOUN
(at a station) der Fahrkartenschalter (PL die Fahrkartenschalter)

to tickle VERB
kitzeln

ℱ**tide** NOUN
1 (high) die Flut (PL die Fluten)
  at high tide bei Flut
  When is high tide? Wann ist Flut?
2 (low) die Ebbe (PL die Ebben)
  The tide is out. Es ist Ebbe.

ℱ**tidy** ADJECTIVE
ordentlich

to tidy VERB
aufräumen SEP
I'll tidy (up) the kitchen. Ich räume die Küche auf.

ℱ**tie** NOUN
1 (necktie) die Krawatte (PL die Krawatten)
2 (in a match) das Unentschieden

to tie VERB
1 binden◇
  to tie your shoelaces sich (DAT) die Schnürsenkel binden
2 **to tie a knot in something** einen Knoten in etwas (ACC) machen
3 (in a match) unentschieden spielen
  We tied two all. Wir haben zwei zu zwei gespielt.

tiger NOUN
der Tiger (PL die Tiger)

tight ADJECTIVE
(close-fitting) eng
The skirt's a bit tight. Der Rock ist etwas eng.
These shoes are too tight. Diese Schuhe sind zu eng.
She was wearing tight jeans. Sie hatte enge Jeans an.

tight ADVERB
Hold tight! Halt dich fest!

to tighten VERB
anziehen◇ SEP (a screw, knot)
He tightened his belt. Er schnallte seinen Gürtel enger.
He tightened his grip. Er griff fester zu.

A B C D E F G H I J K L M N O P Q R S T U V W X Y Z

659

ℱ indicates key words

tightly ADVERB
fest

ℰ **tights** PLURAL NOUN
die **Strumpfhose** (PL die **Strumpfhosen**)
a pair of purple tights eine lila Strumpfhose

WORD TIP In German die Strumpfhose is singular.

tile NOUN
1 *(on a floor)* die **Fliese** (PL die **Fliesen**)
2 *(on a wall)* die **Kachel** (PL die **Kacheln**)
3 *(on a roof)* der **Ziegel** (PL die **Ziegel**)

ℰ **till¹** PREPOSITION, CONJUNCTION
1 bis
They're staying till Sunday. Sie bleiben bis Sonntag.
till then bis dann
till now bis jetzt
2 *(when 'till' is followed by a noun it is usually translated as bis zu +DAT)*
till the evening bis zum Abend
3 not till erst
She won't be back till ten. Sie kommt erst um zehn zurück.
We won't know till Monday. Wir werden erst am Montag Bescheid wissen.

till² NOUN
die **Kasse** (PL die **Kassen**)
Please pay at the till. Bitte zahlen Sie an der Kasse.

ℰ **time** NOUN
1 *(on the clock)* die **Zeit**
It's time for breakfast. Es ist Zeit zum Frühstücken.
2 What time is it? Wie viel Uhr ist es?
At what time does it start? Um wie viel Uhr fängt es an?
ten o'clock German time zehn Uhr, deutsche Zeit
3 on time pünktlich
They arrived on time. Sie kamen pünktlich.
4 in time (for something) rechtzeitig (zu etwas)
They arrived just in time for the main film. Sie kamen gerade rechtzeitig zum Hauptfilm.
Will we be in time for the train? Werden wir den Zug noch schaffen?
5 *(an amount of time)* die **Zeit**
We've got lots of time. Wir haben viel Zeit.
I haven't got time now. Ich habe jetzt keine Zeit.
There's no time left to do it. Dafür bleibt keine Zeit mehr.
from time to time von Zeit zu Zeit
for a long time lange

6 *(moment)* der **Moment** (PL die **Momente**)
This isn't a good time to discuss it. Das ist kein guter Moment, um darüber zu sprechen.
at the right time im richtigen Moment
for the time being im Moment
any time now jeden Moment
7 at times manchmal
8 *(in a series)* das **Mal** (PL die **Male**)
eight times achtmal
for the first time zum ersten Mal
the first time I saw you das erste Mal, als ich dich sah
three times a year dreimal im Jahr
9 Three times two is six. Drei mal zwei ist sechs.
10 to have a good time sich amüsieren
We had a really good time. Wir haben uns richtig gut amüsiert.
Have a good time! Viel Vergnügen!

ℰ **timetable** NOUN
1 *(in school)* der **Stundenplan** (PL die **Stundenpläne**)
2 *(for trains or buses)* der **Fahrplan** (PL die **Fahrpläne**)
bus timetable der Busfahrplan

ℰ **tin** NOUN
die **Dose** (PL die **Dosen**)
a tin of tomatoes eine Dose Tomaten

tinned ADJECTIVE
in Dosen
tinned peas Erbsen aus der Dose

tin opener NOUN
der **Dosenöffner** (PL die **Dosenöffner**)

tiny ADJECTIVE
winzig

ℰ **tip** NOUN
1 *(end)* die **Spitze** (PL die **Spitzen**)
2 *(money)* das **Trinkgeld**
3 *(useful hint)* der **Tipp** (PL die **Tipps**)
to **tip** VERB
(give money) ein Trinkgeld geben◇ (+DAT)
We tipped the waiter. Wir haben dem Kellner ein Trinkgeld gegeben.

tiptoe NOUN
on tiptoe auf Zehenspitzen

ℰ **tired** ADJECTIVE
1 müde
I'm tired. Ich bin müde.
You look tired. Du siehst müde aus.
2 to be tired of something etwas satt haben
I'm tired of London. Ich habe London satt.
I'm tired of watching TV every evening.

◇ irregular verb; SEP separable verb; for more help with verbs see centre section

Ich habe es satt, jeden Abend fernzusehen.

tiring *ADJECTIVE*
ermüdend

tissue *NOUN*
(*a paper hanky*) das **Papiertaschentuch**
(*PL* die **Papiertaschentücher**)

title *NOUN*
der **Titel** (*PL* die **Titel**)

ℱ **to** *PREPOSITION*
1 (*to a country or town*) **nach**
   to go to London nach London fahren
   the motorway to Italy die Autobahn nach
   Italien
2 (*to the cinema, theatre, school, office*) **in**
   (*+ACC*)
   I'm going to school. Ich gehe in die Schule.
   She's gone to the office. Sie ist ins Büro
   gegangen.
   We want to go to town. Wir wollen in die
   Stadt gehen.
3 (*to a wedding, party, university, the toilet*)
   auf (*+ACC*)
   She's gone to the toilet. Sie ist auf die
   Toilette gegangen.
4 (*addressed or attached to*) **an** (*+ACC*)
   a letter to my parents ein Brief an meine
   Eltern
5 **Give the book to her.** Gib ihr das Buch.
   He said to me that ... Er hat mir gesagt,
   dass ...
6 (*to somebody's house, a particular place, or
   person*) **zu** (*+DAT*)
   I went round to Paul's house. Ich bin zu
   Paul nach Hause gegangen.
   We're going to the Browns' for supper.
   Wir gehen zu Browns zum Abendessen.
   I'm going to the dentist tomorrow.
   Morgen gehe ich zum Zahnarzt.
7 (*talking about the time*)
   It's ten to nine. Es ist zehn vor neun.
   from eight to ten von acht bis zehn
   from Monday to Friday von Montag bis
   Freitag
8 (*in order to*) **um zu** (*+ INFINITIVE*)
   **He gave me some money to buy a
   sandwich.** Er hat mir Geld gegeben, um ein
   Sandwich zu kaufen.
9 (*in verbal phrases with the infinitive*) **zu**
   I have nothing to do. Ich habe nichts zu
   tun.
   Have you got something to eat? Hast du
   etwas zu essen?

> **WORD TIP** Note that with countries that have
> 'die' as part of their name, 'to' is translated by
> in + *ACC*: Sie fahren in die Schweiz. Wir fliegen
> in die Türkei.

ℱ **toast** *NOUN*
1 der **Toast** (*PL* die **Toasts**)
   two slices of toast zwei Scheiben Toast
2 (*to your health*) der **Toast** (*PL* die **Toasts**)
   to drink a toast to somebody auf
   jemanden trinken

toaster *NOUN*
der **Toaster** (*PL* die **Toaster**)

ℱ **tobacco** *NOUN*
der **Tabak**

ℱ **today** *ADVERB*
heute
Today's her birthday. Sie hat heute
Geburtstag.

ℱ **toe** *NOUN*
der **Zeh** (*PL* die **Zehen**)

toffee *NOUN*
der **Karamell**

together *ADVERB*
1 **zusammen**
   We did it together. Wir haben es
   zusammen gemacht.
2 (*at the same time*) **gleichzeitig**
   They all left together. Sie sind alle
   gleichzeitig weggegangen.

ℱ **toilet** *NOUN*
die **Toilette** (*PL* die **Toiletten**)
She's gone to the toilet. Sie ist auf die
Toilette gegangen.

toilet paper *NOUN*
das **Toilettenpapier**

toilet roll *NOUN*
die **Rolle Toilettenpapier** (*PL* die **Rollen**)
Toilettenpapier

token *NOUN*
1 (*for a machine or game*) die **Marke** (*PL* die
   Marken)
2 (*voucher*) der **Gutschein** (*PL* die **Gutscheine**)
   gift token der Geschenkgutschein

tolerant *ADJECTIVE*
tolerant

ℱ **toll** *NOUN*
1 (*payment*) die **Gebühr** (*PL* die **Gebühren**)
2 (*for a bridge or road*) die **Maut** (*PL* die
   Mauten)
3 (*number*) die **Zahl**
   The death toll has risen to 25. Die Zahl der
   Todesopfer liegt jetzt bei 25.

ℱ **tomato** *NOUN*
die **Tomate** (*PL* die **Tomaten**)
tomato salad der Tomatensalat
tomato sauce die Tomatensoße

♁ tomorrow ADVERB
1 morgen
I'll do it tomorrow. Ich mache es morgen.
tomorrow afternoon morgen Nachmittag
tomorrow morning morgen früh
tomorrow night morgen Abend
2 **the day after tomorrow** übermorgen

tone NOUN
(on an answerphone, of a voice or letter) der
Ton *(PL die Töne)*

♁ tongue NOUN
die Zunge *(PL die Zungen)*
to stick your tongue out at somebody
jemandem die Zunge herausstrecken SEP
It's on the tip of my tongue. Es liegt mir auf
der Zunge.

♁ tonight ADVERB
1 *(this evening)* heute Abend
What are you doing tonight? Was macht
ihr heute Abend?
I'm going out with my friends tonight. Ich
gehe heute Abend mit meinen Freunden
weg.
See you tonight! Bis heute Abend!
2 *(after bedtime)* heute Nacht

tonsillitis NOUN
die Mandelentzündung
Ahlem's got tonsillitis. Ahlem hat eine
Mandelentzündung.

♁ too ADVERB
1 zu
It's too expensive. Es ist zu teuer.
too often zu oft
2 **too much** zu viel
I've spent too much. Ich habe zu viel
ausgegeben.
3 **too many** zu viele
4 *(as well)* auch
Karen's coming too. Karen kommt auch.
Me too! Ich auch!

tool NOUN
das Werkzeug *(PL die Werkzeuge)*

tool kit NOUN
das Werkzeug

♁ tooth NOUN
der Zahn *(PL die Zähne)*
to brush your teeth sich *(DAT)* die Zähne
putzen

toothache NOUN
die Zahnschmerzen *(PLURAL)*
I've got toothache. Ich habe
Zahnschmerzen.

♁ toothbrush NOUN
die Zahnbürste *(PL die Zahnbürsten)*

♁ toothpaste NOUN
die Zahnpasta *(PL die Zahnpasten)*

♁ top NOUN
1 *(highest part)* die Spitze *(PL die Spitzen) (of
a tree)*
2 **at the top of** oben auf *(+DAT)*
at the top of the ladder oben auf der Leiter
It's on top of the chest of drawers. Es liegt
oben auf der Kommode.
3 **at the top** oben
There are four rooms at the top. Oben sind
vier Zimmer.
from top to bottom von oben bis unten
4 *(of a mountain)* der Gipfel *(PL die Gipfel)*
5 *(a lid)* der Deckel *(PL die Deckel) (of a
container, jar, or box)*, die Kappe *(PL die
Kappen) (of a pen)*, der Verschluss *(PL die
Verschlüsse) (of a bottle)*
6 *(of a garment)* das Oberteil *(PL die
Oberteile)*
7 *(in sport)*
the top of the table die Tabellenspitze
Arsenal are top of the table. Arsenal steht
an der Tabellenspitze.
8 **and on top of all that** und obendrein
9 **It was a bit over the top.** Es war leicht
übertrieben.

top ADJECTIVE
oberster/oberste/oberstes *(step or floor)*
on the top floor im obersten Stockwerk

topic NOUN
das Thema *(PL die Themen)*

topping NOUN
der Belag *(PL die Beläge)*
Which topping would you like? Welchen
Belag hättest du gerne?

torch NOUN
die Taschenlampe *(PL die Taschenlampen)*

torn ADJECTIVE
zerrissen

tortoise NOUN
die Schildkröte *(PL die Schildkröten)*

torture NOUN
1 die Folter *(PL die Foltern)*
2 **The exam was torture.** Die Prüfung war die
Hölle. *(informal)*

to torture VERB
(use torture) foltern

Tory NOUN
der/die Konservative *(PL die Konservativen)*

ℙ **total** NOUN
1 (number) die **Gesamtzahl** (PL die **Gesamtzahlen**)
2 (result of addition) die **Summe** (PL die **Summen**)

total ADJECTIVE
gesamt

totally ADVERB
völlig

ℙ **touch** NOUN
1 (contact)
to get in touch with somebody sich mit jemandem in Verbindung setzen
to stay in touch with somebody mit jemandem Kontakt halten◇
2 **We've lost touch.** Wir haben keinen Kontakt mehr.
I've lost touch with Peter. Ich habe keinen Kontakt mehr zu Peter.
3 (a little bit)
a touch of salt eine Spur Salz
It was a touch embarrassing. Es war ein bisschen peinlich.

to **touch** VERB
1 berühren
2 (get hold of) anfassen SEP
Don't touch that. Fass das nicht an.

touched ADJECTIVE
gerührt

touching ADJECTIVE
rührend

touchscreen NOUN
der **Touchscreen** (PL die **Touchscreens**)

tough ADJECTIVE
1 hart
She's had a tough time. Sie hat eine harte Zeit hinter sich.
a tough guy ein harter Kerl
2 zäh
The meat's tough. Das Fleisch ist zäh.
3 fest (material, shoes, etc.)
4 **Tough luck!** Pech!
Tough, you're too late. So'n Pech, du bist zu spät dran.

tour NOUN
1 die **Besichtigung** (PL die **Besichtigungen**)
a tour of the city eine Stadtbesichtigung
We did a tour of the castle. Wir haben das Schloss besichtigt.
2 **guided tour** die Führung
3 **package tour** die Pauschalreise
4 (by a band or theatre group) die **Tournee** (PL die **Tournees**)

to go on tour auf Tournee gehen (PERF sein)
to **tour** VERB
(performer) auf Tournee sein◇ (PERF sein)
They're touring America. Sie sind auf Tournee in Amerika.

tour guide NOUN
der **Reiseleiter** (PL die **Reiseleiter**), die **Reiseleiterin** (PL die **Reiseleiterinnen**)

> **WORD TIP** Professions, hobbies, and sports don't take an article in German: Er ist Reiseleiter.

tourism NOUN
der **Tourismus**

ℙ **tourist** NOUN
der **Tourist** (PL die **Touristen**), die **Touristin** (PL die **Touristinnen**)

tourist information office NOUN
das **Fremdenverkehrsbüro** (PL die **Fremdenverkehrsbüros**)

tournament NOUN
das **Turnier** (PL die **Turniere**)
tennis tournament das Tennisturnier

to **tow** VERB
to be towed away abgeschleppt werden◇ (PERF sein)

ℙ **towards** PREPOSITION
zu (+DAT)
She went off towards the lake. Sie ist zum See gegangen.
to come towards somebody auf jemanden zukommen◇ SEP (PERF sein)

ℙ **towel** NOUN
das **Handtuch** (PL die **Handtücher**)

tower NOUN
der **Turm** (PL die **Türme**)

tower block NOUN
das **Hochhaus** (PL die **Hochhäuser**)

ℙ **town** NOUN
die **Stadt** (PL die **Städte**)
to go into town in die Stadt gehen (PERF sein)

town centre NOUN
die **Stadtmitte** (PL die **Stadtmitten**)

town hall NOUN
das **Rathaus** (PL die **Rathäuser**)

ℙ **toy** NOUN
das **Spielzeug**
a lot of toys viel Spielzeug

toy shop NOUN
das **Spielzeuggeschäft** (PL die **Spielzeuggeschäfte**)

ℙ indicates key words

trace NOUN
die **Spur** (PL die **Spuren**)
There was no trace of the thieves. Es fehlte
jede Spur von den Dieben.

to **trace** VERB
1 (find) **finden**◇
2 (follow) **verfolgen**
3 (copy) **durchpausen** SEP

tracing paper NOUN
das **Pauspapier**

ℙ **track** NOUN
1 (for sport) die **Bahn** (PL die **Bahnen**)
cycling track die **Radrennbahn**
racing track (for cars) die **Rennstrecke**
2 (a path) der **Weg** (PL die **Wege**)
3 (song) das **Stück** (PL die **Stücke**)
This is my favourite track. Das ist mein
Lieblingsstück.

tracksuit NOUN
der **Trainingsanzug** (PL die
Trainingsanzüge)

tractor NOUN
der **Traktor** (PL die **Traktoren**)

trade NOUN
1 (a profession) das **Gewerbe**
2 (skill, craft) das **Handwerk**
to learn a trade ein Handwerk erlernen

trade union NOUN
die **Gewerkschaft** (PL die **Gewerkschaften**)

tradition NOUN
die **Tradition** (PL die **Traditionen**)

traditional ADJECTIVE
traditionell

ℙ **traffic** NOUN
der **Verkehr**
There was a lot of traffic. Es war viel
Verkehr.
We were stuck in traffic. Wir steckten im
Stau.

traffic island NOUN
die **Verkehrsinsel** (PL die **Verkehrsinseln**)

traffic jam NOUN
der **Stau** (PL die **Staus**)

traffic lights PLURAL NOUN
die **Ampel** (PL die **Ampeln**)
The traffic lights were red. Die Ampel war
rot.

WORD TIP In German die Ampel is singular.

traffic warden NOUN
der **Verkehrsüberwacher** (PL die

Verkehrsüberwacher), (female) die
Politesse (PL die **Politessen**)

WORD TIP Professions, hobbies, and sports
don't take an article in German: Sie ist Politesse.

tragedy NOUN
die **Tragödie** (PL die **Tragödien**)

tragic ADJECTIVE
tragisch

trail NOUN
(a path) der **Pfad** (PL die **Pfade**)
a nature trail ein Naturlehrpfad

trailer NOUN
der **Anhänger** (PL die **Anhänger**)

ℙ **train** NOUN
der **Zug** (PL die **Züge**)
He's coming by train. Er kommt mit dem
Zug.
I met her on the train. Ich habe sie im Zug
getroffen.
the train for York der Zug nach York
train crash das Zugunglück

to **train** VERB
1 (somebody for a career) **ausbilden** SEP
badly trained staff schecht ausgebildetes
Personal
2 She's training to be a nurse. Sie macht eine
Ausbildung zur Krankenschwester.
3 (in sport) **trainieren**
The team trains on Wednesdays. Die
Mannschaft trainiert mittwochs.

ℙ **trainee** NOUN
der/die **Auszubildende** (PL die
Auszubildenden)
Lisa is a trainee. Lisa ist Auszubildende.

ℙ **trainer** NOUN
1 (of an athlete or horse) der **Trainer** (PL die
Trainer), die **Trainerin** (PL die **Trainerinnen**)
2 trainers die **Turnschuhe** (PLURAL)
a new pair of trainers neue Turnschuhe

WORD TIP Professions, hobbies, and sports
don't take an article in German: Sie ist Trainerin.

ℙ **training** NOUN
1 (for a career) die **Ausbildung**
2 (for sport) das **Training**

train ticket NOUN
die **Zugfahrkarte** (PL die **Zugfahrkarten**)

train timetable NOUN
der **Bahnfahrplan** (PL die **Bahnfahrpläne**)

tram NOUN
die **Straßenbahn** (PL die **Straßenbahnen**)

◇ irregular verb; SEP separable verb; for more help with verbs see centre section

We went by tram. Wir sind mit der
Straßenbahn gefahren.

tramp NOUN
der **Landstreicher** (PL die **Landstreicher**),
die **Landstreicherin** (PL die
Landstreicherinnen)

trampoline NOUN
das **Trampolin** (PL die **Trampoline**)

trampolining NOUN
das **Trampolinspringen**

transfer NOUN
das **Abziehbild** (PL die **Abziehbilder**)

to **transform** VERB
verwandeln

to **translate** VERB
übersetzen
to translate something into German etwas
ins Deutsche übersetzen

translation NOUN
die **Übersetzung** (PL die **Übersetzungen**)

translator NOUN
der **Übersetzer** (PL die **Übersetzer**), die
Übersetzerin (PL die **Übersetzerinnen**)

WORD TIP Professions, hobbies, and sports
don't take an article in German: Sie ist
Übersetzerin.

transparent ADJECTIVE
durchsichtig

transplant NOUN
die **Transplantation** (PL die
Transplantationen)

ℓ **transport** NOUN
der **Transport** (PL die **Transporte**)
the transport of goods der Warentransport
public transport die öffentlichen
Verkehrsmittel (PLURAL)
We use public transport if possible. Wir
fahren nach Möglichkeit mit öffentlichen
Verkehrsmitteln.

trap NOUN
die **Falle** (PL die **Fallen**)

ℓ **travel** NOUN
das **Reisen**
foreign travel die Auslandsreisen (PLURAL)

to **travel** VERB
reisen (PERF sein)

travel agency NOUN
das **Reisebüro** (PL die **Reisebüros**)

travel agent NOUN
der **Reisebürokaufmann** (PL
die **Reisebürokaufleute**), die
Reisebürokauffrau (PL die
Reisebürokauffrauen)

WORD TIP Professions, hobbies, and sports
don't take an article in German: Er ist
Reisebürokaufmann.

ℓ **traveller** NOUN
1 der/die **Reisende** (PL die **Reisenden**)
2 (gypsy) der **Zigeuner** (PL die **Zigeuner**), die
Zigeunerin (PL die **Zigeunerinnen**)

ℓ **traveller's cheque** NOUN
der **Reisescheck** (PL die **Reiseschecks**)

travel-sick ADJECTIVE
reisekrank
I get travel-sick. Ich werde reisekrank.

tray NOUN
das **Tablett** (PL die **Tabletts**)

to **tread** VERB
to tread on something auf etwas (ACC)
treten◇ (PERF sein)
I trod on a nail. Ich bin auf einen Nagel
getreten.
She trod on my foot. Sie ist mir auf den Fuß
getreten.

treasure NOUN
der **Schatz** (PL die **Schätze**)

treat NOUN
1 **I took them to the circus as a treat.** Ich
habe ihnen eine besondere Freude gemacht
und sie in den Zirkus eingeladen.
2 (food) der **Leckerbissen** (PL die
Leckerbissen)

to **treat** VERB
1 **behandeln**
He treats his dog well. Er behandelt seinen
Hund gut.
the doctor who treated you der Arzt, der
dich behandelt hat
Don't treat me like a baby. Behandele mich
nicht wie ein Baby.
2 **to treat somebody to something**
jemandem etwas spendieren
I'll treat you to an ice cream. Ich spendiere
euch ein Eis.

treatment NOUN
die **Behandlung** (PL die **Behandlungen**)

ℓ **tree** NOUN
der **Baum** (PL die **Bäume**)

to **tremble** VERB
zittern

trend NOUN
1 (a fashion) der **Trend** (PL die **Trends**)
2 (a tendency) die **Tendenz** (PL die **Tendenzen**)

trendy ADJECTIVE
modern

trial NOUN
(in court) der **Prozess** (PL die **Prozesse**)

triangle NOUN
das **Dreieck** (PL die **Dreiecke**)

triathlon NOUN
das/der **Triathlon** (PL die **Triathlons**)

ℓ **trick** NOUN
1 (a joke) der **Streich** (PL die **Streiche**)
to play a trick on somebody jemandem einen Streich spielen
2 (a knack or by a conjuror) der **Trick** (PL die **Tricks**)
There must be a trick to it. Da muss ein Trick dabei sein.

to **trick** VERB
hereinlegen SEP
He tricked me! Er hat mich hereingelegt!

tricky ADJECTIVE
verzwickt
It's a tricky situation. Das ist eine verzwickte Situation.

tricycle NOUN
das **Dreirad** (PL die **Dreiräder**)

to **trim** VERB
schneiden◇ (hair)

ℓ **trip** NOUN
1 die **Reise** (PL die **Reisen**)
a trip to Florida eine Reise nach Florida
He's going on a business trip. Er macht eine Geschäftsreise.
2 (a day out) der **Ausflug** (PL die **Ausflüge**)
a day trip to France ein Tagesausflug nach Frankreich

to **trip** VERB
(stumble) stolpern (PERF sein)
Nicky tripped over a stone. Nicky ist über einen Stein gestolpert.

triple jump NOUN
der **Dreisprung**
He won a medal in the triple jump. Er hat eine Medaille im Dreisprung gewonnen.

triumph NOUN
der **Triumph** (PL die **Triumphe**)

ℓ **trolley** NOUN
1 (for shopping) der **Einkaufswagen** (PL die **Einkaufswagen**)

2 (for luggage) der **Kofferkuli** (PL die **Kofferkulis**)

trombone NOUN
die **Posaune** (PL die **Posaunen**)
Amy plays the trombone. Amy spielt Posaune.

WORD TIP Don't use the article when you talk about playing an instrument.

troops PLURAL NOUN
die **Truppen** (PLURAL)

trophy NOUN
die **Trophäe** (PL die **Trophäen**), (in competitions) der **Pokal** (PL die **Pokale**)

tropical ADJECTIVE
tropisch
tropical fruits die Südfrüchte (PLURAL)

to **trot** VERB
traben (PERF sein)

ℓ **trouble** NOUN
1 (general difficulties) der **Ärger**
to make trouble Ärger machen
to get into trouble Ärger bekommen
We had trouble with the travel agency. Wir hatten Ärger mit dem Reisebüro.
2 (problem) das **Problem** (PL die **Probleme**)
The trouble is, I've lost his phone number. Das Problem ist, dass ich seine Telefonnummer verloren habe.
Steph's in trouble. Steph hat Probleme.
What's the trouble? Was ist los?
It's no trouble! Das ist kein Problem!
3 (difficulty, effort) die **Mühe**
to have trouble doing something Mühe haben, etwas zu tun
I had trouble finding a seat. Ich hatte Mühe, einen Platz zu finden.
It's not worth the trouble. Das ist nicht der Mühe wert.
I took a lot of trouble over the essay. Ich habe mir mit dem Aufsatz viel Mühe gegeben.

ℓ **trousers** PLURAL NOUN
die **Hose** (PL die **Hosen**)
my old trousers meine alte Hose
a new pair of trousers eine neue Hose

WORD TIP In German die Hose is singular.

trout NOUN
die **Forelle** (PL die **Forellen**)

truant NOUN
der **Schulschwänzer** (PL die **Schulschwänzer**), die **Schulschwänzerin** (PL die **Schulschwänzerinnen**)

◇ irregular verb; SEP separable verb; for more help with verbs see centre section

truck — Turkish

She's playing truant. Sie schwänzt die Schule.

ℙ **truck** NOUN
der **Lastkraftwagen** (PL die **Lastkraftwagen**)

ℙ **true** ADJECTIVE
1 **wahr**
a true story eine wahre Geschichte
2 **Is that true?** Stimmt das?
It's true that she's absent-minded. Es stimmt, dass sie sehr vergesslich ist.

trump NOUN
der **Trumpf** (PL die **Trümpfe**)
Hearts are trumps. Herz ist Trumpf.

trumpet NOUN
die **Trompete** (PL die **Trompeten**)
Sam plays the trumpet. Sam spielt Trompete.

WORD TIP Don't use the article when you talk about playing an instrument.

trunk NOUN
1 (of a tree) der **Stamm** (PL die **Stämme**)
2 (of an elephant) der **Rüssel** (PL die **Rüssel**)

trunks PLURAL NOUN
swimming trunks die Badehose
a new pair of trunks eine neue Badehose

WORD TIP In German die Badehose is singular.

trust NOUN
das **Vertrauen**

to **trust** VERB
1 **to trust somebody** jemandem vertrauen
Can we trust her? Können wir ihr vertrauen?
2 **Trust me!** Glaub mir!
3 **Trust Mike to be late!** Mike kommt wie immer zu spät.

truth NOUN
die **Wahrheit**

ℙ **try** NOUN
der **Versuch** (PL die **Versuche**)
It's my first try. Es ist mein erster Versuch.
to have a try es versuchen
Give it a try! Versuch's doch mal!

to **try** VERB
1 **versuchen**
to try to do something versuchen, etwas zu tun
I'm trying to open the door. Ich versuche (PL die Tür aufzumachen.
2 (taste) **probieren**
• **to try something on**
etwas anprobieren SEP (a garment)

ℙ **T-shirt** NOUN
das **T-Shirt** (PL die **T-Shirts**)

tube NOUN
1 die **Tube** (PL die **Tuben**)
2 (the Underground) **the Tube** die U-Bahn

tuberculosis NOUN
die **Tuberkulose**

ℙ **Tuesday** NOUN
1 der **Dienstag** (PL die **Dienstage**)
on Tuesday (am) Dienstag
I'm going to the cinema on Tuesday. Ich gehe Dienstag ins Kino.
See you on Tuesday! Bis Dienstag!
every Tuesday jeden Dienstag
last Tuesday vorigen Dienstag
next Tuesday nächsten Dienstag
2 **on Tuesdays** dienstags
The museum is closed on Tuesdays. Das Museum ist dienstags geschlossen.

tuition NOUN
1 der **Unterricht**
piano tuition der Klavierunterricht
2 **extra tuition** die Nachhilfestunden (PLURAL)

tulip NOUN
die **Tulpe** (PL die **Tulpen**)

tumble-drier NOUN
der **Wäschetrockner** (PL die **Wäschetrockner**)

tumbler NOUN
das **Becherglas** (PL die **Bechergläser**)

ℙ **tuna** NOUN
der **Thunfisch**

tune NOUN
die **Melodie** (PL die **Melodien**)

ℙ **tunnel** NOUN
der **Tunnel** (PL die **Tunnel**)
the Channel Tunnel der Eurotunnel

turkey NOUN
die **Pute** (PL die **Puten**)

Turkey NOUN
die **Türkei**
from Turkey aus der Türkei
in Turkey in der Türkei
to Turkey in die Türkei

WORD TIP In German, this is always used with the article.

Turkish NOUN
(language) das **Türkisch**
Turkish ADJECTIVE
türkisch
the Turkish coast die türkische Küste
He is Turkish. Er ist Türke.

ℙ indicates key words

ENGLISH—GERMAN

667

She is Turkish. Sie ist Türkin.

WORD TIP Adjectives never have capitals in German, even for regions, countries, or nationalities.

ℓ **turn** NOUN
1 *(in a game)*
It's your turn. Du bist an der Reihe.
Whose turn is it? Wer ist an der Reihe?
It's Jane's turn. Jane ist an der Reihe.
2 **to take turns** sich abwechseln SEP
to take it in turns to do something abwechselnd etwas tun
3 *(in a road)* die **Abbiegung** (PL die **Abbiegungen**)
to take a right/left turn nach rechts/links abbiegen◇ SEP (PERF **sein**)
Take the next turn on the right. Nehmen Sie die nächste Straße rechts.

to **turn** VERB
1 drehen
Turn the key to the right. Dreh den Schlüssel nach rechts.
Turn your chair round. Dreh deinen Stuhl herum.
2 *(person, car)* abbiegen◇ SEP (PERF **sein**)
Turn left at the next set of lights. Biegen Sie an der nächsten Ampel links ab.
3 *(become)* werden◇ (PERF **sein**)
She turned red. Sie wurde rot.
• **to turn back**
umkehren SEP (PERF **sein**)
• **to turn off**
1 *(from a road)* abbiegen◇ SEP (PERF **sein**)
2 *(switch off)* ausmachen SEP *(a light, an oven, a TV, or radio)*, zudrehen SEP *(a tap)*, abstellen SEP *(gas, electricity, or water)*, ausschalten SEP *(an engine)*
• **to turn on**
anmachen SEP *(a TV, radio, or light)*, aufdrehen SEP *(a tap)*, anschalten SEP *(an oven)*, anlassen◇ SEP *(an engine)*
• **to turn out**
1 **to turn out well** gut ausgehen◇ SEP (PERF **sein**)
The discussions turned out badly. Die Gespräche sind schlecht ausgegangen.
It turned out all right in the end. Am Ende ging alles gut aus.
2 **It turned out that I was right.** Es stellte sich heraus, dass ich Recht hatte.
• **to turn over**
1 umdrehen SEP
She turned the meat over. Sie drehte das Fleisch um.
Turn over the page! Bitte umblättern!
2 sich umdrehen SEP
I turned over and went to sleep. Ich drehte

mich um und schlief ein.
• **to turn up**
1 *(arrive)* aufkreuzen SEP (PERF **sein**)
They turned up an hour later. Sie sind eine Stunde später aufgekreuzt.
2 *(make louder)* lauter machen

turning NOUN
die **Abbiegung** (PL die **Abbiegungen**)
Take the third turning on the right. Nimm die dritte Abbiegung rechts.

turnip NOUN
die **Steckrübe** (PL die **Steckrüben**)

turquoise ADJECTIVE
türkis *('turkis' never changes)*

turtle NOUN
die **Schildkröte** (PL die **Schildkröten**)

TV NOUN
das **Fernsehen**
I saw her on TV. Ich habe sie im Fernsehen gesehen.

tweezers PLURAL NOUN
die **Pinzette** (PL die **Pinzetten**)
a pair of tweezers eine Pinzette

WORD TIP In German die Pinzette is singular.

ℓ **twelfth** NUMBER
zwölfter/zwölfte/zwölftes
on the twelfth floor im zwölften Stock
the twelfth of May der zwölfte Mai

ℓ **twelve** NUMBER
1 zwölf
Tara's twelve. Tara ist zwölf.
2 **at twelve o'clock** um zwölf Uhr

ℓ **twenty** NUMBER
zwanzig
Marie's twenty. Marie ist zwanzig.
twenty-one einundzwanzig

twice ADVERB
1 zweimal
I've asked him twice. Ich habe ihn zweimal gefragt.
twice a day zweimal täglich
2 **twice as much** doppelt so viel

twig NOUN
der **Zweig** (PL die **Zweige**)

ℓ **twin** NOUN
der **Zwilling** (PL die **Zwillinge**)
Helen and Tim are twins. Helen und Tim sind Zwillinge.
her twin sister ihre Zwillingsschwester

◇ **irregular verb;** SEP **separable verb; for more help with verbs see centre section**

to **twin** VERB
Richmond is twinned with Konstanz.
Richmond und Konstanz sind
Partnerstädte.

twin room NOUN
das Zweibettzimmer (PL die
Zweibettzimmer)

to **twist** VERB
1 (bend out of shape) verbiegen◇
2 verdrehen (words, meaning)
3 **to twist your ankle** (DAT) den Knöchel
verrenken

ℰ**two** NUMBER
zwei
Ben's two. Ben ist zwei.
two by two zu zweit

type NOUN
die Art
What type of computer is it? Welche Art
Computer ist es?

to **type** VERB
(on a typewriter or computer) Maschine
schreiben◇, tippen (informal)
I'm learning to type. Ich lerne Maschine
schreiben.
How fast can you type? Wie schnell kannst
du tippen?
I'm just typing some letters. Ich tippe
gerade ein paar Briefe.
Type in your password. Geben sie ihr
Passwort ein.

typewriter NOUN
die Schreibmaschine (PL die
Schreibmaschinen)

typical ADJECTIVE
typisch

ℰ**tyre** NOUN
der Reifen (PL die Reifen)

Uu

ℰ**ugly** ADJECTIVE
hässlich

UK NOUN
(United Kingdom) das Vereinigte
Königreich

ulcer NOUN
das Geschwür (PL die Geschwüre)

Ulster NOUN
Ulster
from Ulster aus Ulster, aus Nordirland

ultraviolet ADJECTIVE
ultraviolett

ℰ**umbrella** NOUN
der Regenschirm (PL die Regenschirme)

umpire NOUN
der Schiedsrichter (PL die Schiedsrichter),
die Schiedsrichterin (PL die
Schiedsrichterinnen)

UN NOUN
(United Nations) die UN (PLURAL)

unable ADJECTIVE
to be unable to do something etwas nicht
tun können◇
He's unable to come. Er kann nicht
kommen.

unavoidable ADJECTIVE
unvermeidlich

unbearable ADJECTIVE
unerträglich

unbelievable ADJECTIVE
unglaublich

uncertain ADJECTIVE
1 (not sure)
to be uncertain whether ... sich (DAT) nicht
sicher sein, ob ...
2 (unpredictable) ungewiss (future or result)

ℰ**uncle** NOUN
der Onkel (PL die Onkel)

ℰ**uncomfortable** ADJECTIVE
1 unbequem (shoes, chair, or journey)
2 unangenehm (situation, heat)

unconscious ADJECTIVE
(out cold) bewusstlos

ℰ**under** PREPOSITION
1 (underneath) unter (+DAT, or, with movement
towards a place, +ACC)
The dog's under the bed. Der Hund ist
unter dem Bett. (DAT)
The ball rolled under the bed. Der Ball ist
unter das Bett gerollt. (ACC)
2 **under there** da drunter
Perhaps it's under there. Vielleicht ist es
da drunter.
3 (less than) unter (+DAT)
under £20 unter zwanzig Pfund
children under five Kinder unter fünf

underage ADJECTIVE
to be underage minderjährig sein

underclothes PLURAL NOUN
die Unterwäsche (SINGULAR)

undercooked ADJECTIVE
nicht gar

to **underestimate** VERB
unterschätzen

♪ **underground** NOUN
(railway) die U-Bahn (PL die U-Bahnen)
I saw her on the underground. Ich habe sie in der U-Bahn gesehen.
Shall we go by underground? Fahren wir mit der U-Bahn?

underground ADJECTIVE
unterirdisch (cave)
underground car park die Tiefgarage

to **underline** VERB
unterstreichen◇

♪ **underneath** PREPOSITION
unter (+DAT, or, with movement towards a place, +ACC)
It's underneath the newspaper. Es ist unter der Zeitung. (DAT)
I put it underneath the newspaper. Ich habe es unter die Zeitung gelegt. (ACC)

underneath ADVERB
darunter
Check underneath. Sieh darunter nach.

♪ **underpants** PLURAL NOUN
die Unterhose (PL die Unterhosen)
my underpants meine Unterhose
a new pair of underpants eine neue Unterhose

> **WORD TIP** In German die Unterhose is singular.

underpass NOUN
die Unterführung (PL die Unterführungen)

♪ to **understand** VERB
verstehen◇
Do you understand? Verstehst du?
I don't understand. Ich verstehe nicht.
I couldn't understand what he was saying. Ich konnte ihn nicht verstehen.
I can't understand why she doesn't want to see him. Ich kann nicht verstehen, warum sie ihn nicht sehen will.

understandable ADJECTIVE
That's understandable. Das ist verständlich.

understanding NOUN
das Verständnis

understanding ADJECTIVE
verständnisvoll

underwear NOUN
die Unterwäsche

to **undo** VERB
aufmachen SEP

undone ADJECTIVE
to come undone aufgehen◇ SEP (PERF sein)

♪ to **undress** VERB
to get undressed sich ausziehen◇ SEP

♪ **unemployed** NOUN
the unemployed die Arbeitslosen (PLURAL)

unemployed ADJECTIVE
arbeitslos

♪ **unemployment** NOUN
die Arbeitslosigkeit

uneven ADJECTIVE
1 uneben (surface)
The pitch was very uneven. Der Platz war sehr uneben.
2 **Her pulse is uneven.** Ihr Puls ist unregelmäßig.
3 **Your writing is very uneven.** Deine Schrift ist sehr ungleichmäßig.

unexpected ADJECTIVE
unerwartet

unexpectedly ADVERB
(to happen, arrive) überraschend

unfair ADJECTIVE
unfair
It's unfair on young people. Es ist jungen Leuten gegenüber unfair.

unfashionable ADJECTIVE
unmodern

to **unfasten** VERB
aufmachen SEP

unfit ADJECTIVE
nicht fit
I'm terribly unfit. Ich bin überhaupt nicht fit.

to **unfold** VERB
1 (a map) ausbreiten SEP
2 (develop) spielen
The story unfolds in Africa. Die Geschichte spielt in Afrika.

♪ **unfortunate** ADJECTIVE
unglücklich

♪ **unfortunately** ADVERB
leider

unfriendly ADJECTIVE
unfreundlich

ungrateful ADJECTIVE
undankbar

◇ **irregular verb;** SEP **separable verb; for more help with verbs see centre section**

ℰ **unhappy** *ADJECTIVE*
1 unglücklich
2 *(not satisfied)* unzufrieden
to be unhappy about something mit etwas unzufrieden sein

unhealthy *ADJECTIVE*
ungesund

unhurt *ADJECTIVE*
unverletzt

uni *NOUN*
die Uni (PL die Unis) *(informal)*
My brother is at uni in Bristol. Mein Bruder ist in Bristol an der Uni.

ℰ **uniform** *NOUN*
die Uniform (PL die Uniformen)

union *NOUN*
(trade union) die Gewerkschaft (PL die Gewerkschaften)

Union Jack *NOUN*
the Union Jack die britische Nationalflagge

ℰ **unique** *ADJECTIVE*
einzigartig

unit *NOUN*
1 *(for measuring, for example)* die Einheit (PL die Einheiten)
2 *(in a kitchen)* der Einbauschrank (PL die Einbauschränke)
3 *(a department)* die Abteilung (PL die Abteilungen)
the research unit die Forschungsabteilung

United Kingdom *NOUN*
das Vereinigte Königreich

United Nations *NOUN*
die Vereinten Nationen (PLURAL)

United States (of America) *NOUN*
die Vereinigten Staaten (von Amerika) (PLURAL)

universe *NOUN*
das Universum, das Weltall

ℰ **university** *NOUN*
die Universität (PL die Universitäten)
Bristol University die Universität von Bristol
Do you want to go to university? Willst du studieren?

unkind *ADJECTIVE*
unfreundlich

unknown *ADJECTIVE*
unbekannt

ℰ **unleaded petrol** *NOUN*
das bleifreie Benzin

ℰ **unless** *CONJUNCTION*
es sei denn
unless he does it es sei denn, er macht es
unless you write es sei denn, du schreibst

unlike *ADJECTIVE*
1 im Gegensatz zu (+DAT)
Unlike me, she hates dogs. Im Gegensatz zu mir hasst sie Hunde.
2 It's unlike her to be late. Es sieht ihr gar nicht ähnlich, zu spät zu kommen.

unlikely *ADJECTIVE*
unwahrscheinlich

unlimited *ADJECTIVE*
unbegrenzt

to **unload** *VERB*
1 ausladen◇ SEP *(luggage, car)*
2 entladen◇ *(lorry)*

to **unlock** *VERB*
aufschließen◇ SEP

ℰ **unlucky** *ADJECTIVE*
1 to be unlucky person Pech haben
I was unlucky – the shop was shut. Ich hatte Pech – das Geschäft war zu.
2 *(bringing bad luck)* Unglücks-
Thirteen is an unlucky number. Dreizehn ist eine Unglückszahl.
It's unlucky. Es bringt Unglück.

unmarried *ADJECTIVE*
ledig

unnecessary *ADJECTIVE*
unnötig

to **unpack** *VERB*
auspacken SEP
I'm just unpacking my rucksack. Ich packe gerade meinen Rucksack aus.

unpaid *ADJECTIVE*
unbezahlt

ℰ **unpleasant** *ADJECTIVE*
unangenehm

to **unplug** *VERB*
to unplug the lamp den Stecker der Lampe herausziehen◇ SEP

unpopular *ADJECTIVE*
unbeliebt

unrecognizable *ADJECTIVE*
nicht wiederzuerkennen

ℰ indicates key words

unreliable ADJECTIVE
unzuverlässig
He's unreliable. Er ist unzuverlässig.

unsafe ADJECTIVE
gefährlich (wiring, for example)

unsatisfactory ADJECTIVE
unbefriedigend

to **unscrew** VERB
aufschrauben SEP

unshaven ADJECTIVE
unrasiert

unsuccessful ADJECTIVE
1 erfolglos
an unsuccessful attempt ein erfolgloser
Versuch
2 to be unsuccessful keinen Erfolg haben
I tried, but I was unsuccessful. Ich habe es
versucht, aber ich hatte keinen Erfolg.

unsuitable ADJECTIVE
unpassend

untidy ADJECTIVE
unordentlich
The house is always untidy. Das Haus ist
immer unordentlich.

♪ **until** PREPOSITION, CONJUNCTION
1 bis
until Monday bis Montag
until now bis jetzt
until then bis dahin
I waited until they were ready. Ich habe
gewartet, bis sie fertig waren.
2 (when 'until' is followed by a noun it is
usually translated as bis zu +DAT)
until the tenth bis zum Zehnten
until the morning bis zum Morgen
3 not until erst
not until September erst im September
It won't be finished until Friday. Es wird
erst Freitag fertig sein.
I can't go until I've finished my homework.
Ich kann erst gehen, wenn ich mit meinen
Hausaufgaben fertig bin.

unusual ADJECTIVE
ungewöhnlich
an unusual face ein ungewöhnliches
Gesicht

unwilling ADJECTIVE
to be unwilling to do something etwas
nicht tun wollen♦

to **unwrap** VERB
auspacken SEP

♪ **up** PREPOSITION, ADVERB
1 (out of bed)
to be up auf sein♦ (PERF sein)
Liz isn't up yet. Liz ist noch nicht auf.
I was up late last night. Ich war gestern bis
spät auf.
2 to get up aufstehen♦ SEP (PERF sein)
We got up at six. Wir sind um sechs
aufgestanden.
3 (up on) auf, (+DAT, or +ACC when there is
movement towards a place)
The cat was up the tree. Die Katze war auf
dem Baum. (DAT)
They climbed up the tree. Sie kletterten
auf den Baum. (ACC)
4 up here hier oben
up there da oben
to go up (upstairs) nach oben gehen
I went up. Ich bin nach oben gegangen.
5 to go up the road die Straße
entlanggehen♦ SEP (PERF sein)
It's further up the road. Es ist weiter die
Straße entlang.
6 to go up the hill (on foot) hinaufgehen♦ SEP
(PERF sein), (in a vehicle) hinauffahren♦ SEP
(PERF sein)
(in spoken German the prefix rauf- is most
common) Does the bus go up the hill?
Fährt der Bus den Berg rauf?
7 to come up heraufkommen♦ SEP (PERF sein),
raufkommen♦ SEP (PERF sein) (informal)
8 (wrong)
What's up? Was ist los? (informal)
What's up with him? Was ist mit ihm los?
9 up to bis
up to here bis hier
up to last week bis zur letzten Woche
10 She came up to me. Sie kam auf mich zu.
11 What's she up to? Was hat sie vor?
12 It's up to you. (it's for you to decide) Das
musst du selbst entscheiden., (it concerns
only you) Das ist deine Sache.
13 Time's up! Die Zeit ist um.

update NOUN
die Aktualisierung (PL die
Aktualisierungen)
Here's an update on our plans. Dies ist der
neueste Stand unserer Pläne.

to **update** VERB
1 (revise) überarbeiten (timetables,
information)
2 (modernize) auf den neuesten Stand
bringen♦ (styles, furnishings)

upheaval NOUN
die Unruhe (PL die Unruhen)

uphill ADVERB
bergauf

to **upload** VERB
(onto a website) heraufladen◇ SEP,
uploaden

upper-class ADJECTIVE
der Oberschicht
an upper-class family eine Familie der
Oberschicht

upright ADJECTIVE
aufrecht
Put it upright. Stell es aufrecht.
to stand upright aufrecht stehen

upset NOUN
stomach upset die Magenverstimmung

upset ADJECTIVE
1 (annoyed) ärgerlich
He's upset. Er ist ärgerlich.
2 (distressed) bestürzt, (sad) betrübt

to **upset** VERB
to upset somebody (hurt) jemanden
kränken, (annoy) jemanden ärgern

upside down ADJECTIVE
verkehrt herum

ᗩ **upstairs** ADVERB
1 oben
Mum's upstairs. Mutti ist oben.
2 (with movement) nach oben
to go upstairs nach oben gehen◇ (PERF
sein)

up-to-date ADJECTIVE
1 (in fashion) modern
2 (information) aktuell

upwards ADJECTIVE
nach oben

ᗩ **urgent** ADJECTIVE
dringend

urgently ADVERB
dringend
I need to speak to her urgently. Ich muss
sie dringend sprechen.

ᗩ **us** PRONOUN
1 uns
She knows us. Sie kennt uns.
They saw us. Sie haben uns gesehen.
with us mit uns
2 (in the nominative) wir
Hello, it's us again! Hallo, wir sind's wieder!

US NOUN
die USA (PLURAL)

USA NOUN
die USA (PLURAL)

ᗩ **use** NOUN
1 der Gebrauch
instructions for use die
Gebrauchsanweisung (SINGULAR)
2 It's no use. Es hat keinen Zweck.
It's no use phoning. Es hat keinen Zweck
anzurufen.

to **use** VERB
benutzen
We used the dictionary. Wir haben das
Wörterbuch benutzt.
to use something to do something etwas
zu etwas (DAT) benutzen
I used a towel to dry myself. Ich habe ein
Handtuch zum Abtrocknen benutzt.
• to use up
1 aufbrauchen SEP (food)
2 verbrauchen (money)

ᗩ **used** ADJECTIVE
gebraucht
a used car ein Gebrauchtwagen

ᗩ **used to** ADJECTIVE
1 to be used to something an etwas (ACC)
gewöhnt sein
I'm used to cats. Ich bin an Katzen
gewöhnt.
I'm not used to eating in restaurants. Ich
bin nicht daran gewöhnt, in Restaurants
zu essen.
2 to get used to something sich an etwas
(ACC) gewöhnen
You'll soon get used to the new car.
Du wirst dich schnell an das neue Auto
gewöhnen.
I've got used to living here. Ich habe mich
daran gewöhnt, hier zu wohnen.
You'll get used to it. Du wirst dich schon
daran gewöhnen.

used to VERB
She used to smoke. Sie hat früher
geraucht.
I didn't use to like maths. Früher mochte
ich Mathe nicht.

ᗩ **useful** ADJECTIVE
nützlich

ᗩ **useless** ADJECTIVE
1 unbrauchbar
This knife's useless. Dieses Messer ist
unbrauchbar.
You're completely useless! Du bist wirklich
zu nichts zu gebrauchen!
2 nutzlos (advice, information, or facts, for
example)
useless knowledge nutzloses Wissen
3 (pointless) zwecklos

user NOUN
der Benutzer (PL die Benutzer), die Benutzerin (PL die Benutzerinnen)

user-friendly ADJECTIVE
benutzerfreundlich

user name NOUN
der Benutzername (PL die Benutzernamen)

ℙ **usual** ADJECTIVE
1 üblich
It's the usual problem. Es ist das übliche Problem.
as usual wie üblich
2 It's colder than usual. Es ist kälter als gewöhnlich.

ℙ **usually** ADJECTIVE
normalerweise
I usually leave at eight. Normalerweise gehe ich um acht weg.

Vv

vacancy NOUN
1 (in a hotel)
'Vacancies' 'Zimmer frei'
'No vacancies' 'Belegt'
2 job vacancy die freie Stelle

vacant ADJECTIVE
frei

to **vaccinate** VERB
impfen

vaccination NOUN
die Impfung (PL die Impfungen)

to **vacuum** VERB
saugen
I'm going to vacuum my room. Ich sauge mein Zimmer.

vacuum cleaner NOUN
der Staubsauger (PL die Staubsauger)

vagina NOUN
die Vagina (PL die Vaginen), die Scheide (PL die Scheiden)

vague ADJECTIVE
vage

vain ADJECTIVE
1 eitel
2 in vain vergeblich

valentine card NOUN
die Valentinskarte (PL die Valentinskarten)

Valentine's Day NOUN
der Valentinstag (PL die Valentinstage)

valid ADJECTIVE
gültig

valley NOUN
das Tal (PL die Täler)

valuable ADJECTIVE
wertvoll

value NOUN
der Wert (PL die Werte)

to **value** VERB
schätzen

van NOUN
der Lieferwagen (PL die Lieferwagen)

vandal NOUN
der Rowdy (PL die Rowdys)

vandalism NOUN
der Vandalismus

to **vandalize** VERB
mutwillig zerstören

ℙ **vanilla** NOUN
die Vanille
vanilla ice cream das Vanilleeis

to **vanish** VERB
verschwinden◇ (PERF sein)

variety NOUN
1 die Abwechslung (in a routine diet, or style)
for the sake of variety zur Abwechslung
2 (kind) die Sorte (PL die Sorten)
a new variety of apple eine neue Apfelsorte
3 (assortment) die Auswahl

ℙ **various** ADJECTIVE
verschieden
There are various ways of doing it. Man kann es auf verschiedene Art und Weise machen.

to **vary** VERB
1 (become different) sich ändern
2 It varies a lot. Es ist sehr unterschiedlich.
3 (make different) ändern (a programme or method)

vase NOUN
die Vase (PL die Vasen)

VAT NOUN
die Mehrwertsteuer
Prices include VAT. Die Mehrwertsteuer ist im Preis inbegriffen.

◇ irregular verb; SEP separable verb; for more help with verbs see centre section

VDU NOUN
der **Bildschirm** (PL die **Bildschirme**)

ℰ **veal** NOUN
das **Kalbfleisch**

vegan NOUN
der **Veganer** (PL die **Veganer**), die **Veganerin** (PL die **Veganerinnen**)
She's a vegan. Sie ist Veganerin.

ℰ **vegetable** NOUN
das **Gemüse**
fresh vegetables frisches Gemüse

ℰ **vegetarian** NOUN
der **Vegetarier** (PL die **Vegetarier**), die **Vegetarierin** (PL die **Vegetarierinnen**)
He's a vegetarian. Er ist Vegetarier.

vegetarian ADJECTIVE
vegetarisch

ℰ **vehicle** NOUN
das **Fahrzeug** (PL die **Fahrzeuge**)

vein NOUN
die **Vene** (PL die **Venen**)

velvet NOUN
der **Samt**
a velvet skirt ein Samtrock

vending machine NOUN
der **Automat** (PL die **Automaten**)

verb NOUN
das **Verb** (PL die **Verben**)

verdict NOUN
das **Urteil** (PL die **Urteile**)

verge NOUN
1 (roadside) der **Seitenstreifen** (PL die **Seitenstreifen**)
2 **to be on the verge of doing something** im Begriff sein, etwas zu tun
I was on the verge of leaving. Ich war im Begriff zu gehen.

ℰ **version** NOUN
die **Version** (PL die **Versionen**)

versus PREPOSITION
gegen (+ACC)
Arsenal versus Chelsea Arsenal gegen Chelsea

vertical ADJECTIVE
senkrecht

vertigo NOUN
das **Schwindelgefühl**

ℰ **very** ADVERB
sehr

It's very difficult. Es ist sehr schwer.
very much sehr viel
very little sehr wenig

very ADJECTIVE
1 **The very person I need!** Genau der Mann, den ich brauche./Genau die Frau (PL die ich brauche.
the very thing he's looking for genau das, was er sucht
in the very middle genau in der Mitte
2 **at the very end** ganz am Ende
at the very front ganz vorne

vest NOUN
das **Unterhemd** (PL die **Unterhemden**)

vet NOUN
der **Tierarzt** (PL die **Tierärzte**), die **Tierärztin** (PL die **Tierärztinnen**)

> **WORD TIP** Professions, hobbies, and sports don't take an article in German: Sie ist Tierärztin.

via PREPOSITION
über (+ACC)
We're going to Frankfurt via Brussels. Wir fahren über Brüssel nach Frankfurt.

vicar NOUN
der **Pfarrer** (PL die **Pfarrer**), die **Pfarrerin** (PL die **Pfarrerinnen**)

> **WORD TIP** Professions, hobbies, and sports don't take an article in German: Er ist Pfarrer.

vicious ADJECTIVE
1 bösartig (dog)
2 brutal (attack)

victim NOUN
das **Opfer** (PL die **Opfer**)

victory NOUN
der **Sieg** (PL die **Siege**)

ℰ **video** NOUN
(film) das **Video** (PL die **Videos**)
to watch a video ein Video ansehen
I've got it on video. Ich habe es auf Video.

to video VERB
aufzeichnen SEP
I'll video it for you. Ich zeichne es für dich auf.

video game NOUN
das **Videospiel** (PL die **Videospiele**)

Vienna NOUN
Wien (NEUTER)

to Vienna nach Wien

 VIENNA

Vienna is the capital city of Austria.

p **view** NOUN
1 die **Aussicht**
   a room with a view of the lake ein Zimmer
   mit Aussicht auf den See
2 (opinion) die **Meinung** (PL die **Meinungen**)
   in my view meiner Meinung nach
   point of view der Standpunkt

p **viewer** NOUN
   der **Zuschauer** (PL die **Zuschauer**), die
   Zuschauerin (PL die **Zuschauerinnen**)

vile ADJECTIVE
   ekelhaft

villa NOUN
1 die **Villa** (PL die **Villen**)
2 (holiday home) das **Ferienhaus** (PL die
   Ferienhäuser)

p **village** NOUN
   das **Dorf** (PL die **Dörfer**)

vine NOUN
   die **Weinrebe** (PL die **Weinreben**)

p **vinegar** NOUN
   der **Essig**

vineyard NOUN
   der **Weinberg** (PL die **Weinberge**)

violence NOUN
   die **Gewalt**

p **violent** ADJECTIVE
1 gewalttätig (person, film, behaviour)
2 heftig (jolt, punch)

violin NOUN
   die **Geige** (PL die **Geigen**)
   Jack plays the violin. Jack spielt Geige.

   WORD TIP Don't use the article when you talk
   about playing an instrument.

violinist NOUN
   der **Geiger** (PL die **Geiger**), die **Geigerin** (PL
   die **Geigerinnen**)

   WORD TIP Professions, hobbies, and sports
   don't take an article in German: Sie ist Geigerin.

virgin NOUN
   die **Jungfrau** (PL die **Jungfrauen**)

Virgo NOUN
   die **Jungfrau**
   Robert is Virgo. Robert ist Jungfrau.

virtual reality NOUN
   die **virtuelle Realität**

virus NOUN
   (in medicine and IT) das or der **Virus** (PL die
   Viren)
   anti-virus software das Antivirenprogramm

visa NOUN
   das **Visum** (PL die **Visa** or **Visen**)

visible ADJECTIVE
   sichtbar

p **visit** NOUN
   der **Besuch** (PL die **Besuche**)
   I was in Berlin on a visit to friends. Ich war
   in Berlin bei Freunden zu Besuch.
   my last visit to Germany mein letzter
   Deutschlandbesuch

to **visit** VERB
1 besuchen (a person)
2 besichtigen (a building, town)

visitor NOUN
1 der **Besucher** (PL die **Besucher**), die
   Besucherin (PL die **Besucherinnen**)
2 **We've got visitors tonight.** Wir haben
   heute Abend Besuch.
3 (in a hotel) der **Gast** (PL die **Gäste**)

visual ADJECTIVE
   visuell

vital ADJECTIVE
   unbedingt erforderlich
   It's vital to book a table. Es ist unbedingt
   erforderlich, einen Tisch zu bestellen.

vitamin NOUN
   das **Vitamin** (PL die **Vitamine**)

vivid ADJECTIVE
   lebhaft (colours, memory)
   to have a vivid imagination eine lebhafte
   Fantasie haben

vocabulary NOUN
   der **Wortschatz**
   He has a huge vocabulary. Er hat einen
   riesigen Wortschatz.
   to learn vocabulary Vokabeln lernen

vocational ADJECTIVE
   beruflich

vodka NOUN
   der **Wodka** (PL die **Wodkas**)

p **voice** NOUN
   die **Stimme** (PL die **Stimmen**)

volcano NOUN
   der **Vulkan** (PL die **Vulkane**)

◊ irregular verb; SEP separable verb; for more help with verbs see centre section

volleyball NOUN
der **Volleyball**
to play volleyball Volleyball spielen
beach volleyball der Beachvolleyball

volume NOUN
1 die **Lautstärke**
Could you turn down the volume?
Könntest du es etwas leiser stellen?
2 *(book)* der **Band** (PL die **Bände**)

voluntary ADJECTIVE
1 freiwillig
a voluntary worker ein freiwilliger Helfer/
eine freiwillige Helferin
2 **to do voluntary work** für einen
wohltätigen Zweck arbeiten

volunteer NOUN
der/die **Freiwillige** (PL die **Freiwilligen**)
to **volunteer** VERB
to volunteer to do something sich
freiwillig melden, etwas zu tun

ℓ to **vomit** VERB
sich übergeben◇

ℓ **vote** NOUN
die **Stimme** (PL die **Stimmen**)
He won by five votes. Er gewann mit fünf
Stimmen Vorsprung.
Let's take a vote on it. Lasst uns darüber
abstimmen.
to **vote** VERB
wählen
to vote for somebody jemanden wählen
She always votes Green. Sie wählt immer
die Grünen.

voucher NOUN
der **Gutschein** (PL die **Gutscheine**)

vowel NOUN
der **Vokal** (PL die **Vokale**)

vulgar ADJECTIVE
vulgär

Ww

waffle NOUN
die **Waffel** (PL die **Waffeln**)

wage(s) NOUN
der **Lohn** (PL die **Löhne**)

ℓ **waist** NOUN
die **Taille** (PL die **Taillen**)

waistcoat NOUN
die **Weste** (PL die **Westen**)

waist measurement NOUN
die **Taillenweite**

ℓ **wait** NOUN
die **Wartezeit**
an hour's wait eine Stunde Wartezeit
We had a long wait. Wir mussten lange
warten.
to **wait** VERB
1 warten
They're waiting in the car. Sie warten im
Auto.
She kept me waiting. Sie hat mich warten
lassen.
2 **to wait for somebody** auf jemanden
warten
Wait for me. Warte auf mich.
to wait for something auf etwas (ACC)
warten
We waited for a taxi. Wir haben auf ein
Taxi gewartet.
3 **to wait for somebody to do something**
darauf warten, dass jemand etwas tut
I'm waiting for him to ring. Ich warte
darauf, dass er anruft.
4 **I can't wait to open it.** Ich kann's kaum
erwarten, es aufzumachen.

ℓ **waiter** NOUN
der **Kellner** (PL die **Kellner**)
Waiter! Herr Ober!
WORD TIP Professions, hobbies, and sports
don't take an article in German: Er ist Kellner.

waiting list NOUN
die **Warteliste** (PL die **Wartelisten**)

ℓ **waiting room** NOUN
das **Wartezimmer** (PL die **Wartezimmer**),
(at a station) der **Warteraum** (PL die
Warteräume)

ℓ **waitress** NOUN
die **Kellnerin** (PL die **Kellnerinnen**)
Waitress! Fräulein!
WORD TIP Professions, hobbies, and sports
don't take an article in German: Sie ist Kellnerin.

ℓ to **wake** VERB
1 **wecken** somebody
Jess woke me (up) at six. Jess hat mich um
sechs geweckt.
2 **aufwachen** SEP *(PERF* **sein***)*
I woke (up) at six. Ich bin um sechs
aufgewacht.
Wake up! Wach auf!

A B C D E F G H I J K L M N O P Q R S T U V W X Y Z

♪ **Wales** NOUN
  Wales (NEUTER)
  from Wales aus Wales
  to Wales nach Wales

♪ **walk** NOUN
1 der Spaziergang (PL die Spaziergänge)
  to go for a walk einen Spaziergang machen
  We'll go for a little walk round the village.
  Wir machen einen kleinen Spaziergang
  durchs Dorf.
2 **to take the dog for a walk** mit dem Hund
  spazieren gehen◇ (PERF sein)
3 **It's about five minutes' walk from here.** Es
  ist ungefähr fünf Minuten zu Fuß von hier.

to **walk** VERB
1 (go, not run) gehen◇ (PERF sein)
  He walks very slowly. Er geht sehr
  langsam.
  I'll walk to the bus stop with you. Ich gehe
  mit dir zur Bushaltestelle.
2 (on foot rather than by car or bus) zu Fuß
  gehen◇ (PERF sein)
  It's not far, we can walk. Es ist nicht weit,
  wir können zu Fuß gehen.
3 (walk around) spazieren gehen◇ (PERF sein)
  We walked around the old town. Wir sind
  in der Altstadt spazieren gegangen.
4 (move on foot) laufen◇ (PERF sein)
  to learn to walk laufen lernen
  The child can't walk yet. Das Kind kann
  noch nicht laufen.

walking NOUN
  (hiking) das Wandern
  to go walking wandern (PERF sein)

walking distance NOUN
  to be within walking distance zu Fuß zu
  erreichen sein
  It's within walking distance of the sea.
  Man kann das Meer zu Fuß erreichen.

♪ **wall** NOUN
1 (inside a building) die Wand (PL die Wände)
  There's a picture on every wall. An jeder
  Wand hängt ein Bild.
2 (outside) die Mauer (PL die Mauern)

♪ **wallet** NOUN
  die Brieftasche (PL die Brieftaschen)

wallpaper NOUN
  die Tapete (PL die Tapeten)

walnut NOUN
  die Walnuss (PL die Walnüsse)

to **wander** VERB
  to wander around town durch die Stadt
  bummeln (PERF sein)

  to wander off weggehen◇ SEP (PERF sein)

♪ to **want** VERB
1 wollen◇
  Do you want to come? Willst du
  mitkommen?
  What do you want to do? Was willst du
  machen?
  I don't want to bother him. Ich will ihn
  nicht stören.
  She did not want him to come. Sie wollte
  nicht, dass er kommt.
2 (more polite) mögen◇
  Do you want some more coffee? Möchtest
  du noch Kaffee?
  I want two pounds of apples please. Ich
  möchte gern zwei Pfund Äpfel.

  WORD TIP When you ask for something, ich
  möchte is much politer than ich will. Ich möchte
  gern is particularly used when shopping.

war NOUN
  der Krieg (PL die Kriege)
  The country was at war. In dem Land
  herrschte Krieg.
  civil war der Bürgerkrieg

ward NOUN
  (in hospital) die Station (PL die Stationen)
  in the children's ward auf der
  Kinderstation

♪ **wardrobe** NOUN
  der Kleiderschrank (PL die
  Kleiderschränke)

warehouse NOUN
  das Lager (PL die Lager)

  WORD TIP Do not translate the English word
  warehouse with the German Warenhaus.

♪ **warm** ADJECTIVE
1 warm
  a warm coat ein warmer Mantel
  It's warm today. Heute ist es warm.
  I'll keep your dinner warm. Ich halte dir
  das Essen warm.
  It's warm inside. Drinnen ist es warm.
  I am warm. Mir ist warm.
2 (friendly) herzlich
  a warm welcome ein herzlicher Empfang

to **warm** VERB
  wärmen
  to warm the plates die Teller wärmen
• **to warm up**
1 (weather) warm werden◇ (PERF sein)
2 (an athlete) sich aufwärmen SEP
3 (heat up) aufwärmen SEP
  I'll warm the soup up for you. Ich wärme
  dir die Suppe auf.

◇ irregular verb; SEP separable verb; for more help with verbs see centre section

warmth NOUN
die Wärme

to **warn** VERB

1 warnen
I warn you, it's expensive. Ich warne dich,
es ist teuer.
to warn somebody not to do something
jemanden davor warnen, etwas zu tun
She warned me not to let him drive. Sie
hat mich davor gewarnt, ihn fahren zu
lassen.

2 He warned me to lock the car. Er hat mich
ermahnt, das Auto abzuschließen.

warning NOUN
die Warnung (PL die Warnungen)

wart NOUN
die Warze (PL die Warzen)

ℰ **wash** NOUN
to give something a wash etwas waschen◇
to have a wash sich waschen◇

to **wash** VERB

1 waschen◇
I've washed your jeans. Ich habe deine
Jeans gewaschen.

2 (have a wash) sich waschen◇
to get washed sich waschen

3 to wash your hands sich (DAT) die Hände
waschen
I washed my hands. Ich habe mir die Hände
gewaschen.
to wash your hair sich (DAT) die Haare
waschen

4 to wash the dishes abwaschen◇ SEP

• to wash up
abwaschen◇ SEP

washbasin NOUN
das Waschbecken (PL die Waschbecken)

washing NOUN
die Wäsche
to do the washing Wäsche waschen◇

washing machine NOUN
die Waschmaschine (PL die
Waschmaschinen)

washing powder NOUN
das Waschpulver (PL die Waschpulver)

ℰ **washing-up** NOUN
der Abwasch
to do the washing-up den Abwasch
machen

washing-up liquid NOUN
das Spülmittel (PL die Spülmittel)

wasp NOUN
die Wespe (PL die Wespen)
a wasp sting ein Wespenstich

ℰ **waste** NOUN
die Verschwendung
It's a waste of time. Das ist eine
Zeitverschwendung.

to **waste** VERB
verschwenden

waste bin NOUN
die Mülltonne (PL die Mülltonnen)

waste-paper basket NOUN
der Papierkorb (PL die Papierkörbe)

ℰ **watch** NOUN
die Uhr (PL die Uhren), die Armbanduhr
(PL die Armbanduhren)
My watch is fast. Meine Uhr geht vor.
My watch is slow. Meine Uhr geht nach.
My parents gave me a watch for my
birthday. Meine Eltern haben mir zum
Geburtstag eine Armbanduhr geschenkt.

to **watch** VERB

1 (look at) sich (DAT) ansehen◇ SEP
I was watching a film. Ich habe mir einen
Film angesehen.

2 to watch TV fernsehen◇ SEP

3 (keep a check on, look after) achten auf
(+ACC)
Watch the children. Achte auf die Kinder.

4 (be careful) aufpassen SEP
Watch you don't spill it. Pass auf, dass du
es nicht verschüttest.
Watch out! Pass auf!

5 (observe) beobachten
They were being watched. Sie wurden
beobachtet.

ℰ **water** NOUN
das Wasser
drinking water das Trinkwasser

to **water** VERB
gießen◇ plants

waterfall NOUN
der Wasserfall (PL die Wasserfälle)

watering can NOUN
die Gießkanne (PL die Gießkannen)

watermelon NOUN
die Wassermelone (PL die
Wassermelonen)

waterproof ADJECTIVE
wasserdicht

ℰ **waterskiing** NOUN
das Wasserskifahren
to go waterskiing Wasserski fahren

water sports PLURAL NOUN
der **Wassersport** (SINGULAR)

wave NOUN
1 (in the sea) die **Welle** (PL die **Wellen**)
2 (with your hand)
to give somebody a wave jemandem zuwinken SEP
She gave him a wave from the bus. Sie winkte ihm vom Bus zu.

to **wave** VERB
1 (with your hand) **winken**
2 (flap) **schwenken** (a flag, for example)

wax NOUN
das **Wachs**

ℓ **way** NOUN
1 (a route or road) der **Weg** (PL die **Wege**)
the way to town der Weg in die Stadt
We asked the way to the station. Wir haben gefragt, wie man zum Bahnhof kommt.
on the way back auf dem Rückweg
on the way unterwegs
to be in the way im Weg sein
to be in somebody's way jemandem im Weg sein
to get out of the way aus dem Weg gehen◇ (PERF sein)
2 **to lose your way** sich verlaufen◇ (in a car) sich verfahren◇
3 '**Way in**' 'Eingang'
'**Way out**' 'Ausgang'
4 (direction) die **Richtung** (PL die **Richtungen**)
Which way did he go? In welche Richtung ist er gegangen?
this way in diese Richtung
5 (side)
the right way up richtig herum
the wrong way round falsch herum
the other way round andersherum
6 (distance)
It's a long way. Es ist weit weg.
We still had a little way to go. Wir mussten noch ein kleines Stück gehen.
7 (manner) die **Art und Weise**
my way of learning German meine Art und Weise, Deutsch zu lernen
He does it his way. Er macht es auf seine Art und Weise.
I've done it the wrong way. Ich habe es falsch gemacht.
in a way in gewisser Weise
8 **No way!** Auf keinen Fall!
9 **by the way** übrigens

ℓ **we** PRONOUN
wir

We're going to the cinema tonight. Wir gehen heute Abend ins Kino.

ℓ **weak** ADJECTIVE
1 (feeble) **schwach**
in a weak voice mit schwacher Stimme
2 **dünn** coffee or tea

wealthy ADJECTIVE
reich

weapon NOUN
die **Waffe** (PL die **Waffen**)
weapons of mass destruction die Massenvernichtungswaffen (PLURAL)

ℓ **wear** NOUN
children's wear die Kinderkleidung
sports wear die Sportkleidung

to **wear** VERB
tragen◇, anhaben◇ SEP
She often wears red. Sie trägt oft Rot.
Tamsin's wearing her jeans. Tamsin hat ihre Jeans an.

ℓ **weather** NOUN
1 das **Wetter**
What's the weather like? Wie ist das Wetter?
in fine weather bei schönem Wetter
The weather is terrible. Das Wetter ist furchtbar.
2 **in wet weather** wenn es regnet
The weather was cold. Es war kalt.

ℓ **weather forecast** NOUN
die **Wettervorhersage**
The weather forecast says it will rain. Der Wettervorhersage zufolge soll es regnen.

ℓ **web** NOUN
1 (spider's) das **Spinnennetz** (PL die **Spinnennetze**)
2 (World Wide Web)
the Web das Netz, das Internet

webcam NOUN
die **Webcam** (PL die **Webcams**), die **Netzkamera** (PL die **Netzkameras**)

web page NOUN
die **Webseite** (PL die **Webseiten**)

website NOUN
die **Website** (PL die **Websites**)
I found the information on their website. Ich habe die Informationen auf ihrer Website gefunden.

ℓ **wedding** NOUN
die **Hochzeit** (PL die **Hochzeiten**)
When is the wedding? Wann ist die Hochzeit?

◇ irregular verb; SEP separable verb; for more help with verbs see centre section

a wedding ring ein Ehering

ₚ **Wednesday** *NOUN*
1 der **Mittwoch** (*PL* die **Mittwoche**)
on Wednesday (am) Mittwoch
I'm going to the cinema on Wednesday.
Ich gehe Mittwoch ins Kino.
See you on Wednesday! Bis Mittwoch!
every Wednesday jeden Mittwoch
last Wednesday vorigen Mittwoch
next Wednesday nächsten Mittwoch
2 on Wednesdays mittwochs
The museum is closed on Wednesdays.
Das Museum ist mittwochs geschlossen.

weed *NOUN*
das **Unkraut**

ₚ **week** *NOUN*
die **Woche** (*PL* die **Wochen**)
last week vorige Woche
next week nächste Woche
this week diese Woche
for weeks wochenlang
a week today heute in einer Woche
a week on Monday Montag in einer Woche.
in three weeks' time in drei Wochen

weekday *NOUN*
on weekdays wochentags

ₚ **weekend** *NOUN*
das **Wochenende** (*PL* die **Wochenenden**)
last weekend voriges Wochenende
next weekend nächstes Wochenende
They're coming for the weekend. Sie
kommen übers Wochenende.
I'll do it at the weekend. Ich mache es am
Wochenende.
Have a nice weekend! (Ein) schönes
Wochenende!

ₚ to **weigh** *VERB*
1 wiegen◇
to weigh something etwas wiegen
to weigh yourself sich wiegen
2 How much do you weigh? Wie viel wiegst
du?
I weigh 50 kilos. Ich wiege fünfzig Kilo.

ₚ **weight** *NOUN*
1 das **Gewicht** (*PL* die **Gewichte**)
2 to put on weight zunehmen◇ *SEP*
3 to lose weight abnehmen◇ *SEP*

weightlifting *NOUN*
das **Gewichtheben**

weird *ADJECTIVE*
seltsam

ₚ **welcome** *NOUN*
They gave us a warm welcome. Sie haben
uns herzlich empfangen.

welcome *ADJECTIVE*
1 willkommen
You're welcome any time. Du bist immer
willkommen.
2 'Thank you!' – 'You're welcome!' 'Danke!'
– 'Bitte!'

to **welcome** *VERB*
1 begrüßen
to welcome somebody jemanden
begrüßen
2 Welcome to Oxford! Herzlich willkommen
in Oxford!

ₚ **well**[1] *ADJECTIVE, ADVERB*
1 to be well gesund sein
when I'm well again wenn ich wieder
gesund bin
She wasn't well. Es ging ihr nicht gut.
I'm very well, thank you. Danke, es geht
mir gut.
Get well soon! Gute Besserung!
2 gut
Terry played well. Terry hat gut gespielt.
It's well paid. Es wird gut bezahlt.
Well done! Gut gemacht!
3 as well auch
Kevin's coming as well. Kevin kommt auch.
4 na ja
Well, never mind. Na ja, macht nichts.
Oh well, I'll try again later. Na ja, dann
versuche ich's später noch einmal.
5 gut
It may well be that ... Es ist gut möglich,
dass ...
Very well then, you can go. Also gut, du
kannst gehen.

well[2] *NOUN*
der **Brunnen** (*PL* die **Brunnen**)

well-behaved *ADJECTIVE*
artig

well-done *ADJECTIVE*
durchgebraten (*steak*)

wellington (boot) *NOUN*
der **Gummistiefel** (*PL* die **Gummistiefel**)

well-known *ADJECTIVE*
bekannt

ₚ **well-off** *ADJECTIVE*
wohlhabend

ₚ **Welsh** *NOUN*
1 the Welsh (*people*) die Waliser (*PLURAL*)
2 (*language*) das **Walisisch**

ₚ indicates key words

Welsh ADJECTIVE
  walisisch
  the Welsh coast die walisische Küste
  He's Welsh. Er ist Waliser.
  She's Welsh. Sie ist Waliserin.

> **WORD TIP** Adjectives never have capitals in German, even for regions, countries, or nationalities.

ℰ **Welshman** NOUN
  der **Waliser** (PL die **Waliser**)

ℰ **Welshwoman** NOUN
  die **Waliserin** (PL die **Waliserinnen**)

ℰ **west** NOUN
  der **Westen**
  in the west im Westen

west ADJECTIVE
  westlich, West-
  the west side die Westseite
  west wind der Westwind

west ADVERB
1 (towards the west) nach Westen
  to travel west nach Westen fahren◇ (PERF sein)
2 **west of London** westlich von London

ℰ **western** ADJECTIVE
  westlich, West-
  on the western side of the mountain an der Westseite des Berges

western NOUN
  (film) der **Western** (PL die **Western**)

West Indian NOUN
  der **Westinder** (PL die **Westinder**), die **Westinderin** (PL die **Westinderinnen**)

West Indian ADJECTIVE
  westindisch
  the West Indian team die westindische Mannschaft
  He's West Indian. Er ist Westinder.
  She's West Indian. Sie ist Westinderin.

> **WORD TIP** Adjectives never have capitals in German, even for regions, countries, or nationalities.

West Indies PLURAL NOUN
  die **Westindischen Inseln** (PLURAL)
  in the West Indies auf den Westindischen Inseln

ℰ **wet** ADJECTIVE
1 nass
  We got wet. Wir sind nass geworden.
2 **a wet day** ein regnerischer Tag

whale NOUN
  der **Wal** (PL die **Wale**)

ℰ **what** PRONOUN, ADJECTIVE
1 (in questions) was
  What did you say? Was hast du gesagt?
  What's she doing? Was macht sie?
  What did you buy? Was hast du gekauft?
  What is it? Was ist das?
  What's the matter? Was ist los?
  What's happened? Was ist passiert?
  What? Was?
2 **What's your address?** Wie ist Ihre Adresse?
  What's her name? Wie heißt sie?
  What was it like? Wie war's?
3 (asking for an amount) wie viel
  At what time? Um wie viel Uhr?
4 (that which) was (relative pronoun)
  She told me what had happened. Sie hat mir gesagt, was passiert ist.
  Do what I tell you. Tu, was ich dir sage.
5 (which) welcher/welche/welches
  What country is it in? In welchem Land ist es?
  What colour is it? Welche Farbe hat es?
  What make is it? Welche Marke ist es?
6 **What for?** Wozu?
7 **What if ...?** Was ist, wenn ...?
  What if I can't find it? Was ist, wenn ich es nicht finden kann?

wheat NOUN
  der **Weizen**

wheel NOUN
  das **Rad** (PL die **Räder**)
  the spare wheel das Reserverad
  the steering wheel das Lenkrad

wheelbarrow NOUN
  die **Schubkarre** (PL die **Schubkarren**)

wheelchair NOUN
  der **Rollstuhl** (PL die **Rollstühle**)

ℰ **when** ADVERB
  wann
  When is she arriving? Wann kommt sie an?
  When's your birthday? Wann hast du Geburtstag?

when CONJUNCTION
1 (with the past) als
  I was out shopping when you rang. Ich war beim Einkaufen, als du anriefst.
2 (with the present or future) wenn
  When she comes I'll ring. Wenn sie kommt, rufe ich an.
  I'll call you when I'm ready. Ich rufe dich, wenn ich fertig bin.

ℰ **where** ADVERB, CONJUNCTION
  wo
  Where do you live? Wo wohnst du?

◇ irregular verb; SEP separable verb; for more help with verbs see centre section

Where are you going? Wo gehst du hin?
I don't know where they live. Ich weiß
nicht, wo sie wohnen.

whether CONJUNCTION
  ob
  I don't know whether he's back. Ich weiß
  nicht, ob er schon zurück ist.
  We'll play whether it rains or not. Wir
  spielen, ob es regnet oder nicht.

℘ **which** DETERMINER, PRONOUN
1 welcher/welche/welches
  Which hat did you buy? Welche Hut hast
  du gekauft?
2 which (one) welcher/welche/welches
  (depending on the gender of the noun the
  question refers back to) (PLURAL) welche
  'I met your brother.' – 'Which one?' 'Ich
  habe deinen Bruder getroffen.' – 'Welchen?'
  'I met your sister.' – 'Which one?' 'Ich habe
  deine Schwester getroffen' – 'Welche?'
  'Have you seen my book?' – 'Which one?'
  'Hast du mein Buch gesehen?' – 'Welches?'
  **'Have you seen my shoes?' – 'Which
  ones?'** 'Hast du meine Schuhe gesehen?' –
  'Welche?'
3 *(relative pronoun)* der/die/das *(depending
  on the gender of the noun 'which' refers to)
  (plural)* die
  the film which is showing now der Film,
  der gerade läuft
  the lamp which is on the table die Lampe
  die auf dem Tisch steht
  the book which I lent you das Buch, das ich
  dir geliehen habe
  the books which I've read die Bücher
  (PL die ich gelesen habe)

℘ **while** NOUN
  for a while eine Weile
  She worked here for a while. Sie hat eine
  Weile hier gearbeitet.
  after a while nach einer Weile

while CONJUNCTION
  während
  **You can make some coffee while I'm
  finishing my homework.** Du kannst Kaffee
  kochen, während ich meine Hausaufgaben
  fertig mache.

  WORD TIP Do not translate the English word
  while with the German weil.

whip NOUN
  die **Peitsche** (PL die **Peitschen**)
to **whip** VERB
  schlagen◇ *(cream)*

whipped cream die Schlagsahne

🔵 **WHIPPED CREAM**
In Austria whipped cream is also called
Schlagobers or Schlag.

whisker NOUN
  das **Schnurrhaar** (PL die **Schnurrhaare**)

whisky NOUN
  der **Whisky** (PL die **Whiskys**)

whisper NOUN
  das **Flüstern**
  in a whisper im Flüsterton
to **whisper** VERB
  flüstern
  She whispered the answer to me. Sie
  flüsterte mir die Antwort zu.

whistle NOUN
  die **Pfeife** (PL die **Pfeifen**)
to **whistle** VERB
  pfeifen◇

℘ **white** NOUN
  das **Weiß**
  egg white das Eiweiß

white ADJECTIVE
  weiß
  a white shirt ein weißes Hemd

Whitsun NOUN
  Pfingsten (NEUTER)

℘ **who** PRONOUN
1 *(in questions)* wer
  Who wants some chocolate? Wer möchte
  Schokolade?
2 *(in the accusative)* wen
  Who did you ring? Wen hast du angerufen?
3 *(in the dative)* wem
  Who did you give it to? Wem hast du es
  gegeben?
4 *(relative pronoun)* der/die/das *(depending
  on the gender of the noun 'who' refers to)
  (plural)* die
  my uncle who lives in Liverpool mein
  Onkel, der in Liverpool wohnt
  my aunt who lives in Berlin meine Tante (PL
  die in Berlin wohnt)
  the child who's staying with us das Kind,
  das bei uns wohnt
  **the friends who are coming to see us
  tonight** die Freunde (PL die heute Abend zu
  Besuch kommen)

℘ **whole** NOUN
  the whole of the class die ganze Klasse
  the whole of Germany ganz Deutschland
  on the whole im Großen und Ganzen

whole ADJECTIVE
ganz
the whole family die ganze Familie
the whole morning den ganzen Morgen
the whole time die ganze Zeit
the whole world die ganze Welt

wholemeal ADJECTIVE
Vollkorn-
wholemeal bread das Vollkornbrot

whom PRONOUN
den/die/das (PLURAL) (PL die)
the man whom I saw der Mann, den ich sah
the woman whom I saw die Frau (PL die ich sah)
the child whom I saw das Kind, das ich sah
the children whom I saw die Kinder (PL die ich sah)
5 (in the dative) dem/der/dem, (plural) denen
the girl to whom I wrote das Mädchen, dem ich geschrieben habe
6 (in questions) wen
Whom did you see? Wen haben Sie gesehen?
7 **To whom did you give it?** Wem haben Sie es gegeben?

whose PRONOUN, ADJECTIVE
1 (in questions) wessen
Whose is this jacket? Wessen Jacke ist das?
Whose shoes are these? Wessen Schuhe sind das?
2 **Whose is it?** Wem gehört das?
I know whose it is. Ich weiß, wem es gehört.
3 (as a relative pronoun) dessen/deren/dessen (depending on the gender of the noun 'whose' refers to) (plural) deren
the man whose car I'm buying der Mann, dessen Auto ich kaufe
the woman whose bag I found die Frau, deren Tasche ich gefunden habe
the girl whose sister I know das Mädchen, dessen Schwester ich kenne
the people whose children he teaches die Leute, deren Kinder er unterrichtet

why ADVERB
1 warum
Why did she phone? Warum hat sie angerufen?
Why not? Warum nicht?
2 **That's why I don't want to come.** Deswegen will ich nicht kommen.

wicked ADJECTIVE
1 (bad) böse
2 (brilliant) geil (informal)

wide ADJECTIVE
1 breit
It's a very wide road. Es ist eine sehr breite Straße.
The shelf is 30 cm wide. Das Regal ist dreißig Zentimeter breit.
wide screen das Breitbild
2 groß
a wide range eine große Auswahl

wide ADVERB
weit
The door was wide open. Die Tür stand weit offen.

wide awake ADJECTIVE
hellwach

widow NOUN
die Witwe (PL die Witwen)
She's a widow. Sie ist Witwe.

widower NOUN
der Witwer (PL die Witwer)
He's a widower. Er ist Witwer.

width NOUN
die Breite

wife NOUN
die Ehefrau (PL die Ehefrauen), die Frau (PL die Frauen)
his wife seine Frau

WiFi NOUN
das WLAN

wig NOUN
die Perücke (PL die Perücken)

wild ADJECTIVE
1 wild
wild animals wilde Tiere
2 (crazy) verrückt (idea, party, person)
3 **to be wild about something** scharf auf etwas (ACC) sein

wildlife NOUN
die Tierwelt
a programme on wildlife in Africa eine Sendung über die afrikanische Tierwelt

wildlife park NOUN
der Wildpark (PL die Wildparks)

will NOUN
1 der Wille
He's got a very strong will. Er hat einen sehr starken Willen.
2 das Testament (PL die Testamente)
My gran left us some money in her will. Meine Oma hat uns in ihrem Testament Geld hinterlassen.

will *VERB*
1 *(in German the present tense is often used to express future actions and intentions)*
I'll wait for you at the bus stop. Ich warte an der Bushaltestelle auf dich.
He'll be pleased to help you. Er hilft dir gern.
That won't be a problem. Das ist kein Problem.
I'll phone them at once. Ich rufe sie sofort an.
2 *(the German future tense is used when firm intention is stressed, when referring to the more distant future and when some doubt about the future is expressed)* **werden**◇
He will definitely come. Er wird ganz bestimmt kommen.
She'll probably ring before leaving. Sie wird wahrscheinlich anrufen, bevor sie geht.
3 *(in questions and requests)*
Will you have some more tea? Möchten Sie noch Tee?
Will you help me? Hilfst du mir?
'Will you write to me?' – 'Of course I will!' 'Schreibst du mir?' – 'Ja, natürlich!'
'He won't like it.' – 'Yes he will.' 'Es wird ihm nicht gefallen.' – 'Doch.'
4 *(be willing)* **wollen**◇
He won't help us. Er will uns nicht helfen.
The car won't start. Das Auto will nicht anspringen.

willing *ADJECTIVE*
to be willing to do something bereit sein, etwas zu tun
I'm willing to pay half. Ich bin bereit (*PL* die Hälfte zu zahlen.)

willingly *ADVERB*
gern

willow *NOUN*
die Weide (*PL* die Weiden)

willpower *NOUN*
die Willenskraft

℗ **win** *NOUN*
der Sieg (*PL* die Siege)
our win over Everton unser Sieg über Everton

to win *VERB*
1 gewinnen◇
We won! Wir haben gewonnen!
2 **to win a prize** einen Preis bekommen◇

℗ **wind¹** *NOUN*
der Wind (*PL* die Winde)

to wind² *VERB*
1 wickeln *(a wire or rope, for example)*
2 aufziehen◇ *SEP (a clock)*

wind farm *NOUN*
der Windpark (*PL* die Windparks)

wind instrument *NOUN*
das Blasinstrument (*PL* die Blasinstrumente)

℗ **window** *NOUN*
1 das Fenster (*PL* die Fenster)
to look out of the window aus dem Fenster sehen◇
2 *(in a shop)* das Schaufenster (*PL* die Schaufenster)

window-shopping *NOUN*
to go window-shopping einen Schaufensterbummel machen

℗ **windscreen** *NOUN*
die Windschutzscheibe (*PL* die Windschutzscheiben)

windscreen wiper *NOUN*
der Scheibenwischer (*PL* die Scheibenwischer)

℗ **windsurfing** *NOUN*
das Windsurfen
to go windsurfing windsurfen gehen◇
(PERF **sein)**

windy *ADJECTIVE*
windig
It's windy today. Heute ist es windig.

℗ **wine** *NOUN*
der Wein (*PL* die Weine)
a glass of white wine ein Glas Weißwein
red wine der Rotwein

wing *NOUN*
der Flügel (*PL* die Flügel)

to wink *VERB*
to wink at somebody jemandem zuzwinkern *SEP*

winner *NOUN*
der Sieger (*PL* die Sieger), die Siegerin (*PL* die Siegerinnen)

winning *ADJECTIVE*
siegreich

winnings *PLURAL NOUN*
der Gewinn *(SINGULAR)*

℗ **winter** *NOUN*
der Winter (*PL* die Winter)
in winter im Winter

℗ indicates key words

winter sports *PLURAL NOUN*
der **Wintersport** *(SINGULAR)*

ℐ to **wipe** *VERB*
1 **abwischen** *SEP*
I'll just wipe the table. Ich wische schnell den Tisch ab.
to wipe your nose sich *(DAT)* die Nase abwischen
2 **to wipe the floor** den Boden wischen
3 **to wipe your feet** sich *(DAT)* die Schuhe abtreten◇ *SEP*
• **to wipe up**
aufwischen *SEP*
I wiped up the milk I had spilt. Ich wischte die Milch auf (die ich verschüttet hatte.)

wire *NOUN*
der **Draht** *(PL* die **Drähte)**
electric wire die Leitung

ℐ **wise** *ADJECTIVE*
weise

wish *NOUN*
1 der **Wunsch** *(PL* die **Wünsche)**
to make a wish sich *(DAT)* etwas wünschen
Make a wish! Wünsch dir was!
2 **Best wishes on your birthday.** Alles Gute zum Geburtstag.
3 *(in a letter)*
With best wishes Mit freundlichen Grüßen
to wish *VERB*
1 **I wish she were here.** Ich wünschte, sie wäre hier.
2 **to wish for something** sich *(DAT)* etwas wünschen
3 **to wish somebody a happy Christmas** jemandem frohe Weihnachten wünschen
I wished him happy birthday. Ich habe ihm alles Gute zum Geburtstag gewünscht.

witch *NOUN*
die **Hexe** *(PL* die **Hexen)**

ℐ **with** *PREPOSITION*
1 **mit** *(+DAT)*
with me mit mir
with pleasure mit Vergnügen
He went on holiday with his friends. Er ist mit seinen Freunden in die Ferien gefahren.
a girl with red hair ein Mädchen mit roten Haaren
2 *(at the house of)* **bei** *(+DAT)*
We're staying the night with friends. Wir übernachten bei Freunden.
3 **vor** *(+DAT)*
to shiver with cold vor Kälte zittern
to tremble with fear vor Angst zittern
4 **I haven't got any money with me.** Ich habe

kein Geld dabei.

ℐ **without** *PREPOSITION*
ohne *(+ACC)*
without you ohne dich
without a sweater ohne einen Pullover
without knowing ohne zu wissen

witness *NOUN*
der **Zeuge** *(PL* die **Zeugen)**, die **Zeugin** *(PL* die **Zeuginnen)**

witty *ADJECTIVE*
geistreich

wizard *NOUN*
der **Zauberer** *(PL* die **Zauberer)**

wolf *NOUN*
der **Wolf** *(PL* die **Wölfe)**

ℐ **woman** *NOUN*
die **Frau** *(PL* die **Frauen)**
a woman friend eine Freundin
a woman doctor eine Ärztin

wonder *NOUN*
das **Wunder** *(PL* die **Wunder)**
It's no wonder you're tired. Es ist kein Wunder, dass du müde bist.
to wonder *VERB*
1 **sich fragen**
I wonder why she did that. Ich frage mich, warum sie das getan hat.
2 **I wonder who?** Wer wohl?
I wonder where Jake is. Wo Jake wohl ist?
3 *(in polite requests)*
I wonder if you could tell me? Könnten Sie mir vielleicht sagen?

wonderful *ADJECTIVE*
wunderbar

ℐ **wood** *NOUN*
1 das **Holz**
The lamp is made of wood. Die Lampe ist aus Holz.
2 *(place with trees)* der **Wald** *(PL* die **Wälder)**
The children played in the wood/woods. Die Kinder spielten im Wald.

wooden *ADJECTIVE*
Holz-, hölzern
wooden toys das Holzspielzeug

woodwork *NOUN*
(craft) die **Tischlerei**

ℐ **wool** *NOUN*
die **Wolle**

woollen *ADJECTIVE*
Woll-

◇ **irregular verb;** *SEP* **separable verb; for more help with verbs see centre section**

ℱ **word** NOUN

1 das **Wort** (PL die **Wörter**) (the plural Wörter is used when the words are unrelated)
a long word ein langes Wort
words in the dictionary Wörter im Wörterbuch
I've learned ten German words today. Ich habe heute zehn deutsche Wörter gelernt.
What's the German word for 'window'? Wie heißt 'window' auf Deutsch?

2 das **Wort** (PL die **Worte**) (the plural Worte is used when the words are connected in a text or conversation)
He wanted to say a few words. Er wollte ein paar Worte sagen.
in other words mit anderen Worten
to have a word with somebody mit jemandem sprechen◇

3 (promise) das **Wort**
to keep your word sein Wort halten◇
He broke his word. Er hat sein Wort gebrochen.

4 **the words of a song** der Text von einem Lied

word processing NOUN
die **Textverarbeitung**

word processor NOUN
das **Textverarbeitungssystem** (PL die **Textverarbeitungssysteme**)

ℱ **work** NOUN

1 die **Arbeit**
I enjoy my work. Meine Arbeit macht mir Spaß.
She's looking for work. Sie sucht Arbeit.
I've got some work to do. Ich habe noch etwas Arbeit.
He's out of work. Er hat keine Arbeit.
to be off work nicht arbeiten
Ben's off work. (sick) Ben ist krank.
to go to work on the tube mit der U-Bahn zur Arbeit fahren

2 **to be hard work** anstrengend sein
It's hard work learning vocabulary. Es ist anstrengend, Vokabeln zu lernen.

to work VERB

1 **arbeiten**
She works in an office. Sie arbeitet in einem Büro.
Mum works as a dentist. Mutti ist Zahnärztin.
He works part-time. Er arbeitet halbtags.

2 (operate) **sich auskennen**◇ SEP **mit**
Can you work the photocopier? Kennst du dich mit dem Kopierer aus?

3 (function) **funktionieren**
The washing machine's not working. Die Waschmaschine funktioniert nicht.

4 (a plan or idea) **klappen**
That worked really well. Das hat prima geklappt.

• **to work out**

1 (understand) **verstehen**◇
I can't work out why. Ich kann nicht verstehen, warum.

2 (exercise) **trainieren**

3 (go well) **klappen**

4 (calculate) **ausrechnen** SEP (a sum)
I'll work out how much it would cost. Ich rechne aus, wie viel es kosten würde.

5 (solve) **lösen** (a problem)

worker NOUN
der **Arbeiter** (PL die **Arbeiter**), die **Arbeiterin** (PL die **Arbeiterinnen**)

ℱ **work experience** NOUN
das **Praktikum** (PL die **Praktika**)
to do work experience ein Praktikum machen

working-class ADJECTIVE
aus der **Arbeiterschicht**, **Arbeiter**-
a working-class family eine Arbeiterfamilie

working hours PLURAL NOUN
die **Arbeitszeit** (PL die **Arbeitszeiten**)

work of art NOUN
das **Kunstwerk** (PL die **Kunstwerke**)

worksheet NOUN
das **Arbeitsblatt** (PL die **Arbeitsblätter**)

workshop NOUN
die **Werkstatt** (PL die **Werkstätten**)

workstation NOUN
das **Computerterminal** (PL die **Computerterminals**)

world NOUN
die **Welt**
the biggest tree in the world der größte Baum der Welt
all over the world auf der ganzen Welt
the Western world die westliche Welt

World Cup NOUN
the World Cup die Weltmeisterschaft

world war NOUN
der **Weltkrieg** (PL die **Weltkriege**)
the Second World War der Zweite Weltkrieg

worm NOUN
der **Wurm** (PL die **Würmer**)

worn out ADJECTIVE

1 (person) **erschöpft**

2 *(clothes or shoes)* **abgetragen**

ℱ **worried** ADJECTIVE
1 **besorgt**
   his worried parents seine besorgten Eltern
2 **to be worried about somebody** sich *(DAT)*
   um jemanden Sorgen machen
   We're worried about Susan. Wir machen
   uns um Susan Sorgen.

ℱ **worry** NOUN
   die **Sorge** (PL die **Sorgen**)
to **worry** VERB
   sich *(DAT)* Sorgen machen
   Don't worry! Keine Sorge!
   Don't worry about it. Mach dir darum
   keine Sorgen.

worrying ADJECTIVE
   beunruhigend

ℱ **worse** ADJECTIVE
1 *(more unpleasant)* **schlimmer** *(problem,
   pain, illness)*
   Things couldn't be worse. Es kann nicht
   schlimmer kommen.
2 *(less good)* **schlechter**
   It was even worse than the last time. Es
   war noch schlechter als letztes Mal.
   to get worse schlechter werden
   The weather's getting worse. Das Wetter
   wird schlechter.
   She's getting worse. *(in health)* Es geht ihr
   schlechter.

worst ADJECTIVE
1 *(most unpleasant)* **schlimmster/
   schlimmste/schlimmstes**
   the worst der/die/das schlimmste
   It was the worst day of my life. Es war der
   schlimmste Tag meines Lebens.
   if the worst comes to the worst wenn es
   zum Schlimmsten kommt
2 *(least good)* **schlechtester/schlechteste/
   schlechtestes**
   It's his worst film. Das ist sein schlechtester
   Film.
   French is my worst subject. In Französisch
   bin ich am schlechtesten.

worth ADJECTIVE
1 **to be worth** wert sein
   How much is it worth? Wie viel ist es wert?
2 **It's worth it.** Das lohnt sich.
   It's not worth it. Es lohnt sich nicht.
   It's worth buying. Das lohnt sich zu kaufen.
   It's not worth starting now. Es lohnt sich
   nicht, jetzt anzufangen.

ℱ **would** VERB
1 **Would you like something to eat?**

Möchtest du etwas essen?
What would you like? Was möchten Sie?
2 **I wouldn't do it.** Ich würde das nicht
machen.
**I would buy it, but I haven't got any
money at the moment.** Ich würde es
kaufen, aber ich habe zur Zeit kein Geld.
I'd like to go to the cinema. Ich würde gern
ins Kino gehen.
She said she'd help us. Sie hat gesagt, sie
würde uns helfen.
3 **That would be a good idea.** Das wäre ein
gute Idee.
**If we had asked her she would have helped
us.** Wenn wir sie gefragt hätten, hätte sie
uns geholfen.
4 *(be willing)*
He wouldn't answer. Er wollte nicht
antworten.
The car wouldn't start. Das Auto wollte
nicht anspringen.

wound NOUN
die **Wunde** (PL die **Wunden**)
to **wound** VERB
verwunden

wow! EXCLAMATION
wow!, Wahnsinn!
Wow! That's great! Wahnsinn! Das ist toll!

to **wrap** VERB
einpacken SEP
I'm going to wrap (up) my presents. Ich
packe meine Geschenke ein.
Could you wrap it for me please? Können
Sie es bitte in Geschenkpapier einpacken?

wrapping paper NOUN
das **Geschenkpapier**

wreck NOUN
1 das **Wrack** (PL die **Wracks**)
2 **I feel a wreck.** Ich bin völlig kaputt.
to **wreck** VERB
1 **zerstören** *(a building or machinery)*
2 **kaputtfahren**◇ SEP *(a car)*
3 **verderben**◇ *(a party, holidays)*
It completely wrecked my evening. Das
hat mir den Abend völlig verdorben.
4 **zunichte machen** *(PLANS)*

wrestler NOUN
der **Ringer** (PL die **Ringer**), die **Ringerin**
(PL die **Ringerinnen**)

WORD TIP Professions, hobbies, and sports
don't take an article in German: Er ist Ringer.

wrestling NOUN
das **Ringen**

◇ *irregular verb;* SEP *separable verb; for more help with verbs see centre section*

wrist *NOUN*
   das **Handgelenk** (*PL* die **Handgelenke**)

ℓ to **write** *VERB*
   schreiben◇
   to write to somebody jemandem schreiben
   I'll write her a letter. Ich schreibe ihr einen Brief.
   to write to a firm an eine Firma schreiben
• **to write down**
   aufschreiben◇ *SEP*
   I wrote down her name. Ich schrieb ihren Namen auf.
   She wrote it down for me. Sie hat es mir aufgeschrieben.

writer *NOUN*
   der **Schriftsteller** (*PL* die **Schriftsteller**), die **Schriftstellerin** (*PL* die **Schriftstellerinnen**)

   WORD TIP Professions, hobbies, and sports don't take an article in German: Er ist Schriftsteller.

writing *NOUN*
   die **Schrift**
   I can't read your writing. Ich kann deine Schrift nicht lesen.
   Please answer in writing. Bitte antworten Sie schriftlich.

ℓ **wrong** *ADJECTIVE*
   1 *(not correct)* **falsch**
      the wrong answer die falsche Antwort
      It's the wrong address. Das ist die falsche Adresse.
   2 **You've got the wrong number.** Sie haben sich verwählt.
   3 **to be wrong** *(be mistaken)* **sich irren, unrecht haben**
      I must have been wrong. Ich muss mich geirrt haben.
      He's wrong. Er hat unrecht.
   4 *(out of order)*
      to be wrong nicht stimmen
      There's something wrong. Etwas stimmt nicht.
   5 *(dishonest)* **nicht richtig**
      It's wrong to make him pay for it. Es ist nicht richtig, dass er dafür zahlen muss.
   6 *(bad)* **unrecht**
      But I haven't done anything wrong! Aber ich habe nichts Unrechtes getan!
   7 **What's wrong?** Was ist los?

wrong *ADVERB*
   1 *(false)* **falsch**
      He's got it wrong. Er hat es falsch gemacht.
   2 **to go wrong** *(break)* **kaputtgehen**◇ *SEP* (*PERF* **sein**)
   3 **to go wrong** schiefgehen◇ *SEP* (*PERF* **sein**) **plan**

Xx

Xmas *NOUN*
   Weihnachten *(NEUTER)*

ℓ **X-ray** *NOUN*
   die **Röntgenaufnahme** (*PL* die **Röntgenaufnahmen**)
   to have an X-ray geröntgt werden◇ (*PERF* **sein**)

to **X-ray** *VERB*
   röntgen
   They X-rayed her ankle. Sie haben ihren Knöchel geröntgt.

xylophone *NOUN*
   das **Xylophon** (*PL* die **Xylophone**)
   He plays the xylophone. Er spielt Xylophon.

   WORD TIP Don't use the article when you talk about playing an instrument.

Yy

yacht *NOUN*
   1 *(sailing boat)* das **Segelboot** (*PL* die **Segelboote**)
   2 *(large luxury boat)* die **Jacht** (*PL* die **Jachten**)

to **yawn** *VERB*
   gähnen

ℓ **year** *NOUN*
   1 das **Jahr** (*PL* die **Jahre**)
      six years ago vor sechs Jahren
      the whole year das ganze Jahr
   2 **for years** jahrelang
      They lived in Moscow for years. Sie haben jahrelang in Moskau gewohnt.
   3 **to be seventeen years old** siebzehn Jahre alt sein
      a two-year-old child ein zweijähriges Kind
   4 *(in school)* die **Klasse** (*PL* die **Klassen**)
      I'm in Year 10. Ich gehe in die zehnte Klasse.
      He'll be in Year 11. Er kommt in die elfte Klasse.
   5 *(all the pupils in a year)* der **Jahrgang** (*PL* die **Jahrgänge**)
      There are 100 pupils in my year. In meinem Jahrgang sind 100 Schüler.

to **yell** *VERB*
   schreien◇

ℓ **yellow** *ADJECTIVE*
   gelb

A
B
C
D
E
F
G
H
I
J
K
L
M
N
O
P
Q
R
S
T
U
V
W
X
Y
Z

ℓ **indicates key words**

yes ADVERB
1 **ja**
yes please ja bitte
'Is Tom in his room?' – 'Yes, he is.' 'Ist Tom in seinem Zimmer?' – 'Ja.'
2 (answering a negative) **doch**
'You don't want to come with us, do you?' – 'Yes, I do!' 'Du willst nicht mitkommen?' – 'Doch!'
'You haven't finished, have you?' – 'Yes, I have.' 'Sie sind noch nicht fertig, oder?' – 'Doch!'

yesterday ADVERB
1 **gestern**
I saw her yesterday. Ich habe sie gestern gesehen.
yesterday afternoon gestern Nachmittag
yesterday morning gestern früh
2 **the day before yesterday** vorgestern

yet ADVERB
1 **not yet** noch nicht
It's not ready yet. Es ist noch nicht fertig.
2 (in questions) **schon**
Has she mentioned it yet? Hat sie es schon erwähnt?

yoga NOUN
das **Yoga**
to do yoga Yoga machen

yoghurt NOUN
der **Joghurt** (PL die **Joghurt**)

yolk NOUN
das **Eigelb** (PL die **Eigelbe**)

you PRONOUN
1 (as the subject of the sentence and in comparisons) **du** (familiar form, singular) **Sie** (polite form, singular and plural) (du is the familiar way of talking to family members, close friends, and people of your own age; Sie is more polite) **Do you want to go to the cinema tonight?** Möchtest du heute Abend ins Kino gehen?
Can you tell me where the station is, please? Können Sie mir bitte sagen, wo der Bahnhof ist?
He's older than you. Er ist älter als du./Er ist älter als Sie.
2 (the object form of du and Sie, in the dative) **dir** (familiar form, singular), **Ihnen** (polite form, singular and plural)
I'll lend you my bike. Ich leihe dir mein Rad.
I'll write to you. Ich schreibe Ihnen.
I'll come with you. Ich komme mit Ihnen mit./Ich komme mit dir mit.
3 (the object form of du and Sie, in the accusative) **dich** (familiar form, singular) **Sie** (polite form, singular and plural)
I saw you. Ich habe dich gesehen./Ich habe Sie gesehen.
4 (as the subject of the sentence) **ihr** (familiar form, plural)
Do you all want to come? Wollt ihr alle kommen?
5 (the object form, in the accusative and the dative) **euch**
I'll invite you all! Ich lade euch alle ein!
I'll give it to you later. Ich gebe es euch später.

young ADJECTIVE
jung
young people junge Leute
He's younger than me. Er ist jünger als ich.
Tessa's two years younger than me. Tessa ist zwei Jahre jünger als ich.

your DETERMINER
1 (familiar form, singular) **dein** (this is the familiar way of talking to family members, close friends, and people of your own age; Ihr is more polite)
I met your brother. Ich habe deinen Bruder getroffen.
I met your sister. Ich habe deine Schwester getroffen.
I drove your car. Ich bin mit deinem Auto gefahren.
I know your brothers. Ich kenne deine Brüder.
2 (familiar form, plural) **euer**
your brother euer Bruder
your sister eure Schwester
your car euer Auto
Your friends are waiting downstairs. Eure Freunde warten unten.
3 (polite form, singular and plural) **Ihr**
your brother Ihr Bruder
your sister Ihre Schwester
Your car is in the garage. Ihr Auto ist in der Garage.
You can all bring your friends. Sie können alle Ihre Freunde mitbringen.

yours PRONOUN
1 (familiar form, singular) **deiner/deine/deins** (this is the familiar way of talking to family members, close friends, and people of your own age; Ihrer/Ihre/Ihrs is more polite)
My brother's younger than yours. Mein Bruder ist jünger als deiner.
My sister is older than yours. Meine Schwester ist älter als deine.
I enjoyed that book - is it yours? Das Buch hat mir gefallen - ist es deins?

◇ **irregular verb;** SEP **separable verb; for more help with verbs see centre section**